OF PERMANENT VALUE

THE STORY OF

WARREN BUFFETT

UPDATED AND EXPANDED EDITION

BY ANDREW KILPATRICK

McGraw-Hill

New York Chicago San Francisco Lisbon London
Madrid Mexico City Milan New Delhi San Juan
Seoul Singapore Sydney Toronto

McGraw-Hill

A Division of the **McGraw-Hill** Companies

1 2 3 4 5 6 7 8 9 0   DOC/DOC   0 9 8 7 6 5 4 3 2 1

ISBN 0-07-137080-3

Printed and bound by R.R. Donnelley & Sons Company.

McGraw-Hill books are available at special quantity discounts to use as premiums and sales promotions, or for use in corporate training programs. For more information, please write to the Director of Special Sales, Professional Publishing, McGraw-Hill, Two Penn Plaza, New York, NY 10121-2298.

For Frances Kilpatrick

My mother died of a stroke on November 25, 1999 at age 85. She was the hardest working person I ever saw. In my youth we had a summer home in Peru, Vermont. Once, after playing tennis and going fishing all day, I got home at dark and found Mother at the top of a ladder finishing a painting job. From dawn to dusk she had single-handedly painted the entire *inside* and *outside* of the house. In one form or another, every day of her life was like that.

Frances Williams Kilpatrick

When she found out I was working on this book, which had no prospect of publication, she wrote: "You're throwing away your life." False starts in this world were not her bag. I took her to a Berkshire Hathaway annual meeting, where she was very impressed with Warren Buffett. Later, she helped all she could with the book.

For Mary Anne Adams

My wife Pat's great friend Mary Anne Adams lost her 10-year valiant battle with breast cancer on November 7, 1999 at age 51. Mary Anne was world class as a wife to her husband Richard and as a mother to her four children: Britt, Kate, Bo and Charlie. She was chosen as a Community Hero to run in the 1996 Summer Olympics Torch Run. She will forever be a hero to her family and friends.

(Courtesy of Richard Adams)

Mary Anne Adams

(Photo courtesy of ABC News/Steve Fenn © 1999)

Warren E. Buffett

Table of Contents

Table of Contents

Table of Contents

Table of Contents

Table of Contents

Table of Contents

IRS TO AKPE: A GREEN LIGHT

The IRS (Internal Revenue Service) invited AKPE (Andy Kilpatrick Publishing Empire), publisher of this book, in for an audit in 1998. The IRS, thank heavens, found nothing wrong with the empire's tax filing. It turned out that AKPE's problem was that losses on the 1996 book needed explanation. Sales somehow failed to match the 28 million copies sold of *Gone With The Wind* although the epic about Scarlett O'Hara is a mere 1,024 pages. Clearly quality counts.

After the greetings notice from the IRS, there was a mad scramble to get the records in orderly form in the required 10 days. So a particular thanks to my wife, Pat, who managed to find the records and arrange them in neat, organized folders that saved us from the Federal Government. Indeed the IRS auditor complimented us on the good order of the records. "Sometimes I get records in grocery bags," she said. Well, Pat pretty much started with a bunch of my records in grocery bags.

Pat "Book Widow" Kilpatrick

Each time the auditor would say, "Let's see invoices from Cherie Kosak...Nancy Jacobs," Pat pulled out the right folder and all was well. Talk about getting blood from a turnip. The final IRS tally showed that Uncle Sam owed AKPE a refund.

Buffett talks about Berkshire shareholders "giving at the office" because of Berkshire's large taxes. AKPE also came to the aid of our country in a tiny way.

The IRS was really no problem. The next close encounter, however, was of the worst kind. The two "gentlemen" who had offices to either side of me, in a joint business, summarily booted me out after finding out from the landlord that AKPE had a 30-day lease (for the past 10 years). Legal, but crummy. The empire gets no respect. The worst of the move came when I had to yank down hundreds of photos, cartoons, articles—even book notes that I had tacked or taped to the walls. These guys perfectly fit the adage: "Some men are born great, some achieve greatness, and some just grate upon you." The good news was that the 200-square-foot headquarters moved down the hall to slightly more glamorous quarters. But then months later AKPE got kicked out a second time and found a home in a big, old storage room in the same building. So it was almost a case of "AKPE has left the building."

Another in a series of indignities happened when a Galveston flood destroyed several hundred books. Pat said that was the only good thing

(Photo courtesy of Ann Eady)

Don Pippen

about the two feet of water in our basement. The water-logged versions *Of Permanent Value*—double its usual size—was a terrifying sight.

Yet another slight was that AKPE managed to sell only 4,000 copies of a 20,000 run. The rest went to the remainder table or charity.

Anyway, thanks always to Don Pippen who helped this book in every way. Don died May 11, 1997, after years of battling cancer. He loved Sewanee, books, and Smyer Lake near Birmingham, Alabama. Never once did I hear him complain about anything, including his disease, not even on his deathbed. Don was 44.

He was a perfect gentleman. There was little in this book for Don. The night before the final typeset for the 1994 version went to press, I mentioned to him there were still too many typos. Late that afternoon Don came by the humble headquarters and said, "Well, Andy, give me half."

He took half and I took half and we worked until late at night giving the book its final proofreading. This is probably not the way it's done at big publishing houses, but we had a ball.

Writing a book is an odyssey and I needed help. My thanks first to my mother, Frances Kilpatrick, and my wife, Patricia Ann Burgess Terrell Kilpatrick, who says she's become a "book widow." She identifies with Tom Wolfe's wife because after the exasperating length of time to compose *The Right Stuff,* he told her he still had to get the men to the moon. "Not in this house," she replied.

I've enjoyed writing this book so much I've told Pat I want to be buried in the book office. She says that can be arranged. Pat's own wishes are to be buried across the country from me, sitting beside the pool at The Peninsula hotel in Beverly Hills, California—cell phone in hand.

Some say the B in her name is for Burgess; I say it's for Borsheim's where we bought her wedding ring. Pat and I are interchangeable partners as shipping clerks at AKPE which is so little known that some of the incoming calls are for a local hospital, others for "Kilpatrick Trailer Park." One disturbing call was about getting my psychiatrist bill current. Although I probably need to see a psychiatrist, I haven't *yet*. Other calls included: "Is this the Andrew Kilpatrick with Allstate?" and "Can I speak to Grandma?"

Thanks to Charles Munger, Berkshire's vice chairman; Don Keough, former president of Coca-Cola; Miami Dolphins' Coach Don Shula; Ann Landers; New Mexico state legislator George Buffett; Howard

Buffett, and others for interviews.

I would like to thank Harvey Terrell (who died at 92 in 1997), Birmingham's Mr. Birmingham who gave almost everyone in town a first loan, and who all along was reassuring, convinced that I had a worthwhile project.

The person who was the most helpful with editing was Michael Assael of New York City, a door-to-door floor wax salesman at age 14 and later a Columbia Business School graduate, now a lawyer, accountant, author, and investor who has Warren Buffett's autograph on a 1934 edition of *Security Analysis*. (The asking price at Julian's Books in New York for a first edition, second printing copy signed by author Ben Graham is $24,000.) Michael is my idea of a Renaissance man. He is the spiritual guide for this book. Thanks also to his wife, Eiko.

With the page count of this monster edition now surpassing *Gone With the Wind*, the new standard is now *War and Peace* which has *Of Permanent Value* beat by about 300 pages. I'll shoot to overtake it in the Millennium Plus Two Edition. Then the benchmark will be *World Book*. Twenty-five editions from now maybe I'll publish a set of Warren Buffett encyclopedias. Michael is worried that its *table of contents* might be as long as *Gone With the Wind*.

In the decade of working on this book, Michael and I have had only one disagreement. He thinks quality counts whereas I think what matters is the quantity of items in the table of contents.

Thanks to Phil McCaull of Greenwich, Connecticut, Allan Maxwell, a one-man clipping service, and Terry Haney, both of Omaha, Nebraska, and ace photographer Michael O'Brien of Austin, Texas. Computer buffs Lonnie Drew and Sabrina Ward of Birmingham, Alabama, fashioned the index. Writing a book is one thing. Creating an index is quite another.

LaVerne Ramsey of Birmingham, George Morgan of Omaha, Nebraska, commander-in-chief of Buffett Wannabes were with me along the journey. Nancy Line Jacobs of Omaha, Jane Liss of Columbus, Nebraska and Nancy Burgess of Acworth, Georgia, were all real friends of the book. Many thanks to the folks at the Omaha Public Library and the *Omaha World-Herald* which was particularly helpful with stories and photos.

Cherie C. Kosak deciphered my hieroglyphics and typed every word of this major monster millennium unabridged edition into her computer. God bless Cherie. Thanks to Lori Leath Smith, Tommy and Jane Johnson, Earl Bloom, Bobby Luckie, Andy Campbell, Steve Edmondson, and Beverly Valin, Lisa Nichols, Pam Conley, and Karen Salerno, all of Birmingham, Alabama; Ellen Oakes of Vincent, Alabama; Russ Fletcher of Cohasset, Massachusetts; Chris Robinson of Cullman, Alabama; David Hayden of Los Angeles; David Hardee of

Santa Barbara, California; Ken Mills of Lakeland, Florida; Stevin Hoover of Boston, Massachusetts; and particularly longtime Berkshire follower Bill Scargle of San Francisco; Ken Monroe of Merritt Island, Florida; Ian Darling, Sydney, Australia; Jim Maves, Woodbury, Minnesota; John Zemanovich, Toronto, Canada; Anthony Breckner, of Buffalo, New York; Don Danly, Buffett's early partner in the Wilson Coin-Operated Machine Co., of Pensacola, Florida, and Charles Page, of Carmel, California.

Thanks to Dr. Frank Kilpatrick, Mary Jo, Robert, John and Sarah of Madison, Wisconsin and to Judith Goodnow Prus: Grosse Pointe Farms, Michigan; talk about class.

Here's a salute to my children, Jack and Anna, both far better writers than I, who should one day write their own books (Jack has started two novels and developed an interest in Berkshire. Who knows? Maybe this book will have sequels into the next millennium.) and to Pat's children, rock stars: Tommy, Michael and Mark (on the drums, keyboard, piano and guitar).

Thanks to Floyd Jones of Seattle, Steve Wallman of Madison, Wisconsin, Peter Bradford of Peru, Vermont. And a tip of the hat to Barbara Finch of EBSCO Media in Birmingham, Alabama, for printing the book. She would have made the U.S. women's soccer team proud the night of the delivery of the 1998 edition. She pitched in with a big assist along with Steve Edmondson and several stronger backs from a trucking company in unloading and stacking thousands of books. But when the sweaty effort was over about midnight, Barbara, a former Junior League president, did *not* pull off her shirt.

Thanks to Gladys Kaiser retired as Berkshire Hathaway's administrative assistant, who long ago patiently endured fact-checking missions. Also a bow to Saint Debbie Bosanek whose duties can range from momentarily running Berkshire to being an usherette at Omaha Royals games. She is "db" on Buffett's typed correspondence.

Finally, the book is self-published (yep, totally home baked). I want to encourage other writers to take up self-publishing, a go-it-alone style that long has been downplayed, but now is coming more into vogue.

I took as my heroes James Joyce, Mark Twain, Sigmund Freud, and Walt Whitman who self-published the first edition of *Leaves of Grass*. D.H. Lawrence's *Lady Chatterly's Lover* was self-published as was Mark Twain's *Huckleberry Finn*. Carl Sandburg set type, rolled presses, hand-pulled galleys and bound his books himself.

Well, Buffett says: "Have fun."

Note: To paraphrase P. G. Wodehouse's dedication in *The Heart of a Goof*: To my wife Pat without whose never-failing sympathy and encouragement this book would have been finished in half the time.

PREFACE
SHREWDNESS OF GORILLAS

This book, revised every two years, is about legendary investor Warren Buffett, his spectacular investment vehicle Berkshire Hathaway Inc. and the range of businesses he and Berkshire own.

The work is a look at Buffett's transcendent career as well as his wit and wisdom. This is the Monster Millennium Edition published because so much has happened at Berkshire during the last two years.

(In a clear attempt to feed off the flowing riches of this book, Microsoft has named a computer operating system after this book called Windows Millennium Edition.)

Mr. Buffett has neither approved nor disapproved of the book, which is an attempt to portray him as he really is—a remarkable person by almost everyone's account.

Buffett told me in 1990 that he contemplates writing a book of his own, which probably will be in the style of his annual reports, and therefore doesn't plan to help others with works about him.

Later I wrote Berkshire shareholder Ann Landers asking for an interview. She forwarded my letter to Buffett, who then sent me a copy of his reply to her and added a note.

In his reply to Ann Landers, Buffett said:

Andy Kilpatrick is a decent and well-intentioned fellow, but I am not personally cooperating on the book. On the other hand, whatever my friends decide to do is up to them.

My reason for not helping Andy personally is that someday I'll write my own book—if I can get Carol Loomis to do about 90% of the work—and I don't see any sense in giving away any of the punch lines.

I hope you're coming out for the Annual Meeting next year, but it would be better if you would come by much sooner for dinner.

Best wishes,
Warren E. Buffett

His note at the bottom said: "Andy, as you can see, I wish you well, but not too well. Actually everything I do is public, so I am trying to save a few things for a fresh look at some time. Warren."

He later got me back for writing a book about him with a note, "Wait till I write a book on you!" My heart stopped. So I know how he felt. My reply was, "I wish you well, but not too well."

This one-liner from Buffett has taken on a life of its own. Here's a portion of a letter to Buffett from James Manis of Ooltewah, Tennessee:

The author reports that you included the following words in a note to him, "I wish you well, but not too well." Regarding the Nebraska Cornhuskers and the Fiesta Bowl, I will use your phrase in a slightly altered manner. I wish them well, but not too well. Our local newspaper reports that Nebraska is about a three-point favorite, which is not difficult to understand with its impressive 11-1 season. Both teams have solid records in recent years which should make for a fun and exciting game.

In Knoxville, Tennessee, we pack Neyland Stadium with over 100,000 fans on game day, have an old hound dog for a mascot, play and sing Rocky Top, bleed orange when we lose, and LOVE THOSE VOLS, affectionately known as THE BIG ORANGE.

I hope you enjoy the Nebraska/Tennessee game, but not too much.

I make no claim to have access to Buffett, although I have had lunch with him twice and have watched him, mainly at Berkshire annual meetings and related functions, for 15 years. In all, I have been around him about 100 hours while he was operating at full throttle.

You'll want to read *his* book some day. But in the meantime, there will be many books about Buffett. This one is offered as a look at how things now stand for Buffett and Berkshire.

This book is not intended as an investment guide. Bear in mind that any investment mentioned here as held by Berkshire already may have been sold.

These pages should be read in the following light: I'm a Berkshire shareholder and this book, in part, is an ordinary shareholder's journey of discovery about Berkshire. I'm like the fellow who once posted this on a "Berkshire message board" on the Internet: "What is Berkshire Co? [sic] Saw this stock for the first time last night and it was selling for 46,600." The answer on the Internet: "[Berkshire] is like getting a drink of water...from a fire hydrant."

Years ago I became interested in Buffett as a result of his investment in The Washington Post Co., where my father, Carroll Kilpatrick, was White House correspondent during the Kennedy through Ford administrations (1961 to 1975).

My father and I were always amazed that one person could own such a huge piece of The Post, which seemed to us such a mighty enterprise.

I regard Buffett, as do many people, as an extraordinary human being, combining in a single package financial genius, impeccable ethics, and a priceless sense of humor. Pound for pound, he is one of the funniest people alive. He is a role model for anyone wanting to live life to the fullest.

My relationship with Buffett is reporter to public figure, but we have had a few conversations and laughs along the way. Once we talked about the grand, but imperfect world of publishing and he mentioned that typos drive him nuts. I had the feeling if he found a typo in the Berkshire Annual Report he'd jump off Kiewit Plaza, the modest office building in downtown Omaha where he works.

So I hope he, and you, may enjoy my book. When I took bids to print this book in 1996, I wrote out the title and received a bid to print *Permanent Valve*. That sounds like something that would help a heart patient. Still, that's better than the wit who calls it: *Of Limited Value*. Undervalued? Overvalued? My opinion is that the intrinsic value of the book is $30. The opinion of the head of one remaindering company I called to sell off unsold 1998 editions was that he didn't want them at any price. That was after he asked: "Who's Warren Buffett?"

One fellow, during Berkshire's stock price plunge in early 2000, came up with the title of: *Of Permanent Value?*

The self-publishing effort overall has been about a financial wash—okay a bit less than that. To counter my wife Pat's being on the war path about that, I told her that a McGraw-Hill paperback version of the '98 book was to make about a buck a book. Fine, she said, "*A Buck a Book* will be a good title for the next version." She also calls it *The Final Edition*.

Editor Michael Assael had nicknamed the book *A Permanent Wave* which is something a stadium full of football fans do. In 1998 he coined the phrase *The 30 Billion Pound Gorilla*. Now he's calling it *A Permanent Gorilla*.

Do you have any idea what a group of gorillas is called? It's a "shrewdness of gorillas." Make of that what you will.

The gorilla is the most powerful of the great apes. An adult gorilla can weigh about 500 pounds. They are shy, intelligent and vegetarian.

The aberrational gorilla under study here weighs 30 billion pounds and definitely is not vegetarian. He feeds largely on hamburgers and drinks Cokes constantly. His idea of a well-rounded meal is a big box of See's peanut brittle.

In any event, I offer this book—*Of Permanent Value: The Story of Warren Buffett/Monster Millennium Collector's Item Edition*. It is generally chronological, although the fast-paced chronology sometimes is interrupted to group together Berkshire's major, "permanent" investments, and its "sainted" businesses. Some of the early chapters fall into a "breaking news" category. Like the man himself, some chapters stand alone. All the chapters are a humble effort to track ("stalk," my wife says) Buffett's fast-paced odyssey.

IMAGINARY BOOK REVIEWS

"Unusual."—*Newsweek*

"Really unusual."—*Time*

"Unbelievable sex scenes."—*Playboy*

"Unbelievable number of stock splits."—*Business Week*

"Unbelievable number of words."—James Michener

"A little skimpy."—Warren Buffett

"Has a photo of a secretary in a small office."—Debbie Bosanek

"I have nothing to add."—Charles Munger

"Shameless. Doesn't make a dent."—Ann Landers

"Avoid the poetry section in this book."—Nikos Kazantzakis

"Clear...concise...but has no point."—*Fortune*

"Best annual meeting in all of commerce."—Don Keough

"Short Berkshire."—Merrill Lynch

"No thank you."—PaineWebber

"Our opinion is negative. Downgrading possible."—Salomon Smith Barney

"What's the big deal? It's an okay story about just another fellow in Omaha."—*Omaha World-Herald*

"Take this one to the beach and deep six it."—*Los Angeles Times*

"Lacks financial sophistication."—*Money* magazine

"Phone book makes better reading."—*Harvard Business Review*

"The chapter which mentions Steve Forbes is outstanding. The other chapters are not presidential material."—*Forbes*

"The play failed to gain."—Coach Don Shula

"A political setback."—U.S. Sen. Bob Kerrey

"Has a large newshole."—*The Buffalo News*

"No comment."—*The Washington Post*

"It's ok."—*USA Today*

"Bizarre."—*National Enquirer*

"A crashing bore...Who's Warren Buffett?"—*Hustler*

"Has Permanent Value."—*Worth* magazine

"Difficult to value."—*Wall Street Journal*

"Of dubious value."—*Barron's*

"Better book in paperback."—*McGraw-Hill*

"Things to incorporate in other chapters. Is someone playing a practical joke on me with this book?"—Michael Assael

"Damndest typing job of my whole life."—Cherie Kosak

"Sweeping, monumental, historic, timeless literature...but please feel my pain for living through it."—Pat Kilpatrick

"Know-what-I-mean, Vern?"—Pat Kilpatrick

"Better than *Moby-Dick* and *Gone With The Wind*. Well, at least longer."—Andy Kilpatrick

"No one will ever finish it."—*Financial Times*

"It's a gorilla!"—*New York Times*

1
OF PERMANENT VALUE
$10,000 INTO ABOUT $200 MILLION—AFTER TAX

If you had handed Warren Edward Buffett $10,000 in 1956, today it would be worth about $200 million. AFTER TAX!

But by no means has the ride for his shareholders been a straight moon shot. Berkshire took a terrible hit in the severe recession of 1973-1974 when the stock dropped from about $90 to $40 a share. And it took a whipping in the 1987 stock market crash, dropping from roughly $4,000 to $3,000 and it got clobbered in the months leading up to the Gulf War in 1990-1991 plummeting from $8,900 to $5,500.

Berkshire also nosedived in the 1998-2000 period after it said it would buy reinsurer General Re. Soft pricing and an unusual number of disasters rocked General Re's performance and a number of Berkshire's high profile investments such as Coke and Gillette stumbled badly. Rising interest rates whacked Berkshire's big bond portfolio at the same time. A 100-year storm, even a perfect storm, battered the walls of Berkshire and caused the worst stock slide since the 1973-1975 era when Berkshire lost 60% of its value. Berkshire's stock price this time slumped about 50%.

From mid-1998 Berkshire stock plunged from about $80,000 to $40,800 in early 2000. In short, 1999—an *annus horribilis* was a bummer for Berkshire shareholders—hereinafter referred to as the "Bummer of '99." The stock plunged in early 2000 during a series of rumors about Buffett's health, false press releases on the Internet and dozens of press accounts about how Buffett had finally lost his touch.

Indeed Buffett's value investing approach came under fire as many investors seized on momentum and tech-driven styles. Julian Robertson's Tiger funds, which had a long, successful record of adhering to value investing, shut down because of poor performance and redemptions.

Berkshire's $43,000 (it touched a low of $40,800) price then was only 1.13 times estimated book value, or accounting value, of about $38,000 a share, the lowest ratio since 1983 when it reached 1.04 times, according to PaineWebber analyst Alice Schroeder. So although the stock price had plunged, book value was roughly the same as the previous year. Many analysts thought Berkshire's intrinsic value—its true value in the real world set by rational would-be buyers and sellers rather than the fearful and greedy at the edge of the market—ranged from $60,000 to $80,000. Estimates of Berkshire's intrinsic value vary from $37,000 a share (Credit Suisse First Boston) to $100,000 (Hoover Capital Management).

Berkshire shareholder David Hayden, of Rancho Palos Verdes, California, had this take on Berkshire's 1999:

"What strikes me about 1999, the worst year since the Panic of 1907, is that book value increased, even if by a small amount. That means despite miserable underwriting results, a dramatic drop in the portfolio, the effect of General Re's removal from the S&P, the pawn-shop valuations of value stocks versus pie-in-the-sky for techs, and natural disasters of biblical proportion the underlying value actually increased. Any one of these torpedoes would have been enough to sink the Bismark but Berkshire took them all and was worth more at the end of the year than the beginning. Does this justify a 49% drop in price?"

Still and all, here's what's happened at Berkshire since Buffett bought the struggling textile mill in the 1960s on the cheap. Berkshire at that time was a "used cigar butt," Buffett's term for a dramatically cheap investment with only "one puff left." Today Berkshire is one of the largest publicly traded companies in the world, as measured by standard accounting net worth. In the U.S., Berkshire is third in net worth after AT&T and Exxon Mobil.

If your grandparents didn't give you $10,000 45 years ago and tell you to invest with Buffett, well, consider getting new grandparents. Actually, don't feel too bad. Almost no one else's forebears thought of it either.

Had you invested in his Buffett Partnership—disbanded in 1969—you could have chosen to reinvest in an ongoing business called Berkshire Hathaway, which Buffett also ran.

That's a glittering return of about 20,000-fold on your money in an era when the Dow Jones Industrial Average rose about elevenfold. And the Dow Jones number is a pre-tax figure.

Before fees, a few of which existed back in the original partnership, but still after all taxes, the $10,000 would have mushroomed to $200 million if Berkshire were trading at $60,000 a share. Before all fees and taxes, that $10,000 would have blossomed to more than $250 million! That's why some have called Berkshire: "The gift that keeps hurting." If you didn't invest with Buffett early on, it's enough to make you want to lie face down in the bathtub.

One problem with the Buffett/Berkshire "Buy Low, Don't Sell" story is that it seems improbable. People are skeptical because most investors have trouble just treading water. Therefore, it's hard to relate to making millions upon millions of dollars. Billions of dollars.

It's all a little like Mark Twain's saying, "Of course truth is stranger than fiction. Fiction has to make sense."

Had you arrived late at the party and not invested in Berkshire until 1965 when Buffett took it over, a $10,000 investment then would be worth about $50 million now. Had you put $10,000 in the Standard & Poor's 500 stock index, it would be worth about $500,000 now.

Since 1965 Berkshire is up almost 5,000-fold. During that time the Dow Jones Industrial Average, emanating from the Street of Dreams, rose from roughly 1,000 to about 11,000.

When Buffett took over Berkshire in the spring of 1965, Berkshire's stock price was in the teens; the Dow at almost 1,000. In 1983 Berkshire's stock price and the Dow were both at about 1,000. In the spring of 2000 the Dow was at about 11,000. Berkshire's stock price was about $60,000.

Through his partnership and later through Berkshire, Buffett built a financial empire beyond anyone's wildest dreams. Buffett and Berkshire now own pieces of some of the world's most prominent businesses, including an 8% stake in The Coca-Cola Company.

If your investment made you a millionaire, you may wonder what it did for Buffett. Answer: It made him a billionaire many times over. Buffett, who didn't inherit any money, owns about 34.9%, and combined with his wife, about 38% of the stock of Berkshire, an investment holding company which has vast stock, bond, cash, and silver holdings as well as many operating businesses.

Because of Buffett's huge stake, in many ways Buffett is Berkshire and Berkshire is certainly the creation of Buffett. He calls Berkshire his canvas. "I feel very good about my work. When I go to my office every morning I feel like I'm going to the Sistine Chapel to paint," Buffett told *Women's Wear Daily* (October 10, 1985).

"What could be more fun? It's like an unfinished painting. If I want to paint blue or red on the canvas, I can do it. No one criticizes. Someone else may not like the painting, but I like it," Buffett has said. (*San Antonio Express-News*, March 20, 1999)

This is reminiscent of the adage: "Find a job you like and you'll never work a day in your life." William Faulkner saw it this way: "The ideal job: Landlord of a bordello! The company's good and the mornings are quiet, which is the best time to write."

Of his canvas, Buffett has said, "I hope it's an example in some ways of corporate action that people might emulate over time." (WOWT-TV in Omaha, October 14, 1993) On his canvas, Buffett draws sweeping, nearly priceless investment works of art.

Buffett is the Michelangelo of business. The businesses Berkshire owns with their "mouth-watering economics" are a big piece of the art collection. Buffett, at 70, is erecting business galleries.

Berkshire's record vies with almost anything in American business. Yet Buffett—ultra-famous in financial circles—was still largely unknown until he stepped in to save the Wall Street firm of Salomon Inc in 1991. He manages one of America's largest corporations from a small office in a nondescript building in midtown Omaha, Nebraska—roughly the geographical center of the United States— where Nebraskans themselves joke that the state has two seasons: "winter and construction."

Over the years, as Buffett has sat in the office reading and thinking, he has spawned billions of dollars in shareholder value, making multi-millionaires of dozens of early investors and ordinary millionaires of hundreds more.

Berkshire's stock trades higher than any other stock on the New York Stock Exchange and sky-high above its give-away 1965 price of $12.

So how did Buffett multiply his money roughly 20,000 times in less than half a century?

"We like simple businesses," Buffett says. That means businesses where not much change is expected and which have clear competitive advantages. Buffett invests only in a few sectors of the American economy. There's not a lot of research and development at Berkshire's businesses.

As a persistent corporate acquisitor who loves to buy and hates to sell, he usually stays away from businesses saddled with large plants, lots of fast-changing technology, and those requiring high health costs, and big pension funds and constant product changes. He's not big on employee changes either. In 35 years Berkshire has never lost a manager of any of its operating units, except to death.

Buffett has joked that nothing ever changes at Berkshire. And not much changes with him—same city, same house, same car, same food, same friends. He used the same old battered hip pocket wallet for 20 years before auctioning it off in 1999 for the benefit of a charity, Girls Incorporated of Omaha. (*Wall Street Journal*, December 1, 1999)

As Buffett said, "There's nothing special about the wallet. It goes back a long time. My suits are old, my wallet's old, my car's old. I've lived in the same house since 1958, so I hang on to things." (*Omaha World-Herald*, December 2, 1999)

How much does the owner of one of the world's greatest fortunes carry around in that wallet? "Let me see," he said, getting out his wallet and counting eight or so $100 bills. "I usually carry somewhere around $1,000," he said. (*St. Petersburg Times*, December 15, 1999)

Over the years, he has compounded invested money faster than a speeding bullet. But just how he achieved his remarkable results—through his trademark value-oriented, marathon-distance investing—is even more remarkable.

The Buffett Partnership, in 13 years, never had a down year despite some nasty bear markets. Instead, it forged a 29.5% compound annual rate of return. And Berkshire's own annual increase in stock price, more than 25% a year, has exceeded its annual return on book value of 24% (the best was a 59% return on book value in 1976).

Although in several years Berkshire's stock price has ended lower than it began, Buffett has NEVER EVER had a down year for return on stockholders' equity. In other words, Berkshire has never had a year in which it lost money. But the "Bummer of '99" was a close call as Berkshire's net worth rose only half of one percent. Only an outstanding performance by American Express saved Berkshire from a reduction in net worth.

As Buffett wrote in Berkshire's 1999 Annual Report: "We had the worst absolute performance of my tenure and, compared to the S&P, the worst relative performance as well."

But, he added, "The fallout from our weak results in 1999 was a more-than-commensurate drop in our stock price."

Berkshire's next worst years were 1973 and 1974 when it grew its book value by 4.7% and 5.5%, respectively. Although that sounds mediocre, the S&P was down 14.8% and 26.4% respectively so that Berkshire's results relative to the market were plus 19.5 percentage points in 1973 and plus 31.9 percentage points in 1974—a sensational performance since most money managers cannot beat the market. The average performance is average and with frictional costs like commissions, the average performance becomes below average. Therefore, most money managers, compared against average stock performance, bring no new value to the table, Buffett says.

Buffett rang up a 29%-to-30% return in the partnership days. It was about 29% for the partnership and about 24% for his limited partners after Buffett's slice.

All along the way he created an enterprise *of permanent value*, enormous permanent value.

Back in 1986, V. Eugene Shahan, a Columbia University Business School alumnus and portfolio manager, wrote a follow-up article to Buffett's [classic] *The Superinvestors of Graham-and-Doddsville*. In his piece titled *Are Short-Term Performance and Value Investing Mutually Exclusive?* Shahan posed this question: How appropriate is it to measure a money manager's skill on the basis of short-term performance?

He noted that, with the exception of Buffett himself, many of the people Buffett described as "Superinvestors"—undeniably skilled, undeniably successful—faced periods of short-term underperformance. In a money-management version of the tortoise and the hare, Shahan said, "It may be another of life's ironies that investors principally concerned with short-term performance may well achieve it, but at the expense of long-term results. The outstanding records of the Superinvestors of Graham-and-Doddsville [Columbia teachers Ben Graham and David Dodd] were compiled with apparent indifference to short-term performance." In today's mutual fund performance derby, he pointed out, many of the Superinvestors of Graham-and-Doddsville would have been overlooked.

The Superinvestors of Graham-and-Doddsville

	Number of years of performance	Number of years of underperformance	Underperformance as a % of all years measured
[John Meynard] Keynes	18	6	33
[Warren] Buffett	13	0	0
[Charles] Munger	14	5	36
[Bill] Ruane	27	10	37
[Lou] Simpson	17	4	24

Buffett's Berkshire was created by making a few large, staggeringly successful decisions. More than half his net worth is attributable to fewer than a dozen large investment actions. Buffett almost always buys at distressed times and bargain prices, then holds for the long term. Long term in some investment quarters means settlement date or the posting of the next quarter's earnings. Buffett instead has held on to many of his present investments for years, decades, through good times and bad, for a far sunnier day. When it comes to investing, Buffett is a marathon man still out to capture a greater piece of the world's business pie.

The investment shots he talks about making are layups. He puts money to work in places he's sure about and then holds on. "Our favorite holding period is forever," he says. That's a different attitude from such trader talk as, "I wouldn't go home long tonight" or brokerage squawk box talk such as: "If you're a long-term bull, say, 6 to 12 months..." Buffett is trying to buy companies that will be here decades from now. He's a decade trader, not a day trader.

Berkshire shareholders have largely taken Buffett's lessons to heart. Here's a chart of selected stocks showing the average holding period of freely traded shares, according to Bain & Co. data. (*Business Week*, September 13, 1999):

Company	Average Holding Period of Freely Traded Shares
PRICELINE.COM	4 DAYS
AMAZON.COM	7 DAYS
YAHOO!	8 DAYS
UAL (UNITED AIRLINES)	1.1 MONTHS
DELL	3.7 MONTHS
MICROSOFT	6.3 MONTHS
CISCO	8.5 MONTHS
GILLETTE	11.1 MONTHS
IBM	13.8 MONTHS
PFIZER	18.3 MONTHS
WAL-MART	18.5 MONTHS
MCDONALD'S	22.1 MONTHS
COCA-COLA	26.4 MONTHS
JOHNSON & JOHNSON	30.2 MONTHS
GENERAL ELECTRIC	33.1 MONTHS
BERKSHIRE HATHAWAY	180 MONTHS

Beyond the dollars Buffett has accumulated, beyond the worth of the businesses, stocks, bonds and cash Berkshire owns, there is an even greater value.

The permanent value he has created is a statement—a statement about how to do things right, how to do them ethically, sensibly, simply and inexpensively.

There is, for example, no waste.

Buffett, who would get no objection from Berkshire shareholders were he to pay himself $10 million a year, has kept his annual salary at $100,000 (no options, no bonuses) for the past 17 years, making

Buffett, left, and Berkshire Vice Chairman Charles Munger conduct Berkshire's Annual Meeting in 1999. The meeting lasts 5-10 minutes. The questions go on most of the day.

him one of the lowest-paid chief executives of a major firm and also easily the best price-to-performance money manager on the planet.

I once asked Buffett if he lived within his salary. "Most definitely not!" was the Oracle of Omaha's entire written response.

In Berkshire's 1998 Annual Report, he wrote, "And now a small hint to Berkshire's directors. Last year I spent more than nine times my salary at Borsheim's and EJA [Executive Jet]. Just think how Berkshire's business would boom if you'd only spring for a raise."

For Berkshire's Class A shareholders he's working for less than a dime a share per year and for the Class B shareholders for less than a penny a share. No mutual fund expenses or wrap fees here.

Here's the Big Picture for Berkshire shareholders: Buffett is your partner and he's working for you.

Buffett builds no monuments to himself at shareholder expense.

There is no Buffett Tower, no Buffett Plaza, Airport, Road or Zoo.

There is no touting of Berkshire shares. If anything, Buffett downplays the historic compounding of their worth and tells shareholders next year's return probably won't be as good as last year's. Buffett's style is under-promise, over-deliver.

Cosmetics are not applied by splitting the stock. To Buffett that's a meaningless exercise of valuing ten $1 dollar bills over one $10 bill. And Buffett doesn't want shareholders who don't understand that.

However, in 1996, a "do-it-yourself stock split" was declared with the creation of a Class B, or "Baby Berkshire" share which trades at about $1/30$ of the big Class A share. (see Chapter 178) There are now about 250,000 shareholders.

There is no company logo for Berkshire, unless you count the fist full of dollars emblazoned on T-shirts and caps you can buy at the annual meeting, "a truly 'closet' logo," explains shareholder Michael Assael.

Despite Berkshire's extraordinary success and even Buffett's fame, Wall Street still largely ignores Berkshire. Almost no analyst follows it (although PaineWebber's Alice Schroeder does now) and stockbrokers almost never mention it to investors. It is rarely written up as a stock to consider. In many major Blue Chip corporate lists, it's not even mentioned.

Berkshire itself makes little effort to be known. You have to discover it for yourself.

There are no photos—color or black and white—no bar charts, no graphs in the company's plain looking annual report—which is famous among its fans, but unknown to others. The annual report is the company's only real communication to the public. What it lacks in gloss, it makes up for in permanent value.

Once you have read a Berkshire Annual Report, nothing else in the business world matches it. There is little argument that the report, the bible of business and finance that includes Buffett's famous letter to shareholders, is a brilliant accounting of business.

There is humor, common sense, insight into the business world and human nature, and praise for the managers of the disparate group of businesses Berkshire owns.

Buffett's literary pyrotechnics in the report offer commentary on Berkshire's major properties, huge interests—far north of $1 billion in many cases—in some of the country's major apple pie businesses. The holdings include Coca-Cola, Gillette, American Express, Wells Fargo and Dun & Bradstreet, an extravaganza of brand names.

The reports offer a unique literary style, spiced with wit and wisdom about the human condition.

The Berkshire Annual Meeting also is unique. A happy tribe of about 10,000 to 15,000 shareholders from all over the world now make the pilgrimage to investment mecca in Omaha each spring. After Buffett dispenses with company business in five to ten minutes, he answers questions—all day.

"The meeting of Berkshire Hathaway is adjourned," he announces almost as soon as it has begun, "Any questions?" There are—usually six hours' worth.

Buffett, who is normally self-effacing and leans to an unflamboyant, low-key lifestyle most of the time, describes his principles as "simple, old and few."

He started early from scratch but was buoyed by a family of substance. In addition to starting early, he plans to stay late at his career. After all, it's the compounding of money in the later years that really counts if you want to amass wealth. If Buffett continues compounding at only half his historic rate, he could end up controlling dozens of the world's greatest companies before he stops collecting businesses.

In the early days, young crewcut Buffett operated an investment partnership from his upstairs bedroom and sun porch in his $31,500 home in Omaha, a word which in Native American means "above all others on the water."

He bought a three-story Dutch colonial home in 1958 and has never moved. Homes in his neighborhood today go for about $350,000. That's a lousy return, percentage-wise, compared to the runup in Berkshire's stock price.

Buffett's house, with a "Welcome" sign at the door, is in the Dundee section of Omaha, appropriately near Happy Hollow Boulevard in the Elmwood Park area.

Buffett lives in a "blighted" area

It's hard to believe, but he lives in a "blighted" area of Omaha. That's because a 35.822-acre area of east Omaha was declared blighted in an effort to win tax incentives for the Aksarben (Nebraska spelled backwards) property development nearby. The area includes wealthy as well as deteriorating sections.

In the early days, he sometimes kept track of intricate financial matters literally on the backs of envelopes. His was a "one-room" operation.

Buffett always has lived beneath his means.

He insists on rock-bottom operating costs, plenty of cash on hand and "little or no debt."

For example, it was not until he was in his late 20s and well on his way to being a millionaire that he splurged on a $295 IBM typewriter for the partnership.

"He was always saying he didn't need it," recalls William O'Connor, a vice president of Mutual of Omaha who had been an IBM salesman for 30 years. In his early days, O'Connor made the strenuous sale to Buffett. "It was an IBM Standard Model electric typewriter. He bought the standard model rather than the more costly executive model."

Always tight-fisted, Buffett occasionally has dipped into his fortune for such endeavors as adding rooms to his house, including a handball court.

In his garage and home entranceway, he stores cases of Cherry Coke, which he is so well known for drinking. He buys the Cokes himself—fifty 12-packs at a time, getting a good discount. Fewer trips to the store that way.

His habit helps the bottom line at Berkshire, about a tenth of a penny for every Coke he drinks.

Buffett is a beacon of simplicity and sanity—and probably a genius. Rationality and common sense, actually uncommon sense, are his guiding lights. For example, there are many reasons he bought Coca-Cola stock, but a main one is that human beings, worldwide, get thirsty, and history shows that once exposed to Coke, people continue to drink it.

His three-word job description: "I allocate capital." His verbose explanation: "My job is to figure out which businesses to invest in, with whom, and at what price."

Operating from his spartan office, Buffett is the nerve center—along with business partner Charles Munger, who operates from Los Angeles—of a financial empire whose reach and influence sprawl all across the land and beyond.

Usually Buffett invests when there is some temporary stigma or fear or misunderstanding surrounding a superb business. Such was the case when GEICO, the auto insurance firm, came dangerously near bankruptcy in the mid-1970s. He bought big, made about 40 times on his money and now owns all of GEICO.

A key tenet at Berkshire is to bet big and seldom. You work in what Buffett calls your "circle of competence." You find your edge in life and investing. When on rare occasions you're certain of that edge and you have a "fat pitch" in your "comfort zone," you swing for the bleachers.

And he needs to keep the managers of his businesses happy. Three-fourths of them are worth more than $100 million so they are financially happy already. He just needs to keep them motivated.

Holed up in the heartland of America—a locale for steaks and cornstalks, and peace and quiet—Buffett spends most of his time thinking and reading.

"We read. That's about it," says Buffett, who also says: "We like to buy wonderful businesses at reasonable prices."

Mainly Buffett buys privately owned businesses outright or stock representing pieces of publicly owned businesses.

What Buffett does not do is as important as what he does. He does no program trading (although some Berkshire investees do). He makes no fast bets on a company's upcoming quarterly earnings. He mouths no threats and will not participate in hostile takeovers. And he does not try to force things with debt, loud talk or long shots.

The secret to making money, in his view, is not to take risks, but to avoid risks. "We've done better by avoiding dragons rather than by slaying them," Buffett says.

On the question of ethics and integrity, there is no question.

Operating far from the maddening crowd of Wall Street, Buffett was, just a few years ago, named the country's richest person. *The Forbes* 400 issue of October 18, 1993, listed Buffett as the richest person in the U.S. with $8.3 billion. In 1994 Buffett came in second in *Forbes'* calculation, with $9.2 billion, behind Bill Gates' $9.35 billion.

"The only reason Gates was ahead is that they counted his house," Buffett said during a talk at the University of Nebraska in Lincoln October 10, 1994. In 1995 *Forbes* found Gates to be No. 1 again with $14.8 billion and Buffett No. 2 with $11.8 billion. But later that year Berkshire soared and Microsoft dropped so that it was about a dead heat. In recent years Microsoft has far outstripped Berkshire making both Gates and Microsoft's co-founder Paul "wired world" Allen the two richest people in the world and Buffett third.

If we take Buffett's $30 billion asset figure now, (which makes him A 30 Billion Pound Gorilla) let's consider his debts. There are none.

For years his only debt was a $70,000 mortgage which he has paid off. The mortgage was on a three bedroom, two-bath second home he bought in 1971 in Laguna Beach, California, at Emerald Bay, overlooking the Pacific Ocean, where he goes at Christmas. He bought the home, now enlarged, for $150,000 when the assessed value was $185,000.

Buffett's assets-to-debt ratio clearly qualifies as one of the most important concepts he wants in an investment: "Margin of Safety."

Speaking to Salomon Inc's clients on September 13, 1991, about his distaste for debt, Buffett said, "You're looking at a fellow who owes $70,000 on a second home in Laguna and I've got that because of the low rate...and that's all I've owed for I don't know how many years." [Buffett now owns another home right behind the old one in Laguna to meet the needs of an ever-growing family. Warren Buffett: real estate mogul.]

(John Steinback wrote *Tortilla Flat* in Laguna Beach and Bette

Davis lived there in the 1940s. The area is known for its Mediterranean climate and artsy atmosphere.)

At an R.C. Willey store opening near Boise, Idaho, September 29, 1999 Buffett told a group of people: "I have never sold a house. I live in one that I have owned for 41 years, bought four others but have never sold one," according to Berkshire shareholder Lonnie Johnson of Meridian, Idaho. Buffett owns one house in Omaha, two in Laguna Beach, California and two units in San Francisco.

"If you're smart, you don't need debt. If you're dumb, it's poisonous," he said.

Actually Berkshire's aversion in some sense is overstated. He's happy to borrow money at very low rates or at no rate at all. Indeed Berkshire's insurance operation "borrows" billions of dollars from insurance policy holders and invests much of that money in stocks.

Indeed Berkshire's real secret is that it's a giant sucking margin account where the best investor in the world is buying stocks on margin that is interest free.

In addition to insurance "float" and deferred taxes which might never be paid, Berkshire has a colossal interest-free loan in its hands. It's a rough guess, but it may be that Berkshire's return would be about 15% instead of 24% without the magic of interest-free leverage.

Thus Buffett has a multiplier effect on his investment results while playing it safe.

Samuel Butler once wrote, "All progress is based upon a universal innate desire on the part of every organism to live beyond its income." Buffett is the exception to the rule.

In the late 1980s the Ivan Boeskys and Michael Milkens of the world, using inside information, lots of debt, threats and fraudulent schemes, ultimately ran afoul of securities laws. Buffett's friend, Michael Yanney, chairman of America First Capital Associates in Omaha, refers to that era as a time when "greed on Wall Street exceeded its intellect."

What was Buffett doing in that era of frenzy? He was running businesses such as *World Book* encyclopedias, See's Candies and *The Buffalo News*, and buying Coca-Cola stock, investments he still has. Buffett's general idea is not so much buy-and-hold as it is buy-and-die.

Beyond his wealth, Buffett is the most influential investment mind and voice in the land.

He has two concrete rules for all who seek riches:

Rule No. 1. Never lose money.
Rule No. 2. Never forget Rule No. 1.
One Berkshire fan has posed a new set of rules:
Rule No. 1. Don't sell your Berkshire.
Rule No. 2. Don't forget Rule No. 1.
With an appearance and manner slightly reminiscent of Jack Benny, Buffett remains modest and dryly witty, with knee-slappers whizzing by at 90 miles per hour. Once a Berkshire shareholder, knowing of Buffett's love for bridge, sent him an Omar Sharif bridge tape. He thanked the shareholder in a note saying, "If I listen to it long enough, will I be as handsome as Omar Sharif?"

Another time, before he was to talk to University of Nebraska students he was asked, "Do you want extra security here?" His reply: "We don't need any security; just ask the attendees to check any soft fruit at the door."

In describing Berkshire's acquisition policy, he once told shareholders, "It's very scientific. We just sit around and wait for the phone to ring. Sometimes it's a wrong number."

He lives an extraordinarily independent, stirringly original life. More than 99% of the monetary proceeds and 100% of the human proceeds of his life are to be "returned to society."

There may be a stunning denouement. It's not yet spelled out, but expect a rousing finale when it comes to the eventual use of his fortune.

Buffett has said: "I want my trustees to swing for the fences on a few projects that do not have natural funding constituencies, but that are important to society. I tell them that if they start giving half a million to this hospital and half a million to that college, I will come back and haunt them. But if they spend a ton of money on something and it flops, God bless them." (*Financial Times*, May 17, 1999)

Buffett's Triple-A reputation, built block by block and stock by stock through value investing, has risen to the upper silvery firmament of mythological heroes.

When Buffett, the avatar of modern investing, wings off to money heaven, he has promised to keep in touch with us. He once told author Adam Smith, "I see myself running Berkshire as long as I live and working on seances afterward."

The mystique of Warren Buffett is so out of this world he just may do that.

Buffett was named one of the world's most powerful people by *Vanity Fair* magazine (November, 1997) which says, "His biggest job has become managing his own impact."

Fortune in a survey in 2000 found Berkshire to be the seventh most admired company in the U.S. after General Electric, Microsoft, Dell, Cisco, Wal-Mart and Southwest Airlines.

In 1999 Buffett was named the top money manager of the 20th century, according to a nationwide survey of 300 investment professionals. (*Omaha World-Herald*, November 23, 1999)

David Braverman, senior investment strategy officer for Standard & Poor's Equity Services, has said: "Berkshire Hathaway is the investing success story of the 20th century."

For all his splendid long record—even with the surprising setbacks of the past couple of years—Buffett serves as the business muse of the world.

2
GENERAL RE—A WATERSHED EVENT AND A YEAR FROM HELL

"The welfare and prosperity of a modern developed national economy depends heavily upon the strength and quality of the insurance business serving that economy."—Eric Maynard, author of unpublished A History of General Reinsurance Corporation

Berkshire announced on June 19, 1998 it planned to buy Stamford, Connecticut-based General Re Corp., the largest U.S. reinsurance company and one of the largest in the world.

Reinsurance companies insure other insurance companies, not the sort of thing the young and restless aspire to.

Berkshire offered a 29% premium to General Re's closing price that day of $220.25 a share. The deal paid for in Berkshire stock did not close until December 21, 1998 after a ruling by the IRS that the merger was tax-free.

Judging by Berkshire's sharp stock price decline after the acquisition was known, many General Re shareholders chose not to become Berkshire shareholders. Berkshire is not everyone's cup of tea.

(AP/Wide World Photos)

Berkshire's CEO Warren Buffett, right, and General Re's CEO Ron Ferguson announced on June 19, 1998 in New York that Berkshire would buy General Re for about $22 billion in Berkshire stock.

Berkshire's stock slide wasn't all the fault of General Re's poor performance in a down cycle for the insurance industry. Coke and Gillette, big Berkshire stock holdings which shortly after Buffett had called "Inevitables," took a dive as their foreign sales slumped. And Disney, Wells Fargo, Freddie Mac and Wesco stocks all dropped in mid-1999.

Based on prices at the time of the deal's announcement, General Re's shareholders could have expected about $276.50 per General Re share or a total of about $22 billion. But because the Berkshire—General Re interlinked stock package declined in the six months prior to the closing, General Re shareholders received $204.40 a share or about $16 billion in Berkshire stock, or about 16 times 1998 operating earnings.

Buffett said: "The merger will bring more than $80,000 of investments to Berkshire for each Class A or Class A-equivalent share issued. That's beneficial, being nearly double the existing level, or put another way, the merger brought more than $24 billion of additional investments to Berkshire." General Re owned roughly $19 billion in bonds and about $5 billion in stocks and it had about $15 billion in "float" (premiums paid by clients but not yet paid out for claims).

The amazing deal boosted Berkshire's assets by about 65% while increasing the number of Berkshire shares only by about 22%.

Buffett talked of synergies which he rarely does. He said the merger would remove constraints on earnings volatility at General Re which in the past had forced General Re to hand off some of the business it wrote to other companies. Now wide swings in earnings could be better absorbed by the financially stronger, combined Berkshire-General Re entity. General Re, a Triple-A credit rated company, could develop its global business at whatever pace it saw fit. Also, General Re gained tax flexibility because of the reliability of Berkshire's future large and diverse streams of taxable income. Lastly, Berkshire's huge capital allowed all its insurance units—including General Re—to operate unfettered by worries about a sharp market decline. "These synergies will be coupled with General Re's pristine worldwide reputation, long-standing client relationships and powerful underwriting, risk management and distribution capabilities. This combination virtually assures both Berkshire and General Re shareholders that they will have a better future than if the two companies operated separately," Buffett said.

At a press conference, Buffett said: "We're creating Fort Knox here."

Ron Ferguson, General Re's CEO, was to join Berkshire's board, but then did not at his own request. "Ron notified me he deferred his decision to be on the board," Buffett said at Berkshire's annual meeting in 1999. Buffett explained that serving on a board can be restricting when it comes to matters of stock purchases, compensation packages and taxes. "The invitation to him to be on the board is 100% open to Ron at any time."

There were signs, however, that General Re's management was unsettled by the Berkshire purchase: "Ferguson outraged many of his colleagues by keeping his negotiations secret from but one of them [on the six person office of chairman] until just before the deal was announced.

"Ferguson might have anticipated opposition, in part because of Buffett's well-advocated opposition to the use of stock options as an executive incentive. James Gustafson, General Reinsurance's president and chief operating officer, promptly resigned, and sources say that a number of other senior executives aspire now to nothing more than retirement." (*BusinessWeek*, March 20, 2000)

Here's a letter Gustafson sent *Business Week* (April 17, 2000):

"I read with interest Anthony Bianco's commentary. 'The Sage Has Some Explaining to Do' in the March 20 edition.

"Mr. Bianco made no attempt to contact me but that didn't prevent him from guessing about why I left General Reinsurance. For the record from the moment I learned of Berkshire Hathaway's interest in General Re, I have believed that the combination is a perfect one. And I didn't promptly resign as President and COO because of 'Buffett's well-advertised opposition to stock options.' In fact, I spent seven months following the announcement of the acquisition from June 1998 to February 1999 traveling to Gen Re offices around the world assuring the company's management team, employees and customers that the acquisition was right for them. I resigned for the opportunity to help lead The St. Paul Companies, one of the leading primary commercial insurers in the world. But even when the opportunity presented itself it was still a very hard decision to leave Gen Re, a great company in every respect, after 30 years."

General Re traces its descent from Norwegian Globe Insurance Company, of Christiana, Norway. Norwegian Globe was established in 1911 and began business in New York City in 1917.

In 1921 Duncan Reid founded General Casualty Reinsurance Corp. of New York. In 1945 the Mellon family combined its Mellon Indemnity and the company took over operations, gaining a near

General Re headquarters at the Financial Centre in Stamford, Connecticut. Buffett bought two companies in 1998—General Re and Executive Jet without ever seeing the home office of either. "I've never been to the home office...I hope they have one." (Miami Herald, December 27, 1998, quoting a talk by Buffett to University of Florida business students.)

monopoly in the U.S. reinsurance market. The company bought out its largest competitor, National Re, in 1996 and opened an office in China a year later.

The company, which earned about $1 billion a year before merging into Berkshire, engages in global reinsurance often writing coverage for protection of ships and airplanes. In addition to writing all lines of property/casualty reinsurance directly from primary insurers, General Re's 3,800 employees also provide actuarial, claims, underwriting, financial and investment management services in more than 100 countries. It owns General Reinsurance Corp. and National Reinsurance Corp., the largest property and casualty reinsurance group in the U.S.

General Re writes insurance through its General Star Management Company and offers protection for executives of publicly traded firms through comprehensive coverage, claims attorneys and securities litigation loss services through Genesis Underwriting Management Company. General Re offers reinsurance brokerage services through Herbert Clough, manages aviation insurance risks through United States Aviation Underwriters and acts as a business development consultant and reinsurance intermediary through Ardent Risk Services.

The company also operates as a dealer in the interest rate swap and derivatives market which banks, insurers and other companies use to hedge their exposure to risk—through General Re Financial Products Corp. (GRFP) and offers investment services to the insurance industry.

However, GRFP may be liquidating derivative positions or selling the derivatives unit, according to a *Bridge News* story (January 31, 2000) citing sources familiar with the company. The story quoted a sources as saying, "Buffett had instructed his lieutenants at General Re to get out of derivatives because he 'hates' them." The story said Buffett doesn't like investing in products he doesn't understand. It's not that Buffett hates derivatives because he doesn't understand them; he hates them because he *does* understand them. General Re said on February 2, 2000 it was weighing "strategic alternatives" for its financial products business. But in the end General Re decided not to sell GRFP. After a sale brokered by Goldman Sachs collapsed.

General Re is one of only five nongovernmental U.S.-based financial institutions with a Triple-A senior debt rating from Standard & Poor's. About 70% of its shareholders were institutional investors such as mutual funds, insurance companies and pension funds. It also owns a controlling interest—about 88%—of Cologne Re, of Cologne, Germany, a major international reinsurer.

Cologne Re, formed in 1846, is the oldest reinsurance firm in the world and does business around the world from 37 locations. It was acquired by General Re in 1994. Cologne Re, in turn, owns a 27% stake in Gothaer Re, a small reinsurance firm based in Germany.

Hurricane Georges, which hit the Caribbean and U.S. killing 4,000 people, as well as ice storms in the U.S. and Canada and several large fires at German factories caused Cologne Re to report a $33 million loss in 1998, compared with a strong gain in 1997.

Back in 1988 General Re had part of the risk for Pan Am Flight 103, the airliner destroyed by a bomb over Lockerbie, Scotland.

In more recent years it has suffered losses from fires at the Brussels Airport and flooding along the Oder, affecting mainly Polish and Czech clients. And it was the lead insurer of such high-profile disasters as the 1996 crash of Trans World Airlines Flight 800.

In 1999 General Re had $1.25 in claims for every $1 in premium. General Re was hit by a record-breaking hailstorm in Sydney, Australia and other disasters in a year filled with natural catastrophe losses, including earthquakes in Taiwan and Turkey and storms in Europe.

A storm the day after Christmas, 1999, ravaged France wreaking havoc on the famed gardens of Versailles. "Winds reaching 100 mph uprooted 10,000 of the 250,000 trees on this 2,000-acre estate. About 80% of Versailles' rare tree specimens, some more than two centuries old and therefore fragile, were lost...

"The winds that devastated Versailles took out 7%, or 300 million of France's 8 billion trees and damaged three-fourths of the country's parks and forests." (*Business Week*, April 24, 2000)

General Re was the risk-bearer on the largest house fire in history, a home in Westchester County, in Bedford, New York, about 50 miles north of New York City, formerly owned by music industry executive Tommy Mottola and songbird Mariah Carey. The house burned to the ground and General Re suffered a $20 million loss. The buyer of the home was neighbor Nelson Peltz, chief executive of Triarc Cos. which runs Arby's, Snapple and Royal Crown Cola.

(Photo courtesy of The Journal News/Frank Becerra, Jr.)

This mansion, which belonged to pop singer Mariah Carey, burned to the ground in 1999 when it was being remodeled by the new owner, Nelson Peltz. General Re was the risk-bearer and took a $20 million hit. The gutted home served as a symbol of the bad year for General Re and Berkshire, underscoring one of humanity's age old problems: anything can happen.

To rub more salt in the wounds, losses also included $100 million from insuring box-office sales for a series of five films that turned out to be flops, including Barbra Streisand's "The Mirror Has Two Faces."

PaineWebber analyst Alice Schroeder said: "The insurer is betting that it knows more about what revenues from a Hollywood film are likely to be than the firm's producer and the bank financing the deal."

In a surprise setback, Cologne Re said in 1998 it was setting aside $275 million to cover potential losses in workers' compensation reinsurance in the U.S. through an involvement with an ill-fated insurance pool called Unicover now known as Cragwood Managers. Many other insurance companies involved in the Unicover loss estimated at $1 billion, have not reported potential losses on their part. Many lawsuits were filed against Unicover. The losses were incurred by General Re's U.S. subsidiary, Cologne Life Reinsurance Co.

Here's what happened, according to *Forbes* (January 10, 2000): Unicover Managers, an insurance middleman in South Plainview, New Jersey, wrote workers' compensation coverage passing along most of the risk to insurers and reinsurers.

Unicover's John Pallat and his brokers got a triumvirate of companies—Cologne Life Re, a subsidiary of General Re (now part of Berkshire Hathaway), Phoenix Home Life and Sun Life—to take on most of the expense under the policies. Incredibly, these three reinsurers took on portions of the premium at a ratio of 40%. This meant they were taking on $4 of loss and expenses for every $1 of premium. They underestimated the future payouts.

"But the trash-passing did not stop here. It went on and on, with some brokers entering the equation in more than one place and with some insurers at a remove of several layers from where the insurance originated.

"The daisy chain began to break in late 1998. Sun began hearing rumors about huge volumes of reinsurance. It belatedly realized it was exposed to significant losses, later pegged at up to $910 million.

"In early 1999 both Sun and Phoenix withdrew from Unicover, refusing to accept any more business. They returned the premiums and refused to pay claims. Cologne also refused to accept more business, but continued to pay...

"It appears that Warren Buffett was completely unaware of this workers' comp exposure when he had Berkshire Hathaway buy General Re in 1998..." the *Forbes* story said.

Buffett said at Berkshire's annual meeting in 1999 that it will be years before all the litigation surrounding the issue is sorted out. He said $275 million was the best guess of what the problem will amount to, that it could wind up higher or lower. At the end of 1999 Berkshire kept the $275 million figure unchanged. Such problems are distracting and do involve some mix of mistakes and misinformation, he added. Further, General Re's earnings in 1999 came in at sub-par levels.

Also Buffett immediately put in a cash bonus plan to replace General Re's stock-option plan at a cost of $63 million. Buffett said, "Formerly what counted for these managers was General Re's stock price, now their payoff will come from the business performance they deliver."

The purchase of General Re, in one move, reduced Berkshire's exposure to fluctuations in the stock market on a percentage basis, since General Re has such a large portfolio of fixed-income securities, including a large amount in municipal bonds. Berkshire gained enormous liquidity and General Re won the ability to write far more business. For example, in 1997, General Re laid off $1 billion in business to others, including Berkshire, for a lack of resources. "The biggest advantage [of the deal] is probably the chance to maximize [Gen Re's] investment portfolio," Buffett said. (*Business Week*, July 6, 1998)

With the close of the deal in late 1998, Berkshire had the highest shareholders' equity of all U.S. companies and the second in the world to Royal Dutch. However, a subsequent merger of Exxon and Mobil made that combination the largest in net worth.

The purchase was Berkshire's watershed event in all its fabled history since its early days as a struggling textile mill.

At General Re's meeting September 18, 1998, to vote on the deal, Ferguson said General Re first approached Berkshire about a joint venture, then later Buffett suggested a full combining of the companies. Ferguson said, "The best reinsurance underwriter [is joining] the best investor." And he talked of "strategic homeruns."

At the Berkshire special meeting September 16, 1998, Buffett said he wanted the combined Berkshire-General Re enterprise to become the "premier reservoir of financial strength in the insurance industry for time immemorial."

ЯЯЯЯЯЯЯЯЯЯЯЯЯЯЯЯЯЯЯЯЯЯЯЯЯ

John Steggles, the former president of General Re subsidiary Herbert Clough, recalls how Buffett and Ferguson met in 1985:

"GEICO under [Jack] Byrne's direction was now thriving and Warren had become the biggest individual stockholder—he was also getting more involved in reinsurance deals—General Re was heavily involved with GEICO and Jack Byrne and I thought it would be beneficial all around if Warren Buffett and the General Re Chairman knew one another—so I arranged a private room dinner at my New

York Club—The Metropolitan Club—(1 East 60th Street). I invited Frank Munson, Jack Byrne, Warren Buffett and Frank who was then Chairman of General Re who brought Ron Ferguson who I think was then President and Director. The date was early February 1985. Warren arrived considerably late."

It turned out Buffett had been meeting with 20 or so people including Leonard Goldenson, the head of ABC-TV, on negotiations for Cap Cities to buy ABC-TV. The negotiations got sticky but were resolved. So Buffett was late to the General Re dinner.

"The gestation period for Berkshire/General Re has been long but both have prepared exceptionally well for this great birthing. They are both very strong and great parents—both unique in their blood-lines and growth...," Steggles said.

(Photo by Celia Sullivan)

John Steggles

Steggles, a Berkshire shareholder today via the General Re acquisition, recalls that he looked at Berkshire in 1976 when it was trading at about $40 a share. He shakes his head at the conclusion he drew after reading Berkshire's 1976 Annual Report: "Bunch of cats and dogs. It'll never make any money."

🐾🐾🐾🐾🐾🐾🐾🐾🐾🐾🐾🐾🐾🐾🐾🐾🐾🐾🐾🐾🐾

General Re announced on November 3, 1998 it had agreed to buy U.K.-based insurer DP Mann Holdings, giving the largest U.S. reinsurer a presence in London's big insurance market.

The company, founded by David Mann in 1984, had 1998 premiums of about $390 million. DP Mann has been profitable every year since it was founded. It was one of the last remaining managing agents at Lloyd's of London.

DP Mann and General Re had working relationships for 14 years prior to the buyout. Discussions between General Re and DP Mann pre-dated the Berkshire discussions, according to IBNR *Insurance Weekly* (November 8, 1998). Mr. Mann was quoted as saying: "This deal is about giving us the strength that comes from being part of a major international insurance group." In short DP Mann is General Re's man in London.

The buyout of DP Mann for an estimated $125 million to $165 million gave General Re a larger presence in London, the world's third largest reinsurance market.

General Re claims more than 1,000 clients, most of whom have been with the company for years.

At Berkshire's special meeting September 16, 1998, Buffett said, "We should be number one by a significant margin in the world reinsurance market in ten to fifteen years."

Buffett sold almost all of General Re's stock position, reportedly $3.7 billion after taxes, about the time Berkshire and General Re merged.

In Berkshire's 1998 Annual Report, he wrote: "Once we knew that the General Re merger would definitely take place, we asked the company to dispose of the equities that it held. (As mentioned earlier, we do not manage the Cologne Re portfolio, which includes many equities.) General Re subsequently eliminated its positions in about 250 common stocks, incurring $935 million of taxes in the process. This 'clean sweep' approach reflects a basic principle that Charlie and I employ in business and investing. We don't back into any decisions."

A 150-person investment unit was the only cutback made at the time of the General Re merger. The work of the group was assumed by one person. Who? You get only one guess.

As the financial services industry continues to consolidate in the years ahead, no doubt Berkshire will capture an ever-increasing piece of the global financial action.

In the early 1980s, there were 130 reinsurance companies in the U.S. Today there are only 28. General Re had been the largest U.S. reinsurance company but in 1999 it fell behind Employers Re, a subsidiary of General Electric.

Although General Re got off to a slow start in 1999, it began expanding in Europe and around the world. And with the explosive growth of Berkshire's GEICO auto insurance business and the solid performance of its own insurance operations, Berkshire stands today as an insurance empire.

General Re's Ron Ferguson suffered a subarachnoid hemorrhage outside the brain on November 19, 1999. He recovered.

More than one Berkshire shareholder hurriedly read the original news release as: Berkshire Hathaway Chief recuperating from a hemorrhage whereas the headline really had been about a Berkshire Hathaway unit chief.

General Re and Cologne Re on June 1, 2000 united under the name General/Cologne Re.

Eric Maynard in his *A History of General Reinsurance Corporation* gives an example of the best face of insurance:

Insurance at its Best

The year 1957 saw the inauguration of a rehabilitation advisory service under the direction of Justin A. Harris, who joined the company after many years of experience in the rehabilitation of persons injured in industrial accidents. This service was to be available to all clients. As the annual report stated, the purpose was to help "injured claimants find a road back to a useful and self-supporting life after disabling injuries."

The claim files of the insurance business have always contained a distressingly high number of cases involving disabling injuries. Institutions and the people concerned with the treatment of such cases are invariably overburdened. In addition to taking care of their patients they must also attempt to keep abreast of the latest knowledge and techniques developed elsewhere. For a number of reasons, a person suffering from a disabling injury does not always reach the care of an institution and the people most able to deal with the type of injury involved. And even after doctors and therapists have exercised their highest skills, application of a continuing interest and quite different skills may enable a disabled person to return home to family rather than remaining in an institution.

Reviewing the claim records of General Re and its clients, and applying his own specialized knowledge, Justin Harris brought a new dimension to this aspect of the company's activities. Disabled people were brought in touch with doctors and other professionals possessing an expertise in dealing with the type of disability involved. With the cooperation and support of the client companies, other steps were taken, ranging from remodeling homes and supplying specialized equipment designed for use by handicapped people to the training of family members to provide necessary nursing services.

In a typical case, a disabled man and his family were resigned to his spending the rest of his life in an institution, the cost to be borne by the insurance company concerned and by General Re. Justin Harris discovered that a small general store was for sale on the main street of the small town where the family lived. He arranged for the purchase of the store, the remodeling of the attached living quarters, and the training of the wife to provide the nursing services required by her disabled husband, who could then return to live with his family. Operation of the business by the family, supplemented by continuing but reduced expenditures by the insurance company, provided a livelihood. The disabled individual and the reunited family could then look forward to a more dignified and rewarding future.

A combination of knowledge, resources, and imagination can be a powerful force. Over the years, the rehabilitation service has produced economic savings for General Re and its clients, which have translated into an enhanced quality of life for many disabled individuals and their families.

3
"WHO'S WARREN BUFFETT?"

Before Travelers bought Salomon in 1997, making Berkshire a major shareholder in the combined financial services giant before Berkshire sold its stake, Buffett had spent a tumultuous decade as a major investor in Salomon.

Perhaps his worst moment as a Salomon shareholder came at 6:45 a.m., August 16, 1991, when the phone rang at Buffett's home, waking him up. It was some of Salomon's top officers telling him they planned to resign.

That afternoon news wires were crackling with word of a scandal at Salomon.

"S&P puts Salomon ratings on creditwatch: Negative," flashed one.

A few minutes later came another: "Salomon stock, bonds plunge on spreading scandal news."

"Salomon says Gutfreund, Strauss prepare to resign," flashed another.

At the same minute as the previous bulletin—at 2:27 p.m., as Salomon's world was crashing—yet another bulletin flashed: "Salomon says Buffett to become interim chairman."

Buffett was, of course, Warren Buffett—the multi-billionaire from Omaha, the world's greatest investor.

Throughout his life, people have asked, "Who's Warren Buffett?" A follow-up question sometimes is, "Where's Omaha?" Omaha, shareholders know, is in the state of Berkshire.

With time, Buffett has become better known, but the story is still not out fully. Here's an inquiry from a reporter in late 1995: "Is he American?"

When Buffett was inducted into the Nebraska Business Hall of Fame February 8, 1996, the program featured an irreverent 7-minute video about Buffett narrated by celebrity interviewer Robin Leach.

Leach: "Excuse me, sir, do you know who Warren Buffett is?" Unidentified man: "Yeah, he's that guy who'll paint any car for $99.95."

Despite his private ways, Buffett became vastly famous to an ever growing cadre of investors. He remained largely unrecognized by the rest of the world because of his down-home lifestyle and avoidance of interviews.

It was the bond trading scandal at Salomon—the giant securities firm in which Buffett was holding a $700 million investment—that finally thrust him into the limelight.

In short order authorities wanted 12 sets of fingerprints from Buffett to meet a variety of securities business rules.

"There was also a rule that because I was an officer of a securities firm I had to take the Series 7 exam [for stockbrokers]. I kept delaying it until I left because I wasn't sure I could pass it," Buffett once said.

The scandal at Salomon, caused by illegal trading activities and failure to report them, forced the firm to turn to Buffett. It had no other choice. Buffett was the one person the firm, its clients, the U.S. Government, regulators, investigators and investors all around the world could trust to set Salomon straight. And Buffett already was sitting on the Salomon board.

Who was Warren Buffett, this modest, mild-mannered, tough-minded Midwesterner chosen to save Salomon?

Brilliant graduates of Harvard, Columbia and Stanford, in unsolicited remarks, have used the word "genius" to describe this semi-eccentric, financial wizard.

Buffett's longtime counterpart, Berkshire Vice Chairman Charles Munger—no dim bulb himself—indeed a magna cum laude graduate of Harvard Law School, has said, "There were a thousand people in my Harvard law class. I knew all the top students. There was no one as able as Warren."

Salomon spokesman Robert Baker, who spoke with Buffett often during the Salomon bond scandal crisis said, "He's everything as advertised and more. Everytime I told him something he was waiting at the end of the sentence for me...and his moral compass is due North."

Rich. Smart. Honest? The people who know Buffett best, his children, say he's the most honest person they've ever known.

Within hours of being called upon to serve as Salomon's chairman, Buffett saddled up his corporate jet. It's one of the few expensive worldly trappings the multi-billionaire allows himself.

The airplane he'd dubbed *The Indefensible*—later redubbed *The Indispensable*—(and now Executive Jet) flew from Omaha to Teterboro, New Jersey. From there the billionaire made his way to Seven World Trade Center, Salomon's then one million square foot headquarters in New York City.

As the crisis unfolded, Salomon's own stock plummeted with revelations that the firm's traders bought up more than the legal limit of bonds at Treasury auctions. Salomon's problems were compounded because top management knew about the bond trading violations for months but had failed to report them. This coverup turned the matter into a full-blown scandal, one so intense some thought it capable of bringing down mighty Salomon.

This was the second time, not the first, that Buffett rescued Salomon.

In 1987 when corporate raider Revlon Chairman Ronald Perelman—backed with financing from junk bond king Michael Milken—was threatening a takeover of Salomon, Buffett quickly stepped in with $700 million in cash to halt the Perelman-Milken takeover.

Buffett made his Salomon investment for Berkshire three weeks before the October 19, 1987, stock market crash. The crash itself created deadly air pockets for Salomon and its Wall Street counterparts. Buffett faced no less rocky turbulence in his second effort to save Salomon, this time from a seemingly incomprehensible trading mess that seemed likely to cause the failure of a big engine of Wall Street.

As he prepared to take Salomon's top position, amidst client defections, Buffett met immediately with the managing directors and told them point-blank that Salomon's reputation was on the line. Staying just within the bounds of the rules, Buffett warned, would NOT be acceptable—Salomon's very future depended upon the firm's reputation. No reputation. No Salomon. Indeed, no jobs.

Buffett told Salomon's managers that the firm faced a huge management job in facing fines and litigation, that he would name a new chief operating officer and that—following an emergency board meeting Sunday, August 18, 1991, he would hold a press conference. That was newsworthy because Buffett rarely holds press conferences or grants interviews.

The Salomon executives were so impressed with Buffett's straightforward approach, they burst into applause.

Buffett began preparations for Sunday's dramatic board meeting where he accepted the resignations of Salomon's top executives: John Gutfreund, the chairman once described as "King of Wall Street;" Thomas Strauss, president; and John Meriwether, Salomon Brothers vice chairman—key men who admitted knowing of the violations but who failed to report them.

It would be only hours before the names of the top managers

implicated in the scandal were removed from the glass encased directory on the main floor of the headquarters building. One new name was inserted: Warren E. Buffett.

In combating the scandal, Buffett also fired two men in the bond trading department and later would fire Salomon's law firm, name a new chief operating officer and put into place tighter internal controls.

In the midst of this chaos, Buffett convinced U.S. Treasury Secretary Nicholas Brady to reverse a major portion of a potentially crippling, five-hour-old ban on Salomon's highly profitable government securities trading.

This allowed Salomon to continue bidding at government bond auctions for its own account, even though it was still banned from placing orders for customers. In the process of handling the crisis, Buffett drew Brady's warm praise.

Buffett, already ensconced in Gutfreund's 43rd floor office with a new phone line, next went out to meet the press. He won them over in a split second by saying, "I will attempt to answer questions in the manner of a fellow who has never met a lawyer. We'll stay as long as you wish."

In the next three hours he took a tell-all approach, saying, "It looks to me, like in the case of the two people we fired, there were things done you and I would characterize as a coverup."

In his inimitable homespun style, Buffett described the Salomon atmosphere as "what some people might call macho and others cavalier."

"I don't think the same things would have happened in a monastery," he added.

He was asked if he had read *Liar's Poker*, the book about Salomon's rough-and-tumble corporate culture. Buffett said he had. Well?

"I just don't want there to be a second edition," he replied.

The next day Buffett went to Washington to meet with regulators and to continue his fast-paced mission to save Salomon.

About a week later he was giving the Salomon sales force a 15-minute pep talk beamed to Salomon offices around the world. "I don't want anyone playing close to the lines...," he counseled. "You can do very well hitting down the middle of the court."

Later he added, "If you lose money for the firm by bad decisions, I will be very understanding. If you lose reputation for the firm, I will be ruthless."

Buffett had to form fast judgments about how best to keep clients, how to keep employee defections down, how to reassure Salomon's creditors and the government. He decided to sell some $40 billion of Salomon's securities to finance the firm's operations, keeping it competitive at a very dangerous time.

The government seemed reassured by Buffett's leadership at the firm. Investors and clients breathed a sigh of relief and Salomon's stock, which had lost about one-third of its value during the ordeal, steadied, then rallied.

For Buffett, who far prefers his quiet existence in Omaha, it was an action-packed time of racing from Omaha to New York and Washington and living out of a suitcase.

Asked if such a hectic pace were a problem, Buffett quipped, "My mother's sewn my name in the underwear, so it's all okay."

4
ROOTS
POLITICS, COMMERCE, AND MEDIA

Buffett was born on August 30, 1930, on a hot, humid day in Omaha, just blocks from where he now runs Berkshire. There's no report that money fell from trees that day. It was, after all, the midst of the Depression. The healthy baby arrived at the old Doctors Hospital in downtown Omaha into a family prominent for six generations in the city's political and commercial endeavors.

The first Buffett to reach Nebraska, Buffett's great-grandfather Sidney H. Buffett from Dix Hills on Long Island, New York, opened a grocery store on Omaha's Fourteenth Street on August 20, 1869. In the store's early days, the delivery wagon was mule drawn and the mules were kept in a stable behind the store.

In a story in the *Omaha World-Herald* (August 17, 1998) about the preservation of old documents, one document was a claim filed against an estate for $7.50 for groceries, including chicken, eggs, oranges, lemons and oil bought from the S.H. Buffett store at 486 Fourteenth Street. The store was described as a dealer in "foreign and domestic fruits, groceries, and confectionery."

Ernest Buffett, Sidney Buffett's son, joined his father in working at the store February 1, 1894. The store was moved to Omaha's Dundee section in 1915. Ernest Buffett's son, Fred, joined his father in the business at 5015 Underwood on June 1, 1929.

The *Dundee News* ran an ad for the Buffett & Son grocery store on June 16, 1950, with photos of Sidney, Ernest and Fred Buffett under the headline, "81 years of selling foods in Omaha." All the Buffetts were known as upright citizens.

Warren's father edited the *Daily Nebraskan* at the University of Nebraska, where he met Warren's mother, Leila, in 1924 when she came calling for a job to earn money for college.

She had set type in her family's printshop and was a reporter for her father's weekly newspaper, the *Cuming County Democrat*, in West Point, Nebraska.

Her father had bought that newspaper in 1905 and his family lived on a top level of the newspaper building.

Warren Buffett is the grandson of Ernest Buffett and the son of Howard Homan Buffett, who was a rock-ribbed Republican U.S.

Congressman. In addition to Howard and Fred, Ernest Buffett had an older son Clarence, who was killed in an auto wreck in Texas in 1937, and a daughter, Alice Buffett, who never married and was a revered schoolteacher for years at both Benson High School and Central High School in Omaha. Warren Buffett, through his Buffett Foundation, gives an award of $10,000 each to 15 teachers every year in her honor.

The money has no strings attached. As Buffett told NBC News Anchor Tom Brokaw for a segment about education which aired April 12, 1994, the teacher can blow it all in Las Vegas.

Warren's father, Howard H. Buffett, was a stockbroker who founded Buffett-Falk & Company in 1931. He also sold diamonds to clients who wanted an inflation hedge.

Howard Buffett, an isolationist opposed to Roosevelt's New Deal and to the war, served in Congress from 1942 to 1948 and from 1950 to 1952. He was known as a forceful writer and astute observer of politics and commerce who called things as he saw them. Howard Buffett died April 29, 1964, of cancer at age 60.

In a May 6, 1948, article in the *Commercial and Financial Chronicle*, when gold was illegal to own, Howard Buffett wrote:

"I warn you that politicians of both parties will oppose the restoration of gold, although they may outwardly seem to favor it. Also, those elements here and abroad who are getting rich from the continued American inflation will oppose a return to sound money. You must be prepared to meet their opposition intelligently and vigorously.

"But unless you are willing to surrender your children and your country to galloping inflation, war and slavery, then this cause demands your support. For if human liberty is to survive in America, we must win the battle to restore a return to sound money. There is no more important challenge facing us than this issue—the restoration of your freedom to secure gold in exchange for the fruits of your labor."

In a speech to a group of Omaha businessmen in 1948, Congressman Buffett said: "In a free country, the monetary unit rests upon a fixed foundation of gold or silver independent of the ruling politicians [and is] redeemable for a certain weight of gold, at the free option and choice of the holder of paper money. Our finances will never be brought to order until Congress is compelled to do so. Making our money redeemable in gold will create this compulsion." (*MoneyWorld*, June, 1998) Congress didn't listen to Buffett but his son would one day load up on silver.

Warren Buffett's sister, Mrs. Doris Bryant, says of her father, "Mainly he had a fear of creeping socialism. And he worried about inflation. He was ahead of his time about inflation and wrote about it and was advising clients to hedge against it in 1932. He encouraged people to buy art and jewelry."

Buffett's father, widely regarded for his staunch integrity and conservative views—was an early member of the John Birch Society in Nebraska, attracted to the controversial organization because of its fierce opposition to Communism.

Howard Buffett gave an interview to the *Dundee* and *West Omaha Sun* about why he was a member of the John Birch Society. The article, which ran as the paper's lead story on April 6, 1961, carried the headline, "Why I Joined Birch Society."

The story began, "The John Birch Society, which apparently has had just one member in Nebraska for the past 2½ years, is likely to grow as a result of recent publicity.

"So says the lone acknowledged member, Howard H. Buffett, 2501 N. 53rd, a member of a pioneer family and a former Congressman.

" 'I've had half a dozen people ask me in the past day or so how they could join the society,' Buffett told *The Sun.* 'If my health permits, I plan to seek some new members.' "

(Photo by Allan Maxwell)

This is the home where Buffett grew up in Omaha at 2501 North 53rd Street. He and his family once sang in the living room for one of his father's congressional campaigns. At Berkshire's annual meeting in 1999, Buffett said, "In 1942 my two sisters, who are here today, joined me to sing 'America the Beautiful.' My dad was elected to Congress on the back of that."

Warren Buffett's mother was Leila (Stahl) Buffett, a lively woman with an easy, humorous manner who walked into the Berkshire annual meeting in 1992 and said, "I'm still here." Buffett's mother died August 30, 1996, at age 92, on her son's 66th birthday.

Leila Buffett, twice widowed, took back the Buffett name after the death of her second husband, Roy Ralph, because she was married to Congressman Buffett for more than three decades.

Buffett's parents also had two daughters, Mrs. Doris Bryant, of Morehead City, North Carolina, and Mrs. Roberta Bialek, of Carmel, California.

The three children, who all skipped grades in school, grew up in a respectable red brick home in the popular Country Club area of Omaha at the corner of 53rd and Lake Street, after living first at 4224 Barker.

Warren Buffett's roots and heredity gave him a lifelong love of the newspaper industry in which he has moved from delivery boy to Pulitzer Prize winner to mass media owner.

5

"WARREN COULDN'T PUT A NUT ON A BOLT...
BUT HE COULD ADD 20 TWO-DIGIT NUMBERS IN HIS HEAD." —DON DANLY

Buffett attended Alice Deal Junior High School and Woodrow Wilson High School in Washington D.C. after his father was elected to Congress. Buffett graduated from Alice Deal in February, 1945 at age 14, and graduated from Wilson in June, 1947, at age 16.

Early photo of Woodrow Wilson High School in Washington D.C.

39

Buffett would have been slated to graduate from Wilson in February, 1948, had he gone the normal three years. But he took extra credits and graduated in 2½ years in June 1947. It was considered prudent at the time to graduate in June because so many colleges started in September.

When Buffett was 16, he and a friend, Don Danly, 17, who also was attending Wilson, bought a 1928 Rolls Royce for $350 and rented it out for $35 a day.

Their classmate, Norma Jean Perna, who was dating Danly at the time, recalls bringing the car back: "I was in the car on that trip back from Baltimore. It came from a lot in Baltimore that looked like a junkyard to me. We were all really scared on the way back to D.C. ... We didn't know if the car would make it home and of course there were no tags... We all three painted the car blue. It was originally grey. Don and I did most of the painting, as I recall. Warren's mother usually provided lunch." (Maybe this is why Buffett now says: "We don't do turnarounds.")

Danly, now a retired Monsanto director of technology who lives in Pensacola, Florida, recalls that in 1947 they went to Baltimore to buy the car.

Danly said, "The car was found in a junk yard south of Baltimore. (Norma says it looked like a junkyard—that's because it was a junkyard.) The car had been sold for scrap, having little or no value as transportation. It was called a "lady's shopping car," having a single bucket seat in front for the driver (presumably the chauffeur) and a double-wide seat set back behind the driver.

"Warren, Norma and I drove to Baltimore in my Dad's '38 Buick Special (our only car). The drive back to Washington was interesting, as the fuel system for the Rolls had a one-gallon gravity tank mounted on the fire wall and gasoline was supposed to be drawn into this tank from the rear fuel tank via vacuum from the manifold. This didn't work since the vacuum tank leaked. We had to remove the top from the one-gallon tank and pour in fuel about every six or seven miles. Since we had to drive about forty miles, this turned out to be a rather tedious process. However, with this exception the car did actually run, though not very fast. I drove the Rolls with Warren in the 'lady's' seat and Norma followed in the Buick."

Danly added, "we drove it back, but it didn't have a tag. When we got to D.C., we were stopped by the police because we didn't have a tag. Warren pulled rank and said his father was a congressman and we were let go.

"We put the car in Warren's garage. I'd work on it. I was the technical fellow and he was the finance guy. Some have said we worked on the car together, but Warren couldn't put a nut on a bolt or do anything technical. He sat there and read business books to me. He read 100 business books before he left high school. He read other books, too. One was called *How to Lose Friends and Alienate People.*

"Sometimes he'd have me give him about 20 two-digit numbers to add in his head," said Danly, who went on to Cornell. Danly would add the figures with the aid of paper and pencil. "He'd be right," Danly marveled.

Danly was one of 11 students to tie for first in the 1947 class at Woodrow Wilson. He said Buffett was 16th in the class of about 350. "He did that without even trying. I hit the books hard."

Buffett's bio in the 1947 Woodrow Wilson yearbook is a little thin compared with his classmates: "W. Club, Debate Team, Golf Team. A sportsman...basketball and golf: the favorites...likes math...a future stock broker."

The two youngsters rented out the Rolls a few times. Danly still has a photo of the two entrepreneurs standing by the Rolls. Between them in that photo is Norma Jean Thurston (Perna), bearing a resemblance to another Norma Jean. Norma Jean Thurston was known as "Peroxide," even though she is a natural blonde. Buffett was called Buffett and Danly was called "Duck." So it's fair to say Buffett's early business partner was Donald Duck.

In the photo, Buffett is wearing a coat and tie, the tie stopping about four inches above his belt. "It was rare for Warren to be in a coat and tie," Danly said.

In addition to the Rolls rent-a-car business, the two had other enterprises. "We had a peanut vending machine and

(Photo courtesy of Norma Perna)

This photo from the 1945 Alice Deal Junior High School class album shows blonde Norma Jean Thurston (Perna), about 30 billion style points ahead of her classmate, 14-year old, bespectacled Warren Buffett. Her future husband Bill Perna, and his first cousin, Lou Battistone, were in this class.

(Photo courtesy of Norma Perna)

This photo of the Woodrow Wilson High School class of June 1947 shows Buffett in glasses and a crewcut. Don Danly is wearing a white coat. These two teenage entrepreneurs were the Wilson Coin-Operated Machine Co.

(Photo courtesy of Norma Perna)

Classmates Lou Battistone, Norma Perna and Buffett at their Woodrow Wilson High School 50th reunion October 17, 1997.

(Photo courtesy of Don Danly)

Don Danly, Mrs. Susan Buffett, and Warren Buffett at the Woodrow Wilson High School reunion October 17, 1997.

(Photo courtesy of Don Danly)

Mrs. Vera Danly and Mrs. Susan Buffett at the Wilson reunion

a pinball machine business." They called the pinball machine business Wilson Coin-Operated Machine Co. Danly has said. "I knew then that he was a winner."

Danly said: "A Berkshire stockholder from Laguna Beach, California, Keith Baim, sent Warren the 'Wilson Coin-Operated Machine Co.' frame in January 1998. Warren mailed me a Xerox of it and a copy of the letter he had received from Keith. I then wrote to Keith and explained that I was Warren's partner in this 1947 enterprise and greatly admired the frame he had sent to Warren. I then went on to express a concern as to whether the paper frame I received from Warren would hold up in our humid Florida climate. I asked him if he might be able to acquire a more durable version (at my expense).

"Keith wrote back to me, thanking me for my letter and went on to say, 'I share your concern about the paper frame holding up in the humid Florida climate. Perhaps relocating to a somewhat colder part of the country, say North Dakota, would solve such a problem. Though I'd suggest talking it over with Vera before any final decision.'

"He closed this first letter to me with a P.S., 'Are there any other former partners, employees, suppliers, sub-contractors or shareholders of Wilson I should expect to hear from?'

"After a couple of letters back and forth it was agreed that he would bring another license plate frame to the annual Berkshire meeting in May in exchange for some personal tales of Warren's high school days. I met with Keith and his father at the Embassy Suites during the weekend prior to the meeting, receiving, and immediately mounting my frame."

(Photo by Phil Swigard)

"Wilson Coin-Operated Machine Co." is displayed on Buffett's license plate on his blue Lincoln Town Car.

Buffett's current car license tag has the number of a regular citizen and its frame says nothing about Berkshire. It reads: "Wilson Coin-Operated Machine Co."

Later on Buffett sent Danly a series of letters starting in 1951 telling Danly how he was investing his money for him—about $6,000 Danly inherited after his parents died early. Danly saved Buffett's letters because he thought Buffett was special. "But I didn't know it was going to come to this," he said.

The two have stayed in touch over the years and attended their 50th reunion together at Woodrow Wilson in 1997. Mrs. Perna said that at the reunion Buffett attended, a number of classmates were saying: "I wish I had known him better back then."

Danly has said, "In 1993, on his way to a Coke board meeting, Warren stopped in for dinner. I reminded him that we had agreed (in our early business ventures) we'd split everything 50/50."

Buffett's old pinball machine partner has struggled along very well with a $25,000 investment he made in the Buffett Partnership in 1961. He later took Berkshire stock and never sold a share.

Danly wrote on the "Berkshire message board" on America Online September 13, 1997, "I must confess that I'm one of those who is guilty of checking the BRK price several times each day. I can't sign on to AOL without clicking that crooked arrow that suggests the price is going up. In a way I long for the 'old days' of Buffett Partnership Limited, when I received a statement once a year giving the value of my holding (it was always up). I've had my BRK stock over 30 years and never sold any, so today's price has little significance (no plans to sell). Having said that, I'm sure I'll continue to check the price at least daily."

When Buffett visited them in Pensacola, Danly and his wife, Vera, picked him up and brought him to their home overlooking Mackey Cove. They took him to dinner and came back home, all the while talking about the old days and business.

"Then he excused himself and went to the bedroom and made telephone calls for two or three hours. He was on the phone long after we went to bed," Danly said. "He works very hard."

The next day Buffett and the Danlys boarded Berkshire's plane and flew to Atlanta where Buffett arranged a tour of the Coca-Cola Museum for them while he went off to a Coca-Cola board meeting.

Danly said the two have kept up an interest in antique cars and that in the 1980s Buffett made an offer for Harrah's antique car museum in Reno, Nevada, but a price was not agreed upon.

Buffett told Danly that he had seen Norma Jean Perna in 1993.

Asked if she still looked good, Buffett told Danly she did: "She looked like her daughter, actually her granddaughter."

Mrs. Perna, of Potomac, Maryland, said Buffett's humor was always there. "He hasn't changed at all since I knew him."

"I was never in the businesses they started, but I was interested in them," she said. "We were like the three musketeers. I'd go with them to pick up the money from the pinball machines. Warren was always picking up the money and Don was always repairing the machines."

"I remember when Warren got going on golf balls. He got them from a golf course. He'd clean them and sell them.

"He told me he'd be a millionaire by the time he was 30 and I believed him."

On February 7, 1997, Danly came on the internet with this posting:

"As a BRK-watcher for 27 years (when I discovered I owned the stock upon the liquidation of Buffett Partnership Ltd.), I am delighted to have found this bulletin board. I have tried to find something on BRK in a number of chatrooms to no avail.

"My bit of memorabilia is that this is the 50th anniversary of Wilson Coin-Operated Machine Co., which Warren and I formed during our high school days in Washington. Would you believe that Warren typed up a monthly income/loss statement for this enterprise? Warren provided the capital and I was director of technology (fixed the machines). The company was sold later that year when Warren went off to U. of Penn and I to Cornell.

"I find the bulletin board comments on LTEPS [look-through earnings per share] fascinating, as they tend to give me a warm feeling. Looking forward to more."

Danly's former wife, Charlotte Colby Danly, of Connecticut, recalls getting to know Buffett when he was the best man at her wedding.

"I was 19 and Warren and Susie were recently married." she recalled.

Over the years the Danlys occasionally visited the Buffetts in Omaha. "I remember Susie and Peter jamming on a piano, long after midnight," Mrs. Danly said.

Years later they attended Buffett's 50th birthday party at the Metropolitan Club in New York. "There were [business] leaders from all over there. Gary Cooper's daughter, Maria, an artist, was there who is married to Byron Janis, the famous classical pianist....Buffett's friend, Fred Stanback of Salisbury, North Carolina, a longtime Berkshire investor and Buffett friend, was there. [Fred Stanback is the son of Fred

Stanback, Sr., and the nephew of Tom Stanback, the founder of the Stanback Headache Powder company where Fred once worked. The slogan for their company was "Snapback with Stanback." Fred Stanback, the best man at Buffett's wedding invested $125,000 in 1962 in the Buffett Partnership. (*Forbes*, October 12, 1998)] Susie had written a song for Warren on his birthday and sang it with her piano accompanist from San Francisco. His birthday cake was in the shape of a Pepsi, which he drank at the time. It was one of the most memorable of nights."

She said over the years she's written Buffett on occasion about questions arising about house sales. "He's always written back in three days. I try not to write much. He has a prodigious memory and he's very loyal to old friends."

Mrs. Danly has Berkshire stock which she and Don Danly got as a result of investing in the Buffett Partnership. She said she has rarely sold shares, but has on occasion. The cost basis of some of the stock is $19. On the day she gave the interview Berkshire closed at $43,000. "It's like a money tree," she said.

Danly recalls a couple of motorcycle stories involving him and Buffett. Once when Buffett was at the University of Pennsylvania and Danly was at Cornell, Buffett called Danly to see if he would come to Philadelphia and drive a Harley Davidson to D.C. They did. The wind-swept youngsters arrived after a five-hour ride huddled in the same seat together.

Another time Danly towed Buffett who was behind him on a motorcycle. But at a curve the motorcycle and Buffett took a bad spill. "I almost killed him," Danly said.

Teenage Second-hand Car Dealers

Don Danly, left, and Buffett standing in front of their Rolls Royce outside Buffett's house on 49th street in Washington D.C. in the fall of 1947. The teenagers are dressed up! Buffett is in a racoon fur coat just for the fun of it. Sometimes he wore it to the high school football games. Danly said, "My camel hair coat was my regular winter attire except when I rode my bike to school."

6
YOUTH

"I WAS CONCEIVED DURING THE STOCK MARKET CRASH."

"I was conceived during the stock market crash" in the fall of 1929, Buffett has said, noting that his father was a stock salesman at the time.

"I'm quite fond of 1929, since that's when it all began for me. My dad was a stock salesman at the time, and after the Crash came, in the fall, he was afraid to call anyone—all those people who'd been burned. So he just stayed home in the afternoons. And there wasn't television then. Soooo... I was conceived on or about Nov. 30, 1929 (and born nine months later, on Aug. 30, 1930), and I've forever had a kind of warm feeling about the Crash." (*Fortune*, November 22, 1999)

If his father had enough business to be out making his regular calls at the time, Buffett says there's "no telling what might have happened." (WOWT-TV in Omaha, October 14, 1993)

One of young Warren's first and favorite toys was a metal money changer he strapped around his waist. "He loved it," recalls his older sister, Mrs. Doris Bryant, who describes young Warren as a "typical younger brother."

Like a Good Humor ice cream man, Buffett went around making change. He was fascinated by the process of making change and keeping track of the money. Making math calculations, particularly when it concerned compounding money at a blistering pace, was a pastime that absorbed him from his earliest days.

"As a child he was so cautious he walked with his knees bent so he wouldn't have too far to fall, but as an adult he was capable of grand gestures...It was a broad stroke," Mrs. Bryant said, referring to Buffett's purchase of $1 billion of Coke stock.

Young Buffett's first real business venture was in soft drinks, fitting for a fellow who would one day own billions of dollars of Coca-Cola stock. His mother recalled that her son's first appreciation of free enterprise occurred when Buffett was six years old. The escapade involved peddling, yes, Coca-Colas.

"We were at Lake Okoboji in Iowa. Warren paid twenty-five cents for a six-pack of Coke and sold it for five cents a bottle. Warren always had a fascination for numbers in connection with earning money," Mrs. Buffett recalled. Those 20% returns were about consistent with Buffett's entire business career. And that's why he's a multi-billionaire.

Buffett also bought Coca-Cola from his grandfather's grocery store in Omaha and sold it to neighbors.

In Berkshire's 1989 Annual Report, Buffett wrote: "I believe I had my first Coca-Cola in either 1935 or 1936. Of a certainty, it was in 1936 that I started buying Cokes at the rate of six for 25¢ from Buffett & Son, the family grocery store, to sell around the neighborhood for 5¢ each. In this excursion into high-margin retailing, I duly observed the extraordinary consumer attractiveness and commercial possibilities of the product."

By the time he was 10, Buffett's favorite soft drink to sell was Pepsi. As he later explained to Berkshire shareholder Paul Cassidy of North Andover, Massachusetts, "I originally started on the Pepsi because at the time (1940) Pepsi came in 12-ounce bottles and Coke came in 6-ounce bottles, and the price was the same. That was a pretty powerful argument."

Buffett's recall for numbers, an important facility for any businessman, may have come from both parents—his father was a stockbroker and his mother calculates numbers well, too, according to Ed Conine, who lived near Buffett.

Conine, president of J Bragg women's apparel department store chain in Omaha and Lincoln, before his death in 1993, recalled that Mrs. Buffett once told him that when she was in her late 70s, Buffett gave her both an exercise bike and a Cadillac. "I have 34,000 miles on the bike and 5,600 miles on the Cadillac," Mrs. Buffett quipped.

"While most youngsters were content to get sodas out of machines and never give things a further thought, Buffett was retrieving the discarded bottle caps from soda pop machines, sorting and counting them to find out which soda brand was really selling," says Berkshire shareholder Irving Fenster of Tulsa, Oklahoma, one of Buffett's early investors.

Buffett's auditor's instinct—the ability to get at the real numbers, not the supposed numbers passed along by others—remains one of his trademarks.

And he hasn't relied on traditional wisdom. After all, he says, "Traditional wisdom can be long on tradition and short on wisdom."

The precocious youngster, who could spout off the populations of U.S. cities, was popular, witty, and industrious. But even at Rosehill

Elementary School, a kindergarten through eighth grade school in Omaha where Buffett skipped a grade, young Buffett was known more as an "egghead" than as an athlete. In class photos, his hair is unkempt.

"What I had forgotten, but he remembered, is that he was out for three weeks with appendicitis. He was very ill and the other students wrote him," recalls Marie Madsen, his second grade teacher.

"He was never a problem or I would have remembered that. He was a good boy. . . He was a good student and kept his nose to the grindstone. I don't remember how good he was in math, but I'm sure he was good. I know he was good in English because he corrected me once. It had to do with a contraction of a word and he was right.

"I remember him standing up in the back of the room looking around. If he was funny, I don't remember it. He may have been with his classmates."

She said her overall impression of him during his years at Rosehill was as a young fellow "who wanted to go off and do something himself."

At Rosehill he picked up the nickname, "Bathless Buffett." It didn't stick long. The name was taken from a "Li'l Abner" character of the time.

That's not to say he didn't get along well with his peers. He did. He mixes so well these days that he sits on the board of directors of Coca-Cola, Gillette and The Washington Post Co. But Buffett

(Photo by Allan Maxwell)

At Rosehill Elementary School, Buffett daydreamed about stocks. When he was 12 years old, he left— not very willingly— for Washington, D.C., after his father was elected to Congress in 1942. The school, named after wild roses growing in nearby hills, was torn down in the summer of 2000. There are plans for a new school at the same site.

always has had a private, independent streak.

That streak appeared once when Buffett's father encouraged Warren and his sister, Doris, to spend part of a summer at the Elmer Benne farm near West Point, Nebraska.

The idea, recalls Mrs. Bryant, was that farm values would be instilled in the children. Buffett knows the lessons of hard work and independence, but apparently he didn't learn them by working behind a plow from dawn to drop; others say hot and heavy labor never interested Buffett.

"I never saw him behind a plow. He was reading a lot of the time," said Mrs. Bryant.

Those who knew Buffett were aware of his abilities, but those who knew him only casually may not have taken note because of his lack of outward success. He may have reminded people of Joseph Heller's saying: "He was a self-made man who owed his lack of success to nobody."

Kathryn Haskell Smith, recalling a story her deceased sister Carolyn Haskell Hallquist told her, said, "He wanted to be around the guys and he would play basketball with them and then while the others were still playing, he'd be over reading the *Wall Street Journal*. The others would just say, 'That's Warren.' He'd play a little basketball with the guys, then go off and read the *Journal* and come back and play with them again."

It was Carolyn Haskell whom Buffett often dropped over to see when the Buffett and Haskell families lived a few blocks from one another in the Country Club section of Omaha. The area had a golf course until about 1926 when the Omaha Country Club moved to a new site in northwest Omaha.

Some evenings the young pair struck up a duet with Buffett on the ukulele and Carolyn on the piano.

One hot summer evening, as young Buffett was strumming along, he remarked, "All we need now is some mint juleps," recalls Kathryn Smith.

Mrs. Smith knew the Buffett family as a result of a friendship that her father, John Haskell, and Buffett's father formed back in their days at the University of Nebraska. For years Haskell's stockbroker was Howard Buffett.

"He (Warren Buffett) would come over to our house sometimes and talk finances with my father...My father agreed with Warren's father that you should buy good stocks and keep them for a very long time," she said.

"He was always so quick and witty...He was a great guy, lots of fun but it was obvious he was way ahead of us in brains," she said.

Buffett, Mrs. Smith, and other students all walked to school together. Many of Buffett's friends went on to Benson High School where students were known as Benson High School Bunnies.

Even the school sign says: "Benson High School. Home of the Bunnies."

"Benson High School's mascot is the bunny. Hence, we were known as 'the bunnies.' At the time we didn't think it was funny, but it has been the brunt of many jokes since," said Mrs. Smith, who is the wife of Homer Smith, a football coach who formerly oversaw the offense of the University of Alabama, UCLA and the University of Arizona. Early on he was the football coach at West Point. He is the author of a fast-paced novel, *A Game to Play*.

Coach Smith, who sports degrees from Princeton—where he was a single-wing fullback—Stanford and Harvard, recalls Buffett in his early 20s standing in a yard one day, "talking about stocks, talking about buying businesses," and telling slightly risque jokes.

"It was in the yard of Kathy Haskell, my wife now. Warren was there to see Carolyn, Kathy's older sister.

"Warren was obviously brilliant. Also, he was a great guy. [But] I thought he was young to be trying to teach a class at Omaha University. He was unforgettable [even] early on."

He and his wife remember Buffett as always being funny. Buffett could keep classmates in stitches with his joke-telling.

They think he got that quality from his mother and described his father as absolutely serious and high-minded.

Smith, who played on the same basketball team at Benson High School as former Vulcan Materials Co. Chairman Herb Sklennar, has retired from coaching. He and his wife live in Tuscaloosa, Alabama, where he writes football coaching manuals. He writes them. She types them.

Buffett himself didn't go to Benson because he moved to Washington, but he still attends the 1947 and 1948 high school class reunions because he has friends in those classes.

"I was aware he wanted to make money. He was very industrious and was always trying to get money to buy stocks, but no one ever dreamed it would come to this," Mrs. Smith said.

Even though young Warren was a math prodigy, his fascination with finance came as a surprise to Buffett's religious and frugal father, who had little interest in amassing money for its own sake. He found his son, whom he hoped would one day join the clergy, spellbound by the power of the Almighty Dollar. But young Buffett

(Photo courtesy of Doris Buffett Bryant)

Roberta (Bertie), Doris and Warren Buffett in front of a neighbor's home in Washington, D.C.'s Spring Valley area. Photo was taken when Warren was a skinny 13-year-old; Doris was 16 and Bertie 10.

couldn't really make the leap to religious faith. What mattered was rationality, facts, numbers and money.

Buffett has said he's an agnostic because he doubts the human mind can know whether there is a God, but says his father was very religious. "As a practical matter I think my dad and I came out at about the same place in terms of what we believed behavior should be and how society should operate." And he says, "In my whole life I never saw my dad or my wife ever do anything in their lives you couldn't put on the front pages of a newspaper, written by an unfriendly reporter." (*Omaha World-Herald*, February 22, 2000 from a talk to Midland College business students)

The Buffetts came from a long line of staunch Republicans, but all the Buffetts have an independent streak. Warren Buffett, largely persuaded that Democrats had a better approach to civil rights matters, shocked his family when he and his wife, Susan, became Democrats. Susan Buffett told *Forbes* (October 21, 1991), "It caused great commotion" [in the family].

A cousin of Buffett's recalls family dinners as often centering around rapid-fire political talk. "His sisters have about the same IQ he does," said Katherine Grimm of Akron, Ohio. "If they were at dinner someone would toss out a political idea and the next would say, 'defend your position.' "

Buffett told *Forbes*, October 18, 1993, "I became a Democrat basically because I felt the Democrats were closer by a considerable

(Photo courtesy of Kathryn Smith)

Kathryn and Coach Homer Smith at the Fiesta Bowl in Tempe, Arizona in 1984.

margin to what I felt in the early 1960s about civil rights. I don't vote the party line. But I probably vote for more Democrats than Republicans."

Congressman Buffett was such a straight arrow and fiscal conservative he once returned a $2,500 annual pay raise (from $10,000 to $12,500) to the United States Treasury.

Buffett adored his father, who referred to Warren as "Fireball" because of his energy and precociousness.

"Yes, he called him Fireball and Warren called him Pop. They were the best of friends. When he died, Warren cried for days," Mrs. Leila Buffett once recalled. Buffett was 33 years old when his father died and 66 when his mother died.

Buffett remained close to his mother, and

(Photo by Lee Armstrong)

Kathryn and Coach Homer Smith at festivities surrounding Berkshire's annual meeting in 1999.

(Photo courtesy of Howard Buffett)

Four generations of Buffetts: Warren Buffett and his mother, Leila Stahl Buffett; his son, Howard Graham Buffett; and his grandson, Howard Warren Buffett, a Coke stock accumulator.

once at the height of the Salomon crisis, flew home from New York just in time to be with her when she was honored as Woman of the Year by the Nebraska Chapter of the Arthritis Foundation. Quipped Buffett, "She's been woman of the year for the last 87 years."

While Buffett was still a Rosehill student, he briefly published a racetrack tip sheet, called *Stable-boy Selections*, about handicapping and betting on horses. He printed the sheets in his parents' basement and sold them for a quarter. He and a friend used math to develop a system for picking the winners of horse races. The business was shut down for not having a license.

When Buffett was eight years old, he began reading books about the stock market that his father left around the house. He has said he became interested in stocks when he was 6 or 7. "And I've always been upset that I didn't start earlier." (*Omaha World-Herald*, February 22, 2000)

He continued to be enraptured by the stock market, charting the rise and fall of stock prices. "I was fascinated with anything to do with numbers and money," he has said. (*Los Angeles Times*, Linda Grant, April 7, 1991) Buffett has later called charting and most things away from fundamental analysis of a company just "chicken tracks."

In April, 1942—when Buffett was 11—he began buying stocks in a small way: three shares of Cities Service Preferred, which he bought for $38 a share. That was his net worth at the time.

He talked his sister, Doris, into investing with him.

He recalls that on walks to Rosehill with his sister, "she would remind me I wasn't setting any records." So he sold at $40 a share, making $5 after commissions. A few years later the stock went to $200 a share.

Buffett already had been following the stock market, computing averages, and had begun to realize his views about the markets were more astute than those of others.

He once told *Forbes* (November 1, 1969), "I'd been interested in the stock market from the time I was 11, when I marked the board here at Harris Upham where my father was a broker. I ran the gamut, stock tips, the Magee charting stuff, everything. Then I picked up Graham's *Security Analysis*. Reading it was like seeing the light."

Harris Upham was in the same building as his father's firm, Buffett-Falk & Co.

Young Buffett, ever the student, took in the early stock investment lessons well; that is, do not be guided by what people say and don't tell fellow investors what you are doing at the time you do it.

The lesson was later reinforced by Ben Graham, his teacher at Columbia Business School, who taught that whether someone else agrees or disagrees with you does not make you right or wrong. That hallmark idea never left Buffett, who in 1965 was writing members of the Buffett Partnership: "We derive no comfort because important people, vocal people, or great numbers of people agree with us. Nor do we derive comfort if they don't. A public opinion poll is no substitute for thought."

Buffett added that when you find a situation you understand, where the facts are ascertainable and clear, then act, whether the action is conventional or unconventional and regardless of whether others agree or disagree.

When you are dead sure of something and are armed with all the facts, then everyone else's advice is only confusing and time-consuming. When almost everyone was dismissing the newspaper business as unappealing in the 1970s, Buffett spotted its monopoly-like franchises and bought one media stock after another.

From his early days Buffett rarely showed his hand until he had to. The practice would take on far greater significance later when Wall Street would try to guess what he was doing. Only rarely did his moves in the market leak out. To this day Buffett tries to keep his investments secret until publication of the Berkshire Annual Report each March.

Buffett has said it's not easy to keep secrets, especially when talking to attractive members of the opposite sex.

At the time his father was elected to Congress, 12-year-old Buffett lived with his grandfather, Ernest Buffett, for about four months. President of the Rotary Club in Omaha in 1934 and a grocer by trade, Ernest Buffett was working on a book. Each night he dictated a few pages to his grandson.

The title of the book was *How to Run a Grocery Store and a Few Things I Have Learned About Fishing.* Buffett has joked that he was overexposed at an impressionable age to his grandfather's long-winded literary style.

In 1942 Buffett's father was elected to the first of four terms as a congressman on the Republican ticket, and Buffett's days in Omaha were interrupted.

His family moved to Fredericksburg, Virginia, in January, 1943, and although his two sisters were happy, Buffett felt uprooted and unhappy. The Buffett family lived just across the Rappahannock River from Fredericksburg. For a brief time young Buffett worked for a local baker. "I didn't like the change at all, so I made a real pain of myself over this move. My grandfather was quite keen on me, and he was back in Omaha. I'd write him and tell him how terrible things were. He finally said, 'You'd better send the boy back here.' " (*Regardie's*, February, 1986)

The next month Buffett returned to Omaha to live with his grandfather and his unmarried aunt, Alice Buffett. He continued to attend Rosehill.

He often had lunch with the Carl Falk family. Carl Falk and Howard Buffett had run the Buffett-Falk brokerage firm. In June, 1943, young Buffett rejoined his family in Fredericksburg, but went back to Omaha for much of the summer, staying at a Presbyterian manse while its minister was away. The Buffett family, including Warren, moved to Washington, D.C., in July, 1943, to 4211 49th Street N.W. near Massachusetts Avenue, in Spring Valley. A few years later congressman Richard Nixon moved into the area.

Young Buffett, a crewcut lad in those days, went back and forth from Omaha to Washington so much that one retired executive in Omaha recalls that back then Buffett "was like a phantom."

Buffett told L.J. Davis (*New York Times Magazine,* April, 1990) about his days in Fredericksburg, "I was miserably homesick. I told my parents I couldn't breathe. I told them not to worry about it, to get themselves a good night's sleep, and I'd just stand up all night."

When he was 13, Buffett ran away briefly from his Washington, D.C., home. "He ran away with a friend, Roger Bell. I think they were picked up by the police," his sister Doris Bryant recalls.

Buffett's escapade had to be a little different and of course business related. He ran away to Hershey, Pennsylvania, where he was sent home by the police. Buffett, Bell and another friend had the idea of earning a little money caddying at a local golf course. Also he had the idea of touring the Hershey chocolate plant and getting a free candy bar. But he didn't tour the plant and apparently didn't consider buying the company.

Buffett told this story to *Atlanta Constitution* business writer Melissa Turner who asked him if he might sample Hershey stock some day. His reply: "I've driven a car all my life, but I haven't bought any car companies."

Still, Buffett often mentions the attributes of Hershey when he gets going about the concept of consumer "franchises." He explains that consumer franchises or "name brands," as people call them, such as Coca-Cola, Gillette and Wrigley, have extra value. A valuable consumer franchise exists, he says, when people prefer a certain brand name so much that they would pay extra, even walk out of the store they're standing in, then walk across the street just to buy the "better" brand name. Even if another chocolate bar is five cents cheaper, one is still likely to choose the Hershey name.

In Washington, Buffett attended Alice Deal Junior High School, where his grades were poor. They improved only when his father threatened to take away his cherished paper routes. (While still 13, Buffett began paying taxes on an income of $1,000 he earned from newspaper routes.)

Still rebellious and looking for his place in the world, Buffett hit once again on his main passion—business.

He undertook a series of financial ventures, including retrieving lost golf balls at a country club in Washington, but his main pursuit was being an industrious newspaper boy.

Buffett at one point delivered 500 newspapers on five paper routes, mainly to apartment complexes, according to Robert Dorr of the *Omaha World-Herald*.

Buffett combined two *Washington Post* routes in the Spring Valley area with two rival *Times-Herald* routes and later added the Westchester apartments to his routes.

Usually Buffett left at 5:20 a.m. and caught a bus down Massachusetts Avenue. On the few times young Buffett was ill, his mother did the route. "Collections were everything to him. You didn't dare touch the drawer where he kept the money. Every penny had to be there," his mother said. (*Buffett: The Making of an American Capitalist*, Roger Lowenstein, p. 22)

"Thinking he could better use the time to collect from his customers, he developed an effective scheme for selling magazine subscriptions. He would tear the stickers with the expiration date from discarded magazines, file them, and at the right time ask the customer for a renewal," Dorr wrote in a May 29, 1966, story.

Eugene Meyer would later merge the *Post* and *Times-Herald* into a large, successful newspaper. Buffett would one day make an investment in the Post, an enormously successful move that vaulted him to the top ranks of investors.

Buffett always remained fascinated by the stock market, recalls Mrs. Bryant. "I never had any doubt. I never knew it would amount to this, but even back then everyone recognized he knew about the stock market."

Even when Buffett was starting his partnership in his bedroom, it did not create a stir in the family. "We took it for granted he knew what he was doing," Mrs. Bryant said.

According to stories by his longtime friend, Carol Loomis, a journalist with *Fortune* magazine since 1954, Buffett as a youngster virtually memorized a book called *A Thousand Ways to Make $1,000*, fantasizing in particular about penny-weighing machines. He pictured himself starting with a single machine pyramiding his take into thousands more.

The Loomis connection began in the mid-1960s when Carol Loomis's husband, John, a Wall Street money manager with First Manhattan Corp., in New York, went to Omaha to discuss business with Buffett and reported back to his wife, "I think I just met the smartest man in the country."

Investor Phil Carret, who went to Harvard, once called Buffett, "The smartest man in the U.S." (*Bottom Line/Tomorrow*, June, 1998)

Buffett was constantly running calculations in his head. In church he calculated the life span of the composers of hymns, checking to see if their religious calling rewarded them with extra longevity. His conclusion: no.

Perhaps that was the reason Buffett settled on being an agnostic. Buffett has said, "I am an agnostic. That's the person who says I'm an atheist, thank God." (*Financial Times*, May 17, 1999)

Buffett and his friend Don Danly at Woodrow Wilson High School in Washington D.C. began a pinball machine business when they bought a $25 pinball machine which they fixed up. They installed it in a barbershop on busy Wisconsin Avenue.

After the first day of operation, the young entrepreneurs returned to find $4 in a pan full of nickels. Buffett has said, "I figured I had discovered the wheel."

This incident seems analogous to Charles Lindbergh's first flight after a particularly undistinguished youth. Indeed, he had recently flunked out of college. A. Scott Berg, author of *Lindbergh* (p. 64) wrote: "When the plane took flight and banked for the first time, Lindbergh felt as though he had 'lost all conscious connection with the past,' that he lived 'only in the moment in the strange, unmortal space, crowded with beauty, pierced with danger.' "

(Seth Poppel Yearbook Archives)

Buffett's senior year photo at Woodrow Wilson High School

After Buffett found that $4, he was flying.

As more barbers asked for the machines, the youngsters said they would check with their hardnosed boss—"Mr. Wilson," (themselves actually) and wound up installing other machines.

In time, the Wilson Coin-Operated Machine Co. expanded to seven machines and was hauling in $50 a week. "I hadn't dreamed life could be so good," Buffett said. (*The Midas Touch*, John Train, p. 5)

He also was pulling in about $175 a month from paper routes. (*Supermoney*, Adam Smith, p. 184)

While Buffett was still in high school in 1945, he was able to save enough money to buy a $1,200 unimproved 40-acre farm in northwestern Nebraska. His father had bought the farm years earlier. Buffett paid his father in cash and rented the land to a tenant farmer.

The Wilson Coin-Operated Machine Co. was sold in August, 1947 to a war veteran for $1,200. Buffett took his share and headed for Wharton. This extraordinary force—a Nebraska special—was on his way. Buffett became so extraordinary he has been called "a five-sigma event," a statistical aberration so rare it practically never occurs. (*Fortune*, Carol Loomis, April 11, 1988)

I once wrote Buffett that my mother, Frances Kilpatrick, taught at Woodrow Wilson High School, the school he attended. Buffett replied:

...I went to Woodrow Wilson in 1945-1947. I don't remember a Mrs. Kilpatrick, so she must have been teaching one of the harder courses at the time. My high school career was not particularly illustrious—I was more interested in the pinball machines than in the classroom. Best regards, Sincerely, Warren E. Buffett

(Actually, my mother taught there after he left.)

In school Buffett was neither cool nor a nerd, just a maverick. "I would not have been the most popular guy in the class, but I wouldn't have been the most unpopular either. I was just sort of nothing." (*Regardie's*, February, 1986)

Buffett once wrote a Wilson teacher, Miss Grace Carter (letter of June 26, 1998) in part: "I remember my days at Wilson very well though, in all honesty, I was not on my best behavior at the time. If you're going to have a rebellious period, I guess it's a good idea to get it out of your system early. Incidentally, I note from your address that you live only a few blocks away from the Westchester Apartments (3900 Cathedral Avenue) where I got my financial start delivering papers..."

During his high school days, he pursued Carolyn Falk of Omaha, but so too did Walter Scott, now head of the Peter Kiewit Sons' conglomerate, who married her. "Unfortunately, the best man won," Buffett says. (*Forbes*, October 24, 1994)

If Buffett still was trying to establish himself in high school, he already was noteworthy in the business world.

In 1947 when he graduated from high school at 16, in a "chartist" phase in his study of the stock market, he had amassed the extraordinary sum of about $6,000, largely from his paper routes. The youngster was making more than his teachers.

Although he could have, he did not pay for college. His parents footed the bill, letting Buffett keep his money for investing. By the end of 1950, he had $9,800.

At the urging of his father—and it took some doing to convince Buffett to go to college instead of going on with his business pursuits—he headed for the Wharton School of Business at the University of Pennsylvania. There he was president of the Young Republicans' Club and found time to make arrangements to rent an elephant to ride in a Republican victory parade, but Truman upset Dewey and the plans were canceled. At the University of Pennsylvania, Buffett learned to play bridge. (*Forbes*, June 2, 1997) And he pledged Alpha Sigma Phi fraternity his freshman year. He was at Penn from 1947 to 1949 and then transferred in his junior year to the University of Nebraska—Lincoln College of Business Administration, where he earned a B.S. degree in 1950. He breezed through both schools, earning his degree in just three years. Even as he worked at the college paper, played bridge, and made A's in his courses, Buffett found time for money making activities, once submitting a dozen entries trying to win a $100 Burma-Shave jingle contest.

His best entry: "If missin' on kissin'—Hey listen, try thissen—Burma-Shave." (*Buffett: The Making of an American Capitalist,* Roger Lowenstein, pp. 33-34)

At Penn, Buffett became friends with Harry Beja. "The two of them matched A+'s in Industry 1, but Beja couldn't help but notice how much harder he worked in the course then Buffett had." And at Penn Buffett also became friends with Beja's roommate, a student from Brooklyn, who quickly decided Buffett was a "genius." (*Buffett: The Making of an American Capitalist,* Roger Lowenstein, p. 29)

"I didn't feel I was learning that much," he has said of his experience at the University of Pennsylvania.

During college, at Penn and later at the University of Nebraska, he was regional circulation manager for the *Lincoln Journal,* supervising 50 paper boys in six rural counties. He also found time to work for J.C. Penney. While at Penn, he worked at Penney's in Omaha one summer and during a Christmas vacation. He made 75 cents an hour selling men's shirts and has joked, "I became an authority on the Minimum Wage Act." The upside, however, was that Buffett saw firsthand how business worked.

About this time he rounded up 220 dozen golf balls and sold them to Jerry Orans for $1,200. (*Buffett: The Making of an American Capitalist, Roger Lowenstein,* p. 34)

In the summer of 1950, after graduating from the University of Nebraska at age 19 after taking 14 courses in one full year, Buffett applied to Harvard Business School.

And he kept up his constant reading about business by frequent visits to the Omaha Public Library, and absorbing everything he could find about accounting and insurance.

He took a train to Chicago where a Harvard alumnus interviewed him. Years later Buffett told Carol Loomis all the Harvard representative saw was, "a scrawny 19-year-old who looked 16 and had the social poise of a 12-year-old."

When the interview was over, so were Buffett's prospects at Harvard, and so too was the infallibility of the Harvard admissions office.

"The interview in Chicago took about 10 minutes and they threw me back in the water," Buffett said. Harvard told him he was too young and to try again in a year or two.

Buffett wrote his friend, Jerry Orans: "Now for the blow. Those stuffed shirts at Harvard didn't see there [sic] way clear to admit me to their graduate school. They decided 19 was too young to get admitted and advised me to wait a year or two. Therefore, I am now faced with the grim realities of life since I start paying room and board here in four weeks. My dad wants me to go on to some graduate school, but I'm not too sold on the idea."

Two weeks later Buffett wrote again: "To tell you the truth, I was kind of snowed when I heard from Harvard. Presently, I'm waiting for an application blank from Columbia. They have a pretty good finance department there; at least they have a couple of hot shots in Graham and Dodd that teach common stock valuation." (*Buffett: The Making of an American Capitalist*, Roger Lowenstein p. 35)

The rejection stung, but it turned out to be for the best because

(AP/Wide World Photos)

Ben Graham, the father of value investing and Buffett's teacher at Columbia University. "He was my god," Buffett says.

he soon realized that the greatest business professor was teaching at Columbia. Buffett applied to Columbia Business School, was immediately accepted, and graduated in June 1951.

As a senior at the University of Nebraska in 1950, Buffett had read Benjamin Graham's newly published book, *The Intelligent Investor*, which preached "value investing"—finding companies that are undervalued in the stock market, that is, companies whose intrinsic values are substantially greater than the value the stock market assigns to the enterprise. A value investor tries to buy stocks for substantially less than what the underlying business is worth—its

64

true "intrinsic value"—in the real business world. He wants to buy stocks selling at a good discount to the "transactional value" of the business.

Graham also thought investors should buy a stock only if it traded at less than two-thirds of net working capital.

To Graham a sound investment required high net asset values and low earnings multiples. He stressed prices in relation to interest rates.

It is *The Intelligent Investor* that offers one of Buffett's key business beliefs: "Investment is most intelligent when it is most businesslike." That means investments should not be swayed by emotions—hopes and fears—and fads.

Graham, born Benjamin Grossbaum in London in 1894 to a Jewish family in the bric-a-brac trade, encouraged investors to pay attention to intrinsic business value—what a reasonable businessman would pay. Graham once said: "The investor's worst enemy—is likely to be himself."

Also, an investor should keep in mind a "Margin of Safety," being sure the business you're buying is worth significantly more than you pay for it in the stock market. Only price and value count. Buffett would later say "Margin of Safety" are the three most important words in investing.

Buffett would become the world's greatest practitioner of value investing.

For Buffett, reading the book was an epiphany. "It was like Paul on the road to Damascus," Buffett told *Omaha World-Herald* reporter Robert Dorr. (March 24, 1985)

Buffett has said, "I read the first edition of this book early in 1950, when I was nineteen. I thought then that it was by far the best book about investing ever written. I still think it is."

Graham's *Intelligent Investor* is a popular version of *Security Analysis*, the classic study written by Graham and Columbia Professor David L. Dodd. Dodd was fond of saying: "There are no new eras, only new errors."

"I don't want to sound like a religious fanatic or anything, but it really did get me," Buffett told L.J. Davis. (*New York Times Magazine*, April 2, 1990)

Buffett always has recommended the book as required reading for any successful investor. He has said Chapter 8 about investor attitudes toward an erratic, unpredictable stock market and Chapter 20 on "Margin of Safety" about buying at bargain prices are among the most important pieces of investment advice ever written—that the true investor takes advantage of stock prices when they become silly in either direction and he buys at a good price compared to real business value.

Chapter 8 says when approaching the stock market, you should imagine you're in business with "Mr. Market" but you have to watch him because he lets his enthusiasms and fears run away with him. The chapter says, "Basically, price fluctuations have only one significant meaning for the true investor. They provide him with an opportunity to buy wisely when prices fall sharply and to sell wisely when they advance a great deal. At other times he will do better if he forgets about the stock market and pays attention to his dividend returns and to the operating results of his companies."

Chapter 20 talks about "a favorable difference in price on the one hand and an indicated or appraised value on the other. That difference is the margin of safety." Therefore, the margin of safety depends on the price paid.

Buffett also recommends the early works by investment guru Philip Fisher as well as *The Money Masters* by John Train.

Buffett's academic record was one of the best ever at Columbia Business School where he earned a masters in economics in June 1951.

It is said at the time Graham was teaching him, he believed young Buffett would become the greatest financial mind of his time.

Buffett made an A+ under Graham, according to Jim Rogers, who taught finance at Columbia, and John Burton, former dean of the Columbia Business School. Indeed, it is said that Buffett made the only A+ under Ben Graham, but that feat is not documented.

Rogers, born in Demopolis, Alabama, educated at Yale and Oxford, hit Wall Street in the 1970s, hooking up with famed investor George Soros. Their Quantum Fund, which often shorted stocks, assuming prices would fall, did so well that Rogers retired at age 37 with a reported $14 million.

Rogers still has a letter dated March 5, 1987, from Buffett to Columbia University Graduate School of Business Dean John Burton which reads:

"I appreciate the invitation to the Annual Dinner but will have to decline. My extended trip to New York always occurs in May—and even then I like to skip formal dinners as I find I can do a lot more catching up with friends in four- and six-people lunches and dinners. In fact, I'm not sure I can quite remember the last formal dinner I've attended. I enjoyed the Columbia Business School Annual Report. From everything I hear, Jim Rogers continues to be regarded as the best finance teacher in the country."

Dean Burton said, "He [Buffett] was gifted in math, but his ability to perceive economic value is his genius."

Graham himself had enrolled at Columbia on a scholarship and graduated second in his class in 1914. Graham was the sort of genius who masters a wide variety of intellectual disciplines, and Buffett was his greatest student.

Berkshire Vice Chairman Charles Munger, who knew Graham, has said: "Warren had a professor/mentor—Ben Graham—for whom he had great affection. Graham was so academic that when he graduated from Columbia three different academic departments invited him into their Ph.D. programs and asked him to start teaching immediately as part of the Ph.D. program: [those three departments being] literature, Greek and Latin classics and mathematics." (*Outstanding Investor Digest*, December 19, 1997)

Bill Ruane, a Harvard Business School graduate who became interested in the teachings of Columbia's Ben Graham and David Dodd, took one of Graham's courses and thus became a classmate of Buffett's in 1951. Today Ruane heads the Ruane, Cunniff & Co. investment management firm, runs the Sequoia Fund (which has large investments in Berkshire, and other stocks), is also a director of The Washington Post Co. and was a director of GEICO until Berkshire bought the rest of GEICO it didn't already own.

Ruane, who has joked that the only difference between himself and Buffett is billions of dollars and 100 points of IQ, says a kind of intellectual electricity coursed between Graham and Buffett and that the rest of the class was a rapt audience.

"Sparks were flying," recalls Ruane. "You could tell then he (Buffett) was someone who was very unusual." Back in the 1960s, Ruane was Buffett's stockbroker.

At Columbia, Buffett ran into a friend from Nebraska, Bill Christensen, and discovered the two were dating the same girl. Buffett told Christensen he'd back out of the situation.

Christensen, a history professor retired from Midland College in Fremont, Nebraska, laughed, "That girl told me he'd be a millionaire someday." Christensen said the woman married someone else, lives in Colorado, and he has kidded her over the years about not marrying Buffett.

(Photo by Laverne Ramsey)

Buffett's friend Bill Christensen

67

After Columbia, Buffett offered to work for Graham's investment company, Graham-Newman & Co. for free "but Ben," Buffett jokes, "made his customary calculation of price to value and said no."

Rejected, Buffett, armed with a Columbia master's degree at age 20, returned to Omaha to work in his father's brokerage firm, Buffett-Falk & Co., as an investment salesman from 1951 to 1954.

He felt his public speaking was inadequate, so he paid $100 and took a Dale Carnegie course when he was 21.

During that time, he also taught an investment course at the University of Omaha's adult education program. One time he arrived for a course and found only four students; he dismissed the class, saying he was sorry there wasn't enough interest to hold the course. Eventually his class got off the ground. *Omaha World-Herald's* Robert Dorr has written about a student from that course who recalled how class members, whose average age was in the 40s, snickered slightly when they first saw young Buffett. Buffett told Dorr, "I was skinnier then and looked like I could get into a basketball game as a high school student."

The moment Buffett began speaking, the snickering stopped. "After two minutes he had the class in his hands," said the former student.

One of the students was Dr. Carol Angle, a young pediatrician. (*Forbes*, October 12, 1998) "Warren had us calculate how money would grow using a slide rule. He brainwashed us to truly believe in our heart of hearts in the miracle of compound interest," said Dr. Angle. She and her husband, William, also a doctor, invited 11 other doctors to a dinner to meet Buffett.

Buffett remembers (*Forbes*, October 12, 1998) Bill Angle getting up at the end of the dinner and announcing: "I'm putting $10,000 in. The rest of you should too."

Today, Dr. Carol Angle, who clearly doesn't work because of the money, is director of clinical toxicology at the University of Nebraska Medical Center.

As always Buffett kept investing, but not every venture worked out.

"I guess my worst decision was that I went into a service station when I was 20 or 21. And I lost 20% of my net worth. So that service station's cost me about $800 million now, I guess. It's very satisfying when Berkshire goes down because the cost of that service station mistake declines," he said at the Berkshire Annual Meeting in 1992.

In those days he devoured financial books. While he worked for his father's brokerage firm, he would go to Nebraska's capital, Lincoln, and read statistical histories of insurance companies. He told *Forbes*, October 18, 1993, "I read from page to page. I didn't read brokers' reports or anything. I just looked at raw data. And I would get all excited about these things. I'd find Kansas City Life at 3 times earnings, Western Insurance Securities at 1 times earnings. I never had enough money and I didn't like to borrow money. So I sold something too soon to buy something else. I was over-stimulated in the early days and I'm under-stimulated now. I bought into an anthracite company. I bought into a windmill company. I bought into a street railway company, or more than one." Buffett bought cheap and found the stocks were cheap for good reasons.

Buffett now calls his efforts at statistically cheap buys his "used cigar butt" approach.

"When you're buying cigar butts, you've got to get rid of them. There aren't lots of puffs in it," Buffett said in a talk to Columbia business students October 27, 1993, as reported in the *Omaha World-Herald*, January 2, 1994. In the same talk, Buffett added:

"When I got out of Columbia the first place I went to work was a five-person brokerage firm with operations in Omaha (Buffett-Falk & Co., which his father founded). It subscribed to *Moody's* industrial manual, banks and finance manual and public utility manual. I went through all those page by page.

"I found a little company called Genessee Valley Gas near Rochester [New York]. It had 22,000 shares out. It was a public utility that was earning about $5 per share, and the nice thing about it was you could buy it at $5 per share.

"I found Western Insurance in Fort Scott, Kansas. The price range in Moody's financial manual...was $12-$20. Earnings $16 a share. I ran an ad in the Fort Scott paper to buy that stock.

"I found the Union Street Railway, in New Bedford [Massachusetts], a bus company. At that time it was selling at about $45 and, as I remember, had $120 a share in cash and no liabilities.

Nobody's going to tell you about the Union Street Railway Co...or Genessee Valley Gas. Sometimes the management's buying it themselves. You can't do this for big money, but it's somewhat the same principle. You find something that shouts at you."

Buffett later said of Genessee: "When I got out of Columbia University, I went through the Moody's manuals page by page—the industrial manual, the transportation manual, the banks and finance manual—just looking for things. And I found stocks at one times earnings. One was Genessee Valley Gas, a little tiny company in upstate New York. There were no brokerage reports on it, no nothing, but all you had to do was turn the page. It worked out so well I actually went through the book a second time." (*Fortune*, July 20, 1998)

Those early days for Buffett were also courting days. On April 19, 1952, at Dundee Presbyterian Church, he married Susan Thompson of Omaha, a petite brunette with a winning smile and manner, the popular daughter of Dr. William Thompson. "We used to call him 'Wild Bill'," says Buffett's son, Howard. Thompson was a psychology professor as well as dean of the School of Arts and Sciences at the University of Omaha, which later became part of the University of Nebraska. Susan Thompson, whose parents knew Buffett's parents, attended Northwestern University where she roomed with Buffett's sister, Bertie. It was she who introduced Susan Thompson to Warren Buffett.

Both grandparents on Mrs. Buffett's mother's side were deaf. Her grandfather wrote one of the two sign language dictionaries. The royalties from the dictionary go to Gallaudet University in Washington, D.C. Her uncle was head of the California School for the Deaf which Warren and Susie Buffett visited on their honey-

(Photo by LaVerne Ramsey)

This is Buffett's home in Omaha which he bought for $31,500 in 1958. He has never moved, but he has remodeled and added rooms, including a racquetball court. The house has large television screens, bookshelves throughout and stacks of Cokes near the garage entranceway. The home is furnished in early Nebraska Furniture Mart.

70

moon.

Occasionally Susie Buffett and her sister would use sign language to communicate between themselves at parties. Although Mrs. Buffett is not fluent in sign language, she is good enough to be understood.

During their early married years, Buffett and his wife lived in a run-down rented apartment from 1951-1952. Then they moved into a duplex where they lived until 1954, when they moved to New York. In 1956 they moved back to Omaha, renting a house on Underwood Avenue not far from the Buffett grocery store. Some of the early Buffett Partnership letters are written from 5202 Underwood Avenue. In 1958 they moved into the home where Buffett still lives.

(Photo courtesy of John Gass)

Mrs. Susan Buffett's childhood home in Omaha

"When I got married we had $10,000 and two choices. I told Susie that we could (1) buy a house now or (2) she could let me work on this, and that it would hopefully increase. So we waited four years. I bought the house when it represented 10% of my net worth," Buffett said at the Berkshire Annual Meeting in 1998.

All this is not to say Buffett doesn't have some amenities today. A snowstorm in 1997 left many homes near Buffett's without power for days. But did Buffett's home lose power? No.

In the mid 1970s, after her children were grown, Mrs. Buffett, always interested in music, pursued her passion in earnest, singing blues and jazz.

Music had long been a small part of Buffett's life. At age 11, he sang "America the Beautiful" with his sisters as part of a radio campaign for his father's first successful race for Congress.

The singing took place in the living room of the Buffett home at the corner of 53rd and Lake Streets.

And music may have helped Buffett in winning his wife's hand.

During their college days, Buffett won Susie's attention by playing the ukulele with her father, a mandolin player.

"It was obvious I was not number 1 with her. But he [Susan's father] became very pro-me. It was two against one," Buffett is quoted in the Armstrong story.

"That's true. My father really did court her through her father," says Howard Buffett.

Warren and Susan Buffett, who grew up about a mile from one another, have three children. After the children were grown, and shortly after their 25th wedding anniversary, Buffett and his wife followed their own paths and have lived apart since late 1977. Mrs. Buffett moved to San Francisco and still lives there. She and her husband remain on very close terms. In 1991 she was named to Berkshire's board, replacing Ken Chace of Maine, who retired.

Astrid Menks, a vivacious woman 17 years younger than Buffett and once a hostess in the same cafe where Buffett's wife sang, has lived with Buffett since 1978, the year after Mrs. Buffett left for San Francisco. Buffett and Astrid Menks live together in the standard sense of the term living together.

"Astrid was not around until after my mother left for San Francisco," said Buffett's daughter, Susan Buffett.

Buffett and his wife see each other about once a month and at Christmas with the family at Laguna Beach. She travels with him on many non-business trips.

"My dad was so involved with his work, which is his fun. My mother had a very different life...We have such great parents. They are very affectionate. They still have strong relations. Once the kids were raised, my mother didn't want to sit home," Buffett's daughter said.

Buffett's wife was interested in her musical career and in travel.

Buffett, his wife and Ms. Menks all showed up at a party held for shareholders at Borsheim's, the jewelry store Berkshire owns, the day before the annual meeting in 1990. As usual they were all cordial to one another and have attended the same annual meeting events every year. The three send presents to relatives from "Warren, Susie and Astrid." (*Salon*, August 31, 1999)

Astrid Menks and Buffett are clearly very close. Buffett has given her bejeweled mementos, including a gold piece in the form of a Berkshire stock certificate, and other gifts, some bought at Borsheim's. Astrid Menks has been a Berkshire shareholder for many years.

Buffett has said his arrangement with his wife and Astrid Menks is unusual. "But if you knew everybody well, you'd understand it quite well." (*Regardie's*, February, 1986)

Buffett finally landed a job with Graham at Graham-Newman on Wall Street in 1954.

"Between 1951 and 1954, when I was pestering Ben Graham for

a job (he turned me down when I got out of school, even though I offered to work for him for nothing), he mentioned me to Bill Rosenwald (son of Julius Rosenwald who developed Sears, Roebuck into a mass merchandiser) with the result that I received an exploratory letter about going to work for the family. I couldn't follow through at the time because National Guard obligations kept me in Omaha. I will never know if Ben was trying to do Bill Rosenwald a favor, or whether he was just trying to get me off his own doorstep." (from a letter Buffett wrote July 24, 1985, to Maria Anagnos, author of "Financial Theory and the Formation of an Investment Empire", a thesis for an MBA degree at New York University Graduate School of Business Administration in 1986.)

Today Buffett gets many requests to work for him, some even offering to pay him their salary. Buffett says, "O.K., fine. I'll even double your salary." (Anagnos thesis)

"When Warren Buffett became a junior employee at Graham-Newman in the 1950s, he made a detailed study of arbitrage earnings from 1926 to 1956—the entire life span of the company. He discovered that unleveraged returns from arbitrage averaged 20% per year. Buffett soaked up the tricks of arbitrage used at Graham-Newman and has used and improved on them ever since." (*Benjamin Graham on Value Investing*, Janet Lowe, p. 75)

Buffett stayed there two years until Graham closed the business in 1956 and retired. Graham never gave Buffett money to invest. Buffett later said, "He couldn't have cared less. That was my frustration with Graham. He had no intensity for money." (*Forbes*, October 12, 1998) Graham's wife, Estelle, invested $20,000 with Buffett early on. During his stay in New York, Buffett taught an adult education course on the stock market in Scarsdale in 1955. Buffett and his wife, who was pregnant with their second child, rented an apartment in White Plains, New York. Both Graham and his partner, Jerome Newman, died wealthy. Ben Graham who lived his last years in a La Jolla, California, condominium overlooking the Pacific Ocean, died in 1976.

The Graham-Newman firm was small. "It operated with $6 million in capital," Buffett said at Berkshire's Annual Meeting in 1992.

In addition to Buffett, the Graham-Newman firm hired Walter Schloss and Tom Knapp who became famous value investors.

Irving Kahn, head of Kahn Brothers & Company, Inc. in New York, worked for Graham for 27 years at Columbia and Graham-Newman, and recalls young Buffett at Graham-Newman as Graham's prized protégé.

"He was much the same as he is now but he was a brash, cocky young guy...He was always busy on his own. He has tremendous energy. He could wear you out talking to you. He was very ambitious about making money," said Kahn, adding that Buffett had an extraordinary understanding of how business worked.

Kahn said Buffett's father knew Ben Graham and that both men, seared by the Depression, sought ways to restore old values and to find ways that would ensure price stability.

"Warren's father was at the forefront of the Depression in Omaha, and for farmers he had a deep feeling that the system had broken down...It was a widespread farmbelt feeling. He was also in the securities business. Coming out of the Depression he met Ben Graham in Washington who was a sort of Renaissance man. They talked a lot about tying price stability to commodities and what could be done for lesser developed countries."

In addition to having an eye for business and value investing, Graham also had an eye for the catch of the day in the form of willowy blondes. As Buffett said in a 1988 *Fortune's Investor's Guide* interview: "It was all open and everything, but Ben liked women. And women liked him. He wasn't physically attractive—he looked like Edward G. Robinson, but he had style."

During his time with Graham-Newman, young family man Buffett commuted by train from his Westchester County apartment in White Plains.

"It didn't seem like much of a life," he told Linda Grant. "People kept coming up to me all the time, whispering into my ear about some wonderful business. I was getting excited all the time. I was a wonderful customer for the brokerages. Trouble was, everyone else was, too."

He decided to strike out on his own, never again to have a boss. Along the way, Buffett discovered that he and Graham had somewhat differing views of practical investing.

"Ben was not that interested in going deeply into corporate analysis as I might have been," Buffett told Davis. Buffett, at Berkshire's annual meeting in 1992, said Graham—seeking simple ways to provide safety for investors—focused on measures of cheapness in selecting stocks. Graham was after such benchmarks as buying stocks for two-thirds of the net working capital of a company.

Buffett began to look beyond only measures of cheapness. "I tried hard to get business insights," he said, adding that he began looking at stocks as businesses and that while he looked for value, as do all investors, he also looked at growth as another part of value.

Berkshire shareholder Michael Assael explains, "It's the classic case of Buffett getting *two* for the price of *one*. Buffett teaches us that 'growth is always a component in the calculation of value, constituting a variable whose importance can range from negligible to enormous.' Just look at the worldwide growth of The Coca-Cola Company Berkshire bought in the 1980s when Coke's PE ratio and earnings were a fraction of what they are today."

Buffett ultimately became interested in not only strict value investing, emphasizing a company's balance sheet, but also in the fundamentals and growth prospects of a company, taking into account its competitive position.

At age 25, Buffett returned to Omaha where he expects to live the rest of his days in the midwestern city 1,100 miles from Wall Street. In the spring of 1956, he rented a home on Underwood Avenue not far from the Buffett grocery store.

In 1996, serving as a poster boy for a campaign to promote Nebraska's business climate, Buffett said: "I chose to stay in Nebraska because it has a great deal going for it. For one thing, Nebraska's pro-business climate makes real economic sense for any type of business. And, of course, there are all those characteristics we are known for here in Nebraska: clean air, low crime rate, good schools and a Midwestern work ethic." (*Omaha World-Herald*, August 1, 1996)

Buffett got little encouragement about going into the investment business in 1951 after his days at Columbia. "The two people I respected the most were my dad and Ben Graham and they both said it was a bad time to go into it," Buffett said at the Berkshire Annual Meeting in 1992.

To begin working at home in his bedroom took courage. Not many young people would make much of an impression if they announced they were going to their bedroom to start a business.

"I first met him when he came home after working for Ben Graham," recalls William O'Connor, the former Mutual of Omaha executive. O'Connor got to know Buffett in investment club circles in Omaha. "I invited him to our investment club. Like most of us he was about our age of 24, but unlike us he was so profound when it came to business and finance. He was so well received we invited him back the next year and each time he played a little penny-ante poker and he left some small sums. He would say it was against his better judgment, but frequently said, 'I'll call.' "

O'Connor took Buffett's 10-week investment course at the University of Omaha, now the University of Nebraska. During breaks Buffett and the students would drink a Pepsi and students soaked up Buffett's investment insights.

"He rarely gave specific advice, but he gave you a lot to think about. He left his students well grounded in the principles of compounding," O'Connor said.

O'Connor sold Buffett an IBM typewriter for the Buffett Partnership in December, 1958. "I installed it at his home. Over the years I sold him an office replacement typewriter and a dictating machine. Perhaps what he got the most use from was the dictating machine I sold to his wife, Susie, who used it for her correspondence with 60 or 70 minority children she helped with college and moral support."

In late 1958 O'Connor sold about $16,000 of his IBM stock and some other small holdings, and on January 1, 1959, invested $18,600 in the Buffett Partnership.

Over the years he added to his holdings, occasionally selling some holdings for family needs.

"My wife, Jean, questioned my judgment" about putting so much with Buffett, but O'Connor told her that if she knew what he knew about Buffett, she'd understand.

O'Connor's faith paid off and he became one of Buffett's many millionaires in Omaha. Good thing—William and Jean O'Connor have 10 children. "Warren really is a very uncomplicated person. He's a super nice guy who just keeps things simple," O'Connor said.

"He is truly a remarkable person. His technical knowledge and his humor are unique. It's truly entertaining to be associated with him...He has an insatiable thirst for knowledge. He reads from all the sources and he has a photographic memory that helps him recall and reconstruct things in an orderly, logical fashion...

"He plays a little tennis and golf, but I think he'd rather read—and play bridge—than anything."

Over the years Buffett has changed little. He reads. He plays bridge. But above all, despite a wide range of intellectual pursuits, his most consuming passion is business.

In 1956, at age 25, he was married with two children. His personal kitty jumped from $9,800 in 1950 to $140,000 in 1956. "I thought it was enough to retire on...I had no master plan," Buffett told reporter L.J. Davis. Before that, in his first year out of college, the net worth of Buffett's investments had soared 144% when he was dealing with about $10,000. He started fast.

In those days, he was approached by family members who wanted investment advice. As a result he founded the Buffett Partnership in 1956 telling investors, "I'll run it like I run my own money, and I'll take part of the losses and part of the profits. And I won't tell you what I'm doing."

Buffett managed the partnership while the other members were limited partners who made none of the decisions. Buffett's investors always have been in the dark about what he's up to until an earnings report is filed.

He pooled $105,100 from friends and relatives to form his partnership. Other than going around town trying to solicit money, mainly from doctors, Buffett rang up only a few expenses. The price of the rent was right. Buffett always would hold dear his low-cost operating habits.

He ran the partnership from the sun porch located just off his upstairs bedroom. If ever someone lived over the store—in the store actually—Buffett did in the early days as he began his unmatched career in money management.

The man who would become known as the Wizard of Omaha, the Oracle of Omaha, the Sage of Omaha was on his way.

"What I like about him is that he started from nothing," said teenage stock picker Matt Seto, from Troy, Michigan, who later was written up in the *Wall Street Journal* and widely interviewed for his prowess in running the Matt Seto Fund.

"So many of the wealthy people you read about started out wealthy. Buffett didn't," Seto said.

(Photo courtesy of Matt Seto)

Teenage stock-picker Matt Seto: "What I like about him is that he started from nothing."

One day in the summer of 1956 Homer Dodge, a physics professor and president of Norwich University in Vermont who heard of the wunderkind as a result of being a friend of Ben Graham's, arrived in Omaha after a canoe trip, sought out Buffett and became the first outside partner.

The canoe trip was apparently incidental. Dodge had driven

(Courtesy of Walter Schloss; photo taken in 1968 at Del Coronado in San Diego)

Members of the "intellectual village" of Graham and Dodd

Ben Graham and his disciples—From left: Warren Buffett, Bob Brustein, deceased friend of Ben Graham's. (Brustein's widow, Hannah, married Alan Pakula, the movie producer of To Kill A Mockingbird, All the President's Men, Sophie's Choice and many other movies. Pakula was killed in a car accident in 1998.) Ben Graham, David "Sandy" Gottesman, Tom Knapp, Charles Munger, Jack Alexander, Henry Brandt, Walter Schloss, Marshall Weinberg, Ed Anderson, Buddy Fox and Bill Ruane.

1,500 miles alone in hopes of persuading 25-year-old Buffett to manage his family's savings. (*Fortune/1990 Investors Guide*)

Buffett came to the door of his home in his socks and invited Dodge in for an informal chat. Dodge gave Buffett $120,000 to invest for his family. (*Forbes*, October 12, 1998)

Recalls Buffett for the *Fortune* piece, "Homer told me, 'I'd like you to handle my money.' I said, 'The only thing I'm doing is a partnership with my family.' He said, 'Well, I'd like one with you.' So I set up one with Homer, his wife, children and grandchildren."

Dodge invested for his family in the Buffett Partnership and when Dodge died in 1983, that sum had multiplied into tens of millions of dollars.

Dodge's son Norton, a University of Maryland expert on the Soviet economy, had contributed $40,000. *Forbes* (October 12, 1998) said Norton Dodge decided to use his wealth for worthwhile purposes. On his frequent trips to the Soviet Union, Dodge learned about the many talented artists who couldn't exhibit their works because they did not celebrate the glories of the Communist state so Dodge sold some Berkshire and used the money to buy their work and publicize them. Dodge later donated about $20 million worth of the art to Rutgers University. He has said it could be called, "The Buffett Collection."

Dodge has said, "My father saw immediately that Warren was brilliant at financial analysis. But it was more than that."

The elder Dodge saw a uniquely talented craftsman who loved the process of investing and who had mastered all the tools. The same *Fortune* article quoted Berkshire Vice Chairman Charles Munger, "His [Buffett's] brain is a superbly rational mechanism. And since he's articulate, you can see the damn brain working."

In the early to mid-1960s a fellow named Laurence Tisch, later to become chairman of Loews and CBS, sent Buffett a check for $300,000 and a note saying, "Include me in."

Tisch, no slouch as an investor, would later describe Buffett as "the greatest investor of his generation." Adds Michael Assael, "That's an understatement. As Berkshire's web of wealth expands exponentially, Warren Buffett will come to be seen as one of the greatest architects of economic value a free society has ever known." Tisch later told *Forbes* (October 12, 1998) he sold his Berkshire to avoid being criticized for being a Buffett investor when both men might be interested in the same stocks.

In those early days some investors signed on with Buffett, but others didn't. John Train wrote (*The Money Masters*, p. 10): "I made the opposite decision when, looking for a good place to park some capital, I first met Buffett. At that very early stage he had no office at all, and ran things from a tiny sitting-room off his bedroom—no secretary, no calculator. When I found that the holdings could not be revealed, I decided not to sign up."

One day Buffett called on his neighbor, Donald Keough, then a Butter-Nut Coffee executive. To do so Buffett just had to walk across the street. That the two lived so close is as odd as Truman Capote (*In Cold Blood*) and Harper Lee (*To Kill a Mockingbird*) once living next door to one another in the small town of Monroeville, Alabama. Monroeville had a population of 6,993, according to the 1990 Census. And why that number of people? Well, a city with a population of at least 7,000 located in a "dry county" can vote wet. But all that is some other book.

Keough came to Coca-Cola as a result of a series of acquisitions. Keough eventually became president of The Coca-Cola Company as well as a board member of The Washington Post Company and McDonald's Corp. In any event, young Keough, partly because Buffett sat around in a T-shirt reading all day, declined Buffett's offer to invest:

"I had five small kids and left for work each day," Keough recalled for a profile of Buffett by Bernice Kanner in *New York* magazine (April 22, 1985): "Buffett had three and stayed home. He had this marvelous hobby, model trains, and my kids used to troop over there and play with them. One day Warren popped over and asked if I'd thought about how I was going to educate these kids...I told him I planned to work hard and see what happened. Warren said if I gave him $5,000 he'd probably do better (for me). My wife and I talked it over, but we figured we didn't know what this guy even did for a living—how could we give him $5,000? We've been kicking ourselves ever since. I mean, if we had given him the dough, we could have owned a college by now."

By the time Buffett was 31 in 1961, he was a millionaire. However, by the time Microsoft's Bill Gates was 31, Gates was a billionaire. Comedian Jay Leno once said of Gates: "This man is so successful, his chauffeur is Ross Perot."

"I had a lot better ideas back then than I do now," Buffett told *Money World's* Adam Smith, whose real name is George J.W. Goodman. Smith took his nom de plume from the 18th-century Scottish economist who outlined the mechanics of capitalism.

In 1965, through his Buffett Partnership, Buffett acquired a controlling interest in Berkshire Hathaway, a New Bedford, Massachusetts, textile mill, for about $14 million.

At the time, Berkshire was suffering from a prolonged slide and Buffett bought its unimpressive operations for the proverbial song.

Despite hard work and a new management, the textile operations never paid off.

It would become one of the few businesses that never really made it under Buffett and in 1985, after years of struggling to keep it afloat, he sold it for scrap.

In 1969, Buffett determined that he could no longer find real values—buying a business or part of a business at wide discount to its intrinsic business value—and he decided to dissolve the highly successful partnership.

The partnership—after 13 years of average annual 30% growth—was worth $100 million; Buffett's stake about $20 million. Buffett, then 38, wrote his limited partners:

"I am out of step with present conditions. When the game is no longer played your way, it is only human to say the new approach is all wrong, bound to lead to trouble, and so on...On one point, however, I am clear. I will not abandon a previous approach whose logic I understand (although I find it difficult to apply) even though it may mean foregoing large, and apparently easy, profits to embrace an approach which I don't fully understand, have not practiced successfully, and which possibly could lead to substantial permanent loss of capital."

He distributed to his investors their stakes in the partnership and their pro rata shares in Berkshire.

John Train wrote a chapter about Buffett in his book, *The Money Masters.* Of the partnership he wrote, "He never had a down year, even in the severe bear markets of 1957, 1962, 1966 and 1969. That achievement stands alone in modern portfolio management."

Three years after the Buffett Partnership was disbanded, the market suffered one of its worst periods in decades, the 1973-74 collapse.

Guess who was buying in 1973? In the spring and summer of 1973, Buffett picked up media and advertising stocks at rock-bottom prices, including $10.6 million in Washington Post Co. shares.

7
CHESS WITH FIVE-YEAR-OLD
JONATHAN BRANDT

Henry Brandt, Harvard's top student in 1949 and long a senior vice president with Shearson Lehman Hutton, made the mistake of selling more than 1,500 of the family's Berkshire shares for millions of dollars less than they are worth today. "I'm very embarrassed about that," Brandt once told *Fortune*.

His embarrassment was more acute when he discovered the buyer of his shares was a Berkshire subsidiary, Rockford Bancorp, which later was spun off.

Brandt and Buffett were friends from the early days and their families have remained friends since.

An unbelievable gatherer of information, Brandt would spend his days writing out his investment thoughts on yellow pads. Everyone recognized his extraordinary fact-gathering abilities and on this Buffett did not go against the crowd. "He still does that [writes out everything on yellow pads]," says his wife, Roxanne.

For a time the two men shared an apartment during the week and then returned to their wives on the weekends.

"So Buffett has slept in my bed," laughs Roxanne Brandt.

When the families did get together at the Brandt home in Manhattan, the men, after dinner, would settle in chairs or sit on the floor and listen to Buffett talk. Even back then, recalls Roxanne Brandt, it was "Jesus and the apostles."

Mrs. Brandt wrote in her daughter's baby book at the time: "Three greatest minds of the era: Einstein, Schweitzer and Buffett."

Once Buffett played chess with the Brandt's five-year-old son, Jonathan. "Buffett has always said he lost to Jonathan," Mrs. Brandt said. "The truth is he beat Jonathan, but barely. He was sweating it."

Jonathan, who went to Harvard and Stanford, wound up working for Buffett's long time friend, Bill Ruane at the Ruane, Cunniff firm. "I always had the feeling that Buffett looked at Jonathan thinking: when he grows up where will he fit in my picture."

Well, Jonathan is alive and well at Ruane, Cunniff where he is an expert on banks and, of course, Berkshire.

8
"I MAKE NO FURTHER PROVISION FOR MY SON, WARREN."

Congressman Howard H. Buffett signed his last will and testament on August 5, 1963, the year before he died. After his death, an inventory of his estate amounted to $563,292.77, of which $334,739.00 was invested in the Buffett Partnership.

The elder Buffett bequeathed $20,000 to The Nebraska Methodist Hospital, $10,000 to The Immanuel Deaconess Institute and $5,000 to Harding College of Searcy, Arkansas.

He left the rest of his estate to his "Beloved Wife," Leila. He named her as executrix and his son as trustee.

Howard Buffett's instructions were, "Upon the death of my wife and myself, the Trustee shall divide the trust into as many equal shares as there are then living daughters of mine and deceased daughters of mine who have left issue then surviving."

Warren Buffett was to receive nothing, except a few personal effects.

Congressman Buffett explained why he was leaving nothing to his son: "I make no further provision for my son, Warren, not out of any lack of love for him but because he has a substantial estate in his own right and for the further reason that he has advised me that he does not desire the same and has requested that I not make any further provision for him."

At his death the elder Buffett, in line with the probity of his life, had checking accounts at local banks with a total of about $7,000, about $30,000 in Treasury bonds, a 1961 Buick automobile worth $1,800 and

(Omaha World-Herald)

Congressman Howard Buffett

a solid stock portfolio with such holdings as 300 shares of DeBeers Consolidated Mines, the diamond company, 300 shares of Dome Petroleum, 200 shares of Handy and Harmon, 500 shares of Kewanee Oil Co. and 100 shares of Weyerhaeuser—all positions reflecting concern about inflation.

He also had some investments in agriculture, such as 185 shares of South Omaha Feed & Supply Co., and 208 shares of Government Employees Insurance Co., (GEICO) one of Warren Buffett's favorite stocks, indeed a company where one day Buffett would own all the shares.

The 208 shares and a few other positions were sold by Mrs. Buffett after her husband's death to be invested elsewhere, according to court documents. What Congressman Buffett started as a compiling of solid wealth, Warren Buffett finished. But none of Warren Buffett's wealth was inherited from his father.

9
BUFFETT PARTNERSHIP
A $100 INVESTMENT AND A 49-CENT LEDGER FROM WOOLWORTH'S

Flashback to the Buffett Partnership days, the Fabulous Fifties. To talk to Buffett face to face during the first years, "You went in the back door of his home, walked through the kitchen, the living room and went up the stairs to the bedroom," the *Omaha World-Herald* quoted one partner in a May 5, 1986, story. "If you were impressed with show and image, Warren was not your man."

During the life of the partnership—from 1956 to 1969—average annual returns were 30%, before fees. $10,000 became $300,000.

At the partnership's inception, Buffett had been married for four years and had two small children. He was fresh off a brilliant academic career and a two-year stint on Wall Street. But Buffett, calling on his pioneer spirit and self-reliance of the agrarian Midwest, shunned Wall Street and would forever operate from his beloved Omaha.

At one point in his career, when Buffett was testifying before Congress about the Salomon scandal, he was introduced to the House Energy and Finance Subcommittee by U.S. Representative Peter Hoagland (D.-Nebraska) who said it was his pleasure to introduce one of his state's most illustrious and inspiring citizens.

Hoagland attributed Buffett's success "to growing up in Omaha, a beginning that instilled in him the old-fashioned values of integrity, discipline and character."

Above all, Omaha is a town where almost everything is dedicated to economic activity. It is the home of such no-nonsense enterprises as Mutual of Omaha, Union Pacific, ConAgra, Woodmen of the World Insurance, a Campbell's Soup plant, Creighton University, a large health care industry and the nearby Strategic Air Command (SAC) headquarters.

Born of a substantial family fully involved in the community, blessed with extraordinary mental gifts and operating in a perfect economic soil of capitalism, Buffett arose one morning and entirely on his own founded the Buffett Partnership.

Organized May 1, 1956, when Buffett was 25, the tiny partnership had seven limited partners—four family members and three close friends—who contributed $105,000 but had no voting power, no say in the running of the partnership.

For the history books, according to a certificate of limited partnership filing at the Douglas County Courthouse in Omaha, the following limited partners were the real lottery winners of 1956:

Charles E. Peterson, Jr.	$5,000	(friend)
Elizabeth B. Peterson	$25,000	(Charles' mother)
Doris B. Wood	$5,000	(sister)
Daniel J. Monen, Jr.	$5,000	(attorney friend)
William H. Thompson	$25,000	(father-in-law)
Alice R. Buffett	$35,000	(aunt)
Truman S. Wood	$5,000	(brother-in-law)

(Truman Wood, an Omaha native, married Doris Buffett in the early 1950s. They were divorced in 1965. Wood died in Fort Lauderdale, Florida, in 1998.)

Buffett says: "The first investors just believed in me. The ones who had faith stayed on—you couldn't get my Aunt Katie to sell if you came at her with a crowbar." (*Forbes*, October 11, 1999)

Attorney Daniel Monen drew up all Buffett Partnership papers.

The first meeting of the partners was held at the Omaha Club in downtown Omaha.

General Partner Warren Buffett, listed as residing at 5202 Underwood Avenue where he rented a home, chipped in $100 and so the partnership actually began with $105,100. "Buffett's initial investment for the partnership (not including the $100) was the purchase of a 49-cent ledger from Woolworth's." (Maria Anagnos thesis) He would add more of his own money later to the successful enterprise. As manager, Buffett received 25% of the profits above the 6% investors could receive in savings accounts annually, with deficiencies carried forward. The override amounted to a good income for young Buffett.

"I got the idea for my partnership form because I had worked for Ben. I was inspired by the example. I changed certain things, but it was not original with me. That has never been recognized," Buffett says. *(Benjamin Graham on Value Investing, Janet Lowe, p. 170)*

Over the life of the partnership, the setup made Buffett rich.

Two additional single-family limited partnerships were formed in 1956. By January 1, 1957, combined assets were $303,726.

To seek new money, Buffett called on investors, sometimes approaching them with his tax return asking, "Don't you wish you could pay this much in taxes?"

Dorothy Davis, a wealthy neighbor, invited Buffett over to her apartment one evening in 1957, according to *Forbes* (October 12, 1998). " 'I've heard you manage money,' she said. Buffett recalls, 'She questioned me very closely for two hours about my philosophy of investing. But her husband, Dr. Davis, didn't say a word. He appeared not even to be listening. Suddenly, Dr. Davis announced, 'We're giving you $100,000.' 'How come?' I asked. 'Because you remind me of Charlie Munger.' " Who's Charles Munger? Buffett didn't even know Munger yet. Two years later Dr. Davis introduced the two.

Buffett approached one Omaha businessman in the early partnership days and asked for a $10,000 investment. The businessman told his wife he wanted to do it, but his wife told him they didn't have $10,000. "We could borrow it," he said. "Like hell," she replied.

Today that businessman's son bemoans that his parents didn't make the investment and missed out on being millionaires, adding: "We've all been working our asses off ever since."

Among the early partners was Charles Heider who today is general partner of Heider-Weitz Partners in Omaha. Heider says: "I told my family. 'Look, Warren is going to think about how to invest our money seven days a week.' "

Another was investor Fred Stanback who met and was impressed with Buffett at Columbia. Stanback is known for his long term holdings in Berkshire, Food Lion and other stocks.

As time passed, some original partners added money and other partners came on board. Later there were other partnerships, amendments to the original partnership and at year end 1961, Buffett merged 10 of his partnerships and changed the name from Buffett Associates to Buffett Partnership.

In 1957, the partnership had recorded a gain of $31,615.97—a 10.4% increase. That may not sound so hot, but compared to the Dow Jones Industrial Average that slumped 8.4% that year, it was splendid.

Here are the Dow and partnership results in percentage terms as presented in *The Intelligent Investor* (Fourth Revised Edition, 1973):

	Dow	Buffett Partnership
1957	-8.4	10.4
1958	38.5	40.9
1959	20.0	25.9
1960	-6.2	22.8
1961	22.4	45.9

1962	-7.6	13.9
1963	20.6	38.7
1964	18.7	27.8
1965	14.2	47.2
1966	-15.6	20.4
1967	19.0	35.9
1968	7.7	58.8
1969	-11.6	6.8

Buffett, worth about $100,000 when he started the partnership in 1956, was worth about $400,000 by 1959.

(Buffett's net worth ballooned to about $250 million by 1982 when *Forbes* magazine listed Buffett as one of the 400 wealthiest people in America. By 1984 Buffett was worth about $700 million.)

The partnership never failed to beat the Dow. It never had a down year. On average, from 1957 through 1962, while the Dow grew 8.3% a year, the partnership grew 26% a year.

Net assets of the partnership, compiled by Buffett while still under his own roof at home, were $7,178,500!

In November 1962, the partnership, which along the way had invested in windmill makers and anthracite producers, began buying shares of a textile mill: Berkshire Hathaway. The stock price had dropped below book value, indeed, even the cash in the bank.

Buffett bought his first shares of Berkshire at a price of $7.60 and kept on buying between $7 and $8 a share. By 1965 he gained financial control of Berkshire and became a director.

From the beginning, Buffett knew his mission was to compound his cash at a hefty, steady clip.

In 1963 Buffett wrote his partners the following epistle about the "Joys of Compounding":

"I have it from unreliable sources that the cost of the voyage Isabella originally underwrote for Columbus was approximately $30,000....Without attempting to evaluate the psychic income derived from finding a new hemisphere, it must be pointed out that even had squatter's rights prevailed, the whole deal was not exactly another IBM. Figured very roughly, the $30,000 invested at 4% compounded annually would have amounted to something like $2,000,000,000,000 (that's two trillion for those of you who are not government statisticians) by 1962."

He adds, "Historical apologists for the Indians of Manhattan may find refuge in similar calculations. Such fanciful geometric progressions illustrate the value of either living a long time, or compounding your money at a decent rate."

In the same letter Buffett told partners he had moved from an office off his bedroom "to one a bit (quite a bit) more conventional. Surprising as it may seem, the return to a time clock has not been unpleasant. As a matter of fact, I enjoy not keeping track of everything on the backs of envelopes."

Buffett moved the partnership in 1962 to 810 Kiewit Plaza and by then had splurged by hiring his first employee, Bill Scott, who managed Berkshire's bond portfolio until his retirement in 1993. Scott still works part-time at Berkshire and oversees his own charity interests.

(Photo by Nancy Line Jacobs)
Bill Scott

In 1964 Buffett Partnership listed 440 Omaha partners with an average investment of $98,430. Assuming those investments have remained, the $98,430 has grown to $112 million. (*Omaha World-Herald*, July 12, 1998)

In 1965 Buffett was telling partners, "If our record is better than that of these (market averages) we consider it a good year whether we are plus or minus. If we do poorer, we deserve the tomatoes."

By 1969 the partnership's assets had grown to $104,429,431.

From the beginning, partnership expenses were worrisome. From 1963 to 1969 rent soared from $3,947 to $5,823. Dues and subscriptions skyrocketed from $900 to $994. "At least the situation hasn't gotten completely out of control," Buffett wrote in his partnership letter of January 22, 1969.

Along the way—in 1963—a Dun and Bradstreet Report dated November 13, 1963, gave approval of the fledgling enterprise: "Volume steady. Condition sound."

The partnership received this one-sentence description of its creditworthiness: "Due to the nature of this business subject is not a general seeker of mercantile credit however maintains a prompt local pay record."

As for its finances, the report found that at the start of 1963, the partnership had a worth of $9.4 million, "consisting of cash resources, income-producing securities and other investments. A sound condition continues. Cash averages a low to moderate six-figure amount in two local depository [sic] with a high six figure amount owing secured and relations satisfactory...Employs one. Location: Rents office space on eighth floor of multi-story brick office building located [in an] outlying business district. Premises orderly."

At that time there were more than 90 limited partners.

In his January 18, 1964, letter, Buffett reports the partnership began the year with assets of $17,454,900. "Susie and I have an investment of $2,393,900 in the Partnership. For the first time, I had to withdraw funds in addition to monthly payments, but it was a choice of this or disappointing the Internal Revenue Service."

Two years later he wrote, "Susie and I have an investment of $6,849,936, which should keep me from slipping away to the movies in the afternoon."

At this time Buffett kept telling of three main investment categories the partnership was engaged in:

1. "Generals"—Undervalued stocks generally to be held for a long time.
2. "Workouts"—Securities with a timetable, arbitrage situations arising from sell-outs, mergers, reorganizations and the like.
3. "Controls"—Owning such a sizeable block that the partnership gains control of the business.

In the midst of all this Buffett was saying, "We like good management—we like a decent industry—we like a certain amount of 'ferment' in a previously dormant management or stockholder group. But we demand value."

One undervalued investment that had started as a "general" in 1956 was Dempster Mill Manufacturing Co., a farm equipment maker. Buffett reported that the stock was selling at $18 a share with about $72 in book value.

One Berkshire shareholder thinks the overall play at Dempster was along these lines: buy the company at a quarter of book value, liquidate a substantial portion of the book value to generate funds for investment, borrow money on the unleveraged company for further investment and then spin off the core business.

Buffett continued buying the stock in small quantities for five years. By mid-1961 the partnership owned more than 70% of the company.

Things didn't go particularly well and that's when Buffett called in Harry Bottle, who later became an investor in Berkshire, to run things. Bottle still pops up at times to get some operating doldrums moving for Buffett. Two years later, the business, later named First Beatrice Corp., was sold.

Because it was the largest employer in Beatrice, Nebraska, the city helped finance the acquisition of Buffett's stake.

By 1965, the partnership's net assets—through contributions and growth—had grown to $26 million from $105,100 ten years earlier.

Buffett celebrated in the spring, renting an additional 227 square feet of space at headquarters, about the size of an ordinary room.

"Our War on Poverty was successful in 1965. Specifically, we were $12,304,060 less poor at the end of the year," began Buffett in his January 20, 1966, letter to partners.

For the year (1965), when the Dow was up 14.2%, the Buffett Partnership orbited the world. A 47.2% return! That was about the time Buffett started saying, "Democracy is great but not in investment decisions."

Although Buffett had told partners his goal was to beat the Dow by 10 percentage points, in reality he was beating it by nearly 20 points. From 1957 through 1965, the Dow rose 11.4%, on average. The partnership returns were 29.8% a year! Goal achieved and surpassed.

"I now feel that we are much closer to the point where increased size may prove disadvantageous," he said.

He would say it almost every year afterwards. He's been saying it for more than 30 years. Yet average returns have continued coming in at more than 20% a year.

In 1962, Buffett Partnership began buying Berkshire Hathaway at under $8 a share when Berkshire had about $16 a share in working capital alone.

Of Berkshire, Buffett wrote January 20, 1965:

> Our purchases of Berkshire started at a price of $7.60 per share in 1962. This price partially reflected large losses incurred by the prior management in closing some of the mills made obsolete by changing conditions within the textile business (which the old management had been quite slow to recognize). In the postwar period the company had slid downhill a considerable distance, having hit a peak in 1948 when about $29½ million was earned before tax and about 11,000 workers were employed. This reflected output from 11 mills.

> At the time we acquired control in the spring of 1965, Berkshire was down to two mills and about 2,300 employees. It was a very pleasant surprise to find that the remaining units had excellent management personnel, and we have not had to bring a single man from outside into the operation. In relation to our beginning acquisition cost of $7.60 per share (the average cost, however, was $14.86 per share, reflecting very heavy purchases in early 1965), the company on December 31, 1965, had net

working capital alone (before placing any value on the plants and equipment) of about $19 a share.

Berkshire is a delight to own. There is no question that the state of the textile industry is the dominant factor in determining the earning power of the business, but we are most fortunate to have Ken Chace running the business in a first-class manner, and we will have several of the best sales people in the business heading up this end of their respective divisions.

While a Berkshire is hardly going to be as profitable as a Xerox, Fairchild Camera or National Video in a hypertensed market, it is a very comfortable holding. As my West Coast philosopher [Buffett also has called on an East Coast philosopher] says, 'It is well to have a diet consisting of oatmeal as well as cream puffs.'

In a July 12, 1966 letter, Buffett reported that the partnership, with two 10% partners, had purchased all the stock of Hochschild, Kohn & Co., a privately owned Baltimore-based department store chain, for about $5 million.

Buffett's partnership bought 80% of Diversified Retailing Co., and Diversified purchased Hochschild.

The chain, which never did well, was sold on December 1, 1969, to Supermarkets General for about the same price.

The partnership continued its astounding success in 1966. In his January 25, 1967, letter Buffett wrote: "The Partnership had its tenth anniversary during 1966. The celebration was appropriate— an all-time record (both past and future) was established for our performance margin relative to the Dow. Our advantage was 36 points which resulted from a plus 20.4% for the Partnership and a minus 15.6% for the Dow."

His January 24, 1968, letter began: "By most standards, we had a good year in 1967. Our overall performance was plus 35.9% compared to plus 19.0% for the Dow, thus surpassing our previous objective of performance ten points superior to the Dow. Our overall gain was $19,384,250 which, even under accelerating inflation, will buy a lot of Pepsi [which in those days he was spiking with cherry syrup]. And due to the sale of some long-standing large positions in marketable securities, we had realized taxable income of $27,376,667, which has nothing to do with 1967 performance but should give you all a feeling of vigorous participation in The Great Society on April 15."

This was also when he reported that through the partnership's two controlled companies, Diversified Retailing and Berkshire, two other companies were acquired—Associated Cotton Shops, later named Associated Retail Stores, and National Indemnity, along with National Fire & Marine, an affiliated company.

Associated was bought by Diversified Retailing and National Indemnity was purchased by Berkshire.

"The office group, spouses and children have over $15 million invested in BPL on January 1, 1968, so we have not had a need for NoDoz during business hours."

In his July 11, 1968, letter, Buffett is clearly worried about a speculative blowoff for the market:

> I make no effort to predict the course of general business or the stock market. Period. However, currently, there are practices snowballing in the security markets and business world which, while devoid of short-term predictive value, bother me as to possible long-term consequences.
>
> ...Spectacular amounts of money are being made by those participating (whether as originators, top employees, professional advisors, investment bankers, stock speculators, etc.) in the chain-letter type stock-promotion vogue.

From 1957 through 1968, the Dow's compound annual growth rate was 9.1%; Buffett Partnership's rate was 31.6%. Buffett wrote:

> The investment management business, which I used to severely chastise in this section for excessive lethargy, has now swung in many quarters to acute hypertension. One investment manager, representing an organization (with an old established name you would recognize) handling mutual funds aggregating well over $1 billion, said upon launching a new advisory service in 1968:
>
> The complexities of national and international economics make money management a full-time job. A good money manager cannot maintain a study of securities on a week-by-week or even a day-by-day basis. Securities must be studied in a minute-by-minute program.

"Wow!" wrote Buffett. "This sort of stuff makes me feel guilty when I go out for a Pepsi."

In his January 22, 1969 letter he wrote:

> I still sometimes get comments from partners like: "Say, Berkshire is up four points—that's great!" or "What's happening to us, Berkshire was down three last week?" Market price is irrelevant to us in the valuation of our controlling interests. We valued B-H at 25 at yearend 1967 when the market was about

20, and 31 at yearend 1968 when the market was about 37. We would have done the same thing if the markets had been 15 and 50, respectively. ("Price is what you pay, value is what you get"). We will prosper or suffer in controlled investments in relation to the operating performances of our businesses—we will not attempt to profit by playing various games in the securities markets.

By May 29, 1969, he wrote, "About 18 months ago I wrote to you regarding changed environmental and personal factors causing me to modify our future performance objectives."

He said the investing environment was becoming more negative and frustrating and, further, "I know I don't want to be totally occupied with out-pacing an investment rabbit all my life. The only way to slow down is to stop."

Of course today, in a slightly different business structure, Buffett remains occupied with outrunning that investment rabbit for the best investment carrots.

"Buffett ended the partnership in 1969, because he was tired of the pressure of being the league leader in mutual funds, he thought that the stock market was overvalued, and the number of partners had grown to where he would have to register as an investment company, subject to government regulations. Most importantly, he no longer needed other people's money to play the game." (*Spinner*, 1988, p. 187)

From 1957 to the end of 1969, the partnership had rung up a 29.5% annual compound return while the Dow had a 7.4% annual return!

Buffett liquidated the partnership and distributed to the investors their profits and their pro rata interest in Berkshire. He gave them a range of options, maintaining proportional interests in Diversified Retailing or in Berkshire. Or the partners could take cash. Also he offered to help investors make bond investments.

He even recommended another money manager, his old friend, Bill Ruane, who established the Sequoia Fund on July 15, 1970, to serve limited partners when Buffett Partnership closed.

The successful Sequoia Fund has long invested in some of the same stocks that Berkshire has, such as Freddie Mac. About a quarter of Sequoia's money is in Berkshire.

The 100-member Buffett Partnership was terminated at the end of 1969 and the market was well into a long tailspin culminating in the collapse of 1973-74. Perhaps Buffett was familiar with Shakespeare's stage direction in *The Winter's Tale*: "Exit, pursued by a bear."

Buffett's caution about conditions and his withdrawal were perfectly timed.

When the partnership closed, Berkshire had 983,582 shares outstanding. Buffett Partnership owned 691,441 of them.

Berkshire's market value had grown to about $105 million and Buffett's own stake was worth about $25 million, much of which he quietly invested in Berkshire Hathaway. His interest, managerial and financial, had increased in Berkshire, which in 1969 had bought the Illinois National Bank and Trust of Rockford, Illinois.

Berkshire started business on August 1, 1970 on the 14th floor of Kiewit Plaza.

Berkshire then had three main businesses: the textile operation, the insurance operation conducted by National Indemnity and National Fire & Marine, and the Illinois National Bank and Trust. It also owned Sun Newspapers, Inc., Blacker Printing Company and 70% of Gateway Underwriters, but these operations were not financially significant. Berkshire also bought the *Omaha Sun*, along with a string of weeklies in 1969, and sold them in 1981, two years before the *Sun* folded.

In a final letter to partners on February 18, 1970, Buffett thanked his partners for giving him a free hand.

"My activity has not been burdened by second-guessing, discussing non sequiturs, or hand holding. You have let me play the game without telling me what club to use, how to grip it, or how much better the other players were doing.

"I've appreciated this, and the results you have achieved have significantly reflected your attitudes and behavior. If you don't feel this is the case, you underestimate the importance of personal encouragement and empathy in maximizing human effort and achievement."

"Herein lies the motivational and management aspects of Buffett's genius," says Michael Assael.

"But Warren Buffett's business and investment genius goes deeper. It now revolves around three elements, and the interplay among them:

1. Finance. Buffett understands *return on investment* is paramount. He inputs capital efficiently and gets the most bang for Berkshire's buck.

2. Economics. Buffett is sensitive to the evolving economic landscape and invests in long-term trends to Berkshire's advantage. He reads the mind of the consumer and senses which businesses have the greatest competitive strengths. Globally, he

understands civilization's hierarchy of desires.

3. People Management. Buffett is touched by the importance of human sensitivity and empathy in motivating people and maximizing human achievement. He's careful to plant and nurture the seeds of human capital and goodwill.

"Combining these talents makes Buffett unique," Assael continues. "He views his work in a multi-dimensional way, much as Einstein viewed space, time and gravitation, and Freud the depths of the mind and nervous system. The gifts of Buffett's genius speak for themselves."

As the partnership closed out, a young man with a bizarre offbeat manner was planning bigger things.

But first, here's a look back at two partnership letters:

Warren E. Buffett
5202 Underwood Ave.
Omaha, Nebraska

SECOND ANNUAL LETTER TO LIMITED PARTNERS

The General Stock Market Picture in 1957

In last year's letter to partners, I said the following:

My view of the general market level is that it is priced above intrinsic value. This view relates to blue-chip securities. This view, if accurate, carries with it the possibility of a substantial decline in all stock prices, both undervalued and otherwise. In any event I think the probability is very slight that current market levels will be thought of as cheap five years from now. Even a full-scale bear market, however, should not hurt the market value of our work-outs substantially.

If the general market were to return to an undervalued status our capital might be employed exclusively in general issues and perhaps some borrowed money would be used in this operation at that time. Conversely, if the market should go considerably higher our policy will be to reduce our general issues as profits present themselves and increase the work-out portfolio.

All of the above is not intended to imply that market analysis is foremost in my mind. Primary attention is given at all

98

times to the detection of substantially undervalued securities.

The past year witnessed a moderate decline in stock prices. I stress the word "moderate" since casual reading of the press or conversing with those who have had only recent experience with stocks would tend to create an impression of a much greater decline. Actually, it appears to me that the decline in stock prices has been considerably less than the decline in corporate earning power under present business conditions. This means that the public is still very bullish on blue chip stocks and the general economic picture. I make no attempt to forecast either business or the stock market; the above is simply intended to dispel any notions that stocks have suffered any drastic decline or that the general market is at a low level. I still consider the general market to be priced on the high side based on long term investment value.

Our Activities in 1957

The market decline has created greater opportunity among undervalued situations so that, generally, our portfolio is heavier in undervalued situations relative to work-outs than it was last year. Perhaps an explanation of the term "work-out" is in order. A work-out is an investment which is dependent on a specific corporate action for its profit rather than a general advance in the price of the stock as in the case of undervalued situations. Work-outs come about through sales, mergers, liquidations, tenders, etc. In each case, the risk is that something will upset the applecart and cause the abandonment of the planned action, not that the economic picture will deteriorate and stocks decline generally. At the end of 1956, we had a ratio of about 70-30 between general issues and work-outs. Now it is about 85-15.

During the past year we have taken positions in two situations which have reached a size where we may expect to take some part in corporate decisions. One of these positions accounts for between 10% and 20% of the portfolio of the various partnerships and the other accounts for about 5%. Both of these will probably take in the neighborhood of three to five years of work but they presently appear to have potential for a high average annual rate of return with a minimum of risk. While not in the classification of work-outs, they have very little dependence on the general action of the stock market.

Should the general market have a substantial rise, of course, I would expect this section of our portfolio to lag behind the action of the market.

Results for 1957

In 1957 the three partnerships which were formed in 1956 did substantially better than the general market. At the beginning of the year, the Dow-Jones Industrials stood at 499 and at the end of the year it was at 435 for a loss of 64 points. If one had owned the Averages, he would have received 22 points in dividends reducing the overall loss to 42 points or 8.4% for the year. This loss is roughly equivalent to what would have been achieved by investing in most investment funds and, to my knowledge, no investment fund invested in stocks showed a gain for the year.

All three of the 1956 partnerships showed a gain during the year amounting to about 6.2%, 7.8% and 25% on year end 1956 net worth. Naturally, a question is created as to the vastly superior performance of the last partnership, particularly in the minds of the partners of the first two. This performance emphasizes the importance of luck in the short run, particularly in regard to when funds are received. The third partnership was started the latest in 1956 when the market was at a lower level and when several securities were particularly attractive. Because of the availability of funds, large positions were taken in these issues whereas the two partnerships formed earlier were already substantially invested so that they could only take relatively small positions in these issues.

Basically, all partnerships are invested in the same securities and in approximately the same percentages. However, particularly during the initial stages, money becomes available at varying times and varying levels of the market so there is more variation in results than is likely to be the case in later years. Over the years, I will be quite satisfied with a performance that is 10% per year better than the Averages, so in respect to these three partnerships, 1957 was a successful, and probably better than average, year.

Two partnerships were started during the middle of 1957 and their results for the balance of the year were roughly the same as the performance of the Averages which were down about 12% for the period since inception of the 1957 partnerships.

Their portfolios are now starting to approximate those of the 1956 partnerships and performance of the entire group should be much more comparable in the future.

Interpretation of Results

To some extent our better than average performance in 1957 was due to the fact that it was a generally poor year for most stocks. Our performance, relatively, is likely to be better in a bear market than in a bull market so that deductions made from the above results should be tempered by the fact that it was the type of year when we should have done relatively well. In a year when the general market had a substantial advance I would be well satisfied to match the advance of the Averages.

I can definitely say that our portfolio represents better value at the end of 1957 than it did at the end of 1956. This is due to both generally lower prices and the fact that we have had more time to acquire the more substantially undervalued securities which can only be acquired with patience. Earlier I mentioned our largest position which comprised 10% to 20% of the assets of the various partnerships. In time I plan to have this represent 20% of the assets of all partnerships but this cannot be hurried. Obviously, during any acquisition period, our primary interest is to have the stock do nothing or decline rather than advance. Therefore, at any given time, a fair proportion of our portfolio may be in the "sterile" stage. This policy, while requiring patience, should maximize long term profits.

I have tried to cover points which I felt might be of interest and disclose as much of our philosophy as may be imparted without talking of individual issues. If there are any questions concerning any phase of the operation, I would welcome hearing from you.

February 6, 1958

Buffett's letter in 1961 said:

The General Stock Market in 1960:

A year ago, I commented on the somewhat faulty picture presented in 1959 by the Dow-Jones Industrial Average which had advanced from 583 to 679, or 16.4%. Although practically all investment companies showed gains for that year, less than

10% of them were able to match or better the record of the Industrial Average. The Dow-Jones Utility Average had a small decline and the Railroad Average recorded a substantial one.

In 1960, the picture was reversed. The Industrial Average declined from 679 to 616, or 9.3%. Adding back the dividends which would have been received through ownership of the Average still left it with an overall loss of 6.3%. On the other hand, the Utility average showed a good gain and while all the results are not now available, my guess is that about 90% of all investment companies out-performed the Industrial Average. The majority of investment companies appear to have ended the year with overall results in the range of plus or minus 5%. On the New York Stock Exchange, 653 common stocks registered losses for the year while 404 showed gains.

Results in 1960:

My continual objective in managing partnership funds is to achieve a long-term performance record superior to that of the Industrial Average. I believe this Average, over a period of years, will more or less parallel the results of leading investment companies. Unless we do achieve this superior performance there is no reason for existence of the partnerships.

However, I have pointed out that any superior record which we might accomplish should not be expected to be evidenced by a relatively constant advantage in performance compared to the Average. Rather it is likely that if such an advantage is achieved, it will be through better-than-average performance in stable or declining markets and average, or perhaps even poorer-than-average performance in rising markets.

I would consider a year in which we declined 15% and the Average 30% to be much superior to a year when both we and the Average advanced 20%. Over a period of time there are going to be good and bad years; there is nothing to be gained by getting enthused or depressed about the sequence in which they occur. The important thing is to be beating par; a four on a par three hole is not as good as a five on a par five hole and it is unrealistic to assume we are not going to have our share of both par three's and par five's.

The above dose of philosophy is being dispensed since we have a number of new partners this year and I want to make sure they understand my objectives, my measure of attainment of these objectives, and some of my known limitations.

With this background it is not unexpected that 1960 was a better-than-average year for us. As contrasted with an overall loss of 5.3% for the Industrial Average, we had a 22.8% gain for the seven partnerships operating throughout the year. Our results for the four complete years of partnership operation after expenses but before interest to limited partners or allocation to the general partner are:

Year	Partnerships Operating Entire Year	Partnership Gain	Dow-Jones Gain
1957	3	10.4%	-8.4%
1958	5	40.9%	38.5%
1959	6	25.9%	19.9%
1960	7	22.8%	-6.3%

It should be emphasized again that these are the net results to the partnership; the net results to the limited partners would depend on the partnership agreement that they had selected.

The overall gain or loss is computed on a market to market basis. After allowing for any money added or withdrawn, such a method gives results based upon what would have been realized upon liquidation of the partnership at the beginning of the year and what would have been realized upon liquidation gains and losses and is different, of course, from our tax results which value securities at cost and realize gains or losses only when securities are actually sold.

On a compounded basis, the cumulative results have been:

Year	Partnership Gain	Dow-Jones Gain
1957	10.4%	- 8.4%
1958	55.6%	26.9%
1959	95.9%	52.2%
1960	140.6%	42.6%

Although four years is entirely too short a period from which to make deductions, what evidence there is points toward confirming the proposition that our results should be relatively better in moderately declining or static markets. To the extent that this is true, it indicates that our portfolio may be more conservatively, although decidedly less conventionally, invested than if we owned "blue-chip" securities. During a strongly rising market for the latter, we might have real difficulty in matching their performance.

Multiplicity of Partnerships:

A preceding table shows that the family is growing. There has been no partnership which has had a consistently superior or inferior record compared to our group average, but there has been some variance each year despite my efforts to keep all partnerships invested in the same securities and about the same proportions. This variation, of course, could be eliminated by combining the present partnerships into one large partnership. Such a move would also eliminate much detail and a moderate amount of expense.

Frankly, I am hopeful of doing something along this line in the next few years. The problem is that various partners have expressed preferences for varying partnership arrangements. Nothing will be done without unanimous consent of partners.

Advance Payments:

Several partners have inquired about adding money during the year to their partnership. Although an exception has been made, it is too difficult to amend partnership agreements during mid-year where we have more than one family represented among the limited partners. Therefore, in mixed partnerships an additional interest can only be acquired at the end of the year.

We do accept advance payments during the year toward a partnership interest and pay interest at 6% on this payment from the time received until the end of the year. At that time, subject to amendment of the agreement by the partners, the payment plus interest is added to the partnership capital and thereafter participates in profits and losses.

Sanborn Map:

Last year mention was made of an investment which accounted for a very high and unusual proportion (35%) of our net assets along with the comment that I had some hope this investment would be concluded in 1960. This hope materialized. The history of an investment of this magnitude may be of interest to you.

Sanborn Map Co. is engaged in the publication and continuous revision of extremely detailed maps of all cities of the United States. For example, the volumes mapping Omaha would weigh perhaps fifty pounds and provide minute details on each structure. The map would be revised by the paste-over method showing new construction, changed occupancy, new fire protection facilities, changed structural materials, etc. These revisions would be done approximately annually and a new map would be published every twenty or thirty years when further paste-overs became impractical. The cost of keeping the map revised to an Omaha customer would run around $100 per year.

This detailed information showing diameter of water mains underlying streets, location of fire hydrants, composition of roof, etc., was primarily of use to fire insurance companies. Their underwriting departments, located in a central office, could evaluate business by agents nationally. The theory was that "a picture was worth a thousand words" and such evaluation would decide whether the risk was properly rated, the degree of conflagration exposure in an area, advisable reinsurance procedure, etc. The bulk of Sanborn's business was done with about thirty insurance companies although maps were also sold to customers outside the insurance industry such as public utilities, mortgage companies, and taxing authorities.

For seventy-five years the business operated in a more or less monopolistic manner with profits realized in every year accompanied by almost complete immunity to recession and lack of need for any sales effort. In the earlier years of the business, the insurance industry became fearful that Sanborn's profits would become too great and placed a number of prominent insurance men on Sanborn's board of directors to act in a watch-dog capacity.

In the early 1950s, a competitive method of underwriting known as "carding" made inroads on Sanborn's business and after-tax profits of the map business fell from an average annual level of over $500,000 in the late 1930s to under $100,000 in 1958 and 1959. Considering the upward bias in the economy during this period, this amounted to an almost complete elimination of what had been sizable, stable earning power.

However, during the early 1930s Sanborn had begun to accumulate an investment portfolio. There were no capital requirements to the business so that any retained earnings could be devoted to this project. Over a period of time about $2.5 million was invested, roughly half in bonds and half in stocks. Thus, in the last decade particularly, the investment portfolio blossomed while the operating map business wilted.

Let me give you some idea of the extreme divergence of these two factors. In 1938 when the Dow-Jones Industrial Average was in the 100-120 range, Sanborn sold at $110 per share. In 1958 with the Average in the 550 area, Sanborn sold at $45 per share. Yet during that same period the value of the Sanborn investment portfolio increased from about $20 per share to $65 per share. This means, in effect, that the buyer of Sanborn stock in 1938 was placing a positive valuation of $90 per share on the map business ($110 less the $20 value of the investments unrelated to the map business) in a year of depressed business and stock market conditions. In the tremendously more vigorous climate of 1958 the same map business was evaluated at a minus $20 with the buyer of the stock unwilling to pay more than 70¢ on the dollar for the investment portfolio with the map business thrown in for nothing.

How could this come about? Sanborn in 1958 as well as 1938 possessed a wealth of information of substantial value to the insurance industry. To reproduce the detailed information they had gathered over the years would have cost tens of millions of dollars. Despite "carding," over $500 million of fire premiums were underwritten by "mapping" companies. However, the means of selling and packaging Sanborn's product, information, had remained unchanged throughout the years and finally this inertia was reflected in the earnings.

The very fact that the investment portfolio had done so well served to minimize in the eyes of most directors the need for rejuvenation of the map business. Sanborn had a sales volume of about $2½ million per year and owned about $7 million worth of marketable securities. The income from the investment portfolio was substantial, the business had no possible financial worries, the insurance companies were satisfied with the price paid for maps, and the stockholders still received dividends. However, these dividends were cut five times in eight years although I could never find any record of suggestions pertaining to cutting salaries or director's and committee fees.

Prior to my entry on the Board, of the fourteen directors, nine were prominent men from the insurance industry who combined held 46 shares of stock out of 105,000 shares outstanding. Despite their top positions with very large companies which would suggest the financial wherewithal to make at least a modest commitment, the largest holding in this group was ten shares. In several cases, the insurance companies these men ran owned small blocks of stock but these were token investments in relation to the portfolios in which they were held. For the past decade the insurance companies had been only sellers in any transactions involving Sanborn stock.

The tenth director was the company attorney, who held ten shares. The eleventh was a banker with ten shares who recognized the problems of the company, actively pointed them out, and later added to his holdings. The next two directors were the top officers of Sanborn who owned about 300 shares combined. The officers were capable, aware of the problems of the business, but kept in a subservient role by the Board of Directors. The final member of our cast was a son of a deceased president of Sanborn. The widow owned about 15,000 shares of stock.

In late 1958, the son, unhappy with the trend of the business, demanded the top position in the company, was turned down and submitted his resignation, which was accepted. Shortly thereafter we made a bid to his mother for her block of stock, which was accepted. At the time there were two other large holdings, one of about 10,000 shares (dispersed among customers of a brokerage firm) and one of about 8,000. These people were quite unhappy with the situation and desired a separation of the investment portfolio from the map business, as did we.

Subsequently our holdings (including associates) were increased through open market purchases to about 24,000 shares and the total represented by the three groups increased to 46,000 shares. We hoped to separate the two businesses, realize the fair value of the investment portfolio and work to re-establish the earning power of the map business. There appeared to be a real opportunity to multiply map profits through utilization of Sanborn's wealth of raw material in conjunction with electronic means of converting this data to the most usable form for the customer.

There was considerable opposition on the Board to change of any type, particularly when initiated by an "outsider," although management was in complete accord with our plan and a similar plan had been recommended by Booz, Allen & Hamilton, Management Experts. To avoid a proxy fight (which very probably would not have been forthcoming and which we would have been certain of winning) and to avoid time delay with a large portion of Sanborn's money tied up in blue-chip stocks which I didn't care for at current prices, a plan was evolved taking out all stockholders at fair value who wanted out. The SEC ruled favorably on the fairness of the plan. About 72% of the Sanborn stock, involving 50% of the 1,600 stockholders, was exchanged for portfolio securities at fair value. The map business was left with over $1¼ million in government and municipal bonds as a reserve fund, and a potential corporate capital gains tax of over $1 million was eliminated. The remaining stockholders were left with a slightly improved asset value, substantially higher earnings per share, and an increased dividend rate.

Necessarily, the above little melodrama is a very abbreviated description of this investment operation. However, it does point up the necessity for secrecy regarding our portfolio operations as well as the futility of measuring our results over a short span of time such as a year. Such "control situations" may occur very infrequently. Our bread-and-butter business is buying undervalued securities and selling when the undervaluation is corrected along with investment in "special situations" where the profit is dependent on corporate rather than market action. To the extent that partnership funds continue to grow, it is possible that more opportunities will be available in "control situations."

The auditors should be mailing your financial statement and tax information within about a week. If you have any questions at all regarding either their report or this letter, be sure to let me know. *Warren E. Buffett*

1-30-61

In 1969 when Buffett ended the partnership, he channeled all his own $25 million into a strange and unlikely firm, a textile company called Berkshire Hathaway.

10

BUFFETT'S EARLY INVESTORS

Jim Rasmussen wrote the following story about Buffett's early investors which ran in the *Omaha World-Herald* August 16, 1998:

To live in Omaha in the late 1950s and know Warren Buffett was to hold a ticket to incredible wealth.

To punch this ticket, you needed at least $5,000 to invest. And you had to have confidence in the twenty-something investor, who worked out of his modest house and drove a Volkswagen bug.

Those who did invest never regretted it. They became very rich simply by keeping their money with Buffett and watching it grow. Now the world's second-richest person, Buffett has compiled one of the greatest investment records in history.

Consider the numbers. An investor who put $10,000 with Buffett in 1957 saw it multiply to $160,000 by 1970, the year Buffett dissolved his investment partnership.

If that investor then converted the $160,000 into stock in Berkshire Hathaway Inc.—the company that Buffett has used since then as his investment vehicle—it would be worth *$259 million* today.

At least 16 Omahans who invested in limited partnerships with Buffett in the 1950s and '60s still live in Omaha. Dozens more are scattered across the country. The fortunes of some have grown so big that they confess to having trouble deciding what to do with their money.

Even though most of Buffett's early partners did not reinvest all their money in Berkshire, many put significant sums in the company. Even after selling some of the stock and giving some away to family or charity, many of these Buffett partners retain fortunes in the tens of millions, perhaps more than $100 million in some cases.

Yet, at least in Omaha, most of Buffett's partners live in relatively ordinary houses, drive ordinary cars and show few outward signs of being among the city's superrich.

For example, Leland and Dorothy Olson live in a simple but comfortable one-story home southeast of Westside High School. It's been their address for the past 45 years.

They've also given millions to the University of Nebraska Medical Center and other charities.

Leland Olson said their lifestyle is probably the same as if he'd never invested with Buffett.

"I'd probably live in the same house," said Olson, a retired obstetrician, "I just wouldn't be giving away a lot of money."

The Olsons and several others of Buffett's partners have quietly established their own charitable foundations. They're giving to universities, hospitals, churches and other charities.

Some of these World War II-generation investors are certain to leave large gifts to charity when they die.

The size of some of the estates will be mind-boggling. That became apparent after Nebraska natives Donald and Mildred Othmer, early Buffett partners, left a fortune of more than $650 million at their deaths.

They left nearly all to charity. Among the beneficiaries was the University of Nebraska-Lincoln, scheduled to receive about $100 million from Mildred Othmer's estate. That would be the largest bequest in the university's history.

Buffett has said that even larger bequests from some Berkshire investors are sure to come.

The Buffett millionaires are among a growing number of super-rich in Omaha, say financial professionals who advise the wealthy. By one estimate, more than 120 Omaha families and individuals have a net worth of at least $100 million.

Their ranks have been swelled by stockholders in successful Omaha companies such as Berkshire Hathaway and Peter Kiewit & Sons' Inc.

Although hundreds of Omahans have become millionaires investing in Berkshire, few can claim to be among those who invested in Buffett's early partnerships. These early investors had the best opportunity to profit from the investment wizard's skill since they had their money growing with him for the longest. During the first 10 years of Buffett's investment partnership (from 1957, the first full year of partnership, through 1966) it earned a total return of 1,156 percent, nearly 10 times the return on the Dow Jones Industrial Average.

Later investors also were pleased, as Berkshire Hathaway's returns have consistently thrashed the stock-market averages.

Many of the early Buffett investors were his family, friends and acquaintances. Others included students of investment night courses that he taught at Omaha University (now the University of

Nebraska at Omaha). Still others heard of Buffett's reputation by word of mouth.

When Buffett ended the partnerships in 1970, the list included 99 partners, the limit allowed by law at the time. There were more, though, because Buffett grouped some of his investors into single entities to stay under the 99-partner limit. Douglas County records include a list of the partners and their holdings for each year of the partnerships.

While several declined to be interviewed, 10 of those on the list agreed to share their recollections of Buffett and how investing with him has changed their lives.

They share a freedom from financial worry and an opportunity to allocate large sums of money—whether to family, charity or their own use.

Omahan Dick Holland, a Buffett investor, puts it this way: "We're lucky as hell. That's all there is to it."

Buffett, 67, continues as chairman of Berkshire Hathaway Inc. He owns $33.3 billion in Berkshire stock. He has built the company's wealth by buying good companies cheap, and then holding on.

Some of his early partners remain friends with Buffett, although increasing demands on his time have reduced their contact with him. Most of their memories of him come from those early days, when the man in the VW bug set out to make them, and himself, rich.

Dan Monen—One of the original seven investors in Buffett's first partnership in 1956, made his first killing on a Buffett idea in the late 1950s.

Buffett had analyzed an Omaha company, National American Fire Insurance. The company's management was buying up National American stock for $50 a share, but Buffett knew it was worth a lot more. He sent his friend Monen, an Omaha lawyer, on a journey across Nebraska. His job: to buy as much stock from ordinary share-holders as he could find, for $100 a share.

Monen spent three weeks on the road, buying shares from small-town bankers and farmers. By the time National American's management heard about their activities, Buffett and Monen were well on their way to buying 10 percent of the company. They later sold their stake to a New York investor and split a profit of $100,000.

"That was my first big stake," Monen says.

Now 70, Monen lives in a retirement apartment complex in west Omaha. Investing with Buffett enabled him to retire from his law practice at age 55. He bought a farm and a bank. Monen, who is divorced, eventually sold both the farm and the bank and bought a California company that makes women's sportswear.

He sold that business about two years ago and moved back to Omaha to be near his children and grandchildren.

(Omaha World-Herald)

Investing with Buffett in 1956 enabled Dan Monen to retire at age 55. "By almost anybody's standards, I've got a lot of money to give away," he says.

Monen recalls digging dandelions with Buffett at about age 4 in the yard of Buffett's grandparents in Omaha.

Monen later worked in the grandfather's Omaha grocery store but saw little of Warren growing up. They eventually became friends as young adults.

When Buffett formed his first investment partnership in 1956, Monen put in $5,000 that he borrowed from his mother-in-law.

He kept investing. By 1969, he had $384,000 with Buffett. After the partnership was dissolved the next year. Monen says, he kept most or all of the money in Berkshire stock and held on.

When a visitor noted that such a stake would have grown to hundreds of millions today, Monen nods. He says he's trying to decide where his money should go after his death.

Last year he gave $500,000 toward construction of an addition to Creighton University's law library.

"By almost anybody's standards, I've got a lot of money to give away," he says.

Robert Soener—A retired stockbroker, Soener still watches the

(Omaha World-Herald)

Bob Soener of Omaha used a bonus from his company to invest with Buffett in the 1950s instead of paying off his mortgage.

market on CNBC in the afternoons, checking Berkshire's stock price and chatting with his broker on the phone from his upstairs den.

He and a son live in the two-story brick house near 38th and Cuming Streets that Soener bought in 1961. It was there that he and his wife, Mary, raised seven children. She died in 1980.

Today, even after sending seven kids through private colleges and giving away money to charity and family, Soener says he still holds millions of dollars worth of Berkshire stock. He says his wealth has allowed him to give significant sums to charity but hasn't changed much else in his life.

"I live in the same house," he says. "I drive a 1990 Buick Regal. My lifestyle hasn't changed to speak of."

In a golf shirt and shorts, Soener is the picture of relaxed retirement at age 74. He became acquainted with Buffett when the future billionaire was selling stocks for his father's Omaha brokerage in the early '50s.

A few years later, Buffett was lining up investors for his own limited partnerships. One day Soener got a bonus check for $10,000 from his firm, Cruttendon & Co. Buffett stopped by the Cruttendon office that day.

"I said, 'Look what I got from Cruttendon,' " Soener recalled. "He said, 'What are you going to do with it?' "

Soener, who could have paid off his mortgage with the $10,000, decided to put it with Buffett instead. He had become familiar with Buffett's abilities when they taught an investment course together at Omaha University.

Soener later added an additional $9,000 to his holdings with Buffett as the investment began to grow. After Buffett closed the partnership in 1970, Soener kept some of his money in Berkshire Hathaway. "It just kept getting better and better," he says.

He has established the charitable Soener Foundation, and he and his children designate the charities to which it contributes. The foundation had assets of $1.7 million at the end of 1997 and contributed $90,600 last year to 39 charities across the Midwest, its tax return shows.

Of that, $39,400 went to Omaha-based groups. Recipients included a number of Catholic churches, schools and colleges, as well as hospitals and disease research funds.

Investing with Buffett, Soener says, "has had a beneficial effect on not only myself but my whole family. The grandkids will have it for their college education."

Soener once told *Forbes* (October 12, 1998): "There are three things in my life. God, Warren Buffett and my wife, and I'm not sure about the order of the first two."

Charles E. Peterson Jr.—Holds the distinction of being one of the original investors in Buffett's first partnership in Omaha in 1956.

(Omaha World-Herald)

Charles Peterson displays the original partnership agreement with Buffett Associates in his office, along with documents showing he sold all his stock in 1970.

114

He proudly displays the original partnership agreement for Buffett Associates Ltd. on his office wall at Byron Reed Co. Peterson is president and owner of the Omaha company which manages real estate and employee relocations.

The document on the wall shows he put $5,000 into Buffett Associates, the minimum Buffett would accept.

"That was a lot of money to me," says Peterson, who had been Buffett's roommate at the University of Pennsylvania in 1950.

The other original investors were Peterson's mother, Elizabeth; Buffett's sister, Doris Wood, and her husband, Truman Wood; Monen; Buffett's father-in-law, William Thompson; and Buffett's aunt, Alice Buffett. Together the Omaha group invested $105,000.

Peterson had seen Buffett's exceptional mind in action at Penn. He says Buffett read all the textbooks for his courses, cover to cover, by the end of September. "Then he'd throw 'em aside the rest of the semester and still earn A's," Peterson says.

A few years later in Omaha, Peterson was having lunch with his former college roommate. He asked Buffett what one of their professors at Penn had said about a certain aspect of contract law.

"Warren said, 'Well, that was on page 221, paragraph 3,' and he started to recite the book." Peterson checked the textbook and found the paragraph as Buffett had recited it. "It was a little intimidating," Peterson says.

They have remained friends. Peterson, a robust man of 71, says he bought Berkshire stock again and again over the years. He declined to discuss the size of his Berkshire holdings.

By 1969, Douglas County records show, Peterson's investment in Buffett's partnership totaled $662,000. Another framed document on his office wall shows he sold all his Berkshire Hathaway stock to Buffett—4,228 shares—for $42 a share in 1970 when the partnership ended.

"Pretty smart, huh?" he said. At Friday's closing price of $69,710 a share, the Berkshire stock he sold is worth $295 million.

Peterson says he reinvested in Berkshire again a few years later and kept buying. He says his investments with Buffett over the years have earned an average annual return of about 32 percent.

Investing with Buffett enabled Peterson and his wife, Marjorie, to take up flying airplanes as a hobby and to travel the world. She died in 1996.

Peterson's advice to anyone considering buying Berkshire Hathaway stock: "Get your feet in the water because you're never going to win until you do."

The Hollands—Richard and Marilyn Holland met Buffett in the '50s through Monen, a mutual friend.

"He (Buffett) was the first person I ever ran into who made investment ideas make sense," says Richard Holland, a retired Omaha advertising executive.

As Holland remembers it, Buffett explained his method of buying stocks at less than half of what he believed they were really worth. "Eventually the asset value would be realized," Holland says.

The Hollands live in the one-story house they built in 1957 near 84th and Pacific Streets. Partially hidden by trees, it's a modest home for a couple of considerable wealth.

Although the Hollands decline to disclose the size of their fortune, tax returns of their charitable Holland foundation provide a glimpse. The foundation held $26.1 million in assets at the end of last year, including $22.1 million in Berkshire Hathaway stock.

The foundation gave away $812,700 in 1997, including $602,700 to Opera Omaha and $100,000 to Quality Living Inc., an agency that provides care to people with brain injuries or severe physical disabilities.

Earlier this year they donated $2.5 million to All Our Kids, a program that provides mentors for at-risk youths.

Being a long-term investor with Buffett has left them with more money than they need, Richard Holland says. That has presented them with a choice: Give some of their money to charity, or let more than half of it go to estate taxes at their deaths.

"If you aren't charitably minded, you've got a terrible problem, because you're going to wind up handing it on and letting 60 percent pass to the estate tax," Holland says.

They plan to give away some money to their three children, but the bulk will go to charity, he says. They plan to leave it to Midlands-area causes that benefit children, education and the arts.

The Olsons—Leland Olson, an obstetrician, took Buffett's investment course at Omaha University in the mid-1950s. Olson was so impressed he took the course twice, the second time bringing his wife, Dorothy.

"The basic theory was that you're not smart enough to do your own investing unless you spend seven days a week studying it," Olson says. "So you've got to get somebody else to help."

For the Olsons, that somebody became Buffett. They invested in a partnership that Buffett had established with a dozen other physicians.

Once a year, Buffett and his wife, Susan, were hosts at a catered dinner for the partners at their home. It was the partners' one chance for the year to hear what Buffett had been doing with their money. To minimize distractions, he did not allow partners to ask questions about the investments during the year.

"We'd have a good social hour and then after dinner, he'd take us into the den and open it up to questions," Olson says. "It was a fascinating occasion."

At the University of Nebraska Medical Center the Olsons' gifts helped establish the Olson Center for Women's Health. The center conducts research and educational programs focusing on women's health issues.

Although they continue to live in the same house they've owned for 45 years, the Olsons have traveled the world and have homes at the Lake of the Ozarks in Missouri and in Arizona.

The income from his medical practice (he's now retired) and other successful investments meant they didn't need to sell much of their Berkshire stock.

"It's made it possible for us to be able to give fair amounts to certain charities," he says.

Warren Buffett—Like many of his partners, Buffett has lived a modest lifestyle considering his wealth. He drives a 1991 Lincoln Town Car and lives in the same house near 55th and Farnam Streets that he bought for $31,500 in 1958. The house is valued for tax purposes at $419,700.

The tax return for his Buffett Foundation listed charitable contributions of nearly $10 million in the 12 months ending June 30, 1997. Contributions included $10,000 apiece to 15 Omaha public school teachers who received Alice Buffett Outstanding Teacher Awards, named for his late aunt. An additional $370,000 went to the Boys' and Girls' Club of Omaha.

As it has for years, the foundation gave numerous gifts to groups dedicated to population control. Recipients included a number of local Planned Parenthood groups, including those in Omaha and Lincoln.

Buffett has said that the foundation will be the recipient of the bulk of his fortune after he and his wife die.

(With permission of the Omaha World-Herald)

11

CORNERING THE MARKET
ON 1954 BLUE EAGLE FOUR-CENT AIRMAIL STAMPS—"IF ONE LIKES A NEGATIVE RETURN, PLUS A 40-YEAR TIME SPAN, THIS WAS AN INVESTMENT HARD TO BEAT."—*TOM KNAPP*

Tom Knapp, one of the investors who studied under Ben Graham and who was part of the Tweedy, Browne & Knapp brokerage firm, recalls how he and Buffett once tried to corner the market in 1954 Blue Eagle four-cent airmail stamps, thinking it might become a collectible.

It was in the late 1950s and Ben Graham was to speak at an analyst's meeting being held at Beloit College in Wisconsin. "Warren called me from Omaha and said, 'let's go to the analysts' meeting!' I asked him how were we going to get to Beloit. He said, 'Easy, come to Omaha and we'll drive. We'll see a lot of cornfields.' "

"We got in his car. It took all day. We were talking about deals and I said I had been reading in Linn's Stamp News about a 4-cent Blue Eagle stamp that was being taken off the market for a 5-cent Red Eagle stamp."

Knapp kept telling Buffett about it and on the drive home to Omaha the two began stopping at post offices to buy the stamps. "We stopped at one place and I found it had 23 stamps. Warren said, 'go buy them.' "

"The big hit was Denver," Knapp said where the two bought about 200,000 stamps through the mail. Buffett and Knapp wrote to all the big post offices to see if any of the stamps were left. In all they came up with some 400,000 stamps. "We split them up and held them for some years. But we could see problems occurring. They were sticking together because of the cheap glue. A few sheets I had in Long Island stuck together. The ones in Omaha didn't stick."

As the years went by Knapp and Buffett found no great demand for their stamps. "Warren was looking at the time value of money and saw things were evening out. He found the one buyer in the world. The fellow bought a lot of them at 10% from face value. I kept a few sheets of them for old times sake."

Knapp said he found a use for some of them. "When I was at

Tweedy, Browne we'd send a set of pink sheets [stock quotes for thinly traded companies] to Warren so he could check the quotes that were not in the newspapers."

Knapp, a Princeton University chemistry major, who is to the day 10 years older than Buffett, says he may be Berkshire's oldest shareholder. I got my shares when Dempster Mill [a windmill company Buffett owned] was liquidated. I received Berkshire stock which was one of its holdings. My cost basis was between five and ten dollars a share. I never sold a share and bought some for my family and they seem happy with it... I don't know of a better company."

Knapp has homes in New York and Vero Beach, Florida. Buffett has joked about a friend who likes the beach adding, "Now he owns the beach." The friend, of course, is Tom Knapp.

Knapp said even though he was in his 30s and Buffett in his 20s when they were young fellows trying to corner the stamp market, "he was definitely ahead of everyone. His grasp and concentration were so incredible. And his integrity was 100%. If it was a matter of 10 cents, he'd report it. He wanted everything right straight in line."

Noted value investor Walter Schloss of New York, who became friends with Buffett during Buffett's Columbia days and worked with him under Ben Graham, recalls: "I got out of the Army Signal Corps at the end of 1945...In 1960 I was feeling sentimental about my buddies and I decided to write all of them. It was about 140 people. Knapp saw that I had all these letters and he said he had stamps for them," recalled Schloss. Schloss recently said, "Most of the 833rd

(Photo courtesy of Walter Schloss)

Walter Schloss in his New York office

Signal Service fellows I had written to in 1960 who had been with me in Iran during World War II have now departed."

Schloss put the stamps on all his letters and mailed them. Soon, "I got a call from the postmaster asking if I was the guy using airmail stamps on the letters." Schloss said he was, and the postmaster said he wouldn't send the letters because they were airmail stamps for postcards so he couldn't use them.

Finally, the postmaster said he'd mail the letters if Schloss would come to the post office and write "not an airmail letter" on each letter. "I remember the story as if it was yesterday. A 4-cent postcard is now 20 cents and going up which is better than the 4-cent regular stamp which now goes for 32 cents," Schloss said. Schloss said he knew back then that Buffett was an unusual person. "I could tell he was brilliant and would be successful, but I never thought he'd be this successful. He's very focused. He's always thinking of the future...He's been like a shooting star."

"There's never been anything like him...The continued growth will be very hard. Maybe he'll merge it [Berkshire] with Canada."

Buffett has said of Schloss, known for his tight cost controls, "I think his operational style should be a lesson for us all (one Charlie has already mastered). In effect, he is running an office for a year on what it costs Berkshire to start the engines on The Indefensible." (*Warren Buffett Speaks,* Janet Lowe, p. 102, quoting a letter Buffett wrote Schloss, October 3, 1994)

Was the investment in the four-cent Blue Eagle stamps worthwhile? Not really, according to Tom Knapp's view of it in a letter more than 40 years later:

Dear David Leib,

Warren sent me a copy of your letter regarding the C-48 4¢ Blue Eagle Air Mail stamp. The current update on the stamp was most interesting.

If one likes a negative return, plus a 40-year time span, this was an investment hard to beat.

We held these stamps for some years and then looked around for a buyer. Warren located a dealer who specialized in a "control mail" business. A control mail dealer purchases large amounts of mint stamps (at a discount from face). He will remove the plate blocks (usually worth a premium over face), and use the remainder as postage. He has some control over the recipients of the mail who return the cancelled stamps to the dealer. His profit consists of (1) the original discount from face value at time of purchase, (2) premium for plate blocks, and (3) sale of the retrieved canceled stamps.

As you may observe by the franking on this letter, I still have a few remaining copies of C-48.

Sincerely yours,
Tom Knapp

12
APPEARANCE AND STYLE
SIMPLE TASTES; FRUGAL HABITS

Buffett is a genial, pleasant-looking, rather muscular man with large horn-rimmed glasses—glasses which the *New York Times* has called "Margaret Thatcher issued."

He is 5 feet 11 inches tall, has a medium build, and weighs 175 pounds. However, he occasionally bulks up to about 30 billion pounds. When I spoke with him briefly at Borsheim's before the Berkshire Annual Meeting in 1998, I congratulated him on his weight loss, from 190 to 175. He said: "My goal is to weigh less than your book!" He also told my wife he found that about 62% of shareholders who return admission forms for the annual meeting actually show up. My wife, imitating him, had the presence of mind to say: "62.1384...."

With a pale complexion and buttery-soft hands, Buffett easily could pass for a clerk, accountant, banker, or the next guy in line at Wal-Mart. Buffett once made a nonspeaking, cameo appearance in 1988 as a bartender in an ABC-TV soap opera, *Loving*.

In 1991 Buffett and his friend, Cap Cities Chairman Thomas Murphy, made a four-minute appearance on ABC's soap opera *All My Children*. Playing themselves, they were beseeched by femme fatale Erica Kane (Martin Brent Cudahy Chandler Montgomery Montgomery because she supposedly married Montgomery twice, etc., etc.) played by Susan Lucci, the actress many thought should have won an Emmy long before she did in 1999. Lucci asked the financiers for advice about her cosmetics company. Buffett's recommendation: "Go public."

For their advice, Ms. Kane gave Buffett and Murphy big hugs and Buffett said, "Murph, Erica Kane gives a whole new meaning to the word 'takeover.' "

Buffett would later say of his brief showbiz appearance, "If we run against the test pattern on the other two networks, I expect to do very well." He followed up with flowers to the show's producer and a note saying he wanted to renegotiate his contract.

In 1993 he made another cameo appearance on *All My Children*. A Cap Cities spokesman said Buffett changed the scripted line when he called his office for messages from "Hi, Marie. Any messages?" to use the real name of his assistant, Debbie Bosanek.

During the segment Buffett is approached by the outrageous Opal Cortlandt (Jil Larson) who wants Buffett to finance her husband's company. Buffett, on the phone from ABC headquarters says, "Debbie, don't go anywhere. I may need your help."

After Cortlandt, vamping in a wild hairdo, leaned over the desk, cooing, "Is this kismet, or what?" Buffett put her off, first asking if she left her medication behind and finally telling her, "Cap Cities is not a lending institution."

At the Berkshire Annual Meeting in 1992, Buffett said that because of union rules he was paid $300 for his 1991 appearance and given a $10 wardrobe allowance, adding that the allowance was appropriate.

On the wall across from his desk at Berkshire headquarters, there's a small photo of Buffett, Murphy and Susan Lucci, accompanied by documentation of the fees he received.

Showing a visitor the $10 wardrobe fee, Buffett once said, "My daughter thinks that's about what I spend on my wardrobe."

And Berkshire Vice Chairman Charles Munger has said, "Buffett's tailoring has caused a certain amount of amusement in the business world." (*Los Angeles Times Magazine*, April 7, 1991)

"He looks like an old college professor," says Omaha stockbroker Cliff Hayes, who for years executed some of the stock trades—including The Washington Post Co. and GEICO—that were to make Buffett a famous billionaire. "He's often just in casual clothes." He looks like a dressed up farmer," says one observer.

Someone once said, "I wouldn't recognize him if he walked in with a group of three people, except for the halo over his head." His manner of dress is rumpled. His tie often comes up short, several inches above the belt. His shoes are sometimes scuffed. Coat and tie rarely match. If he has a suit on, it is off-the-rack conservative—few Continental cuts here, thank you, although his family has given him a few to improve his appearance.

His hair is not blow-dried or brushed to the last strand, rather there's sort of a morning hair effect.

Buffett is the first to kid about his appearance, once telling Salomon clients during a telephone conference call that they were in a "preferred position" because they could hear him but not see him.

Buffett's view of clothes corresponds to his view of most things. "There's nothing material I want very much," he has said. (*Esquire,*

June 1988)

But while his material desires are pedestrian, his personality is ablaze, making Johnny Carson seem catatonic. Various people have described Buffett's offbeat, brilliant personality in different ways: "has an almost photographic memory"..."used to read encyclopedias"..."his mind is encyclopedic, has tremendous concentration"..."fast reader"..."has no peer in security analysis."

There must be some downside. Ask people to cite criticisms of Buffett and this is the sort of reply: "He needs help turning on the radio"..."Can barely start a car"..."Wouldn't know if a new piece of furniture or a rug were put in his home"..."I don't think he understands how to use the fax machine." Buffett admits: "I have a little trouble turning on a light switch."

Buffett can give the appearance of being every inch the absent-minded professor—tousled hair, rumpled clothes, a high Midwestern cackle and laugh. Once when he was out of town, Mrs. Buffett redecorated the house. The story goes that when he came home, Buffett didn't notice any change.

It is when he opens his mouth that people snap to attention with awe because of the crystal clarity, penetration and facile summary he can bring to a complex problem. He is a master communicator whose verbal and written skills are unique. What he says is informative, useful, wise or funny. It's not passing chatter about what's for dinner.

Buffett speaks to people as if they were as intelligent as he; somehow he makes the person believe for a moment that he is with Buffett in his reasoning. The feeling is conveyed because Buffett is so articulate that most listeners actually do understand what Buffett is talking about—even if it involves complicated business concepts.

One day in 1986 Buffett showed up at Omaha's Red Lion Inn for an interview with *Channels* magazine (November, 1986). West Coast Editor Patricia Bauer reported Buffett was wearing khakis and a jacket and a tie. "I dressed up for you," he said, smiling sheepishly.

Although it's been reported he wears $1,500 Italian suits, that is true only on rare occasions.

As his daughter Susan, says, "My mother was in town one day and said, 'Let's get him a new suit.'...We were so sick of looking at those clothes that he's had for 30 years."

"So we bought him a camel-hair blazer and a blue blazer, just to get some new ones. And he had me return them. He said, 'I have a camel-hair blazer and a blue blazer,' and he was serious. I sent them back.

"Finally I went out, unbeknownst to him, and picked out a suit. I didn't even look at the price tag. I looked for something that would be comfortable and conservative looking. He won't wear anything that isn't extremely conservative.

"And he tried it on. It was comfortable. He didn't even look at the price tag. The suit was very boring and conservative, and he bought a few of them."

Susan added, "He'll wear clothes until they are threadbare."

Of course, virtually no one could care whether Buffett wears a tux or a swimsuit to work.

Occasionally, Buffett buys a suit that's somewhere between off the rack and custom made, requiring some slight alterations.

One Berkshire shareholder, who says he talked with a tailor who has fitted Buffett, once asked why Buffett's suits always looked so ill-fitted. The Omaha tailor replied, "He's the hardest guy in the world to fit. Basically he has no butt."

His low budget style is well known to all. Washington Post's Katharine Graham says of her business teacher:

"He was parsimonious in the extreme. Once, when we were together at an airport I asked him for a dime to make a phone call. He started to walk some distance to get change for a quarter. 'Warren,' I exclaimed, 'the quarter will do,' and he sheepishly handed it over." (*Personal History*, Katharine Graham, p. 536)

Mrs. Graham recalled another incident:

"I am sitting down in Virginia with Ben Graham's beginner's book and *How to Read a Financial Report* by someone called Merrill, Lynch, Pierce, Fenner and Smith. I am told I have to finish Ben Graham very soon because Warren is unwilling to pay the small fine involved in having the book out of the Omaha public library too long." (*Personal History*, Katharine Graham, pp. 535-536)

A cowlick and an unruly thatch of thinning hair, that seems to fly around, stand atop a round, open, owlish face that somehow says, "I am from the Midwest," and that often has an eager, quizzical look. His head is somewhat egg shaped, dotted with hazel eyes that need the help of thick bifocals, hooked around ears reminiscent of Lyndon Johnson.

His gait is loping (yes, even slightly gorilla-like). In his eagerness to get where he's going, he seems to overstep slightly what would be a normal stride, looking a bit ungainly as if he were trying to step across a room in one less stride than normal.

The forehead is high above rather wild, bushy eyebrows. His

mouth is large, the smile wrinkles are deep and an impish grin comes easily. His face is usually animated, but can become positively grim at the bridge table where he concentrates so hard.

He has a fast, dry wit, a sunny disposition and folksy manner; he comes across as a mix between Jack Benny and Will Rogers.

When he speaks, his talk comes in a rapid, fully-edited form in a Midwestern twang delivered in total intellectual honesty.

He has great energy and determination and a zest for life.

"He is neither strikingly handsome nor particularly charismatic: on the contrary, he seems rumpled most of the time," wrote *Money* columnist Joseph Nocera (July 1998).

But he added: "One of the most important reasons for this difference between Buffett and the rest of humanity goes almost entirely unacknowledged among those who hope to find in Buffett an easily reproducible investing style. He is a genius when it comes to numbers. 'Accounting,' he likes to say, 'is the language of business.' It is a language in which his own fluency is unsurpassed, and which gives him an enormous competitive advantage. Usually, all he needs is a quick glance at a balance sheet to know whether he's interested in buying a company or not—because he finds meaning in numbers that the rest of us don't."

At annual meetings shareholders can see Buffett's insatiable thirst for the numbers. He constantly talks about the number of people in attendance, wants to know the number of people at various parties, the number of people at the baseball game. He wants to know how many books some wretched author sold. And of course there are the numbers associated with the sales at Borsheim's and the Nebraska Furniture Mart. With Buffett, it's numbers, numbers, numbers.

In the manner of a wise teacher searching restlessly for the truth, he seems to be trying with all his heart to pass on to others his homespun wisdom about how to cope in an imperfect world that features an imperfect stock market. Buffett teaches that the true investor swings at the misappraised stock price, the one that offers great value, as if it were the perfect pitch. As Buffett has said, you wait as long as it takes for the right pitch and when the delivery is "two inches above the navel," you swing for the fences.

Like all great teachers, he remains an eager student. The reasons for his success are his common sense, his own genius, and his lifelong intense study of his area of greatest interest—business. It's as though Buffett has two brains, one of which is always thinking about business. It never sleeps. The other brain works on public policy questions, talks with friends and plays bridge and golf.

But his immersion in business has done nothing to hamper a great sense of fun and sophisticated sense of humor, whether it be needling himself, Wall Street, or general human conduct.

A large worry line runs straight down his forehead just to the left of center. One would guess it's the result of intense study over the years, of reading the *Wall Street Journal, Value Line* and *Moody's,* the mainline business magazines such as *Forbes, Fortune* and *Business Week* as well as trade publications such as American Banker and annual reports by the hundreds and the works of classical economists such as David Ricardo. Buffett is a subscriber to Henry Emerson's *Outstanding Investor Digest,* joking that reading it is a good way to keep up with what Munger, Berkshire's number two man, is doing. As part of his weekend reading, Buffett often stops in Cris' Rexall Drugstore, now Kohll's Pharmacy, to buy a *Barron's.*

Buffett is an avid reader of a huge range of annual reports, who wants the reports mailed directly to him and not through the slow bureaucracy of brokerage firm mailings that often take several weeks longer. And he tells shareholders to do the same, to have at least one Berkshire share registered in one's own name.

His aw-shucks attitude is genuine and his manner is open and straightforward. Most often it is described as folksy, corn-fed, homespun.

Once a Peter Kiewit & Sons, Inc. pilot, who flew the Berkshire plane, called Buffett's office to inquire if Buffett needed lunch reservations anywhere. Buffett's administrative assistant at the time, Gladys Kaiser, said not to bother, that Buffett wouldn't need a thing.

"He arrived with his mother and a picnic lunch when he came to the airport," says Omaha stockbroker George Morgan. (It so happens Morgan works for the Omaha brokerage firm of Kirkpatrick, Pettis. Buffett's father, Howard Homan Buffett, was with the Buffett & Falk brokerage firm founded in 1931 that merged into the Kirkpatrick firm in 1957.)

For lunch Buffett often has popcorn, potato chips and Cherry Coke. He munches from a Cracker Jack box at ball games. The menu has not impressed his doctors, but they declare him healthy. Lately, Buffett has taken up walking on a treadmill and he has cut back a little on the junk food.

One Sunday in the mid-1980s, Buffett found himself unable to pay a small bill.

"He was in his grubbies having a malt and chips or something, and I realized there was some problem in paying the bill," recalls Virginia Lee Pratt, a retired schoolteacher in Omaha who was a longtime bridge playing friend of Buffett's mother.

"I said, 'Warren, could I help?' and he said, 'This is pretty embarrassing.' "

The bill at Goodrich Dairy was $3.49 and Buffett was unable to pay, he said, because he had given his children his small bills and had only a $100 bill on him that the little dairy shop couldn't change. Pratt stepped in and paid the bill.

"He sent a check the next day with a letter saying that since he had established credit could he up his line of credit to five dollars," she said.

She said she was so honored to have a check signed by Buffett that she didn't cash it and wrote him that he should check his books because he'd be off by the amount of the bill. (No one would cash Picasso's checks either.)

"At our next bridge game, his mother brought me $3.50 in cash," Pratt said.

Buffett is conscientious about paying his bills, but he also wants full payment when he's on the receiving end, even to the point of taking advantage of discount coupons.

Once Buffett was having dinner at the French Cafe. Before dinner Buffett had presented a coupon for $3.95 off the dinner to the waiter, Chris Nisi. "I want this to show up on the check," Nisi recalls Buffett telling him. "When the bill came, he checked it over and found it was there. He had kidded about it all along. He was half kidding, but he was half serious, too."

Using coupons is not a one-time event for the Wizard of Omaha. In 1990, at a time when Berkshire's stock price was heading south, Buffett showed up at Bronco's, a hamburger drive-in in central Omaha. He presented a coupon and said, "This [stock dip] isn't going to stop me from buying lunch here, is it?"

A waitress at Ross's steak house (across from the Nebraska Furniture Mart until the steak house closed in 1996) where Buffett often had dinner with the Blumkin family that runs the mart, recalls serving Buffett in early 1993.

"He was through dinner and the check had come and he wanted a Shirley Temple. He said just run a new tab and I did. It was for $1.50 and he forgot to pay it. The joke around here is that I had to buy Warren Buffett a drink," she laughed.

A Berkshire employee with Buffett at dinner one time at an Omaha restaurant said Buffett saw a cockroach on the wall. "I got to watch an international icon take a swipe at a cockroach," the employee said.

Taxicab drivers and waiters say Buffett tips adequately, but not generously.

For all his folksy ways, it's the high and mighty who seek his advice. Back in 1984 when the Getty family was embroiled in complex merger talks, Ann Getty flew to Omaha to seek Buffett's counsel.

Buffett's easy manner and down-home ways mask a highly sophisticated man. Occasionally he does put on a black tie as he did to escort The Washington Post Co.'s Katharine Graham to her 70th birthday party. He has had dinner with Ronald and Nancy Reagan and been seated next to both Barbara Bush and Jane Muskie at a dinner party. He has been to small, private dinners with President Bill Clinton at the White House.

But he does not try to make every social occasion and in September, 1993, declined an invitation from Mrs. Graham for dinner with President Clinton on Martha's Vineyard. (*Forbes*, October 18, 1993)

However he showed up at Martha's Vineyard August 27, 1994, for a golf game with Clinton. "I can give you a scoop," he told the *Omaha World Herald.* (August 29, 1994) "The president had a 39 on the front nine with a couple of birdies." Buffett said he played only the front nine with Clinton, who finished the 18 with Microsoft's Bill Gates. "The president finished with an 83," Buffett said. "He played better with me than he did with Gates."

In early 1998 Buffett was among the rich and powerful to show up at a formal dinner in the East Room of the White House as President Bill Clinton hosted Britain's Prime Minister Tony Blair. Mrs. Buffett sat next to Clinton, with Mrs. Blair on the other side. Among those invited: Steven Spielberg, Barry Diller, Jack Welch, Tom Hanks, Ralph Lauren, John F. Kennedy, Jr., Tina Brown, Anna Wintour, Barbara Walters and Peter Jennings. (*Time*, February 16, 1998)

(Photo courtesy of the Omaha World-Herald)

Hillary Rodham Clinton enters Borsheim's in the Regency Shopping Center in Omaha March 9, 2000

Buffett, Sen. Bob Kerrey and InfoUSA founder Vinod Gupta

hosted a fund-raiser for Hillary Rodham Clinton in Omaha on March 9, 2000. Buffett took the First Lady to Borsheim's where she shopped for china and silverware for her new house in New York. She left Borsheim's with three shopping bags. She joked she may have left as many dollars as she would take back to New York for her Senate race. (*Omaha World-Herald*, March 10, 2000)

Buffett has popped up at fancy watering holes such as Lyford Cay. He showed up at the 1988 Winter Olympics in Calgary, Alberta, where Agnes Nixon, creator of "All My Children" talked him into his first soap opera appearance.

In New York on March 16, 1993, Buffett showed up at The "21" Club celebrity-studded party for the opening of the TV version of *Barbarians at the Gate*, the story of the RJR Nabisco takeover.

James Garner, who played RJR Chairman Ross Johnson in the movie, was there along with Lauren Bacall, Robert and Georgette Mosbacher and Carl Icahn. Oreo cookies and caviar were served.

A photo of Buffett pops up in the book *Lilly* which is about playwright Lillian Hellman of Martha's Vineyard. There's Buffett, in sneakers, slacks, golf shirt and white hat, standing on a dock, with Lillian Hellman, Barbara Hersey (wife of writer John Hersey), and author William Styron.

Each summer, Buffett shows up in Sun Valley, Idaho, for a media conference hosted by investment banker Herbert Allen. Over the years the participants have included Gerald Levin, chairman of Time Warner, Sumner Redstone of Viacom International, H. Wayne Huizenga of Blockbuster Entertainment, Tom Pollock of Universal Pictures, Jeffrey Katzenberg, the "K" of DreamWorks SKG, Robert Wright of NBC, John Malone of Tele-Communications, Inc. (the nation's largest cable operator), and Barry Diller of QVC as well as top officers of Coca-Cola, McDonald's, Fidelity Investments and J.P. Morgan. Other attendees have included AT&T's C. Michael Armstrong, Amazon.com's Jeff Bezos, AOL's Steve Case, Washington Post's Donald and Katharine Graham, Playboy's Christie Hefner, Yahoo's Jerry Yang, Oprah Winfrey, and Robert Strauss, former Democratic National Chairman. Buffett has had talks with Intel's Andy Grove.

ComCast Cable's Brian Roberts says he had a letter from Buffett following a golf outing at Sun Valley after Roberts and Buffett beat Gates at golf and Buffett won $7. Buffett wrote that he wanted to make Roberts a permanent golf partner because it was the first time he had won money from Gates. (*CNN*, January 9, 2000)

In his book *Work in Progress*, Disney's Michael Eisner describes one scene (p. 12) from the 1994 Herb Allen conference in Sun Valley, Idaho:

"I spent most of dinner talking with Warren Buffett, while Jane spoke to his wife Susie. Warren hardly looked the part of one of the wealthiest men in the world. Casually dressed and understated in manner, he exuded a quiet self-assurance but had no interest in drawing attention to himself. At one point, David Geffen, who had made a lot of money selling his record company to MCA, walked into the room and spotted Buffett. He walked over and immediately dropped to his knees, genuflecting. 'Oh my lord,' he said. 'I'm at the feet of the king.' Warren seemed amused, but said nothing."

In September, 1995, he took a trip to Ireland, went on a train trip in China with Microsoft Chairman Bill "A Computer on Every Desk and in Every Home All Running Microsoft Software" Gates and showed up in Switzerland for a Coca-Cola board meeting.

Buffett, the Rev. Jesse Jackson (by phone) and Sen. Bob Kerrey led a forum on October 9, 1999 at Omaha's Doubletree Hotel to help high school students attain economic literacy.

The name of the forum was changed to the Nebraska Education Forum because some invitations for the originally named "Financial

(Photo by Pat Kilpatrick)

Microsoft Chairman Bill Gates at Microsoft's Annual Meeting in 1997. Buffett of Gates: "He may be the smartest guy I ever met." Gates of Buffett: "Favorite CEO...he thinks." Gates has said, "I think Warren has had more effect on the way I think about business and the way I think about running it than any business leader." Gates also has said: "People really underestimate what he has created at Berkshire." (Business Week, July 5, 1999)

Fitness" forum were misdirected to physical education teachers. (*Omaha World Herald*, October 1, 1999) Buffett's advice to the teenagers: develop integrity and avoid credit card debt.

Buffett is a member of the Alfalfa Club (the name comes from a plant whose roots would do anything for a drink). The group of about 225 heavy hitters assemble once a year to drink Scotch and trade quips. President Bill Clinton asked the group at its 1997 dinner meeting to join him to build a "bridge over the 22nd Amendment," the law that limits presidents to two terms. Buffett, and such luminaries as Colin Powell, Supreme Court Chief Justice William Rehnquist, Disney's Michael Eisner and Jack Valenti, head of the Motion Picture Association of America, were on hand that night. (*The Washington Post*, January 27, 1997)

Buffett, no hayseed, can talk for hours about business, politics, literature or public policy.

In an article for the *Washington Post* (September 14, 1993), he wrote that one way to keep the federal deficit under control was to pass an amendment making legislators ineligible for re-election if during any year they served the deficit is more than 3% of GDP.

He was among 19 CEO's who appeared in a *Wall Street Journal* ad, July 14, 1997, calling for an end to soft money donations to political campaigns. (*Omaha World-Herald*, August 29, 1997)

Lisa Gildehaus, of Bloomington, Indiana, who produced a documentary about Buffett called "Oracle of Omaha," relates this anecdote from her friend, Buffett's son Peter. It seems once that someone asked Warren about the Y2K problem and Peter said, "Why are you asking him? He can't set his VCR."

Buffett once told Gates that explaining technology to him was a waste, that Gates would have "better luck with chimps."

There is kidding about how little he knows about technology. Still Buffett has spent hours at a time swapping stories with Bill "Reach Out to the World of Information" Gates. Former *Washington Post* editorial page editor Meg Greenfield introduced the fellow billionaires July 5, 1991 at a picnic at Gates' parents' home. The two have attended Nebraska-Washington football games together and they spent a week together in Bermuda with other business leaders in the fall of 1993 in connection with a reunion of "The Buffett Group," a close circle of his friends that meets every two years to discuss world affairs. Buffett, who has visited Microsoft several times, has encouraged Gates to study Ben Graham.

On occasions, Buffett and Gates have played bridge together on the internet for an entire day.

> At the Comdex convention in 1999 Gates showed a video in which he and Buffett appeared before television's Judge Judy to resolve a $2 dispute over a bridge game the two played on the Internet. The event was filmed in a county courthouse in Monterey, California. In the video, Buffett tells Judge Judy: "We were playing bridge on the Internet and I was cleaning his clock as I always do. This miserable little cheat unplugged his computer to avoid losing."
>
> Judge Judy found in favor of Buffett: "Mr. Gates, pay the man his $2. Maybe he'll invest it and make something of himself."

Gates was once asked (*Forbes* ASAP, December, 1992): "Who's your favorite CEO outside Microsoft?"

Billion-Dollar Bill replied: "Warren Buffett. The guy thinks. I love people who just think. The conventional wisdom, they don't fall into it."

Buffett, who calls Gates and himself "the odd couple," returned a compliment in a *Fortune* story December 29, 1992 about Gates, saying, "I'm not competent to judge his technical ability, but I regard his business savvy as extraordinary. If Bill had started a hot dog stand, he would have become the hot dog king of the world. He will win in any game. He would be very good at my business, but I wouldn't be at his."

Buffett told *Forbes* (October 18, 1993), "Bill Gates is a good friend, and I think he may be the smartest guy I've ever met. But I don't know what those little things [computers] do."

"I bought 100 shares of Microsoft personally [not for Berkshire] the day I met him to get the reports," Buffett said at Berkshire's Annual Meeting in 1995. But Buffett said that doesn't mean Berkshire and Microsoft will be doing business with one another. Buffett said he doesn't understand computers. "I'd walk by a PC and be afraid it might bite me, but once I got started it was easy. Bridge is the only thing I know how to do with the machine." (*Warren Buffett Speaks*, Janet Lowe, p. 18) Still, the media is a consuming common interest for the world's two richest people.

Buffett told "Nightline's" Ted Koppel (March 2, 1999): "He spent nine hours explaining Microsoft to me. Couldn't have been a better teacher. Couldn't have had a dumber student. But I still understood a fair amount of what he was saying because he is a good teacher and I bought 100 shares when I got all through it. That shows you how many dumb things you can do in this world."

Gates has said he wrote his book, *The Road Ahead*, with a bit of the non-technical Buffett in mind as his audience:

Warren Buffett, who's famous for his investment savvy, is a good friend of mine. For years I kept trying to think of how to induce him to use a personal computer. I even offered to fly out and get him started. He wasn't interested until he found he could play bridge with friends all over the country through online services. For the first six months he would come home and play for hours on end. Despite the fact that he had studiously stayed away from technology and technology investing, once he tried the computer, he was hooked. Now, many weeks, Warren uses online services more than I do. (p. 207-8)

Buffett means it when he says he's no expert in the computer business. Early in his career he passed up an offer from a relative to buy into fledgling Control Data, the large computer firm in Minneapolis. (*Regardie's*, February, 1986)

At a *Fortune* seminar in Palm Springs in the spring of 1995, Carol Loomis surprised a breakfast gathering by introducing Buffett and Gates, saying: "One of these men is the richest man in America and

(Photo by Kiley Christian Cruse)

Peter Kiewit Chairman Walter Scott, left, Buffett and Gates attended the Nebraska-Washington football game in 1997. "I offered to bet my house against his, but he turned me down," Buffett said. Gates has a $47 million home on Lake Washington. Buffett's home in Omaha is valued at $385,000. (Omaha World-Herald, September 20, 1997) Yes, that item between the world's two richest people is a Pepsi cup. The Huskie Stadium in Washington served only Pepsi. Buffett said the Pepsi belonged to Gates, adding "I knew the game was in the bag when I saw that Pepsi was Washington's official drink." (Omaha World-Herald, September 23, 1997)

the other is second." (*Fortune*, May 1, 1995)

Gates, in an article he wrote about his friendship with Buffett for *Harvard Business Review*, January-February, 1996, said:

> We recently vacationed in China with our wives. I think his jokes are funny. I think his dietary practices —lots of burgers and Cokes —are excellent. In short, I'm a fan...
>
> When you are with Warren, you can tell how much he loves his work. It comes across in many ways. When he explains stuff, it's never, 'Hey, I'm smart about this and I'm going to impress you.' It's more the 'This is so interesting and it's actually very simple. I'll just explain it to you and you'll realize how dumb it was that it took me a long time to figure it out.'
>
> We are quite candid and not at all adversarial. Our business interests don't overlap much, although his printed *World Book Encyclopedia* competes with my *Microsoft Encarta*. Warren stays away from technology companies because he likes investments in which he can predict winners a decade in advance—an almost impossible feat when it comes to technology...

Buffett once said he didn't eat a bite of Chinese food during his China trip with Gates. Gates' entourage asked Buffett what he'd like to eat on the trip. Buffett wrote: "Hamburgers and french fries. And nothing else." He underlined "and nothing else."

Time did a cover story (January 13, 1997) about Gates and called Buffett for an interview: "Buffett's secretary apologetically explained that Buffett isn't giving interviews these days and at the moment is traveling, but she promises to pass along the request. Less than three hours later, Buffett calls to say he happens to be in the Time Life Building with some free time between meetings in Manhattan, and he would be happy to come by to be interviewed. He likes to talk about Bill Gates."

Buffett shared stories about Gates' family who visited Warren and Susan Buffett in San Francisco. They ended up playing bridge for nine hours.

Time's story said: ... "Gates made a movie for Buffett's birthday. It featured Gates, pretending to wander the country in search of tales about Buffett and calling Melinda with them from pay phones. After each call, Gates is shown checking the coin slot for loose change. When she mentions that Buffett is only the country's second richest man, he informs her that on the new *Forbes* list Buffett had (at least that year) regained the top spot. The phone suddenly goes dead. "Melinda, Melinda," Gates sputters, "you still there? Hello?"

In his early days Buffett served on some civic boards, furthering the cause of organizations like Planned Parenthood or the local Boys Club—but he has so many self-imposed demands on his time that he doesn't do a lot in the way of civic or charity functions, and there is some grumbling about that in Omaha. But he has given to the local United Way, education generally and a little to AIDS education, specifically. He has backed some fundraising activities in Omaha. For example, he bid $44,000 for a polar bear necktie. The tie, decorated with large, white animals, was auctioned at the Henry Doorly Zoo's 1997 fundraiser by Peter Kiewit's Chairman Walter Scott. The first bid was for $5,000, but the bidding escalated to Buffett's bid of $44,000 of his own money. (*Omaha World-Herald*, September 6, 1997)

Here's how things went at the Zoofari '99 fundraiser which raised about $1 million for the zoo. "During the auction, Walter Scott bought back his polar bear necktie from Warren Buffett for $59,000. Buffett had bought it from him at the previous Zoofari. Then Buffett bought the animal print Scott was wearing for another $59,000. The bidding brought a rousing round of applause and ovation from the crowd." (*Omaha World-Herald*, September 11, 1999)

At one fund-raiser for breast cancer survivors held at the Nebraska Furniture Mart the most popular auction items were sheets of $2 bills signed by Buffett and Bill Gates.

The main focus of his charity efforts is toward reproductive freedom (pro-choice). His efforts for civic and charity causes may be just beginning. After all, he is leaving his fortune to the Buffett Foundation which will give it back to society.

Some have described him as almost reclusive.

"He's not comfortable around people he doesn't know. He's even a little shy. He doesn't like parties...He would be happy in a one-room apartment with his *Wall Street Journal*, his TV and a Pepsi [now Coke]," said his daughter, Susan. (*Register*, February, 1984) One of Buffett's pals who attended a New Year's party with him in the early 1980s has said Buffett spent the bulk of the party off in a corner, killing time until he could leave. Neighbors rarely see him. He is not much of a yardman and doesn't work in his well-tended yard himself. Instead he spends time indoors reading or attending board meetings related to Berkshire's far-flung empire. At his office, very few people drop in—maybe two or three people a week will get a short audience—and they do not include stockbrokers or analysts.

But he has an extraordinarily wide range of friends with whom he stays in contact by phone and letter. He occasionally lectures at colleges such as Columbia, Stanford, Harvard, Yale, Notre Dame,

Vanderbilt, M.I.T., and Creighton University in Omaha. Dartmouth's Amos Tuck School induced him to speak in May 1993 for the dedication of the business school's Byrne Hall. It's in honor of his longtime friend, Jack Byrne, a top figure in the insurance world who once headed GEICO and later Fund American Enterprises.

In the fall of 1998 he addressed the Warrenton [not named for Warren] College of Business at the University of Florida. His talk was sponsored by the Graham-Buffett Teaching Endowment funded by Florida business alumnus O. Mason Hawkins. For the occasion Buffett was decked out in a SunTrust Banks T-shirt. SunTrust, which has a major presence in Georgia and Florida, is also a Berkshire investee.

Buffett almost never goes on television and rarely grants an interview. However, he's gregarious around friends. He hoards a good portion of his time for reading and studying. Although some people have described him as shy, he can talk up a storm and dominate conversations.

And if he is shy, it does not mean he doesn't have confidence in his own abilities. After all, he has said he has known all along, even as a youngster, that he would be rich. Anyone starting an investment partnership in his own bedroom has to have confidence and ignore those pushing him to get a real job.

Buffett is not physically imposing, yet when he starts talking people stop to listen to his every word. His commanding personality is a reflection of his electrifying intellectual powers. In person, Buffett is totally unpretentious, though well aware he is a folk hero and that Wall Street—and others in the room—watch his every move.

"I watch my every move and I'm not that impressed," he quips.

Even where his fame might be obvious, sometimes it is not. Who's Who in America carries just a brief mention of him, describing him as a "corporate executive," the equivalent of saying Babe Ruth played baseball. *The World Almanac* (1994, p. 317) lists Buffett among "noted personalities" but misspells his name!

In person, though, he doesn't particularly care for small talk, Buffett is open, accessible, forthright, speedy and cheerful. Munger has said despite Buffett's amazing memory, he's not as good at remembering names as one would expect.

"He's like talking to a neighbor," says Ronald K. Richey, chairman of Torchmark, an insurance and financial services company in Birmingham, Alabama, in which Berkshire has a small investment—about $10 million. By Berkshire's standards, that's small.

"He called up one day and said he'd like to meet with us," Richey recalls. Richey, who was in Torchmark's New York office at the time, said he'd be glad to meet with Buffett wherever he liked, including Omaha. Buffett, in New York at the time, said, "Oh, no, I know where you are. I'll just walk over."

Richey said a short time later Buffett walked in, basically told him and Jon Rotenstreich, then Torchmark's president, that he was not a threat to the company, just an investor, and left.

Herbert Sklenar, president of Birmingham's Vulcan Materials, the nation's foremost producer of crushed stone, grew up on a farm near Omaha, attended Benson High School and is among those who see Buffett at class reunions. "He (Buffett) was the second person I ran into at the reunion in 1988," Sklenar recalls.

During the reunion, attendees were asked to update their lives and Sklenar said he was with a company "that makes big stones into little stones." Buffett himself got up before the group and offered a little witty investment advice.

Sklenar, who went to Harvard and has hefty experience on the financial side of corporations, admits he'd want to think twice about any possible business proposition with Buffett. "He's just so darn smart," Sklenar said.

Buffett's style is to tackle problems his intellectual brilliance can solve but to steer clear of problems it cannot. Often he has said he's trying to step over one-foot obstacles, not jump over seven-foot obstacles. He strives to make things as easy as possible by seeking sensible, efficient ways of doing things, making the layups he talks about. There are no high-percentage shots from half court. He works hard at the possible and avoids the impossible. One of his great messages is to avoid trouble. In the stock market, that means staying away from capital losses. Ben Franklin-like, Buffett is generally early to bed and early to rise although his sleep hours do vary.

He watches television about seven hours a week, keeping abreast mainly of news and sports. He is a statistics nut and his recall of baseball batting averages and trivia is nearly encyclopedic. However, his baseball interest was most intense in high school.

Whether watching baseball games or not, you can bet his eyeballs would rather be glued to ABC-TV than to any other channel because of his large stake in Disney, which owns Cap Cities, which owns ABC-TV.

Whatever he's doing, it's with self-confidence. "I've never had any self-doubt. I have never been discouraged," he says. (*U.S. News & World Report*, June 20, 1994)

An occasional trace of ego slips through. L.J. Davis wrote in a *New York Times Magazine* story (April 2, 1990) that Buffett has no calculators, no Quotrons, and no computers in his office. "I am a computer," Buffett flatly told Davis.

For better or worse, a lot of Berkshire's records are kept in Buffett's head. Once John Hillery, a Canadian investment advisor, wrote Buffett for a breakdown of Berkshire's bond portfolio—what was taxable, tax free, which bonds were convertible and what the maturities were.

Buffett replied in a letter December 15, 1980: "We may be able to put something in the reports, such as you suggest, relating to bond types and maturities. We get very little in the way of formal reports, and most of that sort of information is in my head rather than in any computer print-out. But I may try to give some general impressions if I have a section on bond investments again this year."

Buffett's small office is located in Omaha's Kiewit Plaza, a modest building, far less imposing than the nearby headquarters of Mutual of Omaha, whose annual returns are in turn less imposing than Berkshire's. For a haircut, Buffett goes down to the basement to the Kiewit Plaza Barber Shop where he is described as "a regular man." Berkshire's headquarters have been expanded and upgraded so everything's roomier—but still under 4,000-square-feet. Headquarters has been described as "linoleum floors and throw rugs." That's a slight exaggeration, but it is far from some plush corner office with mahogany paneling. On the outside of the door is a sign saying, "No admittance except by appointment."

Russ Fletcher, an insurance executive, who is now executive vice president of Homesite Group, Inc. in Boston, had an appointment one day in the mid-1980s to see Berkshire's Michael Goldberg. Fletcher arrived for his appointment set for a Saturday morning. "I walked in and he (Buffett) was behind his secretary's desk opening the mail," Fletcher recalls. "He was dressed in blue jeans and a turtleneck...He said 'Hi' and we exchanged pleasantries...He's very unassuming."

Another fellow who got into the inner sanctum once in 1988 was Michael O'Brien of Austin, Texas. "I was there to shoot a picture of him for *Esquire*...I asked him about the crash, if that made him fearful. He said no, that if the market had dropped another 500 points, he'd really have found bargains."

Inside world headquarters there is a mini-conference room and places for about a dozen people to operate.

Berkshire does have other locations for its team of accountants responsible for insurance subsidiaries, and a data processing building elsewhere in Omaha to track the insurance operation's complex finances, but Berkshire's operations are lean beyond belief.

Buffett runs Berkshire's empire from a rather small desk near the corner of his office piled with reading material such as the *Wall Street Journal* and the *Omaha World-Herald* and magazines. The desk, at times, sports notepads that read, "In case of nuclear war, disregard this message."

He has other notepads as well. Buffett once sent me a photo of Coca-Cola's President Don Keough (now chairman of Allen & Co.). A number of Berkshire shareholders had their picture taken with Keough at the Berkshire annual meeting in 1991. Coke folks sent Buffett the photos and he forwarded them to shareholders. Mine came with a little Post-it note saying he thought I'd enjoy the photo. It was signed in his usual way with a large W, a legible "a" and a sort of loop representing two r's, to form a scrawled "Warren."

What was unusual about the note was the inscription at the bottom, which read:

"An absolutely brilliant memo"—*NY Times*
"Clear...concise...to the point"—*Fortune*
"Masterful use of the language"—*Atlantic*

Sometimes Buffett will jot messages on sticky notes like these:

A message from

GOD!

There's nothing like
OLD MONEY™

RECYCLED U.S. CURRENCY

Visitors to his pale emerald-green office in the building owned by privately held construction conglomerate Peter Kiewit Sons', Inc., are greeted by a small porcelain plaque given to him by his wife. The inscription, hanging just inside the door of his headquarters, reads, "A fool and his money are soon invited everywhere."

Mementos of the stock market abound, particularly from the crash of 1929. Scattered about are miniature sculptures of bulls and bears. On the walls are stock quotations from the crash, a portrait of Buffett's father and a photo of Ben Graham. There is a Pulitzer Prize for the exposé of Boys Town by his now defunct Omaha Sun newspapers.

His desk is neither clear nor messy. "It's in between," says Dr. Ronald W. Roskens, former president of the University of Nebraska, who has occasionally called on Buffett at his office about civic or charitable missions. "It's what makes sense...He's trying to keep things simple. There's a sofa here, his desk is over there. It's not a dump but it's not ornate either," he added.

His tiny staff of a dozen people for years included his administrative assistant, Gladys Kaiser, with him from December 1967, when she walked in as a "temporary" Kelly Girl. She retired in 1993, and Debbie Bosanek was named to her job. Mrs. Kaiser still has lunch with Buffett every month or so.

Of her he once said, "Things just wouldn't quite work around here without her...I wish her immortality. If Gladys can't have it, I'm not sure I want it either." (*Fortune*, April 11, 1988)

One of the few people working close to Buffett is Michael Goldberg, an intense, hard-driving man who long headed Berkshire's disparate, far-flung nationwide insurance operations, and remains a vice president. "He's so damn smart and quick that people who are around him all the time feel a constant mental pressure trying to keep up. You'd need a strong ego to survive in headquarters," Goldberg has told Buffett's friend and chronicler, Carol Loomis of *Fortune* magazine.

Goldberg, who attended Columbia, Northwestern and Stanford Business School, came to Berkshire as a young man already a top executive with the Pacific Stock Exchange. He told Loomis, "I've had a chance to see someone who can't be believed. The negative is: How do you ever think much of your abilities after being around Warren Buffett?"

Goldberg later told Linda Grant (*Los Angeles Times*, April 7, 1991): "Warren Buffett is a person who, the closer he gets, the more extraordinary he gets. If you tell people about him, the way he is, they just think you were bamboozled."

Precisely. A lot of things about Buffett and Berkshire are so unbelievable—such as its five-digit stock price—that at first people are skeptical.

Buffett's one acknowledgement of modern technology is a bank of two telephones that connect him with different brokerage firms when the need arises. Berkshire has gone high tech and has a fax machine.

Buffett roams around the five-room suite of offices at Kiewit Plaza getting his own Cherry Cokes, pulling his own files from the office storeroom. He doesn't mind if someone brings him a hamburger for lunch so he can stay and answer the telephone. Not all calls to Buffett are about billion-dollar deals. "Sometimes it's a wrong number," Buffett has joked.

And sometimes it's a request for an annual report. "I called Berkshire in 1988 because I didn't get my annual report. I cannot prove this in a court of law, but I'm 99% sure I got him...He had a clipped, fast voice. He said 'That's awful' that I didn't get the report," recalls Dr. Wallace Gaye, a Berkshire shareholder who lives in Durham, New Hampshire.

Dr. Gaye, a former medical school teacher, left the medical world, in part, to track the ticker tape and his Berkshire shares.

"I started to ask if he was Warren Buffett, but I just couldn't...He was fast. He said something like he'd fix it. Two days later I got the report," Gaye said.

Gilman Gunn, of Wellesley, Massachusetts, who in the late 1970s sold securities for Mabon Nugent, once called Buffett, got him on the phone and tried to sell him some Doubleday publishing stock, 600 shares of the stock which was trading at $13,000 a share.

"He said send the information and that he'd take a look. I called him a few days later and he said he had reviewed it and decided, 'It wasn't cheap enough for us,' " said Gunn, surprised Buffett took his calls.

Other folks have encountered Buffett's quick responses. As his fame has grown, well-meaning people have besieged Buffett with investment advice. But only rarely does he want it. Once a large Berkshire shareholder, Ernie Williams of Village of Golf, Florida, called him, excited about an investment publication he wanted to share with Buffett. Buffett's reply: "Please don't send it."

Buffett is basically a homebody, preferring to stick close to his own office and home and counsel. But he also has to travel, as he serves on a number of corporate boards, and occasionally he manages to get away to his second home in Laguna Beach, California.

There is rarely any pomposity or moodiness in this multi-billion-aire. People who have known him for years say they have never seen him angry. His response to things is not anger, but rationality. His reply to things that are okay with him is usually: "Yeah, sure." If something displeases him, his reply can be, "We don't need any of that."

He responds to the world by examining it thoroughly and in a positive and witty way. He often delivers self-deprecating humor as in "Your Chairman has blundered again," or offers stories about how he studied the soft drink industry for more than 50 years and eventually determined that the industry's two main rivals, Coca-Cola and Pepsi-Cola, have both done well.

Those who have worked with him describe him as almost unfailingly upbeat and supportive, practically never testy. He works hard. "He's thinking about three things at a time. He's thinking about it [Berkshire] 24 hours a day," says an employee of a Berkshire subsidiary. And yet he says his work is not work, but fun. Fun to Buffett is studying the world of business through voracious reading. His health has always been good although he suffers somewhat from a back problem, the result of playing handball years ago. It forced him to cut back his tennis.

Buffett, a member of Augusta National, site of The Masters, has played golf over the years and these days occasionally shows up at the Seminole golf course in Palm Beach, Florida, or with Bill Gates or Charles Munger at Pebble Beach or Palm Springs in California. He has a 22 handicap. Those who have played with him describe his game as so-so, but they say he is very competitive, improving as the round progresses and most likely to come through in the clutch, say, when things are tied up on the 18th.

His style in golf is to save his two mulligans for the last two holes, says a golfing partner.

Bob Hancock, head of Robert Hancock Investments in Omaha, once asked Buffett how he'd play Augusta and Buffett said, "I'd tee it up and hit it directly into the water."

Once a fellow asked Buffett how he had managed to shoot a round of 108. Buffett replied: "I three putted 18."

Golf Digest (March 2000) figuring Buffett's golf handicap at 18.2 listed him as 157th of the top 200 CEOs. The top ranking went to Sun Microsystem's Scott McNealy with a 3.3 handicap. McNealy, once captain of Harvard's golf team, jokes that it is "kind of like being the Florida State ski captain." (*Fortune*, February 21, 2000)

Buffett seems practically oblivious to temptation—living a modest lifestyle marked by few parties, no cigarettes, and very little drink other than the Cherry Cokes he craves. Buffett carries no moral outrage about smoking or drinking. He just doesn't find much point to either.

He shuns fancy restaurants, settling on Gorat's steakhouse in Omaha, with its "Go Big Red" signs (that's only one notch below a "Go, God, Go" cheer) for a dinner of steak and potatoes. Linda Grant described his eating habits this way: "He orders Cherry Coke for his aperitif and consumes steaks and thick, juicy hamburgers with no regard for the current cholesterol phobia. Heavily salting his T-bone one recent evening at Gorat's steakhouse, his favorite Omaha hangout, Buffett said, 'You know how our life span depends on how long your parents live? Well, I watch my mother's exercise and diet very carefully. She has 40,000 miles on her bike.' Chuckling, he dives into sides of hash browns and spaghetti."

One Friday evening in January, 1993, Buffett attended a function for the powers-that-be of Omaha's Emmy Gifford Children's Theater, now the Rose Blumkin Center for the Performing Arts. Everyone except Buffett had a Greek buffet. He had a cheeseburger, fries and a Coke.

Buffett just says no to all drugs except one: caffeine. The man is fairly wired on the stuff. To satisfy his caffeine habit, bolstered by a desire to give wings to Coke stock, Buffett constantly drinks Cokes and has an occasional piece of See's candy. Before Coke, it was Pepsi. His wife once said: "Everyone who knows Warren knows he doesn't have a bloodstream—it's a Pepsi stream; he even has it for breakfast." (*Warren Buffett Speaks*, Janet Lowe, p. 19)

Over the years a slight paunch has developed in his middle, but it's one that might be attached to someone 15 years younger. He

(Omaha World-Herald)

Buffett, who invested little in his game for a celebrity tennis match in Omaha in 1992, plays here with tennis champions Pam Shriver and Martina Navratilova and former NFL quarterback Danny White. Buffett said his preparation for the match was to learn to say, "yours" in Czech to Navratilova. Even that didn't work because Miss Shriver and White won the match on a one-point tie-breaker.

admits his diet and exercise habits are not all they should be. Once at the height of the Salomon bond trading crisis in the early 1990s, Buffett called his friend James Burke, the former chairman of Johnson & Johnson. Buffett said he was having trouble sleeping and asked Burke for help. When Burke said he ran three to five miles a day during Johnson & Johnson's Tylenol crisis, Buffett hesitated and then said, "Any other suggestions?" (*Wall Street Journal*, November 14, 1991)

Even so, Buffett is the picture of health and is enormously energetic.

His house is fixed up these days into a perfectly respectable home, with a well-kept yard, surrounding trees and a roomy driveway. Over the years he has furnished the home largely with items from Omaha's Nebraska Furniture Mart, a business he bought in 1983. In short, his nice, rambling house—with a 40 by 20-foot racquetball court and exercise equipment in the basement—is a pleasant addition to the quiet, tree-lined neighborhood. Ostentatious it is not.

The house is plainly furnished and has only a few luxuries such as 30-inch, 40-inch and 50-inch television screens, according to Nebraska Furniture Mart salesman Doug Clayton, who sold him two of the big screens.

Harvey Lipsman of Omaha recalls that his son, Rocky, used to visit the Buffett home to see Buffett's son, Howard. Their talk was often about girls, not money. Later in life Rocky—realizing Warren Buffett's success—got him to sign a book. Warren Buffett wrote: "Rocky, you should have talked to me instead of Howie."

Once Washington Post Co. Chairman Katharine Graham visited Buffett's modest home and joked, "Warren, is this all you can afford?"

His home is full of books, including a shelf of Bertrand Russell (Buffett says: "Because he thought like Graham") tomes from which Buffett can quote long passages. Here's a sample of Russell's writings. This is the prologue to the *Autobiography of Bertrand Russell* written in 1956:

Three passions, simple but overwhelmingly strong, have governed my life: the longing for love, the search for knowledge, and unbearable pity for the suffering of mankind. These passions, like great winds, have blown me hither and thither, in a wayward course, over a deep ocean of anguish, reaching to the very verge of despair.

I have sought love, first, because it brings ecstasy—ecstasy so great that I would often have sacrificed all rest of life for a few hours of this joy. I have sought it, next, because it relieves loneliness—that terrible loneliness in which one shivering consciousness looks over the rim of the world into the cold unfathomable lifeless abyss. I have sought it, finally because in the union of love I have seen, in a mystic miniature, the prefiguring vision of the heaven that saints and poets have imagined. This is what I sought, and though it might seem too good for human life, this is what—at last—I have found.

With equal passion I have sought knowledge. I have wished to understand the hearts of men. I have wished to know why the stars shine. And I have tried to apprehend the Pythagorean power by which number holds sway above the flux. A little of this, but not much, I have achieved.

Love and knowledge, so far as they were possible, led upward toward the heavens. But always pity brought me back to earth. Echoes of cries of pain reverberate in my heart. Children in famine, victims tortured by oppressors, helpless old people a hated burden to their sons, and the whole world of loneliness, poverty, and pain make a mockery of what human life should be. I long to alleviate the evil, but I cannot, and I too suffer.

This has been my life. I have found it worth living, and would gladly live it again if the chance were offered me.

Buffett admires the writings of British economist (and investor) John Maynard Keynes such as *Essays in Persuasion*. Keynes was known for investing only in a very few companies in which he had full confidence. Buffett particularly likes biographies. He has read such books as *Father, Son and Company; McDonald's, Behind the Arches; The Big Story, Influence; Bonfire of the Vanities; Liar's Poker; Den of Thieves and Barbarians at the Gate.* "He's read all the usual books but they are usually financially related," said his daughter, Susan.

For investors he says required reading includes the chapters about "Margin of Safety" and about investor's attitudes towards the market in *The Intelligent Investor*, the 1934 edition of *Security Analysis*, *The Money Masters* and investor Phil Fisher's first two books. Buffett wrote *Forbes* (October 7, 1996): "How lucky I have been to have Phil [Fisher] and Ben Graham write down their ideas when they had no financial incentive to do so. I am leagues ahead richer than I would be if I hadn't read Phil. I can't even calculate the compound rate of return from the few dollars spent buying his books 35 years ago."

And he recommends Pete Peterson's *Will America Grow Up Before*

I Grow Old? about the looming Social Security crisis. "Send it to your congressman," says Buffett.

From his house, Buffett can nose down Farnam Street in less than five minutes to his spartan office. Another several minutes away is downtown Omaha, should he need to go that far. One of his mantras is that it's much easier to stay out of trouble now than to get out of trouble later. Along with keeping things simple, he wants to keep distractions to a minimum and to be consistent. If you can live close to the office, do. If the restaurant serves a hamburger or steak you like, why search out a restaurant across town?

> The Stage Delicatessen restaurant in New York has a sandwich in Buffett's honor. It's one of his favorites, roast beef on white, with extra mayo. It's listed on the menu as "The Oracle of Omaha." (*Omaha World-Herald,* May 11, 1999)

One Wall Streeter, Marshall Weinberg, a stockbroker with Gruntal & Co., recalled going to the old Ruben's restaurant in New York for a meal with Buffett.

"He had an exceptional ham-and-cheese sandwich. A few days later, we were going out again. He said, 'Let's go back to that restaurant.' I said, 'But we were just there.' 'Precisely. Why take the risk with another place? We know exactly what we're going to get.' "

One of Buffett's tenets is don't run all around without a good reason. You can do most of what you need to do right where you are. "I'll be in Omaha as long as I live," Buffett has told Berkshire shareholders.

(Photo by Nancy Line Jacobs)

Buffett, Carol Loomis, Sharon Osberg and Charles Munger settle in for a bridge game the day before Berkshire's annual meeting in 1996.

Another lesson is to do things yourself. He drove himself to the Berkshire Annual Meeting in 1989, parking his car around back of the Joslyn Art Museum. Just before he got in to drive away after the meeting, a Berkshire shareholder came up to him with a thick pile of papers and asked him if he would look at them. He said he would and she asked if she should mail them to him.

"Oh, no. I'll just take them and read them back at the office." He took the papers, got in his 1983 dark blue Cadillac and no doubt drove back to the office and read the papers.

It was not until 1991 that Buffett actually bought himself a new car, a Lincoln Town Car four-door sedan that he still owns. "I think he's getting a little mellower," said Omaha stockbroker George Morgan of the purchase. When filling up, Buffett uses the self-serve pump to fill his unwashed car.

Morgan has another story about the car. There was a big event one night in the summer of 1999 to celebrate the opening of the Kiewit Institute of Information Sciences, Technology and Engineering at the University of Nebraska in Omaha. More than 1,000 of Omaha's finest were invited for the big event at a museum south of Omaha which included dinner as well as entertainment by Liza Minnelli. Valet parking was the order of the evening for most of the attendees. When the event was over, Morgan saw Buffett walking over a little grassy knoll toward his old Lincoln Town Car which he had parked himself.

> Buffett owns a blue Lincoln Town Car because it has dual air bags. Actually Buffett didn't buy the car. His daughter, Susan, shopped for it in the early 1990s. "I bought it for him (he paid!) without any consultation about color, make, anything except that the two requirements he had were that it had airbags and that it weighed a certain amount of pounds (obviously both safety issues.) Anyway, the big bonus was that I ended up paying less because it was hail damaged....The damage had been fixed when I bought it, but they couldn't sell it for the regular new price because of the hail."

After GM CEO Jack Smith pointed out a Cadillac has air bags for the passenger, the driver and a person in the middle, Buffett told Smith his next car will be a Cadillac. (*Fortune*, May 2, 1994)

In earlier years, Buffett, already wealthy, picked up friends in a baby blue Volkswagen bug. "My father loved that car," Susan said. One Berkshire shareholder recalls a time in the early days when he visited Buffett in Omaha. "He picked us up in a Volkswagen and was sort of apologetic about it," the visitor said.

In addition to tennis, golf, and racquetball, Buffett's hobbies include Scrabble, but his particular passion is for bridge—played at times with a deck of cards inscribed, "Make checks payable to Warren Buffett." Bridge, he is fond of saying, is better than a cocktail party.

Buffett jokes that once he asked his bridge partner how he should have played a hand and was told: "Under an assumed name."

"I always say I wouldn't mind going to jail if I had three cellmates who played bridge," says Buffett, whose bridge partners have ranged from Peter Lynch to George Burns. The ageless Burns played Buffett (and Munger and others) at a table reserved for Burns at the Hillcrest Country Club in Los Angeles under a sign that reads, "No Cigar Smoking if Under 95." Burns's team beat Buffett's.

At the Berkshire Annual Meeting in 1998, Buffett repeated a joke Burns told when he was 98. Burns, surrounded by five or six beautiful, young women at a hotel one night said: "At my age, one of you is going to have to leave tonight."

In 1993-1995 Buffett was captain of a corporate team that for three years topped a team from Congress in bridge matches.

Buffett likes to play bridge with Sharon Osberg of San Francisco, twice a member of the world's women's championship team and silver medalist in Greece in October 1996 in world mixed teams.

Ms. Osberg, an executive vice president at Wells Fargo Bank for online financial services until she left that job in early 2000, said, "I met him about three years ago at a celebrity bridge tournament through Carol Loomis." Later Ms. Osberg gently tried to convince Buffett to play computer bridge. Finally Buffett agreed.

"We bought a computer at the Nebraska Furniture Mart, of course, and set it up in his home. We play a couple of times a week in the evenings. He really loves it," Ms. Osberg said.

"T-Bone" is Buffett's handle for games on his IBM Aptiva PC. Gates plays under the name "chalenger." [spelled with one l] They play at the website OKbridge.

Buffett has since become so entranced by the computer he's now regularly surfing the Internet, Ms. Osberg said, adding that he sends and receives E-mail messages and looks up corporate filings.

Early one Saturday morning Buffett called Ms. Osberg for a game. "T-Bone" and "Sharon O" searched cyberspace for partners coming across a couple of players from Israel who recognized "Sharon O." Ms. Osberg asked, "Who are your group?" The players explained they were part of the Israeli national bridge team practicing for the world championships. "T-Bone" and "Sharon O" took them on anyway. "We lost, but held our own," Ms. Osberg said. She and

Buffett have found other partners all over the world, in such places as Europe and South America.

Ms. Osberg, Buffett's bridge teacher, says his game has improved to the point of being a world class player. "We played in the World Championship recently. We had to drop out because he had a business emergency, but we made it to the finals. He is moving toward holding his own at the world level. He can play with anyone. It's because of his logic, his ability to solve problems and his concentration." Ms. Osberg, through her friendship with Buffett, has played with Bill Gates, Katharine Graham and U.S. Supreme Court Justice Sandra Day O'Connor (who graduated No. 3 in her class at Stanford Law School).

"The most intense game I've ever played was a six hour game with Bill Gates. We played Buffett and Munger. We lost $28. Warren named the stake of ½ cent a point. I thought Charlie would pass out " [from the low stakes] Ms. Osberg added.

The game, which started about noon, took place at Gates' house. Buffett said, "Seven hours later, dinner guests were knocking at the door, but Bill wanted to keep on playing." (*Forbes*, June 2, 1997)

Buffett says of bridge: "It's got to be the best intellectual exercise out there. You're seeing through new situations every ten minutes... In the stock market you don't base your decisions on what the market is doing, but on what you think is rational. ...Bridge is about

(Photo by Nancy Line Jacobs)

Do not play bridge against this man.
The Oracle of Omaha, whose idea of downtime to rest his gray matter is an intense game of duplicate bridge, plays here at the Omaha Bridge Studio in November 1993. A can of Coke, another fraction of a penny to Berkshire's bottom line, is on the floor.

weighing gain/loss ratios. You're doing calculations all the time..."
(*Forbes*, June 2, 1997)

At festivities connected with Berkshire's 1996 Annual Meeting, Osberg and Loomis played Buffett and Munger. "We won," Osberg said proudly.

Often Buffett plays bridge with his sister, Bertie, and her husband, Hilton Bialek, of Carmel, California, or with William H. Gates, Sr., the Seattle attorney and father of Microsoft's founder. And he occasionally plays bridge with his Omaha friends. One is Richard Holland, a retired advertising executive who says, "Warren's an excellent bridge player. If he had time to play enough, he'd be one of the best in the country." (*Omaha World-Herald*, October 30, 1993)

Perhaps there is a link between the intuitive abilities common to great bridge players and great security analysts as they both try to figure probabilities. They trust their decisions relating to intangible factors. And they always are being dealt new hands.

The San Francisco Chronicle (August 27, 1998) in a story about Osberg and Buffett playing online bridge said, "Buffett, who has played the game since childhood, has become an Internet bridge junkie, known to play all night until the stock market opens. In response to a question typed in by Osberg, T-bone said he plays about 12 hours a week. 'I'm glad you asked about quantity rather than quality,' T-bone wrote back." The article went on to say "Buffett's game gives little insight into his investment strategies. Buffett routinely declines press interviews, but agreed to answer several questions posed through Osberg."

Buffett said, "The approach and strategies are very similar in that you gather all the information you can and then keep adding to that base of information as things develop. You do whatever the probabilities indicated based on the knowledge that you have at that time, but you are always willing to modify your behavior or your approach as you get new information.

"In bridge, you behave in a way that gets the best from your partner. And in business, you behave in the way that gets the best from your managers and your employees."

But when the reporter asked whether his bridge game resembles how he plays the stock market, Buffett said, "I don't play the market. I buy businesses."

Buffett concentrates hard when he works or plays bridge. Once Nancy Line Jacobs of Omaha asked if she could take his picture playing bridge, hoping it wouldn't distract him. Buffett replied, "It won't distract me, but I'll pretend it will."

Afterwards Mrs. Jacobs sent him some photos to sign with a note that she had "crashed" the previous annual meeting as a member of the press, though she didn't write an article, but was now a Berkshire shareholder and would be at the next meeting in an honest way. "He even returned my pen," Mrs. Jacobs said.

Buffett signed a photo for her, "To Nancy, Finally, an honest woman." For a photo for Omaha stockbroker George Morgan, who says his net worth is no different from Buffett's except for some zeros, Buffett wrote, "To George, here's to more 0's." To me he wrote, "To Andy, You have treated me better than I deserve—thank God!"

Instead of drinking and dancing at some big city disco, he takes an interest in his family, gets some exercise and stays in touch with friends.

When he is in New York, he often stays at Katharine Graham's apartment and usually calls on John and Carol Loomis and George Gillespie, III. Gillespie, a close friend, is a partner in the Cravath, Swaine & Moore law firm in New York which has such clients as IBM, Time Warner and Salomon. Also the firm helps with Buffett's estate planning and has advised The Buffett Foundation. Gillespie is a large Washington Post Co. shareholder and a supporter of the fight against Muscular Dystrophy.

The foursome passes the evening playing bridge and eating peanuts, ice cream and deli sandwiches—Buffett's idea of a big night in the Big Apple.

Buffett has no aides, no advance team. When he was already the richest person in the country, he once arrived at National Airport in Washington, D.C., walked up to the corporate jet counter and asked: "How do I get a taxi?"

The same flavor was captured by *Business Week* (July 5, 1999) reporter Anthony Bianco: "Warren Buffett is returning to the U.S. from Europe in a private jet. As his plane nears its destination, the flight attendant gives out landing cards and a warning to all eight passengers aboard. 'The customs inspector here is utterly humorless,' she says, 'so no wisecracks or he will tear the plane apart from fore to aft.' Buffett, who quips as reflexively as he breathes, takes his card without comment.

"In the terminal a surly looking man with a crewcut and a pistol on his hip sits behind a small table. Buffett hands over his passport and landing card to the inspector, who does not seem to realize that the professorial-looking 68-year-old standing before him is America's second-richest man. Or perhaps he just gets a kick out of trying to take the high and mighty down a peg. 'You left some things blank,' the inspector says peevishly. 'Do you have $10,000?'

"The question could have launched a dozen snappy retorts, but Buffett restrains himself. 'I have what I left with,' he says carefully. The inspector furrows his brow—was that some kind of joke?—but does not press the issue. He asks Buffett if he has anything else to declare. 'I was given two books,' Buffett says. 'Well, you have to put it down, then,' snaps the agent, who fills in the blanks himself.

"Buffett shows not a flicker of annoyance at being treated like a misbehaving child. He stands mute and impassive before the inspector, who, after a few more curt remarks, can think of nothing else to do but let the 'Oracle of Omaha' be on his way."

There are no airs. His shoes are scuffed. The pen is a Bic. Buffett does his own taxes, saying they are really quite simple. He's even kept all his tax returns since 1944. Buffett is anything but simple, though his tastes are. And things at Berkshire seem and are simple. But the reality of what's been built, which Buffett created with a unique combination of simplicity and genius, is something to behold.

13
TOMATO SOUP AND A
STRAWBERRY MILKSHAKE

Here's Buffett's idea of a good meal, found in a recipe he provided for William D. Orr's *First Gentleman's Cookbook* (p. 178):

My ideas about food and diet were irrevocably formed quite early—the product of a wildly successful party that celebrated my fifth birthday. On that occasion we had hot dogs, hamburgers, soft drinks, popcorn and ice cream.

I found complete gastronomical fulfillment in this array and have seen no reason subsequently to expand my horizons. In fact, I am thought to be so expert in this specialized area of food preparation that I am often called upon to act as a consultant for pre-puberty dinner parties. The loudest applause at such affairs is invariably rendered when I sculpt my Dusty Sundae.

This sophisticated-sounding delicacy is really quite simple in preparation: First pour generous quantities of Hershey's Chocolate Syrup over vanilla ice cream, and then build a mountain of malted milk powder atop the chocolate.

The caloric consumption produced by this concoction is inconsequential. Assume that your basal metabolism rate is 2,800 calories per day. Simple arithmetic tells us that you can—indeed you must—consume slightly over one million calories per year. In my own case—with a life expectancy of about 25 years—this means that, in order to avoid premature death through starvation, I need to eat some 25 million calories. Why not get on with it?

A neighbor swears he once saw Buffett down a bowl of tomato soup and then drink a strawberry milkshake.

14
GOLF OUTINGS
(WARREN'S WORLD)

Each year Buffett hosts a day-long golf event known as Omaha Golf Day for the benefit of Omaha charities, including the Rose Blumkin Performing Arts Center where his daughter Susan heads the foundation.

Those attending the golf and tennis outing at the Omaha Country Club have included top officers of Salomon Brothers, Merrill Lynch, AT&T, Sprint, *The New York Times*, Bozell Inc., ConAgra, Coopers & Lybrand, Deloitte & Touche, Caterpillar, Schering Plough, U.S. West, Bank One, the *Omaha World-Herald* and others.

The event, a mini-Warren's World, in 1993 raised $175,000, in 1994 $900,000 and in 1995 $350,000 to help pay the center's operating expenses. Buffett personally matched the 1994 and 1995 contributions.

(Omaha World-Herald)

Sporting a Cherry Coke hat, Buffett hosts an annual golf outing, a benefit for the Rose Blumkin Performing Arts Center in Omaha.

For one outing, Buffett sported not only a Cherry Coke hat, but also a golf shirt displaying a fistful of money inside the Berkshire Hathaway name.

U.S. Senator Sam Nunn of Georgia and about 100 political and business leaders often attend the event. Participants are invited by the event co-chairmen, Walter Scott, chairman of Peter Kiewit Sons' and Michael Yanney, chairman of America First Companies.

Former Treasury Secretary Nicholas Brady, Jack Byrne of Fund American, Nebraska's U.S. Senators Bob Kerrey and J. James Exon have found time for the event, which includes dinner with Buffett.

Buffett told Nunn he'd attend a conference of Nunn's to discuss ideas for overhauling the federal tax system. (*Omaha World-Herald,* August 31, 1993)

"Buffett said Nunn's effort to overhaul the tax system could bring a consumption tax 'one notch closer' to reality.

"Buffett said he favors a 'progressive consumption tax' to replace the federal income tax. The schedule would allow people to pay for basic living expenses and to deduct what they save or invest. They would pay taxes on the rest of the money they spend on consumption."

"As the amount spent on consumption increases, the taxed amount would increase," he said.

"I personally would prefer to make it steeply progressive as a matter of social equity," Buffett said.

Shortly thereafter, on November 8, 1993, Buffett, saying Kerrey was, "good for Nebraska, good for business," announced he would serve as honorary chairman of Kerrey's re-election bid for the Senate.

In the summer of 1993, Kerrey turned to Buffett for advice about President Clinton's economic plan. Kerrey was the last and deciding vote in the Senate and he finally voted for the president's package. Buffett's recommendation to Kerrey was: "Hold your nose and vote for it." (*The Agenda,* Bob Woodward, p. 306)

Among those attending the event in 1996 were former Dallas Cowboys quarterback Roger Staubach, former U.S. Defense Secretary Dick Cheney and former U.S. Senator Lloyd Bentsen. Buffett reminded Bentsen that when he ran for vice president in 1988—it was in Omaha that he said his famous line to Dan Quayle: "Senator, I served with Jack Kennedy. I knew Jack Kennedy. Jack Kennedy was a friend of mine. Senator, you're no Jack Kennedy." Bentsen said he wished he had copyrighted the line.

Buffett, in 1997, played in a golf tournament hosted by St. Louis Cardinals pitcher Bob Gibson, an asthma sufferer who lives in Omaha. About 40 former athletes—including Sandy Koufax, Vida Blue, Gale Sayers and Stan Musial—played in the tournament. Collectively, the athletes owned nine Hall of Fame plaques, 10 Cy Young Awards, 13 season and World Series most-valuable-player trophies and four rookie-of-the-year honors. (*Omaha World-Herald*, June 15, 1997)

Bryant Gumbel and comedian Bill Murray were among those who played in the tournament benefiting the American Lung Association.

Buffett and Gary Wiren, a golf teacher in North Palm Beach, Florida played 18 holes together at the Elmwood Park public golf course in Omaha on October 12, 1998.

The two hadn't played the course in 50 years, according to the *Omaha World-Herald* (October 13, 1998).

"There were no golf carts, no fancy golf bags and no caddies. The two friends slung well-worn canvas golf bags over their shoulders and walked Elmwood, a short-yardage course that ranks high in scenery and low in difficulty," wrote Jim Rasmusson of the two men recalling childhood memories of the course.

"Buffett readily agreed to play Elmwood, joking that he'd get to play holes No. 1 and 18 for the first time. He said he and other boys used to skip the first and last holes to avoid paying the 25-cent greens fee."

(Omaha World-Herald)

Golf pro Gary Wiren and Buffett use well-worn canvas bags to carry their golf clubs at Elmwood Park golf course.

"On the first tee, Buffett waggled his Calloway Big Bertha driver, pulled it back slowly and swung. The 'tink' of the metal-headed club signaled a solid shot. His drive soared down the middle of the fairway, finishing 230 yards away and just 30 from the green."

"Go away, fellas. That's typical." Buffett said jokingly to the reporters and photographer.

(Omaha World-Herald)

Wiren hands Buffett a penny to mark his ball on the first green. "He's not getting it back," Buffett quipped. "I didn't say anything about a loan."

(Omaha World-Herald)

Host of the event: Warren Buffett, left, chats with Joe Ford, chairman and CEO of Alltel Corp.

BY JIM RASMUSSEN
WORLD-HERALD STAFF WRITER

When Warren Buffett arrived Tuesday at his charity golf and tennis event at Omaha Country Club, he first had to duck into the clubhouse for a quick phone call.

He emerged five minutes later to say that he had given a price quote over the phone for $50 million worth of insurance against damage from Hurricane Floyd, which at that minute was bearing down on the Florida coast. "The quote's good for 15 minutes," the billionaire investor said, in complete seriousness. "That storm could change direction in a hurry."

Conversations soon turned lighter for Buffett, chairman of Omaha-based conglomerate Berkshire Hathaway Inc. He served as host for about 140 guests—including corporate chief executives from across the country—at an event that raised more than $1 million for Girls Inc. in Omaha.

Many attendees got their first look at Omaha at the fund-raiser, which Buffett and other local leaders said is good for the city's image.

"They get a favorable impression of Omaha," Buffett said. "It can't hurt for people to come here and see friendly people and what a great town it is."

As it has for all eight years, Buffett has hosted his annual Omaha Classic, the weather cooperated, with sunny skies and temperatures in the mid-60s.

But several executives who attended this year's event said they don't come to Omaha for the weather. They come to hear Buffett speak at an evening dinner, and to relax for a day.

"Warren's the catalyst," said Dan Cook, a former Nebraskan who works in Dallas as a senior director with investment bank Goldman, Sachs & Co. "There are a lot of high-powered egos here, and they learn from Warren. Everyone looks forward to Warren's speech at night."

Cook sponsored a golf foursome that included Harold Simmons of Dallas, chief executive of Contran Corp., a conglomerate that includes chemical and steel companies.

"I've always been an admirer of

161

Warren Buffett," Simmons said in explaining why he made the trip. "And this is just a good time. The main thing is to raise money for charity, and you get the opportunity to meet a few people."

The guest list was sprinkled with celebrities from the worlds of business, sports and entertainment. There was investment guru Peter Lynch of Fidelity Management, remarking to Buffett on Omaha's "New England weather." There was baseball Hall of Famer George Brett, hitting drives on the practice range. There was Chuck Norris, star of TV's "Walker, Texas Ranger," talking with Jack Valenti, president of the Motion Picture Association of America.

Pat Summerall of Fox Sports, who has long been one of pro football's top TV play-by-play announcers, waited to meet Buffett as reporters interviewed the Omaha billionaire on the country club lawn.

When they finally shook hands, Buffett quickly turned the conversation to University of Nebraska football.

"We're out here where real football is played." Buffett told Summerall. He added that about half the team's players come from Nebraska, including many from "little tiny towns."

"Yeah, they seem to grow some out here," Summerall replied. "They're very successful."

Bill Fairfield, chief executive with Omaha-based computer company Inacom Corp., said Buffett makes the event special for executives and celebrities.

"The real hit is listening to Warren pontificate at the evening dinner," he said. "He's almost a natural stand-up comedian."

Valenti used movie-industry terms in explaining why guests find Buffett entertaining.

"He's such a compelling character," Valenti said. "He's the only business titan I know who's genuinely witty. He doesn't need a screenwriter to inject life into what he's saying."

Bob Bell, president of the Greater Omaha Chamber of Commerce, called the event "priceless" exposure for the city. He noted that many of the guests had eaten breakfast at the University of Nebraska's new Peter Kiewit Institute for Information Science, Technology and Engineering Tuesday morning.

"The Kiewit Institute made an impression on Buffett guest Joe Cappy, chief executive with Dollar Thrifty Auto Group, "I think it's fantastic," he said. "It's something I wasn't aware of."

Golfer David Duval was to have attended but couldn't make it because of mechanical troubles with the plane he was to take.

This year marked the second time Girls Inc. has been the event's beneficiary. It takes turns as the recipient with three other youth-oriented charities—the Omaha Children's Museum, the Boys and Girls Club of Omaha, and the Omaha Theater Company for Young People.

Sponsors of each golf foursome donated at least $15,000, and tennis doubles team gave at least $7,500. Their donations were matched by Buffett.

Most of the sponsors are Omaha businesses and local business people, said Buffett and his daughter, Susie Buffett, who helps organize the event. Most of the out-of-town guests are sponsored by their Omaha hosts, but some guests also donate money.

BUFFETT GOLF LIST

Golfers at Buffett's Omaha Classic:

Roger Ackerman, chairman and CEO, Corning Inc.; Beau Armstrong, president of Stratus Properties; Joe Armstrong, partner, Kutak Rock; former astronaut Neil Armstrong, now CEO of AIL Corp.; Robin Barr, chairman, A.G. Barr; Glen Barton, chairman and CEO, Catepillar Inc.; Bob Bates, chairman and CEO, Guarantee Life Cos.; Jack Baum, president, Sagebrook Investments; Bob Bell, president, Greater Omaha Chamber of Commerce; Dennis Berman, chairman, Denitech Corp.; George Brett, vice president of baseball operations, Kansas City Royals; Stan Bright, vice chairman, MidAmerican Energy Holdings Co.; Dick Callahan, president and CEO, Callahan Associates International.

Michael Capellas, president and CEO, Compaq Corp.; Joe Cappy, CEO, Dollar Thrifty Auto Group; Bob Cochran, chairman and CEO, Financial Security Assurance; Dan Cook, senior director, Goldman, Sachs & Co.; Bob Crandall, chairman emeritus, AMR Corp.; Tom Cruikshank, chairman emeritus, Haliburton Co.; Dave Daberko, chairman and CEO, National City Corp.; Harris Diamond, CEO, BSMG Corp.; Irl Engelhardt, chairman and CEO, Peabody Group; Ike Evans, president, Union Pacific Railroad; Bill Fairfield, president and CEO, Inacom Corp.; Tom Fisher, chairman and CEO, Nicor Inc.; Don Fites, chairman emeritus, Catepillar Inc.; Joe Ford, chairman and CEO, Alltel Corp.; Fabio Freyre, publisher, Sports Illustrated; Lee Gammill, retired vice chairman, New York Life Insurance Co.; Joe Gasper, president, Nationwide Life Insurance Co.; David Goode, chairman and CEO, Norfolk Southern Corp.; Vin Gupta, chairman and CEO, InfoUSA Inc.; Stedman Graham, president, S. Graham & Associates; Grant Gregory, chairman, Gregory and Hoenemeyer.

Tom Hacking, president, Hacking & Co.; Darryl Hansen, chairman and CEO, Guide One Insurance; Phil Heasley, president, U.S. Bancorp; Charlie Heider, general partner, Heider-Weitz Partners; Tom Hicks, chairman and CEO, Hicks, Muse, Tate & Furst; Tim Hoeksema, president and CEO, Midwest Express Airlines; Dick Holland, retired; Paul Horn, president, RDO Equipment; Ralph Horn, chairman and CEO, First Tennessee National Corp; Jim Houlihan, assessor, Cook County, Ill.; David Hunerberg, regional managing partner, Deloitte & Touche; Clark Johnson, chairman emeritus, Pier 1 Imports; Joel Johnson, chairman and CEO, Hormel Foods Corp.; Clarke Keough, vice president, Allen & Co.; Tom Kincaid, president and CEO, Kincaid Capital Group.

John Kizer, president, Central States Indemnity; John Leinweber, chief executive officer, Imagine Technology Group; Jim Leslie, president, Staubach Co.; Mike Lindley, CEO, HotLink Marketing; Ben Love, retired chairman, Texas Commerce Bancshares, Peter Lynch, vice chairman, Fidelity Management; Harold Marshall, retired president, Associates First Capital; Brad Martin, chairman and CEO, Saks, Inc.; Dennis McClain, president, Temerlin McClain; Jim McFarlane, president and area chairman, Arthur J. Gallagher; Joe Moeller, president, Koch Industries; Ellen Moran, executive vice president, Bozell Worldwide; George Muller, president, Subaru of America; Lance Munger, office managing partner, Deloitte & Touche; Stan Musial, former baseball star; Aaron Norris, executive producer, Amadea Film; Judy Owen, president and CEO, Norwest Bank Nebraska; Susan Parks, president and general manager U.S. West Business & Government Services; Chuck Peebler, chairman emeritus, True North Communications; Jeff Raikes, group vice president, Microsoft Corp.; Dick Reiten, president and CEO Northwest Natural Gas; David Rismiller, president and CEO, America First Financial Institutions Investment Management.

Rich Santulli; chairman, Executive Jet Aviation; Jack Schneider, managing director, Allen & Co.; Walter Scott Jr., chairman Level 3 Communications Inc.; Rick Seibert, vice president and general manager, Omaha World-Herald; Bobby Shackouls, chairman and CEO, Burlington Resources Inc.; Harold Simmons, chairman and CEO, Contran Corp.; John Simons, president, ConAgra Beef Cos.; Mickey Skinner, chairman and CEO, New World Pasta; David Sokol, chairman and CEO, MidAmerican Energy Holdings Co.; Warren Staley, president and CEO, Cargill Inc.; Mike Starnes, chairman and CEO, MS Carriers; Ken Stinson, chairman and CEO, Peter Kiewitt Sons', Inc.; John Sturgeon, president, Mutual of Omaha Cos.; Pat Summerall, sports anchor, Fox Sports; Bill Strauss, chairman emeritus, Enron Corp.; Frank Swan, CEO Nationwide Foods/Brookfield Farms; Al Ueltschi, president, FlightSafety International; Jack Valenti, president and CEO, Motion Picture Association of America; Chris Volk, executive vice president and chief operating officer, Franchise Finance Corporation of America; Willliam Welsh, president and CEO, Election Systems & Software; Gary Wiren, president, Golf Around the World; and Mike Yanney, chairman and CEO, America First Cos.

Tennis participants:

Graham Arader, owner, Arader Galleries; Zoe Baird, president, Markle Foundation; Mogens Bay, chairman and CEO, Valmont Industries; Dick Berry president, United Seeds; Eddy Blanton, president, Edison Interests; Jack Blanton, chairman, Houston

Endowment, Inc.; Mariann Byerwalter, vice president and chief financial officer, Stanford University; Michael Carns, retired general, U.S. Air Force; Hank Chiles, retired admiral, U.S. Navy; Myrv Christopherson, president, Dana College; Ed Cox, chairman, Edwil L. Cox.; Arthur Diedrick, chairman and CEO, Communications International; Peter Duerr, president and CEO, BFD Capital Beteiligungs; Elias Eliopoulos, executive vice president, First National Bank of Omaha; Al Fasola, CEO, Jumbo Sports; Russell Glass, president, ICAHN Associates Corp.; John Golden, president, Stephen Gould Co.; Rudiger Gunther, executive vice president, Class KGaA; Jim Hebenstreit, president, Bartlett and Co.; Hugh Hunt, president, HunTel Systems; Francis Jelensberger, Alstom; Kelly Jelensberger, Myron Kandel, financial editor, CNN; David Kames, president and CEO, Fairmont Group.

Jeff Love, partner, Locke, Liddell & Sapp; Louis Marx Jr., chairman and CEO, Hudson River Capital; David McCourt, chairman and CEO, RCN Corp.; Gregor Medinger, president, HVB Capital Markets, Inc.; Scott Miller, executive vice president, Hyatt Development Corp.; Chuck Norris, chairman and founder, Kick Drugs out of America; Tom O'Neill, chairman, McDermott/O'Neill & Associates; Whitney Quillen, chairman and CEO, Q Properties; Bill Quinn, president, AMR Investment Services; Allen Salmasi, chairman and CEO, NextWave Telecom; Charles Stevenson, chairman and CEO, Navigator Group; Sol Trujillo, president and CEO, U.S. West Inc.; John Veiner, senior partner, SHH Christy and Veiner; Edward Wanaandi, chairman, Trailmobile; and Richard Ware II, president, Amarillo National Bank.

(Source: Omaha World-Herald, September 15, 1999 with permission)

Hollywood players: Actor Chuck Norris, left, jokes with Jack Valenti, president of the Motion Picture Association of America.

(Photos by Omaha World-Herald)

Neil Armstrong, first man on the moon

15

DINNER AT SENATOR DANIEL MOYNIHAN'S HOME

Buffett, along with U.S. Senator Bob Kerrey and some health care CEOs, had dinner at Senator Daniel Moynihan's home in Washington, D.C., on November 24, 1993.

One person at the dinner/health reform workshop was Richard Scrushy, chairman of HealthSouth Rehabilitation Corp. in Birmingham which specializes in treating sports and head injuries.

Scrushy, who came in thinking Buffett could not possibly be as good as advertised came away saying, "I was really taken with him."

The two shared a ride from the airport to the dinner and Buffett told him about his early paper route and pinball machine days in Washington. Scrushy wound up seated next to Buffett for a time as Buffett, Kerrey and Moynihan rotated among the several tables.

"He did not know about my company, but he asked a lot of questions. He was fascinated by the rehabilitation aspect of our company," says Scrushy.

The dinner conversation centered on health care reform and how to pay for it. Also, there was discussion about how to revamp the entire tax system.

"He wanted the tax code to be more consumption-based instead of income-based...He felt the tax system should be more progressive, that it's actually regressive as it is. He said it's discouraging to entrepreneurs and wealth building, that incentives should be in place to encourage entrepreneurs and wealth building," Scrushy recalls.

The talks covered a number of issues, even the importance of fighting the drug problem, all agreeing it was a huge health care cost.

HealthSouth Rehabilitation CEO Richard Scrushy and Buffett in a car after dinner at Senator Moynihan's; Buffett reenacts his trademark of pulling out his wallet and handing it over whenever he meets a politician.

(Photo by Barry Morton)

165

At the end, Buffett and Scrushy had photos taken of themselves tugging at Buffett's wallet.

"He's not only brilliant. He's very funny," Scrushy said.

Another person at the dinner, Barry Morton, CEO of Robins & Morton, a health care construction firm in Birmingham, Alabama, said that Buffett, on meeting a politician at dinner, would pull out his wallet and say, "Here, take all my money."

In 1997 HealthSouth signed an exclusive five-year partnership with Coca-Cola, Berkshire's biggest investee. The $5 million deal means HealthSouth serves only Coke products at its facilities in all 50 states.

Scrushy is a Diet Coke junkie.

16
MRS. SUSAN BUFFETT
WIFE, BOARD MEMBER, HEIRESS, SINGER, AND ANONYMOUS DONOR

Buffett and Susan Thompson married in 1952. Their parents had been friends and she roomed with Buffett's sister Bertie at Northwestern University.

When Buffett dropped in, courting her, she dropped out of college to marry him. Mrs. Buffett grew up a block and a half from Buffett's present home.

After the Buffett children were raised, Mrs. Buffett was briefly a cabaret singer at the French Cafe, a fancy restaurant in downtown Omaha.

Singing has long been her passion. In 1997 she recorded a CD. She sang such songs as "Come In From The Rain," "Up Where We Belong," and "Send In The Clowns."

In the brochure accompanying the CD entitled "What Is There To Do With Such A Heart But Sing," she thanks her producer, Dave Stryker and says: "Thank you W.E. for the love and encouragement—Thank you Peter for the joy of making music together. Thank you Howard for the beautiful photography." Howard shot the photos for the brochure.

Mrs. Buffett, who says her husband would be happy with "a book and 60-watt light bulb," radiates a calm, empathetic demeanor. Once in the late 1970s during the Christmas season, she came into a Little Professor bookstore in Omaha, dressed in full-length mink coat and blue jeans, and bought about $70 worth of books, recalls Martha Line, who waited on her.

"I knew who she was, but the store manager explained to her he would have to run a credit card check because the amount was more than $50. She was not indignant or insulted, quite calm about it. She handled it a lot better than I would have," Mrs. Line said.

Mrs. Buffett, an open, friendly and dignified woman, lives apart from her husband, although she has described him as the most interesting person she's ever met. "He's like a color TV instead of black and white. Most people come in black and white," she has said. (*Register*, February, 1984)

She has indicated that a factor in her move from Omaha was getting "hit from all sides" by community groups in Omaha looking for help. *(Regardie's,* February, 1986)

For a long time she has lived in San Francisco, although she has said she really lives everywhere because she travels so much, often for a variety of civic causes, especially civil rights and Planned Parenthood and has volunteered to help people in Omaha housing projects. She has worked with minority youths, keeping in touch with them by letters over the years and encouraging their studies.

She and Buffett remain close. They are separated but by no means estranged. They travel and socialize together, seeing each other about once a month

Of the separation Buffett has said, "It works well this way. She sort of roams; she's a free spirit." *(Forbes,* October 21, 1991)

Howard Buffett says, "If the comment 'behind every good man there is a good woman' has any truth to it, then you absolutely must give my mother credit for a good share of my dad's success. She is the most understanding and kind person I have ever known, and her support throughout his career has been very important to him."

Her daughter, Susan, says her mother was long active in race relations and women's causes in Omaha, but in recent years has had less time to work for causes.

She devoted much time to Susan who had a difficult pregnancy with her son, Michael. She helped her own son, Howard, campaign for the county commission, and was on hand when her sister faced a lengthy battle with cancer.

Mrs. Buffett is a major Berkshire shareholder, owning 34,478 shares—about 2.6% of the company. The block of stock is worth about $2 billion.

In 1991, Mrs. Buffett was named to Berkshire's board, and Buffett has said that she shares his views about maintaining the character of Berkshire.

Should Mrs. Buffett outlive her husband, she would inherit his stake and with 38% of the company would effectively control Berkshire, making her one of the richest people in the world. Bill Gates, with his enormous stake in Microsoft and a personal portfolio of more than $5 billion, has been holding on to the number one spot. After Mrs. Buffett's death, her Berkshire stock is slated to go to charity, through The Buffett Foundation (where Mrs. Buffett is president and to which she devotes much of her time), and eventually back to society.

Buffett has no written contract with his wife that the shares will go to the foundation, but there is an understanding between the two that it will. *(Forbes,* October 18, 1993) "The deal is whoever dies last will leave the Berkshire Hathaway shares with no strings attached. I've got this fund that's growing at a rate of 25 to 30%.

"When I'm dead, I assume there'll still be serious problems of a social nature as there are now. Society will get a greater benefit from my money later than if I do it now."

Buffett has said leaving his Berkshire stock to his wife first, before it goes to the foundation, preserves the most flexibility in terms of reacting to changes in the laws. Wives are not taxed on inheritance from their husbands, no matter how large the amount.

(Photo by Nancy Line Jacobs)

Mrs. Susan Buffett before Berkshire's annual meeting in 1997

Mrs. Buffett has said, "Our foundation is focused on population (problems), and my other giving is very personal." (*Warren Buffett Speaks*, Janet Lowe, p. 168)

Mrs. Buffett was inducted into Omaha's Central High School Hall of Fame in 1999 and told the *Omaha World-Herald* (September 30, 1999): "For me, Central has always been symbolic of what you want an urban school to be. It's all-inclusive, academic and socially diverse, as a school ought to be. It's full of all kinds of kids living different lives but coming together and learning together.

The story also said: "To protect her privacy, Susan Buffett—sometimes called "Susie Sr." to distinguish her from daughter Susie Buffett—a community activist in Omaha rarely gives interviews. Susie Sr. declined to talk Wednesday about the Buffett Foundation, of which she is president, except to say she chose to be in Omaha

(Photo by Marlin Stockwell)

Buffett's daughter, Susie, and his wife, Susie Sr.

tonight instead of in Vietnam for the foundation.

"She lives in San Francisco but says she is there only 20% of the time. She travels widely, kidding that she's a 'geriatric gypsy.' "

She also said, "Warren's parents and my parents were great political and personal friends. They were a little to the right of Queen Victoria. Warren and I fell far from that tree."

Once asked for comments about her mother, daughter Susan Buffett said: "I don't want to add anything...about my mother because she really tries to keep her life private. The only thing I will say is that she is one of the best people I know. She's one of the first people my father names when he's asked to list his heroes. And my parents have a wonderful relationship. They are very close and have a deep respect and love for each other. Actually my dad would say that my mother and his father are the two people who have had the most influence on his life."

(Photo by Nancy Line Jacobs)

Warren and Susan Buffett before Berkshire's Annual Meeting in 1999

17

"ALL MY CHILDREN"...
"THOUGHT HE CHECKED ALARM SYSTEMS."

The Buffetts have three energetic, grown children: Susan Buffett, born July 30, 1953; Howard Graham Buffett, born December 16, 1954, (named after Buffett's father, Howard Buffett, and Ben Graham) and Peter Buffett, born May 4, 1958.

As with any family raising children, things have at times been like a soap opera. All of Buffett's children attended college, but none finished. All are healthy, intelligent and productive.

Susan, sometimes called "Little Miss Muffett" in elementary school, worked as an assistant to the CEO of Century 21 in California before she worked for the *New Republic* and later as an administrative assistant to the editor at *U.S. News and World Report* in Washington, D.C. Then she returned to Omaha where she heads the Rose Blumkin Center for Performing Arts foundation.

Susan recalls a time she needed cash to pay for airport parking in Washington, D.C. Her father was there. But to get the money, Susan had to write him a $20 check.

"Sometimes it's frustrating, but unfortunately, I basically agree with him," Susan said. (*Omaha World-Herald*, May 26, 1996)

"What makes my dad happy," she added, "is hanging around the house, reading, playing bridge and talking with us. He's about as normal as you can get."

While Susan was in Washington, she and her daughter, Emily, often saw Katharine Graham, longtime chairman of The Washington Post Co. "I remember Mrs. Graham being impressed with Emily because she could eat avocados and caviar. That's unlike my father and me. All we want is hamburgers," Howard Buffett said.

Howard Buffett, a Republican who served most of one term as chairman of the Douglas County Commission, where he was known as an advocate of programs for the disadvantaged, has a 406-acre farm north of Omaha where he raises corn and soybeans.

He long has been outspoken on behalf of the state's ethanol industry. He drove a 1988 Corvette convertible with "Ethanol" printed on the license plate.

And he has been an avid speaker promoting the benefits of using the corn- and sugar-based fuel additive. He served on the Nebraska

Gasohol Committee and served as chairman of the Nebraska Ethanol Authority and Development Board until 1991, when he was named to the International Policy Advisory Committee on International Trade which advised the Bush administration on trade issues.

Howard was elected to the board of Archer-Daniels-Midland Co., the food processing company, known as "Supermarket to the World," based in Decatur, Illinois. Howard replaced Robert Strauss after Strauss was named ambassador to the Soviet Union and later to the Commonwealth of Independent States. (Strauss was renamed to the board in 1993.)

It was early 1992 when Howard resigned his county commission post to take a job under ADM's Chairman Dwayne Andreas as corporate vice chairman and assistant to the chairman.

"This is a big decision. It's probably the largest one I've ever made in my life," Howard said.

"For someone like me who is interested in agriculture," said Howard, "the opportunity to work under him would be like someone who is interested in investments getting to work under my father."

Howard asked for his father's advice. Warren called the job, "a once-in-a-lifetime opportunity."

In 1995 Howard resigned from ADM, apparently troubled by a price fixing investigation of the company. He is now the chairman of the board of The GSI Group, a farm equipment firm in Assumption, Illinois.

A lot of people hated to see Howard leave Omaha.

"He's a rare breed of a young politician," says Buffett family friend Michael Yanney. "He has excellent intellect and a high degree of political sensitivity, but more importantly he exhibits his father's integrity."

Howard has recounted a time when as county commissioner he backed a project to bring basketball immortal Michael Jordan to Omaha for two days of events on August 23, 1990.

Berkshire's corporate jet was called into action to pick up Jordan in Lawrence, Kansas.

Howard, who had worked for 18 months to organize Jordan's trip, showed Jordan the long list of activities and Jordan said, "Man, I'm not doing all this stuff."

Howard said, "I was about to die."

Then Jordan winked and after two full days of activities, which raised $47,000 for youth agencies, told Howard, "Howie, I want you to remember one thing. You really owe me one."

At one of the events, a celebrity basketball game, Jordan ejected Howard for not wearing Nike (a stock tip?) shoes.

"Michael Jordan...did more for Omaha in two days than most people could do in two years," Howard said.

In addition to his political and agribusiness careers, Howard Buffett is an accomplished photographer and his photos have captured wildlife around the globe. His pictures have been published by Wildlife Conservation Society, World Wildlife Fund, The Nature Conservancy, The Wilderness Society, and *Prairie Farmer* and *World Book Publications.* Also he

(Photo courtesy of Howard Buffett)

Photographer Howard Buffett

has written a number of articles about conservation which have been published in *The Washington Post, Chicago Tribune,* and *The Wall Street Journal.* He has published a brochure of his photos called *BioImages.*

Buffett's daughter, Susan, when asked about her father being a Democrat and her brother being a Republican said that both her father and brother are more concerned with principles than politics. "My father and my brother are very principled. Politics does not come between them." In fact, she added, they kid each other about it.

Susan said she would never have any idea what stocks her father was buying. "He might ask a consumer question about what kind of candy I liked, or something, and maybe three years

photographic images by
Howard G. Buffett

BioImages

(Photo courtesy of Howard Buffett)

Award winning photo by Howard Buffett

later you could see why." But she said he would never walk around the house and say some stock was a great buy.

Peter Buffett, who studied photography, physics and music at Stanford University for two years, is a successful musician/businessman in Milwaukee. He recorded the sound track for an award-winning eight-hour miniseries, "500 Nations," about the history of Indians, directed by Kevin Costner and aired by CBS. Peter writes commercials that he says, "support me and my habit, which is my studio." (*Fortune*, August 24, 1992)

A New Age composer whose creations include a synthesized musical score for the Infiniti 20 television spots, Peter also scored the fire-dance scene for Costner's Oscar-winning movie, *Dances with Wolves*. Most of Peter's business is recording commercial jingles for companies like DuPont, Infiniti, CNN and Levi Strauss.

(Omaha World-Herald)

Peter Buffett and his wife, Jennifer, stand outside Warren Buffett's home, where Peter stayed while preparing for his concert at the Rose Blumkin Performing Arts Center. Sounding like his father, Peter said, "It's home and it's cheaper than a motel."

In 1996 Peter Buffett performed at Omaha's Rose Blumkin Performing Arts Center at a benefit for the James Redford Institute for Transplant Awareness. Actor Robert Redford's son underwent two liver surgeries at the University of Nebraska Medical Center in 1993 after being on a national organ transplant waiting list for seven months. Since then Robert Redford has led efforts to inform people about organ donation. Both Redfords attended the benefit.

Peter Buffett's "Spirit-A Journey in Dance, Drums and Song" which grew out of his work on "Dances With Wolves" was aired on PBS in 1999 and toured nationally.

Peter told Linda Grant of *The Los Angeles Times* (April 7, 1991),

"My dad says the money is not important to him, but it is. Not because he wants to spend it, but because it makes him a winner. My dad casts a big shadow. I remember sitting at the dinner table with him, and there was nothing you could tell him that he didn't already know. But I always got the impression he would support me in whatever I chose."

Peter has said his father calls and visits frequently and enjoys hearing about the music industry.

"It's neat to be able to talk to him about what's happening in my life. I read about what's happening in his," Peter said. (*Omaha World-Herald*, August 30, 1991)

His childhood was nothing unusual, Peter told *The Lincoln Nebraska Journal* (August 8, 1991). "It was incredibly normal, almost to a fault. He (Warren Buffett) really didn't reach notoriety until the 80s. When I was a kid, I never thought twice about who he was and what he was doing. We didn't live in what would be considered a special neighborhood, we didn't go to a special school, we didn't have special friends. So I never really noticed anything out of the ordinary."

Peter Buffett told *Worth* magazine (April, 1996): "For as long as I can remember, he thought all three of us should do what made us happy. He was great that way. He is, essentially, the same way he was 30 years ago. He'll ask me, 'What do you get paid for something like *The Scarlet Letter*?' 'Well, I got this or that,' and he'll be like, 'Wow, that's a lot of money!'"

According to his sister, Susan, Peter picked up music naturally. "This is a kid who can't read music. He just sat down at the piano at age 7 and started playing a lot better than his sister who had 8 years of piano lessons."

Peter also told the magazine he long ago had sold his Berkshire stock, an amount that would be about $30 million today.

Warren Buffett, who doesn't plan to leave much money, relatively speaking, to his children, has said his reasoning is this: "As Jesse Owens' child, your development would not be facilitated by letting you start 100-yard dashes at the 50-yard line."

Peter has asked his father for a loan only once—when he was moving to Milwaukee. His father turned him down.

"He just said: 'Look, I want our relationship to stay clean. Once money gets into it, it will get complicated.' It was great. It wasn't great then. I learned a lot more going through the bank and dealing with it than if I had gotten a free ride." (*Omaha World-Herald*, November 3, 1996)

BERKSHIRE HATHAWAY

Activewear

Titleist
HP2

Titleist HP2TOUR / One Dozen Balls
(4 sleeves of 3 balls each)

Currency not included.

BERKSHIRE HATHAWAY 1998

Actual Size: 4" x 4"

(Photo handout at Berkshire Annual Meeting in 1998)

Buffett and Buffett's daughter Susan, right, model Berkshire's activewear sporting the company's fist full of dollars logo. Until a Fortune story ran (December 8, 1997), Berkshire had sold only 2,300 shirts. The reporter did a "test-drive" of the activewear at bars in New York City's financial district. One Lehman trader was quoted as saying, "Oh, Warren Buffett—he sings that Magaritaville song!" Proceeds from the sales of T-shirts, sweatshirts and golf shirts go to Berkshire's bottom line. The fine print under Buffett says: "Currency not included." Buffett wrote in Berkshire's 1998 Annual Report, "Our 1999 apparel line will be unveiled at the meeting, so please defer your designer purchases until you view our collection."

Buffett's daughter, Susan, has told any number of jokes about vague disgruntlement with her father's tight-fisted policy about not leaving his wealth to his children.

Susan says she understands his reasoning, but indicates that now that his children are grown he can lighten up on the heavy lessons.

As Howard says, "I still think there is hope for him yet. He has demonstrated a little more flexibility in the last few years."

Susan told Linda Grant that because Buffett is her father, everyone assumes she is rich. Not the case, she has told reporters. "They don't understand that when I write my dad a check for $20, he cashes it. If I had $2,000 now, I'd pay off my credit card bill."

Howard says, "I told her I'd loan her the money! Someone in the family has to have deep pockets, even if they have holes in them."

Buffett doesn't believe in leaving it all to his children and has set aside only a few million for each, all told less than .1% of his net worth. The rest will go to The Buffett Foundation.

Susan tells many stories about her father, perhaps the most amusing being the one about what her early classmates thought her father did for a living.

She has told Adam Smith, "For years I didn't even know what he did. They asked me at school what he did, and I said he was a security analyst, and they thought he checked alarm systems."

18

"MY DAD COULDN'T RUN A LAWNMOWER..

(BUT) HE ONCE TOLD ME IT TAKES A LIFETIME TO BUILD A REPUTATION AND FIVE MINUTES TO RUIN IT."—HOWARD BUFFETT

Buffett's son, Howard Graham Buffett, met Ben Graham in Warren Buffett's New York days. Howard was just a toddler then and has but one recollection of him.

"He gave me a stuffed animal...a stuffed dog," recalled Howard Buffett. "Obviously, he had a lot more impact on my father than he did on me."

Howard Buffett's wife, Devon, came into the marriage with four children. The couple added Howie Buffett. Howie Buffett's middle name is Warren and it may be that he has inherited the family's financial genes.

"He owns 10 shares of Coke, it may be more now, and he's always asking his grandfather for advice about Coke stock," said Howard Buffett. "He called my dad the other day to ask him about it."

"I sometimes talk to him about investments...I do take his advice. We have some Coca-Cola stock," said Howard Buffett.

Howard Buffett, says of his father, "He learned it all from me." Howard said he never really regarded his father as different in most respects. "I never thought of him as any different, just as my dad, just as anyone else would." But Howard Buffett admits there were a few puzzling things going on even in his youth.

"I really remember him up in his office (at the house) reading *Moody's* or something. He worked really hard. He could work 18 hours a day."

"I do remember once when we were on vacation in California and he was constantly on the phone with Stan Lipsey of *The Buffalo News* for about three days straight. There was a strike at the paper and my father was going through every business calculation," he said. His father was nearing the conclusion it was going to be more economical to close the paper than keep publishing, Howard added.

(Photo courtesy of Howard Buffett)

Warren Buffett, Howard Buffett and former Cap Cities Chairman Tom Murphy

It never came to that, but those on the other side underestimated how seriously his father was thinking of closing it because reason dictated it, said Howard Buffett. "I've watched him go through the process...He takes all the emotion out of a decision. He just goes through the fundamental reasons when he makes a decision. He doesn't deviate."

Buffett is a caring person, but when it comes to business decisions he just boils it all down to facts and reasons.

"My father couldn't run a lawnmower...I never saw him cut the grass, trim a hedge or wash a car," Howard Buffett said. "I remember that used to be irritating and only when I got older and understood the value of time did I realize why he did things the way he did. His time is so valuable."

Howard Buffett said in his own life he tries to save time for different interests. "I want time to farm and do other things."

The younger Buffett said his father cares nothing for comfort or style. "He had an old Volkswagen for years and only gave it up when he thought it was unsafe. He's had other cars but he doesn't care a thing about them...It could be a car or a horse. All he cares about is getting there."

Once Buffett was returning from an East Coast trip on the company jet when it developed hydraulic problems and landed in Indianapolis, leaving Buffett temporarily stranded. So how did he get back to Omaha?

"He flew coach," his son said. "He was proud he flew coach and I'm not sure he may not have wanted to go first class, but I'm sure he couldn't have stood it if he had been spotted on first class."

180

Howard once told *Forbes* (October 12, 1998):

"When I graduated from high school in 1973, all I wanted in the world was a new Corvette," the young Buffett begins.

Dad didn't just say no. Neither did he reach for his checkbook. He offered a deal.

Warren would pay $5,000 toward the car, but it counted for three years of birthday presents, three years of Christmas presents, his entire graduation gift, and Howard would have to come up with the $2,500 balance on his own.

Howard got the car. Then somebody backed into it.

Buffett overheard a bystander exclaim: "No big deal! That's the Buffett kid, there's lots more where that came from."

Fat chance. Howard paid for the repairs himself.

He attended Augustana College in 1974, Chapman College in 1975 and the University of California at Irvine in 1976.

After a few jobs—operating a bulldozer; working for See's Candies, one of his dad's companies; and farming—Howard thought he'd take a stab at politics. It was 1988, and he ran for commissioner of the Douglas County board that oversees the Omaha district.

"I asked my dad one question that, if he had answered differently, I might not have run for office. I asked him if he thought voters would think less of you if you ran for political office and lost. Dad instantly responded: 'Not at all. People will respect you if you are willing to participate and put yourself on the line,'" he told *Forbes*. (October 12, 1998)

During the campaign there was a community meeting in one of Omaha's poorer districts. Howard was nervous. "They're all going to think I'm just some rich kid from West Omaha," he confided to his dad, again asking for advice. "Just go down there, shake hands, be friendly," Warren responded. "They're all going to think you're going to be a jerk, and so long as you're not a jerk, you win."

Howard Buffett says his father often offered guideposts to live by. "I remember once, we were on Dodge Street near a McDonald's that's no longer there, and my father told me, 'It takes a lifetime to build a reputation and five minutes to ruin it.' "

"He's so basic and so very fast paced," he said.

"All the stories about him sticking to basics are true. A lot of CEOs are flamboyant, not all, but many are. He's not. He's not phony. He's totally sincere."

Howard says there's just one real problem being around his father. "He's so smart, it's frustrating."

"He's a walking *Almanac*...When I was a kid it was discouraging. In fact, it was overwhelming," said Buffett, who found it was almost impossible to tell his father anything he didn't already know or achieve some success that ever compared with that of his father.

Howard Buffett told *Fortune* magazine (September 10, 1990) about how he farmed 406 acres and loved the work: "I've been farming nine years. It's a very independent type of activity—everything's up to you. It teaches you a value system and gives you the instrument to achieve that."

But Howard probably has heard: "... There are three easy ways of losing money—racing being the quickest, women the most pleasant, and farming the most certain."

However, "Dad owns the land. I pay him a percentage of the gross income as rent. The rent is based upon my weight. I'm 5 foot 8, and I weigh around 200 pounds. He thinks I weigh too much—that I should weigh 182.5. If I'm over, my rent is 26% of gross income. If I'm under, 22%. It's the Buffett family version of going to Weight Watchers. I don't mind it, really. He's showing he's concerned about my health. Even at 22%, he's getting a bigger payback than almost anybody around..."

Back in 1985 Buffett once financed a 30-day shopping spree for his daughter as a bribe for her pledge not to gain weight in the coming year. However, the agreement was canceled because Susan became pregnant. (*Fortune*, August 24, 1992)

Howard Buffett said later that although his father is receiving the high end of a normal return on farm ground rental, that's OK.

After all, said the younger Buffett, "I feel very fortunate that my dad has enough interest in my farming activity that he was willing to purchase a farm. It's my dream, but it's his farm, and it's his privilege to determine how he wants to rent it to me."

As things turned out, when Howard Buffett moved to Decatur, Illinois, he sub-leased the land at a good profit above what he pays his father. But he missed the tractor and the plowing. There's a story about Howard that occurred after he moved to Decatur. On some snowy days, Howard's neighbors would find their driveways cleared. A man discovered Howard snow plowing one day and asked him why he was doing it. Howard said he missed being on his tractor so much that he got one out to be on it and was happy to play snow remover.

Before Howard moved, he had lunch with his father every Tuesday. "We have a great relationship. He has been a great instructor, a great teacher. I never look at my dad as the Warren Buffett that you see in *Forbes* magazine. All I see him as is my dad. But at the same time, I realize he has so much experience and knowledge to offer," he told the *Omaha World-Herald.* (October 31, 1993)

Finally, in the son's eyes, what is it that makes Warren Buffett tick?

"I think it stems from his basic philosophy that you ought to want to give back to society and not just be a consumer of it. That's totally consistent with what he does," he said. "He does want to be a success and he likes to be creative. He's extra creative and intelligent...He has all the tools and all that's combined with a drive and determination...There's an inside drive. He wants to do good things. He wants respect and to be in a position to have a positive influence."

"What he really likes is a challenge. What he's really about is finding a better way to do it," he said in an interview several months before the Salomon scandal occurred.

In June, 1993, Berkshire expanded its board from five to six members and Howard Buffett was named to the board. Howard is a director of Lindsay Manufacturing Co., an irrigation equipment maker in Lindsay, Nebraska, and he's a director of Coke's 43% owned Coca-Cola Enterprises Inc. board, a modern-day version of Buffett & Son continuity.

19
WARREN BUFFETT, JIMMY BUFFETT
PARROT HEADS, "BERK" HEADS

Warren Buffett's name—that's double f and double t—is often misspelled with one t, as in breakfast buffet. It's misspelled "Buffet" in such prominent places as the 1992 Nike Annual Report, major newspapers and by top stock jock commentators.

(Photo by George Lange)

Jimmy Buffett in coat and tie and Warren Buffett in laid back attire share musical talent, business instincts and possibly ancestors from the same penal colony. This photo was taken in Warren Buffett's Plaza hotel room in New York May 10, 1999.

Here's a news item from *Bloomberg News Service,* October 11, 1995:

DETROIT—Chrysler Corp. made a meal [sic] out of billionaire investor Warren Buffet's [sic] name when it tried to take a slap at Kirk Kerkorian, its largest shareholder.

Jerome York, vice chairman of Tracinda Corp., said in a speech in New York that his company, of which Kerkorian is chairman, follows the same tight staffing regimen that Buffett imposes in his investment firm, Berkshire Hathaway.

The Detroit auto maker sent out a press release objecting to any comparison between Buffett and Kerkorian, who launched an abortive $21 billion bid for Chrysler in April.

"We know Warren Buffett" the Chrysler release said, "and believe us, Kirk Kerkorian is no Warren Buffet." [sic]

The line, which mirrored Sen. Lloyd Bentsen's famous putdown of that other great speller, Vice President Dan Quayle, had a typographical error, a Chrysler spokesman said.

"Ooh, we do have a typo there, don't we?" Harris said.

It's Buffett—double f, double t—as in singer/songwriter and author Jimmy Buffett. There must be a strong business gene that runs in the family.

(Omaha World-Herald)

Jimmy Buffett, head Parrot Head and quite a businessman in his own right.

Jimmy Buffett, is the author of *Tales from Margaritaville, Where is Joe Merchant?,* and *A Pirate Looks at Fifty* and hit songs such as *Come Monday, Cheeseburger in Paradise* and *Margaritaville.* In a style similar to his "uncle" Warren, he has created his own brand recognition and built a successful string of restaurants and retail outlets by selling the laid back image of Margaritaville.

Jimmy Buffett, who calls himself a mediocre musician has said he picked up the guitar to meet women. Margaritaville is not a real place, but one that exists only in your imagination. In a small way then it shares the attributes of any other brand name. Walt Disney built a powerful brand by harnessing the power of imagination, yet ironically Jimmy Buffett has spurned offers from Disney to open Margaritavilles in their theme parks. (*Forbes,* January 16, 1995)

Fans of Jimmy Buffett are known as Parrot Heads. Fans of Warren Buffett are known as "Berk" heads. Both groups are devoted fans and some are in both camps.

When President Clinton was having knee surgery, he chose to listen to Jimmy Buffett's music. So that makes even the President of the United States a Parrot Head.

It is clear that Jimmy Buffett's own personal image of Margaritaville was largely shaped during his time in Key West, Florida where he lived for many years as a struggling musician. Today the successful entertainer owns two houses, a recording studio and the Margaritaville Store and Cafe on Duval Street in Key West.

On February 6, 1996 while eating a "cheeseburger in paradise" at the Margaritaville Cafe, Parrot Heads and Berkshire shareholders Ken Monroe and Linda Hannett met (Jimmy) Buffett, who was in town recording his recent album, *Banana Wind.* "Since I am a fan of both Buffetts I asked Jimmy if he was related to Warren. He said he thought he was but wasn't sure of the exact genealogy," said Monroe. "Although Jimmy Buffett continues to make millions in Margaritaville, I think the real test of the business gene would be whether Jimmy has been smart enough to invest in Berkshire Hathaway."

(Photo courtesy of Ken Monroe)

Jimmy Buffett, left, and Berkshire shareholder Ken Monroe meet up at the Margaritaville Cafe in Key West in 1996.

In 1997 Jimmy Buffett sued two restaurant owners for naming their restaurants "Cheeseburger in Paradise," the title of Jimmy Buffett's 1978 hit song. (*People,* April 14, 1997)

In any event, Warren and Jimmy, of Palm Beach Florida, are distantly related. Warren's son, Peter, a musician, says it took the family a long while to discover Jimmy Buffett was a cousin.

Genealogy buffs in the Buffett family say the men owe their kinship to John Buffett, who in the 1600s lived on an island in the

South Pacific and took 14 wives. "And now there are hundreds of Buffetts on this island," says Peter Buffett. (*The Capital Times Wisconsin State Journal*, April 3, 1997)

And there is some confusion between the two. The Buffett of business fame can sing a little and the one of singing fame has done some investing.

Don Bohmont of Omaha, a math professor at the University of Nebraska, says as famous as Buffett is, he's still confused with Jimmy Buffett, even by some people who work in the securities business.

Bohmont often calls his daughter Amy Scott, a stockbroker in St. Petersburg, Florida, sometimes leaving a message to call a famous person.

"I've left messages to call Ted Turner or Larry Tisch in Omaha. This time I left her a message to call Warren Buffett in Omaha. If I say Omaha she knows I'm calling."

When his daughter returned and got the message from "Warren Buffett," an awed co-worker said, "You mean you know him?"

"Of course, he lives in my hometown of Omaha," Bohmont's daughter replied.

It turned out, however, her brokerage house colleague still thought the caller was Jimmy Buffett, not Warren Buffett—double t. Jimmy, with all his flourishing book, movie and retailing interests, occasionally calls Warren for advice.

"He calls from time to time for advice, but I should be calling him," says Warren Buffett. (*Forbes*, January, 16, 1995)

Forbes, reported July 31, 1995, that Warren, Jimmy and Peter Buffett were planning an album. It quoted Peter Buffett saying, "My dad will play the ukulele and sing a bit, too." Oh, God.

Fortune (June 21, 1999) concluded Warren and Jimmy probably are related, possibly from an inbred family in an old penal colony:

Are they related? *Fortune* believes, but cannot prove beyond a doubt, that Warren and Jimmy are kin. It was Warren's sister Doris, the family geneologist, who first raised the subject. Two years after mailing out questionnaires to all 125 Buffetts in the U.S., she got a call from a curious Jimmy. "He said, 'I want to be related to your family because they're rich and famous,' " Doris recalls. "And I said, 'That's funny, we want to be related to you because you're rich and famous.' " Doris' research has unearthed three possible ancestral links: John Buffett, a poor 17th century pickle farmer from Long Island; a Newfoundland sailor whom Jimmy honors in "Son of a Son of a Sailor"; and Norfolk Island in the South Pacific, which is inhabited by hundreds of Buffetts (as well as a good many descendants of the mutineers of the *Bounty*).

When Doris and Jimmy discovered that Norfolk Island used to be a penal colony, however, they lost hope: centuries of inbreeding have blurred family lines.

Despite the lack of absolute proof that they're related (as of press time, no DNA testing had been conducted), Warren and Jimmy have become friends. While Jimmy insists Uncle Warren doesn't slip him any investing tips, the two have been known to break out in song. "I think he's angling to get into my will," the billionaire Buffett jokes. "But the way things are going, I'd rather be in his."

20
BERKSHIRE'S HISTORY
A TEXTILE GIANT THAT WENT BUST

To find out where Buffett's billions came from, let's start at the beginning.

Back in 1929, several textile operations with common ownership were joined together with Berkshire Cotton Manufacturing Co. (incorporated in 1889) and renamed Berkshire Fine Spinning Associates.

Berkshire's roots can be traced to Samuel Slater who built the first U.S. textile mill about 1790 in Rhode Island.

The earliest of the Berkshire corporations—founded by Oliver Chace, a carpenter who worked for Slater, an ancestor of current Berkshire Hathaway board member Kim Chace—opened its doors in 1806 in Providence, Rhode Island. The resulting operation was a textile giant that once spun a quarter of the nation's fine cotton.

(Photo courtesy of the Old Dartmouth Historical Society—New Bedford Whaling Museum/Joseph S. Martin)

Hathaway Manufacturing Company about 1925

191

The Hathaway Mill about 1912

HATHAWAY MANUFACTURING COMPANY
NEW BEDFORD, MASSACHUSETTS

The Hathaway Manufacturing Company about 1920

(Photos courtesy of the American Textile History Museum in Lowell, Massachusetts)

The roving frame machines for yarn manufacturing at Hathaway Manufacturing Company of New Bedford, Massachusetts.

192

In the 1930s its many mills used about 1% of the electric output in the New England states. However, the company was not a money maker and therefore preferred dividends were omitted in late 1930 and for the next six years. World War II and the immediate postwar years, however, brought profits.

Hathaway Manufacturing Co., a New Bedford, Massachusetts - based textile firm, was founded in 1888 by Horatio Hathaway as part of the local economy shifted from low profit whaling to higher profit textiles. "Capital heeded the call of King Cotton and prospered in New Bedford." From 1881 to the beginning of the First World War, 32 cotton manufacturing companies were incorporated." (*Spinner*, Volume IV, p. 185). In World War II the company specialized in producing parachute material. After the war it became the largest maker of rayon suit linings.

"After the destruction of one of its mills and severe damage to its largest building complex from the hurricane of 1954, Hathaway was merged with Berkshire Fine Spinning." (ibid, p. 186)

The merger was overseen by Malcolm Chace, father of today's board member, Kim Chace. The name was changed to Berkshire Hathaway Inc.

Berkshire itself was a product of consolidation of a number of mills in Rhode Island and Western Massachusetts, under the direction of Malcolm Chace. "In 1962, the Berkshire/Hathaway Company operated seven plants, employed 6,000 people, annually produced one quarter of a billion yards of material that sold for more than $60 million, but most importantly had money in the bank. The company, and especially the money in the bank, caught the eye of Warren Buffett, an up-and-coming stock market wizard from Omaha, Nebraska" (ibid, p. 186)

Kim Chace has recalled a summer he spent working at the mill as "absolutely terrible...I think they call it character-building." (*Forbes*, October 11, 1999)

Although Berkshire has no relation to Hathaway shirts made famous by ads featuring a man with a patch over his eye, Buffett has said when he first bought Berkshire Hathaway, "I must have had seven calls in Omaha asking if I had to wear an eye patch."

Once *Barron's* Editor Alan Abelson described Berkshire this way: "Warren Buffett, for recent émigrés from Minsk and Pinsk, is the investor who runs a funny company called Berkshire Hathaway, which everyone thinks makes shirts but really makes money."

Back in 1948 the combined Berkshire Hathaway companies had profits of $18 million and had 10,000 workers at a dozen large mills

She's 6 years old
...and so are the
Hathaway Nylon *curtains!*

After six years of wear in many homes all over the country, HATHAWAY NYLON curtains are still giving excellent service ... still looking luxurious and beautiful.

Six years ago, it was HATHAWAY who made the first nylon marquisette available for curtains! In these six years, many millions of yards of HATHAWAY NYLON have been decorating American windows, and not one yard has ever been returned because of damage by sunlight!

HATHAWAY NYLON with its high thread count has *everything* you want (and need) in a curtain fabric. It is easy to wash, quick to dry, beautiful, strong, non-inflammable, heat-resistant. It shrinks less than 1%. Its wonderful properties are "sealed in" by an exclusive HATHAWAY process.

So, look for the label "HATHAWAY 100% NYLON MARQUISETTE" when you shop for curtains. Feel HATHAWAY NYLON curtains, hold them to the light...*see* the difference! *Buy* them, and *know* the difference! Always ask for HATHAWAY NYLON!

HATHAWAY NYLON
MARQUISETTE

— — — — — FREE! "ALL ABOUT CURTAINS" — — — — —

HATHAWAY MFG. CO., Dept. D103, New Bedford, Mass.

Send for this free booklet of decorating ideas. Shows how to use standard curtains to achieve beautiful effects.

NAME_____

ADDRESS_____

(Ad courtesy of Alan Sears)

throughout New England. That was at a time when IBM's earnings were $28 million.

But by 1964 the business was reduced to near rubble—two mills and a net worth of about $22 million.

The Hathaway Manufacturing firm claimed Hetty Green among its early shareholders.

Henrietta Howland Robinson Green (1834-1916), of Quaker stock, grew up in New Bedford, Massachusetts. In her 20s, she inherited a fortune in trading and shipping interests. Later she became a successful operator in the stock markets causing bull movements when word got out of her investments, most notably in railroads.

She also loaned money and amassed large land interests around Chicago. Rich and cheap, she left an estate of more than $100 million she accumulated through "investing, forgery and lending to speculators" (*Fortune*, July 5, 1999) to her children when she died in New York. This financier avoided the outstretched hands of strangers by living a simple and obscure life. Known for wearing a black, unwashed mourning dress, and for living like a transient to avoid residency taxes, she became known as the "richest and most detested woman in America." For her unparalleled stinginess, she earned the title of "The Witch of Wall Street." (*The Wealthy 100*, Michael Klepper and Robert Gunther, p. 139)

Once asked why she had taken out a license to carry a revolver, she replied, "Mostly to protect myself against lawyers. I'm not much afraid of burglars or highwaymen."

Buffett never has been so harsh on lawyers. After all, his right arm is lawyer Charles Munger, but his own preference is to steer clear of legal entanglements and lawyers whenever possible.

In 1955, Berkshire's stockholders' equity was $55,448,000.

During the next nine years, stockholders' equity fell to $22,139,000. But as late as 1961 its managers were still calling it a strong company with a bright future.

In an address to the Newcomen Society that year, Berkshire President Seabury Stanton said that World War II was a turning point for the company:

> When the war came, we were equipped to do well, and did. Production was shifted over to powder bags, camouflage cloths, ponchos, mosquito netting and many other military items—but for us, the big chance to serve came through parachute fabric.

The Quartermaster Corps called textile manufacturers

from all parts of the country for a meeting. They wanted us to develop and manufacture nylon parachute fabric. Since none of us had had much experience with nylon fabrics, there was marked hesitancy about accepting such a commitment.

The Government official in charge of the meeting read off the list of companies represented there, one by one, and, in turn, each agreed to produce so many yards of the fabric. Because they were reluctant to plunge into this new field, most of the offers were relatively small, perhaps 25,000 yards or something of the sort. When they came to us, we said firmly, 'Three million yards' and you could have heard a pin drop in that room.

After that, a good many of those present agreed to take more and we increased our initial commitment to five million yards at the Quartermaster's request.

Today, [1961] Berkshire Hathaway is the largest textile manufacturer of cotton and synthetic fabrics in New England. A total of about a million spindles and approximately 12,000 looms each year produce 225,000,000 yards of fabrics, consisting of fancy colored dress goods, handkerchief fabrics, lawns, voiles, dimities, combed and carded sateens, rayon linings, dacron marquisette curtain fabrics and dacron cotton blends.

The total employment numbers approximately 5,800 people. All seven plants operate on a three-shift basis and Berkshire Hathaway does an average annual business of better than $60 million.

But business kept sliding in the early 1960s. Buffett began buying shares of Berkshire Hathaway.

Item from the Internet: The Rosetta stone of modern investing

This amendment No. 49 is being filed solely to report in this schedule 13D the voting agreement among Warren E. Buffett, for himself and The Howard Buffett Family Trust (The "Trust"), Susan T. Buffett, and Berkshire Hathaway Inc. electronic filings.

Item 3. Source and amount of funds or other consideration.

The 474,998 shares of Common Stock described in Item 5 over which Mr. Buffett has sole voting and investment power were purchased at a cost of $15,415,044. The 4,204 shares of Common Stock described in Item 5 and owned by the Trust, of which Mr. Buffett is sole trustee but in which he has no economic interest, were purchased at a cost of $88,294. The 36,985 shares described in Item 5 and owned by Mrs. Buffett were purchased at a cost of $1,964,491. No borrowed funds were used for such purchases.

"It was in 1962 that Buffett first started acquiring for BPL [Buffett Partnership Limited] Berkshire Hathaway stock at seven dollars per share. After a few years, Seabury Stanton, the then president of Berkshire, promised Buffett that he would tender the remaining Berkshire Hathaway shares at 11$\frac{1}{2}$. Three weeks later the shares were tendered but at 11$\frac{1}{8}$. This was one time that a Buffett 'handshake and trust' deal did not materialize. Annoyed at Stanton for not keeping his word, Buffett began buying up Berkshire stock from Stanton's brother-in-law, and from Malcolm Chace, the then chairman of the board of Hathaway. Chace, who was also apparently annoyed with Stanton, sold Buffett a large chunk of his Berkshire Hathaway issues. It was at this time in 1965 that Buffett was able to acquire control of Berkshire Hathaway." (Anagnos thesis, quoting Buffett)

The stock price had dropped below book value. According to Buffett, "Berkshire had no net cash at the time we bought control. All of the net worth was tied up in the textile business at the time."

"In 1965, with the help of Chace and Otis Stanton, Buffett bought control of the company; Seabury Stanton, President, and his son Jack, Treasurer and heir apparent, were out. With the sale of [Berkshire Hathaway] to a stock market speculator the company was following the road, trodden by many other old line manufacturing companies: from merchant trading in primary commodities to investment manufacturing, and finally, to pure finance. The company's main product became money for speculation. After 80 years in the textile business, the textile division wasn't doing very well." (*Spinner*, 1988, p. 188)

A business downturn continued and Berkshire's balance sheet on October 3, 1964, showed assets of $27,887,000 and stockholders' equity of $22 million. Berkshire's shares outstanding then were 1,137,778. Today there are 1,512,899 equivalent Class A shares.

Buffett kept buying and by 1965 his partnership had a 70% interest in the company, whose textile operations included about 4,700 looms. Buffett's total stake in Berkshire was acquired for about $14 million (*Forbes*, October 21, 1991). Buffett took control of Berkshire on May 10, 1965, when Berkshire had a market value of about $18 million. In the late 1960s Berkshire had about 1,200 shareholders. Today there are about 250,000.

Buffett became chairman of the board in 1970 but the economic characteristics of the textile business began to fade by the late 1970s.

"Berkshire's textile division lost money throughout the recession of the early 1980s. There was a modest recovery in 1983, but the losses in 1984 totalled $2 million. The cycle was repeating." (*Spinner*, 1988, p. 188)

"Late in 1984, Gary Morrison, President of the Textile Division, sent a detailed plan to Buffett, asking for a small investment in new machinery. Without it, he said, the mill couldn't be profitable. When Buffett didn't respond, he knew the end was near. On May 1, 1985, Morrison told local management that the mill was closing. The employees weren't told in order to keep up their morale, while they ran out the mill. On August 12, the workers were informed and shut-down began by departments. Just before Christmas, the mill ceased operations, having used up all raw materials, satisfied all orders, and sold or salvaged the equipment.

On that day, Berkshire Hathaway stock stood at $2,600 per share, up from $11, the average price Buffett had paid 20 years before." (*Spinner*, 1988, p. 189)

He kept the textile business until 1985, although, after a brief burst of prosperity, it gradually failed. He wrung cash out of the period of brief prosperity and out of working capital downsizings. This cash was invested in better businesses. At last, he sold the more than 100-year old business for a pittance. It turned out to be one of the few business quagmires into which Buffett ever sank money. As Yogi Berra has said: "A nickel isn't worth a dime today."

Buffett would explain at the Berkshire Annual Meeting in 1991 that the textile business was a commodity business and although a large number of men's suits had Hathaway linings in World War II, it all came to mean nothing when a foreign business could make the linings more cheaply. Now he knows to go with the low-cost producer.

"I knew it was a tough business...I was either more arrogant or innocent then. We learned a lot of lessons, but I wish we could have learned them somewhere else," he said.

> Buffett once joked of Berkshire's textile business that the assets weren't worth what he thought they were, "but the liabilities were solid."

Buffett would later say: "We went into a terrible business because it was cheap." (*Fortune*, July 20, 1998)

At Berkshire's Annual Meeting in 1998, Buffett said: "Berkshire itself was a mistake, believe it or not. We went into Berkshire because it was cheap statistically just as a general investment back in the early sixties. In the previous 10 years, it had earned less than nothing. It had accrued a significant net loss over the previous 10 years. [But] it was selling well below working capital. So Berkshire itself was a cigar butt.

"And had we been able to do the things we've done since from a neutral base rather than a negative base, it would have worked out better. But it's been a lot of fun..."

That's in line with a comment in a letter Jerry Zucker, of Encino, California, once wrote. He signed the letter: Jerry Zucker, Retired, West Coast Sales Manager, Berkshire Hathaway Textiles, "A Cigar Butt Investment."

Berkshire's textile business survived until 1985 when Buffett closed the declining business. Machinery that had cost $12 million was sold for less than $200,000. Buffett didn't sell the two million square feet of space which he rented out for $2 to $5 per square foot. (*Spinner*, 1988, p. 189)

He got $163,000 for machinery with a book value of $866,000. Looms that were bought a few years earlier for $5,000 were sold as scrap for $26 each, less than the cost of taking them away. (*The Midas Touch*, John Train, p. 67) But long before then Berkshire's other businesses, financed by textile mill cash, were flourishing.

Today the sites of the Berkshire mills in New Bedford are relics, part of a scene of economic devastation.

The old red buildings are about worthless. But under the management of Bill Betts, who leased parts of them as office space and warehouse storage, they provided Berkshire a small stream of income until the office complex was sold in early 2000. (see Chapter 22)

A surviving complex of 31 buildings, just inland from the harbor side hurricane wall, is home to 28 tenants who occupy about 35% of the business incubator space. (*The Business Journal*, June, 1996) "Berkshire Hathaway rents to all types of businesses, especially since Stride Rite Shoes moved out in 1992, after 11 years. It had grown to occupy 800,000 of the million square feet, and employed up to 500 of the local work force." Stride Rite was lured by an attractive incentive package to relocate in Kentucky.

From tiny beginnings, great things followed. Buffett, in 1986, calculated that 52 people in the Omaha area owned enough Berkshire stock to be millionaires. Berkshire stock has soared since then. (*Omaha World-Herald*, August 17, 1991) It's now thought there are about 200 Buffett millionaires in Omaha.

Other shareholders have been lucky. There's also a story of an unwitting beneficiary from New Jersey. Paul Laplante once got a letter from a finder's service saying it had found his deceased father's account—with 66 shares of Berkshire in it. It turns out Laplante's father had once done some legal work for Parker Mills, which paid him in warrants. Parker Mills was acquired by Berkshire Fine Spinning, later Berkshire Hathaway. "Those once nearly worthless warrants had blossomed into 66 shares of what had become Warren Buffett's investment company." *(Forbes, May 6, 1996)*.

Although the textile business with headquarters in New Bedford, a west coast office in Los Angeles and an office in New York City didn't last, the Berkshire Hathaway name did. Perhaps the original name should have been BerkshireHathaway.com.

Omaha stockbroker George Morgan, whose motto is "money doesn't come with instructions," says, "He named the company after his biggest mistake." Buffett bought his first shares of Berkshire Hathaway in 1962. His first order, executed by the Tweedy, Browne firm, was for 2,000 shares at $7.50. Berkshire Vice Chairman Charles Munger has described the Tweedy, Browne firm, known for its strict approach to value investing, as a place where Buffett "used to hang out when he was young and poor." (*Worth*, April, 1997) That $15,000 investment is worth more than $100 million today.

Berkshire was once described by Munger as "a small, doomed New England textile enterprise."

Indeed Berkshire's textile operations folded in 1985 as a result of foreign competition, lower foreign wages and obstacles encountered in the mass clothes business. In short, Berkshire was unable to distinguish itself from its competitors. Its products became a commodity easily bought elsewhere. From such ashes, a phoenix arose.

Even Buffett, in looking back over what he said were the mistakes of the first 25 years, said his first mistake was buying Berkshire. Although he recognized it as an unpromising business, he bought in because of the low price, figuring that, at worst, he could wring out more cash than he paid and use it to buy other businesses.

In 1965 Buffett Partnership informed Berkshire it held 500,975 shares, or about 49% of Berkshire's stock. Buffett's partnership had become Berkshire's largest shareholder and it kept right on buying. By January 1967, it owned 59.5% and as of April 1968, it owned almost 70% of Berkshire, according to documents filed with the Securities and Exchange Commission.

Berkshire Under Buffett

Meanwhile Berkshire, now under Buffett's management, was making acquisitions, venturing into the insurance business with a tender offer for National Indemnity Co. on February 23, 1967.

In early 1969 Berkshire bought 97% of The Illinois National Bank and Trust Co. and about the same time bought Sun Newspapers, Inc. and Blacker Printer, Inc., Berkshire's first entry into the publishing business.

Sun Newspapers published five weekly newspapers in Omaha with a circulation of about 50,000. The related printing businesses were run by Stanford Lipsey.

In 1970 Buffett Partnership ceased to be a stockholder and parent of Berkshire and distributed, pro rata to its partners, 691,441 Berkshire shares. After the liquidation, Buffett quietly bought Berkshire shares for himself.

An SEC document says:

> Subsequent to the above liquidating distribution, Warren E. Buffett purchased during January, 1970, an additional 87,591 shares of common stock of the registrant from other partners of Buffett Partnership Ltd. who had received these shares on the liquidating distribution. Also, during January, Mr. Buffett purchased in the open market an additional 2,100 shares of common stock of the registrant. Warren Buffett himself on January 31, 1970, owned beneficially a total of 245,129, or approximately 25%, of the registrant's 979,582 shares of presently outstanding common stock. As a result of these transactions, Warren E. Buffett may be regarded as the parent of the registrant (Berkshire).

When Buffett was 40 years old, he controlled Berkshire from his office in Omaha.

Robert Cope, a bond underwriter from Montgomery, Alabama, called Berkshire in New Bedford, Massachusetts in the early 1970s to try to sell some industrial revenue bonds. He was told to call Buffett in Omaha.

"I called and got Bill Scott who told me he wasn't buying anything except industrial revenue bonds and I told him that was the only thing I was selling," Cope said. "He gave me to Buffett and I explained what I had. He understood corporate credits. He didn't have to go look anything up in *Moody's* or *S&P*. He said he was interested in the tax-exempt bonds I had."

When Cope asked how much he could take, Buffett replied,

"Well, all of it." "I was used to selling 100 bonds. He took three or four million!" Cope said.

Cope continued to sell bonds to Berkshire. "I'd call and either Scott or Buffett would answer. Frankly, I always was relieved when I got Buffett. Scott was tough and would ask 'Whatcha got?' "

"Buffett was always a prince of a guy. He was cordial. He said, 'Good morning, tell me what you're working on.' Then he'd say he liked the company or that he didn't and would say he'd pass on it or he would take it."

Cope said, "I went out to Kiewit Plaza a few times and I'd go up to his little office. He'd stick his head out and say come in and let's talk a while."

There was once a day when Buffett couldn't even get Berkshire's earnings listed in the *Wall Street Journal.* Buffett wrote the *Journal* about it, but was rejected. (*Omaha World-Herald,* July 9, 1998)

"In 1973 and 1977, the *Journal* sent polite turn-downs to Buffett. At the start of '77 his holding company, Berkshire Hathaway, had a net worth of about $100 million when compared to today's net worth of $100 billion.

"Buffett, in pleading his case, had written that the *Journal* was printing the earnings of several companies whose annual sales are less than Berkshire Hathaway's annual earnings." Yes, the editor replied, but Berkshire wasn't listed by NASDAQ, the quotations of the National Association of Securities Dealers. And NASDAQ was the standard."

Today Berkshire is a far-reaching investment holding company. It is an insurance empire with large stock, bond, cash and silver holdings. It also has a number of operating businesses.

Berkshire fits no category—in corporate listings it variously is lumped with insurance, candy, media, diversified, nonbank financial, investment, miscellaneous or conglomerate firms. Berkshire is a hybrid company: it is all of the above. Here's a typical description of Berkshire: "Berkshire is an investment holding company that offers property and casualty insurance, publishes magazines and provides other services."

In *Business Week's* July 7, 1997, issue Berkshire was listed as the 32nd largest company in the world and the 21st largest in the U.S. in market value. *Forbes* (April 19, 1999) ranked Berkshire overall as the 34th U.S. company. Sales ranked 109th, net profits ranked 32nd, assets ranked 23rd and market value ranked 18th. Still, practically no analyst tracks it although in 1998 Alice Schroeder, an insurance analyst with PaineWebber, started following it. Until then, if you punched up Berkshire in the Bloomberg newswire and went to recommendations you found: "No recommendations available for this company."

To find out about the company, you have to make your own effort. Several times a year the company will issue one-sentence announcements of a new investment. About the only way to get a picture of how Berkshire stands is to ask the company for an annual report.

Beyond its plain looks—its largely hidden-from-view chairman, its tiny headquarters in Omaha at Kiewit Plaza at 36th and Farnam Streets, its plain-bound annual report, its largely no-comment policy—lies a constellation of beautiful businesses.

They're not sexy businesses—uniforms, shoes, vacuum cleaners—that sort of thing. Retraction. They are sexy businesses, if you're talking profitability. Some of the businesses earn a return on capital of 20%. That's outstanding by any measure. And sometimes they earn 30% to 40%.

Buffett's prosaic businesses in bad years sometimes rang up a 50% return on equity on operations alone, and in 1989, reached an astronomical 67% return based on historical cost, a figure almost no one in the business world has ever heard about or seen! Most businessmen talk happily in terms of a 10% to 15% return on equity. The number is so far beyond the range of most business numbers that generally it would be deemed a misprint.

Dry-sounding businesses supply these heavenly numbers: *The Buffalo News*, a newspaper firm in upstate New York; Fechheimer, a uniform company based in Cincinnati; Scott Fetzer Manufacturing Group, of Chicago, which has a variety of manufacturing businesses; *World Book*, also of Chicago, the encyclopedia maker; Kirby, a vacuum cleaner maker based in Cleveland, Ohio; Nebraska Furniture Mart, a large furniture store in Omaha; See's Candies, a San Francisco candy maker with more than 200 stores mainly on the West Coast and H.H. Brown Shoe Company, Inc. of Greenwich, Connecticut, which owns Lowell Shoe of Hudson, New Hampshire. Berkshire also owns Dexter Shoe Co. of Dexter, Maine; Helzberg's Diamond Shops of Kansas City, Missouri; R.C. Willey Home Furnishings of Salt Lake City, Utah; FlightSafety International of Flushing, New York; Star Furniture Co. of Houston, Texas; International Dairy Queen of Minneapolis, Minnesota; Executive Jet of Montvale, New Jersey; Jordan Furniture Company of Avon, Massachusetts; MidAmerican Energy of Des Moines, Iowa, CORT Business Services, of Fairfax, Virginia, and Ben Bridge Jeweler, of Seattle.

(Photo by Nancy Line Jacobs)

Kiewit's Walter Scott, Jr., and former Cap Cities Chairman Tom Murphy are close friends of Buffett.

Berkshire-owned Borsheim's, a jewelry store in Omaha, might not sound like a big deal until you find it may have more sales than any other single jewelry store in the country with the exception of Tiffany's flagship New York store.

Further, Berkshire's Wesco Financial Corp., of Pasadena, California, in some ways a baby Berkshire, in turn owns a handful of businesses.

In addition to Berkshire's operating businesses, there is a large, separate insurance group of businesses.

It is the property and casualty insurance business—Berkshire's largest operating business—that is the vehicle through which Buffett usually makes his investments.

It's the money from Berkshire's businesses, particularly from the insurance operations as well as the income from Berkshire's stock and bond investments, that gives Buffett the ready cash for new investments to bring in more money.

Berkshire has about 60,000 full-time employees. The company is listed on the New York Stock Exchange and trades under the symbols BRK.A and BRK.B and is listed as BerkHaA and BerkHaB in newspaper listings.

With Berkshire's acquisition of FlightSafety in late 1996 and the acquisition in early 1996 of the half of GEICO that Berkshire did not already own, and the smaller purchases of Star Furniture Co. in 1997 and International Dairy Queen in 1998 and particularly with its purchase of General Re in 1998, Berkshire transformed itself in a big way.

Berkshire, often thought of as a bunch of stocks, is now also a collection of wholly owned operating businesses of real size.

Berkshire now walks on three very long but stable legs: a large insurance business, a large stock and bond portfolio and a large collection of fully owned operating businesses—all throwing off cash, cash, cash.

Berkshire's Owners

Buffett's 477,166 shares (35.6%) of Berkshire's 1,520,562 equivalent Class A shares is by far the largest ownership position. Buffett's wife, Susan, owns 34,478 shares (2.6%) of the stock. Her voting and investment power is shared with her husband.

Most top officers have a substantial portion of their net worth in Berkshire. Buffett's description is apt when he tells people, "We eat our own cooking."

It is a happy, wealthy group that has known the feeling expressed in the Josh Billings quote, "The happiest time in a man's life is when he is in red-hot pursuit of a dollar with a reasonable prospect of overtaking it."

About 18% of Berkshire's stock is held by institutions.

The rest of the stock is in the hands of about 250,000 individual shareholders, who don't trade the stock much. Berkshire has less turnover than any stock on the New York Stock Exchange.

About 80% of Berkshire's shares were bought at $100 or less, giving the company an old wealthy family air.

"There are 125 shareholders in my zip code in Omaha, so I can go out and trick-or-treat on Halloween and be assured of good treatment," Buffett said on Adam Smith's *Money World* show October 21, 1993.

By one estimate there are 300 to 400 Omahans with more than $1 million in Berkshire stock. (*Omaha World-Herald*, July 12, 1998)

Berkshire shareholders almost all come from the United States, the United Kingdom, Germany, India and Canada. Many shareholders own 10 shares or less. Some consider it an honor to own one share.

Berkshire Vice Chairman Charles Munger, Buffett's friend Sandy Gottesman, who heads the First Manhattan investment firm in New York and Dr. William Angle of Omaha—until his death—have been among the major shareholders. Malcolm Chace, a private investor, and a former chairman of Berkshire, who died in 1996 at age 92 was a large stockholder whose cost basis for some of his Berkshire shares was about 25 cents.

Berkshire's Board

Berkshire, operated by Buffett and just a handful of people, operates in such a lean manner it's a parody of other firms. In keeping with its lean structure carefully devised by Buffett, there are only seven directors on the board, which has no standing committees and gets little in the way of outside advice.

Munger has said that long ago Berkshire was subpoenaed for its staffing papers in connection with one of its acquisitions. "There were no papers. There was no staff," Munger said at Berkshire's Annual Meeting in 1991.

Berkshire's board includes Buffett; his wife, Mrs. Susan T. Buffett; Munger; Malcolm G. (Kim) Chace III, a private investor and chairman of BankRI, a community bank in Rhode Island, who replaced his father on the board in 1992; Howard G. Buffett, Buffett's son; and Walter Scott, Jr., chairman emeritus of Peter Kiewit Sons' Inc., a privately held construction conglomerate firm in Omaha whose record is so good that Buffett has said he won't recount it for fear of making Berkshire shareholders restive. Scott is also chairman of Level 3 Communications, a fiber-optics network which is a successor to some of Kiewit's businesses. Scott has been Buffett's friend since boyhood.

Berkshire's proxy statements indicated that Chace's holdings changed from 13,030 to 2,167 shares during 1998, but Chace may have sold little or no stock. There are many Chace trusts and some apparently were transferred in ways that no longer require reporting.

Ronald L. Olson, a partner with the Munger, Tolles & Olson law firm in Los Angeles, California, was named to the board in 1997.

The directors are paid a whopping $900 a year.

Buffett began the Berkshire Annual Meeting in 1998 by saying: "The meeting will now come to order. I'm Warren Buffett, chairman of Berkshire Hathaway, and this hyperactive fellow is Berkshire's vice chairman, Charlie Munger. Incidentally one of our directors is one of the singers during the [company] movie. We keep costs down here at Berkshire...Susan T. Buffett, the vocalist. Howard G. Buffett, the non-vocalist..."

Kim Chace's ancestor, Oliver Chace, founded the Berkshire textile mill in 1806 in Providence, Rhode Island. Chace's father, Malcolm, oversaw the merger with Hathaway in 1955.

The Chace family was at first ambivalent about Buffett's buying, which began in 1962 and the takeover completed in 1965.

"We sort of sat there and smiled and watched [Buffett] do his thing," Chace said. (*Forbes*, October 14, 1996)

Chace, at one time, owned more than 13,000 Berkshire shares and is also chairman of the Bank of Rhode Island. "I do consider myself lucky, he said." (*Forbes*, October 14, 1996)

The folks on Berkshire's board are the "WORST" board in corporate America, according to *Chief Executive* magazine. *USA Today* in its May 6, 1994, issue said the magazine had come up with a list of the best and worst boards and that Berkshire's was at the bottom. Apparently the conclusion was reached because Berkshire's board is small, family-oriented and has no real outside directors. Giri Bogavelli, an investor in San Francisco, offers this rebuttal:

> Two of the more important factors in evaluating any board of directors are corporate governance and enhancement of shareholders' value. Berkshire's record on the issue of corporate governance is unblemished. Few philosophers in the arena of corporate governance ever get a chance to translate their well-articulated theories into practice. Mr. Buffett has done just that at Berkshire.
>
> As to the enhancement of shareholders' value, Berkshire's record is matched by very few in corporate America. What is more important is that this was achieved with clearly enunciated principles and the highest ethical standards.

Munger is the chairman of Wesco and vice chairman of Berkshire. Buffett is chairman of the board, chief executive officer, and Berkshire's heart and soul and maximum leader.

21

BERKSHIRE IN 1970

A Standard & Poor's sheet about Berkshire from 1970 said:

Position: The company produces fine cotton materials and has increased its emphasis on synthetic blends and finished fabrics and, through acquisitions in 1967 writes insurance with major emphasis on automobile lines. Subsequent diversification moves include the purchase of a group of newspapers and an Illinois bank.

Berkshire Hathaway produces fine cotton fabrics, including organdies, handkerchief cloth, shirtings, and sateens; box loom fabrics; and rayon, nylon, dacron, and other synthetic fabrics. Diversification into insurance underwriting was accomplished in 1967 through the acquisition of National Indemnity and National Fire & Marine Insurance of Omaha. In early 1969, Sun Newspapers and Blacker Printing were purchased, and Illinois National Bank & Trust Company of Rockford, Illinois, was acquired.

Because of industry-wide overproduction, the company phased out production of cotton staple grey goods in 1969. At the same time it was substantially increasing output of synthetic blend fabrics in which it had, or could develop, a semi-proprietary interest. Also, new marketing programs were developed, including that of the Home Fabrics division, which sells finished fabrics for home sewing.

National Indemnity and National Fire & Marine derive over 80% of their premium volume from automobile lines of insurance.

Sun Newspapers publishes five weekly newspapers in the Omaha, Nebraska, area with paid circulation of about 50,000. A related printing business is conducted by Blacker Printing Company.

As of December 31, 1969, Illinois National Bank had total deposits of $99,554,818 up from $99,085,440 a year earlier.

At January 3, 1970, the company's portfolio consisted of U.S. Treasury bills carried at a cost of $294,165, with a market value of $297,120. At December 28, 1968, the portfolio consisted primarily of marketable common stocks carried at a cost of $5,421,384, and having a market value at that time of $11,824,000.

		Earnings-Dividend Forecast			
Yr. End.	aNet	Per	Share		Data($)
Dec. 31	Sales	Earns.	Divs.		Range
1970	...	...	...	45	32
1969	40.43g	4.32fg	Nil	42	31
1968	46.00	f3.41	Nil	37	20 1/2
1967	39.06	f1.02	0.10	20 3/4	16
1966	49.37	2.71	Nil	27	17
1965	49.30	2.24	Nil	21 5/8	13 1/8
1964	49.98	0.15	Nil	13 1/2	8 7/8
1963	50.59	d0.43	Nil	10 1/2	6 1/4
1962	53.26	d1.34	0.10	9 3/8	6

a. In millions of dollars. b. Calendar year; bid prices. c. Before estimated loss on properties to be sold of $1,400,000 in 1962, $1,500,000 in 1963, $3,000,000 in 1964, and $300,000 in 1965; after normalization charges equivalent to federal income taxes of $50,000 in 1964 and $2,040,000 in 1965. d. Deficit. e. Yrs. ended Sept. 30 in 1967 and prior years. f. Bef. invest. gains of $3.87 in 1969 and $1.49 in 1968; bef. spec. chgs. of $0.12 in 1969 and $0.17 in 1968; bef. spec. cr. of $0.10 in 1967. g. 53 weeks.

Recent Developments

Net sales from textile operations for the 52 weeks ended January 3, 1970, declined 12% from those for 1968 (52 weeks). Margins widened on cost-reduction efforts, and the decline in operating income was pared to 6.6%. Lower other income and substantially increased interest charges more than offset reduced depreciation, and pretax income dropped 43%. After taxes at 40.7%, versus 45.7%, and the equity in the after-tax earnings and investment gains or losses of unconsolidated subsidiaries, net income was up 27%.

For the six months ended July 4, 1970, sales fell some 41%, year to year, but net income advanced 2.7%. Earnings on fewer shares outstanding were $1.89 a share up from $1.81. Results were before nonrecurring credits of $0.14 and $4.08 a share, respectively.

Stock Data

The company was formed in 1889 as Berkshire Cotton Manufacturing; the present title was adopted in 1955 on merger with Hathaway Manufacturing, also founded in 1889.

In 1947, authorized common was raised to 3,000,000 shares for a three-for-one split. In 1952, par value of the common was changed from no par to $5.

In the 1955 merger, four common shares were issued for each of the 100,000 Hathaway shares outstanding.

Authorized stock was reduced to 2,312,816 shares in December 1962, when 687,184 treasury shares were canceled and retired; and to 1,843,214 in December 1964, when 469,602 shares were repurchased during the year, mainly under tenders at $11.37-1/2, were canceled and retired. Another 120,231 shares were repurchased in 1965, and authorized stock was cut to 1,722,983 shares.

W. E. Buffett owns 70% of the stock.

Finances

On September 24, 1969, the company reported that it had signed a three year term loan agreement with four banks for $7.5 million. Proceeds would refinance short term debt, which, along with liquidation of its securities portfolio was used to purchase the stock of Illinois National Bank & Trust Co.

At January 3, 1970, the combined adjusted investment in unconsolidated insurance subsidiaries was $15,314,965, and the investment in the unconsolidated bank subsidiary was $18,868,404.

Dividend Data

No dividend action has been taken since the resumption of cash payments on January 3, 1967, following omission after 1961-62. Previously, distributions had been made from 1929 in all years except 1931-36, 1938-40 and 1957-58.

Capitalization

Long Term Debt: $5,891,300.

Common Stock: 979,582 shs. ($5 par)

22

BERKSHIRE HATHAWAY SOLD

Berkshire Hathaway was sold in February, 2000. That's right, the original company complex of buildings in New Bedford, Massachusetts was sold, following the sale of the textile machinery in 1985. Berkshire sold its large, historic southend complex to Niche Corp., according to Berkshire's William Betts. (New Bedford *Standard-Times*, February 6, 2000)

Niche, a leather goods manufacturer, had become one of the complexes major tenants in 1999.

The price was not disclosed but it wasn't much. Betts said, "What Niche paid is what it cost us to close the deal." And that was fine with Berkshire which for a long time had sought to get the 112-year-old buildings off its books. In recent years the old complex had served as a home to several dozen tenants.

For Betts (the chief operating officer of Berkshire Hathaway Realty Corp. and in recent years the caretaker of the complex) and Berkshire the sale closed a chapter on the life of a textile company which began in 1888, was purchased by Buffett in 1965 and closed in 1985, selling off its machinery, as imports and cheap labor in the South made the mills less profitable. About 400 workers were laid off in 1985. At peak production in the 1960s, the Berkshire textile mill employed 2,200 workers.

In the end, Berkshire was faced with the cost of demolishing the complex or selling it off and was glad to find a buyer.

From this aerial photo, Berkshire's old textile mill complex, sold in 2000, can be seen in the lower part of the photo. Berkshire's textile mill operations took place in the long, large buildings.

Bill Betts, who went to work for Berkshire in 1966, stands in front of the original Berkshire textile mill complex in New Bedford, Massachusetts.

23

HOW FAR WILL BERKSHIRE GO?

"THROUGH CHANCES VARIOUS, THROUGH ALL VICISSITUDES, WE MAKE OUR WAY."

After the Berkshire Annual Meeting in 1989, Buffett showed up at Borsheim's. There he attracted a small band of shareholders and was going through his often repeated litany about how Berkshire's increasing size was forging its own anchor on growth, and how as Berkshire continues to grow the pace of growth is bound to slow.

Then Buffett said, and there really was a twinkle in his eye, "Well, it will be fun to see how far we can take it."

Soon Berkshire's stock price took one of its biggest leaps ever, moving in a few months from $5,900 a share to more than $8,000 a share. Over the years, Berkshire's 24% average annual return on book value and nearly 30% average annual advance in stock price has put it near the top of the investment charts.

Berkshire, like any other stock, takes its lickings, but it keeps on ticking. It's a case of, "Through chances various, through all vicissitudes, we make our way," as Virgil said in his *Aeneid.*

Can Berkshire keep such a pace? Clearly not. Since the 1960s Buffett has been saying that size is its own drag. In 1963 he wrote: "A considerably more moderate annual edge over The Dow will be satisfactory." In 1964 he said: "I believe our margin over The Dow cannot be maintained." Buffett is the first to say Berkshire can't maintain its growth rate.

After all, should Berkshire over the next 35 years keep up its annual 30% pace in stock price rise, the per share price would be in the hundreds of millions of dollars. Berkshire's stock market worth would be hundreds of trillions of dollars—many times larger than today's U.S. gross national product. Berkshire would own the planet.

Newsweek's Wall Street Editor Allan Sloan wrote in 1996:

> Anyone who buys Berkshire at today's price expecting the next 31 years to match the past 31 is betting on a miracle. Buffett is still brilliant; it's a question of math. Berkshire's stock is valued at more than $40 billion in the market, up

from around $18 million when Buffett took control on May 10, 1965. To match that rate of increase, Berkshire's stock...would have to be worth $75 trillion by the fall of 2027. That's trillion, with a 'T'. Some 10 times the current GNP of the U.S. Ain't gonna happen.

Buffett put it this way at the 1995 annual meeting, saying that if Berkshire could grow at 23% of its book value annually, "it could gobble up the GDP. We think about it occasionally, but it won't happen."

And there are parts of the world Buffett doesn't care to own. But he clearly has set out to own some of the best parts and he may see Berkshire having some role in the world. But many investors simply do not believe the stock can go higher.

In my early days as a stockbroker, I tried to sell a share of Berkshire to a fellow. After much back and forth, he wrote, "When I get some mad money, I'd like to buy a share or two. It's hard to justify $12,000 for a share that pays no dividend. How high can it go? We will do some business together." I never heard from him again.

Take this as you wish, but although Berkshire does not have a company logo (unless you count the fist full of dollars insignia on some items Berkshire sells), it may have a secret symbol. A letter dated September 13, 1991, which Buffett wrote to shareholders explaining that year's shareholder designated contribution plan—if held up to the light—reveals a large circle surrounding the letters BH.

Berkshire actually has no secret symbol. Still it's curious.

"I don't think it means anything," says one skeptical Berkshire shareholder. "It'd be unlike him to go to the expense."

Is Buffett having some fun? Is he trying to tell us something about where Berkshire is going? In a circle? From zero to zero in stock price; ashes to ashes? Peace on earth?

Skipping the occult, here are the facts about how far Berkshire has come in terms of its stock price. Phoenix-like, it has risen from $12 in 1965 to $80,000 in 1998, then sinking much of 1999.

24
THE STOCK PRICE
BERKSHIRE CLASS A: DOWNPAYMENT ON A HOUSE

A share of Berkshire (Class A) won't buy a house, but it might make a downpayment on one. Heck, it might make a downpayment on a castle.

A woman once called her broker and said she had $2,500 in her checking account and would like to buy a share of Berkshire. "Honey, you're missing a zero," the broker replied.

Another time at a party a stockbroker asked a Berkshire shareholder the price of Berkshire. "33" was the reply. The broker leaned over to his wife and exclaimed, "He means 3,300!" Yet another zero was omitted.

One of the most unusual things about Berkshire is its 5-digit stock price. A share of Berkshire would buy a BMW. At least a share of the Class A stock. Even the Class B stock, worth 1/30 of the A stock, might buy a jalopy.

"I never bought Berkshire because I always thought it was too high," said the late Ed Conine, who headed J Braggs, the women's clothing chain in Omaha. Conine knew Buffett and was familiar with his record.

Echoes a man who sports a Harvard MBA, has one of the top jobs at one of the largest securities firms on Wall Street, is well aware of Berkshire and has met Buffett: "I just couldn't buy the stock because of the price...I realize it's what's behind the price but I just can't think in terms other than round lots." The man said he looked at the stock once and it was more than $1,000 a share.

"I couldn't recommend it," a number of stockbrokers have said.

Other reasons investors have offered for not buying Berkshire include:

"It's too rich for my blood."

"That's the one that doesn't pay a dividend."

"That's the one where he doesn't split the stock."

"That's the craziest thing I've ever heard of."

"It doesn't make any sense to me."

"I plan to wait and buy it the day he dies."

You can go down the list on the New York Stock Exchange past many stocks selling for $30 or $40 a share. Then you work through the B's and find Berkshire trading in five figures.

"When Berkshire Hathaway's stock was first to be listed in the *Wall Street Journal*, Buffett received a call and was asked if there were any plans for a stock split in the near future, and if such plans did exist would he please let the *WSJ* know now. Apparently in order to list the stock, the OTC section of the paper had to be reprogrammed to handle the four digit numeric value of the shares. Buffett promised that no stock split would occur and advised *The Wall Street Journal* to go ahead and reprogram the columns. Still concerned, the *Journal* programmer told Buffett that Berkshire's stock was growing too fast and he planned to reprogram the section for five digits, just in case." (Anagnos thesis)

The price itself has left many an investor and stockbroker aghast. "What the hell is that?"..."There's some mistake" are refrains from many brokers over the years after getting the Wall Street inquiry of "How's Berkshire?"

For fun, call your broker and ask for a quote on Berkshire.

"What's that? There's something wrong with my machine," will probably be the reply.

Here's an unhappy story from Rich Rockwood, a Berkshire shareholder from Rumford, Maine: "When I went to work at a major (?) brokerage firm, as an intern, I was asked to conduct research for two weeks and to recommend a stock purchase to my boss when finished. I conducted my research and recommended BRK.B. My broker told me that Berkshire was a horrible company with an inflated value due to Warren Buffett. He further added he didn't trust Mr. Buffett and related him to Al Dunlap. So he decided to position himself (and his clients) in a steel stock, LTV Corp. (NYSE:LTV) at approximately 12. Then he made a bet with me that LTV would outperform BRK.B. BRK.B went up approximately 20% and LTV went down 55%. I won the bet but lost a job because he wasn't getting any new orders coming in...".

There is no other stock like Berkshire. Many brokers just don't know the stock. Most brokerage firms don't follow the stock, have no opinion about it and thus its brokers can't solicit orders for Berkshire unless they convince their firms they have researched it. Here's a normal finding when a broker calls up on his quote machine for a report about Berkshire: "ERROR-BRK. INVALID INPUT— NO REPORT."

Commissions on the stock are unusually low and trying to convince someone to buy a stock trading in five digits isn't worth it for most brokers.

Berkshire is the highest priced and one of the least traded issues on the New York Stock Exchange. Because of its high price, a few shares make a big trade. A quirk in brokerage commission schedules, which usually don't go above $100 a share, involving the combination of the price and number of shares, creates only a tiny commission on trades of Berkshire stock.

At some discount brokerages you can buy 100 shares of Berkshire for a $38.50 commission, or even half that. Trades of that dollar volume for lower-priced shares of another stock would be in the hundreds of dollars, thousands at a full-service brokerage.

Trades for one to 100 or more shares of Berkshire at full-service firms carry a commission of about $100.

"Berkshire is mutual fund-like, and (because of its low commission structure) it's basically no load," says Tim Callahan, a stockbroker in Birmingham. In fact, Berkshire is really a no-load fund with low expenses.

Once investors are in Berkshire, most don't sell. Therefore, a broker is less likely to enjoy a round trip on commissions. Berkshire stock just does not fit into the scheme of things for stockbrokers.

"I began buying Berkshire in the early 1980s. I bought from 1981 until 1987," said Chad Brenner, a lawyer in Cleveland, Ohio, who said Buffett's insistence on quality management and long-term outlook appealed to him. "I'm not a smart seller. I've never sold any shares...My kids will inherit my stock and I'm 37."

Buffett said in 1984 that more than 90% of Berkshire shares were held by the same people who were shareholders five years before that and that 95% of the shares were held by investors for whom the next largest investment was less than half the size of their Berkshire holdings. Thus, Berkshire has a loyal group of shareholders and ones with a big percentage of their net worth riding on Berkshire's fortunes.

The float is so thin and shares traded so infrequently that one can stand with Jim McGuire, chairman of Henderson Brothers, at his post on the floor of the New York Stock Exchange where Berkshire and more than 80 other companies trade and find there's an hour or two between Berkshire trades. Or a day. Henderson Brothers is the oldest continuing specialist firm on the Exchange.

Buffett once recalled that on the day Berkshire was listed on the New York Stock Exchange in 1988, he told McGuire: "I will consider you an enormous success if the next trade in this stock is about two years from now." Buffett joked that McGuire wasn't too enthusiastic about his comment. (*The Essays of Warren Buffett: Lessons for Corporate America*, Lawrence A. Cunningham, Cardozo Law

Review, p. 17-18)

On July 25 and 26, 1991, there were no Berkshire trades. The streak was broken the following day when 10 shares changed hands, giving new meaning to the Wall Street term "trades by appointment." Buffett likes that.

"Our goal is to attract long-term owners who, at the time of purchase, have no timetable or price target for sale but plan instead to stay with us indefinitely," Buffett wrote in the 1988 Berkshire annual report.

Brokers and journalists often are embarrassed by their lack of knowledge about Berkshire's high stock price.

One day in 1989 when Berkshire was up $100 to $8,550, an office worker at one brokerage firm said, "Something's wrong here. I need to get you a broker...Boy, I was about to blow my mind!"

Frequently, the first digit gets left off and any number purporting to be the actual price can be suspect. For example, Associated Press on November 18, 1989, listed the price-earnings ratio as 11,100. Ouch! On September 2, 1990, the P/E, actually about 17, was still higher at 11,636. But that was nothing compared to the listing March 22, 1991, which carried the P/E at 112,857, hardly in range for value investors.

The high P/E business never seems to get fixed. On July 1, 1991, the P/E was listed as 248,525 and on July 14, 1991, *Barron's* carried the P/E as 258,625! The price of Berkshire shares is so high, many newspapers have trouble squeezing the full price into their listings. In December 1989, at the Associated Press, a computer program that processes stock prices had to be modified when it was discovered the share price exceeded the program's previous per-share ceiling of $8,192.

For a string of days in late 1989 the Stock Phone stock quote service in Atlanta carried Berkshire at minus $83.

In September, 1990, when the early trading volume was 10 shares, Berkshire was listed as trading 6,000 shares. It would be a rare day indeed if Berkshire were to trade 6,000 shares because the stock has a very low turnover rate of about 4% a year. It trades on average about 250 shares a day.

At the same time that a brokerage firm's quote machine indicated 6,000 shares were trading, it correctly listed the high for the year in 1990 as $8,725, but listed the low at $175. 1990 was a bad year, but not that bad.

Another day Berkshire's share price shot up $175 to a new all-time high of $8,300. The next day the *Wall Street Journal* tables reported the previous day's high was $158, the low $8, and the closing price $108, down $801 for the day. Say what?

A Berkshire stock quote one morning in 1995 on the *Bloomberg* wire read: 37,000 + 15,000! One day in 1998 the Class B shares were listed at 254, down 2294.

All the volatility reminds one of a *Barron's* cartoon (February 5, 1990): "The stock market rocketed up a big four-thousand points today, and then zoomed back down a hefty fifty-six hundred points, before rebounding in the final two minutes of trading to close up one-point-three-two points."

The *Journal* also said Berkshire's 1993 operating earnings were $413,000 a share when they were $413 a share.

One time during a nasty spill in the market, Berkshire shareholder George Eyraud of Birmingham called a broker for a quote and was told that Berkshire was down $700, trading at $200 a share. Eyraud's next stop: debtor's prison.

"I went and got a bowl of soup and tried to pull myself together, but I couldn't eat anything," he said hoping that once again the quotes were awry, which they were.

Another time he called a discount brokerage in Birmingham and asked to transfer $3,000 to his bank account.

"Sir, you only have $2,400 and you owe us $45,000. You'll be getting a big bill from us," the person at the other end of the line said.

"How can that be when I have 32 shares of Berkshire in the account?" he asked.

"Well, your Berkshire stock is selling at $77.50," the broker replied.

"Ma'am, that stock is selling for seven thousand seven hundred and fifty dollars," Eyraud said.

"Well, we'll check into it," a skeptical brokerage firm hand said.

Once Eyraud, who calls Buffett the Bear Bryant of investing, suggested to a woman stockbroker she buy a share of Berkshire. Her reply was "$8,000! I could get a full-length mink coat for that. You've got to get your priorities straight."

Eyraud also recalls talking to a fellow, suggesting Berkshire was a good investment.

"I would never invest in that," the fellow replied.

"Why not?" Eyraud asked.

"Well, it's just the principle."

"What principle is that?" inquired Eyraud.

"Well, it's just too high," the fellow explained.

Once a young stockbroker, seeing Berkshire's high stock price for the first time said, "Boy, am I going to short that thing!"

He could have shorted it and could have been burned. The short position in Berkshire usually runs about 2,000 shares and as of August 1994, was 3,586 shares. In 1995 it leaped to about 15,000 shares before settling at about 8,000 shares short.

Investors entering the land of Berkshire simply cannot get over the stock price. Once Joanne Englebert of Birmingham, a Berkshire shareholder, suggested to a friend, Dr. Martha Wingfield of Chapel Hill, North Carolina, that she buy a share of Berkshire, then trading at about $7,000. That way, Mrs. Englebert reasoned, she too could go to the Berkshire Annual Meeting in Omaha.

"I think $7,000 is a little much for a weekend in Omaha, don't you?" Wingfield replied.

One shareholder tells of a time he called a stockbroker who punched up a Berkshire quote. The broker took a hard look at the four-digit figure, then suddenly began apologizing, saying he couldn't read his screen. "I recently had an eye operation," he explained.

The price has thrown off investors, even experienced ones. One lifelong lawyer/investor who took a look at a Berkshire report and kept hearing about the stock price pronounced one day in 1988, "All the gravy's been taken out of that thing." The price then: $4,200.

Years later that person bought a share for $16,000.

Wyomissing, Pennsylvania, money manager Tom Weik recalls that in 1985 a young accountant came to him (back when Weik was a stockbroker in Reading, Pennsylvania) with $2,500 when Berkshire happened to be trading at just about that price. "It took me several days to convince him to invest it all in one share, but we bought the one share," Weik said.

Weik, who has written articles about Berkshire for local publications since the stock traded at $200 a share back in the 1970s, showed up at the Rotary Club soon after the purchase. He was accosted by a fellow who had read one of his columns about Berkshire and said, "God, I sure wouldn't buy something at that price."

"I looked around and saw the accountant I had sold the share of Berkshire to standing next to him," Weik said.

"I did not blanch because I was that confident about Berkshire, but the accountant looked like he might have difficulty digesting his dinner."

A similar incident occurred in 1988 when Berkshire was trading at about $4,800. "But who would buy it now?" a woman asked

Weik.

Weik said, "Well, I just bought it for your retirement plan."

Berkshire has its slow periods and its down periods. Sometimes long-time shareholders who know better wind up selling.

Charles Akre, managing partner of Braddock Capital Partners, L.P., in Arlington, Virginia, wrote to his partners September 20, 1995:

> Back in 1977, when I was a young retail broker, I came across Berkshire Hathaway in the course of my research and I bought one share for $120. Over the next four years I accumulated a total of 40 shares, buying them a few at a time. Also during the late 1970s I tried my hand at real estate development. By 1981 I was in the midst of a "condo conversion" project which, owing to the 21% prime rate level, needed to have the construction loan refinanced. The lenders were aware, of course, that I had some liquidity away from the project, and the rest is history; I sold 39 shares for $500 per share. The single original share I still have sells today at an astounding <u>241 times the purchase price</u>.

Akre made up for his mistake by loading up on Berkshire and International Speedway shares in Braddock Capital Partners.

An investor first having a look at Berkshire usually is floored by the price and then put off again because it pays no dividend. Of course, the price is high because the underlying value is high and because Buffett has never split the stock, reasoning that such actions are cosmetic, involve paperwork and attract the kind of investor interested in meaningless stock splits rather than those concerned about what the company is really worth. Buffett wants investors, not speculators.

Although it's fun when dividends arrive, dividends are after-tax money from the corporation which then is taxed again when an individual pays taxes. Dividends may look good and they may feel good, but Buffett's not about looking or feeling good. It makes more sense—and that is what Buffett is about—not to have dividends, particularly if Buffett is your money manager.

With Berkshire, the investor is leaving his share of the retained earnings within the company for Buffett to reinvest which he has compounded on the order of 25% a year. Or would you prefer, say a 3% paid-out dividend that would be taxed?

Investor John Slater of New York says he first bought a share of Berkshire at $425. "I had sent away for the annual report and I thought that was a good price for a lifetime subscription to the annual report."

About the same time, he gave a share of Berkshire to Gil Gunn, the newborn son of his friend, Gilman Gunn.

"By the time his second child came along, Berkshire was at $1,000 and I said that it was too much for me, that he ought to buy a share for the second child." Gunn, a widely recognized international investor, never did, although he later became a Berkshire shareholder himself.

Once the following conversation took place between a stockbroker and his sales assistant about Berkshire's stock price:

Stockbroker: "How about calling up a quote on BRK." [now BRKA]

Sales assistant: "It's trading at $15."

Stockbroker: "Are you sure?"

Sales assistant: "Well, there are some extra zeros."

Stockbroker: "Check again. Isn't it $15,000 a share?"

Sales assistant: "No, there's no stock that trades at $15,000."

At that time, a customer calling Merrill Lynch for a quote was told: "Could that be right?"

A fellow called in early 1998 and asked if Berkshire's price were about $36,000. He was given a quote of more than $50,000. About three seconds later the phone went dead.

25

AMERICAN EXPRESS
BUFFETT PEEKS IN THE CASH REGISTER

One of Buffett's greatest decisions in the early 1960s was to invest in a big way in American Express.

Late in 1963 the Anthony De Angelis salad oil scandal occurred when an American Express subsidiary mistakenly issued warehouse receipts for salad oil fraudulently certified to exist in storage tanks in Bayonne, New Jersey.

White collar crook De Angelis came up with the scam to invent the salad oil holding, then borrowed money, bet on vegetable oil futures, and lost. It turned out the tanks were mostly full of water. American Express had been storing the containers and issuing receipts that could be traded as financial instruments. The company had been defrauded but, at great cost, made sure no innocent third party suffered a loss. American Express found itself possibly liable for hundreds of millions of dollars. A crisis brewed which could have wiped out shareholder equity and left the company with a negative net worth. Buffett viewed the incident as a one-time loss of a dividend to shareholders but the company itself remained whole.

"A great investment opportunity occurs when a marvelous business encounters a one-time huge, but solvable problem," Buffett says.

The ultimate advocate of a franchise business, Buffett liked the American Express charge card and travelers check businesses and concluded their strengths were unassailable, and powerful enough to carry the company through troubled times.

Buffett already understood the principle of "Other People's Money." He knew American Express was a good business because of the huge cash "float" generated by American Express' travelers checks.

Buffett knew the float, like a low-cost loan, was valuable. So he went about making sure the underlying business was not hurt by the cloud overhanging American Express. In Ross' steak house in Omaha—one of his favorite haunts—and in other establishments, Buffett stood behind the cashier and peeked into the cash register to see if people were still using American Express cards and checks.

He found that merchants still were accepting the cards. Because the cards were still honored and the American Express empire remained intact, Buffett bought the battered stock. In 1964, investing 40% of the net worth of the Buffett Partnership, or roughly $13 million, Buffett bought 5% of American Express stock, which had collapsed to $35 a share from $65.

In doing so he violated his rule of not investing more than 25% of the partnership money in one investment, but he wrote a new rule of buying great companies when they temporarily stumble. In the next two years American Express stock tripled and the Buffett Partnership reportedly sold out with a $20 million profit. Apparently his partnership made even more because Buffett told the *Omaha World-Herald* (August 2, 1991) he held the stock for four years although published reports indicated he sold out after two years. Over a five year period the stock quintupled from $35 to $189. Buffett's investment lesson: when a great company falters, have a look.

26
GRINNELL COLLEGE
AN EDUCATION IN INVESTING

In 1968, not many years after the American Express investment, Buffett became a trustee of Grinnell College in Grinnell, Iowa, when the school's liquid endowment was about $12 million. He soon gave the college some good investment advice. Rule No. 1: Act fast. Rule No. 2: If someone else owns what you want, then buy a piece of their company.

It was at the urging of his friend Joseph F. Rosenfield of Des Moines, a lawyer, investor and retired chairman of Younkers department stores, that Buffett went on the Grinnell board. In 1967, Rosenfield, a member of Grinnell's investment committee, urged the endowment fund to buy 300 shares of Berkshire at $17.50 a share. That $5,250 investment would now be worth millions.

"We bought 300 shares and we sold 100 shares of it at $5,000," says Rosenfield. "We have since bought back more shares but I can't disclose how much. Of course, we bought them back at much higher prices."

Rosenfield, now 96, has turned $11 million in 1968 into $1 billion now. Most of that figure has been made for Grinnell College. (Money.com, June, 2000) By 1999 Grinnell, with 1,300 students and 108-acre campus, had the largest endowment, at $1.02 billion, of any private liberal arts college in the U.S.

In 1976 while attending a conference in New Orleans about the economics of newspapers, Buffett discovered that AVCO Corp. had decided to sell its television stations.

Under FCC rules Buffett couldn't buy the stations for Berkshire because of the number of television holdings already held by The Washington Post Co. So he proposed to Rosenfield that Grinnell College try to buy one of them. Buffett called Rosenfield, told him AVCO was having some financial difficulty and that Grinnell could buy a television station. "It was his idea," Rosenfield said.

Buffett's first choice was to buy a television station in Cincinnati, but the Grinnell board spent so much time discussing the financing that Multimedia, not Grinnell, bought the station for $16 million. Under Buffett's guidance, Grinnell did respond by buying $315,000 of Multimedia stock. The stock soared.

Buffett's second investment deal for the college was AVCO's television station in Dayton. Without waiting for financing, he bid $12.9 million, two and a half times the station's sales. He got it in the late 1970s and in late 1984 Grinnell sold the station to Hearst Corp. for about $50 million. Again, nice work if you can get it.

The transaction about doubled Grinnell's endowment which rose to about $120 million in 1984. "It turned out very well," Rosenfield said. "I got to know him 25 or 30 years ago through some mutual friends in Des Moines and he visited here."

If Buffett has some financial advice for Grinnell's board, he usually just calls Rosenfield.

"I see him every so often. He's still on the Grinnell board. He came to the board meetings for a while, but then stopped," Rosenfield said. "He really doesn't like meetings. Long-winded meetings are not his forte." Buffett was named a life trustee of Grinnell in 1968.

Grinnell's trustees have done very well with another Buffett connection, Bill Ruane's Sequoia Fund.

Grinnell, which celebrated 150 years of existence in 1996, is the largest shareholder, with about 13% of Sequoia which has about 29% of its money in Berkshire.

The trustees could consider a name change to Grinnell College and Bank.

Little wonder Buffett is a life trustee of Grinnell College. He is also a life trustee of the Urban Institute; trustee of the Business Enterprise Trust, Stanford, California; trustee of the Wellness Council of the Midlands (Nebraska), and is a member of the American Academy of Arts and Science.

Another interesting Grinnell investment was described by Buffett during the Berkshire Annual Meeting in 1997.

"...Bob Noyce, one of the two primary founders of Intel, grew up in Grinnell, Iowa. I think he was the son of a minister in Grinnell, went to Grinnell College and was Chairman of the Board of Trustees at Grinnell when I went on their board back in the late 1960s. And when Noyce left Fairchild to form Intel with Gordon Moore, Grinnell bought 10% of the private placement that...was actually the initial funding for Intel.

"...So we did buy 10% of the original issue [for Grinnell]. But the genius who ran Grinnell's investment committee managed to sell those shares a few years later—although I won't give you his name. And there's no prize for anybody who calculates the value of those shares today."

27
THE BERKSHIRE HATHAWAY INSURANCE GROUP

FLOAT THAT IS "TANTAMOUNT TO EQUITY"

Even Don Wurster, the company president, admitted running a nervous finger down the columns of fine print in the morning newspapers until he found a particular team," wrote Melinda Norris in a May 13, 1990, story for the *Omaha World-Herald.*

"He'd pore over the inning-by-inning scores to make sure the team didn't score four runs or more in a single inning. National Indemnity was betting $1 million that no one on the team would hit a grand slam home run."

National Indemnity, Berkshire's main non-GEICO direct insurance operation, was underwriting a television contest that offered contestants a chance to win $1 million for predicting the station's secret Grand Slam Inning.

"If the guy hits a grand slam (during that inning), we write a check and some fan is rich," Wurster said. "Fortunately, they never hit a grand slam."

The same willingness to write unusual business—whether prize indemnification or inland marine cargo policies—at the right price still exists at Berkshire.

Buffett wrote in Berkshire's 1995 Annual Report: "We insured (1) the life of Mike Tyson for a sum that is large initially and that fight-by-fight, gradually declines to zero over the next few years; (2) Lloyd's against more than 225 of its 'names' dying during the year, and (3) the launch, and a year in orbit, of two Chinese satellites. Happily, both satellites are orbiting, the Lloyd's folk avoided abnormal mortality, and if Mike Tyson looked any healthier, no one would get into the ring with him."

In 1996 Berkshire, in a joint venture with the huge American International Group, entered another insurance area: writing policies for product liability coverage for pharmaceutical companies.

The coverage, called "PharmaCat", is offered through Johnson and Higgins, an international insurance broker.

• Also in 1996 Berkshire entered into a large contract with Allstate Insurance Company covering property risks in Florida.

• In July, 1999 Berkshire's National Indemnity Co. agreed to provide protection to ACE Ltd. which was acquiring Cigna's property-casualty business. ACE obtained from National Indemnity $1.25 billion in protection against unexpected losses at the Cigna business. The agreement protects Bermuda-based ACE against adverse reserve development at Brandywine Holdings, a Cigna unit that was created to pay off the claims on the company's discontinued asbestos and environmental businesses. This meant that $1.25 billion in premium went to Berkshire and meant that Berkshire would also record large losses.

The ACE contract provided $2.5 billion in protection in exchange for the premium. How the contract will work out depends on the amount and speed of the claims—the slower the better for Berkshire—and how well Berkshire invests its $1.25 billion.

• In 1999 AXE Re Group bought a $300 million, 5-year, second-event retrocession index cover, which in English is the protection that a reinsurer buys from another reinsurer (retrocession) to guard against a second catastrophe, or event, striking in one time frame. The rates are set for five years and the limits of liability fluctuate with an economic index.

• Countrywide Credit Industries, of Calabasas, California, a leading residential finance company announced February 3, 2000 it had agreed that National Indemnity would provide Countrywide's Balboa Life and Casualty unit with an extra layer of protection against property and casualty risk. The agreement called for National Indemnity to buy up to $100 million in newly issued shares of a special purpose class of Countrywide preferred stock if certain events took place. The primary trigger would be weather and fire related catastrophic events. The agreement lasts until January 1, 2003.

Back in early 1967 Berkshire paid about $8.6 million for two small Omaha insurance companies, National Indemnity and National Fire & Marine. "The two tiny underwriters had $17.3 million in so-called float—or double the companies' acquisition cost." (Forbes, January 22, 1996)

Berkshire entered the reinsurance business in the 1960s because the rate on line (price per dollar of coverage provided) for aviation hull risk was 3%. Doing some simple math in his head, Buffett concluded that 3%—or even 1% —of the world's aircraft were not

(Photo by Nancy Line Jacobs)

This is the National Indemnity cafeteria where the early Berkshire annual meetings were held which had an attendance of about a dozen people.

going to crash and the insurance product was offering big margins. (PaineWebber report, September 22, 1998)

Today Berkshire's largest business is insurance—property and casualty insurance—conducted nationwide by a dozen insurance companies that operate with tiny organizational resources, but huge financial strengths. Huge. In 1998 Berkshire overtook State Farm's leading position as the largest property/casualty insurer in terms of surplus.

Capital expenditures for all the insurance businesses in 1997 were about $29 million. Identifiable assets for 1997 were almost $50 billion! For all of Berkshire, identifiable assets were about $56 billion. Assets were $131 million at the end of 1999.

National Indemnity alone ranks among the top ten U.S. reinsurers, based on net premiums written and is among the most highly capitalized insurers in the world.

(Photo by Nancy Line Jacobs)

Berkshire's former Chief Financial Officer Verne McKenzie showed reporters the National Indemnity cafeteria during Berkshire's annual meeting weekend in 1999.

(Photo by Andrew Kilpatrick)

Nondescript headquarters of National Indemnity Co. in Omaha, Berkshire's leading insurance firm. Many of Berkshire's investments are bought by National Indemnity. Technically, this little building's operations house billions.

Munger at the Wesco Annual Meeting in 1993 talked about Berkshire's low expenses: "I'm sure we have the lowest ratio of headquarters cost to stockholders' capital of any insurance operation in the country, if not the world.

"In fact, Warren once considered buying a building on a distressed basis for about a quarter of what it would have cost to duplicate it. And tempting as it was, he decided that it would give everybody bad ideas to have surroundings so opulent. So we continue to run our insurance operation from very modest quarters."

The Duff and Phelps Rating Co. in late 1999 gave National Indemnity and its units its highest credit rating saying: "National Indemnity estimates its maximum after-tax exposure to a single event to be $600 million. With almost $40 billion in surplus, National Indemnity could easily absorb such a loss, which might even be a boon to its business if it firms up pricing in this competitive segment or causes a 'flight to quality'; that would benefit the best capitalized competitors."

Normally Berkshire writes insurance for commercial vehicles and workers' compensation. But it has insured carnivals, free-throw contests, basketball and hockey games. It offers coverage for commercial trucks and truckers, autos, garages and dealers, price information, general liability, inland marine cargo and reinsurance.

Buffett says Berkshire may be the largest writer of super-catastrophe (super-cat—insurance on cats and dogs, some say) business in the world. He writes multi-million dollar policies against earthquakes and offers coverage other insurance companies buy to protect themselves against a catastrophe. Maybe Berkshire should write a policy for its own ultimate super-cat: Buffett's demise.

In 1993 Berkshire entered the life insurance business, writing annuity policies for injured people who win insurance contract settlements. The firm got its risk-taking philosophy from founder Jack Ringwalt, who died in 1984. Ringwalt founded the company in 1940 for two Omaha cab companies that couldn't get insurance. In 1967 Buffett bought the company, which still had a hefty commercial vehicle business.

Charles Heider, general partner of Heider-Weitz Partners in Omaha, says that Ringwalt called him one day about the possibility of selling National Indemnity for $10 million. Heider called his friend Buffett who told him he was interested. When Heider asked when would be a good time to get together to talk about it, Buffett replied, "What about this afternoon?"

(Photo by Nancy Line Jacobs)
Charles Heider

"Warren liked everything about National Indemnity and had followed it with interest for some years. Warren recognized Jack Ringwalt as a very intelligent person and his respect was confirmed when he learned that Jack made sure all the lights were out before leaving for the day. I also believe Warren was well ahead of his time in recognizing the value of 'float,' i.e., in the insurance business and specifically at National Indemnity—the opportunity to manage the company's not insignificant investment account in his own style."

Ringwalt's memoirs said Buffett was about 20 years old when the two first met. Buffett was trying to raise $100,000 to start an investment pool. Ringwalt said he offered to invest $10,000. Buffett, however, said he would accept nothing less than $50,000.

"I remarked, 'If you think I am going to let a punk kid like you handle $50,000 of my money, you are even nuttier than I thought,'" Ringwalt wrote. Ringwalt took back his offer of the $10,000. "If I had put in $50,000 at the time he so desired, I could have taken out $2 million after taxes 20 years later. I did pretty well with National Indemnity Co., but not that well."

Although it covers risk, insurance itself can be a risky business as even Buffett's sometimes spotty insurance record can attest. Insurance companies always have a huge potential for liabilities should claims come due. And that potential problem exists for Berkshire, too.

Buffett wrote in Berkshire's 1988 Annual Report, "The property-casualty insurance industry is not only subnormally profitable, it is subnormally popular. (As Sam Goldwyn philosophized: 'In life, one must learn to take the bitter with the sour.')" Occasionally, Buffett has misjudged the business known for its boom-and-bust cycles, and is the first to admit it. Overall, his predictions about industry trends have been remarkable, often predicting years ahead how things would turn out.

"It's only when the tide goes out that you learn who's been swimming naked," Buffett said at the Berkshire Annual Meeting in 1993.

Berkshire has shown discipline in not writing policies unless it can get good prices. When prices are not attractive, Berkshire simply doesn't write the business. Buffett once said in a talk to Notre Dame students that when prices are unattractive, "We have a lot of people doing crossword puzzles."

Berkshire has $45 billion in insurance capital and could write far more business than it does. The ability to turn bad news into good news exists because Berkshire's untapped capacity is huge.

At the Wesco Annual Meeting in 1993, Munger said he's often asked why Berkshire doesn't write more insurance. "People are always saying to Berkshire, 'Gee, why don't you write a lot more volume in relation to capital? Everyone else is doing it. The rating agencies say that you can write twice as much in annual volume as you have capital.' And they look at our $10 billion in insurance capital and say, 'That's $20 billion a year. What are you doing writing only $1 billion?'

"But then...somebody else comes in and asks, 'Why did everybody get killed last year but you?' Maybe the questions are related."

In 1996 Berkshire's net premiums were 16% of the insurance group's year-end statutory surplus, compared to an industry average premiums-to-surplus ratio of about 130%.

The appeal of the insurance business is that premiums come up front—cash in the form of other people's money arriving every day at the office for you to invest. Essentially, the insurance business provides "float" (not to be confused with a Southern ice cream dish) somewhat akin to deposits in a bank, that can be invested. It brings Berkshire low-cost money. Basically, it's a free margin account.

"Float, per se, is not a blessing," says Buffett. But it is a blessing if you can get it in increasing amounts and above all if you can get it cheap, he adds.

"It has been a big mistake by some analysts to think of the value of the insurance operation as its book value alone, without regard to the value of the float." (Annual Meeting in 1996)

Essentially, the insurance group has provided 30 years of free money.

In Berkshire's 1997 Annual Report, Buffett, writing about float, which is insurance premiums collected, but not yet paid out for insured losses, said: "Unless you understand this subject, it will be impossible for you to make an informed judgment about Berkshire's intrinsic value."

He wrote, "Since 1967, when we entered the insurance business, our float has grown at an annual compound rate of 21.7%. Better yet, it has cost us nothing, and in fact has made us money. Therein lies an accounting irony. Though our float is shown on our balance sheet as a liability, it has had value to Berkshire greater than an equal amount of net worth would have had."

Buffett told shareholders at the Berkshire Annual Meeting in 1998: "Float comes to us at a negative cost, with a cost less than zero. It comes with a profit attached." He added, "But the real key is what the float will be in 10 years."

"We have $7 billion of float presently," Buffett said at Berkshire's annual meeting in 1996. "And if I were offered $7 billion for that float and did not have to pay tax on the gain, but would thereafter have to stay out of the insurance business forever—a perpetual non-compete in any kind of insurance—would I accept that? The answer is no.

"That's not because I'd rather have $7 billion of float than $7 billion of free money. It's because I expect the $7 billion to grow." Berkshire had more than $22 billion in float as a result of its 1998 acquisition of General Re. At the end of 1999 Berkshire had more than $25 billion in float. When that "float" hits Berkshire's doorstep, it's immediately invested in stocks, bonds, and businesses, or whatever.

Buffett has called the float "tantamount to equity." And the growth of float can be roughly regarded as income. There are no carrying charges and possibly no repayments.

Buffett wrote in Berkshire's 1998 Annual Report that float "has had more economic value to us than an equal amount of net worth would have had. As long as we can continue to achieve an underwriting profit, float will continue to outrank net worth in value."

Although in many years Berkshire has had no cost for its float, it mushroomed in 1999 to 5.8% mainly because of large losses at General Re.

Berkshire usually writes "long tail" insurance policies most likely to be paid off in the distant future. Clearly, it's good to have the policyholder's money for as long as possible, but Buffett also has warned that long tail policies are tricky because by the time it comes to pay policyholders, inflation and regulations may have raised costs so much that profits are elusive.

Court-awarded judgments far in excess of what was contemplated at the time the policy was written also can hurt insurance profits.

Insurance is an important business, especially in Nebraska where the business has received favorable treatment by state lawmakers. Mutual of Omaha, one well-known business made better known by Marlin Perkins' exploits on *Wild Kingdom*, is based near Berkshire's headquarters, its own version of a wild kingdom. It is a jungle out there, you know.

Starting in March 1967, when Berkshire made a tender offer for National Indemnity and National Fire and Marine Insurance managed by Jack Ringwalt, Buffett bought the more than a dozen insurance businesses Berkshire now owns.

Berkshire entered insurance for diversity and for increased profits. National Indemnity, which even in the late 1980s was still using old IBM card sorters, occupies a six-story, 35,000-square-foot building in Omaha and owns an adjoining 9,600-square-foot building, not far from Berkshire's headquarters.

In addition to National Indemnity in Omaha, which has a reinsurance division in Stamford, Connecticut, the Berkshire insurance empire owns the following companies:

—General Re Corp., Stamford, Connecticut (which has many
  subsidiaries)
—GEICO, Chevy Chase, Maryland (which has many
  subsidiaries)
—Aksarben Life Insurance, Omaha, Nebraska
—Berkshire Hathaway International Insurance Limited,
  United Kingdom
—Berkshire Hathaway Life Insurance Company of Nebraska and
  its affiliate IdeaLife (which has branched into selling
  annuities on the Internet, a business developed by Ajit Jain)*
—Central States Indemnity, Omaha, Nebraska
—Central States of Omaha Companies, Inc., Omaha, Nebraska
—Columbia Insurance, Omaha, Nebraska
—Continental Divide Insurance, Englewood, Colorado
—Cornhusker Casualty, Omaha, Nebraska
—Cypress Insurance, Pasadena, California
—Fairfield Insurance, Connecticut
—Gateway Underwriters Agency, St. Louis, Missouri

—Kansas Bankers Surety, Topeka, Kansas
—National Fire and Marine Insurance, Omaha, Nebraska
—National Indemnity, Omaha, Nebraska
—National Indemnity Company of the South,
 St. Petersburg, Florida
—National Indemnity Company of Mid-America,
 St. Paul, Minnesota
—National Liability and Fire Insurance, Nebraska
—National Liability and Fire Insurance, Chicago, Illinois
—Northern States Agency, St. Paul, Minnesota
—Oak River Insurance, Omaha, Nebraska
—OCSAP, Ltd., Maine
—Redwood Fire and Casualty Insurance, Omaha, Nebraska
—Resolute Reinsurance, New York
—Ringwalt and Liesche, Omaha, Nebraska
—U.S. Investment Corp., Wayne, Pennsylvania
—Wesco-Financial Insurance, Omaha, Nebraska

*An Internet notice on Berkshire's home page at www.berkshire-hathaway.com for the Berkshire Hathaway Life Insurance Company of Nebraska, says: "The Berkshire Hathaway group of insurance companies is the most highly capitalized insurance group in the world, in terms of net worth, and utilizes minimal leverage."

"The people who will be most interested will be those who want to set aside a portion of their assets to build a safety net for the future, and who want those assets invested with an institution that can be totally relied upon to fulfill its promises to pay decades in the future."

The main annuity products are the single Premium Immediate Annuity (SPIA) which ensures the buyer a guaranteed income for a lifetime in exchange for an upfront investment and the Single Premium Deferred Annuity (SPDA), a wealth accumulation product that allows one to save in a tax-deferred environment essentially through investing in tax-deferred zero coupon bonds.

Berkshire's "Homestate Businesses" are based in Colorado, Nebraska and California with branch operations in several other states.

The underwriting activities of these businesses include the handling of almost all forms of property and casualty insurance through agents, in the District of Columbia and in all 50 states except Hawaii.

The main business of the insurance group is the sale of auto insurance, which accounts for about half of all the business. The busi-

(Photo by LaVerne Ramsey)

Ajit Jain, shown here before the Berkshire annual meeting in 1995, and Buffett are friends. They are on the phone daily discussing Berkshire's super-catastrophe reinsurance business which Jain heads. In Berkshire's 1999 Annual Report, Buffett said: "It's simply impossible to evaluate Ajit's value to Berkshire: He has from scratch built an outstanding reinsurance business, which during his tenure has earned an underwriting profit and now holds $6.3 billion of float."

nesses also sell trucking insurance, workers' compensation, homeowners', fire, and even insurance policies for those who serve as officers and directors of companies. For many years Berkshire wrote insurance for taxicabs in Omaha, but it no longer handles that business.

The insurance group also writes insurance for farm owners, business owners and garage owners. It writes insurance for luxury cars, marine accidents, earthquakes, cargo damage, and burglaries. It sells personal and commercial package policies.

Berkshire-owned See's Candies sometimes buys its workers' compensation insurance at discount rates through Berkshire.

The Berkshire insurance companies do a hefty reinsurance business, taking on the insurance risk and reward of insurance written by other companies. The reinsurance operations are run from National Indemnity's offices in Stamford, Connecticut, by Harvard Business School graduate Ajit Jain. Born in India, Jain worked for IBM and the McKinsey & Co. consulting firm before joining Berkshire.

Folks at Berkshire's annual meeting kidded Jain about all his brains. He replied: "There is only one brain at this company."

"I talk to Ajit Jain about reinsurance deals every night. I do it as much for enjoyment as anything else. He could do it just as well without me," Buffett says.

Jain says: "Warren and I might have a 30-second conversation or a 30-minute one, but he has been involved in every piece of business I've done." (*Business Week*, July 5, 1999)

Reinsurance involves insuring other insurance companies and exists so no one company will get hit with the total cost of something like an earthquake, which might bankrupt a primary insurance company with thousands of dependent, individual policyholders.

Reinsurers repackage and then parcel out the really big risks to someone, spreading the risk around as well as taking some of it themselves. To be in reinsurance means one better be able to take a big loss. Berkshire is just that sort of company, and its unusual financial strength is a good marketing tool for seeking both insurance and reinsurance business. The Berkshire folks will write the policies and charge a stiff price for them, but if there is a catastrophe Berkshire could take a big hit. "When a major quake occurs in an urban area or a winter storm rages across Europe, light a candle for us," Buffett wrote in Berkshire's 1990 Annual Report.

Still Berkshire itself is willing to take these big risks for its own account. "One reason we never 'lay off' part of the risks we insure is that we have reservations about our ability to collect from others when disaster strikes," Buffett wrote in Berkshire's 1996 Annual Report.

At least the super-cat policies have caps on the possible losses although in some cases Berkshire has an obligation to renew the policy at once. Buffett has said Berkshire could be exposed to a $600 million loss if a hurricane were to slam the east coast, particularly New York.

Munger has said, "So if we have real disaster—if you had Hurricane Andrew followed one week later by another one just like it—Berkshire would have a very unpleasant year."

Berkshire is choosy about the business it writes, rejecting 98% of what it's offered.

Indeed, in the third quarter of 1992 Berkshire had to pay out $125 million in claims in connection with Hurricane Andrew damage in Florida. Buffett wrote a letter to shareholders reminding them of the volatility of the business:

> At this point, Berkshire may be the largest writer of super-cat policies in the world, an activity that will continue to make our quarterly earnings volatile. But that is of no concern to us: The gold medal in a marathon is awarded to the runner with the best time for the entire race and not to the one who ran the steadiest pace. Whenever the choice is offered, we welcome the chance to forfeit stability of quar-

terly or annual earnings in exchange for greater long-term profitability.

In 1994 Berkshire underwrote a $400 million reinsurance policy for 20th Century Industries, the California auto insurer.

"We will quote prices for coverage as great as $500 million on the same day that we are asked to bid. No one else in the industry will do the same," Buffett said in the 1994 Annual Report.

Buffett long has wanted to expand the insurance business. In 1985 he joined with American Express's Sanford Weill and some senior Fireman's Fund executives in a plan to buy Fireman's Fund from American Express. But the plan, organized by Weill, was rejected by American Express.

Berkshire's insurance companies own many of the investments Buffett makes, investments that provide such enormous financial strength that it's clear Berkshire can pay policyholders. Carrying far more assets than normally required by the insurance regulators, all the Berkshire insurance companies carry an A+ (superior) grade from A.M. Best & Co., the highest rating offered by that insurance rating firm.

Buffett wrote in the 1992 Annual Report:

> Currently Berkshire is second in the U.S. property-casualty industry in net worth (the leader being State Farm, which neither buys nor sells reinsurance). Therefore, we have the capacity to assume risk on a scale that interests virtually no other company...Charlie and I continue to like the insurance business, which we expect to be our main source of earnings for decades to come. The industry is huge; in certain sectors we can compete world-wide; and Berkshire possesses an important advantage. We will look for ways to expand our participation in the business...

In the early days Buffett himself oversaw the insurance business, but he later turned over operations to Berkshire's Mike Goldberg, who is one of the few people who work at Berkshire headquarters with Buffett. His office is next to Buffett's.

A story in *Business Week* (July 5, 1999) said:

"The office next to Buffett's is occupied by Michael Goldberg. A former McKinsey & Co. consultant, Goldberg was hired in 1981 to bring order to Berkshire's far-flung insurance interests and essentially functioned as chief operating officer for the next 11 years. The single-minded intensity Goldberg brought to the job created friction in the ranks—and gave him a bad case of burnout. In 1993, Buffett

(Photo courtesy of Omaha World-Herald)

Buffett, right, and William Kizer, Sr., center, and Kizer's son Richard, of Central States, at a press conference in 1991 when Berkshire bought Central States Health and Life. William Kizer said, "The price he quoted us was that he buys companies for 10 times earnings. I suggested, 'Well, last year we made $10 million, so...that's $100 million,' and I gulped. And he said, 'OK.' And I said, '$125 million?' He said, 'You're too late.' "

reassigned Goldberg to 'special projects' and eliminated his old position. The line managers who once reported to Goldberg, now 53, have reported directly to Buffett ever since—as do the chiefs of all 22 of Berkshire's operating companies...

"And Buffett's respectful treatment of his managers has instilled in them an ambition to 'make Warren proud,' as one puts it. 'Somehow, Warren has been able to keep a diverse cast of characters working harder for him than they did for themselves,' Goldberg says. 'I see it every day—and I still don't know how he does it. But I do know that all of us feel this incredible responsibility to him.' "

Because the insurance group is not publicly listed, it's tough to tell exactly what the insurance business is worth. Buffett has never put a figure on it other than to say it's difficult to do because of the nature of the business.

On October 20, 1992, Berkshire said it agreed to buy an 82% interest in Central States Indemnity Co. of Omaha for $82 million.

The main line of the business, a unit of Central States Health and Life Insurance Co., is credit card insurance distributed through card issuers nationwide. The company pays the scheduled minimum payments on the credit card balance should the policyholder become disabled or lose a job.

Its products help customers with monthly payments in the event of death, disability and involuntary unemployment.

"It's a business I like, run by people I like and it's located in a city I like," Buffett said at a press conference announcing the deal.

Central States founder, William Kizer, Sr., said, according to the *Omaha World-Herald* (October 21, 1992), that his negotiations with Buffett were straightforward.

"The price he quoted us was that he buys companies for 10 times (annual) earnings. I suggested, 'Well, last year we made $10 million, so if my multiplication is right, that's $100 million', and I gulped. And he said, 'OK.' "

"And I said, '$125 million?' He said, 'You're too late.' "

At a Berkshire Annual Meeting, Buffett was asked about the problems at Lloyd's of London. He said:

> For a century, syndicates of Lloyd's have operated in such a way that its members have unlimited liability. They were a center for certain types of insurance—and a very important center.
>
> The liabilities that have accrued to certain members because of things like asbestos—where they had no idea of the huge scale in which the costs would occur—have caused a number of the people who were willing to be Names to dramatically decrease. And Lloyd's is groping around for some system that handles the problem of the long-tail liability and unlimited liability.
>
> I don't think that they've got any easy answers to that. So I think that they'll still be groping to some extent a year or two hence. Quite clearly, all of that is a benefit to us.
>
> I'll tell you what really benefits us...The hurricane in Florida looks like it will ultimately prove to have caused $16 billion or so of damage....But it's very easy to visualize a hurricane that comes up and hits Long Island that could triple or quadruple that amount.
>
> Well, when you start talking about $50 or $60 billion of losses and very major companies in this business only have a couple billion of dollars of net worth—Berkshire has a significant advantage to be able to sustain significant losses. We should be able to get the appropriate premium.
>
> I'm not sure what Lloyd's total capital is, but I don't think that they have as much capital in aggregate as we do—and most of theirs is psychological, whereas ours is real.

Sequoia Fund's Bill Ruane says: "That insurance company is really a sleeper. Don't expect it to wake up. But if we're ever unfortunate to have true catastrophes that are anything like Andrew, there is one insurance company out there that can write 20 times what it's writing now very capably. Berkshire's got $10 billion or so in capital. Currently he's writing only about $200 million in regular business and about $500 million in reinsurance and catastrophe business." (*Outstanding Investor Digest*, June 23, 1994)

Buffett wrote in the 1996 Annual Report: "We are currently getting sizable "standby" fees from reinsurers that are simply nailing down their ability to get coverage from us should the market tighten."

Financial World (November 9, 1993) said: "While Berkshire Hathaway has long been active in reinsurance, that part of the company's business remained fairly small until 1988. That year, Buffett began to expand both the property and the casualty—or liability—side of his reinsurance business very aggressively. Berkshire's reinsurance premium revenues shot from just $83 million in 1988 to $676 million in 1992. Reinsurance now represents nearly three-quarters of Berkshire's net written premiums."

But even as reinsurance prices have shot up in recent years, many firms still have been hit.

"Since 1988 property insurers have lost 10 cents on every premium dollar, but during the same period, Berkshire Hathaway paid out only $312 million in claims on $379 million in earned premiums. In crude terms that's a five year average return, before expenses, of 17.8%," the *Financial World* story said.

"But Buffett's real genius becomes apparent in casualty reinsurance. Unlike property claims, casualty claims often take years to settle. So here Buffett plays a complicated game that employs both a tax shelter and the float on funds before they're paid to settle claims.

"Berkshire's record in casualty reinsurance may look terrible, but it isn't. Over the past five years it has incurred losses averaging 138% of premiums earned. Add in 5% or so for expenses, and you wonder why anyone in his right mind would be writing casualty reinsurance like this.

"But don't forget the float. Unlike U.S. property reinsurers, U.S. casualty reinsurers get the use of the money for five or more years, compounding it in a tax-free reserve set up in anticipation of future losses. And here is where Buffett's stock market genius comes in. By compounding his cash through common stocks, he can increase the money at prodigious rates: 24% per year for the past 28 years. At that rate, $100 million in premiums becomes $288 million in five years' time, more than enough to pay even large claims with profit to spare."

The article goes on to say the average property and casualty insurer keeps 79% of its capital and reserves in high-grade corporate and government bonds so they can be liquidated without a loss when a catastrophe hits.

"Yet Berkshire Hathaway needs no such cushion, thanks to the rapid rate at which Buffett has been able to build Berkshire's equity portfolio. So Buffett can maintain, as he does, 85% of Berkshire's liquid assets in common stocks. In fact, Berkshire's actuaries may be overestimating their losses, in order to create larger reserves to shelter even more of the compounding assets.

"That is why most casualty reinsurers can't hope to keep up with Berkshire."

One of the early Berkshire reinsurance executives was George Young, who met Buffett in 1962 at a financial seminar. In 1969 Buffett asked Young to come to work for him. The two men started Berkshire's reinsurance business. Young, a Ph.D. in political science and regarded as brilliant, viewed Buffett as a mental giant.

"He once told me Buffett was the only fellow who made him feel retarded," says Mrs. Willie Young, Young's widow, a former Eastern Airlines flight attendant who lives in Omaha.

Bill Lyons, National Indemnity's retired general counsel, recalls Buffett's wit: "He once asked me to check out a no-fault insurance business in Florida and I reported back that the business was in awful shape and that it would be stupid to invest in it. He said, 'Don't spare me just because it was my idea.' "

In the spring of 2000, Berkshire purchased U.S. Investment Corp., a Wayne, Pennsylvannia-based insurance company. The price was not disclosed. U.S. Investment owns three insurance companies—United States Liability Insurance Co., Mount Vernon Fire Insurance Co., and U.S. Underwriters Insurance Co.

28
PROTECTION AGAINST
THE BIG ONE

In late 1996 Berkshire agreed to sell California's state-run earthquake insurance agency $1.5 billion of reinsurance for four years for a premium of $590 million which is paid in equal parts to Berkshire during the four year period of the coverage.

Therefore Berkshire is betting that no big earthquake will hit California before March 31, 2001. The policy went into effect April 1, 1997. If the damage from any quake until that time exceeds $5 billion in homeowners' claims, Berkshire will pay the next $1.5 billion in claims.

Certainly Berkshire would take a big hit if the Big One were to occur. But then Berkshire can try to make the best of investing its premiums during that time, and if a loss were suffered of $1.5 billion minus $590 million, or $910 million, it would amount to quite a bit less than that after tax-loss deductions.

Still, it's a huge bet there won't be a large quake in California through March 2001.

The California Earthquake Authority's actuary, John Drennan, said that calculations of annual quake probabilities indicate that there is only one chance in 20 that Berkshire would have to pay out even a penny in return for the big premium. (*The Los Angeles Times*, November 18, 1996) Drennan said the annual probability of a big California quake is only 1.27%.

"In an 80-year period, you would expect to have one year where the losses exceeded $7 billion," Drennan was quoted as saying. So in four years, the chances would be one in 20, but of course the Big One could hit tomorrow.

Although the premium appeared high, California officials were quoted in the story as saying that it would still be cheaper than paying interest on bonds which the earthquake authority originally had planned to sell to shore up its resources.

The $7 billion figure relates only to damage that would be paid by the quake authority. In the 1994 Northridge earthquake, private insurance firms paid $8.5 billion in residential damage claims.

Under a new state law designed to provide more bare-bones coverage and limit the state authority's liability, new limits were placed on coverage of a home's contents. Garages, pools, and fences were exempted, and deductibles raised to 15%. With these changes the state authority's payout in a quake the size of Northridge would be about $4 billion, rather than $8.5 billion.

Total damages to all public and private facilities in the Northridge quake were $27 billion.

The Los Angeles Times story said of the $27 billion, a little more than half of the relief came from private insurers, a little less than half came from the federal government. After Northridge, private insurers mounted an effort to lessen their exposure by forming a state agency for homeowners insurance.

The story noted that selling earthquake insurance was profitable for the companies in every California quake but one. But damages from that one—Northridge—far exceeded all the earthquake premiums ever paid. In the end, the quake would have to be very big to affect Berkshire. Still, it could happen.

Maybe that's why some of the boilerplate in Berkshire's reports says it has "significant liquidity and above average capital strength."

It turned out the earthquake authority abandoned a $1.5 billion bond offering even as its banker, Morgan Stanley, was in the middle of marketing it. (*Barron's*, January 6, 1996) The agency shelved the offering after it suddenly received better terms from Berkshire.

"The bond deal was getting to be too expensive. We were able to save anywhere from $20 million to $40 million a year with reinsurance from Berkshire," said Greg Butler, head of the earthquake authority.

The *Barron's* story quoted Berkshire's Ajit Jain as saying: "The problem with these [bond] deals is that investors are being provided fixed-income type returns for equity-type risk. Since we take on the risk and put aside capital for it, we can provide a lower cost."

Berkshire demonstrated here the business advantage of its enormous capital strength, speed and savvy.

Butler was quoted in the *San Francisco Chronicle* (November 19, 1996) as saying that Berkshire, unlike other reinsurers, didn't use sophisticated statistical models to assess its risk and determine its premiums.

"I have no idea how Buffett did it," Butler said. "Maybe by the corn on his foot."

Buffett wrote in Berkshire's 1996 Annual Report of the California policy: "So what are the true odds of our having to make a payout during the policy's term? We don't know—nor do we think computer models will help us, since we believe the precision they project is a chimera. In fact, such models can lull decision-makers into a false sense of security and thereby increase their chances of making a really huge mistake. We've already seen such debacles in both insurance and investments. Witness 'portfolio insurance,' whose destructive effects in the 1987 market crash led one wag to observe that it was the computers that should have been jumping out the windows."

Berkshire also has a contract—about half the size of the California contract—with Allstate that covers Florida hurricanes.

Said Buffett in the 1996 Annual Report: "Large as these coverages are, Berkshire's after-tax 'worse-case' loss from a true mega-catastrophe is probably no more than $600 million, which is less than 3% of our book value and 1.5% of our market value."

At the annual meeting in 1997, Munger said such a loss for Berkshire would be, "irritating," but no major catastrophe.

29

SKIP THIS CHAPTER
ONLY FOR THE VERY HARD CORE

Here's a post from The Motley Fool by EliasFardo@yahoo.com who is Berkshire shareholder Paul Hartman of Oklahoma City, Oklahoma, delving into some of Berkshire's insurance accounting:

This will be a discussion of the insurance accounting for various types of transactions of BRK. I will say up front that this is just my understanding and may not be perfect. I will try to explain the way I think a BRK shareholder should look at these transactions. I do not have any understanding of the insurance contracts themselves other than what is in the annual report.

All of these transactions are entered into by the Berkshire Hathaway Reinsurance Group, so these are deals structured by Ajit Jain and Buffett. The reason I think these deals are important is because they were very large in 1999, and they have accounting results that can easily be misunderstood. We have been instructed to view the value of an insurance company by the amount of float it generates and the cost of that float. If the shareholder does not understand the accounting behind these deals, he will overestimate the cost of the float, thereby getting a distorted picture of financial results. The deals I will discuss here involve contracts in which the time value of money is a prime consideration. What happens for financial accounting is that large underwriting losses are recognized by BRK, but large amounts of float are created, thus the opportunity for investment income. I, as a shareholder, feel very comfortable with this activity. We have Ajit Jain determining the timing and amount of the expected claims' payouts, and Warren Buffett determining the proper discount rate to use to price such claims.

I call all of these transactions "purchased float" but I am sure that is not technically correct from the standpoint of an insurance professional. But to the BRK shareholder, that is what the net economic effect seems to be. There are two broad types of contracts.

Retroactive Reinsurance Contracts, Including Structured Settlements

Premiums earned from retroactive reinsurance contracts, including structured settlements, were $1,508 million in 1999, $343 million in 1998 and $144 million in 1997. Premiums earned in 1999 included $1,250 million related to a single contact entered into with an affiliate of a major U.S. property/casualty insurer. [Portions in italics are from Bershire's 1999 Annual Reprot]

As you can see, the amount of these contracts increased substantially in 1999, most of it from one contract.

Generally, retroactive reinsurance contracts indemnify the ceding company, subject to aggregate loss limits, with respect to past loss events that were insured by the counterparty. It is generally expected that losses ultimately paid under these arrangements will exceed the premiums received, possibly by a wide margin. Premiums are based in part on time-value-of-money concepts because loss payments are expected to occur over lengthy time periods. However, retroactive contracts do not significantly impact earnings in the year of inception. Consistent with Berkshire's accounting policy, the excess of the estimated ultimate losses payable over the premiums received is established as a deferred charge and amortized against income over the estimated future claim settlement periods.

This is what I understand happens. BRK will assume the payment liability for a past loss in return for a smaller amount of cash. For instance, BRK will assume a $1,000 loss for the receipt of $900 in cash. We will profit from the investment of the $900 while paying off the $1,000 loss. On the books, $1,000 is recognized as premium income and $100 is recorded as a deferred charge in "other assets" on the balance sheet. This $100 deferred charge will be charged against income over the life of the contract, resulting in underwriting losses.

The deferred charges are subsequently amortized using the interest method over the expected settlement periods of the claim liabilities. The periodic amortization charges are reflected in the accompanying Consolidated Statements of Earnings as losses and loss adjustment expenses. The unamortized balance of deferred charges is included in other assets and was $1,518 million at December 31, 1999 and $560 million at December 31, 1998.

So you can see how the large increase in these transactions in 1999, going from $343 million in 1998 to $1,508 million in 1999, resulted in a large increase in the deferred charges on the balance sheet; going from $560 million at the end of 1998 to $1,518 at the end of 1999. This $1,518 will be amortized and shown as an underwriting loss in future years, offsetting some, but hopefully not all, of the investment income earned by the cash paid to BRK by the ceding company. You can also see especially how the one large $1,250 million contract found its way through all of the company. For the Berkshire Hathaway Reinsurance Group, in 1999 premiums increased by $1,424 million and float increased by $1,980 million.

These types of contracts do not impact the income statement in the year in which the contact is issued because the underwriting loss is amortized over the life of the policy. *Net underwriting losses with respect to retroactive reinsurance contracts were $97 million in 1999, $90 million in 1998 and $82 million in 1997.* Because of the $1,508 million of activity in 1999, I would expect the amortization in 2000 to be substantially more than the $97 million in 1999.

The important thing to remember with these contracts is that while they increase the amount of the reported underwriting losses, such losses are factored into the transaction and do not necessarily indicate poor pricing or a high cost of float. We more than make up for the underwriting losses with investment income.

Non-catastrophe Reinsurance Contracts

Premiums earned from non-catastrophe reinsurance contracts totaled $560 million in 1999, $310 million in 1998 and $513 million in 1997.

*Net underwriting losses from the non-catastrophe reinsurance business were $355 million in 1999, $86 million in 1998 and $73 million in 1997. BHRG incurred a net loss of approximately $220 million from a single aggregate excess contract during the fourth quarter of 1999. Also, the 1999 underwriting loss includes $126 million of net losses on reinsurance assumed from General Re's North American property/casualty businesses. As with retroactive reinsurance contracts, the premiums established for non-catastrophe reinsurance contracts are based on time-value-of-money concepts because loss payments are expected to occur over lengthy time periods. Loss reserves for this business are established without such time discounting but, **unlike retroactive reinsurance contracts, no deferred charges are established. Consequently, significant under-***

writing losses result. This business is accepted because of the large amounts of investable policyholder funds ("float") that is produced. It is anticipated that Berkshire will derive significant economic benefits over the lengthy period of time that the float will be available for investment.

These are really interesting because no deferred charges are established, so the entire underwriting loss flows to the bottom line in the year in which the contract is written. This is where BRK recognizes all of the losses in the current year, and most of the income in subsequent years as investment income is earned. I am assuming that the $220 million 4th quarter contract mentioned above is with GE. When Buffett writes *We enthusiastically welcomed $400 million of the loss because it stems from business that will deliver us exceptional float over the next decade,* he is talking about some, or all, of the $355 million loss from the non-catastrophe reinsurance and the $97 million from the retroactive reinsurance contracts.

I believe it is important to understand at least the accounting behind these types of contracts in order to get a proper understanding of the economic performance of the Berkshire Hathaway Reinsurance Group. In 1999, there was $2,068 million of premiums on these type of time value weighted contracts. When you consider that the total premiums earned for the Berkshire Hathaway Reinsurance Group in 1999 was $2,382 million, you can see how important these types of contracts are. They make up 87% of the total.

30

MORE FROM ELIAS FARDO
"I'M FEELING BETTER," SAYS VALUE.

Elias Fardo, who is Paul Hartman, offered this post on The Motley Fool message board at a time when value stocks were making a slight rebound from a severe slump:

At a press conference this morning, Value insisted that regardless of reports to the otherwise, he is still alive and well. Looking fit and tanned, Value opened the conference with a prepared statement.

Value: There have been many times in the past when I have been forced to reintroduce myself to the public. At those times I usually quoted Mark Twain who once quipped, "The report of my death was an exaggeration." Today I would like to also quote from a more contemporary comedy group, Monty Python, and say, "I'm not dead yet." In fact, I am feeling better than ever.

Today, I want to make two specific points and then open the conference for questions. First, value is. It exists. What I mean by value is a determinable worth independent of price. To me, it is embarrassing that I should feel compelled to call a news conference to make a point that is clear on its face. I feel like a NASA scientist defending his belief in the existence of gravity. But when I read the comments of the financial pundits, I discover that this self evident idea is, for some inexplicable reason, in dispute. And even worse than that, even though I have not been closely following the price mania in the stock market, this lack of belief in value's existence seems to have carried over into the actions of many investors; enough investors anyway to dictate the current valuation of almost all common stocks. So I stand before you today to state, uncategorically, that I, Value, exist.

Secondly, I want to remind the public that value is not just a philosophical idea, but a concept that can be used for profit in the investment process. I leave it to the individual investor to find the methods that work best for him; the ways to employ value are varied and vast. But what I want to tell people today, especially to the newcomers to the investment process, is that price is not value and value is not price. And to confuse the two is detrimental to your financial wellbeing.

Questions?

Reporter: You mention that you feel the need to reintroduce yourself. Does that mean that you have been intentionally absent?

Value: In a way, yes. I have known Momentum for much longer than any of you have. We go way back. I have noticed a difference between the two of us. I try to work my will every day, but Momentum is an opportunistic fellow; he only strikes when the timing seems exactly perfect for his brand of madness. Therefore, when Momentum is acting out he has all this stored energy to project, and he does so with wild abandon. He will work himself to exhaustion, flame out, and sanity will return to whatever market he was involved with.

The lesson I have learned from the past is that when Momentum is obsessing, I need to step aside, for I will not be heard. So I decided that I can be here and be ignored, or I can be gone and be ignored. The result is the same. So I took a vacation.

But there is another reason as well. I quoted from Mark Twain earlier. He also said, "A man who carries a cat by the tail learns something he can learn in no other way." So I decided to just let investors lug that cat around by its tail for a few months. I believe that investors need the opportunity to experience the full consequences of their actions. Sometimes that is the only way to learn a lesson. If nothing succeeds like excess, let us have excess.

Reporter: What are those full consequences?

Value: Momentum investing actually is just Greater Fool theory in disguise. When investors buy a security not because they want to enjoy the profits from its assets, products and services, but simply because they think the price will be higher tomorrow than it is today, they are simply hoping that someone more foolish than they will bail

254

them out. What many eventually learn is that they are the greatest fool of all.

I witness stockholders claiming that they own a business that has many wonderful products and services that will be in increasing demand for many years. And all of that may be true. But at the same time they are happily ignorant of the market capitalization of this wonderful enterprise. Is it $100 million, $1 billion, $10 billion, $100 billion? They don't know or care. So unsustainable, unreasonable expectations occur until Momentum eventually becomes exhausted and the stock price crashes. Some people can learn that lesson in no other way.

Reporter: Why are you returning now?

Value: There is a zen saying, "When the student is ready, the teacher will appear." I had a growing feeling that people either were or soon would be experiencing enough pain to become teachable. I believe that day is today.

But even I can take only so much. The confusion between price and value had become so rampart that I was becoming very annoyed. For instance, when I heard an investor insist that he was a value investor because the current price was less than what he expected next week's price to be, I knew something had to be done. For those reporters among you who see no problem with the logic of this particular investor, I am here for you too.

Reporter: Would there be any truth to a claim that you are coming back because people were laughing at you?

Value: Whoever they may be, I have been laughed at by funnier people than them. They can laugh at me and shift all the paradigms they desire. That doesn't bother me at all.

Reporter: You said in your opening remarks that you would leave it to each investor to use value in his own way, but surely you have some ideas on what investors should do.

Value: The way I see it, there are two different ways to determine when a particular security should be purchased or sold. The investor can compare today's price to today's value, or today's price to tomorrow's price. Once an investor accepts that a security has a determined worth independent of price, and computes such worth, he has an amount that can be compared to today's price. An exact determination of value may not be realistic, but an estimate can be had. And then armed with this estimate of value, the investor can act. What the evidence does show, however, is that tomorrow's price is unknowable. So the investor has a choice: he can make decisions based on something that is at least subject to estimation, today's value, or he can make decisions based on something that is unknowable, tomorrow's price. To me the choice seems obvious.

As an aside, the argument I have heard that value is just another word for price and therefore has no separate existence, is a polemic that borders on nihilism. And for people who would base decisions on something like future price, which is entirely unknowable, nihilistic arguments represent very strange reasoning indeed.

Reporter: In what way is this argument nihilistic?

Value: Nihilism is the denial of the existence of any basis for knowledge. When someone insists that the worth of something is entirely dependent on market price, they are denying that other forms of inquiry, such as the use of reason and logic, will reveal any valid information. Whether they are aware of it or not, they are making an epistemological argument.

And all kinds of things have an existence separate from prices. As far as I know, there is not a quote for sunsets, clouds or a mother's love for her child, yet these things are real; they exist; they have value.

But if you want to hold the discussion to financial assets, let me give the following example. Imagine that Michael Jordan is six years old and his family is in need of money. So his parents make you an offer. They will sell you half of Michael Jordan's future earnings from playing basketball and making product endorsements for only $1,000. Now, Michael is only six and his oncourt potential may or may not be evident, so you might protest that $1,000 is too much and make a counter offer for $500. What if they accept? If value has no existence separate from price, does this mean that the true present value of half of Michael Jordan's future earnings from playing basketball was indeed worth only $500? Or what if they don't accept? Does that mean that his future earnings are worthless? Today, we know that such a conclusion is nonsense. Yet to argue that something is only worth what someone will pay for it demands such a conclusion.

Reporter: In your opening remarks you said that you have not been closely following the mania. But surely you have some opinion on the Internet stocks that make up most of this mania?

Value: When I say I am not following the mania closely, what I mean is that I am watching it obsessively. My thoughts on the Internet stocks are very simple. I believe that to succeed, a business needs products, sales and earnings; and most internet stocks have all but three of those things.

Reporter: What have you been doing while away?

Value: Getting sun and playing tennis. I found an excellent doubles partner in Mr. Market. Sometimes, however, Mr. Market is not a desirable partner. He can be manic and bouncing off the ceiling, or he can be so depressed that he has to look up to see bottom. But when he is balanced, we make a killer team. I have grown to like Mr. Market a lot. He is actually the one who should be holding this press conference.

Hartman said,
"In real life I am a retired CPA and living in Oklahoma City with my wonderful wife and two cats. I bought my first shares of Berkshire Hathaway in 1981 and still own them. I am 50 years old, so with the help of Warren Buffett, I got off to an early retirement...

"Elias Fardo is a name I made up in high school. I had a friend who was always inventing names. He and I were doing some silly thing that seemed to demand fake names. So I made up Elias Fardo and have used it for silly stuff like signing birthday cards, donating books to libraries, and posting on Internet message boards. It has no meaning. But the good thing is that I am probably the only Elias Fardo in the world. It is full of Paul Hartmans but there is only one Fardo."

31
BOYS TOWN
"GIVE AN ACCOUNT OF THY STEWARDSHIP."

Buffett made his first newspaper purchase in 1969 when Berkshire bought The Sun newspapers, neighborhood weeklies in Omaha from Stan Lipsey. Buffett's role in his many media properties has been almost exclusively devoted to the business side, but in at least one case he had a very definite impact on the editorial end, when he played a key role in helping disclose the financial scandal at Boys Town in Omaha.

Back in 1917, Father Edward J. Flanagan, a lanky Irish Catholic priest, paid $90 to rent a drafty Victorian house to shelter five home-less Omaha boys. The home expanded greatly and was the subject of a 1938 hit movie starring Spencer Tracy and Mickey Rooney, mak-ing Father Flanagan a hero. With growth and strong leadership the institution also became a financial powerhouse. It helped children, but it could have helped more with the huge stock portfolio it began accumulating from fundraising.

(Photo by Pat Kilpatrick)

Boys Town in Omaha

In 1972, as Buffett described it to then *Wall Street Journal* reporter Jonathan Laing for a March 31, 1977 story, "I knew of an IRS regulation that required charitable foundations to publicly disclose their assets for the first time, so I told our editor to get a copy of the Boys Town filing. I'd heard a lot of rumors during my fund days about Boys Town's large stockholdings, but even I was staggered when we found that the home, which was constantly pleading poverty and caring for less than 700 kids, had accumulated assets of more than $200 million."

In a letter to the author, *Buffalo News* Publisher Stan Lipsey wrote:
The idea for the Boys Town story came from Warren Buffett. Warren, Paul Williams, editor of *The Sun*, and I would meet at Warren's house and brainstorm ideas for

investigative or enterprise stories for *The Sun* newspapers. As weeklies, it was hard to report breaking news against a daily and the electronic media, so we had to come up with our own enterprise pieces.

In one of these sessions, Warren talked about Boys Town, and Paul and I went to work on it. Paul headed the team and organized the investigation. He and I would develop strategy, timing of interviews, and review information we secured.

At one point, we had a good story, but not the ultimate one. Warren was crucial because he told us about the IRS Form 990 regulation which Congress had just passed requiring foundations to disclose their assets. When we secured the Boys Town Form 990 in Washington, it totaled 100 pages that revealed holdings of $219 million.

While I helped brainstorm the story, and read everything several times, Paul Williams developed it. Near the end of the investigation, so there would be no leaks, we moved four reporters with telephones, desks and tape recorders into the basement recreation room of Paul Williams' house.

Without Warren, there was no story, no Pulitzer. It was his idea, he told us about the Form 990, and then he analyzed the vast Boys Town holdings that totaled $219 million.

The 8-page story won a Pulitzer Prize in May 1973, for special local reporting. Buffett came up with the headline for the story citing Luke 16 from the Bible: "Give an account of thy stewardship."

Buffett sold Sun Newspapers in 1981 and they ceased publication in 1983.

One fellow who recalls working for the weekly as a newspaperboy is Allan Maxwell, now a medical sales representative with Searle Laboratories in Omaha. "I was a carrier for about five years and the pay was great for a 15-cent newspaper. I was able to keep five cents, as I recall," said Maxwell, adding, "I only wish I'd put my profits into Berkshire."

Today Boys Town is a well regarded institution helping thousands of youngsters. From its single campus it has expanded its youth-care services to 17 other cities. Its trust fund in 1998 amounted to $733 million. (*Omaha World-Herald*, June 28, 1999)

Buffett had told *Wall Street Journal's* (March 31, 1977) Laing why he felt that newspapers are more interesting than most businesses.

"Let's face it. Newspapers are a lot more interesting business than say, making couplers for rail cars. While I don't get involved in the editorial operations of the papers I own, I really enjoy being a part of institutions that help shape society.

32
MEDIA CONNECTIONS
CHARLES PETERS, JAY ROCKEFELLER,
KAY GRAHAM, ET AL.

Buffett's first tip about the Boys Town scandal was not to his own paper, but to his friend Charles Peters, publisher of *The Washington Monthly* in which Buffett had a small investment.

"I passed it [the tip] on [to his newsmen]...they decided not to pursue the story, largely, on the grounds, I suspect, that an investor's article idea had to be suspect. Warren then gave the story to an Omaha newspaper, which won a Pulitzer for it." (Charles Peters's autobiography, *Tilting at Windmills*, p. 196)

Peters gives an account of how Buffett, Jay Rockefeller and Louis Marx became investors in the magazine and said that Buffett asked him (Peters) for an introduction to Katharine Graham:

> Jay Rockefeller and Louis Marx got us to $100,000 with additional pledges. Then Jay introduced me to Warren Buffett...
>
> In October [1969] he [Buffett] flew into Washington with two friends, Joseph Rosenfield, from Des Moines, and Fred Stanback, a North Carolinian who was heir to a headache remedy fortune. Together, they agreed to put up the remaining $50,000. We took all that money and blew it.
>
> The magazine, praised for its literary efforts, always struggled financially. Jay and Warren Buffett went to New York to ask James Kobak, a prominent magazine consultant, if there was any hope for the *Monthly*....Warren was impressed with Kaplan [Gilbert Kaplan of *Institutional Investor*] and said that he might be willing to put up another $50,000 if Kaplan took over the direction of the *Monthly's* business affairs long enough to get us straightened out.
>
> But in early September came a fifty-minute phone conversation with me in which it was clear that Warren's two sides were still at war. I was grateful for what he had already done for us and could understand his suspicion that the magazine was at best doomed to a life on the fiscal margin. So I wasn't angry when, at times during the conversation, he

tried to withdraw from further involvement. But if I wasn't angry, I was desperate, because I knew I had to hold him in if the magazine was to survive. The conversation went back and forth: Warren would come within an inch of pulling out, and I would slowly try to pull him back. Then the dance would be repeated. Warren, who did not get to be a billionaire by being slow-witted, kept finding new escape routes, each of which had enough instant plausibility to put me into a state of near panic. My mind went into its highest gear as I tried to block the exits.

Finally, he agreed to stay in. I have never been more keyed up than at that moment...Warren's sympathetic side had won out over the hard-boiled investor. (pp. 174-5)

Peters said his investors rarely called for favors, and when they did, they were innocent. "Warren, for example, asked me to introduce him to Kay Graham, which I did, and it turned out to be a very good thing for both of them. He became her principal financial advisor and the leading minority holder of Washington Post Co. stock. They have made each other a lot richer than either was before they met. I should have asked for 10%." (pp. 196-7)

33

THE WASHINGTON POST
A PERFECT PITCH

Buffett bought his stock in The Washington Post Company during the spring and summer of 1973 for $10.6 million, making Berkshire the largest shareholder of The Post Co. outside the Graham family.

"Did it with about 20 orders over a several-month period," he said later. "Sometimes in life things happen very fast."

He knew Post Chairman Katharine Graham, saw the stock had gone public and wasn't doing well, "and I knew that the *Post* was going to outdo *The Star*, not necessarily make it fold, but outdo it."

In her book, *Personal History*, a Pulitzer Prize winner, Mrs. Graham wrote: "Warren Buffett, whose company, Berkshire Hathaway, bought about 10% of the company's B shares in 1973, later told me he didn't think we really had to go public but was glad we had. In fact I was glad we had, too, although I still dislike some of the responsibilities being public entails. The advent of Warren was only one of the positive things that resulted from our going public. The date of the stock offering was set for June 15. In a ceremony on the floor of the American Stock Exchange, I bought the first share for $24.75, and we went public at $26 a share." (p. 442)

Buffett's stake would turn out to be one of his most remarkable investments, one that he bought early when there was no particular interest in media stocks and that he held even after the *Post* had a near monopoly in Washington, D.C. The Post Co. went public in 1971. Its Class B common stock was issued at $6.50 a share, split adjusted, and over the years has risen to about $550 a share, compounding about 16% a year. The Class A stock, which controls elections of two-thirds of the board and therefore the company, is held by the Graham family.

Buffett's lifelong interest in media properties—epitomized by his purchase of Post Co. shares—always has gone far beyond cash flows. He is genuinely interested in media businesses, claims top journalists as friends and has said that if business had not been his calling, journalism might have been.

After all, his parents met while they worked at the school news-

(AP/Wide World Photos)

Washington Post's Donald Graham, left, Katharine Graham and Ben Bradlee are FOBs—Friends of Buffett. Donald Graham once said of Buffett, "In finance, he's the smartest guy I know. I don't know who is second."

paper and Buffett was once an industrious *Post* delivery boy.

He has a reporter's instinct for the story, and his search for under-valued businesses combines a sharp business sense and a reporter's detective skills. Had Buffett become a journalist, he would have been a terrific one, but no matter what, he would not have made a tiny fraction of what he has earned as an investor.

In 1973 there were about 14 million shares of Post Co. stock out-standing, of which 2.7 million Class A controlling shares were owned by Mrs. Graham. She is the daughter of the late Eugene Meyer, a wealthy Republican Wall Street industrialist and financier who bought the paper in 1933 for $825,000, when his daughter was 16. Meyer named her husband, Philip Graham, publisher, in 1946.

By 1973, the beginning of the severe 1973-74 stock market slump, Post Co. stock had dropped from its original $6.50 issue price to $4 a share, adjusted for later stock splits. Buffett struck, buy-ing his $10.6 million of Post stock, a 12% stake of the Class B stock or about 10% of the total stock.

The $4 price implied about $80 million evaluation of the whole company, which was debt free at a time when Buffett figured the enterprise had an intrinsic worth of $400 million. Yet it was not until 1981 that the market capitalization of The Post Co. was $400 million.

Buffett, in a talk to Columbia business students October 27, 1993 said:

> If you had asked anyone in the business what their properties were worth, they'd have said $400 million or something like that. You could have an auction in the middle of the Atlantic Ocean at two in the morning, and you would have people to show up and bid that much for them. And it was being run by honest and able people who all had a significant part of their net worth in the business. It was ungodly safe. It wouldn't have bothered me to put my whole net worth in it. Not in the least.

The Post Co.'s revenues in 1973 were about $200 million. Subsidiaries included the *Washington Post* newspaper, *Newsweek* magazine, the Times-Herald Company, four television stations and a paper company that provided most of its newsprint.

Since one rule of thumb is that good newspapers may sell for about two and a half times annual revenues, The Post Co. was worth four times what Buffett paid. Buffett has said the reason he could buy Post stock at a great price was because people just weren't very enthusiastic about the world at the time.

After Buffett's purchase, the stock fell for the next two years, and Buffett's investment sank from $10 million in 1973 to $8 million in late 1974. Post Co. stock did not move solidly ahead of Buffett's purchase price until 1976. Now the stake is worth about $1 billion.

Mrs. Graham tried to get a fix on this fellow from Omaha. "I scurried and said 'Who is he and what's he like and is he a threat?' "

In the beginning Buffett was not a welcome guest. Andre Meyer, a family friend of Mrs. Graham's, (but no relation to her parents, Eugene and Agnes Meyer) was upset when he found out Buffett had taken a big stake in the Post Co. (*Financier, The Biography of Andre Meyer*, by Cary Reich, 1983, p. 90)

"He was irate when one of the country's most successful private investors, Warren Buffet [sic], took a substantial position in Post Co. shares. As someone who had done that sort of thing himself, Meyer was naturally suspicious of Buffet's [sic] motives...

"Andre kept warning me about Warren Buffett," Mrs. Graham recalled. "He regarded all people who bought into companies uninvited as threats. But I checked Warren out rather carefully and decided that we were quite lucky, in that he was a very hands-off and honorable man."

Although Buffett convinced Mrs. Graham, Meyer kept after her, asking, "How is your boss?"

After his investment, Buffett wrote to Mrs. Graham, who still had much concern about this largely unknown man who was buying so much Post Co. stock. Buffett told her he was no threat to her position and he fully understood she controlled the company through her ownership of the company's Class A stock.

"I recognize that the *Post* is Graham-controlled and Graham-managed. And that suits me fine," he wrote her. The letter was later jokingly referred to as the "Dear Mrs. Graham" letter. (*Regardie's*, February, 1986)

One thing that may have broken the ice: Buffett was able to remind her he had worked for the *Post* as a paperboy 25 years earlier. By the way, in delivering the *Post* in the 1940s, Buffett earned about half of his initial investment money as a youngster.

"Buffett had asked Charles Peters, an acquaintance of Kay's, to make the introduction in 1971. Buffett had a specific reason for wanting to meet her: he owned stock in *The New Yorker*, which he believed might be for sale, and he wanted to interest Kay in attempting a takeover, arguing that the *Post* would be the perfect owner for the magazine. Kay dismissed his suggestion." (*Power, Privilege and The Post*, Carol Felsenthal, p. 321)

Katharine Graham, in her book *Personal History* (p. 531) said they had not met again until 1973, at the office of the Los Angeles *Times*. This was after Buffett's Post Co. purchase. Reassured by the encounter, Mrs. Graham asked Buffett to come to dinner in Washington and take a look at the *Post*. A strong friendship and a profitable relationship were born as Buffett became her business mentor.

> In late June 1974... "I combined an analysts' meeting in Los Angeles with a visit to Warren and Susie at their house in Laguna Beach. Warren's family was convulsed with laughter about my visit, because Warren, who theretofore had never been known to go near water despite having vacationed in Laguna since 1962, actually bought a beach umbrella and swimsuit so as to make my visit more enjoyable. He said this was the 'source of enormous merriment in our house...because of this incredible—compared to what my family was used to—standard of flexibility I would show around you.' The visit was an intense and happy two days, during which he and I talked about many things, including the possibility of his coming on the board of The Washington Post Company.

In 1974 Buffett was named to the Post Co. board and, appropriately, chaired its finance committee. Soon he suggested the board buy back Post Co. stock. Few companies in the 1970s were doing stock buybacks and very few, if any, in the media business were buying back their own shares.

Warren's advice and steady communication with me were critical to a number of actions I took in these years. Crucially, he persuaded me of the benefits of buying in our own stock. I had been suspicious of the idea. Repurchasing stock is a commonplace today, but only a handful of companies were doing it in the mid-1970s. I felt that, if we spent all of our money buying in our own stock, we wouldn't be able to grow. Warren went through the numbers with me, showing me what this action could do for the company in the long run, or even in the short run. He re-emphasized how low the stock was compared with its real value and how this was a better business move than many we were contemplating. He gradually made his point: if we bought in 1% of the stock in the Post Company, everyone owned a larger share of our stock at a bargain price. I decided we should do it. (*Personal History*, Katharine Graham, p. 577)

Mrs. Graham has since said Buffett is: "eternally interesting and fun to be with." (*The New Yorker*, March 20, 2000)

Here's how what was to become Buffett's hallmark—the stock buy-back—worked for the Post Company. Between 1975 and 1992, the Post Co. bought back about 43% of its outstanding shares. Average cost: $60 a share. So it bought back more than 40% of its business at roughly a tenth of its present price. By 2000 The Post had bought back half of its stock meaning shareholders owned twice as much of its properties.

Also, Buffett suggested that the Post's pension fund switch from a large bank to managers with a value orientation. After the move to value managers, returns rose substantially even though The Post told the managers to keep at least 25% of the money in bonds.

Warren and I were driving down to Glen Welby for the weekend [one day in 1979] when, as tactfully and gently as he could, he broke the news to me that Bill Ruane and Sandy Gottesman, close friends of his and investors who had bought a lot of *Post* stock for themselves and for their clients, were going to sell tens of millions of dollars' worth of it. Ruane managed the Sequoia Fund, and Gottesman was a managing partner at the First Manhattan Company, and these groups were about to sell all or half of their Post stock.

Warren had pondered how best to deliver this news, and he tried sugar-coating it in every way he could. I have to admit that my immediate response was to burst into tears. Here were these terribly clever investors, reputed to have such great judgement, who no longer believed in us; others surely would be leaving in droves. I considered their move a referendum on my management of the company, and it was clear I was found wanting.

Warren did his desperate best to console me, explaining that Bill considered he had done so well on Post stock that it added up to too much of some of his portfolios. He was keeping his own stock. "You don't know Wall Street," Warren tried to reassure me. "People don't think in a longterm way there. When your stock reaches $100, Wall Street will buy it." Naturally, I thought he was just trying to make me feel better; it was absurd to think that the stock would ever reach $100. I was not consoled.

Warren, of course, had a totally different perspective from mine on what Bill and Sandy were doing. He viewed it as an enormous plus in the lifetime of the company, almost like the *Times-Herald* merger. Though he knew I'd be profoundly distressed by the idea, he realized right away how much the company would benefit in future profits by their selling their stock. He tried to convince me that we should be holding a party, adding, "Don't worry. We'll just buy what they sell. It will be good for us and they'll regret it." Although I didn't stop worrying, we did buy in the stock at an average price of $21.91, which Sandy and Bill had bought before two splits at an equivalent price of $6.50.

Once, much later, Warren and I discussed women bursting into tears in business situations and I reminded him of our ride to Glen Welby. "Well," he said, smiling, "we made several hundred million dollars then. The next time you burst into tears call me first." He added, "Look at it this way, Kay. If you hadn't bought it in, I would have burst into tears, so one of us had to cry." (*Personal History*, Katharine Graham, pp. 591-592)

Buffett served on The Post Co. board until 1986, when he resigned after Berkshire committed $517 million to help Cap Cities buy ABC. The resulting company became media giant Cap Cities/ABC and Buffett was invited on its board.

Buffett had to leave The Post Co. board because Federal Communications Commission rules prohibited an individual from serving simultaneously as a director both of a company that owns a television network (Cap Cities/ABC) and also one that owns cable television systems.

A similar prohibition applies to overlaps of television signals from stations owned by different companies such as Cap Cities' New York station and The Post Co.'s Hartford, Connecticut station. This overlap also prohibited Buffett from serving on both boards at the same time.

If Mrs. Graham ever had reservations about Buffett or his intentions, they have long since vanished. "Our board was just devastated by his departure. They really miss him," she was quoted in *The Wall Street Journal.* (September 30, 1987)

The devastation did not last forever. After Disney bought Cap Cities in 1996, Buffett was re-elected. He was back on board. Buffett and Mrs. Graham remain close friends and today she sings his praises. "He has wisdom, human sensitivity and above all humor. I think it's a unique combination," Mrs. Graham told Adam Smith, host of *Money World,* in a show about the Berkshire annual meeting of April 30, 1990.

In 1987 Buffett gave a talk to the Center for Communicators in New York where Mrs. Graham was the guest of honor. Buffett recounted the success of the Post. "Warren also joked to the group that he had once found a sheet of paper prominently displayed on my desk that said, "Assets on the left, liabilities on the right." (*Personal History*, Katharine Graham, p. 620)

Buffett joked, not very convincingly, about his lack of influence at The Post Co., citing as an example his lack of a role in The Post Co.'s decision to sell some cellular phone properties. "My only role with Washington Post Co.'s sale of the cellular phone properties was to recommend against the original purchase of the properties at one fifth of the price they sold it for. And that's the last time they asked. They didn't pay attention to me the first time and they didn't ask the second time," he said at Berkshire's 1987 Annual Meeting.

But it's apparent Buffett remains a trusted friend of Mrs. Graham's.

Mrs. Graham's son, Donald Graham, is publisher and Rhodes Scholar Boisfeuillet (looks like the most difficult word in a spelling bee. The preferred spelled is Bo.) Jones is associate publisher and a classmate of Graham's at St. Albans and Harvard. Graham was editor of the Harvard *Crimson,* graduated from Harvard, served in

Vietnam and later worked as a policeman in Washington, D.C. He became a *Post* reporter in 1971. About 95% of Donald Graham's net worth is in Post stock.

Donald Graham has said of Buffett, "In finance, he is the smartest guy I know. I don't know who is second." He has since said: "I quickly saw that this was the smartest person I had ever met. Warren talks so clearly that, in a way, he's very deceptive. A lot of us flatter ourselves that we are all influenced by him, but we always know there are deeper layers within him that we can't see. It's like saying my chess is influenced by Gary Kasperov or my basketball by Michael Jordan." (*The New Yorker*, March 20, 2000)

Buffett thinks Graham is a smart fellow himself and over the years has spent time tutoring him, "sending him annotated balance sheets and teaching him how to judge the value of acquisitions." Graham adopted Buffett's business philosophy of paying for quality and skimping on frills. (*Washingtonian*, August, 1992)

"Once, a group of Post board members was standing around kibitzing, waiting for Donald Graham to show up, and Robert McNamara bet them nobody could name Abraham Lincoln's first vice president. Nobody could. Buffett then bet $5 that Don would know the answer. 'Sure,' Graham said when he arrived, 'It was Hannibal Hamlin.'

"Don is incredibly smart, and his memory is off the charts," says Buffett. "If I try to remember something from my annual reports, he can quote it back. It's easier to call him than to look it up myself." It was The Post Co. investment—a more than 50-fold return on his money—that locked up Buffett's reputation as a master investor. Over the years the *Post* strengthened its dominance of the city's newspaper industry, but the path was not always easy. Coverage of the Watergate scandal, particularly by Bob Woodward and Carl Bernstein, did bring the paper enormous acclaim, including a Pulitzer Prize in 1973 for their stories that led to President Nixon's resignation in 1974.

"Deep Throat," the anonymous source of some of the "Woodstein" stories became synonymous for anything smacking of investigative journalism.

Once Woodward asked Buffett a good way to make more money and Buffett suggested investing. Woodward told Buffett, "I don't know anything about investing."

"Yes, you do." Buffett said, "All it is, is investigative reporting."

In 1954, the *Post*, then the third-ranking newspaper in the capital city, bought *The Times-Herald*—buying its 3,500 shares for $1,600 a share or $5.6 million. The paper's rapid growth swept it past the *Washington Star*, which wilted under the competition from the *Post* and folded in 1981.

But before that, The Post Co. faced in rapid order three major problems: the stock market plunge of 1973-74, the Watergate crisis, with all the glory and headaches it brought the *Post*, and a crippling strike in 1975. In 1972 and 1973, The Post Co.'s stock price was sinking because of withering criticism the paper was receiving from the Nixon White House for its Watergate coverage.

At the height of Watergate, according to the Nixon tapes, Nixon encouraged talk of revoking the licenses for The Post Co.'s two Florida television stations, WJXT/TV4 in Jacksonville and WPLG/TV in Miami, the station whose call letters are taken from the initials of Philip L. Graham, the deceased husband of Mrs. Graham.

The license revocations were pushed by a number of people with associations to the Nixon administration, but they were never successful, according to Chalmers Roberts, a long-time *Post* reporter who has written *In the Shadow of Power: The Story of The Washington Post*.

The Watergate scandal was one financial blow; the bitter strike that occurred at the paper in 1975 was worse. Even as the paper prevailed in the Watergate crisis, a new problem was brewing—relations with its unions. In late 1975 the unions went on strike. The strike's ugliest moment came with the trashing of the pressrooms, a blow to both the finances and pride of the mighty newspaper.

Mrs. Graham was uneasy about the risk of holding out, particularly in view of competition from the *Star*.

The strike helped cement the relationship between Buffett and Mrs. Graham. "Characteristically, Buffett—who was 'omnipresent at the *Post*,' according to a former employee—plays down his role. 'I was around,' he says." (*Regardie's*, February, 1986)

Mrs. Graham said, "The strike was terribly hard on me, in the sense of judging how dangerous it was [financially] for us to be on strike with the *Star* publishing. He said, 'Look, if I think it's dangerous, I'll tell you.' He was very supportive." Buffett and Mrs. Graham worked side by side in the *Post's* mailroom more than once, sometimes staying until 3 a.m. to assemble the Sunday papers for distribution.

In her book *Personal History*, Katharine Graham wrote:

> It was a tough job that left us filthy, sweaty, and covered with paste. We had to roll up each individual paper in a

brown wrapper, paste on an address label, seal the whole thing shut, and throw the finished, wrapped package into the big, smelly, heavy, and unwieldy canvas bags at the side of the worktable, which we then dragged over to another station from which they were finally hauled off to the post office. This was the only time in my life that I regretted the substantial circulation the *Post* had outside of Washington. The whole job was so tedious and interminable that we came to look on it as our supreme service for the cause, the ultimate sacrifice. Warren Buffett, who spent several Saturday nights in the mailroom with us, said it made him rethink the price of the Sunday paper—no price was sufficient. (*Personal History*, Katharine Graham, p. 550)

We were all there at the *Post* on the night of November 4. It was a dramatic moment, with rumors of printers and pressmen carrying guns. Coincidentally, Warren Buffett and his wife Susie, were right across the street from the paper, staying in the Madison Hotel, having come to town for their close-up look at The Washington Post Company and for a dinner in their honor at my house the next night. They were looking out their window all night at the commotion, the lights, and the television cameras. It wasn't a very auspicious beginning for this new stockholder to observe what was happening at *The Washington Post.* (p. 523)

We had made a serious mistake in letting the pressmen back into the pressroom, but amazingly, they had printed a paper totally prepared by nonunion labor and cold type. The wildcat strike had taught both the unions and management quite a bit. Nevertheless, when the printers came back to work, they resumed slowdowns and production disruptions.

I went home that morning at about six, tired and depressed, and only then did I remember that I had forty people coming to a black-tie dinner that night at my house for the Buffetts. Since I had been up all night I thought of canceling, but it seemed easier to go ahead with it. Warren still recalls his introduction to Washington life, sitting between Barbara Bush and Jane Muskie.

We had scheduled a lunch at the *Post* the next day so that Warren could meet with various people on both the business and editorial sides of the paper. There was some talk of acquisitions, and someone mentioned the problem of amortization of goodwill being a disadvantage in a company like ours, because of its accounting impact. Howard Simons, always a delightful but mischievous goad, looked at me and said, "Now Katharine, how does that amortization of goodwill work?" The conversation stopped for a second, Warren recalled, and "I could see this look on your face like he'd asked you to explain Einstein's theory of relativity with several corollaries. Here was my chance to be a hero. So I jumped in and explained in a fairly succinct way how it worked." When Warren finished his explanation, I looked at Howard and said, "Exactly." (p. 524)

Buffett kept encouraging Mrs. Graham and guiding her business education. "Warren saw how little I knew about business. He would bring about 25 or 30 annual reports and take me through them," Mrs. Graham has said.

During these tumultuous events, Buffett hung steadfast and in the end his investment grew mightily.

In 1984 Buffett wrote Mrs. Graham:

Berkshire Hathaway bought its shares in *The Washington Post* in the spring and summer of 1973. The cost of these shares was $10.6 million and the present market value is about $140 million....If we had spent this same $10.6 million at the same time in the shares of...other media companies...we would now have either $60 million worth of Dow Jones, $30 million worth of Gannett, $75 million worth of Knight-Ridder, $60 million worth of *The New York Times* or $40 million of *Times Mirror*.

So—instead of thanks a million—make it thanks anywhere from $65 to $110 million. (*The Midas Touch*, John Train, p. 77)

Now make it thanks a billion—and still growing.

Throughout the 1980s, The Post Co. racked up tremendous financial gains and journalistic recognition in the form of Pulitzer Prizes. Today the Post Co. oversees a vast journalistic enterprise with a stock market value of well above $5 billion. The Post Co.'s interests include the *Washington Post*, by far the most influential paper in one of the world's most important cities. Daily circulation of the *Post* is about 800,000 and Sunday circulation is 1.1 million.

The Post Co. owns *The Herald*, in Everett, Washington.

In recent years, the *Post* has surpassed its bigger archrival, *The New York Times*, in profitability and stock market value. In addition to the *Post* newspaper which accounts for about half of The Post Co.'s profits, the company owns *Newsweek*, the national news weekly with

3.2 million subscribers which has long run second in circulation to its main competitor, *Time* magazine. The Post Co. bought *Newsweek* in 1961 for $15 million. In 1995 *Newsweek* made that much in operating profit and $38 million in 1997.

The Post Co., which has about 6,000 employees, also owns six television stations: WDIV/TV4 in Detroit, WPLG/TV10 in Miami [traded stations with Meredith Corp.], WCPX in Orlando, changed to WKMG in honor of Katharine Meyer Graham in 1998 [after trading CBS stations with Meredith Corp. in 1997], WJXT/TV4 in Jacksonville. It bought KPRC-TV in Houston and KSAT-TV in San Antonio in 1994 for $253 million. Also, it owns a large cable television franchise it bought from Cap Cities in 1986 for $350 million when the franchise had about 360,000 subscribers. Buffett was a central figure in the transaction. The Post Co.'s Cable One cable operations are based in Phoenix, Arizona, and have grown through acquisitions and new subscribers to about 739,000 subscribers. The cable business is vastly more profitable than when it was acquired.

Kaplan and the Internet are two fast-growing areas of The Washington Post Company, according to its president, Alan Spoon.

In a presentation in 1999 to the Mid-Year Media Review, Spoon said: "This year, for the first time, we're breaking out Kaplan's financial results. Because Kaplan itself is composed of a number of different operations, I'd like to give you a brief overview of the companies' activities and their relative contribution to Kaplan. I can't promise we'll provide this level of detail on a regular basis—no doubt we'll soon return to our normal, more reticent mode. But this can be a benchmark for you to understand and evaluate Kaplan's progress."

Kaplan's revenues more than tripled in the past three years with revenues of about $280 million in 1999. The sales were produced by six Kaplan units:
- Test Prep and Admissions
- Kaplan Professional
- Score! Educational Centers
- Kaplan Learning Services
- Kaplan University (a long distance learning operation)
- Kaplan Interactive

The Post Co. owns the Stanley H. Kaplan Company (now called the Kaplan Educational Center), bought in 1984 from founder

Stanley Kaplan for a reported $33 million. Its locations prepare students for licensing exams and admissions tests, including the revamped Scholastic Aptitude Test. In turn, Kaplan owns Crimson and Brown Associates of Cambridge, Massachusetts, a collegiate recruiting firm that helps employers identify, interview and hire hard-to-find candidates. Kaplan also owns Score, a San Francisco firm that provides after-school educational services for children in grades K through 12. Score, renamed Score@Kaplan, has centers nationwide. Kaplan is headed by Jonathan Grayer, a young Harvard business school graduate. The 1996 Post Annual Report referred to Grayer as the "aging president" of Kaplan. He was 32 then.

In 2000 Kaplan, digging deeper into "Webucation", launched Kaplan College.com, a site offering 500 courses across nine professions.

The Post Co. owned 28% of Cowles Media Company which publishes the *Minneapolis Star Tribune* and other properties which were sold to McClatchy in 1997. It owns one half, as does *The New York Times*, of the *International Herald Tribune* newspaper published in Paris and printed in eight cities, which circulates both *Post* and *New York Times* stories in almost 200 countries. *The International Tribune* has a circulation of about 200,000.

Also the Post's media subsidiary—Washingtonpost Newsweek Interactive (WPNI) is responsible for about half of the company's Internet-related efforts which include Washingtonpost.com and Newsweek.com.

Spoon said there is extraordinary growth of internet usage in the Washington, D.C. area. "Not only is Washington home of the internet—after all, as everyone knows Vice President Al Gore invented it right here in D.C.—Washington also has the largest Internet penetration of any market in the country...

"And not surprisingly, we're home to a large and growing number of Web-based companies too long to list. Employment in Washington's 'InfoComm' industry now totals over 345,000. It has surpassed the federal government and will never look back!"

The Post Co. owns half of the Los Angeles-Washington Post News Service which supplies news, features and commentary to more than 768 clients in 50 countries.

In March 1992, The Post Co. acquired an 80% stake in Gaithersburg Gazette, Inc., the parent firm of Gazette Newspapers which now has 32 weekly newspapers in Maryland. The weeklies have a combined circulation of 493,000.

The Post also has 12 weekly newspapers at military bases in the region, including the *Beam* at Bolling Air Force Base, the *Trident* at the U.S. Naval Academy, and *Stripe* at Walter Reed Army Medical Center.

Berkshire now owns about an 18% share of all the Post Co.'s wonderful businesses, up from the original 10% of the company Buffett bought in 1973. Over the years, with the Post Co. buying back a portion of its own stock, Buffett's ownership percentage has bloomed.

🐿 🐿 🐿 🐿 🐿 🐿 🐿 🐿 🐿 🐿 🐿 🐿 🐿

The Washington Post was founded at the end of Reconstruction in 1877 by young Stilson Hutchins, a restless man originally from Whitefield, New Hampshire.

"That first edition of *The Washington Post* had four pages, each with seven columns, printed on rag paper," wrote Chalmers Roberts in his book, *In the Shadow of Power.*

As a journalist, Hutchins was on top of the breaking story that Thomas Edison was making headway with his invention of an electric lamp. He interviewed Edison on the last day of 1879 and on January 2, 1880, a front-page story by him began:

> New York, January 1, 1880,—I went over to Menlo Park (New Jersey) yesterday afternoon and evening to see Edison and his electric light. The workshop was crowded with people, who arrive and depart by almost every train. They are inquisitive and troublesome, but, notwithstanding the annoyance they frequently cause, they are treated with consideration and politeness. Edison is not only a great inventor, but has as much patience as Job.
>
> In all about sixty lights are constantly maintained and others are being added daily. The first lights are still burning, having been in steady operation for twenty-two days. The little carbon horseshoe, as it is called, seems not to have lost an atom of its weight or abated a particle of its illuminating power. If it will last twenty-two days without deterioration or loss there seems no reason why it should not last twenty-two years or an age. So far as the experiment has gone it is literally indestructible. Mr. Edison considers this feature of his invention as perfected, and, as is well known, it was the one over which he has spent the most time and which the world considered unattainable...

Hutchins was so taken with the coming of electricity that he was largely responsible for the electrification of Washington, D.C. Hutchins' was the first of three ownerships before the paper began its modern life in 1933 when Meyer bought it at auction in a bankruptcy sale at the depth of the Depression.

A lawyer, George E. Hamilton, Jr.—representing Meyer, the undisclosed principal, who authorized his representative to bid as high as $2 million— won the paper with a bid of $825,000.

The *Post* on Friday, June 2, 1933, carried the headline: "*Washington Post* sold for $825,000."

Chalmers Roberts wrote: "Rumors of the real buyer's identity floated about the capital but Hamilton would disclose nothing...On June 4 The [*Washington*] *Star* carried a Meyer denial to the AP story in New York that he was the buyer. There was a ten-day delay for the necessary court approval...On Tuesday, June 13, *The Post* carried at the top of page 1 a two column box headed: "Eugene Meyer announced as *Washington Post* buyer.*"

Meyer dedicated his time, energy and considerable fortune to making the *Post* viable. The *Post* rang up a long string of losses. But Meyer's integrity, hands-on management and constant financial support saved the *Post*.

Roberts again: "The *Post's* deficits were massive: $323,588 for the last half of 1933 after Meyer took over: $1,191,597 in 1934; $1,279,262 in 1935; $857,156 in 1936 and $838,937 in 1937. 'One year,' Meyer later remarked to a friend, paying the *Post's* losses 'took more than my entire income.' To another he said, 'No one is rich enough to keep that up.' But not only did Meyer keep on paying the losses, he plunged ahead to improve his paper."

The losses continued through the early World War II years. After nine and a half years of losses under Meyer, it finally rang up profits of $247,451 from 1942-1945. In 1946 President Truman asked Meyer to be the first president of the World Bank.

Enter Philip Graham, who had married Meyer's daughter, Katharine. Meyer was so impressed with the vitality and charm of Graham, who had graduated 10th in a class of 400 at Harvard Law School in 1939 and had been head of the Law Review, that Meyer prepared to hand over the reins of the Post Co. to young Graham.

In 1948 Meyer announced the transfer of voting stock to Philip and Katharine Graham saying that Graham would hold 3,500 shares and his wife 1,500 shares of the 5,000 voting shares.

Meyer explained to Graham: "You never want a man working for his wife." (*In the Shadow of Power*, Chalmers Roberts, p. 258)

The relationship between Meyer and Graham was very close and Graham quickly became a brilliant leader of the Post Co. He set out to make it a journalistic and financial success and succeeded at both.

The real turning point for the *Post* came in 1954 when it bought the *Times-Herald* and became the sole morning paper in the nation's capital. The purchase doubled its circulation and sent ad revenues jumping.

"The purchase capped Eugene Meyer's two-decade gamble with the *Post* and it left no doubt that Philip Graham, now 39, would be a major figure in American journalism," Roberts wrote.

At the time Meyer said: "The real significance of this event is that it makes the paper safe for Donnie (his grandson)."

Philip Graham was a publisher bursting with ideas: pushing The Post Co. into television in a big way, buying *Newsweek* in 1961 and buying an interest in Bowater Mersey Paper Co.—the firm that supplies most of the paper's newsprint. Graham also developed a close friendship with President John Kennedy. Everything was going his way, but then something went terribly wrong.

Graham began suffering periodically from a manic-depressive illness in 1957; on August 3, 1963, he was allowed to leave a psychiatric care facility, and with Katharine Graham, drove to Glen Welby, their farm near Marshall, Virginia, for a weekend outing.

As the *Post* reported the next day: "Shortly after 1 p.m. while Mrs. Graham was in her room upstairs, Mr. Graham killed himself with a .28-gauge sportsman's shotgun. He was alone in a first-floor room." Graham was 48.

Responsibility for The Post Co. fell immediately upon Mrs. Graham, who had worked as an editor at the paper, but her interest in journalism or business was limited at the time. Her main credentials: her father had owned the paper and her husband had run it.

"When my husband died I had three choices," she has said. "I could sell it. I could find somebody to run it. Or I could go to work. And that was no choice at all. I went to work...It was simply inconceivable to me to dismantle all that my father and my husband had built with so much labor and love."

Once asked if she wasn't terrified, she replied, "congealed." Nevertheless, she built the *Post* into one of the best newspapers in the country, one known for investigative reporting, stylish prose and business success.

Under her leadership, the newspaper and its reporters won 18 Pulitzer Prizes. One Pulitzer had to be returned in 1981 because the winning entry turned out to be a fictitious story by Janet Cooke about a young drug user ("Jimmy's World").

Her first major change at the *Post* was to name self-confident Benjamin Bradlee as managing editor, moving longtime friend and managing editor Al Friendly upstairs to the London bureau. Bradlee, who later occasionally played tennis with Buffett, energized a highly talented and competitive newsroom.

Bradlee was fond of "holy s—" stories. So what's a "holy s—" story? Here's an example from *Bird by Bird* (p. 13-14), a book about how to write by Anne Lamott:

> My son, Sam, at three and a half, had these keys to a set of plastic handcuffs, and one morning he intentionally locked himself out of the house. I was sitting on the couch reading the newspaper when I heard him stick his plastic keys into the doorknob and try to open the door. Then I heard him say, "Oh, s—." My whole face widened, like the guy in Edward Munch's *Screams*. After a moment I got up and opened the front door.
>
> "Honey," I said, "what'd you just say?"
>
> "I said, 'Oh, s—,' " he said.
>
> "But, honey, that's a naughty word. Both of us have absolutely got to stop using it. Okay?"
>
> He hung his head for a moment, nodded, and said, "Okay, Mom." Then he leaned forward and said confidentially, "But I'll tell you why I said 's—.' " I said Okay, and he said, "Because of the f—ing keys!"

Some years later Bradlee was one of the heroes of both the 1971 publication of the Pentagon Papers, top-secret documents about Vietnam, and the Watergate scandal from 1972 to 1974.

Publishing the Pentagon Papers in 1971 gave The Post Co. plenty to worry about. The decision to do so came in the midst of plans for the privately held company to make a multi-million-dollar public stock offering. Indeed the day before the public offering, Bradlee asked Kay Graham to publish the Pentagon Papers story.

"The Justice Department had sent her a pre-publication message threatening to prosecute the company, which could have resulted in the forfeiture of its broadcast licenses if convicted," wrote Donald Graham in the company's 1991 annual report in a tribute to his mother.

Bradlee argued nonpublication would make the *Post* appear cowardly and also said the *Post* could start running the story the next day or get a new executive editor. *(Newsweek,* July 1, 1991) Mrs. Graham's response to Bradlee was "Okay, go ahead, go ahead!"

The *Post's* finest hour came with its coverage of Watergate. For the *Post*, Watergate began with a call from Joseph A. Califano, Jr., then general counsel of the Democratic National Committee, to Howard Simons, the paper's managing editor, telling him of a break-in at the party headquarters at the Watergate office building.

Simons put the paper to work immediately after the June 17, 1972, break-in.

The *Post* ran a story the next day on the top left side of page 1 of the 306-page Sunday *Post* with the headline: "5 Held in Plot to Bug Democrats' Office Here."

Two of the eight reporters contributing to the lengthy account were Bob Woodward and Carl Bernstein, a duo with a definite nose for news. A new era in investigative journalism was underway. "Deep Throat"—taken from the title of a pornographic movie of the time—epitomized the critical importance of confidential sources.

Later some reporters on a medical story developed a source who came to be known as "Sore Throat." That one didn't stick.

A new age in journalism spawned a new age in counterattack as evidenced by Roberts' account (pp. 437-8):

> As the Nixon tapes would show, the attack on the *Post* had been planned at least as early as September 15, 1972. On that day, in a conversation between Haldeman and John Dean, the President had said of the *Post*, "It's going to have its problems...The main thing is The Post is going to have damnable, damnable problems out of this one. They have a television station...and they're going to have to get it renewed." When Haldeman added, "They've got a radio station too," Nixon went on, "Does that come up, too? The point is, when does it come up?" Dean replied, "I don't know. But the practice of non-licensees filing on top of licensees has certainly gotten more...active in this area." And Nixon: "And it's going to be God damn active here...Well, the game has to be played awfully rough."

In January 1973, challenges were filed before the Federal Communications Commission against the renewal of The Post Co.'s two Florida television stations.

Mrs. Graham noted that all the challenges were filed by Nixon administration supporters, and in an affidavit said she believed the challenges were "a part of a White House-inspired effort to injure the...company in retaliation for its Watergate coverage."

The challengers denied the contention. In any event, The Post Co. kept its stations, but Post stock fell by nearly half. "During

Watergate, friends of the Nixon administration filed challenges to our television licenses in Florida. These cost a fortune to defend and caused our stock to plummet," Mrs. Graham said. (*Wall Street Journal*, March 20, 2000) As always, Buffett hung in there.

Woodward and Bernstein went on to write the book *All The President's Men*. The movie starring Robert Redford (Woodward), Dustin Hoffman (Bernstein) and Jason Robards (Bradlee) made the *Post* more famous.

Buffett, as were most Americans, was absorbed by the Watergate scandal and followed it closely on television and in the newspapers.

Much later in early 1998, The *Post* was the first to print the Monica Lewinsky story and *Newsweek* reporter Michael Isikoff had the first reports of the Monica Lewinsky investigation.

All through the bear markets, the Watergate scandal, and the strike, Buffett never sold one share of Post Co. stock. For his patience, he was well paid.

For decades the *Post* had struggled in its competition with the *Star*, but with the purchase of the *Times-Herald*, it became a much stronger competitor, soon racing by the *Star*. In 1981, the *Star* folded, making the *Post* essentially a monopoly newspaper in one of the world's most important cities, the U.S. capitol.

For Buffett and Berkshire shareholders, the 1980s were boom times as Buffett rode the tiger of one of his great ideas: that monopoly newspapers are bullet-proof "toll-bridges" that advertisers have to cross. Buffett seized on the monopoly, "toll-bridge" concept earlier and with more dramatic results than any other investor.

When customers can satisfy their buying needs by crossing only a particular monopoly toll bridge, there's nowhere else to cross. If you want to advertise, through the printed word at least, there's no other place to get your message across. It's the only game in town, a monopoly bulletin board.

Although the late 1970s and 1980s were boom times for The Post Co., its annual meetings were next to unbearable, marred by unreasonable questions from Accuracy in Media and other advocates, (questions often designed simply to embarrass Mrs. Graham and Donald Graham), and also dominated by harangues from corporate gadfly Evelyn Y. Davis.

One could go to a Post Co. Annual Meeting and hear several hours of political bickering and learn little about Post Co. businesses. The annual meeting aside, almost everything else at The Post Co. had the mark of great success during the 1980s. But by 1990 newspapers were facing the worst advertising environment in 20 years.

The recession of the early 1990s even caught up with Washington, D.C., and with retailing and real estate in tailspins, the *Post's* ad linage declined, earnings for the year fell, and Mrs. Graham was forced to write in the 1990 annual report that financial results were "very disappointing." Donald Graham later called 1991 a terrible year.

In 1991 both Mrs. Graham and Bradlee retired from their main jobs at the *Post* and were contemplating their memoirs. Bradlee's best-selling book, *A Good Life: Newspapering and Other Adventures* came out in 1995. Mrs. Graham came out in 1997 with *Personal History* which was also a bestseller.

The short-term air pockets that triggered the well-publicized nationwide recession in advertising were outlasting Buffett's expectations, but The Post Co. has remained a mighty enterprise even though it has become increasingly apparent that newspapers are no longer the only advertising game in town.

Big city newspapers, with advertising nosediving, were underpriced by small newspapers and magazines, by direct mail campaigns, more cable television channels and new technologies such as videotext.

The Post is well known for being savvy in journalism and business, but it is not perfect. In 1998 it sold its interest in Junglee, a facilitator of internet commerce. "With impeccable timing, we sold most of the Amazon.com stock we received for our Junglee interest just days before Amazon tripled," wrote Donald Graham in the Post's 1998 Annual Report.

He also wrote: "Because of brilliant management of our pension funds provided in great part by Bill Ruane over the past 20-plus years, The Washington Post Company's operating income now includes more than $60 million of pension credits. These earnings are real in that we will avoid spending that much of the company's money in the future on retirement benefits."

Graham added: "Shareholders also should know that late last year we invested $165 million in the stock of Berkshire Hathaway Inc. This was a late-breaking revelation. Had Messrs. Graham and Spoon made the same investment when they assumed their present jobs in 1991, the investment would be worth almost $1.5 billion. Berkshire's management needs no endorsement from us. Berkshire's purchase of General Re and the increasing strength of Berkshire's position in several industries attracted our interest. (Warren Buffett, our director, played no role whatever in our analysis or our decision to invest.) We hope to be long-time participants in the continued rise of this unique company."

The Post Co. and Buffett have treated one another well. Buffett is often invited to dinners at Mrs. Graham's home. It's an invitation for a formal dinner only the high and mighty get. But when she serves a gourmet meal, Buffett passes it up for a hamburger, fries and a sundae. "He has a limited palate," says Mrs. Graham. (*USA Today*, September 18, 1991)

The Buffett-Graham friendship goes far beyond dinner. Occasionally Buffett has written an article for the paper and when he first testified before Congress in connection with the Salomon scandal, Katharine Graham had a front row seat. Buffett was surrounded by reporters and photographers throughout his testimony and as he left the hearing room, they pursued him. But he eluded them and slipped into a limousine that took him to the *Washington Post*, where he met with the editorial board.

Buffett and the *Post* know all about scoops.

The story of the Post is one in which growth and value coincided. The Post was a perfect pitch.

Post Buys Berkshire Stock

And maybe buying Berkshire via General Re will turn out to be a perfect pitch for The Post. Actually, The Post swung too early, but then so did Buffett when he bought into The Post.

In 1998 The Post bought about $124 million of General Re stock as a roundabout and cheap way to get Berkshire stock.

"It was a very good opportunity" [read perfect pitch] said John Morse, the CFO at The Post, according to a *Bloomberg* news story (November 19, 1998).

Because the deal had not yet closed there was a small, but significant discount between General Re and Berkshire stock. For example, Berkshire closed at $59,000 on September 21, 1998. Buying an equivalent amount of Gen Re stock that day would have cost only $57,285. Therein lies an arbitrage bet, the risk being that the deal might not close.

Post officials said Buffett was not consulted about the investment. "He was not involved in that at all," Morse was quoted. "We told him of our decision to do it after the fact."

Of course it wasn't as though Buffett needed to be consulted. He's on the board and been a friend of the Post for decades. And it's not an investment idea about which Bill Ruane (on the Post board) or Katharine Graham or Donald Graham would be unaware.

Consulted or not, Buffett still came out ahead on the deal. That's because with Berkshire's 17% in the Post, that percentage of Gen Re shares was indirectly repurchased on behalf of Berkshire. Thus Berkshire was indirectly buying back its own stock via Gen Re at a discount.

The Post's 10-K statement said: "At January 3, 1999, the company's ownership of 747,100 shares of General Re Corporation ("General Re") common stock and 20 shares of Berkshire Hathaway, Inc. ("Berkshire") Class A common stock account for approximately 72 percent of the total fair value of the Company's investments in marketable equity securities. The investment in General Re and Berkshire common stock was acquired by the Company throughout the third and fourth quarters of 1998 from the open market for a total cost of $164,955,000. The gross unrealized gain on the General Re and Berkshire common stock totaled $19,485,000 at January 3, 1999."

It appears The Post added slightly to its Berkshire position in 1999. At yearend it owned 2,634 A shares and 9,845 B shares.

Also Washington Post employees have an unusual 401(k) option. They may buy Berkshire stock. (*Fortune*, October 25, 1999)

34
GEICO
"EACH WEEK 10,000 DRIVERS SWITCH TO GEICO."

Always looking for that edge, Buffett early on took a fancy to GEICO, the auto insurance company that sells by mail and telephone. In a seminal event, Berkshire now owns all of GEICO with the purchase in early 1996 of the half of GEICO it didn't already own. "We'll own GEICO forever," Buffett has said.

"[Ben] Graham paid $720,000 [in 1948] for the same percentage of GEICO for which Buffett in 1995 paid $2.3 billion." (*Value Investing Made Easy*, Janet Lowe, p. 170)

"When I first got interested in GEICO, Graham was chairman of Government Employees Insurance [GEICO] at the time. I took his class here at Columbia," Buffett said in a talk to Columbia business students, October 27, 1993.

"I went to the library...and looked it up... and it said it was located in Washington, D.C. So I went down there on a Saturday in January from Columbia. And I got there fairly early, 11 or so o'clock, and the door was locked. And I banged on the door for a while and finally a janitor came. And I said, is there anybody here I could talk to except you? Well, there was a guy up on the fifth floor, and the janitor said if you like, go up and see him.

"So I went up and met him. He's 90 or 91 years old now. His name's Lorimer Davidson. [Davidson died in 1999 at the age of 97.] At the time he was the investment officer there. He later became CEO. He spent about five hours with me that day. He explained the whole insurance business to me, how it worked and how GEICO worked. And I became totally enamored of it."

(Davidson said in a taped presentation at the Berkshire Annual Meeting in 1998 that he told young Buffett that day: "Next time please make an appointment and don't come on Saturday morning.")

"And then I came back to New York, back at school, and I went downtown to talk [to]...big insurance specialists. And every one of them told me that [GEICO] was way overpriced compared to these other companies, for all kinds of reasons. And it didn't make any sense to me..."

Only 21 at the time, Buffett invested $10,282 in GEICO in

1951. In 1952 he sold out for $15,259 mainly to switch the money into Western Insurance Securities selling at one times earnings.

Buffett told *Forbes*, October 18, 1993, "It [GEICO] was a company selling insurance at prices well below all the standard companies, and making 15% profit margins. It had an underwriting cost then of 13% or so, whereas the standard companies had probably 30% to 35% cost. It was a company with a huge competitive advantage, managed by the guy that was my god."

Eventually Buffett pitched the idea of buying GEICO to stockbrokers and found little interest. He sold his first 100 shares to his Aunt Alice. He could not convince investors of the promise of the business that sold directly to customers, bypassing agents and thereby making a 20% profit on its underwriting activities compared to the normal 5%.

In 1971 Jerome Newman, following Ben Graham into retirement, nominated Buffett to take his place on the board, but because Buffett had sizeable insurance investments, the SEC had reservations and the idea was dropped. (*Benjamin Graham on Value Investing*, Janet Lowe, p. 152)

The entire company, when Buffett bought in, had a market value of $7 million.

In 1976, because of a miscalculation of its claims and underpricing, GEICO was nearing bankruptcy. The stock had dropped from $61 to $2 a share.

That year Ben Graham was interviewed about GEICO and gave this reply:

Hartman L. Butler, Jr., C.F.A.: Do you think GEICO will survive?

Graham: Yes, I think it will survive. There is no basic reason why it won't survive, but naturally I ask myself whether the company did expand much too fast without taking into account the possibilities of these big losses. It makes me shudder to think of the amounts of money they were able to lose in one year. Incredible! It is surprising how many of the large companies have managed to turn in losses of $50 million or $100 million in one year, in these last few years. Something unheard of in the old days. You have to be a genius to lose that much money. (*Financial Analysts Journal*, November/December 1976. Copyright 1976, Financial Analysts Federation, Charlottesville, Va. as found in *The Rediscovered Benjamin Graham*, Janet Lowe, pp. 267-268)

GEICO founder Leo Goodwin left his stock to his son, Leo, Jr., who margined his shares and was hit by the stock's slide. Leo, Jr. committed suicide.

But Buffett believed that the company's competitive advantages were intact. Further, he had great confidence in a newly named chief executive, John J. Byrne (who retired as CEO of Fund American Enterprises in 1997).

In 1976 and during the following five years, Buffett invested $45.7 million in GEICO. Buffett's cost basis was $1.31 per share (adjusted for a 5-1 stock split in 1992). Buffett and Byrne, who went off to run Fireman's Fund in 1985, now called The Fund American Companies, became close friends. GEICO became a cornerstone of Berkshire's growth.

Byrne has said, "In a sense, GEICO sort of made Warren's financial career." (*Chicago Tribune*, December 8, 1985)

During its brush with bankruptcy, GEICO needed the help of an investment banker. Salomon Brothers' John Gutfreund backed the turnaround as did General Re.

"Charlie and I like, admire, and trust John. We first got to know him in 1976 when he played a key role in GEICO's escape from near bankruptcy," Buffett wrote in Berkshire's 1987 Annual Report.

Buffett has described his thinking on the GEICO purchase this way (*Investing in Equity Markets*, pp. 11-12):

> It wasn't necessarily bankrupt but it was heading there. It was 1976. It had a great business franchise which had not been destroyed by a lot of errors that had been made in terms of exploiting that franchise. And it had a manager...I felt he had the ability to get through an extraordinarily tough period there and to re-establish the value of that franchise. They still were a low-cost operator. They made all kinds of mistakes. They still didn't know their costs because they didn't know what their loss reserves should be and they got captivated by growth: they did all kinds of things wrong but they still had the franchise.
>
> It was similar to American Express in late 1963 when the salad oil scandal hit it. It did not hurt the franchise of the travelers check or the credit card. It could have ruined the balance sheet of American Express but the answer of course was that American Express with no net worth was worth a tremendous amount of money.
>
> And GEICO with no net worth was worth a tremendous amount of money too except it might get closed up the next

day because it had no net worth, but I was satisfied that the net worth would be there. The truth is a lot of insurance companies for the ownership of it would have put up the net worth. We would have put it up. But they were trying to save it for the shareholders, which is what they should have done. It had a very valuable franchise. Take away all the net worth. Let's just say that GEICO paid out a $500 million dividend right now which would eliminate the net worth of GEICO, would it still have a lot of value? Of course, it would have a lot of value. You'd have to do something, you'd have to be part of another entity that kept insurance regulators happy, but the franchise value is the big value in something like that...

GEICO is the nation's sixth largest insurer of private passenger vehicles with 6.6 million cars insured and 4.5 million policyholders. The policyholders pay GEICO about $1,200 a year on average for the promise of car insurance. It relies on direct marketing and offers a 24-hour, seven-day-a-week telephone line for customers to call in. "Each week, 10,000 drivers switch their car insurance to GEICO," said a GEICO flier inserted in Berkshire's 1995 Annual Report. And 30,000 drivers a week inquire about a switch and most of those continue to stay with GEICO with only a relatively small percentage leaving, often because they are too old to drive or have died.

The company has 500,000 policyholders in Florida and about 225,000 in Texas. Currently State Farm has about 20%; Allstate 12%; Farmers 6%; Nationwide 4%; Progressive 4%; GEICO 3½%; USAA 3%, and Travelers about 2%. "Warren has told us that in 10 years, he wants GEICO to have a 10% market share," according to GEICO CEO Tony Nicely. (*St. Petersburg Times*, December 15, 1999)

In July, 1999, a GEICO lawyer complained to Progressive that it was using such web sites as "www.geigo.com." It and a number of other mistypes led to a Progressive web site. A Progressive spokesman was quoted as saying the site was not approved by Progressive and that it had been set up by an online marketing partner called carsearch.com that gets fees for referring auto insurance shoppers to Progressive. The site was deactivated.

Since GEICO doesn't have to pay commissions to agents and sells directly to customers, it can undercut its competition because paying agents can cost about 15% of a company's premiums. GEICO markets by direct response methods in 48 states and the District of

Columbia.

Although most property and casualty companies usually lose money in some years on their underwriting, GEICO failed to make an underwriting profit only once in almost two decades. That means that almost every year the company is generating huge amounts of money to invest without having to pay anything for the money. For GEICO, that float is essentially an interest-free loan.

Insurers generally overcome their underwriting losses (There is drinking, bad weather and road rage out there.) by making profits from their investments, and here GEICO is well known for savvy investments. It is willing to invest more heavily in the stock markets than most insurance companies, usually outdistancing stock performance averages because of the stock-picking abilities of its co-CEO, Lou Simpson. Buffett has called Simpson the best investment person in the property-casualty industry.

GEICO was founded in 1936 in Texas by Leo Goodwin, an accountant for an insurance company, USAA, in San Antonio, Texas. By studying accident statistics, Goodwin learned that federal, state and municipal employees had fewer accidents than the general population. Of course, GEICO now insures good drivers in many occupations.

Buffett once said, "GEICO was founded by an official of USAA and his wife, Leo and Lillian Goodwin, in 1936. We stole the idea from (San Antonio based) USAA which insured military officers." (*San Antonio Express-News*, March 20, 1994)

And Goodwin also learned that the largest overhead expense for most casualty insurance companies is the cost of advertising and selling. He saw that if you could cut out the middleman and insure better-than-average drivers, you could sell a $30 car insurance policy at a large savings of $6 or $7. Today, GEICO advertises widely and heavily.

In 1936, Goodwin chartered Government Employees Insurance Company in Fort Worth to sell car insurance to government workers and military employees, and it eventually grew from that niche into a nationwide writer of coverage for autos and homes.

In those early days, Goodwin sought out Fort Worth banker Cleaves Rhea, who believed in his idea. Rhea agreed to invest $75,000 if Goodwin could put up $25,000 to capitalize the fledgling company. Goodwin received 25% of the stock and Rhea 75%.

In the difficult early years, Goodwin and his wife, Lillian, worked 12 hours a day, 365 days a year for a combined monthly salary of $250. Goodwin devoted weekends to writing responses to customers' inquiries or complaints.

The Goodwins targeted government employees as safe drivers with steady incomes. There were more of them in Washington, D.C., so the company was moved there and rechartered in 1937.

The company's underwriting losses declined each year until a $5,000 underwriting gain was achieved in 1940, with a $15,000 net income. This was the first of 35 consecutive profitable years.

In the fall of 1941, a hailstorm damaged thousands of cars in the Washington, D.C., area. Goodwin arranged with repair shops to work 24 hours a day exclusively for GEICO policyholders. Anticipating glass shortages, Goodwin had truckloads of glass shipped to Washington, D.C.

Cars of GEICO's policyholders were repaired in days while policyholders with other companies waited weeks.

In 1948 the Rhea family sold its 75% stock holding to Graham-Newman and a small group of private investors. The value of the company was about $3 million. Later that year, Graham-Newman distributed its stock to its shareholders and the company became publicly owned.

In 1949 GEICO passed the $1 million profit mark and began to expand its operations. In 1952 the company broadened its business to include all state, county and municipal employees, thus gaining a larger group of prospects.

Leo Goodwin retired in 1958 and became founder chairman. He had seen his novel concept—with its operating principles of selling direct and marketing to preferred-risk customers—grow from $104,000 in written premiums in 1936 to $36.2 million in 1957.

Investors fared well, too. If one had bought $2,000 worth of GEICO shares in 1948, that investment would have grown to $95,000 at Goodwin's retirement ten years later.

But by 1975 GEICO was at the brink of bankruptcy. Enter Buffett. Between 1972-74 the introduction of no-fault insurance and public clamor over skyrocketing insurance rates had resulted in states requiring prior rate approvals.

In May, 1976, the board of directors elected John Byrne as chairman, president and chief executive officer. Byrne took three drastic steps to turn the company around:

First, Operation Bootstrap—This included rate increases, vigorous cost controls and a reunderwriting of the entire book of business.

Second, Reinsurance—Byrne convinced 27 GEICO competitors that providing reinsurance relief was in their best interest.

Third, New Capital—The investment banking firm of Salomon Brothers agreed to underwrite a $76 million stock offering, increasing common stock to an equivalent of 34.3 million shares.

Operating profit returned in 1977. No wonder Buffett has called Byrne his "meal ticket."

The company created "sister companies" in 1949, and in 1977 it began to buy back stock of those sister companies.

GEICO, long headed by Chairman William B. Snyder (who retired in 1993) is now headed by Tony Nicely, co-CEO of insurance operations and Lou Simpson, co-CEO of capital operations.

The emphasis at GEICO, based in Chevy Chase, Maryland, is on stellar driving records; if anything goes wrong with that record, Snyder has said, "We can be fairly unforgiving."

The company has kept its underwriting ratios below 100 for all but one year in the past decade, meaning that the company takes in more in premiums than it pays out in claims and expenses.

(Photo courtesy of GEICO)

That sets it apart from most other property-casualty companies, which pay out more in claims and expenses than they collect in premiums, and rely on investments alone for profits. In general, the industry is substantially dependent on investment income for profits.

Most of GEICO's employees are on the underwriting side along with just a handful of people under Simpson who make up the investing team.

In 1991 when Berkshire already owned 48% of the stock, the stake was duly noted by Snyder at GEICO's Annual Meeting held at a regional office in Dallas.

Buffett showed up for the meeting, taking a seat in the back row. More than 90% of the stock was represented in the room. With

GEICO's Tony Nicely. Buffett wrote in Berkshire's 1998 Annual Report: "Quite simply there is no one in the business world who could run GEICO better than Tony does. His instincts are unerring, his energy boundless, and his execution is flawless." Nicely also was mentioned by Bill Gates as one of four CEOs who offered help with Gates' second book, Business @ the Speed of Thought.

Buffett in the room, about half the stock was present and accounted for.

Snyder, conducting the meeting and spotting Buffett in the back of the room said, "Warren Buffett is here (applause). Together Warren Buffett and I own 48% of the company."

Actually, Snyder owned well over 1% of GEICO's stock himself.

The prospect of being controlled by Berkshire never seemed to bother Snyder, who said, "Warren Buffett is such an enlightened owner that we frankly wouldn't be distressed. We thought about this back when he had 35-37% of the stock and we see no problem. Nothing will change." Snyder said Buffett exercised no control over the company at that time.

Simpson and Nicely said then: "Absolutely nothing changes."

In late 1995 GEICO had a $900 million stock portfolio of such stocks as Freddie Mac, Nike, Reebok and about 1,300 shares of Berkshire. GEICO had more than a $3.7 billion bond portfolio consisting of tax-exempt municipal bonds and Treasury securities. GEICO sold its three million shares of Reebok in late 1995, but kept its 2,350,000 shares of Nike. (*Wall Street Journal*, April 23, 1996)

Its portfolio has included such stocks as Burlington Northern, Nike, Mattel and Manpower.

GEICO, however, puts most of its money in bonds. "GEICO prefers not to invest much in equities. Instead, the giant auto insurer sinks most of its $6.5 billion investment portfolio into safe, stodgy federal, state and municipal bonds that yield about 6% a year." (*Washington Post*, March 30, 1998)

Unlike many insurance firms, GEICO has no exposure to real estate and little to junk bonds.

The company's earnings have continued to be solid, with really just a few fender-benders along the way. And it has the ability on the investment side to be wise with its money. After all, its investment folks are occasionally in touch with Buffett.

HOLY COW! NEWS FLASH ON AUGUST 25, 1995! Berkshire will buy all the rest of GEICO for $2.3 billion. By this time Berkshire owned 51% of the stock and agreed to buy the remaining 49% and to make GEICO a wholly owned unit of Berkshire. GEICO is operated independently of Berkshire's other insurance operations.

Buffett said Berkshire and GEICO officials had been talking earlier about a purchase paid for with securities, but although "it looked like it might work, it was very complicated," and there were tax problems.

"So Thursday of last week management said they would be satisfied if we could do it for $70 [a share]...I gulped and squirmed and said okay," Buffett said. "They got the last penny out of me." (*Washington Post*, August 26, 1995)

Of his investment in GEICO back in 1951, Buffett said, "I felt very comfortable with that commitment, and I feel equally comfortable with the major commitment that Berkshire Hathaway made today."

In the early days, Buffett bought GEICO on the cheap, but to buy the whole company he was willing to pay full dollar for a one-of-a-kind business. What accounts for the change? *Business Week* (July 5, 1999) says: "The Buffett psyche is notoriously labyrinthine. I could easily spend a lot of time trying to analyze Warren if I didn't consciously try not to," says Olza M. Nicely, CEO of auto insurer GEICO Corp., one of Berkshire's largest subsidiaries. 'There are certain mysteries you just have to accept."

Here's how Berkshire bought the rest of GEICO, according to a *Washington Post* story which ran in the *Omaha World Herald* on November 7, 1995, quoting proxy information filed with the SEC:

> ...For years, Buffett had mentioned to top GEICO officials that his company, Berkshire Hathaway, should consider acquiring 100% of GEICO. But no discussions took place until August 17, 1994. That was the date on which Buffett met in Washington with Louis A. Simpson, co-chief executive of GEICO and the company's longtime financial whiz, and Samuel C. Butler, chairman of the GEICO board's executive committee.
>
> Buffett suggested that Berkshire acquire GEICO in a tax-free transaction, with GEICO shareholders swapping their shares for Berkshire common stock. Simpson and Butler said they were concerned about the proposal. First, because Berkshire stock did not pay a dividend, as did GEICO. Second because they thought it would be difficult to accomplish the stock swap in a fair way.
>
> Berkshire Hathaway stock, one of the highest-priced stocks on the market, was then selling for $18,700. A GEICO stockholder who had 200 GEICO shares would have received only a fraction of a Berkshire share-and since no fractional shares would be issued, the GEICO stockholder would wind up with taxable cash.
>
> The conversation then turned to the possible use of a new

Berkshire convertible preferred stock having a dividend equal to GEICO's dividend. Buffett indicated that he'd be willing to swap one share of the preferred stock—with a stated value of $55 a share—for each share of GEICO. Butler replied that, while he would talk it over with GEICO's financial advisors, he would not recommend any such deal to the GEICO board unless the fair market value of the Berkshire preferred was at least above $60...

Meanwhile, Buffett raised questions about tax issues involved in a tax-free stock swap, and the two companies started to research those issues.

On March 1, 1995, Simpson and Butler met in New York with Buffett and his partner, Charles T. Munger. Again they talked about a deal, but each side held firm to its position on price. Butler and Simpson noted that since August, Berkshire stock had climbed to $22,500 a share. And they expressed serious concern about how that lofty price might affect the fair market value of a share of Berkshire preferred stock, especially if something should happen to Buffett...

GEICO officials asked Butler to call Buffett and tell them they would go for a $70-a-share cash transaction or for a convertible preferred stock deal that was worth $70 in the market. Two days later Butler made the call. Buffett asked if the price was negotiable. Butler said no. Buffett then said he really did not want to issue preferred stock at $70 a share. Moreover, he said, he would prefer a cash deal.

Buffett then said he wanted to talk to his partner, Munger, about

(Photo by LaVerne Ramsey)

The GEICO booth at Berkshire's Annual Meeting in 1996.

the deal, which he did. Later in the day, Buffett called Butler and said yes, he would agree to do the deal for $70 in cash.

GEICO, which has an agreement with H&R Block to provide car insurance information to Block's tax preparation customers, is a real Buffett Classic. The purchase of all of GEICO was a huge event for Berkshire.

"To sum up, we entered 1995 with an exceptional insurance operation of moderate size. By adding GEICO, we entered 1996 with a business still better in quality, much improved in its growth prospects, and doubled in size. More than ever, insurance is our core strength," Buffett wrote in Berkshire's 1995 Annual Report.

In his "Owner's Manual" to shareholders in June, 1996, Buffett wrote "... Berkshire has access to two low-cost, non-perilous sources of leverage that allow us to safely own far more assets than our equity capital alone would permit: deferred taxes and float," the funds of others that our insurance business holds because it receives premiums before needing to pay out losses. Both of these funding sources have grown rapidly and now total about $12 billion.

"Better yet, the funding to date has been cost-free. Deferred tax liabilities bear no interest. And as long as we can break even in our insurance underwriting—which we have done, on the average, during our 29 years in the business—the cost of the float developed from that operation is zero. Neither item, it should be understood, is equity; these are real liabilities. But they are liabilities without covenants or due dates attached to them. In effect, they give us the benefit of debt—an ability to have assets working for us—but saddles us with none of its drawbacks.

"Of course, there is no guarantee that we can obtain our float in the future at no cost. But we feel our chances of attaining that goal are as good as those of anyone in the insurance business. Not only have we reached the goal in the past (despite a number of important mistakes by your Chairman), but have now, with our acquisition of GEICO, materially improved our prospects for getting there in the future."

At Berkshire's Annual Meeting in 1996, Buffett said: "Five years from now, I think you'll be very happy with the fact that we own 100% of GEICO." It hasn't taken five years for shareholders to realize GEICO is one of Berkshire's most promising growth opportunities. Here's a huge hidden value at Berkshire. There's no stock quote for GEICO and some forget to value it fully. GEICO just may be worth twice what Buffett would have paid for the whole company. (about $4.6 billion). Sold off in whole now it's worth perhaps $13 billion. Maybe more.

Asked why it took him so long to acquire all of GEICO, Buffett said, "It takes money, you know." (*Omaha World-Herald*, August 26, 1995)

Buffett told shareholders in 1996: "The real news at Berkshire this year is the exceptional performance of GEICO."

In Berkshire's 1996 Annual Report, Buffett wrote: "GEICO gets more than one million referrals annually and they produce more than half of our new business, an advantage that gives us enormous savings in acquisition expenses—and that makes our cost still lower..."

"GEICO's sustainable cost advantage is what attracted me to the company way back in 1951, when the entire company was valued at $7 million. It is also why I felt Berkshire should pay $2.3 billion last year for the 49% of the company we didn't then own."

GEICO's voluntary auto policies grew 10% in 1996, the best rate ever to that point. That was nothing compared to 1997 when they grew 16%. By mid 1999, policies were growing at the rate of 23.3%.

After the acquisition Buffett put a new incentive plan in place with half of the bonuses and profit-sharing to employees based on earnings of business that has been on the books more than a year and half tied to policyholder growth.

With GEICO, little dots and stray brush marks that Buffett made on his canvas years ago now form a complete picture, one big part of his masterpiece in the making.

GEICO—which has a Triple-A credit rating with S&P—is tearing up the road.

GEICO has 16,000 employees at its headquarters in Washington, D.C. and regional offices in Fredericksburg, Virginia; Woodbury, New York; Macon, Georgia; Dallas, Texas; and San Diego, California; and its service centers in Coralville, Iowa; Honolulu, Hawaii; Lakeland, Florida, and Virginia Beach, Virginia.

Buffett wrote in Berkshire's 1997 Annual Report: "GEICO is flying, and we expect that it will continue to do so." No wonder he titled his insurance segment in the report: "Insurance—GEICO (1-800-555-2756) and Other Primary Operations." In the 1998 report the section simply became GEICO (1-800-847-7536). The 1999 Annual Report added GEICO.com.

Buffett also wrote: "GEICO's underwriting profitability will probably fall in 1998, but the company's growth could accelerate. We're planning to step on the gas: GEICO's marketing expenditures this year will top $100 million, up 50% from 1997. Our market share today is only 3%, a level of penetration that should increase dramatically in the next decade. The auto insurance industry is huge—it does about $115 billion of volume annually—and there are tens of millions of drivers who would save substantial money by switching to us."

At the opening of GEICO's West Coast headquarters in Poway, California, Buffett recounted his earlier interest in GEICO about that long ago Saturday visit to the headquarters in Washington D.C. when he met with Lorimer Davidson: "When I got there, the doors were locked, so I pounded on them until a janitor came...It probably all goes back to that janitor who opened the door, but I didn't get his name." (*San Diego Union-Tribune*, September 23, 1999)

After his appearance he met with employees and signed autographs. As the crush of people grew, GEICO officials tried to get Buffett away, but he said he was fine, adding: "I don't mind. I just pretend I'm signing insurance policies." (*San Diego Union-Tribune*, September 23, 1999)

In March 2000 he visited the Woodbury Long Island office to congratulate employees on their superior performance. A third-hand account of the event had it that Buffett signed a ton of autographs on $1 bills and remembered people's names.

This was a short time after the false reports that he was on his death bed in an Omaha hospital. Guess he made a quick recovery.

GEICO under Berkshire has transformed itself into a huge force as the low cost producer in the industry. Buffett changed the compensation structure with profitability of the business factored into uncapped bonus plans (16.9% of employee compensation in 1996, 26.9% in 1997 and 32.3% in 1998). A big effort has been put into

GEICO salesman Buffett during the Berkshire Annual Meeting weekend in 1999

(Photo by Nancy Line Jacobs)

advertising (GEICO is one of the largest advertisers on cable TV) and the company's infrastructure. Telephone inquiries jumped five-fold from 1993 to 1998.

GEICO is putting the pedal to the metal.

Buffett has promised even a greater push at GEICO with $300-350 million for advertising alone in 2000. "Tony [Nicely's] foot is going to stay on the advertising pedal (and my foot will be on his)," Buffett said in Berkshire's 1999 Annual Report.

Buffett also wrote: "GEICO is acquiring a direct relationship with a large number of households that, on average, will send us $1,100 year after year. That makes us—among all companies, selling whatever kind of product—one of the country's leading direct merchandisers."

Value Line (March 31, 2000) said: "The magnitude, and rate of growth of Berkshire Hathaway's investment in the private passenger automobile insurance business is awesome in scope. To be sure, the impact of the aggressive marketing program on profitability has been significant and not well received by investors. But we think the company will stay the course, much to the dismay of its peers in the business, since Berkshire Hathaway is taking a calculated risk in building a known brand name. In fact management described GEICO as one of the largest direct merchandisers in the nation. The strategy could reshape the industry and have ramifications above and beyond the personal automobile sector. The business model still allows the company to generate cash, while the potential synergies as the company's brand is built are enormous. We think these items are the most important factors in evaluating Berkshire's future."

This GEICO ad was an insert in Berkshire's 1999 Annual Report.

35

A LOOK AT GEICO BY A NOT-YOUR-AVERAGE 21-YEAR-OLD

In 1951 Buffett wrote an article about GEICO for the "The Security I Like Best" column of a New York publication. It's a look at GEICO by a not-your-average 21-year-old:

Reprinted from

THE COMMERCIAL AND FINANCIAL CHRONICLE
Thursday, December 6, 1951

The Security I Like Best
Warren E. Buffett
Buffett-Falk & Co., Omaha Nebr.

Government Employees Insurance Co.

Full employment, boomtime profits and record dividend payments do not set the stage for depressed security prices. Most industries have been riding this wave of prosperity during the past five years with few ripples to disturb the tide.

The auto insurance business has not shared in the boom. After the staggering losses of the immediate postwar period, the situation began to right itself in 1949. In 1950, stock casualty companies again took it on the chin with underwriting experience the second worst in 15 years. The recent earnings reports of casualty companies, particularly those with the bulk of writings in auto lines, have diverted bull market enthusiasm from their stocks. On the basis of normal earning power and asset factors, many of these stocks appear undervalued.

The nature of the industry is such as to ease cyclical bumps. Auto insurance is regarded as a necessity by the majority of purchasers. Contracts must be renewed yearly at rates based upon experience. The lag of rates behind costs, although detrimental in a period of rising prices as has characterized the 1945-1951 period, should prove beneficial if deflationary forces should be set in action.

Warren E. Buffett

Other industry advantages include lack of inventory collection, labor and raw material problems. The hazard of product obsolescence is also absent.

Government Employees Insurance Corporation was organized in the mid-30's to provide complete auto insurance on a nation-wide basis to an eligible class including: (1) Federal, State and municipal government employees; (2) active and reserve commissioned officers and the first three pay grades of non-commissioned officers of the Armed Forces; (3) veterans who were eligible when on active duty; (4) former policyholders; (5) faculty members of universities, colleges and schools; (6) government contractor employees engaged in defense work exclusively, and (7) stockholders.

The company has no agents or branch offices. As a result, policyholders receive standard auto insurance policies at premium discounts running as high as 30% off manual rates. Claims are handled promptly through approximately 500 representatives throughout the country.

The term "growth company" has been applied with abandon during the past few years to companies whose sales increases represented little more than inflation of prices and general earnings of business competition. GEICO qualifies as a legitimate growth company based upon the following record:

Year	Premiums Written	Policy holders
1936	$ 103,696.31	3,754
1940	768,057.86	25,514
1945	1,638,562.09	51,697
1950	8,016,975.79	143,944

Of course the investor of today does not profit from yesterday's growth. In GEICO's case, there is reason to believe the major portion of growth lies ahead. Prior to 1950, the company was only licensed in 15 of 50 jurisdictions including D.C. and Hawaii. At the beginning of the year there were less than 3,000 policyholders in New York State. Yet 25% saved on an insurance bill of $125 in New York should look bigger to the prospect than the 25% saved on the $50 rate in more sparsely settled regions.

As cost competition increases in importance during times of recession, GEICO's rate attraction should become even more effective in diverting business from the brother-in-law. With insurance rates moving higher due to inflation, the 25% spread in rates becomes wider in terms of dollars and cents.

There is no pressure from agents to accept questionable applicants or renew poor risks. In States where the rate structure is inadequate, new promotion may be halted.

Probably the biggest attraction of GEICO is the profit margin advantage it enjoys. The ratio of underwriting profit to premiums earned in 1949 was 27.5% for GEICO as compared to 6.7% for the 133 stock casualty and surety companies summarized by Best's. As experience turned for the worse in 1950, Best's aggregates profit margin dropped to 3.0% and GEICO's dropped to 18.0%. GEICO does not write all casualty lines; however, bodily injury and property damage, both important lines for GEICO, were among the least profitable lines. GEICO also does a large amount of collision writing which was a profitable line in 1950.

During the first half of 1951, practically all insurers operated in the red on casualty lines with bodily injury and property damage among the most unprofitable. Whereas GEICO's profit margin was cut to slightly above 9%, Massachusetts's Bonding & Insurance showed a 16% loss, New Amsterdam Casualty an 8% loss, Standard Accident Insurance a 9% loss, etc.

Because of the rapid growth of GEICO, cash dividends have had to remain low. Stock dividends and a 25-for-1 split increased the outstanding shares from 3,000 on June 1, 1948, to 250,000 on Nov. 10, 1951. Valuable rights to subscribe to stock of affiliated companies have also been issued.

Benjamin Graham has been Chairman of the Board since his investment trust acquired and distributed a large block of the stock in 1948. Leo Goodwin, who has guided GEICO's growth since inception, is the able President. At the end of 1950, the 10 members of the Board of Directors owned approximately one-third of the outstanding stock.

Earnings in 1950 amounted to $3.92 as contrasted to $4.71 on the smaller amount of business in 1949. These figures include no allowance for the increase in the unearned premium reserve which was substantial in both years. Earnings in 1951 will be lower than 1950, but the wave of rate increases during the past summer should evidence themselves in 1952 earnings. Investment income quadrupled between 1947 and 1950 reflecting the growth of the company's assets.

At the present price of about eight times the earnings of 1950, a poor year for the industry, it appears that no price is being paid for the tremendous growth potential of the company.

36

COCA-COLA'S DON KEOUGH

"WARREN, ARE YOU BUYING A SHARE OR TWO OF COCA-COLA STOCK?"

Shortly before Buffett would make stock market history by buying a billion dollars worth of Coca-Cola stock, he took a call from then Coca-Coca President Don Keough.

"I asked how things were and I said, 'Warren, are you buying a share or two of Coca-Cola stock?' "

"He said yes and he said it enthusiastically," recalled Keough, chairman of Notre Dame's board of trustees. Keough is known for standing ovations as an after-dinner speaker.

"It wasn't too long before the announcement that he [Warren] was buying when I called him. We knew somebody was buying the stock. We figured it out by deduction," said Keough, indicating the conclusion was reached by folks at Coke who follow the stock's trading patterns.

"As the stock started regaining its lost ground [after the 1987 stock market crash], an inordinate amount of activity came from a relatively obscure midwestern brokerage. [Coke Chairman Roberto] Goizueta and Keough were studying Coke's stock activity one day in the fall of 1988, when Keough suddenly saw the light. 'You know, it could be Warren Buffett,' " he told Goizueta. (*I'd Like The World To Buy a Coke: The Life and Leadership of Roberto Goizueta*, David Greising, p. 176)

"We knew he had an interest in The Coca-Cola Company," said Keough, admitting that one of the tips occurred when "Warren became America's number-one fan of Cherry Coke which we introduced in 1985."

"He really understands the company. He's a terrific board member. He knows the company. He knows the numbers. He's an informed and stimulating director. He has a clear understanding of the inherent value of global trademarks."

And what did Mr. Keough do after Mr. Buffett bought Coke stock? "I became a modest Berkshire shareholder after his purchase of Coca-Cola stock," said Keough, who had had an opportunity more than 30 years earlier to invest in the Buffett Partnership but passed up Buffett's invitation.

"I wish I had invested back then," Keough said. Had he done so, Buffett would have turned the $5,000 he asked of Keough into something on the order of $60 million. Oh, well.

In 1958 Keough, the son of a Sioux City, Iowa, cattleman and Irish-American mother, and a graduate of Creighton University where he was an award-winning debater, moved into the house directly across from Buffett on Farnam Street in Omaha.

Buffett has said Keough's extraordinary personality is one reason he invested so heavily in Coca-Cola.

For a while Keough worked at a fledgling television station in Omaha, WOWT-TV announcing football games where he got to know Johnny Carson and later the investment broker Warren Buffett. Keough left his TV job to take an advertising job at Paxton and Gallagher, maker of Butter-Nut Coffee.

The Swanson family bought Paxton and Gallagher and sold the renamed Swanson Foods to Duncan Coffee Company, which in turn was bought by the Coca-Cola Co. (*I'd Like the World to Buy a Coke: The Life and Leadership of Roberto Goizueta*, David Greising, p. 66)

The future Mr. Coca-Cola, who drinks his Coke in diet form, was one of many people Buffett solicited to join the Buffett Partnership. Although Keough was late investing with Buffett, he was early on another Berkshire investment. "My wife Mickie and I bought furniture from Mrs. Blumkin at the Nebraska Furniture Mart when we were early married in Omaha. We've been married over 40 years," Keough said.

Keough says he can't recall exactly how he met Buffett, just that they were neighbors in Omaha. "I don't remember how we were introduced...He was about 25 and I was about 30.

"He was exactly the same then as he is now...What you see is what you get. He had the same values. His story really is not money. It's values. People should know about his values....What he said at the [Berkshire] annual meeting [in 1991] in his response to a question about choosing careers says it all. He said enjoy your work and work for whom you admire."

Keough, the marketing whiz, and the late Roberto Goizueta, the chemical engineer, began working together in the 1960s and both were on a management fast track. Goizueta joined Coke in 1954 after answering an ad for a bilingual chemist.

On the evening of February 14, 1980, at a birthday party for then Coke Chairman J. Paul Austin at The Four Seasons restaurant in Manhattan, both arrived as rivals to succeed Austin.

Keough told Goizueta: "Nobody knows how this is going to work out. The two of us are quite compatible, and we have different skills. So let's sleep at night. Whoever comes out on top, let's put the other one to work immediately."

Goizueta was picked as chairman and chief executive officer and he and Keough became one of the top management teams in American business. After retiring in 1993, Keough became chairman of the Allen & Co. investment banking firm. Goizueta, long a heavy smoker, died October 18, 1997 of complications from lung cancer. At Goizueta's death, the *Atlanta Journal Constitution* (October 19, 1997) devoted an entire section to his life. Buffett was quoted as saying, "His greatest legacy is the way he so carefully selected and nurtured the future leadership of the company."

M. Douglas Ivester was named Coca-Cola's chairman and chief executive officer shortly after Goizueta's death, serving two rocky years.

37

THE COCA-COLA COMPANY
LESS FIZZ

A brief announcement came over the Dow Jones news wire on March 15, 1989: Berkshire had bought 6.3% of the stock of The Coca-Cola Company! That stake, because of Coke's own stock repurchases and Buffett's additional buying in mid-1994, now represents about 8% of the company. Berkshire owns 200 million shares of Coca-Cola, the most widely distributed product on the planet.

Berkshire owns more than twice as much Coke stock as the entire mutual fund industry—200 million shares versus 90 million. (*Barron's*, November 17, 1997) Coca-Cola is Berkshire's holy water. Buffett calls the sugar and caffeine Coke product the "nectar of the gods."

Some viewed it less favorably in 1999 when Coke stumbled badly. E-mails then noted that a good way to clean a toilet was to pour a can of Coca-Cola in the toilet bowl. "Let 'the real thing' sit for an hour, then flush clean." In any event, Coke, after the stock market crash of 1987, was a perfect pitch to the center of Buffett's "circle of competence." It was "two inches above the navel." He swung big and hit a 500-foot home run high over the center field fence.

That's more than a big stake by a 30 Billion Pound Gorilla. That's an investment from King Kong.

With Buffett's Coke purchase, a grandiose era of permanent value was born for both Berkshire and Coke. Buffett, making his largest investment ever, struck during an unusually long period when Berkshire doesn't report—from the quarter ending in September until March when the annual earnings and annual report are issued.

He had spent months in late 1988 and early 1989 secretly putting in buy orders and had just finished guzzling down a $1 billion-plus ocean-size helping of Coca-Cola. "Can't Beat The Feeling."

Buffett's investment, "The Real Thing", made him Coke's largest shareholder. He went on the board where he serves with former U.S. Senator Sam Nunn, entertainment industry investor Herbert Allen, former Major League Baseball commissioner Peter Ueberroth and others.

Former Coca-Cola Chairman M. Douglas Ivester wrote in Coke's 1997 Annual Report: "The pioneers who built this Company scarcely could have imagined it. About the time you are reading this letter, your Company will achieve an amazing milestone—sales of Coca-Cola and other Company products will exceed 1 billion servings per day. It took 22 years for us to sell the first billion servings of Coca-Cola. And now we're selling a billion drinks a day." That amounts to 2% of the daily beverage consumption on earth.

"I wish we had bought more," Buffett has said, reminiscent of the view of an anonymous wit: "There are more important things in life than a little money, and one of them is a lot of money."

Now Coke sells a billion servings a day to the world's six billion people. Berkshire's 8% ownership claim of a billion servings is about 80 million servings.

Perhaps the first tipoff about Buffett's interest in the world's largest soft drink maker came in Berkshire's 1985 Annual Report when he wrote, "After 48 years of allegiance to another soft drink" (Pepsi) he was switching to Cherry Coke. He even declared Cherry Coke "the official drink" of Berkshire's annual meetings. That should have registered with Berkshire shareholders as a stock tip.

Kent Hanon, a teacher and actor in Omaha, recalls the days of Buffett's allegiance to Pepsi. His mother Elizabeth was an early secretary to Buffett and she recalls going across Farnam Street each afternoon to get Buffett a Pepsi. "It was a great source of amusement to my parents that Warren Buffett bought Coca-Cola which he had totally refused to drink," recalls Kent Hanon. (*Omaha World Herald*, September 27, 1997)

In Buffett's words, the switch happened when "Don [Keough] sent me a trial sample of the formula for Cherry Coke very early on—and I loved it. I wrote him back saying he could save all his test-marketing money, send me a portion of what he'd spend otherwise and that it was going to be a great success."

"As Coca-Cola test marketed Cherry Coke in late 1984, Don Keough sent Buffett a case of the new drink." (*I'd Like The World To Buy a Coke: The Life and Leadership of Roberto Goizueta, David Greising*, p. 176)

Later Buffett would tell *Forbes* a key reason he bought Coke was that its stock price did not reflect the all-but-guaranteed growth in international sales in a world that is increasingly uniform in its tastes. Throughout the world, for more than a century, fountain clerks have mixed an ounce of Coca-Cola syrup with six and a half ounces of carbonated water. No product is so universal.

Even the Queen of England drinks Coke. Greta Garbo, John F. Kennedy, the Beatles and Fidel Castro have been Coke fans.

President Bill Clinton constantly swigs Cokes. Vice President Al Gore likes Diet Coke. British Open champion John Daly, celebrating victory in 1995, turned down champagne for a Diet Coke. Bill Gates—a Coke drinker himself—has starred in an ad, scrounging for change to buy a Coke.

The most widely recognized and esteemed brand names on earth, by far, are Coca-Cola and Coke. In a *Financial World* story (July 8; 1996), it was calculated that Coca-Cola's brand name alone is worth more than $43 billion.

Coca-Cola, according to the 1995 Coca-Cola Annual Report, is the world's second most widely recognized expression after "OK." Coke annual reports are among the best of the genre. The 1996 Coke Annual Report was an award winner using the theme of thirst to communicate Coke's motivation and opportunity.

John Tilson of Roger Engemann & Associates, says, "The Coca-Cola brand name is worth over twice what it generates in annual sales because its worldwide recognition and established marketing generate both superior operating margins and high market shares." (*Outstanding Investor Digest,* October 7, 1993)

In Coke, Sprite, Tab and Fanta, Coke has four of the five top carbonated drinks in the world. Coke sells more than two billion gallons every year of soft drink syrup and concentrate to bottlers. And Coke's value may rise because it's habit forming, a business trait Buffett likes.

Buffett wannabe George Morgan tells the story of Buffett running into a youngster wearing a Coca-Cola outfit at a mall. Buffett asked him how much he paid for it. The youngster replied $75. "That's a lot to pay to advertise someone else's product," said Buffett, even more convinced of Coke's valuable franchise.

From Australia to Zimbabwe, from Omaha to Osaka, from the Great Wall of China to the Great Barrier Reef, millions of people are drinking a billion servings a day.

The company sells half of the soda pop consumed ON EARTH, more than twice as much as its nearest rival, PepsiCo. In the U.S., the Coke and Pepsi empires claim about three-fourths of the $50 billion-a-year soda business.

Coca-Cola USA accounts for 10% of all of America's liquid consumption.

Coke supplies its syrups and concentrates to about 1,000 bottling partners in almost 200 countries. In many of those countries Coke has little competition.

The sun never sets on the world of Coca-Cola, still Berkshire's biggest stock investment. Buffett's stake in Coca-Cola stock is his master stroke. In many nations, "Coca-Cola" is synonymous with "U.S.A."

Buffett says: "If you run across one good idea for a business in your lifetime, you're lucky, and fundamentally this is the best large business in the world. It has got the most powerful brand in the world. It sells for an extremely moderate price. It's universally liked—the per capita consumption goes up almost every year in almost every country. There is no other product like it." *(Fortune,* May 31, 1993)

As far back as May 15, 1950, Coca-Cola appeared on the cover of *Time* magazine (20 cents an issue then) over the title "World and Friend" with the drawing of a happy-faced, thirsty Earth drinking a Coke.

Coca-Cola's former Chairman, Cuban-born, Yale-educated, Atlanta booster Roberto Goizueta, who died in 1997, once said the "C" in kitchen sinks should deliver Coke, not cold water.

Often saying, "God is in the details," Goizueta knew something about growth. The only property he held onto after the emergence of Cuba's Castro (while on vacation in Miami in 1960 he and his wife defected and never returned to Cuba) was 100 shares of Coca-Cola he had bought in a custodial account with $8,000 loaned to him by his father. Those shares, which he still owned at the time of

(Photo by Phil Skinner
The Atlanta Journal-The Atlanta Constitution)

Former Coca-Cola Chairman and CEO, M. Douglas Ivester, left, and the late Coca-Cola Chairman Roberto Goizueta in a 1996 photo.

his death, were worth about $3 million. In the years he was chairman he guided the growth of Coke from a market worth of $4 billion to about $150 billion. Talk about liquid assets!

Goizueta, at the time of his death, was a Coke billionaire!

(Shortly after the Berkshire Annual Meeting in 1994 Goizueta said he called Buffett, and Buffett told him there had been only one question about Coca-Cola and kidded Goizueta that it was about management.)

(Photo courtesy of The Atlanta Journal-Constitution/Ben Gray)

Coca-Cola's new leadership: Chairman and CEO Douglas Daft, right, and President and Chief Operating Officer Jack Stahl

Ivester served as Coke chairman for 2½ tumultuous years after Goizueta's death. Ivester shocked Wall Street December 6, 1999 saying he would retire in April 2000. Ivester's tenure was marked by a downturn in many foreign markets (effective hedging became difficult as many foreign currencies plummeted) and a massive product recall in Europe. In June 1999 Coke products were pulled from shelves in Luxemburg and parts of France and the Netherlands in a health scare that began in Belgium where a number of children became ill after drinking Cokes. Coke said it found the contaminations were due to the carbon dioxide used in bottles made in a plant in Antwerp, Belgium and to a fungicide found on the outside of cans made at another plant in Dunkirk, France.

In the end a Belgium authority concluded the cause was psychosomatic, the result of youngsters influenced by a bad odor.

Also Ivester's time was marred by a racial discrimination lawsuit in the U.S. and a failed buyout of France's Pernod-Richard Orangina drinks brand. And Coke had to scale back its proposed purchase of Cadbury Schweppes to win regulatory approval. A string of earnings shortfalls finally led to a huge restructuring of the company involving 5,200 layoffs and big writedowns of business in such places as Russia, India and Vietnam.

Increasingly Coke has been beset by changing tastes in drinks, problems with bottlers, foreign government opposition and international anti-Americanism.

313

History of One Share of Stock	
One Share 1919 (value $40)	
Result of splits/stock dividends 1919-1994	2,304 shares
Price 12/31/94	$51.50
Total value of 1 original share on 12/31/94	$118,656.00
Dividends paid 1919 through 12/31/94	16,942.01
Dividends: Class A	$129.00
Class A redeemed (2 shares @ $52.50)	$105.00
	$135,832.01

Stock Splits		
Date	Activity	Cumulative Stock
April 25, 1927		1
	1-for-1 stock dividend	2
November 15, 1935	4-for-1 stock split	8
January 22, 1960	3-for-1 stock split	24
January 22, 1965	2-for-1 stock split	48
May 13, 1968	2-for-1 stock split	96
May 9, 1977	2-for-1 stock split	192
June 16, 1986	3-for-1 stock split	576
May 1, 1990	2-for-1 stock split	1,152
May 1, 1992	2-for-1 stock split	2,304
* [1994	2-for-1 stock split	4.608]
* [1996	2-for-1 stock split	9,216]

(Consumer Information Center, The Coca-Cola Company, April 1995)

Thirty-year Coke veteran Douglas Daft; a former math teacher, was called on to lead Coke and Daft soon named Jack Stahl president. *Fortune* (January 10, 2000) reported that Coke and directors Buffett and Herbert Allen met with Ivester in Chicago December 1, 1999, and told him they had lost confidence in his leadership. Ivester returned to Atlanta, called an emergency board meeting and quit.

Before Coke's severe stumble in the late 1990s, its return on equity in 1990 was 39%. It has risen each year since to 61.3% in 1997, but dropped to 45.1% in 1998, but dropped to 27.1% in Coke's tumultuous "Bummer of '99."

Just what is Coke selling? Berkshire's Vice Chairman Charles Munger has quoted Keough as saying: "The business of The Coca-Cola Company is to create and maintain conditioned reflexes." (*Outstanding Investor Digest*, December 29, 1997) Coke really is selling its brand of refreshment. Nothing so vital as food or energy. Just refreshment. And although you might say it's just a sugar water company peddling tooth decay, let's stick with the refreshment idea. Over the years Coke has offered so many moments of tasty refreshment it has become entrenched as the world's leading thirst quencher.

Buffett's original investment in mere cans of Coke came to

$1,023,920,000. For that money, he bought 23,350,000 shares of Coca-Cola stock, which split 2-for-1 in 1990, giving Berkshire 46,700,000 shares. And with another 2-for-1 split in 1992, it had 93,400,000 shares. His mid-1994 refills boosted Berkshire's stock to exactly 100 million shares. Nice round number. The number became, as mentioned, 200 million with the 2-for-1 stock split in 1996.

The day after Berkshire's first Coke announcement, Buffett told *Wall Street Journal* reporter Michael J. McCarthy (March 16, 1989) that the purchase of Coke was "the ultimate case of putting your money where your mouth is."

"Coke is exactly the kind of company I like," Buffett told him. "I like products I can understand. I don't know what a transistor is, for example." Further, he said, "More and more in recent years, their superb decision-making and the focus of their strategy have emerged more clearly to me."

The story suggested that analysts saw Buffett's move as protection against recession. "There could be 10 recessions between now and the time we sell our Coke stock. Our favorite holding period is forever," Buffett replied.

Shortly after the Coke purchase was revealed, trading in Coke's stock was halted because of a flood of buy orders. A year and half later the $1 billion stake in Coke was worth $2 billion. Now there's a real return on some mighty large dollars.

Another large Coke shareholder, SunTrust Banks, holds almost 8% of Coke stock, but that is split between stock it owns—about 2%—and about 6% of Coke stock the bank holds in fiduciary accounts. SunTrust itself owns about 48 million Coke shares. So what if it's taken a lifetime to rise from $110,000, or less than half a cent a share—the price the old Trust Company of Georgia took in stock instead of cash for its services as its fee in 1919 when it helped underwrite Coca-Cola's first stock offering. The Coca-Cola stock is a nice fat percentage of the worth of SunTrust which, by the way, has in its vault the only written copy of the Coke formula.

The secret formula for Coca-Cola, Merchandise 7x, is kept in a bank vault at Trust Co. of Georgia (now SunTrust Banks). But it is never touched there. Instead, the formula is passed by word of mouth, almost as if it were the ritualistic cant of a secret fraternal order. (*I'd Like the World to Buy a Coke: The Life and Leadership of Roberto Goizueto*, David Greising, p. 42)

Emory University in Atlanta, whose business school is named after Goizueta, owns about 40 million shares of Coke, and its dividends have gone to build the campus and to fund scholarships and professorships at the well-endowed school.

Back in 1922 tobacco farmers in Quincy, Florida, plowed profit from a bumper crop into Coca-Cola stock at the urging of local banker Mark Monroe. "Coke had just come public and Daddy liked the taste," said Julia Woodward, Monroe's daughter. "Plus, he figured the stock would be good collateral because folks would always have a nickel to buy a bottle." (*Bloomberg News Service*, December 13, 1996) Today, the descendents of the farmers who heeded the banker own 7.5 million shares of Coke, which adjusted for splits, cost them 2 cents a share. The same 25 Coke millionaires have generously shared their largess with their well-off town located near Tallahassee.

Remember, Buffett began his business career when he was six years old, buying six-packs of Coke for a quarter at his grandfather's Buffett & Son family grocery store. Selling the Cokes around the neighborhood for five cents a drink was among his earliest business ventures; he found margins to be good.

Despite making pocket money as a Coke salesman, he was drinking Pepsi-Cola and would not change his taste habits for almost half a century when he, too, joined the ranks of "Cokeaholics." Buffett has said "his eyeballs connected with his brain" in the summer of 1988 and he began buying Coke all the way through March 1989. Coke itself was buying back shares so there were two huge buyers of Coke stock in the marketplace.

What Buffett saw, and what made him thirst for Coke, was the world's greatest brand name. The Coca-Cola name was being carried for zero on the balance sheet of a company with stunning international possibilities for profit growth and efficient global advertising. Buffett discovered—and it was right there in front of everybody's eyes—a worldwide seemingly bulletproof franchise.

Coca-Cola dominates the fountain portion of the U.S. soft drink business and is the primary supplier for many of the major fast food chains, including McDonald's, Wendy's, Burger King, and Pizza Inn restaurants. Where McDonald's goes, for example, so goes Coke. McDonald's is Coke's largest customer.

Delta Airlines, Continental Airlines, and US Airways and AirTran serve Coca-Cola.

Its vending business covers the world. Coke machines are all over Europe and the U.S. There are even Coke machines at the Berkshire-owned Borsheim's jewelry store and Nebraska Furniture Mart in Omaha.

About 70% of Coke's sales and about 80% of its profits come from its vastly expanding overseas operations. Pepsi derives about 70% of its sales and 80% of its income in the U.S.

Pepsico, itself a mighty consumer products company, still bedevils Coke in the United States where Americans drink more pop than water. Somewhat stalemated in its domestic profitability by fierce competition from Pepsico, Coca-Cola is always looking to the rest of the world for growth. Yet Coke has now extended its lead over Pepsi in the U.S. by 44.5% to 31.4%. Coke has 50%—half of the world's soft drink market—while Pepsi only has 20%.

Coke and Pepsi are huge competitors who together have beaten back competitors trying to fight their way on the shelf. "When cows and buffaloes fight, the flies are usually the ones that die," goes an old Vietnamese saying.

Overseas, Coke is way ahead of Pepsi. In Europe, home to 347 million people, 39% more than the U.S. population, Coke's sales are exploding and surpass Pepsi's sales by a wide margin.

Coke has made huge inroads in Europe and the Pacific Rim. Coke's domination of Europe is being extended into Poland and what was East Germany.

When the Berlin Wall fell in November, 1989, Coke made an immediate foray into East Germany, setting up vending machines by the thousands. Delivery trucks gave away thousands of cans of Cokes. By early 1991 Coke was buying bottling and distribution plants all over Germany. East Germans knew of Coke from television even before the Berlin Wall came down, and Coke is even more popular than soft drink beverages made by the old East German government.

In early 1991, Coke officials were saying East Germans were swallowing an average of 30 servings a year and that the company was aiming to match West Germany's rate of 190 servings within a few years. Coke quickly expanded operations in East Germany. German unification has been a boon to both Pepsi, with strong operations in a number of Eastern European countries, and to Coke with its strong operations long established in Europe.

Coca-Cola has consolidated the company's European bottling network, including the sale of franchises in France, Belgium and Britain to Coca-Cola Enterprises, Coke's largest bottler.

Coke makes more money in Japan than in the United States because of much higher margins. Coke's army of vending machines, which includes more than 760,000 of Japan's two million soft drink machines, helps Coke claim about 30% of the soft drink market there. Coke's Georgia brand of canned coffee is also a huge seller in Japan.

"Our international opportunity is obvious," said Coke's 1989 Annual Report. "As a market develops, as any market develops, people drink more soft drinks. It's only a matter of time. And the time it takes us to develop a market is growing shorter."

Goizueta wrote in Coke's 1993 Annual Report: "When people ask me about the growth prospects of The Coca-Cola Company, I always respond with three simple facts. First, every day, every single one of the world's 5.6 billion people will get thirsty. Second, only in the last few years have world events allowed us true access to more than half of those people. And third, as the world's foremost beverage company, we are in the best position to satisfy their need for refreshment."

The opportunity for Coca-Cola is apparent overseas where foreigners consume only a fraction as much soda pop as do Americans. Although the mature U.S. market consumes 395 servings a person a year, the average person worldwide consumes 64 servings. The U.S. per capita consumption is many times the worldwide average. And the gap is now being filled to Coke and Berkshire's advantage.

In Indonesia, the yearly per capita consumption is 8 servings, in Russia 22, in China seven and in India three. *Half of the world's population drinks less than two servings per person per year!* Consider the growth prospects!

The overseas consumption average is growing rapidly. Coca-Cola's aim is to be ubiquitous. Its red and white logo shows up at sports events around the world—at bullfights in Spain, camel races in Australia, sheep-shearing contests in New Zealand, and the Super Bowl in the U.S. It has long been a sponsor of the Olympics.

Along the way, Coca-Cola has been making huge investments in bottlers around the world. In Europe particularly, Coca-Cola is consolidating many of its bottling operations to capitalize on the industry deregulation expected from the economic unity of the European community.

Since bottling is a high fixed-cost business, manufacturing and distributing products from fewer locations will enable Coca-Cola to enjoy significant economies of scale and solidify its position as the low-cost soft drink producer. The financial folks at Coca-Cola seem to have their heads on straight, making careful hedges to international currency exposures and making good use of what little debt they have.

Business Week (November 12, 1990) has described one aspect of

Coke's use of debt this way:

> Coca-Cola shows how leverage can be played like a fine instrument. In 1986, the once debt-averse Coke borrowed $2.5 billion to buy up many of its bottlers. Then it sold 51% of the new bottling unit to the public. Coke moved the acquisition debt to the balance sheet of the new unit, which in turn used the proceeds of the offering to help slash its debt. The result: Coke wound up with 49% of a $3.9 billion company—and gained marketing clout by consolidating once-independent bottlers.

Keep this in mind the next time you go to the philharmonic!

You can talk about Coke's splendid balance sheet with lots of cash and little debt and you can even talk about its world empire and how many servings of Coke there are around the world on any given day.

But here may be the most stunning of all the remarkable statistics about Coca-Cola, again noted in its 1989 annual report:

"The Coca-Cola Company began to transform itself into a global enterprise in the early 1920s. For more than 60 years, we have been developing business relationships and investing in a system that today carries an estimated replacement cost of more than $100 billion."

One hundred billion dollars!

Let's say you wanted to enter the soft drink business and match Coke. You can't raise $100 billion. Buffett can't raise $100 billion.

Speaking of $100 billion, Buffett says: "If you gave me $100 billion and said take away the soft drink leadership of Coca-Cola in the world, I'd give it back to you and say it can't be done." (*Fortune*, May 31, 1993)

The 1995 Coca-Cola Annual Report says: "If our Company burned to the ground, we'd have no trouble borrowing the money to rebuild, based on the strength of our trademarks alone."

No brand name is totally immune from competition. GM and IBM weren't. A handful of Japanese tigers took huge bites out of GM and zillions of ants did damage to IBM. Still, in the late 1990s Coke's growth slowed. But if there's an impregnable business franchise on earth, it's Coca-Cola. It is little wonder that in Berkshire's 1990 Annual Report, Buffett says he regards Coca-Cola as "the most valuable franchise in the world."

One Berkshire shareholder said of the Coca-Cola investment, "He really doesn't ever have to make another investment."

In other words, Buffett can basically rely on his huge investments in Coke and Gillette and if they do well, they will carry Berkshire for years to come even if Berkshire makes no new investments.

What Buffett saw in Coca-Cola was a bulletproof international brand name growing quickly, with high margins, domiciled in the United States, right there in good old understandable Atlanta, Georgia, home of the 1996 Summer Olympics, a happenstance upon which Coke capitalized.

When Buffett bought Coca-Cola stock, it was trading at only 12 times earnings.

Buffett gave a number of reasons for buying and others supplied other reasons for him, but in the end, it may be more than just a list of reasons.

"It's like when you marry a girl. Is it her eyes? Her personality? It's a whole bunch of things you can't separate," he said.

When Buffett courted Coke, he did so in a quiet but huge way. For months he had three brokers at the other end of his phones picking off whatever large blocks of Coke stock they could find.

About a week after the March 1989 announcement, *Atlanta Constitution* business writer Melissa Turner interviewed Buffett at his office in Omaha. She asked him why he hadn't bought sooner and he replied, "You wonder what pushes the needle, don't you? Must have just dawned on me."

He also told her, "Let's say you were going away for 10 years and you wanted to make one investment and you know everything you know now, and you couldn't change it while you're gone. What would you think about?

"If I came up with anything in terms of certainty, where I knew the market was going to continue to grow, where I knew the leader was going to continue to be the leader—I mean worldwide—and where I knew there would be big unit growth, I just don't know anything like Coke."

Pausing for a sip of Cherry Coke, he continued, "I'd be relatively sure that when I came back they'd be doing a hell of a lot more business than they are doing now."

He told her that Hershey Foods would also be here but that humanity wouldn't raise its intake of Hershey bars as it will Coke.

"But people are going to drink eight servings of something every day, and history shows that once they are exposed to it [Coke], and I'm living proof, they like drinking it."

She reported that Buffett's portable office refrigerator is stocked full and that there are three unopened Cherry Coke 12-packs on the counter waiting to be chilled.

"I drink five a day and that's 750 calories, which means really a pound every five days and 70 pounds a year..." he told Turner. At the Berkshire Annual Meeting in 1992, he gave things a slightly different spin: "I drink five Cokes a day. That's 750 calories. I would have lost 70 pounds a year if I didn't drink them. Really, it's been a life-saver."

Five Cokes a day? A fib? A white lie from Mr. Squeaky Clean? Does he drink five Cokes a day? "He drinks eight to 10 a day," says Deep Throat, who sees Buffett almost every day.

Buffett told Turner that the night before their chat, it was so hot in his house that he'd hopped out of bed at 2 a.m. and gone downstairs to the refrigerator. After guzzling a Cherry Coke, he felt a lot better and went back to bed.

Shortly after Buffett completed his huge Coke purchase, he flew to Atlanta, Coke's headquarters, and took Goizueta and Keough to lunch.

(Photo by Andrew Kilpatrick)

Coca-Cola headquarters in Atlanta background supplies sugar water to the world. The nearby Varsity restaurant, where Buffett, Goizueta and Keough have eaten together, offers a big supply of Cokes, onion rings and burgers.

So, fellow Coke drinkers, where did Buffett, Goizueta and Keough go for lunch in Atlanta? The Varsity restaurant. The what? The Varsity restaurant.

The Varsity, near Georgia Institute of Technology and Coke's North Avenue headquarters, is a popular, low-priced, fast food restaurant billed as the world's largest drive-in. The trio came to The Varsity at the request of Buffett, whose culinary interests are largely along the lines of straight Crisco washed down with a Cherry Coke. The Varsity does not serve Crisco, but there are few non-cholesterol items and the greasy onion rings are sensational.

The restaurant is a crowded, busy place with a number of rooms, some with school desk chairs lined in front of a television set where fans often watch ballgames. Buffett, Goizueta and Keough did not just pop in. "I called," Keough remembers.

Gordon Muir, personnel director of the restaurant, said, "We knew they were coming...Buffett came in and I met him briefly. You could never tell he was rich."

Muir's mother, Nancy Simms, owner of the restaurant that her father founded in 1928, sat with Buffett, Goizueta and Keough at a round table by a window with a perfect view of Coca-Cola's world headquarters several blocks away. The Varsity is the world's biggest non-chain server of Coca-Cola. It's as if Coke were piped from Coke headquarters.

"Our colors are red and white and so I put a checked red and white tablecloth on the table and put some red begonias in a Varsity carry-out box on the table," Mrs. Simms said. "They are all down-to-earth, people-oriented people...He [Buffett] ordered hot dogs, onion rings and fries. He just loved them...We ate on paper plates...They brought a six-pack of Cherry Cokes with them. That's what he likes," she said.

"They stayed about an hour or an hour and a half. He talked about his businesses, about See's and Nebraska Furniture Mart. He said he likes to buy businesses with good managements and then let them run things as they always have."

"There is something in his personality that comes out that says he's a unique and fun person," she said, adding, "I was hoping he'd buy me out with his last billion."

Sale of The Varsity to Buffett has been kidded about but Buffett's reply was, "She's too smart to sell."

The Varsity is frequented by college students in search of hamburgers, hot dogs and onion rings as well as such people as Jimmy Carter, George Bush and Bill Clinton in search of votes. Former heavyweight boxing champion Evander Holyfield, now a Coke spokesman, has dropped in and so have Burt Reynolds and the late Lucille Ball and Arthur Godfrey. At one point Nipsey Russell worked there. Buffett made his trip to Atlanta about the time he was named to Coke's prestigious board.

After the Berkshire Annual Meeting in April, 1989, Buffett dropped by Borsheim's jewelry store and was surrounded by a band of shareholders.

Buffett had completed his $1 billion purchase of Coca-Cola stock and was asked if he intended to make it a permanent holding. In the annual report it had not been listed as a permanent holding.

Replied Buffett, "Well, I don't want to move it to that category too fast." But it wasn't very long before he was calling it a permanent holding. There was little doubt it was headed toward being a huge holding of permanent value for Berkshire.

Coca-Cola has been a part of people's lives for more than 100 years. The world's best-known trademark originated on May 8, 1886, when, legend has it, pharmacist Dr. John Styth Pemberton first made the syrup for Coca-Cola in a three-legged brass pot in his backyard at 107 Marietta Street in Atlanta.

He carried a jug of the new product down the street to Jacobs Pharmacy, one of Atlanta's leading soda fountains (located not far from today's Underground Atlanta area), where it was sold for a nickel a glass. Willis Venable at Jacobs Pharmacy was the first person to sell Coca-Cola. In its first year, Coke sales averaged six drinks a day. Total sales for the first year were $50. The year's expenses were $73.96; so Pemberton took a loss.

Soon the drink was "Delicious and Refreshing."

Pemberton placed an ad for Coca-Cola in the May 29, 1886, edition of the *Atlanta Journal* claiming the drink was "Delicious, Refreshing, Exhilarating, Invigorating."

On November 15, 1886, legend has it, a man with a hangover asked for something that would ease his headache. Pemberton had touted his drink as a cure for a headache. Whether by design or accident, carbonated water was added with syrup, producing a drink that eased the customer's headache. (*The Real Ones*, by Elizabeth Candler Graham, great-great-granddaughter of Asa Candler, and Ralph Roberts. p. 6)

Mrs. Graham wrote that Asa Candler had sought a cure for headaches all his life since suffering an accident as a child when he fell out of a loaded wagon and a wheel ran over his head.

"One of Pemberton's goals in formulating Coca-Cola was to present a cure for headaches. During almost all of its first decade of life, Coca-Cola was considered a medicine. Candler himself advertised it in the 1890s as 'The Wonderful Nerve and Brain Tonic and Remarkable Therapeutic Agent.' "

In 1887 a patent was filed for a product listed as "Coca-Cola Syrup and Extract."

Thinking that two C's, derived from two of the drink's ingredients—flavoring extracts from the coca leaf and the cola nut—would look nice together in advertising, Pemberton's bookkeeper, Frank M. Robinson, with an ear for alliteration, suggested the name and penned "Coca-Cola" in the flowing Spencerian script now world-famous.

Pemberton also started Coca-Cola's push into advertising, making it one of the first American companies to make substantial use of it.

His early ad efforts began when he painted squares of oilcloth to hang from drugstore awnings. One oilcloth sign over Jacobs' store said "Drink Coca-Cola."

Pemberton sold 25 gallons that first year, shipped in bright red wooden kegs. Red has been the distinctive color associated with the drink ever since.

By 1891, Atlanta businessman Asa G. Candler had acquired complete ownership of Coca-Cola for $2,300. "He essentially bought the whole Coca-Cola Company for $2,000. And that may be the smartest purchase in the history of the world," Buffett said at Berkshire's Annual Meeting in 1997. Within four years, Candler's merchandising skill helped extend availability of Coca-Cola to every state.

Candler, who like Pemberton, developed a number of consumer products, now had the task of mixing the syrup for Coca-Cola. To water he added natural ingredients as well as what came to be known as "Merchandise 7x," the most jealously guarded ingredient in a recipe and trade secret in the world.

Some say the ingredient is cocoa. (*The Real Ones*, Elizabeth Candler Graham and Ralph Roberts, p. 22)

Along the way, looking for a way to serve beverages at a picnic, candy merchant Joseph A. Biedenharn of Vicksburg, Mississippi, became the first person to bottle Coca-Cola, using syrup shipped from Atlanta. His 1894 innovation was a marketing concept that led to wider distribution of the beverages.

In 1899 large-scale bottling became possible. Joseph B. Whitehead and Benjamin F. Thomas of Chattanooga, Tennessee, landed the exclusive right to bottle and sell Coca-Cola to much of the United States.

The contract launched Coca-Cola's independent bottling system that remains the foundation of the company's soft-drink operations. Today the syrups and concentrates for the company's soft-drink products are sold to bottlers around the world, bottlers who package, market and distribute Coke products in their areas.

Coca-Cola held its first annual meeting in 1892 in Atlanta. There were four shareholders present. Annual sales were $49,676.30; the balance sheet carried $74,898.12 in assets. Cash on hand was $11.42.

In 1919, the company was sold to a group of investors headed by Ernest Woodruff for $25 million. His son, Robert W. Woodruff, became president of the company in 1923. For more than six decades his leadership took the business to new heights.

"If you're right about the business, that's really the thing," Buffett said at the Berkshire Annual Meeting in 1992. A classic case he said—noting the pun—is that you could have bought a share of Coca-Cola in 1919 for $40 a share. "A year later it was $19.50," Buffett said. "Sugar prices went up and you lost half your money. Today that $40, if you had reinvested all dividends, is worth $1.8 million [more than $5 million in 1998] and that's with depressions and wars. How much more fruitful it is to invest in a wonderful business."

Coca-Cola is a wonderful business buying back its stock. From 1984 through 1995, Coke repurchased 483 million shares, about 30% of the company. In 1992 Coke authorized a plan to buy back up to 100 million shares of stock, a nice round number again, through the year 2000.

Buffett said at the Berkshire Annual Meeting in 1998 that Coca-Cola's repurchase of its stock, even at 40 times earnings, is a good use of the company's capital. "It sounds like a very high price, when you name it in terms of P/E to buy back stock at that kind of number," Buffett said. Still, "it's the best large business in the world. I approve of Coke's repurchases. I'd rather have them repurchase at 15 times earnings, but it's a very efficient way of using capital."

Berkshire has done even better than Coke. Berkshire's annual increase in stock price since Buffett took over is between 25% and 30%, whereas Coke's average annual increase—from $40 to about $4 million—is less than 20%. But, as Buffett says, Coke has been through depressions and wars. Berkshire under Buffett has yet to live through a world war. Coke survived two of them.

Among Woodruff's contributions during many of those years were the six-pack and open-top cooler, vending and dispensing equipment and displays and promotions. Under him commercially successful Coca-Cola eventually became an institution the world over.

Coca-Cola, which already had gone international in the 1890s by branching out to Canada and Cuba, began its association with the Olympics in 1928, when an American freighter arrived in Amsterdam carrying the United States Olympic team and 1,000 cases of Coca-Cola. In the 1920s it penetrated Europe and even amid World War II, it opened 64 bottling plants abroad with government help.

In 1941, as the United States entered World War II, Woodruff decreed that, "every man in uniform gets a bottle of Coca-Cola for five cents, wherever he is and whatever it costs the company."

As Mark Pendergrast, author of *For God, Country and Coca-Cola*, wrote in a *New York Times* article August 15, 1993, successful companies need dedicated consumers, "People like the World War II soldier who wrote home that 'the most important question in amphibious landings is whether the Coke machine goes ashore in the first or second wave.'"

The presence of Coca-Cola not only lifted troop morale, it also gave foreigners their first taste of Coke and paved the way for future bottling operations overseas. Even after the troops left, Coke stayed, establishing its own beachhead as one of the first American products widely available overseas. Naturally this increased the value of its name.

Coca-Cola is the official soft drink of the Super Bowl, the National Football League and its teams.

The trademark "Coca-Cola" was registered with the U.S. Patent and Trademark Office in 1893, followed by "Coke" in 1945. The bottle so familar to consumers was designed by Root Glass Co. of Terre Haute, Indiana, in 1916.

In 1982 The Coca-Cola Co. introduced Diet Coke, marking the first extension of the company's trademark to another product. Today, Diet Coke is the nation's top one-calorie soft drink and the third best-selling soft drink of any kind. Cherry Coke, Buffett's particular favorite, was rolled out in 1985, a year most famous for the introduction of New Coke. Diet Cherry Coke came out in 1986.

Later, other drinks were to join a powerful line of Coke products. In addition to Sprite, introduced in 1960 and now the world's number one lemon-lime soft drink, Coca-Cola's brands include Mr. Pibb, Mello Yello, Fanta, Tab, Fresca, Powerade, Five Alive, Fruitopia, Hi-C, and Bacardi Tropical fruit mixers. Coke also owns The Minute Maid Company, the leading maker of juices and juice drinks.

Although over the years Coke has expanded to other businesses, more and more it is shedding extra businesses to concentrate on being a worldwide soft drink company. And in 1999 Coke came out with its bottled water product, Dasani.

Coke sold its minority interest in Columbia Pictures, the movie and television studio it bought in 1982, to Sony Corp. for $5 billion in late 1989. It invested much of the money in new bottling systems as well as buying back its own stock, almost always a hallmark of Buffett's investees.

(With permission of The Coca-Cola Company)

Goizueta spearheaded Coke's buy of Columbia Pictures seven years earlier. But he later sold Columbia Pictures and the businesses not related to the beverage industry, and once said, "There's a perception in this country that you're better off if you're in two lousy businesses than if you're in one good one—that you're spreading the risk. It's crazy."

In 1990, Coke opened a $15 million museum to itself in Atlanta called "The World of Coca-Cola," located next to Underground Atlanta. Its visitors have even included Tibetan monks.

The World of Coca-Cola exhibits include the original patent for Coke, a 1930s soda fountain, Coke's well-known Santa Claus ads, and a gift shop. Among the 1,000 artifacts displayed is the prototype of the famous 6½-ounce curvy bottle. Wider than the one that was actually adopted, the bottle is one of only two in existence and worth about $10,000. Almost 200 flags that line the lobby show the markets where Coke is sold.

As you move through the exhibits, you encounter bathing beauties, sports heroes and movie stars who have popularized Coke's advertising through the years. There are cardboard cutouts featuring such celebrities as Jean Harlow and Cary Grant pitching Coca-Cola.

Besides the displays of print advertising, there is a retrospective look at Coke's television commercials. There is, probably to the delight of Pepsi fans, a 1969 commercial featuring Ray Charles, who later pitched Pepsi's popular ads—"You Got The Right One, Baby. Uh Huh."

The museum admission fee is $6.00. Each visitor gets a complimentary Coke served from a futuristic soda fountain. The nearby 1930s style soda fountain was the setting for the photo of the board of directors for Coca-Cola's 1990 Annual Report.

Some surmise Buffett and Coke are planning a CokeWorld on the Moon, a Disney-like concept, which, if successful, could be exported to other orbiting bodies.

Although Coke has only about 10,000 employees in the U.S. and about 23,000 outside the U.S., around the world about one million people have employment in some connection with Coke's products.

Coca-Cola, so admired for its marketing skills, committed the ultimate marketing fiasco in 1985 when it changed its famous 7x formula, which has been in an Atlanta bank vault for 99 years. Over the years the formula has been tinkered with at times but only to accommodate better forms of the original ingredients or better ways of processing them. This was a radical change—a whole "new" Coke.

In the research leading up to the introduction of New Coke, one question was never asked: "How would you feel if we took your Coke away?" (*I'd Like to Buy The World a Coke: The Life and Leadership of Roberto Goizueta*, David Greising, p. 112) One focus group participant, however, summed things up this way: "What do you mean you're taking away my f—ing Coca Cola?" Others were less polite. (ibid, p. 114)

Public outcry over the Black Tuesday announcement was swift and massive. The public relations disaster was immortalized by songwriter George Pickard who recorded, "Coke Was It."

Three months later the company went back to the original formula with Coca-Coca Classic and also kept New Coke. "Coke Are It," said some. The fantastic episode worked in Coke's favor as its overall market share bubbled to 40% from 37.5%. The day Coke announced it was bringing back its original formula, ABC News interrupted "General Hospital" with the news flash, and 18,000 gleeful Coke fans lit up Coke's switchboard in Atlanta.

The museum display explaining this to visitors quotes then Coke President Keough: "Some critics will say Coca-Cola made a marketing mistake. Some cynics will say that we planned the whole thing. The truth is we are not that dumb and we are not that smart." Speaking of smart and dumb, a Trust Company of Georgia director once said, "Our dumbness in not being smart enough to diversify

(Photo by Tommy Terrell)

Large Coca-Cola bottles on display during the 1996 Olympics in Atlanta.

has been the smartest thing any dumb people ever did." (*Secret Formula*, Frederick Allen, p. 422)

It's not unusual for Coca-Cola to come up with great marketing ideas. In 1923 it introduced a marketing revolution with the carry-out six-pack container. But in 1990 its ill-conceived MagiCan promotion was ended after paper money failed to pop out of a few of the special cans.

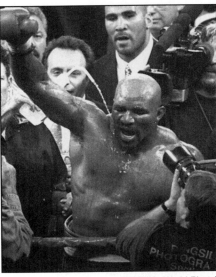

(AP/Wide World Photo)

Evander Holyfield

But all along, Coke has continued to, in Buffett's words, "blanket the world."

Throughout the 20th Century, Coke has played a part in national celebrations and global happenings, and Coke has been linked to World's Fairs and national expositions since 1905.

And only an alien would not have foreseen that Coke was planning a massive marketing campaign at the 1996 Olympics in Atlanta, a city where, an Associated Press reporter once wrote: "Four out of five dentists recommend their patients rinse with Coca-Cola." Indeed, Coke's "The World Together—Always" ads started appearing on Atlanta billboards in early 1994. Coca-Cola is the longest-running and largest corporate sponsor of the Olympics.

To assist in that event, Coca-Cola was never unaware that Evander Holyfield, fittingly of Atlanta, could make a knockout ad. Indeed, in November, 1990, Coke and Pepsi were vying for Holyfield's endorsement. You guessed it, Coke signed Holyfield for a six-year agreement—an agreement billed as "The Real Thing" signing with "The Real Deal." The agreement was probably for a real cost, too, but the amount was not disclosed.

It was no accident that Holyfield warmed up for his fight with big George Foreman April 19, 1991, wearing a red Coca-Cola Classic T-shirt, conveniently visible to fans watching the fight on cable television.

The contract called for Holyfield to appear in advertising for company products as well as to make personal appearances on behalf of

Coca-Cola Slogans

1886	Drink Coca-Cola
1904	Delicious and Refreshing
1905	Coca-Cola Revives and Sustains
1906	The Great National Temperance Drink
1917	Three Million a Day
1922	Thirst Knows No Season
1925	Six Million a Day
1927	Around the Corner From Everywhere
1929	The Pause that Refreshes
1932	Ice-Cold Sunshine
1938	The Best Friend Thirst Ever Had
1939	Coca-Cola Goes Along
1942	Wherever You Are, Whatever You Do, Wherever You May Be, When You Think of Refreshment, Think Ice-Cold Coca-Cola
1942	The Only Thing Like Coca-Cola is Coca-Cola Itself. It's The Real Thing
1948	Where There's Coke, There's Hospitality
1949	Coca-Cola...Along The Highway To Anywhere
1952	What You Want Is A Coke
1956	Coca-Cola...Making Good Things Taste Better
1957	Sign of Good Taste
1958	The Cold, Crisp Taste Of Coke
1959	Be Really Refreshed
1963	Things Go Better With Coke
1970	It's The Real Thing
1971	I'd Like To Buy The World A Coke
1975	Look Up America
1976	Coke Adds Life
1979	Have A Coke And A Smile
1982	Coke Is It!
1985	We've Got a Taste For You (Coca-Cola and Coca-Cola Classic) America's Real Choice
1986	Catch the Wave (Coca-Cola) Red, White and You (Coca-Cola Classic)
1989	Can't Beat The Real Feeling
1990	Can't Beat The Real Thing
1993	Always Coca-Cola
2000	Coca-Cola Enjoy.com

(Source: Coca-Cola's Website)

the company. Holyfield worked with the company on its Olympic Games activities. Even with Holyfield and whatever ads Coke dreams up in the future, Coke will be hard put to beat the success of some of its previous efforts.

Curiously, Holyfield pulled a Buffett-like investment, scoring a financial knockout, buying more than a million dollars worth of Coke stock in early 1991. (*Forbes*, December 23, 1991) So Holyfield may have taken Buffett for one round, but there has been no conjecture—even from ABC Sports—about how Buffett would fare, even for a round, in the boxing ring against Holyfield. Mike Tyson himself didn't fare well against "The Real Deal" in 1996 or 1997 although both increased their net worth enough to afford a few shares of Coke. Baseball's Ty Cobb began investing in 1908 and did very well on the stock.

Getting back to Coke's sports ads, the early 1980s saw the "Mean" Joe Greene Coke ad. As the lineman from the world champion Pittsburgh Steelers limped out of a stadium he was trailed by a timid young fan carrying a bottle of Coca-Cola.

The boy's offer of a cold Coke was at first refused, then accepted as "Mean" Joe downed the bottle without a pause. Refreshed, he straightened up, flashed a smile and tossed his jersey to the youngster.

Other celebrities who have endorsed Coke or Diet Coke are Sugar Ray Leonard, Elton John and Ted Turner, whose CNN empire is not far from the Coke headquarters in Atlanta.

But perhaps no ad beats the one aired during Super Bowl XXIV when Coke premiered its "Hilltop Reunion," the new version of one of the most famous television commercials of all time with "I'd Like to Buy the World a Coke." In 1971, the company's Hilltop commercial brought together young people from around the world to the Italian countryside near Rome for the expression of world unity and, incidentally, to advertise Coke. Many original cast members and their children were located for the new, 60-second spot in 1990. The response to the original ad was so overwhelming the company pressed 45 rpm versions of it.

To satisfy an increasing number of requests from disc jockeys, the company put out a second, slightly reworded version, "I'd Like to Teach the World to Sing." Renditions of "I'd Like to Teach the World to Sing" propelled their way to the pop music charts, selling a million copies by the end of the year.

Like the original spot, the contemporary version focused on the simple, but striking imagery of people from around the world joining together on a mountaintop to offer a message of hope.

Finding the young, blond, British woman who opened the 1971 spot with the lyric, "I'd like to buy the world a home and furnish it with love..." is a story in itself. Her name was Linda Higson, but old files incorrectly listed her as "Hipson," which temporarily foiled detectives, including Pinkerton's best, scouring Europe for the missing woman.

With production set to begin in Italy, she still had not been found. As a last resort, an advertisement was placed in the classified section of several international and British newspapers. (Buffett has long proclaimed the "billboard" benefits of newspapers.) The newspaper ad read: "Linda Hipson where are you? If you're the Linda Hipson who was in the Coca-Cola commercial 20 years ago, please call U.S. (212)-984-2611. We'd love to hear you sing again."

In Stockholm, a friend of Ms. Higson's was waiting at the airport and came upon the ad in the *International Herald Tribune* (appropriately owned in part by another Berkshire investee, The Washington Post Co.). The similarity of the names, he figured, was enough. He called Linda in Cheshire, England. Linda—like E.T. phoning home—called McCann-Erickson in New York and Coke's ad agency called the producers in Rome.

As the central character was on her way to Italy, "Hilltop Reunion" was quickly redesigned around her appearance. Linda Higson Neary, now married with four daughters, again opened the 1990s version of the commercial, this time with daughter Kelly, who celebrated her 10th birthday on location. Coke got a great plug out of it.

Buffett has called Coke his favorite stock. Five months after he announced the Coke investment, Buffett filed a statement with the Securities and Exchange Commission for clearance to more than double his stake to up to 15% of Coke's common stock. J. Verne McKenzie, Berkshire's chief financial officer at the time, said, "This does not say there are plans now to buy," noting that purchase plans would be made based on stock price and market conditions. "This gives us a flexibility to buy to match our flexibility to sell...There are no plans to sell now."

Suggestion: Keep your eye on KO, Coke's stock symbol. Even Buffett's grandson, Howie, owns a few shares of Coca-Cola.

"Things Go Better with Coke" and "You Can't Beat the Real Thing." Buffett surely believes it. In the year 2000, tune in to see how many billions Buffett's original $1 billion plus Coke stake is worth.

Buffett has, as Elvis would say, "a hunk a hunk of burning love" for Coke.

When Coke reported a 13-14% increase in volume in the first quarter of 1998 instead of the expected 9-10%, with an accompanying pop in the stock, a posting on AOL's "Berkshire message board" flashed: "200,000,000 shares x 3.125=$625,000,000, I'll drink to that."

When Coke's stock price was slammed by the international financial crisis of the summer of 1998, Buffett stood steady in the quarterback's pocket telling *The New York Times* (November 1, 1998): "In given countries at given times there will be hiccups. But that doesn't take your eye off where you want to be 10 or 15 years from now, which is to have everybody drinking nothing but Coke."

Buffett related a story about taking his grandson out for a pizza at an Omaha restaurant and discovered the place served Pepsi, not Coke.

"I mentioned it to Atlanta, and World War III broke out. They're now serving Coke."

On December 11, 1998 Cadbury Schweppes, the world's No. 3 soda maker, agreed to sell most of its soft-drink businesses outside the U.S. to Coca-Cola for about $1.85 billion. However, the deal went through only partially.

The agreement included Schweppes, Dr Pepper, Canada Dry and the Crush brand in a number of countries.

After Coca-Cola's annual meeting in 1999 Ivester and Buffett signed autographs. Buffett, asked if he was happy with his Coke investment, said: "We'll have it 10 years from now, 20 years from now and 30 years from now." (*Wall Street Journal*, April 22, 1999)

The Wind

Jill Silverman of New York City has a story about Buffett, Coke and a children's book she wrote featuring Coca-Cola. She and her husband, Josh, have been Berkshire shareholders since 1994.

In 1996 they visited some friends in Italy and found their two-year-old son Marco wanted a Coke every time he saw the red and white logo. Jill wrote a short children's book about a "wind" that brought Josh and Jill and Coca-Cola to young Marco.

Jill sent the story to Buffett who replied immediately: "I really enjoyed your book about Marco. In fact, it's so good I've sent it along to Doug Ivester, the CEO of Coke. "I'm enclosing a little something for Marco (not as good as a Coke, however) and maybe the "wind" can deliver it to him at some appropriate time.

"Come up and say hello at one of the weekend events prior to the annual meeting. Sincerely, Warren E. Buffett."

The gift to Marco was a note saying: "Hi Marco—keep drinking Coca-Cola. Warren E. Buffett."

Berkshire share-holders Celia and Bob Sullivan, of Springfield, Massachusetts, at Berkshire annual meeting festivities in 1999 with their favorite beverage. Bob says, "I can't believe I drank the whole bottle."

(Photo courtesy of Bob Sullivan)

38

DEFINING BRAND NAME
IN VIETNAM AND ITALY

Berkshire shareholder Lyle McIntosh, of Missouri Valley, Iowa, offered this post on the "Berkshire's Internet message board" April 11, 1999. This is the meaning of brand name:

This winter in Vietnam I had a humorous experience on a day trip out of Hanoi to the Perfume Pagoda. After a two-hour minibus ride out of Hanoi, we prepared to embark on an hour's canoe ride before an hour-and-a-half hike up a mountain to the Perfume Pagoda. Four of us were about to enter a canoe, when we were approached by two boys, 16-year-old Hoa, and a 13-year-old I called Felix, because of his Felix the Cat T-shirt. They each had a small container containing about 3 Cokes each and asked if they could accompany us for the day, hoping to sell us one coke each at the top of the mountain. They were likable and friendly boys, and we said "hop in." We found out later, that they spend the whole day going up and down the mountain, considering it a success if they can sell a couple of Cokes.

There was a Viet woman paddling each canoe for the hour up the river. It was hot so the boys took turns relieving them some.

Departing from the canoes, the one and a half hour hike up the rather steep trail was also demanding, as it was becoming much more hot and humid. All the way up the mountain, Hoa stuck close to me telling me constantly that "Don't worry, Mister, I have Coca-Cola. It make you feel good. No problem. Don't worry. I have Coca-Cola." He must have told me this about a hundred times. We finally got to the top, and everyone was tired and sweating. I sat down on a rock and Hoa then approached me, dripping with perspiration, and said, "Now sir, you are very tired, but Hoa sell you Coca-Cola, and you feel much better. No problem. You will see." After paddling for an hour, and climbing for an hour and one half, he anticipated his reward.

I couldn't resist teasing him a little, and I just looked at him and very seriously said, "Sorry, Hoa, but I only drink Pepsi."

His brow immediately furrowed, and looking very worried, he

immediately went into his sales pitch, "Please, sir, you don't understand, Americans only like Coca-Cola. Coca-Cola make you feel good. Last year I t.ing 2 Pepsi-Cola up the mountain, and nobody buy, they say Americans no like Pepsi. They tell me Americans only like Coca-Cola. So now I only sell Coca-Cola. Coca-Cola very good. Please, sir."

So as I was only human, and very hot and tired, I said "OK, Hoa, I think I'll take a Coke." And, lo and behold, it was very good and it made me happy.

In Italy

Jack "The Italian Stallion" Benvent, of Haworth, New Jersey, gave this version of brand name power in a post July 8, 1999:

I have just returned from about a month in Italy. The places I visited included sojourns to the villages where my grandfathers were born and raised. Very emotional experiences. I will be writing it up for my family when time permits.

In the case of my father's father (the man for whom I am named), there had been little or no contact between the new world and the old world for over 50 years. He died when my Dad was a small boy. I'll spare you all the gory details, but I set out to find the house of my grandfather's family armed with nothing but a 50-year-old postcard (that I learned later was of the wrong village) and a 52-year-old snapshot of his house. It took quite awhile and I ended up having to hike for miles up the side of a mountain, but I found it. A miracle. Euphoria.

As I was taking photos of the house to show my father, a woman comes out and asks me in Italian what I was doing. I explained and in the process learned that she was my father's first cousin! Amazing. First shock, then tears followed. She graciously invited me into her home and offered me food and drink. We talk. She explained that the only person from their small mountaintop village to ever even visit America was my grandfather (in the 1920s)—and that I was the first American to visit their village since 1952, just after the war (hyperbole I'm sure—but, then again, there really isn't a reason for an American to visit Teriasca unless you are really into mountain climbing and chickens).

Anyway, here's the point. She sees I'm exhausted and offers food and drink. I only ask for water. That isn't good enough to give a visitor who has journeyed so far, she says, and she hands me a bottle of Coke! I like Coke, don't I?"

39
WRITING COKE PUTS

When brand-name stocks, including Coca-Cola, took a hammering after Philip Morris' April 2, 1993, "Marlboro Friday" announcement that it was lowering prices by 20% for its Marlboro cigarettes to better compete with generic cigarettes, Buffett did the unusual.

Despite his distaste generally for options, in April 1993, he wrote (sold) out-of-the-money put options, for $1.50 apiece, to buy three million Coca-Cola shares. The options expired December 17, 1993, and were exercisable until then at about $35 a share.

At the Berkshire Annual Meeting in April 1993, Buffett confirmed the move and said he had added another two million shares in a similar move.

What all this meant was that Buffett got $7.5 million in cash up front, and consequently, had the stock gone down from the roughly $40 range where it was then trading, to roughly $35 a share, he would have had to buy five million shares of Coke at roughly that $35 price. Since Buffett had already received $1.50 a share, his effective cost would have been about $33.50.

His only risk under this "put" contract, was that if Coke stock dropped below $33.50 in December he would have had to pay $35 for the stock, rather than whatever lower price Coke was selling for in the stock market at the time. But if the stock were lower, he might also have bought more Coke stock anyway, because he was willing to buy Coke stock at $35 a share.

For Buffett, it was pretty much a win-win situation, a case of getting cash and having your Coke stock, too. The options worked and Buffett pocketed the $7.5 million. But don't try this at home, unless you're an experienced investor.

40

QUICK, HOW COULD YOU TURN $2 MILLION INTO $2 TRILLION?
CHARLES MUNGER SEEKS EDUCATIONAL REFORM BY POSING A RIDDLE

Let's say you were to imagine that it is still 1884 and you had 15 minutes to plausibly explain how to go into the beverage business and turn $2 million into $2 trillion. You are secretly aided by your 1996 knowledge of all the past progress of The Coca-Cola Company. Even with the help of this vast hindsight, can you persuasively lay out the right business plan under 1884 conditions? And, if you can't do it well, what are the educational implications?

These are the questions Berkshire Vice Chairman Charles Munger posed on July 20, 1996 to a group including CEOs and educators. Munger's talk was as follows:

The title of my talk is "Practical thought about practical thought?"—with a question mark at the end.

In a long career I have assimilated various ultrasimple general notions that I find helpful in solving problems. Five of these helpful notions I will now describe. After that I will present to you a problem of extreme scale. Indeed, the problem will involve turning start-up capital of two million dollars into two trillion dollars, a sum large enough to represent a practical achievement. Then I will try to solve the problem, assisted by my helpful general notions. Following that, I will suggest that there are important educational implications in my demonstration. I will so finish because my objective is educational, my game today being a search for better methods of thought.

The first helpful notion is that it is usually best to simplify problems by deciding big "no-brainer" questions first.

The second helpful notion mimics Galileo's conclusion that scientific reality is often revealed only by math, as if math was the language of God. Galileo's attitude also works well in messy practical life. Without numerical fluency, in the part of life most of us inhabit, you are like a one-legged man in an ass-kicking contest.

The third helpful notion is that it is not enough to think problems through forward. You must also think in reverse, much like the rustic who wanted to know where he was going to die so that he'd never go there. Indeed, many problems can't be solved forward. And that is why the great algebrist, Carl Jacobi, so often said: "Invert, always invert." And why Pythagoras thought in reverse to prove that the square root of two was an irrational number.

The fourth helpful notion is that the best and most practical wisdom is elementary academic wisdom. But there is one extremely important qualification: You must think in a multidisciplinary manner. You must routinely use all the easy-to-learn concepts from the freshman course in every basic subject. Where elementary ideas will serve, your problem solving must not be limited, as academia and many business bureaucracies are limited, by extreme Balkanization into disciplines and subdisciplines, with strong taboos against any venture outside assigned territory. Instead, you must do your multidisciplinary thinking in accord with Ben Franklin's prescription in Poor Richard: "If you want it done, go. If not send."

If, in your thinking, you rely entirely on others, often through purchase of professional advice, whenever outside a small territory of your own, you will suffer much calamity. And it is not just difficulties in complex coordination that will do you in. You will also suffer from the reality evoked by the Shavian character who said: "In the last analysis, every profession is a conspiracy against the laity." Indeed, a Shavian character for once understated the horrors of something Shaw didn't like. It is not usually the conscious malfeasance of your narrow professional adviser that does you in. Instead, your troubles come from his subconscious bias. His cognition will often be impaired, for your purposes, by financial incentives different from yours. And he will also suffer from the psychological defect caught by the proverb: "To a man with a hammer, every problem looks like a nail."

The fifth helpful notion is that really big effects, lalapalooza effects will often come only from large combinations of factors. For instance, tuberculosis was tamed, at least for a long time, only by routine combined use in each case of three different drugs. And other lalapalooza effects, like the flight of an airplane, follow a similar pattern.

It is now time to present my practical problem. And here is the problem:

It is 1884 in Atlanta. You are brought, along with twenty others like you, before a rich and eccentric Atlanta citizen named Glotz. Both you and Glotz share two characteristics: first, you routinely use in problem solving the five helpful notions, and second, you know all the elementary ideas in all the basic college courses, as taught in

1996. However, all discoverers and all examples demonstrating these elementary ideas come from dates transposed back before 1884. Glotz knows nothing about anything that has happened after 1884 and you must pretend that you share his ignorance.

Glotz offers to invest two million 1884 dollars, yet take only half the equity, for a Glotz Charitable Foundation, in a new corporation organized to go into the non-alcoholic beverage business and remain in that business only, forever. Glotz wants to use a name that has somehow charmed him: Coca-Cola.

The other half of the new corporation's equity will go to the man who most plausibly demonstrates that his business plan will cause Glotz's foundation to be worth a trillion dollars 150 years later, in the money of the later time, 2034, despite paying out a large part of its earnings each year as a dividend. This will make the whole new corporation worth two trillion dollars, even after paying out many billions of dollars in dividends.

You have fifteen minutes to make your pitch. What do you say to Glotz?

And here is my solution, my pitch to Glotz, using only the helpful notions and what every bright college sophomore should now know.

Well Glotz, the big "no-brainer" decisions that, to simplify our problem, should be made first are as follows: First, we are never going to create something worth two trillion dollars by selling some generic beverage. Therefore we must make your name "Coca-Cola," into a strong, legally protected trademark. Second, we can get to two trillion dollars only by starting in Atlanta, then succeeding in the rest of the United States, then rapidly succeeding with our new beverage all over the world. This will require powerful elemental forces. And the right place to find such powerful elemental forces is in the subject matter of elementary academic courses.

We will next use numerical fluency to ascertain what our target implies. We can guess reasonably that by 2034 there will be about eight billion beverage consumers in the world. On average, each of these consumers will be much more prosperous in real terms than the average consumer of 1884. Each consumer is composed mostly of water and must ingest about 64 ounces of water per day. This is eight eight-ounce servings. Thus, if our new beverage, and other imitative beverages in our new market, can flavor and otherwise improve only 25% of ingested water worldwide, and we can occupy half of the new world market, we can sell 2.92 trillion eight-ounce servings in 2034. And if we can then net four cents per serving, we will earn $117 billion. This will be enough, if our business is still growing at a good rate, to make it easily worth two trillion dollars.

A big question, of course, is whether four cents per serving is a reasonable profit target for 2034. And the answer is yes, if we can create a beverage with strong universal appeal. 150 years is a long time. The dollar, like the Roman drachma, will almost surely suffer monetary depreciation. Concurrently, real purchasing power of the average beverage consumer in the world will go way up for reasons well explained by Adam Smith. Moreover, the customer's proclivity to inexpensively improve his experience while ingesting water will go up considerably faster. Meanwhile, as technology improves, the cost of our simple product, in units of constant purchasing power, will go down. All four factors will work together in favor of our four-cents-per-serving profit target. Worldwide beverage-purchasing power in dollars will probably multiply by a factor of at least forty over 150 years. Thinking in reverse, this makes our profit-per-serving target, under 1884 conditions, a mere one fortieth of four cents or one tenth of a cent per serving. This is an easy-to-exceed target as we start out if our new product has universal appeal.

That decided, we must next solve the problem of invention to create universal appeal. There are two intertwined challenges of large scale: First, over 150 years we must cause a new-beverage market to assimilate about one fourth of the world's water ingestion. Second, we must so operate that half the new market is ours, while all our competitors combined are left to share the remaining half. These results are lalapalooza results. Accordingly, we must attack our problem by causing every favorable factor we can think of to work for us. Plainly, only a powerful combination of many factors is likely to cause the lalapalooza consequences we desire. Fortunately, the solution to these intertwined problems turns out to be fairly easy, if one has stayed awake in all the freshman courses.

Let us start by exploring the consequences of our simplifying "no-brainer" decision that we must rely on a strong trademark. This conclusion automatically leads to an understanding of the essence of our business in proper elementary academic terms. We can see from the introductory course in psychology that, in essence, we are going into the business of creating and maintaining conditioned reflexes. The "Coca Cola" trade name and trade dress will act as the stimuli, and the purchase and ingestion of our beverage will be the desired responses.

And how does one create and maintain conditioned reflexes? Well, the psychology text gives two answers: (1) by operant conditioning, using rewards, and (2) by classical conditioning, often called Pavlovian conditioning to honor the great Russian scientist. And, since we want a lalapalooza result, we must use both conditioning techniques—and all we can invent to enhance effects from each technique.

The operant-conditioning part of our problem is easy to solve. We need only to (1) maximize rewards of our beverage's ingestion, and (2) minimize possibilities that desired reflexes, once created by us, will be extinguished through operant conditioning by proprietors of competing products.

(Photo by LaVerne Ramsey)

Munger drinks to Coke's future.

For operant conditioning rewards, there are only a few categories we will find practical:

(1) Food value in calories or other inputs;

(2) Flavor, texture and aroma acting as stimuli to consumption under neural pre-programming of man through Darwinian natural selection;

(3) Stimulus, as by sugar or caffeine;

(4) Cooling effect when man is too hot or warming effect when man is too cool.

Wanting a lalapalooza result, we will naturally include rewards in all the categories.

To start out, it is easy to decide to design our beverage for consumption cold. There is much less opportunity, without ingesting beverage, to counteract excessive heat, compared with excessive cold. Moreover, with excessive heat, much liquid must be consumed, and the reverse is not true. It is also easy to decide to include both sugar and caffeine. After all, tea, coffee and lemonade are already widely consumed. And it is also clear that we must be fanatic about characteristics that will maximize human pleasure while taking in the sugared water and caffeine we will provide. And, to counteract possibilities that desired operant-conditioned reflexes, once created by us, will be extinguished by operant conditioning employing competing products, there is also an obvious answer: we will make it a permanent obsession in our company that our beverage, as fast as practicable, will at all times be available everywhere throughout the world. After all, a competing product, if it is never tried, can't act as a reward creating a conflicting habit. Every spouse knows that.

We must next consider the Pavlovian conditioning we must also use. In Pavlovian conditioning powerful effects come from mere association. The neural system of Pavlov's dog causes it to salivate at the bell it can't eat. And the brain of man yearns for the type of beverage held by the pretty woman he can't have. And so, Glotz, we must use every sort of decent, honorable Pavlovian conditioning we can think of. For as long as we are in business, our beverage and its promotion must be associated in consumer minds with all other things consumers like or admire.

Such extensive Pavlovian conditioning will cost a lot of money, particularly for advertising. We will spend big money as far ahead as we can imagine. But the money will be effectively spent. As we expand fast in our new-beverage market, our competitors will face gross disadvantages of scale in buying advertising to create the Pavlovian conditioning they need. And this outcome, along with other volume-creates-power effects, should help us gain and hold at least 50% of the new market everywhere. Indeed, provided buyers are scattered, our higher volumes will give us very extreme cost advantages in distribution.

Moreover, Pavlovian effects from mere association will help us choose the flavor, texture and color of our new beverage. Considering Pavlovian effects, we will have wisely chosen the exotic and expensive-sounding name "Coca-Cola," instead of a pedestrian name like "Glotz's Sugared, Caffeinated Water." For similar Pavlovian reasons, it will be wise to have our beverage look pretty much like wine, instead of sugared water. And so we will artificially color our beverage if it comes out clear. And we will carbonate our water, making our product seem like champagne, or some other expensive beverage, while also making its flavor better and imitation harder to arrange for competing products. And, because we are going to attach so many expensive psychological effects to our flavor, that flavor should be different from any other standard flavor so that we maximize difficulties for competitors and give no accidental same-flavor benefit to any existing product.

What else, from the psychology textbook, can help our new business? Well, there is that powerful "monkey-see, monkey-do" aspect of human nature that psychologists often call "social proof." Social proof, imitative consumption triggered by mere sight of consumption, will not only help induce trial of our beverage, it will also bolster perceived rewards from consumption. We will always take this powerful social-proof factor into account as we design advertising and sales promotion and as we forego present profit to enhance present and future consumption. More than with most other products, increased selling power will come from each increase in sales.

We can now see, Glotz, that by combining (1) much Pavlovian conditioning, (2) powerful social-proof effects, and (3) a wonderful-tasting, energy-giving, stimulating and desirably cold beverage that causes much operant conditioning, we are going to get sales that speed up for a long time by reason of the huge mixture of factors we have chosen. Therefore, we are going to start something like an auto-catalytic reaction in chemistry, precisely the sort of multi-factor-triggered lalapalooza effect we need.

The logistics and the distribution strategy of our business will be simple. There are only two practical ways to sell our beverage (1) as syrup to fountains and restaurants, and (2) as a complete carbonated-water product in containers. Wanting lalapalooza results, we will naturally do it both ways. And, wanting huge Pavlovian and social-proof effects, we will always spend on advertising and sales promotion, per serving, over 40% of the fountain price for syrup needed to make the serving.

A few syrup-making plants can serve the world. However, to avoid needless shipping of mere space and water, we will need many bottling plants scattered over the world. We will maximize profits if (like early General Electric with light bulbs) we always set the first-sale price, either (1) for fountain syrup, or (2) for any container of our complete product. The best way to arrange this desirable profit-maximizing control is to make any independent bottler we need a subcontractor, not a vendee of syrup, and certainly not a vendee of syrup under a perpetual franchise specifying a syrup price frozen forever at its starting level.

Being unable to get a patent or copyright on our superimportant flavor, we will work obsessively to keep our formula secret. We will make a big hoopla over our secrecy, which will enhance Pavlovian effects. Eventually food-chemical engineering will advance so that our flavor can be copied with near exactitude. But, by that time, we will be so far ahead, with such strong trademarks and complete, "always available" worldwide distribution, that good flavor copying won't bar us from our objective. Moreover, the advances in food chemistry that help competitors will almost surely be accompanied by technological advances that will help us, including refrigeration, better transportation, and, for dieters, ability to insert a sugar taste without inserting sugar's calories. Also, there will be related beverage opportunities we will seize.

This brings us to a final reality check for our business plan. We will, once more, think in reverse like Jacobi. What must we avoid because we don't want it? Four answers seem clear:

First we must avoid the protective, cloying, stop-consumption effects of aftertaste that are a standard part of physiology, developed through Darwinian evolution to enhance the replication of man's genes by forcing a generally helpful moderation on the gene carrier. To serve our ends, on hot days a consumer must be able to drink container after container of our product with almost no impediment from aftertaste. We will find a wonderful no-aftertaste flavor by trial and error and will thereby solve this problem.

Second, we must avoid ever losing even half of our powerful trade-marked name. It will cost us mightily, for instance, if our sloppiness should ever allow sale of any other kind of "Cola," for instance, a "Peppy Cola". If there is ever a "Peppy Cola," we will be the proprietor of the brand.

Third, with so much success coming, we must avoid bad effects from envy, given a prominent place in the ten commandments because envy is so much a part of human nature. The best way to avoid envy, recognized by Aristotle, is to plainly deserve the success we get. We will be fanatic about product quality, quality of product presentation, and reasonableness of prices, considering the harmless pleasure we will provide.

Fourth, after our trademarked flavor dominates our new market, we must avoid making any huge and sudden change in our flavor. Even if a new flavor performs better in blind taste tests, changing to that new flavor would be a foolish thing to do. This follows because, under such conditions, our old flavor will be so entrenched in consumer preference by psychological effects that a big flavor change would do us little good, and it would do immense harm by triggering in consumers the standard deprival super-reaction syndrome that makes "take-aways" so hard to get in any type of negotiation and helps make most gamblers so irrational. Moreover, such a large flavor change would allow a competitor, by copying our old flavor, to take advantage of both (1) the hostile consumer super-reaction to deprival and (2) the huge love of our original flavor created by our previous work.

Well, that is my solution to my own problem of turning two million dollars into two trillion dollars, even after paying out billions of dollars in dividends. I think it would have won with Glotz in 1884 and should convince you more than you expected at the outset. After all, the correct strategies are clear after being related to elementary academic ideas brought into play by the helpful notions.

How consistent is my solution with the history of the real Coca Cola Company? Well, as late as 1896, twelve years after the fictional Glotz was to start vigorously with two million 1884 dollars, the real Coca Cola Company had a net worth under $150 thousand and earnings of about zero. And thereafter the real Coca Cola Company did lose half its trademark and did grant perpetual bottling franchises at fixed syrup prices. And some of the bottlers were not very effective and couldn't easily be changed. And the real Coca Cola Company, with this system, did lose much pricing control that would have improved results, had it been retained. Yet, even so, the real Coca Cola Company followed so much of the plan given to Glotz that it is now worth about $125 billion and will have to increase its value at only 8% per year until 2034 to reach a value of two trillion dollars. And it can hit an annual physical volume target of 2.92 trillion servings if servings grow until 2034 at only 6% per year, a result consistent with much past experience and leaving plenty of plain-water ingestion for Coca Cola to replace after 2034. So I would guess that the fictional Glotz, starting earlier and stronger and avoiding the worst errors, would have easily hit his two trillion dollar target. And he would have done it well before 2034.

This brings me, at last, to the main purpose of my talk. Large educational implications exist, if my answer to Glotz's problem is roughly right and you make one more assumption I believe true—that most Ph.D. educators, even psychology professors and business school deans, would not have given the same simple answer I did. And, if I am right in these two ways, this would indicate that our civilization now keeps in place a great many educators who can't satisfactorily explain Coca Cola, even in retrospect, and even after watching it closely all their lives. This is not a satisfactory state of affairs.

Moreover—and this result is even more extreme—the brilliant and effective executives who, surrounded by business school and law school graduates, have run The Coca-Cola Company with glorious success in recent years, also did not understand elementary psychology well enough to predict and avoid the "New Coke" fiasco, which dangerously threatened their company. That people so talented, sur-rounded by professional advisers from the best universities, should thus demonstrate a huge gap in their education is also not a satis-factory state of affairs.

Such extreme ignorance, in both the high reaches of academia and the high reaches of business, is a lalapalooza effect of a negative sort, demonstrating grave defects in academia. Because the bad effect is lalapalooza, we should expect to find intertwined, multiple academ-ic causes. I suspect at least two such causes.

First, academic psychology, while it is admirable and useful as a list of ingenious and important experiments, lacks interdisciplinary synthesis. In particular, not enough attention is given to lalapalooza effects coming from combinations of psychological tendencies. This creates a situation reminding one of a rustic teacher who tries to sim-plify school work by rounding Pi to an even three. And it violates Einstein's injunction that "everything should be made as simple as possible—but no more simple." In general, psychology is laid out and misunderstood as electromagnetism would now be misunder-stood if physics had produced many brilliant experimenters like Michael Faraday and no grand synthesizer like James Clerk Maxwell.

And, second, there is truly horrible lack of synthesis blending psy-chology and other academic subjects. But only an interdisciplinary approach will correctly deal with reality—in academia as with The Coca-Cola Company.

In short, academic psychology departments are immensely more important and useful than other academic departments think. And, at the same time, the psychology departments are worse than most of their inhabitants think. It is, of course, normal for self appraisal to be more positive than external appraisal. Indeed, a problem of this sort may have given you your speaker today. But the size of this psy-chology-department gap is preposterously large. In fact, the gap is so enormous that one very eminent university (Chicago) at one time simply abolished its psychology department, perhaps with an undis-closed hope of later creating a better version.

In such a state of affairs, many years ago and with much that was plainly wrong already present, the 'New Coke' fiasco occurred, wherein Coke's executives came to the brink of destroying the most valuable trademark in the world. The academically correct reaction to this immense and well publicized fiasco would have been the sort of reaction Boeing would display if three of its new airplanes crashed in a single week. After all, product integrity is involved in each case, and the plain educational failure was immense.

But almost no such responsible, Boeing-like reaction has come from academia. Instead academia, by and large, continues in its Balkanized way to tolerate psychology professors who mis-teach psychology, non-psychology professors who fail to consider psychological effects obviously crucial in their subject matter, and professional schools that carefully preserve psychological ignorance coming in with each entering class and are proud of their inadequacies.

Even though this regrettable blindness and lassitude is now the normal academic result, are there exceptions providing hope that disgraceful shortcomings of the educational establishment will eventually be corrected? Here, my answer is a very optimistic yes.

For instance, consider the recent behavior of the economics department of The University of Chicago. Over the last decade, this department has enjoyed a near monopoly of the Nobel prizes in economics, largely by getting good predictions out of "free market" models postulating man's rationality. And what is the reaction of this department, after winning so steadily with its rational-man approach?

Well, it just invited into a precious slot amid its company of greats a wise and witty Cornell economist, Richard Thaler. And it has done this because Thaler pokes fun at much that is holy at the University of Chicago. Indeed, Thaler believes, with me, that people are often massively irrational in ways, predicted by psychology, that must be taken into account in microeconomics.

In so behaving, the University of Chicago is imitating Darwin, who spent much of his long life thinking in reverse as he tried to disprove his own hardest won and best loved ideas. And so long as there are parts of academia that keep alive its best values by thinking in reverse like Darwin, we can confidently expect that silly educational practices will eventually be replaced by better ones, exactly as Carl Jacobi might have predicted.

This will happen because the Darwinian approach, with its habitual objectivity taken on as a sort of hair shirt, is a mighty approach. Indeed, no less a figure than Einstein said that one of the four causes of his achievement was "self criticism," ranking right up there with curiosity, concentration, and perseverance.

And, to further appreciate the power of self criticism, consider where lies the grave of that very ungifted undergraduate, Charles Darwin. It is in Westminster Abbey, right next to the headstone of Isaac Newton, perhaps the most gifted student who ever lived, honored on that headstone in five Latin words constituting the most eloquent praise in all graveyard print: "Hic Iacet Quod Mortale

Fuet."—"Here lie the remains of what was mortal."

A civilization that so places a dead Darwin will eventually develop and integrate psychology in a proper and practical fashion that greatly increases skills of all sorts. But all of us who have dollops of power and see the light should help the process along. There is a lot at stake. If, in many high places, a universal product as successful as Coca-Cola is not properly understood and explained, it can't bode well for our competency in dealing with much else that is important.

Of course, those of you with 50% of net worth in Coca-Cola stock, occurring because you tried to invest 10% after thinking like I did in making my pitch to Glotz, can ignore my message about psychology as too elementary for useful transmission to you. But I am not so sure that this reaction is wise for the rest of you. The situation reminds me of the old-time Warner & Swasey ad that was a favorite of mine: "The company that needs a new machine tool, and hasn't bought it, is already paying for it."

41
MIDNIGHT AT MCDONALD'S

Warren Buffett ordered a Big Mac, fries and a Coke at a McDonald's in Hong Kong just about midnight between October 1 and 2, 1995.

"He was walking back from the counter when I saw him. I had seen him before," said Mark Langdon of Omaha. "I jumped up and basically used the Omaha connection to introduce myself. He stopped and chatted and then set his tray down at my table. He looked around and said, 'I have some friends here and I don't want to miss them.' "

"My brother and I had heard that Buffett had been in China with [Microsoft Chairman] Bill Gates," Langdon said. "Then Bill Gates walked up and Warren introduced Gates to me and my brother. I had to scrape my jaw off the floor."

"Buffett said to Fred and me, 'This is Bill Gates,' like you have to do that," Langdon said of the introduction.

Then Gates' wife, Melinda, and Gates' father, Bill Gates, Sr., came over to the table. "It was crazy," said Langdon, then a 33-year-old application analyst with Applied Communications Inc., in Omaha, a company which writes software for the transfer of electronic funds.

Buffett explained to Gates that it was companies like Applied Communications that kept Omaha's jobless rate so low.

"The six of us sat at the table for about 20 minutes," Langdon said.

Langdon was returning from a trip to Jakarta. His brother, Fred, 35, was on his way from Omaha back to his job as an engineer with Procter & Gamble in Kobe, Japan. The brothers decided to meet and tour Hong Kong.

"We had been sightseeing all day and came back to the hotel. We watched TV and fell asleep and woke

(Photo by LaVerne Ramsey)

Mark Langdon of Omaha had a late night dinner at McDonald's with Buffett and Gates.

up hungry so we went to McDonald's," Langdon said.

Buffett's party was preparing to leave for home the next day after their trip through China together and Buffett explained they had come to McDonald's "to get some familiar food."

As the six ate, Buffett made a point of the familiarity and consistency of McDonald's servings worldwide. Langdon felt that Buffett was, to some extent, analyzing the meal, as well as eating it.

"He picked up the bun a little and looked at the bun and the meat and said, 'the bun is the same [whether in the U.S. or Asia], the meat is the same and the fries are the same. And the price is about the same,' " Langdon reported.

Buffett said his group also had eaten at McDonald's in Beijing during their trip to China.

"I knew he was a Coke junkie so I asked him, 'What do you think of the Coke?'" Buffett joked: "It might be a slightly richer mixture for my taste, but it'll do."

"I was talking to him like any other person. It was hard to believe these were the two richest people in the world," Langdon said.

Buffett, he said, was dressed in a white polo shirt bearing a small insignia: "Nebraska 1994 National Champions." Gates was in a button-down shirt. Both wore casual pants. "I knew Buffett was this way [casual], but I didn't know Gates was. He was kind of the same way."

Langdon was struck that apparently there were no bodyguards around, that Buffett and Gates were out at midnight and that nobody recognized them.

"I saw just one gentleman turn and look a couple of times." said Langdon, adding that most people in McDonald's that night were Asian.

The Buffett group was staying at the famous old Peninsula Hotel, but never said how it traveled from the hotel to McDonald's. "I saw no evidence of a driver," Langdon said.

There was some talk between Gates and Fred Langdon about the Internet, but the main thing Mark Langdon recalled about Gates was that he ate two Big Macs. He devoured his and one that his wife brought over. "He inhaled them," Langdon said.

Buffett paid for the meals with McDonald's gift certificates and gave the Langdon brothers certificates that were left over. Buffett said, "They gave us these," without saying exactly who gave them to him, according to Langdon. After Buffett handed over the gift certificates, he cracked, "You don't have any frequent flier coupons, do you?"

Buffett and Gates had a late night dinner at this McDonald's near the Peninsula Hotel in Hong Kong.

Langdon said he had heard the rumors that Buffett was buying McDonald's stock, but had no proof from the late night meal with him.

"My brother and I did come away with the impression, just vibes, that Buffett and Gates both were interested in McDonald's. The two of them were talking about McDonald's," Langdon said.

42
MISTAKE: CLIMBING THE FAST-FOOD CHAIN AND THEN SELLING

Rumors were rampant in 1995 and 1996 that McBuffett was taking a big stake in McDonald's. During that time a friend was driving in a car with Buffett and asked him if he were buying McDonald's.

> Buffett said to his friend: "Have you ever been to Egypt?"
> Friend: "Yes."
> Buffett: "Did the sphinx say anything?"
> Friend: "No."
> Buffett: "Well, that's the answer."

The rumors were true as confirmation first came March 6, 1996, that an SEC filing showed Berkshire owned 4.9 million shares of McDonald's at the end of 1994.

A filing in late 1996 for the third quarter of 1995 said Berkshire owned 9.34 million shares, or about 1.3% of McDonald's and Berkshire's 1996 Annual Report showed that Berkshire beefed up its stake to 30,156,600, or 4.3%, of McDonald's shares.

Several years ago Buffett was at it again, taking a stake in a universally recognized brand name, a company with exploding overseas growth, even as growth in the U.S. seemed mature and growth of McProfits were slowing.

Because McDonald's stock was not listed in Berkshire's 1997 Annual Report as one of Berkshire's holdings worth more than $750 million, it appeared that Buffett had sold some or all his McDonald's stake. A *Bloomberg* story (August 3, 1999) said Buffett had reduced the McDonald's stake to 6.6 million shares by the end of the first quarter of 1998 and later reports showed he was entirely out of the stock in the third quarter of 1998.

About 60% of Mickey D's income comes from overseas and some 80% of that comes from seven countries. The China and Russia markets remained virtually untapped. Lots of potential McFamilies out there.

It all began with the McDonald brothers, Dick and Mac, in 1937 in California where drive-in restaurants were becoming a craze for Californians on the go in their automobiles.

The first restaurant was opened in a parking lot just east of Pasadena and then a grander one was opened in San Bernadino in 1940. It was a huge success.

Ray Kroc, a high school dropout who was an excellent salesman, met the McDonald brothers in 1954. The brothers were a good account for Kroc who sold them Multimixers to make milk shakes.

John F. Love's book, *McDonald's: Behind the Arches* best describes how history was made.

"He (Kroc) had parked his rental car in the McDonald's lot a full hour before noon, but already lines were forming at the two front windows, where the main orders were filled, and the side window, where orders for french fries were handled separately...It was not the shape of things that caught his eye, but the speed of them."

"What Kroc was so excited about on that first visit was that one in three orders included milk shakes made with his Multimixers.

"The McDonalds were making milk shakes so fast that they...cut a couple of inches off the spindles on Kroc's Multimixer so that they could mix shakes right in the twelve-ounce paper cup, not in the sixteen-ounce stainless steel mixers the soda fountains used...

"He was bubbling over with enthusiasm as he walked inside to introduce himself... 'My God, I've been standing out there looking at it all but I can't believe it,' he told the brothers. Dick and Mac assured him that his reaction was normal—and as typical as that day's business. 'When will this die down?' Kroc asked. 'Sometime late tonight,' Dick replied. 'Some way,' Kroc declared, 'I've got to get involved in this.' When I saw it working that day in 1954, I felt like some latter-day Newton who'd just had an Idaho potato caromed off his skull. That night in my motel room I did a lot of heavy thinking about what I'd seen during the day. Visions of McDonald's restaurants dotting crossroads all over the country paraded through my brain." (*Forbes Greatest Business Stories of All Time*, Daniel Kross, p. 180, quoting Kroc's autobiography *Grinding It Out*.) The new company became Kroc's obsession. "I believe in God, family, and McDonald's—and in the office, that order is reversed." Kroc was fond of saying. (p. 182)

Later Kroc, well into his middle age, bought out the McDonald brothers and led the company to enormous success. Kroc, who had dropped out of high school after his sophomore year, had come a long way.

When World War I had started, he went overseas, joining the Red Cross at age 15 and working in the same company as Walt Disney. Each liked one another but they were opposites. Love's book quotes Kroc as saying, "He was always drawing pictures while the rest of us were chasing girls. Therein lies a lesson, because his drawings have gone on forever - and most of those girls are dead now."

Late in life Kroc opened his first McDonald's in Des Plaines, Illinois, and Kroc perfectly caught the fast-food craze in the country. He insisted on low prices for his hamburgers and on quality, service, cleanliness and training.

The rest is now history. As Love's book points out:

- Fully 96% of American consumers have eaten at one of its restaurants in the past year.
- Slightly more than half of the U.S. population lives within a three-minute drive to a McDonald's.
- McDonald's has served far more than 100 billion hamburgers.
- McDonald's captures 14% of all restaurant visits in the United States—one out of every six—and has a 6.6% share of all dollars spent on eating out.
- McDonald's sells 34% of all hamburgers sold by commercial restaurants and 26% of all french fries.
- Control of such a market share has given McDonald's a big impact on the food processing business in the U.S.
- McDonald's is the country's largest purchaser of beef and sells so many french fries it buys 5% of the entire U.S. potato crop harvested for food.
- McDonald's stores account for 5% of all Coca-Cola sold in the U.S.
- McDonald's has enjoyed an average return on equity of 25% and a 24% earnings growth annually since becoming a public company in 1965.
- An initial investment of $2,250 for 100 shares of stock has grown through 11 stock splits and one stock dividend to 27,180 shares worth more than $1 million in mid 1994.
- **Key item:** McDonald's is the world's largest owner of retail real estate.

Also, McDonald's provides one in 15 Americans with his or her first job.

When McDonald's opened a store in Moscow on a cold day on January 31, 1990, more than 30,000 people showed up, the most customers a restaurant had ever served in a single day. The Moscow restaurant served 15 million customers in its first year of operation—a number the average U.S. restaurant takes 30 years to achieve. McDonald's opening in Beijing on April 23, 1991, shattered the opening day record that had been set in Moscow, attracting 40,000 customers.

McDonald's is widely known for its Ronald McDonald House which has dozens of houses throughout the world, providing a home-away-from home for families of seriously ill children receiving treatment at nearby hospitals.

Buffett's close friend, Donald Keough, the former Coca-Cola president, serves on McDonald's board and another of Buffett's close friends, Bill Ruane, who heads the Ruane, Cunniff investment firm, disclosed in early 1998 his firm owns 4.6 million shares of McDonald's.

"Warren has been known to speak eloquently of the joys of a Big Mac." Keough has said. (*Fortune*, April 4, 1997) In fact, Buffett eats breakfast or lunch at McDonald's about 50 times a year, paying cash despite a special gold card created for him by McDonald's that would allow him to eat free at its restaurants. (*Wall Street Journal*, March 2, 1998) He still carries the card proudly which allows him to eat at McDonald's free for the rest of his life. Home run sluggers Mark McGuire and Sammy Sosa, who have done ads for the company, should ask for the same privilege.

"Did somebody say McDonald's?"

"Did somebody sell McDonald's?"

Somebody did sell McDonald's and he regretted it. In Berkshire's 1998 Annual report, Buffett wrote, "My decision to sell McDonald's was a very big mistake. Overall, you would have been better off last year if I had regularly snuck off to the movies during market hours."

A report in 1999 said Berkshire owned 895,800 shares of McDonald's as of June 30, 1998.

McDonald's chairman Jack Greenberg says: "Whether he is a shareholder or not, Warren has always been one of our best customers. He once told me he eats at McDonald's four times a week." (*Worth Online*, July, 1999) But now, he may be an even bigger fan of Dairy Queen.

43

THE WALT DISNEY COMPANY
SELLING A STAKE

After holding more than 51 million shares of The Walt Disney Co. at the end of 1998, Berkshire showed no shares of Disney at the end of 1999, meaning it apparently sold down below its $750 million cutoff for listing its large holdings.

Falling in and then out of love with the Mouse? Over the years Buffett has been a big fan of Disney and was a central figure when Disney bought Capital Cities.

"Walt Disney, Capital Cities agree to merger."—Dow Jones news wire, 7:56 a.m., July 31, 1995. The jokes started flying immediately. "I knew Cap Cities was a Mickey Mouse operation...My new boss is Mickey Mouse." Headlines read: "The Mouse that Roared" or "The Mouse that Scored." But underneath the jokes, the largest merger of entertainment and media companies in history was being launched.

It was a big day for everyone. Disney Chairman Michael Eisner, Cap Cities/ABC Chairman Tom Murphy and Buffett held a press conference to talk about the $19 billion merger being paid for in Disney stock and cash. By the way, Murphy has said a key to Eisner's success is that Eisner is: "A boy in a man's body."

In any event, the deal got cracking at investment banker Allen & Co.'s annual summer getaway for media executives held in Sun Valley, Idaho, in the middle of July 1995. Eisner and Murphy had talked before about a possible deal, but Murphy wanted Disney stock and Eisner wanted to offer cash. Soil for such deals had been watered by expectations that Congress would remove some restrictions on

(Photo by Nancy Line Jacobs)

Disney's Michael Eisner, the head Mouseketeer, at the Berkshire Annual Meeting in 1998.

Buffett and his wife, Susie, celebrating as Mickey and Minnie Mouse with Disney CEO Michael Eisner and Michael Ovitz at a Cap Cities management meeting in Phoenix, Arizona, about the time of the Disney-Cap Cities merger.

TV ownership. It sounds Goofy, but here's how the megadeal occurred.

Eisner, bumping into Buffett who was on his way to a golf game with Murphy, asked Buffett if Cap Cities were for sale. Buffett said, "I think so, let's ask Murphy."

Here's Eisner's version of the event from his book, *Work in Progress* (p. 363-364):

> I was still digesting the conversation [with Larry Tisch about the possibility of buying CBS] when I looked up and saw Warren Buffett coming toward me. He, too, stopped to tell me how impressed he had been by our presentation.
>
> "The funniest thing just happened," I told him. "I ran into Larry Tisch and we ended up talking about our buying CBS. Unless, of course, you want to sell us Cap Cities for cash." I was hoping that the possibility of Disney's buying CBS might make Buffett, the largest shareholder in Cap Cities, more eager to sell the company.
>
> "Sounds good to me," he said without hesitation, "Why don't we go talk to Tom about it?" He was referring to Tom Murphy.
>
> "I don't know where he is," I said.
>
> "I'm just going to meet him," Buffett told me, "We have a

date to play golf with Bill Gates. Why don't you walk over with me?"

When we caught up with Murphy, Buffett made the pitch for me. "Michael wants to pay cash for Cap Cities," he said. "I think he's right. Any time we ever bought anything at Berkshire that worked out, it was in cash. What do you think, Tom?"

Murphy seemed slightly taken aback. Just three months had passed since our last negotiation ended unsuccessfully. "I'd have to think about it," he said. We talked some more about the deal and I slipped in, as casually as possible, the story about what had just occurred with Tisch. Murphy knew that we were seriously interested in a network, and that CBS was in play. Whatever doubts he still had about selling Cap Cities, Disney remained one of the few potential buyers with whom he felt comfortable.

Eisner later told Murphy that both companies were running on all cylinders. The two men came to terms in a few weeks after Murphy consulted with Buffett and Eisner consulted with Sid Bass, a big Disney investor. A contract was drawn up over a three-day period.

Investment bankers had only a slight hand in the merger. The deal was presented to the Cap Cities board on Sunday afternoon, July 30. It was approved the next morning and the merger was announced.

The deal was for Disney to buy Cap Cities (now ABC Inc. in the Disney empire) for about $127 a share in cash and stock. ABC Inc. is headed by Robert Iger, who is Disney's No. 2 man and married to broadcaster Willow Bay. She worked for ABC before joining CNN where she is now a co-anchor with Stuart Varney on "Moneyline." They took over after Lou Dobbs resigned in 1999.

A stock swap seemed advantageous for many investors who were long term Cap Cities investors because a stock swap is tax free. At the end of 1997 Berkshire owned 21,563,414 Disney shares and at the end of 1998 it owned 51,202,243 after a three-for-one split and some selling.

Murphy joined the Disney board and Buffett was back in an investment he had touched on in the 1960s, buying 5% of Disney in 1966. He sold the stake in 1967 for $6 million, scoring a nice gain. Huge mistake.

Buffett has said: "In the 1960s, the entire Walt Disney Company was selling for only $80 million. At that time, they put $17 million into their pirate ride. So the company was selling at only five times rides. We took a stake for $5 million and sold it a year later for $6 million. Had we kept it, that $5 million would have been worth over a billion dollars in the mid-1990s."

The day of the announcement Cap Cities stock soared about $20 from $96. Even the stock of Disney, the acquiring company rose. It's unusual for the stock of an acquiring company to go up, but Buffett won a $100 bet with a Disney official that Disney's stock would rise.

And Berkshire's stock spiked up $550 to $24,750.

It was a good day for Buffett. Since Berkshire owned 20 million shares of Cap Cities which was up about $20 on the day, about $400 million rolled in for Berkshire that day.

The Dow Jones wire service pointed out that it would take 16,000 Americans making the U.S. average of $25,000 a year to earn that.

There had been no flurry of options trading, no news report or any hint the megadeal was coming. The announcement shocked Wall Street, unlike the long rumored and widely reported takeover of CBS by Westinghouse which came the next day.

Eisner, Murphy and Buffett—those three Mouseketeers—were suddenly telling the world about the blockbuster combination.

"Exportation of U.S. intellectual product has been going on forever, but now it can be more organized," said Eisner, who once worked for ABC. "This is the real beginning of U.S. companies being global."

Murphy said: "On a personal basis...this is the high point of my career: seeing these two great companies go forward together."

Buffett explained the deal was a boon for the shareholders of the companies involved: "It's a wonderful marriage of the No. 1 content company and the No. 1 distribution company."

The merger, the second largest ever at that point after the takeover of RJR Nabisco, created the largest entertainment and media company in the world, at the time, but in the late 1990s Time Warner surpassed Disney as Disney slumped. Two weeks after the merger announcement, Michael Ovitz of Creative Artists Agency, was named Disney's president. However, Ovitz lasted only 14 months in the job.

Disney, home of the world's most recognized mascot—Mickey Mouse—and Donald Duck, has sales of more than $10 billion a year that it reaps from its theme parks, movies, music, books, stores, sports and other properties such as Disney Interactive, Disney Cruise Line and GO.com. Cap Cities brought in more than $6 billion a year from its ABC television network, 225 affiliate stations and a range of other media properties such as the globe-spanning ESPN sports channel thought to be worth more than $10 billion. "An estimated 80 million people a day are touched in some way by

Disney." (*Barron's*, July 26, 1999)

How did it come to pass that one of the great business mergers in all history ran through a fellow from Omaha, a man fabulously famous in some circles, yet still widely unknown?

Michael Eisner asked Buffett about whether such a deal was possible and probably figured the deal was done when Buffett again replied, "Sure, but you should go find Tom [Murphy]."

Michael found Tom who got with Warren and the triumvirate marched off into the "Wonderful World of Disney."

Later at a party held in Phoenix, Arizona, to celebrate the merger, Buffett brought hundreds of Cap Cities and Disney executives to their feet when he and his wife appeared on stage in full costume—as Mickey and Minnie Mouse.

Buffett said: "I thought I would prepare a little by checking out the Academy Awards to see how they did it. I would at this time like to thank my hairstylist, my wardrobe consultant and, of course, my personal trainer."

Still donning his mouse ears and while Wall Street waited to hear whether Buffett would take Disney stock or cash as a result of the merger, he sang:

> *"Shall we go for stock or cash?*
> *Paper money turns to trash.*
> *Stocks, however, sometimes crash.*
> *Shall we go for stock or cash?"*

His magical decision was made known on March 7, 1996.

Here's how it happened: On March 5, 1996, Buffett walked into Harris Trust in New York and handed a trust officer two envelopes.

"Envelope No. 1 was stock worth, gulp, $2.5 billion: Berkshire's 20 million shares of Capital Cities/ABC , being delivered to that company's purchaser, Walt Disney Co.

"In envelope No. 2, sealed and marked, 'Do not open until 4:30 p.m. on March 7,' were Buffett's wishes—kept secret from even the management of Disney and Cap Cities..." (*Fortune*, Carol Loomis, April 1, 1996)

Buffett asked for as much stock as possible. With the stock he received and with some additional purchases in the open market, Buffett wound up with about 3½% of Disney's shares. Suddenly he was a large shareholder in another of the greatest brand name companies on earth.

When Buffett gave a talk to Harvard Business School March 21, 1996, he was asked why he liked Disney stock.

His reply: "The mouse doesn't have an agent."

At Berkshire's Annual Meeting in 1996, Buffett continued:

"The Mouse is yours. He's not in there renegotiating every day or every month saying: 'Look how much more famous I've become in China.' If you own the Mouse, you own the Mouse."

Here's a condensed version of the background leading up to Walt Disney's acquisition of Cap Cities, according to a Cap Cities' letter to shareholders:

•In the fall of 1993 Michael Eisner and Sid Bass, whose Bass Management Trust owns 31,125,578 shares, or 5.95% of Disney's stock, met with Cap Cities's Tom Murphy and Daniel Burke and Buffett, a director of Cap Cities, to discuss a potential business combination. Nothing came of the talks.

•In March 1995, Eisner and Murphy met again. Murphy suggested that Cap Cities might consider a stock-for-stock transaction, Eisner said Disney would not be interested in an all stock transaction. Nothing developed.

•While attending an industry conference, Eisner met on July 14, 1995 with Buffett and Murphy. Again, Murphy said Cap Cities would be interested only in Disney stock. But they agreed to talk again.

•On July 21, 1995, Eisner asked if Cap Cities would consider a cash offer. Murphy said no. Eisner suggested the companies consider a strategic alliance involving, among other things, the provision by Disney for the ABC Television Network of Saturday morning programming and certain other programs. Murphy said he'd consider it.

•On July 25, 1995, Murphy called Eisner, and suggested that instead of the strategic alliance, Disney and Cap Cities enter a merger for cash and stock.

•From July 25 through July 31, senior management of Disney, Cap Cities and Buffett hammered out the stock and cash agreement. The boards agreed July 30, 1995, and the $19 billion deal for Disney to buy Cap Cities was announced.

Eisner wrote in Disney's 1999 Annual Report that although Disney had a poor year because of slumps in its home video and consumer products business the purchase of ABC/Cap Cities was a success: "Outside estimates have valued our cable assets alone—not including the Disney Channel—at more than we paid for the entire Capital Cities/ABC acquisition. In addition, the ABC-TV stations and radio group have been valued at more than half the cost of the overall acquisition. On top of that, we have generated roughly $4 billion from the sale of ABC's publishing assets."

The Walt Disney Company operates Disneyland in California and Walt Disney World in Florida which includes the Magic Kingdom, Epcot Center, Disney-MGM Studios and Animal Kingdom. It also earns royalties from Tokyo Disneyland and owns 39% of Euro-Disney located on a 4,800 acre site near Paris.

The Burbank, California-based giant supplies entertainment via its Buena Vista, Touchstone, Hollywood Pictures and Miramax outlets to theaters, television and video. It publishes books, records music and sells its consumer products through a chain of more than 500 Disney stores worldwide. Disney has launched ESPN stores and *ESPN Magazine*. Disney owns Hyperion Press which published *Make the Connection* by Bob Greene and Oprah Winfrey, a number one best-seller about fitness. Disney owns the Anaheim Angels baseball team, the Mighty Ducks of Anaheim hockey team and the stage productions of *Beauty and the Beast* and *The Lion King*. It operates the widely viewed Disney Channel and Radio Disney.

Disney has been famous throughout its history for its movies which include *Cinderella* (the single most profitable movie for television ever produced), *Aladdin, The Lion King, Pocahontas, The Little Mermaid, Toy Story, 101 Dalmatians, Evita, Hercules* and *Tarzan*.

Disney owns E! Entertainment Television. And it has a stake in the Internet through ESPN.com and ABC.com web sites.

ABC and Disney have long had connections, not to mention Eisner's 10-year stint early in his career at ABC.

Walt Disney's brother, Roy, and ABC's Leonard Goldenson agreed back in the 1950s that Disney would supply a one-hour television series to ABC in return for a $500,000 investment in the Disneyland park.

"In early 1954, Disneyland, Incorporated, which Walt had founded three years before, was reconstituted with Walt Disney Productions and American Broadcasting Company-Paramount Theaters each owning 34.48% with investments of $500,000 a piece." (*Walt Disney*, Bob Thomas, 1994, p. 249)

Later ABC aired *The Mickey Mouse Club* show watched by three-quarters of the nation's television set owners between five and six o'clock each weekday.

"Children and adults everywhere were singing the club's anthem—'M-I-C, K-E-Y, M-O-U-S-E.' The mouse-ear caps worn by the Mouseketeers sold at the rate of 24,000 a day; two hundred other items were merchandised by seventy-five manufacturers. The Mouseketeers became national figures, and millions of children could recite 'Darlene,' 'Cubby,' 'Karen' and all the other names during the daily roll call. The most popular of the Mouseketeers proved to be Annette Funicello, a gasoline-station operator's daughter who had been discovered at a children's dance recital. She attracted the most fan mail—as many as six thousand letters a month." (p. 275) From those days Disney, which employs 69,000 people, grew into a business with a global brand name which is buying back its stock.

At Disney's Annual Meeting in 1997 shareholders expressed concerns about the pay to the departed Michael Ovitz, about the pay package for Eisner himself and about the board being Eisner-controlled. Eisner brought Buffett on stage who said, "We think it's [Disney] one of the great brand names in the world. I advise you to keep your stock."

Disney's growth rate, however, slowed in the late 1990s and its image was marred by a trial between Disney and former studio head Jeffrey Katzenberg. The bitter suit was settled in 1999 but only after negative headlines about the war between Eisner and Katzenberg. *The Los Angeles Times* (July 8, 1999) quoting sources said that Murphy and Buffett had pushed for a resolution to the case.

Capital Cities/ABC

Buffett was in Washington one day in 1985 when an urgent call came from his office to get in touch with his friend, Cap Cities Communications Chairman Tom Murphy. Murphy said he needed advice about financing a $3.5 billion purchase of giant American Broadcasting Companies, Inc. At the time, the Cap Cities acquisition of ABC-TV, announced March 18, 1985, was the largest media purchase in history.

That night, Peter Jennings began *World News Tonight* with, "To paraphrase Pogo, we have seen the news and it is us." (*The House that Roone Built*, Marc Gunther, p. 214)

Neither Murphy nor Buffett at first thought of Buffett being personally involved, but the Wizard of Omaha quickly became a key figure in the acquisition. His role in the huge business combination probably helped Wall Street give its nod to the deal, as the stock prices of both companies shot up.

Buffett's great interest in media stocks, evident since the early 1970s, culminated with word that Cap Cities would buy ABC with Berkshire owning almost a fifth of the new media powerhouse.

Without putting pen to paper, Buffett agreed to invest $517.5 million in cash to buy three million shares of Cap Cities at $172.50 a share. (That's before a 10-for-1 stock split in 1994.) That raised the money that contributed to the merger that spawned Cap

(AP/Wide World Photos)

Former Cap Cities Chairman Tom Murphy, left, and former CBS Chairman Laurence Tisch also are FOBs. "Murph" is what Buffett calls Murphy, and Murphy calls Buffett a "400-pound gorilla." Later Buffett would grow into a Thirty Billion Pound Gorilla.

Cities/ABC, Inc., in January, 1986.

Buffett's part of the deal was wrapped up one mid-afternoon of March, 1985. "It took about 30 seconds to work. It's all in a page or two," Buffett said of his investment. *(Regardie's,* February, 1986)

Two hours later Buffett was engrossed in a six-hour bridge game with three New York friends, putting the deal out of his mind.

"I don't think about anything else when I play bridge," he told *Omaha-World Herald's* Robert Dorr.

The call from Murphy came because he and Buffett had long been friends. Buffett has always had high regard for Murphy, whom he calls "Murph," and of whom he has said, "I think he is the top manager in the U.S." *(Fortune,* April 15, 1985) Murphy has returned the compliment and has said of Buffett, "If I were around him all the time, I'd have a huge inferiority complex...He's one of the greatest friends. He will try and do anything he can to help you. Without him, I wouldn't have been able to buy ABC." *(USA Today,* September 18, 1991)

Buffett once told *Channels* magazine's West Coast Editor, Patricia Bauer (November 1986), "I love being associated with Murph. I literally do not work with anyone I don't like. I'm fortunate to be able to spend the rest of my life working with people that I like and admire. And here's Murph up at the top of that list with a terribly interesting business."

But did Buffett plan to shape opinion or tell ABC what programs to air? "No," he told Bauer, "I'm not the right guy to ask about those things." He said it again at the Berkshire Annual Meeting in 1991: "I'm a director of Cap Cities/ABC, but they don't ask me for my suggestions on shows. That's not my end of the game."

At a Berkshire Annual Meeting (1987), Buffett was asked if he thought there was too much sex on television. "I don't see anything wrong with sex on television, but there ought to be a few shows where the gal says no."

Buffett met Murphy in the late 1960s when a former Harvard Business School classmate of Murphy's seated them together at a lunch in New York. Murphy was so taken with Buffett that he invited him to be on the board of Cap Cities. Buffett declined but the two remained fast friends.

In 1985, ABC's magisterial Chairman Leonard Goldenson, who founded ABC in 1953 and ran it until 1986 when he was 79, decided that Murphy and Murphy's number two man, Daniel Burke (also a Harvard MBA via the University of Vermont and military service), would be the right men to run his company. (Murphy was a graduate-school roommate of James Burke, Daniel's other brother, who was later chairman of Johnson & Johnson.)

Murphy and Burke were known as cost-cutters. There is an oft-repeated story that at the old Cap Cities when an Albany station needed repainting, Murphy had only the sides facing the main road spruced up. (*The House that Roone Built*, Marc Gunther, p. 214)

Goldenson, who was preparing to turn ABC over, is the man who presided over "Charlie's Angels," "The Dating Game," "Monday Night Football," instant replay, and the first miniseries.

In 1991 Goldenson's autobiography, *Beating the Odds*, appeared. Buffett wrote a foreword saying, "Business management can be viewed as a three-act play—the dream, the execution, and the passing of the baton. Leonard Goldenson will be remembered as a master of all three." Buffett told about getting a call from Murphy who said, "Pal, you're not going to believe this. I've just bought ABC. You've got to come and tell me how I'm going to pay for it." Buffett did just that, telling Murphy he needed "a nine-hundred-pound gorilla" investor to keep raiders at bay, and then kicked in $517 million.

But there was still a problem. There was an FCC "cross-ownership" rule banning a company from owning a television station and a newspaper in the same town. Buffett told Murphy he didn't want to sell the *Buffalo News* which meant Cap Cities had to sell a television station in Buffalo. In the Goldenson book, Buffett said he told Murphy he was committed to the *Buffalo News*: "I promised the people there that I would never sell it. I told them, when they wrote my obituary it would say, 'He owns the *Buffalo News*.'"

"This deal popped up three weeks ago. Four weeks ago I had no idea it was about to happen," *New York Times* reporter Vartanig G. Vartan wrote March 20, 1985, quoting Buffett. Buffett summarized to *Atlanta Constitution* business writer Melissa Turner (April 2, 1989) the final conversation that clinched Buffett's investment. "I was up there on a Thursday morning. I said, 'How many shares do you want me to buy?' He said, 'What do you say?' I said, 'How's three million?' He said, 'Fine.' I said 'What price should I pay?' He said, 'What do you think?' I said, '$172.50.' He said, 'Done.'"

To shareholders at the time, Buffett inserted just one paragraph in his 1985 annual report—a subsequent event note explaining the agreement had come a week after his annual report had gone to the typographer but shortly before production.

Buffett became a director of Cap Cities. He also agreed to vote with management for 11 years as long as either Tom Murphy or Daniel Burke was in charge. It turned out that the decision to buy Cap Cities reversed a previous one Buffett made in the late 1970s to sell the very same stock.

His explanation: "Of course some of you probably wonder why we are now buying Cap Cities at $172.50 per share given that this author, in a characteristic burst of brilliance, sold Berkshire's holdings in the same company at $43 per share in 1978-80. Anticipating your question, I spent a lot of time working on a snappy answer that would reconcile these acts.

"A little more time please."

Cap Cities was a good investment, despite a long struggle to get the ABC network turned around.

Back in the late 1940s and 1950s, ABC was the third-rated network. Attempts to buy ABC by CBS and 20th Century Fox failed, but in 1953 the struggling network merged with United Paramount Theatres. United Paramount's Leonard Goldenson hired Disney Studios and others to produce programming.

About that time Hudson Valley Broadcasting, owner of a struggling television station, went public, becoming Capital Cities Television Corp.

Under Murphy's guidance, Cap Cities bought Fairchild Publications, publisher of *Women's Wear Daily*—a real franchise in the fashion industry—and made a steady march of buying other media properties.

Still in third place in the 1960s and known as the Almost Broadcasting Co., lagging behind NBC and CBS, ABC fended off takeover attempts by Norton Simon, General Electric and Howard Hughes. But by the 1970s with hits like "*Love Boat*" and "*Happy Days*" (developed by Michael Eisner when he was at ABC in program development) ABC became the top network.

As a result of the 1986 merger, Cap Cities owned and operated ABC Television Network, seven ABC Radio Networks serving 2,200 affiliates (radio's largest advertising medium) drawing on ABC News as well as respected radio commentator Paul Harvey, eight television stations and 80% of the highly successful ESPN sports cable channel acquired in 1984.

ESPN, through its 24-hour-a-day sports cable television programming service reaches 73 million U.S. households, making it the most widely distributed cable network in the country. ESPN reaches more than 150 million homes in 150 foreign countries in 21 languages—more than any other cable network—and has been highly successful.

ESPN is a powerful vehicle for Disney to expand overseas because the Disney Channel can piggyback ESPN's worldwide penetration. ESPN2, after only a few years of operation, reaches 50 million U.S. homes.

The ABC Television Network has more than 200 primary affiliated stations reaching more than 99% of all U.S. television households.

The company owns 38% of Arts and Entertainment Network, a cable service devoted to cultural and entertainment programs and known for its excellent *Biography* series which drew 20 Emmy nominations in 1999 and won five. A&E has 81 million subscribers. Disney's History Channel reaches 61 million homes.

Also, ABC owns one-half of Lifetime Television, a cable program service devoted to women's lifestyle and health shows reaching 70% of U.S. households with its movies and specials. ABC also owns half of Tele-Munchen GmbH. This Munich, Germany-based television and theatrical production/distribution company has interests in cinemas and minority interests in a Munich radio station and a German cable television program service.

In early 2000, SoapNet, a 24-hour soap opera channel, was launched.

Good Morning America and ABC News' *World News Tonight* with Peter Jennings are top-rated shows. Ted Koppel's *Nightline* and

20/20, have also been very successful. Koppel had worried that with the Cap Cities buyout of ABC, the news side might be subject to cost-cutting.

Both Murphy and Buffett went by Koppel's house for lunch to assure him that they cared about the news side and *Nightline*. (*The House That Roone Built*, Marc Gunther, p. 257)

In 1989 ABC News premiered *PrimeTime Live* and in sports ABC's *Monday Night Football* was the most popular prime-time program among men who were mesmerized in its heyday by the announcing trio of Howard Cosell, Frank Gifford and Dandy Don Meredith. *Wide World of Sports* was the most popular anthology series. *Home Improvement* starring Tim Allen has been a hit as has *America's Funniest Home Videos*. *Who Wants To Be a Millionaire* with Regis Philbin has been a huge hit.

In 1993 Cap Cities announced it planned to buy back 12% of its stock in a Dutch auction at prices somewhere between $590 and $630 a share. And Berkshire said it would tender a million of its three million shares on condition the entire million shares were bought back.

As it turned out, Buffett sold a million shares back to Cap Cities for $630 a share. Berkshire, with its cash pile bulked up to the $2 billion range, continued to own 2 million shares, or about 13% of the 15.4 million shares of Cap Cities. With the 10-for-1 stock split, Berkshire owned 20 million shares.

A "Mistake Du Jour" is how Buffett later described his sale of Capital Cities shares:

> Late in 1993 I sold 10 million shares of Cap Cities at $63; at year-end 1994, the price was $85¼. (The difference is $222.5 million for those of you who wish to avoid the pain of calculating the damage yourself.) When we purchased the stock at $17.25 in 1986, I told you that I had previously sold our Cap Cities holdings at $4.30 per share during 1978-80, and added that I was at a loss to explain my earlier behavior. Now I've become a repeat offender. Maybe it's time to get a guardian appointed. (1994 Annual Report)

We'll check in the Millennium Plus Ten Edition to see if Buffett needs that guardian in this case.

Overall, Cap Cities/ABC turned out to be a good fit with Disney, a truly worldwide brand name franchise.

44

DIVERSIFIED RETAILING

A SMALL STREAM RUNS INTO A MIGHTY RIVER, AND ULTIMATELY INTO AN OCEAN.

Way back in time and space, long before Buffett was making billion dollar investments, he was fishing in far smaller investment streams—bringing those small streams together into a river of income and ultimately into an ocean of assets. Toward the end of 1978, Diversified Retailing was merged into Berkshire.

Buffett, long the largest shareholder of Berkshire, was by this time also the majority stockholder in Diversified, holding 56% of Diversified's stock. He began buying Diversified stock not long after he started buying Berkshire stock.

He became chief executive officer of Diversified in 1966. By 1976, then chairman of both companies, Buffett owned about 36% of Berkshire and 52% of Diversified.

At the time, Berkshire's main executive offices were in New Bedford, Massachusetts, while those of Diversified were in Baltimore, Maryland.

Diversified, incorporated in 1966, was the parent of Associated Retail Stores, Inc.'s more than 80-store chain. Also Diversified owned a large amount of Berkshire stock as well as Blue Chip Stamps stock.

Associated, based in New York, was acquired by Diversified in 1967. Its stores operated in 11 states under such names as York, Amy's, Goodwin's Gaytime, Fashion Outlet, Madison's, Yorkster, Lanes and Tops and Bottoms. The Gap, it was not!

In one of its rare business sales, Berkshire sold Associated Retail Stores to Joseph Norban, Inc. of New York in 1987.

Buffett's early retailing efforts never were winners. In the 1970s he owned shares of Munsingwear and the stock was unspectacular.

In the proposed merger of Berkshire and Diversified, Buffett and his wife agreed to vote for the merger only if a majority of the other shareholders did. With this combination Buffett was trying to bring the far-flung elements of his financial empire under one house: Berkshire.

In the negotiations, Berkshire was represented by Malcolm G. Chace, Jr., Berkshire's former chairman. Diversified was represented by David S. (Sandy) Gottesman, a director of Diversified who would become one of Buffett's close friends and a wealthy Berkshire shareholder.

Gottesman, because of his large ownership in Diversified, emerged from the Berkshire-Diversified merger with 17,977 shares of Berkshire.

A number of people at the investment firm he heads, First Manhattan in New York City, also had been Diversified investors and came away collectively owning another 13,158 Berkshire shares.

It's traditional for Gottesman to stand up at the end of Berkshire's annual meeting and eloquently thank Buffett on behalf of shareholders for Buffett's stewardship.

Small wonder Gottesman feels so ebullient and Buffett usually looks bemused or embarrassed when Gottesman gushes forth. Buffett responded to Gottesman's outpourings one year by saying nothing and another year by saying, "Well, thank you, Sandy."

Because Buffett owned big positions in both Berkshire and Diversified, the negotiations took place without him and were conducted by independent directors of each corporation.

The proxy statement relating to the merger explained:

> Berkshire and its subsidiaries are engaged in the underwriting of property and casualty insurance throughout the United States, in the manufacture and sale of woven textiles in the United States and Canada, and, through a subsidiary which Berkshire is required to divest by 1981, in the commercial banking business in Rockford, Illinois. Berkshire and its subsidiaries additionally maintain long-term investments in a number of other businesses...Berkshire owns approximately 18.8% of the outstanding common stock of Blue Chip, whose shares are traded in the over-the-counter market. And Berkshire's insurance subsidiaries hold in their investment portfolios approximately 22.6% of Blue Chip's outstanding common stock.

Blue Chip in turn owned a number of businesses such as See's Candy, the *Buffalo News* and Wesco, which in turn once owned 22% of Detroit International Bridge Co., operator of the Ambassador toll bridge between Detroit, Michigan, and Windsor, Ontario. Berkshire no longer has any ownership in the bridge.

Here's what the proxy statement had to say about Diversified:

> Diversified is a holding company which renders financial and operating advice to Associated Retail Stores, Inc., a

wholly-owned subsidiary engaged in retailing of popular-price women's and children's apparel, to Associated's wholly-owned subsidiary, Columbia Insurance Company, which is engaged in the fire and casualty insurance business primarily through accepting portions of reinsurance contracts from Berkshire's insurance subsidiaries, and to Southern Casualty Insurance Company, a wholly-owned subsidiary of Columbia engaged in Louisiana in providing workers' compensation insurance, almost exclusively to the forest products industry. In the opinion of Diversified's management, Diversified's most significant asset, other than its Berkshire stock, is its beneficial ownership of approximately 16.3% of the outstanding common stock of Blue Chip...

The merger called for little management change, although Munger, who had become chairman of Blue Chip in 1976 and was a director of Diversified, was to serve as a director of Berkshire.

For years, Buffett had wanted to combine the two companies. He particularly wanted to bring together the two corporations' holdings of Blue Chip, to simplify the corporate structure under Berkshire.

With the merger, Berkshire owned 58% of Blue Chip and Buffett and his family owned another 13% of the stock. It was not until 1983 that Blue Chip was fully merged into Berkshire.

A little stream was merging with other little streams and turning into a mighty river, running toward an ocean. The following chart shows the pre-merger and post-merger ownerships:

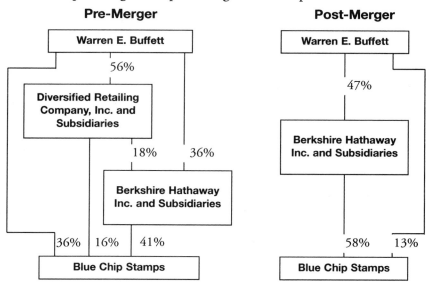

The intricate arrangement meant Buffett was investing on behalf of Berkshire, Diversified and Blue Chip. In 1972 Blue Chip began buying Wesco stock.

To complicate things, Wesco entered a merger agreement which was later called off. It all called into question prices Blue Chip was paying for Wesco.

And Buffett and Munger were trying to merge Diversified into Berkshire.

The Securities and Exchange commission launched an investigation into Berkshire, Blue Chip and Buffett.

Buffett had to explain the whole puzzle to the SEC. In 1976 the matter was settled without admitting or denying guilt.

Because the SEC found that the Wesco shareholders had been hurt by Blue Chip's trades, they were paid $115,000.

45

BLUE CHIP STAMPS
"MAYBE WE SHOULD BUY INTO ANOTHER DYING BUSINESS."

Over the years, through the Berkshire subsidiary, Blue Chip Stamps, Buffett bought such businesses as See's Candy Shops, and *The Buffalo News*, both future Berkshire cash cows. Blue Chip of Los Angeles, California, started as a trading stamp business and in 1973 bought Wesco Financial Corp. In the late 1960s Berkshire, and separately Munger, began accumulating Blue Chip and by 1983 Berkshire owned about 60% of the company.

When Buffett began buying the stock in 1968, its float was about $60 million in outstanding, unredeemed stamps. In 1972 Buffett took $25 million of the money and bought See's, which had annual sales then of $35 million.

In 1977 Buffett, through Blue Chip, bought *The Buffalo News* for about $33 million from the estate of Mrs. Edward H. Butler, Jr.

When Buffett was 46 years old, he owned about $35 million worth of Berkshire stock and about $10 million worth of Blue Chip stock (according to *Fortune* magazine which in May 1977 ran an article by Buffett about how inflation swindles the equity investor).

In 1983 Blue Chip, headed by Munger, was entirely merged into Berkshire. Blue Chip offers two main kinds of promotional services: those used by businesses to attract or retain customers; and, those used by businesses to motivate their employees. Often the stamps are given as supermarket premiums.

Blue Chip started its trading stamp business in 1956 and for years that was a successful business. There was a time when a ladies' quartz watch could be purchased for 17 books of stamps. Although the stamp business is still in existence, it has withered. But the company has managed to shrink profitably.

Blue Chip sales hit a peak of more than $124 million in 1970, then dropped to little more than $9 million in 1982, and to $200,000 a year currently.

Munger, at the Berkshire Annual Meeting in 1994, said of the more than 99% decline: "We're waiting for a bounce."

Most of the decline occurred in the early 1970s, when many

supermarkets converted to discount merchandising, and service stations, facing the first major gas shortage, decided they didn't need trading stamps for promotion.

The stamp business was dealt an all but fatal blow when a supermarket chain that accounted for 51% of trading stamp revenues discontinued the stamps in 1982. The only benefit the stamp business offered was some continuing float, the cash received in advance of need, which was invested.

Blue Chip Stamps headquarters in Los Angeles. The stamp business was virtually wiped out but its investments in See's Candies and the Buffalo News brought sweet and newsworthy riches.

(Photo by Andrew Kilpatrick)

Blue Chip Motivation, operated as a separate division, struggled in a competitive environment offering motivation programs for organizations. It uses awards of merchandise and travel to stimulate sales and productivity, promote attendance and safety and otherwise motivate their employees. Today the stamp operations of Blue Chip are tiny. In the 1983 Blue Chip Annual Report, Munger wrote:

> We began the 1970s with a single business, trading stamps, which was destined to decline to a small fraction of its former size, and a portfolio of securities, offsetting stamp redemption liability, which had been selected by previous owners and would have led to a disastrous result if held through the present time. (The portfolio, for instance, contained a substantial amount of very long-term, low-coupon municipal bonds of issuers with declining credit ratings.)

> We began the 1980s with five constituent businesses instead of one. In order of acquisition they are: (1) trading stamps and other promotional services, (2) See's Candy

Shops, Incorporated, (3) Mutual Savings, (4) *Buffalo Evening News*, and (5) Precision Steel.

Munger says the businesses have in common both good management and some resistance to inflation.

> The second of these two common characteristics gets more important every year as inflation continues. Many businesses, once good investments when inflation was low, are now, under inflationary conditions, unable to produce much, if any, cash even when physical volume is constant...

> Inflation is a very effective form of indirect taxation on capital represented by holdings of common stock. We know of no countermeasure...But, even so, we think a habit of always thinking about and trying to serve shareholders' interests in real terms, instead of rationalizing growth of managed assets regardless of real effects on shareholders, is quite useful and may fairly be expected of corporate managements.

Later he signed off, saying:

> This may well be the last annual report our shareholders will ever receive from Blue Chip Stamps as a separate corporation, because work is in progress on a proposal that our corporation be merged with Berkshire Hathaway Inc., long a 59.6%-owner of Blue Chip Stamps.

At the time of the merger, Buffett personally owned more than 10% of the outstanding shares. After Berkshire itself he was the company's second largest shareholder. Munger owned 2.2% of Blue Chip. Berkshire had 986,509 shares outstanding held by about 1,900 shareholders, and Blue Chip had 5,178,770 shares outstanding held by about 1,500 shareholders.

At Wesco's Annual Meeting in 1993 Munger kidded Bob Bird about his managerial record at Blue Chip. He said Bird had helped take sales of Blue Chip from $120 million a year down to $300,000 a year. "This is a managerial record that not everybody would be proud of.

"Even so, there is some success. If you trace Blue Chip stock, it's way over a billion dollars now."

When Buffett and Munger bought the stock in 1968 and 1969, it was worth about $40 million. (*Outstanding Investor Digest*, June 30, 1993)

Munger said:

Years ago, before Warren and I bought any stock, Blue
Chip Stamps mailed minor amounts of Blue Chip stock out
to filling station operators as a class action settlement of
some kind. My wife told the guy where she gets her car
washed to hold onto it. Well, the other day he dragged her
out of the car and kissed her. So maybe we should buy into
another dying business.

In 1997 some former Blue Chip shareholders sued Berkshire, saying their shares had become lost in transfer agent records. Thus
they were unaware when Blue Chip merged with Berkshire in 1983
that they had become Berkshire shareholders and had later been
damaged by having their Berkshire shares transferred to various
states under escheat laws. But escheats are reversible, and each of the
suing shareholders had been able to recover about $31,000 per "lost"
Berkshire share by reversing escheats to the State of California, and
most or all these shareholders had thus been lucky that they had
become "lost," forcing their retention of Berkshire shares during a
long holding period while the share price increased by over thirty-
fold to the roughly $31,000 per share they recovered. Late in 1997
the court threw out this shareholders' litigation against Berkshire,
ruling that the litigation was barred by the applicable statute of limitations.

46
WESCO
"A TOURIST-CLASS TICKET"

Wesco Financial Corp. was written up in a *Wall Street Journal* article on April 17, 1990, as a "tourist-class ticket" way to invest in a Berkshire-like way because Wesco, which has many of the same investments as Berkshire, trades in a price range of three digits rather than five. With no Berkshire B shares then outstanding, the article argued Wesco could then be thought of as a poor man's Berkshire.

Wesco, of Pasadena, California, is 80.1% owned by Berkshire through Blue Chip Stamps which bought Wesco in 1973. Buffett and Munger convinced Elizabeth Caspers Peters, the daughter of Wesco's founder to cancel a merger so they could buy the company. The Peters family owns about 1.3% of Wesco stock. (*New York Times*, June 8, 1997)

Would Berkshire ever buy the remaining Wesco stock? "Chances are low, but not nil," Wesco Chairman Charles Munger said at Wesco's Annual Meeting in 1997.

In 1996 Wesco bought Kansas Bankers Surety company, which insures community banks, for about $80 million. Munger wrote in the 1997 Wesco Annual Report: "KBS is run by Donald Towle, Chairman, assisted by 13 dedicated officers and employees." (See next chapter)

And in 2000 Wesco bought CORT Business Services, a large furniture rental company based in Fairfax, Virginia.

Wesco owns Precision Steel, a steel service center and branded metal specialty products firm bought in 1979 for about $15 million. Precision has locations in Franklin Park, Illinois, and in Charlotte, North Carolina. Precision earned about $2.5 million in 1999. Precision had begun business as a supplier of precision steel in the Chicago area. The company was founded by George C. Tinsley in 1940. It started up in a rented office space of 5,000 square feet. The first years were difficult because of shortage of metal as a result of World War II. After the war years, steel became more plentiful and the company grew.

And, Wesco, since 1959, had owned Mutual Savings and Loan Association in Pasadena, California. Mutual Savings was co-found-

(Photo by Andrew Kilpatrick)

This is the office building in Pasadena, California, owned by Wesco's property unit. Wesco's Annual Meeting used to be held in a cafeteria in the company owned building. In 1998 Wesco's Annual Meeting was held at the nearby McCormick & Schmick's Seafood Restaurant. Munger explained that the cafeteria tenant had left. He apologized for the opulent surroundings of the seafood restaurant room, but said it would have been more expensive to cater the event in an empty office space. The 1999 and 2000 Wesco meetings were held at the nearby University Club.

ed in 1925 by Rudolph W. Caspers, the father of William T. Caspers. Bill Caspers, a Wesco director, died in 1999. His sister, Elizabeth Caspers Peters, remains a Wesco director. Also, Salomon's former chairman, Robert Denham, was named to the Wesco board in early 2000.

For years, in the lower level of Mutual's nine-story building, Munger held the Wesco Annual Meeting for a small band of shareholders.

In the 1992 Wesco Annual Report, Munger wrote, "We have decided that Mutual Savings will shortly give up its status as a regulated savings and loan association. To achieve this objective, Mutual Savings is negotiating to sell to another financial institution..." (Cenfed Financial).

As a result, about $300 million in capital was transferred to Wes-FIC (Wesco-Financial Insurance Co.) in Omaha where its place of business is in the headquarters office of Berkshire's National Indemnity. That doubled the capital of Wes-FIC, which writes super-cat insurance policies with Berkshire's insurance group, one of the world's largest insurance organizations in terms of capital, stronger than Lloyd's of London.

"So why shouldn't we do more of what works well for us and what's less complicated?" Munger said. (*Omaha World-Herald*, April 22, 1993)

Munger has noted that the move would result in a cost savings in a less regulated environment. The plan also included transferring Mutual Savings real estate to a newly formed Wesco subsidiary. Afterwards, Mutual Savings retained a majority of its former assets such as its Freddie Mac stock and was merged into Wesco's subsidiary, Wesco-Financial Insurance Co., regulated by the Nebraska Department of Insurance. "After all, there are practical advantages in moving hundreds of millions of dollars of assets (at market value) from a high-cost, low-flexibility environment to a low-cost, high-flexibility environment."

"After Wes-FIC's capital and claims-paying capacity have been greatly augmented by the merger into Wes-FIC of Mutual Savings, Wes-FIC plans, through subcontracts with the Berkshire Hathaway Insurance Group, to enter the business of super-catastrophe ("super-cat") reinsurance."

So Wesco left the heavily regulated S&L industry and joined up with Berkshire to boldly enter the more profitable arena of reinsurance.

"It [the S&L] took up time disproportionate to the capital involved," Munger said.

In November 1993, Wesco said although its Wes-FIC unit had planned to enter the super-cat business, a flood of capital into the reinsurance market had resulted in lower prices and Berkshire might not have enough extra business to give to the unit. Wesco said it would seek other insurance opportunities.

"But what are the predictions of man!" Munger wrote in Wesco's 1993 Annual Report. He said that in February 1994, Wes-FIC was offered five unusual super-cat reinsurance participations by National Indemnity.

Buffett has no office at Wesco but he is a director of Wes-FIC.

Wesco's headquarters is not far from Cypress Insurance Corp. of Pasadena, one of Berkshire's insurance businesses that sometimes does some business with Wes-FIC. Wes-FIC, which carries a rare AAA rating from Standard and Poor's, wrote only 1% of its statutory surplus compared to an industry average of about 113% in 1995, Munger wrote in Wesco's 1996 Annual Report.

He added, "On super-cat reinsurance accepted by Wes-FIC to

date (March 7, 1995) there has been no loss whatever that we know of. Our accounting policy requires contract expiration before super-cat underwriting profit is recognized. Needless to say, we would not have similar reticence to report losses before contract expirations. Our super-cat accounting is not intentionally super conservative, although it may amount to 'best-practice' accounting."

Wes-FIC has sometimes reinsured some of the book of the workers' compensation insurance business of Cypress. Cypress has written some insurance business for See's. More synergy at Berkshire?

Berkshire owns about 5.7 million of the 7.1 million Wesco shares outstanding. The stock is thinly traded with an average of 1,300 shares a day changing hands on the American Stock Exchange. Many of the other shares are held by the Caspers and Peters families, who have family members on Wesco's board.

In many ways Wesco, which has about 5,000 shareholders, is indeed something of a baby Berkshire and holds some of the same securities as Berkshire. It owns positions in American Express, Coca-Cola, Gillette and Wells Fargo stock. Its main holding is 28.8 million shares of Freddie Mac. Wesco's cost for the stock bought in late 1988 was $71.7 million, now worth far more than $1 billion.

In the 1995 Wesco Annual Report, Munger wrote of the Freddie Mac position: "For us, at least, our experience in shifting from savings and loan operation to ownership of Freddie Mac shares tends to confirm a long held notion that being prepared, on a few occasions in a lifetime, to act promptly in scale in doing some simple thing will often be enough to make the financial results of that lifetime quite satisfactory."

As a result of a foreclosure in 1966, Wesco long owned about 22 acres of oceanfront property near Santa Barbara, California originally carried on the books at $2 million. The land was slowly developed for about 32 houses and recreation facilities, causing a grossly unsatisfactory return, far below interest levels on government bonds.

Other properties include several buildings in a small shopping center in Upland, California, leased to small businesses.

About the time Mutual Savings was sold to Cenfed, Wesco organized MS Property Company, a real estate subsidiary that was slowly selling some of Mutual's old troubled assets. "Wesco still retains a recently formed real estate subsidiary that, mostly, it does not want," Munger wrote in the 1994 Wesco Annual Report.

Wesco's Chief Financial Officer Jeffrey Jacobson portrays Wesco as a company where nothing fancy happens, where management just tries to keep things in the middle of the road. In short, things are on track.

"We still have the Freddie Mac stock," he said.

During the long work of trying to make something of the Santa Barbara property, Jacobson said, "We're starting to sell some of the units. A number of the houses have been built."

Munger and his wife took a fancy to the land, paying Mutual Savings $2.1 million in cash for two lots in the Montecito real estate development just south of Santa Barbara where Munger built a palatial home overlooking the Pacific Ocean. The home is impeccably appointed. Little, except several magazine covers of Munger suggests he lives there. Tucked back in a small study is a *New Yorker* cartoon saying: "In Charlie's hands, wealth just never seems obscene no matter how big it gets." In a spacious library there are such books as a set of *World Books, Encyclopedia Britannica,* volumes by Learned Hand, Graham Greene, Charles Dickens, and Mark Twain. Also on the shelves are *The Last Lion, The Age of Federalism, The Life of Herbert Hoover, Eleanor Roosevelt, Citizen Turner,* and *Bonfire of the Vanities.* And there is a photo of Munger's hero, Ben Franklin.

At Wesco's meeting in 2000, Munger recommended reading *The Selfish Gene.*

Buffett has dubbed the house, "Munger's Folly." Others call the area "Mungerville."

"He keeps a low profile," Jacobson said of Munger, adding that Munger has lots of irons in the fire. He's Chairman of the Board of Good Samaritan Hospital in Los Angeles and he's chairman of The Daily Journal Corp., an over-the-counter firm that publishes the *Los Angeles Daily Journal,* a sort of *Wall Street Journal* for the area's legal profession.

Each year Munger writes to Wesco's small band of shareholders much in the same vein that Buffett does. There's no pulling of punches. Usually there's heavy criticism and sarcasm about such things as the S&L crisis or leveraged buyout operators. Still Wesco has not enjoyed fast growth nor has it found enough of the right acquisitions.

In Wesco's 1989 report Munger said how hard it is for Wesco to find good acquisition candidates, and he likened that search to catching muskies.

"To Wesco, as a non-LBO operator, the good-corporate-acquisition game was always tough. And that game in each recent year has become more like fishing for muskies at Leech Lake, in Minnesota, where the writer's earliest business partner, Ed Hoskins, had the following conversation with his Indian guide:

"Are any muskies caught in this lake?"

"More muskies are caught in this lake than in any other lake in Minnesota. This lake is famous for muskies."
"How long have you been fishing here?"
"19 years."
"And how many muskies have you caught?"
"None."

Munger said: "Wesco continues to try more to profit from always remembering the obvious than from grasping the esoteric. It is remarkable how much long-term advantage people like us have gotten by trying to be consistently not stupid, instead of trying to be very intelligent. There must be some wisdom in the folk saying, 'It's the strong swimmers who drown.' "

In 1989 Wesco, with a stinging letter from Munger, resigned from the United States League of Savings, in protest of the league's reluctance to call for proper reforms in light of the national S&L crisis. Wrote Munger, "It is not unfair to liken the situation now facing Congress to cancer and to liken the League to a significant carcinogenic agent. And, like cancer, our present troubles will recur if Congress lacks the wisdom and courage to excise elements which caused the troubles."

Wesco is a steady, if unglamorous, part of Berkshire, and perhaps can be thought of as having the safety and about the same steady and sure return of a money market account. In fact, once a Berkshire shareholder suggested to Munger he might want to turn Wesco into a money market account one day. Munger did not totally dismiss the idea.

That should not suggest he is about to liquidate things, but then Munger has no problems with cash in the bank earning sure money either.

Munger has always thought that high-quality businesses and stocks will carry the day. Buffett says that Munger has influenced him greatly towards being concerned about the quality of a business rather than just buying for a cheap price.

The Wall Street Journal story about Wesco also noted that Wesco's businesses were not considered as good as Berkshire's. Munger has said much the same thing himself. He wound up saying, "We'd be fine if we had bought quality stocks, instead of Wesco, in 1972."

Berkshire acquired Wesco at about $6 a share. With the stock selling at more than $300 per share in 1998, that's on the order of 17% on his money annually, a "money fund" Buffett could be proud of, even with Wesco's drop in 1999.

At Wesco's Annual Meeting in 1993, Munger was asked who really makes the decisions for Wesco; he threw a compliment to Buffett saying, "Well, the most important person is in Omaha."

And in response to another question, Munger said, "I always like to see the nerds win."

Wesco's stock continues to do well though Munger downplays it. At one time he said: "An orangutan could figure out that the stock is selling for miles above the value of the company if it were liquidated. I keep telling people this, but they keep on buying the stock. It may be that Berkshire groupies see us as a way to buy into the [Berkshire] complex." (*Washington Post,* November 28, 1993)

In the 1995 Wesco Annual Report, Munger calculated Wesco's intrinsic value at $149 a share compared to the stock price of $182 on December 31, 1995. In the 1996 Wesco Annual Report, Munger calculated Wesco's intrinsic value as $196 a share compared with $187 stock price at the end of 1996. "This comparison indicates that Wesco stock was then selling about 5% below intrinsic value," Munger wrote. In Wesco's 1997 Annual Report, Munger calculated Wesco's intrinsic value at $273 at yearend 1997 compared with a stock price of $300 a share. In the 1998 Wesco Annual Report, Munger calculated Wesco's yearend 1998 intrinsic value to be $342 a share compared to the yearend stock price of $354 ¾, about 4% above intrinsic value.

Munger calculated in Wesco's 1999 Annual Report that yearend 1999 intrinsic value was $286 a share compared to Wesco's stock price of $245, about 14% below intrinsic value.

And he wrote: "Wesco is not an equally-good-but-smaller version of Berkshire Hathaway, better because its small size makes growth easier. Instead, each dollar of book value at Wesco continues plainly to provide much less intrinsic value than a similar dollar of book value at Berkshire Hathaway."

At the Wesco Annual Meeting in 1998, Munger said he calculates Wesco's intrinsic value because it's a lot easier to figure than Berkshire. At the 1998 meeting with Berkshire trading at about $70,000, Munger said Berkshire's stock price was "not crazy" when compared to most other stocks.

NOTE FROM THE INTERNET: Here's a posting on the "Berkshire message board" from February 16, 1998:

"...I decided to do some half-baked 'back of the envelope' figuring. What follows is the Wesco common stock portfolio as listed in the 1996 Annual Report (and confirmed by the latest 10Q) On the left is the 'Quoted Market (Carrying) Value' as of 12/31/96 for each security. On the right is the value as of the close last Friday, assuming no major changes to the portfolio in the interim.

Stock	12/31/96	2/13/98
Freddie Mac	$794,700,000	$1,319,400,000
Coca-Cola	$379,195,000	$494,033,950
Gillette	$248,800,000	$327,800,000
Wells Fargo	$45,679,000	$55,310,677
American Express	$36,595,000	$57,200,000
Travelers (Salomon)	$20,000,000	$45,999,800
Total of Above	**$1,529,772,000**	**$2,299,745,000**

"That portfolio shows an increase in value in the past 13½ months of almost exactly 50% (if I did it correctly). Not too shabby. To extrapolate one step further, there are 7,119,807 shares outstanding. Dividing the current value of the common stock portfolio by the outstanding shares, you get a per share value of $323.00

"Please remember that this doesn't even look at Wesco's other businesses (insurance, steel, etc.) and the rest of its holdings, and that when CM [Charles Munger] calculates Wesco's IV [intrinsic value], he factors in the tax consequences of the cost of liquidating those assets (which is pretty hefty). But as Wesco is currently selling for about $305 a share, this should make you feel a little better about your investment."

Wesco's 10-K for the period ending December 31, 1999 showed Wesco's stock portfolio as follows:

	Shares	Cost
Freddie Mac	28,800,000	$71,729,000
Coca Cola	7,205,600	$40,761,000
Gillette	3,200,000	$40,000,000
American Express	647,700	$20,687,000
Wells Fargo	169,340	$11,351,000
		$184,528,000

Munger said at the Berkshire Annual Meeting in 1998: "Per unit of book value, Wesco is not a clone of Berkshire. It's an historical accident. We will do our best for Wesco, but most opportunities will be with Berkshire."

Maybe Wesco shares are really Berkshire's Class C shares.

In the first quarter of 2000, Wesco sold some of its Freddie Mac shares, reports said.

(Photo by John Gartmann)

Munger at Wesco's annual meeting in 2000. To left is Cathy Hayden, a Berkshire and Wesco shareholder, from Rancho Palos Verdes, California.

47

KANSAS BANKERS SURETY CO.
GO TO A PARTY; BUY A BUSINESS

Berkshire through Wesco acquired Kansas Bankers Surety Co. of Topeka, Kansas, for $80 million in 1996. Kansas Bankers, founded in 1909, insures community banks throughout middle America.

The company's stock, which had been listed on the OTC bulletin board and traded infrequently, was at $19 a share before the announcement. The price Berkshire paid in cash was about $24.50 a share.

"He just flat made an offer to us out of the blue," said Don Towle, CEO of Kansas Bankers, of a letter Buffett wrote to the company in February, 1996. (*Topeka Capital-Journal*, April 12, 1996)

Buffett wrote the letter to Roy Dinsdale, a Kansas Bankers director who is also chairman of Pinnacle Bancorp Inc. of Central City, Nebraska.

Towle, who runs the company with five other people, said he was initially "shocked," then finally "flattered" that Buffett would make an offer.

Buffett explains in Berkshire's 1996 Annual Report: "You might be interested in the carefully-crafted and sophisticated strategy that allowed Berkshire to nab the deal. Early in 1996 I was invited to the 40th birthday party of my nephew's wife, Jane Rogers. My taste for social events being low, I immediately and in my standard gracious way began to invent reasons for skipping the event. The party planners then countered brilliantly by offering me a seat next to a man I always enjoy, Jane's dad, Roy Dinsdale—so I went.

"The party took place on January 26. Though the music was loud—why must bands play as if they will be paid by the decibel? I just managed to hear Roy say he'd come back from a director's meeting of Kansas Bankers Surety, a company I'd always admired. I shouted back that he should let me know if it ever became available for purchase."

Dinsdale sent Buffett the company's financials and Buffett made the offer.

Most of the 600 stockholders of Kansas Bankers—most of whom

were banks or bankers—sold out to Berkshire.

Kansas Bankers insures bank deposits beyond limits of the federal government and it insures banks against burglaries, robberies, and forgeries.

The company insures more than 1,200 banks and about 70% of the banks in Nebraska and is the only bonding firm owned by the banks it serves, according to the *Topeka Capital-Journal.*

Kansas Bankers was founded by a group of bankers who shunned government programs designed to insure their banks' deposits. The company started as Bankers Deposit, Guaranty and Surety Co. Its main purpose was to guarantee the deposits of the banks that formed it. By 1922, the company changed its focus, deciding it was no longer profitable to issue deposit insurance. The company's stock, on a pro-rata basis, was placed in more than 700 Kansas banks and the name was changed to Kansas Bankers Surety Co.

By 1979 the company had captured all the market share in Kansas it could and it expanded to other Midwestern states.

Kansas Bankers had a net income of $6.4 million in 1999. The company has a Triple-A claims paying rating from Standard & Poor's.

48
BERKSHIRE'S "SAINTED SEVEN," EIGHT, NINE...BUSINESSES

"Last year we dubbed these operations the Sainted Seven: Buffalo News, Fechheimer, Kirby, Nebraska Furniture Mart, Scott Fetzer Manufacturing Group, See's and World Book. In 1988 the Saints came marching in."

—1988 Berkshire Annual Report.

BERKSHIRE OPERATING COMPANY PROFILE

See's Candies

The Buffalo News

Nebraska Furniture Mart

Scott Fetzer Manufacturing Group

Kirby

World Book

Fechheimer

Borsheim's

H.H. Brown, Lowell, and Dexter

Helzberg's Diamond Shops/Ben Bridge Jeweler

R.C. Willey Home Furnishings

FlightSafety International

Star Furniture

International Dairy Queen

Executive Jet

Jordan's Furniture Company

MidAmerican Energy

CORT Business Services

Finance and Financial Products Businesses

Other

"If Berkshire's directly owned manufacturing, publishing and retailing businesses alone were separated as an independent company, its financial profits would be impressive. The 'company' would have sales of $2.4 billion, net income of over $200 million, and rank in the Fortune 500. In fact, in terms of profitability defined as return on assets, it would rank in the top 5 of the Fortune 500!" (*Sequoia Fund Quarterly Report, March 31, 1995*)

49
SEE'S CANDIES
IMPROVES YOUR CHANCES OF GETTING SEX

Buffett once sent a box of See's Candies at Christmas time to a Berkshire stockholder. The box was accompanied by an item from *USA Today* (December 8, 1998) which noted that: "Twenty-nine percent of men believe that giving boxed chocolates improves their chances of getting sex and 8% of women agree, according to the American Boxed Chocolate Manufactures.

Next to the newspaper item, Buffett scrawled: "Much higher with See's. Please verify and report."

Candy companies are fun and in the case of See's Candies, both fun and profitable and Buffett watches the numbers obsessively. "We fax him a sales report *daily*," says Dave Harvey, a See's executive at the 350,000-square-foot plant in Carson, California. Buffett is so devoted to See's that his Laguna Beach, California, home has a portrait of a box of See's that for a long time hung over a couch in the family room, according to Buffett's long-time stockbroker, Arthur Rowsell.

Buffett is proud of a photo he has of Nancy Reagan boarding Air Force One carrying a large box of See's candy under her arm.

Actress Sally Field is a big See's Candy fan.

The See's Candy Shops, wholly owned by Berkshire, have been making candy for sweet-toothed customers for more than 78 years. Buffett, at Munger's suggestion, bought See's on January 3, 1972, for $25 million, buying it through Berkshire's Blue Chip Stamps affiliate. Buffett's decision to buy

(Courtesy of See's Candies)

See's President Chuck Huggins, 75, has served longer than any other head of a Berkshire operating business. He's worked at See's for 50 years.

397

This See's Candies shop in Pasadena, California, is typical of the more than 200 shops in black and white décor of the West Coast firm serving chocoholics. Buffett hopes customers wash things down with Coke, then grab their Gillette Oral-B toothbrushes.

the company was easy. "It was a no-brainer. I wish I could find 50 more like it.

"Most of the businesses we've bought on the first visit. See's Candy, I went out there one time to see the grandson of Mary See. His name was Harry See...We had a deal. We understood the kind of position they held in consumers' minds and pricing flexibility and so on.

"Did I think they could charge 20 cents a pound more for candy? Sure. And sure enough, they could," he said in a talk to Columbia business students, October 27, 1993.

See's, which made 12 cents a pound profit in 1972, now makes more than a $1 a pound largely because it has been able to raise prices. Buffett has said that while Blue Chip's sales dropped from about $100 million in 1972 to about $1 million in 1991, See's revenues more than made up for things. They rose from $29 million to $196 million during that time. Profits in 1999 were $36 million when See's sold 33 million pounds of boxed chocolates. Brand quality counts.

When Buffett bought See's for chocoholics everywhere—a company that may be a subtle plug for Gillette's Oral-B toothbrushes—he put Charles Huggins in charge.

Buffett said it took him five minutes to name Huggins and that with the record Huggins has notched, one could wonder what took him so long. Buffett said in the 1991 Annual Report that the compensation agreement was "conceived in about five minutes and never reduced to a written contract—that remains unchanged to this day." Over the years Huggins and Buffett have talked about once every 10 days although Huggins said during the Salomon crisis it was more on the order of once a month. (*Wall Street Journal*, November 8, 1991)

See's was founded in 1921 by a 71-year-old grandmother, Mary See, who went into the business with little more than an apron and a few pans, at a small neighborhood candy shop in California. See's candy boxes still bear the logo of a smiling Mrs. See, a logo designed by her son Charles.

During the Great Depression, See's lowered the price of its chocolates from 80 to 50 cents a pound. "Be Thrifty. Pay Fifty," was See's slogan. Fortunately, See's landlords lowered rents, so See's was able to stay in business.

In the 1920s, a time when there were only a few See's shops, See's delivered to many of its customers by Harley Davidson motorcycles hitched to an enclosed sidevan. (*Ironworks*, August, 1997) (Maybe this is why Sequoia Fund, managed by Buffett's friend Bill Ruane, owns a large stake of Harley Davidson stock.) David H. Ramsey, president/co-publisher of Hatton-Brown Publishers, Inc., of Montgomery, Alabama, which publishes *Ironworks* magazine, sent Buffett the magazine piece about the connection between See's and Harley cycles. Buffett wrote Ramsey: "Thanks for your nice letter and the article. Fifty years ago, I had an Indian [motorcycle] for a short while, which I lost enthusiasm for after I drove it over the cobblestones of Baltimore (they made them a little different in those days).

"During the festivities last year, they let me sit in the driver's seat of the See's Harley, but they pushed it out on stage rather than trust me to rev it up. Somewhat humiliating!"

Today See's candy is delivered in a variety of ways, including 40-foot tractor trailers and 747 jet aircraft.

See's makes boxed chocolates and other confectionery goodies in two large kitchens, one in Los Angeles and the other in South San Francisco.

See's distributes candies through its own distinctive white and black retail stores in many western and midwestern states and Hawaii. About 40% of See's candies are made in Los Angeles and about 60% in San Francisco. The Los Angeles plant concentrates on hard-centered candies. An "enrober moves the centers—the toffees and carmels through various chocolate baths, and a drying period. They are then boxed in brown cardboard... Women crowd the head and foot of the enrober, keeping the candies upright, then getting them off the machine without marring the shiny surfaces. Yes, this is the same type of machine that Lucy and Ethel worked on in the famous "I Love Lucy" episode." (*Los Angeles Times*, July 19, 1999)

The scene is reminiscent of the famous one in the *I Love Lucy* TV show with Lucille Ball and Ethel Mertz working in the chocolate factory. Huggins has been asked if this scene was filmed at See's: "What actually happened is one of the producers toured out factory to see how candy was really made. Then they re-created part of the assembly line in a studio in Los Angeles. It was filmed there." (*Sacramento Bee*, August 11, 1999)

The great majority of them, more than 165 stores, are located in California where the company gets about 80% of its profits. The stores have a variety of chocolate goodies. The mouth-watering names are kept simple: Walnut Cluster, Peanut Cluster, Almond Square, Milk Patties, Molasses Chip and Milk Cherry. Maybe Death by Chocolate will be offerings in this new millennium. And there are lollipops in chocolate, butterscotch and a variety of flavors.

Many sales are made through direct shipments nationwide from a seasonally varying number of order distribution centers. Significant seasonality exists in the business—heavy sales in cold months and light sales in hot months. Most of each year's sales come in the last two months of the year when quantity discounts add to extremely high Christmas and New Year's sales. Half of its chocolate sales are made between Thanksgiving and New Year's Eve. About 90% of its profits are recorded in December.

See's gift-wraps its boxes, the perfect Christmas present. For years, a few Congressmen have sent boxes of See's to friends.

Many customers report pleasant experiences with See's. Karen Salerno says when she grew up in Houston, See's had a shop downtown. "It was one of the first businesses I ever knew that let me always try the candy to decide if I liked it before buying. I could go in, try four or five and then buy as little as two or three individual pieces, or as many gift-wrapped boxes, but was always treated courteously. That is how they won my loyalty and business."

In March 1982, Berkshire received a bid for See's from a British firm for $120 million in cash. Buffett didn't bite. See's net income has grown from about $6 million in 1981 to well over five times that much—about $31 million in 1996. But it has difficulty expanding.

"We've looked at dozens of ideas of how to expand," Buffett said at the annual meeting in 1988. "And in the end we haven't found how to do it...It's a tough business." Shareholder Michael Assael wonders, "Maybe Dairy Queen, or even McDonald's or Starbucks could get together with See's. Maybe the Disney characters could join in, too."

Recently See's has opened a few sites in New York, Pennsylvania and in a few international locations such as Hong Kong (back in 1976). And more recently in Singapore and Guam. See's, which calls itself a "Happy Habit," can now be ordered over the Internet.

Buffett himself is a big See's eater—probably just taste testing of course. But even when it comes to delicious chocolates, Buffett strives for discipline, limiting himself to one box a month. Still, it's another example of, "We eat our own cooking."

That two-pound box arrives at Berkshire headquarters once a month. Everyone at the office shares it.

In every box of See's, you'll find the following message of See's philosophy:

> For over 75 years we have worked hard to maintain the tradition of quality which literally millions of faithful See's candy eaters have come to expect, year after year.
>
> Our philosophy is quite simple: Be absolutely persistent in all attitudes regarding quality—buy only the best ingredients obtainable—offer the most delicious and interesting assortments of candies available in the United States—own and operate all See's sparkling white shops, while providing the highest level of customer service.
>
> This may seem old-fashioned, if not unusual, in this day and age—but it works. At the same time we fully believe that we can always do a better job at what we try to do— ultimately making people happy!

See's does some things the old-fashioned way. For example, it had long refused to honor credit cards in its stores. But all that has now changed, according to this ad in the *Los Angeles Times* on November 18, 1997:

> After some lengthy debate, the Accounting Department at See's has concluded that credit cards are here to stay. So now we've begun accepting American Express, Visa, MasterCard and Discover cards at all of our shops. We want to make it easier for you to make your purchases, especially during the holiday season. Other than that, nothing has changed. Your cash and personal checks are still gladly wel-

(Photo courtesy of See's Candies)

A See's packing plant in Carson, California, where workers are packing one-pound boxes of Assorted Chocolates.

come. And when it comes to making candy, and to our friendly service, we're happy to stay behind the times. Forty years behind at least.

Presumably Buffett's still top-secret plan for synergy at Berkshire calls for all that candy to be washed through everyone's digestive track with Cokes.

And that includes the Tim Moylan family of Omaha. Moylan keeps a stock of See's at his office for visitors, and one day the candy caught the fancy of Moylan's four-year-old son, Dan.

"Remember our friend, Howard Buffett?" asked Moylan. "Well, Howard's father owns the factory that makes the candy." Replied Dan, "You mean Howard's dad is Willy Wonka?" The writer of the story, Robert McMorris, promptly got a note from Buffett saying he planned to pass out samples of See's candy at the Berkshire annual meeting. (*Omaha World-Herald*, April 8, 1992)

"When business sags," Buffett wrote, "we spread the rumor that our candy acts as an aphrodisiac. Very effective. The rumor, that is; not the candy."

The aphrodisiac theme has come up before in the annals of chocolate: " 'Twill make Old women Young and Fresh; Create New Motions of the Flesh,

And cause them to long for you know what,

If they but taste of chocolate."

(James Wadsworth's quatrain as contained in *A Curious History of the Nations of Chocolate* as quoted in the *Emperors of Chocolate: Inside the Secret World of Hershey and Mars, Jöel Glenn Brenner*, pp. 94-95)

Buffett said at Berkshire's Annual Meeting in 1997: "Here we were in 1972—and we know a fair amount about candy; in fact, I know more than when I sat down this morning. I've eaten about 20 pieces already.

"But does their face light up on Valentine's Day when you hand 'em a box of candy of some nondescript origin and say, 'Here,

Honey, I took the low bid'?

"You've got tens of millions of people, or at least many millions of people, who remember that the first time they handed that box of candy to someone, it wasn't long thereafter that they got kissed for the first time or something. The memories are good. The associations are good."

Munger said at the meeting in 1997: "See's is the first time we paid up for quality. If they had wanted just $100,000 more for See's we wouldn't have bought it."

Buffett added, "If we hadn't bought See's, we wouldn't have bought Coke. So thank See's for the $12 billion. We've had the luck to buy whole businesses that taught us a whole lot. We've had windmills, well, I've had windmills. Charlie was never in the windmill businesses. I've had second rate department stores, pumps and textile mills..."

Munger ended the discussion saying: "I don't think it's necessary to be as dumb as we were."

Buffett loves See's: "I find companies fascinating. We've had See's since 1972, but I can tell you what its sales are day by day. We had 1,800 orders yesterday off the Internet, for example." (*St. Petersburg Times*, December 15, 1999)

See's sold 182,000 pounds of candy on the Internet in 1999 for $2.7 million. Coming off a small base, See's Internet sales were growing rapidly in early 2000, See's officials say.

In late 1999 Buffett toured the See's Candies plant in Carson, California. When he walked by the area where Internet orders are received, he noticed a sign that said: "WEB orders." "Oh, thanks, you've got my initials up there," he quipped.

So how did the Internet come to old-fashioned See's where each piece of candy is placed by hand in boxes?

"Buffett called Huggins and told him to get on the Internet," said See's Dave Harvey. See's set up the website on July 28, 1998, moving very cautiously at first.

A big piece of See's business, in addition to 70% of its sales through its retail outlets, is bulk orders for fundraisers or for corporations. In a Berkshire synergy note, GEICO employees get a discount at See's. "We love GEICO," said a See's employee.

Where does See's get its chocolate? From Guittard in San Francisco which is just down the street from the See's factory. 50,000-gallon tanker trucks deliver the melted chocolate which is held at 120 degrees. During Christmas and Easter, See's gets several tanker truck deliveries a day. Yum.

A cardboard cutout of Mrs. See and Dave Harvey who is with the See's plant in Carson, California.

The See's candy Barbie Doll made by Mattel was introduced at Berkshire's annual meeting in 2000. There were 1,000 orders in the first few days after Buffett announced the product was to be available in September 2000.

See's plant at Carson, California shows number of orders handled—225 orders by 9:42 a.m.

Entrance to See's facility in Carson, California has portraits of Buffett, Munger and Huggins.

50
THE BUFFALO NEWS
A LARGE NEWSHOLE

Buffett bought *The Buffalo News*—sight unseen—in 1977 for $34 million from the estate of Mrs. Edward H. Butler, Jr.

The newspaper made about that amount in annual after-tax income in 1999.

Buffett negotiated the purchase and Munger, dropping quarters in a pay phone near his home in Minnesota, dictated the contract to Buffett.

Because of his knowledge of newspapers, Buffett could tell how the paper was doing by looking at its financial statements. It wasn't necessary, in his view, to go look at the plant. He already knew what a printing press looked like.

He bought the newspaper, not through Berkshire, but through the other company he controlled, Blue Chip Stamps. The *Washington Post* and the *Chicago Tribune* had turned down purchase of the paper.

In her book *Personal History*, Katharine Graham wrote:

> I started to look into properties that I'd hear were available. Warren was of especial help on acquisitions, knowing to some degree about almost every deal that was taking place or had taken place in the previous ten years. One potential acquisition we considered was a television station in Buffalo. Warren advised me that the newspaper, which was also for sale, would be a better buy, and if we didn't want it, he did. Although dominant in its market, the paper had strong competition, strong unions, and no Sunday edition. When we decided not to pursue it, Warren bought it and after considerable struggle managed it to great success. I still feel we made the right decision for us. (p. 581)

The Buffalo News had a very slow start after coming into the Berkshire fold. Here are small excerpts from the 1981 Annual Report of Blue Chip Stamps written by Charles Munger:

> Our 100%-owned subsidiary, Buffalo Evening News, Inc. was acquired in April 1977 for approximately $34 million. It now constitutes only approximately $28.5 million of our con-

solidated net worth, as a result of about $5.5 million of aggregate after-tax operating losses after acquisition. This translates roughly into $11 million of aggregate operating losses before taxes.

However, the operating loss, before taxes, of the News in 1981 was lower than than that of 1980, having declined to $1,091,000 from $2,805,000 in the previous year, which in turn had declined from $4,617,000 in 1979.

...We predicted accurately the financial improvement in 1980 and 1981. For 1982 we confidently predict a lack of improvement. We anticipate terrible market conditions for the News in 1982.

...Economic forces are at work which are plainly beyond anyone's control, and we are catching at least our share of a widespread malaise. We know of no easy solution.

It is of course a temptation when writing an annual letter to shareholders to gloss over difficulties, like those in Buffalo, and comment extensively concerning successes. We recommend exactly the opposite emphasis to business managers who report to us, and we believe in practicing what we preach. Accordingly, year after year, we re-tell and extend the history of the News, creating the largest single section of our annual letter. This year we surpass all previous records.

...While convention doesn't require reporting of "opportunity cost" losses to shareholders, we believe they are just as important as conventional reported losses and should be faced just as squarely. If we hadn't purchased the News in 1977 but had simply earned returns on the unspent purchase price comparable with the average earning power of the rest of our shareholders' equity, we would now have about $70 million in value of other assets, earning over $10 million per year, in place of the Buffalo Evening News and its current red ink. No matter what happens in the future in Buffalo we are about 100% sure to have an economic place lower than we would have occupied if we had not made our purchase.

...The News remains a salable property, even with its current troubles, so long as its share of circulation and advertising is stable-to-inching-ahead, and we could easily improve our consolidated operating earnings and the percentage return we earn on our shareholders' investment by selling the News and reinvesting the proceeds, after tax effects, in profit-earning assets. That we are not even slightly tempted to do so demonstrates our conviction that Buffalo will have a reasonably felicitous future as a city and that the fine people who work at the News will ultimately succeed in making it a sound business for its owners and employees, through continued provision of sound service to its customers. We still plan to stay with the News until it either expires, or far more likely, becomes a solid earner and employer.

Buffett saw that the Buffalo paper might be a good business if it could launch a Sunday edition, so he bought the property. It has been wholly owned by Berkshire since 1983 when Blue Chip was merged into Berkshire.

The News quickly decided to launch a Sunday paper and its special introductory offers to subscribers and advertisers brought a reaction—a lawsuit on the grounds the introductory practices were improper—from its competitor, the morning *Buffalo Courier-Express*, later a Cowles Media paper that published seven days a week.

The News eventually beat back the lawsuit, but both papers continued to lose money for years. From the time of Buffett's purchase, *The News* lost about $12 million, before taxes, through December 31, 1982. Then in 1982 the *Courier-Express* folded, and what Buffett had was a flourishing monopoly, his favorite kind of business. *The News* began putting out a morning edition and today the successful

(Courtesy of The Buffalo News)

The Buffalo News, an early Berkshire investment, now earns in a year about what Buffett originally paid for the newspaper.

paper publishes Sunday and eight editions each weekday.

Munger has often said that buying *The News* was not at all sure to work out well. While it was a gamble at favorable odds, the quick and favorable outcome came partly from luck.

The Buffalo News, which has 1,000 employees, serves the large city and surrounding area long regarded as the eastern end of the Rust Belt, an industrial outpost on the Canadian border. It is the only metropolitan paper within its 10-county distribution area and has a high percentage of household penetration in that area.

A dominant newspaper with great penetration, *The News* has turned into a quintessential Buffett business. It has a return on assets of "an astonishing 91.2%," according to a January, 1991, story in *NewsInc* magazine. "*The Buffalo News* may well be the most profitable newspaper company in the country," it said. The paper has a circulation of 240,000 a day.

Indeed, the paper has the highest profit margin of the nation's publicly owned newspapers, better than 35 cents on each dollar the paper takes in, according to *Editor and Publisher*, said the *Columbia Journalism Review* November/December 1998 which portrayed *The News* as a respectable, if not outstanding paper.

It said although it was a huge success as a business, "Journalistically, Buffett gets a B in Buffalo."

The story said Buffett is not involved in the paper's political endorsements, but did interview Barbara Ireland in 1989 for two and a half hours before she was hired as editorial page editor.

Now at the *New York Times*, Ireland told the *Columbia Journalism*

THE BUFFALO NEWS

Opinion

WARREN E. BUFFETT		STANFORD LIPSEY
Chairman		*Publisher and President*
	MARGARET M. SULLIVAN	
	Editor	
EDWARD L. CUDDIHY	GERALD I. GOLDBERG	STEPHEN W. BELL
Managing Editor	*Editorial Page Editor*	*Managing Editor*

(From the *Buffalo News*, 1999)

408

Review: "You could do a helluva lot worse than Warren Buffett as owner. He definitely was not the standard business conservative. I saw a humane attitude on social issues. He had just two major issues: world population and nuclear weapons control. Because he doesn't impose his politics, most people don't even know what they are."

The article quoted *News* Editor Murray Light as saying: "In his first meeting with me he told me he would not interfere with newsroom operations. He never has."

Buffett is on the masthead, listed as chairman of *The Buffalo News*, and is followed by Stanford Lipsey, publisher and president, and Margaret Sullivan, the editor replacing Murray Light who had been with the newspaper 50 years and editor for 30 years before retiring in September 1999.

Publisher in the press room. Buffalo News Publisher Stan Lipsey is shown here as the presses run.

Former Editor Murray Light worked at the News exactly 50 years, retiring September 19, 1999.

(Photos courtesy of The Buffalo News)

Margaret Sullivan was named editor after Light's retirement saying: "My goal is for the Buffalo News to be the best regional newspaper in the country."

(Photo by Nancy Line Jacobs)

Buffett near a Buffalo News display before Berkshire's Annual Meeting in 1994.

Just before Light's 71st birthday in 1996, Buffett wrote: "From both a professional and a personal standpoint, you are a perfect person to be editor of *The Buffalo News*. I've always considered myself very lucky in having you there when I arrived in 1977." (*Buffalo News*, August 9, 1999)

After Light's retirement, news managing editor Margaret Sullivan was named editor.

Slight of build, the curly-haired Lipsey has been with Buffett since Berkshire bought the now defunct *Sun Newspapers* of Omaha in 1969. Lipsey owned that business when Berkshire acquired it, and later took over management of the much larger *Buffalo News*. Lipsey is a close friend of Buffett. They talk on the phone frequently.

Tim Medley, president of the Medley & Company investment counsel/financial planning company in Jackson, Mississippi, tells this story about meeting "Stan" at a Berkshire shareholder party at Borsheim's the day before the annual meeting in 1990: "While you all were over talking to those bigwigs, I was talking to some regular fellow named Stan who said he was with *The Buffalo News*," he told a small band of fellow shareholders.

Informed that it must be Stan Lipsey, publisher of the paper and a Pulitzer Prize winner, Medley demurred, doubting the fellow was really the publisher since he said he'd be glad to drop off a couple of copies of the newspaper at Medley's hotel room the following morning. Medley had the impression "Stan" might be with the newspaper's circulation department. The end of the story is that Lipsey left two copies of *The Buffalo News* at Medley's hotel doorway the following morning.

Generally a newspaper has great difficulty enjoying better economic times than the area it serves. But someone forgot to tell Lipsey.

(Photo courtesy of The Buffalo News)

New York Governor George Pataki, Buffalo Bills' owner Ralph Wilson, Buffett and Buffalo News Publisher Stan Lipsey at a function September 9, 1998 to boost the cause of the Buffalo Bills. Buffett's effort (and 5' 9 3/4" Doug "The Pass" Flutie's quarterbacking) helped keep the Bills in town for at least five more years.

"We don't budget at the *News*," he told *NewsInc*. "We maintain a living, everyday awareness of expenses, and thereby we save an enormous amount of time and aggravation that goes into budgeting." This attitude is common but not everpresent in Berkshire's subsidiaries.

Buffalo lost 23% of its manufacturing jobs in the early 1980s as its industrial base declined, hit by such closings as Bethlehem Steel in 1983. But life recovered gradually for the heavily blue-collar city after the U.S.-Canada free trade agreement of late 1988. The unemployment rate dropped from a high of 13% in the 1980s to a respectable 5% by the early 1990s.

Buffalo, located on the Niagara River separating the United States and Canada, is just a 90-minute drive along Queen Elizabeth Way to Toronto, the highly congested and expensive business hub of Canada. Real estate prices have been improving, and many Canadian businesses have opened offices in Buffalo, once home for NBC's Tim Russert.

It also hasn't hurt that the Buffalo Bills professional football team improved to the point that they were the first team to appear in four straight Super Bowls in the early 1990s for the sports-happy town.

Businesses still are not enthralled with Buffalo's bitterly cold, snow-belt winters, but local boosters of the city are fond of saying that the city does have four seasons. What businesses do like is that

411

Buffalo's industrial land costs are far below those of Toronto, as are taxes and electricity.

All this has not been lost on *The Buffalo News*, which has been enjoying steadily rising profits even in a sluggish ad environment. Among newspapers published in major markets, *The Buffalo News* claims the highest percentage of area household coverage, 66% on weekdays and 81% on Sundays.

Buffett has said he believes the large "newshole" (percentage of the paper devoted to news versus advertising) of *The Buffalo News* to be greater than any other dominant paper of its size or larger.

In 1997 *The Buffalo News* won a George Polk Award for excellence in journalism. The reporting of Kevin Collison linked the death of a teenager run over on a highway on her way to work at a suburban shopping mall with an alleged policy of denying some city buses access to the mall to discourage minority customers.

The paper had profits of $32 million in 1998.

On September 9, 1998, Buffett made an appearance to help sell luxury boxes and club seats for the Buffalo Bills to help keep the team in Buffalo. *The Buffalo News* (July 15, 1998) reported that team owner Ralph C. Wilson, Jr. and Buffalo News Publisher Stan Lipsey collaborated on the invitation to Buffett. "I think it's important for Buffalo to keep the Bills, so I'm happy to do it for Buffalo and Ralph. I think it would be a terrible mistake for Buffalo to lose the Bills."

In his folksy way, Buffett said it was important to keep the Bills in Buffalo. "It's a little like virginity," he said of the National Football League franchise. "It can be preserved, but not restored. If this community loses it, you're not going to get it back."

And if Buffalo lost the Bills and somehow managed to earn another franchise, he said, it would pay a lot more for the privilege. (*The Buffalo News*, September 19, 1998)

51
NEBRASKA FURNITURE MART
1.2 MILLION SQUARE FEET

"He [Buffett] walked into the store and said, 'Today is my birthday and I want to buy your store. How much do you want for it?' I tell him '$60 million.' He goes, gets a check and comes back right away," Mrs. Rose Blumkin, known as Mrs. B, once said.

Buffett's final purchase price made in 1983 was $55 million for 80% of the store in Omaha, with the other 20% held by management. Berkshire originally had bought 90% of the store, but later management upped its stake to 20%.

At the time of the purchase, Nebraska Furniture Mart had sales of $500 a square foot in the 200,000-square-foot store.

A few of the sales over the years have been to NBC Anchor Tom Brokaw who worked in Omaha in the early 1960s.

(Photo by Nancy Line Jacobs)

Today's Nebraska Furniture Mart operates on 1.2 million square feet.

Although Buffett just walked in and bought the store, it is not as though he hadn't thought about it for a long time.

More than 10 years before the purchase, he was telling journalist Adam Smith it was a good business.

"We are driving down a street in Omaha and we pass a large furniture store. I have to use letters in the story because I can't remember the numbers. 'See that store?' Warren says. 'That's really a good business. It has "a" square feet of floor space, does an annual volume of "b," has an inventory of only "c," and it turns over its capital at

Here's the Nebraska Furniture Mart in Omaha that Buffett bought in 1983 from Rose Blumkin after saying, "I'd like to buy your store." When she said okay, he gave her a check for $60 million. No lawyers, no accountants, no investment bankers. No due diligence. The See's sign signals synergy at Berkshire.

"d," Smith wrote in *Supermoney*, p. 196.

"Why don't you buy it?" I said.

"It's privately held," Warren said.

"Oh," I said.

"I might buy it anyway," Warren said. "Someday."

The Nebraska Furniture Mart, founded in 1935, is a whopper of a furniture store—the largest single home-furnishings complex in the United States.

The store, which in 1993 expanded by building an electronics and appliance superstore, serves a trade area within a radius of about 300 miles from Omaha. It sells everything from rugs, sofas, lamps, to tile, lawn furniture, and grandfather clocks, electronics to cellular telephones.

"Anybody would learn a lot more from watching this business for a few months than from going to business school," Buffett says. (*New York Times*, June 17, 1994)

When Buffett was buying the store, he did not even order an inventory check until the deal was completed; and when Mrs. B, who never spent a day of her life in a school room, asked where were his accountants, lawyers, and investment bankers, he replied, "I trust you more." The contract was one page long and Mrs. B signed by simply making a mark. She never learned to read or write English.

Rose Blumkin, the former Rose Gorelick, one of eight children born to a rabbi and a mother who ran a small grocery store during the reign of czars, was born December 3, 1893. Later she talked her way past a border guard in her native Russia, assuring the guard she would be back after buying leather for the army and a bottle of vodka for him. She made her way to this country and forever after did only two things: run her business and raise her family.

Mrs. B, a feisty 4-foot-10, came to the U.S. in 1917 at the age of 23, began selling furniture in her basement in 1936 and started Nebraska Furniture Mart in 1937 with only $500. "Just imagine what she could have done with more," Buffett jokes. And following her own advice of "Sell cheap and tell the truth," she eventually made the Nebraska Furniture Mart the success that drew Buffett's attention.

By controlling costs and offering value to the customer, the business flourished. It's now the dominant furniture store in the region. In fact, when Mrs. Blumkin was sued by a competitor for selling too cheap, the judge not only ruled in her favor, he also decided to buy $1,400 worth of carpet from her.

For years Buffett brought friends by to see her and he bragged at annual meetings and in the annual reports about how she was picking up speed as she got older. His portrait of Mrs. B was of a business heroine. But in 1989, at age 96, following a dispute with her family about the remodeling and running of the Nebraska Furniture Mart's carpet department to which she was so devoted in her later years, she quit.

Further, she demanded and got from Berkshire $96,000 for unused vacation time. Although she received every penny of it, she stormed out and set up shop across the street from the Nebraska Furniture Mart. She called her new store Mrs. B's Warehouse. "Their price $104; our price $80," a sign in her store used to read.

"I got mad. I expect too much," she later told *Forbes.* (April 26, 1993)

At the time she was still moving around on her famous motorized cart and for a while gave interviews saying Buffett was not her friend and that she was running her store to get revenge. For years her family members preferred not to talk about it.

Buffett was once asked how he was able to inspire such loyalty in such a range of business managers and he joked that he tended to have trouble with them in their 90s.

In his annual report, Buffett told it straight to shareholders and he was more than gracious in his remarks about Mrs. B. Nevertheless, it was a distressing moment in a storybook business relationship.

But the story would have a happy ending when Berkshire bought her out again in 1992.

The Nebraska Furniture Mart is always a must-visit for Berkshire shareholders. Once I wandered in the Furniture Mart a day prior to the annual meeting and happened to be told that Buffett had been in earlier. I assumed he had left.

But when I turned into the carpet section, I saw a scene that would have warmed the heart of any Berkshire shareholder. There in the middle of the carpet section was Buffett with a man I would learn was his longtime friend Sandy Gottesman, chairman of the First Manhattan investment firm in New York and a large Berkshire shareholder.

The two were talking to Mrs. B as she sat in her cart. One had the feeling that if Buffett and Mrs. B were really on the carpet section floor talking business, things were as they ought to be.

Normally shy, I walked up to Buffett years ago and introduced myself as a Berkshire shareholder. He said, "Good, come to the annual meeting. Ask questions."

We had a very brief chat in which, instead of asking about business, I asked how his tennis game was and he said he wasn't playing much any more because he had hurt his back.

He and Gottesman wandered around the carpet section inspecting the operations and so I wandered around inspecting (stalking?) them.

One year I asked a Nebraska Furniture Mart employee if Buffett had been in lately. She said yes that he was with a friend. Naturally, I inquired who the person was and she replied, "Some guy named Tisch." I asked whether it might be Larry or Preston Tisch. She said she had no idea.

Yet another year I found Charles Munger, wearing a well-worn casual travel jacket, blue shirt and dark slacks, wandering around in the lower level of the store.

That same year, standing again in the carpet section, I saw an energetic young man in casual clothes come up to Mrs. B's grandson and Nebraska Furniture Mart's executive vice-president Robert Batt, and ask to use the telephone. The man was Buffett's son, Howard Buffett, then county commissioner of Omaha's Douglas County.

He talked politics for a time and then I said hello and asked him a question he's heard a time or two in his life.

"What's your father like?" The younger Buffett replied, "He's great. I've been working on him a long time and he's improving a lot."

Buffett and Mrs. B were inducted into the Omaha Chamber of Commerce Business Hall of Fame in 1993. Mrs. B is driving a souped-up motorized cart. She was famous for driving around the warehouse in a cart after both knees were replaced.

(Omaha World Herald)

Batt, who had just been talking about Buffett said: "I often fly in the plane with Buffett to go to New York to buy rugs.

"Buffett will talk to all of us. Actually he does the talking and we listen. We really don't talk to Buffett. We listen...and then he'll read a lot of the way.

"He knows more about our business than we do. He knows about our business and he knows about competitors. It's not just that he knows about See's. He knows about Russell Stover's. He knows all about Coca-Cola, but then he also knows all about Pepsi, too."

He also said Buffett has told him that he should have bought a huge stake in Disney, that he recognizes Michael Eisner's talents.

Batt, who is heavy-set, once fell at a garage sale held by Sen. Bob Kerrey who was moving from one home to another. He and Kerrey are friends and Kerrey asked him to help with the sale. Batt arrived to help and stumbled, hurting his back and knees and smashing a chest of drawers. "I massacred it," Batt said. "But what's really embarrassing is that I'm our company's safety officer." (*Omaha World-Herald*, August 26, 1997)

Batt says the mart now has 1.2 million square feet—500,000 of which is selling space—or 80 acres.

Both the *Washington Post's* Katharine Graham and *The Buffalo News'* Stanford Lipsey have visited the Nebraska Furniture Mart.

Of late, Berkshire-style synergy has come to the store. There is now a See's Candy shop on the premises. As Buffett wrote in Berkshire's 1990 Annual Report to shareholders, "While there, stop at See's Candy cart and see for yourself the dawn of synergism at Berkshire."

Installed October 21, 1990, the See's Candy cart—the first See's outlet east of Colorado—sold 1,000 pounds of candy in its first week. It didn't hurt sales when Buffett went on an ABC affiliate in Omaha notifying chocoholics of the See's Candy cart's existence.

Now Borsheim's sometimes also offers a small See's candy box with its advertising materials. And See's is now offered in Wells Fargo's online banking service as a gift idea selection. Expanded synergy? Who knows, maybe one day See's and Coke will be combined into a Berkshire Foods Division based at the Nebraska Furniture Mart.

In October 1991, the Nebraska Furniture Mart opened a new store called Trends just behind the Mart. The store sells mainly ready-to-assemble contemporary furniture, including leather sofas, day beds, children's furniture and cribs.

Buffett was on hand for the ribbon cutting and predicted the store would become the second largest furniture store in sales in the Midwest, second only to the Nebraska Furniture Mart itself.

With synergy apparently still on his mind, Buffett went over to the store's soda fountain and asked for a Cherry Coke.

On December 1, 1991, just before Mrs. B's 98th birthday, Buffett paid a call and presented her with two dozen pink roses and a 5-pound box of See's candy. (*Omaha World-Herald*, February 2, 1992)

Mrs. B was quoted as saying, "He's quite a gentleman." Rapprochement? Could be. The story said Louie Blumkin had recently asked his mother whether she might be willing to sell her business to Berkshire.

The rapprochement was well on its way when Rose Blumkin told the *Omaha World-Herald*, July 14, 1992, that she planned to sell her furniture business to her son, Louie Blumkin.

"I do a very good business there, but it's hard to manage it," she said. "My son offered to buy me out, and I'm going to sell."

She said her son is buying the business for the Nebraska Furniture Mart owned by Berkshire.

Under the agreement of December 31, 1992, did Mrs. B contemplate early retirement? No way. She kept selling carpet.

Mrs. B was having her headaches at her store because there had been some theft and she was getting cantankerous with employees and customers.

"I am delighted that Mrs. B has again linked up with us," Buffett wrote in Berkshire's 1992 Annual Report. "Her business story has no parallel and I have always been a fan of hers, whether a partner or a competitor... But, believe me, partner is better.

"This time around Mrs. B graciously offered to sign a non-compete agreement—and I, having been incautious on this point when she was 89, snapped at the deal. Mrs. B belongs in the Guinness Book of World Records on many counts. Signing a non-compete at 99 merely adds one more."

Explaining his oversight a decade earlier in not thinking of the non-compete agreement then, 62-year-old Buffett conceded to *Forbes,* April 26, 1993, "I was young and inexperienced."

"Maybe I was wrong. Maybe I was too hard on them," Mrs. B said in an interview (*Omaha World-Herald,* April 24, 1993) when Buffett and Mrs. B held dedication ceremonies for Mrs. B's after the Nebraska Furniture Mart bought it.

As the start of an era of better feelings, Buffett pulled out a stuffed bee, playfully putting it in Mrs. B's hair and mugging for photographers. Shortly afterwards, she said, "He's an honest person. He's never stuck-up. He's straight."

Riding around in her cart in the carpet section, Mrs. B, who never even attended kindergarten, said, "You can't get good help these days," adding that she had recently threatened some wayward employees by bluffing that she was going to throw acid in their eyes.

Then her tough side gave way and she said, "I live alone now and so that's why I work. I hate to go home. I work to avoid the grave." *At the age of 100, Mrs. B was still working at the store 60 hours a week.*

"Rose Blumkin's going to be 100 years old in December. Incidentally, she still works 7 days a week. The nights the store's open until 9 o'clock, you'll find her there at 9 o'clock. She rides around in a little golf cart, and if the salesperson isn't waiting on someone and she gets a little disgusted, she goes up and rams him with her cart and makes her point," Buffett told an audience at Columbia University's Business School on October 27, 1993.

"We'll do $200 million (in sales) in that store this year. A very remarkable woman, remarkable family. She has done it by having a terrific mind, an incredible desire." Only toward 103 in 1997 after fighting pneumonia did she come to work less often, dismissing her slowdown with: "I'm not sick. I'm lazy." She died August 9, 1998 at the age of 104. She would have been 105 on December 3, 1998. Remarkably three of her siblings were at her funeral. Afterwards she went to the great warehouse in the Business Hall of Fame in the sky. At her death Buffett said, "She came over unable to speak the language. They'll be studying her in business history books for decades."

Sales at Nebraska Furniture Mart are now about $300 million a year.

Buffett said: "It was brains, intelligence, her wouldn't-be-stopped drive. It wouldn't have happened with anybody except Mrs. B and it had to happen in America. It was the right qualities, the right soil." (*Omaha World-Herald*, August 10, 1998)

The Furniture Mart also owns a flooring business in Lincoln, Nebraska, and a commercial sales office in Des Moines, Iowa.

Nebraska Governor Ben Nelson, Senator Bob Kerrey, Representative Peter Hoagland and Omaha Mayor P.J. Morgan all showed up at Mrs. B's Clearance and Factory Outlet for her 100th birthday celebration.

Kerrey said, "We all have noticed that sometimes we, as a consequence of profession, are held in somewhat low regard. So what we try to do is appear in photographs with people who are held in very high regard."

Buffett couldn't make the party because he was in New York for a Cap Cities board meeting. But that weekend Buffett gave her a $1 million check for the Rose Blumkin Performing Arts Center in Omaha.

The check was written on the Buffett Foundation account at FirsTier Bank. It was folded up, rumpled and had a Coke stain on it.

At Berkshire's Annual Meeting in 1994, Buffett offered a display of Berkshire's products, including a See's candy assortment commemorating Mrs. B's 100th birthday, featuring her picture rather than Mrs. See's on the package.

Buffett, at the annual meeting in 1995, wondered aloud why students of business don't study Mrs. B. "She started a business with $500 with not a day of school... Look what she accomplished...Who is studying her?" Buffett said business schools are preoccupied with teaching things like "Economic Value Added," and just see Mrs. B. as a curiosity. Buffett said it was probably asking too much for folks to come out to the Nebraska Furniture Mart and "study a woman in a golf cart."

In the 1996 Annual Report, Buffett wrote of Mrs. B: "She's 103 now and sometimes operates with an oxygen mask that is attached to her cart. But if you try to keep pace with her, it will be you who needs oxygen." In 1997 Mrs. B was fitted with a pacemaker. Her grandson said, "She'll probably be back [at work] before the doctor will allow." (*Omaha World-Herald*, May 21, 1997)

In the fall of 1994, the furniture mart opened the Mega Mart, billed as the "Greatest Store on the Planet". The 102,000-square-foot store carries more than 50,000 items, mainly electronics, computer equipment and appliances. The items include built-in refrigerators, microwaves, cameras, video games, whirlpool baths, Cuisinarts and coffee makers. CDs, normally $14, sell for about $10.

At the opening ceremony Buffett said, "The Nebraska Furniture Mart is never finished."

In 2000 the Furniture Mart completed a $23 million expansion, but the project had another cost. Thomasville, one of the Mart's longtime brands and the Mart parted ways. Mart officials said Thomasville wanted to dictate how its display areas would be set up.

Still and all, the Nebraska Furniture Mart was the launching pad of Berkshire's furniture empire.

(Photo by Nancy Line Jacobs)

Nebraska Furniture Mart's Mega Mart carries it all from CDs to coffee makers.

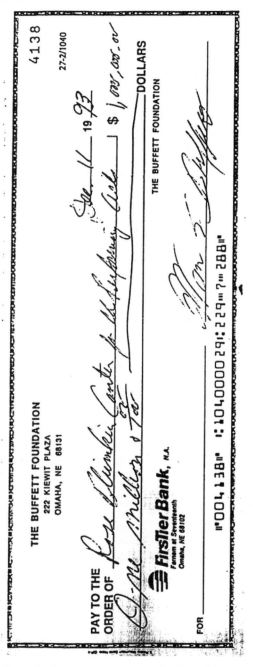

Here's a $1 million check Buffett wrote to the Rose Blumkin Center for the Performing Arts.

52

SCOTT & FETZER

"SCOTT FETZER TO ACQUIRE BERKSHIRE HATHAWAY"

Berkshire bought The Scott & Fetzer Company of Cleveland, Ohio, in early 1986 for $315 million. Scott Fetzer doubled Berkshire's sales to about $2 billion. Scott Fetzer had been on the auction block since 1984, but nothing had clicked. Finally a plan involving heavy Employee Stock Ownership Plan participation was approved by shareholders. But when difficulty arose in closing, the plan was dropped.

Buffett's ever watchful eye tracked the progress, or lack thereof, in the newspapers. He phoned Chief Executive Ralph Schey and asked for a meeting. Schey is an unusual businessman who has found the time to be actively involved with The Cleveland Clinic, Ohio University, Case Western Reserve and a venture capital firm that has backed a number of Ohio firms.

Buffett and Munger dined with Schey in Chicago on October 22, 1985. The following week, a contract was signed.

Buffett wrote in Berkshire's 1999 Annual Report: "Unfortunately, Scott & Fetzer's letter of engagement with a banking firm provided it with a $2.5 million upon sale, even if it had nothing to do with finding a buyer. I guess the lead banker felt he should do something for his payment, so he graciously offered us a copy of the book on Scott & Fetzer that his firm prepared. With his customary tact, Charlie responded: 'I'll pay $2.5 million *not* to read it.' "

Word of Berkshire's purchase of Scott Fetzer was carried by the Dow Jones news service, which startled Berkshire shareholders: "Scott Fetzer to acquire Berkshire Hathaway." The report was quickly corrected to show that Berkshire was buying Scott Fetzer.

At Berkshire's Annual Meeting in 1987, Munger and Buffett said they were presented an inch-thick notebook prepared by Scott Fetzer's investment bankers before the purchase. But they handed it back saying they didn't want to get confused. As usual, they just wanted to keep things simple. They saved some time and energy.

With Scott Fetzer, Berkshire acquired such businesses as *World Book* encyclopedias and the Kirby, Douglas and Cleveland Wood divisions of the Scott Fetzer Company. Campbell Hausfeld, which makes powered equipment "Built to Last" employs more than 1,200

(Photo courtesy of *World Book*)

Ralph Schey heads Berkshire's Scott Fetzer unit which includes World Book, Kirby vacuums, Campbell Hausfeld and other businesses.

people in manufacturing and distribution facilities in the U.S. The product line-up includes air compressors, air tools, generators, painting systems, pressure washing and welders.

Other Scott Fetzer businesses include Adalet, Carefree, Douglas/Quickut, France, Halex, Kingston Meriam Instrument, Northland, Scot Laboratories, Scottcare and Western Enterprises.

These businesses are lumped with Berkshire's other small businesses, collectively referred to as "other businesses."

Talk about dull businesses!

There's nothing very sexy about any of them, but together they're another little stream winding its way into Old Man River. The main business, and clearly Buffett's favorite of the businesses from the Scott Fetzer acquisition, is *World Book*.

But he likes Kirby, too.

More and more Berkshire's subsidiaries are experimenting with E-commerce. "The No. 1 topic Warren and I talk about now is whether retail selling is going to move over to the Internet," says Schey. (*Business Week*, July 5, 1999)

Scott Fetzer has been a big cash cow for Berkshire "Since 1986, when Berkshire paid $315 million for Scott Fetzer, its earnings have risen by only 5.5% a year on average. Yet Buffett repeatedly has praised it as a model of capital efficiency. In 1998, Scott Fetzer net-ted $96.5 million after taxes on its $112 million in equity, a return on equity of 86%. This is all the more breathtaking considering that Buffett has been milking it for 13 years, extracting more than $1 billion all told. (*Business Week*, July 5, 1999)

53
KIRBY
"IT LEAVES THE OTHERS IN THE DUST."

With the acquisition of Scott Fetzer, Berkshire became the owner of Kirby vacuum cleaners.

The company was founded by Jim Kirby, an inventor. Known for the vacuum cleaner that bears his name, his goal in life was to reduce drudgery wherever it existed. After watching his mother's cleaning result in dust settling back on everything, he came up with the concept for a vacuum cleaner. In 1906 he invented his first cleaner which used water for dirt separation. He later improved the system that used centrifugal action and cloth to filter out the dirt.

After World War I, Kirby designed vacuum cleaners exclusively for George Scott and Charles Fetzer. More than 200 patents that are used today are attributed to Kirby.

"See, it actually picks up the carpet...it collects sand," says Hank Smith, vice president of Kirby South in Birmingham, Alabama, demonstrating the vacuum cleaner's prowess.

"If we get in the home, we usually make the sale," Smith explains.

In one consumer survey after another, Kirby ranks at the top. "It leaves the others in the dust," Buffett likes to say.

Kirby, headed by Gene Windfeldt, tends to cost more, about $1,300 for its Generation 3 model with a power-assisted drive. But users say the strong engine, the space-age materials, the strength and durability are all worth it. Generation 4 and 5 have come out since.

Mrs. Beryl Erickson, of Cleveland, Ohio, wrote a letter in a Kirby online ad: "My daughter let me borrow her Kirby G3. I must tell you how great it is. I have arthritis, but I can use this cleaner with so little effort and the way it cleans is unbelievable. I am 84 years old, but if I were younger, you would have another salesperson."

Kirbys are sold all over the world. Indeed almost a fourth of its sales are overseas. Kirbys are so powerful that they are often used for commercial use (not recommended by the company) as well as in homes. Kirby sells to about 835 factory distributors. They in turn sell the Kirbys to a network of area distributors and dealers. Some of these independent dealers sell the vacuum cleaners door-to-door using in-the-home demonstrations. A recent innovation is "Micron Magic" filtration which cleans the air, helping individuals with asthma or allergies.

Although Berkshire's home cleaning segment is led by Kirby, it also includes Douglas Products, Cleveland Wood, and a host of other profit centers. The segment has been solidly profitable for Berkshire.

Douglas makes specialty hand-held electric and cordless vacuums and distributes through department and hardware stores and catalog showrooms.

Cleveland Wood manufactures vacuum cleaner brushes. It distributes through discount, hardware and department stores and catalog showrooms.

Kirby, which has been in business more than 80 years, has cleaned up a lot of dust in that time. Kirby earned about $40 million in 1996.

Kirby vacuum cleaner representative Mathew Maniaci shows a Kirby vacuum cleaner at the display booth at Berkshire's annual meeting in 2000.

(Photo by Nancy Line Jacobs)

However, in a page one story (October 4, 1999), *The Wall Street Journal,* said Kirby dealers, selling door-to-door often were too aggressive in their sales tactics. It said salesmen, who are self-employed, often called on the elderly, stayed in the home until a sale was closed and sometimes set up financing of the $1,500 vacuum cleaners at high rates of interest.

"Of 22 state consumer-protection agencies queried, 15 have received a total of more than 600 complaints in recent years about Kirby distributors and their sales techniques," the story said.

Buffett did not comment for the story but Ralph Schey, CEO of Kirby parent Scott Fetzer said: "Why does a Porsche cost more than a Chevy?" He said salesmen call door-to-door because that's the best way to demonstrate the quality of a Kirby.

Debbie Bosanek, Buffett's assistant, told the *Omaha World-Herald* (October 14, 1999) that Buffett receives about 100 complaining letters a year about products and services of Berkshire's companies. On average, only one in 100 comes from a disappointed Kirby customer.

428

54
WORLD BOOK
"I BOUGHT WORLD BOOK, TOO."

After Bob Kerrey was governor of Nebraska and before he was elected to the U.S. Senate from the Cornhusker State, he visited Birmingham, Alabama. Following an interview, I asked if he knew Buffett. He related this story:

Kerrey, the Navy SEAL Vietnam-veteran Medal of Honor winner who for a time dated actress Debra Winger, said he once told Buffett he had bought a set of *The World Book Encyclopedias* for his two children.

"I bought *World Book,* too," replied Buffett, meaning, of course, he had bought the whole company. Kerrey has said, if ever elected President, he'd turn to Buffett for economic advice. The two men occasionally have dinner at the French Cafe in Omaha, and Kerrey calls Buffett for advice about economic matters, including tax, healthcare reform, finance and trade policy.

World Book issued its first edition in 1917 with eight volumes and 6,300 pages. By 1997 *World Book* had multimedia and online information.

Buffett, an avid reader of encyclopedias as a youngster, did not read *World Book* then, but in 1962 he bought a set for his children and has used them since.

Bill Gates read *World Book* from beginning to end when he was only seven or eight years old. In later years Buffett would confess: "Bill was reading *World Book* at that time. He has since put it out of business [with Microsoft's *Encarta*]." (*Fortune,* July 20, 1998) Walter Cronkite's mother sold *World Books* and Cronkite himself spent hours as a child reading *World Book.*

World Book is available on a compact disk version, *Infofinder.* It contains 17,000 articles, 1,700 tables, 150,000 index entries, 60,000 cross references, 1,600 reading lists and 229,000 entries from *The World Book Dictionary.*

Other products include the 16-volume *Childcraft,* a children's resource, and Early World of Learning, a preschool educational program.

One fact, according to *World Book* brochures, is that the average

16-year-old has spent about 20,000 hours watching television—more hours than it takes to earn a bachelor's degree. Solution: read *World Book*.

Almost 10 million pounds of paper were used to print the 1993 *World Book*, according to the company so fond of compiling facts. The paper would stretch 106 million feet—nearly 20,000 miles—or across the continental United States more than 7 times.

The paper would fill 70 railroad cars, which means every day during the printing of the 1993 *World Book*, a carload of paper moved from Luke, Maryland, where it was loaded, to the Crawfordsville, Indiana, printing plant.

There are about 100 million characters of type in a *World Book* set.

Competing in a $500 million encyclopedia industry, *World Book* is found in four of every 10 homes in the U.S. and Canada that own an encyclopedia. And it's estimated that $1 of every $10 spent for books is spent on encyclopedias.

However, *World Book*'s profits sank in 1993 to $13.5 million, down from $19.5 million in 1992. They were $17.3 in 1994 and plummeted to $7 million in 1995 in the face of tough competition from CD-ROM and on-line offerings. *World Book* belatedly brought out a CD-ROM version, distributed by IBM and created in collaboration with IBM.

Once Microsoft offered to form a partnership with *World Book* to market a multimedia encyclopedia, according to *The Microsoft Way* by Randall Stross.

> In 1989, as Microsoft received the tapes that contained the Funk & Wagnalls text, it discovered that its new partner had failed to clean up the tapes and remove internal codes as it had promised in its contract. Some Microsoft managers lobbied to reopen the question of who should supply the text for Microsoft's multimedia encyclopedia, and a delegation was dispatched to talk again to World Book. Peter Mollman, the president of World Book Publishing, listened to the pitch with some interest. Microsoft offered to invest $7 to $12 million over the next two years to develop a multimedia encyclopedia based on World Book's text, but World Book hardly was desperate for funds. Mollman mentioned in passing just how little World Book had to spend annually to update and maintain the source of its mainstream revenue. (Microsoft representatives were astounded to learn how small the figure required to sustain the franchise was, but they could have seen the same phenomenon within

Microsoft, such as in the Word or Excel groups, where an astonishingly small team of a few dozen developers was needed to update mature programs that brought in hundreds of millions of dollars a year.) Mollman pointed out that World Book's commissioned salesforce of over 25,000 representatives remained a sticky problem, and he wondered how a truly multimedia encyclopedia could be compressed into one CD-ROM. Microsoft replied obligingly that it would keep an open mind about the question—perhaps multiple discs would be offered.

In a formal offer to create a partnership that Microsoft tendered to World Book after this meeting, Microsoft presented a number of ingenious arguments... (p. 82)

In the fall of 1993, after Encarta's initial release, Gates asked Peter Mollman [who after retiring from World Book went to work for Microsoft] to look into the possibility of purchasing World Book, a possibility to which Mollman and another manager coincidentally had also recently given some thought—all continuing to feel that the Funk & Wagnalls provenance of Encarta's text was a handicap. Mollman's inside sources had reported that World Book's sales had been sliding downward in recent years—from 330,000 sets in 1988 to perhaps fewer than 150,000 sets in 1992. At Mollman's urging, Gates spoke to his friend Warren Buffett about a possible sale, but they did not arrive at a satisfactory arrangement. (p. 91)

Buffett, at Berkshire's Annual Meeting in 1997, kidded Gates, saying: "Microsoft's *Encarta* is the old Funk & Wagnalls. Bill Gates hates it when I tell people that, but it's true. Gates had a lot of success with *Encarta* [on CD-ROM] so we copied him." But Buffett said, "in some versions of *Encarta,* the moon collides with the Earth. In the *World Book* CD-ROM, the moon never collides with the Earth."

A *World Book* [yearbook] is published annually to update the set and is marketed by mail to owners of earlier editions. Otherwise products are marketed primarily through demonstrations at homes, schools, and libraries by a commissioned sales force of more than 20,000 throughout the U.S. and Canada, Australia and the British Isles and distribution points in many other countries.

A set of *World Book* includes a 32-page article with color maps and color photographs on many aspects of Russian life; from religion, family life, government to natural resources, the ballet and architecture. More than seventy other major references in various volumes include biographies and photographs of Russian leaders and articles on major Russian cities and physical features.

World Book products have been translated into many languages including Arabic, Chinese, Finnish, French, Indonesian, Japanese, Korean, Malay, Portuguese, Spanish, and Swedish. *World Book* has printed a Chinese-language edition for distribution by the Chinese government.

Education is *World Book*'s best selling point. And about half of *World Book*'s sales force consists of current or former teachers.

The encyclopedia industry has a number of major players, including *Encyclopaedia Britannica* (which Ben Franklin helped write and which is now free on-line, the catch being you have to wade through the ads), *Grolier* and *Collier's*. *World Book* is a market leader. But Microsoft's *Encarta* CD-ROM format now far outsells *World Book*. A large portion of encyclopedia sales is made on an installment basis. Buyers can finance their purchases through *World Book* Finance, Inc., a Scott Fetzer subsidiary.

In 1988, *World Book* made a major revision of its format. The 70th anniversary edition was three years and $7 million in the making, featuring its most extensive revision in 26 years. Every revised edition of *World Book* involves more than 500 scholars, specialists, editors, artists, researchers, cartographers, contributors, production specialists and illustrators, who check about 5,000 information sources and review 5,000 to 10,000 photographs.

The publication is known for extensive fact checking. At *World Book*'s request, an official of Quebec's Department of Transportation measured the width of the Sous-le-Cap Street (8 ft. 10 in.) in Quebec, Canada, reputedly North America's narrowest street. The 22-volume *World Book* includes 14,000 pages and 7,000 articles by some 3,900 of the world's leading experts in their fields, such as Sir Edmund Hillary, "Mount Everest" contributor, and Georgetown University Coach John Thompson, "basketball" contributor. The encyclopedia also includes 28,000 photographs and illustrations and 2,200 maps.

It's estimated that more than 100 million people have grown up with *World Book* since 1917 and that there are 12 million *World Book* sets in use worldwide. *The World Book Encyclopedia* was introduced by J.H. Hanson of the Hanson-Bellows Co. in Chicago in 1917 as *The World Book-Organized Knowledge in Story and Pictures*. He created *World Book* by spending $150,000 to revise his then popular encyclopedia, *The New Practical Reference Library*. In 1918,

Hanson's money ran out and he sold *World Book* to one of his former accountants, W.F. Quarrie, also of Chicago, and the company flourished.

Celebrities such as the late FBI Director J. Edgar Hoover, etiquette expert Emily Post and Bishop Fulton J. Sheen became *World Book* contributors.

In 1945, Marshall Field III bought *World Book* to be the flagship of a new company that ultimately became Field Enterprises Educational Corp. Field believed that "education is the keystone of the democratic form of government" and that *World Book* was a key tool for education. In 1978, *World Book* was bought by Scott Fetzer.

There are many stories about the gentle persistence of dedicated *World Book* sales agents, not the least of whom is Joyce Fishman of Marshfield, Massachusetts, a top *World Book* saleswoman who was once bitten by a dog and still managed to make the sale (perhaps because the potential customer feared a reprisal).

World Book's part-time and full-time sales consultants make anywhere from $100 to more than $30,000 a year and generally have the luxury of flexible hours. They get a minimum $100 commission for a set of *World Book* which in 1999 cost $829 a set. Managers, who get a cut from all the sales force under them, make substantially more, and a top branch manager can make as much as $250,000 a year.

Munger, at the Berkshire annual meeting in 1994, said, "I give away more of that product than any other product that Berkshire Hathaway makes...It's a perfectly fabulous human achievement. To edit something that user-friendly with that much wisdom encapsulated is a fabulous thing."

Ever the advocate of eating one's own cooking, Buffett has gently pushed sets at his children and grandchildren. He keeps a set of *World Book* at both his home and office.

Here's the *World Book* entry about Buffett:

Printed from The World Book Multimedia Encyclopedia
BUFFETT: WARREN EDWARD

BUFFETT, WARREN EDWARD (1930-...), an American business executive, is chairman of the board of directors of Berkshire Hathaway, Inc., a major U.S. holding company. Berkshire Hathaway's holdings consist of insurance companies and manufacturing, retail and publishing businesses—including the publisher of The World Book Encyclopedia. Buffett is known for buying into undervalued firms. Buffett was born in Omaha, Nebr. He received a bachelor's degree from the University of Nebraska in 1950 and a master's degree in business administration from Columbia University in 1951. After graduation, Buffett worked first as an investment salesman with his father's brokerage firm in Omaha, then as a security analyst in New York City. In 1956 Buffett borrowed money from relatives and friends and formed an investment firm, the Buffett Partnership. By the time he dissolved the firm in 1969, the investors had received 30 times their original investment. Buffett then turned his attention to building up Berkshire Hathaway, a Massachusetts textile firm he had bought control of in 1965. The textile business eventually failed and Buffett closed it in 1985. By that time, he had developed Berkshire Hathaway into a profitable holding company.

In 1996 Berkshire's World Book Finance unit sold $100 million worth of bonds in Europe, Berkshire's debut in the Eurobond market.

"It is a routine issue, replacing a maturing issue," said a Berkshire spokesman.

The proceeds went to refinance part of a $120 million bond issue by World Book Finance, a Scott Fetzer subsidiary, which matured September 1, 1996. Berkshire paid cash for the rest.

At Berkshire's Annual Meeting in 1997, shareholder Nancy Jacobs of Omaha asked Buffett: "Does purchasing *World Book* over a competitor give someone an improved chance of becoming a brilliant billionaire investor?"

Buffett: "It practically guarantees it!"

Jacobs: "I'm buying it."

55
J.P. TAN'S ANALYSIS OF SCOTT FETZER

Jui Pah Tan, of Singapore, who really lives at his e-mail address
of writejp@hotmail.com, holds a Master's of Business
Administration degree with distinction from the State University of New York at Buffalo. He is founder of Bizlike.Com LLC
in the U.S. and Bizlike.Com Investments Private Limited in
Singapore (bizlikedotcom@yahoo.com). Tan sent his analysis of
Scott Fetzer in 1996 to Buffett, who wrote back: "Thanks for your
nice letter. Your analysis of Scott Fetzer is very much on the money.
I just wish we could find another situation like it. I can't do one-on-one meetings, but you are welcome to come to the Annual Meeting
next year on May 5 (with preliminary ceremonies starting May 3)."

Here's Tan's analysis of Berkshire's purchase of Scott Fetzer:

Buffett's Showcase: A Private Business with 86% Return on Equity Without Debt

Scott Fetzer was an obscure Ohio-based conglomerate. Its three
most important units are Kirby vacuum cleaners, *World Book
Encyclopedia* and Scott Fetzer Manufacturing Group which makes a
range of products related to the transmission of air and fluids. In
1984, its Chairman Ralph Schey tried to buy it at $50 a share in a
leveraged buyout. His offer was only $5
above market. Within a fortnight Ivan
Boesky, an arbitrageur, bid it up to $60.

Schey was repelled both by the
thought of having Boesky as his boss and
by Boesky's insistence on a $4 million
"break-up fee." Schey put up a new LBO
at $62 but it fell apart. It drove the company into the hands of speculators whose
first, last and only interest was to sell the
business.

By October 1985,[1] Buffett had accumulated 250,000 shares or about 5% of
the company. He had a discussion with

(Photo courtesy of J.P. Tan)

J.P. Tan

435

Schey and eventually bought the entire company with $60 cash per share at a total cost of $315.2 million. Thus, Scott Fetzer became a private subsidiary of Berkshire Hathaway.

Scott Fetzer Illustrates Buffett's Investment Principles

Buffett used Scott Fetzer in his 1994 annual report merely to explain the difference between book value and intrinsic. On closer examination, however, the data he unveiled illustrates several of his investment principles better than most other companies in his portfolio.

Return on Equity Increased Steadily From 46% to 86%

The first principle we shall discuss is the return on equity which increased from 46% in 1986 when he first took control to a high of 86% in 1994.

To assure us that no gimmicks have been deployed, Buffett tells us the following:

Scott Fetzer is a collection of 22 businesses. It has exactly the same businesses as it had when it was first purchased—with no additions or disposals.

Berkshire paid $315.2 million for Scott Fetzer which had $172.6 million of book value at that time. The $142.6 million premium Buffett paid indicated his belief that the company's intrinsic value was almost double the book value.

Because it had surplus cash when the deal was made, Scott Fetzer was able to pay Berkshire $125 million dividends in 1986 even though it only earned $40.3 million. Since the purchase, the company has gone from very modest debt to virtually no debt at all (apart from debt its finance subsidiary uses). Furthermore, Buffett had not sold plants and leased them back or sold receivables and the like. Throughout Berkshire's ownership of Scott, the company was operated as a liquid and conservatively financed enterprise.

The extraordinary returns were not due to monopolistic position, leverage or cyclical peak in earnings. Buffett, as usual, gives the credit to his manager, in this case CEO Ralph Schey.

One Hundred Percent Payout Ratio

Scott has a high dividend payout ratio that ranged from a high of 122% in 1989 to a low of 55% in 1990. The difference in ending book value between 1986 and 1994 was only 7% or $6 million. On the average, the dividend payout ratio was about 100% per year if we ignore the 310% payout in 1986 when the company was first acquired.

Why Return on Equity Is A Splendid Thermometer

The company's ability to double its income on almost the same amount of equity illustrates the kind of business Buffett hungers after. He does not judge the quality of a business by its increase in absolute earnings but by its ability to increase return on capital. For this reason, he considers return on equity in the light of the debt level. In the case of Scott, it is virtually debt-free.

The fact that he could pull out $84.7 million[2] cash from the original $172.5 million equity shows that the ROE before Buffett's purchase disguised the real ROE capability of the business. If the $84.7 million cash had not been pulled out, the ROE would have been merely 26%[3] rather than 46%.

There are only five ways Scott could have improved its return on equity to 86%. One is to increase asset turnover. Two is to improve operating margins. Three is to increase leverage. Four is to reduce the cost of leverage. Five is to pay less tax.

Since debt and tax are irrelevant here, the main causes for Scott's increase in return on equity are due to higher asset turnover and higher operating margins. The dramatic increases in asset turnover and operating margins needed to produce an 86% return on equity indicates the desirability and pricing power of Scott's products. These are tell tale signs of a strong franchise likely to sustain its pricing power for a long time to come.

Strong Businesses Don't Need To Borrow

Buffett has a strong disdain for debt and prefers companies that have little or no debt. In fact, he is convinced that a fundamentally good business with consistent and sustainable high returns on equity has little or no need for debt. It is the fundamentally poor business with low returns on capital that has to face the bankers often. Scott is his kind of company with so much free cash that it is able to release all its earnings to its parent company.

High Returns On Equity Makes Growth Enriching

High returns on equity also indicate that the company can grow with little incremental capital. The growth thus entails lower risk and higher reward. Such growth is healthy and enriching. Conversely, a company that grows with low returns on equity requires high incremental capital. Such growth entails higher risk and lower rewards. It is thus unhealthy and "enrisking." It enlarges the business but it may not enrich the shareholders.

Born Winners and Born Losers

He notes that the nature of some businesses forbids them to produce high returns on equity no matter how superb the management may be. Thus he seeks after businesses whose very nature allows high returns on equity. He considers business fundamentals as far more important than management though management can maximize or minimize the fundamentals.

Compensation Scheme That Maximizes Business Fundamentals

In this regard, he provides an executive compensation scheme that rewards managers like Schey who maximize the fundamentals of the businesses they run.

When a Berkshire manager employs a significant amount of capital in his operation, Berkshire charges the manager a high rate for incremental capital the manager employs and credits the manager with an equally high rate for the capital he releases to Berkshire. The manager's bonus increases when income on incremental capital exceeds a certain hurdle rate. Conversely, if additional capital yields income below the hurdle rate, the shortfall penalizes both the manager and Berkshire.

As a result, managers of Berkshire strive to achieve increasingly higher rate of return rather than just absolute returns which may be due to increased retained earnings rather than better returns on equity. Thus, it pays managers—and pays them well—to send any cash they can't use effectively in their own businesses to the parent company.

Given the consistently high rate of returns Buffett has been getting, it is likely that he imposes an unusually high hurdle rate for his managers.

Buffett Bought Scott For a Price-Earnings Ratio of Only 5.7

At first look, one may think that Buffett bought Scott at a 7.8 PE. This is because the acquisition cost of $315 million divided by the first year earnings of $40.3 gives us 7.8.

On closer look, one may argue that Berkshire's acquisition cost of Scott Fetzer was not $315.2 million but only $230.5 million. This is because in 1986, Scott paid Berkshire a dividend that exceeds its earnings by $84.7 million. This $84.7 million was deployed by Berkshire for other purposes. Hence, the effective cost required to generate the first year earnings was only $315.2 million minus the $84.7 million which gives us $230.5 million. Scott's price-earnings ratio in the first year was therefore only 5.72—an astonishingly low P/E for a growing company with such high return on equity.

Patience and Margin of Safety

This clearly provides Buffett a huge margin of safety. It gives us an indisputable number to see what he means when he says he waits patiently for a company that can be bought at a large discount to value. This is all the more amazing because he has often said that it is more difficult to buy an entire company at a discount than to buy a portion of it at a discount.

Buffett Took Only Six Years to Recoup Actual Cost of Acquisition

When we consider the fact that Scott paid virtually all its earnings out as dividends to Berkshire, Berkshire has already more than recouped its cost of investment from pure cash. Even if we use a discount rate of 10%, the January 1986 present value of nine years' earnings[4] from 1986 to 1994 would have amounted to $339 million. This is more than $100 million above the actual acquisition cost of $230.5 million. The value of this money as of 1996 is far greater, especially when Buffett has the track record of compounding money at more than 20% per annum.

In any case, it took Buffett only six years of earnings discounted by 10% to recoup the January 1986 present value acquisition cost of $230.5 million.

Got a More Than $1.6 Billion Money Machine for Free

Most important of all, after recouping all his investments, he still has a powerful cash-generating machine that made him $79.3 million operating income in 1994. This machine has a long, positive track record of improving return on equity and has an average compound earnings growth of 8.8% per annum. Given the high ROE fundamental of this business, if Scott should decide to expand its business, it could do so with high return on incremental capital. The dividend payout ratio is likely to stay around 100% for the rest of its business life assuming no incremental capital investment and no change in return on equity.

Meanwhile, the market will continue to assign a multiple value on its operating earnings. Assuming discount rate of 10%, perpetual earnings growth of 5% without incremental capital expenditure and 100% dividend payout, the business would deserve a P/E of 20. This means an intrinsic value of $1.6 billion for Scott Fetzer's operating earnings.

The Present Value of Scott's Future Operating Earnings Is Only a Fraction of Scott's Total Intrinsic Value to Berkshire

Meanwhile, since all its earnings are freely distributable, they will

439

be deployed by Berkshire for other high return opportunities. Presently, Scott's earnings come purely from operations. If Scott were to retain its earnings, its total future earnings would consist of both operating earnings and investment income. Since the earnings are fully paid out, the present value of the future cash flow from the redeployed earnings is not yet accounted for.

If we assume an operating earnings growth of 5% per annum that is fully paid out and redeployed at a 15% compound rate, the future value of 20 years' redeployed dividend flow would be $12.5 billion 20 years later. Using a discount rate of 10%, the present value of this redeployed dividend flow over the next 20 years is $1.86 billion.

That is only an estimate of its present value over 20 years. If we assume the business is a perpetuity, the present value is far greater. The 15% returns per annum will have to be compounded over infinity.

What Does a Company Do With the Money It Makes?

The present value of the redeployed dividend flow demonstrates why Buffett considers capital allocation as a top priority. If Scott merely retains its earnings and places them in fixed deposits, the value of the investible cash flow would be drastically reduced.

Freely Distributable Earnings

Buffett wants earnings that are truly and freely distributable like that of Scott. The norm of companies reporting earnings without accounting for capital expenditure is unacceptable to him. Why should investors pay taxes for dividends only to plow these after-tax earnings back into the same heavy capital expenditure companies that are forever hungry for fresh equity or debt capital?

He thus uses his own definition of "owner earnings" which is net income plus depreciation, depletion and amortization minus capital expenditure and additional working capital.

He advises investors to look for companies that would yield the highest possible owner earnings a decade or so from the date of purchase.[5] In this way, investors would focus on long-term prospects of predictable businesses rather than short-term market prospects which he thinks are impossible to predict.

Focus on Intrinsic Value Rather than Book Value

Compare the intrinsic value of Scott to the book value and the discrepancies become apparent. While its earnings have doubled, its value on Berkshire's book has been halved.

To illustrate the lack of correlation between book value and intrinsic value, Buffett explains what is done to the $142.6 million premium paid to purchase Scott. It was first recorded on Berkshire's balance sheet and written off through annual charges. These charges appear as costs in Berkshire's earnings statement.

By the end of 1994, the premium had been reduced to $54.2 million. When the $54.2 million is added to Scott Fetzer's 1994 book value of $94 million, the total is $148.2 million. This $148.2 million is the 1994 value of Scott Fetzer carried on Berkshire's books. It is less than half Berkshire's carrying value for the company when it was first acquired at $315.2 million. Yet what Scott Fetzer earned in 1994 was twice what it earned when it was acquired. The intrinsic value of Scott Fetzer has grown consistently even though its carrying value has been marked down.

Ironically, while the marking down of carrying value reduces Berkshire's earnings[6] and net worth, the true value of Scott Fetzer has been increasing.[7]

Buffett is not upset with such mismatches. So long as intrinsic value increases, the greater the mismatch, the happier he will be.

While the emotions of the market are outside the control of a manager, the earnings potential is within the manager's control.

---

[1] Notice that there was easily a one year time lag between 1984 when Schey tried the leveraged buyout, and October 1985, when Buffett had his discussion with Schey. If he had started the discussion in 1984, the stock may have been bid up further.

[2] $125 million minus 40.3 million or $172.6 million minus $87.9 million

[3] If we assume 5% returns on the $84.7 million cash, the cash returns would be $4.235 million. This will bring total earnings to $44.535 million on total equity of $172.6 million. Thus, the return on equity would be 26%.

[4] Since the after-tax earnings were virtually paid out as dividends, we may use them to represent owner earnings or "look-through" earnings.

[5] 1991 Berkshire Report. This writer draws a parallel between owner earnings and look-through earnings.

[6] This is because the charges appear as costs in Berkshire's earnings statement.

[7] Furthermore, the premium purchase charges that he makes annually receive 14% tax rebate. As at end 1994, the tax rebate amounts to a simple total of $12 million. There is another $7.6 million tax rebate down the line.

56
FECHHEIMER
BRAD KINSTLER ON THE SCENE

Berkshire bought its 84% ownership in Fechheimer Brothers Co., a uniform company in Cincinnati, Ohio, in June, 1986. This was after Bob Heldman, a longtime Berkshire shareholder, wrote Buffett that he ran a business he believed met Buffett's famous acquisition tests.

Buffett frequently has referred to his "ad" for what he is looking for in businesses: large purchases; demonstrated, consistent earning power; businesses earning good returns on equity while employing little or no debt; management in place ("we can't supply it"); simple businesses ("if there's lots of technology, we won't understand it") and an offering price.

Heldman, a longtime reader of the Berkshire Annual Report, and well aware of what Buffett was looking for, convinced Buffett his company was a good fit for Berkshire. He wrote Buffett about Fechheimer, a uniform manufacturing and distribution business owned and operated by the Heldman family—Bob and his brother, George, and a subsequent generation of Heldmans. George Heldman is retired and Bob Heldman has died.

"We wrote several times and I think convinced him the business fit the tests he lists in his ad. I had a meeting with him in Omaha," recalled Bob Heldman.

"We had the parameters of a deal set and met just one last time. It turned out it was in Middle Fork, Idaho, on the Snake River. There are no roads. You have to fly in. We had planned a board meeting at a lodge there and decided that was a good time to settle it.

"He (Buffett) flew into Boise and I met him and then we got on a little plane and went to Middle Fork. Munger flew in from California and we all met most of the afternoon with our lawyers and we were going to meet the next day but a storm warning came up and we left," Heldman said.

Heldman recalled that Munger asked him, "What are you least proud of?" Heldman said.

"I really couldn't think of anything. We have made a few bad deliveries," Heldman recalled.

Buffett never went to Cincinnati, either before or after Berkshire's purchase of the concern there, but once complimented Bob Heldman saying, "He knows the size uniform every prisoner needs."

The buyout of Fechheimer closed shortly afterwards with Buffett paying about $46 million for a stake based on a $55 million valuation for the whole company.

Buffett has said the only problem with Fechheimer is its small size, but it remains a steady contributor to Berkshire's earnings stream and has been expanding. It now has more than 50 stores nationwide.

The uniforms are mainly for police, fire, postal and service industry workers and Fechheimer makes uniforms for schools and bands. It also offers socks, belts and jackets.

Fechheimer, founded in 1842, makes uniforms at plants in Kentucky, Ohio, Tennessee and Texas, for marketing through its stores and by independent dealers who together serve more than 200 of the country's major metropolitan areas.

Fechheimer stores go by different names. For example, the stores in Birmingham and Mobile, Alabama, are called McCain Uniform Co.; in Arizona they are Pima Uniforms; in Tennessee, Kay Uniforms and in Texas, Uniforms of Texas stores.

The Heldmans are hands-on managers known for starting their day sitting around a table and personally opening the company's mail whether it be bills, a complaint, a compliment or a new business idea. A stockbroker showed up once to make a pitch while the Heldmans were opening the mail. He was told to go ahead and make his case as the Heldmans went right on reading the mail. The inscrutable Heldmans, hardly looking up, finally nodded approval to the idea and went right on poring over the mail, which they believe keeps them in close touch with every aspect of the company.

Not much gets by the circumspect, play-it-close-to-the-vest Heldmans.

During the cocktail party at Borsheim's the day before the annual meeting in 1990, Buffett and the Heldmans slipped off to a back office room of Borsheim's for a game of bridge.

Buffett teamed up with his friend, lawyer George Gillespie of the New York law firm of Cravath, Swaine & Moore, and they squared off against the Heldman brothers.

Afterwards, one shareholder had the audacity to ask Buffett if he had won. Grimacing a bit, he said no, adding, "Hard to believe, isn't it?"

The slightly built Heldmans had bettered their boss at the bridge table, but later would not confirm it. Two years later, Bob Heldman said with quiet pride, "Well, we don't like to talk about it, but we did win."

They just grinned ever so slightly.

You will not get a lot of fast and loose talk when the Heldmans are around. And you simply cannot tell what their bridge or business hand holds.

In 1994 Fechheimer won a 3-year contract to supply uniforms and accessories to the New York Fire Department.

The Alabama High School Athletic Association requires all baseball and softball umpires in the state to wear Fechheimer slacks so that all umpires will have identically colored slacks.

In 1997 Buffett named Patrick Byrne president of Fechheimer's. Byrne, son of Jack Byrne, retired CEO of Fund American Enterprises and once head of GEICO, went to Dartmouth College and Beijing Teachers College. Patrick also earned an M.A. from Cambridge and a Ph.D. in philosophy from Stanford University. He is also is a director of Fund American Enterprises.

Byrne, who boxed as a youngster, was diagnosed with cancer shortly after college and had 20 surgeries from 1985 to 1988, but recovered to pursue a professional boxing career—even though his 6-foot 5-inch frame had lost some ribs and about 75 pounds to cancer. After he cut off his boxing career, he became a businessman.

In 1997 he left his company, Centricut, a tool-and-die firm in West Lebanon, New Hampshire, for Cincinnati to run Fechheimer for Berkshire.

At the Berkshire Annual Meeting in 1998, Byrne, identifying himself only as a Berkshire shareholder, asked a question. In his response, Buffett pointed out Byrne now heads Fechheimer, adding: "He's doing a sensational job."

Buffett also said he had hired Byrne's brother, Mark, to run a new office in London and Bermuda. Buffett didn't say what sort of office. It turned out to be West End Capital that operates like a hedge fund. It's engaged mainly in fixed-income arbitrage. Buffett put $270 million into the fund originally and it's now much larger. Mark Byrne in 2000 was also named CEO of General Re Financial Products. (GRFP).

Buffett also said there is a third Byrne brother, John, and indicated he might have to go to work on him.

In 1999 Byrne, who had been with Berkshire on a temporary basis, left to go to China to honor a previous commitment to teach Chinese and American students there. Byrne, who speaks five foreign languages and has bicycled across the U.S. three times, is now

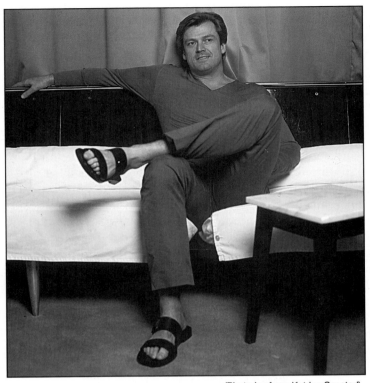

(Photo by Anne Katrina Senstad)

Patrick Byrne survived cancer to become a professional boxer, a Berkshire subsidiary head and a successful businessman.

CEO of Overstock.com, an e-commerce business in Salt Lake City. (*Fortune*, February 7, 2000)

So Patrick, what's it like to work for Buffett?

"It's like trying to get a drink from a firehose. It was absolutely one of the highlights of my life to be able to call him up and ask about different business issues and get on a couple of dozen of business issues how he sees inventory control or marketing or hiring and so on. It was definitely one of the great privileges of my life.

"There was a physicist Richard Feynman who died some years ago and another physicist said of him that there are two kinds of geniuses in the world. There's the kind that you and I would be if we were just a lot smarter. And there's the kind we'd never be no matter how much smarter we were. They are somewhere off to the side. That's Buffett."

Brad Kinstler, long a mainstay in Berkshire's insurance operations, now runs Fechheimer.

446

57

BORSHEIM'S

A JEWEL

Borsheim's, the jewelry store in Omaha, with an inventory of 100,000 pieces of jewelry, that Buffett bought 80% of in February 1989, is now the site for the shareholder shopping spree and cocktail party during the annual meeting weekend.

One grown woman, Mrs. Deedee Walter, a former Borsheim's employee, jokes: "I want to get my big girl ring here."

Each year at Borsheim's the store hosts a special exhibit for Berkshire's stockholders. The one in 1996 featured the world's largest polished diamond. The 545-carat Golden Jubilee Diamond is a gift to the King of Thailand from the people of Thailand. King Bhumibol Adulyadej, who has been on the throne more than 50 years, is the world's longest reigning monarch.

Buffett himself shows up for the Borsheim's party and so do the likes of Katharine Graham and Ann Landers.

Some years a string quartet played and champagne and salmon were served. In recent years, the goodies have been cut to wine and Cokes—more cost cutting at Berkshire. Whatever is served, shareholders spend the afternoon swapping Buffett stories. My story is that years ago I walked up to him, as scores of shareholders do, to shake hands. Thinking he could not possibly know me or where I was from, I told him my name. His instant reply was, "Up from Birmingham, are you?"

His memory is so widely regarded that if it ever fails, people are shocked. One shareholder at the same party, relating that he had a brief chat with Buffett about bridge, came away shaking his head, "Gosh, he didn't remember I sent him a bridge hand (last year)."

The party is great fun. Everyone peers at the merchandise, which ranges from $10 items and inexpensive coffee cups to jewelry priced at hundreds of thousands of dollars. Borsheim's carries pens, rings, watches, bracelets, china, crystal and a myriad of other items. At the store—a Berkshire gem—you can pay as little as $15,000 or as much as $115,000 for a Patek Philippe Swiss watch.

A 35-karat diamond ring has sold for $450,000. Some of the sapphires are almost the size of golf balls.

(Photo courtesy of Borsheim's)

In 1986 this golden yellow diamond weighing 755.50 carats was discovered in the DeBeers Premier Diamond Mine in Transvaal, South Africa. Two years in the cutting, the resulting 545-carat diamond—about the size of a baseball—is the largest polished diamond in the world.

Berkshire shareholders Wayne and Alice Murphy, of Vancouver, Washington, checked out Borsheim's the weekend before the annual meeting in 1999. Murphy, a retired Delta pilot, was out in the nearby mall, leaving his wife in Borsheim's. Huge mistake.

Alice Murphy passed by the store's center aisle when Borsheim's Marvin Cohn said, "Could I interest you in something?" "He left me with a 3½-carat and then a 4½-carat. It was making me nervous," laughed Alice. "Then he gave me a 6-carat in tweezers but he didn't fasten the tweezers."

When she was handed the rock, in her excitement she squeezed the diamond. It popped high in the air and fell to the floor under the milling crowd.

"The color drained from my face." Alice said. "I dropped to the floor." She said Cohn said to stay calm. Down on her hands and knees, she quickly found the diamond worth about $40,000. "I had no intention of buying it," said Alice, who did wind up buying a gold bracelet.

When she told her husband about her near disaster, he said, "Well, you would have found it anyway when someone twisted their ankle on it."

(Photo by LaVerne Ramsey)

Buffett and the author at Borsheim's April 29, 1990. I broke the news here that I planned to write a book about him. He did __not__ say: "Boy, that's great to hear." He cordially declined an interview. Later he said, "I wish you well, but not too well." Years later he kidded me, "Are you up to 1,000 pages yet?"

(Photo by Marsha Tate)

Author and Warren "The Whip" Buffett meet up May 1, 1999. Earlier in the day The Whip said: "Andy thinks he gets paid by the word."

For Berkshire shareholders, Borsheim's held a special event in April 1992, an exhibition which included a $6 million Patek Philippe watch. Made of gold and 126 jewels, it's the most expensive watch ever made. The watch had 1,800 parts and was equipped with a chime, moon phases, a calendar and a century leap year correction that turns once every four hundred years.

The company produces only 15,000 pieces a year. The collection also included pocket watches owned by Queen Victoria, Albert Einstein and Rudyard Kipling.

The day before the Berkshire Annual Meeting in 1992, the usual party at Borsheim's was held, but with a twist. Buffett and Patek Philippe President Philippe Stern, held a 1 p.m. Sunday press conference at the store to introduce the watch exhibit. Borsheim's President Donald Yale said "good morning" and introduced Stern, who in a thick Swiss accent proclaimed the watches his company makes as "the finest watches in the world." Buffett then addressed the party: "Good afternoon—my watch is keeping more accurate time."

After the press conference, Harvey Knowles, a stockbroker with Merrill Lynch in Cincinnati who is co-author of *The Dividend Factor*, a book touting the importance of high dividends, asked Buffett to sign his book.

Buffett, well known as no fan of dividends because corporate reinvestment can work better, dutifully signed Knowles's book, then shouted, "Throw him out!"

Also after the press conference, Dr. Michael Prus and his wife, Judith Goodnow Prus, of Grosse Pointe Farms, Michigan, and their daughter, Elizabeth, met Buffett. Elizabeth Prus, then a senior at Princeton University, had received a number of job offers from Wall Street firms, including Salomon and J.P. Morgan; she had accepted the Morgan offer. Buffett said to Elizabeth, "Maybe you could send us some of your extra business."

Borsheim's offers it all. If you are interested in—you know, something special for your "significant other"—a Fabergé egg, gold chains, Lalique crystal, a Cartier necklace, gemstones or pearls the size of marbles, Borsheim's has them. At the 1993 event at Borsheim's, some items from Joan Crawford's collection were on display.

Maybe you want a Waterman pen. After all, it's made by Gillette. Synergy at Berkshire is coming along.

At the 1991 meeting some jewelry was priced in Berkshire stock. Cute little signs: two shares of Berkshire for this diamond, three shares will get you that necklace. One diamond ensemble went for 15 shares—$120,000 at the time.

In 2000 Borsheim's shareholder shopping day was sponsored by Tag Heuer. Berkshire's annual meeting notice said: "Shop exquisite jewelry, watches, fine gifts, and explore World Championship

McLauren Formula One Racing courtesy of Tag Heuer, the Official Formula One Timekeeper."

Borsheim's was founded in 1870 by Louis Borsheim, and in 1947 it was bought by Louis Friedman and his wife, Rebecca, the younger sister of Rose Blumkin of Nebraska Furniture Mart fame. Their son, Ike Friedman—who once worked at the Nebraska Furniture Mart—took over the business after his father. Ike, his son, daughters, and sons-in-law owned and managed the business when Buffett bought it.

But later Berkshire redeemed Alan Friedman's (Ike Friedman's son's) share of the business so that Berkshire now owns 85.72% of Borsheim's. The (Donald) Yales and (Marvin) Cohns each own half of the remaining 14.28% of the business.

Between Thanksgiving and Christmas in 1991, 58,500 customers—an average of 2,250 a day—bought 38,500 items. (*Omaha World-Herald*, February 23, 1992)

In 1986, Borsheim's moved from its 6,800 square-foot location with its 35 employees in downtown Omaha to what is now a 45,000 square-foot site in the Regency Fashion Court Mall.

The store—which carries about $60 million to $75 million in merchandise—claims more than half the jewelry market in Omaha. About 55% of Borsheim's customers are from the Omaha area, and on a normal Saturday more than 2,500 people show up at the store, gazing at an inventory of more than 75,000 pieces of finished jewelry, 400 china patterns, 375 flatware patterns and thousands of loose gems.

The other 45% of its sales comes from out of state, partly from a catalog business.

Borsheim's or Borsheim's.com, with 300 employees, is the largest jewelry store in the country other than Tiffany's Fifth Avenue flagship store. Borsheim's customarily sends trusted customers a custom-made smorgasbord of the store's collection, say $40,000 watches, to look over. You can look them over, buy what you want and send back the rest. Buffett had said there had never been a case of dishonesty in connection with this honor system.

But that clean record was spoiled in 1998 when a man posing as a wealthy Asian businessman deceived Borsheim's into shipping him nearly $410,100 worth of merchandise. In late 1999 John Dewey Lim, 36, of Kansas City, Missouri was sentenced to 57 months in prison and fined, but none of the jewelry, which included diamond earrings and cufflinks, was recovered. (*Omaha World-Herald*, December 28, 1999)

Borsheim's is a single-unit giant jeweler. Employees do not work for commissions, as management feels that would force them to worry more about making the sale than serving the customer.

The store traditionally has advertised little, but does more now and even offers a special bridal package. Borsheim's first catalog in 1989 was sent to 23,000 people around the U.S., including 11,000 preferred customers, as well as Berkshire shareholders who get a discount at the store. Now the catalog is sent to about 250,000 people.

The store buys in great volume, often directly from the source, and sometimes cuts its own stones. Also, the store is a part-owner of an amethyst mine in Brazil, which explains the large pile of geodes on the floor by an entrance to Borsheim's.

Donald Yale, Friedman's son-in-law who came to Borsheim's management team after a successful accounting practice, played a role in the business going to Buffett.

When Buffett was looking at a ring while Christmas shopping at Borsheim's in 1988, Yale yelled out, "Don't sell Warren the ring, sell him the store!"

After the first of the year, Buffett called and asked if a sale were possible. A short time later Buffett bought the store from Ike Friedman, Borsheim's president, after a brief meeting at Friedman's house with Friedman and Yale.

"The substantive part of the talk was 10 minutes," Yale said. "He asked us five questions and Ike had a price. The three of us later met at Buffett's office and Ike and Warren shook hands on the sale."

"The contract was a short document in which the signatures were longer than the contract. The legal costs for both parties in total was $1,100," Yale said.

Buffett and Friedman agreed not to disclose the price, but it's believed to have been more than $60 million. (*Lear's*, James Traub, October, 1991)

Traub interviewed Friedman about doing business in Omaha and Friedman told him the following story:

"Guy calls from Geneva and says where the hell is Omaha, Nebraska. Guy says, 'Do you think you could use three million dollars worth of diamonds?' "

Replies Friedman, "If you can come up with thirty million dollars worth of diamonds, or three hundred million dollars worth, if it's the right price, we'll buy 'em all." Friedman said the fellow couldn't believe it.

Friedman told Traub, "We buy it right. We sell it right. That's the difference between us and the other stores. I would say that 70% to

80% of our jewelry is cheaper than what a jeweler would pay to buy it. We make money on volume. And compared to other jewelers' expenses, ours are nil."

Of his purchase of Borsheim's, Buffett has said, "I neglected to ask Mrs. B a question that any schoolboy would have asked. That is, 'Are there any more at home like you?' "

Here are the five questions Buffett asked about the business: What are sales? What are gross profits? What are expenses? What's in inventory? Are you willing to stay on?

"He already knew we had no debt," Yale said.

Without referring to books, Friedman answered the questions. Although we now have the questions, we do not have the answers except whether Friedman would stay—yes.

As usual Buffett wrote a check, paying cash. Friedman was suddenly a cash-rich man and a happy, fruitful business partnership with Berkshire was born.

Buffett said at the time: "Ike, there are only a handful of people I do business with this way. And none of them is a Fortune 500 company."

Friedman told Buffett, "I'd never have guessed when I was selling newspapers downtown that I would one day sell a business for this kind of money! I'm a lucky man."

Once the agreement was reached, Yale has recalled: "Buffett said, 'Now, forget that it happened, and just keep doing what you were doing.' There was no discussion of future growth and absolutely no discussion of changing our way of making decisions, planning expansion or bringing in additional profits. He made it very clear that he was not in this as a quick-return deal."

In delineating the fundamentals of Borsheim's business, Buffett has listed these attributes:

1. *Huge inventories and enormous selection across all price ranges.*
2. *Daily attention to detail by top management.*
3. *Rapid turnover.*
4. *Shrewd buying.*
5. *Incredibly low expenses.*

"The combination of the last three factors," he says, "lets the store offer everyday prices that no one in the country comes close to matching." (*The Goldsmith*, November, 1989)

"Ike has a big smile on his face today," Buffett announced at the annual meeting in 1990. That was because the previous day's sales figure was $1.5 million. Not bad for an afternoon Berkshire shareholder get-together.

Berkshire's 10-K form explains: "The size of this operation, like several of the Scott Fetzer operations, currently precludes its classification as a 'reportable business segment' of Berkshire. However, it contributes meaningful added diversity to Berkshire's activities."

(Photo by Nancy Line Jacobs)

The crowd outside Borsheim's the day before Berkshire's annual meeting in 1996. A number of shareholders try to get Buffett's autograph.

The day before the 1991 annual meeting, *Buffalo News* Publisher Stan Lipsey and his girlfriend spent hours checking out practically everything in Borsheim's. The moment Buffett passed by the couple (giving her a quick kiss on the cheek), they finally settled on an emerald ring.

Once at Borsheim's a shareholder asked Buffett to sign a two-share Berkshire stock certificate. Buffett did so, saying, "I'm not sure they'll cash it if I sign it." The young man said, "Well, I'm never going to sell it."

Buffett replied, "I haven't sold any of mine either."

Those were happy moments.

But on a terribly sad note, Ike Friedman, long a heavy smoker and seriously ill with lung cancer, died September 12, 1991.

Yale was named president and chief executive officer, and Marvin Cohn, also a son-in-law of Friedman's, was named executive vice president. Buffett was named chairman of the board of Borsheim's at a time when he was already chairman of Berkshire and interim chairman of Salomon.

454

(Photo by Nancy Line Jacobs)

Susan Jacques, who joined the store in 1983 as a $4 an hour salesperson and became CEO in 1994, mans (womans) the center counter of the jewelry store Buffett bought after asking five questions.

Due to family obligations, Yale left in early 1994. Yale told the *Omaha World-Herald*, "I have family responsibilities and business responsibilities, and it got to the point I couldn't do both. My family responsibilities are my priority...This was my decision solely. Warren was very understanding and supportive of my decision." Yale remained on the board.

Buffett named as president and CEO 34-year-old Susan Jacques, who had joined the firm as a gemologist and appraiser. A native of Zimbabwe, she came to the United States in 1980 and once won a prize as the outstanding gemology student worldwide. She joined Borsheim's in 1983 at age 23, making $4 an hour. She is married to Gene Dunn, of Omaha, owner of Mica Mecca, a cabinetry casework firm.

She said, "Becoming a subsidiary of Berkshire Hathaway opened our market to a whole new group of people who previously may not have been aware of us...We've drawn thousands to shop here and at the Nebraska Furniture Mart, with the added attraction of seeing Warren at the stockholders' meeting." (*Midlands Business Journal*, February 4-10, 1994)

At the Berkshire Annual Meeting in 1994, Buffett introduced Susan Jacques, saying she had a record day at the Berkshire party the day before. "Keep it up, Susan," Buffett implored.

Once George Morgan introduced his son, Adam, and Adam's fiancée to Buffett and they told him they planned to buy a wedding ring the next day at Borsheim's.

"Good. We'll open the store early and send a cab," Buffett said.

During the 1995 cocktail party at Borsheim's, sales popped up 15% over 1994 sales which were up 40% over 1993 sales. "You're a sporty crowd," Buffett said at the annual meeting the next day. Sales during the annual meeting party in 1996 were 60% higher than those in 1995. Sales were about flat in 1997 with no exceptional exhibit on display that year. Sales took a moon shot in 1998, doubling over the comparable day in 1997, with so many more Berkshire shareholders attending Woodstock.

A shareholder came up to Munger at the Borsheim's party in 1996 and asked for Munger's autograph on his sales slip from Borsheim's for a $54,000 watch the shareholder had purchased. "That is the kind of autograph we like to give," laughed Munger. A remodeling of Borsheim's was completed in 1997, adding 7,000 square feet of operations and showroom space, making a total of 50,000 square feet, including a second-floor corporate office.

Buffett wrote in Berkshire's 1998 Annual Report: "The store's volume on Sunday [of the 1998 annual meeting weekend] greatly exceeded volume for any day in Borsheim's history. Charlie attributes this to the fact that he autographed sales tickets that day and, while I have my doubts about this proposition, we are not about to mess with a winning formula. Please give him writer's cramp."

Bill Gates shops for an engagement ring at Borsheim's

Microsoft Chairman Bill Gates shopped for an engagement ring for his fiancée at Borsheim's on Easter Sunday, April 11, 1993. Buffett, stepping in with an assist, met Gates and his fiancée, Melinda French, at the airport and drove them to Borsheim's to get the ring.

The story was that Gates told his fiancée they were flying to Seattle. When the plane arrived in Omaha, she was very surprised to see Buffett meeting the plane.

During a talk at the University of Nebraska in Lincoln, October 10, 1994, Buffett confirmed the story saying that as he drove Gates and Melinda French from the airport to Borsheim's, he said, "It's none of my business—who am I to give you advice?—but when I bought an engagement ring for my wife in 1951, I spent 6% of my net worth on it! We didn't have quite as big a day that Sunday as I had hoped."

Buffett said he was disappointed in Gates' ticket, that it did not come up to 6% of his net worth.

Gates, a Harvard dropout who brought Windows to the world and whose E-mail address is "billg," met his wife at the Microsoft offices in 1987.

Buffett was one of 130 guests who attended Gates' wedding, New Year's Day 1994, held at a Jack Nicklaus-designed golf course in Hawaii. Gates was the second richest person at his wedding because Buffett was atop the U.S. rankings then. Other luminaries included Microsoft co-founder Paul Allen—whose 154-foot yacht was the site of a champagne brunch before the wedding—Microsoft's Steve Ballmer (known as Boom Boom Ballmer for his supercharged voice and personality) and singer Willie Nelson.

Afterwards, the couple honeymooned in Fiji.

Buffett has said of Gates' marriage: "She's (Melinda) not a junior partner, she's not a senior partner—she's an equal partner." (*Newsweek*, August 30, 1999)

Here's a post from Morriss Partee of Holyoke, Massachusetts, on September 23, 1998:

"WEB was disappointed that Gates did not spend 6% of his net worth on the ring, as he did when he bought an engagement ring for his wife in 1951.

"Frankly, I was shocked that WEB spent so much of his net worth on a ring. I'm glad to hear of it. It makes him seem more human. But I wouldn't have been surprised if he had not spent such a large part of his net worth on an engagement ring. After all, he and Susie rented their dwellings three years beyond the time when they could have bought a house so that WEB could build up his net worth some more before spending the cash on the down payment.

"While I don't know that anyone knows what 6% of WEB's net worth was in 1951, we can say how much Warren loves Susie in that if Warren hadn't bought the ring, he would now have an additional $200 million or so. That is one expensive ring!"

58
H.H. BROWN SHOE
"WHEN A SINGLE STEER TOPPLES, THEY KNOW."
LOWELL SHOE/ISABELA SHOE

It was a case of the ultimate in dull businesses, a case of Buffett as a shoe salesman.

Berkshire said it had agreed on June 10, 1991, to buy all of H.H. Brown Shoe Company, a closely held shoe business based in Greenwich, Connecticut, with annual sales of about $200 million.

In 1992, H.H. Brown acquired Lowell Shoe Inc., of Hudson, New Hampshire, with yearly sales of about $90 million and a manufacturing facility in Puerto Rico. Lowell makes Nurse Mates, a line of shoes for nurses, and has other shoe lines such as Soft Spots and Day Lights. The Nurse Mates shoes are comfortable, durable and amuse nurses because of the hearts on the shoe boxes and the shoes.

In 1997 H.H. Brown bought Dicon Technologies, an engineering and research firm enabling Brown to improve its footwear.

H.H. Brown was founded in 1883 by Henry H. Brown when he opened his first shoe factory in Natuck, Massachusetts.

Berkshire bought H.H. Brown from the estate of the owner and board chairman, Ray Heffernan, who had been with the company since 1927 after buying it then for $10,000. His daughter, Frances Heffernan, married Frank Rooney, who became the longtime boss of what is now Melville Corp. (formerly Melville Shoe).

Before Heffernan's death, he asked Rooney to run H.H. Brown. When the Heffernan family decided to sell the company, Rooney sold to Berkshire after Buffett's friend John Loomis told Rooney (during a golf game in Florida) that Brown might fit comfortably at Berkshire.

Brown Shoe operates as an independent Berkshire unit run by Rooney, chairman of the board and chief executive officer, and James E. Issler, president and chief operating officer. Employing more than 2,000 people, Brown markets its shoes under the H.H. Brown, Born, Carolina Shoe, Corcoran, Double H Boot, Matterhorn and other names. It also owns Isabela Shoe Corp., an offshore company. A faded red Double H Boot plant in Womelsdorf, Pennsylvania, gives new meaning to the words nondescript and no frills. At that location about 300 people turn out about 10,000 pairs of boots and work shoes each week.

H.H. Brown is the leading U.S. producer of steel-toe safety work shoes. Cyclists and cowboys often buy Brown shoes. Bikers prefer their rugged harness boots for their cross country trips. The company's Ranch Wellington work boots are among its best sellers. About 40,000 pairs a year are sold for $110 each. H.H. Brown is the leading North American manufacturer of work shoes and boots, according to Buffett, who says the shoe business in the U.S. is tough since 85% of all shoes sold in America are imported.

Buffett called H.H. Brown "exactly the type of business Berkshire strives to acquire: a leader in its industry and already staffed with tested and trusted management."

The company is not related to Brown Group, Inc., a large shoe company in St. Louis that a number of Berkshire shareholders raced to buy a few shares of, thinking it was Buffett's purchase.

H.H. Brown makes, imports and markets work, safety, outdoors, western and casual shoes through 15 company-operated retail stores around the country. The company sells a variety of men's and women's shoe lines including walking and hiking shoes, cowboy boots and a businessman's shoe called Comfa.

Many of H.H. Brown's work and military boots are sold to the United States and Canadian military PXs, as well as to such retailers as Wal-Mart, Kmart and Payless Shoe Co. The company competes in the middle-price markets where the consumer is often an industrial laborer required by OSHA to wear certain footwear. The company has plants in Morganton, North Carolina; in Womelsdorf and Martinsburg, Pennsylvania; and in Canada.

At the Berkshire Annual Meeting in 1991, Buffett said he was then looking at a business that had some international operations because it did business in Canada. Shareholders did some rifling through the usual publicly held stock information guides but couldn't figure out his tip about some firm which had foreign interests. Since the Brown stock was privately held, he was hardly giving anything away.

Buffett said at Berkshire's Annual Meeting in 1992 that Brown management is so good that, "When a single steer topples, they know."

A tidbit from *Fortune* (February 20, 1998): "Warren Buffett may have found a use for the 129.7 million ounces of silver he bought, right inside Berkshire Hathaway! Turns out Buffett was recently at a shoe show in Las Vegas of all places—remember, Berkshire owns several shoe businesses—when some executives from one of his own companies, H.H. Brown Shoe, showed him a new product which fights the bacteria that causes foot odor. The active ingredient in that product, is, you guessed it, silver..." [Berkshire announced a large silver purchase in 1998.]

59
DEXTER SHOE
OUCH!

Extending his reach in the shoe industry, Buffett bought Dexter Shoe Company in late 1993. Buffett, who rarely gives away stock, did so in this case to the tune of $420 million.

The announcement came on September 30, 1993, and the Dow Jones wire said Berkshire was trading at $6,600 a share. Then Dow Jones ran a correction: Berkshire was trading at $16,600.

Berkshire and Dexter agreed that privately held Dexter, with about $250 million in annual sales and headed by sports philanthropist Harold Alfond, part-owner of the Boston Red Sox since 1978, would merge into Berkshire for 25,203 Berkshire shares.

The purchase increased the number of Berkshire shares by 2.2% to about 1.2 million shares.

Born in Lynn, Massachusetts, Alfond, the son of Polish immigrants, began his career in the shoe industry in Maine in the 1930s for 25 cents an hour. He founded Dexter in 1957 with $10,000 and was joined by his nephew, Peter Lunder, in 1958. Their business now makes more than 7.5 million shoes a year, even in a declining domestic shoe industry.

Alfond, in his 80s, says, "Buffett won't let me retire. He's the smartest man in America." (*Forbes,* October 16, 1995)

Alfond has been generous in his gifts to a number of sports facilities in Maine, including the Alfond Arena at the University of Maine campus in Orono.

Early in 1993, at the suggestion of Frank Rooney, head of Berkshire's H.H. Brown Shoe Co., Buffett met with Alfond and Lunder at an airport in West Palm Beach, Florida. "We went to some little restaurant based on a World War II theme, had a hamburger, and talked about shoes," Buffett said. (*Forbes,* October 10, 1994)

Buffett made a cash offer on the spot, but Alfond, not wanting to give a third to the government in capital gains, wanted Berkshire stock. Buffett told Alfond he'd think about it.

Several months later Buffett, with Berkshire stock trading near an all-time high, met Alfond and Lunder in Lunder's apartment in Boston. There with no lawyers, accountants or investment bankers, the deal was struck.

Buffett didn't wear Dexter shoes until he bought the company. "Well, I'd never heard of him before, either," Alfond said. *(Forbes,* October, 1994) The Alfond and Lunder families suddenly owned 2% of Berkshire's stock, becoming the largest shareholders other than the Buffett family. Their 25,203 shares would have grown to more than $1 billion now. And neither Alford nor Lunder have ever sold a share of Berkshire.

"Dexter is exactly the type of business Berkshire Hathaway admires," Buffett said. "It has a long profitable history, enduring franchise and superb management."

The Dexter, Maine-based company has about 3,900 employees. About 2,400 work in four factories in Maine and the rest work in a Puerto Rico plant. Dexter makes a variety of men's and women's dress, casual and athletic shoes, golf shoes particularly, at plants in Maine and Puerto Rico. Dexter sells classic "New England casual" shoes, including moccasins and boat-type footwear. Nordstrom and J.C. Penney are big buyers of Dexter shoes. Dexter has 90 factory outlet stores from Maine to California in such locales as Manchester, Vermont.

Dexter's main customers are department stores, better grade independents and specialty retailers such as Sibley's and military PX's.

A pair of Dexter shoes retails for about $80, women's for about $60. The brand appeals to the broad middle range of the shoe industry. "That's where the volume is," Alfond said. *(Forbes,* October 10, 1994)

One observer of the company said, "It's well run. Its margins are good. It has good relations with employees and it makes mid-to lower-quality shoes. It makes $40 loafers that last a year."

Dexter is a major provider of bowling shoes.

With more Berkshire shares on the market as a result of the Dexter purchase, Berkshire shareholders owned a slightly smaller percentage of Berkshire. But then presumably Dexter is worth what Buffett paid or more, since Buffett has often said he will never give away Berkshire shares unless he's getting equal value in return.

The purchase for stock could be read that Buffett saw Berkshire shares as a bit on the high side. And the stock had indeed had a runup in 1993 without intrinsic value going up as significantly.

But a Berkshire official said, "We could have done it for either cash or stock, but Dexter shareholders wanted it in stock."

With the acquisitions of Brown, Lowell and Dexter shoe companies, Buffett's shoe size was extra large in the shoe world.

Again Buffett was looking for that everyday, necessary product—and one that has to be replaced from time to time.

Buffett used Dexter as an example of long-term holdings in a talk he gave to Columbia business students October 27, 1993.

"We're just buying something called Dexter Shoe, which is a big shoe company. It's a little like a romance for a while. You spend some time with them, and you know, you have your first date. And then, finally, the big moment comes (laughter). The next day, do you want to start thinking about if somebody offers me "2X" for this or "3X" for this, would I sell it?

"I think that's kind of a crazy way to live. It's a little like marrying for money. It's probably a bad idea under any circumstances but absolutely nuts if you're already rich."

In Berkshire's 1993 Annual Report, Buffett said 1994 sales from Berkshire's shoe operations would top $550 million, with pre-tax earnings of more than $85 million. The prediction was right on the money.

"Five years ago, we had no thought of getting into shoes. Now we have 7,200 employees in that industry, and I sing, *There's No Business Like Shoe Business*, as I drive to work. So much for strategic plans."

In 1994 Berkshire bought a small chain of 11 retail stores in Maryland, Pennsylvania and Virginia which carries H.H. Brown and other shoes.

But profits at the shoe companies slumped in 1995 and 1996 amidst fierce industry competition.

Still Berkshire makes more money out of non-athletic shoes than anyone else in the United States.

In a video show before the Berkshire Annual Meeting in 1997, one clip includes a shot of Bill Clinton campaigning in Maine and telling voters: "I'm wearing my Dexter shoes."

In the late 1990s the shoe business became increasingly subject to foreign competition. At Berkshire's special meeting September 16, 1998, Buffett said the shoe segment was "not a big winner" for Berkshire.

But, of course, Buffett continues to wear Dexter shoes.

Still, the shoe business declined further in 1999 and Buffett wrote in the Annual Report: "We manufacture shoes primarily in the U.S. and it has become extremely difficult for domestic producers to compete effectively. In 1999, approximately 93% of the 1.3 billion pairs of shoes purchased in this country came from abroad, where extremely low-cost labor is the rule.

"Counting both Dexter and H.H. Brown, we are currently the leading domestic manufacturer of shoes, and we are likely to continue to be. We have loyal, highly-skilled workers in our U.S. plants, and we want to retain every job here that we can. Nevertheless, in order to remain viable, we are sourcing more of our output internationally. In doing that we have incurred significant severance and relocation costs ..."

60
HELZBERG'S DIAMOND SHOPS

The next business to join Berkshire's sainted business fold was privately held Helzberg's Diamond Shops, of North Kansas City, Missouri. The national retail specialty chain, now has more than 220 fine jewelry stores located in 28 states, mainly in malls. Helzberg's is the fifth largest jewelry chain in the U.S.

The purchase of Helzberg's was with Berkshire stock.

Buffett said at the annual meeting in 1995 that the acquisition had come about this way: in the spring of 1994 Buffett was in New York walking near 58th Street and Fifth Avenue near the Plaza hotel when a woman stopped him to talk about how she enjoyed the annual meeting. Barnett Helzberg who had four shares of Berkshire in his IRA (first one bought in 1985), and who had also been to the annual meeting, overheard her talking to Buffett and came up and said he might have a business to sell him.

"I hear this quite a bit so I asked him to write me," Buffett said.

Helzberg said, "I walked over to Buffett, and we had a very detailed 20-second meeting." Later a deal was struck.

So how does one negotiate with Warren Buffett about the sale of a business? Said Helzberg: "Basically the way to negotiate with Warren Buffett—you don't negotiate. He tells you the deal and that's the deal." You accept or walk away.

Helzberg, Jr., former chairman and owner of Helzberg's, said Buffett's deal was fair and was particularly attractive because Buffett promised to retain the employees and keep the business intact. "I did not want a lot of people spitting on my grave," Helzberg said.

Helzberg's position in the market is similar to Zales or Gordon's, but its sales per store is twice theirs.

Helzberg, whose grandfather Morris opened the first store in 1915, said the original store was located in a 12-foot building at 529 Minnesota Avenue in Kansas City, Kansas.

"In the first year, Morris' landlord offered to spend $500 fixing up the store front if he could raise the rent from $25 to $29 a month. After much deliberation, the family decided to accept the offer. From the outset, the concerns of the small store belonged to the family. Serious matters, such as the $4 rise in rent, were debated and dis-

(Photo courtesy of Helzberg's)

Barnett Helzberg

cussed for hours. The voice of each family member counted," Helzberg said.

Morris' youngest son, Barnett, succeeded his father. His son, Barnett Jr., who succeeded his father in 1963, recalls "An artistic pal by the name of Walt Disney was constantly drawing pictures and did a sketch of my father in one of his textbooks." Who could have guessed that ownership of their companies would totally or partially wind up with Buffett?"

Helzberg said that Berkshire's ownership of Helzberg's would allow the jewelry firm continued growth and continuity of its culture. Also it would assure that the headquarters is still in Kansas City and would allow him time to pursue non-profit community interests.

Helzberg said: "I am extremely pleased with the fact that we have been able to take a three-generation business and allow it to continue its growth and prosperity under the respected umbrella of Berkshire Hathaway. I believe this ownership change is a win for the associates of Helzberg's Diamond Shops, a win for the investors of Berkshire Hathaway, a win for our family, and most importantly, a win for the customers of our fine company."

Buffett said, "I am proud that Berkshire Hathaway is adding Helzberg's Diamond Shops to our family of businesses. I have great confidence in the present management team. The talent pool represented by the Helzberg management and its associates is one of the reasons I place such a high value on this acquisition. It goes without saying that the long term financial stability and very bright outlook for the future of Helzberg Diamonds were also major factors in our decision."

Jeffrey W. Comment, formerly president of Wanamaker's, became chairman and chief executive officer of Helzberg's.

Comment told *The Kansas City Star* (March 11, 1995) "The thing I told our associates, and what's so beautiful about the deal, is that Mr. Buffett likes his subsidiaries to run as their own business... He told me, 'I don't call my presidents, but I like hearing from you guys once in a while.'"

Comment has written a book, *Jonathan—Through Santa's Eyes*, a compilation of stories of children and families facing life's toughest situations. The book was inspired by Jonathan, an 11-year-old boy dying of AIDS who Comment met when he went for a visit as Santa to a hospital. Proceeds from the book available at Helzberg's stores are donated to the Elizabeth Glaser Pediatric AIDS Foundation.

Buffett wrote in Berkshire's 1996 Annual Report: "Our only disappointment last year was in jewelry. Borsheim's did fine, but Helzberg's suffered a material decline in earnings. Its expense levels had been geared to a sizable increase in same-store sales, consistent with the gains achieved in recent years. When sales were instead flat, profit margins fell. Jeff Comment, CEO of Helzberg's, is addressing the expense problems in a decisive manner..."

Helzberg, "in retirement," teaches management excellence courses, works with a mentoring program, oversees a variety of charitable activities, helps to obtain licenses for children's television programs, skis, fishes, and is working on a book with the working title of *What I Learned Before I Sold to Warren Buffett*.

Helzberg recalled that at the time he asked Buffett about selling to him, Buffett had said to send him some information but then Helzberg hesitated, telling *The Kansas City Star* (March 11, 1995):

(Photo courtesy of Helzberg's)

A Helzberg's Diamond store at Lenox Square in Atlanta

"I'm the kind of guy who likes to get someone's Social Security number before I tell them the time. But finally, I said to myself, 'You idiot, send him the stuff.' "

Later Helzberg asked Buffett if he could use his name ("in vain") in the book Helzberg plans. Buffett told Helzberg he certainly could use his name— and even his Social Security number.

BEN BRIDGE JEWELER

Berkshire moved deeper into the jewelry business when it said on May 18, 2000 that it had agreed to buy Seattle-based Ben Bridge Jeweler headed by Ed and Jon Bridge.

The company, which employs 750 people, operates 63 jewelry stores in 18 U.S. markets and competes with Helzberg's in Seattle and throughout the West.

"...This arrangement will provide for the smooth transition from this generation to the next—a concern that has been at the center of this action," Jon Bridge said in a press release. "We're pleased to have the opportunity to become a part of what we believe to be the finest family of companies ever assembled under one corporate name," said Ed Bridge.

In the release, Buffett said: "I can't tell you how pleased we are to enter into association with Ben Bridge. Run by an outstanding management team, Ben Bridge will be a great addition to the Berkshire family."

Ben Bridge Jeweler was founded in 1912 by Samuel Silverman, a watchmaker in downtown Seattle who later sold the business to his son-in-law, Ben Bridge. Bridge ran the company for 25 years before turning it over to his sons, Herb and Bob, who later sold it to their sons, Ed and Jon. Today the company is run by the Bridge family, including President/Co-CEO Ed Bridge and Vice Chairman/Co-CEO Jonathan Bridge. His wife is Judge Bobbe J. Bridge who serves on the Washington State Supreme Court.

Guess what you see if you call up the company's website, BenBridge.com? Answer: A gift wrapped box with the caption: "Think inside the box."

61
R.C. WILLEY HOME FURNISHINGS

Berkshire, widening its reach in the home furnishings business, announced May 24, 1995, it would buy R.C. Willey Home Furnishings of Salt Lake City, Utah.

The fast-growing company, with eight stores, including a clearance center and a carpet center in Utah, has more than $300 million in annual sales—with 56% of the state's market share in furniture and 28% of the state's electronics market. (*Utah Business*, February, 1997) The firm is the 20th largest furniture firm in the country and has about 1,650 employees.

Buffett said: "Bill Child and his family have built a business that is the envy of merchants throughout the country." Child built the business from $250,000 in sales in 1954 to $342 million in 1999.

Child and his brother Sheldon and their children, who owned the company, sold to Berkshire, in part, for estate planning reasons. Sheldon retired to lead missionary work for the Mormon Church in the Philippines.

"Bill Child was talking to a friend [about possibly selling] and the friend [Nebraska Furniture Mart's Irv Blumkin] knew Buffett. Two days later Buffett called and the deal was wrapped up in two months," said Roger Pusey, business writer for the *Deseret News* in Salt Lake City.

Bill Child, Utah's Master Entrepreneur of the Year, and Blumkin had talked while at a fabric industry conference in California. Child said Buffett called and told him, "You've got a jewel of a company. We'd be very interested. I'll have you a price within three days." (*Omaha World-Herald, May 26, 1995*)

Within three days a two-page Federal Express letter came with what Child called "a very fair price."

"I called him and said I was flattered," Child said, inviting Buffett to visit the stores.

"I know you, I know your reputation. I know a lot about your company. I really don't need to," Child said Buffett told him. (*Omaha World-Herald,* May 26, 1995)

But Child did talk Buffett into an eight-hour visit and Buffett found all was well. Child asked for time to work out some tax issues

R.C. Willey owner William Child and his brother, company President Sheldon Child, sold Utah's largest furniture business to Berkshire.

and to think about whether to take the cash or Berkshire stock that Buffett offered.

Child, who said he always had wanted to buy Berkshire stock but delayed because the price kept going up, told Buffett: "We'll go with the stock." *(Omaha World-Herald, May 26, 1995)*

It turned out that Berkshire overpaid Child by several shares and Child called Berkshire to point out the error. "Warren gave him a call back, thanked him for pointing out the error, and said he wanted Bill to keep the $100,000." *(Phil Swigard Newsletter*, Spring, 1996)

R.C. Willey, Child's father-in-law, had long been known in the community as "someone who started out in the back of his truck," Pusey said. "Then he got a small building, a garage really, and sold appliances to folks."

He was known as someone who could fix anything. He would come over and wire your house and wind up selling you a stove.

In 1932 Rufus Carl Willey started selling appliances door-to-door. He and his wife, Helen, started out selling appliances to their friends and neighbors in Syracuse, Utah. The customers had a choice of an electric range or refrigerator. R.C. Willey did this for almost 20 years and made a good living. He let customers buy on an extended finance term program called Farm Plan where customers paid one-third each fall for three years. Customers were delighted because they could keep their food from spoiling and cook their meals without overheating their homes in summertime.

In 1950 R.C. Willey built his company's first building which was 600 square feet. The building was located next to his home. A nine-party telephone line ran from his home to the store. He had one employee. In 1954 Willey became ill and his son-in-law, William H. Child, who had just graduated from college was asked to run the business for a short period until Willey recovered. However, he passed away and Bill Child has been running the business since.

"It's a beautiful concern," said Hugh Coltharp, a stockbroker and Berkshire shareholder in Salt Lake City. "They have a big warehouse and they were smart to get a stop light where you turn into it."

There was no change in name or management and no jobs were affected by the transaction.

The company, which is planning new ventures in-state and out-of-state, is known for a well-trained sales force encouraged to call shoppers back and write thank-you notes. And its credit card operations ensure a healthy cash flow.

With the Nebraska Furniture Mart having annual sales of more than $250 million a year and with R.C. Willey's $300 million, Berkshire was solidly into the furniture business in America's heartland. R.C. Willey, like the Nebraska Furniture Mart, also sells appliances, electronics, computers and carpets.

A footnote: As part of R.C. Willey's sales promotions, the company offers free hot dogs and soft drinks to customers on many Saturdays.

Child said the soft drink henceforth is Coca-Cola. *(Deseret News, May 25, 1995)*

Child told *Utah Business* (February, 1997):

> We have a wonderful business partner in Warren Buffett. He knows how to manage people. He only has 13 people at headquarters, and 35,000 employees in companies he owns or controls. So, rather than tell us how to run our business, he gives us a big vote of confidence, 100 percent support and total trust. We don't have anyone looking over our shoulder. He's interested in the long haul, and he supports whatever market strategy that we feel is best. If we were to sell every appliance and electronic product we have at a very low margin for the next four years to protect our market share, he would probably not say a thing. He's the perfect partner.
>
> I've learned a lot from Warren. He is one of the brightest men I've met. He's a delightful individual, a fabulous per-

R.C. Willey sign for its new 850,000-square-foot warehouse

son. We just love him, and he likes our company and this state. He enjoys coming to Utah. He's been in Utah five times—and he owns companies in other states that he has never visited. He comes here to give us a shot in the arm. Our relationship is great. He is easy to talk with when I call him, or he calls me.

When Warren called to ask about purchasing our company, he asked me what I wanted for it. I just said that I want a fair price and that I want the buyer to get a great deal. I want it to be fair for Berkshire Hathaway and the shareholders.

In Berkshire's 1999 Annual Report, Buffett told a story about Bill Child's desire to open a new store in Boise, Idaho.

R.C. Willey, operated largely by Mormans, doesn't operate on Sunday. Buffett wrote: "I was highly skeptical about taking a no-Sunday policy into a territory where we would be up against entrenched rivals open seven days a week. Nevertheless, this was Bill's business to run. So despite my reservations, I told him to follow both his business judgment and his religious convictions.

"Bill then insisted on a truly extraordinary proposition: He would personally buy the land and build the store -- for about $9 million as it turned out -- and would sell it to us at his cost if it proved to be successful. On the other hand, if sales fell short of his expectations, we could exit the business without paying Bill a cent. This outcome, of course, would leave him with a huge investment in an empty building. I told him that I appreciated his offer but felt that if Berkshire was going to get the upside it should also take the downside. Bill said nothing doing: If there was to be failure because of his religious beliefs, he wanted to take the blow personally.

"The store opened last August and immediately became a huge success. Bill thereupon turned the property over to us -- including some extra land that had appreciated significantly -- and we wrote him a check for his cost. And get this: *Bill refused to take a dime of interest on the capital he had tied up over the two years.*

"A footnote: After our 'soft' opening in August, we had a grand opening of the Boise store about a month later. Naturally, I went there to cut the ribbon (your Chairman, I wish to emphasize, is good for something). In my talk I told the crowd how sales had far exceeded expectations, making us, by a considerable margin, the largest home furnishings store in Idaho. Then, as the speech progressed, my memory miraculously began to improve. By the end of my talk, it all had come back to me: Opening a store in Boise had been *my* idea."

62

LANDING FLIGHTSAFETY

Berkshire entered a pact to buy all FlightSafety International Inc. for $1.5 billion in stock and cash on October 15, 1996.

At first this purchase might have seemed outside Buffett's "circle of competence," but on closer look it seemed to qualify as a brand name, high-entry-barrier business. FlightSafety is the world's largest non-airline, non-government aviation trainer with virtually no competition in its niche.

The pilot training company, which mainly trains corporate pilots, provides a pathway into the growing worldwide travel and transportation market. FlightSafety, based at the Marine Air Terminal at LaGuardia Airport in Flushing, New York, provides high-technology simulator-based training to airlines and ship owners throughout the world. Its marine division trains ship captains. In addition to pilots and sea captains, the company trains aviation ground crew members. FlightSafety trains about 55,000 pilots and aviation personnel each year. It also makes full-motion flight simulators and other training equipment.

Unlike many Berkshire businesses, FlightSafety is capital intensive. While the business requires little inventory, the simulators are very expensive and become obsolete over years, not decades. Therefore, the business earns high return on capital only so long as market dominance permits high profit margins on services sold.

Buffett wrote in Berkshire's 1999 Annual Report: "FSI must lay out huge amounts of capital. A single flight simulator can cost as much as $15 million—and we have 222. Only one person at a time, furthermore, can be trained in a simulator, which means that the capital investment per dollar revenues of FSI is exceptionally high. Operating margins must therefore be high, if we are to earn a reasonable return on capital. Last year we made capital expenditures of $215 million at FSI and FlightSafety Boeing, its 50%-owned affiliate."

The acquisition let Buffett make a play on the future of the booming travel industry. Over the next 20 years, airlines are expected to order about 16,000 jetliners, and private aviation is expected to grow at a roughly similar rate.

FlightSafety benefits from a rising need for new aircraft and huge growth is expected from the international express-cargo business.

Under the merger, FlightSafety shareholders could take either $50 a share in cash or $48 a share in Berkshire stock. And most analysts thought Buffett got a good price for it, buying the company in a bumpy time of sluggish earnings growth.

FlightSafety's chairman, Albert Ueltschi, now 83, who founded the company in 1951, was the company's largest stockholder. He said, "I believe that this merger is in the best interests of FlightSafety, its customers, employees and shareholders. My family and I will vote our entire 37% holding in FlightSafety in favor of the merger. Further, I will elect to receive Berkshire common stock for the FlightSafety shares owned by me. I personally consider Berkshire shares to be one of the finest investments that I could make and anticipate holding the shares indefinitely. I look forward to continuing to run FlightSafety as part of Berkshire and working with Warren Buffett."

(Photo courtesy of FlightSafety)
FlightSafety Chairman Al Ueltschi

Buffett said: "FlightSafety is a business that I like, run by a man I like and admire. Al Ueltschi and FlightSafety will fit perfectly in the Berkshire family."

Ueltschi, raised on a Kentucky dairy farm, began his aviation career as a barnstorming wing-walker in the 1930s. "From the moment he first heard the distant blattering of an old OX-5 engine and saw the twin wings soaring overhead, he was hooked. It was that simple. He yearned to be a part of it, to be a pilot." (*Flying*, March, 1998) With a $3,500 loan he bought an open cockpit biplane and gave flying lessons. He joined Pan Am in 1941 and found that the industry lacked good pilot training. Once he piloted Charles Lindbergh and they became friends. Ueltschi founded the company in 1951 when airlines relied on propeller-driven aircraft. That year he rented a small office at La Guardia's Marine Air Terminal. Ueltschi mortgaged his house to start his budding flight training company. FlightSafety went public in 1968.

"The company is expected to benefit in the future from the airline industry's resurgence, the introduction of new aircraft models and the decline in military-trained pilots entering commercial aviation." (*Wall Street Journal*, October 16, 1996)

Customers include corporations, commercial airlines and government agencies including the military. It has about 2,500 employees.

FlightSafety, which has margins of about 30%, operates about 40 learning centers in the U.S., Canada, Europe, and China and has the largest civil aviation simulator fleet in the world with more than 170 simulators and training devices. Pilot training makes up about 94% of the sales and equipment sales make up the other 6%.

So how did Berkshire's purchase of FlightSafety happen?

Buffett said in Berkshire's 1996 Annual Report: "The heroes of the story are first, Richard Sercer, a Tucson aviation consultant, and second, his wife, Alma Murphy, an ophthalmology graduate of Harvard Medical School, who in 1990 wore down her husband's reluctance and got him to buy Berkshire stock. Since then, the two have attended all our Annual Meetings, but I didn't know them personally.

"Fortunately, Richard had also been a long-time shareholder of FlightSafety, and it occurred to them last year that the two companies would make a good fit."

It turns out that Sercer approached Salomon Chairman Robert Denham suggesting the merger. Denham wrote Buffett and Ueltschi at the same time.

Denham contacted FlightSafety's counsel—Skadden, Arps, Slate, Meaghen and Flom to see if Ueltschi would be willing to meet with Buffett about a possible buyout by Berkshire. Ueltschi and Buffett met on September 18, 1996. The next day Buffett sent Ueltschi a letter saying Berkshire was interested in buying FlightSafety.

It's a good thing Buffett moved swiftly on the FlightSafety acquisition. It turns out that a unit of Boeing was studying a purchase of FlightSafety when Berkshire bought it. (*Bloomberg News*, April 29, 1997)

In 1997 FlightSafety and Boeing Co. founded a joint venture—FlightSafety Boeing Training International to train commercial jet pilots and aircraft maintenance workers. The venture has a contract to provide 737 systems training to the Federal Aviation Administration's airworthiness inspectors.

FlightSafety and Boeing each contributed about $100 million in assets to launch the venture and each owns 50% of the training company.

In 1998 the Boeing/Berkshire joint venture announced it would build a $100 million dollar flight-training center in Miami to instruct pilots for Latin American routes. The Miami center, to open in 2000, is to be the largest flight-training facility not owned by an airline. It will house 18 flight simulators. It's expected that the center will train 7,000 pilots and 3,000 maintenance technicians annually. The training center will be run by FlightSafety Boeing Training International, the joint venture which runs the training centers.

A simulator at FlightSafety where the motto is: "The best safety device in any aircraft is a well-trained pilot."

The joint venture now has 15 locations and more than 600 employees. The company specializes in aircraft with 100 seats or more, including Boeing, McDonnell Douglas, Airbus and Fokker models. Also the company is the trainer for the Boeing Commercial Airplanes Group.

Buffett, who rarely takes part in testimonials or ads, took an active role in an ad with him touting FlightSafety. The ad featured a photo of him aboard Berkshire's jet (*The Indispensable*) drinking a Coke and eating a McDonald's hamburger. The caption read: "Warren Buffett's FlightSafety-trained pilots give him safe returns on his investments." (*Wall Street Journal*, September 10, 1997)

Going even further into testimonials, Buffett appeared in an ad in the *Wall Street Journal* (September 30, 1997) touting Gulfstream's Executive Jet program which allows owners to buy fractional shares in jets. Buffett said, "Berkshire Hathaway owns a jet. It more than pays for itself. That's why I recently changed its name from 'The Indefensible' to 'The Indispensable.' (Buffett has since sold the company plane and uses Executive Jet.)

"But Berkshire's plane is for business purposes. For my family, I bought a 25% interest in Executive Jet's Net Jets program. And do they love it! Both the service and the pilots of Executive Jet are absolutely first class. My wife, Susie, came up with the name for this plane, 'The Richly Deserved.' "

There can be little doubt that Buffett would like to see Executive Jet's pilots trained at FlightSafety. FlightSafety had profits of about $84 million in 1997.

It turned out that Berkshire not only bought Executive Jet in 1998, but it also bought General Re which happens to be the insurer for FlightSafety and Executive Jet.

FlightSafety trained John F. Kennedy, Jr., whose small plane crashed off the coast of Martha's Vinyard July 16, 1999, killing Kennedy, his wife, Carolyn Bessette Kennedy and her sister, Lauren Bessette.

(Photo by AP/Wide World Photos)

John F. Kennedy, Jr.

The tragedy drew comment on "Berkshire's message board" varying from sorrowful to sick. The appropriate response was this post: "Any man's death diminishes me, because I am involved in mankind. And therefore never send to know for whom the bell tolls. It tolls for thee."—John Donne.

There have been thin but so far unsubstantiated rumors that Kennedy was a Berkshire shareholder.

63

STAR FURNITURE CO.

Berkshire agreed to buy Star Furniture Co. of Houston on June 24, 1997. The 85-year-old retailer, with annual sales of about $110 million, was Berkshire's third purchase of a furniture firm, following the 1983 acquisition of the Nebraska Furniture Mart in Omaha and the 1995 purchase of R.C. Willey in Salt Lake City.

Now Berkshire also owns Jordan's Furniture Co. and CORT Business Services, a furniture rental company.

Under the agreement with Star, Chairman Melvyn Wolff, said he and his family, including his sister and co-owner Shirley Toomin, received Berkshire stock in payment for their business which has 550 employees.

"We've made most of our deals in one meeting. This one took two hours and 20 minutes in a hotel room in New York. That's par for the course," Buffett has said. (*San Antonio Express-News*, March 20, 1999)

(Photo by Ken Monroe)

Star Furniture in Houston, Texas

Wolff told the *Omaha World-Herald* (June 24, 1997) that Buffett gave him the choice of taking either stock or cash and that he chose stock because "we like what he has done with his company and how he makes his stock values grow."

Star, which was founded in 1912, consists of 12 stores, ten in Houston and one each in Austin and Bryan and had plans to open one in San Antonio.

The transaction was revealed during a company-wide breakfast at the George R. Brown Convention Center in Houston where Buffett and Wolff spoke about it.

Buffett wrote in Berkshire's 1997 Annual Report: "On the Thursday before last year's annual meeting Bob Denham of Salomon told me that Melvyn Wolff, the long-time controlling shareholder and CEO of Star, wanted to talk. At our invitation, Melvyn came to the meeting and spent his time in Omaha confirming his positive feelings about Berkshire. I, meanwhile, looked at Star's financials and liked what I saw.

"A few days later Melvyn and I met in New York and made a deal in a single, two-hour session. As was the case with the Blumkins and Bill Child, I had no need to check leases, work out employment contracts, etc. I knew I was dealing with a man of integrity and that's what counted."

Wolff said, "We couldn't be more pleased than to have the opportunity to become a part of what we believe to be the finest family of companies ever assembled under one corporate name. Warren Buffett has demonstrated a legendary track record for growth, and we want to be part of it."

Star Furniture was listed as the 32nd largest furniture store in the country at the time it sold to Berkshire. The Nebraska Furniture Mart was listed as 27th and R. C. Willey as the 20th largest in the top 100 list of *Furniture Today*.

64

SCOOPING UP
INTERNATIONAL DAIRY QUEEN

A s usual it was a busy day for Buffett. On the morning of October 21, 1997 Buffett, along with the likes of Jimmy Carter, attended the funeral in Atlanta of Coca-Cola Chairman Roberto Guizueta. Then he attended a Coke board meeting and that night shared his wisdom with students at Caltech in Pasadena, California.

In the middle of the day Berkshire and International Dairy Queen announced a merger. Berkshire would buy, for about $585 million in Berkshire stock and cash, the entire ice-cream-and-hamburger chain. Again, Buffett was following his gut instincts, much as he has with See's, Coke and McDonalds.

When the word got out that Buffett was buying Dairy Queen, (the merger was effective January 7, 1998) more than one person was heard to ask, "Which one?"

"Buffett has loved ice cream and burgers since he was little. It's the nature of the product," says Berkshire shareholder Michael Assael. "And since you can't download this food from cyberspace, it'll be difficult for the tech capitalists to eat much into Dairy Queen's profits."

The Minneapolis-based chain operates about 6,000 Dairy Queen stores which feature soft-serve ice cream. The chain franchises almost all its fast food/dessert stores in 49 states (What's the prob-

(Photo by Ruth J. Muchemore)

At this Dairy Queen in Omaha at Dodge and 114th Street you can get a "Buffett Banana No-split Blizzard." Dairy Queen sells such items as Buster Bar, Dillywich, Dilly Bar and Peanut Butter Parfaits. The first Blizzard was whirled in 1985. In a year, 200-million sold. (Boston Globe, July 28, 1999)

485

lem Rhode Island?) and 25 foreign countries. There are 729 Dairy Queens in Texas. Illinois is second with 282. Only 34 of the stores, which serve hamburgers, hotdogs, dairy desserts and beverages, are company owned. Most of the stores, known for their red roofs and simple logos, are located in small towns and suburbs of larger cities. Most of Dairy Queen's operating income comes from franchise fees paid by franchise stores. It's the ninth largest U.S. restaurant chain.

Among Buffett's favorite offerings is the Blizzard, a dish of soft-serve ice cream with candies mixed in. Buffett has been a customer of the Dairy Queen at the corner of Dodge and 114th Street in Omaha since 1963. The operation is run by sisters, Coni Birge and Deb Novotny. This is one of 12 Dairy Queens in Omaha. In Berkshire's 1997 Annual Report Buffett invited shareholders to join him at the Dodge Street Dairy Queen for a Dusty Sundae dessert after the traditional dinner at Gorat's steakhouse the night before the Berkshire Annual Meeting. Shareholders were given a coupon for a free five ounce cone.

(Photo by Robert Sullivan)

These young people at an Omaha Dairy Queen are happy to serve you "The Warren Buffett Original 'Dairy Queen' Dusty Sundae."

Dairy Queen has about 409 Orange Julius stores, 43 Karmelkorn shoppes featuring caramel-coated popcorn and other treats and 21 Golden Skillet restaurants. It also has a Treat Centers format and a fledgling Just Juice format. Buffett particularly likes to have an Orange Julius, sometimes going to a mall to get one.

Berkshire paid $27 a share in cash or $26 in stock for a company whose stock was trading at $24 a share at the time the merger was announced.

Dairy Queen's roots go back to 1939 when a Green River, Illinois, ice cream maker joined forces with a refrigerator inventor. The company started when J.F. "Grandpa" McCullough and his son, Alex, invented a machine in Green River, Illinois in 1938 for making soft ice cream and named it after his cow. The McCulloughs unveiled their product at Sherb Noble's ice cream parlor on August 4, 1938. "We dished up over 1,600 servings in about two hours," Noble recalled in a Dairy Queen corporate history. (*Boston Globe*, July 28, 1999) A year later, McCullough joined up with Harry Oltz, who came up with a way to keep ice cream at a constant temperature. The two sold franchises the right to use the machines and the company soon flourished. The first Dairy Queen opened on June 22, 1940 in Joliet, Illinois.

As the middle-class thrived in the 1950s and 1960s, flocked to the suburbs and filled the highways, the company grew. In 1970 a group of investors led by John Mooty bought Dairy Queen for $5 million.

Dairy Queen had about 600 employees and about 1,200 shareholders at the time of the buyout.

"I did a double take when I saw it," press reports quoted John Roberts, an analyst with Louisville, Kentucky-based brokerage J.J.B. Hilliard, W.L. Lyons. "It doesn't sound like the normal investment [Buffett] makes."

What's normal is that most people upon hearing of a new Buffett investment do a double take. The truth is nothing ever sounds like the normal investment Buffett makes. True enough, Dairy Queen isn't the biggest brand name in the world, but it is a brand name and has its niche markets in small corners of the country.

John W. Mooty, Dairy Queen's Chairman, said in a press release: "Our family will vote our entire 35% of the voting shares of Dairy Queen in favor of the merger and will elect to receive Berkshire common stock for all the Dairy Queen shares owned by us. We are not interested in trading our Dairy Queen shares for any other securities. I personally consider Berkshire shares to be one of the finest investments that our family could make and we anticipate holding the shares indefinitely."

Mooty told the *Wall Street Journal* (November 5, 1997) that the idea of selling to Buffett had originated a year earlier, and was rekindled when Minneapolis car dealer Rudy Luther, a Dairy Queen director and big shareholder, died in early 1997.

The story said when executors tried to sell some of Luther's shares to Buffett to cover estate taxes, Buffett indicated he'd rather buy the whole company. Mooty said Buffett neither precluded other unsolicited bids for Dairy Queen nor did he seek any breakup fees for Berkshire if the deal didn't go through.

Buffett said in a press release: "Dairy Queen is a business that I like, run by an outstanding management team. Dairy Queen will be a great addition to the Berkshire family."

Buffett wrote this letter to the editor of the *Wall Street Journal* which appeared November 6, 1997:

The Heard on the Street column yesterday on the Berkshire Hathaway-International Dairy Queen merger misstates a vital point, an error that led to several incorrect conclusions. We are offering IDQ shareholders $27 in cash or $26 in Berkshire stock, just the opposite of what the reporter stated ($26 in cash and $27 in stock). Ironically, the *Journal* had reported the correct figures in its original news story of Oct. 22.

Your error led you to conclude that IDQ has been trading above the cash offer and to speculate about the implications of that premium. In reality, the stock has been trading at a normal arbitrage discount.

The story also has quotes to the effect that John Mooty, IDQ's chairman, may be benefiting to the detriment of other shareholders. That is wrong: The Class B shareholders with whom the voting power resides—Mr. Mooty among them — are receiving no premium whatsoever relative to the Class A shareholders. Furthermore, Mr. Mooty is electing to receive Berkshire shares having an immediate cash value below the cash price being offered to all.

You also characterize our acquisition of FlightSafety as "low-priced." The FlightSafety shareholders who elected to receive Berkshire stock now have for each share they exchanged about $65 in value. Looking at the 1996 and 1997 earnings of FlightSafety, I estimate that this significantly exceeds what FlightSafety stock would now be selling for had the company remained independent.

Warren E. Buffett
Chairman
Berkshire Hathaway Inc.

Omaha, Neb.

Buffett told "Nightline's" Ted Koppel (March 2, 1999), in an interview at a Dairy Queen in Omaha: "It was a business that I could understand. Now, there's all kinds of businesses I can't understand and I try not to buy into those because ..., why should I expect to make money on something I can't understand? So I'm not in any high tech businesses, for example. But I understand, you know, an ultimate hamburger or, you know, a Peanut Buster or a Dilly Bar and I can handle that. And I like the people that run it. I like the economics of the business. It's a good business."

At Berkshire's annual meeting, Buffett was asked about the possibility of investing in software. Unwrapping a Dilly Bar and taking a bite, Buffett said: "The Dilly Bar is more certain."

On a sour note, Berkshire's first quarter report said the company took a $27 million pre-tax charge for "costs to be incurred in connection with the settlement of litigation (that pre-dated Berkshire's acquisition of Dairy Queen) by certain franchisees and provisions for losses in connection with the bankruptcy of a major supplier."

(Photo courtesy of ABC News/Steve Fenn© 1999)

"Nightline's" Ted Koppel interviewed Buffett at a Dairy Queen in Omaha on March 2, 1999.

Putlizer Prize-winning novelist Larry McMurtry (*Lonesome Dove*) wrote a short book in 1999 called *Walter Benjamin at the Dairy Queen*. He used as a springboard an essay by the German literary critic Walter Benjamin that he first read at a Dairy Queen in Archer City, Texas. McMurtry writes of small-town life and his love of books and bookstores.

His book begins:

In the summer of 1980, in the Archer City Dairy Queen, while nursing a lime Dr Pepper (a delicacy strictly local, unheard of even in the next Dairy Queen down the road— Olney's, eighteen miles south—but easily obtainable by anyone willing to buy a lime and a Dr Pepper), I opened a book called *Illuminations* and read Walter Benjamin's essay *The Storyteller*, nominally a study of or reflection on the stories of Nikolay Leskov, but really (I came to feel, after several rereadings) an examination, and a profound one, of the growing obsolescence of what might be called practical memory and the consequent diminution of the power of oral narrative in our twentieth-century lives.

The place where I first read the essay, Archer City's Dairy Queen, was apposite in more ways than one. Dairy Queens, simple drive-up eateries, taverns without alcohol, began to appear in the arid little towns of west Texas about the same time (the late sixties) that Walter Benjamin's work began to arrive in the English language—in the case of *Illuminations*, beautifully introduced by Hannah Arendt. The aridity of the small west Texas towns was not all a matter of unforgiving skies, baking heat, and rainlessness, either; the drought in those towns was social, as well as climatic. The extent to which it was moral is a question we can table for the moment. What I remember clearly is that before the Dairy Queens appeared the people of the small towns had no place to meet and talk; and so they didn't meet *or* talk, which meant that much local lore or incident remained private and ceased to be exchanged, debated, and stored as local lore had been during the centuries that Benjamin describes.

The Dairy Queens, by providing a comfortable setting that made possible hundreds of small, informal local forums, revived, for a time, the potential for storytelling of the sort Walter Benjamin favored.

65
EXECUTIVE JET

B erkshire agreed to buy Executive Jet Inc. on July 23, 1998 for $725 million in stock and cash for the privately held company.

Executive Jet, based in Montvale, New Jersey, but which has its operations headquarters in Columbus, Ohio, pioneered the idea of "time sharing" for corporate jets. Customers can buy "fractional ownership" of business jets through the company's "NetJets" program. (Maybe "NetYachts" is Berkshire's next business.)

The idea is that private jets, a great convenience for the wealthy, can be shared with fellow rich folks thus bringing down the cost by not leaving a plane idle.

Berkshire doesn't own the planes, the customers do. Essentially Berkshire is paid a stream of royalties on the business.

Executive Jet Chairman Richard Santulli had been looking for a way to cash out while being pressed to go public. He asked Buffett's advice, who replied: "Well, what if I buy the company?" (*Forbes*, September 21, 1998)

(Courtesy of the *Columbus Dispatch*)
Executive Jet Chairman Richard Santulli with Buffett at a groundbreaking ceremony in Columbus, Ohio August 25, 1998.

Buffett first heard of Executive Jet from Frank Rooney, the manager of H.H. Brown. "Frank had used and been delighted with the service and suggested I meet Rich to investigate signing up for my family's use. It took Rich about 15 minutes to sell me a quarter (200 hours annually) of a Hawker 1000. Since then, my family has learned first hand—through flying 900 hours on 300 trips—what a friendly, efficient and safe operation EJA runs," Buffett wrote in Berkshire's 1998 Annual Report.

Buffett now flies Executive Jet about 225 hours a year and is the sole passenger on about 85% of his flights.

When Buffett bought the company he said, "It's clearly a field that is going to explode over the next decade." He also predicted it would become the fastest growing of any of the Berkshire businesses, being lumped into an aviation section of Berkshire's businesses along with FlightSafety, a Berkshire unit which happens to train Executive Jet pilots.

Executive Jet, fully airborne, flew 145,000 hours in 1998, up from 95,000 in 1997.

About 15 employees are at headquarters and about 1,000 employees are in the operations center at Port Columbus International Airport.

Buffett first became familiar with Executive Jet and became convinced of its growth potential in 1995 when he first looked into it for his family's use. And since that time he's been an unpaid spokesman for the company.

His wife, Susie, has a one-quarter interest in an Executive Jet plane and Buffett said, "My Aunt Katie now has a 1/16 interest. She's 92 years old, and still lives in the same house she has had for the past 65 years and she's in love with this program." (*Wall Street Journal,* July 23, 1998) "Aunt Katie's become a real swinger now," he would say. (*Omaha World-Herald,* April 14, 1999) Other customers include Tiger Woods and Pete Sampras and companies such as General Electric, Gillette and Texaco.

In 1997 Buffett appeared in a testimonial magazine ad for Executive Jet's Santulli who holds two advance degrees in mathematics. In the 1970s he helped Goldman, Sachs & Co. develop some of the earliest computer programs that applied quantitative techniques to investment banking. He later headed a Goldman leasing operation, before leaving to found an aircraft-leasing concern of his own. In 1984 his company acquired then struggling Executive Jet which was founded in 1964 by some former U.S. Air Force officers. (*Wall Street Journal,* July 23, 1998) Actor/pilot James Stewart and

TV personality Arthur Godfrey were on the original board.

Among the early investors was one Jack Nicklaus. "It struggled for a while and I got out. Look at it now, typical of my luck," the Golden Bear told *Golf Digest* (May 1999).

Santulli was raised in Brooklyn, attended Polytechnic Institute of Brooklyn, taught math, and served a stint at Shell Oil before joining Goldman. His hobby is investing in race horses.

Santulli rolled out Executive Jet's NetJets program in 1986 after using his math background to examine plane usage data to determine that a time-share program for aircraft was viable. He had to figure out how many jets and how many owners are needed that can be assured a jet within four hours notice.

"A plane is an expensive piece of equipment." Buffett said. "If you only use an airplane 100 hours a year, you're only getting one-eighth the use. This makes a plane available for somebody who wants to use a plane 100 or 200 hours a year." (*Wall Street Journal,* July 23, 1998)

For a one-eighth share of a Citation VII, which allows as much as 100 hours of usage and guarantees the owner access to a piloted craft within a matter of hours, clients pay $1.37 million, as well as $9,600 a month in management fees and hourly operational costs.

Among the jets available are Cessnas, Hawkers, Gulfstreams, Dassault Falcon, Raytheon and Boeing Business Jets.

Brigadier General Paul Tibbetts, who dropped a nuclear bomb on Japan from the Enola Gay (named for his mother) was a long-time president of Executive Jet.

Today Executive Jet has:
- 400 million miles of flight experience
- 265 NetJets aircraft, with 549 more on order
- 1,000 employees, including 400 pilots
- More than 1000 customers

In 2000 NetJets planned to fly more than 180,000 flights to more than 90 countries.

NetJets offers its customers MedAire's Medlink Worldwide passenger care services that include medical services.

On August 25, 1998 Santulli and Buffett turned over the first shovels of soil at groundbreaking ceremonies for the continuation of Executive Jet's new operational headquarters at Port Columbus International Airport.

The 200,000-square-foot, $25 million facility opened in 1999.

The company's old offices were retired by Executive Jet and converted into a training facility for pilots, technicians and support staff.

In a *Forbes* story (September 21, 1998) about the Executive Jet purchase, Buffett told the reporter: "Look, I drink the same Coke that you do. I eat the same McDonald's and I bet our houses are not that different. But the big difference is that for sure I travel one hell of a sight better than you do!"

In a story about Executive Jet expansion in *Aviation International News* (October 1, 1998), Buffett was quoted as saying: "I've never done what you could call real due diligence when buying a company. I look for people who are in love with their businesses. Anyone who spends five minutes with Rich Santulli can tell that about him. Rich is a managerial artist. It's my job to bring him the canvas, paint and brushes. He was the one who, in 1986, saw an opportunity over the horizon for something that didn't exist yet, and made it work—through tough times. That's the kind of vision and commitment I look for."

And Santulli said: "Obviously my best choice was to get backing from someone like Mr. Buffett. Warren is a long-term player with the capital and independence to make it work. And he is a hands-off manager. Not that we don't talk all the time. We do. But, it's like this. He asked me, 'Who's the competition in Europe?' I said, 'No one.' He said, 'What do you need to make sure it stays that way?' "

In Berkshire's 1998 Annual Report, Buffett wrote: "The *piece de resistance* of our one-company trade show will be a 79-foot-long, nearly 12-foot-wide, fully-outfitted cabin of a 737 Boeing Business

(Photo by Nancy Line Jacobs)

Here's the tradeshow display of an Executive Jet outside Aksarben, meeting place for Berkshire's annual meeting in 1999. In 2000 Berkshire displayed a number of types of jets at the airport in Omaha. Maybe next year Buffett will order up the whole Executive Jet Fleet.

Jet ("BBJ"), which is NetJets' newest product. This plane has a 14-hour range, is designed to carry 19 passengers, and offers a bedroom, an office, and two showers. Deliveries to fractional owners will begin in the first quarter of 2000.

"The BBJ will be available for your inspection on May 1-3 near the entrance to the Aksarben hall. You should be able to minimize your wait by making your visit on Saturday or Sunday. Bring along your checkbook in case you decide to make an impulse purchase."

In April 1999 Buffett made a trip to London, Frankfurt, and Paris to promote Executive Jet in Europe which operates 15 aircraft and plans to add 10 more in 2000. "He flew on a Gulfstream IV-SP to London, had lunch in Frankfurt and dinner near Paris...then returned to Boston for a board meeting of Gillette...all within three days. Says Buffett, fractional-jet salesman: "Difficult to do that flying commercial."

In 1999 National Air Service, the Saudi affiliate of Executive Jet, was set up. It serves a region including 22 Arab states and also Turkey and Greece. Plans were under way for service in Asia and South America.

Competitors of Executive Jet are Canada's Bombardier Inc. and Raytheon.

"The customer owns the planes so that it's not a capital-intensive business, even though we move large amounts of capital around. Our customers have the capital investment, but less than if they bought the whole plane," Buffett said at Berkshire's annual meeting in 1999.

A *Business Week* story (July 5, 1999) said:

"As for Santulli's business, Buffett is intrigued not just by the novel challenges posed by EJA's rapid growth, but also by the logistical complexities of the fractional-shares business. 'He likes the mental challenge of it,' says Santulli, a former mathematics professor. 'He calls it 3-D chess.' Even so, Buffett is careful not to impinge on Santulli's operating authority. EJA's chief once asked Buffett for advice in making a decision and was rebuffed. 'Don't bother with that!' Buffett told him. 'Just decide.' "

Who are Executive Jet's customers? Often they are celebrities from entertainment and sports. "From the big screen, there's Sylvester Stallone and Arnold Schwarzenegger. TV provides David Letterman and Kathy Lee Gifford. Golfer Tiger Woods and tennis star Pete Sampras also are in the club. And to dress them all, there's Calvin Klein." (*The Columbus Dispatch*, December 12, 1999)

"It allows you to go places that you normally wouldn't be able to go," said Executive Jet customer and national radio personality Don Imus... "The limo is there. They take your luggage. You can take your gun on the plane.. It's great."

Kevin Russell, Executive Jet senior vice president, said the company has more than 40 entertainers among its customers, as well as a similar number of professional athletes, mostly pro golfers. (*The Columbus Dispatch*, December 12, 1999)

The newspaper said golf pro Davis Love, III told *Golf Digest* that Executive Jet allowed him an extra 25 nights a year at home. Besides Love and Woods, Executive Jet's golf pro customers include Ben Crenshaw, Curtis Strange and Tom Kite.

One of Executive Jet's new customers is Charles Munger—not a golf pro. In Berkshire's 1999 Annual Report, Buffett wrote:

"Still, most of the planes we fly are owned by customers, which means that modest pre-tax margins in this business can produce good returns on equity. Currently, our customers own planes worth over $2 billion, and in addition we have $4.2 billion of planes on order. Indeed, the limiting factor in our business right now is the availability of planes. We now are taking delivery of about 8% of all business jets manufactured in the world, and we wish we could get a bigger share than that. Though EJA was supply-constrained in 1999, its recurring revenues -- monthly management fees plus hourly flight fees -- increased 46%.

"The fractional-ownership industry is still in its infancy. EJA is now building critical mass in Europe, and over time we will expand around the world. Doing that will be expensive -- very expensive -- but we will spend what it takes. Scale is vital to both us and our customers: The company with the most planes in the air worldwide will be able to offer its customers the best service. 'Buy a fraction, get a fleet' has real meaning at EJA."

Buffett showed up at a charity auction at the Silicon Valley home of investor Ron Conway on May 19, 2000, along with some 300 fellow billionaires. Buffett took the opportunity to plug NetJets which was offering round trip flights to Orlando, Florida, for a little golf with NetJets customer Tiger Woods. The chance to play with Woods and have Buffett serve as caddy brought $650,000 to charity coffers.

- -

Buffett, dressed casually, once attended a promotional event for Executive Jet. When he got cold, Executive Jet employee Sandra Gibson asked fellow employee Dan Dugger for the ultimate sacrifice—his coat. Buffett returned to Omaha before realizing that the coat belonged to an employee. He asked Debbie Bosanek personally to return the coat to the employee when he came to Omaha. With the coat was a Berkshire shirt and a note from Buffett thanking the employee for giving him "the shirt off his back."

(Courtesy of Executive Jet)

This ad for Executive Jet features such customers as Buffett and tennis star Pete Sampras.

66

JORDAN'S FURNITURE COMPANY

"NOT TO BE CONFUSED WITH JORDAN-MARSH"

If ever an iconoclastic, irreverent company existed, it's Jordan's Furniture Company of Massachusetts. On October 11, 1999 Berkshire announced that it was buying the privately held firm run by two brothers with a flair for the unusual, particularly in advertising.

Buffett said: "Jordan's Furniture is truly one of the most phenomenal and unique companies that I have ever seen. The reputation that Eliot and Barry [Tatelman] have earned from their employees, their customers, and the community is unparalled. This company is a gem!"

Barry Tatelman said, "Nothing in the company will change…except for the fact that our growth potential is huge with the financial support of Berkshire Hathaway."

(Photo by Michael O'Brien)

The Tatelman brothers Eliot and Barry sell furniture via witty, goofy ads, such as this one shot on the wing of an airplane.

He added, "We wanted to share the excitement of this merger with our incredible group of employees. Therefore, we are rewarding every single J-Team member with 50 cents for every hour that they have ever worked for us. Many of our people have been with us for 10 years, 20 years." That meant long-time employees each received $10,000 to $20,000. Earlier in the year Jordan's flew all 1,200 employees to Bermuda for a one-day beach party to reward workers for their hard work.

Jordan's was founded in 1918 by Samuel Tatelman in Waltham, Massachusetts. He sold furniture out of the back of his truck until 1926. In the late 1930s his son Edward joined the effort, but it was Edward's sons, Eliot and Barry, who put the store on the map.

When Barry and Eliot joined the firm in the 1950s and 1960s to help out on the weekends, Eliot got 10 cents an hour and Barry 5 cents to dust. Barry said that Eliot was overpaid. In any event, they took the firm from eight employees to 1,200 today.

In 1983 a store built in Nashua, New Hampshire, was wildly successful. When one was built in Avon, Massachusetts, in 1987 it created the largest traffic jam ever on Route 24. Messages from the store on the radio begged people not to come.

There are also stores in Natick and Waltham, Massachusetts. Jordan's sells more furniture per square foot than anyone in the United States. An average furniture store turns over inventory one to two times a year. Jordan's turns over inventory 13 times a year.

Jordan's (known for greeters who race to cars to wash customers' windows), operates a "shoppertainment" within its store. The Avon location has a 48-seat flight simulator movie theater called Motion Odyssey Movie Ride (M.O.M.), a full blown movie theater with a giant screen and seats that move while you watch.

In the Natick store, customers walk through a recreation of New Orleans' Bourbon Street, complete with a riverboat, a "Streetcar Named Dessert," a man handing out beads, full-scale French building facades, and a 9-minute multi-media Mardi Gras show. Every 45 minutes a Louie Armstrong doll emerges from a wall and plays "When the Saints Go Marching In."

At other times animatronic versions of Elvis Presley, the Supremes and the Village People pop out.

A screen displays some of the Tatelmans' goofy ads. In one, the brothers ride up a ski lift in one of their easy chairs and in another they play drums, then close saying, "Just trying to drum up some business."

It was Buffett who approached the Tatelmans about selling. They had not planned to sell until Buffett came calling and they took him through the Natick store. "We never put the company up for sale. Ever," said Barry Tatelman.

The sales price was not disclosed, but some say the top furniture stores often sell for the same amount as their annual revenues—in this case $250 million.

Jordan's ads are known as irreverent, sometimes spoofing the ads of other products. For example, in one the Tatelman brothers dropped a ball bearing on a couch to mimic a Lexus ad that did the same thing to bring attention to the luxury car's sleek lines and precision engineering. Another ad featured a woman sitting on a Jordan's couch, making uncomplimentary remarks—in Swedish—about the brothers who couldn't understand what she was saying. In all, it's retailing entertainment.

In the early days when they were not well known and when Jordon-Marsh was a big retailer in the area, their motto was: "Jordan's Furniture, not to be confused with Jordon-Marsh."

Back in 1983 when Buffett bought Nebraska Furniture Mart, he asked the Blumkin family "Are there any others like you out there?"

The Blumkins gave him the names of three stores, according to Stevin Hoover, head of Hoover Capital Management in Boston, Massachusetts.

"But at that time not one of the three was for sale. So he waited patiently, stepped forward when the families were finally ready to sell, and Berkshire now owns all four of what may arguably be the most profitable home-furnishings retailers in the nation," Hoover said.

Here are Berkshire's furniture acquisitions:

1983 Berkshire acquires 90% of Nebraska Furniture Mart

1995 Berkshire acquires R.C. Willey

1997 Berkshire acquires Star Furniture

1999 Berkshire acquires Jordan's Furniture

And the beat goes on:

2000 Berkshire acquires CORT Business Services

Hoover added:

"Berkshire's furniture-company acquisitions have followed a simple consistent pattern: Buffett learns, through word-of-mouth from friends in the business, of established, family-owned furniture operations that have (1) a dominant presence in their region. (2) hands-on family owner/managers of proven capability, and (3) profitablility well above industry norms. When the family members are ready to sell, he is ready to buy.

"For these businesses there are three key benefits from being owned by Berkshire: (1) access to capital to grow store-count and inventory; (2) complete autonomy in running the business; and (3) a collective buying power advantage. Each of the four [now five] Berkshire-owned companies will continue to have a strictly regional presence (and thus not compete with each other) but they will come together for the purpose of 'Wal-Marting' their suppliers. That is, they will use their collective purchasing power to buy in size from manufacturers and suppliers at a lower cost than the competition. Lower costs translate into lower prices to customers, which in turn translate into increased sales, and so the cycle goes providing Berkshire with another 'virtuous circle' business."

67

MIDAMERICAN ENERGY
GETTING ELECTRICITY FROM BERKSHIRE

Berkshire launched into an entirely new business on October 25, 1999, saying it planned to buy MidAmerican Energy Holdings Co., a utility company based in Des Moines, Iowa.

Many customers are now getting their electricity from Berkshire: shocking.

The $9.35 billion Berkshire-led buyout, closed on March 14, 2000.

Buffett wrote in Berkshire's 1999 Annual Report: "Acquisitions in the electric utility industry are complicated by a variety of regulations including the Public Utility Holding Act of 1935. Therefore, we had to structure a transaction that would avoid Berkshire gaining voting control. Instead we are purchasing an 11% fixed-income security, along with a combination of common stock and exchangeable preferred that will give Berkshire just under 10% of the voting power of MidAmerican but about 76% of the equity interest. All told our investment will be about $2 billion."

The deal, including assumed debt, gave MidAmerican greater financial strength because Berkshire became the parent assuring a better credit rating so MidAmerican could borrow more cheaply. But what really happened was the deal increased the power company's competitiveness in the energy sector as that industry was being deregulated. MidAmerican gave Berkshire a platform to make acquisitions in a fragmented, consolidating industry wracked by inefficiencies—an industry which was becoming more deregulated after a century of regulation.

(Photo courtesy of the Omaha World-Herald)

MidAmerican Energy Chairman David Sokol

Joining Berkshire in the buyout were Walter Scott, former chairman of Peter Kiewit Sons' and David Sokol, chairman of

MidAmerican. Both were big shareholders of the power generating company. Scott, who is on Berkshire's board, brought the deal to Buffett.

Sokol told CNBC (October 25, 1999) that the deal was a "leveraged buyout (LBO) without the L." Known for his deal making, Sokol said it may be the dealmaking was just beginning. There are about 150 utility firms in the U.S., but that in five to 10 years there may be only 20, he said. "We will buy as many as we can," he added.

Sokol told other reporters, "This may be very much a transforming transaction in the industry."

The buyout group of Berkshire, Scott and Sokol, bought MidAmerican's equity for $2.3 billion in cash. The ownership group assumed $7 billion in debt from MidAmerican and paid the rest in cash by buying common and preferred stock.

Berkshire wound up with a 75% stake in MidAmerican. Scott and Sokol received the other 25%, with Scott getting about 20%.

Buffett said, "We buy good companies with outstanding management and good growth potential at a fair price, and we're willing to wait longer than some investors for that potential to be realized. This investment is right in our sweet spot. If I only had two draft picks out of American business, Walter Scott and David Sokol are the ones I would choose for this industry."

MidAmerican, which kept that name after CalEnergy bought the company, had annual revenues of $4.4 billion, $11 billion in assets and 9,800 employees. CalEnergy was formed to tap the electricity-generating potential of superhot underground water in California. MidAmerican owns MidAmerican Energy and United Kingdom-based-Northern Electric. CalEnergy paid $1.3 billion for Northern Electric in 1996.

MidAmerican had been hit by CalEnergy's exposure to Asia, particularly Indonesia. After the government fell there, Indonesia's state-owned electric company refused to buy power from two plants CalEnergy had built there.

Sokol was working for Kiewit when it bought into CalEnergy in 1991. He headed CalEnergy which in early 1999 bought MidAmerican.

Sokol told the *Omaha-World Herald* (October 26, 1999) that Buffett already had researched the energy industry when Scott first talked to him a month before about the possibility of buying MidAmerican. Most of the discussions were about determining a fair price. Scott came up with the idea of approaching Buffett.

"He had some knowledge that Warren had an interest in getting his arms around this industry," Sokol said.

He added that MidAmerican's decision to seek such a buyer stemmed from the fact it had to turn down a number of acquisition possibilities because MidAmerican's slumping stock price gave the company only a weak currency to buy another company.

MidAmerican's stock peaked at $40 a share in 1997 only to slip back to $27 a share in the fall of 1999—about ten times earnings.

The company's shares had been hit by industry tumult even though MidAmerican's earnings were steadily rising.

To stay competitive, Sokol said (*Fortune*, March 6, 2000) MidAmerican needed to make acquisitions fast at a time when that might depress earnings and hurt the stock more. "We were afraid the confusion factor among shareholders was going to slow us down right when the long-term strategy called for taking advantage of acquisition opportunities." MidAmerican sold to Berkshire for $35 a share, a 29% premium, taking itself private into the Berkshire fold.

MidAmerican's board on August 19, 1999 authorized a look at finding ways to increase shareholder value. Following the meeting Sokol discussed a buyout possibility with Walter Scott, a director of MidAmerican. At a social gathering September 23, 1999 Scott asked Buffett if Berkshire would be interested in looking at a possible

(Photo courtesy of Omaha World-Herald)

MidAmerican Energy plant south of Council Bluffs, Iowa

investment and Buffett expressed preliminary interest, according to a notice of a meeting for a shareholder approval vote.

Although MidAmerican is based in Des Moines, Sokol's office is across the street from Kiewit Plaza in Omaha where Berkshire rents office space from Kiewit.

Innovative MidAmerican offers power generation in the U.S., the U.K., the Philippines and Indonesia. It supplies electricity to about 2 million customers and natural gas to 1.2 million customers. It supplies energy from a variety of sources including geothermal, natural gas, hydroelectric, nuclear and coal.

With Berkshire's access to cheaper capital for MidAmerican, the power company can focus on the continuing wave of deregulation that will open most markets to MidAmerican which might bundle utility, telecommunications and household services to its customers.

MidAmerican owns a majority stake in HomeServices.com, one of the largest residential real estate brokerages in the U.S. with more than 140 offices in 10 Midwestern states. The service, which offers the latest news on decorating, remodeling, gardening and home security, is involved in the sale of more than 80,000 homes a year.

MidAmerican owns CBS Home Real Estate in Omaha. So MidAmerican could offer the ability to broker your home, help buy a new one and arrange for home utilities.

MidAmerican plans to play on the whittling down of the industry and bundling of services.

The MidAmerican shareholder vote approval notice said: "Because our common stock will be privately held, we will enjoy certain efficiencies, such as the elimination of the time devoted by management and certain other employees to comply with the reporting obligations of the Exchange Act with respect to the common stock, and the directors, officers and beneficial owners of more than 10% of the common stock will be relieved of their reporting requirements and restrictions under Section 16 of the Exchange Act. In addition, we will be relieved of certain listing and reporting requirements under the rule of the stock exchanges on which our common stock is listed. We will be able to reduce certain costs, which we expect will result in combined savings of approximately $1 million per year, including the costs of preparing, printing and mailing annual reports and proxy statements, the expenses of a transfer agent and registrar, the costs associated with the number of members of our Board and the costs of certain investor relations activities."

Just a few more advantages of joining Berkshire's extended family which also include Buffett's lobbying abilities.

In April 2000 Buffett personally made the rounds at Congress on behalf of restructuring the nation's utility industry, arguing for deregulation: the Dow Jones News Wires (April 7, 2000) reported:

...This alternative consensus for restructuring the industry, which largely overlapped with the Department of Energy—brokered principles, was hand-delivered to members of Congress by billionaire investor Warren Buffett.

Buffett, an icon of value investing, used his Berkshire Hathaway Inc., holding company to take MidAmerican Energy Holdings Co. private in a deal completed earlier this year.

The acquisition is reported to be just the first foray into the electricity sector that Buffett intends to take.

But before he can easily accomplish any further acquisitions, he needs Congress to repeal the 1935 Public Utility Holding Company Act, which restricts the geographic and business operations of multi-state utility holding companies.

And Buffett knows that politics dictate that any holding company act repeal must be part of a comprehensive bill promoting power market competition.

Buffett and MidAmerican have hired former Rep. Robert Livingston, R-La. to lobby Congress on their behalf.

On Wednesday, Buffett had personal meetings with (Rep. Thomas] Bliley, the Commerce Committee chairman, and Rep. John Dingell, D-Mich., the committee's ranking Democrat and former chairman.

At the meeting with Bliley, Buffett was accompanied by Kenneth Lay, chairman of Enron Corp., an ardent proponent of congressional action to restructure electricity markets.

Buffett further hosted a luncheon for Commerce Committee Democrats and a dinner for Republican members of the panel, and met with Energy Secretary Richardson to discuss restructuring legislation.

Industry officials advocating congressional action this year saw Buffett's visit as significant in that it helped focus lawmakers' attention to the issue...

68

RED ROOF INNS

Berkshire and another buyer, U.S. Realty Advisors, bought about half of the Red Roof Inn properties in the summer of 1999 from the French firm Accor SA. (*The Columbus Dispatch*, December 2, 1999)

Accor, the world's fourth largest hotel company, planned to lease back the properties from the buyers to run the hotels from its headquarters in Dallas, the Ohio newspaper said.

The story quoted Accor officials saying they had sold 145 Red Roof properties for $500 million, but had no plans to sell their other 177 Red Roof Inns.

Such deals have become common in the hotel industry. The deals amount to a way to finance expansion.

Accor also owns Motel 6, an economy hotel chain. Earlier Accor had raised nearly $1 billion selling 40% of its Motel 6 properties in a sale-lease back arrangement, according to *The Columbus Dispatch*.

(Photo by third-rate photographer Andrew Kilpatrick)

A Red Roof Inn in Birmingham, Alabama

69
CORT BUSINESS SERVICES

Berkshire's Wesco announced on January 14, 2000 it was buying CORT Business Services, Corporation in a cash transaction valued at $467 million, including about $83 million of assumed debt.

The purchase of CORT makes Berkshire a large player in the furniture industry with its ownership already of Nebraska Furniture Mart, R.C. Willey Furnishings, Star Furniture and Jordan Furniture Company.

CORT, of Fairfax, Virginia, is the leading provider of rental furniture, accessories and related services in the growing "rent-to-rent" furniture rental industry.

CORT went public in 1995 after 23 years in business.

As the industry's biggest renter of residential and office furniture, it estimates that more than 80% of the Fortune 500 companies rent from it. The company rents to business executives in need of temporary furnishings for either office or home. Warner Brothers, EDS, Exxon and Pepsi are among its customers. CORT also rents furniture, including conference tables and chairs, for tradeshows and meetings.

(Photo courtesy of CORT Business Services)

CORT Business Services showroom in Pleasanton, California

After an average of three rentals, the furniture is moved to CORT's clearance centers and sold.

(Photo courtesy of CORT Business Services)

CORT President Paul Arnold

Wesco bought CORT for $28 a share. Citigroup Venture Capital (CVC), which owned about 44% of CORT's shares, agreed to tender its shares.

Wesco's Munger said: "CORT is a classic example of a fine company that can be even better as a result of the strength and stability that result from inclusion in the Berkshire Group of companies."

Buffett said: "CORT is the kind of 'best in class' business that Charlie and I like to add to the Berkshire Group of companies. Paul Arnold and his managers are exactly the kind of people with whom we like to be associated in business. We are certain this is going to be a great relationship."

CORT operates 118 showrooms, 87 clearance centers and 75 warehouses in 34 states and the District of Columbia and has Internet sites relocationcentral.com, cort1.com and corttradeshow.com.

Beginning in the second half of 1998, CORT's board began talking about ways to increase shareholder value.

In the spring of 1999 top executives hooked up with a leveraged buyout firm and offered to buy CORT from shareholders at $26.50, but shareholders showed insufficient support. The stock had hit a peak of $48 in April 1998.

Another offer for the company had come from Fremont Partners and Brook Furniture Rental Inc. but the offer was rejected.

"On November 23, 1999, Mr. Arnold received a call from Bruce Cort, an acquaintance of Mr. Arnold. Mr. Arnold returned the call later that day. In their discussions Mr. Cort informed Mr. Arnold that earlier that day he had forwarded a recent *Washington Post* article about the Company to Warren E. Buffett, Chairman of Berkshire Hathaway, and that Buffett had responded that Berkshire would be interested in a friendly transaction for the Company at $28.00 per share. Mr. Arnold requested that Mr. Cort arrange a meeting with Mr. Buffett," Wesco's filing said.

Exterior of a CORT showroom in Louisville, Kentucky

"Mr. Arnold, who was accompanied by Mr. Cort, met Mr. Buffett in Omaha on November 29, 1999. They talked about the business of the Company and the Company's recent history. Mr. Buffett indicated an interest in acquiring the Company at $28.00 per share, and said he would need to talk to the company's largest shareholder, CVC."

CORT was on track to have about $350 million in revenues in 1999 and had net income of about $21 million in the first nine months of 1999.

Things worked out and Berkshire made its merger agreement known on January 14, 2000.

The same day Lou Simpson, GEICO's CEO, told Buffett he owned 200,000 shares, and that members of his family and their trusts owned up to 100,000 shares, all acquired in February and March 1999 that he anticipated tendering in the offer.

The total Simpson investment of roughly $5 million quickly turned into about $8 million.

CORT bought Cost Plus Enterprises' rental contracts and certain other assets on February 14, 2000. The privately held company based in Stamford, Connecticut rents furniture to accounts in New York, New Jersey and Connecticut. Annual sales were almost $7 million in 1999.

CORT and NextOffice.com, an online source for business furnishings, announced a strategic partnership March 29, 2000 which includes development of an online rental center, a co-marketing agreement and investment by CORT in NextOffice.com of San Francisco.

Berkshire was turning into a furniture powerhouse.

70

BERKSHIRE'S FINANCIAL BUSINESSES

Berkshire has a business segment called "finance and financial products businesses."

Very little is said or known about this segment, but it is increasingly showing up on Berkshire's balance sheet as a money maker.

It earned $205 million pre-tax in 1997.

Some years back the unit was described as consisting of Scott Fetzer Financial Group, Berkshire Hathaway Credit Corporation and Berkshire Hathaway Life Insurance Company of Nebraska.

Berkshire's 1998 Annual Report described it this way: "Berkshire's finance and financial products businesses consist primarily of the financial products businesses of General Re, the finance businesses of Scott Fetzer Financial Group and a life insurance subsidiary in the business of selling annuities. General Re's financial products businesses consist of General Re Financial Products ("GRFP") group and a collection of other businesses that provide investment, insurance, reinsurance and real estate management and brokerage services." GRFP has been put up for sale.

In this collection are General Re's Financial Products which is a derivatives dealer acquired with the buyout of General Re at the end of 1998. The Scott Fetzer Financial Group finances sales of Scott Fetzer, Kirby and *World Book* products and Berkshire. Berkshire Life Insurance, established in 1993, sells structured settlement annuity products which make periodic payments to personal injury claimants.

Berkshire's Mike Goldberg who heads "special projects", has a hand in these increasingly important operations.

Occasionally there are rumors about buying Florida land loans or financing real estate projects, but the segment seems a "mystery wrapped in an enigma" because so little is known about it.

THE WALL STREET JOURNAL, TUESDAY, FEBRUARY 8, 1994

This announcement appears as a matter of record only.

$110,000,000

First Mortgage Financing

One and Two Arizona Center
Phoenix, Arizona

Two office buildings totalling 786,000 square feet

A Project of

The Rouse Company

Financing provided by an affiliate of

Berkshire Hathaway Inc.

Placement Agent

Citicorp Securities, Inc.

December 1993

CITICORP

This notice from the Wall Street Journal, found by Berkshire shareholder Bill Scargle, appears to be about a financing by Berkshire's financial business.

Berkshire Hathaway wants to see real-estate finance opportunities in excess of $100,000,000

In a market where most real-estate lenders are looking to accumulate diversified portfolios of small loans, Berkshire Hathaway is looking to assemble a small portfolio of very large real-estate loans. In fact, we have closed several transactions exceeding $100 million over the past few years and just closed a $500 million net lease transaction. We would like to see your real-estate financing opportunity if it exceeds $100 million.

WE ARE INTERESTED IN:

(1) traditional financings related to large single assets or portfolios if cross-collateralized;

(2) financings or equity investments related to net lease transactions; and

(3) REIT re-capitalizations (potentially debt or equity).

We are flexible concerning asset types and will consider office, retail, industrial and multi-family. We are also interested in operating real estate such as hotels if an income stream is guaranteed by an acceptable corporate credit. We prefer providing long-term fixed-rate loans and are not interested in transactions with a maturity of less than five years. Our loans require significant levels of amortization over the term and are priced at a substantial spread to Treasuries. We are less interested in acquiring equity interests in multi-tenant real estate and will not lend on development projects.

Our underwriting approach is most likely unique in the industry. We require that you submit summary information regarding the real estate and the significant elements of the financing such as principal amount, maturity, loan to value, coverage, amortization, etc., as well as indicate the price you are willing to pay (we generally think in terms of spreads over Treasuries of comparable duration). We will then accept your proposal subject to due diligence or we may counter if the price and terms are close to those we believe appropriate. If our ideas and yours with regards to pricing are far apart, we will turn the offering down with the understanding that we will not entertain any additional proposals on the same transaction. This simple procedure disciplines both of us and saves time.

Virtually no transaction is too large. And we will respond quickly. We rarely take more than a few days to answer. Often our response is immediate.

For more information, contact
Bob Bennett, Senior Vice President, Berkshire Hathaway Credit Corporation
Phone: 1-781-659-2432; Fax: 1-781-659-2491; Email: rebbhcc@aol.com

(The Wall Street Journal, February 22, 2000)

71

"OTHER"

IT'S NOT A BAD BERKSHIRE SUBSIDIARY IF A $20 MILLION PROFIT IN 1999 MEANS ANYTHING TO YOU.

Berkshire has an interesting "subsidiary" called "Other," which includes about two dozen small businesses.

In 1977, "Other" made $48,000. Here's how "Other" has done since in annual profits:

1978	$261,000
1979	$753,000
1980	$1,255,000
1981	$1,513,000
1982	$1,780,000
1983	$8,490,000
1984	$3,476,000
1985	$2,102,000
1986	$8,685,000
1987	$13,696,000
1988	$27,177,000
1989	$12,863,000
1990	$35,782,000
1991	$47,896,000
1992	$36,267,000
1993	$15,364,000
1994	$22,275,000
1995	$24,400,000
1996	$42,200,000
1997	$37,000,000
1998	$29,000,000
1999	$20,000,000

That's more than a lemonade stand. But "Other" is a nice business.

The group's largest business is Campbell Hausfeld, the country's leading producer of small and medium-sized air compressors, with annual sales of about $100 million.

Berkshire's "other" small businesses:

OPERATOR	PRODUCT/SERVICE/ACTIVITY
ADALET	Electrical enclosure systems and cable accessories
BLUE CHIP STAMPS	Marketing motivational services
BORSHEIM'S	Retailing fine jewelry
BUFFALO NEWS	Daily and Sunday newspaper
CAMPBELL HAUSFELD	Air compressors and air tools, painting systems, pressure washers, welders and generators
CAREFREE	Comfort and convenience products for the recreational vehicle industry
CLEVELAND WOOD PRODUCTS	Vacuum cleaner brushes and bags
DEXTER SHOE COMPANIES	Dress, casual and athletic shoes
DOUGLAS PRODUCTS	Specialty cordless vacuum cleaners
EXECUTIVE JET	Fractional ownership programs for general aviation aircraft
FECHHEIMER BROS. CO.	Uniforms and accessories
FLIGHTSAFETY	High technology training to operators of aircrafts and ships
FRANCE	Ignition and sign transformers and components
H.H. BROWN SHOE	Work shoes, boots and casual footwear

HALEX	Zinc die cast conduit fittings and other electrical construction materials
HELZBERG'S DIAMOND SHOPS	Retailing fine jewelry
INTERNATIONAL DAIRY QUEEN	Licensing and servicing Dairy Queen Stores
JORDAN'S FURNITURE	Retailing home furnishings
KINGSTON	Appliance controls and actuators
KIRBY	Home cleaning systems
LOWELL SHOE, INC.	Women's and nurses' shoes
MERIAM	Pressure and flow measurement devices
NEBRASKA FURNITURE MART	Retailing home furnishings
NORTHLAND	Fractional horsepower electric motors
POWERWINCH	Marine and general purpose winches, windlasses, and hoists
PRECISION STEEL PRODUCTS	Steel service center
QUIKUT	Cutlery for home and sporting goods markets
SCOTTCARE	Cardiopulmonary rehabilitation and monitoring equipment
SCOT LABS	Cleaning compounds and solutions
SEE'S CANDIES	Boxed chocolates and other confectionery product

STAHL	Truck equipment including service, flatbed and dump bodies, cranes, toolboxes and hoists
STAR FURNITURE COMPANY	Retailing home furnishings
WAYNE COMBUSTION SYSTEMS	Oil and gas burners for residential and commercial appliances and equipment
WAYNE WATER SYSTEMS	Sump, utility and sewage pumps
WESTERN ENTERPRISES	Medical and industrial compressed gas fittings and regulators
WESTERN PLASTICS	Molded plastic components
R.C. WILLEY HOME FURNISHINGS	Retailing home furnishings
WORLD BOOK	Printed and multimedia encyclopedia and other reference materials

K&W Products, an automotive compounds business, acquired in the mid-1970s, was sold in February 1996 to a group of investors which included the former president of K&W Products.

72

WPPSS BONDS

"IF WE WANTED MOODY'S OR STANDARD & POOR'S TO RUN OUR MONEY, WE'D GIVE IT TO THEM."

Buffett quietly bought $139 million worth of Projects 1, 2, and 3 of Washington Public Power Supply System bonds in 1983 and 1984.

In Berkshire's 1984 Annual Report, Buffett stunned Berkshire shareholders, revealing he had bought bonds issued by the Washington Public Power Supply System (WPPSS), a nuclear power plant construction corporation in Washington state so troubled it was dubbed "Whoops."

The shock deepened when Buffett explained how WPPSS had defaulted on $2.2 billion worth of bonds issued to help finance Projects 4 and 5. That stigma stained other projects and Buffett was able to buy the bonds at a steep discount.

Naturally, ratings of the bonds indicated they were a high risk. "We don't make judgments based on ratings. If we wanted *Moody's* or *Standard & Poor's* to run our money, we'd give it to them." (*Omaha World-Herald*, April 14, 1985)

Steve Wallman, head of Wallman Investment Counsel in Madison, Wisconsin, says: "Our day-to-day lives don't prepare us in the least for going against the crowd. In almost everything we do, success is a function of how well we go along with the crowd, not how well we go against it. As a result, going against the crowd, and ignoring what psychologists call social proof, is contrary to our nature. Little wonder value investing is so tough, and so little used. Most people just don't have the psychological musculature to carry the burden of negative opinion that goes with fifty-cent dollars like WPPSS 1, 2, and 3."

The bonds had a special appeal, however, offering a fixed 16.3%, after tax current yield, a $22.7 million annual return on the investment.

As usual, the investment worked out profitably for Buffett. The projects went well and the bonds rose to the occasion. The 16.3% after-tax payoff arrived like clockwork into the Berkshire account.

Buffett said he bought the bonds because he probably would have had to pay almost twice his WPPSS purchase price for a business bringing in that much after-tax money.

Many of Berkshire's "Whoops" bonds have been called, but Berkshire still holds a portion of the bonds.

Although Buffett is not a great fan of bonds, he will buy them under special circumstances. He has a history of buying bonds of troubled companies. In the 1970s he bought the depressed bonds of Chrysler when the firm was near collapsing, and Penn Central bonds for about 50 cents on the dollar after the railroad went bust. Both companies rallied back.

In 1986, he bought an additional $700 million of medium-term, tax-exempt bonds, which he considered the least objectionable alternative to stocks.

Berkshire's bond purchases for decades were handled by Bill Scott, the first employee Buffett ever hired.

73
RJR NABISCO BONDS
"JUNK BONDS WILL ONE DAY LIVE UP TO THEIR NAME."

In 1989 and 1990, Buffett bought junk bond offerings of RJR Nabisco. The tobacco and food giant known for Winston cigarettes, Life-Savers candy, Ritz crackers, Fig Newtons and Oreo cookies was the subject of a leveraged buyout by Kohlberg Kravis Roberts in 1988.

It was the largest takeover in Wall Street history, with a $25 billion pricetag—a cap to the Decade of Greed.

The first hint that Buffett might be entering the junk bond market came at the annual meeting in 1990 when a shareholder asked if the junk bond market could ever become a fruitful place for a professional investor. "I'll let you know in a year or two," said Buffett, known for saying, "Junk bonds will one day live up to their name."

In late 1989 Buffett started accumulating the RJR bonds issued to help finance the takeover, and in 1990 he added heavily to the holding. No one knew it until the Berkshire Annual Report came out in 1991.

Even then, you could have missed the news because it was not until page 17 of his letter that Buffett made a one-paragraph mention of it.

He wrote, "Our other major portfolio change last year was large additions to our RJR Nabisco bonds, securities that we first bought in late 1989. At yearend 1990 we had $440 million invested in these securities, an amount that approximated market value. [As I write this, their market value has risen by more than $150 million.]"

Had almost any other company made a quick $150 million, it would have been, in newspaper parlance, the "lead" paragraph of the chairman's letter.

Buffett wrote in Berkshire's 1990 Annual Report: "In the case of RJR Nabisco, we feel the Company's credit is considerably better than was generally perceived for a while and that the yield we receive, as well as the potential for capital gain, more than compensates for the risk we incur (though that is far from nil). RJR has made asset sales at favorable prices, has added major amounts of equity, and in general is being run well.

"However, as we survey the field, most low-grade bonds still look unattractive. The handiwork of the Wall Street of the 1980s is even worse than we had thought: Many important businesses have been mortally wounded. We will, though, keep looking for opportunities as the junk market continues to unravel."

Fortune reported the Nabisco purchase and asked Buffett if he wished he had bought more. "There are lots of things I wish I'd done in hindsight. But I don't think much of hindsight generally in terms of investment decisions. You only get paid for what you do," he said.

Many of the RJR Nabisco bonds were paying about 15%, so Buffett was hauling in a splendid return while he waited for management to sell some assets and keep their Oreo cookies stocked at the stores.

As junk bonds tanked, Buffett spotted a gem. But he didn't just wing it and buy large well-known company bonds at random. Only after intensive study of the massacred junk bond market in which he said he found more carnage than he expected, did he pick RJR as offering the best hope of a good return.

Junk bonds, called high-yield bonds for their double-digit interest rates, were popularized in the 1980s by firms trying to find money to finance takeovers.

The bonds were risky because the issuers were saddled with debt. But again Buffett's reading of the overall financial landscape and his precise timing produced another bonanza for Berkshire. Just about the time his RJR investment was made public, financial writers began offering stories about a comeback in the junk bond market.

Not only that, RJR was beginning to get more notice for paring down its debt. Its losses were dropping dramatically; its creditworthiness improved. And RJR was refinancing at lower rates.

RJR seemed on its way back to life under Louis Gerstner, who left a top job at American Express to run things at RJR, then exited to head IBM.

On May 3, 1991, RJR announced it was retiring most of its junk bonds used to finance the buyout, using money it had raised in a stock offering. The company said it planned to redeem the bonds at face value, bonds that Buffett had purchased at a steep discount.

Buffett had made a large and quick profit and now apparently he would have back a lot of cash, which he knows how to deploy. Once again, Buffett was creating permanent value for Berkshire shareholders.

At yearend 1992, Berkshire held more than $1 billion of bonds in such entities as Washington Public Power Supply System and ACF

Industries.

The bonds of ACF Industries, the rail-car manufacturing and leasing firm Carl Icahn owns, gave Buffett a handsome profit when they were called in 1993.

74

$30 BILLION IN FIXED-INCOME SECURITIES

"Our largest non-traditional position at yearend was $4.6 billion at amortized cost, of long-term zero-coupon obligations of the U.S. Treasury... Since rates fell in 1997, we ended the year with an unrealized pre-tax gain of $598.8 million in our zeros," Buffett wrote in Berkshire's 1997 Annual Report.

This was after disclosing "non-traditional" investments in oil and silver.

Over the years Berkshire has accumulated bonds as well as stocks. Berkshire got about $3 billion in fixed-income securities when it bought GEICO and Berkshire raised its stake in bonds significantly in 1997 and inherited a massive amount of bonds with the General Re acquisition of 1998.

Buffett made real money in Chrysler Financial, Texaco, Time Warner, WPPSS and RJR Nabisco bonds.

There have been bonds ranging from U.S. Treasury strips to Birmingham, Alabama, Industrial Water Board bonds and Scottsboro, Alabama, water and gas bonds.

He's got bonds from Los Angeles County to the Suffolk County, New York, sewer district; Cripple Creek, Texas, water and sewer revenue bonds to Utah Housing Authority bonds; Peoria, Illinois, economic development bonds to Massachusetts Turnpike Authority bonds.

And he has bonds ranging from $5,000 to millions of dollars in value. He has bonds ranging from less than a year to more than 20 years in maturity. He has bonds paying from 1% to 15%. But there was little bond buying between 1987 and 1992.

It may have been that Buffett's interest in run-of-the-mill bonds evaporated when convertible preferreds of his own making, such as in Salomon and Gillette, became available, or perhaps he thought interest rates were getting too low for bonds to be an attractive alternative to stocks.

Berkshire now has more than $31 billion in fixed-income investments.

According to *Forbes* (September 8, 1997), Buffett was buying a large amount of zero-coupon treasuries with maturities of 20 to 23 years.

Berkshire bought $10 billion face value of U.S. bonds for a little more than $2 billion, according to the *Wall Street Journal* (September 15, 1997). So give the *Journal* credit. Right on the story. A tad low on the amount.

If rates don't change from the time Berkshire bought them, they would pay about 7% although no actual interest payment is made during the life of the discounted bond.

Wall Street firms created zero-coupon bonds by separating the principal and interest portions of U.S. Treasury bonds. The investments are sold at deep discounts to their principal amount. They pay no interest over the life of the bond, only the principal amount at maturity.

Each year the cost basis for the bondholder is accreted (increased) for tax purposes. The accretion represents taxable income to the holder even though it has not been received. This is called "phantom income" since tax liability exists even though income has not actually been received.

Should a zero-coupon bond be held to maturity, the bondholder's cost basis would increase to par. Therefore, there would be no capital gain. A capital gain would occur if the investor sold the bond prior to maturity for more than the accreted basis. If sold for less than the accreted basis, the difference would be a capital loss.

Zeros are volatile, reacting to change in the course of interest rates, resulting in swings in their value. If rates rise, zero-coupon bonds fare poorly because investors don't receive interest payments to reinvest at new, higher rates. On the other hand, if interest rates fall, the locked in reinvestment level helps them outperform other fixed-income instruments.

A zero-coupon bond eliminates reinvestment risk because interest payments are not received by the investor but are automatically reinvested at the yield-to-maturity. As with any bond, they lose value if interest rates rise, but bonds are beautiful when rates fall in disinflationary and deflationary environments.

One would buy zeros if one thinks inflation is under control and interest rates likely to trend down.

Buffett wrote in Berkshire's 1997 Annual Report that he had sold, net of some purchases, about 5% of Berkshire's stocks. The sales were made "changing our bond-stock ratio moderately in response to the relative values that we saw in each market, a realignment we have continued in 1998."

With the 1998 second quarter earnings report, Berkshire announced that it had sold its entire position in long-term zero coupon bonds and that a substantial portion of its $864 million investment gain that quarter was due to the sale.

That's adult money. And nice work, if you can get it.

In the second quarter of 1999, Buffett moved about $10 billion from the cash position to the fixed-income position bringing the fixed-income position to more than $30 billion. No explanation was given as to what sort of fixed-income securities they were. Treasuries is one guess.

Berkshire's fixed-income investments include about $4 billion in Treasuries, more than $8 billion in obligations of state, municipality and political subdivisions, about $2 billion in obligations of foreign governments, more than $5 billion in corporate bonds, a small amount of preferred stocks and almost $10 billion in mortgage-backed securities.

Buffett hired two hedge fund managers from Dublin-based EuroPlus Alternative Investments to manage fixed-income investments. They were Daniel Donovan and Richard Grindon. (*Bloomberg News*, March 20, 2000)

The two now work with Mark Byrne at West End Capital which has London and Bermuda offices. Byrne, as previously mentioned, is also CEO of General Re Financial Products (GRFP) and is based at GRFP's London office.

West End Capital manages more than $800 million in net assets, mainly for Berkshire's subsidiaries.

75

THE SALOMON SAGA
A CITIGROUP STAKE

After a lifetime of denouncing Wall Street's demented short-term mentality, Buffett made a $700 million preferred stock investment in Salomon Inc on September 28, 1987.

"It's a huge commitment. We'll know in ten years whether it was a great idea," he said then. He was fortunate to allow himself such an un-Wall-Street-like time frame. The investment, at best, turned out so-so, not counting huge headaches. In 1997 Salomon was sold to Travelers Group which merged with Citicorp in 1998.

"Without borrowing, it pretty much empties the piggy bank for now," he told *The Wall Street Journal.* (September 30, 1987)

Buffett long had been a critic of Wall Street's short-term trading fixation as well as its excesses ranging from corporate jets to swanky dining rooms. So why Salomon? Why did Buffett invest in the heart of Wall Street? And why particularly in a firm widely known for aggressiveness and shrewd, hair-trigger trading?

"Why are we vocal critics of the investment banking business when we have a $700 million investment in Salomon? I guess atonement is probably the answer," he said at the Berkshire Annual Meeting in 1991.

The real answer may be that he got a sweet deal in a worldwide franchise. Salomon, founded in 1910, had been one of the largest and most profitable brokerage firms in the United States. In 1996 Salomon managed more than $310 billion in fixed-income offerings for issuers in 47 countries.

Before looking at Buffett's transaction with Salomon, let's examine the timing which, in hindsight, simply could not have been worse.

The stock market crash of 1987 was only three weeks away—the day the market would drop 508 points—or almost 23%—its worst single-day loss in modern times.

The crash sent almost all stocks nosediving. Brokerage stocks particularly were hit because of their cyclical nature and partly because overexpansion in the securities industry had knocked down margins. The crash triggered a lasting tailspin for brokerage stocks dragging

Salomon's stock price down with it.

Salomon's common stock was trading at about $32 a share when Buffett bought the preferred stock. After the crash, the common stock eventually sank to a low of $16 a share. (Called "S— Brothers" by some at that price).

Instead of buying Salomon stock, Buffett and then Salomon Chairman John Gutfreund (pronounced Good Friend) agreed that Berkshire would buy a newly issued preferred stock—a Salomon financial instrument that would pay Berkshire a 9% annual dividend.

Preferred stock is a hybrid investment, containing characteristics of both stocks and bonds.

Common stock is a security representing ownership in a company, and although common stockholders can benefit most if business is good, they assume the primary risk if the business goes sour.

Preferred stockholders, on the other hand, get dividends paid before any are paid to common stockholders. If the company goes under, a preferred stockholder also has a claim to the assets before a common stockholder.

Berkshire never lost a cent on its investment in Salomon even though Salomon common stock languished for years after Buffett's purchase. Thus, Berkshire was insulated, short of bankruptcy, through its preferred investment. Buffett has called such investments, "Treasury bonds with lottery tickets attached."

And Salomon's 9% dividend paid to Berkshire was largely exempt from corporate taxes because corporations don't have to pay taxes on 70% of their dividend income on preferred stocks.

Perhaps it was the attractiveness of the deal that triggered Buffett into making a move that could have been a severe miscalculation of upside potential. Berkshire shareholders were surprised. After all, they had listened to him deride Wall Street for years.

In any event, Buffett got into bed with Salomon and it literally caused Buffett some sleepless nights.

Gutfreund had to do some hard selling to the Salomon board to get it to bite on the deal clearly so favorable to Berkshire.

Salomon was under pressure from a takeover threat from Revlon Chairman Ronald Perelman in 1987. Perelman was trying to buy a 14% stake in Salomon stock held by Mineral Resources, a Bermuda-based company controlled by the South Africa Oppenheimer family who decided to sell its stake. Buffett got his investment and Perelman backed off. The Mineral Resources stake was repurchased by Salomon.

For this and his subsequent preferred stakes in Gillette, US Airways and Champion International, where there was a real or a perceived takeover threat, Buffett became known as a "White Knight," stepping in to save the takeover targets.

In Michael Lewis's *Liar's Poker*, (p. 227) an account of his bond trading days at Salomon, he quoted Gutfreund as saying that if Buffett's plan were rejected in favor of Perelman, he, Gutfreund, would resign.

"I never stated it as a threat. I was stating a fact," Lewis quoted Gutfreund telling a companion.

The book's most telling moment of the money madness and loose ways that would ultimately lead to the Salomon scandal in 1991, is Gutfreund, a cigar-smoking, gruff, hard-edged man, challenging his chief trader, John Meriwether (who later founded Long-Term Capital Management), to a hand of liar's poker, a game where a series of players each hold a dollar bill. Bidding begins over what serial numbers are held by the players until a point when all the players challenge a single player's bid.

The particular game—Lewis says it took place in early 1986—started when Gutfreund approached Meriwether for a million-dollar hand, but supposedly Meriwether—realizing a game against his boss was a no-win proposition—outbluffed Gutfreund by saying he'd play only for $10 million, at which point Gutfreund backed off saying, "You're crazy."

At Salomon, the incident was denied.

The buccaneer spirit at Salomon was exemplified by Gutfreund's description of a good trader as someone "ready to bite the ass off a bear." Tom Wolfe, author of *Bonfire of the Vanities*, did some of his research for the book at Salomon's trading floor, encountering there some "Masters of the Universe." (*New York Times*, September 30, 1997)

The high living of Gutfreund and his socialite wife, Susan, was publicized in articles describing an estimated $20 million fix-up of their $6 million duplex on New York's Fifth Avenue. They spent millions more on a home in Paris.

Buffett may have had second thoughts about Gutfreund along the way. A *Los Angeles Times Magazine* piece (February 16, 1992) said Buffett "hit the roof" in October, 1990, when Gutfreund came to a Salomon board of director's compensation committee with a plan to boost bonuses by $120 million at a time when Salomon was struggling.

Buffett asked Gutfreund to lower the figure, but Gutfreund countered with a request for $127 million. Buffett voted against the plan, but it passed anyway.

Even operationally, Salomon had a record of overexpansion, exorbitant bonuses, and an overly ambitious plan to invest in and occupy a dramatic new office tower at New York City's Columbus Circle that Mortimer Zuckerman hoped to build. Salomon decided to scrap its plans, causing it to forfeit about $100 million.

In February, 1991, Salomon moved from One New York Plaza, known for the football-sized trading rooms that Gutfreund roamed, to 7 World Trade Center.

A number of Salomon's investments had done poorly. Its forays into merchant banking using its own money for investments in leveraged buyouts of Revco and Southland, which wound up in bankruptcy proceedings, were lackluster. Finally, for all Salomon's worldwide business expertise and range of deep talent apparent from the gilt-edged résumés of its employees, Salomon hadn't done much for its shareholders. Its stock price had changed little from where it was a decade earlier although its book value tripled in that time, up from about $11 a share to about $50 a share.

Buffett has thrown a lot of business Salomon's way just on behalf of Berkshire. Berkshire's zero-coupon bond was underwritten by Salomon, and Salomon and Berkshire have traded huge amounts of securities back and forth.

In 1996 Berkshire (and its affiliates including GEICO) bought about $4 billion in securities from Salomon and sold $3.7 billion, paying fees of about $10.4 million. Berkshire and Salomon have done business for a long time. Salomon sold some debt for Berkshire in 1973 and conducted business with Berkshire even before that.

When Buffett needs a stockbroker, he calls Salomon.

On August 9, 1991, Salomon, a Wall Street powerhouse largely from trading government bonds, disclosed that it had uncovered "irregularities and rule violations" in connection with its bids at Treasury securities auctions, the most important of all financial markets. It's not the sort of thing that gets you votes for the vestry. The Salomon scandal was underway.

The firm had been buying more than its fair and legal share at auctions of Treasury securities, the bonds sold to finance the government's debt.

Salomon said bids were submitted in the names of firms which had not authorized Salomon to make them and that the 35% threshold—intended to keep one buyer from dominating the market—was in some instances deliberately breached. Although the firm itself revealed the infractions and suspended four employees, it was hardly out front with the disclosures, making them known only after the government was six weeks into an investigation of a "squeeze" in the May auction of two-year Treasury notes. A squeeze occurs when a group of buyers controls a disproportionately large amount of securities and forces other buyers to pay more for securities later, thus undermining fairness in the market. In this case, Salomon was investigated for "cornering," but was never charged with this.

A government probe was launched after competing firms complained that Salomon had corralled too big a piece of the $12.26 billion notes sold in May and then squeezed competitors by driving up prices. (*Wall Street Journal*, August 12, 1991)

But even though Salomon had time to think things over, the Gutfreund management team released information about only part of its maneuvers.

On August 14, the firm said that although top Salomon officials, including Gutfreund, President Thomas Strauss and Vice Chairman John Meriwether, knew in April of an earlier illegal bid, they had not reported it to authorities. Salomon had disclosed nothing until faced with a federal investigation. It was Munger who alerted Buffett that information was being withheld from the board. (*Fortune,* October 27, 1997)

Salomon also said it bought $1.1 billion in government securities from customers under questionable arrangements and further that a bogus bid for $1 billion of bonds was carried out inadvertently as a result of a botched practical joke!

Salomon officials later reported that Paul Mozer put a client up to making a false bid that he would later stop and then have the client call to complain that the order had not been filled. The client was to call and rattle a soon-to-retire saleswoman on whom Mozer was trying to play a joke. But the joke was on Mozer. Although Mozer crossed out the bid, a clerk did not understand that it was canceled and submitted it anyway. Some joke.

Early reaction to the scandal was summarized best by William Simon, former Treasury secretary and former Salomon partner: "Good God. I'll be damned. Good God. That can be my only reaction." (*Wall Street Journal*, August 15, 1991)

Within days Salomon's stock fell from $36 to $25 a share, eventually plummeting to a low of $20 a share in September, 1991. Its bonds plunged as credit agencies threatened lower ratings; some big investors ceased to do business with Salomon as many corporations gave their underwriting business to rival firms.

The Treasury Department yanked Salomon's status as a primary dealer in the Treasury market. However, hours later that fateful day of August 18, 1991 Salomon was allowed to retain its role as a primary dealer, but was temporarily suspended from submitting bids for its customers at Treasury auctions.

The New York Times lead story the next day began under the headlines: Treasury Punishes Salomon Brothers and then Relents—Buffett Now Chairman—Resignations and Dismissals, an Appeal to Brady, End Suspension of Firm: "In an extraordinary action, the Treasury Department yesterday suspended Salomon Brothers Inc., one of Wall Street's biggest trading and investment houses from bidding at Treasury auctions because of the scandal involving the firm's alleged bidding in that market. But hours later, the department largely reversed itself after a personal appeal to Nicholas F. Brady, the Treasury Secretary, by Warren E. Buffett, who was named chairman and chief executive officer of the scandal-torn firm at a dramatic weekend board meeting yesterday."

"In the four hours of suspense between the two actions [the Treasury's ban and partial reversal], Buffett struggled passionately to ward off a tragedy he saw threatening to unfold. In Buffett's opinion, the ban put Salomon...in sure danger of having immediately to file for bankruptcy. Even more important, he believed on that day, as he does now, that the collapse of Salomon would have shaken the world's financial system to its core."

"Buffett told Brady of his deep concerns, adding, 'Nick, this is the most important day of my life.'"

"Brady said, 'Don't worry, Warren, we'll get through this.'"

Of the final result of the Salomon investment, Buffett said "I'd say we hit a scratch single, but not before the count got to 0 and 2." (*Fortune*, October 27, 1997)

During the meeting about Salomon's fate, Fed Chairman Alan Greenspan said, "The trouble, unfortunately, is that what we can't do is suspend them temporarily as a primary dealer. It's like executing somebody technically and then resuscitating them." (*Wall Street Journal*, January 10, 1997)

Still a crisis swept the firm with investigations underway into every facet of its activities while lawsuits in droves were stamped in at the courthouse.

Gutfreund said he would resign, and a frantic call was placed to Buffett, "Mr. Clean," who offered to tackle the top job. He immediately flew to New York.

From that moment of management overhaul forward, Buffett

would be unknown no more. But that was hardly the point. Buffett had to face Salomon's life-threatening mess.

Gutfreund told a colleague that reading the *Wall Street Journal* story about top Salomon officials knowing about illegal bidding was like reading his obituary. (*Institutional Investor*, September, 1991) He called Buffett and said that he and Strauss were going to resign. Later that morning, Buffett called Gutfreund back and volunteered to head the firm on an interim basis. In the same interview, Buffett said:

"You won't believe this—because I don't look that dumb—but I volunteered for the job of interim chairman. It's not what I want to be doing, but it will be what I will be doing until it gets done properly."

> Salomon owed more money than any other institution in the United States, with the exception of Citicorp, the big bank...Salomon's total liabilities were just under $150 billion. Now $150 billion was roughly equal to the profits of all of the companies on the New York Stock Exchange that year...The problem about this $150 billion was that basically, it almost all came due within the next couple of weeks...so we were faced with the fact all over the world, because the money was owed all over the world, that people on that Friday and the following Monday were going to want us to pay back $140 odd billion or something close to it, which is not the easiest thing to do. (Buffett talk to University of Nebraska students, October 10, 1994)

Buffett faced the complex issues of appeasing investors and clients, dealing with criminal and civil investigators, and worrying about some new bomb exploding on his watch. But Buffett was the logical person to turn to, and got things off on the right foot when he quickly met with Salomon's managing directors at the World Trade Center, telling them that the firm's reputation for staying just within the bounds of the rules would *not* be acceptable. (*New York Times*, August 17, 1991) He told them he would be open, that the firm faced a huge management job in dealing with fines and litigation costs.

The story was covered by everyone including *Barron's* Alan Abelson, who took his usual satirical approach (August 19, 1991), saying, "The caretaker appointed to look after Salomon in the absence of Gutfreund and Strauss is an out-of-towner, from Omaha, Nebraska, to be exact, and he runs a textile company. But he's supposed to be a fast learner, so we've no doubt he'll pick up enough about the securities business while on the job to keep the traders from sneaking off to play paddle ball or catch the 3 p.m. showing of *Terminator 2.*"

Here's what Buffett did on the Sunday afternoon of August 18, 1991: 1) Accepted the resignations of Gutfreund, Strauss and Meriwether; 2) Fired government-bond trading chief Paul Mozer as well as Thomas Murphy; 3) Named Deryck C. Maughan, the former Tokyo-based chairman of Salomon Brothers Asia Ltd., chief operating officer, telling Maughan minutes before a press conference he was to be Salomon's CEO; 4) Successfully appealed to Treasury Secretary Nicholas Brady to partially lift an hours-old government suspension of Salomon trading in Treasury securities auctions.

"I had no idea," Maughan said at Borsheim's before the Berkshire Annual Meeting in 1994 when asked if he knew Buffett would pick him. "He called 12 of us in for 10 minutes each and asked each of us who should run the firm. I told him I was not a U.S. national and was not a trader.

"We got in an elevator. He punched a button and he said, 'Deryck, you're the one.' " Two minutes later they met with the press.

Maughan said Buffett immediately had to keep up his constant calls to Nicholas Brady and that he, Maughan, had to be on the trading floor supervising massive selling.

"We were selling out. Our CEO was gone," Maughan said as the firm faced a sudden loss of business and funding. Salomon even had quit trading its own paper.

Buffett and Maughan met with the press for about three hours August 18, 1991, saying the illegal trading first came to the attention of Salomon in April, when Mozer received a Xerox copy of a letter indicating the Treasury was aware of a problem in one of

(AP/Wide World Photos)

Buffett, left, and Deryck Maughan hold a press conference August 18, 1991, explaining Salomon's bond-trading scandal. Shortly before, Interim Chairman Buffett named Maughan chief operating officer telling him, "Deryck, you're the one."

its auctions. The letter from a federal regulator was sent to a customer whose name Salomon had used without authorization to make a bid.

Mozer approached Meriwether and "showed him a letter which was clearly going to lead to Mr. Mozer being in trouble," Buffett said.

Top management discussed the matter with its lawyers and determined that the government should be told, Buffett said, but it was not done.

"I cannot explain the subsequent failure to report," Buffett said, adding that he had long been an admirer of Gutfreund but that he was distressed by management's actions. "The failure to report is, in my view, inexplicable and inexcusable." Buffett and Gutfreund, on September 3, 1991, agreed not to talk to one another during the investigation.

Buffett pledged to root out the scandal and improve the firm's reputation. The next few days were unusually hectic, with the Soviet Union coup and its collapse in the several days following Buffett's press conference. The fast-paced events led to a photo mix-up at the Asbury Park (New Jersey) *Press,* which ran a purported photo of Gorbachev's momentary successor, Gennady Yanayev. Actually it was a photo of Buffett.

And Salomon itself was acting under intense pressure during the crisis. Once a reporter called to speak to Salomon's spokesman, Robert Baker, and was told, "I'll have Mr. Buffett call you." The reporter replied, "Gosh, that'd be great."

When Baker called back, he suddenly broke-off saying he'd have to hang up and call back. "Warren's on the line," he blurted. Later Baker said Buffett had set the company on a new path, even while working both from New York and Omaha. During the crisis, Buffett was in New York several days a week and then began to come about one or two days a week. "He's found he can run things from Omaha pretty well," Baker said.

"Warren has given the company its strategic direction...He has kept his focus on the regulators and the capital structure."

Buffett focused most of his attention on matters in Washington. "It's our belief that those who misbehaved are gone. New management dealt with that very swiftly. Warren has cleaned house. I see no reason for the government to shut us down...We are cooperating with the government in an unprecedented way. We are cooperating to a greater degree than in any case in the history of Wall Street," Baker added.

Salomon's business, he said, began rebounding with the return of such clients as the World Bank and the state of Massachusetts.

"Our bond underwriting is returning fast. We still have some trouble on some of the equity underwritings because of the two-, three-, four-month lead time. Some clients don't want to deal with the uncertainty for that long. This has to hurt us in getting some new business," Baker said. As for a *Wall Street Journal* story that Buffett stayed at the Plaza hotel and wore expensive suits, Baker said Buffett doesn't stay at the Plaza, that he stays at either Katharine Graham's apartment or at the Marriott hotel near the World Trade Center.

"He stays at the Marriott for $190 a night so he can walk to work," Baker said. Okay, said Baker, he has a couple of expensive suits.

(Photo courtesy of Salomon Inc)

Former Salomon Chairman Robert Denham

"They're not even tailored and he jokes that when he wears an expensive suit, he makes it look like a $300 suit."

As for staying at the Plaza, Buffett has stayed there in years past on spring trips to New York, largely because Mrs. Buffett liked to stay there, says Buffett's daughter, Susan.

She said he did not stay at the Plaza during the Salomon crisis. "He'd just as soon stay at Motel 6...He's been staying at either the Vista or the Marriott."

In subsequent days of the Salomon scandal, Buffett fired Salomon's top lawyer, Donald Feuerstein, and replaced him with Robert Denham, a 1971 Harvard Law School graduate who was the managing partner of the Los Angeles-based Munger, Tolles & Olson law firm founded by Charles Munger, Berkshire's vice chairman.

Buffett said at the Berkshire Annual Meeting in 1994 that he quickly called Robert Denham, living a peaceful life in California. "I told him I was in a mess." And he called Salomon's treasurer, John MacFarlane, who was competing in a triathlon. "Not a practice Charlie and I follow," Buffett quipped. MacFarlane now works for

Tutor Investments Corp.

Buffett described Denham, who was the top student in his freshman law class, as his first and only choice. For 17 years Denham had worked with Buffett on such Berkshire acquisitions as Scott Fetzer and such investments as American Express, Champion and Salomon itself. (*Business Week*, September 9, 1991)

Soon Buffett told the Salomon sales force, "It's my job to deal with the past. It's your job to maximize the future, and it can be a huge future."

"Everyone must be his own compliance officer. That means that everything you do can be put on the front page of the newspaper, and there will be nothing that cannot stand up to scrutiny," he added.

Buffett even accepted the resignation of Salomon's outside counsel—the Wachtell, Lipton, Rosen & Katz law firm—a highly regarded firm that had represented Salomon for years, and had helped Gutfreund bring in Buffett as an investor in 1987. (*Wall Street Journal*, September 3, 1991)

As for the number of lawsuits the firm faced, Buffett later said, "I may be the American Bar Association's Man of the Year before the year is over."

Buffett slashed bonuses, making them payable largely in stock rather than cash, reduced debt and had every Treasury auction bid cross-checked at least twice.

He told Salomon's Phibro Energy unit to cut all ties with Marc Rich & Co., a major client of Phibro's, saying Salomon wasn't going to do business with Marc Rich, a U.S. fugitive.

Amidst the crisis, what about Berkshire?

"Berkshire works pretty well, some say, without me," Buffett said. "It really is a lot less complicated operation than Salomon. I've always said I could run (Berkshire) working five hours a week. Maybe we'll test that. But I hope not for too long." Added Buffett, "I was practically looking for a job" when the crisis broke. That's because Berkshire's managers run things so well for him.

"The only thing I am is an addressee on the envelope when they send me the check," he added. "...I can spend whatever time is needed...If I quit thinking about this, I'd probably just have a big hole up there."

Buffett's selection of Maughan quickly took hold as he rose to the occasion, calling for integrity by all at the firm. And Maughan began picking up Buffett's lead on humor.

Maughan pointed out he was not from Salomon's trading culture and there was no way he could be. "You cannot graft the head of an investment banker onto the body of a trader and not get tissue rejection," Maughan said.

Soon Buffett was testifying before Congressional committees. On September 4, 1991, he testified before the House Energy and Commerce finance subcommittee; at the end of the session subcommittee chairman Edward Markey asked him to sum up his recommendations in one minute.

"I'm not sure I can drag it out for one minute," Buffett replied. "Integrity is paramount."

Here's what he told Congress on September 11, 1991:

> A week ago when I testified before the House subcommittee, I began by apologizing for the misdeeds of Salomon employees that have brought us here. Normally I would not wish to be repetitious. But in my opinion this particular message bears repetition many times over. The nation has a right to expect its rules and laws to be obeyed, and Salomon did not live up to this obligation.
>
> Our customers have a right also to expect that their names will not be drawn into some underhanded scheme. So to you and them and the American people I apologize on behalf of more than 8,000 honest and decent Salomon employees as well as myself.
>
> Mr. Chairman, I also want to thank you for holding these hearings in such a timely manner. You and the American people have a right to know exactly what went on at Salomon Brothers and I am here to tell you the full truth as I know it to date. When and if I learn more it will immediately be disclosed to the proper authorities.
>
> Many decades ago J.P. Morgan stated the objective of his firm: 'First-class business run in a first-class way.' I have yet to hear of a better goal. It will guide me at Salomon Brothers and I invite you to measure our future conduct by that yardstick.

Salomon took out an unusual two-page newspaper ad October 29, 1991, in the *Wall Street Journal, The New York Times* and *The Washington Post*, at a cost of about $600,000, running Buffett's letter to shareholders as well as the firm's newly shrunken balance sheet.

It was solid good news for Salomon, whose stock price rose 8% that day, and shortly thereafter the World Bank, after a three-month suspension, resumed business ties with Salomon, a major plus for the firm.

But even under Buffett, Salomon still frequently had its snakebit days. On March 25, 1992, a clerk mistook a customer's order to sell $11 million of stock as an order to unload 11 million shares, some $500 million. The huge sale in the closing minutes of the trading day wiped out a 12-point rally on the Dow, which closed instead with a one-point loss.

But remember, Buffett said he'd be forgiving of honest mistakes. The clerk was not fired. Buffett said it was an honest mistake; in fact, Buffett asked that he not be told the clerk's name.

At the three-hour Salomon Annual Meeting in May, 1992, corporate gadfly Evelyn Y. Davis asked Buffett how he could justify charging Salomon $158,000 for his corporate jet flights from Omaha to New York during the crisis.

Buffett replied that he was working for $1 a year for Salomon. "I work cheap, but I travel expensive," he said.

When she asked him whether the company's $25 million in legal fees to deal with the scandal was too much, Buffett deadpanned, "I would be delighted to have you negotiate with them, Evelyn. And I think the mere mention of that would be enough to induce a little moderation." On May 20, 1992, Salomon reached a $290 million settlement with the government.

Salomon agreed to pay $190 million in fines and forfeitures relating to the cheating in the Treasury auctions, and another $100 million fund was established by Salomon to compensate victims who lost money as a result of the wrongdoing.

As part of the settlement, Salomon was suspended from trading with the Federal Reserve for a two-month period ending August 1, 1992. Also, the Treasury Department said sanctions imposed on Salomon would be lifted, allowing the firm to resume submitting bids for customers. The settlement was one of the largest ever for wrongdoing in the securities industry, but the good news for Salomon was that it escaped criminal charges.

"We believe," Buffett said, "that the intense regulatory and investigative focus on Salomon has ended. We can now move forward to show that high ethical standards and meaningful profits are not only compatible objectives, but ones that can reinforce each other."

"I believe Salomon would have gone under without Warren Buffett," said Steve Forbes, head of the Forbes publishing empire and a Republican presidential candidate in 1996 and 2000. "There is no question he saved it."

That view is supported by someone in the midst of the crisis, Don Howard, Salomon's chief financial officer who oversaw the sale of

$50 billion in assets and a total balance sheet restructuring.

"I never thought, 'We aren't going to make it'...I did wonder how in the hell we were going to get through." *(CFO,* March, 1992)

Howard said if the firm had replaced Gutfreund from within, it might not have survived.

"Warren's reputation gave the market confidence," said Howard, adding, "He's incisive, he knows what he wants, he understands very quickly, he goes to the essence of the problem very quickly."

For years people had asked, "Who's Warren Buffett?" Now the world knew. In the end Buffett really did save Salomon.

He ousted the old management and overhauled the firm with a new management—emphasizing ethics, openness and compliance rather than risk-taking and bravado.

Overseeing Robert Denham's legal team in its strenuous negotiations with the government, Buffett managed to guide Salomon, against heavy odds, by avoiding criminal penalties that could have brought the firm to its knees.

Indeed, Salomon—while settling civil matters for $290 million—was able to keep criminal charges at bay in part because it fully cooperated with government investigators.

Late in 1993 Mozer pleaded guilty to two counts of making false statements about two illegal $3 billion bids at a 1991 Treasury auction. Mozer's fine and sentence seemed light to Buffett: "Mozer's paying $300,000 and is sentenced to prison for four months. Salomon's shareholders—including me—paid $290 million, and I got sentenced to ten months as CEO." *Fortune,* January 10, 1994)

"If he had not repositioned the firm, he would not have been able to get anything in the negotiations with the government," said Omaha stockbroker George Morgan.

Buffett's impeccable reputation helped smooth potentially acrimonious talks with the Treasury Department, the SEC and the Justice Department.

Taking a more conservative fiscal stance, Buffett reduced Salomon's balance sheet by selling about $50 billion in assets, lowering Salomon's exposure to huge borrowings. His message was that ultra-easy access to funding often leads to undisciplined decision-making.

Buffett has pointed out that Salomon's finances are extraordinary and subject to great volatility with market fluctuations. The balance sheet of $170 billion can change dramatically—a one-tenth percentage point change in market conditions is a $170 million change on Salomon's financial statements.

(Fred R. Conrad /New York Times Pictures)

Former Salomon Brothers CEO Deryck Maughan on the firm's equity trading floor. He's now a top executive at Citigroup.

Slashing bonuses, Buffett set up fairer compensation standards. He restructured Salomon's stock and bond trading units, cutting back on stock trading and moving the firm back to its bond-trading roots, the source of its prominence.

He assuaged clients, employees, shareholders and the government itself, asking all to look for a new Salomon, setting the highest standards in its business dealings. Here he teaches us that good profits and good behavior go hand in hand.

Salomon had learned an expensive lesson but was ready to move forward as both an ethical and profitable company, as those elements should complement and reinforce one another.

Buffett kept his pledge about staying on with the firm until the investigations were completed. Better yet, he kept his pledge about turning the firm around and rebuilding its reputation.

"We have managed to preserve a firm with a proud history and promising future," he wrote Salomon shareholders. "You have our pledge that we will conduct our business in the future so as to merit your continued trust."

Along the way, Buffett had setbacks. There were many defections from the firm, and there was some grousing about Buffett's not wanting to play near the edge of the court. There was kidding about his "Jimmy Stewart" ways, his supposed naiveté about Wall Street's quick-buck ways.

But in the end the mild-mannered, straight-arrow, determined Midwesterner had come to town and put a stop to Salomon's brash,

cut-corners mentality. The emphasis would be on solid business relationships and understandings—not on rigging Treasury market bids
or hiding wrongdoing. Buffett was able to bring about a corporate
culture metamorphosis at Salomon by imposing his values of openness and fair-mindedness. As a result, Salomon righted itself and its
stock steadily rebounded.

Buffett believes you shouldn't cut corners. You should do things
simply, ethically, and without a lot of loud talk. You should do
things in a way that would not be embarrassing if you appeared on
page one of a newspaper. You should try to be a good guy.

"He demonstrated that an honest person could come in and clean
up Wall Street's ways. He showed that honesty, hard work, good relationships, and openness are good—that honesty works," George
Morgan said. "That *Liar's Poker* stuff scares me and that's what the
world perceived those guys as being...He put in a compensation plan
that rewards honest money-making for the firm—not money just
because you are there or are generating a lot of activity."

When Buffett stepped down, he named Deryck Maughan to head
Salomon Brothers.

There was much speculation about who Buffett would name as
chairman of the parent firm, Salomon Inc. But Buffett's "sole recommendation" for the job was Robert Denham, the lawyer who
had served Buffett so well during the Salomon crisis.

Denham was certainly the person to oversee the remaining lawsuits against the firm, and Buffett said Denham's job—exactly in line
with Buffett's philosophy of running things—would include evaluating the performance of the Salomon units, setting compensation
for top executives, ensuring legal compliance, allocating capital and
avoiding undue risk.

Having imposed boundaries on a wayward firm he had reined in,
Buffett returned to Omaha to carry out his duties for Berkshire.

At Salomon's Annual Meeting in 1993, Denham addressed
Buffett's $1 pay, saying that on a prorated basis Buffett was due 79
cents, but Buffett merited a dollar anyway saying, "given pay for performance, and in light of our belief in pay for performance, I think
we should award him the whole dollar."

Buffett replied, "Bob may look at this as pay for performance, but
I look at it as interest for late payment. Twenty-one cents for four
months is 80% interest, which is a rate I extend only to my best
credits."

At the Salomon Annual Meeting in 1993, Denham presented
Buffett his salary for saving Salomon, a $1 bill encased in Plexi-glass.
Chief Financial Officer Don Howard said, "Don't think you don't

have to pay taxes on it, just because it's in Plexi-glass."

Two years to the day after the Salomon scandal broke, Berkshire announced it planned to raise its stake in Salomon. The plan was to boost it to 15%, up from the 14.3% it holds by way of the preferred stock investment. And Berkshire announced it was seeking clearance from federal regulators to allow it to buy up to 24.99% of Salomon. Permission was granted.

Under the Hart-Scott-Rodino Act, institutional investors must get clearance before buying more than 15% of a company for investment purposes.

Forbes (October 18, 1993) reported that Buffett waited as long as he did to boost his stake because he felt it wasn't fair to buy more shares when he was involved in Salomon's turnaround.

Buffett later lifted his Salomon's stake to slightly above 20%. That gave him a tax break on his Salomon preferred investment. But Salomon stock spent a lot of 1994 declining. "The move was not my most brilliant investment to date," Buffett said. *(Forbes,* December 5, 1994)

Indeed, Salomon Chairman Robert Denham began the 1994 Annual Report saying: "Your Company's results were awful." Salomon had been hit by a world-wide bond market crash.

In 1996 word came that Buffett would not convert his preferred stock into common stock. Instead he took $140 million in cash and said:

> I am making a single decision about whether I want to put $140 million into Salomon common stock at $38 today or whether there is something else I would rather have Berkshire do with the money.
>
> Every day the stock market offers Berkshire an option to buy shares of Coca-Cola, Gillette, Salomon or thousands of other companies. So far this year, Berkshire has not exercised this 'market' option to buy shares of any of the three mentioned companies (including Salomon when it was trading below $38).
>
> Obviously, the fact that Berkshire has not exercised its market option to buy more Coca-Cola or Gillette does not mean that I am negative on these companies nor should that interpretation be placed upon the non-exercise of a 'company' option to purchase more Salomon common shares.

In 1996 Berkshire converted its slice of the preferred stock into Salomon common stock. Still Buffett left his options open. Berkshire said at some future time it might sell some Salomon common stock. In late 1996 Berkshire issued $440 million of 5-year exchangeable notes—Berkshire notes exchangeable into Salomon common stock.

It was a way to get cash up front for a portion of his investment in Salomon. Berkshire had planned to issue $400 million of notes, but investor demand pushed it up to $500 million. The notes amount to an insurance policy on Buffett's decision to commit into Salomon's common shares. They would let him bail out of some of his Salomon stock in three years and have cash instead.

Buffett said at Berkshire's Annual Meeting in 1997: "It's a way of taking the capital out of that block of stock at a very low interest cost to use elsewhere while we take a limited position of the upside in the Salomon stock. We just decided... that we might have good opportunities at some point to use the money. And we thought that raising the money at a current cost of a little over 1% and a cost to maturity of 3%—and we think the actual cost is likely to be closer to 1%—made sense."

If Salomon (now a unit of Citigroup) stock is trading above the notes' conversion price of $54.47 in 1999, Buffett could choose to reduce his stake to 10.4% based on full conversion of his preferred holdings, through the exchange of stock for notes. (*Wall Street Journal*, December 3, 1996)

Buffett said: "I feel that Salomon has made a great deal of progress since I was looking at the decision a year ago." Salomon rebounded, but never fully recovered from the bond trading scandal.

Buffett's ultimate decision about his Salomon stake came in 1997 when he sold it to Travelers and swapped Salomon stock for Travelers stock. Travelers and Citicorp merged in 1998.

The largest shareholder of Citicorp is Saudi Arabian Prince Alwaleed Bin Talal. Buffett once wrote Prince Alwaleed: "In Omaha, I'm known as the 'Alwaleed of America'—quite a compliment." (*Fortune*, December 6, 1999)

However, in Berkshire's 1998 Annual Report there was no listing of Citigroup in investments worth more than $750 million and later reports indicated that all Berkshire's Travelers stock had been sold.

But reports on February 14, 2000 showed that Berkshire owned about 8 million shares of Citigroup. It was not clear whether this was a new purchase or possibly the result of a holdover from a slice of Solomon preferred stock that Berkshire once owned.

Don Keough, Coca-Cola's former president and Buffett's friend, has said the Salomon crisis "measured the man more than any other event." (MSNBC, April 7, 2000)

76
THE GILLETTE COMPANY
LOSING ITS EDGE

"He's glad there are more people growing hair on their face," says one Berkshire employee. After all, it has to be shaved off. From a Berkshire view, shaving should be done with a Gillette razor. Twice a day! The stock symbol for The Gillette Company is G, but it once was "GS" for Gillette Safety Razor Company. Some suggest it was for a Good Shave.

Every day, more than 1.2 billion people around the world use a Gillette.

"It's pleasant to go to bed every night knowing there are 2.5 billion males in the world who have to shave in the morning... Gillette was invented almost 100 years ago. These nations are upscaling the blade. So the dollars spent on Gillette products will go up," Buffett told *Forbes*. (October 18, 1993)

"There are 20 to 21 billion razor blades used in the world a year. 30% of those are Gillette, but 60% by value are Gillette. They have 90% market shares in some countries—in Scandinavia and Mexico. Now, when something has been around as long as shaving and you find a company that has both that kind of innovation, in terms of developing better razors all the time, plus the distribution power, and the position in people's minds... You know, here's something you do every day—for $20 (per year) you get a terrific shaving experience. Now men are not inclined to shift around when they get that kind of situation." (The University of North Carolina, Center for Public Television, 1995)

Berkshire's nick-free investment in Gillette —until the sting of profit warnings in 1999—is a direct result of Buffett's voracious reading of annual reports.

Buffett once told reporter Sue Baggarly of WOWT-TV in Omaha, (October 14, 1993) that he buys 100 shares of many companies. He does it for the purpose of getting the annual reports on time, "not lost at some brokerage house."

At home in his favorite reading chair one night, Buffett was looking through the 1988 Gillette Annual Report, when it occurred to him Gillette could use more capital. "It was my thought that they might be interested in a big investment in their shares because they had used up all their capital in repurchasing shares," Buffett has said. (*Cutting Edge*, Gordon McKibben, p. 225)

He checked the list of directors, called one (Joe Sisco, who served with Buffett on GEICO's board), and asked if he might talk with management about an investment.

Buffett created the investment by proposing to Sisco, "an equity issue that might make sense." (*Business Week*, August 7, 1989)

Sisco had served as undersecretary for political affairs in the Ford administration and had negotiated the Egypt-Israel ceasefire of 1970. He later served as chancellor and president of American University in Washington D.C. (*Cutting Edge*, Gordon McKibben, p. 225)

Sisco immediately got in touch with then Gillette Chairman Colman Mockler and a few days later Mockler, returning from a business trip to Mexico, landed in Omaha. Buffett picked him up and drove him to the Omaha Press Club for a lunch of hamburgers, Cokes and an ice cream dessert. "We hit it off, a couple of Midwestern boys. I liked him, the chemistry was good." (p. 226) Buffett suggested a preferred stock investment. "I do know that I told him, 'any amount between $300 million and $750 million, and he could pick the number, whatever he felt was appropriate.' " (p. 227) Negotiations ensued.

"Gillette had in the summer of 1989 a higher long-run value than its low market price. Looking at Gillette's consistent earning power, good cash flow, its management in place, and its everyday products, such as razors and blades and pens, it would have been hard for Warren Buffett to miss that Gillette was a real opportunity for his investment arm, Berkshire Hathaway." (*Resisting Hostile Takeovers: The Case of Gillette*, Rita Ricardo-Campbell, p. 208)

Ricardo-Campbell said Gillette's board was happy to accept Buffett's investment, but the terms remained to be negotiated. Buffett and Mockler began talks, found they liked one another, but Mockler didn't like Buffett's initial proposal. Final negotiations between Berkshire's Vice Chairman Charles Munger and lawyers for Gillette's board took place and then an agreement was reached between Buffett and Mockler. (*Resisting Hostile Takeovers: The Case of Gillette*, Rita Ricardo-Campbell, p. 211)

In July 1989 when Buffett invested $600 million in a preferred stock stake in Gillette, which was subsequently converted into an 11% common stock stake, Buffett said, "Gillette is synonymous with highly successful, international consumer marketing and is exactly the sort of business in which we like to invest for the long term."

With about 70% of its sales and profits from overseas, Gillette is a global firm that offers personal care products. It's the dominant producer of razors and blades for men and women worldwide. The company for decades has been known for its huge cash flow mainly derived from its razor and blade business. The company has 54 facilities in 20 countries and does business in more than 200 countries.

Gillette's edge is sharper because it is the world leader in selling toothbrushes and oral care appliances. It claims 22% of the global toothbrush market. It offers electric shavers and Oral-B oral care products. As a major force in providing grooming aids, Gillette is also looking sharp. The company sells toiletries and offers stationery products, and correction fluids (Liquid Paper).

Gillette bought the Liquid Paper Corporation in 1979. First named Mistake Out, it came into existence from the kitchen of a young Dallas divorcee, Bette Nesmith. She worked as an executive secretary to support her nine-year-old son, Michael, who a decade later achieved stardom as one of The Monkees (*"Hey, hey. We're The Monkees"*) in a TV sitcom about a rock group of the same name. (*Cutting Edge*, Gordon McKibben, p. 83) Michael Nesmith is founder and owner of Pacific Arts, a video-distribution company in Los Angeles.

Ms. Nesmith sat down at her kitchen table one evening and mixed up a watery paint which would "white out" her mistakes. Nesmith had dabbled in art and knew that artists corrected their mistakes by painting over them with white paint. She tried the technique to correct her typing errors, and this led to the development of Mistake Out. Later she went to work for IBM but was still absorbed at night with her fledgling company. One day she signed an important document dictated by her boss with the name "Mistake Out Company" rather than IBM. She was fired on the spot. That's okay because her company grew into a typewriter ribbon and correction fluid business which Gillette purchased and at her death, she left $25 million to her son. (p. 84-85)

Gillette owns Paper Mate and Waterman pens, and in 1993 it bought privately held Parker Pen Holdings of Britain (the sole supplier of pens to the Queen since 1962) for $561 million. Parker, which offers mid-priced lines of writing instruments, complements Gillette's low-price Paper Mate and its luxury Waterman lines. The Parker purchase made Gillette the world's largest writing instruments seller. But pen sales have slumped in recent years and in early 2000 Gillette called on Merrill Lynch to find a buyer for its writing products business. And Gillette retained J.P. Morgan to see what to do about its Braun unit.

Its distribution network sets Gillette apart. "Think there's little synergy between an Oral-B toothbrush, a stick of Right Guard deodorant and a Paper Mate ballpoint pen? Look closer. They all share distribution channels. That means Gillette can keep costs low by warehousing and shipping products together." (*Financial World*, April 8, 1996)

(Photo courtesy of The Gillette Company)

Former Gillette Chairman and CEO Alfred Zeien

(Photo courtesy of The Gillette Company)

Michael Hawley, Gillette's Chairman and CEO, has been with Gillette since 1961.

As with his investment in Coca-Cola, Buffett again picked a U.S. domiciled company running a huge overseas business, from its Boston headquarters.

Gillette Chairman Colman C. Mockler, Jr., a Harvard Business School graduate who took over management of Gillette in 1975, died of a heart attack in Gillette headquarters on January 25, 1991. Mockler had fended off takeover attempts and stabilized Gillette after a brief period of negative net worth in the late 1980s; he lived to see the extraordinary success of its magical Sensor razor.

Forbes, in its February 4, 1991, issue that arrived at subscribers' homes the day Mockler died, carried a cover picture of Mockler reaching the top of the mountain against competitors, in a cover story highlighting Gillette's many achievements.

Buffett has referred to Mockler as one of those people we "like, admire and trust." Mockler had planned to retire at the end of 1991 and Alfred Zeien (pronounced Zane) had been named president. Zeien, a graduate of Webb Institute of Naval Architecture, who designed and built his new home on Cape Cod, took over Gillette's top job shortly after Mockler's death. Gillette's president was Michael Hawley who became chairman and CEO in 1999 when Zeien retired.

Gillette executives check the competition to be sure of keeping their dominant market share. Actually, every day at a Gillette plant in South Boston, 200 men lather up and shave, evaluating razors of the future.

Mockler told shareholders in April 1990 of Gillette's push into the former Soviet Union, "The potential of the Soviet project is encouraging on a number of fronts. First, the large and growing market is estimated at about two billion blades per year. The Soviet Union currently imports about one billion blades, almost half of which this year will be supplied from seven Gillette international plants—in Argentina, Brazil, Colombia, Egypt, India, Mexico and Morocco.

"Secondly, from the outset of the talks, the Soviet negotiating team has been aware of Gillette's position that profit remittance from the operation would have to be paid in hard currency. The ongoing joint team effort between the Soviets and Gillette will verify the means to accomplish this.

"With the dramatic changes in Eastern Europe opening up good long-term growth possibilities, Gillette International also is exploring opportunities to expand its previously limited presence there." For example, Gillette owns an 80% interest in Wizamet, S.A., a leading razor blade maker in Poland.

Gillette has a joint venture in the former Soviet Union for razor blade operations.

It is making inroads into a number of emerging countries as well by following an astute strategy. As was mentioned in *Financial World* (March 2, 1993), Gillette introduces its oldest U.S. technologies and then upgrades the market gradually by rolling out its newer products. The equipment used in producing these products is already depreciated on its books, and hence the setup costs are very low, allowing the new operations to be profitable within a short period of time. And the inroads sliced into these markets by the razors may lead to piggybacks in the company's other businesses.

Gillette was founded in 1901 as The American Safety Razor Company by King C. Gillette, an entrepreneur and dreamer of a social utopia, whose safety razor was a landmark invention. The company began operations in an office located over a fish market on the Boston waterfront. (*Resisting Hostile Takeovers: The Case of Gillette*, Rita Ricardo-Campbell, p. 74) The company became Gillette Safety Razor Company in 1904.

Gillette's founder made business history by inventing the disposable razor blade and making a fortune on replacements. He was working for Crown Cork & Seal as a salesman and dabbling with inventions when his boss, William Painter, advised him: "Why don't you invent something that is thrown away, once used, and customers will have to come for more?"

It is said some men do their best thinking while shaving. Apparently this was true for 40-year-old Gillette because while shaving one morning in 1895, the idea of a razor with disposable blades popped into his head.

Gillette later described how the whole idea of a small, thin piece of steel came to him:

> ... the way the blade could be held in a holder: the idea of sharpening the two opposite edges of the thin piece of steel: the clamping plates for the blade, with a handle halfway between the two edges of the blade. All this came more in pictures than conscious thought, as though the razor were already a finished thing, and held before my eyes. I stood there before that mirror in a trance of joy. My wife was visiting Ohio, and I hurriedly wrote to her. 'I've got it! Our fortune is made!' Fool that I was, I knew little about razors and nothing about steel, and I could not foresee the trials and tribulations I was to pass through before the razor was a success. But I believed in it with all my heart. (*The Book of Business Anecdotes*, Peter Hay, p. 269)

In 1903, Gillette's firm began selling the Gillette safety razor and 20 blades for $5. Its annual sales in 1904 were 91,000 razors and 124,000 blades. (*Resisting Hostile Takeovers: The Case of Gillette*, Rita Ricardo-Campbell, p. 46) Gillette grew into a multi-national company well before World War I.

In 1926, Gillette said: "There is no other article for the individual use so universally known or widely distributed. In my travels, I have found it on the most northern town in Norway and in the heart of the Sahara Desert."

For all his success, Gillette died broke in 1932 as a result of poor investments and debts in the 1920s.

By 1960, the firm developed a way to apply a silicone coating to the blade edge, vastly improving shaving quality.

Gillette was riding high on its new Sensor razor—the world's first razor that continuously senses and automatically adjusts to contours of the face. The Sensor features twin blades that are individually mounted and "float" on tiny springs. The revolutionary Sensor razor was launched in January, 1990, hyped by $3 million worth of ads that claimed Gillette is "The Best A Man Can Get." The ads were first aired during the 1990 Super Bowl. (The company has been known for its "Cavalcade of Sports" advertising campaign and its efforts to reach men have included ads in connection with boxing events and sponsorship of World Cup soccer.)

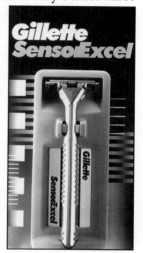

(Photo courtesy of The Gillette Company)

Gillette's SensorExel

Gillette's two major razor factories in South Boston and Berlin were running seven-day weeks and three shifts a day. (*Resisting Hostile Takeovers: The Case of Gillette*, Rita Ricardo-Campbell, p. 66)

By October, 1991, Gillette had made its one billionth Sensor replacement cartridge. In its history, Gillette has made more than 325 billion blades. The first billion were produced between 1901 and 1917. The Sensor captured 9% of the U.S. razors and blades market in 1990 and more than 15% by the end of 1991. Now Sensor and the new SensorExcel shaving system introduced in 1993 account for hundreds of millions of razors and billions of blades sold, enough to give Gillette 68% of the U.S. market in wet shaving. Schick has about 16%, Bic about 9% and American Safety Razor has about 6%. Gillette has about 70% of the female market.

Sensor for Women was introduced in 1992 when for the first time Gillette designed a product solely for women.

The Sensor was 13 years in preparation and cost about $300 million—$200 million in research, engineering and tooling and another $100 million for advertising. Carrying the code name "The Flag" (acronym for "floated angle geometry"), the Sensor was developed at Gillette's south Boston factory behind eight-foot walls.

The project was peaking in 1988 just when Coniston Partners was waging a proxy fight for the company.

To speed things along Gillette executive Donald Chaulk rounded up a nine-person crisis team of product designers, R&D people and engineers. "I put them away and said, 'This is your life. Let us know when you finish it.' " (*Financial World*, January 8, 1991)

Before the Sensor was introduced, top executives were using it for a smooth, clean shave. But they left it at home when they traveled.

The Sensor launch was so successful that Gillette was able to delay some advertising costs while production caught up with demand.

The Sensor has been a big hit, and as the world's economies become more linked, Gillette's value as the leading brand name in razors can only rise. Gillette has won more than 700 million shavers around the world from its operations in 200 countries. Gillette gets $7 of every $10 that the North American man spends for blades and razors.

Gillette's constant barrage of cutting-edge products includes deodorants, antiperspirants, shave creams, hair sprays, shampoos, conditioners, home permanents and styling aids.

1999 was the sixth consecutive year in which at least 40% of Gillette's sales came from products launched within the previous five years, according to Gillette's 1999 Annual Report. In 1999 Gillette launched its Oral-B Cross Action toothbrush.

Technology inclined Zeien says: "Good products come out of market research. Great products come out of market research. Great products come from R&D. And blockbusters are born out of the lab at the same time people want it." (*Fortune*, October 14, 1996)

The company claims about a fifth of the U.S. deodorant market with its Right Guard, Dry Idea and Soft & Dri brands, second behind giant Procter & Gamble.

Gillette's Braun small household products and electric shaver lines have been among international leaders over the years, but in recent years sales have faltered. Braun is the top marketer of electric shavers in Germany and is among the leaders in Europe, North America and Japan. Braun's Flex Control electric razor was the first pivoting swivel-headed electric razor. Gillette bought the Braun unit in 1967 for only $68 million.

After fending off a series of major takeover attempts in three years—three by Revlon's chieftain Ron Perelman in 1986 and one by now-defunct Coniston Partners in 1988, Gillette restructured. The workforce was reduced by 8% and under-performing operations were sold. To escape the takeovers, Gillette bought back almost 30% of its common stock, ballooning its debt from $436 million to nearly $2 billion. It has been paying that down quickly.

Although Gillette's balance sheet for a while looked like that of an LBO, Gillette paid down debt because of its superior cash flow and the help of Berkshire's $600 million investment.

Buffett's privately arranged transaction was for $600 million worth of Gillette's 8¾% convertible preferred stock. The stock was convertible after two years into 12 million shares at $50 a share, with the stock trading at about $41 a share at the time. If not converted, the preferred stock would have been required to be redeemed by Gillette within 10 years.

"One thing changed quickly when Buffett joined the Gillette board. Coke replaced Pepsi at Gillette cafeterias and vending machines around the world." (*Cutting Edge*, Gordon McKibben, p. 231)

Gillette enjoyed strong gains in earnings throughout the 1990s, but as with many multi-national companies in 1998, it suffered a year of flat sales.

Buffett said that the Gillette preferred investment would be the best of Berkshire's preferred category of investments. He was right.

Newsday columnist Allan Sloan, who has followed Buffett's career off and on since Buffett was buying (and selling) Detroit bank stocks some 20 years ago, argued that Buffett's stake in Gillette was immediately worth about $40 million more than Buffett paid for it, although a Gillette spokesman disagreed.

Sloan said:

> The stock bought by Buffett's Berkshire Hathaway Inc., carries a dividend of 8.75% a year, and he can trade $50 worth of it for one share of Gillette common stock. In other words, he agreed to pay "a conversion premium" of 8⅜ a share over the 41⅝ that regular investors were paying for Gillette at the time the deal was negotiated.
>
> But look. Buffett is getting 4⅜ a year in dividend income (the 8.75% interest times $50) for each Gillette share he controls. The holder of a share of Gillette common stock gets a dividend of only 96 cents a year. So, while Buffett has agreed to pay a premium of $8.375 a share for Gillette, he gets an extra $3.415 a year in dividend income ($4.375 minus 96 cents) while he's waiting. Work it out, and in less than 2½ years, the extra dividends that Buffett will receive make up for the premium he has agreed to pay.
>
> You still with me? Now watch. In the arcane world of convertible securities, three and a half years is the norm for breaking even in a security such as this Gillette convertible. Run the numbers through Gillette's black box, which the company graciously did for me, and you'll find that to reach

the break-even point in three and a half years, Buffett would have had to pay 53¼ a share, rather than 50. That's a 7% difference. Now, multiply that by $600 million, and Buffett is $42 million ahead...

Sloan reported that Buffett and Gillette agreed with the math, but not the interpretation.

"Gillette claims that certain aspects of the stock—the fact that Gillette can call it in for early redemption, that Gillette has the right of first refusal to buy the stock should Buffett decide to sell, and other arcana—offset the relatively high dividend and relatively low conversion price." He reports that Buffett told him, "We thought we made a good investment or we wouldn't be in it," and noted that Gillette was getting his services. "Charlie and I agree to work on the company for 10 years. We don't charge a fee, we don't even bill for transportation services to come to board meetings."

Gillette redeemed Berkshire's preferred stock investment of $600 million in 1991 and Berkshire converted its stake into 12 million shares of Gillette stock, about 11% of the stock. With a 2-for-1 stock split in 1991, Berkshire had 24 million shares and with a 2-for-1 split in 1995, it had 48 million shares. And with a 2-for-1 split in 1998, Berkshire owned 96 million shares.

Gillette's stock in the past 10 years has given a smooth average annual return of 29%.

Meanwhile Gillette focused on its international blade business, making inroads in China, India, Poland, the former Soviet Union, Turkey and Latin America. In 1995 Gillette bought Thermoscan Inc, of San Diego, California, a marketer of infrared ear thermometers which was merged into Gillette's Braun unit based in Germany.

Gillette employs about 40,000 people, most of whom work outside the U.S.

In 1996 Gillette bought battery maker Duracell International Inc. The purchase wound up being for $7.8 billion in stock and debt. It was Gillette's largest acquistion ever. The buyout came after Zeien approached Duracell in January, 1996. Gillette thought of buying Duracell in 1987 but didn't offer a high enough price. Duracell was sold to Kolhberg Kravis Roberts in 1988 for $1.8 billion. When Gillette bought Duracell, it was a case of one brand name buying another brand name. The combined company would have the advantages of using Gillette's formidable sales channels to further extend Duracell's products. Gillette has exceptional warehousing and merchandising capabilities around the world.

It turned out that Buffett abstained from the Gillette board's vote about the merger, objecting to the investment banking fees. Buffett felt that the $30 million fee was excessive. However, Buffett did favor the merger. (*Wall Street Journal*, November 26, 1996) Of the fees, $10 million went to Morgan Stanley and Co. and $20 million to Kohlberg Kravis Roberts and Co., the buyout firm which owned 34% of Duracell.

Analysts said the buyout was a perfect fit for the two consumer products companies. Less than half of Duracell's sales were oversees, compared with about 70% for Gillette. Since 1987 Duracell has grown even faster than Gillette.

(Photo courtesy of Duracell)

Duracell battery

"Duracell and Gillette share numerous characteristics, including global brand franchises, common distribution channels, exceptional merchandising opportunities and geographic extension potential. Given the distribution similarities of blades and batteries, we expect the Duracell business will gain significant economies of scale and greater market penetration through Gillette's worldwide distribution network," said Gillette's 1996 Annual Report. "With only 20% of Duracell's sales outside North America and Western Europe, there are significant growth opportunities ahead."

Duracell, based at Berkshire Corporate Park—named Berkshire because it's located in the foothills of the Berkshire mountains—in Bethel, Connecticut, makes alkaline, lithium and specialty batteries. It has about 8,000 employees. It is the world's biggest maker of alkaline batteries, a disposable energy source that powers a range of consumer products. Duracell opened alkaline battery plants in China and India in 1997, markets that together consume about five billion household batteries annually, or about one-fourth of the world's total. Duracell, with annual sales of about $2.3 billion, has about 50% of the U.S. alkaline battery market, significantly above archrival Eveready/Energizer spun off by Ralston-Purina.

In 1998 Duracell introduced a new line of alkaline batteries—called Duracell Ultra—in AA and AAA sizes for use in high-technology products such as digital cameras, small computers, remote-controlled toys, and cellular phones.

Since Gillette bought Duracell, Duracell's operating profit margin has risen more than three points.

On April 14, 1998, Gillette announced its flagship Mach 3 three-bladed razor. The Mach 3 was the result of a 7-year, $750 million research effort. Its introduction into the marketplace was supported by a $300 million marketing effort.

In the first six months, Mach 3 sales in the U.S. were triple those of the Sensor system in the first six months of its launch.

"I've been using it since about November 1 [1997]," Buffett said at Berkshire's annual meeting festivities in 1998. "Just look at this," he said, rubbing his chin. "It's an amazing razor."

Gillette's stock price had soared 15-fold from the end of 1986 to the end of 1996, but in the past several years Gillette's international profits have slowed with 1999 being a particularly disappointing year as it kept missing profit expectations as inventories backed up. Gillette's Braun and stationery units did poorly in 1999.

Gillette bought $1.18 billion of its stock in the second quarter of 1999 as its shares plummeted by more than a third after a warning that profits would miss forecasts. The company bought back 25 million shares at an average price of $47.32 a share, according to a regulatory filing.

77
US AIRWAYS
"PHONE MR. WOLF."

Berkshire made its $358 million preferred stock investment in USAir on August 7, 1989. USAir had merged with Piedmont Aviation just two days earlier.

"It is unusual for Berkshire Hathaway to invest in a capital-intensive, labor-intensive industry, such as the airline industry. Our enthusiasm for the investment in USAir Group preferred stock is dramatic evidence of our high regard for Ed Colodny's management," Buffett said. "I like Ed."

Still Buffett saw the USAir (name changed to US Airways in 1996) stake as a senior security, not a great business. Buffett's strategy may have been spotting an industry which had a few large players which he hoped might consolidate, with good financial results for shareholders.

But in this case Buffett's strategy backfired on the runway as many factors hastened USAir's stunning decline amidst turbulence in the airline industry. On May 8, 1996, Berkshire announced it planned to sell its USAir stake, offering first to sell it back to the company, but in the end Berkshire held on to the stake.

It was Buffett's decision to buy into the Arlington, Virginia-based airline, which was about 8% owned by Michael Steinhardt's Steinhardt Partners who was raising its stake in USAir, the fourth largest U.S. airline.

The investment was a jet-propelled descent. With its jumbo-jet-sized problems, the airline lost about $3 billion from 1988-1994. Buffett once told a group of business students at Columbia University not to invest in airlines, saying it's one of the worst businesses in the world, loaded with costs and overcapacity.

Asked by a Columbia student why he invested in the airline, Buffett quipped, "This is my psychiatrist asking this. Actually I have an 800 number now which I call if I ever get an urge to buy an airline stock. I say my name is Warren. I'm an air-aholic and then they talk me down."

It all reminds one of theatrical producer Billy Rose's investment advice: "Never invest in anything that eats or needs repairing."

US Airways started life as Allegheny Airlines ("Agony Airlines") in the East, acquired Mohawk Airlines in 1972, established a hub in Pittsburgh in 1978 and became USAir in 1979 before acquiring PSA and Piedmont. US Airways now has hubs in Pittsburgh, Philadelphia, Baltimore, Charlotte and Indianapolis.

When Buffett invested, the common stock was trading at about $50 a share. Each of the $1,000 face value preferred shares was convertible after two years from the purchase date at a conversion price into $16^2/3$ common shares when and if the price hits $60 a share. The investment, which represents about a 12% stake, paid Berkshire a 9.25% tax-advantaged dividend a year.

The airline could buy back or call the preferred stock after August 7, 1991, for $100 a share higher than the $1,000 purchase price. Berkshire had until August 7, 1999, to convert its stock, selling any remaining shares of the preferred stock to the airline at the original $1,000 a share price. US Airways redeemed the stake in 1998.

What Buffett saw, through his preferred stake, was a way to gamble safely. If he lost, he would earn a tax-advantaged 9%. If he won, he would own a significant portion in an airline in a consolidating industry. "My mistake was I didn't think price competition would get that bad. The cost side, of course, has been abysmal as well as the result of events in the Middle East," Buffett said at the annual meeting in 1991.

And he added, "You get six or eight competitors, some of whom are operating in bankruptcy. Once an airline goes into bankruptcy, they're in effect debt-free. Eastern picked up hundreds of millions of dollars essentially by selling off gates and other assets to subsidize operating losses at a time when they were effectively debt-free— because they weren't paying anything on their debt. And USAir can't compete with that. To compete with someone who's bleeding copiously, you need a blood bank."

Even before that, it did not help when two passengers were killed as USAir Flight 5050 skidded off a rain-slicked runway at New York's LaGuardia Airport, bellyflopping into the water on an abortive takeoff for Charlotte on September 20, 1989. And on February 1, 1991, a USAir flight and a commuter plane collided on the runway at Los Angeles International Airport leaving 34 passengers dead. That was also the effective date of the airline's decision to cut back on its insurance coverage for its fleet.

When it rains, it pours...On March 22, 1992, a USAir flight during inclement weather crashed at LaGuardia, killing 26 of the 51 people aboard.

After the merger with Piedmont, things were slow to mesh and the airline racked up an unimpressive on-time record. Planes were late. Bags were lost. "Useless Air" and "U.S.-scare" became monikers. But gradually during 1990 its on-time performance improved from No. 6 of the major airlines in January, 1990, to No. 1 by June, 1990, and it maintained a number-two rating through 1991. Competition was fierce, and when Iraq invaded Kuwait on August 2, 1990, jet fuel prices soared and moneymaking USAir turned in a string of quarterly losses.

Layoffs and discontinued service dominated headlines about the airline. The industry was in disarray as airlines such as Midway retreated and Eastern and others crashed and burned. Chairman Colodny said in the 1989 Annual Report conditions were deteriorating because of industry fundamentals and merger-related problems. Eventually 7,000 furloughs were announced: 14% of the work force. Orders for planes were deferred, the number of flights reduced. At one point the payroll was met by selling some airplanes.

The airline industry has been described as an industry where perhaps only four or five carriers will survive. All airlines have faced severe pressures that remind one of a cartoon that ran in *Barron's*. It read: "Arrivals, Departures, Bankruptcies."

Indeed, in the year prior to mid-1991, six of the top dozen airlines in the nation filed for bankruptcy protection.

Colodny retired in June, 1991, after 34 years with the company. Seth E. Schofield succeeded Colodny as president and in early 1996 Stephen Wolf, who formerly ran UAL Corp., was named chairman and CEO. In 1991 Buffett was calling the USAir investment "an unforced error" and Colodny was starting his annual report letter to stockholders with, "The year 1990 was the most difficult in the Company's history. The soft domestic traffic and weak economy, skyrocketing fuel prices, fear of travel due to the Persian Gulf crisis, and widespread, sharply discounted fares all contributed to the $454 million net loss for the year."

"Buffett still walks on water. He just splashes a little bit," said Marshall Lewis, senior vice president of the Blunt, Ellis & Loewi investment firm. (*Omaha World-Herald*, October 20, 1991)

Losses continued to stack up. At yearend 1991 Buffett wrote down his estimation of the $358 million investment to $232.7 million. Meanwhile employees, officers and board members walked or took pay cuts.

In 1992, British Airways agreed to buy a 44% stake in the airline for $750 million, creating a formidable competitor in the increasingly global airline industry. Although that deal fell through, British

Airways eventually invested $300 million in the airline.

In January 1993, Buffett and Munger, taking on a huge new challenge in a weak link of their empire, went on the board of the company. Buffett wrote that the British Airways investment would help in "assuring survival—and eventual prosperity."

Apparently Buffett never has said, as one wag has warned: "Don't invest in anything with wheels on it."

USAir did not turn out to be Buffett's finest hour. In short, it was not the preferred way to fly. "We could not have been more wrong...I mean I could not have been more wrong. Charlie was not consulted on the buying." (*Financial Times*, May 15, 1998)

At the Wesco Annual Meeting in 1993, Munger said of the USAir stake, "We cut that a little fine, but it's not over."

In March 1994 British Airways said it was suspending plans to invest further in USAir. By then British Airways had invested $400 million with plans to invest another $450 million. The decision sent the stock crashing and burning to a single digit share price.

The tragedy of errors continued on July 2, 1994 when a USAir jet crashed near Charlotte, killing 57 people. In a seeming last straw for the company, a USAir jetliner crashed near Pittsburgh September 8, 1994, killing all 132 people aboard. It was the fifth fatal crash in five years for the beleaguered airline. A short time later USAir deferred its preferred stock dividend to Berkshire due September 30, 1994.

For the fourth quarter of 1994 Berkshire wrote down its investment in the airline, taking a $268.5 million pre-tax charge. The write-down was to $89 million, about 25 cents on the dollar.

In early 1995 Buffett and Munger stepped down as directors after they had said they would do so if the airline couldn't reach a timely agreement with its labor groups about cost-savings.

The first ray of sunlight for the airline came with a profit in 1995, its first profit in seven years. The company and the stock rebounded in 1996.

The investment was written up to $214.8 million at the end of 1995 and up to $322 million in 1996. Buffett said in Berkshire's 1995 Annual Report: "Though we have not been paid dividends since June, 1994, the amounts owed us are compounding at 5% over the prime rate. On the minus side is the fact that we are dealing with a weak credit." USAir began catching up on its preferred dividends in 1996. In late 1996 British Airways said it wanted to sell its stake back to the company.

Lesson: do not invest in airline stocks.

At the Berkshire Annual Meeting in 1995, a stockholder asked if an investment in another airline would be considered. The stock-holder, because of the crowd, had not been able to get into the main room and was watching the meeting on a screen.

"Thanks for the question. We're putting everyone who asks us questions about USAir in the other room," Buffett replied.

With new CEO Stephen Wolf's arrival in 1996, the company and the stock rebounded.

Buffett tried to sell his stake in the airline. "Fortunately, I was unsuccessful," Buffett wrote in Berkshire's 1996 Annual Report. He said the airline was doing better and in 1997 it paid up on its dividends which had been in arrears to Berkshire.

"Early in 1996... I tried once more to unload our holdings—this time for about $335 million. You're lucky: I again failed in my attempt to snatch defeat from the jaws of victory."

In another context, a friend once asked Buffett: "If you're so rich, why aren't you smart?"

At Berkshire's Annual Meeting in 1997, Buffett said: "When Charlie and I left the board, the fortunes of [US Airways] went abruptly upward."

Buffett has said he failed to foresee both the downturn and the upturn of USAir.

Berkshire gained leeway to sell its US Airways stake in 1997 under a revised agreement when Berkshire swapped its Preferred A shares into H shares as part of an agreement to restructure debt of US Airways. As part of the deal, US Airways gave Berkshire greater choice in selling the securities, if Berkshire so chose.

US Airways continued to come out of its tailspin. Indeed it even began flying in fine formation. By 1997-1998 US Airways surpassed the $50 and $60 a share price levels, bailing Buffett out of what looked for years like a losing investment. And as Charles Munger has said, "It's not over."

On February 3, 1998 US Airways said it would redeem Berkshire's $358 million in preferred stock. The conversion was for about 9.24 million common shares, worth roughly $660 million. And US Airways authorized a large common stock buyback as it retired debt and piled up cash. Buffett's "mistake" became quite a winner.

Buffett reduced Berkshire's common stock holding in US Airways to 3.83 million shares, according to an SEC filing of May 11, 1998, leaving Berkshire a 3.79% stake in the airline's stock.

And that's the story of the fall and rise of US Airways.

Buffett wrote in Berkshire's 1997 Annual Report: "Our preferred has been called for redemption on March 15 [1998]. But the rise in the company's stock has given our conversion rights, which we thought worthless not long ago, great value. It is now almost certain that our US Airways shares will produce a decent profit—that is, if my cost for Maalox is excluded—and the gain could even prove indecent.

"Next time I make a big, dumb decision, Berkshire shareholders will know what to do: *Phone Mr. Wolf.*"

As the years went by, US Airways made a complete turnaround climbing, by some reports, from the worst to the best airline, but has had its troubles lately.

UAL Corp., the parent of United Airlines, on May 24, 2000, agreed to buy most of US Air.

78
M&T BANK CORP.
"CONVERT AND KEEP"

In 1991 with the banking industry in shambles and Buffett sensing consolidation, he returned to Buffalo for a new investment.

M&T Bank Corp., based in Buffalo, New York, was known until 1998 as First Empire State Corp. It agreed March 15, 1991 to issue 40,000 shares of 9% preferred stock to Berkshire's National Indemnity Co. for $40 million. With that $40 million M&T bought two bankrupt Buffalo thrifts.

For the second time, Buffett made an investment in Buffalo. His first one was in *The Buffalo News*. M&T stock was trading at about $63 a share when the deal was struck and began climbing steadily thereafter. The preferred stock was convertible at any time into shares of M&T's common stock at an initial conversion price of $78.91 per share.

Based on the 6,637,138 shares of common stock outstanding as of March 13, 1991, complete exercise of the conversion privilege would be equal to 506,930 shares, or about 7% of the common stock outstanding following conversion, M&T said.

M&T had the right to redeem the preferred stock without premium on or after March 31, 1996. In other words, Buffett had five years, a long time, to make his investment work—that is, for M&T's price to reach about $79 a share, which it did in short order. In the meantime the perfectly satisfactory 9% return kept arriving at Berkshire's doorstep.

In Berkshire's 1995 Annual Report, Buffett said that on March 31, 1996, Berkshire would "convert and keep" its First Empire common shares. At the end of 1999 Berkshire owned 510,310, or 6.65% of the stock.

M&T historically has carried low debt levels and has an excellent long-term record. In the past decade its stock is up many times from the $7 to $10 a share level where it traded in 1981, according to Standard and Poor's.

M&T's subsidiaries are Manufacturers and Traders Trust Co., The East New York Savings Bank and M&T Bank, National Association.

The upstate New York bank, with assets of $20 billion at the end of 1998, has a clean balance sheet. It is heavily owned by its officers and directors and institutional investors.

569

(Photo courtesy of M&T Bank Corp./Robert L. Smith)

Robert Wilmers

The message to shareholders in M&T's 1990 Annual Report is one of the more articulate looks at the U.S. banking scene. It's in plain English.

In 1991 the FDIC closed Goldome, a Buffalo-based savings and loan, dividing its assets between competitors KeyCorp and M&T. Wall Street apparently liked the deal. M&T stock jumped right through the conversion point so that Buffett, in addition to getting the 9%, is way in the money on the stock side.

M&T, headed by Robert Wilmers, was a steady performer in the early 1990s and by early 1998, with the company buying back its own shares, the stock had hit $500 per share.

Wilmers is a French-speaking Harvard graduate from an affluent Manhattan family. (*Wall Street Journal*, July 1, 1998)

In the early 1980s he left his job as head of private banking in Belgium with Morgan Guaranty. Assisted by other investors, he began buying shares of M&T, then a troubled bank. He became chairman after what was was essentially a hostile takeover. "He set about cleaning the place up, dumping its moribund loans to Venezuelan car dealers and Mexican department stores. Henceforth, the bank would concentrate on knowing and lending to its New York neighbor." (*Wall Street Journal*, July 1, 1998)

"The thing that hits you in the face is that insiders own 23% of the stock. When a financial institution has that much of its officers' money in it, it's not going to make risky loans, and it won't make acquisitions just for the sake of growing, because the company's entire worth is dependent on the price of the stock. Warren Buffett is a big shareholder." (Blaine Robbins of Janus Balanced Fund, *Kiplinger's Personal Finance Magazine*, November 1996)

In 1997 M&T announced it would buy ONBANCorp for about $872 million in stock and cash, creating the largest bank in upstate New York. M&T bought 29 branches in upstate New York from the Chase Manhattan Bank in 1999.

The combined bank became the 38th largest bank in the U.S. with about $22 billion in assets and more than 200 branches serving New York and Northern Pennsylvania.

On May 17, 2000 M&T and Keystone Financial, Inc., of Harrisburg, Pennsylvannia, said they would merge with M&T paying $1 billion in stock and cash for Keystone.

79

AMERICAN EXPRESS REDUX
PLAYING ITS CARDS RIGHT

Amerian Express announced on August 1, 1991 that it would accept a cash infusion of $300 million from Berkshire.

To the *Omaha World-Herald*, Buffett landed this punchline: "He [American Express Chairman Jim Robinson] has not offered to let me pay for this transaction on my credit card."

Buffett had returned to American Express, the scene of one of his early investment victories. With his newly acquired stake, Buffett became a major shareholder in the giant company known for its credit cards, travelers checks and struggling Shearson Lehman Brothers brokerage firm into which American Express had recently pumped more than $1 billion to restructure. The hard-hit subsidiary had lost $900 million the year Buffett invested.

American Express was founded in 1850 by Henry Wells and William Fargo, who also founded Wells Fargo, another major Berkshire investee.

American Express began as a freight forwarding company, later became a travel company, then was known for its credit cards and today is a global financial and travel services company.

American Express credit cards are accepted as far away as the Mongolian People's Republic, and are honored in 180 countries. Travel and tourism may be the largest industry in the world and American Express is the world's largest travel company with a related network of more than 1,700 offices around the globe.

The company is also a leader in financial planning, securities brokerage, asset management, international banking, investment banking and information services.

This time Buffett had a much larger amount invested in American Express. Recall that in 1964, during the American Express salad oil scandal, Buffett invested only about $13 million. In 1991 it was $300 million. And American Express was pledged to pay him an 8.85% dividend, a return made even better because of the 70% corporate-tax exemption on the dividend income: Berkshire was earning more than 11% on a taxable equivalent basis.

This investment, called a "Perc," was somewhat different from Buffett's earlier convertible preferred stakes in Salomon, Gillette, US

Airways and Champion; in the end it offered Buffett less potential upside and gave American Express more control over its outcome. Although the arrangement gave Buffett a much heftier dividend on its American Express shares than common shareholders receive, the deal limited Buffett's capital gains.

The preferred shares were exchangeable into common shares at the option of American Express, not Buffett, making them different from convertible shares.

"There's not much upside potential with this one. I'm not sure why he did it," said *Newsday* columnist Allan Sloan.

"Convertible preferred shares have unlimited upside," Buffett told the *Wall Street Journal* (August 2, 1991). "With this, we get less of an investment opportunity."

The Berkshire-American Express agreement called for Buffett's non-transferable preferred shares to be exchanged for common stock within three or four years under terms of the investment, a private placement.

American Express would redeem the securities issued to Berkshire no later than maturity by exchanging common shares for the preferred stock. The number of common shares to be issued were to be determined by the American Express share price at the time of the redemption. If American Express didn't redeem before maturity, (three years, with the possibility of a year extension if American Express stock was below $24.50 at the time) it would exchange about 12 million common shares for the preferred stake, about a 2.5% stake in American Express. Amex stock was trading at about $25 a share when Buffett bought his preferred stake.

"When I heard they needed some equity funds, I told Jim [Robinson, then chairman of American Express] that Berkshire would be interested in investing $500 million. I was willing to buy more, but Jim didn't want to sell more than $300 million," Buffett told the *Journal.*

In this case, Buffett did not join the board, as he often does when he invests. Robinson told *USA Today* (August 2, 1991), "I don't think he needs to be on the board to provide that [counsel]. We would have welcomed him on our board, but he's on a number of boards. He has a full plate. Also, he's on the Salomon board and we own [rival] Shearson."

As for Buffett, he told the Associated Press he wouldn't play a role in running American Express, but that he would "speak when spoken to."

Taking on numerous interviews in connection with the

announcement, Buffett told the *Omaha World-Herald* (August 2, 1991) that the then-recent losses at Shearson were temporary.

"It really doesn't take any of the luster off the really great franchises—the cards, the travelers checks and the information systems," Buffett said, shortly before the company's setbacks in its Optima card operations.

As usual, when Buffett made his investment, things did not look good at American Express.

To make matters worse for American Express, but to create the perfect buying opportunity for Buffett, a wave of merchants (initially a group of restaurants in Boston that were subsequently dubbed the "Boston Fee Party") was complaining that American Express cards had been taking too large a commission from sales billed to its cards. The entire credit card industry was becoming more competitive than ever, with a number of other credit cards, including AT&T's (now owned by Citigroup), being introduced. Visa and Mastercard all along were gaining market share.

Value Line at the time said, "These shares seem unexciting...not confident that the stock will show any special strength for the year ahead. And prospects for 1994-96 aren't well defined." Enter Warren Buffett.

Omaha World-Herald columnist Robert McMorris ran this item August 2, 1991:

> Lunch-table conversation overheard at a west Omaha restaurant: I understand Warren Buffett is investing $300 million in American Express.
>
> That so? You know, American Express owns Shearson Brokerage, and Warren already has Salomon.
>
> Yeah, pretty soon he'll own all of Wall Street. Think he'll move there so he can be close to his money?
>
> I doubt it. Warren would probably say Wall Street is a nice property to own, but he wouldn't want to live there.

Over the next several years Buffett continued to follow events at American Express. In an unsuccessful effort to become a "financial supermarket" during the 1980s, American Express had become a disjointed collection of mergers and acquisitions. It lacked a clear focus, but it still had terrific cash flow, one of the greatest brand franchises in the world, and generated huge amounts of float. The stock price had drifted sideways for nearly a decade.

Buffett converted his American Express investment into 14 million common shares in the summer of 1994 and began buying more American Express stock, and more and more and more and more. By the end of 1994 he was up to 27.76 million shares and added another 20.7 million in the first month and a half of 1995.

Just over 30 years after his first investment in American Express, Berkshire announced that it owned 9.8% of American Express. The announcement came across the wire as a one liner:

> **02/15 WSJ Buffett Boosts American Express Stake to 9.8%**

Here's how Buffett explained the move in Berkshire's 1997 Annual Report:

> In addition to the convertible preferreds, we purchased one other private placement in 1991, $300 million of American Express Percs. This security was essentially a common stock that featured a tradeoff in its first three years: We received extra dividend payments during that period, but we were also capped in the price appreciation we could realize. Despite the cap, this holding has proved extraordinarily profitable thanks to a move by your Chairman that combined luck and skill—110% luck, the balance skill.
>
> Our Percs were due to convert into common stock in August 1994, and in the month before I was mulling whether to sell upon conversion. One reason to hold was Amex's outstanding CEO, Harvey Golub, who seemed likely to maximize whatever potential the company had (a supposition that has since been proved—in spades). But the size of that potential was in question: Amex faced relentless competition from a multitude of card-issuers, led by Visa. Weighing the arguments, I leaned toward sale.
>
> Here's where I got lucky. During that month of decision, I played golf at Prouts Neck, Maine with Frank Olson, CEO of Hertz. Frank is a brilliant manager, with intimate knowledge of the card business. So from the first tee on I was quizzing him about the industry. By the time we reached the second green, Frank had convinced me that Amex's corporate card was a terrific franchise, and I had decided not to sell. On the back nine I turned buyer, and in a few months Berkshire owned 10% of the company.

The investment amounted to 48.5 million shares of American Express. Also he said he wanted clearance to buy above 10% of the company. Late in 1995 Berkshire raised its stake in American Express to 49,456,000 shares. By December 1995 Berkshire had invested a staggering $1.4 billion and owned 10.5%, now 11.3%, of the company because of stock buybacks, making American Express Buffett's largest allocation of new capital to date. It was even larger than the initial investment in Coca-Cola which had a cost basis of $1.3 billion.

Most significant is American Express' contribution to "look-through" earnings. In Berkshire's 1996 Annual Report, Buffett wrote, "Reported earnings are a poor measure of economic progress at Berkshire...dividends typically represent only a small fraction of the earnings attributable to ownership...on balance we regard the undistributed earnings of our investees as more valuable to us than the portion paid out. The reason is simple: Our investees often have the opportunity to reinvest earnings at high rates of return. So why should we want them paid out?" He estimated Berkshire's share of undistributed operating earnings from American Express as $132 million. Of all of Berkshire's major investees only Coca-Cola delivers a greater contribution in the form of undistributed "look-through" earnings. At yearend 1999 Berkshire's "look-through" portion was $228 million.

Harvey Golub, the hard-nosed CEO of American Express is joined by Kenneth Chenault as president who is to succeed Golub as CEO when Golub retires in 2001. As long as Harvey Golub remains CEO, Berkshire has agreed to vote its shares in accordance with the wishes of the American Express board. Buffett agreed to limit his stake and influence at American Express as part of an agreement with the Federal Reserve Board that allowed him to buy more than 10% of the stock of American Express.

Because American Express owns a bank, the Fed could decide Berkshire had a controlling interest in American Express and thus was subject to regulations for bank holding companies.

Buffett would have to get out of everything banks aren't allowed to do, such as owning newspaper and candy companies.

With the agreement to be a passive investor, Berkshire can continue its other operations. Under the agreement Berkshire said it will keep its stake under 15% if it receives board representation and below 17% if it doesn't. (*Bloomberg News Service*, November 16, 1995) Berkshire has the right to own up to 17% of American Express.

In the 1994 Annual Report, Buffett wrote:

> My American Express history includes a couple of episodes: In the mid-1960s, just after the stock was battered by the company's infamous salad-oil scandal, we put about 40% of Buffett Partnership Ltd.'s capital into the stock —

the largest investment the partnership had ever made. I should add that this commitment gave us over 5% ownership of Amex at a cost of $13 million. As I write this, we own just under 10% which has cost us $1.36 billion. (Amex earned $12.5 million in 1964 and $1.4 billion in 1994.)

My history with Amex's IDS unit, which today contributes about a third of the earnings of the company goes back even further. I first purchased stock in IDS in 1953 when it was growing rapidly and selling at a price-earnings ratio of only 3. (There was a lot of low-hanging fruit in those days.) I even produced a long report—do I ever write a short one?—on the company that I sold for $1 through an ad in *The Wall Street Journal.*

Obviously American Express and IDS (recently renamed American Express Financial Advisors) are far different operations from what they were then. Nevertheless, I find that a long-term familiarity with a company and its products is often helpful in evaluating it.

"The key will be in how the credit card does," Buffett said of American Express at the Berkshire Annual Meeting in 1995. "Credit cards are going to be a very competitive business over time, and American Express needs to establish special value for its card in some way, or it gets commodity-like."

Its card faces huge competition from Visa and Mastercard. As airlines, oil companies, car makers and telephone companies issue cards, increasingly American Express cards offer more deals than in the past. "The AmEx card now gets you deals on hotels, car rentals, retail merchandise and airlines including Delta, USAir and Swissair." (*Forbes*, July 1, 1996).

As for American Express Financial Advisors: "Today it sells financial and estate planning, annuities, its own mutual funds, life insurance, pension plans, 401(k) plans, loans and accounting services to individuals and business through 8,000 financial advisors in 50 states. It's a nice business, producing a third of AmEx's net income." (*Forbes*, July 1, 1996)

Later in 1996 it was disclosed that American Express had talked to Citicorp about the possibility of selling American Express to Citicorp. But nothing came of the talks.

When there are merger talks, guess who probably knows about them. *Barron's* (April 27, 1998) quotes money manager Kurt Feuerman: "Berkshire is tough...because we can't talk to management, and that breaks one rule we have. It's a unique situation where you own a portfolio of growth stocks where the management can influence the holdings. You get Warren Buffett and his ability to act. Was he involved in Travelers-Citicorp? I don't know. But he was involved in selling Cap Cities to Disney. I own American Express and once asked Harvey Golub how often he spoke to the Great One. He said, 'every week'. That made me feel good about American Express and great about Berkshire."

In 1997 golf superstar Tiger Woods signed a multiyear, multimillion dollar deal to be a spokesman for American Express, and comedian Jerry Seinfeld starred in an American Express commercial he had written. The commercial, which aired during the Super Bowl, depicted Jerry "rescuing" Lois Lane at the check-out line of the store when his friend and superhero, Superman, is shown to be helpless without an American Express card.

Don't leave home without it!

In October, 1998, after American Express had been hit by that international financial crisis, Buffett bought a little more than one million shares at just about the stock's low point, upping Berkshire's stake to 50,536,900 shares, or slightly more than 11% of American Express.

As the crisis blew over and Berkshire's new purchase rebounded strongly into 1999, American Express and Costco, a leading wholesale warehouse club operator, began to issue co-branded credit cards. It was the first time American Express shared its brand with a retailer, so that consumers could use an American Express card that doubled as a Costco membership card.

Berkshire, with its large position in American Express, also has a small stake in Costco. Munger, Berkshire's vice-chairman, serves on the board of Costco and has a personal investment in the giant retailer, too.

"American Express and Costco make a powerful fit. And there may be other natural affinities among Berkshire and her investees," says Berkshire devotee Michael Assael. "Though the business synergies today may seem minor and incidental, the occasional blending of brands and resources could prove increasingly valuable in the years ahead. As markets develop and industries evolve to serve new customers worldwide, Berkshire and her investees will be there, combining competitive products and services and attractive prices."

American Express is a financial services supermarket serving more than 70% of the *Fortune* 500 companies with the American Express Corporate Card.

And the company has a large Internet presence. Its American

Express@Work site allows customers to manage their AmEx Corporate card. Also, AmEx is an online bank with its Membership B@nking aimed at retail customers. Another Internet initiative is Blue, a card with a smart chip and special security for online shopping. AmEx operates American Express Brokerage which offers commission-free trades for accounts over $25,000. Futhermore, AmEx operates 9,000 ATMs making it the largest off-site offerer of ATMs in the U.S.

Lastly, the average card member spent $7,758 in 1999, up from $6,885, in 1998. Americans' love of spending with plastic continued. The average annual spending of an AmEx card is almost four times that of the average Visa or MasterCard.

American Express, the single ray of sunshine in Berkshire's stock portfolio in 1999, one day may be the center of everything.

80
FREDDIE MAC

In late 1988 Berkshire's Wesco unit beefed up its minor stake to 7.2 million shares of the stock of Federal Home Loan Mortgage, now known as Freddie Mac.

Buffett and Munger decided to make the investment after conferring for about three hours. *(Forbes,* January 22, 1996)

It was the maximum amount, at the time, that any single shareholder could own under federal rules. The cost of the purchase was $71.7 million.

Explaining the investment to *Fortune* (December 19, 1988), The Sage of Omaha said, "Freddie Mac is a triple dip. You've got a low price/earnings ratio on a company with a terrific record. You've got growing earnings. And you have a stock that is bound to become much better known to equity investors."

When Buffett made the investment, some investors were asking themselves, "Who is Freddie Mac?" Freddie Mac, a key part of the nation's housing finance system, is chartered by the federal government as a private company to provide liquidity to the mortgage market. It buys mortgages, then pools and packages them into securities that it sells to investors. It insures mortgages on about five million homes for a fee of ¼ of 1%.

Freddie Mac helps make the American dream (or nightmare, depending on your mortgage rate. You know the line: "Why is there so much month left at the end of the money?") of owning a home come true by ensuring the flow of credit to home buyers. Over the years, Freddie Mac has helped finance one in six American homes, including more than 700,000 apartment units. Freddie Mac buys a home loan every several seconds of every business day. With lower interest rates in recent years, more homeowners are refinancing their mortgages and more people are finding home mortgages more affordable.

About 97% of Freddie Mac's business is with single-family mortgages. Since 1970 it has financed the homes of about 25 million Americans, financing more than 2 million homes in 1999.

Freddie Mac has a 16% market share of a $4 trillion growing market.

Freddie Mac was chartered by Congress in 1970 during a credit crisis to keep savings and loans liquid and enable more Americans to afford home ownership. The stockholder-owned company buys home mortgages from lenders, guarantees the mortgages against default, packages them as securities and sells them to investors such as S&Ls. It creates a continuous flow of money to mortgage lenders in support of home ownership and rental housing. The company has been profitable every year of its existence.

In 1984, it issued about 15 million shares of participating preferred stock to Federal Home Loan Board-member S&Ls, with trading generally restricted to board members.

In 1988, Freddie Mac stock began trading on the New York Stock Exchange. The company had been owned by thrifts that owned the stock through the country's Federal Home Loan Bank System and were allowed to resell the stock starting in January, 1989. The lifting of trading restrictions on Freddie Mac preferred stock allowed public investors to come in.

So what is Freddie Mac with its 3,000 employees (70% of whom are Freddie Mac shareholders) and how does it work to link the nation's mortgage markets with its financial markets?

Freddie Mac, based in McLean, Virginia, provides stability in the secondary market for home mortgages. The moment you drop your monthly mortgage payment in the mail is the start of a long journey for your money.

If your lender has kept the loan on its books, your payment will be processed, your check deposited and the money used to pay interest on deposits and make more loans to new borrowers in your area.

But let's say you take out a 7.5% fixed-rate home loan of $150,000 from your bank and the bank doesn't want to carry it on its books for the next 30 years. One reason it might not want to carry the loan: the bank may wind up losing money if rates skyrocket in the future. To eliminate the risk, the bank sells your loan to an entity like Freddie Mac. Freddie buys your promise to pay, and your local bank gets immediate cash.

Freddie Mac's only real competition is Fannie Mae, making them duopoly businesses, both of which benefited from the decline of the S&L industry nationwide. If Buffett can't locate a true monopoly business, he's usually glad to settle for a duopoly.

The secondary market accomplishes several things. Lending institutions can make long-term mortgage loans knowing they can sell them to someone like Freddie Mac, and at the same time mortgage-backed securities make it easier and safer for more investors to participate in the mortgage market.

After Buffett made the investment in the stock at a cost per share of about $30, it rose in 1990, but then began to plummet along with anything smacking of the suddenly suspect world of real estate.

At its low in 1990, the stock had lost two-thirds of its value from the 1989 peak and was trading at a price/earnings ratio of about five.

The Freddie Mac plunge rocked the stock of Wesco, which owns the Freddie Mac stock directly, and didn't help Berkshire in the tempestuous stock market of 1990.

In late 1990, Freddie Mac was reporting problems in its apartment-backed mortgage business, particularly in New York and Atlanta, but even so profits from the company's single-family mortgage business remained strong and the stock began to rebound.

In its 1990 year-end report, Freddie Mac Chairman Leland Brendsel said, "We estimate that property values underlying our single-family mortgage portfolio stood at approximately $600 billion at year-end, reflecting a decade of home price appreciation. This means, on average, there is almost two dollars of property value underlying every mortgage dollar represented in our single-family portfolio."

In 1991, Freddie Mac stock rebounded strongly as fears about real estate eased and interest rates dipped dramatically. Despite the 1990 scare, Steady Freddie has been profitable in every quarter since 1971. Again Buffett's strategy of patience paid off.

Berkshire's 1997 Annual Report showed 63,977,600 shares of Freddie Mac worth about $2.7 billion. At the end of 1999 the figure was 59,559,300 shares, or 8.6%.

Years ago Bill Ruane, who heads Sequoia Fund which also has a large Freddie Mac stake, said, "Here's a company that has been growing—and they predict will continue to grow—at a mid-teens growth rate selling at about 12 times earnings with a very high return on capital...

"If you were to take Freddie Mac and look at the simple numbers—it's selling at 12 times earnings versus 18 to 20 times earnings for the S&P. It probably has a double-digit earnings growth rate versus an average growth rate over nine years of 7% or even less for the S&P. Its return on equity is 20% or better against an average return of 12½% to 13% for the S&P. So by any simple statistical measure, it's a very attractive stock."

Fast forward to the late 1990s. Freddie Mac had strong earnings gains in 1999 and a sharp stock decline. Overall, though, its stock has been one of the cornerstones of Berkshire's growth.

81
THE BODY OF HIS WORK
"COMMON SENSE IS GENIUS DRESSED IN ITS WORKING CLOTHES."—*Ralph Waldo Emerson*

From the beginning, common sense is the trait that has most characterized Buffett's body of work.

"We don't buy and sell stocks based on what other people think the stock market is going to do. The course of the stock market will determine, to a great degree, when we will be right, but the accuracy of our analysis of the company will largely determine whether we are right. In other words, we tend to concentrate on what should happen, not when it should happen," he wrote in a Buffett Partnership letter, July 22, 1966.

Common sense may be the most important factor helping Buffett to make more money in the stock market than anyone; he is the only person on the *Forbes 400* richest Americans list who got there entirely by investing.

"One piece of advice that I got at Columbia from Ben Graham that I've never forgotten: You're neither right nor wrong because other people agree with you. You're right because your facts are right and your reasoning is right. That's the only thing that makes you right," Buffett said at the Berkshire Annual Meeting in 1991.

Buffett's corporate strategy often is, "hoping the phone rings." He wants bad news out quickly; good news will take care of itself. He wants red tape and meetings cut out in favor of by-the-seat-of-your-pants judgments. He wants action, not paperwork. He likes people who want to manage a business, not one another.

In the words of Ralph Waldo Emerson, "Common sense is genius dressed in its working clothes."

Buffett's emphasis on common sense could remind one of Mark Twain's approach to common sense: "I would rather go to bed with Lillian Russell stark naked than with Ulysses S. Grant in full military regalia."

Stick To Your "Circle of Competence"

Ben Graham, who liked to dance, once gave Buffett certificates to take dance lessons. Buffett never went to the classes. Apparently dancing is outside Buffett's "circle of competence."

In the world of business, Buffett sticks to what he knows and what he can do. He does not try to do what he cannot. He knows he understands media, financial and consumer product companies and has concentrated his assets particularly in those areas over the years.

Mental Discipline

You need mental discipline to stick to what you're about and not go down some side trail nor take chances where things aren't your game. Buffett's friend, Jack Byrne, once recalled a story about Buffett's attitude toward betting:

The bet was the kind that rich golfing buddies like. Investment wizard Warren Buffett's $10 against $20,000 that he wouldn't score a hole-in-one over the three-day outing.

Eight of us had gotten together to play Pebble Beach, and in a loose moment, after dinner and a couple bottles of wine, I offered the bet. It was meant as a fun thing, and the other six took me up on it. Everyone except Warren.

Well, we heaped abuse on him and tried to cajole him—after all, it was only $10. But he said he had thought it over and decided it wasn't a good bet for him. He said if you let yourself be undisciplined on the small things, you'd probably be undisciplined on the large things, too. (*Chicago Tribune*, December 8, 1985)

It doesn't hurt to be gifted either. The same story quoted Byrne:

He works at his trade awfully hard. And he has the most amazing memory I've ever encountered. Someone can bring up some obscure company, and what Warren knows about it will leave you slackjawed. He'll tell you the number of shares outstanding, the square footage of retailing space they have in Minneapolis.

Let me tell you. I follow the insurance industry pretty closely and Warren still will bring up important facts from some annual report that I've missed completely.

Although a stratospheric IQ probably accounts largely for Buffett's success, so too does plain old hard work. He's a combination of a sort of genius squared who pushes very hard. Those who work with him in his office say he has a great ability to focus hard, to concentrate completely on the task at hand. "He focuses very hard on the task at hand and then he focuses very hard on the next task," said a Berkshire employee.

Be Your Own Reporter

Buffett's unique ability is to separate what's true from what merely seems true. The practical manifestation of Buffett's ability in the stock market is to buy a good out-of-favor business. Buffett wants to buy a great business—or, in his words, a "wonderful business," at a time when its price is temporarily depressed due to some unwarranted stigma, fear or misunderstanding about the company.

His purchases of American Express, GEICO, and Wells Fargo are examples. He bought American Express the first time when scandal surrounded that high-quality business and he bought Wells Fargo when it seemed its real estate loans might cripple the bank.

Being your own reporter means keeping up not only with the business you own, but also with competitors.

At the Berkshire Annual Meeting in 1993, talking about the number of annual reports he reads, Buffett said, "And we'd be interested not only in any business that we own or are thinking of owning, but we'll be interested in reading their competitors.' I get the Bic Annual Report. I get the Warner-Lambert Annual Report to read about Schick. I get the Pepsico Annual Report. I get the Cott Beverage report. Cott Beverage makes more of the generic colas than anybody—at least in this hemisphere. I want to know what competitors are doing and talking about, what results they are getting and what strategies seem logical to them."

The Market is Not Always Efficient

One notion that Buffett has shot holes through is the so-called "efficient-market" theory, which holds that every stock price is fairly priced because it already incorporates all known information about a company. The theory argues there's nothing to be gained by digging for new information.

> Here's a thought that's analogous to Buffett's thinking about supposedly efficient markets: Two University of Chicago professors were walking down the street when one of them spotted a $100 bill lying on the sidewalk. "Hey, I think that's a $100 bill. Let's stop and pick it up," said one. "No, don't bother," replied the other. "That's not a real $100 bill. Since the market is efficient, a real $100 bill would have been picked up long ago." (*Business Week*, November 9, 1998)

According to the theory, since market prices at any given moment reflect all knowledge, the prices in the stock tables are the right prices. There are no bargains. The efficient-market theory says it's useless to try to outperform the market. Further, all future prices are subject to new, random information. At Berkshire's Annual Meeting in 1997 Buffett summarized his problem with advocates of an efficient market theory. "Observing correctly that the market was frequently efficient, they went on to conclude incorrectly that it was always efficient."

Many times Buffett has said, "It has been helpful to me to have tens of thousands turned out of business schools taught that it didn't do any good to think."

Buffett often has joked that he wished more people would subscribe to the efficient-market theory so there would be fewer investors trying to figure out where the market has gone astray, where it does not reflect intrinsic value. It is in this murky arena that Buffett thrives, doing his lab work, capitalizing on fear and uncertainty while other investors are panicked into selling. That's how Buffett has become the second richest person in the world. Buffett thinks the theory is absurd, that it's better to turn the theory on its head, believing that the market can be inefficient, subject to fear and greed, fads and herd behavior—in short—subject to temporary insanity.

Buffett does not maintain the market is always wrong. Indeed, it is often correct, he says. The trick is figuring out when, on occasion, it's wildly off base.

"The man is a living refutation of the random walk theory," says *Newsday's* Allan Sloan.

Buffett wrote an article for *Barron's* (February 23, 1985), outlining the investment results of a number of value investors who have consistently beaten the market. What one has to wonder about the efficient-market theory is how anything can be efficient when fear and greed infect Wall Street. Although that is not a mathematical refutation of the theory, there is still a sure way to refute it—just present the record of Buffett, who has consistently beaten the market over a lifetime.

And consider that the market dropped 23% on October 19, 1987. That was the day they were throwing rocks at the stock market. But did the underlying economic world change 23% that day?

> Buffett says: "When the price of a stock can be influenced by a 'herd' on Wall Street with prices set at the margin by the most emotional person, or the greediest person, or the most depressed person, it is hard to argue that the market always prices rationally.

> In fact, market prices are frequently nonsensical." ("The Superinvestors of Graham-and-Doddsville," *Hermes*, Fall, 1984)

Buffett has said: "I'd be a bum on the street with a tin cup if the market were always efficient."

Price vs. Value

Early on, Buffett's common sense led him to the simple premise that there is a difference between price and value. "Price is what you pay. Value is what you get." Ben Graham taught Buffett that concept.

"Price does not imply that you got a thing equal in value to what you paid," Buffett Wannabe George Morgan wrote in *Buffett and I Have Zero in Common: He Just Has More of Them Than I Do*. Morgan also recalls a story told by Joe Garagiola:

"Yogi Berra once told his friend Whitey Ford that he had just purchased a valuable house. Ford replied that he was familiar with the house and didn't think it was very valuable. Yogi responded with, 'You may not think it's valuable now but you will after I tell you the price.'"

In a different way, Buffett seeks to buy a valuable house for a bargain price.

People who have talked with those who have traded with Buffett describe him as very tough on pricing. "You know people who want to argue about a 32nd on a trade, well, he'll try to get the last 100th out of it," is one description of Buffett's focus on price.

However, Buffett does not like to haggle. Buying or selling, he has one price, then it's take it or leave it.

Inflation

Another part of Buffett's approach is to keep in mind what havoc inflation can wreak. An investment that can't beat inflation is useless. Only gains in purchasing power count.

Buffett says, "If you forego the purchase of ten hamburgers and place those dollars in the bank for two years, you will receive interest which after tax will buy two hamburgers. Then at the end of the two years, you will receive back an amount equal to the number of dollars in the original deposit but which will only purchase eight hamburgers. You will feel richer but you won't eat richer."

The hamburger parable is an example of Buffett's genius. You do not have to read a textbook or some economist's bloated explanation about inflation. It's all there, simply put, in one paragraph.

And, said Buffett at the Berkshire Annual Meeting in 1986, about valuations: "I always crank through something for inflation."

Compounding

Something else Buffett understands is the beauty of compounding. Buffett ruminates, "$1,000 invested at 10% for 45 years grows to $72,800. At 20% the same $1,000 becomes $3,657,262. This difference strikes me as a significant difference that might conceivably arouse one's curiosity."

Albert Einstein once said: "What is the greatest miracle known to man? Compounding!" And Bernard Baruch once said: "Compounding is the eighth wonder of the world."

George Morgan's example of compounding is this: "You start a company by issuing 100 shares at $10/share. The company is now worth $1,000 (equity). During your first year, you make a $200 profit, which is equal to 20% of your company (equity). You put your profit back into the company and it is now worth $1,200 (in equity). Next year, you experience an additional 20% return on equity which is now $240. This increases your total equity to $1,420. Do this for 79 years and the original investment (equity of the shareholders) of $1,000 is now worth (equity) $1,800,000,000."

Berkshire, since 1965, has averaged a 24% annual return on equity. That is how Buffett has pulled off his monumental achievements.

Ben Franklin once wrote of compounding: "...'tis the stone that will turn all your lead into gold .... Remember that money is of a prolific generating nature. Money can beget money, and its offering can beget more."

Good vs. Bad Businesses: Company A vs. Company E

In addition to nuggets of wisdom, Buffett really does know almost all the people, the numbers, the facts, and even the minutiae involved in an investment decision. He makes a dogged, detailed study. But the art of investing centers on the search for value—not gimmicks, not hunches. For all his intellectual powers, Buffett long has been boiling things down to investing in good businesses at reasonable prices, rather than bad or so-so businesses even at a bargain-basement price.

No smokestack industries please. There's too much chance for high costs and obsolescence.

On occasion, Buffett has talked about good and bad businesses and has described their characteristics, often talking about a hypothetical "Company A and Company E."

Companies A&E? "That's Agony and Ecstasy," Buffett once told Kiewit Construction's Mike Faust, the assistant to Walter Scott, head of the huge privately held conglomerate. Buffett has owned companies in both categories.

But Buffett has had a lot more Company E's than Company A's and now runs one of the greatest Company E's on earth.

In some ways Buffett adds value to a business when he buys it because then it's not just a business. It's a Berkshire business. Kahn Brothers' Irving Kahn says, "His skill is finding private companies that are revalued when public."

So many times Buffett has bought an unrecognized business and given it a halo with just a one-paragraph mention in the Berkshire annual report.

Old-Fashioned Values

If great achievement comes from both natural talent and the environment of one's upbringing, then Buffett has it all. No one disputes Buffett's natural mental gifts, his recall for facts and numbers, his energy.

But he also had advantages: growing up in a family engaged in the commercial and political affairs of its community, and growing up in a place best known for its economic pursuits—mainly meat packing and grain handling in the early decades of this century and now a telemarketing and hotel reservations center. Omaha is no longer a place where the buffalo roam. But tall corn still grows outside the city unmarked by the complaints of bigger cites: rush hour traffic, pollution and high crime rates. Omaha today is also an insurance center. It all provided the right locale for a passionate businessman like Buffett.

Omaha is also near the Strategic Air Command (SAC). *Forbes* (May 31, 1999), listing Omaha as one of the best cities to live in, said of the U.S. Nuclear command: "Shielding Warren Buffett?"

Omaha folks are straightforward, open, friendly and businesslike, just as Buffett himself is open and very quick to respond to matters as they arise. He takes his calls. He responds as quickly as possible to mail. He does not leave people hanging for answers. There is no show, pretense or dissembling. Old-fashioned values prevail. Honesty and decency are assumed.

With Berkshire's financial clout, Buffett could easily pull a lot of tricks—threaten takeovers, corner markets or create market turmoil to his advantage. But there's none of that. Buffett does not go where he's not wanted.

He once took a relatively small stake in a company and expressed interest about a larger stake to the company. A top executive told Buffett the company wanted to buy back its stock and asked him not to buy any more shares. Buffett stopped on the spot and did not buy another share.

Had Buffett wanted he could have bought the whole company; instead he honored the wishes of management.

Look Around You; Work on What's on Your Desk

There's little doubt Buffett subscribes to Theodore Roosevelt's saying: "Do what you can, with what you have, where you are."

Omaha provides a stable, comfortable home for Buffett where he can operate without a lot of distractions. "Successful analysis, like successful investment, requires a fairly rational atmosphere to work in and at least some stability of values to work with," Ben Graham wrote in *Security Analysis*.

Buffett took on the qualities of his traditionally agribusiness and insurance community—hard work, honesty, a pioneer's independent streak and most of all common sense—and mixed them thoroughly with his natural gifts to become both an original personality and the world's best investor.

Buffett appreciates Omaha, which has a metro-area population of 700,000 and which has produced down-home folks, and famous folks (such as Ted Sorensen, Dick Cavett, Dorothy McGuire, Fred Astaire, who was the son of an Omaha brewery worker, Montgomery Clift, Malcolm X, Gerald Ford, Bob Gibson, Paula Zahn, Nick Nolte and Marlon Brando as well as Academy Award winner Henry Fonda and NFL Hall of Famer former Chicago Bears running back Gale Sayers, who both attended Central High School in Omaha.

Buffett understands that Omaha has contributed to his success: "I can be anywhere in three hours—New York or Los Angeles...This is a good place to bring up children and a good place to live. You can think here. You can think better about the market; you don't hear so many stories, and you can just sit and look at the stock on the desk in front of you. You can think about a lot of things." (*Supermoney*, Adam Smith, p. 182)

Not everyone is clear that Buffett is from Omaha. Here's a quote from a wire service story: "Buffett's office in Kansas City said he could not be reached to elaborate."

Good Management

Buffett has earned success through a love of what he's doing, an ability to keep on learning as well as through extraordinary day-to-day persistence. But for all his ability, he knows what he cannot do. "I don't run the businesses. Can you imagine me doing what [Borsheim's former president] Ike Friedman does?" he has said.

Buffett takes a common sense approach about letting others run the businesses, but he does assert himself in some ways. "I set the price on See's Candy every year. I set the circulation prices at *The Buffalo News*. There are certain things, with certain managers who want me to do it, in which it's better to have it centralized.

"Because a person who is too close to a business probably would not tend to price as aggressively as they can," he told Columbia business students on October 27, 1993.

Value Investor, Part Contrarian, Deal-Maker

Buffett is part value investor, part contrarian and part deal-maker.

He's shown it's better to buy a great business when fickle Mr. Market values it unreasonably low.

It is Buffett's genius that leads him to simple solutions. In *The Money Masters* (pp. 40-41) John Train relates the following story: "Buffett once met a leading executive of a capital-intensive business giant at a time when the company was selling in the market for one-quarter of its replacement value."

Buffett asked the executive, "Why don't you buy back your own stock? If you like to build new facilities at one hundred cents on the dollar, why not buy the ones you know best and were responsible for creating at twenty-five cents on the dollar?"

Executive: "We should."

Buffett: "Well?"

Executive: "That's not what we're here to do."

It is through rationality that Buffett, sometimes at the expense of less rational people, has made investing his art form. There is common sense, even genius, but there is an overriding ingredient: a love of what you're doing.

"Buffett loves the investing process in the same way an artist loves his creation," says Omaha stockbroker George Morgan.

Buffett is intensely passionate about what he does. One version of his supposed employment application form other than, "What's your IQ?" is, "Are you a fanatic?"

Genius, love of what you do, and common sense. Stir well and the result can be huge success.

KISS—"Keep It Simple, Stupid" is another Buffett tenet. His passion is for analysis and problem-solving. His aim is to simplify.

No Stock Splits

It makes no sense to pay dividends automatically or split a stock. Berkshire did have a back-door split in 1996 (see Chapter 178). Buffett has said there's no sense splitting because transactional costs would be greater and it would draw more speculation to the stock. Besides, he says, splitting the stock is like asking for a pizza to be sliced into five pieces because you can't possibly eat seven.

"I disagree with him about not splitting the stock," says Dr. Wallace Gaye of Durham, New Hampshire. "One, I don't think the transactional costs are less. And I don't think there would be speculation if he split it 10 to 1... but that would make it easier to deal with. My dad left $5,000 for each kid and with that I can't buy a share of Berkshire for them," Dr. Gaye said.

Michael Assael thinks total transactional costs and speculative turnover are less on the unsplit stock, but he also thinks there may come a point when the shares becomes too unwieldy.

"Hopefully, if Berkshire's price passes Pluto and the shares look as though they are becoming irretrievably illiquid, Buffett will reconsider. But not to worry—there are always mutual funds that could buy shares at $100,000 apiece," Assael said.

"And perhaps someone will start a fund to invest solely in Berkshire for a pure play on Buffett. Just think of it. Kids could shovel snow, sell lemonade or babysit and then invest in Buffett for as little as say, five hundred bucks." Indeed there are new investment vehicles which invest in Berkshire and Berkshire related stocks. "There is no substitute though, for Berkshire itself and the total shareholder experience," Assael said.

For now and perhaps for always, splitting a stock is just another charade that makes no particular sense to Buffett, at least for Berkshire. To him splitting a stock is only a cosmetic exercise. It involves paperwork and creates unnecessary stimulation and a false sense of progress.

What is the difference whether you have one share of Berkshire at price x or 100 shares at 100th of x? Stock splits are something stockbrokers like because they increase trading, giving speculators a false energy and feeling of wealth.

Each year Buffett is asked about the possibility of splitting Berkshire's stock. At the annual meeting in 1990, one shareholder asked if he could see splitting the stock in the foreseeable future. "I don't see a stock split in the unforeseeable future," Buffett replied.

"I have a stockholder friend of mine who is 60. I just sent him a telegram on his birthday that said, "May you live until Berkshire Hathaway splits," Buffett remarked at the Berkshire annual meeting in 1987.

With the issue of the new Class B shares in 1996 (Class B shares sell at 1/30th of the price of the Class A shares), Buffett may have to revise his salutation to: "May you live until Berkshire's Class Z shares are issued."

No Dividends

Buffett doesn't believe in paying dividends so long as retained earnings are compounding at a high rate.

Berkshire paid a 10-cent dividend back in early 1967. Buffett said later, "I must have been in the bathroom at the time." (*Forbes*, October 21, 1991) Berkshire has not paid a dividend since.

Arbitrage

Perhaps one of the least understood areas of Buffett's success is his use of arbitrage—again an area that calls for common sense, judgment, sizing up the odds on discrepancies in the marketplace.

Arbitrage, a French term for profiting risklessly, involves trading on the differences in prices in different markets. Arbitrage, or "workouts," applies to a range of pursuits, but these days often to stock traders' betting on the outcome of a merger deal or reorganization plan. Buffett enters the field of arbitrage only after a deal has been announced. He does not place bets on rumors.

Buffett makes his evaluations on information, not rumors. He looks at the probability of the announced event occurring, the length of time the money will be tied up, the opportunity cost of losing out on a better use of the money and the probability of loss if the announced deal collapses.

After the takeover announcement when the stock of the target firm often soars to just below the takeover price, Buffett might step in, buy the stock and hold it until it reaches its full takeover price achieved when the deal finally goes through. This technique enables him to make a tidy percentage in a relatively short time.

In 1962 arbitrage saved the Buffett Partnership from a down year. The market was declining, but earnings from the workouts allowed the partnership to have a decent year. "They allowed the partnership to be up 13.9% compared to the Dow's miserable performance of being down 7.6%." (*Buffettology*, Mary Buffett and David Clark, p. 253) In years of declining markets, successful arbitrage can provide a competitive edge.

Here's an example of arbitrage. On February 13, 1982, Bayuk Cigars Inc., announced that it had approval from the Justice Department to sell its cigar operations to American Maize Products Co. for $14.5 million, or about $7.87 a share. It also adopted a plan of liquidation and said it would distribute the proceeds to shareholders. Shortly after the announcement Buffett bought about 5.7%

of Bayuk Cigar's stock for $572,907, or $5.44 a share. Buffett concluded the whole plan had a high likelihood of going through in a reasonable amount of time. (*Buffettology*, Mary Buffett and David Clark, pp. 756-757)

The Bayuk Cigar arbitrage went through successfully. The deal must go through or the investor/arbitrageur can be axed, if he isn't nimble.

Since Buffett is a good judge of the probabilities of these deals occurring, he has consistently brought Berkshire a little extra return. He describes one of his earliest arbitrage moves, which was not a takeover arbitrage, in the 1988 Annual Report.

> I participated in one of these when I was 24 and working in New York at Graham-Newman Corp. Rockwood & Co., a Brooklyn-based chocolate products company of limited profitability, had adopted a LIFO inventory valuation in 1941 when cocoa was selling for five cents per pound. In 1954 a temporary shortage of cocoa caused the price to soar to over 60 cents. Consequently Rockwood wished to unload its valuable inventory—quickly, before the price dropped. But if the cocoa had simply been sold off, the company would have owed close to a 50% tax on the proceeds.
>
> The 1954 Tax Code came to the rescue. It contained an arcane provision that eliminated the tax otherwise due on LIFO profits if inventory was distributed to shareholders as part of a plan reducing the scope of a corporation's business. Rockwood decided to terminate one of its businesses, the sale of cocoa butter, and said 13 million pounds of its cocoa bean inventory was attributable to the activity. Accordingly, the company offered to purchase its stock in exchange for the cocoa beans it no longer needed, paying 80 pounds of beans for each share.
>
> For several weeks I busily bought shares, sold beans, and made periodic stops at Schroeder Trust to exchange stock certificates for warehouse receipts. The profits were good and my only expense was subway tokens.
>
> Moral: *Know the tax code.*

In 1981 Berkshire bought the stock of Arcata, a forest products and printing firm, at about $33.50 a share. Arcata was the subject of a buyout by KKR. In 1978 the U.S. Government had seized more than 10,000 acres of redwood timber to expand the Redwood National Park. The government was to pay Arcata for the trees, but the question was how much.

Buffett, who has said he "couldn't tell an elm from an oak tree", added that he coolly evaluated the claim at somewhere between zero and a whole lot. The deal with KKR fell apart, but Arcata sold out in a later offer. Berkshire made about 15% on its investment, selling at about $37.50 a share, but in 1988 received an additional $19.3 million, or $29.48 a share, when the government agreed to pay a total of $519 million for the timberland. (*The Warren Buffett Way*, Robert Hagstrom, pp. 166-167)

At the end of 1993 Berkshire held $146 million worth of Paramount Communications stock. If Berkshire held through the Viacom takeover of Paramount, Berkshire apparently made money through arbitrage. Buffett is at ease with whatever makes money, be it arbitrage, dealmaking, value investing or understanding the importance of brand names.

After money manager George Michaelis joined Source Capital in 1971, Buffett and Munger through Berkshire bought 20% of the closed-end investment fund. (*Forbes*, August 21, 1989)

Michaelis, much influenced by Buffett and Munger, told *Forbes*, "I think of myself as an investor in really great businesses, whereas Ben Graham was really a purchaser of cheap assets. In that sense Buffett has really evolved away from pure Ben Graham."

Forbes said, "The Buffett-Michaelis version goes beyond tangible assets to count such intangibles as brand names or the kind of "franchise" that makes a newspaper or television station valuable. Such businesses tend to have a high return on book equity. Why? Because they are earning not only on their tangible assets but on the intangible ones as well." Michaelis died in a biking accident in 1996.

Buffett is always looking for value, and value may come in many forms; the Coca-Cola and Gillette brand names, for example.

And Buffett admits that growth is not separate from value, but is instead an important component of value investing.

Buffett focuses not only on price but value, the mission of any investor. Business folks in Omaha talk about business and value, not price and certainly not about wild bets, program trading and options.

It has been estimated that Buffett has added several percentage points a year to Berkshire's returns through his workings in arbitrage.

No Derivatives, Please

Buffett has let his horse sense tell him some other things; one result is he doesn't care much for program trading.

He has often told the story that if a group of people were stranded on an island you might well set a certain number to farming, a certain number to building shelter, even some to figuring out how to get off the island, but you would not select several of the people to trade options based on the output of the other workers. Whenever he tells that story, if Munger is around, Munger will say of program traders, "I like them less than you do."

There are no securities on Gilligan's Island either. In our world, at least, there is no options trading available on Berkshire's stock.

Buffett generally deplores options, program and derivatives trading and anything else that brings a casino-like atmosphere to the marketplace, especially where a little leverage can control a lot of assets.

In a March 1982, letter to John Dingell, chairman of the House subcommittee on Oversight and Investigations that was considering whether to allow the Chicago Mercantile Exchange to trade futures, Buffett wrote:

> We do not need more people gambling on the nonessential instruments identified with the stock market in the country, nor brokers who encourage them to do so. What we need are investors and advisers who look at the long-term prospects for an enterprise and invest accordingly. We need the intelligent commitment of investment capital, not leveraged market wagers. The propensity to operate in the intelligent, pro-social sector of capital markets is deterred, not enhanced, by an active and exciting casino operating in somewhat the same arena, utilizing somewhat similar language and serviced by the same work force.

Buffett's investments are straightforward—no hot tips, no betting on the next quarter's earnings report. Using his meticulous research and common sense, he comes to decisions to buy common stocks themselves, be they 20th Century Industries, the insurer in California, or National Service Industries, the lighting equipment company in Georgia, or negotiated purchases of pieces of businesses, such as Bowery Savings of New York, which Berkshire had some ownership in from 1985 to 1987.

A Time to Hold, A Time to Fold

Back when Buffett decided to buy shares of The Washington Post Co., he got in touch with Omaha broker Cliff Hayes, now with Wallace Weitz & Co. in Omaha.

"He asked me to buy Post shares," recalls Hayes. Hayes said when he raised a question of what price to try to buy them for and how much to buy, Buffett told him, "You don't understand, I just want to buy."

"It was just totally expected for me to use my best professional judgment in making the purchases. We'd buy a third or a half of the day's volume, then step back."

Hayes said it was understood that the buyer should not rile the market with big orders or alert the market to a big purchaser in the wings.

Offering his version of a verse from *Ecclesiastes*, Buffett told Hayes, "There is a time to bid for them and there is a time to take them."

Does common sense in the stock market always pan out right away? No. "We started buying The Post at $20 (at 1973 prices) and we were buying it at $12 when we were done," Hayes said.

Even though Buffett was a big purchaser, the Post's share price steadily declined. All the better for Buffett in the long run.

"He does a lot of his trading now at Salomon—but he often asked me to accumulate small positions, sometimes over a two-or three-year period," Hayes said.

"I did the GEICO buying...We bought baskets of it when it was an almost busted company," Hayes said. Again, Hayes bought a healthy percentage of the day's volume but not so much that the market could detect a big buyer.

As for the question of secrecy of the trades, it was understood things were to be kept quiet, says Hayes. "He didn't say keep it a secret. It was just implied," Hayes said, adding it was also understood everything was to be on the up and up. "We never traded ahead of him."

Hayes said if there was something amiss, it was best to tell Buffett immediately and not let any problem fester. Once, Hayes said, word leaked about what Buffett was buying, and Hayes said he told Buffett about it right away. He wound up trading for Buffett for years.

But other brokers who did not report problems quickly to Buffett were not used again. "He's dropped brokers," Hayes said.

Hayes emphasized that it would be very rare for a broker to leak a trade, but leaks in the brokerage community often can happen in the back office, through the stock transfer agent—or anyone else along the way who may have access to the trade or stock delivery process.

Buffett has a rule against trading while he's in the frenetic city of New York. He makes his trades in the peace and calm of Omaha. (*Fortune*, November 27, 1995)

Business Franchise

Buffett discovered early the importance of a business franchise.

A franchise is a business that for one reason or another has a dominance in the marketplace—a leading business such as Pinkerton's in a difficult-to-breach market. It can be a monopoly newspaper such as the *Washington Post* dominating its market, or a strong brand name such as General Foods—a stock Buffett held for years before selling for a big profit when Philip Morris bought it in the mid-1980s—or the ultimate brand name, Coca-Cola—it is always a business with a superior competitive edge. Such a business is so formidable that it is difficult for those wishing to compete with it even to get into the business.

Something Buffett has tried to do, especially in recent years, is to seek out businesses with extremely strong franchises, impregnable but unrecognized franchises.

Buffett saw an archetype of this idea in the monopoly newspaper. He explains:

> The test of a franchise is what a smart guy with a lot of money could do to it if he tried. If you gave me a billion dollars, and you gave me first draft pick of fifty business managers throughout the United States, I could absolutely cream both the business world and the journalistic world. If you said, "Go take *The Wall Street Journal* apart," I would hand you back the billion dollars. Reluctantly, but I would hand it back to you.
>
> Now, incidentally, if you gave me a similar amount of money and you told me to make a dent in the profitability or change the market position of the Omaha National Bank [forerunner of FirsTier Bank] or the leading department store in Omaha, I could give them a hard time. I might not do much for you in the process, but I could cause them a lot of trouble. The real test of a business is how much damage a competitor can do, even if he is stupid about returns.
>
> There are some businesses that have very large moats around them and they have crocodiles and sharks and piranhas swimming around in them. Those are the kind of businesses you want. You want some business that, going back to my day, Johnny Weissmuller in a suit of armor could not make it across the moat. There are businesses like that. Sometimes they're regulated. If I had the only water company in Omaha, I'd do fine if I didn't have a regulator. What you're looking for is an unregulated water company. The trick is to find the ones that haven't been identified by someone else. What you want is a disguised

television station or newspaper. (Investing in Equity Markets, Summer, 1985)

The reason one would like a monopoly television station or newspaper: most other businesses have to go through that business to advertise.

That amounts to what Buffett calls a royalty on the other guy's gross sales—a payment that almost every business in town must pay. If you have the only newspaper, television or radio station in town, you have to get a good percentage of the advertising business.

This was a major reason, one not recognized by many in the 1970s, that Buffett was buying such stocks as The Washington Post Co., Time Inc., Knight-Ridder Newspapers, Media General, Multimedia, and Affiliated Publications, which owns the *Boston Globe*.

Other huge business franchises Buffett recognized are the large advertising firms. It is the large ad agencies with global interests that the giant global firms wanting to advertise must come to.

An IBM, Coca-Cola or General Motors is going to insist on a worldwide ad campaign, and it doesn't want to fool around with 100 different ad agencies in 100 different countries. Instead it picks an Ogilvy & Mather or an Interpublic Group, two firms Buffett made large profits in before selling in 1985, when he thought their merits were fully recognized.

Another conclusion Buffett reached: there are a number of poor businesses and it's best to steer clear of them.

Buffett has stayed away from big, heavy industries requiring constant new investments, businesses with rising competition, rising labor costs and rising need for more capital [except US Airways].

Also, Buffett tries to examine the opposite of a proposition—there are some good businesses with little need for new capital, businesses that have little competition and hence ultimately throw off new cash.

Buying Part of a Business

Overall, what Buffett sees in the stock market is a way to pick up assets that produce a steady stream of cash. Buffett buys at a good price because he buys only a part—not the whole company, for which he would have to pay a premium.

When a whole company is put on the block, everyone looks at the deal in the open, and it usually sells at full value to the highest bidder.

It is different in the stock market: you can buy shares, portions of the business, often quietly with little competition. Better yet, you can operate at the time of your picking.

You do not have to join what Buffett terms the "Swing, you bum," syndrome. You can wait for the perfect pitch two inches above the navel, as Buffett says.

"Investing is the greatest business in the world because you never have to swing. You stand at the plate; the pitcher throws you General Motors at 47! U.S. Steel at 39! And nobody calls a strike at you. There's no penalty except opportunity. All day you wait for the pitch you like; then when the fielders are asleep, you step up and hit it." ("Look at All Those Beautiful Scantily Clad Girls Out There," *Forbes*, November 1, 1974)

That's the appeal of the stock market to Buffett.

Explains Buffett, "When I buy a stock, I think of it in terms of buying a whole company, just as if I were buying the store down the street. If I were buying the store, I'd want to know all about it. I mean I look at what Walt Disney was worth on the stock market in the first half of 1966. The price per share was $53 and this didn't look especially cheap, but on that basis you could buy the whole company for $80 million when *Snow White, Swiss Family Robinson*, and some other cartoons, which had been written off the books, were worth that much. And then you had Disneyland and Walt Disney, a genius, as a partner."

Buffett's huge network of knowledgeable and influential friends also has been a help along the way. Buffett has been an original thinker, but it cannot have hurt to discuss prospects for a television station with Tom Murphy, chat about a common investment with Laurence Tisch, or talk with Jack Byrne about insurance.

"His network of friends has been very important," says broker Hayes.

Ability to Read People

For all Buffett's understanding of the inner workings of business, his greater understanding may be of human nature. He would certainly subscribe to John D. Rockefeller's warning: "A friendship founded on business is better than a business founded on friendship." And Buffett knows that human nature includes: "Fools rush in where wise men fear to trade." He reads people quickly and accurately and his judgment of their abilities, motives and ambitions is almost always on the money. He can see the first class person in a flash, and the fraudulent person just as fast.

Exhibit A: He was one of the few people to detect that Larry King of Omaha was not all the community thought he was.

King, once manager-treasurer of the Franklin Community Federal Credit Union, ultimately pleaded guilty and is serving a 15-year prison sentence for crimes connected with Franklin's 1988 collapse and the disappearance of $39 million in deposits.

GQ magazine looked at King in its December 1991 issue: "Very few people in Omaha closed their doors to Larry King. One who did was Warren Buffett...In 1978, King asked Susan Buffett if she would be willing to host his and Alice's (King's wife's) tenth anniversary party at her house, an act of chutzpah even by King's standards. Susan Buffett said yes, but her husband said no. 'I knew that King was a phony,' says Buffett, 'and I think that he knew I knew. I'm probably the only person in Omaha he never asked for money.' How did Buffett know? 'It was like he had a big sign on his head that said PHONY, PHONY, PHONY.'"

"No less an authority than John F. Welch, CEO of General Electric Co., considers Buffett a superb judge of managerial talent. Buffett and Welch have gotten to know each other over the years as golf partners and as rivals in auto insurance and other businesses. 'Take 20 people you know quite well but Warren has just met casually,' Welch says. 'If you ask Warren his opinion about them, he'll have each one nailed. He's a master evaluator of people, and that's the biggest job there is in running a company.' " (*Business Week*, July 5, 1999)

Avoid Technology and Drug Stocks

Once a shareholder asked Buffett what he thought of pharmaceutical stocks; he said that was not the sort of thing Berkshire had expertise in. (Of course that was before he bought some Bristol-Myers Squibb stock in 1993.)

Buffett added, "That does not mean there are not good ones."

What Buffett was driving at is that while pharmaceutical firms were beyond Berkshire's expertise, no doubt Merck is a superb firm. But Buffett cannot predict what drug is going to be a winner and which one will wind up drawing lawsuits.

In a way they are like his forbidden category of technology stocks, a group whose performance Buffett says he has no way of predicting, because he knows little about present technology and even less about future competitors' technologies.

Buffett would say there are others who can make those determinations better than he about technology or pharmacology—but then he is not sure their determinations are so hot either. It's too tricky an area for a sensible investor trying to cut risks and guesswork.

Buffett said at Berkshire's Annual Meeting in 1998: "I've been an admirer of Andy Grove, and Bill Gates and I wish I'd translated that admiration into action by backing it up with money. But when it comes to Microsoft and Intel, I don't know what the world will look like 10 years from now and I don't want to play in a game where the other guy has an advantage. I could spend all my time thinking about technology for the next year and still not be the 100th, 1,000th or even the 10,000th smartest guy in the country analyzing those businesses. There are people who can analyze technology, but I can't."

Debt is Poisonous, Cash is Good

Buffett's sparing use of debt has been a hallmark of his from the start. When much of the rest of the investing world, burdened by debt, encounters some new crisis forcing a panic, Buffett is usually calmly standing there with little debt and a loaded gun of cash ready to "bag rare and fast-moving elephants."

Little debt and lots of cash give him an ability to respond quickly when the right investment comes in his sights. He does not have to call bankers to get a loan. After dogged investigation in the 1950s, Buffett bought Western Insurance at $16 when it was earning $16 a share, and National American Insurance at one times earnings. (*Forbes*, November 1, 1969)

Then in 1962 he found Gurdon Wattles American Manufacturing selling at a 40% discount from net worth. 'If you went to Wattles of American Manufacturing or Howard Ahmason of National American Insurance and asked them to be partners, you could never get in at 1 times earnings,' Buffett told *Forbes*.

When the reading puts him on to something, he'll do some informal field research. In one case in 1965, Buffett says he spent the better part of a month counting tank cars in a Kansas City railroad yard. He was not, however, considering buying railroad stocks. He was interested in the old Studebaker Corp., because of STP, a highly successful gasoline additive. The company wouldn't tell him how the product was doing. But he knew that the basic ingredient came from Union Carbide, and he knew how much it took to produce one can of STP. Hence, the tank-car counting. When shipments rose, he bought Studebaker stock, which subsequently went from 18 to 30.

On occasion Buffett has asked Omaha cab drivers how their business is doing. He's always watching, asking, reading, and looking for investment possibilities.

Don't Over-Diversify

For all his conservative, sure-footed ways, Buffett is also capable of remarkable boldness when he sees an opening. It's not that he's throwing caution to the wind. It's that his intensive research usually has ferreted out an investment with excellent prospects.

No investment is a sure thing—including Berkshire—and in the early days when he committed so heavy a percentage of his worth to American Express and The Washington Post Co., he had to be right.

Be Bold and Be Original When the Fat Pitch Comes

Later in life, no matter how wealthy he was, it was a bold move to take $1 billion and buy stock, even if it was Coca-Cola at a down time.

In addition to being bold, he is original. What else is it when, at a time the industry is spooked about writing officers' and directors' liability insurance due to the lack of any statistical history and the unpredictability of court awards, Buffett takes out an ad in an industry publication saying that Berkshire will write the insurance?

"To those paying or who are willing to pay over one million dollars for this O&D coverage—you tell us the amount of liability coverage you want and what premium you are willing to pay—and we will tell you if we wish to write the coverage."

Perhaps because he's in the business, Buffett often comes up with ideas on how to sell insurance. In the fall of 1990 when the S&L crisis and banking problems were front-page news, he came up with a suggestion to help the federal government with depositor's insurance—have private insurers write a piece of the action.

"What is needed is a system that combines the ability of private insurers to evaluate risk with the ability of government to bear it. Co-insurance arrangements, varying by size of bank, would appear to be the way to go," he wrote in a piece that ran in the *Washington Post*.

Later Buffett said Berkshire would be happy to write that kind of insurance.

Over the years he has made investments in scores of companies ranging from insurance firms to R.J. Reynolds and Philip Morris to National Presto, the pressure cooker and appliances firm, to National Service Industries.

Handy and Harman has been one as well as 20th Century Industries, General Foods, Affiliated Publications, Interpublic Group, Time Inc., City National Corp., the bank holding company in Beverly Hills, Melville Corp., and the retailer and pet food maker

Ralston Purina.

Has Buffett made a few mistakes? Yes. There was too much devotion to buying really cheap companies in the early days. Remember Berkshire's textile operation failed.

And he told *Forbes* (October 18, 1993) he left $2 billion on the table by not buying enough Fannie Mae, then selling his small position too early. "It was easy to analyze. It was within my circle of competence. And for one reason or another I quit. I wish I could give you a good answer."

Also, he said he sold Affiliated Publications stock because he didn't fully understand the value of Affiliated's big position in McCaw Cellular. "I missed the play in cellular because cellular is outside of my circle of competence."

Still, Buffett has great trust in his thinking. People often write him with their investment ideas and he has replied, "With my idea and your money, we'll do OK."

For all Buffett's monumental achievements, he still was not known to the ordinary citizen and not universally known even in the business world until he stepped in to resolve the scandal at Salomon.

On October 12, 1986, Alan Gersten, an *Omaha World-Herald* reporter, called a Burroughs executive to inform him that Buffett owned 9.9% of the company's stock, an arbitrage position Buffett soon sold. The spokesman asked, "Who's Warren Buffett?" People were still asking that question when Buffett became interim chairman of Salomon.

Because of Buffett's wisdom, his counsel (and money) are often sought. When Salomon was considering taking part in the bidding for RJR Nabisco, Salomon Chairman Gutfreund called Buffett for advice.

"I'll tell you why I like the economies of the cigarette business," he said. "It reminds me of the ideal business where the product costs a penny to make sells for a dollar, is habit-forming, and there's fantastic brand loyalty."

Gutfreund asked if Buffett wanted to invest in the deal with Salomon. Not this time, Buffett said, not willing to be an active participant in the Death Merchant aspects of cigarettes. "I don't need to own a tobacco company." Says one Berkshire shareholder who is a doctor, "I appreciate that." Hence, Coke.

Salomon made its own bid, but the Kohlberg, Kravis & Roberts firm eventually won the tobacco giant.

Buffett has many views on raising children and the lessons they should learn. Probably his most famous view, regarded as eccentric by many parents, is that children should not inherit great wealth. He believes children should be left enough to cope with necessities, but not really large amounts.

Buffett has said he refuses to leave his children "a lifetime of food stamps just because they came out of the right womb." (Richard J. Kirkland, "Should You Leave It All to the Children?" *Fortune* September 29, 1986) Susan recalls a time when she had a car wreck and had to tell her father.

"He was reading *Moody's*. I told him I had had a wreck and he said, 'Anybody hurt?' I told him no. He later came in and said the other guy's always the jerk. What he meant was drive defensively."

Buffett taught her other lessons along the way. One day when young Susan approached her father for a loan, he suggested she go to the bank.

And Howard Buffett has said his father is fixated on finances: "If he drives out to my place (when Howard had a farm) and sees I have $30,000 invested in a tractor, it drives him nuts, especially when it's financed at 15%. But I'd have a hard time getting through life without a John Deere tractor sitting in the garage." (*Register*, February 1984)

Buffett can concentrate so hard on something that he can also be absent-minded on occasion, forgetting momentarily to take his baseball cap off during the National Anthem.

Susan recalls a time when her mother was sick and she asked Buffett to go to the kitchen and bring her a pan. He did and returned with a colander. His mechanical inabilities and his childrens' stories about his tight-fisted ways are representative of the height of criticism of Buffett before the Salomon crisis.

Occasionally, behind his back, people refer to him as Mr. Rogers or Jimmy Stewart, a jealous knock at his childlike, country-simple honesty. Although occasionally absent-minded in his personal life, in business he is super alert, concentrating with all his powers.

Buffett does not buy the idea held by many corporations that the chief executive should make the decisions about philanthropy. So in 1981 Buffett announced that each Berkshire shareholder could designate $2—raised as the years went by to $18 a share in 1999—of corporate donations for each share owned to the charity of the shareholder's choice. "Lots of companies don't earn or sell at what we give away," says Berkshire shareholder Bill Scargle. Back in 1981, Buffett estimated that if every stockholder contributed, the roughly $2 million in contributions would reduce Berkshire's net by about $1 million and its percentage gain in annual net worth by about one-fourth of 1%. (*Forbes*, November 20, 1981)

Charitable contributions in 1999 amounted to $17.2 million, which went to 3,850 charities.

Here's Berkshire's unusual charity policy: "Each Berkshire share-holder—on a basis proportional to the number of shares of Berkshire that he owns—will be able to designate recipients of char-itable contributions by our company. You'll name the charity: Berkshire will write the check."

Buffett has given most of his donations to the Buffett Foundation.

Buffett, the capital allocator, has said that in examining potential purchases, the area he has probably done most of his thinking about, he has three criteria. First, the business should have good economic characteristics; second it must have an able, trustworthy manage-ment and finally it must be a business that is interesting to him.

Sounds simple, easy, sensible, right? Well, that's the whole point.

Buy Back Stock

Buffett has often been asked about the possibility of Berkshire buying back its stock. Buffett says he has no problem with buying it back.

But rather than just willy-nilly buying back stock, he takes the common sense approach. Clearly, the stock would have to be at a good price, and if Berkshire were selling at a cheap price, it's quite likely that would be at a time when something else is selling even more cheaply.

"We'd go wherever we'd get the most for our money," he said at the annual meeting in 1991.

Above All, Avoid Dragons

Buffett often has said he prefers avoiding dragons to fighting them. It's akin to the advice from the power company: call before you dig. Buffett prefers to avoid some problems, but praises his friend, Jim Burke, the former Johnson & Johnson chairman, known for facing problems.

"I would say Jim Burke is a national asset...There are all kinds of people who have 500 horsepower motors who only get 100 horse-power of output. But Jim has a motor with horsepower equal to anyone else's, and the efficiency is 100%...

"He likes to work on problems; I try to avoid problems." (*USA Today*, February 16, 1993)

Once Buffett was asked just what he does, how he spends his day.

"Well, first of all, I tap dance into work. And then I sit down and I read. Then I talk on the phone for seven or eight hours. And then

I take home more to read. Then I talk on the phone in the evening...We read a lot. We have a general sense of what we're after. We're looking for 7-footers. That's about all there is to it," says Buffett of his search for business superstars.

Buffett's looking for 7-footers to make slam-dunks.

Be Dead Right About the Big Decisions

Buffett has said many times that every investor ought to have a lifetime decision card with just "20 punches." Buffett says his success is due to being right on a few big decisions.

Buffett has made a number of small mistakes and might have just an above average record were it not for the monumental decisions to buy big stock stakes at the right time in American Express, The Washington Post Co., GEICO and Coca-Cola.

He looks for haystacks and not needles in a haystack, as he said at the annual meeting in 1994.

"What I try to do is come up with a big idea [gorilla] every year or so."

Forget the Algebra

Knowing of Buffett's distrust of algebraic formulas, Robert Greene, a stockbroker with Robinson-Humphrey in Macon, Georgia, once sent a brokerage report to Buffett containing an enormously complicated algebraic formula for predicting interest rate risk carried by a given fixed-income security.

Buffett replied: "Thanks for the secret formula. With its help, Berkshire should be able to conquer the world."

"Better Plant the Tree Today"

At a conference for analysts June 22, 1998 shortly after Berkshire announced it would buy General Re, Buffett was asked if this was a good time for General Re to expand its insurance operations in Asia. He said yes, that it's important to build long lasting relationships as soon as possible. He told the story of a fellow who asked his yardman about planting a tree and was told it could be put off because it would take 50 years for the tree to grow. The fellow told the yardman: "Then we better plant the tree today."

82

THE PRESS CLIPPINGS
"INVESTMENT GENIUS...FALLEN ANGEL...SCIENCE FICTION...GOD...INTERNATIONAL ICON...FALSE GOD...FOLK HERO OF U.S. CAPITALISM...A NATIONAL HERO"

Overall the press coverage of Buffett has been laudatory and generally—but not always—accurate.

Sometimes a few writers, enamored with spotting some flaw in Buffett's character, speculate that he hobnobs with celebrities, owns a few expensive suits, and occasionally has stayed in an expensive hotel. Sometimes a story will refer to him as a millionaire. Accurate, but not the full story.

For the first couple of decades of his career there was little press coverage. People who knew him were aware of his brilliance, but he operated in such a publicity-shy style, or at least a style of choosing his publicity, that the press was late with the story.

Buffett rarely gives interviews, and when he buys or sells his stocks—or suits—he doesn't yell it out from Kiewit Plaza.

In the 1960s and 1970s, the *Omaha World-Herald* and the *Wall Street Journal* ran stories about Buffett as an investment wunderkind. The first major story was by Robert Dorr in the *Omaha World-Herald*, May 29, 1966.

"I was the business reporter...I had heard stories about how well he was doing. There were rumors in Omaha. I decided to do a story and approached him and he said he didn't want it done...He was reluctant," recalled Dorr. "He said he didn't know how to deal with the press and that it was going to be hard to write an accurate story about what he was doing."

When Dorr said he was going ahead with the story, with or without Buffett's help, Buffett read the story and helped with facts. Dorr got in to see Buffett about the story, several years after Buffett had moved his partnership operations to Kiewit Plaza. "He made a few corrections," said Dorr, still a newsman with the *Omaha World-Herald*. "I believe I was the first person to write a story about him."

Adam Smith in *Supermoney* (1972) wrote a highly favorable chapter about Buffett's investment abilities. And Jonathan Laing wrote a long piece for the *Wall Street Journal*, March 31, 1977.

Buffett's reputation surged in the 1980s as authors Adam Smith and John Train described his endeavors.

More recently some reporters have taken the tack that Buffett is overly famous. A number of press accounts have begun to pick at him—okay, he's an investment genius, but there are some flaws.

One of the first critical pieces (of Berkshire's worth, not Buffett) was a *Barron's* story that suggested Berkshire's stock price was way overvalued. Berkshire shareholders naturally thought the story was off base. (see Chapter 148)

Then almost overnight with the Salomon scandal, the press became aware of Buffett and everyone wrote stories, with some taking the view that Buffett had little experience in running businesses. An odd thing to say about a fellow who founded his own business, runs Berkshire, ran Berkshire's insurance business for years and has tinkered for years with businesses such as The Washington Post Co. and *The Buffalo News*. Further, he speaks constantly with Berkshire's managers.

Most press coverage has been accurate. *Institutional Investor* had a balanced and detailed article on Salomon (September 1991), as did Bernice Kanner in a cover story about Salomon for *New York* magazine. (December 9, 1991)

Other articles (e.g., *Business Week,* February 17, 1992) said that Buffett did well in stepping in to save Salomon; but in running the firm he had not set a clear strategy, employee defections were rampant, policy was inconsistent on bonuses, and Buffett was wrongly trying to run New York-based Salomon from Omaha.

As for Buffett spending only a day or so a week at Salomon, Berkshire's then Chief Financial Officer J. Verne McKenzie said, "We have telephones in Omaha."

But the story that really got under the skin of Buffett fans was Michael Lewis' cover piece in the February 17, 1992, issue of the *New Republic* entitled "The Temptation of Saint Warren," depicting Buffett as a "fallen angel."

Lewis, author of *Liar's Poker* detailing Salomon's excesses, seemed to favor the theme that because Buffett is not a saint, therefore he's a sinner. At no point has Buffett taken a vow of poverty.

"Suddenly there was a delicious gap between what the moralist said and what he did," wrote Lewis, saying Buffett—a critic of Wall Street—had suddenly accepted all its excessive ways because Salomon dealt in leveraged buyouts, junk bonds, and all the rest. Lewis portrayed Buffett as on a moral crusade to save Salomon when what Buffett had said is that he hoped to put the stigma on the dishonest Paul Mozers and get it off the good employees of Salomon.

He had talked about changing the corporate culture at Salomon but he had not talked about becoming a saint himself, and there seems little un-American in Buffett's efforts to save Salomon and help Berkshire. Lewis cast Buffett's efforts as merely trying to save Berkshire's money there.

Lewis maintained that Buffett, as proof of his new fast-buck Wall Street ways, had recently become an arbitrageur speculating on pending takeovers.

Munger, interviewed by the *Omaha World-Herald* (February 12, 1992), said that Berkshire has no rule restricting its activities solely to long-term investing, and that Buffett has practiced arbitrage on publicly announced takeovers every year for the past 40 years and has said so many times. Buffett long has explained in annual reports that Berkshire, from time to time, practices arbitrage.

Further, Lewis portrayed Buffett's financial success as pure luck in the same way that someone could win 40 coin tosses in a row.

Newsday's Allan Sloan says Buffett naturally isn't a saint. "He hasn't ever said he didn't want to make money." And at times, particularly with Gutfreund (rightly so, in Sloan's opinion), Buffett can be very tough on people. He will drop accountants and brokers in an instant if they don't see things his way. "But he is an honorable businessman," Sloan said.

Munger also told the *Omaha World-Herald* (February 12, 1992) that Buffett is not some changed fellow who is a fallen angel.

"I've known a lot of people for a long time," Munger said. "I would say that Warren has changed less in many decades than almost anybody else I know."

Munger was asked at the Berkshire Annual Meeting in 1995 how much Buffett had changed over the years. Munger said, "about one stone...it takes one to know one.

"What he (Lewis) says is that Buffett has lost his soul. He thinks there's some huge change in the way Warren's mind works, and of course there isn't any big change in the way Warren's mind works."

Munger went on to cite a number of errors in the Lewis story. Lewis, for example, said Buffett considered backing the Ross Johnson bid for RJR Nabisco. Munger said Berkshire turned down a chance to participate in the RJR takeover.

Buffett says emphatically:

> I neither offered nor gave financial backing to Ross Johnson or anyone else involved in the RJR buyout. Berkshire was invited to participate in an early attempt by Hanson Industries to enter the bidding and declined.

Salomon elected to support Johnson and I, as a director, said I believed the transaction would work well at $90 a share. Neither I nor other outside directors were consulted about future escalations in price...

On a Sunday in 1988, I was called in Omaha by Salomon and was asked if Berkshire Hathaway would participate in a small way in a purchase offer that Salomon and Hanson Industries might make for RJR. The reason they needed us (or somebody) in the deal was that each partner wished, for some reason, to keep its interest just below 50%. I said I had previously concluded that I did not want Berkshire to own a direct interest in the tobacco business (a decision I made when we were offered a chance to buy Conwood Co., a maker of smokeless tobacco products). But I said I had no problem if Salomon itself wished to proceed and indeed thought it a good economic decision at the price being talked about.

In the process of this discussion about economics of tobacco, I related a story told years before by Father Reinert, then president of Creighton University, as he introduced me to a Creighton class as someone who was going to tell them a lot about investments. But, he said, the real secret of investing was to buy into a business that had a product that "cost a penny, sold for a dollar, and was habit-forming." I have told that story many times in speeches to business schools, and also at the Berkshire Annual Meeting, to make the point about the economic characteristics of certain companies, among them tobacco companies.

As to Lewis' suggestion that Buffett's success is a coin-flipping matter, Munger fired this cannon: "He's got the idea that Warren's success for 40 years is because he flipped coins for 40 years and it has come up heads 40 times. All I can say is, if he believes that, I've got a bridge I'd like to sell him."

After Buffett saved Salomon, *Business Week* (June 1, 1992) said, "By coming clean with both investigators and customers, Buffett kept the firm alive."

Probably no CEO in the country has been more a subject of the press or understands the press better. He certainly knows how reporters work. Buffett's view is that reporters, like people in almost all professions, range from superb to unethical.

"Some people are very talented; some are not talented at all; and you get a lot in the middle," he said in a talk to the Omaha Press

Club. (*Omaha World-Herald*, September 3, 1992). "You get some people who are super-ethical. You get a great majority who are reasonably ethical, but if the story's big enough, they might forget to mention they are a reporter for just a few minutes into the interview.

"And you get a few who are patently unethical...The tough part about it is, essentially, there is no one, virtually with the exception of an assassin, that can do you as much damage as somebody can in the press if they do something the wrong way." (As Mae West once said: "The curve is more powerful than the sword.")

In the same talk, Buffett also said that over the years a number of reporters have interviewed him about Berkshire and written glowing accounts about the merits of Berkshire.

He said the same reporters who wrote the stories have called back asking him to name a good company to invest in.

"Somehow, their brains aren't quite connected to their eyeballs sometimes," Buffett said.

After *Forbes* proclaimed Buffett the richest person in the U.S. in 1993, Buffett made the *National Enquirer*. (October 26, 1993) But there were no aliens, no scandals in the story. The article portrayed the richest man in the country as a regular Joe.

In 1994 Robert Hagstrom, a principal with the Lloyd, Leith & Sawin money management firm in Philadelphia, wrote *The Warren Buffett Way*, a book which looked particularly at Buffett as a value investor influenced by Phil Fisher and Ben Graham. It made the best-seller lists.

In 1999 Hagstrom, now with Legg Mason Focus Capital, wrote a second book, *The Warren Buffett Portfolio: Mastering the Power of the Focus Investment Strategy*.

In 1995 Roger Lowenstein, a *Wall Street Journal* reporter, came out with *Buffett: The Making of an American Capitalist*. It also made the best-seller lists. Lowenstein became a director of the Sequoia Fund in 1998.

A Creighton University administrator, Richard Blankenau, once spotted Hagstrom's book at the Denver airport. He was taken aback at the way the store categorized the book.

It was in the "Science Fiction" section.

Close to it was a book called *History of God*. (*Omaha World-Herald*, March 22, 1995)

In its April 1995 issue, *Money* magazine said Berkshire was overvalued and quoted the "*Overpriced Stock Service*" newsletter as saying Berkshire's stock price "makes sense only if the company is run by God."

In its December 1995 issue, *Money* remained unrepentant:

> In April we told you not to buy Berkshire Hathaway, the firm run by Warren Buffett. The stock was trading in the nose bleed zone of $22,500 per share, a price that made sense, we said, only if your portfolio were run by God. Well, in late October, the stock was up 31% to a staggering $29,500. We're a little red-faced, that's for sure; but we're still not about to run out and start the First United Church of Warren.

The day the issue arrived at homes, Berkshire jumped $1,100 and then another $1,500 the next day to close at $31,600.

At Berkshire there is some confusion between Buffett, Science Fiction and God.

As Buffett's reputation ballooned ever larger, phrases like these popped up in the press: "living saint of value investing, "near-mythical stock-picking success" and "international icon."

Then on June 16, 1997 *Barron's* came with one article saying Berkshire was worth $40,000 a share, not $48,000. Fair enough opinion, but worse was a second story reviewing the Janet Lowe book *Warren Buffett Speaks*.

After mentioning the likes of Jim Jones, Jim Bakker and David Koresh, Liscio declared Buffett also was a "false god." Then he called Buffett a "disingenous elitist," dismissed Janet Lowe as an "apparent sycophant" and then weighed in with another final blow: "Indeed, Lowe even makes Buffett's living arrangement sound like an act of philanthropy. He persuaded wife Suzie [sic] to conquer her fears and move to San Francisco to pursue a singing career, leaving him free to move in current 'companion' Astrid Menks. Ever the canny businessman, Buffett manages to get some on the side, avoid a costly divorce and have his wife praise him for loving her enough to let her follow her lifelong dream. Hey, the guy is a genius."

Although the story hit below the belt, Berkshire's stock dropped only $2,500 that day.

Barron's has been consistently wrong about Buffett and Berkshire. Were *Barron's* ever to run a bullish story about Berkshire, unload all your stock at the opening bell!

On a different note, a *Forbes* story (July 28, 1997) called Buffett the "folk hero of U.S. capitalism."

In 1996 Robert V. Keeley, through his Five and Ten Press in Washington, D.C., published 500 copies of a 49-page pamphlet entitled *Annals of Investing: Steve Forbes vs. Warren Buffett*. Keeley recounted three years of dismal results following the recommendations of the *Forbes Special Situation Survey* stock-picking service published by Steve Forbes' company.

After following several dozens of the survey's selections and making only about 1% a year, Keeley put all his IRA money—$61,404 into Berkshire. "On January 4, 1995, that bought me exactly three shares, at $20,450 each." Keeley reported that he paid $54 to a discount broker and never looked back.

In 1997 *Buffettology* by Mary Buffett and David Clark was published. Mary Buffett is Buffett's former daughter-in-law who was married to Peter Buffett for 12 years. She and Clark, an attorney in Omaha, wrote how Buffett uses "business perspective investing."

Mary Buffett wrote: "While married to Peter, I was instructed more than once not to speak to anyone outside the family about Warren and his investment operations. Writing this book simply would have been out of the question."

"But in 1993 Peter and I were divorced, which shattered my heart into a thousand tears." (p. 15)

She recalled: "In the early years of my marriage, Warren celebrated Christmas morning by tossing out to each of his children and their spouses envelopes with a gift of $10,000. Like a jolly billionaire version of old Saint Nicholas, he would fling the envelopes across the living room, laughing 'Merry Christmas' to each of the delighted recipients. Later he decided that we should be taking a stronger interest in the family business and replaced the $10,000 with $10,000 worth of stock in a business in which he had recently invested. The stock of Capital Cities, Americus Trust for Coca-Cola (a publicly traded trust, no longer in existence that held Coca-Cola stock) Freddie Mac, and ServiceMaster were some of the great companies I found in my Christmas stocking." (pp. 16-17)

In 1997 Janet Lowe wrote a book about Buffett, *Warren Buffett Speaks*, a collection of Buffett's wit and wisdom.

In 1997 the Cardozo Law Review published a volume of *The Essays of Warren Buffett: Lessons for Corporate America*. The September-November 1997 issue features Berkshire's annual reports and has many excellent articles about corporate governance, accounting, boards of directors and other business and legal subjects.

Lawrence A. Cunningham, a professor of law at Benjamin N. Cardozo School of Law in New York City, selected, arranged and introduced a professional summary of Buffett's letters to shareholders. The work was compiled with Buffett's blessing.

The publication hit home with this writer because it's a 30 billion pound, 800-page gorilla.

Thoughts of Chairman Buffett, a small book of Buffett's best quotes, compiled by Simon Reynolds, was published in 1998.

Forbes, in a story October 12, 1998, proclaimed Buffett, "a national hero."

A *New York Times* story (January 17, 1998) looked at why Berkshire's stock had declined at the time and concluded: "Investors say Berkshire's relative weakness is mostly a temporary result of its $22 billion acquisition, announced last summer of General Re, the giant reinsurance company.

"As it turned out, General Re stockholders did not jump at the chance to become Buffett's investment partners by exchanging their shares for Berkshire."

Wall Street on Sale by Timothy Vick in 1999 is a book about value investing and has a chapter about Buffett.

Also in 1999 *Buffett: Step by Step* by Richard Simmons was published and Robert Miles self-published a short book called *The World's Greatest Investment: 101 Reasons to Own Berkshire Hathaway.*

A number of authors spoke at two conferences, one sponsored by *Analyst* magazine in London in January, 1999 and one sponsored by Berkshire Securities, no relation to Berkshire Hathaway, in Toronto in September, 1999. At the same time in the same hotel where the Toronto conference was held, there were also conferences about reproduction and about how to make a living trading stocks...at home.

As 1999 turned into a poor year with Berkshire's positions in Coke and Gillette slumping at the same time as a soft insurance cycle hit, stories began to crop up taking the tune of "Has Buffett Lost His Touch?" and "Is Buffett Washed Up?" *Time* (October 25, 1999) weighed in with "Berkshire's Buffett-ing" saying: "This might be the year the rest of us got smarter than Warren Buffett."

The New York Times (December 25, 1999) ran a story entitled "Investing Diary: A Three-Decade Legend Loses Some Luster."

In late 1999 Jay Steele's *Warren Buffett: Master of the Market,* a short paperback book, was published. And in 2000 Timothy Vick's *How to Pick Stocks Like Warren Buffett: Profiting from the Bargain Hunting Strategies of the World's Greatest Value Investor* came out— certainly one of the longest titles ever.

In early 2000 *Warren Buffett,* a short book by Robert Heller was published. A book about Charles Munger called *Damn Right* by Janet Lowe was slated to come out in the fall of 2000.

And in late 2000 the Monster Millennium Edition of *Of Permanent Value: The Story of Warren Buffett,* an extraordinary masterpiece, a timeless work, took the literary world by storm.

83

"I WOULDN'T WANT TO OWN BERKSHIRE."

"Call it a looming bear market in Warren Buffett stocks," blared a *Wall Street Journal* story August 20, 1997.

The story recited a litany of misfortunes with Berkshire's stocks. Coke and Gillette had warned of disappointing results. Wells Fargo was off. Disney was off. McDonald's was down.

"Even Mr. Buffett's best performers this year, American Express and Washington Post, are down from their peaks." [no mention naturally that Berkshire's stake in the Post had risen from $4 to $440 a share in the past quarter of a century]

The story quoted folks saying it'd be best to sell Coke, that Berkshire had dropped only 8% compared to bigger drops in its largest holdings. The story made an obligatory pass saying that GEICO was doing well and quoted a money manager saying he wouldn't bet against Buffett.

The story ended by quoting one Wall Streeter with a hedging, difficult to fathom statement: "I wouldn't want to bet against Buffett. But I wouldn't want to own Berkshire either."

Berkshire shareholders were used to all this and the stock closed down only 200 for the day to $44,800.

Lesson: Buffett buys businesses based on their intrinsic value and does not sell merely because the market price exceeds intrinsic value. The fact that a number of Berkshire stocks were down probably has little, or no bearing on Buffett's decision to sell. People keep judging Buffett (with a certain amount of self-satisfaction) on inbred, short-term standards which aren't relevant. Yes, the stocks were down at the time. But, yes, Berkshire's stock performance was outpacing the Dow at the time. And yes, the stocks recovered.

Famed financial writer Andrew Tobias, in a story for *Money* magazine (1998 Forecast Issue), said he'd looked at Berkshire since it was $300 a share in 1979. He never could bring himself to buy the stock. He concluded all along it was too high. His advice in late 1997 with Berkshire's stock price at $44,000: "I would hold off."

(With possible apologies to Mr. Tobias, depending on the stock price—and depending on whether or not he bought Berkshire during the lows of Y2K)

84

A THINLY TRADED STOCK

Berkshire is a thinly traded stock and the purchase or sale of a relatively few number of shares can move the stock price dramatically. Here's what happened when an investment bank sold 290 "A" shares, according to the *Omaha World-Herald* (November 22, 1997):

A big stock trade late in the day left Berkshire Hathaway "A" shares down $1,600 apiece Friday, or 3.5%.

Henderson Bros. Chairman James Maguire Sr., who handles trading of Berkshire stock on the New York Stock Exchange, said the sale of 290 shares by a large investment bank caused the dip.

As the trading specialist on the exchange floor, Maguire matches buyers and sellers of Berkshire stock. In the absence of competing bids and to ensure an orderly market, he buys and sells shares for his company's account.

Maguire said a lack of buyers caused him to buy the investment bank's shares for $44,000 a share, $1,900 below the last trade.

"All interest to buy the stock below the $44,000 level was explored," he said. "There were very few orders, and they didn't choose to step up (in price), he said. "Consequently, the price of $44,000 was something we pretty much agreed on would be fair to all parties."

The $12.76 million trade came about 20 minutes before the market closed for the day, and Berkshire shares quickly recovered $500 to finish at $44,500.

The company's "B" shares finished down $43 a share, 2.8%, at $1,493...

85

OVERSEXED MAN

Steve Forbes, who inherited the *Forbes* magazine publishing empire after his father's death February 24, 1990, says his father and Buffett were good friends. Indeed, they played bridge together the night before globe-trotter (by balloon, motorcycle or yacht) Malcolm Forbes' fatal heart attack.

"They were playing in Britain against British Parliament members," recalled the younger Forbes of the Corporate America vs. British Parliament game. The name of the corporate America team was Corporate America's Six Honchos (CASH).

It took place at a 17th century riverside mansion, Old Battersea House, the London home of Malcolm Forbes, a Victorian art-filled house said to have been built by Sir Christopher Wren.

The Corporate America team was headed by former CBS chairman Laurence Tisch, Buffett, Malcolm Forbes, and Bear Stearns' Chairman Alan "Ace" Greenberg. (Buffett wrote a short foreword for Greenberg's book *Memos from the Chairman*. In it Buffett writes: "Ace Greenberg does almost everything better than I do—bridge, magic tricks, dog training, arbitrage—all the important things in life.") James Cayne, president of Bear Stearns, George Gillespie III, partner of the Cravath, Swaine and Moore law firm and Milton Petrie, chairman of the Petrie Stores, played against the Dukes, Sirs and Lords of England on February 23, 1990. The British team was headed by Sir Peter Emery.

Corporate America played 16 hands against the House of Commons in the morning and 16 hands against the House of Lords in the afternoon. The House of Lords team soundly beat the Americans and the Americans squeaked by the House of Commons team.

In those matches, Tisch was Forbes' partner and Buffett and Gillespie played together.

Buffett came up with the idea for the game after a similar one between Corporate America and Congress. (U.S. Senator Bob Kerrey was on the congressional team.)

Buffett arrived in London with his wife. The Buffetts and Gillespies went to dinner and theater the night before the bridge game.

(AP/Wide World Photos)

Forbes magazine's Steve Forbes about Buffett: "I think he's a market timer...We interviewed him in 1969...and he said the market was too high...We interviewed him again in 1974... He said it was a time to buy."

After the bridge games, Malcolm Forbes hosted a dinner for the bridge teams, friends and press members. "My father came home (Far Hills, New Jersey) the next day and died there," said Forbes. "Warren Buffett wrote me a nice letter about how much my father had enjoyed the bridge game and how he seemed to be in such a festive mood."

"My father was not all that great a bridge player but he felt he had played well that night. He (Buffett) is an excellent bridge player. If he had taken up bridge as a career he would have done very well. It's math, a card sense and he just sees some extra dimension...He has a superb mind."

"Warren Buffett is one of the few people to make their fortunes through investing," Forbes said in an interview in Birmingham, Alabama. Forbes sported a money green tie that said, "Capitalist Tool."

"We know Buffett as a value investor but I think he's a market timer, too...We interviewed him (for *Forbes*) in 1969 when he was a virtual unknown and he said the market was too high and that he was selling everything. We said, gosh, he sure called that one right. We interviewed him again in 1974 when the market had declined two-thirds in value in real terms, after inflation. He said it was a time to buy and that he felt like a sex-starved man in a harem."

Buffett, talking about the high-priced stock market in 1973, said "I felt like an oversexed guy on a desert island. I (didn't) find anything to buy." (*Forbes 400*, October 18, 1993)

Forbes said (July 7, 1997): "To observe the niceties of the times [1974] we had censored Buffett a bit. What he actually said was: "I feel like an oversexed man in a whorehouse."

86

PHIL CARRET
"THE GRANDFATHER OF VALUE INVESTING"

Phil Carret, who turned 100 years old on November 29, 1996, was the grandfather of value investing. He lived through more than 30 bull markets, more than 30 bear markets, 20 recessions and the Depression. Carret, born in Lynn, Massachusetts, died May 28, 1998, at the age of 101.

Interviewed on the *Today* show on his 100th birthday, he said his best piece of investment advice was never to go into debt and that his greatest achievement was making his wife happy all the years of their marriage. Carret says there are six words which can lead to a happy marriage: "Please, thank you and I love you."

Carret (rhymes with hurray) was born in 1896, the same year as the Dow Jones Industrial Average and got to know Buffett about a half a century later, around 1952.

Carret wasn't much on handing out unsolicited advice, but when his son, Don, joined the Navy during World War II, he offered the following fatherly advice: "I'm not going to tell you not to drink because I know you're going to and I'm not going to tell you not to chase women, because I know you're going to. Just don't do both at the same time." (*Investor's Business Daily*, January 14, 1999)

Carret once found that he and Buffett both owned stock in the retailer Vornado and called Buffett to tell him he knew Vornado's chairman and to ask Buffett if he would like to meet him the next time he was in New York. Buffett said he'd like that.

The three men had lunch and afterwards Buffett told Carret he wasn't all that taken with the chairman's discussion of the business scene. "I guess I didn't understand retailing as well as I thought," Buffett told Carret. "He sold the stock," Carret laughed.

Carret who put in a 40-hour week until near the end of his life, but drew no salary, said in an interview several years ago that Buffett was one of the two great investors he'd seen. The other was Fred Abbe, three years ahead of Carret at Harvard where Carret graduated in 1917. "There are no reunions for me," Carret cracked shortly before attending the Berkshire Annual Meeting in 1997.

"Abbe was a registered representative who never made more than $10,000 a year as a broker. His strategy was to buy and hold. He'd buy for himself some of the stocks he bought for his customers. He would hold on. He was worth millions later... Among his greatest coups was buying $1,400 worth of stock when he was 25 or thereabouts. Sixty years later he still had it and it was worth $2 million," Carret said.

Carret, of course, was a great investor himself. He owned Grief Brothers, which makes fiberboard containers, for more than 50 years. It was a steady winner. It so happens Carret bought the stock in 1946 on the recommendation of Buffett's father.

The mutual fund pioneer spotted one of his best investments of the 1970s during a business trip. During his stay at a Boston hotel he was impressed by a glycerine soap he used. It rinsed easily, smelled good and didn't irritate his skin. He tracked down the soap maker, studied the company and bought stock in Neutrogena Corp., which became a 30-bagger before it was sold to Johnson & Johnson in 1994. (*Investor's Business Daily*, January 14, 1999)

Carret said Abbe was often needled for holding so long and was told he should keep a closer eye on his stocks rather than just let them sit. According to Carret, Abbe's reply was: "If you buy them cheap enough, they watch themselves."

Later Abbe asked Carret if he'd be the executor of his will and Carret said he'd be honored. Abbe picked five people to back up Carret, but when one of them about the age of Abbe died, Abbe tossed out the whole first team, fearing they might predecease him, for a younger team. "So I never did handle his estate," laughed Carret. This reminds one of a joke about a couple in their late 90s who were asked why they hadn't made estate plans. The 99-year-old husband replied: "Well, we're waiting for the children to die."

In later years, Carret tried to get Buffett to make a contribution to Harvard, taking the approach that Buffett likes to invest in businesses that are No. 1 in their field run by a management he "likes, trusts and admires." "I told him Harvard was No. 1 and that I could introduce him to folks at Harvard that I knew he would like, trust and admire." Nice try. No luck.

Carret, full of anecdotes, sitting in his unpretentious office in New York City, said he had a plaque that reads: "A cluttered desk is a mark of genius." When Carret looked through his desk, he quipped, "Well, I can't find it. My desk is too cluttered."

In curmudgeonly fashion, Carret has told reporters, in talking about government securities, "I don't like to invest in the operations of insolvent organizations," or "trading in and out of the market is the pinnacle of stupidity." (*New York Times*, November 19, 1995)

Carret, like Buffett, worked without a computer. Asked why, Carret replied, "It's up here," he said, pointing to his head. "It works fairly well."

In long hand on yellow legal pads, Carret was well into writing his fourth book, to be called *The Patient Investor*, at his death. Among his earlier books is *The Art of Speculation*, a business classic published in 1930.

Except for a stint as an Air Force pilot in World War I in France and one as a reporter in Boston for Clarence Barron, founder of *Barron's*, Carret was "seduced by Wall Street."

In 1928 he started the successful Pioneer Fund with $25,000 in assets and for years ran Carret & Company, now run by David Olderman and a group of associates including Carret's son, Donald Carret. The fund is up about 450-fold since 1928.

As for planning his 100th birthday, Carret once said he hoped to have about 150 friends over for dinner, which he did. "Of course, I've already celebrated it a few times in case I don't make it," said Carret, who likes parties.

Carret & Company's Frank Betz explained that Carret started celebrating his centennial when he was 93. A mock newspaper head-line in Carret's office reads: "Phil Carret celebrates his 100th birth-day again!"

As Carret, Betz and a visitor headed out for a lunch several years ago, Carret, instead of waiting for a revolving door, skipped quickly to beat it through, leaving Betz and the visitor in stitches.

In talking about Carret's age, Betz says: "Phil remembers when T-shirts didn't say anything and bicycles had one speed."

Carret, who used to take the subway to work, later had a driver who brought him from his home in Scarsdale. Although he accept-ed that luxury in his old age, he still refused to fly first class, men-tioning it in connection with an upcoming trip to England and France.

Carret often crossed the street from his office at quarter past noon for lunch, and made his way to the Waldorf-Astoria Hotel where he entered the Marco Polo Club, a club started by Carret's friend Lowell Thomas, the explorer. This day Carret related stories about an early investment in H&R Block. He said someone told him not to buy the stock because taxpayers could have the returns done by the IRS instead. Carret countered that argument with: "Are taxpayers going to get their worst enemy to fill out their returns?"

(Photo by Frank Betz)

Phil Carret, who loved the markets and parties celebrating his 100th birthday, and Buffett, the day of Berkshire's Annual Meeting in May, 1996.

Carret made a killing in the stock.

He talked about the Detroit International Bridge Co. in which Berkshire once had a stake. "It was for the toll-bridge concept...Of course it had auxiliary businesses such as a liquor store on the American side and some souvenir shops."

Carret became a Berkshire shareholder because he had been a Blue Chip shareholder since 1968 and converted that stock into Berkshire at about $400 a share. Carret has had huge winners with Merck, reinsurer Exel and municipal bond insurer MBIA.

Carret talked about his book, saying there would be a chapter about arrogance—a fatal flaw among many executives.

"IBM was a classic example," he said. Carret noted that former IBM Chairman John Akers demonstrated arrogance in 1991 when he told shareholders the $4.20 dividend was "very safe." It was cut to $1.00. Akers also said earnings were in good shape. IBM had losses the next year. "When Lou Gerstner took over IBM, he talked about the prospects of a comeback at IBM: "I *think* that we can do it." That's the reverse of arrogance and Carret was so impressed by that statement that he bought the stock.

He said Buffett has self-confidence, but is not arrogant. "That there's no arrogance is the remarkable thing about him," Carret said.

In the spring of 1995, Carret, during an appearance on *Wall $treet Week with Louis Rukeyser* said that his favorite stock was Berkshire Hathaway.

After lunch a visitor said, "Just one more question. What's your secret for longevity?" Carret's answer: "Pick your parents well, don't smoke and never worry." Carret said the only time he had worried

626

was during the Depression.

Buffett once wrote Carret:

Dear Phil, Although I know you are still investing for long-term growth, here is the annual dividend on Berkshire Hathaway. [a box of See's Candies]

It was good to have you at the annual meeting last year and I hope you can make it next April. The group is upgraded by your presence.

Happy Holidays and all the best in 1992.

Warren

For decades Carret was interested in solar eclipses and traveled worldwide to view many of them.

Buffett also wrote Carret:

Dear Phil, You are the Lou Gehrig of investing and, like him, your record will never be forgotten.

Come out to the annual meeting: I'll try to arrange an eclipse. Happy Holidays.

Warren

On *Wall $treet with Louis Rukeyser* on April 28, 1995, Rukeyser asked Carret: "What is the single most important thing that you learned about investing over the past three-quarters of a century?"

Carret: "Patience."

87
SEQUOIA FUND'S
BILL RUANE

Bill Ruane, Buffett's longtime friend, attended Harvard Business School, Class of 1949, a class which produced a remarkable number of business leaders.

This is also the class Buffett applied to and was rejected. "To its eternal embarrassment, Harvard Business School rejected Buffett as too young to join its class of 1949." (*Forbes*, October 18, 1999)

The *Forbes* story caught up with a few of the graduates for their 50th anniversary. Among those in the class were Tom Murphy, also Buffett's longtime friend and creator of ABC/Cap Cities, former Johnson and Johnson CEO Jim Burke, Xerox's Peter McCullough and Bloomingdale's Marvin Taub. There were no women in the class. Of the 648 students, 292 ended up as a president, CEO or chairman. One in seven became a majority owner of a business.

Ruane mustered out of the Navy in 1947, worked in a General Electric training program for $49 a week and discovered he was a "mechanical idiot."

But he was good at math and attended Harvard and afterwards worked at Kidder, Peabody. On June 6, 1969 he and Richard Cunniff set up their business which has always been a small operation. Even today it has only 40 employees and about $10 billion under management. (*Forbes*, October 18, 1999)

Ruane, chairman of Ruane, Cunniff & Co. in New York City which manages the Sequoia mutual fund, closed in 1982 to new money from investors, can recall a time when no one showed up at Sequoia's annual meetings although the fund now has such cachet that one Berkshire shareholder paid $500 for a share which he bought through Ebay, the Internet auction house.

Ruane's partner, Richard Cunniff, told the following story at the 1997 Sequoia Annual Meeting: Cunniff said Ruane asked him before one of Sequoia's early meetings, "Do you think anybody's going to show up?"

The two men kicked around the question and finally decided to rent 12 chairs just in case. "So we rented 12 chairs and nobody showed up," Cunniff said. They should have showed up because from 1971 through 1997 Sequoia outstripped the S&P 500 with average annual returns of

Bill Ruane, right, and Phil Carret, chat at festivities before Berkshire's Annual Meeting in 1997.
(Photo by Bob Sullivan)

19.6% compared to 14.5%.

The no show story is reminiscent of Berkshire's early annual meetings held in a cafeteria.

Ruane has described his relationship with Buffett as being like "the caddy for Tiger Woods."

Ruane's modesty continues with comments such as: "We don't go in much for titles at our firm, but if we did, my business card would read Bill Ruane, research analyst."

Over the years Ruane, who has called Ben Graham the old testament and Buffett the new testament, has made many of the same investments as Berkshire and his observations about the market are similar.

In Sequoia's report for the second quarter of 1995, Ruane discussed the craze surrounding the initial public offering of Netscape Communications, a company which allows customers to access the Internet:

> Lest you think that we are going the way of Neanderthals however, we think you should know that your Chairman, out of sheer curiosity resulting from all the media hype, asked a young technophile to lead him into the Internet one day last year. In search of something familiar, he further asked if there was an Internet "room" or "bulletin board" (our terminology may not be quite accurate here) designated for items relating to Berkshire Hathaway. Believe it or not, there is! And a gratuitous remark on this "bulletin board" read: I think Warren Buffett is highly overrated and Berkshire is a short, any comments? The stock was then about $18,000 per share (today's price: $24,850), permitting your Chairman to depart the Internet with the com-

fortable thought that technological sophistication does not necessarily equate to investment acumen.

It must be added, of course, that a comparison of the 1995 performances of Netscape and Berkshire stock prices was not a happy one for Berkshire shareholders.

Berkshire's performance was terrific. Netscape's was off the charts. By 1998, however it was Berkshire's shareholders who were smiling all the way to the bank, with Berkshire's stock price hitting the $70,000 mark.

About 29% of Sequoia Fund's money is in Berkshire stock. Berkshire remains a permanent holding for Sequoia unless totally irrational exuberance were to erupt in Berkshire's stock price.

At Sequoia's Annual Meeting in 1997, Ruane was asked how he would value Berkshire. Ruane replied:

> Well, how much time do you have? This discussion can expand to fill any amount of time available, but to keep it simple, we look at the company a number of different ways, but we focus primarily on earnings. In the latest annual report, Warren Buffett provides a rough estimate of $1.5 billion for the company's 1996 "see-through"—or real economic as opposed to accounting—earning power. Remember this is a bottoms up earnings estimate constructed by "looking through" to Berkshire's economic earnings interests in its many individual holdings, which arguably eliminates the need to decide whether the P/E multiple for Coke common is appropriate. On earnings, I think you're not far from the market multiple level and certainly Berkshire's earnings quality and earnings growth prospects are superior to that of the market. Then you just have to take a look at the sources of the earnings. How much do you think the earnings from the banks it owns or its wholly-owned businesses are worth? If you attribute your own multiples, you will come up with your own figure. It's really not as complicated as some people make it out to be. I think if you start off with the simple idea that it's selling on an earning power basis at around a 5% earnings yield, and then consider the really brilliant management that's in place at both headquarters and most of the operating companies, you will understand why we're very comfortable with our investment.
>
> And then you can go at it from an asset standpoint, and add up the market value of the portfolio and then try to

evaluate the privately owned operations. In doing that, I think you will come up with a number that's not dramatically different from that derived from the earnings power method. On an asset basis, you'll find that there's a premium for Buffett's ability, but it's my feeling that the premium is deserved. When Warren wrote the shareholder's letter in the annual last month, he said that he and Charlie Munger thought that Berkshire's price, relative to the company's business value, was much more appropriate than it had been a year ago.

I think it's really amazing when you just look at what Buffett's done. If you read the annual report carefully, it's there. If you were to evaluate his money management ability or results—these numbers are somewhat inaccurate but they're not far off—the portfolio that he ran in 1995 reported on a comparable basis to the reporting of Sequoia Fund and the S&P 500 was up over 60%, versus the S&P, which was up about 38% and Sequoia, up 41%. And last year the S&P was up about 23% and we did 22%. It gets a little complicated because most of Berkshire's Disney holding was not owned for the whole year, but on a comparable basis, Buffett was up well over 30%. Over a long period of time he's been the Tiger Woods or Michael Jordan of the investment field, and he still is. That mind is still whirring. And I think, also, there's something going on there that I think is interesting. In the past, if you were to take the last 20 annual reports and analyze them, you would find that this is a master portfolio manager at work, creating enormous leaps of value. With the addition of GEICO, FlightSafety, catastrophe insurance, etc., you now have very significant, well run, wholly-owned operations. I personally think that the umbrella of Berkshire Hathaway and its substantial resources permits GEICO to be far more aggressive than it was able to be as a stand alone operation. If you take GEICO and compare it to other great businesses, it would rank very high among them. Maybe it's not an "Inevitable", but—what's that second rank—"Highly Probable"? It's a beautiful business. And Lou Simpson and Tony Nicely are just doing a great job. And that wholly-owned business is now a very significant part of Berkshire Hathaway.

In Sequoia's 1997 Annual Report, Ruane wrote:

Probably unique among fund shareholders, holders of each fifteen shares of Sequoia can now claim that 'Warren Buffett bought me one ounce of silver in the last six months.' Mr. Buffett's recent highly publicized silver investment is a fascinating, if modest, example of the manifold attractions of our major position in Berkshire Hathaway. Buffett continually amazes by thinking and acting "outside the box." Berkshire's recent silver purchases further illustrate the enormous economic diversification that our so-called concentrated holding in Berkshire brings to our portfolio. Each of the components of Berkshire, including its holdings in American Express, Coke and Gillette, among numerous others, has a direct effect on the value of the company we own. While we have long known that Mr. Buffett had no peer in the investment field, it took us far too many years to do something about it and buy his stock on the theory that if you can't beat him, join him. As they say, age is a heavy price to pay for insight, but we are pleased that we did get there eventually.

One would think Ruane has a real interest in money, right? Apparently not so. *Forbes* (October 12, 1998) quotes Buffett as saying: "Ruane just isn't interested in money. And he's the most generous guy I know."

The following is an anecdote about Buffett that Ruane told at the Sequoia Fund's 1999 Annual Meeting:

Warren was asked to testify by Cravath, Swaine & Moore who was defending IBM in the government's antitrust suit. He was on the stand for two days before a very tough judge who clearly felt no warmth for IBM and was pretty outspoken about it. And this one prosecutor said, 'Mr. Buffett, you believe that everything Ben Graham said is accurate, don't you?' Warren said, 'Absolutely.' And the lawyer said, 'Well, let me read you this definition of depreciation...' And he read this definition of depreciation, which was pertinent to the business issue that was being raised at the time, from Graham and Dodd.

The lawyer then looked at Warren and said, 'Do you agree with that definition?' And Warren said, 'No.' 'Well it's straight from Graham and Dodd.' And Warren said, 'What edition was that?' The prosecutor paused and said. 'May I have an adjournment for a few minutes?'

And the lawyers came back the next day and they still didn't have an answer. Finally, Warren said, 'I think you'll find that it was from the fifth edition—and that particular chapter on depreciation wasn't written by Ben Graham. It was cited as having been written by an expert on utility companies. And that happens to be the definition of this other gentleman, not Ben Graham. And I don't agree with it.'

And I can still remember the judge, a hardhearted guy, just looked over the bench at Warren, 'Hmmm'. And then, 'Mr. Buffett, thank you.' I thought he was going to ask Warren for a tip on the stock market. And you know, sometime thereafter, IBM was exonerated. I'm not saying it was due to Warren. But it was a great courtroom scene—right out of Perry Mason...

Irwin Eisinger, with Spectrum Advisors, Inc. in Rancho Santa Fe, California, has been a Sequoia shareholder since the early days. "My big problem has been that I have never been able to find a mutual fund as good as Sequoia despite 25 years of looking. I mentioned this to Buffett last year and asked his advice. His advice was—'Stop looking, you're not going to find it.' "

88

A WHO'S WHO
SHAREHOLDER LIST

OTIS BOOTH, ROGER STAUBACH, TED KOPPEL,
BILL GATES, GEORGE SOROS; CONNECTIONS TO
FORREST MARS, JR., AND RONALD AND NANCY
REAGAN. CALL GIRLS.

Few things give Buffett more pride than knowing the names of the shareholders he has drawn to his unusual enterprise. The shareholders are a wide-ranging lot, everyone from yuppies all over the country, investment bankers and money managers of all stripes, to corporate executives, and sports and media stars, and a number of shareholders who have known Buffett for years.

The Berkshire shareholder list also includes some of the outright rich and famous and mainly people of achievement. This is not a bunch of lounge lizards.

Franklin Otis Booth, Jr., cousin of the Los Angeles Chandler family and great grandson of Time Mirror Co. founder Harrison Gray Otis is a shareholder. Booth has 18,000 A shares. (*Forbes*, October 22, 1998) The amount is a little under that which his friend Charles Munger owns. Booth, who entered college at 16 and has a Stanford M.B.A., has one home in Santa Barbara, California, near Munger's. Both Munger and Booth's homes overlook the Pacific Ocean. The two men met in the 1960s during negotiations to buy a printing outfit used by the *Los Angeles Times*. The deal fell through, but they remained friends. (*Forbes*, October 11, 1999)

In 1963 Munger told Booth, of Bel Air, California, about Buffett. Booth flew to Omaha to meet the largely unknown Buffett. They stayed up until midnight talking about investments. (*Forbes*, October 12, 1998) Shortly afterwards, Booth invested $1 million. That stake has blossomed into a $1 billion fortune even after Booth sold off a bit for living expenses, other investments and charity.

In 1977 Booth gave the Museum of Natural History in Los Angeles about 6,000 shares of Diversified Retailing, then worth about $350,000. He told the museum not to sell the stock. Later,

Diversified was bought by Berkshire. The Booth endowment, down-sized only by small sales for the museum's budget, is now worth $80 million. (*Forbes*, October 12, 1998)

To continue name droppping: U.S. Senator Bob Kerrey, (D.-Neb.); Washington Post's Katharine Graham as well as The Washington Post Company; Coca-Cola's former president Don Keough; General Re CEO Ron Ferguson; former Cap Cities' executives Tom Murphy and Daniel Burke; GEICO's William Snyder; Tony Nicely and Lou Simpson; former USAir's chairman Ed Colodny; Sequoia Fund's Bill Ruane; First Manhattan's Sandy Gottesman; Wells Fargo's Paul Hazen; PS Group's Rick Guerin; Wall Street's Mario Gabelli and Archie MacAllaster; children's author Martha Tolles, wife of Roy Tolles of the Munger, Tolles law firm in Los Angeles; Ann Landers; and investment banker John Loomis and his wife, *Fortune's* Carol Loomis.

A major shareholder is Stewart Horejsi, of Paradise Valley, Arizona who owns 5,000 A shares. (See next chapter.)

Another shareholder is Edwin Pope, the longtime sports editor of *The Miami Herald*. Other shareholders are Dr. and Mrs. John Houbolt. He was a NASA engineer who helped do the math that allowed the U.S. to land on the moon in 1969. A friend of the Houbolts is Berkshire shareholder Marlin Stockwell of New Port Richey, Florida, who says, "I was in computer simulation years ago. I used to program missiles by computer. We also did simulations of the Apollo spacecraft so I know something of what he (John Houbolt) was doing."

(AP/Wide World Photos)

Roger Staubach

Former Dallas Cowboys quarterback Roger Staubach is a Berkshire share-holder who says, "I am one of the lucky ones who has been able to participate in Warren Buffett's golf outings."

Staubach, chairman and CEO of The Staubach Company, a real estate firm headquartered in Dallas, said, "Buffett's success with Berkshire is unmatched and his style is unique which provokes the curiosity of many.

"John Parks in my office is one of the curious. When he heard that I would be traveling to Omaha for one of the golf outings, he said he would die if he could just get to shake hands with Mr. Buffett.

I made arrangements for an introduction, but to get there in time, John had to fly to Kansas City and drive a car on up to Omaha to meet Buffett at a lunch.

"He did get to shake Warren's hand and even got to have his picture taken with him. It was the thrill of John's life, and topped all the opportunities he has had to meet the various athletes who have been in my office over the years," Staubach said.

Ted Koppel, ABC's host of *Nightline,* is a shareholder.

Bill Sr., the father of Microsoft's Bill Gates, is a shareholder. Microsoft's Gates himself has about a $10 million stake in Berkshire. (*Time,* January 13, 1997) Former General Dynamics Chairman William Anders and *Outstanding Investor Digest* publisher Henry Emerson are shareholders.

(AP/Wide World Photos)

Ted Koppel

Frank Kurtz, the Olympic diving medalist, aviation pioneer and World War II combat hero, who died at 85 in 1996, was a Berkshire shareholder. His daughter, Swoosie, the actress, is named after The Swoose, a jury-rigged aircraft Kurtz fashioned out of parts salvaged from planes destroyed in the Philippines in World War II. The plane became a symbol of American determination in the war.

Sharon Osberg, the bridge champion, is a Berkshire shareholder. "In November, 1993, when I met Warren, he invited me to the annual meeting. I was very excited, but didn't feel like I would belong without being a shareholder so I bought a share at $16,000."

Benjamin Graham's son, Benjamin Graham, Jr., is also a shareholder as is Gifford Combs, a noted money manager in Los Angeles. Tom Russo, a partner in Gardner Investments in Lancaster, Pennsylvania, is another shareholder. Teenager Sarah Park, of Tulsa, Oklahoma, who scored a perfect 1600 on her SATs, has one share of Berkshire's Class A stock.

Bruce Wilhelm, a silver medalist weightlifter in the 1976 Olympics known for "Wide World of Sports" appearances, has been a shareholder since 1992. In his competitive days, Wilhelm weighed 357 pounds. Maybe he's really Berkshire's largest shareholder.

"I believe Buffett is a genius. The only thing about him that both-

(Photo courtesy of Bruce Wilhelm)

Berkshire shareholder Bruce Wilhelm, Olympic silver medalist in weightlifting in 1976, kids about Buffett: "I believe he's a genius. The only thing that bothers me is he drinks too many Cokes and he needs to start lifting weights and hitting the treadmill." Recently Buffett has been hitting the treadmill.

ers me is I think he drinks too many Cokes and he needs to start lifting weights and hitting the treadmill more," says Wilhelm.

Former Federal Communications Commission Chairman Newton "television is a vast wasteland" Minow and Voice of America's Geoffrey Cowan, author of *The People v. Clarence Darrow*, are shareholders. Chicago billionaire Lester Crown is another shareholder.

Noted investment expert and writer Charles D. Ellis, managing director of Greenwich Associates, Paul Samuelson, an M.I.T. Nobel Prize winning professor and author are significant shareholders. Richard Russell, author of *Dow Theory Letters*, has been a shareholder since the 1960s. Louis Lowenstein, a professor of law at Columbia University who wrote *What's Wrong With Wall Street* is a shareholder as is his son, Roger Lowenstein, the *Wall Street Journal* reporter who wrote *Buffett: The Making of an American Capitalist*. Morgan Stanley's Byron Wien is another shareholder.

Also, Agnes Nixon, creator of *All My Children*, the ABC-TV soap opera where Buffett appeared, is a shareholder.

William Orr, husband of Kay Orr (former governor of Nebraska) and author of *First Gentleman's Cookbook* for which Buffett supplied his Dusty Sundae recipe, is a Berkshire shareholder.

And so is Ruth Owades, head of Calyx & Corolla, which sells fresh flowers by catalog. Her company's biggest investor is Cap Cities, now Disney, making it indirectly a Berkshire business.

Investor Fred Stanback is a longtime Berkshire shareholder as is his nephew George W. Brumley III. Brumley and David Carr are the founders of Oak Value Capital Management Inc. of Durham, North

Carolina, which holds Berkshire shares as a core investment.

Rita Ricardo-Campbell, the first woman board member of Gillette and author of *Resisting Hostile Takeovers: The Case of Gillette*, says in her book that she's a Berkshire shareholder.

Another Berkshire shareholder is Miami Dolphins' former Head Coach Don Shula.

"Yes, I'm a shareholder," Shula said in the early 1990s.

"I had heard about Warren Buffett and a couple of years ago John Loomis of First Manhattan, who handles my finances, arranged for me to meet him. I was on my way to a league meeting in Dallas and I stopped off in Omaha," recalls Shula.

(AP/Wide World Photos)

"We were supposed to have dinner, but my plane was late so we had breakfast the next morning," he said. "It was at the Red Lion." Shula, another friend of Loomis,' and Buffett shared eggs and issues that morning. Shula recalls that Buffett interspersed much of his conversation with sports references.

"I mostly enjoyed his anecdotes. He knows a lot about football. He knew even more about baseball," Shula said. "He was interested in our accomplishments."

Former Miami Dolphins' Coach Don Shula. "You can take what Buffett says and apply it to your own profession."

"Of course, he's a big University of Nebraska fan," the coach said.

"After breakfast he took us over and showed us his office (Shula agreed that the description of throw rugs and linoleum is not far off the mark) and to the Nebraska Furniture Mart.

"I enjoyed it. I came away from meeting him thinking that his message is simplicity. What he says helps you in your own profession, in your own life. You can take what he says and apply it to your own profession," he said, agreeing that blocking and tackling—the kind of message Buffett delivers—even at the Miami Dolphins' level should always be kept in mind.

"I think Berkshire is as solid as ever. It's been down lately but I remain a shareholder...I'm pleased with the investment."

And Shula, a savvy stock market investor, admits to keeping a pretty close eye on the stock market.

"I don't live or die over it," he said with the tone of voice of a man who might say the same thing about the outcome of a Super Bowl involving the Miami Dolphins.

Another shareholder, a book in himself, is Patrick Byrne, son of Jack Byrne, the former head of GEICO. Patrick Byrne, after a year's stay in a hospital and three years battling cancer, recovered to become a prize fighter. Also, he earned a doctorate from Stanford University after writing a 700-page thesis about the lot human beings are born into, whether rich or poor, black or white. Harvard's John Rawls has written in more academic terms of "original position." Buffett's term for all this at extensive annual meeting discussions is: "ovarian lottery." For a time Patrick Byrne was president of Berkshire's Fechheimer unit.

Another Berkshire shareholder, Rabbi Myer Kripke of Omaha, became one of the richest men of the cloth in history. He and his wife, Dorothy,—who met at the Jewish Theological Seminary in New York City—moved to Omaha in 1946 to take over the pulpit of Beth El Synagogue. A chance meeting in the 1950s led to a friendship with Buffett. It turns out Susie Buffett liked the books that Mrs. Kripke wrote. The two couples often played bridge and celebrated Thanksgiving together. Mrs. Kripke encouraged her husband to invest with Buffett but Kripke resisted, telling his wife, "Look, I'll be silly to go up there. He doesn't want the kind of money we have." In 1966, however, Kripke showed up at Buffett's office. He said, "I'll take whatever you have, and I'll make money on you!" Kripke said. "And he did. And we did." The Kripkes invested in the partnership and then kept stock in Berkshire. In 1997 the Kripkes wrote a check for $7 million to the NYC Jewish Seminary. (*Omaha World-Herald*, February 27, 1997)

Also a possible Berkshire shareholder is Dirk Ziff, who oversees a family fortune of about $4 billion, according to the *Wall Street Journal* (March 3, 1997). The story said Buffett is Ziff's role model and that Ziff keeps a collection of Berkshire's annual reports.

Another admirer of Buffett is Jennifer Schulte of Omaha. A *Wall Street Journal* story (September 8, 1998) devoted its lead story to the remarkable work ethic of the 18-year-old, already an office supervisor at Sears.

Texas billionaire Sid Bass was slated to come to Berkshire's annual meeting in 1999, but did not make it. Holiday decorations impressario Christopher Radko, who has decorated the White House foyer and Vice President Al Gore's home, is a friend of Buffett's daughter Susan. They met when Radko made an appearance at Borsheim's and they have stayed in touch. He is not a share-holder, but was a guest of Buffett's at 1999 annual meeting festivities.

Former world bridge champion Bob Hamman is Buffett's friend and present at Berkshire's annual meeting festivities, sometimes slipping in a game of bridge with Buffett and his pals.

Joe Mansueto, founder of Morningstar, which tracks mutual funds, is an admirer of Buffett and credits following Buffett's business principles for helping him run his business. Mansueto has been to a Berkshire annual meeting and met Buffett once. He became a Buffett devotee after reading a chapter about Buffett in *The Money Masters*, by John Train. (*Inc. Online*, July 7, 1999)

Soros Fund Management, the investment advisory business founded by billionaire George Soros, in a report for the second quarter of 1999, said it owned some Berkshire shares. A *Bloomberg* story (August 18, 1999) said new holdings included about $300 million in insurers, including Aetna, AIG, Cigna, Chubb and Berkshire.

(AP/Wide World Photos)

Billionaire investor George Soros

Guess who was at the 1993 Berkshire Annual Meeting: Forrest Mars, Jr., of the Mars, Inc., candy company (M&M's, Snickers, Milky Way, etc.), the sixth largest privately held company in the U.S. Mars has sales of $15 billion a year. That's nearly twice as large as Hershey's sales. Berkshire shareholder Mark Holloway, of Portland, Oregon, recalls: "The second half of the meeting had only a few hundred people. I was standing at the edge of the stage after the meeting. Forrest Mars, Jr., walked by. They exchanged niceties...Buffett called him Forrest. I believe Mars had others with him." It turned out that it was Munger who recognized Mars. Buffett and Mars had not met, but did exchange pleasantries at that point. Then Mars went on to Borsheim's.

Mars, Jr., left the company in 1999 and Forrest Mars, Sr., died in 1999 at the age of 95.

Here's what *The Guardian* (May 10, 1999) wrote about Holloway in a feature story about Berkshire's annual meeting in 1999. "Mark

Holloway, a burly, gregarious character from Portland, Oregon, is doing very nicely as a result of his interest in Buffett. An investment adviser, Holloway first became fascinated with Buffett in 1970, when he was still an unknown. Most investment advisers would have steered clear because of the unconventional nature of a company which paid no dividends and was run by a bunch of unknowns from Omaha. But the young Holloway was fascinated and, over the years, has acquired more than 20 'A' shares now worth $1.6 million, as well as hundreds of cheaper 'B' shares.

"Just as important, however, he created a cluster of wealth in Portland by advising up to 300 of his clients to buy into Buffett over the last three decades. Holloway tells me privately of one of his clients who had come to him in the 1970s after selling his compressed gas business for $2 million. 'I told him to invest most of it in Berkshire Hathaway,' he says. 'He bought 6,250 shares at between $300 and $500 each. That portfolio would now be worth $450 million."

Among Berkshire's youngest shareholders are Emily and Alison Tilson, daughters of Susan and Whitney Tilson. He is president of Tilson Capital Partners in New York City.

One foreign shareholder, apparently is Prem Watsa, head of Fairfax Financial—sometimes dubbed "Berkshire North"—an insurance company listed on the Toronto Exchange. The company is known as a mini-Berkshire in Canada. Historically it has had a fast growth rate, lots of float per share and a literate annual report. Watsa has attended a number of Berkshire annual meetings.

(Photo courtesy of Whitney Tilson)

Among Berkshire's youngest shareholders are Emily Tilson, born April 16, 1999, and Alison Tilson born April 24, 1996.

The largest block of Berkshire stock in Canada is held by AIC Group of Funds which is headed by Michael Lee Chin. His funds own about $500 million worth of Berkshire stock.

Scott Servias, a catcher for the San Francisco Giants is a Berkshire shareholder. (*Fortune*, October 11, 1999)

Harvey Eisen, chief equity strategist for Travelers Group and a frequent guest panelist on *Wall $treet Week* with Louis Rukeyser, is a Berkshire shareholder.

Is former President Ronald Reagan a Berkshire shareholder? It's difficult to say, but not impossible to believe. *Money* magazine (July 1999) quotes Donald Regan, the former Merrill Lynch Chairman and Treasury Secretary under Reagan as saying that in their retirement years Ronald and Nancy Reagan received "some [investment] advice from Warren Buffett."

Business writer Allan Sloan, a Washington Post employee, who is *Newsweek's* Wall Street Editor, owns Berkshire in his 401(k) plan.

Ben Stein, the Yale lawyer, who is an econo-mist, writer, actor and game-show host, appar-ently is a Berkshire shareholder. A *Newsweek* (December 6, 1999) profile of the former Nixon speechwriter and family man quotes Stein as saying: "Aside from a few practicing pimps, nobody knows as many call girls as I do." When he was a columnist for the *Wall Street Journal* he spent afternoons by the pool in his West Hollywood apartment building, which was populated by call girls. "I think I put a couple of them in Berkshire Hathaway and they made a lot of money."

Harvey Eisen
(Photo courtesy of Sharon Sommerhalder)

Nancy Reagan watches as her husband Ronald Reagan takes the oath of office at the Capitol January 20, 1981.

(AP Photo)

89

STEWART HOREJSI
RAGS TO RICHES

Stewart Horejsi (pronounced Horish), a welding supplier who grew up in Salina, Kansas, who bought his first batch of 40 shares, at $265 each in 1980 and continued buying now owns about $360 million of Berkshire stock. Horejsi owns 5,800 of Berkshire's Class A shares at an average cost of $1,879.21. The *Wall Street Journal* (August 23, 1999) said he was trying to get himself named manager of the Preferred Income Management Fund of which he owned 41.6%. He took control of that fund and changed its name to Boulder Total Return Fund. He wanted the fund to buy more common stocks. His family is also the largest shareholder of two other closed end mutual funds, First Financial Fund and USLife Income Fund.

The story asked: "Where does Mr. Horejsi plan to invest once he gains control of Preferred? You guessed it, right where he started out: in Berkshire Hathaway. 'Other than that, I'm not sure,' he said."

Horejsi said in a letter April 1, 2000: "As you may know, I took over as the adviser to a closed-end fund, Boulder Total Return Fund (BTF) August 29. The SEC limits to 25% how much a fund can own in one stock. Fortunately, this dip in Berkshire's price has allowed us to achieve that 25% level at an average cost of about $56,000."

BTF owns 750 A shares and 9,010 B shares, according to Horejsi.

Horejsi grew up rather poor in a family in the welding supplies business. As a child he delivered gro-

(Photo by Celia Sullivan)

Stewart Horejsi

ceries, and later made his way through school. He earned a B.S. degree in business at the University of Kansas in 1959 and a master's in money and banking at Indiana in 1961 and taught industrial management for a year at the University of Kansas. He served with the Army and then worked for the family business.

Besides running the Boulder Total Return Fund, he has a foundation aimed at helping minorities, flies by Executive Jet and owns a house in Barbados that once belonged to Claudette Colbert (1935 Academy Award winner for *It Happened One Night* with Clark Gable). Colbert, at age 92, died in 1996. In her day such people as Ronald Reagan and Frank Sinatra visited her home called Bellerive. It turns out Hollywood mogul David Geffen was about to buy the house, lost interest, and Horejsi picked up Geffen's offer.

Something surely happened?

"I had worked in the family business then took a year off and studied. It began with Adam Smith's *Supermoney*, then I read the *Intelligent Investor* which was the most interesting thing I ever read," he said. Horejsi said Buffett has said you either get value investing right away or you never get it. Apparently Horejsi got it pretty quickly.

"[In 1980, when he was 43] I began buying Berkshire. I bought 40 shares at $265 and then 60 shares at $295 and several hundred shares at $330," he said. "I've bought Berkshire 54 times in my life and in 15 of 19 years I calculate the lowest return was 24%. It really didn't make much difference when I bought, just that I bought. I always bought on dips."

Horejsi continued his buying in the 1980s and 1990s and never sold.

Horejsi, who now lives in Paradise Valley, Arizona, thought early on, Blue Chip Stamps was even a better investment than Berkshire and started buying Blue Chip. "Someone asked Warren [at the 1982 meeting] whether Berkshire or Blue Chip was a better investment and he said Berkshire. But I thought Blue Chip was and kept buying Blue Chip [which merged into Berkshire] and it came out slightly better than Berkshire."

Over the years, Horejsi has attended most of the Berkshire annual meetings. He says his fund can no longer buy Berkshire because 25% of the money is in the stock, but that he still occasionally buys Berkshire for his own account.

This is Bellerive (under renovation), the home Horejsi purchased in Barbados which was once owned by former actress Claudette Colbert.

90

OIL CHECK:

SOME STAYED AND SOME LEFT MOTHER BERKSHIRE

Along the way a number of people have sold or been forced to sell Berkshire. Many have given to charity or have helped their children. Even so, selling usually turned out to be a big mistake.

Forbes (October 12, 1998) said:

Marshall Weinberg, a Columbia classmate of Buffett's who became a stockbroker at Gruntal & Co., sold some stock to make contributions to various causes. William (Buddy) Fox left Wall Street and cashed in his Berkshire stock to move to Australia. Buffett's close associate Tom Knapp was prohibited from building a major position in Berkshire shares because his firm Tweedy Browne was Buffett's broker during the early stage of Buffett's accumulation.

Laurence Tisch sold his position to avoid, he has said, being criticized for being a Buffett investor when both men might be interested in the same stocks.

At least one member of the Berkshire Bunch was forced out [of some of his Berkshire holdings] by circumstances. He is J.P. (Rick) Guerin, vice chairman of PS Group Holdings, an aircraft-leasing and oil-and gas production outfit. His PS Group had to sell 5,700 shares of Berkshire at a relatively low price to pay off bank debts.

The *Omaha World-Herald* had a story (August 16, 1998) telling of some early investors, a few of whom sold:

Investing with Warren Buffett in the late 1950s and early '60s proved to be a highly profitable move for his early partners.

These investors now are scattered across the country. Some held on with Buffett and got rich. Some died. Others sold their investment after just a few years, to their regret.

Here's how some of the investors have fared:

Ethel Bjornsen and her husband, Olaf, of Colome, South Dakota, invested $10,000 with Buffett in 1962. They acted on a tip from a daughter, who worked as a secretary to one of Buffett's friends.

By 1970 when Buffett dissolved the investment partnership, the Bjornsens' stake totaled about $50,000.

They could have held onto stock in Berkshire Hathaway, Buffett's successor investment vehicle, but they sold it, missing out on eventual millions as Berkshire shares soared.

Olaf Bjornsen died in 1991. Ethel Bjornsen, now 83, says she can only laugh now about passing up a fortune.

"I wish to heck I would have had the sense to stay with him," she says of Buffett. "We were young. We thought, shoot, maybe we could do better with it ourselves."

They spent some of the $50,000 and invested the rest. Today Bjornsen says she has about $100,000 invested, including the recent purchase of three Class B shares of Berkshire Hathaway.

John Dobson, an Ann Arbor, Michigan lawyer, heard about Buffett's investing skill from a client. He and three siblings invested in Buffett's partnership. Records show they invested $65,000 with him in 1962.

Dobson has stayed with Buffett. He said he has about $17 million in Berkshire stock. "The whole thing is so unreal," he says of the investment's growth.

He said he has given some money away to family and has made substantial gifts to colleges and universities.

He had a second home in Florida but sold it. "I didn't get down there enough," he said. "I don't have an airplane. I don't have a boat or a second home. I drive a Buick Riviera. I don't need a BMW. My wife drives an Olds Cutlass."

Dobson, 79, still does estate planning for clients and serves as a trustee of some charitable foundations.

Don Danly and Buffett were high school buddies at Woodrow Wilson High School in Washington, D.C. when Buffett's father was serving in Congress.

While in high school, Buffett and Danly bought used pinball machines and placed them in barber shops. Eventually, they were making $50 a week from the venture.

They moved on to bigger things, Buffett to his financial career and Danly to engineering. In 1962, after Danly's family sold a farm in Nebraska, he put $25,000 of the proceeds in Buffett's partnership.

When the partnership was dissolved in 1970 he kept some stock in Berkshire. [Actually he kept all his stock in Berkshire, but not all his stock in Blue Chip Stamps and Diversified Retailing.]

"I've still never sold any," said Danly, who retired from Monsanto Co. in Pensacola, Fla., in 1989. "I've given some away to kids."

He declined to say how much Berkshire stock he's got now. "It's given me the financial confidence to do whatever I want, buy a vacation home or a boat," he said.

William A. Milanese Jr.'s father, of Long Island, New York, invested with Buffett after hearing about him through a business partner.

The elder Milanese sold most of his 2,000 shares of Berkshire Hathaway in 1970. It proved a costly decision but one that he liked to joke about over the years.

He died a few years ago as a successful businessman. His family is more secure financially because of the investment with Buffett, his son said. The family still owns most of the more than 200 shares of Berkshire that his dad kept—more than $14 million worth.

"It added to my estate, but my children will be mostly the beneficiaries of it," said William Milanese Jr., who lives on Long Island.

Richard Kimmel, an orchard owner in Nebraska City, Nebraska, was a client of Buffett's stockbroker father, Howard Buffett. He later invested with Warren Buffett's partnership.

In 1961, he had $32,000 with Buffett. By 1969, his investment had grown to $371,000.

By the time he died in 1996 at the age of 98, Kimmel had amassed a fortune in the tens of millions, said Bill Carroll, a retired pharmacist who is on the board of the charitable foundation established by Kimmel and his wife, Laurine, who died in 1993.

The foundation has given millions in grants to a range of Nebraska charities since Richard Kimmel's death. Among $1.3 million in grants announced last November were gifts of $500,000 each to Midland Lutheran College in Fremont, Nebraska, and the Homestead Girl Scout Council, as well as $100,000 for restoration of the Nebraska Governor's Mansion.

Like many of Buffett's partners who became wealthy, the Kimmels showed few signs of being rich, Carroll said. They lived in "a very modest home in the middle of the orchard."

Richard Kimmel drove a Chevrolet S-10 pickup. They also owned a Buick LeSabre. Their wealth enabled them to travel extensively, Carroll said.

Casper Offutt was a close friend of Truman Wood, who married Buffett's older sister, Doris.

When Buffett was selling stocks for his father's Omaha brokerage in the early '50s, Offutt became a client. In 1959, the Carpenter Paper Co. salesman invested $10,000 in one of Buffett's investment partnerships.

Offutt, the nephew of the World War I flier for whom Offutt Air Force Base is named, moved to California in 1963 and later started his own paper company.

Now a resident of Atherton, California, he said he still owns Berkshire stock. "I've sold off a little here and there. I've given some to charity. It's been a wonderful cushion."

91

GEORGE BUFFETT AND A BEAUTY PAGEANT

George Buffett, of Albuquerque, New Mexico—Warren Buffett's first cousin—is the son of Clarence Buffett. Clarence Buffett—the eldest son of Ernest Buffett—was in the oil business in different states and died in a car wreck in Alvin, Texas in 1937.

But George Buffett's fortunes would pick up thereafter. He was encouraged to start his own business by his mother, Irma, who died at 95 in 1993.

"I had always wanted to be in the candy business," he said. But he wanted to start at the bottom, learn the business and work with his hands. "I went to California (after graduating from college in 1951) and told them when I applied I had finished the 11th grade which was true."

It turned out the company was See's, long before Warren Buffett bought the company.

"In 1952 I went into a concession business with $250. My partner had $200 and four years later I bought him out for $4,000 because he thought we'd never get anywhere," he recalls.

In 1956 George Buffett opened a candy store, Buffett's Candies ("Our Candy is Made to Eat—Not to Keep!") in Albuquerque, a one-store business he has run while also serving in the state legislature since the late 1970s.

Over the years Buffett's candy and other businesses flourished, but of course there were some problems at the store.

"I had a 58-year-old chocolate dipper who liked to party, but I often had to go get her out of jail for partying too much. It would be $40 a pop. And then once I had to get her out three times in one week before one Easter, but I needed her so bad, I did it.

"Then I heard about a machine chocolate dipper in Kansas City and drove there a month after Easter," he said.

After seeing the dipper, George Buffett decided on the spot to drive to Omaha to see his uncle, Howard Buffett.

"Howard Buffett always had me on his mailing list when he was in Congress. He couldn't let me be a liberal so he sent me all his stuff.

(Photo courtesy of Warren Buffett)

Cousins George Buffett and Warren Buffett at an Omaha Royals game in 1995. Buffett quipped: "Mirror, mirror, on the wall, who's the fairest of them all?" This beauty pageant is…"No contest!"

And he would advise me to save money also."

"I drove to Omaha and went to his office and told him how I was putting a third of my money in stocks, a third in property and a third in the business. He said that was great. Then he said 'why not let Warren take care of your money in stocks. He's honest and he's as good as anybody else.' "

George Buffett said, "That was the understatement of the century."

"So I invested $3,000 in the partnership in 1958 and $5,000 in 1960 and I later bought some more in Berkshire. I put some cash in Sequoia when he closed the partnership.

"I guess you could say I got in because of a partying chocolate dipper," he said.

George Buffett demurred when asked what his investment in Berkshire is worth, saying, "Well, you can say it's more than a half million." That's another understatement.

Asked if he ever sold any Berkshire, he confessed to selling on two occasions. "My wife wanted a condo and I sold some to buy it and I once sold some to buy her a ring from Borsheim's. I figured that was much cheaper than a divorce."

George Buffett had no idea in the early days that Warren Buffett's investing would amount to what it has. "I knew he was honest and I knew he was good, but I didn't know he'd turn out to be the best." He says it dawned on him about ten years ago that he was the best.

"Some people have said we look alike. He's smarter than I am, but my wife says I'm the better looking and I feel like I'm the lucky one."

After the annual meeting in 1995, George wrote Warren:

"Do you remember the night at the ballgame when they were taking our picture? I think you said that you would have our pictures in the next annual report to show that you're better looking. I take it that this means that if there are no pictures you've conceded?"

After the picture was developed Warren Buffett said, "No contest!"

Pressing his point home, George sent Warren a different photo saying, "I wouldn't want you to think the outcome was the fault of your photographers...I know it's tough coming in second twice in one year (Gates), but keep trying. Considering my investment, I'll be rooting for you in the Gates' contest."

Buffett asked his cousin George how he prices his candy. "I told him I price it 10 to 20 cents below See's. I let them do all the figuring and then underprice them because I can make it cheaper.

"There's a See's store in Albuquerque, but I know too many people to go in," he laughed.

George Buffett sent me two boxes of candy for Christmas in 1994 with a note: "Here's one for home and one for the office with the name 'Buffett' on it. From: The Good Looking Buffett."

During the weekend of Berkshire's Annual Meeting in 1995, George Buffett told this story on himself. He writes a conservative newsletter called "Buffett's Bullets." Because of its popularity, folks began sending in donations to support the letter. Buffett wanted to thank those who did and settled on sending a key chain with a bullet. He located a distributor of the items in Montana who asked George Buffett if he were related to Warren. The distributor said he had bought Berkshire at $17 a share and sold at $35. George Buffett said he had bought at about $18, but had not sold.

"Why the hell are you working?" the distributor asked.

92

ANN LANDERS HAS A DATE WITH BUFFETT...

"BEHAVES SHAMELESSLY."

From her Sioux City, Iowa, home, Ann Landers (Eppie Lederer) used to visit her sister, Helen Brodkey, in Omaha to date the Nebraska boys.

"No. I didn't date Warren Buffett," she laughed during a telephone interview, but in the mid-1980s when the advice columnist went to Omaha she did indeed have a date with him.

Landers—who has answered thousands of letters from such people as Anxious in Akron, Fed Up in Fresno and Lonely in Laredo— was invited to a function that involved skits at the Omaha Press Club Gridiron. "I was asked to perform and wrote a little skit which had me doing the shimmy in a fringed evening gown. I think Warren was struck by the incongruity of it all—an advice columnist doing the shimmy.

"He came up afterwards and asked if he could take me to lunch the next day. When I told him I already had a luncheon date, he asked, 'Do you think you can get me included?' "

"I told him I was sure that I could since I was having lunch with people from the *Omaha World-Herald*."

The host was Harold Andersen, the publisher, an old friend of Buffett's. "Of course they were thrilled to include Warren Buffett."

"We went to the lunch and sat next to each other and behaved shamelessly. We hardly spoke to anyone else. Warren is a fascinating man and has a marvelous sense of humor. He said 'let's stay in touch' and we have. One of the fringe benefits is See's Candies, which is not available in Chicago. He owns the company, you know."

"I bought Berkshire Hathaway stock immediately after I met Warren. I'm not a plunger in the market, but I do buy when I know the management. I thought if Warren is running a company, then I want to be in on it. When I saw the price, I almost flipped."

"I've been in his home and met Astrid Menks who is a very warm and winning person. I also know his delightful daughter Susie and the grandchildren. I attended a formal party in Lincoln given by Kay

(Photo by Nancy Line Jacobs)

Buffett's daughter, Susan, and Ann Landers at Borsheim's in 1994. Ann Landers: "I suggested that perhaps he ought to give some of his money away while he's alive, but I don't think I made a dent."

Orr who was then the governor and we all went in our formal attire on a bus. I sat with Warren's wife, who is totally captivating and a real stunner. He wanted me to get to know her. He's very proud of Susie and well he might be. Not only is she a knockout, she has all the right values. They have a remarkably warm and pleasant relationship for a married couple who live apart.

"I've talked to Warren about his immense wealth and asked the logical question: 'What are you going to do with all that money?' He told me it's going into The Buffett Foundation and when he dies he's going to leave the largest foundation in the world. I suggested that perhaps he ought to give some of it away while he's alive, but I don't think I made a dent."

In her column of April 25, 1999, Landers mentioned that some readers thought it outrageous for dentists to charge folks with just a few teeth the same amount as they would charge patients with all their teeth.

Here was a response from Laguna Hills, California: "This is for your reader with only six of his original teeth. I am 79 years old and have had less than 20 percent of my original hair since I was 39. That's 40 years. I get a haircut every two weeks, or 26 times a year. In 40 years, I have had 1,040 haircuts and have yet to have a barber offer me a discount. If a haircut costs $8 plus a $2 tip, that's $10 a cut. Had I received an 80 percent discount based on the amount of hair I had, I could have saved $8 a cut, or $8,320. If I had invested that savings with Warren Buffett, I would have about $23 million today. So let's not hear any more complaints."

At every party there are two kinds of people—those who want to go home and those who don't. The trouble is, they are usually married to each other. — Ann Landers

93
MARY AND JOHN HOUBOLT
A MOON LANDING

NASA Engineer Dr. John Houbolt, of Williamsburg, Virginia, who through his math calculations helped the U.S. land on the moon in 1969, is a Berkshire shareholder. It was his equations and rocket trajectory work that paved the way for the historic moon landing. James Michener, in his book *Space,* talks about Houbolt. Also, *Life* magazine (March 14, 1969) ran a piece about Houbolt.

Houbolt's wife, Mary, got her husband interested in Berkshire. She was a member of a women's investment club for years and became interested in Berkshire and makes postings to the AOL Berkshire message board as "Nanaondnet." (Her grandkids call her Nana. So she's known as "Nana on the net", using "d" instead of "the".

"Around 1991, I found Berkshire and began to follow it but only to study what kind of companies Buffett invested in. It never occurred to me to buy it! At *that* price? Of course not! How out-landish a price could there be??!! Then two or three years ago, the computer came into my life. I discovered the Berkshire board and the Yellow BRKers, soon became addicted, studied like crazy and realized Berkshire should be bought—by then, of course, at an even *higher* price!

(Photo courtesy of Mary and John Houbolt)

Mary and John Houbolt

"John still does some consulting work which he loves, and learning about stocks is not his favorite thing to do, but since he's the brains of the family, he was force-fed a lot of what I was learning because I kept taking questions to him when I didn't understand things. I jumped in first, but he was not far behind. The pity is, that we didn't buy when I first found it. I still have the

659

Value Line sheet that I printed at the time. I look at the price on it and cry!

"Oh, well, I'm grateful for having found the Berkshire board and getting in when I did. And now it really is an all-consuming hobby." Mrs. Houbolt said, "The women 'collected' other female posters for awhile and wrote quietly amongst themselves. We were all timid about posting on the board which was, and still is, largely male."

One woman whom Mary contacted in her search for women interested in Berkshire, Susan Warnock (Mommalion) of Windsor, California, recalls that, "Our e-mail conversations had the feel of 'the girls sneaking around the boys' club to me. I pictured a boys' club-house with us girls spying on them without them being aware of us."

"The men never did anything to make us feel unwelcome. I doubt they were even aware of us. And certainly they weren't aware of our behind the scenes discussions. In my early lurking days on the board, the intrinsic value discussions were like Greek to me, but continued reading and study led me to a better understanding of intrinsic value."

Mrs. Houbolt adds: "Who would ever have thought this senior citizen, who just took up the computer two years before, would ever fly all the way to Omaha, Nebraska lugging ten pounds of decorated bricks (gifts for Doshoes) to meet about 40 cyber friends, Yellow BRKers, for the first time along with the second richest man in the country, chairman of the company about which we read and write all the time, and then sit through a whole day's shareholders' meeting thoroughly enjoying it? Or, Finnigan l who lugged two leis all the way from Hawaii for Marlinls' wife and for Doshoes?

"And how many John Gartmanns do you find walking around in two foot high yellow hats? Or semi-amateurs financially analyzing Berkshire Hathaway in a way that even Buffett himself is impressed?

"Or the story of when the one 'bad egg' started posting with bad manners and insults, and the whole group temporarily fled to the unused Zond board to get rid of him. But ultimately, all came back, the nuisance left, and peace reigned once again. This kind of rude behavior is typical on most boards, but so conspicuously absent on this one. It really is a unique group."

Houbolt, who studied at the University of Illinois, originally joined the old National Advisory Committee for Aeronautics at Langley Field, Virginia, where he worked on research and development of aircraft. Around 1957 a group began to look into space flight. "I worked on equations for orbits and trajectories for rockets," Houbolt said.

Mrs. Houbolt says her husband didn't exactly get us to the moon, as one Yellow BRKer has said, but he played an important role. He convinced the government that of the three proposed ways of going to the moon—direct from earth to moon; earth orbit and then to moon (German rocket pioneer Werner von Braun's proposal); or, earth to moon with lunar orbit before landing (Houbolt's proposal)—his way, Lunar Orbit Rendezvous (LOR), was the fastest, cheapest, and most practical way. Convincing the government, of course, was done with a lot of engineering research and mathematical proof, not just verbal arguments.

The *Life* magazine story began:

Its official designation is an unpronounceable, vowel-less LM—for Lunar Module—but it is known to nearly everyone as the Bug or Spider or LEM. It was hatched in controversy from a handful of rough sketches, and for a while it was nothing more than a wooden body with paper-clip legs that looked like a half brother to a yo-yo. Even now, fully grown, it's paper-thin aluminum flanks could never survive high-speed exposure to the earth's atmosphere, and its landing ladder, designed for the one-sixth gravity of the moon, is so fragile it would break if used on earth. Last week this most complex and daring of man-made flying machines rode through space with Apollo 9, a mission that would determine if it was ready to perform the task it was built for—to land two U.S. astronauts on the moon, then send them safely homeward.

The concept that produced the LM is even more audacious than the machine itself. It calls for a descent to the lunar surface from the orbiting mother ship, then a launch from the moon to a dangerous rendezvous before the trip home. Eight years ago the scheme seemed so bizarre that the obscure engineer who first suggested it was ridiculed. His lonely and courageous battle saved the U.S. billions of dollars, prevented years of delay and, if all goes well, will make a moon landing possible this summer.

A quote from the *Life* story says:

"It occurred to me then that rendezvous around the moon was like being in a living room," Houbolt said. "Why take the whole darn living room down to the surface when it is easier to go down in a little tiny craft. As soon as I saw it in that broad context, the concept looked very appealing." Houbolt scribbled some quick back-of-the-envelope calculations. "Almost spontaneously," he says, "it became clear that LOR offered a chain reaction of simplifications: development, testing, manufacturing, launch and flight operations. All would be simplified." I said, "Oh my God, this is it. This is fantastic! If there is any idea we must push, it is this one."

Even before President John Kennedy set the goal of landing a man on the moon, NASA scientists and others were in a debate over the most practical way to achieve a manned landing on the moon. Most agreed on a direct approach.

Time magazine (February 28, 1969) said, "Houbolt's plan was to leave the mother craft in orbit around the moon while a light, ferry-like craft descended from it to the lunar surface carrying only one or two of the astronauts. Later, the little craft could blast off, rendezvous and dock with the mother ship, and then be left behind in lunar orbit as the astronauts returned to earth.

"Houbolt argued that the concept would save an immense amount of fuel. Because the lunar lander would not need a heavy heat shield for a return through the earth's atmosphere and would not have to carry additional equipment and supplies for the long trip to and from the moon, it could be tens of thousands of pounds lighter than other lunar landing vehicles...

"During a visit to Huntsville, President Kennedy stood in embarrassed silence while von Braun argued heatedly with Presidential Science Adviser Jerome Wiesner, the last important holdout against LOR. Pressed for a final decision, Kennedy overruled Wiesner in

(Photo courtesy of Mary Houbolt)

Top Secret: NASA engineer John Houbolt was an unsung hero of the U.S. space program.

October 1962 and gave NASA permission to proceed with the design and construction of a lunar module."

Sputnik had jolted Congress into action and NASA had come into being.

The original concept of the Johnson Space Center for going to the moon was to fly the entire spaceship to the moon, but Houbolt realized that Lunar Orbit Rendezvous was a far better way to succeed than flying directly all the way to the moon or taking the Earth Orbit approach. "By my pushing, we began to give more attention to Lunar Orbit Rendezvous." In the end, it has been said that Houbolt's plan saved the government $20-25 billion [the government should have invested the savings in Berkshire] and enabled the U.S. to accomplish the mission within President Kennedy's time frame.

From 1959-1962, Houbolt, "somewhat as a voice from the wilderness", fought for his idea, finally convincing Werner von Braun whose backing was crucial. "My notion was that the descent to the moon should be in a small lander."

Houbolt was at Cape Canaveral the day the moonshot was launched. "I watched the lift-off at Cape Canaveral, then went to Mission Control in Houston."

As Neil Armstrong landed on the moon July 20, 1969, Houbolt was both worried and thrilled. "They waited a little too long to land. The public didn't know it. Finally man landed. There was clapping, then shushing to keep everyone quiet. We didn't want to miss history. Von Braun turned to me and gave me an A-OK sign and said, 'Thanks, John.' "

[Exactly 27 years later, to the day, Munger gave his famous Coke speech. Maybe Buffett said, "Thanks, Charlie." Shareholders certainly would.]

94

PAUL HARVEY

ABC networks' radioman extraordinaire, Paul Harvey, got to know Buffett because of his work at ABC Radio. "I met him at Cap Cities' meetings. "It was actually my wife (Angel) who invested with him first at about $6,000 or $7,000 a share," Harvey said.

"She invested with him because of his sense of humor," laughed Harvey in an August 26, 1998 telephone interview, adding that he was dubious about that being the best way to make an investment decision.

Harvey became a Berkshire shareholder later and a Buffett fan.

Today 24 million people "stand by" for Paul Harvey and his distinctive radio voice. That's the number of listeners who tune in every week to hear his blend of news and views.

Harvey, the most listened to personality on all radio, grew up in radio newsrooms. Born in Tulsa, Oklahoma, he made his own radio sets while still a boy. In high school he frequented KVOO radio until the station manager hired him.

(Courtesy of Paul Harvey)

Paul Harvey

In St. Louis Harvey became special events director and newsman at KXOK, but the most important event there was his meeting of the girl he called Angel. She had come to the station for a school news program when he invited her to dinner and proposed to her that evening.

After their marriage they lived in Chicago, combining their talents in a news career with Angel producing many of his radio shows and later his television series *Paul Harvey Comments* which ran for 20 years.

"And now you know the rest of the story."

95

EDWIN POPE

Edwin Pope, the longtime sports editor of *The Miami Herald*, has been a Berkshire shareholder since 1994.

Called "the best writer of sports in America," Pope was reared in Athens, Georgia, and in 1943 became the youngest sports editor of any daily newspaper at age 15. He later worked for the *United Press, The Atlanta Constitution*, and *The Atlanta Journal*. In 1956 he joined *The Miami Herald* and has been sports editor there since 1967. He has covered every Super Bowl game.

Pope probably became a sportswriter because that's what he does best. After all, he jokes, his father once told him: "Edwin, put down that wheelbarrow. You know you don't understand machinery."

Pope, 71, has been a working journalist for 60 years. Pope told *The Wall Street Journal* (January 28, 2000): "My daddy had an Underwood typewriter in the office of the cotton warehouse he ran, and I taught myself to use it. I loved to type anything. When I was 11, I listened to the Orange Bowl game on the radio and banged out a verbatim copy of

(Photo courtesy of Edwin Pope)

Edwin Pope, already a veteran sports writer at the age of 19, interviews Joe Louis for the Atlanta Constitution in 1950. It wasn't in this interview, but Louis once said: "I don't like money, but it quiets my nerves."

(Courtesy of Edwin Pope)

Miami Herald Sports Editor Edwin Pope

the broadcast, commercials included. Then I got on my bike and took it down to the *Athens Banner-Herald* and asked the editor if he could use it as a story. He said no, but asked me if I wanted a job as a reporter. I said sure, and he had me—at no pay—cover the local high school and YMCA." At 15 Pope was named sports editor of the *Banner-Herald*.

In an interview in 1999, Pope said, "I'm sitting in Don Shula's Miami Dolphins head coaching office one day in 1987 and we start talking stocks. I was always trying to tout him on my own company, Knight Ridder; Shula had had some Knight Ridder stock but I believe he gave it to his kids. Anyway, that day, he says he has bought shares in a company that has big media holdings. He mentioned Berkshire, and I didn't know what he was talking about. I checked around and found out it cost $3,300 (I don't remember precisely, but I would surmise I probably didn't want to show my ignorance by asking Shula what he paid for it). The next time I saw him I said, 'That's too rich for my blood.'

"I started following it, though, and up and up it went, until I finally said to myself, 'Hey, the boat's pulling out, jump for it.' I bought one share around $18,000 in 1994. Then I kept adding little by little.

"Funny thing, I think it was around the college draft before his last season, 1995, I was talking to Don in the lobby of the Dolphins General Headquarters in Davie, Florida. He had remarried by then (his first wife, Dorothy, died of breast cancer a few years earlier). He said, 'Say, Mary Anne (his new wife) is asking me if I think SHE ought to buy some Berkshire. What do you think?'

"It was still in the low 20's and I said, 'I think it's just digging in for a long run.'

"I'm not sure whether she bought any, but Don had a nice chunk of shares he bought at $3,300.

"I believe Don's financial advisor is (or was, anyhow) one John

Loomis, who is married to Carol. That's how he got onto it. And he really got me into it, so I'm grateful for that.

"A few years later, when a grandson was born, I took a picture of him on the floor posed with *Of Permanent Value* just as though he was reading it. I sent the picture to Buffett and said, 'I am trying to teach my grandson to be rich.'

"To my great surprise Buffett responded by return mail. He wrote, 'Your letter and the picture made my day. Tell the kid I am going to give a quiz on the book when he finishes reading it.'

"Buffett also knew I had written a book on Ted Williams [*The Splendid Splinter*] back in the 1960s, and mentioned his many allusions to Ted Williams and his 'comfort zone.'

"So that's my story with Berkshire and it's not over yet, I'm happy to say."

Will Edwin Pope be at the next Berkshire Annual Meeting? Probably not. Unfortunately it's the weekend of the Kentucky Derby which Pope covers.

Pope once said his son David, as a small boy, asked him why he had to leave home a week early for a Kentucky Derby that lasts only two minutes.

96

"I ASKED IF HE KNEW OF MY FATHER, HANK GREENBERG,

AND HE SAID '1938—HIT 58 HOME RUNS, HAD 183 RBI'S IN 1937'..." *GLENN H. GREENBERG*

" I met him at a Columbia Business School Forum in 1986 in a hotel in New York. There were a bunch of...[financial speakers] and I went along because he's my hero," said Glenn Hank Greenberg, managing director of Chieftain Capital Management in New York, who earned an MBA degree from Columbia in 1973.

"He was surrounded by people and I felt toward him the way some people felt toward my father. There's some human instinct to reach out and make some connection with someone you admire and often it doesn't amount to much," Greenberg said.

"I knew he liked baseball and I asked him if he knew of my father, Hank Greenberg, and he said, '1938—hit 58 home runs, had 183 RBIs in 1937'...heck, I didn't even know them and he repeated three or four statistics. I thought he was trying to show off his memory. As far as I knew they were correct. He has a photographic memory. He was reeling off the statistics...He wasn't telling me [the statistics] because he thought he was coming close."

"My father [Detroit Tigers slugger Hank Greenberg] did hit 58 homers in 1938, eleven years after Babe Ruth hit 60. It was not as big a deal as when Roger Maris hit 61, years later...and my father was always humble about it and [to fans] would say how much he appreciated that they remembered or that the pitchers were hoping he'd break Ruth's record anyway.

"Meeting him [Buffett] was somewhat disappointing from a personal standpoint. There was a crowd around him...but he is without a doubt the best in the investment world. He's done it with no leverage, no cheating...He is my hero."

97

"FROM MARGIN CLERK TO MILLIONAIRE"

THE DIFFERENCE IN BILL SCARGLE'S LIFE

Bill Scargle, a PaineWebber executive in San Francisco, California, started out life as a margin clerk and wound up a millionaire. How? By discovering Warren Buffett. "It started with a $2,000 investment in Blue Chip in 1969 because it looked like a growth company."

Later as Berkshire bought up Blue Chip and Scargle heard more about Buffett, it was off to the races. "In 1974 and 1975 I poured another $10,000 into Blue Chip which was all the money I had at the time," said Scargle, who was making about $12,000 a year in those days. Scargle, who went to the University of Florida and is a big Gators football fan, said:

> Then in 1978 and 1979 I purchased about $4,000 worth of Berkshire at $165 to $175 a share. At that point, my entire life savings was invested in Buffett companies. (Blue Chip merged into Berkshire in 1983.)
>
> As any investor with all his eggs in one basket, I wanted to meet in person the man who held the basket. I attended the Blue Chip annual meetings during the 1970s because Buffett was a director, but he was never there. In the late 1970s...I went to the Berkshire Annual Meeting. It was held in the cafeteria of the National Indemnity Building. It was attended by a half a dozen shareholders, several employees and a couple of Buffett's relatives.
>
> It lasted a few minutes. Buffett said he had about an hour if anyone would like to stick around to talk about investing. That hour changed my life. I knew at once this guy was one very smart investor. Nothing has ever changed my mind since.
>
> After the meeting, I introduced myself to Buffett and he said, 'You came all the way from San Francisco for this?'
>
> I also fly to the Wesco Annual Meeting to hear Charlie Munger talk.

(Photo by LaVerne Ramsey)

Early investor Bill Scargle

I always knew they [Buffett and Munger] knew what they were doing. I've thought about it [Berkshire] every day. I've collected almost everything written about it.

I never sold a share until Berkshire was about $7,000 or $8,000. I sold some then because I decided I should pay off my mortgage and all my debts and invest in some 10% Treasuries for my retirement. Sure, I made a mistake. As it turns out, I'd have done better holding on to the stock.

I've given to charities. I even asked Buffett if I could give to The Buffett Foundation and he said not to, that the foundation has plenty of money.

I guess you could say I was a margin clerk who became a millionaire. It's been a fantastic ride and I don't think it's over yet.

Scargle's other gifts to charity really include his many clients who own Berkshire. Bill would be too modest to say so, but a close friend says his book of Berkshire stock over the years has created about $300 million in wealth. Pointedly pressed for the actual figure, Scargle finally said, "Well not quite that much" at a time when Berkshire was trading at about $73,000.

At Scargle's 60th birthday party on August 17, 1998, Scargle received a note from Buffett which said: "Bill, congratulations on your 60th. May you live until Berkshire ("A") splits."

98

HIGH SCHOOL DROPOUT, MALE MODEL, CONSTRUCTION WORKER, FIREFIGHTER

"I'M A MILLIONAIRE, THANKS TO WARREN."—NEIL MCMAHON

"**I** first learned about Berkshire in 1973 from Adam Smith's *Supermoney,*" says Neil McMahon of New York. "I owned 100 shares of Berkshire by 1979 at an average cost of $220. I sold the 100 shares at a profit in the early 1980s and regret it."

"I bought Berkshire back in 1982. Then in 1986 and 1987 I bought 18 more shares. I own 36 shares now, or almost $2 million of Berkshire and about 2,000 shares of Sequoia Fund so I have more Berkshire indirectly. I got into the Sequoia Fund just before it closed in 1982," he added. "I'm a millionaire, thanks to Warren."

McMahon's portfolio in 1999 stood at 36 Berkshire Class A shares, 8 B shares and more than 2,000 shares of Sequoia.

McMahon, a high school dropout who later earned a high school equivalency degree, has had long careers as a construction worker, firefighter and as a male model.

In 1962 New York City fireman McMahon saved a two-month old baby from a burning building in Queens after he climbed a ladder with a filter-mask on and found the baby squirming. The baby's mother was out shopping at the time of the fire.

Handsome and solidly built,

Photo of models Evelyn Kuhn and Berkshire shareholder Neil McMahon.

(Photos courtesy of Neil McMahon)

McMahon and Virginia Jasper, the 1963 Orange Bowl Queen. An early romance didn't lead to marriage and McMahon became a lifelong bachelor.

McMahon has posed for hundreds of modeling jobs over the years including a six-page spread for an executive style living ad in *Forbes* in 1982.

Now in his 60s, McMahon is a lifelong bachelor who once was engaged to the 1963 Orange Bowl Queen. "But I always stayed a bachelor and live a simple life," he said.

McMahon, who never inherited a penny, was able to save money because for years he worked as both a fireman and a construction worker and did his modeling jobs on the side.

"I'm like Warren in that I'm very frugal with my money. I buy straw hats in the winter or eight pairs of shoes at one time at discount. I have a home in Connecticut that I rent, but I live in a rent controlled apartment in Queens."

After a problem with GEICO one time, McMahon wrote Buffett. Buffett replied February 26, 1997: "Thanks for your nice letter posting me on the problems you've had with GEICO. Generally speaking, their service is quite good, but you clearly have been involved in a foul-up. I hope it has gotten straightened out to your satisfaction and look forward to keeping you a happy GEICO policyholder and shareholder of Berkshire."

If you reread this chapter enough, you'll be as handsome as Neil.

99

RECOLLECTIONS OF A JOY RIDE FROM ED PRENDEVILLE,
A TRAIN COLLECTOR

"**I**first learned of Warren Buffett in Adam Smith's book, *Supermoney* in the late 1970s," said Berkshire shareholder Ed Prendeville of New Vernon, New Jersey. "Unfortunately, I did not invest in Berkshire at that time because I had a young business buying and selling old toy trains and all my money was invested there," added Prendeville, owner of Train Collectors Warehouse, Inc., in Parsippany, New Jersey.

"Because Warren's approach to business and investing was rational and most others were not, it made a lasting impression on me. Then in December 1981, I bought a toy train collection in Salt Lake City, Utah, for $280,000, virtually my entire life's savings plus a lot more.

"The collection was all packed in a U-Haul truck and I was driving home through Omaha. It was 3 a.m. and I remembered that Warren Buffett, the man I had read about, lived there. I remember thinking then I had better look into buying some shares of Berkshire when the train business produced some profits.

"A couple of years later when I had some money, I bought some shares of Berkshire and have held them and added more ever since. It has been a hell of a nice ride.

"The longer I own Berkshire, the more I realize what terrific businesses it owns and invests in. Of course, you have probably the best business and security analyst and capital allocator in a generation, possibly of all time as your partner. You would have to be a fool not to go into business with Warren and can do so any day the New York Stock Exchange is open.

"Fortunately, the most important investment decision I will ever have to make is when to sell Berkshire and I may never have to make that decision."

(Photo by LaVerne Ramsey)

Train collector Ed Prendeville

100
ARTHUR ROWSELL
A TRADER FOR BUFFETT, MUNGER AND GUERIN
"DOES WARREN BUFFETT HAVE AN ACCOUNT AT THE BANK?"...
"WELL, HE OWNS THE BANK."

"I started trading for Warren Buffett in about 1963. I got to know him through Rick Guerin," says Arthur Rowsell of Encinitas, California, known as "the flower capitol of the world," especially for its poinsettias.

I really didn't know who he was and he was putting in big orders saying he'd pay for them with funds at Illinois National Bank.

He called one day and said he was going to Europe but that he wanted to keep buying Blue Chip at under $16 a share, Rowsell recalled.

At that point my boss asked me who the hell Warren Buffett was and told me to check him out. I called Illinois National to ask if he had an account there and the fellow said, 'Well, you're putting me in an embarrassing position. He owns the bank.'

Most people buy stocks as they are going up. As they go down, people get fearful. Buffett, Munger and Guerin come alive in a bad market when they are the only bid in the world, Rowsell said.

Warren is so different from anyone else. Some people, if they want to buy 100,000 shares, just put in an order and they get the right amount. They buy it going up. Buffett wants the market to come to him. He's very patient...He's always buying a stock that's going down.

Buffett wants to participate in the market, not move the market. Buffett puts in orders a bit below the market, and doesn't say how much he wants, meaning he wants all he can get at that price or better.

I once asked Rick Guerin how much stock he wanted and he said, 'Look, Art, I want to get enough to get on the board and make a whole lot of money.'

That's the last time I asked that question of any of those guys.

Rowsell said Buffett is the same way. You buy all you can and you are not finished buying until the last share has been bought. "If you told Buffett he could buy all the stock of a company at his price, he'd say send it in. If he could buy all of a Salomon or Wells Fargo at his price, he'd take it." Continuing, Rowsell, added:

> He's highly ethical. Buffett never buys near a news announcement or on either side of a quarterly earnings report.
>
> I ran trading departments. Mind you I was a market maker in these stocks and the lead market maker in Berkshire. The way Buffett buys goes something like this: I'd say something was trading 30 to 30¼ He would say do the best you can but that did not mean paying 30¼ or supporting the stock. If it wanted to go lower, then I was to buy it cheaper.

Over the years Rowsell worked at Hayden Stone, Doyle O'Connor and Cantor Fitzgerald. Before becoming a private investor, he bought for Buffett such investments as American Express, California Water, Source Capital, Blue Chip, Doyle Dane, Interpublic Group, General Foods, Affiliated Publications and many others.

> Affiliated was interesting. First Boston did an IPO of 500,000 shares in the depths of the down market in the early 1970s, I believe at $13 per share. The selling shareholders were the founding families of the *Boston Globe*. By the time they listed the stock on the American Stock Exchange a couple of months later Warren had bought 350,000 to 400,000 of the 500,000 share issue. You will recall that some years later he sold the stock near $100 after a 2-for-1 split. The stock subsequently sold down to $8 after his sale.
>
> One of the founders of Intel, Robert Noyce, was a graduate of Grinnell College. Buffett was running the Grinnell endowment fund—for gratis, by the way. Noyce came to Grinnell and asked if they could invest $100,000 in Intel's original venture deal. Buffett told Noyce that if he could get his classmates to contribute $100,000 to their college, the fund would match the $100,000 thereby getting a $200,000 participation. This was accomplished and Grinnell some years later sold the stock, in a decision not made by Buffett, for about $18 million, a tiny fraction of its value in 1997.

At Berkshire's annual meeting in 1997, Buffett said: "We did buy 10% of the original [Intel] issue [for Grinnell]. But the genius who ran Grinnell's investment committee managed to sell those shares a few years later—although I won't give you his name. And there's no prize for anybody who calculates the value of those shares today."

Rowsell executed a lot of over-the-counter and arbitrage trading for Buffett. "He does a lot of trading," Rowsell said.

Over the years it was Rowsell's practice to call Gladys Kaiser at the end of the day with a record of the day's trades.

"I've talked with Buffett thousands of times over the years. When he was really buying something, we'd talk five to eight times a day," Rowsell said.

Rowsell was playing tennis with Buffett at the compound near Buffett's Laguna Beach home one day when he realized Buffett was the greatest investor ever.

> Four of us were sitting around afterwards having a Pepsi and someone mentioned Dunkin' Donuts. I thought I knew Dunkin' Donuts. I mean I worked hard at these things...He said, 'You know, I've looked at that a few times.' And he started talking about how the company would be more valuable if it split off its real estate into a REIT, that it was only making 80 cents a share. I mean he had all the facts and figures. He knew Dunkin' Donuts up one side and down the other. That was when I sold my Dunkin' Donuts and bought Berkshire at $300 and $500 a share.
>
> Warren's intellectual capacity and his memory are better than anyone I've ever known. He has the ability to absorb a large number of facts and come out with simple but very effective decisions.

The only person Rowsell's ever met in Buffett's league intellectually was Teledyne's Henry Singleton.

"The difference between the two is interesting. Singleton is just raw daunting brain power but Buffett is just as comfortable as an old shoe. Buffett is equally intelligent but he just presents himself so smoothly."

Rowsell got to know Singleton when they were pitching Teledyne stock to brokers.

"Because I was a market maker in Berkshire, Buffett was kind enough to steer business my way including the liquidation of Ben Graham's estate," Rowsell remarked.

Rowsell said Buffett, on occasion, read the entire S&P sheets and the 2,500-page Walker's Manual [which was a sort of Moody's of

West Coast securities]. The publication, based in Lafayette, California, in a reformed way, still exists.

"He once told me he reads the *Walker's Manual* by starting at the back. He knows about stocks you've never heard of...You could think the earnings of a company were $1.85 and he could tell you they were $1.82. Believe me, they'd be $1.82."

"I Like Oddball Securities"

Walker's Manual Editor & Publisher Harry Eisenberg knows first hand Buffett reads the publication and has this letter from Buffett:

Dear Harry:

You're terrific to think of me in connection with the manual. A quick glance this morning convinces me that I'm going to enjoy perusing it. In fact, if you ever find an offering of some "sleeping beauty" that you don't want to buy for yourself, drop me a fax and I will quickly check it out in the manual and perhaps purchase it for my collection. (I like oddball securities.)

Sincerely,
Warren E. Buffett

101

"HEY, JERRY, DRIVE SLOW...
I WANTED TO INTERVIEW HIM AS LONG AS POSSIBLE."
OMAHA WORLD-HERALD'S JIM RASMUSSEN

O*maha World-Herald* newsman Jim Rasmussen requested an interview with Buffett shortly before a *Forbes* article in October, 1993 proclaimed Berkshire's chairman the richest person in the country.

Buffett told Rasmussen he was amenable to it, but first said, "Let's see what *Forbes* has to say."

After the story ran, Rasmussen got back in touch with Buffett who demurred a bit: "I don't see what else there is to write." But Buffett said okay and that a way to do it was to get together before he gave a talk to Columbia University business students on October 27.

"I met him outside Salomon's headquarters [Buffett was there for a board meeting] at the World Trade Center. I was to meet him at 5 p.m. and I was outside 10 minutes early because I didn't want to miss my shot at the interview," Rasmussen said.

"He walked out the door at 5 p.m. and we had to be at Columbia before 6. We got into a Lincoln Town Car. I think it was a Salomon car, and he introduced me to the driver, Jerry. I said, 'Hey, Jerry, drive slow,' because I wanted to interview him as long as possible."

"I asked him how he felt about the *Forbes* ranking and he said he was glad about it for Berkshire, that if he'd gotten it and Berkshire had done only so-so, it wouldn't have meant as much."

As a result of the story, Berkshire was getting a lot more mail, Buffett said, much of it asking for money. "One guy wrote this long letter asking for $10,000. And then at the end he said, 'Well, why don't you make it a million?' " Buffett told Rasmussen.

"I asked him about the polar bears on his tie in the *Forbes* piece— if that was any subliminal message and he said no that the folks at Coca-Cola gave him the tie as a memento of its ad campaign.

"But he seemed nervous about the question. I don't think he likes questions about his views of the market," Rasmussen said.

Buffett said he needed to be at Columbia 17 minutes before his 6 o'clock appointment. "He had it down to the minute. We got there a little early and he had the car pull around and park and we continued to talk," Rasmussen said.

"I asked him about his personal worth [besides Berkshire] and he said rankings aren't perfect and don't go into other worth, or debt."

Rasmussen pressed, trying to put a figure as an estimate of Buffett's net worth beyond his Berkshire holdings. But Rasmussen said he didn't get the slightest hint about whether the figure was high or low. "He didn't even touch the question...It was as if he said, 'Nice try, Jim.' "

Then Buffett got out and met Carol Loomis of *Fortune*, and talked to the students for two and a half hours, devoting his first remarks to the subject of integrity.

"I mean, I can go hear a speech and I know whether I'm entertained or not, but I probably won't change anything I do," Buffett has said of his preference to talk to students, rather than adults who are unlikely to be as impressionable as students.

"He was swamped by the students and signed annual reports," Rasmussen added.

The 80 students gave Buffett a 40-second ovation.

Afterwards, Buffett left with Carol Loomis, but asked Rasmussen if he needed a ride and Rasmussen said he'd get a cab back to his hotel to write his story.

"I was pretty pumped up the whole time," Rasmussen said.

102

ARTHUR CLARKE

2+2=4

Arthur Clarke first became interested in Buffett because he wanted money from him, not for himself but for the University of Chicago where he was director of corporate giving in the 1970s.

Clarke, who has had a 22% compound annual return for 15 years running his eponymous investment firm of Arthur D. Clarke & Co., in Boston, Massachusetts, said Buffett once asked him what he liked about fundraising. Clarke replied it was easy enough to figure out who has money; the challenge is to figure out how to approach that person. "Warren's eyes brightened and he said, 'I can see how that could be fun.' I should add also, however, that he realized one had to be deeply committed to the cause for it to be lasting fun."

One day Clarke was doing his detective work and spotted an item while leafing through the latest issue of *Official Summary of Security Transactions*, the SEC's monthly publication of insider transactions. "At the time we were probably the only development office subscribing to it," Clarke said. Lights flashed when he saw that Berkshire had made an investment in The Washington Post Co.

Ed Anderson, a Chicago alumnus who at the time, was managing partner of Tweedy, Browne & Knapp, had put Clarke onto Buffett's trail. "Ed recommended I read the chapter on Warren in Adam Smith's book. I did straight away and was hooked. Here was a man who had his life put together in a remarkable way. It may sound strange, but I put Warren, Milton Friedman and Socrates in the same class: each lets reason be his guide. Emotion leads to false expectations, and therefore, disappointment and mean spiritedness."

Buffett became Clarke's role model, which only intensified his drive to find a way to interest Buffett in the University of Chicago. "The Berkshire purchase of Washington Post stock was the key I was looking for. Most people would have passed right by this item, but I knew that Warren was behind Berkshire and Katharine Graham was behind The Washington Post."

"Katharine Graham is an alumna and was, at the time, a trustee of the University of Chicago." This connection gave Clarke the lead he was looking for. "The next day I called Ed to ask him what was going on between Warren and Kay. 'How did you find out about that?' was his surprised response."

The story continued from there, but before long Clarke left the university to raise money for the Urban Institute, a think tank in Washington, D.C. "I had never heard of the place, but Warren (as well as Kay Graham) was a director and that piqued my interest. That's how I finally met him."

When Clarke did meet Buffett, he told him the University of Chicago story. "I told him the experience brought home to me his oft made comment that arithmetic is not the hard part in life. We learn 2+2=4 early. The hard part is that the 2's rarely come together in the real world. Unless you are paying attention, you miss those few times when you have four.

"Of course, everybody's looking for 5," continued Clarke, "and that's why they end up disappointed. Like Socrates, Warren is very wise because he is rational. Therein lies his happiness."

103
NOTES FROM THE DESK OF CHRIS STAVROU

Chris Stavrou of New York—a large Berkshire shareholder since the mid 1980s—has had brief conversations with Buffett over the years and shares these thoughts:

Background: "I went to Wharton and from there straight to Wall Street to work as a brokerage house security analyst servicing the more aggressive institutional money managers, such as Fidelity, the Acorn Fund, Robert Wilson, and George Soros...Later I founded a Buffett-style partnership, Stavrou Partners, in 1983, and among other things built up a massive position in Berkshire Hathaway. I have to pinch myself when I think how well it has all worked out. A great turning point for me as an analyst was studying Warren's methodology; and I was so impressed with his character, honesty, and intellect, that I christened my son Alexander Warren, although I named him after Leonard Warren, the opera singer, as well."

How I First Heard About Warren: "One day in the early 1970s Lou Vincenti, president of Wesco Financial, started talking about Warren and became very enthusiastic. I'll never forget what he said: 'Warren Buffett is the greatest financial genius I've ever met. A new book has just come out called *Supermoney* by Adam Smith. Chris, don't walk, run to the bookstore and get it. There's a chapter in it on Warren. It will be the greatest lesson on investing that you can get.'"

Conversations with Warren: "Finally I met Warren in the mid-1980s...Warren has this way of lightheartedly answering questions, almost seeming to deflect the questioner at times, but really getting to the heart of the question and its relevance to investing. I had heard he had a photographic memory and that he never used a computer or even a calculator, so I asked him whether it was true he never used a calculator, and he said: 'I never owned one and wouldn't know how to use one if I did.'"

"Really? Well, then, say, could you give me an example of how you do division?"

"Ten percent is real easy."

"Seriously, how do you do more complicated calculations? Are you gifted?"

Berkshire shareholder Chris Stavrou and his son, Alexander Warren Stavrou

(Courtesy of Chris Stavrou)

"No, no. It's just that I've been working with numbers for a long time. It's numbers sense."

"Is there a trick? The great mental calculators like von Neumann and Feynman used to do some math operations like addition from left to right instead of right to left. Is there some way like that that you make the math easier?"

"Yeah. You don't have to go four places beyond the decimal point."

"No, seriously give me an example. Like what's 99 times 99?"

"9,801."

"How do you know that?"

"I read it in Feynman's autobiography."

(Sure enough, if you read *Surely You're Joking, Mr. Feynman*, you will see the exact same question asked and answered in the middle of the book.)

"If you have the price of a painting go from $250 to $50 million in 100 years, what's the annual rate of return?"

"13.0%"

"How did you do that?"

"The Union Carbide compound interest tables. They only go out 50 years. You'll do somewhat better in stocks, and a lot better if you live long enough." Needless to say, those tables were nowhere in sight.

"I'm astounded you remember that. (The Union Carbide tables were the first computer generated compounding tables and haven't been published since the mid 1960s.) If they only go out 50 years, how do you do a 100-year calculation? (Here he went through a calculation that I couldn't quite follow. But the point is he didn't just splice two tables together mathematically as you normally would using square roots. He used other simple algorithms I'd never heard of before or since.) But let's say you don't know the compound interest tables or algorithms for using them."

"Then you just go by the number of times it doubles." ($250 doubles about 17.6 times to get $50 million, a double every 5.7 years, or about 13% a year.)"

"Do you use any of this stuff when calculating present values of cash flows?"

"No, no. Forget all the complicated formulas. Just go through *Value Line* and when you find a company you really like and understand and selling for half what it's worth, buy it. And if you can't find it, wait. You'll get your chance."

"You were a supporter of the Pugwash group. (It was an anti-nuclear war association founded by Bertrand Russell. Its efforts led to the first nuclear nonproliferation treaty between the superpowers and the ban on atmospheric testing in 1963.)

"Did you know Bertrand Russell?"

"No, I never actually met him. I saw him on TV and read a number of his books."

"Like *Principia Mathematica*?"

"No, no. Not that sort of thing. The philosophical ones. Like *Has Man a Future?*

"Why?"

"Because he thought like Graham."

"I had an occasion to visit Warren's office once when he wasn't there. Sure enough, there were no Quotrons or computers. What stood out for me was the file room. There were 188 file drawers. When I subsequently saw him, I said, 'What's in all those files?'"

"Annual reports."

"How about 13Ds?"

"No. It's mostly annual reports and quarterly reports (filed by industry)."

"Do you have them going back, say, 15 years?"

"No. We cull them regularly, although I have some, like Coca-Cola, going back more than 15 years. But you don't have to read 15 years of Coca-Cola annual reports to conclude it's a wonderful company."

"How do you wind up with so many?"

"If I'm interested in a company, I'll buy 100 shares of all its competitors to get their annual reports."

"How do you find time to read them all?"

"I skim a lot. But if I'm really interested, I'll read every single word cover to cover."

Intrinsic Value: "Intrinsic value is the discounted value today, of all future distributable cash generated by an entity less the additional capital, including retained earnings, that the owners must put in to generate that cash. A simple way to get at how much a company is worth is to ask how much you would get for it if you sold it today...

"But in the case of Berkshire, we'd get a much better result if we actually made estimates of intrinsic value for both the 80% to 100% owned parts of each business group within the company, as well as for the lesser percentages owned of the investee companies ...Berkshire's intrinsic value is not only composed of See's intrinsic value; it's also composed of Coca-Cola's intrinsic value. A very interesting characteristic of these companies is that they can grow without the addition of much owners' capital, which, remember, includes retained earnings.

"This, by the way, means that Coke can take its excess cash and repurchase its shares, such that Berkshire's original 6% stake is now 8%. A nice little plus.

"If your discount rate is 10%, you are saying you have the low-risk alternative of putting $10 in, say, government bonds that pay you $1 of interest, which *never* grows. But if you have a company that has $1 in distributable cash that will grow 5% per annum *forever*, you would be happy to own that company and pay up to $20 for it. If that $1 in cash flow grew 8% a year forever, you could pay up to $50 for it. If it grew 9% a year forever, you might even pay up to $100 for it. What you are paying as a multiple of cash flow is equal to 1 divided by (the discount rate less the growth rate). Multiple = 1 divided by $(k\text{-}g)$.

"In other words when you are paying $10 for that bond that pays $1 of interest you are paying $1 \div (.10\text{-}.0)$ or 10 times interest income; when you pay $20 for the 5% grower, you are paying $1 \div (.10\text{-}.05)$ or 20 times. And when you pay up to $50 for $1 in cash flow growing 8% a year forever, you are paying $1 \div (.10\text{-}.08)$. Now you can see why you would theoretically pay 100 times cash flow for a 9% grower, and perhaps some phenomenal multiple for a company that grew 11% forever. The only problem is that there are no companies that grow their distributable cash flows at these high rates forever. But of all companies what company or companies come closest to the ideal in terms of high, real, long-term growth of cash flow without massive infusions of new capital? The master found many of them before us. And they are concentrated in the Berkshire portfolio. Of course there are all sorts of caveats. But clearly these companies are worth some big number. We don't really know what it is. High growth rates, above a certain point, become too vulnerable to vicissitudes. More realistically, Berkshire's intrinsic value is within a wide, albeit high, range.

"The other important matter is the issue of float. Warren bought National Indemnity in 1967 for $7.8 million when it had $17 million in float. It is conceivable that he could have turned around in the heated late 1960s and sold it to some insurance company for the price of its float, and made a killing. But clearly, that would have been shortsighted. Today, Berkshire has $7 billion in float, half of which was internally grown at 20% a year at Berkshire. The other half was essentially internally grown at GEICO...

"Think of it this way. What would you pay for a $7 billion mutual fund, where not only could you keep all of the say 10% profits you could make each year with the money of the fund, but each year, the mutual fund shareholders would contribute 20% more money to the fund?...

"I once said on the Adam Smith TV show that Warren Buffett is certainly the greatest investor in the post World War II period and probably the greatest investor in history. I still think this is true, although I'd now say 'allocator of capital' instead of just 'investor.' And as a human being he is more. He's an original. He's philosophically stimulating, skeptically superwise and witty as hell. He's part Aristotle, part Ben Franklin and part George Burns."

Letter to Stavrou Partners: April 1, 1999

Dear Partner:

...Note the figurative word "worldwide" above. Some people are surprised by the size of our operation. I sometimes say, "We have an office in every major industrialized country in the world where English is the national language, south of Canada and north of Jamaica." The catch is that this roundabout statement totals just one office—World Headquarters at the above address.

Our Headquarters campus sprawls over a generous 206 square feet. 1/5 of our space (The Outer Wing) houses our standup library and does extra duty as an entry way. 4/5 (The Inner Atrium) has both reading and culinary comforts in mind: Near our 6 capacious cabinets (containing 22 file drawers of annual reports) our 2 executive dining areas quickly reconvert to desktops when we're done with the paper trays and Dixie cups...

I'll only point out that although we aimed carefully at cost control in 1998, we missed the bulls-eye hit by Berkshire Hathaway: Its corporate costs were under 1 basis point (1/100 of 1.0%) of assets. By comparison, our new compensation expense was 8 basis points of assets. The bad news is that this high but improving number masks a 30.1% rise in office and other expenses (World Headquarters again!) to $12,900. The good news is that we may have the highest profits per square foot of any company in the world, so our approach has its compensations."

In his May 4, 1999 letter, Stavrou started what he calls a "Books for Schools" program. He says:

Last week I was "Principal for a Day" at an inner-city elementary school, which I "adopted." 89% of the parents have incomes under $9,000. The salient parent is a young single mom, abused by those around her in ways difficult to imagine in a more civil or affluent neighborhood. Uninformed and illiterate, she knows little of child-rearing skills and nothing of vouchers, scholarships, PCs or the Internet. She knows domestic violence, drugs, and fatal shootings and doesn't fully appreciate this is very unusual. The school is an oasis. Its high staffing and inefficient construction spending nevertheless render the social services her kids can't get at home. In some surprising ways the student body compares favorably to national numbers. For example, there's a much higher percent of kids with IQs over 130 than nationally. The good news is many people—the teachers (who are the real heroes), the Gateses, George Soros (who now funds the Children's Aid Society at my school), and the more modestly endowed of us—are mounting up to ride to the rescue. (See the enclosed flyer, distributed by World Book at the Berkshire Hathaway annual meeting)

"Books for Schools" is what I call the informal program I started whereby a donor buys and donates to each of as many schools as he or she wants a new World Book Encyclopedia ("WBE") plus computer-related add-on products. These add-ons include the WBE on CD/ROM, software to pipe the WBE to every computer in the school, and Internet access to a World-Book-editor-approved website updated daily. I'm the only donor in my little universe. But I think other individuals would start a Books for Schools set-up on their own, once they knew how it was done. Furthermore I think lots of outside funding could eventually be obtained.

I always thought the WBE is an extraordinary product. I taught myself how to fly a plane when I was 9 years old by reading about planes in a library. In my investment business I made a small fortune by reading. So I'm a believer in the power of reading good books. Bill

Gates of Microsoft began reading through the WBE when he was 8 years old. So he's a believer too.

An encyclopedia is a uniquely good book set and WBE is a uniquely good encyclopedia. Furthermore, the beauty of the WBE is it's a great product that can be used over and over again by every student in a school, and to the extent computers are available on the school network, the WBE can be used by all students at the same time.

One day I noticed the WBE sets in my 9-year-old son's suburban Connecticut elementary school library were out of date. So I called the World Book, Inc. ("WBI") Regional School and Library Director, ordered and paid $1,760 for a new WBE set plus the computer related add-ons for delivery directly to the school, and I received a full tax deduction for this donation. A good deal for all."

Part of Stavrou's letter to his partners March 1, 2000 said:

When Berkshire stock started its long trip down to nearly 50% under its old high, these institutional funds suffered from actual or feared redemptions in favor of technology funds. (The momentum player formula is simple: If stock A is going down and B is going up, then sell A and buy B.)

Also investment banks acting as derivative specialists created privately traded designer options in Gen Re and sold them to those institutional investors. These options differ from publicly traded options in a very important way. Every public option has 100 shares of stock reserved for guaranteed delivery to the holder of the option. But the private option creates leverage on leverage because it normally initially has far fewer than 100 shares held in reserve. (The banker is unprotected, or "naked," as they say.) This permits the banker to sell many more options than otherwise. But here's where a whipsaw effect can come in:

If the stock goes up and thereby creates an obligation to deliver stock to the option holder, the banker must buy that stock in the open market. Conversely, if the stock goes down, there is no obligation to deliver stock to the option holder, so the banker who is now holding the bag begins selling the stock to reduce his loss. As a consequence, when the banker buys and sells stock it exaggerates the stock's volatility in both directions and therefore creates forced selling.

It's important to note that the naked banker doesn't have to know anything about the underlying company to sell private options. Indeed, the automatic buying and selling is done by mathematical formula, irrespective of price or anything fundamental about the company.

In my opinion, the mechanical factors outlined above (in addition to other concerns that mostly are almost surely misplaced or transient, as I shall shortly discuss) are making Berkshire—one of the 10 most admired companies in the United States (according to *Fortune*) and the 12th most Internet-ready of 100 major financial companies (according to *PC Week*)—sell at its *cheapest valuation since 1990* ...

I leave you with this final thought on Berkshire. Berkshire currently has about $60,000 a share in investible capital (shareholders' equity plus deferred taxes, plus insurance float). Could they have 50% more in 5 years or so (i.e., increases in above components of invested capital), an increase of about 8 or 9% a year, to $90,000? I think so. Could they earn in cash 10% after taxes and in securities appreciation on that $90,000? I think so. That's $9,000 a share. At its recent low of $43,000 Berkshire was selling at 5 times that number. Is that cheap? I really, really think so.

104
BUFFETT HAS LUNCH WITH MATTHEW TROXEL

Buffett gets many requests about matters that often have nothing to do with finance. In the case of Matthew Troxel, it involved simply writing an encouraging letter for his recovery from a near fatal illness.

Matthew, 24 at the time and now 29, was a compliance officer for Lind-Waldock & Company, the nation's largest discount commodity futures and options brokerage house, and enrolled in graduate school courses full time at the Illinois Institute of Technology at the time of his illness.

On April Fool's Day 1995 Matthew, of Downers Grove, Illinois, suffered an allergic reaction to amoxicillin, a form of antibiotic he had taken a number of times and this time for a throat infection. Matthew was diagnosed as critically ill with Toxic Epidermal Necrolysis Syndrome.

The journey since then has reminded Matt of Jerry Garcia's words, "What a long, strange trip it has been."

His illness caused burning and blistering of six layers of skin from head to knee. He suffered heart, lung, and kidney failure. This was caused by a necrotic bowel, a part of his intestine that died. He was left deaf in his left ear. He had permanent nerve damage to his feet and wrists and his throat was burned and scarred shut. If that were not enough, he was rendered blind.

Buffett and Troxel after lunch at the Omaha Club September 16, 1998

(Photo by Pat Kilpatrick)

After five months in the hospital enduring many surgical procedures and complications, Matthew was sent home on August 25, 1995 with a temporary ileostomy, bi-lateral nerve damage in his feet and wrists, reduced pulmonary ability, hearing loss, and a tube in the side of his stomach to receive nutrition because his throat was shut.

Matthew was told he would never see again. But after many visits to doctors about his eyes, he found a surgeon who operated and restored his sight. After his eye surgery when the bandages were removed, Matthew told his mother Cheryl: "Mom, I can see my hand again."

Matthew said: "Although this illness has resulted in enormous destruction to my body, I am grateful for my life and the restoration of my sight. Prior to my illness, my vision was 20/20. The scarring and vascularization caused by TENS resulted in blindness. I could only detect hand motion at approximately one foot. After two surgical procedures to both eyes, the vision in my right eye has been restored to 20/40 and the vision in my left eye is currently 20/100."

On March 31, 1996 he wrote Buffett of his condition and said he had plenty of time in the past year to listen to audio books about him and was inspired by his success. In part Matthew wrote: "My chances of survival were less than 5% and only one in a million get this syndrome in the manner I did. Since stock market theorists consider you a statistical 5 Sigma Event, I guess we share something in common."

So what can anyone possibly write to Matthew under the circumstances? Here's Buffett's reply to him of April 4, 1996: "Dear Mr. Troxel: You are indeed a '5 Sigma Event.' I admire your spirit enormously and know that you are going to lead a productive life. Best of luck to you. Sincerely, Warren E. Buffett."

Matthew said, "His response to my correspondence made me feel very special because someone like Warren Buffett does not often make time for an ordinary person to provide inspiration and encouragement to lead a productive life. It is not every day that a person who has achieved such profound success writes to an average person and tells him or her they have value." Matthew added, "When Warren Buffett told me I was valuable, believe me, it was motivating and inspiring."

Matthew owns two shares of Class B Berkshire stock and his two year old niece (his goddaughter) owns three shares of Class B stock held in a UGMA account for her college education.

Matthew faces pain and other medical complications that keep him from working in the normal workplace. Still he runs his own limited liability company called Lexort Capital Group (Lexort is Troxel spelled backwards). Matthew also oversees his The Troxel TENS Foundation, a non-profit organization dedicated to fighting TENS. He reads and writes and is contemplating writing a book about his life.

He's engaged to be married to Terri Modrzyk, a nurse at Loyola University in Chicago. "We met during my hospitalization ... She has been by my side throughout my whole illness and was the first face I saw when I regained consciousness in intensive care. She has been my best friend and support throughout this ordeal."

Occasionally he drives a car in daylight hours and when weather and his health permit, he plays golf.

In April 1998, Matt's illness took a turn for the worse and his doctor informed him he had only 2½ years to live unless he received a double lung transplant.

The severity of the syndrome's attack had caused a form of pulmonary fibrosis in Matt's lungs.

Given the grim news, Troxel wrote Buffett again to ask if he could spend a day with him. Matt received the surprise of his life when Buffett invited him for lunch. The invitation extended to his mom Cheryl, his stepfather, Tom Kehoe and his fiancee Terri. He also let the author tag along. The lunch took place at the Omaha Club after the special General Re merger meeting September 16, 1998.

At the lunch Buffett ordered a Coke but the waitress, who apparently didn't recognize him, asked Buffett how about a Pepsi instead. Buffett replied how about a Coke. The waitress said she didn't have a Coke and Buffett said: "Make it an iced tea." Matt tried to console Buffett about it and said it would be okay if he had a Pepsi.

Buffett ordered a bacon, lettuce and tomato sandwich with an "extra order of bacon" and for dessert had an ice cream concoction with "extra chocolate."

During the luncheon Matt told Buffett of some of his medical problems pointing out that some of his body parts belonged to women and some to minorities. Buffett told Matt: "You're an equal opportunity recipient."

Buffett told Matt of one of the two times he had ever been in the hospital. He said it was in early 1970, shortly after a dinner with Ben Graham. He had been prescribed penicillin for a sore throat and suddenly his body went into a terrible reaction. Buffett was hospitalized for several days and to this day carries a card in his wallet saying not to give him penicillin.

Buffett also told a story about an Italian publication which gave the impression he would be glad to contribute to any charity. He said Berkshire began to receive a lot of requests, "but they were written in Italian."

Buffett told a string of jokes, talked a little about the General Re merger (that he expected it to close in the fourth quarter of 1998) and said he was leaving in two days for two weeks, that he was going to an exotic place. (It turned out to be Alaska and some national parks with Bill Gates.)

Matt was so thrilled with the lunch he wrote the following post to the Berkshire message board:

I want to take this opportunity on behalf of myself and my family to say "Thank You" to everyone who made my journey to Omaha to meet and have lunch with WEB a special memory that will stay with me all my days. The dinner at Gorat's and the hospitality we received was very genuine, sincere and kind. My illness has taken me to many different places, but this event will be the most memorable because it restored my belief in the golden rule that people treat others the way they would like to be treated themselves. By feeling so welcomed we all felt at ease to just be ourselves.

Lunch with our Chairman produced such a high for me I didn't need the plane or any of my pain medication to fly home. Mr. Buffett not only treated me like a fellow shareholder, but more importantly like a regular human being, which I believe speaks volumes about the quality of his compassion and character. The only tense moment occurred when drinks were ordered and I found out much to my surprise, that the Omaha Club does not serve Coke. I gave an inquisitive look to our

Terri Modrzyk, Matt Troxel, Tom Kehoe, and Cheryl Troxel at Gorat's with a Yellow BRKer group the evening before Berkshire's special meeting September 16, 1998.

(Photo by John Gartmann)

698

Chairman and said, "It's okay. You can order a Pepsi." After I placed my order, I told WEB he needed to meet with the management about the soft drinks offered. When I originally contacted Mr. Buffett in 1996, the "B" shares did not exist. I wrote to him only out of admiration and to be his friend. I believe that the time spent during lunch created a foundation of a friendship that I hope we both will enjoy for many years to come.

Health permitting, I plan to attend the annual pilgrimage to the Mecca of Capitalism for the annual meeting in May of 1999. Should the "Master Trader" in the sky call me home before lungs become available for transplant, I will be with you all in spirit and I know that our Chairman will always do his best to increase Berkshire Hathaway's intrinsic value from which I have benefited. However, the greatest benefit I received from my association with Berkshire Hathaway has been the true friendship our Chairman has extended to me.

With best wishes and warm regards,

Matthew Troxel

On May 7, 1999 Troxel wrote Buffett that he hoped to make the annual meeting, but his doctors had advised against it. It turned out Matt had to make a visit to the emergency room the day before but was released "which means death and I returned to our respective corners in the ring."

Here's Buffett's reply of May 18, 1999:

Dear Matt:

I've been away for almost two weeks or you would have heard from me sooner. At annual meeting time I kept inquiring about you. When I found out you weren't in attendance, I knew you must be having health problems. It's great to know that once again you have proven your superiority over illness and that—though it may be a 15-round fight—you're going to emerge the winner.

As you may have read, we had a great time at the meeting, but it will be better next year when you can make it. I'm enclosing my most recent claim to fame [a short item about being one of Nebraska's sexiest men]. You can tell Terri, however, that if the contest were being held in Chicago, I would not stand a chance against you.

On July 2, 1999, Troxel wrote Buffett a letter documenting his frustrations in finding a lung transplant and added, "Although I know you claim to be an agnostic, I believe with all my heart that my Lord and Savior, Jesus Christ, had His hand involved in us becoming friends. The odds are great that I will be waiting with St. Peter for your arrival some day, and I hope you will want to play a game of bridge, share a Coke or a DQ Dilly."

On July 6, 1999 Buffett wrote Matt sympathizing about his lung transplant search adding, "I'm sending along a copy of your letter to Charlie to see if he has any suggestions. [Munger is board chairman of a hospital in Los Angeles.] You're right that it ain't over til it's over. I'll probably meet St. Peter before you do, and he's not expecting me for another 30 years."

Although Matt's health continued to give him fits, he and Terri married on July 9, 2000.

105

A VIEW FROM AUSTRALIA

Two Australian investors—Ian Darling and Mark Nelson—make the journey half way around the world each spring to Omaha to catch up on Buffett's thinking.

Darling and Nelson are managing director and chief executive officer, respectively, of Caledonia, an investment firm in Sydney.

Says Darling, "We first heard about Warren Buffett during the early 1980s when a new Australian company modeled itself after Berkshire Hathaway and quoted Buffett extensively in its annual report." Darling immediately sent away for the 1983 report. "We soon discovered that it was the most exciting piece of investment literature we had ever read. It instantly made us Buffett 'disciples.' It soon became clear that imitating Buffett is one thing, but being able to invest like him is quite another. The Australian company soon disappeared from existence."

"We first went to the Berkshire Annual Meeting in 1995 at the suggestion of our friend Gifford Combs. Combs, a California-based investor, for many years had joined a group of other professional investors in Omaha for a weekend of fun and investment discussion. In simple terms, Combs said, 'one day this will no longer happen—so grab it while you can.' "

Darling added, "We first met Buffett while watching the Omaha Royals at the baseball game in 1995. We sat down beside him in the stand, introduced ourselves, and explained that we were from Australia. He shouted with delight, 'Hey, these guys have come all the way from Australia.' He genuinely seemed excited by our visit. We got the distinct impression that we were the first Australians Buffett had ever met, both from his greeting and the warm letter we received from him back in Australia after the event: 'You both are great sports to come all the way from Australia and I hope you continue to make the trip.' With an invitation like that how could we possibly let him down? We have returned every year since."

"We got the impression on our first visit that very few Australians had actually ever made the journey to Omaha. At last year's meeting [1997], Buffett informed us that as many as 14 shareholders had made the journey from Australia," Darling said. "There can be no doubt that now his fame is truly international."

Australian investors Mark Nelson and Ian Darling and their friend, California investor Gifford Combs, sit in the stands on "Berkshire Hathaway Night" with Warren "Casey Stengel" Buffett.

Darling said the long trip is worth it. "If we were two ambitious Australian golfers who had the opportunity to get a lesson from Jack Nicklaus or Tiger Woods on a golf course in the United States, we wouldn't hesitate to make the trip. The weekend in Omaha gives us an opportunity to learn from the best and every year we return to Australia with valuable lessons, actionable ideas and new insights into the world of investments."

Darling's partner, Mark Nelson, said of their first trip to Omaha, "We were delighted to meet Mrs. B, who upon learning we were Australians exclaimed, 'My, my, what a small world, what a small world.' We were charmed by Charlie Munger during our brief encounter with him at Borsheim's and surprised to see he is much taller in real life than we expected from seeing his pictures. We had our first tasting of See's Candy and encouraged the relevant parties to establish an operation in Australia. We also had our first tasting of Cherry Coke, but it was too sweet, too 'foreign' for us." The two checked out everything in Omaha that had any relation to Buffett, checking out Buffett's home, his office and even where he eats. They were most impressed to run across Buffett driving himself to his own meeting in his rather modest car and struggling to find a parking space!

Nelson added: "The wisdom of Warren Buffett can be applied anywhere in the world. His highly disciplined, common-sense approach to investment has no national boundaries. There are some very fine investors in Australia to learn from, but there is only one Warren Buffett in the world. So it's pretty easy to justify to ourselves why we make the trip. The great lessons from the world of investment are still primarily generated in the U.S., as are the lessons about shareholder returns and progressive management. So, in simple terms, we are happy to go where the 'action is.' "

Nelson said, "We spend the entire weekend prior to the meeting in Omaha. During that time we catch up with the same group of friends each year who are all owners and managers of their own U.S. investment management businesses. Some of the greatest investment minds converge on Omaha over the course of the weekend and we have gained a great deal from our discussions with such investors. We have particularly enjoyed our encounters with the likes of Gifford Combs, Tom Russo, Lou Simpson, Steve Wallman, Fred Whitridge, Jimmy Armstrong, Bill Strong, Gene Gardiner, Bill Scargle, Peter Fang and Palmer Murray, to name a few. On our last visit we formalized the discussions somewhat and arranged a debate titled: 'This time it's different.' It was quite bizarre to see a group of disciplined stockpickers trying to solve this insolvable macro question, but it was great fun nevertheless."

Darling and Nelson said they plan to keep coming to Omaha as long as they continue to get valuable investment insights.

106

"WHO WAS GOING TO GO INTO A FOXHOLE WITH ME?"

Buffett once told Columbia business students about the first moments of the Salomon crisis and how he picked Deryck Maughan because of Maughan's integrity.

"I faced the immediate problem of deciding who was going to run Salomon Brothers, the institution, while essentially, I had to deal with regulators and the public and the politicians, etc.

"On Friday night and again on Saturday morning, I met with about 12 people. These 12 people were top-level managers at Salomon. And essentially, I had to pick from that group of 12 someone to run a $150 billion institution that was going to be under great stress and who could lead 8,000 people under very trying conditions.

"It may be of interest to you what went through my mind because you're going to be hired. And how would you develop yourself in some way that you be the one?

"This was the most important hire of my life.

"I interviewed those people Saturday morning over a couple-hour period, knowing that I was going to pick one when I got all through. I didn't have time to do a lot of psychological tests or anything. The good news is I did not ask them what their grades were in business school (laughter).

"They all had the IQ, just like everybody in this room. It doesn't make any difference whether your IQ is 140 or 160 if you're running Salomon or doing most things in this world. They all had the energy level and the desire.

"The question was: Who would be the best leader? Who was going to go into a foxhole with me? Because whoever went into the foxhole with me could stick a gun to my head.

"If they wanted to come around and say they got an offer from Goldman Sachs or something, for twice as much money as they were making, or wanted special personal indemnification because of lawsuits—a million things could happen and would happen with some people.

"In the end I picked someone and fortunately, it was not only the most important decision of my life, but probably as good a business decision or hiring decision as I could make.

"I devised this little system in getting you to think about how you might attack that problem yourself, or how you might be the person that would be chosen under those circumstances.

"Imagine that you have just won a lottery I conducted. And by winning it, you had a very unusual prize. The prize you get is the right to pick within the next hour one of your classmates. And you get 10% of the earnings of that individual for the rest of your life.

"What starts going through your mind? Are you going to give an IQ test, or look up their grades and take the person with the highest grades? Are you going to try to measure desire or energy or something? I think you'll decide that those factors tend largely to cancel. They could be important up to some threshold limit, but once you hit those levels, you're OK.

"I think you'll probably start looking for the person that you can always depend on; the person whose ego does not get in his way; the person who's perfectly willing to let someone else take credit for an idea as long as it works; the person who essentially wouldn't let you down; who thought straight as opposed to brilliantly.

"And then, let's say there's a catch attached. For the right to buy this 10% interest, you had to go short 10% of somebody else in the room. So in effect, you get the 10% of the first person's earnings, but you have to pay out 10% of the second person's.

"Now again, do you look around for the person that's a little slippery, the one that everything has to be his or her idea, the one that never quite does what's expected of them, or pretends to do things that they don't. You really get back to things that interestingly enough...are things that you can control.

"You have these—what I would call—voluntary items of character, behavior. Essentially, you can pick out those qualities of behavior, and if you want them, you can have them yourself.

"Take that one person where you would go short, and if you find a few of those qualities creeping into your own behavior, they are things you can get rid of.

"If you're taking all the credit for things when other people do it, you can do something about that. You can make yourself into the person that you would buy the 10% of, and you can make very sure that you're not the one that you would sell short 10% of.

"And I would say that most of it's habit.

"It's just as easy to have good ones as bad ones, and it makes an enormous difference.

"Deryck Maughan simply behaves well and he behaves in a high-grade manner. He doesn't give up his independence or his ability to think independently or any of those qualities whatsoever.

"I'll give you an example. Deryck, two or three months after he took the job, had never asked me how much he got paid, let alone had a lawyer around negotiating for him or anything of that sort.

"Deryck, when he came in, had one thought in mind and that was keeping the place initially together, and then building a business that fit his image of what he wanted it to be.

"He never asked me for a dime of indemnification, and he could have been targeted. He could have gone broke. There were dozens of suits. He was working 18-hour days. He could have been making more money someplace else.

"Somebody once said that in looking for people to hire, you look for three qualities: integrity, intelligence and energy. And if they don't have the first, the other two will kill you.

"You think about it, it's true. If you hire somebody without the first, you really want them dumb and lazy (laughter).

"Pick the kind of person to work for you that you want to marry your son or daughter. You won't go wrong." (*Omaha World-Herald*, January 2, 1994)

107

AN UNSUCCESSFUL BID FOR LONG-TERM CAPITAL MANAGEMENT
("LONG-GONE CAPITAL")

A Buffett-led group made a bid September 23, 1998 for the ailing and secretive Long-Term Capital Management LP hedge fund after its highly leveraged positions came under pressure during the world financial crisis in the "summer from hell" of 1998.

The low-ball offer was rejected and Long-Term Capital (nicknamed Long-Gone Capital) accepted a bid that was orchestrated by Goldman Sachs with the help of the Federal Reserve and a number of banks.

Buffett's offer from a partnership that would have included Berkshire, American International Group led by chairman Maurice Greenberg and Goldman Sach's chairman Jon Corzine was for $250 million. Berkshire would have put in $3 billion in capital, AIG $700 million and Goldman Sachs $300 million. Buffett's bid, which only lasted for 50 minutes, or so, also called for the ouster of Long-Term Capital's founder John Meriwether who once was the head of bond trading for Salomon. After he left Salomon following the company's bond-trading scandal, Meriwether started Long-Term Capital in 1994. He and an elite group of investors including Nobel Prize winners and Harvard, MIT, Stanford and Berkeley graduates ran the firm which for years was very successful.

But the crash of 1998 caught them and their lenders came calling.

"Long-Term Capital...used leverage to magnify returns for investors. At the end of August [1998], the hedge fund had $2.3 billion in capital, which it had used as collateral to borrow securities worth about $125 billion. It had then used those securities as collateral to buy derivatives and forward contracts, whose value was tied to assets worth $1 trillion." (*Bloomberg News*, December 29, 1998)

Long-Term Capital had bet that bond yields in Asia, Latin America, Europe and the U.S. would converge as the world became a safer place. However, the world in the summer of 1998 became a riskier place. Bond prices were diverging, not converging.

Buffett mentioned Long-Term Capital in a talk to University of Florida students: "They relied on mathematics to try to make money they didn't need. I think that's madness. You know. It's easy to go broke. It happens to those who know nothing and those who know everything." He said it was a case of "smart people doing dumb things." (*Miami Herald*, December 27, 1998)

Buffett also has been quoted as saying, "Underneath the mathematical elegance, underneath all those betas and sigmas, there was quick-sand."

Here's a copy of the Buffett bid which appeared in *The Wall Street Journal*, September 30, 1998:

HIGHLY CONFIDENTIAL
September 23, 1998

Mr. John Meriwether
Chief Executive Officer
Long-Term Capital Management, LP.
One East Weaver Street
Greenwich, CT 06331-5146

Dear Mr. Meriwether:
Subject to the following deal structure, the partnership described below proposes to purchase the assets of Long-Term Capital Management (and/or its affiliates and subsidiaries, collectively referred to as "Long-Term Capital") for $250 million.

The purchaser will be a limited partnership whose investors will be Berkshire Hathaway for $3 billion, American International Group for $700 million and Goldman Sachs for $300 million (or each of their respective affiliates). All management of the assets will be under the sole control of the partnership and will be transferred to the partnership in an orderly manner.

This bid is also subject to the following:

1) The limited partnership described herein will not assume any liabilities of Long-Term Capital arising from any activities prior to the purchase by the partnership.

2) All current financing provided to Long-Term Capital will remain in place under current terms and conditions.

The names of the proposal may not be disclosed to anyone. If the names are disclosed, the bid will expire.

This bid will expire at 12:30 p.m. New York time on September 23, 1998.
Sincerely,

Warren Buffett   Maurice R. Greenberg   Jon S. Corzine
Agreed and Accepted on Behalf of Long-Term Capital

John Meriwether

From here, the story is best tracked by *Fortune's* Carol Loomis (October 26, 1998):

As the Long-Term Capital crisis mounted, Buffett became more involved, but he "was trying to leave his office [September 18, 1998] to get to a granddaughter's birthday party. That night he was scheduled to fly to Seattle to join Bill Gates' group that was going to spend nearly two weeks touring Alaska and a galaxy of Western parks. It was a highly uncharacteristic move; Buffett ordinarily has no interest in scenery of any kind. But his close friendship with Gates had lured him and his wife, Susan, into signing on for the trip.

"The bid took place over the next few days as Buffett used quite a lot of vacation time on the phone, so much so that friends staged a shot of him on the phone ignoring Old Faithful.

"The bid was faxed to Meriwether at 11:40 on [September 23, 1998] and he was advised it would expire within an hour, at 12:30."

"Buffett didn't want his bid shopped around.

"But Meriwether showed no interest in the bid and the fund was bailed out by bank loans."

The negotiations were not aided by Buffett's cell phone going out toward the end of the talks. (*Vanity Fair*, October 1999) And Buffett has said his efforts might have faired better had he been in New York rather than at Old Faithful. (Buffett joked that a photo taken of him at Old Faithful was of a geezer and a geyser.)

He joked that he didn't want to call Munger about it. "Charlie was in Hawaii. I didn't want to bother him with a little thing like a bid for $100 billion worth of securities...We made a very firm bid for over $1 trillion worth of derivative contracts."

It turns out Buffett has had some experience with hedge funds, according to Mark Byrne who manages West End Capital in Bermuda. Byrne, who is the son of Jack Byrne (former chairman of GEICO) and the brother of Patrick Byrne, former president of Berkshire's Fechheimer uniform unit, told *The Financial Times* (October 15, 1998) that Berkshire made a $270 million investment in West End Capital in July, 1998 which amounts to 90% of West End's capital. West End limits its leverage to 10 to 15 times its capital whereas Long-Term Capital's leverage was closer to 50 times. Mark Byrne is the former head of fixed-income arbitrage at Credit Suisse First Boston.

Byrne told the newspaper that West End had lost less than 10% of its assets in 1998. Byrne said although West End does not use the same type of investment strategy as Long-Term Capital, both try to profit from the convergence of interest rates on different types of bonds.

Long-Term Capital suffered losses after it bet that yields of certain corporate bonds would converge with those of U.S. Treasury bonds. Instead, when financial turmoil worsened in the international markets in the summer of 1998, the spread between the yield widened as investors fled to super-safe Treasuries.

Berkshire's bid for Long-Term Capital probably helped calm markets at the time. Berkshire investor Chris Stavrou thinks so: "I think Berkshire's attempt to rescue LTC by bidding for it will eventually go down as one of the most stabilizing financial aids since J. Pierpont Morgan stabilized the New York Stock Exchange during the panic of 1907."

108

THE BERKSHIRE ANNUAL MEETING

"BUFFETT HAS LEFT THE BUILDING."

Doors opened at 7:00 a.m., the earliest arriving at 3:15 a.m. for the 9:30 a.m. Berkshire Annual Meeting in 2000 attended by 10,000 people. It's the world's best attended stockholders meeting even though attendance had dropped from 15,000 the year before. Crowds were there long before 7:00 a.m. When the auditorium opened, the Buffetteers—grown men and women—ran inside to get the best seats. It was like a rock concert. Buffett calls the annual meeting: "Our capitalist's version of Woodstock." Some have suggested it's a Capitalist Psych Ward.

In 1997 a comical video shown before the annual meeting ended with the Crosby, Stills, Nash and Young rousing song "Woodstock." It can't be long until Berkshire shareholders are spotted with bumper stickers saying: "Wild women don't get the blues."

Before the 1995 meeting, huge video screens re-ran the come-from-behind victory of Nebraska over Miami in the Orange Bowl. Buffett, in a Husker Red coat, walked on stage shortly after victorious Nebraska

(Photo by John Gass)

Buffett in front of the Executive Jet trade show display on May 1, 1999 during the weekend before Berkshire's annual meeting.

(Photo by Nancy Line Jacobs)

Buffett and his daughter, Susan, arrive for Berkshire's Annual Meeting in 1997

(Photo by Nancy Line Jacobs)

The crush around Buffett seated between his daughter, Susan, and his wife, Susie, before the annual meeting in 1997

Left - The Berkshire Annual Meeting is usually held the first Monday in May. Here in 1992 Adam Smith of Money World was preparing to air a show about the meeting.

Below - Always a two-fisted Cherry Coke drinker, Buffett gets fortified for his more-than-three-hour annual meeting in 1992.

(Photos by LaVerne Ramsey)

Above - Buffett, decked out in a Coca-Cola apron, signs annual reports before Berkshire's annual meeting in 1992. The next year he wore a See's Candy cap during the annual meeting.

715

Buffett at 1994 Annual Meeting in front of a portrait of the cover of the Berkshire Annual Report.

(Photo by Nancy Line Jacobs)

Don Keough, former president of Coca-Cola, in Coke apron, chats with Sequoia Fund's Bill Ruane; both are longtime FOBs. Ruane, a Harvard alumnus, has joked there's little difference between him and Buffett except billions of dollars and 100 IQ points.

(Photo by LaVerne Ramsey)

716

(Photo by Paul Fleetwood)

Frank Betz, with Carret & Co., Phil Carret, Buffett, Bank of Granite Chairman John Forlines and "Ollie the Trolley." On Sunday before the 1997 annual meeting, Buffett picks up some shareholders by trolley for a brunch.

football coach Tom Osborne, who retired in 1998, was carried off the field by the National Champion Cornhuskers.

The pre-meeting video features Buffett in some soap opera and Omaha Press Club appearances. One segment has a take-off of "The Graduate" where Dustin Hoffman is told the future is in "plastics." In this case the word "plastics" was substituted with: "GEICO."

One clip in the 1997 video showed Post's Katharine Graham complaining that Berkshire-related businesses were so cheap they didn't offer dental programs until you were 90 and that she was being forced to continue work and had decided on a discount furniture business: "Mrs. G's." Her talk was accompanied by an ad saying: "Mrs. G's blow-out discount on furniture."

Other clips showed joking tributes from Bill Gates and NBC's Tom Brokaw.

In 1997 more than 7,000 shareholders, who gave Buffett and Munger a standing ovation came to the new meeting site—Aksarben (Nebraska spelled backwards). It's a facility at an old horse racing track and betting place. "I used to come here as a boy for the circus. Now we have a circus of our own," Munger said.

The highlight of any year for a Berkshire shareholder is the annual meeting usually held the first Monday in May in Omaha which now draws press coverage from CNN, CNBC, Brazil, Germany,

England, Switzerland, France, Japan and Canada and shareholder attendance from as many as 32 countries. About 75 reporters and photographers attended a press conference Buffett held the day before Berkshire's annual meeting in 1998, attended by 8,000 to 11,000 people. Also, there were more than 100 corporate jets at the airport in Omaha for the meeting in 1999.

At the annual meeting in 1991, Buffett and then Coca-Cola President Don Keough donned bright red Coca-Cola aprons to serve shareholders Cokes as they arrived for the meeting. From their perch in front of a display of Coke cases, Buffett and Keough provided a small sip of Coke from the Fountain of Wealth. Buffett sipped on a Cherry Coke, chatted and signed annual reports. Keough sipped a diet Coke, bear-hugged and lavished good humor on any shareholder within reach. A number of surprised shareholders got a handshake or a word with the men and in some cases a quick photo opportunity.

Early into the meeting Buffett will give a report about sales at Borsheim's from the previous day (usually a record) and point out that Berkshire has its products for sale. And in the 1999 Annual Report, Buffett said: "So, overcoming my normal commercial reticence, I will see that you have a wide display of Berkshire products at the Civic that you can *purchase*. As a benchmark, in 1999 shareholders bought 3,059 pounds of See's candy, $16,155 of World Book Products, 1,928 pairs of Dexter shoes, 895 sets of Quikut knives, 1,752 golf balls with the Berkshire Hathaway logo and 3,446 items of Berkshire apparel. I know you can do better."

"The [Berkshire] annual meeting is the best thing I've ever seen in all of commerce," Keough said.

In 1992 Buffett and See's Candy Chuck Huggins donned caps with a See's logo and passed out small boxes of See's candy to shareholders.

Happy Berkshire pilgrims now journey to the event featuring Buffett and Munger at the dais. As they share Cokes and See's candies, they guide an adoring shareholder group through a quick course in the wisdom of the financial ages.

Not that many people came in the early days. As few as seven to a dozen people showed up for the annual meetings in the 1960s when they were held in New Bedford, Massachusetts, home of the early Berkshire textile business. Later they were held in a fourth floor cafeteria amidst its vending machines at Berkshire's National Indemnity office in Omaha.

Soon the meetings were held in the cafeteria of Kiewit Plaza with

10 to 30 shareholders showing up, and then at the Red Lion Inn (now Doubletree) where about 250 shareholders gathered in 1985. A number of Berkshire shareholders still stay at the Doubletree on their annual pilgrimage.

There were about 1,000 Berkshire shareholders at the time Diversified was merged into Berkshire at the end of 1979. There were about 1,900 shareholders in 1992 and 2,900 in 1993, many of those coming in with the Blue Chip merger. Now about 14,000 of some 250,000 attend. Why? "They come because we make them feel like owners," Buffett says. (*Personal Finance*, Janet Lowe, February 26, 1997)

Over the years, with Berkshire's growth and the spread of Buffett's reputation for wit and wisdom, more shareholders came. In 1996 shareholders came from all 50 states as well as from foreign lands—Australia, Greece, Israel, Portugal, Singapore, Sweden, Switzerland and the United Kingdom creating the need for ever larger meeting places.

Eventually, the annual meetings were held at the Joslyn Art Museum ("Temple of Culture," as Buffett calls it) in Omaha where 580 shareholders met in 1988. The meetings for several years were held at the Orpheum Theatre, then at the Holiday Inn Convention Center and then at Aksarben, an old horse racing track and betting facility. It was at Aksarben that Buffett, as a very young kid, would go to search through discarded stubs on the floor, sometimes finding a winning ticket. (*Buffett: The Making of an American Capitalist*, Roger Lowenstein, p. 4)

One year he welcomed his audience to the new meeting site, the Orpheum Theatre in Omaha, explaining, "Most of you know we held our annual meetings at the Joslyn Art Museum the past several years until we outgrew it. Since the Orpheum Theatre where we're meeting today is an old vaudeville theatre, I suppose we've slid down the cultural chain. Don't ask me where we'd go next."

In 1994, with the theater full, Buffett said the next meeting might have to be elsewhere and that sliding down the cultural pole would continue. He thought it might be held at Aksarben where there is keno and horse-racing.

Indeed, the downwardly mobile trend continued, first at a Holiday Inn in 1995 and 1996, and then it really was moved to Aksarben.

In 2000 the meeting was held at the Omaha Civic Auditorium on Saturday, April 29, because Aksarben, due to budget restraints, scaled back the operation of its coliseum reducing its seating capacity. It was held on Saturday rather than Monday to allow for more parking.

It may be that future meetings will be held in a dimly lit dance hall where the music is loud, and Guinness by the keg is served.

When Adam Smith, who covered the Berkshire Annual Meeting in 1990 for his *Adam Smith's Money World* television program, asked shareholder Charles Dennison of Princeton, New Jersey, why he was coming to the meeting, Dennison said: "I hear it's a great show."

Robert Baker, a retired lawyer from Chagrin Falls, Ohio (who died in 1992), was among the Berkshire shareholders who regularly made the annual trek to Omaha.

Baker had read about Buffett in the early 1980s. "I read enough to know he was terrific and then on April 8, 1983, the 'Heard on the Street' column in the *Wall Street Journal* quoted from his annual report. On April 11th I went and bought five shares. I asked to get them at $920. The broker called back and said I had bought them for $910."

A year later Baker started going to the annual meetings.

"They are fully worth it for the wisdom...It's worth every penny," Baker said. "He always expresses the great truths so simply. We're always too busy making things so complex. He reminds us not to play games or make things complex...I think he looks at the bottom line and looks to see if the managers are having fun, if they love what they do."

Another regular to attend the Berkshire meetings over the years was stockholder Lloyd Wilson until he was hit by a car in late 1994 and left a quadraplegic and partially blind. Wilson, who split his time between Colorado Springs, Colorado, and Santa Cruz, California, still tracks the financial markets. Buffett wrote him shortly after the accident: ... "It's hard to keep a good Berkshire shareholder down, so I know you will be ready for another Annual Meeting before long. I wish you the best in your recovery."

Wilson died in early 2000.

On a personal note: Wilson gave me an off-the-record interview about Berkshire over a long breakfast at the old Red Lion hotel in Omaha in my early days of writing about Buffett. I don't think its much of a journalistic violation to say he talked mainly about the significance of Berkshire's then fresh investment in Coca-Cola.

There is great camaraderie among shareholders who spend the annual meeting weekend swapping Buffett stories. For example, Rob Sullivan of Long Meadow, Massachusetts, once told of writing Buffett that he had named his dog after him. Buffett wrote back that

(Photo by LaVerne Ramsey)

Buffett and Robert Sullivan near Borsheim's the day before Berkshire's annual meeting in 1995. Buffett asked Sullivan if he brought his dog, "Buffett." Sullivan said instead he brought a friend, a stockbroker. Buffett joked, "That's a bad trade."

if Sullivan ever got another pet, he should name it Munger. Sullivan got another dog and named it Munger, but Munger died and Sullivan wrote Buffett: "Buffett's still alive, Munger's six feet under."

(Photo by Bob Sullivan)

"Warren," the Boston terrier

The annual meeting is a communion for kindred spirits who have found investment heaven. "It's the Club Med for investors," says Berkshire shareholder Pat Mojonnet of San Francisco. "And when you come home and tell people about it, nobody believes you."

For example, Buffett himself picks up a batch of invited guests for a Sunday country club brunch. Arriving in "Ollie the Trolley," a converted bus that looks like a streetcar, Buffett will shake hands with shareholders as they get aboard at a hotel stop or two.

Usually, the only real status check during the annual meeting weekend comes from the query, "How long have you been a Berkshire shareholder?" The longer you've been, the wiser you are.

For the uninitiated, seeing Buffett in action can be a jolt.

It's not the usual annual meeting where the chairman drones on, overstating progress with a studied rosiness. And Berkshire's meetings don't have public relations folks who dread questions from disgruntled shareholders. While most ordinary meetings are forgotten within seconds, Berkshire shareholders still delight in what Buffett said years ago.

At Berkshire, shareholders get no excuse of how the sluggish economy led to disappointing results, or some pie-in-the-sky story about how fabulous the following fiscal year will be. You get no gadfly—no Evelyn Y. Davis—questioning the chairman's motives or pay package.

With Buffett and sidekick Munger you get what you see: the precise opposite of what you get at most ordinary annual meetings. First Buffett and Munger walk on stage. Buffett carries up his Coke supply. Berkshire's duo sits at a plain table adorned by See's candy.

Buffett normally starts off with a joke or two, sometimes ostensibly testing the microphone: "Testing...testing...one million...two million...three million."

Buffett distrusts complicated technology, and his instincts were confirmed at the annual meeting in 1990 when Berkshire's Chief Financial Officer Verne McKenzie tried to fix the faulty microphone system. "Verne McKenzie is our resident technology expert. Can you hear me? Can you hear me?...This is why we don't buy technology stocks."

In 1993, with so many people, a giant screen was set up so people could see Buffett and Munger better, and when at first there was noise and flickering, Buffett teased, "We're masters of technology here."

Buffett's sister, Mrs. Doris Bryant, recalls sitting with her mother at the meeting in 1992 when Buffett started on one of his Bartles and Jaymes routines with Munger. "There was a heavy man sitting in front of us who thought it was so funny his whole body was shaking. My mother loved it."

In 1992, in anticipation of a question about how long he intends to be at Berkshire, Buffett said, "We plan to be here until we're both sitting here wondering, 'Who's that guy sitting next to me?'"

Buffett usually introduces Munger, sometimes saying, "It's no breach of etiquette to walk out during his answers." And he'll make witty introductions of the Berkshire managers.

He will jokingly warn the audience to be careful not to say anything off-color about him because he has relatives strategically placed

(Photo by Celia Sullivan)

From left: Jamie, Ceily Mae holding Buffett the dog, Michael holding Munger the turtle, and Charles. The Sullivan children are a combination of Berkshire, Wesco and Coca-Cola shareholders.

throughout the audience.

In 1993 Buffett explained that the meeting would go until noon or until Munger said something optimistic. However, Munger, known for dour, laconic answers, never did say anything cheery, and after each sobering Munger answer, Buffett kept saying, "We'll be here until noon."

(Photo courtesy of Robert Sullivan)

Robert and Celia Sullivan with NBC News Anchor Tom Brokaw at Berkshire annual meeting festivities in 1998. In the early 1960s Brokaw lived in Omaha when he was a reporter for an NBC affiliate. Brokaw's wife, Meredith, was an English teacher then at Omaha Central High School where Buffett's Aunt Alice once taught and where Munger attended school.

723

After Buffett's initial jokes and introduction, he takes up housekeeping matters such as electing his wife to the board of directors. Straight-faced, he may note that attendants "hired from a local modeling agency" are on hand to give you a proxy card should you wish to change your vote.

In 1992, Buffett made his usual introductions of the managers and the board, and when he introduced his wife, Susan Buffett, Buffett said, "It's a name we got out of the phone book." He then introduced his niece, Cynthia Zak, saying she has a son named Berkshire. "That's a not-too-subtle method of trying to get into my will," Buffett joked.

And he'll make his pitch about how shareholders can go to visit Borsheim's or the Nebraska Furniture Mart. In 1991, it went like this: "At noon we'll break. And there'll be buses to take you to Borsheim's, Nebraska Furniture Mart...or anything else that we have an economic interest in."

Voting at the meeting is a moot point since Buffett's block of stock, and the holdings of his wife, insiders, and old friends quickly make up well over 50% of the stock.

In 1997 Buffett said: "All those in favor of the slate signify by saying aye. All those opposed say, 'I'm leaving.' "

Shareholders go along with Buffett's litany of business matters, and after everyone has said aye to some unarguable point, such as dispensing with reading minutes of the prior year's annual meeting, Buffett will say, "You're doing fine."

He notes that Berkshire meetings are not meant to be democratic and take their "Stalinist manner" and autocratic origins from somewhere deep in the old Soviet Union. He says these things almost every year and they always elicit a little chuckle, about a 3 or 4 on the laugh meter.

At the 1994 meeting, Buffett said, "Let's get the business of the meeting out of the way so we can get on to more interesting things."

He then moved the meeting be adjourned, adding, "Democracy in Middle America."

The whole routine takes just 5 or 10 minutes and if you have not been to a Berkshire meeting before, you are surprised at the move to adjourn the meeting. You have come across the country and suddenly it's over. Over?

Well, not really. The fun is just beginning as Buffett leans back from the table a bit and says, "Any questions?"

Then Buffett offers responses stunning in speed, depth and originality.

Mrs. Susan Buffett, left, and Astrid Menks at Borsheim's before the annual meeting in 1992.

(Photo by LaVerne Ramsey)

Once longtime shareholder Irving Fenster, of Tulsa, Oklahoma, got up with a question and started by saying he was from Oklahoma—Nebraska's biggest football rival; Buffett yelled, "Who let you in?"

When he was asked for advice to young investors, he explained, "Look at stocks as businesses, look for businesses you understand, run by

(Photo by Andrea "Andy" Holg/Metro Monthly)

Buffett, Astrid Menks, Sue Scott and Kiewit Chairman Walter Scott at a museum party in Omaha in 1996.

people you trust and are comfortable with, and leave them alone for a long time."

The questions roll on for almost three hours, until lunch, often with shareholders from the Northeast addressing him as "Warren" and shareholders from the South using "Mr. Buffett."

After a fifteen minute lunch break, hard-core fans who want more of Buffett stick around for

(Photo courtesy of Bob Sullivan)

Early Berkshire investor Irving Fenster of Oklahoma

another three hours and even more questions, with Buffett fielding everything shareholders can throw his way.

Munger plays the straight man to Buffett. Sometimes Buffett will describe how some business is deteriorating and Munger will interrupt: "He means it went to hell."

Munger sits stone-faced, arms folded across his chest, usually offering comments like "Yes" or "No" or "No comment" or "I have nothing to add." After one "That's exactly right," from Munger in 1991, Buffett said, "He's learning. Susie take notes," referring to his wife, Susan Buffett, just elected to Berkshire's board. Frequently, Munger will invoke the word "Civilization," comprising America's social and economic fabric, as in "the Civilization needs program trading like it needs more AIDS."

In the midst of the annual meeting in 1992, Floyd Jones of Seattle, praised Buffett's handling of the Salomon scandal. Jones explained that he had worked for the collapsed Drexel Burnham Lambert firm, adding that he felt Buffett had averted what could have been an international financial crisis had Salomon collapsed. "I think you are a hero in world corporate society."

Early in the meeting, for the sake of rotating the questions around the large crowd, Buffett had divided the audience into various zones, and it so happened Jones's question came from zone four. After Jones's eloquent remarks, Buffett said, "Let's stay in zone four for a while."

After the meeting most shareholders make a run for the Nebraska Furniture Mart or Borsheim's before catching a flight out of Omaha.

And Buffett will help you with the transportation to either store— in a rented school bus with no air conditioning. For the meeting in 1989, Buffett hired two old school buses for $100.

After all, Buffett wants those selling, general, and administrative expenses kept below rock bottom.

"It's great to hear Warren and Charlie answer every question openly. And it feels good to know your money is in their hands," says Don Keough.

There is plenty of free-wheeling give and take.

One Berkshire shareholder, LaVerne Ramsey of Birmingham, Alabama, asked at the annual meeting in 1991 what would be revealed if Kitty Kelley wrote an unauthorized biography of him and Munger. Buffett, as quick as a Magic Johnson pass, slyly shunted the question off to Munger.

"I'm afraid not very much," Munger said, "But that wouldn't stop Kitty Kelley." Buffett answered the question, "What you see is what

Right—Susan Buffett, Buffett's daughter, at Borsheim's in 1992. She said her friends in school thought her security analyst father "checked alarm systems."

(Photo by LaVerne Ramsey)

Susan Buffett, striking a Nebraska's national championship theme, near Borsheim's the day before the annual meeting in 1995, with Washington Post's Katharine Graham and Fortune's Carol Loomis

(Photo by Nancy Line Jacobs)

(Photo by LaVerne Ramsey)

Above—Fortune's Carol Loomis near Borsheim's in 1997. She's showing off her bracelet with charms Buffett gives her for editing the Berkshire Annual Report.

Left—Buffett and Always Coke at Borsheim's in 1993.

(Photo by LaVerne Ramsey)

Left - Donald Yale, former president of Borsheim's and Berkshire Vice Chairman Charles Munger at the jewelry store in 1993.

Below - The autograph that counts (and keeps on counting). Buffett signing items at Borsheim's in 1993.

Above - Berkshire's Michael Goldberg oversees Berkshire's commercial finance businesses. He heads BH Credit Corp. Goldberg has said: "The negative is: How do you ever think much of your abilities after being around Warren Buffett?"

(Photos by LaVerne Ramsey)

Left-Buffett, his mother, Mrs. Leila Buffett, and at left, his daughter, Susan Buffett, before the Berkshire Annual Meeting in 1993
(Photo by LaVerne Ramsey)

Below—Berkshire shareholders Michael and Eiko Assael of New York. Michael is holding Buffett-signed "investment guides," including a 1934 edition of Ben Graham's Security Analysis. Such first editions are worth more than $1,000. Eiko sports her personalized "100 BRK" license plate with a message from Buffett. It's a little Buffettabilia for a Berkshire Museum in their kitchen.
(Omaha World-Herald)

Dr. Michael Prus, his wife Judy, and their children, Michael, Elizabeth and Jeff of Grosse Pointe, Michigan are regulars at Berkshire annual meetings.

(Photos by LaVerne Ramsey)

Chad and Carol Brenner of Cincinnati, Ohio, have been irregulars, depending upon whether Carol was pregnant that year. The Brenners have three children.

you get with the two of us." Mrs. Ramsey, a Buffett admirer, explained later she really asked her question as a test of Buffett's wit. "He passed," she said. A small sequel to that story is that later Mrs. Ramsey sent a note and some photos to Buffett explaining the question was just in fun, as Buffett well knew, and he wrote her back, "LaVerne, Thanks for the pictures. I always enjoy them. Charlie should have some Kitty Kelley material for next year; don't let him off the hook."

Later at the meeting, a shareholder asked him how he spent his day and Buffett started out with "More of the Kitty Kelley bit, eh?" Then he said he spends most of the day and night reading and talking on the phone.

After he gave his explanation of how he spent his day, he said, "That's what I do. Charlie, what do you do?"

Munger was not caught off guard: "That reminds me very much of a friend of mine in World War II in a group which had nothing to do. A general once went up to my friend's boss, we'll call him Captain Glotz. He said, 'Captain Glotz, what do you do?' His boss said, 'Not a damn thing.'"

"The General got madder and madder and turned to my friend and said, 'What do you do'?"

"And my friend said, 'I help Captain Glotz.' That's the best way to describe what I do at Berkshire."

One shareholder in 1992 asked Buffett what books he read, and he said that before the Salomon scandal he had read a lot of books. Then he tossed the question to Munger who said one book he'd enjoyed was *The Third Chimpanzee.* "Are we going to add him up here?" Buffett quipped.

When a shareholder asked about billionaire Ross Perot's entry in the presidential race and whether that gave Buffett any ideas, Buffett said it gave him no ideas whatsoever and added, "We'll see if he's a billionaire when it's over."

Buffett's Investor Club Med is all great fun, which includes talking to other Berkshire shareholders on the bus ride to the Berkshire-owned stores. Again, most conversations start with, "How long have you been a Berkshire shareholder?" or some tiny bit of information you may have about Buffett or Berkshire's latest investment.

Sometimes there are sober reminders from Buffett of the dangers of the marketplace. "You shouldn't own common stocks if a 50% decrease in their value in a short period of time would cause you acute distress," he said at the annual meeting in 1988.

After the annual meeting in 1992, Berkshire shareholder Paul

Cassidy said of Buffett, "He's a great education. I bought a couple of shares early on. He gave me the financial security to open my restaurant (The Loft in North Andover, Massachusetts). I try to carry on in my business the ways he talks about. And I tell my children to be long-term investors. They've been buying Coca-Cola stock. I believe that will help send them to college. Our family gets great laughter and enjoyment from Buffett."

A short time later Tom Weik, president of Weik Investment Services, Inc., in Wyomissing, Pennsylvania, was talking in the afterglow of the annual meeting.

Weik, an avid bridge player, has kept up an occasional correspondence with Buffett about bridge, and Weik said Buffett once wrote to him about Ben Graham's relationship with bridge. Buffett said Ben Graham played, but wasn't hard core about it. "This was his only failing." (Bridge champions Bob Hamman and Patrick Wolff are on hand at annual meeting festivities.)

Reflecting on what Berkshire had done for him, Weik said, "It enabled me to have the comfort to start a business from scratch."

Buffett got a ten on the laugh meter at the meeting in 1994 when Allan Maxwell, a Searle Laboratories salesman in Omaha asked: "Now that you're the richest person in the country, what's your next goal?"

Buffett: "That's easy, to be the oldest person in the country." (In 1999 Maxwell asked a variation of his question, that if he weren't himself who would he rather be? "I'd probably want to be Mrs. B. She made it to 104," Buffett replied.)

Later at the 1994 meeting Buffett said he was in pretty good health, then waved at his 2-liter bottle of Coke and said, "This stuff does wonders for you."

(Photo by Gail Wyman)

Buffett signing autographs at Borsheim's before Berkshire's Annual Meeting in 1996

Every year he is asked about splitting the stock and every year he says there are no plans to do so. In 1994 a shareholder asked if he planned a reverse split which leaves fewer shares outstanding. "Now you're talking," Buffett said.

At the 1995 meeting, Buffett announced that shareholders had come

(Photo by Nancy Line Jacobs)

Katharine Graham and Buffett sign books at Borsheim's during Berkshire Annual Meeting festivities in 1997.

from 49 of 50 states with only Vermont not represented. And they had come from Australia, France, Israel, Canada, Sweden and Zimbabwe. Because people had come from such distances, Buffett said he would extend the meeting, which in prior years, lasted until noon or so, until 2:45 p.m.

He began by explaining a proposal to get authorization to issue preferred stock should the board see fit. "There is no downside to the proposal...if we do something dumb we can do it in any form [such as cash]...this gives more forms of currency to make acquisitions."

Buffett said if the acquisitions were huge, like $5 billion, Berkshire would have to come back to the shareholders for another vote and he added if that were to happen, it would come back "with the votes already in hand."

As the questions rolled on, one shareholder asked about having his wife and son on Berkshire's board. Quipped Buffett: "It's terrific for family harmony."

Soon a typical answer of "No" came from laconic Munger and Buffett joked: "I was hoping Charlie would have a near-life experience this morning." Munger shot back with, "No comment."

Later when Munger said Berkshire could be successful even if shareholders didn't get rich as fast as in the past, some shareholders groaned. "It's a tie vote," Buffett said.

During the meeting Buffett asked Katharine Graham, Don Keough and Tom Murphy, who were sitting together, to stand.

When they stood, Buffett said they were responsible for $6½ billion in profits, "so far." (The audience applauded.)

Buffett and Bank of Granite Chairman John Forlines met for the first time the day before the annual meeting in 1996 near the Omaha Marriott. They had only traded several letters beforehand. When they did meet, Buffett said, "I just read your report." Then Buffett began citing figures from the Granite Falls, North Carolina bank's first quarter report. "He was right. I was surprised. I was overwhelmed, to say the least," Forlines said.

Then Buffett made a mention of the bank at the annual meeting saying the bank was one of the most profitable for its size in the U.S.

"We had requests as far away as Hong Kong for annual reports." Forlines beamed. In all, 250 requests came in. The bank had to order and reprint annual reports.

In 1996 the bank was the subject of stories by *Forbes* (October 21) and CBS (November 20).

Forlines, who has headed the bank since 1954 when he was 36 years old, attended Duke University and was a major in the Army's finance unit.

A Bank of Granite share bought for $211 in 1954 has, through splits and reinvested dividends, became 2,948 shares worth more

(Photo by Nancy Line Jacobs)

Astrid Menks, Phil Carret, Mrs. Susan Buffett and Debbie Bosanek at Berkshire Annual Meeting festivities in 1997

(Photo by Frank Kilpatrick)

This is the Dairy Queen in Omaha, with a large Coca-Cola bottle on display, where Buffett and Munger had dessert with shareholders the night before the Berkshire Annual Meeting in 1998.

Buffett having a Dusty Sundae dessert and signing autographs at a Dairy Queen in Omaha the night of May 3, 1998 before the Berkshire Annual Meeting the next day. At the 2000 meeting, Buffett was spotted opening a Dilly Bar package with his teeth.

Berkshire Vice Chairman Charles Munger holds an ice cream cone at the Dairy Queen where about 500 people showed up to see Buffett and Munger.

(Photos by Nancy Line Jacobs)

735

(Photo by Laverne Ramsey)

John Forlines, Bank of
Granite Chairman

(Photo by Linda Hannet)

Bank of Granite "The best little bank in America."

than $78,000. (*Washington Post*, October 25, 1998)

It's "efficiency ratio"—its non-interest expenses as a percentage of its revenues—is 38% versus 60% for similar-sized banks.

At the 1997 meeting Buffett was asked about a small band of anti-abortion protesters who showed up outside Gorat's steakhouse the night before the meeting and again later the next morning outside the Aksarben auditorium. Those demonstrating opposed Buffett's giving to Planned Parenthood and his pro-choice views. Buffett said the protesters had every right to protest and that when it came time for charity giving at Berkshire, some shareholders contributed to pro-choice and some to anti-abortion charities.

Later at the 1997 meeting a woman identified herself as a "very minimum shareholder." Buffett replied: "Don't minimize your holdings. Between the two of us, we control the company."

Here was a typical example of the repartee between Buffett and Munger:

Munger: "Life is a whole series of opportunity costs. You've got to marry the best person who is convenient to find that will have you. And investment is much the same sort of process."

Buffett: "I knew we'd get in trouble after lunch."

Buffett has said of the annual meeting, "We want to make it convenient. We want to make it interesting. And we want people to have fun... I think if you see them [shareholders] at the ballpark or at Gorat's or at Borsheim's, most of 'em are smiling. If people are smiling as they head out to Eppley (Airfield), we're going to see them again." (*Omaha World-Herald*, May 2, 1998)

As the annual meetings have blossomed in size, Buffett has tried to figure out ways to accommodate the crowds. He says he now has a fantasy that one day it'll be held at the Nebraska football stadium and that he'll be the announcer. As the managers run on the field,

736

(Photo by Nancy Line Jacobs)

Hall of Fame baseball player Ernie Banks and Warren "The Whip" Buffett at festivities surrounding Berkshire's annual meeting in 1999. Banks, known for his 19 seasons with the Chicago Cubs at Wrigley Field, was famous for saying: "It's a great day for a ballgame. Let's play two." From 1955 to 1960, Banks hit 248 homeruns—the most of any player in the majors, including Mantle, Mays, and Aaron. One shareholder after meeting both Buffett and Banks said, "I met my lifelong hero—Ernie Banks!"

(Photo by Pat Kilpatrick)

Buffett catching a dinner after the baseball game during the annual meeting weekend in 1999. From left is the back of the head of his sister, Doris Bryant, his daughter, Susan, his other sister, Bertie Bialek, Ernie Banks (his baseball cap, anyway) and Doris Bryant's husband, Al Bryant.

he'll yell: "See's Candy, Chuck Huggins..."

The 1998 meeting was covered by many reporters, including Daniel McGinn of *Newsweek*, who wrapped up his "Woodstock of Capitalism" story this way: "Back at the auditorium the rest of the disciples disperse, their appetite for wisdom sated for another year. The lights go dim. Buffett has left the building."

Even with Berkshire's poor 1999, there were few hostile questions at the meeting in 2000, the worst perhaps being from a shareholder who noted that he had covered his Berkshire losses during the year with his high tech investments.

And one youngster noted that she had bought Berkshire with the hopes of helping to pay for her college education, but had "started to look at correspondence schools" when the stock hit it lows.

Raisins and Turds

The most talked about comment of the day came in the morning session out of the blue from Munger when he was talking about the benefits that the Internet and technology are providing to society compared to the evils of stock speculation in these sections. Munger said: "When you mix raisins and turds you still have turds." Buffett replied: "Now you know why I write the annual reports," and later added, "We'll try to stay away from raisins this afternoon."

(Photo by Bob Sullivan)

Tough duty, but someone has to do it. Nancy Hess, left, of Highland Park, Texas and Carol Padelford of Seattle have a photo op with the Oracle of Omaha at Borsheim's the weekend before the Berkshire Annual Meeting in 1999.

Lionberger, shown here with Buffett, said: "Having been a Bakery Manager at a HyVee in Lincoln for four years while contemplating a business degree, I was accustomed to little sleep. When I realized that I would get little or no sleep whether I tried to or not, I considered the options in a common risk/return, cost/benefit analysis. On one hand, I could be extremely sleepy and possibly dangerous on the road at 7 a.m. (and get a very bad seat). On the other hand, I could get the best seat in the house, and spend several hours with people who no doubt would have the same priorities (investing) and role models (Warren Buffett) as me...I reasoned that in order for someone to get up super-early and stand outside the civic auditorium for hours, they would be of a certain demographic."

(Photo by Joe Lionberger)

(Photo by Mary Houbolt)

Joe Lionberger, center, with big bag off his left shoulder, arrived first at Berkshire's annual meeting in 2000. He showed up at 3:15 a.m. Larry Oberman of Chicago had been the early bird each of the six years before that. Lionberger, 28, originally of Martell, Nebraska, is a finance student at the University of Nebraska-Lincoln.

Buffett gave a few of these autographed fake $100 bills to shareholders during the 1997 Berkshire Annual Meeting festivities.

109

A SPECIAL MEETING
CARDBOARD CUTOUT OF MUNGER

Berkshire held a special meeting on September 16, 1998 to vote the issuance of new stock and to buy General Re.

Munger didn't make the meeting and Buffett joked beforehand that: "I guess he figures that his salary is such that we are entitled to only one appearance per year."

Buffett said Munger told him: "Take off the training wheels and see if you can handle this yourself."

Shortly into the meeting, Buffett got a tough question and said he needed Munger's help. He reached over to Munger's normal seat and pulled up a large cardboard cutout of Munger and placed it in the chair.

To another question, Buffett turned to the Munger cutout and asked for help and they played a taped response from Munger: "I have nothing to add."

At one point Buffett said Munger was more animated than usual. And Buffett continued to play taped responses from Munger such as "no comment" or "no."

(Photo by David Ramsey)

Buffett and his cardboard cutout of Charles Munger at Berkshire's special meeting September 16, 1998. David Ramsey of Montgomery, Alabama, wrote Buffett an apology for taking this photo even though photos of Berkshire meetings are not allowed. He received a letter back from Debbie Bosanek saying, "We received your nice letter and the picture. We're sending it on to Charlie as it is one of his better photos."

110

PHIL SWIGARD'S NEWSLETTER

Phil Swigard, who owns and manages commercial and multi-family residential properties from Kingston, Washington, says that he and his wife Sandy have devoted much of their lives to boats. "We lived aboard full time for 13 years, and over the last 30 years, have sailed around 50,000 miles including most of the Caribbean, both U.S. coasts, the South Pacific, Hawaii, and Alaska.

"We got into the habit of writing these newsletters years ago when we were out of the country on a four-year cruise and only received our mail three times a year. The newsletters were a way of maintaining contact with our friends during such a prolonged absence."

Here are some excerpts from Phil's newsletter in the spring of 1999:

"Our gain in net worth during 1998 was $25.9 billion, which increased the per-share book value of both our Class A and Class B stock by 48.3%." So began this year's letter to shareholders, an epistle looked forward to by just about the entire world's financial community.

As usual, the letter got your attention from the very first sentence. But then, in typical Buffett fashion, Warren explained why this gain was distorted by accounting conventions resulting from issuing shares in connection with several of the acquisitions made this year. I am cynical enough to be sure that a shocking number of today's CEOs would not have bothered with that little detail, and would have instead just basked in the glory of being able to make such a factual, although very misleading, claim.

Not our Warren!

The biggest acquisition was, of course, General Re. This acquisition gave Berkshire the highest book value of any company in the United States, and the second highest of any company in the world, if my information is correct. And yet, you can ask the average person on the street what they know about Berkshire Hathaway and the answer you are likely to get is that they never heard of it. This fascinates me. Here is one of the most important companies in the world and most people, including a surprising number in the financial community, know next to nothing about it. Berkshire's price per A share has been hovering in the mid-seventies lately although it was as high as 84 during the year. That is $84,000 per share, not $84 per share. And the way things are going (with Berkshire's earnings potential—not the stock market), it is close to a certainty that in the not too far future, that price per share will be six figures.

When Berkshire got over $10,000 per share years ago, all the newspapers, including *the Wall Street Journal*, had problems because their financial pages were not set up to show share prices of five figures. I predict that the newspapers are going to have to fix their format again.

Warren warns about making predictions, but I am not too concerned about being wrong about that one.

Warren has made the statement, in various ways over the last 15 years, that Berkshire's growing size is a huge impediment to matching the historical annual returns Berkshire has achieved—around 24% per year. He has managed to prove himself wrong every year so far.

However, Charlie and Warren are now sitting on around 16 billion in cash or equivalents looking for a home. Where can you put that much money to work to earn returns like they have in the past?

With smaller amounts of money to work with, your universe of possible investments is very broad compared to the number of possibilities when you are dealing in such huge sums. Even though these two incredible people have managed the seemingly impossible year after year, it would be wise to heed Warren's advice. To adopt a Pollyanna attitude and blithely assume that they can continue to do the impossible would not be a wise course of action in my not so humble opinion.

In fact, Warren has said that he would be ecstatic if they could achieve 15%.

Of course, all this fades into insignificance compared to what came in the mail along with my annual report. I received another invitation to the annual Sunday Brunch. There is a God!

I dug out my coat and tie, the same one from last year and not worn since, polished up my shoes, stuffed all into my beat up suitcase, gritted my teeth and braced myself for the crowded confines of steerage class on United. I headed for the airport a few days before the meeting, and was squeezed into an absolutely full airplane.

All the flights to Omaha were full. It seemed everyone, including God, was heading to Omaha for the annual Gathering of the Faithful. Well, maybe not God. Many shareholders think God already lives in Omaha.

Just prior to leaving on this trip, I had to make a number of trips to Seattle with its gridlock traffic, and had just come back from a business trip to Florida, also steerage class. These were not my idea of pleasant experiences. Sandy had gone with me to Florida and had to leave for Philadelphia two days after my return. To climb on an airplane again so soon was too much for her, so she decided not to go this year.

Although I had been to Omaha three times before, I was still shocked by the extreme contrast between crowded Orlando and Seattle and the almost empty freeways of Omaha. Especially after all my recent traveling, the contrast seemed even greater. Even the airline terminal was "people sized."

The next morning, suffering from a little jet lag, I realized that in my excitement over getting the invitation, I had forgotten the not-so-small matter of sending in the forms to receive a pass to the annual meeting. No pass—no meeting.

After thinking about what to do and coming up with no creative solutions. I finally gave up and called Berkshire's office. I knew how busy everyone was getting ready for the Big Weekend, and I hated to impose. This year, they expected over 15,000 people to attend.

Besides, World Headquarters for Berkshire Hathaway consists of only 12 people—and one of those is Warren. And they do not hire additional staff to prepare for the annual meeting. These people do the whole show. To say that they were busy would be more than just an understatement...

One of the major acquisitions by Berkshire last year was Executive Jet, a particularly successful enterprise whose purpose is to rationalize the indefensible—owning a private jet. Flying around in a private jet has to be right there up at the top of ways to spend the most money per hour possible. Since corporations and wealthy individuals participate in this financial insanity all the time anyway, Executive Jet has come up with a very good way to make the costs of flying around in luxury significantly less expensive.

They sell fractional interests in a fleet of different jets, and provide the flight crews, training, maintenance, and scheduling. It makes so much sense (relatively speaking, that is) that Warren actually sold his own beloved private jet, appropriately named the *Indefensible*, and bought a fractional interest in one of the jets. Of course, now Berkshire owns the entire caboodle—all the jets, facilities, and cash flow.

Warren had brought the full-sized mockup of the new 737 Business Jet to Omaha for the shareholders to see.

This was not just for the entertainment of the shareholders—this was a very large group of potential buyers of fractional interests...

I was so overwhelmed that I went through the plane twice. It even had two of the four essential food groups tastefully displayed for the passenger's enjoyment—Cherry Coke and See's Candy.

I then went around behind the plane where there were no people standing around to get some pictures. There was a portable generator there that was providing electrical power to the plane. I thought I could get a much better angle for a picture if I climbed up on the generator. So, not having learned from many similar past escapades, I climbed up there and got my picture.

As I climbed down, the generator suddenly stopped. As I stood there looking at the thing wondering why it had stopped, a guy came running around the front of the plane full tilt—this guy was moving at about Warp 9. He got to the generator, whipped open the access doors, and frantically started throwing breakers and twisting valves. He then hit the starter. The thing coughed a little and then lapsed into silence. "Good thing," I thought, "that I got to see the plane before I broke the generator."

About then I fessed up. I told him what I had done. He looked at me briefly. It was a good thing that looks can't kill. He said that Warren Buffett had arrived on the other side of the plane and as he had been about to board, the plane went dark. I thought, "Oops." More frantic lever and valve tweaking followed. He hit the starter again and, and after a prolonged series of gasps and wheezes the thing started. I was grateful.

As we walked around the front of the plane together, he called an armed guard over. He said: "If you see anyone near that generator again, just shoot him."

Warren was indeed on the other side of the plane. There were only a few shareholders around, and he was being his usual jovial self shaking hands and talking to people. I still had my camera in my hand as I walked up to him. Before I knew what was happening the Executive Jet guy had grabbed my camera and there I was standing there with Warren's arm around my shoulder getting my picture taken.

I smiled for the camera, and thought that this was probably not the time to tell him about the generator.

Having had enough excitement for the afternoon, we headed back to our car. It turned out that Warren parked his car just in front of ours. It was an older, blue Lincoln Town Car just like my wife, Sandy's. It was even exactly the same color. Like hers, Warren's car appeared to have aged gracefully. Warren walked over about the same time and got in to drive himself somewhere else. He was alone—no drivers, guards, or anything. Not exactly what you might expect from the second richest man in the world....

Then I took off with the car and made a beeline for the Happy Hollow Country Club and The Brunch. Even though this was not my first time, I was still a little nervous.

As I walked in, I was almost overwhelmed by the greeting from Bill Child and his gracious wife who were standing along with their daughter and her brand new husband by the door. Bill is the CEO of R.C. Willey, the Utah furniture firm acquired by Berkshire a few years ago.

Bill is one of the nicest guys you could ever want to meet, and has been very wonderful to me. He is the fellow I met at my very first annual meeting, and who told me so many stories about his experiences with Warren during the acquisition of his company. Bill qualifies as my absolute favorite CEO—not that I know that many CEOs.

I immediately felt more relaxed.

I found my name tag at the table. It looked like Debbie had not yet talked to Warren. So far, so good.

I saw Tony Nicely, the CEO of GEICO, talking to Stan Lipsey who is editor of the *Buffalo News*, both companies owned by Berkshire. I went over to introduce myself. I particularly wanted to compliment Tony Nicely on what a job he is doing. I feel certain that in the foreseeable future, GEICO will displace State Farm as number one in the automobile insurance field. Tony turned out to be very approachable, and as gracious as he is competent.

I managed to talk to a number of other people I had met in years past before it was time to find a place to sit. I even was able to have a few words with Warren who was talking to Bill Child.

I noticed a table with just five people sitting there, and I went over and introduced myself. The fellow at one end of the group introduced me to everyone at once. He just said that they were the Dairy Queen guys. I thought, "Oh Boy," and asked if I might join them. They said sure, so I grabbed a chair.

Another recent major acquisition by Berkshire was the entire Dairy Queen chain. This was a business I was especially interested in, and here was the entire top management team. What an opportunity to learn!

John and Jane Mooty and their son Chuck sat at one end of the table. John was the patriarch of the group. Next to them was Mike Sullivan, the CEO, and I sat next to Ed Watson, the Executive Vice

President.

I asked them how they liked being a part of Berkshire and they all grinned widely. Then I asked them how they liked the interview Warren and had given Ted Koppel on *Nightline* recently. Then their grins got really wide. They said that the response from their franchisees had been fantastic...

Up early, we left for the stadium by about 6:15 a.m. We arrived to find a very long line already. It turned out that those at the head of the line had been there since about 4 a.m. We got there just as Warren drove off to the "overflow" coliseum a mile or two away. The main stadium holds about 14,000 people, and there were over 15,000 in attendance. And that doesn't count the camera crews, TV reporters, and media from all over the world.

The meeting itself wouldn't start until 9:30 or so, but there was plenty to do until then. Exhibits had been set up all over by See's Candy, GEICO, World Book, and most of the other companies that Berkshire owns including one by Dairy Queen where they were passing out thousands of "Dilly Bars." Plus, the meeting is always preceded by a bunch of funny skits and videos featuring Warren, Charlie, and company. Berkshire had set up a complementary coffee, juice and pastry breakfast upstairs so you could even grab a bite if you felt a little peckish.

I saw Michael Eisner walking around checking out what was happening at the annual meeting of one of Disney's major stockholders—yes, Berkshire owns a good chunk of "The Mouse" too. I also ran across Chuck Huggins, who is CEO of See's, and chatted for a while. I knew that his family had a vacation home on Blakely Island in Washington very near a home that I once made an offer for many years ago. We had something in common besides a love of See's candy.

When Warren and Charlie walked in all 14,000 people present stood and gave them a standing ovation.

The day passed very quickly, and all of a sudden it was 3:30 p.m. and Warren and Charlie adjourned the meeting. It was too soon for me.

So, at the annual Gathering of the Faithful in Omaha, in this, the last year of the millennium, that's the way it was.

111
GORAT'S
"I'LL HAVE WHAT HE'S HAVING."

Beginning in 1996 Buffett wrote in his letter to shareholders they were welcome to join him at Gorat's, his favorite steakhouse, the Sunday night before the annual meeting.

A year later he wrote: "My favorite steakhouse, Gorat's, was sold out last year on the weekend of the annual meeting, even though it added an additional seating at 4 p.m. on Sunday. You can make reservations beginning on April 1st (*but not earlier*) by calling 402-551-3733. I will be at Gorat's on Sunday after Borsheim's, having my usual rare T-bone and double order of hashbrowns. I can also recommend—this is standard fare when Debbie Bosanek, my invaluable assistant, and I go to lunch—the hot roast beef sandwich with mashed potatoes and gravy. Mention Debbie's name and you'll be given an extra boat of gravy." Well, that set things off.

One shareholder called April 1st, before the restaurant opened, barely managing to land a table at 4:30 p.m. No other times were available. The lady answering the phone, clearly swamped, said the restaurant was virtually sold out. With the sounds of the phone ringing and chaos apparent, the lady, exasperated, said: "I think I'll go back home."

(Photo by Nancy Line Jacobs)

Gorat's is Buffett's favorite steakhouse.

(Photo by Bob Sullivan)

Buffett at Gorat's steakhouse the night before Berkshire's Annual Meeting in 1997.

One of those who did get reservations, Ken Mills of Lakeland, Florida, kept his Gorat's menu and sent it to Buffett (the Gorat Entertainer/Educator) to autograph. Buffett replied: "Ken, keep ordering the T-bone—Warren E. Buffett."

About 900 people show up at Gorat's to have dinner with Buffett. In 1998 they included Disney's Michael Eisner and NBC News Anchor Tom Brokaw. In 1997 a fellow named J.P. Tan, of Singapore, was among them. Buffett had invited Tan to the meeting although not as a shareholder. Tan flew 24 hours to attend and wound up only a few feet from Buffett's table saying, "I'm overwhelmed." A waitress asked for his order. "I'll have Mr. Buffett's favorite," Tan says, ordering a T-bone steak. However, Tan decides to have his steak medium. Buffett has his rare. Many other diners ask what Buffett's having and some say, echoing the immortal line from the movie *When Harry met Sally*: "I'll have what he's having."

Buffett wrote in Berkshire's 1998 Annual Report of the shareholders' dinner at Gorat's: "The cognoscenti will continue to order rare T-bones with a double order of hash browns."

Buffett's friend Pal Gorat owns the restaurant. Gorat's daughter Deb told the following story to Berkshire shareholder John Zemanovich of Canada: "Warren had been in the night before to meet some people for dinner. Apparently Warren was early or his guests were late because he waited anxiously at the front door of Gorat's to see them arrive in the parking lot. The funny thing is, that while he stood at the front door, he acted as doorman—opening the door for patrons of the steakhouse. Nobody could believe it. She told me that one patron remarked, 'Isn't that Warren Buffett at the front door?' She answered 'yes' ... She said she told him that if he needed extra work they would hire him. She added that he would get lots of tips."

Berkshire Hathaway Stockholder's
Sunday at

May 2, 1999

Appetizers

Gorat's Famous:

French Fried Onion Rings	$3.50
French Fried Ravioli	$3.50
Shrimp Cocktail	$4.95
Cheese or Garlic Toast	$2.25

Seafood

Jumbo Shrimp (French Fried)	$14.50
Baked Halibut Steak	$14.50
Baked Orange Roughy	$14.50
With Crab Mornay Sauce	

Steaks - *Grilled or Char-Broiled*

Filet Mignon

Small	Large
$15.95	$17.95

U.S. Choice Prime Rib Au Jus

Small	Large
$15.95	$17.95

Warren Buffett's Favorite
T-Bone
$18.50

Omaha Sirloin
Succulent Bone-In Strip
$15.50

New York Blue Ribbon
Strip Sirloin
$18.50

Chicken

Chicken Parmesan	$10.95

Desserts

Spumoni	$2.50
Cheesecake	$3.50
Carrot Cake	$3.50

Entrees are served with Salad, Choice of Salad Dressing (Roquefort .75 Extra); Spaghetti,
Mostaccioli or Vegetable; Baked, Hash Brown or French Fried Potatoes and Coffee or Tea.

Warren has urged us to take an unprecedented number of reservations for this evening. To prevent a backup at later seatings, both Warren and we would appreciate it if you would release your table after a reasonable period. But take your time during dinner and enjoy the meal.

112
GENERICS:
BUSINESS SCHOOL IN AN ELECTRIFYING
TWO MINUTES

The Berkshire Annual Meeting in 1993 occurred just weeks after "Marlboro Friday." Brand managers as well as their ad agencies were shaken badly and many businessmen were wrestling with the question of just how many inroads generic products were making on brand names.

Sitting before a crowd of more than 2,000 people, with no notes, no aides and no idea a question about generics was coming, Buffett stunned the audience with his mastery of the business scene.

Here's how, over a couple of minutes, Buffett answered the question:

"Will developments in the generic brand area hurt Coca-Cola? That's a terribly important question.

"Generic brands have been with us a long time. But lately they've attracted a great deal of attention—partly because they're doing better and in particular because of Philip Morris's actions a few weeks ago—when, in reaction to the threat and the inroads of generics, they cut the price dramatically on Marlboro.

"I wouldn't say Marlboro is the most valuable brand name in the world. Coca-Cola is more valuable—and I think that's been proven by subsequent events. But Marlboro earned more money than any brand name in the world.

"And all of a sudden, Philip Morris took some actions which dramatically reduced the earnings of that brand and changed the pricing dynamic that had existed in the cigarette business for many decades. And since then, Philip Morris has had $16 billion lopped off its market value and RJR's suffered accordingly.

"It's a terribly interesting case study and it illustrates one of the dangers of generic competition. Philip Morris cigarettes got to where they were selling for $2.00 a pack. The average cigarette consumer uses something close to ten packs a week. Meanwhile, the generic was at about $1 or thereabouts. So you really have a $500 a year differential in cost per year to a ten-pack-a-week smoker. And that is a big annual cost differential. You better have something that people think is dramatically better than the generic for the average consumer to shell out an extra $500 a year. It's happening in other areas, too—whether it's corn flakes or diapers or a lot of things...

"In our case, I think the Gillette brand name, for example, is far better protected against generic competition than the main product of Philip Morris—although there always has been generic competition in blades and there always will be.

"The average male purchases something like 30 blades a year. He pays 70 cents each if he buys the best—which is the Sensor. That's $21 a year. The best he can do if he wants something that leaves him Band-Aids on his face and an uncomfortable experience costs him $10 a year. So you're talking $11 for a 365-day experience...

"I think there's a generic threat of some sort in any industry where the leaders are earning high returns on equity. It just stands to reason that that's going to encourage competition.

"And the threat may be accelerating in many industries. But I think that brand names with the right ingredients are enormously valuable. Sometimes infrastructure is a problem for the generics. The worldwide infrastructure for Coca-Cola, for example, is very impressive and very hard for a generic provider to duplicate.

"But if somebody wants to sell a generic box of chocolates in California against See's Chocolates, that's obviously somewhat of a threat. And I just hope that they take them home on Valentine's Day and say, 'Here, Honey, I took the low bid.' "

Then Buffett addressed the question of Coca-Cola point blank:

"Wal-Mart's selling Sam's Cola. And Wal-Mart is a very, very potent force. One thing that's helpful is that they were selling it as cheap as $4.00 a case here. And I don't believe that's sustainable. That's 16⅔ cents a can.

"It's been a while since I looked at aluminum—and it's down. But I think the can is close to a six-cent item by itself. The can is far more expensive than the ingredients...Distribution costs, trucking, stocking and all that sort of thing have to be fairly similar. In a 12-ounce can, there's 1.3 ounces of sugar—which at the domestic price, would be around 1¾ cents per can. And that's got to be the same whether it's Sam's Cola or Coca-Cola.

"The Coca-Cola Company sells about 700 million 8-ounce servings—largely of Coca-Cola, but also of other soft drinks—worldwide every day. If you take 700 million and multiply it by 365 days, you come up with 250 billion or so 8-ounce servings of Coke or its products in the world each year.

"The Coca-Cola Company made about $2½ billion pretax last year. That's one penny per serving. One penny per serving does not leave a huge umbrella. The generic is not going to buy the can any cheaper. And they're not going to buy the sugar any cheaper and so on. Their trucks aren't going to be any cheaper."

Buffett, in an electrifying two minutes, just took you through business school. "Better than business school, I'm in awe," says shareholder Michael Assael.

113
POETRY SECTION

Floyd Jones, principal of First Washington Corp. in Seattle, Washington, which serves many clients who have Berkshire stock, bought his first shares of Berkshire in 1985.

"I kept adding to it over the years and was able to start the Jones Foundation, a dream of mine. Berkshire is 80% of the holdings... The best income stock I know of is a growth stock," Jones said.

Jones was so moved by his experience with Berkshire that he wrote a poem in the middle of the night before the annual meeting in 1993. Jones left his room to write the poem, but did not awaken his wife, Delores.

"She was reaching for the phone in a panic when I went back to the room [at 4:30 a.m.]...At least I know now that she misses me," Jones said.

That morning, after Buffett called on him for a question, Jones read his poem to Berkshire shareholders:

MECCA FOR WALL STREET

They come! They come!
They come to Omaha-O-m-a-h-a
Out on the Western plains,
no hub since wagon trains
They come to see and hear oracles
of Midas fame, Warren and Charlie!
They come for the journey,
to have the feeling,
to be welcome, to say hello
to touch in handshake, to ask the question
to "help."
They come to know fellow travelers, to boast,
debate, to EVALUATE.

Skeptical but analytical minds voice a
challenge to method and even the plan.
The Chairman takes no prisoners
but disposes out of hand.

They come from Alabama and to see Mrs. B.
They love the party at Borsheim's, 'cause
there's none in Tuskegee.

There's Fortune 500's among you.
Warren's their guru too,
Katharine Graham and Senator Kerrey
may say hello to you.
We'll all be at the Orpheum
To the rafters I hear,
it's investors' Mecca and convenes each year.
There'll be lots of See's Candy
and tons of Cherry Coke,
Then it's on to the shareholders
meeting that's uniquely for
the folks.

Another great year has ended,
Another has begun
Warren and Charlie, our warmest
regards... We'll let our
profits run!

An obviously touched Buffett said, "Thanks, Floyd," then asked for the "next question."

Here's another of Jones' poems:

Old red Bricks staring
up at me as I sit on the round tree beneath
Old Omaha, last century
construction...late this century
tourists and habitues seeking
soul, small business providing
protecting the old.

Fred Astaire danced here
Harold Edgerton went to M.I.T.
The Atom bomb would never have won
without him.

Buffett and Munger
Two generations back found they
were living way out on the
tracks
A soulful pair these two,
rational thinkers taking the
long view.

Our annual trek to Omaha,
now virtually a rite of spring,
brings thousands of "sophisticates"
to these old red brick
and antique things.

In early 1995 Berkshire's stock vaulted up to about $25,000 and then with a pounding of stories from *Barron's*, *The New York Times* and *Money* saying Berkshire was overvalued, the stock sank to about $22,000.

Meanwhile Buffett was adding more than $1 billion to his American Express stake, buying about half a billion dollars of PNC bank stock as well as snapping up the Helzberg's Diamond Shops chain.

(Photo by LaVerne Ramsey)

Jones took exception to the overvalued charges with, "Well, hell, he must be making some money."

Someone once asked Jones whether it'd be better to buy Berkshire or Wesco stock. Jones replied, "Always go through the front door, not the back door." So now some Berkshire shareholders call Jones, "Front Door Floyd."

"Front Door Floyd" Jones of Seattle

The Floyd and Delores Jones Foundation financially backed the PBS taping of the session with Buffett and Bill Gates at the University of Washington in 1998.

Computer Mama

Berkshire Shareholder Judy Goodnow Prus of Grosse Pointe, Michigan, was so moved by Berkshire's stock rise in early 1996, she E-mailed her son Michael:

Hark, what is this I hear?
Thirty-seven thousand three!
Our dear old friend Berkshire
Has astounded even me!

Oh, I could truly wax poetic,
Now 'twil be even more renowned!
All other stocks still look pathetic;
We should see that Warren's crowned!

Love, COMPUTER MAMA

Warren's Song
Her cart is rolling on.
Buffett wrote a song and sang it at the Omaha Press Club in 1987:

WARREN'S SONG
(to the tune of "The Battle Hymn of the Republic")

Oh, we thought we'd make a bundle
When we purchased ABC
But we found it's not so easy
When your network's number 3
So now the load at Berkshire
Must be borne by Mrs. B
Her cart is rolling on.
Chorus:
Glory, Glory, Hallelujah
Keep those buyers coming to ya
If we get rich it must be through ya
Her cart is rolling on.
Ideas flop and stocks may drop
But never do I pale
For no matter what my screwups
It's impossible to fail
Mrs. B will save me.
She'll just throw another sale
Her cart is rolling on.
Chorus:
Forbes may think I'm brilliant
When they make their annual log.
But the secret is I'm not the wheel
But merely just a cog.
Without the kiss of Mrs. B
I'd always be a frog
Her cart is rolling on.

And here's a poem from a Berkshire shareholder posted on the
"Berkshire message board" on the Internet February 13, 1998:

To gloat or not to gloat,
Aye, that is the question.
Whether tis nobler in the mind to enjoy the
outrageous fortunes of Warren Buffett

or to take arms against a See of Candy and by
Buying them, eat them.

To compound, to sleep.
Enjoy a dream.
Aye, there's the rub,

For in that time waiting to reach sixty,
after we shuffled up to fifty four,
after that long pause!

And here's one from September 11, 1998:

Ticker in the morning
Ticker in the evening
Ticker at suppertime
Be my favorite Ticker
And I'll love you all the time.
Put your tape around me
and bless the skys above,
You'll be mine forever
The stock ticker of love.
FTSE in the morning,
Cac in the evening
the Nikkei at night.
Be my baby ticker
I'll love you all the time

The Omaha Theater Company
for Young People
Sustaining Fund Drive
presents

Annie

with *A Very Special Scene*
Starring:
Warren Buffett as *Daddy Warbucks*
Monday
December 14, 1998
7:00 p.m.

The ROSE
Blumkin Performing Arts Center

2001 Farnam Street
Omaha, NE 68102
345-4849
Casual Attire
This ticket is good for General Admission
and admits one person

Rose Blumkin Performing Arts Center postcard

(Photo courtesy of the Rose
Blumkin Performing Arts
Center)

Buffett in bald cap as
Daddy Warbucks or
"Daddy Warrenbucks"

Here's Buffett's rendition of "Tomorrow" which he sang as Daddy Warbucks in the play "Annie" December 14, 1998 at the Rose Blumkin Performing Arts Center in Omaha:

The stock won't get split
tomorrow.
You will pay top dollar
on tomorrow for our "A"

No dividend checks tomorrow
If you need some money
just go borrow, day-to-day.

So when the Dow's down
don't frown and worry.
Just cast aside doubt
and shout
Hooray.

The stock'll go up tomorrow
So you gotta hang on
til tomorrow, come what may

This comes to us from Charles Page:

"Two roads diverged in the market,
and I—
I took BRK, not CMGI,
and that has made all the difference
with apologies to Robert Frost—Charles Page

Buffett-Mania by Elizabeth O'Brien

big berks, baby berks
coca cola-whee!
the oracle of omaha's
made a rich girl out of me

i put a ten-note down
in 1953
by 1999 it's worth
three billion forty-three

old warren buffett
has taught me how to save
long-term, not short-term
is what will get his raves

brand names, big moats
his recipe supreme
ben graham he's not, that's not his lot
he has a greater dream

my husband thinks it's crazy
for me to sell a share
to build a pool and deck for us
he says it isn't fair

(Photo courtesy of Wyatt McSpadden)

Elizabeth and Michael O'Brien

he says he's worked so hard
to stockpile As and Bs
the orchard's only started
why cut down any trees?

but i have been so faithful
i've been to omaha
to hear the sage and charlie m
pontificate berkshire's law

I've watched lou dobbs at nighttime
and bitchy willow bay
i've foregone all those manicures
so i could have my day

and now i put my foot down
i want to swim at home
to skinny-dip would be so hip
my husband's such a drone

big berks, baby berks
coca cola-whee!
the oracle of omaha's
made a rich girl out of me

Elizabeth sent her poem to Buffett and drew this reply:
"Tell your husband that even Berkshire holders spend a few dol-

lars now and then—and I definitely recommend a pool. After he gives in, write another poem and send it along. In the meantime, keep coming to the meetings."

[Elizabeth got the pool!]

Yellow Berker "Chamfer" who is Golda Azar of Rockville, Maryland, offered this holiday message in 1999:

Twas the night before X-mas
And all thru the house
Not a creature was stirring
Not even a mouse

The Yellow Berker sat glued to his chair
In the hope that St. Nicholas
Soon would be there

He had made up his list
And checked it out twice
And was sure that it said
"Please bring money tonite"

My BRK stock has had a bad run
And it looks like this X-mas
We won't have much fun.

But true BRKers never complain
They just back up the truck
Again and again.

It's a sign of great faith
To be able to buy
A stock that appears
To be heaving last sighs.

But our faith is unwaivering
And we sleep like a log
And it bothers us not
The stock acts like a dog.

We'll wait the 10 years
Then the whole world will see
That BRK really
Was the place to be

In the meantime I sit here
And think "What the heck"
Why worry about it Santa
I'm sure you bought techs.

Even with these poetic flights of fancy by Berkshire shareholders, the stature of William Butler Yeats seems assured.

114
THE BERKSHIRE ANNUAL REPORT
THE HOLY SCRIPTURE

Buffett often begins his letter for the Berkshire Annual Report at his home in Laguna Beach, California, where he goes at the end of each year. His ex-daughter in law, Mary Buffett, who was married to Peter Buffett for 12 years, says she can remember Buffett starting the report at the Laguna Beach home. "He'd be waiting for a last call from Chuck Huggins at See's Candies. He'd say 'Chuck ought to be calling any minute now.' He would call with a report to say See's sold 500 pounds more than last year, or something."

Usually early in the new year, he sits down with a yellow pad and a black felt pen and imagines he's writing to an intelligent sister who may have been away a lot of the year. He writes with respect, humor and candor.

He did some work on the 1999 Annual Report on the plane to Lakeland, Florida, in mid-December, 1999. "I find that 5% of the time is spent writing it and another 95% just fooling around with it," Buffett said. (*St. Petersburg Times*, December 15, 1999)

In the 1999 report, Buffett blamed himself for the poor results—an increase in book value of just half of one percent. Here are headlines from around the world as to how the report was received:

- *The Independent*: **Warren Buffett Admits to Annus Horribilis**
- *The Australia Financial Review*: **Buffett Apologies for Poor Show**
- *The Guardian*: **Buffett Confesses Blunder: Super-investor Pays Dear for Technophobia but Insists Market Bubble Must Burst**
- *Sydney Morning Herald*: **Buffett Sells Disney, Dodges Dot.Coms**
- *Financial Times*: **Buffett Deserves D Grade**
- *Hong Kong Standard*: **Market Guru Buffett Apologises for Losses**
- *The Courier-Mail*: **Buffett Shoulders the Blame**
- *The Age*: **Buffett Falls on Sword over Poor Earnings**

Here's how Buffett's 1998 letter to shareholders began: "Our gain in net worth during 1998 was $25.9 billion, which increased the per-share book value of both our Class A and Class B stock by 48.3%. Over the last 34 years (that is, since present management took over) per-share book value has grown from $19 to $37,801, a rate of 24.7% compounded annually."

"Normally, a gain of 48.3% would call for handsprings—but not this year. Remember Wagner, whose music has been described as better than it sounds? Well, Berkshire's progress in 1998—though more than satisfactory—was not as good as it looks. That's because most of that 48.3% came from our issuing shares in acquisitions."

The 1997 report had a white cover with red trim in honor of Nebraska's Coach Tom Osborne's retirement. It said: "Given our gain of 34.1%, it is tempting to declare victory and move on. But last year's performance was no great triumph: *Any* investor can chalk up large returns when stocks soar, as they did in 1997. In a bull market, one must avoid the error of the preening duck that quacks boastfully after a torrential rainstorm, thinking that its paddling skills have caused it to rise in the world. A right-thinking duck would instead compare its position after the downpour to that of the other ducks on the pond.

"So what's our duck rating for 1997? The table on the facing page shows that though we paddled furiously last year, passive ducks that simply invested in the S&P Index rose almost as fast as we did. Our appraisal of 1997's performance, then: 'Quack.' "

There is a Baby Berkshire and now we have a Baby Quack.

After the report was issued on the Internet March 14, 1998, Buffett's daughter, Susan, in a posting on the "Berkshire message board" said: "The Head Duck just called me and asked me to pass this message on to all of you: Anyone who printed out the annual report prior to 10:15 EST today should reprint. There was an error on the first page which has since been corrected. The error is the type size for 'quack.' He would also like me to remind you that this error was due to the shortcomings of computers which he has long been aware of, but which seem to have escaped the mind of Bill Gates."

This message was posted on the "Berkshire message board" shortly thereafter: "As one who has used the duck rating system for years in making investment decisions. I can only thank Doshoes...for bringing this change to our attention. At 8:15 CST, based on the original report, all my indicators pointed to BRK as a Strong Buy. At 11:15 CST however, the situation completely reversed itself, and BRK is now a Strong Sell. While parts of my formula are proprietary in nature, I can share the most crucial element is as follows:

$$SP/TS=n$$

Where SP=stock price
TS=type size of animal noise
n=buy or sell indicator

I don't generally give stock recommendations, but in this case it's fairly obvious: DO NOT buy BBK until the Chairman begins quacking up.

Bob in Nebraska

And then there was this posting from Jack Benvent of Haworth, New Jersey, that may quack you up:

(Photo by John Gartmann)

> I just wanted to congratulate the Head Duck for yet another excellent letter. I spent the past few days reviewing the letter and at the risk of ruffling a few feathers, I have made the following de-duck-tions:

Jack Benvent

> First it appears the Head Duck (whose initials are WEB—has any-one checked his feet lately?) made a significant re-duck-tion to his McDonald's holding, presumably because duck soup never made the MCD menu.

> Not to worry though, HD parlayed this money and bought a lot of silver duck-ats and duck-egged coupon bonds, both of which hatched earnings and goosed book value. The HD also wrote about paddling hard to keep up with the rising water. But, as we all know, you have to "float" before you can paddle. If you have any questions about this just ask WEB at the annual meeting—he never ducks questions.

> Next, when I referred to my *World Book* encyclopedia, I learned that scientists have discovered a new genus of ducks. These ducklings are known to spend much of their time molting in front of their computers reading about their favorite company. Not surprising, these new ducks have very little "down" in their portfolios, have tiny "bills" (because they never call their broker to sell) and are easily identified by their distinctive quack, which sounds a little like "brk, brk." No matter how many ugly duckings (silly geese really) predict the swan song of their favorite company, and the swan dive of its stock price, these new ducks just keep wad-

dling along in a row behind their Head Duck. And, like the swallows of San Juan Capistrano, this new genus of ducks migrates on the same date every year, flying in their famous "IV" [intrinsic value] formation, to their favorite watering hole in Nebraska—Mr. Toad's—to have a ducky time. Some ducks are known to preen themselves famously for the occasion (I'll be quaffing my hair in a duck-tail). Best of all, the life spans of these new ducks, (and this is especially true for the head ducks) are really, really long.

Just what are these new ducks called? The Lucky ducks, of course. (insert groan here) Sorry, sometimes, I just quack myself up.

Buffett gained financial control of Berkshire in 1965, assumed policy control that May and became chairman of the board and chief executive officer in 1970—the year for which he first wrote an annual letter to shareholders.

Nothing has brought Buffett more acclaim than his chairman's letter to shareholders in the annual report famous for candor, clarity and humor. For Berkshire aficionados and beyond, they are sublime reading.

Berkshire's owner-related business principles are set out in the first two pages of the report starting: "Although our form is corporate, our attitude is partnership. Charlie Munger and I think of our shareholders as owner-partners, and of ourselves as managing partners. (Because of the size of our shareholdings we also are, for better or worse, controlling partners.) We do not view the company itself as the ultimate owner of our business assets but, instead, view the company as a conduit through which our shareholders own the assets.

"In line with this owner-orientation, our directors are major shareholders of Berkshire Hathaway. In the case of at least four, over 50% of family net worth is represented by holdings of Berkshire. We eat our own cooking..."

"About the time I got to, 'We eat our own cooking,' I was hooked," says Berkshire shareholder Michael O'Brien of Austin, Texas. Berkshire reports are not easy to come by. If you want more than two copies, Berkshire charges $3 for each additional report. Berkshire reports have a tendency to start this way: "Our gain in net worth during 1991 was $2.1 billion, or 39.6%. Over the last 27 years (that is, since present management took over) our per-share book value has grown from $19 to $6,437, or at the rate of 23.7% compounded annually."

The 1995 report began: "Our gain in net worth during 1995 was

$5.3 billion, or 45%. Per-share book value grew by a little less, 43.1%, because we paid stock for two acquisitions, increasing our shares outstanding by 1.3%. Over the last 31 years (that is, since present management took over) per-share book value has grown from $19 to $14,426, or a rate of 23.6% compounded annually."

In these summaries Buffett delivers such jewels as this one from the 1985 Annual Report: "A horse that can count to ten is a remarkable horse—not a remarkable mathematician," quoting Samuel Johnson, and adding, "A textile company that allocates capital brilliantly within its industry is a remarkable textile company—not a remarkable business." Then he repeats one of his most famous statements. "With few exceptions when a manager with a reputation for brilliance tackles a business with a reputation for poor economics, it is the reputation of the business which remains intact." Also, "Gin rummy management behavior (discard your least promising business at each turn) is not our investment style. We would rather have overall results penalized a bit than engage in it."

Through the years, the letters have blossomed in style, substance and originality. The letters are full of humor, uncommon common sense, candor and clarity with wit and wisdom pulled from an array of sources, including the Bible, John Maynard Keynes, Yogi Berra and Mae West. Buffett is fond of quoting John Maynard Keynes: "I'd rather be vaguely right than precisely wrong."

Buffett also loves to quote Mae West, saying in the 1987 annual report, "Currently liking neither stocks nor bonds, I find myself the polar opposite of Mae West as she declared: I like only two kinds of men—foreign and domestic." He repeatedly has drawn on "the prophet" Mae West for her quote, "Too much of a good thing can be wonderful."

Shareholders receive the annual report every year in late March. The plain-looking, bound publication's cover simply says Berkshire Hathaway Inc. Annual Report—no photo of headquarters, board members, or outstanding employees. Not even a glossy of the Ben Franklin of Omaha.

Only Wesco's Munger rivals Buffett in frugally produced annual reports, often filling in numbers from portions of a previous year's report. For decades Munger ran one black and white photo of Wesco's headquarters, using a photo so old it had cars from the 1960s. (*The Warren Buffett Way*, Robert Hagstrom, p. 21)

The only mystery about the report's appearance is what color Berkshire has selected for its cover each year. Silver was the pick for the 1989 report, teal for 1990, uninviting dark blue for 1991, a burgundy red for 1992; in 1993 it arrived in paperbag brown. It was described as looking like a gravy-colored school exercise-book cover by the *London Independent* (February 19, 1995).

The 1994 report came in Husker red as in, "We're national champs! Go. Big Red. Go."

Here's a posting on the "Berkshire message board" from February 17, 1998: "Who cares about intrinsic values or the price of Berkshire on 12/31. What I want to know is will this year's annual report cover be yellow or silver?" Don't judge this book by its cover. The 1998 cover was dark green.

Each winter Buffett begins writing his letter in his scrawl. He turns it over for editing to his longtime friend, Carol Loomis, and Berkshire's Debbie Bosanek for typing.

Says Loomis, "Warren writes it by hand on yellow pads. I weigh in as editor. He's smart enough to know that everyone needs an editor, though sometimes I could kill him for ignoring my suggestions. Anyway, what I do on the report a lot of people who know something about both business and writing could do, as long as they had Warren's trust. What he does nobody else could come close to doing." (*Fortune,* Carol Loomis, April 11, 1988)

Buffett's first letter of March 15, 1971, in the 1970 annual report is a simple summary, less than two pages, of the year's operations. It's a straightforward report that offers little of the brilliance in writing, the wit, or the quotes from such figures as Goethe, Samuel Goldwyn, Yogi Berra and Ted Williams that would come later, along with possibly the most bizarre line ever to appear in an annual report.

In the 1986 report he wrote: "We bought a corporate jet last year." He set it off in diminutive type. Long a critic of aircraft as an example of corporate waste, Buffett backed and filled with a quote from Ben Franklin: "So convenient a thing it is to be a reasonable creature, since it enables one to find or make a reason for everything one has a mind to do."

The 1970 report began: "The past year witnessed dramatically diverse earnings results among our various operating units. The Illinois National Bank & Trust reported record earnings and continued to rank right at the top, nationally, among banks in terms of earnings as a percentage of average assets. Our insurance operations had some deterioration in underwriting results, but increased investment income produced a continued excellent return. The textile business became progressively more difficult throughout the year and the final break-even result is understandable, considering the industry environment."

The following year the letter was three pages. It began:

"It is a pleasure to report that operating earnings in 1971, excluding capital gains, amounted to more than 14% of beginning shareholders' equity. This result—considerably above the average of American industry—was achieved in the face of inadequate earnings in our textile operation, making clear the benefits of redeployment of capital inaugurated five years ago. It will continue to be the objective of management to improve return on total capitalization (long term debt plus equity), as well as the return on equity capital. However, it should be realized that merely maintaining the present relatively high rate of return may well prove more difficult than was improvement from the very low levels of return which prevailed throughout most of the 1960s."

From the early days Buffett has hammered away at getting a good return on capital.

"Buffett's business and investment success hinges on his dedication to return on capital rather than on mere bigness and economies of scale. This, in a nutshell, is what makes Warren Buffett, a capitalist classic," said Michael Assael.

The 1972 letter begins, "Operating earnings of Berkshire Hathaway during 1972 amounted to a highly satisfactory 19.9% of beginning shareholders' equity. Significant improvement was recorded in all of our major lines of businesses, but the most dramatic gains were in insurance underwriting profit. Due to an unusual convergence of favorable factors—diminishing auto accident frequency, moderating accident severity, and an absence of major catastrophes—underwriting profit margins achieved a level far above averages of the past or expectations of the future."

In the 1973 Berkshire report, Buffett notes that Berkshire earned almost $12 million and that the company's directors have approved a merger of Diversified Retailing into Berkshire Hathaway. Diversified operated a chain of retail stores and owned 16% of Blue Chip Stamps at the time.

"Diversified Retailing Company Inc., through subsidiaries, operates a chain of popular-priced women's apparel stores and also conducts a reinsurance business. In the opinion of your management, its most important asset is 16% of Blue Chip Stamps," Buffett wrote.

In addition, Buffett proudly reported that a minor holding, the since-defunct Sun Newspapers Inc., a group of weekly newspapers published in the Omaha area, won the Pulitzer Prize for local investigative reporting, the first time that a weekly had won in that category.

It won for its March 30, 1972, report about Boys Town, delineating the contrast between decreasing services and mounting wealth that had taken place at the home since Father Flanagan's death in 1948.

"Our congratulations go to Paul Williams, Editor, and Stan Lipsey, Publisher, as well as the entire editorial staff of Sun Newspapers for their achievement, which vividly illustrated that size need not be equated with significance in publishing."

In the horrible off-year of 1974, the stock market languished in excruciating torpor, and Buffett was forced to report what every shareholder dreads to hear. Inside that year's royal blue cover, he broke the news:

"Operating results for 1974 overall were unsatisfactory...The outlook for 1975 is not encouraging." From the beginning of 1973 to the end of 1974, Berkshire's stock price took its worst beating ever, falling from $93 a share in the first quarter of 1973 to $40 in the fourth quarter of 1974.

It would touch $38 a share in the first quarter of 1975 before getting back on track.

Things were unsatisfactory, and Buffett explained that the insurance and textile businesses had subpar years; nevertheless the operating business year, comparatively speaking, was fine. Buffett reported that shareholders' equity was up 10.3%, the lowest return on equity realized by the company since 1970. It was actually a stunning performance in a year in which few companies reported any progress at all.

For 1974, his performance was comparatively splendid. Buffett kept a string of increases in stockholders' equity alive, going back to his start in 1956. Through 1998, the record was intact.

Later in the 1974 report what would become vintage Buffett came through.

"Our stock portfolio declined again in 1974—along with most equity portfolios—to the point that at yearend it was worth approximately $17 million less than its carrying value. Again, we are under no pressure to sell such securities except at times that we deem advantageous and it is our belief that over a period of years the overall portfolio will prove to be worth more than its cost. A net capital loss was realized in 1974, and very likely will again occur in 1975. However, we consider several of our major holdings to have great potential for significantly increased values in future years, and therefore feel quite comfortable with our stock portfolio. At this writing, market depreciation of the portfolio has been reduced by half from yearend figures, reflecting higher general stock market levels."

Although his holding in The Washington Post Co. sank from about $10 million to about $8 million in the first few years after the 1973 purchase, The Post Co. has grown 100-fold since.

For the 1975 year, Buffett reported that the property and casualty, and textile businesses were God-awful.

> The property and casualty insurance industry had its worst year in history during 1975. We did our share—unfortunately, even somewhat more. Really disastrous results were concentrated in auto and long-tail (contracts where settlement of loss usually occurs long after the loss event) lines.
>
> Economic inflation, with the increase of cost of repairing humans and property far outstripping the general rate of inflation, produced ultimate loss costs which soared beyond premium levels established in a different cost environment. 'Social' inflation caused the liability concept to be expanded continuously, far beyond limits contemplated when rates were established—in effect, adding coverage beyond what was paid for. Such social inflation increased significantly both the propensity to sue and the possibility of collecting mammoth jury awards for events not previously considered statistically significant in the establishment of rates.

Of Berkshire's textile interests, Buffett wrote, "During the first half of 1975 sales of textile products were extremely depressed, resulting in major production curtailments. Operations ran at a significant loss, with employment down as much as 53% from a year earlier." There was a rebound in textiles in the second half of the year.

During the year Buffett bought more textile operations, Waumbec Mills Inc. and Waumbec Dyeing and Finishing Co. Inc., of Manchester, New Hampshire, only to report the following year that they had not performed well.

"Our textile division was a significant disappointment during 1976," he wrote. Inside the 1976 report, in a five-page letter, he listed main stockholdings of Berkshire at yearend 1976:

141,987 shares
California Water Service Co.   Cost $3,608,711
1,986,953 shares
Government Employees Insurance

Company Convertible Preferred	Cost $19,416,635
1,294,308 shares	
Government Employees Insurance	
Company Common Stock	Cost $4,115,670
395,100 shares	
Interpublic Group of Companies	Cost $4,530,615
562,900 shares	
Kaiser Industries, Inc.	Cost $8,270,871
188,900 shares	
Munsingwear, Inc.	Cost $3,398,404
83,400 shares	
National Presto Industries, Inc.	Cost $1,689,896
170,800 shares	
Ogilvy & Mather International	Cost $2,762,433
934,300 shares	
The Washington Post Co. Class B	Cost $10,627,604
Total:	$58,420,839
All other holdings	$16,974,375

Total equities: *$75,395,214*

He praised Eugene Abegg, chief executive of Illinois National Bank Trust Co., who in 1931 opened the doors of the bank Berkshire later bought.

Buffett wrote: "Recently, National City Corp. of Cleveland, truly an outstandingly well-managed bank, ran an ad stating 'the ratio of earnings to average assets was 1.34% in 1976 which we believe to be the best percentage of any major banking company.' Among the really large banks this was the best earnings achievement, but at the Illinois National Bank earnings were close to 50% better than those of National City, or approximately 2% of assets."

By statute, the bank was divested in 1980, the same year Abegg died. Buffett described him as a man who during Buffett's purchase of the bank put all the negative factors face up on the table, but said as years went by undiscussed items of value popped up. That's quite different from business transactions where the good points are touted up front and negatives surface only after the check crosses over.

Toward the end of the 1976 letter, Buffett said Berkshire had boosted its stake in Blue Chip Stamps to 33% of the company's stock.

Also, he devoted two sentences to K&W Products, an automotive products company. In its first year with Berkshire, Buffett said

K&W had performed well with sales and earnings up moderately.

In 1976 there were 2,000 Berkshire annual reports printed. By 1985 there were 15,500 with a second printing of 2,500 more. Now more than 325,000 a year are printed.

By 1977, Buffett was copyrighting the annual reports and eventually, in response to an increasing demand for back Berkshire reports, the company compiled Buffett's letters into bound volumes.

In the 1977 report, a small position in Cap Cities Communications popped up.

The following year that position was gone, but there was a new holding: American Broadcasting Companies. GEICO and Washington Post Co. were mainstays, as they always would be.

Buffett continued to educate his shareholders about Berkshire's holdings, and about the intricacies of accounting and insurance. But it was not until the middle of the 1979 report that he delivered his first real effort at humor: "Overall, we opt for Polonius (slightly restated): 'Neither a short-term borrower nor a long-term lender be.' "

He never looked back. In subsequent years he got funnier and funnier (as he got richer and richer) quoting pithy, applicable remarks, always with the purpose of helping shareholders better understand their investment.

In later years, the letters accompanying the annual reports have turned into 20-page documents with profound observations and witty asides about everything from the intricacies of accounting to insurance, from the stock market to the fear and greed infecting human nature itself. The reports have become a kind of *Prairie Home Companion* in which Wall Street is a Lake Wobegon and Buffett sets out to tell what awful truths are there.

"Mr. Market"

The 1987 report was in full bloom with a description of "Mr. Market" he picked up from Ben Graham. Buffett says anyone in the stock market should imagine the daily stock quotations coming from a remarkably accommodating fellow named Mr. Market who is your partner in business. Mr. Market flashes you stock quotes for businesses constantly, but there is one thing you need to know about this character: Mr. Market has emotional disorders.

At times Mr. Market feels good and offers high buy-sell prices in the stock market. At other times he is depressed and offers only low buy-sell prices.

You are free to (and often should) ignore Mr. Market and his prices, analogous to the specialist on the market floor and the buyers and sellers, in aggregate, who dictate a stock's price.

Mr. Market will be back tomorrow with another price that may interest you. The trick is to know the difference in Mr. Market's emotional offerings—to buy when he is sad and sell when he is happy—and operate on your own and not under the influence of Mr. Market's manic-depressive personality.

Buffett counsels that Mr. Market is there to serve you, not guide you. It is Mr. Market's pocketbook, his money—not his wisdom—that the true investor is interested in.

People, including Adam Smith, have said that reading the Berkshire Annual Report is a better education than business school itself.

"An investor who reads the letters Buffett has written over the last 16 years will have taken in perhaps the single best 'textbook' that's available on the stock market, corporate finance and investing." (*Forbes*, July 19, 1993)

Says former Younkers department store chairman Joseph Rosenfield: "He [Buffett] sends me some annual reports every year and I give them to my friends. Everything's in there."

Berkshire annual reports usually carry this explanation about why Berkshire doesn't comment about its market activities: "Despite our policy of candor, we will discuss our activities in marketable securities only to the extent legally required. Good investment ideas are rare, valuable and subject to competitive appropriation just as good product or business acquisitions are. Therefore, we normally will not talk about our investment ideas. This ban extends even to securities we have sold (because we may purchase them again) and to stocks we are incorrectly rumored to be buying. If we deny the reports but say 'no-comment' on other occasions, the no-comments become confirmation."

It's all akin to the following divorce court proceeding:

Q: "Did you spend the night with this man in
    Chicago?"
A: "I can't comment."
Q: "Did you spend the night with this man in
    Detroit?"
A: "I can't comment."
Q: "Did you spend the night with this man in
    Miami?"
A: "No."

Any student of Buffett should start with the annual reports. "For the millions of investors who don't come to Omaha [to the Berkshire

Annual Meeting], it [the report] is by far the best window into the way Buffett's mind works." (*Money*, July, 1998)

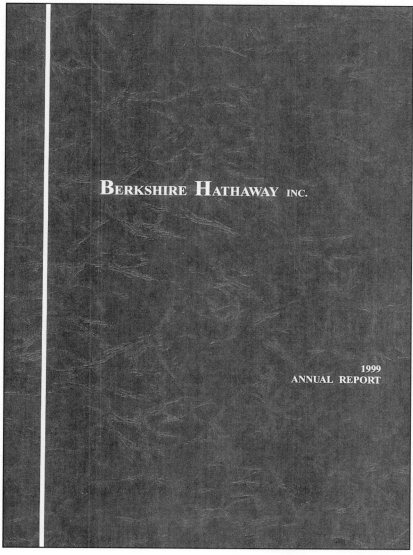

This is the cover of Berkshire's plain looking 1999 Annual Report, the holy scripture of business. The color was deep blue.

115

BERKSHIRE'S WEB SITE
"BUT HOW WILL I KNOW WHAT COLOR THE ANNUAL REPORT IS?"

L aunching its career in cyberspace, Berkshire issued its 1996 Annual Report on the Internet.

"Though it was a close decision, Charlie and I have decided to enter the 20th century. Accordingly, we are going to put future quarterly and annual reports on the Internet, where they can be accessed via http://www.berkshirehathaway.com. We will always post these reports on a Saturday so that anyone interested will have ample time to digest the information before trading begins," Buffett wrote in the 1996 Annual Report.

Berkshire had announced the report would be on Berkshire's website on March 15, 1997. And it was—precisely at midnight. Very hard core Berkshire shareholders were up between midnight and 4 a.m. getting their copies. Other shareholders, who couldn't access the report, let fire some foul language.

Basically the new system went smoothly and fairly. One hitch. The Wall Street Journal Interactive Edition got a copy of the report the day before that had been posted on the World Wide Web but not yet linked to Berkshire's home page.

The site offers Berkshire's annual and quarterly reports, press releases and information and ads about Berkshire's operating businesses.

One wag, who praised Berkshire's entry into the electronic age, said, "But how will I know what color the annual report is?"

With the advent of the Berkshire website, the world had been invited in.

The world could look in on Berkshire and occasionally Buffett could communicate to the world through Berkshire's website. Here's one message from the Oracle of Omaha:

> Thanks for visiting our website. Being a lifelong technophobe, I tiptoed into the computer world only a few years ago. If you have any ideas about how we can make these pages more useful, just drop me a line.
>
> You probably know that I don't make stock recommenda-

tions. However, I have two thoughts regarding your personal expenditures that can save you real money. I'm suggesting that you call on the services of two subsidiaries of Berkshire: GEICO and Borsheim's.

I estimate that about 40% of auto drivers in the country can save money by insuring with GEICO. The figure is not 100% because insurers differ in their underwriting judgments, with some favoring drivers who live in certain geographical areas and work in certain occupations more than GEICO does. I believe, however, that GEICO more frequently offers the low price than does any other national carrier selling insurance to all comers. You can quickly find out whether you can save money by calling 800-555-2756.

Fine jewelry, watches and giftware will almost certainly cost you less at Borsheim's. I've looked at the figures for all publicly-owned jewelry companies and the contrast with Borsheim's is startling. Our one-store operation, with its huge volume, enables us to operate with costs that are fully 15-20 percentage points below those incurred by our competitors. We pass the benefits of this low-cost structure along to our customers.

Every year Borsheim's sends out thousands of selections to customers who want a long-distance opportunity to inspect what it offers and decide which, if any, item they'd like to purchase. We do a huge amount of business in this low-key way, which allows the shopper to conveniently see the exceptional values that we offer. Call Scot Caniglia, Marvin Cohn or Missy Linhart at Borsheim's (800-642-4438) and save substantial money on your next purchase of jewelry.

Sincerely,

Warren E. Buffett

116

THE BERKSHIRE ANNUAL REPORT FOR THE YEAR 2040

Michael Assael, editor of this book, and I imagine this is about the way the Berkshire Annual Report may read for the year 2040:

Berkshire Hathaway

To the Shareholder-Citizens of Berkshire Hathaway Inc.:

Our gain in net worth during 2040 was $40,000,000,000,000 (for those of you who are not World Bank economists, that's $40 *trillion*), an increase of 23.3%. We added some wonders-of-the-world, landmark businesses to our portfolio during the year; I'll tell you about Berkshire's new, brand name colossi later in my letter.

Over the last 76 years (that is, since Charlie and I took over and started putting our two cents in) Berkshire's per-share book value has grown at a rate of 23.0% compounded annually.

Right up front, however, I must make my usual disclaimer: Berkshire's increasing capital base will inevitably forge its own anchor on future growth. I know I've talked about this unfortunate "Inevitable" since the days of President Kennedy and America's first moon landing; my remonstration, though, is not just boilerplate at Berkshire. Consider: fewer than three countries on earth have a net worth greater than Berkshire. Inevitably, we will meet our Maker.

Since virtually all of you are decades-long shareholders, there's no reason to get excited about our heart-throb 2040 book value gain—or, for that matter, any single year's stock market performance. The exuberance of the investment crowd fueling the market one year, often leads to heartaches the next. Just ask Woody Allen. His latest love story—*1929*—a box office smash opening October, fizzled by New Year. (I can't resist recalling one of Woody's lines you may find instructive. Here's Woody: "I took a course in speed reading and finished all nine editions of *Security Analysis* in 20 minutes. It's a love story about money." The lesson here: Stay within your *circle of competence*. Don't fly through Berkshire's annual report at the speed of your ExecuJet.)

Of course, what really counts for the lover of money and security analyst alike—more than stock price—is the rise in *intrinsic value*. Though Berkshire's stock price occasionally flys ahead of its intrinsic value, the good news is that the businesses Berkshire owns—our *investees*—outperformed our stock price in 2040, which brings Berkshire's intrinsic value in line with Berkshire's lofty share price. You may want to read those last two sentences again, just because the relationship between *stock price* and *intrinsic value* is an important one.

Though Charlie and I remain unconvinced our shares are undervalued, I should report that our great-great-grandchildren have dumped their underperforming index funds to buy our new Class U shares. We've tried desperately to talk them out of it. The reason: Your Chairman has a feeling Berkshire's stock price will temporarily nosedive pending a misguided cover story in *Barron's*, which again has forgotten that in addition to our high-flying stock portfolio, we also have an armada of wholly owned insurance, finance, utility, transport, media, food and direct sales businesses.

Why Am I Always Last to Know?

I have it from reliable sources that the upcoming special issue of *Barron's* will make reference to Darwin (one of Charlie's favorites), and call Charlie and me "technology ignoramouses" and "seven-sigma dinosaur fossils." *Barron's* will then set the intrinsic value of Berkshire *Class A* at $40,000 a share. It won't pay to panic though, because if we sink back to our Century 21 low of $40,800, Charlie and I will initiate the long-awaited Berkshire stock buyback. Even better, should the price drop to $39,995, Charlie and I will be keenly focused on the outfield fences. He and I and Babe Ruth will be pointing to the bleachers and swinging at all the easy-to-whack, fat pitches in our grand slam buyback zone. As Yogi Berra said: "90% of this game is half mental."

Charlie and I Feel Younger Than Ever

Charlie, of course, is Charlie Munger, Berkshire's "Silent Slugger"

Vice Chairman, and my partner. He and I, at age 51 and 44, respectively—I mean, the way we actually *feel* as we skateboard to work in our Berkshire baseball caps—have energy that practically outdistances the energy Mrs. B (who was reincarnated in 2000 and is now a spring chicken of 40) brings to millions of her loyal customers at the Nebraska Furniture Mart which now occupies 15% of Omaha and almost 5% of Hong Kong.

Common Stock Investments

Normally, in this mouth-watering section we present our "Sweet Sixteen" common stock investments, itemizing those of our sixteen positions with the largest market values. (You know, Coke, American Express and so forth.)

This year, however, we're adopting a "Sounds of Silence" policy to honor my sometimes silent partner Charlie Munger, who has been elected by Berkshire's Board as Berkshire's Man-of-the-Year.

Those of you who regularly attend our annual meetings are familiar with what I commonly refer to as Charlie's "silent-partner-treatment" during our marathon, Q&A sessions—where Charlie hardly makes a sound, invariably brushing off your thoughtful queries with a "No comment" or "I have nothing to add." In fact though, Charlie would *love* to answer your questions. You see, as *vice*-chairman, Charlie quite properly leaves the heavy lifting to your Chairman.

Just so you don't get the wrong idea about Charlie, I invite all of you to attend a "Charlie Chairman" meeting—the annual meeting of Berkshire's subsidiary, Wesco Financial Corporation in Pasadena, where Charlie serves as chairman. It's in Pasadena you can see and hear Charlie in his natural environment—where he's charming, talkative—and rarely ducks a question—as brilliant a modern man as you'll ever meet. But beware: Charlie and his meetings are habit forming.

Let's get back to our common stock investments: Charlie has permitted me to deviate from his "Don't Ask—Don't Talk" policy to tell you that our Sweet Sixteen remain virtually untouched; in fact, during the year we only slightly increased our holdings in Coca-Cola and in the Microsoft-GE-AT&T conglomerate. My buddy Bill Gates is having fun with his universe of expanding companies—and when Bill is having fun, well, the sky's not the limit. We'll talk more about Gates and Coke later.

One personal item (concerning common stocks) I'm happy to share is a theory I've been working on. (I'm not quite sure whether it qualifies as a *principle*.) My maxim, still a work in progress, goes like this: "A marketable security does not derive its value from its marketability. It's marketability, rather, is derived from its value."

My new aphorism is still in development and I'd appreciate some help with it. If you have a thought, *specifically about this theory*, drop me a short line. (No e-mails please—I still live in the mid 20th century.)

Unconventional Commitments

For years I've been telling you that my real estate investments have failed miserably. From warehouse malls and airport runways, to gaming motels and car lots—I've consistently turned them all into *mud*. *Quicksand* would be too strong a term to use in that last sentence because Charlie says I have the financial savoir-faire to know not to throw *good* money after *bad*.

Now I'm convinced I've landed in financially fertile soil. With Charlie constantly reminding me that the three most important words in real estate are *location, location and moat*—my eyes have finally connected with my brain. The proof: Berkshire entered the bidding for—and our bid was accepted by the French government— and we're now proud owners of the *Eiffel Tower*. Along with the *Statue of Liberty* and the *London Bridge* which we also acquired in 2040, we now operate three of the most famous attractions anywhere. Charlie's first words upon hearing the news: "Three cheers for worldly government privatization."

As an extra, added *bonus* (please excuse my "P.T. Barnum" redundancy): Berkshire's jet helicopter service (piloted by *Mickey*—who else?) will fly you non-stop between the Eiffel Tower and EuroDisney. It's an uplifting experience you won't want to miss. What's the *bonus?*... You shareholders fly *half*-price.

By the way, I recently asked Charlie to take charge of Berkshire's new *Statue of Liberty Doll* line since he's always giving those philosophical speeches about having multiple models in life. Well, needless to say, Charlie seems to be drooling over his new post with never-before-seen animation.

Coca-Cola Enjoy.com

Our fifty year affair with Coke continues: Berkshire increased its lalapalooza position in Coca-Cola last year. We now own 60% of this deliciously unique company, the result of *The Coca-Cola Company's* never-ending share repurchase plan—plus some additional buying we did for our own account.

Each year Charlie and I review thousands of annual reports and brush up on the history of every company in *Value Line* (another enterprise we love not because we *own*, but own because we *love*.) We believe *The Coca-Cola Company* has no equal. In the end we took the investment advice of Mae West: "A girl in a convertible is worth five in the phone book."

The rationale for our additional *Coca-Cola* commitment is simple: People get thirsty. (Who says investing has to be complicated?) *The Coca-Cola Company*—thanks in part to my own drinking habits—is in the midst of another hundred-year sales spurt. This great American institution, *The Coca-Cola Company*, now supplies our civilization with 24% of it's liquid, nutritional intake. So it's only natch that again this year, we've won the top five slots in the Universal Soft Drink Hall of Fame:

#1   Coca-Cola Classic (everyone's favorite)
#2   Diet Coke (Charlie's favorite for obvious reasons)
#3   Cherry Coke (your Chairman's favorite)
#4   The Coca-Marz Fountain-of-Youth Formula
#5   Ginko Cocoba (If *you* aren't worth its rich price, *who* is?)

I'm still drinking five Cherry Cokes and four Banana Cokes a *day* and hope you are, too. (I can't count high enough to tell you how many I drink at *night*.)

Acquisitions of 2040

In the acquisition arena, we continue to play the Clintonian game of "More-Rather-Than-Less, Sooner-Rather-Than-Later." We placed our arms around 52 privately held companies in 2040—everything from the AAA and the Auto Repair Schools of America to the Zoological International Group and their famed Pet & Vet

Centers. Each enterprise is unique. Every one is spirited by the Pablo Picasso or Michael Jordan of its industry.

One of our new superstars and winning teams I'd like to tell you about: "Hap" E. Day and his group of dedicated associates at Hap E. Day Company. As you probably know, it took "Hap" Day fewer than three decades to build his birthday party catering company for children into what Charlie and I believe to be the largest "special occasion" operator in the world.

It's no secret that my own partying (and eating) habits were irrevocably formed quite early—the product of a wildly successful party that celebrated my fifth birthday. On that unforgettable occasion we had hamburgers, Coke, cake, ice cream and candy. (I'm sure you've heard this story before.) To make a long story short: Hap E. Day is my kind of company!

Happy childhood experiences, of course, are important to healthy development and "Hap" takes the cake in applying this "Happy Birthday" principle to real life. "Hap" says that running successful parties for kids is all quite simple, even easy, as his hero is none other than Walt Disney. And when I ask "Hap" how he stays so focused on giving kids peak experiences, he quotes Joe DiMaggio: "I always try my hardest because there probably is a kid in the stands who is watching his first game."

"Hap" and his team give kids from Brooklyn to Bangladesh fat-pitch, peak times so important in growing up. It's the one-on-one relationship between "Hap's" company and each party participant which is the key to "Hap's" past success and bright future prospects. You'll be pleased to know that "Hap" serves Dairy Queen, See's and Coke to kids in every language around the globe. We're proud to be "Hap's" partner.

I might also add that our DP Mann unit that was bought back before the turn of the Millennium, bought out its longtime friend, Lloyd's of London, which greatly bolsters our presence in the U.K., indeed the world, reinsurance market. You all know Mae West's famous line: "I like two kinds of money: foreign and domestic."

The Berkshire Mint and Treasury

Charlie and I are dead serious when we tell you we plan to outshine Fort Knox. Last year we continued to buy gold, silver and other precious resources whose names I can't even pronounce.

When Charlie and I debated whether to buy more gold or silver, instead of just grunting to each other over the phone, we made two calls for advice, one to Woody Allen and the other to Yogi Berra. Woody told us, "Money is better than poverty, if only for financial reasons." Yogi told us, "When you come to a fork in the road, take it." So Charlie and I ended up buying *both* gold *and* silver.

Berkshire's warehouses are packed—that's the way we like them. Storage and rental rates were up again last year and we're happy about that, too. Our purchases add new balance to Berkshire's rich mix of businesses and gives new meaning, we believe, to the term *storehouse of value.*

We hold seven percent of the nation's debt in the fixed-income portion of our portfolio. It's nothing to do handsprings over, but we increased our cash position last year while paying off all our own modest debt.

Charlie and I always want to have our cash bags loaded, ready to engulf fast moving corporate cash cows should one try to sprint past us. It's for this reason that Berkshire's balance sheet is our nation's strongest and shows spectacular liquidity. We continue to be more liquid than Uncle Sam and have more current and ready assets than the Microsoft-GE-AT&T conglomerate.

Pundits have said that a finer global currency than Berkshire shares does not exist. We do not disagree.

Insurance Operations

Our insurance operations reached new heights in 2040. Under the leadership of Ajit Jain, Berkshire Hathaway Insurance Group continues to shine on as the largest insurance diamond in the universe. Our float—the money we hold in trust for policyholders—continues to be attracted to us in ever increasing amounts and at no cost. In fact, we're making more money (holding other people's money) than ever, even on the underwriting part of our business. In today's competitive and disaster prone environment though, we can't count on our insurance group to rocket us much faster. Remember:

we could have a dozen super-catastrophes—monster earthquakes, hurricanes, air disasters, shipwrecks, sex scandals a n d cyclones—*all hit us at once.* It's a tough no-picnic business. Ajit has his work cut out for him. Please light a candle for us if the lights go out in San Francisco, Mexico City or Tokyo.

New Technology

I write to you from the cockpit of our modest headquarters—the *Flying Pleasure Palace* as I like to call it— where we hired our first new temp since the turn of the Millennium and finally upgraded our rather primitive computer system to Windows 2000. This will help with our financial and accounting psychedelics.

As you know, I've never owned a copier but last year I found one for $19.99 at the Nebraska Furniture Mart. Debbie, my invaluable assistant, a great-grandmother now, has been teaching me how to use it. Though the cognoscenti may snicker at my techno-backwardness, Charlie motivates me by telling me I'm at least as talented as his pet chimpanzee.

I've also bought a new calculator. This may sound a bit odd but it's only the second one I've ever owned. I bought my first in 2030 at age 100 and since it still works fine (and rather than auctioning it—I'm attached) I've brought old reliable home to use in the bathroom.

The reason for my recent technological extravagance: I'm having a hard time keeping track of all our colorful, capitalist Woodstock profits in my head. Your Chairman's neurons need help.

The Forbes 400

Since I rarely relish playing second fiddle, I want to give you an explanation as to why "Bet-a-Billion" Gates again was No. 1 and I was No. 2 on the richest lists. *Forbes* counted those fancy new Executive Jet hangers at Gates' house. You know how Bill likes collecting jets, and flying fast.

Though my friend Bill is still Numero Uno, I want to assure you I have never felt better. I love running Berkshire, and if enjoying life promotes longevity, Methuselah's record—as well as Gates' status on the *Forbes* list—is in jeopardy.

Berkshire's Annual Shareholders' Weekend

Charlie and I look forward to entertaining you in Omaha—the cradle of capitalism—on May 5-7 this year for Berkshire's Annual "Woodstock Weekend."

Festivities begin Saturday night when your Chairman takes the mound for the Omaha Golden Spikes who will play the New York Silver Skyscrapers. This year I plan to introduce my sidearm "yellow submarine" which no doubt will rock the sturdy foundation of the Skyscraper offense.

Then the bash at our jewelry store, Borsheim's, will take place, as usual, on Sunday. Oh, I almost forgot to mention: Borsheim's bought Sotheby's Group which will be added to Berkshire's jewelry and collectibles segment. For your shopping convenience, Borsheim's will remain open 24 hours a day straight through "Shareholder Weekend." Just a reminder: Sales records are made to be broken—so stop by and see the chocolate, vanilla and strawberry colored, diamond Dilly Bar display, and let it be your inspiration. As usual, Charlie will be camped out at the cash register to autograph your receipts. Please give him writer's cramp.

And we'll continue our tradition of having dinner together Sunday at my favorite steakhouse, Gorat's. Remember, just mention Debbie's name and you'll be served an extra boat of gravy.

Our annual meeting this year will be held in Omaha's new award-winning Omadome—the football stadium at the University of Nebraska. You'll forgive me if I mention that President Buffett, my grandson, that fellow who recently won re-election by a landslide, will be in the audience at this year's meeting. Last year more than 400,000 of you—including 23 heads of state—journeyed to Omaha. You came from every country on earth. This year we expect a crowd of about 500,000 —as well as a few hundred million more of you via the Internet—and the national championship football team and marching band will run onto the field at high noon. Marc Hamburg, our chief financial officer, will then feature his latest world premiere, multi-media, soap opera, epic 2040 extravaganza: "Classic Follies at Berkshire."

It's at our noontime break when Charlie and I will come around to all of you with Cokes and See's Candies. To speed the lunch hour process, please have the correct change as we come by. Then we'll resume taking your questions until we fall out—or Charlie says something optimistic.

Here's one last piece of good news for Charlie and me and we hope Berkshire Shareholder-Citizens as well. Charlie and I *are* getting older, but we have found a solution in the Woody Allen credo: "I don't want to achieve immortality through my work ... I want to achieve it through not dying."

Though Charlie and I are maturing a bit physically, you can take comfort that we still make a great team. I can see, Charlie can hear and mentally we're feeling sharp as Gillette's new Mach 007s.

So come to Omaha in May and enjoy yourself. Unite with your fellow capitalists during Berkshire's Annual Shareholders' Weekend. We'll see you soon. Young Miss B is lining the streets for all of you Shareholder-Citizens with red carpet!

Best regards,
Your Chairman
February 23, 2041

117

A SHAREHOLDER'S DREAM
COMPOUNDING AT 23%

BERKSHIRE'S TOTAL SHAREHOLDERS' EQUITY ON 12/31/96: **$23,426,300,000**

ANNUAL GROWTH RATE: **23%**

YEAR	SHAREHOLDERS' EQUITY AT END OF YEAR
☑ 1997	$28,814,349,000.00
☑ 1998	$35,441,649,270.00
☑ 1999	$43,593,228,602.10
2000	$53,619,671,180.58
2001	$65,952,195,552.12
2002	$81,121,200,529.10
2003	$99,779,076,650.80
2004	$122,728,264,280.48
2005	$150,955,765,064.99
2006	$18,567,5591,029.94
2007	$228,380,976,966.83
2008	$280,908,601,669.20
2009	$345,517,580,053.11
2010	$424,986,623,465.33
2011	$522,733,546,862.35
2012	$642,962,262,640.69
2013	$790,843,583,048.05
2014	$972,737,607,149.11
2015	$1,196,467,256,793.40
2016	$1,471,654,725,855.88
2017	$1,810,135,312,802.74
2018	$2,226,466,434,747.37
2019	$2,738,553,714,739.26
2020	$3,368,421,069,129.29
2021	$4,143,157,915,029.03
2022	$5,096,084,235,485.70

2023	$6,268,183,609,647.41
2024	$7,709,865,839,866.32
2025	$9,483,134,983,035.57
2026	$11,664,256,029,133.75
2027	$14,347,034,915,834.52
2028	$17,646,852,946,476.45
2029	$21,705,629,124,166.04
2030	$26,697,923,822,724.23

NOTICE OF TEMPORARY INSANITY

118

TORCHMARK

"I'LL LOOK AT TORCHMARK."

In late 1986 I wrote Buffett boldly suggesting he look at the stock of Torchmark, an insurance and financial services company in Birmingham, Alabama.

Several days later I received a note dated December 1, 1986:

> "Thanks for the nice comments—and I'll look at Torchmark. I'm glad you are a shareholder, but you are right—I'm not keen on margin buying. However, we'll try to keep you out of trouble. Sincerely, Warren E. Buffett"

His reply about margin buying came in response to my noting that I liked Berkshire so much I had margined things for more of its shares. He was right about being cautious about margin, and although he tried to keep me out of trouble, even *he* could not swim against the tide. During the crash of 1987, Berkshire stock fell from about $4,000 to under $3,000 a share over a several-day period, about in line with the rest of the market.

But before that disaster, I was the most surprised person in the world when Dan Dorfman reported in August 1987, that Berkshire had amassed a small stake—by Berkshire standards—in Torchmark, a stake not even announced publicly by Berkshire other than through the briefest sort of filings.

Torchmark officials confirmed such a stake and Berkshire filed forms with the SEC acknowledging ownership. There's no proof my letter had anything to do with Buffett's purchase, but it was fun to learn he was in the stock.

Let's put it this way—when I later had lunch with the Oracle of Omaha himself, he did NOT ask me for my best investment idea.

Berkshire owned 863,550 shares of Torchmark at one point. In 1997 Berkshire owned 662,000 Torchmark shares, or about half of one percent of the company.

Torchmark is the parent firm of a battery of insurance companies, the largest of which is Liberty National Life Insurance Co., employing agents who in some cases still go door to door, selling insurance policies, seeking a niche market of customers at the modest end of the income scale.

The company also owns and recently spun off part of Waddell & Reed, a financial services company that manages a group of mutual funds. Waddell and Reed representatives sell life and health insurance policies from another Torchmark subsidiary, United Investors Life, and oil and natural gas partnerships managed by another subsidiary, Torch Energy.

Torchmark's other main subsidiaries are United American Insurance, which sells Medicare supplemental insurance and Globe Life and Accident Insurance, which sells health insurance.

In the past few decades during rocky times for financial services firms, Torchmark has set a record as a model of consistent profitability. For the past 40 years it has compiled both per-share earnings and dividend increases every year, a record unmatched by any other company listed on the New York Stock Exchange.

The company has a reputation for tight control over expenses, and its investments appear solid.

Less than 3% of the company's fixed-maturity investments are in securities of less than investment grade, and three-fourths of the investments are in short-term investments or government securities.

Only slightly more than 2% of total invested assets were in mortgages or real estate.

Since 1986, Torchmark has bought back more than a third of its outstanding stock. Alabama's most profitable company is headed by Ronald K. Richey.

Torchmark's bid to buy much larger American General Corp. for $6.3 billion in 1990 did not come off.

Berkshire's stake in Torchmark has made nice, steady progress as Torchmark's businesses have made nice, steady progress. In the mid-1990s, the stock price suffered in connection with litigation over cancer policy replacements.

"It appears that Mr. Buffett sold approximately a third of his holdings in the fourth quarter of 1993. Nevertheless, Torchmark continues to have many of the characteristics that he looks for in a business: a high return on equity, a low cost structure and cost-conscious management, highly predictable earnings, and a company that repurchases its own stock," said Giri Bogavelli, an investor in San Francisco.

119
TIME WARNER
"IF HE HAD BECOME A MAJOR SHAREHOLDER, WE PROBABLY WOULD NOT HAVE GONE THROUGH WHAT WE DID."
J. RICHARD MUNRO

Buffett, still taken with media franchises, bought shares of Time, Inc., in 1982 at a cost of $45 million. By the end of the year the investment was worth $79 million.

Over the next several years, he lowered, then raised, then lowered his investment and in 1986 he sold out completely. That was the year he also sold a stake in Affiliated Publications, the parent of *The Boston Globe*, for a $51 million profit.

J. Richard Munro, the former chairman of Time, who spearheaded its merger in 1989 with Warner Communications, creating the media giant Time Warner, said he believes Buffett sold his Time stake to help finance his stake in the Cap Cities purchase of American Broadcasting Cos. in early 1986.

"I can tell you I have respect for him far beyond the business aspect. It's as a human being. He's one of the more interesting people of our time. It's his no-nonsense, Midwestern thing. There are just no affectations. He is a legendary figure...What you see is what you get," Munro said.

"When he became a shareholder of Time, the company did not know it...His timing of buying and selling the stock was perfect," he said.

Buffett would drop by Munro's office at the Time-Life Building in New York about once a year for a chat.

"We'd talk about everything. He wanted to know what we knew and of course we wanted to know what he knew. We'd talk about the world and exchange views. He was an admirer of Time," Munro said.

A couple of years after Buffett sold his Time shares, he approached the board for permission to make a major investment in the company, according to Munro.

"He came to us wanting to become a big investor on the order of five to 10%," he added.

Buffett's overture was rejected. Munro said he and Nick Nicholas

(AP/Wide World Photos)

Former Time Warner Chairman J. Richard Munro. "If he had become a major shareholder, we probably would not have gone through what we did."

were for it, "but the board rejected it."

"As I recall it was big shareholders who just didn't want it," said Munro, adding that it was something that was considered very quickly and dismissed as something Time didn't need.

Laments Munro, "If he had become a major shareholder, we probably would not have gone through what we did." What Time soon went through was a $200 a share unsolicited offer for Time from Paramount Communications.

The bid was finally beaten back as Time and Warner agreed to a high debt merger. The combined Time Warner became the largest media and entertainment company in the world and owner of CNN, with huge stakes in magazine publishing such as *Time* magazine and *Sports Illustrated* and in books, cable television (including HBO) and films such as *Batman*.

But the combined company wound up with a debt of more than $10 billion. Buffett didn't think much of that.

"I do not think he (Buffett) approved of the merger, but I will be convinced until I go to my grave that it was right. We would have been acquired or become a second-rate company," Munro said.

In 2000 America Online merged with Time Warner. Rock on.

120

"EXCUSE ME.
AREN'T YOU WARREN BUFFETT?"

One day in 1986, Peter Kenner, who heads Kenner Printing Co. in New York City, saw a man who looked like Buffett at the intersection of Madison Avenue and 55th Street.

"Excuse me. Aren't you Warren Buffett?" asked Kenner. "Yes, how did you know?" replied Buffett.

When Kenner said his father, Morton Kenner, had been an investor since the days of the Buffett Partnership and that he himself was a longtime Berkshire shareholder, Buffett insisted he come to the annual meeting next time around. Kenner had never been, but started going.

Morton Kenner, who attended Berkshire's Annual Meeting in 1992 with his son and grandson, said four generations of his family have invested with Buffett. "I put $80,000 into the partnership at a time you needed to have $100,000 and I got my father (Marcus Kenner) to invest the other $20,000," said Morton Kenner, whose wife was a friend of Ben Graham's.

"I met Buffett in 1964 through Henry Brandt," said Morton Kenner of the former Shearson Lehman executive.

One time Buffett invited Peter Kenner to accompany him on the plane to the annual meeting. Kenner joined Buffett and his wife for the trip to Omaha. "It was that first plane and it had E.T. on it from the movie," Kenner recalled.

By 1990, Peter Kenner's nine-year-old son, Nicholas, a fourth-generation Berkshire shareholder, was pleading to go. "He had been asking me about going to the meeting," says Kenner, who thought it a bit odd.

But he said his son, who inherited 10 shares of Berkshire, explained that if this was his investment for a college education he wanted to go.

At last Kenner told his son he could go, but that it was a grown-up affair and he'd have to be quiet and not ask questions. But young Kenner said he wanted to ask why the Berkshire stock price had dropped from $8,900 to $6,700 a share. His father finally gave in.

The Kenners ran into Buffett just before the meeting, and Buffett encouraged young Kenner to ask whatever question he wanted. So Nicholas, posing the first question at the Berkshire Annual Meeting in 1990, asked the ultimate question of Buffett: "Why did Berkshire's stock go down?"

Buffett, feigning anger, replied, "You're underage! Throw him out!"

The greatest financial mind of our time finally replied that he really did not know, that there was no good answer to that question. Young Kenner had stumped the master.

After an explanation about Berkshire usually trading near its intrinsic value, Buffett ended by saying, "Hold it for your old age."

As it happened, after the meeting Buffett and the Kenners again ran into one another, and Buffett asked Nicholas Kenner if he could pose for a picture with him, a picture that ran with the *Omaha World-Herald's* story about the annual meeting.

Posing for the picture, Buffett said, "Let's do this right" and handed the youngster his wallet. "Can I keep it?" asked Nicholas.

"I was just making a wisecrack," the lad explained later.

A short time later Buffett sent Kenner a copy of the photo with a letter saying to come to future annual meetings and ask more questions.

"He's a nice guy. He's very funny," Kenner said of Buffett.

"I just wanted to ask him why the stock price was down. You know, if it's fallen from over $8,000 you want to know why. I definitely want to hold it unless something absolutely amazing happens and it goes down thousands of dollars," he added.

Kenner, such a hit at the annual meeting in 1990, was allowed the first question at the annual meeting in 1991. Buffett had written in the annual report that he would let young Kenner have first crack at him.

Kenner was ready with two questions: His first was, why did Buffett pick Coke instead of Pepsi as an investment? His second was, why, if Buffett listed Kenner's age as 11 in the Berkshire Annual Report when he was actually 9, should he trust Berkshire's financial numbers in the back of the annual report? That question sent Berkshire shareholders into convulsions of laughter.

Buffett later said he planned "a written response." (*Fortune*, June 3, 1991)

The youngster began his questioning of Buffett by saying he owned 10 shares of Berkshire; Buffett interjected, "I'd like you to meet my granddaughter."

Buffett, calling on the help of then Coca-Cola President Don

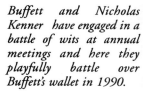

Buffett and Nicholas Kenner have engaged in a battle of wits at annual meetings and here they playfully battle over Buffett's wallet in 1990.
(Omaha World-Herald)

Keough, took on Kenner's first question explaining that Coke is a superb business serving soft drinks in 170 (now almost 200) countries where consumption is increasing. Keough said that consumption internationally was 59 servings per capita a year compared with 300 in the U.S., suggesting Coke's enormous growth potential.

Buffett said he drank five Cokes a day and noted that Munger drinks diet Coke "for obvious reasons."

As for young Kenner's second question about the age discrepancy, Buffett started out with "Charlie wrote that section" and then ducked it with, "That is a very good question. I look forward to seeing you again next year."

Drawing a big laugh, Kenner said, "I'll be back!"

"I know!" Buffett replied.

The repartee was becoming part of Berkshire lore and Buffett wrote at the end of his letter in the 1991 Annual Report: "Nicholas will be at this year's meeting—he spurned my offer of a trip to Disney World on that day—so join us to watch a continuation of this lopsided battle of wits."

In the summer of 1999 Nicholas Kenner worked at the Henderson Brothers post which trades Berkshire's stock on the floor of the New York Stock Exchange. He's now a student at Colgate University.

121

LOW-INCOME HOUSING
WARREN EDWARD BUFFETT TALKS WITH
PRESIDENT GEORGE HERBERT WALKER BUSH

In 1990, Berkshire invested $25 million in the non-profit National Equity Fund to help finance low-income housing. And in 1991, it invested $20 million in low-income housing efforts, split evenly between the National Equity Fund and the Enterprise Fund. By 1994, Berkshire had invested more than $80 million in low-income housing efforts, including small amounts in the Equity Fund of Nebraska. The money went toward creating low-income housing in several cities, including Houston, Los Angeles, Detroit, Chicago and Buffett's hometown of Omaha.

"I look at it as an investment with pro-social aspects," he said at a press conference in 1991. "I don't view it in a philanthropic context."

The investment that Buffett termed "financially and socially responsible" should earn 15% to 20% a year for over a decade in the form of tax credits created through the federal Low-Income Housing Tax Credit Program, part of the 1986 tax law revision.

In its first four years the fund raised $620 million to build more than 14,000 affordable housing units in 62 cities. Buffett's investment is believed to be the largest made in the fund.

He made the investment in part to encourage other firms to make such investments. Salomon also has pledged a similar $10 million investment in the program and American Express has made a small investment.

Berkshire's investment was made through its *World Book* subsidiary, whose encyclopedias, Buffett said, are "in the homes of millions of Americans" in all income groups. Of the law providing for the tax credit, Buffett said, "It seems to me to be a fine marriage between the corporate community and the local community development organizations. The marriage should provide affordable housing for low-income groups." The tax credit was assured when President Bush signed the new housing bill into law at the White House on November 28, 1990.

Before the signing Bush and Buffett had a private chat. The details were not disclosed.

We may never get them, but the discussion was about business, not politics. The President of the United States, George Herbert Walker Bush, peppered Buffett with questions about the economy.

Let's hope the President's secretary didn't erase the White House tapes.

(AP/Wide World Photos)

Former President George Bush

804

122

WHAT DO YOU THINK THE MARKETS WILL DO?...
"WELL, THE PRESIDENT (CLINTON) DIDN'T TELL US ANYTHING ABOUT WHAT THE MARKETS WILL DO."

On June 16, 1993, Buffett and eight other CEOs met with President Clinton at a private lunch. Buffett advised Clinton to raise taxes and cut spending as the only practical way to reduce the deficit.

Interviewed by reporters on the White House lawn afterwards, Buffett said reducing the deficit was important for the economy and the stock and bond markets.

He said he backed Clinton's plan to reduce the deficit and had voted for him.

Clinton and the corporate executives had a two-hour lunch, and afterwards Buffett said the discussion was "quite uninhibited" and that the president was a "good listener."

"The president is articulate and he listens very well. He gets very engaged in the conversation and he is a very engaging person to be with."

Buffett said he endorsed Clinton's proposal to reduce the deficit by $500 billion over five years through a combination of new taxes and spending cuts. The $500 billion figure was significant, although he added he would like to see an even greater reduction via a significant energy tax.

Asked if he were disappointed in the way the White House was functioning under Clinton, Buffett said, "I've been a little disappointed in the way Congress has functioned. I think that maybe it has lost sight of the ultimate goal, which is major deficit reduction."

The markets would evaluate the deficit-reduction package, he said. "Wall Street will evaluate the whole package. In the end, it will look at how business will do five to ten years out, what interest rates are going to do, the credibility of the administration, the ability of Congress to act. There's a whole host of variables it'll be looking at."

Buffett was asked what he thought the markets would do, and replied, "Well, the President didn't tell us anything about what the markets will do."

(AP/Wide World Photos)

President Bill Clinton

Asked if the markets were overvalued, Buffett said, "I've never been a good judge of the markets. I try to evaluate specific businesses. If I could evaluate a few specific businesses every year; half-way correctly, I'd look at it as a successful year. I've never made any money guessing which way the market's going."

Questioned about whether it was harder now to find undervalued investments, he said it is harder now but, "It always seems hard at the present time."

To a question about a rumor he was buying Time Warner stock, he said, "I never comment on rumors, particularly my own."

"Let me ask you outright if you are buying Time Warner stock," a reporter asked. Buffett replied, "I never comment about whether we're buying or selling anything. The only thing I will comment about is that I own Berkshire Hathaway."

To a final question about the possibility of a stock split, Buffett said people shouldn't hold their breath.

There's the old joke about Babe Ruth being paid more than the president because, as Ruth said, "I had a better year."

Clinton's salary is higher than Buffett's, but in 1998, Clinton had a bad year. Buffett's bad year, in a different way, came in 1999. Summing it up at the Gridiron dinner in 1999, Clinton said the previous year had been "awful" then deadpanned: "I want you to know that through it all, I still believe in a place called...Hell."

123

PS GROUP

"NEVER SLEEP WITH ANYONE WHO HAS MORE PROBLEMS THAN YOU DO."

By the end of 1990, Berkshire owned about 20% of PS Group—later reorganized as PS Group Holdings—a San Diego-based enigma long headed by J. P. "Rick" Guerin. For more than 25 years, Guerin has been a disciple and friend of both Buffett and Munger.

Their friendship is both financial and emotional. In 1980 Munger took Guerin and Buffett fishing, using a borrowed small ski boat on a Minnesota lake. Munger put the throttle in reverse, causing water to pour in and sink the craft that was not designed for operation in reverse. He was trying to get in a better casting position.

Tall and lean, Guerin, by far the most athletic (swimmer, tennis player, pilot, sky diver, skier, auto racer, bicyclist and marathoner) of the trio, dove down and freed some life vests from the sunken boat, allowing all three to paddle ashore, fully clothed. That's why Guerin calls Munger, "Admiral Munger."

Munger said in an interview May 21, 1997 that the incident was never life threatening, but that during the accident Guerin, "had the most presence of mind."

Berkshire accumulated about 11% of PS Group in 1990, paying about $32 a share for many of its shares. Afterwards PS Group's board approved Buffett's request to own up to 22.5% of the company, and later in the year granted Buffett permission to buy up to 45% of the stock, which he could do depending on market conditions, price, and the attractiveness of other investments.

Buffett gradually raised his stake in PS Group to about 20% largely by buying a big block of stock from the Tweedy Brown investment firm. During some of the time Buffett was buying PS Group stock, it carried a PE ratio above 50, so there must be something more to stock selection than just searching for low PE ratios.

What was it that Buffett was intrigued by in what appears to be a hard-to-understand firm with a strange mix of businesses?

PS Group traces its roots to Pacific Southwest Airlines, sold to USAir in 1987. After the sale, PS Group was left with an aircraft leasing operation, a fuel distribution unit, and oil and gas operations. Many of the oil and gas operations were sold in 1989 and the remaining oil and gas operations suffered write-downs in 1998. The company's largest investment is in aircraft leasing. It leases aircraft to US Airways. PS Group also has leased aircraft to a number of airlines that landed in bankruptcy court.

In 1987 PS Group, pouring $84 million into the travel agency business (another $49 million would be added in 1989), bought 81% of US Travel Systems, Inc., a large travel management system.

Founder Peter Sontag, a Columbia Business School graduate, and PS Group first came in contact when PS Group was a client of Sontag's firm.

Later, PS Group tried to sell its travel unit agency to the Pritzker family which already owned 15% of the company, but talks fell through. Still later the unit was sold to Dallas investor Murray Holland in 1994.

Guerin has said there were no advance conversations with Buffett before Buffett invested.

At the PS Group Annual Meeting in 1991, Chairman Charles Rickershauser, also a friend of Buffett's, and CEO George Shortley (Guerin had stepped down to vice chairman of the firm) said Buffett remains a friend of the company, is available for counsel at any time, but in no way tells them how to run their business.

PS Group is a combination holding and leasing firm, powerfully strange in its business mix. It is also a major investment for Guerin.

Here's an indication of Guerin's investment record prior to the bad results at PS Group:

"The period 1965-1983, for example, beheld a compound gain of 316% for the S&P and 22,200% for [Guerin] Pacific Partners." (*The Midas Touch*, John Train, p. 92)

And during a 22-year stretch, while the Standard & Poor's 500 was up 510%, Guerin's Pacific Partners Ltd., grew 65,500%, or 34.1% annually.

If Buffett's investing results had an influence on Guerin so too did Buffett's operating style. The influence of Buffett on Guerin is apparent from the annual report: "PSG's full-time officers total four and the overall corporate staff totals thirteen...the policy of not discussing PSG operations except by communications sent simultaneously to all shareholders, and by information through public filings or by questions at the annual meeting remains in effect." Sound familiar?

The company later changed the policy and said it would answer questions in forums other than the annual meeting.

The firm came into 5,750 shares of Berkshire in 1986 as a result of a pension plan reversion. The Berkshire shares were acquired at a cost of $27.6 million, but were sold in 1991 for $47.8 million when PS Group, too leveraged, ran into trouble with its banks, a result of losses it rang up in its airplane leasing business in the early 90s. The airlines were losing planeloads of money, cutting back on flights and filing for bankruptcy.

The sale of Berkshire stock, in a private transaction to Ruane, Cunniff & Co., of New York, was made at Berkshire's market price. Rick Guerin felt he had to sell and Bill Ruane wanted to buy.

At the time of the PS Group Annual Meeting in 1991, the company still held its Berkshire stock, making for cross-ownership of Berkshire and PS Group. Rickershauser, a former head of the Pacific Stock Exchange and a Munger, Tolles law firm partner, said, "I wish we owned 22% of Berkshire."

But the mystery at PS Group, the one that once sent PS Group's stock on a roller-coaster ride, was the story of a fledgling hazardous waste and metals recycling business called Recontek.

Recontek? Again, hardly sounds like something of interest to Buffett, who is so insistent on here-and-now earnings, on fresh cash that can be invested right away.

Recontek developed a proprietary recycling process that takes liquid and solid hazardous waste—generated primarily from the plating, metal finishing, and circuit board industries—and recycles the waste into salable metals and industrial chemicals. It extracts salable commodities such as copper, nickel and zinc from metallic sludge by mixing chemicals with waste.

The process is important because it could provide industry a cheaper disposal method than hazardous waste landfills, deep wells or incinerators. It also reduces the liability for potential cleanup costs for underground and soil contamination.

After operating a pilot facility in San Diego, Recontek built its first recycling plant in Newman, Illinois. The company reached agreements with other communities to build recycling plants.

But in 1994 PS Group sold Recontek which was never successful. It reminds one of the saying: "Ceasar might have married Cleopatra but he had a wife at home—there's always something."

Munger said, "PS Group is another one where we got a little egg on our face. About nine things went wrong at once—including an indirect, huge exposure to USAir. A huge percentage of PS Group's assets depend on USAir's credit. And the shareholders' equity of

USAir touched zero at its low point."

PS Group's performance inspired some people to yell "bankruptcy" in a crowded theater.

Bankruptcy would be a certainty for PS Group by the end of 1992, Gilford Securities President Robert Holmes told *USA Today* columnist Dan Dorfman (April 3, 1992). Holmes was shorting the stock.

At the annual meeting in 1991, Buffett was asked about Berkshire's stake in PS Group. Buffett confirmed a position of about 20% (1.2 million shares, or 19.9% at the end of 1993) but beyond that had no comment. Will we learn more one day? Most likely.

In 1992, when asked about its troubles, Buffett pointed out the company had denied it would file bankruptcy. Pressed about if it were in real trouble and could go bankrupt, Buffett tried to be positive.

"We'll see," he said.

PS Group was still struggling and Berkshire still owned 19.9% of the company in the late 1990s as the company continued to report operating losses. (If Berkshire had a teenage kid, PS Group would be sort of a demented windmill of a teenager.)

It had all been a case of "things aren't as bad as they seem. They're much worse."

In short, in investing: "Never sleep with anyone who has more problems than you have."

In 2000 PS Group merged into Heritage Air Holdings Statutory Trust for $12 a share.

124

WELLS FARGO

"A DEAD DUCK"

Wells Fargo, the California bank that once owned the Pony Express, announced on October 24, 1990, that Buffett had bought five million shares of its common stock, becoming its largest stockholder.

The company's trademark, the Concord stagecoach, is an enduring symbol of reliability, of "coming through." For example, Wells Fargo has been profitable every year of its existence.

Wells Fargo came through in a big way for Buffett. Since its first stake, which Berkshire bought through Salomon, it had raised its position steadily in the bank to almost 73 million shares. With Wells Fargo's acquisition of First Interstate in 1996, Berkshire owned about 8% of the new combined equity. By the end of 1999, Berkshire had lowered its stake in Wells Fargo to about 59 million shares, a $2 billion stake. Berkshire also holds about 280,000 shares of Wells Fargo in defined-benefit plans for some Berkshire employees, assuring them a better-than-anticipated retirement.

Buffett's original investment came, once again, when there was a stigma surrounding the purchase, because 1990 was a terrible time for banks. The very idea of buying a bank stock seemed outrageous at the time he did it. What the word "bank" meant on that day was layoffs, real estate loan writeoffs, slashed dividends—and some smear by association with the S&L crisis. Some pundits were suggesting that rapidly declining real estate prices could bring down the banking system.

The price-to-earnings ratio of Wells Fargo the day of the news of Berkshire's original investment was a minuscule 3.7! Mr. Market was in a crummy mood.

Now, that's an out-of-favor company. Buffett bought his shares of the San Francisco-based bank holding company at about book value, which was just under 6 at the time.

Wells Fargo long has enjoyed a good reputation. Its management was so well thought of that other bankers trained under it. Henry Wells and William Fargo founded the company as an express delivery service and banking operation in 1852, just two years after American Express was founded.

(Courtesy of Wells Fargo Bank)

The Wells Fargo Stagecoach

Dating from the Gold Rush, the company has long provided banking services and an express line, transporting passengers, mail, gold, silver and currency throughout the western United States, Canada and Mexico—by stagecoach and rail.

In those days, a stagecoach traveled only about five miles an hour. Holdups were frequent. The company earned an important spot in the commercial development of the West.

Wells Fargo separated its banking business from its express business in 1905, and the bank established a history of buying other banks. The bank is making a big push toward electronic banking transactions and has made an effort to enter California's supermarkets, opening small branches staffed with a few tellers and an ATM. And through the use of laptop computers, Wells Fargo has streamlined the loan application process for small businesses.

The bank bought Crocker National in 1986, Barclays Bank of California in 1988, the California branch network of Great American Bank in 1990 and others along the way. In all, Wells Fargo has made 150 mergers in the last 45 years.

Throughout his career Buffett has stood by the cash register counting that ever rising, fresh cash pouring in. He probably would concur with the model who once purred, "The nicest thing about money is that it never clashes with anything I wear."

At the time Buffett was buying Wells Fargo stock—he had started with a tiny stake back in 1989—any number of bright investors, including the Feshback Brothers, well-known short sellers, were shorting the stock, that is, betting it would drop. In recent years the stock has been fought over by both short sellers and value investors.

"Wells Fargo's a dead duck," Tom Barton, a money manager for the Feshback Brothers said.

"I don't think it's right to call them a bankruptcy candidate, but I think it's a teenager," he said, meaning the stock price could fall to the teens. "It has one of the highest exposures to real estate of any bank." (*Wall Street Journal*, November 1, 1990)

In one small way the short sellers were right. Soon the dividend was slashed and reserves for bad real estate loans increased dramatically.

Barron's John Liscio weighed in, saying Buffett "won't have to worry about who spends his fortune much longer, not if he keeps trying to pick a bottom in bank stocks." *(Barron's,* October, 29, 1990)

George Salem, an analyst with Prudential Securities Inc., was quoted in the same piece: "He picked the management that underwrites real estate the best. But one thing he didn't realize is that even Mark Spitz (the former Olympic star) can't swim in a hurricane in the middle of the ocean."

So, how were Wells Fargo's earnings at the time? Doing quite nicely, really. However, as commercial real estate prices continued to decline in 1991, Wells Fargo's loan loss provisions rose.

"Despite this extremely difficult environment, Wells Fargo remained profitable, as it has in every year this century, even during the depths of the Great Depression," said Jim McCluskey, an investor in San Francisco.

Buffett's trick is to swim with the tide when it looks to others as though he's swimming against it.

Just what tide did Buffett see? Buffett often kids about how little he thinks about macroeconomics, but Berkshire shareholder Yves Mojonnet thinks in the case of Wells Fargo, Buffett made macroeconomic decisions.

"I think he sees California as one of the largest industrial powers in the world and I think he saw bank consolidation," Mojonnet said. The Country of California-oriented bank is, as is any bank, heavily dependent on the local economy. California's $750 billion economy accounts for about 13% of the nation's Gross National Product and employs almost 14 million people, about 12% of the nation's workforce. California, the world's sixth largest economy, is a vast economy.

Some also see Buffett's Wells Fargo stake as a Pacific Rim economic boom play.

And Mojonnet thinks Buffett saw good management, which Buffett has acknowledged. "Wells Fargo was the first to recognize bad loans to the Third World in 1986-87. Management was on top of it then and is on top of it now, cutting the dividend and increasing loan loss reserves," Mojonnet said soon after Buffett's purchase. Now the dividend is being increased.

Buffett had once again taken an important stake in a major American enterprise, a strong franchise headed then by bank chairman Carl Reichardt, Buffett's friend, and then by Reichardt's successor, Paul Hazen.

Somehow, during the worst of times, as in the recession of 1990, Buffett always manages to generate the cash to become a major shareholder in the country's best businesses. But the Wells Fargo investment did carry with it plenty of risk, plenty of exposure to commercial and real estate loans, as well as HLTs highly leveraged transactions during a virtual depression in real estate in the Golden State.

On the other hand, Wells Fargo traditionally has ranked as one of the most profitable and efficient banks in the country.

And the Wells Fargo earnings stagecoach had always driven through plenty of badlands to avoid robberies. Speaking of the stagecoach, Reichardt and Hazen once gave Buffett a hand-carved two foot high Wells Fargo stagecoach which Buffett keeps at his office.

In 1991, Wells Fargo stock recovered, flying in the face of the shorts, burned in part because of Buffett's heavy buying. It was little wonder that in certain short seller circles, T-shirts proclaimed, "(Expletive deleted) Warren Buffett."

(Photo courtesy of Wells Fargo Bank)   (Photo courtesy of Wells Fargo Bank)

Carl Reichardt   *Paul Hazen*

One more time, while almost everyone else was panicking, Buffett struck gold, this time out on the West Coast.

Forbes (April 15, 1991) quoted Munger about the Wells Fargo purchase: "It's all a bet on management. We think they will fix problems faster and better than other people."

When cost-conscious Reichardt found out one of his executives wanted to buy a Christmas tree for the office, Reichardt told him to buy it with his own money, not the bank's.

"When we heard that, we bought more stock," Munger said at the Berkshire Annual Meeting in 1991. The interest in Wells Fargo continued.

In 1991, Wells Fargo announced that Buffett was seeking permission from the Federal Reserve Board to more than double his stake to as much as 22%. In early August, Buffett got the approval.

Federal change-of-control laws require the Federal Reserve Board to review purchase requests if a buyer intends to acquire more than 10% of a bank holding company stock. One reason Buffett wanted more Wells Fargo was that he knew he could buy some at bargain prices.

In fact, Wells Fargo's gravity-defying ability to stay away from bad loan problems ended in 1991 with a second quarter announcement that the company would post a large loan loss jump and that earnings would be paltry, far below analysts' expectations. The loan loss figure late in 1991 was a stunning $700 million, creating a perfect second buying opportunity.

The stock sank back into Buffett's original buying range, then slowly recovered as a bank consolidation move swept the country.

Buffett's second purchase was made from August 4 to August 10, 1992, at prices a little under $7. Buffett's friend, Walter Annenberg, also disclosed he owned 5.3% of Wells Fargo stock. Annenberg, a wealthy friend of Ronald Reagan and a businessman who has given more than $1 billion to educational projects, owned about 8.6% of Wells Fargo by late 1994.

Late in 1992, Buffett said he had invested another $37 million in Wells Fargo stock.

And Prudential's Salem kept up his sell pitch in late 1992, saying what a terrible stock Wells Fargo was: "When Warren Buffett runs out of money, the stock will plummet," adding that Buffett might as well make "donations to a good cause."

"He's supporting the stock; otherwise it would be much lower," Salem said.

He said the stock would make a good short, that only Buffett was holding the short pants back from a real onslaught. On January 7, 1993, Wells Fargo reported that Buffett had bought another batch of stock in late December, 1992, between $74.46 and $75.43 a share, bringing his total to about 63,000,000 shares.

Prudential's Salem came back that month with, "We reiterate our sell rating on the shares of Wells Fargo & Co...Eventual downside risk appears considerable—perhaps to $60 [$6 at today's adjusted price] or below...The price more than reflects a nearly complete recovery which we don't see."

While some short sellers were predicting a 50% decline in the stock because of predicted writeoffs, Wells Fargo stock solidly crossed $100 a share.

Then the following item appeared in the *The Atlanta Journal/The Atlanta Constitution* on April 30, 1993:

> Calling it the 'strangest stock I have ever covered,' Prudential's Salem dropped coverage of Wells Fargo. A vociferous critic of the San Francisco-based bank, Mr. Salem has been bedeviled for years by Wells Fargo.
>
> The analyst has carried a sell recommendation on the stock since December, 1989...
>
> Mr. Salem, an often-quoted 25-year industry veteran, insists he isn't giving up on a bad call. 'This is not a surrender of any kind, ... It was a business decision based on where I thought I could spend my time more profitably. Wells Fargo is overpriced, volatile and unpredictable and not many people from investment-land care about it.'

Buffett told *Forbes* (October 18, 1993) "I don't want to start touting Wells Fargo stock or anything. I just think it is a very good business, with the best management, at a reasonable price. And usually when that is the case, there is more money to be made."

The stock kept climbing and Buffett bought more in November 1993, hiking his stake to a split-adjusted 6.8 million shares.

A couple of weeks later it was noted that with reserves for bad loans of $2.1 billion, Wells Fargo might be $1 billion over-reserved, money that could go toward profits later on. (*Wall Street Journal*, November 17, 1993)

For Buffett, Wells Fargo delivered. And kept delivering.

On October 18, 1995, Wells Fargo launched a hostile takeover with Buffett's approval, of rival First Interstate Bancorp of Los Angeles.

Why with Buffett's approval when he normally doesn't care for hostile takeovers? It's probably because Buffett doesn't control

Berkshire's investees. Buffett, short of moral turpitude, backs management which has an overriding responsibility to its owners.

The unsolicited bid offered about $10 billion in Wells Fargo stock, the biggest price in banking history, at that time.

Buffett was in on the failed negotiations between leaders of Wells and First Interstate. "Mr. Buffett stated that he had studied both companies in some detail. He also stated that one could come up with positives and negatives of one company compared to the other, but in the end when evaluating each company, one would conclude that they were about equal and that accordingly the exchange ratio of .625 [of a Wells share for each First Interstate share] made sense to him." (First Interstate letter to shareholders announcing on November 6, 1995, that it had entered into an agreement to merge with First Bank System).

The banking combination of Wells and First Interstate created the nation's eighth-largest bank, with more than $100 billion in assets. Wells Fargo was the No. 3 bank in California and First Interstate was No. 2, after Bank of America. Big First Interstate had the largest multistate branch network, operating almost 1,200 branches. It had a large presence in the West and in Texas. The bank had about 26,000 employees before being bought out by Wells Fargo.

Wells Fargo said it could eliminate duplicate California operations and save $800 million in expenses. Indeed, it made huge cuts of First Interstate branches and personnel.

First Interstate Chairman William Siart said: "I am deeply disappointed that Wells Fargo would take this uninvited action."

First Interstate rejected the Wells Fargo offer and agreed to merge with smaller First Bank System of Minneapolis.

But that was not to be the end of the saga. Gradually, as Wells Fargo stock rose faster than First Bank's, the Wells offer became more attractive. And suddenly an SEC ruling ordering First Bank to halt repurchases of its stock for two years made the deal less attractive to First Bank's shareholders.

Soon thereafter the First Interstate board told Siart to begin merger talks with Hazen.

On January 24, 1996, Wells won the hostile fight for First Interstate. Wells planned to cut 7,000 jobs at First Interstate, including Siart's. In the end 8,900 jobs were slashed.

Wells paid two-thirds of a share of its stock for every First Interstate share. The final acquisition price was $11.3 billion in stock.

The integration and conversion of First Interstate into Wells Fargo was completed on schedule in late 1996—one of the fastest full completions of large bank mergers.

Of course, not everything went perfectly: "257 California locations were closed over two weekends in July and August. To add to the logistical challenge, more than two dozen of those moves had to be completed in total darkness, with only flashlights, candles and generators because the largest power outage ever to hit the West Coast struck on Saturday, August 10."

The merger triggered account errors, long lines and employee defections. Paul Hazen finally said of the merger: "It has not been a pleasant year for me and not one that I've enjoyed." (*Business Week*, June 9, 1997).

Wells Fargo now was a western powerhouse of a bank. And California's economy was showing signs of thriving.

On August 21, 1997 reports made national television news that Berkshire had sold its entire stake in Wells Fargo sending the stock down sharply (talk about managing your own impact). But it turned

(AP Photo/Stuart Ramson)

Chairman and CEO of Wells Fargo Paul Hazen, left, and Chairman and CEO of Norwest Richard M. Kovacevich, look over The Wall Street Journal after announcing a merger between their two companies, in New York Monday, June 8, 1998. Wells Fargo & Co. and Norwest Corp. agreed to a $34 billion merger that would create the seventh-largest bank in the United States.

out that Berkshire had received permission from the SEC to keep its holdings of Wells Fargo confidential. Berkshire remained a substantial investor in Wells Fargo.

On June 8, 1998 Wells Fargo and Minneapolis-based Norwest Corp. agreed to merge to form a banking giant in the western U.S. Paul Hazen became chairman of the combined banks and Norwest's Richard Kovacevich became president and CEO.

Norwest bought Wells Fargo but the Wells Fargo name was kept.

The new Wells Fargo has more than 100,000 employees and assets of more than $200 billion, 15 million customers and 5,900 branches. It serves 21 states from Ohio to California. Wells Fargo is the No.1 Internet bank, with almost 1.8 million online accounts and 100,000 new clients coming online each month (*Fortune*, May 15, 2000). Nine of the 21 are among the nation's 10 fastest growing states. The 1998 Wells Fargo Annual Report projects that 50% of the U.S. population growth in the next decade is expected to come from these states. The report said, "California, alone, is the world's seventh largest small business market and the nation's largest farm economy."

Synergy note: Wells Fargo and First Data Corporation (in which Berkshire has a small stake) announced in 1999 the launch of One-Stop Store offering e-commerce solutions for businesses by quickly developing Internet presences.

Wells Fargo said on December 21, 1999 it planned to buy National Bancorp of Alaska, the largest bank in Alaska, for about $907 million in stock and in 2000 Wells Fargo bought First Security Corp. of Salt Lake City for about $2.9 billion in Wells Fargo stock.

Berkshire synergy note: American Express and Wells Fargo announced April 20, 2000 an alliance to distribute investment and annuity products through their retail financial networks. The companies also said they planned two new annuities to be issued by American Enterprise Life Insurance Co., a division of American Express.

125
GUINNESS
A MERGER WHILE WAITING FOR THE
WORLD RECOVERY

In 1991 Buffett quietly struck again, buying about $265 million, or 31.2 million shares of London-based Guinness, one of the world's largest purveyors of liquor. The company is now known as Diageo, after its merger with consumer products giant Grand Metropolitan in 1997. Grand Met, of London, owns such high profile businesses as Burger King, Pillsbury which sells Green Giant frozen foods, Häagen-Dazs, J&B Rare Scotch, and Smirnoff, and seems a perfect fit with Guinness.

The name Diageo ("Drink Is Always Good, Especially Often") is a concoction of the Latin-like "dia" for day and the Greek "Geo" for world. (*Forbes*, September 20, 1999) The company is headed by England's Sir Anthony Greener.

It was Buffett's first significant direct investment overseas and his first major brand-name purchase since Coke and Gillette. Guinness, the beer and record book company, has been slow to deliver the goods to investors.

Buffett compared Guinness to Coca-Cola as a strong franchise, but in the 1991 annual report he wrote: "You'll never get the drinks confused—and your Chairman remains unmovably in the Cherry Coke camp."

Acquisition-minded Guinness is known for its beer, particularly Guinness Stout, a global beer brand, served in some 130 countries—shades of Coca-Cola. Guinness brews Guinness and Harp beers worldwide, and Budweiser and Carlsberg beers in Ireland.

It's well known for such brands as Johnnie Walker scotch whiskey, Bell's, and White Horse. Guinness also is known for its Gordon's vodka and gin and Tanqueray gin and Bailey's Irish Cream liqueur. Indeed, the company is the world leader in scotch and gin.

Guinness got its start when Arthur Guinness leased a small brewery in Dublin, Ireland, in 1759, making ales sold in Dublin. And Guinness is famed for publishing the *Guinness Book of World Records*, the best selling book of all time having sold some 80 million copies—more even than *Gone With the Wind* and *Of Permanent Value* combined. It contains such records as who's won the most

Tony Awards as well as facts about First Ladies. It lists the world's largest octopus, paper clip and watermelon (262 pounds). And we learn that the most cinematic costume changes were made by Elizabeth Taylor when she changed dresses 65 times for the filming of *Cleopatra*. Then there's the *Guinness Book of Olympic Records,* an offshoot of the original, begun by a Guinness executive back in 1955 when the head of the company jumped into a debate over whether the grouse or the golden plume was Europe's fastest game bird. (*Wall Street Journal,* July 30, 1999)

The *Guinness Book of World Records* has been revamped in recent years to reflect modern life with categories such as "biggest divorce settlement" ($950 million to Soraya Khashoggi from Saudi entrepreneur Adhan Khashoggi) and "largest Hollywood home": Manor on Mapleton Drive in Hollywood built for Aaron Spelling. Guinness has more than 30,000 world records on file with new ones arriving at 1,800 a month, but only 4,500 records make it into the book in a year.

Now there is a "Guinness World Records: Primetime" show on the Fox network.

One show in 1999 featured a man who crammed a record 15 plastic straws in his mouth, a man who walked on his hands down the stairs at the Philadelphia Museum of Flight (of "Rocky" fame) and the most yo-yo tricks in a minute—30.

First reported in the *Independent Newspaper* of London, the Guinness stake story was picked up by the Bloomberg News Service and the *Omaha World-Herald* but not by any other major U.S. financial publication until a week and a half later, when Berkshire confirmed that it owned about 1.6% of Guinness.

Under British law, stockholders must identify themselves when they own 3% of a company.

Guinness' largest stockholders are the Prudential of London and LVMH (Louis Vuitton Moet Hennessey), a French maker of beverages, luggage lines, perfumes, beauty and fashion products, including Dom Perignon, Moet & Chandon, Hennessey, Christian Dior and Givenchy. So not only does Buffett buy into brand names, but with Guinness he bought into name-brand partners, because Guinness bought 24% of Moet Hennessey in the late 1980s while that French firm bought a similar stake in Guinness in 1990. The firms share sales operations in the United States and Japan.

Guinness' ties with LVMH date back to 1987 when the firms formed distribution agreements. Guinness invested in LVMH to keep it from splitting apart and to protect its joint ventures when a battle for control broke out for LVMH.

Guinness will celebrate its 250th birthday in Buffett's lifetime, if Buffett's new physical fitness program continues to serve him well.

The stock did poorly following Buffett's purchase and the Bloomberg news service carried a report on January 29, 1993, that Buffett was rumored to be selling his Guinness stake, but there was no confirmation.

Although Guinness had a period of slow going, Buffett was buying more, not selling. Berkshire's 1992 Annual Report, reflecting business as of the end of 1992 said the Guinness stake had increased to 2%, not decreased. It listed the stake as having a cost basis of $333 million and a worth of $299 million.

Bill Ruane, head of the Sequoia mutual fund, which also has had a stake in Guinness, has said, "Guinness...is a wonderful company. It has a phenomenal Scotch business throughout the world. But it's been affected by the worldwide recession—and it's not just in Japan...It has outstanding management and fine brands. Guinness Stout is almost regarded as food in Ireland. I understand it's even approved for medicinal purposes by the government's Group Health Plan there."

However, for years after buying his first shares of Guinness, Buffett remained underwater on this one. Had he gotten too high on Guinness? Or was Guinness about ready to get high itself? As Buffett would say, "We'll know in a few years."

Guinness and LVMH restructured their cross-ownership in early 1994. The change disengaged the British brewer and distiller from LVMH's perfume and luggage businesses while linking it closer to the French company's champagne-and-cognac unit. Also, it made it easier for LVMH to diversify further into businesses that maybe don't interest Guinness. LVMH now owns a large stake in Gucci.

Under the agreement, Guinness sold its 24% indirect stake in LVMH for $1.84 billion and bought 34% of LVMH's Moet Hennessey SA wine and spirits unit. LVMH reduced its stake in Guinness to 20% from 24% by the middle of 1995.

"This is the first good news for Guinness in two years," said Graeme Eadie, an analyst at NatWest Securities, noting that the company has been hurt by the recession and declining consumption of Scotch whiskey. (*Wall Street Journal*, January 21, 1994)

In all, Guinness turned flat, and there remained unconfirmed reports Berkshire's Guinness stock was sold, possibly at a loss. But, as usual, there has been no word from Berkshire of a sale.

If Berkshire hadn't sold its Guinness, it would now have a tiny ownership in Diageo, one of the largest consumer products companies in the world.

Still, stay tuned for the world recovery.

In 1999 Berkshire made an investment in Diageo's competitor, Allied Domecq.

126
GENERAL DYNAMICS
SO MUCH FOR:
"WE-DON'T-UNDERSTAND-TECHNOLOGY."

General Dynamics announced July 23, 1992, that Berkshire had bought 8.7 million shares, counting a 2-for-1 split in 1994, for $312 million. Buffett had bought 15% of the nation's second largest defense contractor.

So much for: "We-don't-understand-technology." Maybe his friendship with Bill Gates had an effect.

But was this any way to invest in the post-Cold War era at a time when everyone knew the defense industry was contracting? Since 1989 more than 1.5 million jobs in the defense industry were terminated.

GD spokesman Ray Lewis explained that Buffett bought the stock in the open market just as the Falls Church, Virginia-based defense giant completed a $957 million repurchase of its own shares. Superb timing for a self-proclaimed non-timer. GD itself bought 30% of its own stock back through a "Dutch auction," a process whereby investors (including the Crown family) tendered their shares, selling them back to the company at a price between about $33 and $38 a share. The company repurchased 26.4 million of its 80 million shares at about $36 a share.

The Crown and Goodman families had reduced their stake to 14.4% of the company, while Berkshire surprised the investment community by becoming GD's largest shareholder.

Under new management headed then by William Anders, a former astronaut who took over the joystick in early 1991, GD had been slimming down and selling off non-core businesses. GD was one of the first defense contractors to take bold action to deal with the end of the Cold War.

The company's military contracts have included the F-16 fighter jet, Atlas and Centaur launch vehicles, M-IA tanks (used extensively in Operation Desert Storm) and M-60 tanks, plus the Trident and Seawolf submarines.

GD sold its Cessna aircraft division for $600 million and disposed of its missile, fighter, space-launch and other units.

GD's Electric Boat unit was vulnerable to cancellation of the

Seawolf submarine, but Congress voted to build a second Seawolf, at an estimated cost of $2 billion.

Buffett saw a well-managed company doing a good job of restructuring in a consolidating industry, and buying back stock. The company had little debt, and planned sales were bringing mounds of cash. However, analysts were seemingly blind to the prudence of Buffett's move, saying the industry had little prospects for growth.

One analyst, the day of Buffett's purchase, said he doubted the stock could reach $40 in 12 months. Hmm. The stock practically reached it a few trading days later.

Along the way Berkshire granted GD its voting rights, and GD officials talked of being open to selling even core businesses. In December 1992, Lockheed agreed to buy fast-shrinking GD's fighter plane unit for about $1.5 billion.

All the while GD held to a strategy of beefing up the core units and selling off others. By January, 1993, the stock was trading at $56 a share, pretty good post-Cold War work. Large cash dividends—a total of $25 a share in 1993—resulted in a lower stock price, but still trading not far below $50.

Buffett explained in the 1992 Annual Report:

> We were lucky in our General Dynamics purchase. I had paid little attention to the company until last summer, when it was announced it would repurchase about 30% of its shares by way of a Dutch tender. Seeing an arbitrage opportunity, I began buying the stock for Berkshire, expecting to tender our holdings for a small profit. We've made the same sort of commitment perhaps a half-dozen times in the past few years, reaping decent rates of return for the short periods our money has been tied up.
>
> But then I began studying the company and the accomplishments of Bill Anders in the brief time he'd been CEO. And what I saw made my eyes pop: Bill had a clearly articulated and rational strategy; he had been focused and imbued with a sense of urgency in carrying it out; and the results were truly remarkable.
>
> In short order, I dumped my arbitrage thoughts and decided that Berkshire should become a long-term investor with Bill. We were helped in gaining a large position by the fact that a tender greatly swells the volume of trading in a stock. In a one-month period, we were able to purchase 14% of the General Dynamics shares that remained outstanding after the tender was completed.

The investment worked very well. In mid-1993 GD was writing shareholders:

> On January 1, 1991, when your new management team first took office, total debt exceeded $1 billion and debt ratings were falling. We reported a cash account of just $115 million and expected cash flow to be negative over the next year. By the end of 1993, we expect your company to be virtually debt free. Similarly, at the end of May your company will have a cash and marketable securities balance of approximately $1.6 billion and an unused $700 million line of credit. This ample liquidity is especially impressive considering that it comes after your new management team—through debt reduction, dividends, share repurchases and special distributions—has already returned $2.2 billion to General Dynamics' lenders and shareholders for them to reinvest in America for competitive strength and new jobs.

In the first two years of Berkshire's stake, as GD raised dividends and bought back stock, Buffett had more than doubled his money. In April 1994, Buffett sold 20% of the GD stake and by the end of August the stake was 5.7 million shares. By the end of 1997 Berkshire's GD stake was 3.98 million shares, or about 6.3%. That amount, with a 2-for-1 stock split in 1998, is 7,959,562 shares. The shares are held by Berkshire's National Indemnity Co. and its National Fire and Marine Insurance Company. A report of a filing in 1999 said Berkshire had trimmed the stake slightly to 7.69 million shares of the company, or 6.1% and a report in 2000 said the stake had been lowered to 2.5%.

GD with its core businesses in nuclear submarines and armored vehicles has two main operating units: Marine Group, which designs and builds nuclear submarines and surface combatant ships, and Combat Systems Group which designs and builds armored vehicles. Also the company makes transmissions, engines, turrets, high speed gun and ammunition handling systems, and ordinance.

In 1999 GD bought Gulfstream Aerospace Corp., the leader in building large cabin, long-range business aircraft, for $5.3 billion. Gulfstream is now GD's most profitable division.

Although GD's stock slumped in 1999-2000, overall it has been a winner for Berkshire.

127

UST/MONEY IN THE WEEDS

JUST SLIDE A PINCH BETWEEN YOUR CHEEK AND GUM.

Philip Morris stunned the market April 2, 1993, saying it would cut prices on its Marlboro cigarettes—the best selling U.S. brand—in an effort to keep customers from buying discount brands.

The "Call for Philip Morris" giant said it expected its domestic cigarette unit's profits to drop as much as 40%. On that word, the stock dropped, slashing about $13 billion off its market capitalization. The stocks of all tobacco companies dived.

Send in Buffett, although it may be controversial with some that he has invested in defense, alcohol and tobacco companies.

On April 13, 1993, *USA Today's* Dan Dorfman reported Buffett had taken almost a 5% stake in UST, formerly U.S. Tobacco, a leading maker of smokeless tobacco.

Not until June 1994, was there confirmation of Buffett's stake in UST when an SEC filing showed Berkshire owned 5.6 million shares, or 2.5% of the firm. Buffett had asked that the stake be kept confidential for a year. In late 1996 the position was 5.2 million shares.

UST is known for its Copenhagen and Skoal products. Copenhagen is the world's best selling brand of snuff. And Skoal is America's favorite wintergreen-flavored moist smokeless tobacco. Just slide a pinch between your cheek and gum.

UST is one of the nation's most profitable companies with 87% of the chewing tobacco market. It also sells wines, including Chateau Ste. Michelle, Columbia Crest, Conn Creek and Villa Mt. Eden and has a sparkling wine made with the Domaine Ste. Michelle label.

Brand loyalty is strong, with discount brands penetrating only 3% of the smokeless tobacco market compared with 27% of the cigarette market. And chewing tobacco costs about a third of what cigarettes do.

UST has a consistently high return on equity, is debt free, and has paid a dividend since 1912, increasing it for more than the past 20 years.

Buffett had struck again under this scenario: when there's a stigma in the industry, locate a brand name cash cow.

UST had the kind of growth that Buffett likes, reflected by a stock market value of $111 million in 1973 and about $7 billion in the early 1990s. Almost makes you wanna chew.

Moist snuff originated in the Scandinavian countries. Due to societal attitudes and restrictions on "spitting" the product was used in the upper lip where there are no salivary glands.

The product was introduced to America when Scandinavian immigrants brought it along with them to the new world. Most of the first wave of immigrants worked in underground mines. Given the prevailing working conditions, they needed to get the dirt out of their mouths constantly so they needed to salivate to spit out the dirt. Thus the product migrated from the upper lip to the lower lip, an area of the mouth which has many salivary glands.

The moist snuff business, which serves only about four million users, has different and stronger fundamentals than the domestic cigarette business. UST operates in an industry with a near monopolistic share of the market, high barriers to entry and few substitute products.

The top two players, UST and Conwood, have a 95% share of the market for smokeless tobacco. The production process is proprietary and secretive—so proprietary that UST designs and makes its own machinery—and not easily duplicated, with the entire process taking about six years.

Also, most of UST's required capital expenses are covered by depreciation and amortization charges. Therefore, a major portion of the cash flow generated is essentially free cash flow available for shareholders.

A controversial issue that remains is pricing flexibility. The fact is Conwood almost always follows a UST-led price increase.

Still in 1995 UST's sales flattened. Its president resigned, and a public health controversy over UST's moist-smokeless-tobacco products ensued as the whole tobacco industry struggled with lawsuits, although smokeless tobacco was drawing fewer suits than cigarette companies.

In 2000 UST was hit with an antitrust ruling ordering UST to pay more than $1 billion.

128

BRISTOL-MYERS SQUIBB
FOR MARKET HEADACHES, TAKE TWO BUFFERIN.

Buffett, after years of saying drug stocks were not up his alley—that they were not in his old "circle of competence"—bought into Bristol-Myers Squibb, a New York company formed by a merger between Bristol-Myers and Squibb Corp. in 1989.

USA Today reported June 9, 1994, that Berkshire owned 957,200 shares that were bought in 1993, according to an SEC filing. The filing wasn't made public for a year so Buffett could have confidentiality. It was reported that Bristol-Myers officials had no idea about Buffett's investment, which is 0.2% of the stock, until the SEC filing was released.

Like all drug stocks, Bristol-Myers was sluggish during the uncertainty of how health reform would play out, but has since recovered strongly from that battering. Bristol-Myers has a worldwide presence, an excellent balance sheet and cash flow. It also pays a good dividend and buys back its stock.

With annual sales of more than $13 billion, Bristol-Myers is one of the world's largest drug firms. It's a major force in offering anticancer and cardiovascular drugs. Flagship drugs are Toxol for some cancers, Pravachol, a cholesterol reducer and Capoten for hypertension.

Bristol-Myers distributes consumer products such as Ban deodorant, Bufferin, Excedrin and Clairol hair products. It is also America's second-largest infant-formula maker.

In recent years Bristol-Myers has cut costs by lowering employee ranks and the firm has introduced a number of new products.

Buffett had a toehold in another of America's great corporations whose stock has been a big winner in the last couple of years.

At the annual meeting in 1997, Buffett explained that Berkshire began buying a drug company during the health reform crisis. "We started buying it a few years ago, but it went up an eighth and we stopped. We should have bought more."

129

GANNETT

EXTRA! EXTRA! NEWSPAPERS STILL MAKE MONEY!

On December 15, 1994, Gannett—the nation's largest newspaper publisher—announced that Berkshire owned 4.9% of its stock.

Buffett had returned to a large media concern as the stock traded near a low after years of sluggishness in the newspaper industry.

His $335 million investment gave him an additional stake in media companies which includes the *Buffalo News* and *Washington Post*.

Arlington, Virginia-based Gannett publishes *USA Today*, the second largest newspaper in the country with an average daily circulation of almost 2.3 million printed at 33 sites. USAToday.com in 1998 had 92 million daily hits and 7 million daily page views. *USA Today* has been dubbed "McPaper," by some, a newspaper offering

(Photo courtesy of AP/Wide World Photos)

USA Today, which came into being September 14, 1982, has had its backers and critics, but its influence has been great. These are weather pages of USA Today, The Washington Post and The Washington Times, right, which are similar, thanks in part to USA Today's original design.

news "McNuggets." *USA Today* is known for short stories with short items set off by bullet marks. And it has drawn its critics: "Many critics, however, thought it simply dumbed down the news. Former editor John Quinn once joked that *USA Today* had become famous for 'bringing new depth to the definition of shallow' and that if it ever won a Pulitzer Prize, it would be for 'best investigative paragraph.' " (*The Washington Post*, August 11, 1997)

Gannett also publishes more than 190 newspapers, including 73 dailies such as *The Detroit News* with a combined circulation of 6.6 million and operates 22 television stations covering about 17% of the U.S. Gannett's cable division was sold to Cox Communications in 1999.

Gannett is the largest consumer of newsprint in North America, using 891,000 tons in 1997. (1997 Gannett Annual Report)

The company, long headed by John Curley, until Douglas McCorkindale took over in 2000, has about 46,000 employees and 14,000 stockholders. Berkshire is the biggest stockholder.

Again, another toe-hold in a major media business which is buying back its own stock.

So what's the strategy here? Maybe, it's to buy all companies beginning with G. Maybe Berkshire's next annual report will be in Green.

In 1995 Gannett bought Multimedia of Greenville, South Carolina, and in 1999 Gannett paid $1.5 billion to buy Newsquest, Britain's third largest newspaper publisher with a portfolio of 180 titles. Publications include 11 daily newspapers with a combined circulation of 450,000. One of its non-daily publications, *Berrow's Worchester Journal* is the oldest continuously published newspaper in the world.

A 1996 filing for 1995 showed Berkshire owned 6,854,500 shares of Gannett. A 1997 filing showed Berkshire had reduced its Gannett stake in 1996 to 2.4 million shares and by the fourth quarter of 1997 to 4.26 million shares on a split adjusted basis.

Headline:

GANNETT MAKES SOLID PROGRESS SINCE BERKSHIRE'S INVESTMENT

130
PNC
AN EAST COAST BANK

On February 14, 1995, the same day Buffett announced Berkshire held 9.8% of American Express, there was a second little noticed news item: "Warren Buffett has 8.3% stake in PNC Bank Corp."

Berkshire had bought 19,453,300 shares of the big Pittsburgh-based bank holding company and the largest in Pennsylvania–the 12th largest bank in the country--at a cost of $503 million.

The bank provides services to more than 300 of the Fortune 500 companies and to the 34 million members of the American Automobile Association coast-to-coast. In 1996 PNC acquired a portfolio of the association's credit-card accounts from Mellon Bank. The portfolio included 1.3 million credit cards from 50 AAA clubs, which provide travel, insurance and auto-related services. AAA is based in Heathrow, Florida.

In the fall of 1994, PNC had announced that rising interest rates had so battered its securities portfolio that 1995 earnings would be 15% below analysts expectations, always a no-no in investment land. The bank also took restructuring charges when it lost six employees in the crash of USAir Flight 427 which went down just outside Pittsburgh on September 8, 1994. The stock sank from about $30 to about $20 a share and Buffett bought in the mid-range of those figures.

Pittsburgh-based PNC Bank, headed by Thomas H. O'Brien, with $75 billion in assets, owns a variety of banking interests.

Buffett has reduced his PNC position to below 5%.

Buffett had again bought a large stake in a bank with presumably temporary setbacks.

Remember Wells Fargo?

131

THE SALE OF MATTEL
NEWLY SHAPED BARBIE, CABBAGE PATCH KIDS, HOT WHEELS

Berkshire's now sold stake in Mattel, Inc., the largest toy maker in the U.S., was acquired by GEICO at the direction of Lou Simpson. When Berkshire acquired GEICO in 1996, the Mattel stake came along with the purchase.

The position of 9.38 million shares amounted to more than 3% of Mattel's stock. A report on June 9, 1998 said Berkshire raised its stake 1.2 million shares in the first quarter of 1997 to 10.6 million shares, or 3.6% of the company.

Mattel, of El Segundo, California, was headed by Chairman and CEO Jill Barad, one of the highest ranking women in corporate America until she departed in 2000 after a string of poor earnings reports. She also serves as a director of BankAmerica and Microsoft.

With Mattel, there was a bit of synergy for Berkshire because Mattel has licenses for the production of Disney's preschool and entertainment toy lines.

In 1993 Mattel acquired Fisher-Price and in 1997 it bought Tyco Toys. The company has about 26,000 employees and 37,000 shareholders.

The toy giant is making headway overseas as it markets its newly shaped Barbie with a less exaggerated bustline [although later with more trendy clothes, lip gloss and a bellybutton], Cabbage Patch Kids and Hot Wheels toy lines. Barbie products accounted for $1.9 billion in sales in 1997.

In 1998 Mattel acquired Pleasant Co., a maker of "American Girl" brand products.

A report in 1999 said Berkshire had unloaded all of its 11 million shares of Mattel in 1998.

132

ARROW ELECTRONICS

Berkshire bought 1.7 million shares of Arrow Electronics Inc. in the second quarter of 1996, according to a filing reported September 11, 1997. The stake of more than $100 million amounts to about 3½% of the shares of the Melville, New York-based firm, the world's largest distributor of electronic components and computer products to industrial and commercial customers. It resells products made by companies such as Intel.

Berkshire's FlightSafety International is among Arrow's customers.

The company has more than 160 selling locations and 17 primary distribution centers around the world. It serves customers ranging from small engineering firms to large original equipment manufacturers.

Arrow has about 7,000 employees and 4,000 shareholders, with annual sales of about $7.4 billion and is headed by Stephen P. Kaufman.

The company enjoys a strong balance sheet, but pays no dividends. It has been buying back its stock.

133

AMERICAN INTERNATIONAL GROUP

Reports in March 1998 showed that Berkshire, at the end of 1996, owned 1.44 million shares of American International Group, the huge insurance company. Buffett later raised the stake to 2.45 million shares as of September 30, 1997.

AIG engages in property, casualty, marine and life insurance underwriting and offers other financial services on a worldwide basis. About one half of its revenues and profits come from overseas.

Headed by Maurice "Hank" Greenberg (he got his nickname from the Detroit Tigers slugger "Hammerin' Hank" Greenberg) for more than 30 years, the company is based in New York City and has about 35,000 employees. It is the largest U.S. financial services company and one of the largest in the world, operating in 130 countries. AIG, with more than 300 subsidiaries, insures a variety of risks related to oil platforms, cargo ships and even a subway system in Hong Kong. A leading insurer of businesses and one of the largest insurers of individuals in Asia, AIG enjoys a Triple-A debt rating.

In the early 1980s, AIG tried but failed to buy GEICO. (*Fortune*, April 27, 1998)

Greenberg, a billionaire, is mentioned in *The Greatest Generation* (p. 323) by NBC's Tom Brokaw as one of the U.S. Army Rangers who stormed Omaha Beach on D-Day in World War II.

Who's What

In Berkshireland the name Greenberg keeps popping up. Here's Who's What:

- Maurice "Hank" Greenberg is the CEO of AIG.
- Alan "Ace" Greenberg is the CEO of Bear Stearns.
- Jack Greenberg is chairman of McDonald's.
- Henry "Hank" Greenberg was the Detroit Tigers slugger.
- Glenn Greenberg is his son and runs Chieftain Capital Management in New York.
- Allen Greenberg is the ex-husband of Susie Buffett and continues to run the Buffett Foundation.

134

STAKES IN OTHER COMPANIES
LIZ CLAIBORNE, JONES APPAREL AND
DUN & BRADSTREET/MICROSOFT PREFERRED STOCK

Berkshire has small stakes in many companies and they add up to well more than $6 billion. Berkshire has warned investors that reports about them can mislead investors. Information about the lesser positions is often long in getting out and positions of the non-permanent holdings are more likely to be traded, even sold off entirely.

Berkshire has told the SEC, "The reports rarely explain in any great degree the staleness of the information and are almost certainly not helpful to potential investors."

Berkshire has acknowledged that a company could try to manipulate the market by moving shares between public and confidential filings. "This is not what Berkshire does nor what it believes to be appropriate corporate behavior."

On March 28, 1994, Dan Dorfman reported that Berkshire held relatively small stakes in three financial services companies: First Interstate Bancorp, a Los Angeles-based bank holding company (later taken over by Wells Fargo), SunTrust Banks, Inc., an Atlanta-based banking firm, and Federal National Mortgage Association (Fannie Mae).

Dorfman, quoting 13F filings with the SEC, said Berkshire held 955,000 shares of First Interstate, 567,000 shares of Fannie Mae and 1.55 million shares of SunTrust. It was later revealed that Berkshire had upped its stake in SunTrust in 1994 to 3.1 million shares and 3.3 million shares in 1995 which split 2-for-1 in 1996. So Berkshire had 6.6 million shares or about 3% of SunTrust's shares.

SunTrust Banks, which owns about $2.5 billion in Coke stock, was formed by the 1985 merger of the Trust Company of Georgia and Florida's SunBank, Inc. SunTrust was headed by James B. Williams, who was also a Coke director. Former Coca-Cola Chairman M. Douglas Ivester is a director of SunTrust. SunTrust, now headed by L. Phillip Humann, acquired Crestar Financial Corp. of Richmond, Virginia in 1998.

(Photo courtesy of SunTrust Banks)

Former SunTrust Banks Chairman Jimmy Williams

With his SunTrust investment, Buffett has more ownership in Coca-Cola and a banking play in the strong, high growth markets of Georgia and Florida.

A 1996 report showed Berkshire owned 8.3 million shares of Fannie Mae and a report in 1999 said the stake in the fourth quarter of 1997 had been trimmed to 6.35 million shares.

In 1995 word came that Berkshire held 1.41 million shares of KeyCorp, the big bank holding company in Cleveland, Ohio. A 1996 filing showed a 1995 position of 3.1 million shares of Key Corp.

Later in 1995 Minneapolis-based First Bank System acquired First Tier of Omaha for about $700 million in stock. Because Berkshire owned about 5% of FirstTier, Berkshire wound up with 858,178 shares of First Bank System stock, now U.S. Bancorp.

With Berkshire's acquisition of GEICO, Berkshire received about 1.9 million shares of U.S. Bancorp that GEICO had in its stock portfolio. Thus Berkshire wound up with about a 2% stake in the old First Bank System known particularly for its credit card and trust services. A report in 1999 said Berkshire had sold 2.4 million shares of U.S. Bancorp in 1998.

In 1994 Buffett bought 262,000 shares of Merrill Lynch & Co. according to a 1995 SEC filing. (*USA Today*, September 28, 1995)

The Wall Street Journal reported on June 14, 1996, that Berkshire acquired a 2.2 million share stake in Sears, Roebuck & Co. (the Seer's Sears) in the first quarter of 1995, according to an SEC filing. Sears is the world's second largest retailer.

The story also said Berkshire cut its holdings in PNC Bank by 3.7 million shares to 16 million shares.

Also, Berkshire raised its stake in Dean Witter, Discover Co. (Dean Witter Discovers Buffett) to 2.8 million shares, (now 4.2 million shares) or just under 2%, in the first quarter of 1995. The financial services company issues and services the Discover credit card and owns the Dean Witter Brokerage firm. In 1997 Dean Witter Discover merged with Morgan Stanley and became Morgan Stanley Dean Witter. A report in 1999 for the fourth quarter of 1997 said Berkshire owned 2.15 million shares of Morgan Stanley Dean Witter.

Further, it said Berkshire trimmed its year-earlier position in Merrill Lynch (Mother Merrill) by 739,600 shares to 205,400 shares (bullish, then bearish on the thundering herd?) and lowered its holdings of Viacom Class B (Viacom Lives!) shares by 495,000 to 512,253 shares.

Reports in 1996 for 1995 showed Berkshire owned more than 2 million shares of Allstate, about 1.6 million shares (later 1.9 million shares) of International Flavors and Fragrance and 853,659 shares or just under 5% of Zenith National Insurance. A report in *Barron's,* July 20, 1998 said Berkshire sold 427,000 shares of IFF in the first quarter of 1997 after unloading 467,500 shares in the fourth quarter of 1996. Another one showed Berkshire owned 239,250 shares of Chrysler which has since had a two-for-one stock split and merged with Daimler. Perhaps this was an arbitrage play by Berkshire about the time Kirk Kerkorian was trying to buy Chrysler.

Buffett was making a large play on bank consolidation and in the financial services industry. He was beginning not only to dominate companies, but industries.

An SEC filing reported June 17, 1997 showed that in the first quarter of 1996, Berkshire (probably through GEICO) acquired 2 million shares of Nike, or about 0.7% of the company; 9.38 million shares of Mattel, or 3.2% of the toy company. Berkshire also owned (then later sold) about 5 million shares of Laboratory Corporation of America, a Burlington, North Carolina company that operates clinical testing labs throughout the country, and 3.7 million shares, or 4.5%, of Manpower Corp. the large temporary help firm. (*Dow Jones* news service, June 17, 1997)

Reports in early 1998 of 1996 filings said Berkshire owned 175,000 shares of Lockheed Martin as of September 30, 1996. In the same period Berkshire sold 124,956 shares of KeyCorp and 729,400 of PNC bank.

Also there have been Internet postings saying Berkshire owns 550,000 shares of discount retailer Costco of Issaquah, Washington, which operates more than 200 warehouses in more than 20 states and has about 12 million members. The Costco investment probably is for Berkshire's future distribution synergy on Mars.

A report on June 9, 1998 said Berkshire owned 4.39 million shares of Wal-Mart Stores as of the third quarter of 1997. Berkshire also held 125,000 shares of Gap, as in "generation gap," a San Francisco-based clothing retailer.

Berkshire also owned 500,000 shares of Tupperware, the Orlando, Florida, manufacturer of food storage products.

According to the *Federal Filings* publication, here is a list of other Berkshire stock holdings:

Company	Shares Held 3/31/97	Market Value 3/31/97 ($MMs)
SunTrust Banks, Inc.	6,641,400	$307.0
Mattel, Inc.	10,583,900	$254.0
Nike, Inc.	4,000,000	$247.5
Fannie Mae	6,764,200	$244.4
American International Group	1,918,900	$225.2
Gannett, Inc.	2,309,900	$198.4
First Bank System	2,608,567	$190.4
First Empire State Corp.	506,930	$162.2
Dean Witter Discover	4,194,200	$146.3
Manpower, Inc.	3,700,000	$133.2
Wal-Mart Stores, Inc.	4,391,700	$122.4
Arrow Electronics, Inc.	1,700,000	$95.8
Int'l Flavors & Fragrances	1,880,350	$82.3
UST, Inc.	2,730,200	$76.1
Burlington Northern & Santa Fe	600,000	$44.4
U.S. Bancorp	483,500	$25.9
Zenith National Insurance Corp.	853,655	$22.9
Tupperware Corp.	500,000	$16.6
Costco Cos.	555,000	$15.3
The Gap, Inc.	125,000	$4.2
York International Corp.	50,000	$2.1

Berkshire, through GEICO, owned more than 8%, or about 4 million shares of TCA Cable of Tyler, Texas, (TCA Cable was bought by Cox Enterprises in 1999) as well as about 7%, or about 4 million shares of Great Lakes Chemical Corp. of West Lafayette, Indiana, the world's biggest maker of chemicals used in flame retardents, according to stories on February 17, 1999 quoting filings. The Great Lakes stake was raised to 7 million shares in 2000.

Berkshire owned about 1.90 million shares of Nucor Corp., according to a filing reported September 16, 1999. Berkshire acquired its stake in the second largest U.S. steelmaker at a time when a growing supply of cold-rolled and galvanized steel had forced the Charlotte, North Carolina, producer to slash prices in order to fend off competitors.

A report April 21, 1999 showed that Berkshire had bought stakes in a health-care real estate investment trust, Omega Healthcare Investors Inc., and affiliate Omega Worldwide.

Berkshire owned 208,378 shares, or 1.7%, of Ann Arbor, Michigan-based Omega Worldwide as of the end of December 1998. And Berkshire owned 60,100 shares, or 0.3%, of Omega Healthcare.

To show the difficulty of interpreting some of the reports about supposed Berkshire holdings, Buffett said at Berkshire's annual meeting in 1999 that he had never heard of the Omega investment although he said possibly it was an investment made by a General Re unit.

Reports in 1999 for the first quarter of 1998 showed minor sales of Morgan Stanley Dean Witter (later all sold), Nucor, AIG, Gannett, International Flavors and Fragrances, Manpower, UST and Wal-Mart. However, a report in late 1999 for the third quarter of 1998 showed Berkshire had more than doubled its stake in Nucor to 4.1 million shares.

Berkshire, through GEICO, owned a position in Burlington Northern Santa Fe, Inc., a holding company for the second largest railroad system in the United States.

The position of 350,000 shares was sold in the first quarter of 1998, according to filings.

Burlington Northern merged with Santa Fe in 1995 and the combined company has about 31,000 miles of track connecting the Midwest, The Pacific Northwest, Canada and the Gulf of Mexico and it serves the Powder River Basin coal mines in Wyoming. Mainly Burlington Northern ships coal and grain.

The railroad, based in Fort Worth, Texas, also owns the Washington Central Railroad which operates lines in the state of Washington.

A filing reported September 16, 1999 for June 30, 1998 showed that Berkshire owned 3 million shares of First Data Corp., which provides back-office processing to credit-card insurers. With annual sales of more than $5 billion, it's one of the world's largest processors of credit card transactions handling about one of every three Visa or Mastercard purchases in the U.S. First Data is a leader in electronic commerce (maybe Buffett knows more about technology than people think) and payment services, processing an average of one million payment transactions every hour and settles more than $3 billion a day. It owns Western Union which accounts for 40% of its sales. Later reports showed the First Data stake at 9.87 million shares.

It also showed minor sales of AIG, Gannett, Morgan Stanley Dean Witter and Wal-Mart.

Berkshire held significant stakes in Liz Claiborne, Jones Apparel and Dun & Bradstreet, according to filings of February 14, 2000. Reportedly Berkshire held about 4.9 million shares of New York apparel maker Liz Claiborne, or an 8.3% stake, 12.1 million shares of Jones Apparel, a 7.5% stake in the Dun & Bradstreet credit-rating service, which owns Moody's, and a 5% stake in GATX Corp., a Chicago-based commercial financing concern specializing in leasing aircraft, railway tankers and *technology* equipment.

Buffett said at Berkshire's annual meeting in 2000 that GEICO's Lou Simpson had made the Jones Apparel investment, but said he [Buffett himself] had made the Liz Claiborne investment. "It was a large block I bought one day when it was offered at a very attractive price," Buffett said.

A group of small stakes was unveiled February 22, 2000 when the Securities and Exchange Commision refused to let Berkshire delay disclosure of the holdings.

Filings showed that Berkshire had 167,500 preferred shares of Microsoft. It's doubtful investors should seize on this as a tech investment, but simply a preferred stake in an excellent credit. The preferred shares worth about $16 million.

Buffett said at a press conference on April 30, 2000 in Omaha in connection with Berkshire's annual meeting that: "That Microsoft preferred stock was just like commercial paper. It had nothing to do with Microsoft. It matured in December and is over already. The press misunderstood and said we were investing in tech stocks. We probably made $200,000 more than in common paper with it... I didn't see one article that understood that the stock had a 7% yield when common paper was at 5.5%."

Berkshire's filings also showed it owned 1.86 million shares of Cox Communications and one million shares of Robert Haft, of Menlo Park, California, which provides staffing services.

Reports on March 10, 2000 showed Berkshire had raised its stakes in four companies. Its stake in GATX rose to 14.9% to 7,340,700 shares. The stake in Dun & Bradstreet was raised to 14.9%, or 24 million shares, and the Jones Apparel stake was raised to 13.1%, or 15,750,000 shares.

If you have kept track of everything in this chapter, you're qualified to run Berkshire!

135

MYSTERY THEATER

In April 1999 when Buffett was in London promoting Executive Jet, he revealed he was building a stake in a British stock. That triggered a big mystery as to which stock it might be.

After weeks of speculation, in which some financial players placed big bets on which company it was, it turned out to be Allied Domecq, a British drinks group. It is the second biggest liquor company whose brands include Ballantine's Scotch whiskey, Canadian Club whiskey, Beefeater gin and Kahlua liqueur as well as Dunkin' Donuts and Baskin-Robbins ice cream chains.

Allied said Berkshire held nearly 22.8 million shares as of April 19, 1999, or 2.2%, of the firm's shares worth roughly $200 million after Allied had issued what's called a 212 notice for the investor to identify itself. In England an investor doesn't have to identify himself until a stake reaches 3%.

Allied Domecq officials reportedly said Buffett sold some of his 2% stake in the company in the summer of 1999.

Allied was in the midst of selling its 3,600-strong pubs unit to Whitehead PLC, but the unit was ultimately sold to Punch Taverns Ltd. for $4.35 billion. So Buffett seemed to be buying into a company with brand names which was in the midst of restructuring to stimulate its slumping shares and better compete with Diageo, the world's biggest beverage firm which owns Guinness. Berkshire made an investment in Guinness in the early 1990s.

The London Stock Exchange Regulatory News Service reported on March 14, 2000 that as of March 10, 2000 Berkshire held 33,618,000 shares of Allied Domecq, or 3.15% of the company.

Buffett apparently sold at a profit in the summer of 1999, then the stock slumped badly and Berkshire bought back in.

136

A SILVER LINING

Tonto: "Gettum-up, Scout."
Lone Ranger: "Hi-yo, Silver! Awaaaaaaay!"
A modern day duo— Buffett and Munger—early in 1998 finished buying a silver bullet worth over half a billion dollars. "Hi-ho, Silver, awaaaaaaay."

Known for buying dollar bills for 50 cents, Buffett this time around may have bought "silver" dollars for half a buck apiece.

Berkshire said on February 3, 1998 it had bought 129.7 million ounces of silver. That's a gleaming silver lining, a case of polishing up Berkshire's portfolio.

It's a lot of silver. Buffett took a shine to the metal between July 25, 1997—a day when silver futures contracts were at $4.32 an ounce—and January 12, 1998 when the price was $5.47 an ounce. Berkshire's precious white metal stake, worth about $850 million at the time of the announcement, was already up about $200 million from Buffett's cost of almost $650 million, or about $5 an ounce. However, by 1999 silver's price had slipped and the investment was roughly a wash.

Berkshire took delivery of the silver which represents about 20% of the world's annual silver mine output. The stash, about 30% of the world's above-ground vault inventories, if melted and poured into a solid block, would fit into a space 26 feet by 26 feet by 26 feet.

The New York Times (February 10, 1998) said: "The booty resides for the moment at one or more London bullion banks which normally store silver for a fee of 5 cents a day per 1,000-ounce bar, including theft insurance. Once Berkshire gets all its silver delivered, it will have 129,710 bars. Perhaps Buffett can get a quantity discount, but if not the storage will cost $6,485.50 a day.

"To avoid that fee Berkshire could take delivery. But finding a place to store so much silver would not be easy. A 1,000-ounce silver bar (actually about 1,097 ounces since silver is weighted in heavier troy ounces), measures 12.5 inches by 5.5 inches by 3.5 inches. To store all that silver, stacked in a building with nine-foot ceilings, Berkshire would need 2,007 square feet of space. That's a couple of one bedroom apartments."

Berkshire had planned the announcement for its annual report of

March 1998, but because of inquiries by silver traders about silver's rising price, Berkshire let the word out early. Berkshire said it was finished buying and had no plans to sell.

Berkshire bought the silver, which cost about $650 million, because bullion inventories had fallen in recent years —according to Berkshire—and "because of an excess of user-demand over mine production and reclamation." Buffett drew the age-old conclusion: Prices should rise if demand exceeded supply.

Demand for silver in 1997 was about 800 million ounces compared with a supply of about 586 million ounces.

Berkshire's press release said: "Therefore, last summer, Mr. Buffett and Mr. Munger, vice chairman of Berkshire, concluded that equilibrium between supply and demand was only likely to be established by a somewhat higher price."

Buffett wrote in Berkshire's 1997 Annual Report: "Inflation expectations, it should be noted, play no part in our calculation of silver's value."

Although accelerating inflation would probably cause silver's price to rise, the real demand for silver comes mainly from jewelry and silverware manufacturers and from makers of photographic and electronics equipment.

Berkshire bought the glittering, malleable metal for delivery in London through a single brokerage, Phibro, the commodities-trading arm of Travelers Group's Salomon Smith Barney unit.

Berkshire said at no time did it own any options. None of its purchases established new highs—all buying came after price dips, a characteristic Buffett buying habit.

The cost of Berkshire's silver represented less than 2% of its investment portfolio.

Berkshire's stake is the largest accumulation of a silver position since the Hunt brothers were accused of trying to corner the silver market at its peak in 1980. That's when Nelson Bunker Hunt and William Herbert Hunt bought with borrowed money huge volumes of silver contracts—about half the world's supply—sending the price soaring. But their financial empire soon rolled off a cliff when the price of silver collapsed from about $50 an ounce to about $10 an ounce after the Hunts failed to meet margin calls. The Hunt brothers lost about $1 billion.

Although Berkshire's stake was more than the inventory available at exchange warehouses, Berkshire did not try to manipulate the market.

"If any seller should have trouble making timely delivery,

Berkshire is willing to defer for a reasonable period upon payment of a modest fee," Berkshire said.

Buffett said at the Berkshire Annual Meeting in 1998: "We didn't want to buy so much that we disrupted the market. We had no intention of replaying any Hunt scenario."

And Munger noted that the silver stake amounted to only about 2% of Berkshire's capital: "This whole episode will have about as much impact on Berkshire's future as Warren's bridge playing. It is close to a non-event."

Berkshire's press release said Buffett had bought some silver 30 years ago. That was a time when the U.S. Government stopped making silver coins and stopped backing dollar bills with the metal. But Berkshire said, "since that time he [Buffett] has followed silver's fundamentals but no entity he manages has owned it."

Berkshire would be required to report a big stake in a stock, but there's no such rule for silver purchases.

At Berkshire's Annual Meeting in 1998, Buffett said: "You can see from looking at the numbers that aggregate demand, primarily from investor and fundamental type uses, is close to 800 million-plus ounces a year, and there are 500 million or so ounces of silver being produced annually, although there will be more coming on in the next couple years. Most of that silver is produced as a by-product, in the mining for copper, lead or zinc. Since it's a by-product, it's not very responsive to price changes. There's been a gap in recent years of perhaps 150 million ounces, which has been filled by inventory bullion above ground, which may have been a billion or two or more ounces a few years back. There's no question that the bullion inventory has been depleted significantly. Which means that the present price for silver does not produce an equilibrium between supply as measured by newly-mined silver plus reclaimed silver, and uses. And eventually something will happen to change that. I figure it could be reduced usage, increased supply, or change in price. That imbalance is significant, even though there is some production coming on, and some digital imaging that will use silver that is targeted. We think that the gap is wide enough so that it will continue to deplete bullion inventories to the point where a new price is able to establish equilibrium. We don't think that price change will necessarily be minor." (*The Monroe Report*, January 30, 1999)

Buffett did not say in Berkshire's 1998 Annual Report whether he had changed the company's stake in silver, saying only that "we have eliminated certain of the [unconventional] positions discussed last year and added certain others."

For Berkshire, the silver story may still be in its early stages. So let's stay tuned to the flight of Berkshire's silver bullet in the months and years ahead. Will new uses of silver be developed? Will inflation return to drive silver's price upward? Will the environmentalists make it difficult to mine silver or require the use of silver-zinc fuel cells for "zero-emission" cars? Will the Asian economies reignite and reinvigorate demand? Will central bankers buy the precious metal as a hedge against currency turmoil? Will investors worldwide diversify into silver as a store of value? Or, as Buffett, the Oracle of Omaha, simply suggests: will equilibrium between supply and demand be established quite routinely, by a somewhat higher price? Time will tell, but one fact remains.

"Hi-yo, Silver! Awaaaaaaay!"

Munger appeared to confirm that Berkshire has maintained some positon in silver. "It's been a dull ride," he said at Berkshire's annual meeting in 2000 when asked about the silver position.

137

WORLD HEADQUARTERS—
"THE PLAYPEN"

Buffett has dubbed Berkshire's tiny headquarters in mid-town Omaha, "World Headquarters." Mission control (There may be no mission statement, but there is a mission. Ken Monroe kiddingly has reduced it to writing: "Make a profit. Buy a great business. Repeat. Continue forever.") has 3,775 square feet of *leased* space.

The office, also variously described by Buffett as the "Playpen," "The Pleasure Palace," "The Temple," and "The Monolith in 2001," is part of a small set of library-quiet offices on the southeast corner of the 14th floor of modest-sized Kiewit Plaza.

"The whole operation could fit inside less than half a tennis court," says Peter Lynch. (foreword of *The Warren Buffett Way* by Robert Hagstrom)

Michael Assael wonders: "Isn't half a tennis court 39 x 36 = 1,404 square feet? How could all those Cokes he drinks even fit inside the service box?"

Buffett once pointed out the "boardroom" to a visitor, saying of the 7-foot by 10-foot room, "We could change it to a closet if we had to."

For another visitor when the subject of bridge came up, Buffett instantly pulled from his files a 1929 newspaper article reporting the acquittal of a woman who killed her husband over a bridge game argument.

Here at headquarters, exactly 20 blocks from Buffett's house, 12 people run Berkshire. In Berkshire's 1995 Annual Report, Buffett said that although through acquisitions in 1995 Berkshire inherited 11,000 new employees, "Our headquarters staff grew only from 11 to 12. (No sense going crazy.)"

By 1998 he did go crazy and had 12.8 people at headquarters, saying in the annual report, "We have enlarged the staff at world headquarters from 12 to 12.8 (the .8 doesn't refer to me or Charlie: We have a new person in accounting, working four days a week.) Despite this alarming trend toward corporate bloat, our after-tax overhead last year was about $3.5 million, or well under one basis point (0.1of 1%) of the value of the assets we manage."

Kiewit Plaza in midtown Omaha. Berkshire's offices are on the 14th floor. Buffett variously calls it "World Headquarters," "The Temple" and "The Pleasure Palace."

(Photo by Pat Kilpatrick)

The people at headquarters are Buffett; Michael A. Goldberg, who oversees the commercial finance businesses; Marc Hamburg, chief financial officer; Daniel J. Jaksich, controller; Jerry W. Hufton, director of taxes; Mark D. Millard, director of financial assets; Debbie Bosanek, Buffett's administrative assistant; Debbie Ray, receptionist; Kelly Muchemore, an administrative assistant whose duties include responsibility for the annual meeting and whose business card reads: "Director of Chaos"; Kerby Ham and Angie Wells, who are in accounting and Ellen Schmidt who is Marc Hamburg's administrative assistant.

The names, in small type on the outside door to headquarters are Buffett's, Goldberg's, Hamburg's and William Scott's, who still works for Berkshire part-time.

Mrs. Bosanek, known for her efficiency, once slowed Berkshire's operations for a moment by causing Buffett to be put on hold.

She had called a fellow who happened to be speaking to Buffett. The man put Buffett on hold and told his secretary he'd take Mrs. Bosanek's call since he wanted to thank her for help on a business matter.

Buffett and a mortified Mrs. Bosanek figured out quickly that she had caused him to wait. "It was probably the first time he's ever been put on hold," she moaned.

Mrs. Bosanek gets many calls for Buffett, but she puts through only a few. Once an insistent caller said he had to get in touch with Buffett. When Mrs. Bosanek refused, the caller said he'd see to it her next job was at Burger King.

Another time a man called saying he was a good friend of Buffett's and demanded to speak to him. Again, Mrs. Bosanek declined. The caller then said he knew Buffett so well he'd "call him on his car phone." Buffett didn't have a car phone although he did get a cell phone at the turn of the new millennium.

(Photo by Nancy Line Jacobs)

Once a caller wanted to speak to Mrs. Bosanek to ask if she ever actu- *Debbie Bosanek, Berkshire's* ally saw Buffett. He happened to be *administrative assistant, fields* standing at her desk. She looked up *many calls, ranging from important* at him and replied to the caller, "Yes, *to peculiar. She once introduced* sometimes I *do* see him!" *herself at a luncheon saying: "I'm a secretary in a small office."*

Debbie Bosanek, Berkshire's administrative assistant, fields many calls, ranging from important to peculiar. She once introduced herself at a luncheon saying: "I'm a secretary in a small office."

Occasionally Mrs. Bosanek writes on sticky notes inscribed: "God's on vacation and I'm in charge."

One time when Buffett took Mrs. Bosanek and Kelly, her friend from the office, to lunch, all forks in the restaurant seemed to stop in mid-air as people stared at Buffett. "I guess they're looking at Kelly and me," Mrs. Bosanek cracked. She says, "I was at Berkshire before we had a fax and when we used to mail the annual report with stamps."

Speaking of Debbie and Kelly, here's an item from the "Berkshire message board" on America Online (See Chapter 145). A fellow named Tony wrote that he was looking for a possible reinsurance deal and wanted to know which "division" of Berkshire he should call.

Buffett's daughter (online name: "Doshoes") Susan answered that query. "There are no divisions at Berkshire. There are almost no people at Berkshire (that was sort of a joke). Call 402-346-1400 and ask Deb or Kelly the question. They can help you."

If you have a question for Berkshire, you can call and probably get a quick yes or no.

> Debbie and Kelly decided that for Buffett's 67th birthday
> August 30, 1997, they would take him to Gorat's for lunch.
> Buffett marked it on his calendar and then brought the calendar
> for them to sign to confirm that THEY were treating.
>
> At lunch they gave Buffett a made up certificate for a free
> lunch at Gorat's. The certificate carried disclaimers in fine print
> saying it could only be used that day and only with Debbie and
> Kelly. Not to be fooled, Buffett tore out the disclaimers.

Once a woman called Berkshire saying she'd like to have a photo
of Buffett. She was told headquarters didn't have any photos of
Buffett.

A shareholder called once and got Buffett's previous assistant,
Gladys Kaiser. The shareholder asked if Buffett would be interested
in buying a certain brokerage firm. Mrs. Kaiser turned to Buffett
and the caller got his answer from Buffett:

"Thanks, but no thanks."

The world headquarters is the home of Berkshire's investor relations department which, of course, doesn't exist. Buffett was once
asked what kind of investor relations Berkshire would have in the
future. Buffett said: "Our performance."

Near an area where Buffett stashes his Cherry Coke supply is a
sign: "Coca-Cola Sold Here Ice Cold."

Buffett buys his own and brings them from his home to the office
when he runs low.

There are no signs, no logos, nothing really to indicate anything
about Berkshire. Even Berkshire's insurance business in Omaha is in
a nondescript building not far from Kiewit Plaza, which modestly
carries a small sign saying National Indemnity Co. It is through
"NICO" that Buffett makes a great number of his investments.

But the heart of Berkshire lies in Buffett's 325-square-foot office
at Kiewit Plaza. It is here that Buffett reads and works the phone,
staying in touch with his managers, friends and brokers and
responding, usually with short, witty notes, to wave after wave of
mail. He is a fanatic about the mail, reading virtually every piece that
comes to him. He sometimes grabs up the mail even before assistants
can get it to him. When Buffett is out of town, Mrs. Bosanek
overnights him the day's new wave of mail.

Buffett often will dictate quick replies to letters. Here's one to
Tom Keegan of Fairfield, Connecticut, who wrote suggesting that
Buffett look at the possibility of "shorting against the box," some of
Berkshire's stock positions. The technique allows postponement of

taxes on stock sales. Buffett replied December 5, 1995: "Thanks very much for your letter. We've looked at the technique you describe, but there are some serious obstacles. We'll look again to see if these can be overcome."

Here's his response of May 20, 1997 to Linda Humes, of Laguna Beach, California, who wrote him that she enjoyed the annual meeting, had been a GEICO policyholder since she was 17 and loved See's candy. "Dear Linda: Thanks for your nice letter. I'm delighted you could make the Annual Meeting and will accept no excuses in the future. In the meantime, double your input of See's and drive carefully. Sincerely, Warren E. Buffett."

(Photo courtesy of Linda Humes)

Shareholder Linda Humes, of Laguna Beach, California, and Buffett at Berkshire's Annual Meeting in 1998.

A shareholder once wrote that he had bought one of Berkshire's Class A shares for his newborn daughter and that as an owner of the company, he'd be watching Buffett. Buffett replied: "You can be sure that I'll tend to business now that I know you're watching."

Many of the letters are pleas for contributions or help, often with the notation that the writer wouldn't tell anybody if Buffett would give to their cause. Buffett is anguished by each request he refuses. He is sensitive to reporter's requests for interviews which he usually turns down. He asks his assistants: "How did he take it?" To his innumerable requests to speak, he replies with a polite note to the effect: "Too many invitations, too little time." He says, "I spend an inordinate amount of time on the mail."

There are no hovering assistants, no computers; there is no typing pool. There are tan metal filing drawers, almost two hundred of them which contain everything from correspondence with Ben Graham to copies of Buffett's own letters and of course annual reports.

Rare photos of Buffett's office and Berkshire's headquarters show little more than a few remarkably plain chairs, desks, couches, framed documents on the walls. There is an original Thomas Edison stock ticker tape given to him by a friend many years ago. A book-

(Photo by Gail Wyman)

Marc Hamburg is Berkshire's chief financial officer and producer of the Hollywood hit: Berkshire's pre-annual meeting videos.

shelf contains financial volumes, several editions of Graham and Dodd's *Security Analysis,* including a worn copy of the 1934 first edition.

Along the walls are displays of Wall Street memorabilia such as a copy of the *New York Times* from October 31, 1929 bearing the headline, "Stocks Mount An All-day Rally: Rockefeller buying heartens market; Two-day closing ordered to ease strain." And there are headlines about the crash and other Wall Street events.

When Adam Smith interviewed Buffett for a *Money World* show which aired after the annual meeting in 1990, the two men simply sat in small, nondescript chairs just a few feet apart facing one another at Berkshire's headquarters.

But very few people ever get access to Buffett's office. Many of the top managers of Berkshire operating units have never been to headquarters in Omaha. Buffett sees a few people a week, and only very rarely gives interviews.

Buffett's aversion to interviews was documented in a four-page story in *Money* magazine by Gary Belsky, who told of not being able to get an interview with Buffett.

Even after Belsky flew to Omaha, he got the same answer when he called Mrs. Kaiser from the lobby of Kiewit Plaza.

He reported that the guard who heard the phone conversation said: "You took that better than most."

Belsky: "Most? Do people drop by like this a lot?"

Guard: "About once a day."

Belsky: "Does she ever let them up?"

Guard: "Sometimes."

Belsky: "Do you think she'll let me up?"

Guard: "No." *(Money,* August, 1991)

The story was reported in the *Omaha World-Herald* under the headline: "Buffett Ignores Money."

One fellow who did get in to see Buffett is Randall Fairchild, an economics teacher at Florin High School in the Elk Grove School

District, according to the *Sacramento Bee* (July 13, 1998). Fairchild had written a paper about Berkshire for an MBA course at UC Davis School of Management. He thought of writing Buffett to see if he could see him and was told to come June 29 at 4 p.m.

"I sent the letter on a Friday and the following Tuesday I received an e-mail from one of Buffett's assistants telling me that, sure enough, he doesn't give interviews but would like to meet me for three minutes for a photo opportunity...

"They buzzed me into the office and within a few minutes Buffett came out from a hallway with a smile on his face and an open hand to greet me. The two talked for three minutes, had their picture taken holding Buffett's wallet. Then Buffett left."

Buffett's aide told Fairchild, "Buffett sees less than one out of every 1,000 people who write him requesting an audience." (*Sacramento Bee*, July 13, 1998)

Another fellow who got an audience in 1998 was Nike Tour golf leader Joe Ogilvie, a young Duke graduate in economics. He had told the *Omaha World-Herald* in an interview Buffett was one of his heroes. Ogilvie was invited for a visit to headquarters where Buffett showed him the ledger sheet from his first stock transaction. The commission was 10 cents. (*Omaha World-Herald*, August 7, 1998)

With few visitors, Buffett hunkers down over his work, often snacking at his desk. The storeroom is filled with staples of Buffett's phoneside lunches—Hawaiian potato chips, Cherry Cokes and See's candy.

Buffett sticks largely to his favorite diet of hamburgers, chips, and Cokes for lunch and rare steaks and a double order of hash browns for dinner. He likes to snack on Planters peanuts and Häagen-Dazs strawberry ice cream.

Then it's back to his reading and phoning. It is all as simple as simple can be.

In Berkshire's 1996 Annual Report, Buffett wrote: "Our after-tax, headquarter's expense amounts to less than two basis points (1/50th of 1%) measured against our net worth. Even so, Charlie used to think the expense percentage outrageously high, blaming it on my use of Berkshire's corporate jet, *The Indefensible* [then *Indispensable*, now *Executive Jet*]."

Buffett said at the Berkshire Annual Meeting in 1998: "Our after-tax cost of running the operation has gotten down to a half a basis point of capital. In contrast, many mutual funds are at 125 basis points. That means they have 250 times the overhead ratio—overhead relative to capitalization—that we do."

138

THE INDEFENSIBLE/ INDISPENSABLE/NOW EXECUTIVE JET

"IT'S SHAMEFUL HOW MUCH I LOVE IT."

Buffett bought Berkshire's first corporate jet in 1986, and it has been the butt of jokes, mostly from Buffett himself, ever since.

"It's shameful how much I love it...I can't explain it. It's a total blank in my mind. I've given speeches against them for years," he says.

"Occasionally a man must rise above principle," he adds.

And Buffett has written, "I find the thought of retiring the plane more revolting than the thought of retiring the chairman.

"In this matter I've demonstrated uncharacteristic flexibility. For years I argued passionately against corporate jets. But finally my dogma was run over by my karma."

Buffett wrote in Berkshire's 1986 Annual Report: "Whether Berkshire will get its money's worth from the plane is an open question, but I will work at achieving some business triumph that I can (no matter how dubiously) attribute to it." Buffett missed his chance to quote Mae West again: "I generally avoid temptation unless I can't resist it."

The first airplane was a 20-year-old Falcon jet that Buffett picked up for only $850,000. It cost about $200,000 a year to operate. The average cost per hour was $1,500. (*Forbes ASAP*, February 24, 1997) In 1989 he turned it in for a really first-class jet, though again a used one, bought for $6.7 million.

"The old plane had lots of problems," said a worker at Omaha's Eppley Airport. The new one—a Canadair Challenger—was a sleek white jet, seating about 10 people. It was housed at the Sky Harbor facilities at Eppley. It had no insignia—nothing to suggest it belonged to Berkshire.

The pilots for the plane were generally from the Peter Kiewit firm in Omaha. One pilot once told a shareholder that it would be normal for Buffett to greet the pilot, talk briefly to any guest aboard, then "stick his head in an annual report."

Buffett uses the plane often because he travels about 60 days a year, mainly tending to the boards on which he sits. (*Business Week,* August 19, 1991) He's glad to share it with people who have Berkshire business.

If passengers are aboard, Buffett will chat briefly and then read, sometimes going through a large pile of mail. "He'll let us piggyback in the plane," says a Borsheim's employee. "He usually reads." Sometimes Buffett talks to a passenger or two about buying their business.

The plane is the one toy of the rich that Buffett accepts for the convenience it provides.

But Munger has never traveled in the jet, refusing to get in it, kidding Buffett that the thing is a monstrosity against shareholder interests and so he refuses to condone its existence.

Munger, who referred to the plane as *The Aberration*, often travels on commercial coach flights and carries his own bags. He showed up at Borsheim's once carrying his own luggage, one suitcase in each hand. Recently Munger has thrown financial caution to the winds and travels Executive Jet.

Privately Munger has said that if any CEO deserves a jet it is Buffett and that for his needs it makes sense. Berkshire shareholder Ed Prendeville recalls overhearing Munger coming out of an annual meeting in the mid-1980s telling someone, "It's the most deserved jet in corporate America."

But Munger's public stance is that the purchase of the airplane is total extravagance and something with which he is not familiar.

With that much needling from Munger, Buffett threatened to name the aircraft *The Charles T. Munger,* but instead dubbed it *The Indefensible,* then *Indispensable,* now Executive Jet.

In a *Fortune* story November 5, 1990, when Berkshire's stock price had fallen to $5,550 a share from a beginning-of-the-year price of about $8,675, Buffett was asked about *The Indefensible* and quipped, "That'll be the last thing to go."

When the Salomon crisis was at its height and Buffett was constantly using the plane to take him from New York to Omaha and back, he re-christened the aircraft *Somewhat Indefensible.* Could it become *The Indispensable?* It did become *The Indispensable* when Munger declared it so at the 1997 annual meeting. His "counterrevelation" occurred after Berkshire's purchase of FlightSafety.

Nothing could beat the punchline in the 1990 Annual Report: Buffett wrote that if he left the scene, Munger immediately would sell the corporate jet, "ignoring my wish that it be buried with me."

If you've ever wondered what would happen to the companies Berkshire owns, such as Coca-Cola, after Buffett dies, consider this: of Coca-Cola Buffett said—Pharoah-like—"There actually will be a short-term bulge (in Coke sales) as I plan to have a large supply buried with me aboard the plane."

In 1995, in his role as pitchman for Nebraska economic development, Buffett posed for photos in front of *The Indefensible* which said "Until Midwest Express came to Omaha this was the only way I could buy a nonstop."

The ad, promoting Midwest's role in Omaha's economic development, quoted Buffett: "Last month I flew Midwest Express to Washington and arrived just as quickly and comfortably as if I had been in Berkshire's corporate jet. (And believe me, it cost a whole lot less!)"

Although Buffett endorsed Midwest Express service, he indicated he wouldn't give up the corporate jet. "Once spoiled, always spoiled," he said. (*Omaha World-Herald*, June 26, 1995)

Buffett likes the plane so much he's said: "I take it to the drugstore now." (*Wall Street Journal*, September 10, 1997)

In 1999 Buffett sold the corporate jet and started using an Executive Jet, telling *The Financial Times* (February 20, 1999): "I'll save a bundle. I have none of the headaches of training or scheduling pilots or waiting on maintenance checks. This way I just call them up and a plane is there when I want it."

Buffett told *Time* (September 13, 1999) that Executive Jet is one of the few luxuries he has. "I sleep in a bed, you sleep in a bed; I go to McDonald's, you go to McDonald's. For most things in life, being rich just isn't that much of an advantage. The one area where money has made a difference for me is the ability to travel efficiently and do things that would otherwise be impossible."

865

139

CHARLES MUNGER
"THE MAIN RISK WE FACE AS WE SCRABBLE ON IS NOT GOING BROKE BUT GOING CRAZY."

Berkshire Vice Chairman Charles Munger says one of the turning points for Berkshire was this: "See's Candy. It was acquired at a premium over book [value] and it worked. Hochschild, Kohn, the department store chain, was bought at a discount. It didn't work. Those two things together helped shift our thinking to the idea of paying higher prices for better businesses." (Interview, May 21, 1997)

With See's Candy, Buffett and Munger learned the real lesson of pricing power.

See's was purchased for three times its book value, far more than Buffett and Munger usually paid for a business. But See's had a quality product and quality service. See's has given Berkshire excellent returns over the years.

Munger said it also helps when you get high returns on a large amount of capital, as was the case with Berkshire's investments in the Washington Post and Coca-Cola.

"The Post took a fair amount of the capital available to us at the time," he added.

At no time, he said, was there a point when Berkshire might have gone off the tracks. "I knew it would do well, but not this well."

Buffett has said, "Charlie shoved me in the direction of not just buying bargains, as Ben Graham had taught me. This was the real impact he had on me. It took a powerful force to move me on from Graham's limiting views. It was the power of Charlie's mind. He expanded my horizons." (*Forbes*, January 22, 1996)

Buffett has said Munger's impact on him has been "huge." (*Omaha World-Herald*, May 2, 1999)

"Charlie has always emphasized, 'Let's buy truly wonderful businesses,' Buffett has said. I fooled around a little more with cigar butts. Too often I was looking at something that was selling at a big discount from working capital...Charlie knows that game and he felt that's not the direction we should go. He was a significant factor in taking me consistantly away from it." (*Omaha World-Herald*, May 2, 1999)

(Photo by LaVerne Ramsey)

Munger is mobbed by Berkshire shareholders the weekend of the Berkshire Annual Meeting in 1995. To the left of Munger is money manager Jim Armstrong, a member of the Lounge Suits Society, a Munger fan club. Lounge suits were worn by upper class Englishmen, in the old days. Among the members are Gifford Combs of Los Angeles, Steve Wallman of Madison, Wisconsin, Bill Scargle of San Francisco, and Mick Moriarty of Omaha.

Still in recent years they have talked less, but some investors were surprised at Buffett's quote in *Business Week* (July 5, 1999) when he said: "Charlie and I don't talk a lot anymore," adding that he didn't consult Munger on the General Re purchase. The *Business Week* story said: "By all accounts, including their own, Munger and Buffett have not fallen out. But while Buffett is wholly devoted to Berkshire, Munger, 75, now spends his time chairing a not-for-profit hospital and serving as a trustee of a private high school. 'Charlie is broader in his interests than I am,' Buffett says. 'He doesn't have the same intensity for Berkshire that I have. It's not his baby.' Munger concurs: 'Warren's whole ego is poured into Berkshire.' "

Still, Buffett told *Forbes* (October 11, 1999): "Our relationship is the same as it has been for 40 years."

The two, of course, have long seen eye-to-eye on investing, particularly on the subject of doing things as conservatively as possible and keeping the balance sheet all but clear of debt. In the early days, Buffett was obsessed with buying assets as cheaply as possible. He has said it was Munger who emphasized to him over the years the importance of buying high-quality businesses for the long run, even if you have to pay a little more.

Buffett has said of his move away somewhat from Graham's bargain basement tactics: "Ben Graham wanted everything to be a quantitative bargain. I want it to be a quantitative bargain in terms of future streams of cash." (*Forbes*, October 18, 1993)

Munger has addressed the question of strict value investing, as long practiced by Ben Graham, versus paying up a little for a high-quality business.

One of Munger's great assets to Buffett was to influence his thinking about moving away from the cheap stuff and paying up a bit for pricing power, brand names, and quality and durability of the franchise. Munger says: "We're not trying to predict the currents, only how things will swim in the currents."

Munger, who receives no compensation as Wesco's CEO, said at the Wesco Annual Meeting in 1991 that, "The basic concept of value to a private owner and being motivated when you're buying and selling securities by reference to intrinsic value instead of price momentum—I don't think that will ever be outdated. But Ben Graham had blind spots. He had too low an appreciation of the fact that some businesses were worth paying big premiums for."

> In a creditable footnote to one edition of *The Intelligent Investor*, he [Graham] sheepishly said that he'd practiced this one value system for a long time and achieved a very respectable record doing it, but he got rich in a hurry by buying one growth stock investment. It amused him that half or more of his fortune came to him from one investment. [GEICO]
>
> Graham was insufficiently aware of the possibility that a company could prove a great holding for a long time—even when it sold at a large multiple of book value. Look at Coca-Cola stock. It has a very minor book value compared to its current price.
>
> You will notice that we're not following classic Graham and Dodd to the last detail as it was in Ben Graham's mind. Both Warren and I sometimes wonder what would have happened if we'd started out in better businesses instead of trading stamps, aluminum, textile companies—we even had a windmill company at one time. It took us a long time to wise up.

Munger is Buffett's friend, soulmate, sidekick and interchangeable partner. Buffett likes to joke that Munger is his "junior partner in good years and senior partner in bad years."

When reporters can't get Buffett, which is most of the time, they'll sometimes call Munger for an observation of Buffett and he'll say something such as, "He takes his work seriously, but he doesn't take himself seriously."

Munger has vision problems. In fact he lost an eye in the early 1980s and wears uncommonly thick and sturdy black frame glasses. But that doesn't stop him from reading such books as *Fermat's Last Theorem*.

In the early 1970s Munger had a cataract operation which went awry. A damaged optical nerve led to excruciating pain and nausea. He had his left eye removed. "It's no big handicap. I play golf and tennis." Also he reads about a book a day, saying he "skims" a fair amount, too.

Munger is a voracious reader. He reads the *Los Angeles Times*, the *New York Times* and the *Wall Street Journal* by the time he finishes breakfast. Also he reads *Forbes*, *Fortune*, and *Business Week* as well as academic writings. He reads "a ton of biographies" and "a lot of expository stuff." Munger says "I don't know anybody I regard as wise, who lives a full-scale life, who isn't a fairly prodigious reader." (*Omaha World-Herald*, May 2, 1999)

He concedes that Buffett is somewhat more talented than he is. But that does not leave Munger in the dummy department. However, Munger says, "The main risk we face as we scrabble on is not going broke but going crazy." (*Personal History*, Katharine Graham, p. 535)

Unlike Buffett, Munger has sold or given away a few thousand shares of Berkshire stock along the way. He has given a few hundred shares to such entities as Los Angeles' Good Samaritan Hospital, Planned Parenthood, Stanford University Law School and the Harvard-Westlake School. (*Forbes*, January 22, 1996)

"I've tried to imitate, in a poor way, the life of Benjamin Franklin. When he was 42, Franklin quit business to focus more on being a writer, statesman, philanthropist, inventor and scientist. That's why I have diverted my interest away from business." (*Forbes*, January 22, 1996)

Munger, who was raised in the Unitarian Church, now attends an Episcopal church. He says he believes in God "in a sense" and has "embraced the ethos" of his church upbringing but not the "technical theology."

"Do you think (Ben) Franklin cared about such things as whether the body of Christ is really present in the sacrament?" Munger asks. "It didn't interest Franklin and it doesn't interest me." (*Omaha World-Herald*, May 2, 1999)

"Warren and I are a little different in that we actually run businesses and allocate capital to them. [John Maynard Keynes] atoned for his portfolio management 'sins' by making money for his college and serving his nation. I do my outside activities to atone, and Warren uses his investment success to be a great teacher." (*Forbes*, January 22, 1996)

One marvels at Buffett and kindred spirit Munger, a curmudgeon of high standards and temperate habits like Buffett: two oldtimers sitting on the porch taking a shrewd, realistic look at an imperfect world and having a ball trying to figure out how to make the most of it. Buffett and Munger have talked with one another almost daily over the years, although less in recent years as both men's schedules are full. They need each other. Munger says: "Everybody engaged in complicated work needs colleagues. Just the discipline of having to put your thoughts in order with somebody else is a very useful thing." (*Forbes*, January 22, 1996)

Buffett said, "I probably haven't talked to anyone on Wall Street one hundredth of the times I speak to Charlie." (*Forbes*, January 22, 1996)

"There are huge advantages for an individual to get into a position where you make a few great investments and just sit back. You're paying less to brokers. You're listening to less nonsense... If it works, the governmental tax system gives you an extra one, two or three percentage points per annum with compound effects," according to Munger. (*Forbes*, January 22, 1996) That's because with a long-term holding you don't pay the tax collector every year.

In many ways Munger is a great foil for Buffett, especially when the two are at the dais conducting the annual meeting. Once Buffett was talking about trying to keep Berkshire's investments quiet. Buffett: "Unfortunately, we have to file certain reports. And it has lately been our policy to list our year-end holdings which total $100 million [now $750 million] or more in our annual reports. But in between, we don't say much. Charlie?"

Munger: "No comment."

Buffett has called Munger, "The abominable no man." *The Washington Post* (March 22, 1998) has called Munger Buffett's "mordant and cerebral sidekick." Munger also is one of the nation's leading thinkers about investing, education and worldly wisdom. Here's a sample from a talk he gave to a Stanford Law School class. "And when law schools do reach out beyond traditional material, they often do it in what looks to me like a pretty dumb way. If you think psychology is badly taught in America, you should look at corporate finance. Modern portfolio theory?! *It's demented.*" (*Outstanding Investor Digest*, March 13, 1998)

Munger also said in his talk: "Each person has to play the game

Harvard Business School students, Class of '97, with Munger at Berkshire's Annual Meeting in 1997. From left, Elizabeth Prus, Ward Glassmeyer, David Tunnel, Tommy Frist, Munger, Allen Thorpe and Jamie Elias. Apparent case study: Coca-Cola.

given his own marginal utility considerations and in a way that takes into account his own pyschology. If losses are going to make you miserable—and some losses are inevitable—you might be wise to utilize a very conservative pattern of investment and saving all your life. So you have to adapt your strategy to your own nature and your own talents. I don't think there's a one-size-fits-all investment strategy that I can give you.

"Mine works for me. But, in part, that's because I'm good at taking losses. I can take them psychologically. And besides, I have very few. The combination works fine." (*Outstanding Investor Digest*, March 13, 1998)

One student asked if he were fulfilling his responsibility to share his wisdom. Munger: "Sure. Look at Berkshire Hathaway. I call it the ultimate didactic exercise. Warren's never going to spend any money. He's going to give it back to society. He's just building a platform so people will listen to his notions. Needless to say, they are very good notions. And the platform's not so bad either. But you could argue that Warren and I are academics in our own way..." (*Outstanding Investor Digest*, March 13, 1998)

In addition to saying "no comment", Munger also says things like, "Just out of our respective graduate schools, my friend Warren Buffett and I entered the business world to find huge, predictable patterns of extreme irrationality. These irrationalities were obviously important to what we wanted to do, but our professors had never

872

mentioned them. This was not an obvious or easy path...I came to the psychology of human misjudgement almost against my will; I rejected it until I realized that my attitude was costing me a lot of money, and reduced my ability to help everything I loved."

Munger's lecture about worldly wisdom as it relates to investments given to the University of Southern California in 1994 is one of the top investment treatises ever. An example:

> It's not given to human beings to have such talent that they can just know everything all the time. But it is given to human beings who work hard at it—who look and sift the world for a mispriced bet—that they can occasionally find one.
>
> And the wise ones bet keenly when the world offers them that opportunity. They bet big when they have the odds. And the rest of the time, they don't. It's just that simple. (*Outstanding Investor Digest,* May 5, 1995)

Another Mungerism: "Understanding both the power of compound return and the difficulty getting it is the heart and soul of understanding a lot of things." (*Forbes,* January 22, 1996)

Additional Mungerisms:

1. A big difference in a life can occur when "a few ideas are thoroughly assimilated."

2. "Life is a whole series of opportunity costs."

Munger noted at the Berkshire Annual Meeting in 1995 how little corporate America has studied Berkshire, despite its success.

(Photo by Dara Zapata)

Central High School in Omaha which Munger attended

"How much of Berkshire has been copied?...People don't want to do it."

At the annual meeting in 1996, Munger noted: "Berkshire's assets have been lovingly put together so as not to require continuing intelligence at headquarters."

At the 1997 meeting Munger said: "People underrate the importance of a few simple big ideas. And I think to the extent Berkshire Hathaway is a didactic enterprise teaching the right systems of thought, the chief lessons are that a few big ideas really work. I think these filters of ours have worked pretty well—because they are so simple."

At the 1999 meeting he commented about the Internet saying great technological advances for mankind do not necessarily turn out to be great investments. He likened the Internet to railroads, refrigeration, radio, television and air conditioning—marvelous advances but often less attractive as investments.

Munger was educated at public schools in Omaha, including Dundee Elementary School and Central High School where he graduated in 1941 and eventually left Omaha for good. Then he attended the University of Michigan (1941-42) and California Institute of Technology (1943) while he was in the Air Force. Thereafter he served as a meteorological officer in World War II.

Munger was admitted to Harvard Law School in 1946 without an undergraduate degree as part of a program favoring veterans. He was one of 12 students in his Harvard Law School class of 335 who graduated magna cum laude in 1948.

He was admitted to the California Bar in 1949.

He was associated with the law firm of Wright & Garrett which later became Musick, Peeler & Garrett. In 1962 a group of lawyers left to found Munger, Tolles, Hills & Rickershauser, which engaged in corporate matters.

Among the seven founders of the firm were Munger, LeRoy Tolles, Roderick Hills, for a time chairman of the SEC, and his wife, Carla Hills, who became U.S. Trade Representative. Munger is no longer a partner in the firm but maintains his office there.

The Munger, Tolles firm has been described by *The American Lawyer* as Los Angeles's most elite law firm—13 of its 103 lawyers at the time being former U.S. Supreme Court clerks.

The publication ran an article in April 1992, headed, "No leverage. No marketing. Consensus compensation. Disdain for management. How Munger, Tolles is breezing through the recession."

The firm's compensation system was described as:

Every January each partner—there are now 52—gets a ballot listing the names of all the partners with a blank after each name. The firm's net income for the previous year is printed at the bottom. Then each partner fills in the amount of money he or she thinks every partner should make, with no rules other than the numbers must add up to the net. No points, no shares. No seniority, no nothing.

Since the early 1970s, the firm has served as Berkshire's chief counsel. Firm partner Robert Denham had done work off and on for Berkshire since 1974 before serving as Salomon's chairman until it was sold to Travelers.

Denham returned to the firm after his stint at Salomon. He focuses on merger-and-acquisition advice, corporate governance issues and crisis management. (*Los Angeles Times*, June 10, 1997)

The *Times* quoted Denham as saying: "When a good company hits a rock, the task of getting it off the rock is critical. Jobs and lives and shareholders' wealth are tied up in succeeding. It's a high energy, high-pressure job where time has value." He added, "Getting the job done [at Salomon] in nine months instead of a year and a half probably made the difference between the company living and dying."

Denham continues to serve as Buffett's main lawyer. Denham and his wife, Carolyn, live in Pasadena, California. She is president of Pacific Oaks College & Children's School.

Munger has distinguished himself as a lawyer, businessman, investor and educator. His investment record suffers in comparison only with Buffett's.

Munger, the grandson of a federal judge and the son of an Omaha lawyer, was born on January 1, 1924, in Omaha and grew up in a house about 100 yards from Buffett's current home. Munger has said that his family and Buffett's knew each other, but that he and Buffett did not actually meet until 1959, introduced by mutual friends, Dr. and Mrs. Edwin Davis.

Dr. Davis, now deceased, set up the meeting. After Buffett made a call on Davis one night, as he did to many doctors in Omaha in the early days, seeking money for his partnership, Buffett asked Davis why he so quickly decided to invest with him; Davis told him it was because Buffett reminded him so much of Munger.

"I knew everyone in the family except Warren," Munger has said of meeting Buffett. Munger once worked Saturdays in the Buffett & Son grocery store belonging to Buffett's grandfather. The small store furnished both credit and delivery services and yet survived the arrival of supermarkets by many years.

Munger had heard about Buffett, but was not prepared to be particularly impressed. Buffett and Munger spent a dinner in July 1959—at Johnny's Cafe in Omaha—talking about the securities markets. But Munger has said that on meeting Buffett he was instantly impressed, recognizing Buffett's sensational abilities on the spot.

"I wasn't just slightly impressed. I was very impressed," Munger has said. (*The Los Angeles Times*, Linda Grant, April 7, 1991) Buffett and Munger became "mental partners."

In an interview Munger joked that he deserves some credit for spotting the abilities of Buffett even though Buffett lacked the outward appearances of success. "He had a crew cut. He was working out of a sun porch at his house, and his dietary [leanings] were toward Pepsi, salted nuts and no vegetables."

Of their first dinner together, yes, they talked about the markets, but "We talked about a lot of things."

The two became fast friends and Buffett kept telling him that investing was a quicker way to riches than the law. Munger became convinced and established a long, successful investment record himself even while keeping one foot in his law practice. He left his law practice in 1965.

"Somewhere along the line, I decided that I would get rich, not so much for the love of money, but for the love of independence. I liked being able to say what I thought instead of what was expected of

(Photo by Nancy Line Jacobs)

Johnny's Cafe in South Omaha where Buffett and Munger first had dinner together in 1959 and became "mental partners."

me," Munger has said. (*Omaha World-Herald*, May 2, 1999)

Independent of Buffett, from 1962 to 1975 Munger managed Wheeler Munger & Co., an investment firm, from a no-frills office in the Pacific Coast Stock Exchange building. "He earned a highly respectable compound return of 19.8% a year before fees and after expenses." (*Forbes*, January 22, 1996)

So why did Munger switch from law to investing?

"I had a huge family. Nancy and I supported eight children... And I didn't realize that the law was going to get as prosperous as it suddenly got. The big money came into law shortly after I left it. By 1962, I was mostly

(Photo by Nancy Line Jacobs)

Munger and his wife, Nancy, at Berkshire's annual meeting in 1997. Munger's first marriage ended in divorce after eight years. He has been married to Nancy for 44 years.

out. And I was totally out by 1965. So that was a long time ago.

"Also, I preferred making decisions and gambling my own money. I usually thought I knew better than the client anyway, so why should I have to do it his way? So partly, it was having an opinionated personality. And partly, it was a desire to get resources permitting independence.

"Also the bulk of my clients were terrific. But there were one or two I didn't enjoy. Plus I liked the independence of a capitalist. And I always had sort of a gambling personality. I liked figuring things out and making bets. So I simply did what came naturally." (*Outstanding Investor Digest*, March 13, 1998)

Buffett and Munger invested together in the mid-1960s, particularly in Blue Chip Stamps, an issuer of trading stamps originally formed by a consortium of grocery store chains. Munger became a Berkshire officer in 1976 and has been vice chairman since 1978 with the Berkshire-Diversified Retailing merger that year.

Munger became a large Berkshire shareholder in the late 1970s when two of his investments, Diversified Retailing and later Blue

Munger, left, and Buffett—Berkshire's dynamic duo—share a moment in a room above Borsheim's the day before the Berkshire Annual Meeting in 1996.

Chip Stamps, were merged into Berkshire. (*Forbes*, January 22, 1996) Five years later Munger became chairman of Wesco Financial.

Munger continues to live in Los Angeles, where he is also chairman, at no salary, of the Daily Journal Corporation, publisher of the *Los Angeles Daily Journal* for lawyers and other small legal newspapers in California, and other western states. Its 19 newspapers have a total paid circulation of about 35,000. It has 14 newspapers in California and five outside California. The Los Angeles and San Francisco Daily Journals, established in the late 1800s, are the largest newspapers the company publishes with about 12,900, and 6,700 paid subscribers, respectively.

In addition to the newspapers, the company offers on-line information, bankruptcy publications and a magazine, *California Lawyer.*

Daily Journal Corporation occupies a certain niche in the newspaper business. It has about 300 employees, headed by Munger and company president Gerald Salzman and had revenues of $37 million and profits of a little more than $2 million in 1999.

In one annual letter to *Daily Journal* shareholders, Munger put things in his usual succinct way in describing a pre-tax loss of $300,000 at the company's *California Lawyer*, a monthly magazine published in cooperation with the State Bar of California.

"The venture plainly (1) is a contribution to the social order, (2) creates the best style of communications between the State Bar and its members and (3) works well for its advertisers. But its economic effects continue to be unsatisfactory to our company as owner."

Munger controls 34.5% of the shares of the over-the-counter company, which he holds through Munger, Marshall & Co., a California limited partnership of which Munger and his family are the largest owners.

Munger's close friend, J.P. Guerin, and his family own about 16% of the shares.

Neither Munger nor Guerin takes any compensation for work on company matters and Munger admits they underpay company president Gerald Salzman. Munger, every bit as cautious with shareholders' money as Buffett, usually flies coach, although he's upgraded to Executive Jet, carries his own luggage, and sometimes replies to shareholder letters by jotting a note back on the letter. Berkshire-like, it saves a sheet of paper and time.

From the early 1970s to the late 1980s, Munger and Rick Guerin ran the New America Fund, which had a terrific record before it was liquidated.

In 1997 Munger was named to the board of directors of Costco Companies, Inc., the retailing company which operates a large string of membership warehouses from its base near Seattle. Costco was formed by the 1993 merger of Price Company and Costco Wholesale. (Maybe See's is planning to sell in bulk.) "I admire the people and the business for what they've invented in retailing," Munger said in an interview. He said Costco has created a revolution in the distribution of consumer goods. Munger owns 91,884 shares of Costco, according to the 1998 Costco Annual Report.

Munger also owns more than 5% of the preferred issue of Price Enterprises, a real estate firm which leases properties to such tenants as Costco. Price was bought out by Excel Legacy Corp. in late 1999.

A *Forbes* story about Costco (August 11, 1997) said Munger knew about the revolution Costco is creating. "Earlier this year the Berkshire Hathaway vice chairman joined Costco's board, at age 73. It's a rare business commitment outside the investment juggernaut he oversees with Warren Buffett. Munger's introduction to Costco wasn't as an investor but as a customer. A man who appreciates the value of a buck, Munger buys everything from meat and wine to office supplies at the warehouse. He even bought his wristwatch there.

"I admire the place so much that I violated my rules [against sitting on outside boards]," says Munger. "It's hard to think of people who have done more in my lifetime to change the world of retailing for good, for added human happiness for the customer."

"Including Sam Walton?" Munger nods.

"Actually, Munger didn't say 'people,' he said 'two people.' One is James Sinegal, 61, president and chief executive officer of Costco. The other is Sinegal's mentor, San Diego's Sol Price, who invented the warehouse concept with the Price Club chain after first transforming mass discounting with his Fed-Mart stores."

Munger is quick with quips and often comes up with important common sense lessons of his own: "The first chance you have to avoid a loss from a foolish loan is by refusing to make it. There is no second chance." Munger is a staunch Republican, Buffett is a Democrat. Munger likes to fish in lakes and stalk big salmon in Alaskan rivers, while Buffett cares little about fishing. Otherwise, the men agree on almost everything else; Buffett has said that if something got by one of them, it might get by both because their "filters" are similar.

Munger and Buffett work quickly and efficiently and have worked together so long, each knows how the other will view something.

Buffett has said, "Charlie Munger and I can handle a four-page memo over the phone with three grunts." (*The Midas Touch*, John Train, p. 70)

"Charlie and I are interchangeable on business decisions. Distance impedes us not at all; we've always found a telephone to be more productive than a half-day meeting," Train has quoted Buffett as saying.

Buffett also has said, "My idea of a group decision is to look in the mirror."

But if Buffett got beyond making the decision himself over the years, Munger was the first person Buffett consulted. "Charlie says everything I do is dumb. If he says it's really dumb, I know it is, but if he just says it's dumb, I take that as an affirmative vote." (*Fortune*, July 20, 1998)

Buffett told *Forbes* (October 18, 1993) that the three people who most influenced him were his father, Ben Graham and Munger. He said his father, "taught me to do nothing that could not be put on the front page of a newspaper. I have never known a better human than my dad."

Buffett said Graham gave him an intellectual framework for investing and a temperamental model, the ability to stand back and not be influenced by a crowd, not be fearful if stocks go down.

Charlie made me focus on the merits of a great business with tremendously growing earning power, but only when you can be sure of it—not like Texas Instruments or

Polaroid, where the earning power was hypothetical. Charlie doesn't have his ego wrapped up in the business the way I do, but he understands it perfectly. Essentially we have never had an argument, though occasional disagreements.

Munger returned a compliment to Buffett in the same *Forbes* story: "One of the reasons Warren is so cheerful is that he doesn't have to remember his lines." Public and private Buffett are the same.

Munger, who claims such friends as Dr. Nathan Myhrvold, Microsoft's chief technology officer, also told *Forbes*, when it rated his net worth at $365 million in 1993 that he was surprised to be on the 400 richest list. "I've been associated with Warren so long, I thought I'd be just a footnote," adding that his life's goal had been to stay below the cutoff for the list.

At Wesco's Annual Meeting in 1997, Munger said: "The beauty of a great business is that it can stand some ruin." He told the story about a mine which had suffered some mismanagement adding, "If it won't stand some mismanagement, it's no mine."

For classic stock picking, he said that one simply needs to try to find mispriced bets where you conclude, through a multi-disciplined approach, you have an advantage. "I need no more than that."

He said, "We don't worry about the Fed...We're a net buyer of stocks as far ahead as we can see."

He ended by saying, naturally, he wants to buy stocks at good prices. "I never want to pay above intrinsic value for a stock—with very rare exceptions where someone like Warren Buffett is in charge. There are people—very few—worth paying up a bit to get in with for a long term advantage."

A *New York Times* story (June 8, 1997) quoted Blair Sanford, an analyst with Hoefer & Arnett in San Francisco, as saying that Wesco has, "if not the smartest investing mind of the 20th Century, then one of the smartest. Warren is more publicized, but Warren wouldn't be Warren had he not met Charlie Munger."

One wag says:
"Warren, Warren. He's our man.
If he can't do it, Munger can."

ႀ ႀ

Mr. and Mrs. Munger showed up at the Borsheim's party in 1997 without a pass. Berkshire shareholder John Zemanovich of Toronto, Canada, witnessed the small saga. Munger and his wife were at first refused entry. "I overheard this and thought I should help out." Zemanovich said. "I explained [to the attendant]: 'This is Charlie

Munger. He's number 2 around here and Warren's best friend. I think he's ok to let in.'

"She looked over at them, then at me, then back to Charlie and said, 'I think I should let you in.'

"Charlie thanked me and said he 'owed me one.' I told him it's simple, 'Let's do a picture and then we're all square.'"

Berkshire Vice Chairman Charlie Munger and his wife are at first refused admittance to Borsheim's in 1997.

With a little help from John Zemanovich, they are admitted.

The payback. Zemanovich gets his photo opportunity with Munger.
(Photos by Zemanovich's wife, Sharon Sommerhalder)

140

MUNGER

INVESTMENT PRACTICES OF LEADING CHARITABLE INSTITUTIONS

Here's a talk Munger gave to a meeting of the Foundation Financial Officers Group in Santa Monica, California on October 14, 1998:

I am speaking here today because my friend, John Argue, asked me. And John well knew that I, who, unlike many other speakers on your agenda, have nothing to sell any of you, would be irreverent about much current investment practice in large institutions, including charitable foundations. Therefore any hostility my talk will cause should be directed at John Argue who comes from the legal profession and may even enjoy it.

It was long the norm at large charitable foundations to invest mostly in unleveraged, marketable, domestic securities, mostly equities. The equities were selected by one or a very few investment counseling organizations. But in recent years there has been a drift toward more complexity. Some foundations, following the lead of institutions like Yale, have tried to become much better versions of Bernie Cornfeld's "fund of funds." This is an amazing development. Few would have predicted that, long after Cornfeld's fall into disgrace, leading universities would be leading foundations into Cornfeld's system.

Now, in some foundations, there are not few but many investment counselors, chosen by an additional layer of consultants who are hired to decide which investment counselors are best, help in allocating funds to various categories, make sure that foreign securities are not neglected in favor of the domestic securities, check validity of claimed investment records, insure that claimed investment styles are scrupulously followed and help augment an already large diversification in a way that conforms to the latest notions of corporate finance professors about volatility and "beta."

But even with this amazingly active, would-be-polymathic new layer of consultant-choosing consultants, the investment counselors, in picking common stocks, still rely to a considerable extent on a third layer of consultants. The third layer consists of the security

885

analysts employed by investment banks. These security analysts receive enormous salaries, sometimes set in seven figures after bidding wars. The hiring investment banks recoup the salaries from two sources: (1) commissions and trading spreads born by security buyers (some of which are rebated as "soft dollars" to money managers), plus (2) investment banking charges paid by corporations which appreciate the enthusiastic way their securities are being recommended by the security analysts.

There is one thing sure about all this complexity including its touches of behavior lacking the full punctilio of honor. Even when nothing but unleveraged stock-picking is involved, the total cost of all the investment management, plus the frictional costs of fairly often getting in and out of large investment positions, can easily reach 3% of foundation net worth per annum if foundations, urged by consultants, add new activity, year after year. This full cost doesn't show up in conventional accounting. But that is because accounting has limitations and not because the full cost isn't present.

Next, we come to time for a little arithmetic: it is one thing each year to pay the croupiers 3% of starting wealth when the average foundation is enjoying a real return, say, of 17% before the croupiers' take. But it's not written in the stars that foundations will always gain 17% gross, a common result in recent years. And if the average annual gross real return from indexed investment in equities goes back, say, to 5% over some long future period, and the croupiers' take turns out to remain the waste it has always been, even for the average intelligent player, then the average intelligent foundation will be in a prolonged, uncomfortable, shrinking mode. After all, 5% minus 3% minus 5% in donations leaves an annual shrink of 3%.

All the equity investors, in total, will surely bear a performance disadvantage per annum equal to the total croupiers' costs they have jointly elected to bear. This is an inescapable fact of life. And it is also inescapable that exactly half of the investors will get a result below the median result after the croupiers' take, which median result may well be somewhere between unexciting and lousy.

Human nature being what it is, most people assume away worries like those I raise. After all, five centuries before Christ Demosthenes noted that: "What a man wishes, he will believe". And in self appraisals of prospects and talents it is the norm, as Demosthenes predicted, for people to be ridiculously over-optimistic. For instance, a careful survey in Sweden showed that 90% of

886

automobile drivers considered themselves above average. And people who are successfully selling something, as investment counselors do, make Swedish drivers sound like depressives. Virtually every investment expert's public assessment is that he is above average, no matter what is the evidence to the contrary.

But, you may think, my foundation, at least, will be above average. It is well endowed, hires the best, and considers all investment issues at length and with objective professionalism. And to this I respond that excess of what seems like professionalism will often hurt you horribly -- precisely because the careful procedures themselves often lead to an overconfidence in their outcome.

General Motors recently made just such a mistake, and it was a lalapalooza. Using fancy consumer surveys, its excess of professionalism, it concluded not to put a fourth door in a truck designed to serve also as the equivalent of a comfortable five-passenger car. Its competitors, more basic, had actually seen five people enter and exit cars. Moreover they had noticed that people were used to four doors in a comfortable five-passenger car and that biological creatures ordinarily prefer effort minimization in routine activities and don't like removals of long-enjoyed benefits. There are only two words that come instantly to mind in reviewing General Motors' horrible decision, which has blown many hundreds of millions of dollars. And one of those words is: "Oops."

Similarly, the hedge fund known as "Long Term Capital Management" recently collapsed, through over confidence in its highly leveraged methods, despite I.Q.'s of its principals that must have averaged 160. Smart, hard-working people aren't exempted from professional disasters from over confidence. Often, they just go aground in the more difficult voyages they choose, relying on their self-appraisals that they have superior talents and methods.

It is, of course, irritating that extra care in thinking is not all good but also introduces extra error. But most good things have undesired "side effects", and thinking is no exception. The best defense is that of the best physicists, who systematically criticize themselves to an extreme degree, using a mindset described by Nobel laureate Richard Feynman as follows: "The first principle is that you must not fool yourself and you're the easiest person to fool."

But suppose that an abnormally realistic foundation, thinking like Feynman, fears a poor future investment outcome because it is unwilling to assume that its unleveraged equities, after deducting all investment costs, will outperform equity indexes, merely because the foundation has adopted the approach of becoming a "fund of funds," with much investment turnover and layers of consultants that consider themselves above average. What are this fearful foundation's options as it seeks improved prospects?

There are at least three modern choices:

(1) The foundation can both dispense with its consultants and reduce its investment turnover as it changes to indexed investment in equities.

(2) The foundation can follow the example of Berkshire Hathaway, and thus get total annual croupier costs below 1/10 of 1% of principal per annum, by investing with virtually total passivity in a very few much-admired domestic corporations. And there is no reason why some outside advice can't be used in this process. All the fee payor has to do is suitably control the high talents in investment counseling organizations so that the servant becomes the useful tool of its master, instead of serving itself under the perverse incentives of a sort of Mad Hatter's Tea Party.

(3) The foundation can supplement unleveraged investment in marketable equities with investment in limited partnerships that do some combination of the following: unleveraged investment in high-tech corporations in their infancy, leveraged investments in corporate buy-outs; leveraged relative value trades in equities, and leveraged convergence trades and other exotic trades in all kinds of securities and derivatives.

For the obvious reasons given by purveyors of indexed equities, I think choice (1), indexing, is a wiser choice for the average foundation than what it is now doing in unleveraged equity investment. And particularly so as its present total croupier costs exceed 1% of principal per annum. Indexing can't work well forever if almost everybody turns to it. But it will work all right for a long time.

Choice (3), investment in fancy limited partnerships, is largely beyond the scope of this talk. I will only say that the Munger Foundation does not so invest, and briefly mention two considerations bearing on "LBO" (leveraged buy-out) funds.

The first consideration bearing on LBO funds is that buying 100% of corporations with much financial leverage and two layers of promotional carry (one for the management and one for the general partners in the LBO fund) is no sure thing to outperform equity indexes in the future if equity indexes perform poorly in the future. In substance, an LBO fund is a better way of buying equivalents of marketable equities on margin, and the debt could prove disastrous if future marketable equity performance is bad. And particularly so if the bad performance comes from generally bad business conditions.

The second consideration is increasing competition for LBO candidates. For instance, if the LBO candidates are good service corporations, General Electric can now buy more than $10 billion worth per year in GE's Credit Corporation, with 100% debt financing at an interest rate only slightly higher than the U.S. Government is paying. This sort of thing is not ordinary competition, but super-competition. And there are now very many LBO funds, both large and small, mostly awash in money and with the general partners highly incentivized to buy something. In addition there is increased buying competition for corporations other than GE, using some combination of debt and equity.

In short, in the LBO field, there is a buried covariance with marketable equities—toward disaster in generally bad business conditions—and competition is now extreme.

Given time limitation, I can say no more about limited partnerships, one of which I once ran. This leaves for extensive discussion only foundation choice (2), more imitation of the investment practices of Berkshire Hathaway in maintaining marketable equity portfolios with virtually zero turnover and with only a very few stocks chosen. This brings us to the question of how much investment diversification is desirable at foundations.

I have more than skepticism regarding the orthodox view that huge diversification is a must for those wise enough so that indexation is not the logical mode for equity investment. I think the orthodox view is grossly mistaken.

In the United States, a person or institution with almost all wealth invested, long-term, in just three fine domestic corporations is securely rich. And why should such an owner care if at any time most other investors are faring somewhat better or worse. And particularly so when he rationally believes, like Berkshire, that his long term results will be superior by reason of his lower costs, required emphasis on long term effects, and concentration in his most preferred choices.

I go even further. I think it can be a rational choice, in some situations, for a family or a foundation to remain 90% concentrated in one equity. Indeed, I hope the Mungers follow roughly this course. And I note that the Woodruff Foundations have, so far, proven extremely wise to retain an approximately 90% concentration in the founder's Coca-Cola stock. It would be interesting to calculate just how all American foundations would have fared if they had never sold a share of founder's stock. Very many, I think, would now be much better off. But, you may say, the diversifiers simply took out insurance against the catastrophe that didn't occur. And I reply: There are worse things than some foundation's losing relative clout in the world, and rich institutions, like rich individuals, should do a lot of self insurance if they want to maximize long term results.

Furthermore, all the good in the world is not done by foundation donations. Much more good is done through the ordinary business operations of the corporations in which the foundations invest. And some corporations do much more good than others in a way that gives investors therein better than average long-term prospects. And I don't consider it foolish, stupid, evil or illegal for a foundation to greatly concentrate investment in what it admires or even loves. Indeed, Ben Franklin required just such an investment practice for the charitable endowment created by his will.

One other aspect of Berkshire's investment practice deserves comparative mention: So far, there has been almost no direct foreign investment at Berkshire and much foreign investment at foundations.

Regarding this divergent history, I wish to say that I agree with Peter Drucker that the culture and legal systems of the United States are especially favorable to shareholder interests, compared to other interests and compared to most other countries. Indeed, there are many other countries where any good going to public shareholders has a very low priority and almost every other constituency stands higher in line. This factor, I think is underweighed at many investment institutions, probably because it does not easily lead to quantitative thinking using modern financial technique. But some important factor doesn't lose share of force just because some "expert" can better measure other types of force. Generally, I tend to prefer over direct foreign investment Berkshire's practice of participating in foreign economies through the likes of Coca-Cola and Gillette.

To conclude, I will make one controversial prediction and one controversial argument.

The one controversial prediction is that, if some of you make your investment style more like Berkshire Hathaway's, in a long term retrospect you will be unlikely to have cause for regret, even if you can't get Warren Buffett to work for nothing. Instead, Berkshire will have cause for regret as it faces more intelligent investment competition. But Berkshire won't actually regret any disadvantage from your enlightenment. We only want what success we can get despite encouraging others to share our general views about reality.

My controversial argument is an additional consideration weighing against the complex, high-cost investment modalities becoming ever more popular at foundations. Even if, contrary to my suspicions, such modalities should turn out to work pretty well, most of the money-making activity will contain profoundly antisocial effects. This will be so because the activity will exacerbate the current, harmful trend in which ever more of the nation's ethical young brainpower is attracted into lucrative money-management and its attendant modern frictions, as distinguished from work providing much more value to others. Money management does not create the right examples. Early Charlie Munger is a horrible career model for the young, because not enough was delivered to civilization in return for what was wrested from capitalism. And other similar career models are even worse.

Rather than encourage such models, a more constructive choice at foundations is long term investment concentration in a few domestic corporations that are wisely admired.

Why not thus imitate Ben Franklin? After all, old Ben was very effective in doing public good. And he was a pretty good investor, too. Better his model, I think, then Bernie Cornfeld's. The choice is plainly yours to make.

(With permission of Charles Munger)

141
THE CHANNEL CAT

During a 2½-year period, Munger oversaw the building of the largest non-metal passenger catamaran in the world.

The boat was built in Florida by 97 workers in a boat yard set up solely for the purpose of its construction. The catamaran encountered Hurricane Mitch on its maiden voyage to its home waters in Santa Barbara, California, near Munger's home there.

After holding up for the hurricane, it cruised the Caribbean, Gulf of Mexico and the Pacific Ocean finally arriving in the Santa Barbara Channel and being dubbed The Channel Cat.

The boat, which has a bird's eye maple bar and pilot's console, is the dream of Munger and its captain, King Williams, a former professional deep sea diver and fishing charter skipper.

Munger says the catamaran "is not crazy opulent or pretentious. I just regard it as a large motor sailing catamaran." (*Santa Barbara News-Press,* May 15, 1999)

The 83-and-a-half-foot-long, 41-foot-wide, 107-ton sailing vessel looms over nearby yachts and other boats.

The large interior resembling a fancy boardroom has cream leather furniture near picture windows and beneath 10 1/2 foot-high

(Photo by Pat Kilpatrick)

This interior view of the Channel Cat shows a birdseye maple bar to the right and on the left is one of several large TV screens.

893

ceilings. Giant TV screens and audio-visual equipment are among the amenities. A kitchen in one of the hulls can cook a sit-down banquet for about 60 people. The catamaran can carry up to 149 people for events ranging from corporate meetings to weddings.

"The thing is for the next 50 years or so, people will get a lot of harmless pleasure out of using the Channel Cat," Munger has said. Munger hopes the boat will be used for day charters and he intends to let the Santa Barbara Maritime Museum use the boat at times. "I'm a bug on education," Munger told the Santa Barbara paper. Munger and his wife previously contributed $600,000 to build the museum's theater, named in his honor.

142
MUNGER'S ATONEMENT

Munger is a man of wide ranging interests. Beyond investments, his interests include a love of fishing in Alaska and an interest in boats. He has read widely and is fascinated by science. He has traveled extensively and owns five homes.

His own wealth hovers near the $1 billion mark. He gives to local causes and has said he has considerable "guilt about making so much with soft white hands." (*Wall Street Journal*, November 19, 1997) He and his wife, Nancy, each have two children from prior marriages, and four together. The Mungers have a wide net of friends in the highest places in the country.

Five sons are graduates of Harvard-Westlake, a private school in Los Angeles and their three daughters attended Marlborough School in Los Angeles or the Westridge School in Pasadena.

None of the Munger children pursued careers in finance.

Munger follows John Maynard Keynes in believing that money management is a "low calling." For that he has tried to make amends to atone for his sins of being one of the world's best investors, instead of spending his time in a profession with more social utility.

One example of his wide ranging charity and community endeavors has been Harvard-Westlake School in North Hollywood.

Munger and his wife have donated more than $10 million to the school, mostly for The Munger Science Building there.

"The state-of-the-art facility, nestled below Seaver on the hillside overlooking Coldwater Canyon, includes a dozen customized laboratory-classrooms, a conference room, a computer center and a theater-style lecture hall with each of the 110 seats wired to accommodate laptop computers," said a story in a Harvard-Westlake publication (Spring 1995).

"The problem with most buildings is that they don't build enough flexibility into them. We tried to assure that it will work, and work well, for the better part of a century. I see no reason why it should become obsolete," Munger told the publication. "We were already short of science facilities before the merger, and then when we doubled up on the advanced grades, we had an enormous need. It was basically a no-brainer. It would have been educational malpractice not to have improved the science facilities."

Munger was involved in every aspect of the building. Teachers were consulted on every item, large and small. Different benches were designed for biology than for chemistry and physics classrooms.

School officials were quoted as saying that Munger, despite his hands-on efforts, left much of the planning to the teachers, but was vehement about first-rate ventilation and heating and that the building far exceed current earthquake standards.

Munger became a trustee in 1969 and served as chairman of the board of trustees of Harvard School (later joined with Westlake in a merger) from 1974 to 1979. His quarter of a century of service on the board is a record.

Munger told the Harvard-Westlake publication that he regarded the school, where a number of his children went, as "one of the best institutions of its type in the world."

With respect to the Munger Science Center, he added: "The best way to get what you want in life is to deserve what you want, and Harvard-Westlake deserves this building."

Munger's other community interests include serving as trustee and chief financial officer of Planned Parenthood of Los Angeles. In 1969, the California Supreme Court had agreed to hear an appeal from Leon Belous, a doctor convicted of referring a woman to an abortionist. Munger read about the case, called Buffett and the two decided to underwrite the appeal. In September, 1969, Belous won a landmark victory. It was the first time an abortion law had been declared unconstitutional. (*Buffett: The Making of an American Capitalist*, Roger Lowenstein, p. 117)

Munger is chairman of the Hospital of the Good Samaritan in Los Angeles and is head of the Alfred C. Munger Foundation. Munger's father, Alfred C. Munger, a Harvard Law School graduate, was the son of Judge Thomas C. Munger, who served as a federal district judge in Lincoln, Nebraska, from 1907 to 1941. Alfred C. Munger was a lawyer who practiced in Omaha from 1915 to 1959, with time out for service in World War I.

Mrs. Munger has served as a trustee to the Marlborough School and Stanford University. The Mungers have donated a 40 x 80 foot swimming pool and shower changing facility to the YMCA Camp Whittle near Big Bear. Mrs. Munger is a longtime member of the board of the YMCA.

143
LOU SIMPSON
"THAT'S THE FELLA."

In Berkshire's 1995 Annual Report, Buffett indicated that GEICO's Louis A. Simpson is the heir apparent at Berkshire. "His presence on the scene assures us that Berkshire would have an extraordinary professional immediately available to handle its investments if something were to happen to Charlie and me," he wrote.

Simpson, born December 23, 1936, who in the past has represented Berkshire's interests on the boards of National Housing Authority and Bowery Savings Bank and who was on Salomon's board, clearly long has had Buffett's confidence. Simpson is co-CEO of GEICO and responsible for its investments.

He is a director of MediaOne Group Inc., Pacific American Income Shares Inc., LM Institutional Fund Advisors 1, Inc., Potomac Electric Power Company, Science International Corp., and, get this, Direct Stock Market, Inc. (DSM.com), a new Internet marketplace for stock sales.

Simpson is a regent of Loyola Management University, Los Angeles, California, and a member of the endowments committee of Ohio Wesleyan University. He also serves as a trustee for the Cote School, the Univeristy of California, San Diego Foundation and the Woodrow Wilson National Fellowship Foundation.

During the 17 years since Simpson began managing GEICO's assets, they have returned a whopping 24.7% average annual return compared with 17.3% for the S&P stock index. (*The San Diego Union-Tribune*, May 11, 1997)

Simpson gets to know managements of the companies he invests in and, like Buffett, makes long term stock picks. A personal investment of his is a 2.3 million share stake in International Dispensing Corp. whose valves keep food and drinks fresh.

Some of Simpson's picks have been Freddie Mac, Nike, Mattel, Manpower, and Burlington Northern Santa Fe.

Simpson lives in Rancho Santa Fe, California, near San Diego and works out of a small office near there. Simpson's idea of good down time is to go hiking in the rolling hills near his home. Rancho Sante Fe is known as horse country and the Rancho Sante Fe Golf Course is the original site of the Bing Crosby Pro-Am. Simpson earlier had

(Courtesy of GEICO)

Berkshire's heir apparent is GEICO's Lou Simpson

moved from GEICO's base in Washington, D.C. to Los Angeles. He has a vacation retreat in Tucson, Arizona.

Simpson "has the ideal temperament for investing," Buffett told *Institutional Investor* magazine in 1986. "He derives no particular pleasure from operating with or against the crowd. He is comfortable following his own reason."

Buffett said at Berkshire's Annual Meeting in 1996: "Investment decisions at GEICO—which has about $5 billion of marketable securities—have been made, are being made and will be made by Lou Simpson."

Simpson grew up in the Highland Park suburb of Chicago and graduated from Ohio Wesleyan University in 1958. He married Margaret Rowley in 1959 and the couple has three grown sons.

He earned a master's degree in economics from Princeton University in 1960 and was an instructor in economics there briefly. One of his students was Bill Bradley, the New York Knicks' basketball star and former U.S. Senator from New Jersey and presidential candidate in 2000. Then Simpson joined Stein, Roe & Farnham investment firm in Chicago. Afterwards he took a job in 1969 in Los Angeles with Shareholders Management in the go-go days of hot funds. But a bear market hit the funds run by Fred Carr and Carr left a month after Simpson arrived. (*New York Times*, April 29, 1997)

Simpson was the chief executive officer at Western Asset Management, a subsidiary of the Los Angeles-based Western Bancorporation in Los Angeles, managing money. In September, 1979 he received a call to come to work for GEICO as senior vice president and chief investment officer.

"The insurer was searching for a new chief investment officer, and its chairman, John Byrne, Jr., had whittled the list of candidates down to four.

"The finalists would travel to Omaha to meet Buffett, who was reviewing a longstanding interest in GEICO..."

"I sent three of the four to meet Warren," Byrne recalled. "And after a four-hour interview with Lou, he called me and said: "Stop the search. That's the fella." (*New York Times*, April 29, 1997)

"It really isn't even succession planning. It's just that if I were to die tonight the fellow who would handle the investments is Lou." (*San Diego Union-Tribune*, May 11, 1997)

Simpson was picked for three qualities: intellect, character and temperament. "Temperament is what causes smart people not to function well," Buffett said. (*San Diego Union-Tribune*, May 11, 1997)

The paper said Simpson's response to being named Buffett's understudy was predictably low key. A friend said, "He was very modest about it and spoke more about the unlikelihood of it being necessary."

"Katharine Graham, retired publisher of the *Washington Post*, who counts Buffett as a longtime friend and mentor, said she has come to admire Simpson enormously in the more than 15 years she's known him. It's understandable, she said, given the type of selective investing Simpson does, that he would want to maintain a level of anonymity. She noted that when Buffett bought an interest in the *Post* in the early 1970s, 'Warren wasn't well known. Louis is very distinguished in his own way. He's not well known but he will be.' " (*San Diego Union-Tribune*, May 11, 1997)

"Like Buffett, Simpson is a voracious reader of annual reports, newspapers and magazines. Plowing through 15 corporate reports in a row is his idea of a satisfying day." (*San Diego Union-Tribune*, May 11, 1997)

The final decision as to whether Simpson would run Berkshire is left to the board after Buffett's demise.

"Buffett acknowledged in the recent interview that upon his passing, the decision would be in the hands of the board of directors, which he and family members control. He's written ten letters to his family expressing his wishes, he said." (*San Diego Union-Tribune*, May 11, 1997)

The story said Buffett and Simpson talk by telephone at least once or twice a week. They discuss GEICO investments in general. They don't share what each is buying or selling. Given their similar philosophies, however, said Buffett, "We certainly go down the same road."

In Berkshire's 1997 Annual Report, Buffett wrote: "Our reported positions, we should add, sometimes reflect the investment of GEICO's Lou Simpson. Lou independently runs an equity portfolio of nearly $2 billion that may at times overlap the portfolio that I manage, and occasionally he makes moves that differ from mine."

Once a woman proudly told him her three sons had GEICO insurance. "Good," he said. "I hope they keep their cars in the garage."

144
TIGHTWAD
"FEES SPECIFIED FOR EXHIBITS ARE $5.00."

Buffett's view about keeping costs low, paying bills and collecting for bills promptly is not just talk. At Berkshire, it's a reality. Buffett has always said good managers know their costs down to how much goes for postage. And better than knowing the cost of a stamp is finding a way around using one in the first place.

Even a sheet of paper is saved. Write Berkshire a letter and you'll generally get a prompt, business-like response. But you may not get it on a new sheet of paper. You may get your answer in a note at the bottom of your own letter to Berkshire!

Once I wrote Berkshire requesting all the back annual reports and received a reply saying Berkshire didn't have back annual reports beyond a certain year. The odd thing about the response: it was typed at the bottom of my own letter! Berkshire had saved a sheet of paper. Perhaps more importantly, it had saved a bit of time, time being more important than money at Berkshire.

On another occasion, I wrote J. Verne McKenzie, Berkshire's former chief financial officer, requesting a Form 10-K Report with related exhibits. Berkshire's annual report had noted these documents were available for a fee.

McKenzie's response, typed at the bottom of my letter—again Berkshire had saved a sheet of letter paper—follows:

4/23/91

Mr. Kilpatrick:
    Enclosed is Berkshire's Form 10-K for 1990 as you requested including exhibits other than Exhibit 13 which was the Annual Report of which you have already received a copy. Fees specified for exhibits are $5.00. Verne McKenzie.

A multi-billion-dollar firm wanted $5 from me. I wrote a check and it was duly signed by McKenzie who typed on the back, "For deposit to the order of Berkshire Hathaway Inc." and deposited it in the Berkshire account at Norwest Bank in Omaha. It would appear that Berkshire officials subscribe to this old saw: "The two most beautiful words in the English language are 'Check Enclosed.'"

Paul Wolsfeld has his own version of Berkshire's terse communications/save-that-piece-of-paper mentality. Wolsfeld, of La Jolla, California, who cycled across America in search of corporate trivia for a book, hit Omaha in 1987 and made his way to the 14th floor of Kiewit Plaza.

"I got up to the door of Berkshire and there was a camera over the door and a speaker came on asking what I wanted. I asked if Mr. Buffett was in and the speaker said he was out of the country," recalled Wolsfeld.

"Then I asked if I could have an annual report and a hand reached out. That's all I ever saw was half a hand that handed me an annual report. I never even got to say hello," said Wolsfeld.

Wolsfeld later wrote Buffett, asking if he would sponsor his bicycle trip around the country.

"He wrote me back a note saying he was not interested in sponsoring me. He wrote the note at the bottom of the letter I sent him. He saved a piece of paper. So cheap."

The point is Berkshire keeps its costs down. At the Berkshire Annual Meeting in 1998, Buffett said, "In relation to corporate overhead, we are at .05% management fee versus 1.25% for the average equity mutual fund."

145

AD TO BUY BUSINESSES
LOOKING FOR A $5-20 BILLION ELEPHANT
[OR GORILLA]

In the late 1980s, Buffett circulated the following ad:

We want to buy businesses worth $100 million or more before December 31, 1986. If you own such a business, there's a vital reason why you should consider selling.

In 44 days the tax you must pay on the sale of your business may soar to 52½%.

All of us know about the change in the Federal capital gains tax rate from 20% to 28%. In most cases, effective state tax rates on capital gains will also materially increase.

A second tax consideration is less well known, but in many cases looms far more important. Effective January 1, the General Utilities doctrine is repealed. This change can produce the equivalent of a 52½% federal capital gains tax on the sale of a business. Ask your lawyer, accountant or investment banker how it will affect your situation.

The change in the General Utilities doctrine will not apply to transactions completed by December 31. Other things being equal, you will net dramatically more money if you close a sale by that date than if you delay.

Berkshire Hathaway will have no problem in completing a transaction by the December 31 deadline. We have the money, and we can act with extraordinary speed. Most of the purchases we have made have been agreed to after one meeting with the owners. If you phone us with a general description of your business and tell us the sort of transaction you are seeking, we can immediately tell you whether we have an interest. And if we do, we will proceed instantly.

Here's what we are looking for:
1. Large purchases (at least $10 million of after-tax earnings, and preferably much more). (Now it's $50 million pre-tax)
2. Demonstrated consistent earning power (future projections

are of little interest to us, nor are "turn-around" situations).

3. Businesses earning good returns on equity while employing little or no debt.

4. Management in place (we can't supply it).

5. Simple businesses (if there's lots of technology, we won't understand it).

6. An offering price (we don't want to waste our time or that of the seller by talking, even preliminarily, about a transaction when price is unknown).

These criteria are firm so we would appreciate hearing only from owners whose businesses fully meet them.

We invite potential sellers to check us out by contacting anyone with whom we have done business in the past. You'll find we are unusual: we buy to keep (no periodic "restructuring" convulsions); we leave subsidiary managements alone to operate in the future as they have in the past; and our own ownership and management structure is predictable for decades to come.

If you are interested, call me at 402-346-1400. Or, if you like, first call Mrs. Kaiser at the same number to request express delivery of Berkshire Hathaway's current annual report. Your inquiry will be totally confidential; we use no staff, and we don't need to discuss your company with consultants, investment bankers, commercial bankers, etc. You will deal only with Charles Munger, Vice Chairman of Berkshire, and with me.

If you have any possible interest, call promptly. Otherwise a 20% tax will become 28% to 52½%.

Warren E. Buffett

Although nothing came of the $47,000 ad, Buffett personally took at least 100 telephone calls.

One caller who wanted to see if Buffett was interested was a native of Pakistan who wished to sell him a newsstand in New York for $185,000. That one didn't meet Buffett's test on size.

Another caller, from Jackson, Mississippi, wanted to sell her antebellum mansion. Buffett turned that one down politely, but quickly. (*Omaha World-Herald*, December 3, 1986)

Other callers offered farms or small-town businesses. Buffett later told his hometown newspaper that the last strong prospect came in on December 20, 1986, from a potential seller in the eastern United States.

Buffett said the business met all the requirements, such as earning

$10 million a year after tax and possessing in-place management. And the price was right. "But it was a business we didn't want to be in," he said, declining to say what kind of business it was. "If you run an ad for a chihuahua, you get a lot of collie replies," and "We're looking for 747s, not model airplanes," he has said.

The ad worked in the sense that the next time people would be more aware of what Berkshire wanted and would be more likely to think of Berkshire.

Also in 1986, Berkshire ran a different ad, published three times in *Business Insurance* magazine, titled, "Berkshire Hathaway wants to see property/casualty risks where the premium is $1 million or more."

As a result of the ads, which cost a total of $20,000, Berkshire's insurance subsidiaries generated new business that produced more than $100 million a year in premiums.

At the Berkshire Annual Meeting in 1993, Buffett granted a brief interview to Linda O'Bryon of *Nightly Business Report.*

One of her questions had to do with whether he was still trying to buy businesses and he said, yes, he was always looking for new businesses to buy.

Then he sneaked in an ad saying if anyone out in television land had a $2 billion to $3 billion business to sell him, to call him collect.

Here's Buffett's later ad. He's looking for an elephant [That's a head fake from Buffett. We know he's looking for a gorilla.] of an acquisition in the $3-5 billion range. Berkshire's 1997 Annual Report said: "The larger the company, the greater will be our interest: We would like to make an acquisition in the $5-10 billion range."

Now it's in the $5-20 billion range.

"If you name almost any big company in the U.S., I can tell you in five seconds whether or not it is within my circle of competence, and if it is I've probably got some sort of fix on it.

"There are probably hundreds of companies in a category and if I got a call from any one of them today, I could tell them whether I was interested or not as soon as the fellow identified himself." (*Financial Times*, May 17, 1999)

146
HIS PERSONAL PORTFOLIO
BUFFETT IS RICHER THAN YOU THINK

In addition to his more than 40% ownership of Berkshire, Buffett also has some smaller but substantial holdings in his personal portfolio.

Lord only knows what the best investor of our time has tucked away in his personal portfolio over the years. Information is skimpy.

In his Buffett Partnership letter of January 25, 1967, Buffett said his investment in the partnership represented more than 90% of his family's worth, so clearly his major personal investment all along has been his stake in the partnership and later in Berkshire stock.

In 1967, Buffett said that most of his money was in the partnership, excluding an investment in Data Documents stock. Buffett told reporter Jonathan Laing for a March 31, 1977, story in the *Wall Street Journal* that his personal portfolio of stockholdings was worth $30 million, but much of that $30 million included Diversified Retailing and Blue Chip Stamps which later became part of Berkshire. So, as he now says, almost all his fortune [99%] is in Berkshire. (In a March 2, 1999 interview with "Nightline" anchor Ted Koppel, Buffett said 99.75% of his net worth was in Berkshire.)

In late 1986, Buffett invested about $38 million in the stock of Illinois's ServiceMaster for his personal portfolio. ServiceMaster cleans hospitals and provides laundry, food preparation and maid services for hospitals, office buildings, colleges and factories.

ServiceMaster runs a variety of cleaning businesses, and the company operates on Christian principles. The name means Service to the Master. There were subsequent reports that Buffett was selling the stake, and ServiceMaster officials have said he is out of the stock.

That investment came to light because Buffett bought slightly more than 5% of ServiceMaster stock, making it a public transaction; when confusion arose as to whether Berkshire bought the stock, Buffett told shareholders the purchase had been made for his personal portfolio, not for Berkshire.

When some shareholders said they wished he had bought ServiceMaster for Berkshire, he explained that the investment, because of tax reasons, was better suited for personal accounts.

Over the years reports of small personal investments, one in

FirsTier Bank in Omaha, another one in Nebraska's sole minority-owned bank, the small Community Bank of Nebraska, and a little investment in the Omaha Royals, have come to light. It's safe to say Buffett is not standing idly by as his own investor, although by all accounts the huge majority of his investment thinking is devoted to Berkshire.

On April 15, 1996, Property Capital Trust, a real estate investment trust in Boston, Massachusetts, said Buffett had bought a 6.7% stake in the company, or 610,800 shares which were trading at about $9 a share. Property Capital Trust planned to sell its real estate investments over the next several years. Reports in 1997 said Buffett bought more shares for his own account bringing his total to 831,600 shares, or 8.9% of the company.

A report October 24, 1998 said Buffett had bought a 5.1% stake, or 700,000 shares, in MGI Properties, another real estate trust in Boston. A report February 17, 1999 said he had raised the stake to 1,141,300 shares, or 8.3% of the company and by April 1, 1999 Buffett held 1.42 million shares, or 10.3% of the company. He raised his stake another 264,000 shares in May, 1999.

MGI planned in June 1998 to liquidate its holdings because the value of its stock was less than the value of its properties.

Reports of April 10, 1999 showed that Buffett personally had bought 417,100 shares, or a 5.3% stake in Greensboro, North Carolina-based Tanger Factory Outlet Centers, the nation's largest factory outlet center owner. Reports in 2000 showed he had raised the stake to 13.5%.

Reports a few days later showed another personal investment in REITs. Buffett owned 797,200 shares of Town & Country Trust, or 5.1% of the REIT based in Baltimore, Maryland—a stake listed in 2000 at 6.7%.

Buffett bought 5.3% (later reduced to 5.2%) or 2.06 million shares of Baker, Fentress & Co. common stock, according to an SEC filing in August 2, 1999. Baker Fentress, of Chicago, Illinois is a non-diversified, closed-end mutual fund investing mainly in stocks, but was planning to sell its securities. Baker Fentress owns nearly 80% of Consolidated-Tomoka Land Co., which owns about 16,000 acres of prime real estate in the Daytona Beach, Florida, area. (*Orlando Sentinel*, August 11, 1999)

In September, 1999, filings showed that Buffett owned 362,729 shares, or 5.7% of Consolidated-Tomoka.

Apparently with the Baker Fentress investment Buffett was making an arbitrage play to capture the difference between the fund's share price and the value of the portfolio after liquidation and return of the proceeds to the shareholders.

As for the REIT investments and the Baker Fentress outing, Buffett appeared to be playing liquidation, not long-term investing.

Reports on December 13, 1999 said Buffett owned a 5.3% stake, or 506,000 shares of Bell Industries, of El Segundo, California. The company, a provider of computer stock services, had said it was open to offers to be bought out.

Buffett told Bell officials in early 2000 he had sold his Bell stock. (*Wall Street Journal*, January 18, 2000)

By March 24, 2000 Buffett had established a 5.05% stake in Aegis Realty, Inc. a New York-based real estate company that invests in neighborhood shopping centers. A short time later a 5% stake was revealed in JDN Realty, an Atlanta-based REIT. He also bought a 5.1% stake in PMC Capital which provides loans to businesses.

The fate of Buffett's personal portfolio is an intriguing question. Something good will come of it. Asked about the fate of his personal portfolio at the annual meeting in 1991, Buffett gave it little recognition, saying his real stake is in Berkshire and that in any case almost all his money will ultimately be returned to society.

"My personal portfolio is Berkshire," he said.

In 1996 he said almost all of his money is in just one stock: Berkshire.

In an "Owner's Manual" to shareholders in June 1996, he wrote: "Charlie's family has 90% or more of its net worth in Berkshire shares; my wife, Susie, and I have more than 99%. In addition many of my relatives—my sisters and cousins for example—keep a huge portion of their net worth in Berkshire stock."

147

THE OMAHA GOLDEN SPIKES
"GRAVITATIONAL WAVES"

In 1991 Buffett and Walter Scott, Peter Kiewit Sons' chairman and Berkshire board member, stepped in to buy a stake in the Omaha Royals, later the Omaha Golden Spikes, a minor league baseball team, when a deal with the previous buyer fell through.

The switch occurred when Philadelphia real estate developer Craig Stein backed out of an ownership plan because he couldn't live with a requirement that gave Union Pacific veto power over any plan to move the franchise from Omaha.

Union Pacific railroad had announced that it would buy 49% of the Omaha AAA franchise with Stein, but when he backed out, Buffett and Scott came to the rescue with $1.25 million each. Union Pacific contributed $2.5 million and the deal was done.

Buffett, a longtime baseball fan, told the *Omaha World-Herald* that he and Scott would sell shares priced at $100,000 of their ownership to interested investors. For Buffett, this was a quick fix to save the local baseball team, not a long-term investment that would add to his billions. Yet Buffett remains one owner of the team.

The franchise, a farm team for the Kansas City Royals, might well have been lost had Buffett not stepped in with what was an act of good citizenship rather than the act of an opportunistic investor.

The hasty announcement was made in the office of Omaha Mayor P. J. Morgan, who said he was surprised to learn that Buffett hadn't visited the mayor's office before then. Buffett replied, "At a million and a quarter a pop, I can't afford it."

Once Buffett asked a lady, Betty Davis, on the elevator at Omaha's City-County Building, "Do you know what floor the mayor's office is on?"

"Third floor," she said.

Buffett thanked her and punched the button.

"I have a favor to ask you," Ms. Davis said. "Do you mind if I tell people I told Warren Buffett where to get off?"

"Not at all," Buffett said, adding, "People are always telling me where to get off." (Robert McMorris, *Omaha World-Herald*, November 25, 1992)

Buffett invited shareholders in 1994 to come to an Omaha

911

Buffett, co-owner of the Omaha Golden Spikes but no threat to Nolan Ryan, winds up for a pitch at Omaha's Rosenblatt Stadium. Right-hander Buffett called his pitch a "humiliating performance...I barely missed my foot."

(Omaha World-Herald)

(Photo by Nancy Line Jacobs)

Mrs. Susan Buffett; their grandson, Howie; Warren "The Whip" Buffett and their granddaughter, Megan, at Omaha Golden Spikes game in 1994. The fistful of dollars insignia on Buffett's shirt is the closest thing Berkshire has to a logo.

(Photo by Nancy Line Jacobs)

The Gloved One threw a perfect strike at an Omaha Golden Spikes game in 1994. Buffett, and the cheering crowd, were shocked.

Golden Spikes game where he planned to throw out the first pitch. He assured folks he would better his "humiliating performance" of last year when "I barely missed my foot."

Buffett walked to the mound, shook off the catcher's sign, wound up and threw a strike! The crowd cheered. The most surprised person was Buffett. The announcer declared the pitch a strike by Warren "The Whip" Buffett, but said it was timed at only eight miles per hour adding, "You'd better keep your day job."

In the 1994 Annual Report, Buffett said, "Opening the game that night, I had my stuff and threw a strike that the scoreboard reported at eight miles per hour. What many fans missed was that I shook off the catcher's call for my fast ball and instead delivered my change-up. This year it will be all smoke."

In 1996 his pitch bounced off the plate. Buffett passed it off as "a premature sinker, but it was hard to hit." (*Omaha World-Herald*, August 16, 1996)

Buffett wrote in Berkshire's 1996 Annual Report: "Though Rosenblatt is normal in appearance, it is anything but: The field sits on a unique geological structure that occasionally emits short gravitational waves causing even the most smoothly-delivered pitch to sink violently. I have been the victim of this weird phenomenon several times in the past but am hoping for benign conditions this year."

After his pitch (low and inside) in 1997, Buffett—decked out in his Royals warm-up jacket—said, "I keep waiting for the year they let me pitch the whole game."

913

After the pitch, Buffett sits in the stands signing T-shirts, programs, $1 bills—anything. One shareholder, Wayne Elmer of New London, Wisconsin, pressed a $100 bill at Buffett and asked, "Will you sign my $100?" Replied Buffett, "I wouldn't sign anything else." (*Money*, July, 1997)

Marvel at the Majestic Arc of my Breaking Ball

In Berkshire's 1997 Annual Report, Buffett wrote: "As usual, your Chairman, shamelessly exploiting his 25% ownership of the team, will take the mound. But this year you will see something new.

"In the past games, much to the bafflement of the crowd, I have shaken off the catcher's first call. He has consistently asked for my sweeping curve, and I have just as regularly resisted. Instead, I have served up a pathetic fast ball, which on my best day was clocked at eight miles per hour (with a following wind).

"There's a story behind my unwillingness to throw the curve ball. As some of you may know, Candy Cummings invented the curve in 1867 and used it to great effect in the National Association, where he never won less than 28 games in a season. The pitch, however, drew immediate criticism from the very highest of authorities, namely Charles Elliott, then president of Harvard University, who declared, 'I have heard that this year we at Harvard won the baseball championship because we have a pitcher who has a fine curve ball. I am further instructed that the purpose of the curve ball is to deliberately deceive the batter. Harvard is not in the business of teaching deception.' (I'm not making this up.)

"Ever since I learned of President Elliott's moral teachings on this subject, I have scrupulously refrained from using my curve, however devastating its effect might have been on hapless batters. Now, however, it is time for my karma to run over Elliott's dogma and for me to quit holding back. Visit the park on Saturday night and marvel at the majestic arc of my breaking ball."

In Berkshire's 1998 Report, Buffett wrote: "It's a real source of irritation to me that many view our annual meeting as a financial event rather than the sports classic I consider it to be. Once the world sees my flutterball, that misperception will be erased."

Steve Pettise, who heads Golden Spikes Resources Group, a marketing firm in Los Angeles, once wrote Buffett a kidding letter that he deserved to be paid off since Buffett's baseball team had taken the name Golden Spikes.

Buffett replied: "Thanks for your threatening note. I would propose as a royalty that we pay you 100% of the profits of the team. In fact, I think I can safely make that 200% of the profits. This would be far cheaper than a 1% royalty based on sales.

Come to the meeting and check out my flutterball. Sincerely, Warren a.k.a. 'The Whip.' "

Buffett tossed his game-opening pitch in 1999 to Hall of Fame player Ernie Banks. Beforehand, Buffett said: "We will face off in what I regard as an extraordinary act of courage on his part," indicating that Banks should be ready to duck.

Banks hit 512 home runs during his 18 seasons with the Chicago Cubs from 1953-1971. Buffett added: "I expect a big crowd in the left-field bleachers." (*Associated Press*, April 24, 1999)

In Berkshire's 1999 Annual Report, Buffett wrote:

"Those who attended last year saw your Chairman pitch to Ernie Banks.

"This encounter proved to be the titanic duel that the sports world had long awaited. After the first few pitches -- which were not my best, but when have I ever thrown my best? -- I fired a brushback at Ernie just to let him know who was in command. Ernie charged the mound, and I charged the plate. But a clash was avoided because we became exhausted before reaching each other...

"I should add that I have extracted a promise from Ernie that he will not hit a 'come-backer' at me since I would never be able to duck in time to avoid it. My reflexes are like Woody Allen's, who said his were so slow that he was once hit by a car being pushed by two guys."

Buffett sent this letter to Seth Swirsky for his book *Every Pitcher Tells a Story* (p. 27):

BERKSHIRE HATHAWAY INC.
1440 KIEWIT PLAZA
OMAHA, NEBRASKA 68131
TELEPHONE (402) 346-1400

WARREN E. BUFFETT, CHAIRMAN

August 26, 1997

Mr. Seth Swirsky
November Nights Music Inc.

Dear Seth:

Thanks for your note. I'm enclosing a copy of Berkshire's 1994 Annual Report where on page five I analogize between our business and investment style and the approach of Ted Williams to hitting.

A few weeks ago, I watched Tony Gwynn and Ted on The Classic Sports Network where he talked of his book, *The Science of Hitting*. I then obtained a copy, which had a diagram prepared by Ted showing what his batting average would be if he swung at balls in various parts of the strike zone. If he waited for a pitch in his "happy zone," he was a .400 hitter; if he swung at one in the lower outside section of the strike zone, his average would be more like .260. This "wait for the fat one" approach is right on the money in terms of making investment decisions, and I may write more about it in next year's report.

A major advantage in investing, however, is that there is no such thing as a called strike. In money-management, the crowd can be screaming "Swing you bum," but even if the pitch is right down the middle, you can wait all day for one that is just a fraction more to your liking. Only if you swing and miss an "investing pitch" is there a penalty. This "no-called strike" aspect to investing is a huge advantage for the patient investor.

Best regards.

Sincerely,

Warren E. Buffett

WEB/db
Enclosures

(With permission of Seth Swirsky)

148

BERKSHIRE'S INTRINSIC VALUE
"RUN NAKED THROUGH THE MONEY."

So-o-o, what's Berkshire really worth?

Well, that's a tricky one because Berkshire isn't the easiest company in the world to pigeonhole with a pricetag. Let's look at some of the methods over recent history, used by clowns as often as financial analysts.

Here's how Beemer, the clown/magician who entertained at the 4th birthday party of Buffett's granddaughter, might have done it at yearend 1991: Step 1. Calculate Berkshire's average investee P/E ratio. Let's call it 20. Step 2. Multiply 20 by the average of the last two years' look-through earnings of $487.50 per share. Poof! Berkshire's stock price should have been $9,750 at yearend 1991 when it was selling at $9,050.

Beemer has now developed a simpler method, the Beemer II Method, so Buffett followers won't have to make but one calculation. Consider 1993. Take the look-through earnings per share ($740 in 1993) and multiply by the growth rate of Berkshire's book value since present management took over (23%) and the worth of Berkshire at yearend is $17,020! The actual yearend close was $16,325.

The calculation for 1994 comes out to about $21,400 when Berkshire was trading at $20,400.

Buffett didn't give look-through earnings in the 1995 annual report because there were so many major yearend changes at Berkshire, but promised them for 1996.

In 1996, look-through earnings of Berkshire and its major investees (including Coke, Gillette, etc.) as given by Buffett were $1,522,000,000. But in 1996 Berkshire also had roughly $3.3 billion in stock it owned in smaller holdings—let's call them *minor* investees—which probably added very roughly another $200 million to look-through earnings.

Add it up, and this brought Berkshire's total look-through earnings to more than $1.7 billion, or look-through earnings per share

Buffett before Berkshire's Annual Meeting in 1994. What is this brainpan worth? Inquiring investors want to know.

somewhere in the $1,400 neighborhood. Accordingly, at the 1996 year-end price of $34,100, Berkshire's price to look-through earnings ratio was about 25.

In 1997 look-through earnings of the *major* investees were $1,930,000,000. But at yearend 1997 Berkshire also had roughly $4.5 billion in stocks it owned in *minor* investees—which probably added very roughly another $225 million to look-through earnings. This brings estimated total look-through earnings to about $2.1 billion dollars, or look-through earnings per share in the $1,700 range. Accordingly, at a yearend price of $46,000, Berkshire's price to look-through earnings ratio was about 29.

Berkshire's 1997 look-through earnings per share of about $1,700 times Berkshire's growth rate in book value (now 24%) equals $40,800 compared to a closing yearend stock price of $46,000.

A lot has happened to Berkshire's book value and stock price since then; General Re was acquired as were a host of other businesses and in the 1998 Annual Report Buffett took a year off from presenting his usual table setting forth look-through earnings. Although author Roger Lowenstein, in a story for the May, 1998, issue of *SmartMoney* put Berkshire's intrinsic value at $53,000 a share, others were saying Berkshire's intrinsic value was solidly in the $60,000-$70,000 range.

But look-through earnings were back again in Berkshire's 1999 Annual Report. Total look-through earnings as presented by Buffett were $1,926,000,000, which included earnings of Berkshire's major investees and operating businesses. At yearend 1999, though, Berkshire had more than $6 billion in stocks it owned in minor investees which probably added very roughly another $300 million to look-through earnings. This would bring estimated total look-through earnings per share to about $1,450 based upon the average number of common shares outstanding which was 1,519,703 for the fiscal year 1999. Accordingly, at a yearend price of $56,100, Berkshire's price to look-through earnings ratio was about 39, about a 20% premium to the price earnings ratio of the S&P 500.

The theoretical way to figure a stock's intrinsic value is by using the John Burr Williams' method—discounting future cash flows—but it's tough to do it accurately because there are too many variables and uncertainties in real life. It all depends on future competitive positions, future demand for a company's products, future prices and costs etc.—things that are hard to quantify until after the fact. It's very vague. Inspector Clouseau couldn't come anywhere close with certainty and most of us would find ourselves in the same boat.

Some say a no-brainer way to get at Berkshire's intrinsic value is simply to take the total assets shown on the balance sheet with no adjustments per share.

By ignoring float and heavily discounting the deferred tax liability, the liabilities left over roughly correspond to the "asset" value of the future float growth.

So here goes, as of December 31, 1996: with assets of about $43.4 billion and about 1.2 million shares outstanding, Berkshire's per share intrinsic value may have been about $36,000. By the end of 1997, Berkshire's assets were about $56 billion.

Another simple route to Berkshire's intrinsic value is to multiply 2 x Berkshire's book value = 2 x about $19,000 a share at yearend 1996 = $38,000 a share. 2 x $25,488—the 1997 book value per share—is $50,976, compared to the closing 1997 stock price of $46,000.

Back in 1996 Buffett had said he and Munger wouldn't buy Berkshire at $36,000. The stock took a big hit, dropping $2,150 the day of that news in March 1996. And the stock then languished all that year in a case of "irrational exuberance" leading to disappointment.

The *San Diego Business Journal* (July 15, 1996) looking at Berkshire as a closed-end mutual fund concluded Berkshire was only worth about $15,000. "So, in my opinion, you gotta be dumber than a bag of ball-peen hammers to pay a $21,000 premium over NAV to own BRKA," wrote columnist Malcolm Baker. (*Warren Buffett Speaks*, Janet Lowe, p. 140)

In 1997 Buffett wrote: "In last year's letter, with Berkshire shares selling at $36,000, I told you: (1) Berkshire's gain in market value in recent years had outstripped its gain in intrinsic value, even though the gain had been highly satisfactory; (2) that kind of performance could not continue indefinitely; (3) Charlie and I did not at that moment consider Berkshire to be undervalued.

"Since I set down those cautions, Berkshire's intrinsic value has increased very significantly—aided in a major way by a stunning performance at GEICO... while the market price of our shares has changed little. This, of course, means in 1996 Berkshire's stock underperformed the business. Consequently, today's price/value relationship is both much different from what it was a year ago and, as Charlie and I see it, more appropriate." In Buffett speak, that's probably a buy.

In Berkshire's "Owner's Manual" in June, 1996, Buffett wrote: "In 1992, our look-through earnings were $604 million, and in that same year we set a goal of raising them by an average of 15% per annum to $1.8 billion in the year 2000. Since that time, however, we have issued additional shares—including the B shares sold recently—so that we now need look-through earnings of $1.9 billion in 2000 to match the per-share goal we originally were shooting for. This is a tough target but one we still hope to hit."

Shareholders and Wall Streeters often take stabs at Berkshire's intrinsic worth, and always the question is posed to Buffett at annual meetings (after all, father should know best). But usually he sidesteps the valuation question by explaining that he doesn't want to "spoil the fun" for shareholders who want to figure it out themselves.

Some say it's not unreasonable if Berkshire were to trade at twice its book value. So if Berkshire had a book value of $18,000 a share at the end of 1996 the price could have been $36,000, but it ended the year at $34,100.

By the end of 1996 the Berkshire rocket scientists running numbers were coming in at no lower than $30,000 and no higher than $40,000 a share.

Buyers and sellers generally have put a pretty fair value price on Berkshire stock. Buffett has said that he wants Berkshire to trade near its intrinsic value, or real business value in the real world, rather than at some inflated or depressed level.

And he adds that reasonable businessmen might value Berkshire 10% higher or lower than its intrinsic worth, that he and Munger might differ by 10% about Berkshire's intrinsic value.

It's doubtful that even Buffett carries around in his head a precise figure for Berkshire's worth, although everyone would like to know his 10% range. Sometimes Buffett takes this tack: "Well, add it all up and then subtract something because I'm running it."

Anyone can see you should tally it up and add something for Buffett's gray matter.

Speaking of addition and subtraction, some people write up Berkshire and after adding it all up they SUBTRACT a huge number because Berkshire owns big stakes in Coke and Gillette.

Presumably the argument is that the Coke and Gillette P/Es are too high.

A unique reason for not buying Berkshire has been offered by *Forbes* columnist Martin Sosnoff who has on several occasions written that Berkshire's glory days are on the wane.

In a piece January 27, 1997, he suggested he would not buy Berkshire because Congress is unlikely to cut the capital gains tax rate.

Occasionally Buffett offers little nudges when the price gets out of whack. After the stock soared to more than $3,000 a share following the excitement over Berkshire's stake in Cap Cities in 1986, he indicated the stock price was too high.

And there were signs he thought Berkshire's stock price too high in late 1989 when it soared to $8,900. That's when he issued zero coupon convertible bonds tied to Berkshire's stock price. Because buyers of Berkshire's convertibles had a right to convert into Berkshire stock and because Buffett does not easily issue new stock, the issuance at that time was probably a sign that he believed Berkshire to be overvalued.

He was right. For about the next two and a half years Berkshire stock, apparently overpriced, went absolutely nowhere.

Buffett said of a *Barron's* piece (February 12, 1990) which set forth the proposition that Berkshire's price was too high, that he did not necessarily disagree with the conclusion, just with some of the calculations employed to reach that conclusion. Besides telling shareholders, Buffett also told *USA Today* that the *Barron's* piece mistakenly undervalued some of Berkshire's holdings. "There's a mathematical error in their numbers," he said. "The figures are wrong."

Berkshire was then off its $8,900 high, trading at about $7,900 a share at the time, and the story had sent the stock down $700 in a single day. The writer, Thomas N. Cochran, concluded that Berkshire was worth only about $4,695 a share and that the $7,900 share price was a 68% premium to Berkshire's real worth, its intrinsic value. Berkshire shareholders and others fired off letters to *Barron's*, which published a few.

One letter, from Berkshire shareholder Dr. Wallace Gaye, said: "Poor Thomas N. Cochran. He apparently wouldn't be able to tell the difference in value between a lump of coal and a diamond because they share a similar structure."

One problem with the *Barron's* story was that it assigned the common stock market value to Berkshire's preferred stock holdings as if the preferred could decrease in value like common stocks. It was true that the stock prices of three of the four preferred stock investments were down sharply. But Buffett explained to shareholders that Berkshire didn't own the common stock of these companies that had taken a beating.

Berkshire owned the *preferred* stock, which had always continued to earn dividends of about 9%, tax-advantaged at that. There's little chance that the preferred could drop in value like the common because the preferred stocks can be redeemed for the original face value—short of bankruptcy—roughly the same amount Buffett paid.

So there was no loss—although later US Airways was doing so poorly that Buffett wrote down that investment on the balance sheet.

And with conversion privileges these investments offer, not to mention the long periods they had to reach their strike price and become more profitable, Berkshire was sitting on nice investments not available to the general public. The only way to own them was through Berkshire.

As Ronald Reagan might say to Thomas Cochran, "There you go again!" Cochran came back with a story in *Barron's*, April 18, 1994, that Berkshire was worth $9,401 a share when it was trading at $16,100.

Letters again were fired off to *Barron's*, most centering on lack of mention of the insurance business. Michael J. Davey, of Sunnyvale, California, wondered why there was no mention of the valuable insurance business when each of the four largest reinsurers in the world buys coverage from Berkshire.

Daniel A. Ogden, president of Dock Street Asset Management in Stamford, Connecticut, wrote, "You may be right that Warren Buffett doesn't deserve a premium to book value, but if that's true, there are very few stocks worth owning. I'll do what I did in 1990 when you came to the same conclusion—hold on to Berkshire and worry more about the other stuff in my portfolio."

Time and again Berkshire has been written off as overvalued or "probable market laggard."

Michael Rhodes, a lawyer in Kansas City, told his Berkshire friends he thought most investors "might like the idea of having the world's best investor working for them with $2 of assets for every $1 of equity, particularly when the liabilities are mostly interest-free (deferred taxes and insurance float)."

In the 1993 Annual Report, Buffett told a story that included the Li'l Abner cartoon temptress Appassionata Van Climax, so one shareholder thought of writing: "Mr. Cochran, If you're right, you must be a pretty rich guy by now. Maybe we could meet for a drink. Signed: Appassionata Van Climax."

Cochran made no mention of $1.85 billion in cash, only half mention of more than $2 billion in fixed-income securities, no mention of Berkshire's valuable insurance businesses and left out about $2 billion in calculating Berkshire's stock portfolio.

Buffett was asked about the Cochran story at the Berkshire annual meeting in 1994. You'd think Buffett would be tempted to say something to Cochran—something like Felix Unger—but ever the gentleman Buffett said: "I hope he hasn't been shorting the stock. It's not the way I'd calculate it...apparently he forgot we were in the insurance business." Then Buffett launched into a dissertation about not making stock market decisions based on what others say, only on what you understand about the business.

Understanding the worth of the rest of Berkshire is a challenge. "The hardest value to figure by far is the worth of our insurance business," said Buffett at the 1991 Annual Meeting. "That doesn't mean it isn't valuable. It just means that it's hard to assess—although it might have a bigger effect on the valuation of Berkshire than See's Candy or *World Book*." Talk about understatement.

He added, "How the insurance table in our annual report (1990) develops over the next 20 years will be a major factor in what the intrinsic value of Berkshire is today...The source of intrinsic value of the insurance business is the ability to generate funds at a low cost. That's what creates value...If you can figure out how that table will look in the next 20 years, you'll have a good handle on our future. We think there is significant potential in it. In terms of dollars, we think that it's bigger than that of our other directly owned businesses."

In the first *Barron's* article, Cochran assigned a P/E of just 12 to Berkshire's operating businesses at a time when the market P/E was 14. (In the second story he said Berkshire's operating businesses were worth $2 billion, probably off by a factor of 2 or 3). Ask Buffett if he'll sell See's, *The Buffalo News* or *World Book* for 12 times earnings and see how long he stays on the phone.

Cochran used an old earnings figure in the first story but had it been the latest, Berkshire's earnings would have already plowed ahead. If you're talking about Berkshire from its latest report, you're probably millions of dollars behind the times.

For one thing, you'd be looking backwards at smaller numbers because Buffett reports as late as possible, about 45 days after the quarter has ended. You're even farther behind if you're citing figures from the annual report that comes out in March and reflects financial conditions prior to December 31.

Also, at the time of Cochran's stories, the market was declining, so Berkshire's tab for deferred capital gains taxes should have been lower than the figure Cochran used.

And are deferred capital gains taxes really a 100% liability as Cochran implied? If Buffett sold everything, he would have to pay Uncle Sam a very large tax bill. No question.

But Buffett tells us he's not selling everything today. In fact, he may hold some investments *forever.* Also, the deferred tax liability is non-interest-bearing and has no redemption date. If it were a bond, it might be sold for 20 cents on the dollar.

In 1993, Bill Ruane, head of Sequoia Fund, made a point about Berkshire's worth and the tax question. "Take its current book value which at the end of the year was $7,850. And that's after a reserve for taxes of about $2,200 or $2,300. If you add that back—and I'm not saying that you should add it back fully—but the prospects of those taxes being paid in the near future are low. So that money's really working for you even though it's not shown in the book value."

He said Berkshire was selling for a below-market price-to-book ratio, adding that many of Berkshire's assets are undervalued on the balance sheet.

With Berkshire, he said, you're getting the "finest security analyst in the world."

Cochran made no mention of Berkshire's substantial "look-through" earnings. You can think of look-through earnings as intrinsic earnings that include important, unrecorded earnings not included on Berkshire's income statement. These invisible, unrecorded earnings are in a sense Berkshire's proportionate ownership of the retained operating earnings of Berkshire's major investees, but under generally accepted accounting principles they are not counted in Berkshire's earnings per share. Coke, for example, earns more than $4 billion a year and Berkshire owns 8% of Coke, but generally accepted accounting rules keep Berkshire from including its share of Coke's income on its income statement.

Berkshire's "look-through" earnings are presumably reflected in the stock prices of the corporations in which Berkshire invests, and hence are included on Berkshire's balance sheet, even if they are not on Berkshire's income statement.

It's a common mistake to dismiss Berkshire as an overvalued

closed end fund, but as Wallace Gaye once said: "Do you know any closed end fund that internally generates its own funds for investment?"

Berkshire is an ongoing enterprise which invests better and borrows more cheaply than most companies.

Berkshire's value cannot be measured by numbers alone. Witness the large stock holdings. There is an extra kicker in Berkshire's commanding stock positions. Some suggest attaching a 20% premium for the huge stock positions. Many of Berkshire's stock positions are so large they are prized for their semi-controlling nature. Such huge positions have a disadvantage of being less liquid than a small position, but overall there's an advantage because their size offers more influence over company performance. Witness GEICO.

The future compounding of dividends from Berkshire's investees could be another fountain of enormous value.

There are other beauties at Berkshire. Consider how Buffett has structured the debt. He's paying 5% to 7.2% on Berkshire's debt. He has very little debt compared to equity.

Berkshire's float, with the buyout of GEICO, became about $7 billion. With General Re it became about $23 billion.

Get this: Buffett himself paid $2.3 billion for slightly less then half of GEICO and then wrote in the 1995 annual report that GEICO doubles Berkshire's growing insurance business. Isn't the worth of Berkshire's insurance businesses in the multi-billions?

And because of the huge capital of the insurance businesses, Berkshire enjoys the capacity to write business at any time propitious to Berkshire. "There is a hidden potential to write huge business in the future."

"And the fact that the insurance business has grown over the years—the fact that he can get to this position is indicative of the strength of the insurance business," said a Berkshire shareholder.

In any case then, what is Berkshire really worth? Adding the worth of the stocks and bonds is easy enough, even fun. Figure that the Coke investment is worth about $10 billion. We won't consider whether the ocean of Coke stock would sell at an even greater premium were it sold as a block to a rich megalomaniac—or to OPEC.

With respect to Berkshire's operating businesses, you should be able to put 20 times earnings on them to estimate their worth.

Berkshire's group of businesses apparently has among the highest return on equity of any group of businesses. That's a high return on equity with practically no debt. So let's loosen up a little and put a healthy P/E on things.

In 1993, *The Schott Letter*, written by Dr. John Schott, figured Berkshire was worth $20,150 a share, and in 1994 it said it was worth more than $21,000. At the annual meeting in 1995, when Berkshire was trading at $21,600, Buffett said the stock price relative to its intrinsic value, "offers as much value, or more, than the majority of stocks I see."

(Photo by LaVerne Ramsey)

Dr. John Schott

Floyd Jones, a principal of First Washington Corp., calculates Berkshire's worth basically by using a comparison to GEICO, which traded at about 2.60 times book value over the years. "GEICO has an outstanding record, but then so does Berkshire," he says.

In April 1998, Jones calculated Berkshire's intrinsic worth at $75,000 compared to a stock price of $66,800, a 12% discount.

What about taxes? Buffett is a keen reader of the tax code. Insurance operations get tax breaks. The dividends on the preferred stock investments are largely tax exempt. (Buffett's investment in low-income housing is another tax break.)

Many of Buffett's investments, such as stocks purchased by Berkshire's non-insurance subsidiaries, are carried at cost. Many businesses he purchased a long time ago are also carried at historical cost. Is See's, bought in 1972 for $25 million, worth more than that today? Of course. Is *The Buffalo News* worth the $33 million Buffett paid for it in 1977? Better to estimate $600 million, although large taxes would be owed if the newspaper were sold. But then Buffett isn't likely to sell See's or *The Buffalo News*. He's going to be buried with boxes of See's, cans of Cokes and a copy of *The Buffalo News* carrying an obituary saying that he still owns the paper.

You can also be sure that Buffett's accounting is as conservative as it comes.

"And there are no hidden liabilities," says one Berkshire shareholder. "So many companies have large pension and health liabilities but Berkshire's pension plan is overfunded."

Berkshire has more than its share of diversity: stocks, bonds, cash, banks, tanks, newspapers, television and radio stations, razor blades, soft drinks, hard drinks, uniforms, ice cream and candy, brokerage and financial services, paper, steel, jewelry, furniture, encyclopedias, air compressors, vacuum cleaners, electricity, and so on. Even cutlery and spray guns. And silver and oil. Oil? Buffett wrote in Berkshire's 1997 Annual Report: "[Berkshire had] derivative contracts for 14.0

million barrels of oil, that being what was then left of a 45.7 million barrel position we established in 1994-95. Contracts for 31.7 million barrels were settled in 1995-97, and these supplied us with a pre-tax gain of about $61.9 million. Our remaining contracts expire during 1998 and 1999. In these, we had an unrealized gain of $11.6 million at yearend."

And Berkshire has flexibility in a number of forms. With Buffett owning almost half of Berkshire's stock, decision-making can be almost instantaneous. Buffett can be on the spot with cash in hand, as when he bought Scott & Fetzer while other bidders were left calculating in the wings.

He has no limits on geography or industry as some other money managers have. He can buy in Akron or Asia and never leave his office. He can decide quickly that Berkshire would gain from more media or soft drink properties, or a shoe or food company, should something attractive be offered at the right price.

Isn't there extra value because Berkshire's managers pay themselves so little and Buffett and Munger serve on the boards of some of the investees? Their talent and time, for a tiny shareholder fee, is most valuable. Witness Salomon.

And Munger as a money manager did outperform the S&P 500 by a factor of about four over a period of about a dozen years, ringing up a 19.8% average annual return from 1962-1975 for his own partnership while the S&P 500 gained only 5.2% annually. For that, let's assign some value. How much, no one knows, but wouldn't you rather have made 19.8% than 5.2% on your money?

There are some technical things that add to Berkshire's worth—Berkshire's corporate structure enabling the insurance vehicle to make investments brings Berkshire some tax breaks. Also, Buffett operates with such size and efficiency that it's difficult to imagine that even his commissions, say, on a billion dollars worth of Coke aren't lower than any other fund manager's per share.

It's Buffett's "financial engineering" that really gives Berkshire an extra edge, says a report by Dominick & Dominick's *The Value Group.* (April 8, 1991) The report says Buffett's record as a stock picker and a runner of businesses has been very good. The report figures that Buffett manages about a 20% return on his stock picking, and his businesses give him about a 21% return: so how has he managed an almost 24% annual return on equity?

Low-cost borrowing is the primary advantage of a public company whose primary operating unit is an insurance company. Since insurance companies are nothing more than a good excuse to assemble a pool of investable assets, many successful investors own an insurance company...

Berkshire Hathaway's second source of long-term no-cost leverage is the U.S. Treasury. Berkshire Hathaway has always used tax laws to its advantage. The most important source of borrowing from Uncle Sam at no cost is a long-term holding period...Combining long-term holding periods with effective use of corporate exclusions for dividends, has permitted Berkshire to generate investment income and capital gains which were taxed at the dividend exclusion rate. Tax law has always permitted an intercorporate dividend exclusion. Currently this exclusion taxes only 20% of a dividend received by one corporation from another. Therefore the effective tax rate of a dividend is approximately 6%. Also, were a shareholder to tender stock back to a company retaining the same percentage of a company after the tender, the sale of the security is taxed as if it were a dividend. This means a corporation can sell a significant piece of a holding and have the gain taxed at 6%, not 29%. Time and again Berkshire Hathaway has used this quirk in tax law to lighten significant positions.

The most obvious examples of this technique were:

1983—GEICO
1984—GEICO
1984—General Foods
1985—General Foods
1985—Washington Post
[1993—Capital Cities]

The Value Group report stresses the advantages of stock buybacks. "Not only did it buy back its own stock in both 1964 and 1965, improving its returns, most of its important long term holdings have been companies that buy back their own stock."

Buffett has gained other "financial engineering" leverage through "tax arbitrage." The after-tax cost of the zero note borrowing is 3.5%; assume Buffett invests that money in a 9.25% investment in Champion International, 80% tax excluded, giving him an after-tax return of about 8.75%. "This gives Berkshire a 250% after-tax return on its money and an "option" to purchase Champion International Corp. at a fixed price for another eight years."

There's more:

The last bit of financial engineering employed by Berkshire Hathaway is its consistent reduction of capital employed to run a business. Almost immediately after assuming control of Berkshire Hathaway, the company reduced its inventory, property, plant and equipment employed in running the business. It was this cash from the reduction of invested capital that produced the first pool of reinvestable cash...when Berkshire Hathaway acquired Kirby, the first move Berkshire made was to reduce its invested capital, thereby reducing the purchase price and raising the returns.

Whatever the advantages, if you could find someone who could bring you a 25% or 30% annual return for years to come, would that not be close to a priceless find? Even 20% or 15% would be a bonanza.

Berkshire might one day sell for $200,000 a share. If you are young enough, you might one day see it reach the $1 million-a-share mark.

Buffett cannot deliver anywhere near the average annual increase of more than 25% in stock price that he did in earlier years, but Berkshire should continue to outperform the market over the long term.

Berkshire is a world-beater investment vehicle. And there is a sort of X factor with Berkshire—some proprietary things that Buffett hasn't explained to shareholders. He has said, "There's not much of that sort of stuff." But there is some and it is unlikely that the worth of it is zero.

And there could be some future synergy. There appears to be very little now at Berkshire—a Coke machine and See's Candy cart at the Nebraska Furniture Mart, some Berkshire insurance sold to See's. But what about selling insurance someday to every Berkshire investee, to Coke, Gillette, Dun & Bradstreet? Who knows?

Does it really make much difference what Berkshire is worth now if it can keep outperforming 90% of the world?

Would it have made much difference whether it was slightly undervalued or overvalued in 1965 when it traded at $12 a share? Wouldn't it have been nice to buy Berkshire at $20 or $200 or $2,000 or $20,000 a share, whether it was a bargain that day or not?

Finally, there is one other value. Buffett is running this operation, not Saddam Hussein. But Glenn Greenberg says there's one negative about Buffett—he will not be there one day. A key to Berkshire's worth is, "Warren Buffett's brain—whether it's alive or dead and he flies around a lot."

So at times there's a "Buffett Premium" in the stock and at times a "Buffett Discount."

But Buffett alive is valuable far beyond his stock-picking and managerial abilities, although those traits may already be built into the stock price. But with access to such business leaders as Tom Murphy, Laurence Tisch, and Katharine Graham, can't something valuable suddenly materialize? Those sorts of people and Buffett are likely to come up with good ideas.

Buffett's elite circle of friends, in fact, retreats every two years to locations such as Lyford Cay in the Bahamas; Dublin, Ireland; Williamsburg, Virginia; the Queen Elizabeth II; Santa Fe, New Mexico; and Victoria, British Columbia. The host for the event gets to pick the location.

The group (originally called the "Hilton Head Group" because it once met there) that Buffett calls the "Graham Group" and others call the "Buffett Group," began in 1968 with 13 people and now has about 60, including Mrs. Graham, Munger, Murphy, Ruane, Tisch, Keough, Gates, Jack Byrne, and Lou Simpson. Sometimes Buffett refers to the group as "Our Gang."

During their retreats, the group holds seminars on public policy, investments, charitable giving (whether to do it early in life or late), life's toughest and silliest moments.

One time Munger gave a lecture on Einstein's Theory of Relativity. Practically no one was interested, but most felt obliged to go, recalls a member. "If Buffett was there, he probably understood it. I don't think anyone else did."

Buffett is friends with such business leaders as Walter Annenberg, and, in fact, advised him to go ahead with the $3 billion sale of his Triangle Publications, which included *TV Guide*, to Rupert Murdoch. Nancy Reagan is another friend. Mrs. Reagan once sent her son, Ron, to Buffett for a little career counseling.

Some descendants of Clarence Barron, one of the early owners of Dow Jones & Co. which publishes *The Wall Street Journal* and *Barron's* have consulted with Buffett about the company's performance and stock price. (*Wall Street Journal*, January 14, 1997)

Some of the country's best and brightest business folks run attractive ideas by Buffett, but usually he just comes up with one or two big ideas a year of his own.

It's a plus that Buffett is on the boards of some of the companies in which Berkshire has investments. He can have some say over how their cash flows are invested, possibly bringing greater value to those companies. On the other hand, companies he invests in may have artificially higher P/Es because of his halo effect.

Finally, Berkshire's sterling reputation has value. Even in the precautionary prospectus for the Class B stock offering, its reputation (as opposed to unit trusts) is explained: "Though the point is impossible to quantify, Berkshire believes that its reputation has added significantly to the Company's intrinsic value over the years. Berkshire believes that its reputation, if it remains unimpaired, will produce substantial gains in the future as well."

If Buffett can keep working his magic at anything approaching his past rate of return, Berkshire will continue to make its way, aided by some value for the brand name of Berkshire Hathaway and Buffett's brains. Still, the true value of Berkshire is in its future cash flows, adjusted for inflation.

If Berkshire could maintain a return of 23% on book annually, (Buffett says he can't do it), then by the Rule of 72 (72 divided by 23 is about 3), you'd double your money about every three years.

"Berkshire's not a company. It's an adding machine," says Berkshire shareholder George Eyraud of Birmingham, Alabama.

When the Florida lottery was at a fever pitch in 1990 because the payoff was more than $100 million, ABC's *World News Tonight* was on the story.

You know how those features go—lots of folks in line giving brief interviews about what dreams might come true for the lucky winner.

Fleeting fame came to a heavyset, middle-aged man when a reporter stuck a mike in his face and asked what he'd do if he won $100 million; the fellow shrugged and replied before Peter Jennings and all the world: "Run naked through the money, I don't know."

After Berkshire's announcement that it would buy General Re and with Berkshire trading toward $80,000, Buffett was asked about the relationship of price to intrinsic value. He said: "There's no question that to date this year, obviously, the price of Berkshire stock has outstripped the gain in intrinsic value. There's no way we could have increased the percentage value at the same percentage rate. But I can tell you also that no member of my family or any of the management of Berkshire that I know of has sold a share and we all think that it's a fine investment for a five or ten year period. And that's the way we think about it. Historically, I think if you look back, we think a good bit of the time Berkshire's been undervalued because people have looked at it, many people have looked at it, on the basis of liquidating value, as they might have looked at a closed end investment company. And frankly they were making a mistake if they were looking at it that way because it was an enterprise that used capital to try to create more value over the years and in most cases it worked out

O.K. so that our intrinsic value has grown at a far faster rate than it would have been anticipated if you'd looked at it as a closed-end company. But because that attitude prevailed and was written about to some extent I think that generally Berkshire was undervalued and I think perhaps the valuation is getting more appropriate now."

Some people underestimate how Berkshire might fare. In short, they can't see where it's all going. That doesn't mean Buffett doesn't know.

It's reminiscent of a story about a young girl drawing a picture and an adult asking her what she's drawing.

"God," she answers.

"But nobody knows what God looks like," the adult said.

"They will when I get through," the girl replied.

149
THE SCHROEDER REPORT
$91,000–$97,000 A SHARE

PaineWebber insurance analyst, Alice Schroeder, concluded in her 54-page report of January 1999 that Berkshire's intrinsic value ranged from $91,000 to $97,000 a share. The stock was trading at $65,000 at the time.

Wow: What gives?

Mrs. Schroeder was the first person from a major brokerage firm to write a report about Berkshire, and more significantly, had Buffett's blessing to do so.

Schroeder told *The New York Times* (January 31, 1999) she "nearly fell out of the chair" when Buffett first called.

"He asked if I would do him a favor," she said. Buffett, with the acquisition of General Re, wanted the company to be less misunderstood.

Schroeder's intrinsic value number was arrived at after exhaustive research and scaling back assumptions to avoid a number so high as to be "absurd," the *Times* story said.

Schroeder rejected the view that Berkshire is really a closed-end investment company whose value is determined by the prices of its securities. She views Berkshire as a holding company whose main business is insurance. She found that 79% of its earnings come from insurance. In addition Berkshire owns

(Photo courtesy of Alice Schroeder)

Alice Schroeder

many fast growing, living, breathing businesses such as its aviation businesses.

Schroeder wrote in her report: "Today, we view the company as primarily an operating company that also has a sizable investment portfolio."

The *Times* quoted a statement from Buffett as saying, "It was clear to me that she was a superior analyst, both in her knowledge of the insurance business and in her willingness to do the legwork to garner facts. I believe that interested investors can obtain all of the information they need about Berkshire from our published materials, but the quantity available may overwhelm them. Alice may fulfill a useful function by organizing and distilling."

Berkshire is "possibly the most-talked about and least-understood company in the world," Schroeder wrote.

She said, "For an insurer that can obtain float at a reasonable cost and hold it in perpetuity, float really is an asset, not a liability."

Buffett has said float is no blessing unless you can get it in increasing quantities and get it cheap.

Schroeder said that Berkshire is getting increasing quantities, and that it appears it can get it cheap for a long time to come in part because GEICO has such a long record of getting it at low cost.

> "An investor should be willing to pay up to the risk-free rate to use float for one year. The investor would, for example, be willing to pay up to $5 to borrow $100 and invest it at 5%.
>
> "Moving on, an investor should be willing to pay up to the amount of float itself for the ability to invest the float at the risk-free rate in perpetuity. For example, an investor would pay up to $100 for the right to invest $100 at the risk-free rate forever."

Berkshire's float at 1998 yearend was almost $23 billion.

Schroeder approached intrinsic value in three ways, by float, book value and earnings and each time came up with about $90,000 a share for her intrinsic value number.

By the way, she valued GEICO alone between $12.8 and $14.5 billion. "The other insurance operations are valued between $23 billion and $26 billion."

The essential message of the Schroeder report was that, at least in Berkshire's case, float is valuable.

Schroeder's report was a literary hit with 10,000 copies printed, three times the usual run. (A second printing was expected of the report, for which some investors paid $540 each.) (*New York Times*, February 7, 1999)

At Berkshire's annual meeting in 1999, Buffett blessed the report but did not comment on the intrinsic value number. "She's a first class analyst. It's the first comprehensive report. We got to a $100 billion in market cap before anybody really published [an analyst report] about the company."

He also said, "It helps to have an analyst who thinks straight. She's a non-paid information officer. We want informed owners."

In an updated report August 16, 1999, she lowered earnings estimates and noted that interest rates had risen in 1999, but that the stock, which had sold off remained attractive. She didn't assign a specific intrinsic value.

After the third quarter report in 1999 when Berkshire was trading at about $60,000, she figured that it was trading at a 25% discount to intrinsic value. She said the company's intrinsic value had dropped about 10% from her original figure largely because interest rates had risen.

In the spring of 2000, Schroeder pegged Berkshire's intrinsic value at $80,000 a share.

150

FAIRHOLME CAPITAL'S BRUCE BERKOWITZ—INTRINSIC VALUE: $62,000-$73,000

Fairholme Capital Management's Bruce Berkowitz of Short Hills, New Jersey, is a longtime Berkshire follower and shareholder. At the end of 1999 Fairholme had a big bet on Berkshire—$369 million of its $515 million stock portfolio—and Bill Aldinger's Household International. Berkowitz said that although Berkshire had its disappointments in the past couple of years Berkshire's stock has been trading below its intrinsic value.

Berkowitz thought Berkshire's intrinsic value in December 1999 ranged from $62,000-$73,000. Here's how he arrives at the figures:

"Berkshire's reported earnings for the third quarter of 1999 were below our expectations due to continued underwriting losses at Gen Re. So far this year, Gen Re has recorded the worst underwriting results in the company's recent history. However, we think the overall results were affected by some one-time factors.

• Stock option plans were converted to cash incentives at significant cost.

• Under Berkshire, Gen Re appears to have adopted more conservative policies regarding the recognition of profit.

• Gen Re appears to be reducing costs substantially, immediately expensing these efforts rather than capitalizing them or reporting the often used 'restructuring charge'."

"There is another very important factor currently affecting Berkshire's short-term earnings. Berkshire has chosen to have certain of its businesses grow rapidly. It is tolerating lower short-term earnings for significantly higher future profits. Among the subsidiaries in this position are GEICO, FlightSafety and Executive Jet.

"We know that the cost to acquire new business in the auto insurance sector can be 25–30¢ in losses per $1 of premium in the first year. But in the second or third year of the policy's renewal, the same customer will generate a profit of close to 10¢ per $1 of premiums. Therefore, $1 billion of new business can cost $300 million in foregone profit at the same time $4 billion of old business earns $400 million—yielding a net profit of $100 million. At its current premium level of roughly $5 billion, GEICO is foregoing roughly $250-300 million of reported profits to grow at its current rate." (*Outstanding Investor Digest*, December 31, 1999)

Here's Berkowitz's view of Berkshire's intrinsic value:

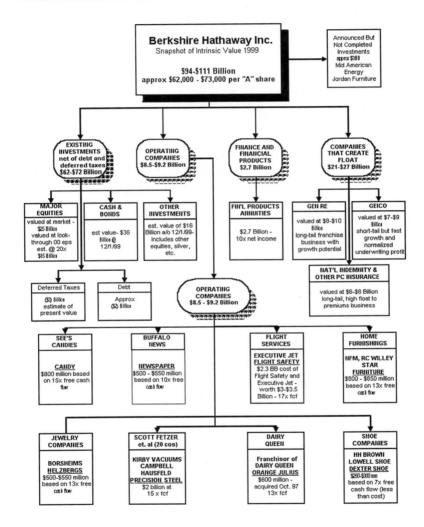

151

WHAT DOES THE FUTURE HOLD FOR BERKSHIRE?

Here's how Darren Weems, an analyst at SouthTrust Bank in Birmingham, Alabama, sees Berkshire's future:

It is widely known that Berkshire Hathaway has been a great investment for more than three decades; however, the past two years have been very difficult for shareholders as the stock price has declined by more than 50%. A closer look reveals that the company's intrinsic value is going in the opposite direction, with strong operating performances from many of its subsidiaries, such as Executive Jet, FlightSafety International, and GEICO. Since the decline in the stock price has led some shareholders to wonder if the best days for Berkshire are in the past, what type of return should shareholders expect to receive?

Warren Buffett has been able to increase Berkshire's book value per share by an annual compounded growth rate of 24% since 1965. With such a large capital base to manage, it will be difficult for Buffett to continue increasing Berkshire's book value per share by 24% per annum. Since the stock price has declined by more than 50%, it is not necessary for Berkshire's book value per share to increase by the same growth rate achieved in the past in order to give shareholders an above-average return. As shown in the chart below, if Buffett can increase the company's book value per share by 10% per annum Berkshire should give shareholders a very satisfactory return.

Furthermore, Buffett has long used the company's cash flow to invest primarily in marketable securities. As a result, Berkshire's stock has historically traded at less than two times book value per share. As Buffett continues to purchase more wholly-owned businesses, the multiple awarded to the company's book value per share will most likely be pushed higher, which should have a very positive impact on the price of its stock. At the current stock price of $41,300, the following chart shows the potential annual compounded returns possible over the next ten years, if Buffett can increase Berkshire's book value per share each year by 10% and by 15%, while using different multiples as shown below:

Scenario 1: Berkshire's book value per share grows by 10% to $98,529 from $37,987.

Multiple of Book Value Per Share	Projected Stock Price in 2009	Potential Compounded Annual Return
1.50 x	$147,793	13.6%
2.00 x	$197,058	16.9%
2.50 x	$246,322	19.6%

Scenario 2: Berkshire's book value per share grows by 15% to $153,679 from $37,987.

Multiple of Book Value Per Share	Projected Stock Price in 2009	Potential Compounded Annual Return
1.50 x	$230,518	18.8%
2.00 x	$307,358	22.2%
2.50 x	$384,198	25.0%

As the chart indicates, Buffett does not have to increase Berkshire's book value per share by similar rates achieved in the past in order to achieve above-average returns. At the current price, Berkshire is extremely undervalued.

152

WHAT'S $25 BILLION OF FLOAT WORTH?

What is $25 billion of float worth? That's very hard to say, but Dr. Sam Park of Tulsa, Oklahoma, gave it a shot in a post on the AOL board January 18 1999:

"This is nothing more than an exercise based on my interpretation of what WEB said on this subject, especially in his 1993 annual letter. 'The value of float funds—in effect their transfer price as they move from insurance operation to the investment operation—should be determined simply by the risk-free long term rate of interest.'

"Let us assume that Berkshire insurance float currently is $25 billion. Let us also assume that the float is expected to grow 12% a year for the next 10 years and stay unchanged without growth thereafter. The cost of float is assumed to be zero, as increasing underwriting profit from GEICO is used to compensate underwriting loss from reinsurance and supercat business. I will use 6% as the LTGB [long-term government bond] rate. These assumptions are open to questions but I am simplifying these assumptions mainly to illustrate the basic thrust of my approach.

"The value of the current $25 billion float is $1.5 billion, 6% of $25 billion, to Berkshire now. At year 1, the value would be $1.68 billion, year 2 $1.88 billion...year 10 $4.66 billion. If I discount these yearly values to present value using 6% discount rate the sum of 10 years' value of float is $20.55 billion.

"The next step is deciding the terminal value at year 10. At year 10, the total float would be $78B, same as $43.6 billion at present value. Since I assumed that the float would not grow any further from year 10 the terminal value of perpetual, no-cost float for Berkshire would be the same as $43.6B at present dollar. $43.6B added to $23.55B is above $60B—the present value of the insurance business' float generating franchise, based on the assumptions mentioned above.

"This exercise illustrates how valuable the Berkshire insurance business could be if, a big IF, the float can continue to grow at low or no-cost. Please notice the fact that I did not even consider the expected superior investment return from Berkshire in valuing the float here. In other words, this is what Munger called 'the institutional momentum' of Berkshire, expected to be present even without the presence of WEB and Munger."

Here's a post from "Ikoborso" who is Robert Kibler of Richmond, Virginia:

"It is absurd to value BRK as if float were fixed or shrinking, particularly now that we own GEICO and Gen Re. While I think it is good to estimate "minimum rational price," what utility is there in making irrational assumptions to get a minimum rational price? You might as well assume that BRK is going bankrupt.

Bobby Kibler, hands down, is the greatest net surfer of all Berkshire's shareholders. For Berk Heads Kibler is like a Library of Congress.

"If we are going to be rational, we should begin by recognizing that one of BRK's biggest assets is its ability to generate float at a very low cost (historically below zero cost). The future growth in low cost float has a present value, for the reasons WEB has explained (and as Schroeder has echoed in her report). The value is a function of the assumptions one makes regarding float growth rate, cost, investment return on float and the discount rate used. One can be very conservative in the assumptions plugged in to the model for valuing future float growth, and derive a minimum rational valuation based on those assumptions, but it is not rational to value BRK as if it were a closed end mutual fund that did not have the ablity to generate internal funds from its insurance operations...

"The 'page 3' snapshots [in Berkshire's Annual Report] only reflect current investments and noninvestment earnings. They don't include the additional cash flow from increments of new float each year. WEB has never said that these two columns on page 3 represent all you need to value BRK. To the contrary, he for many years has been preaching about float's value and he sets out the chart on float growth/cost each year in his report. There is a huge difference between the amount of CURRENT float (which is already counted in the investments column because it finances part of same, and the present value of FUTURE float growth). If you don't include a rational estimate of BOTH elements in your IV estimate you will end up way too low. The 'minimum rational' IV estimates I have seen on this board (50s, 40s, even 30s) are not rational in my opinion."

Kibler later posted: "What if we lay out the variables today—the profits forecast and the growth forecast—and see just what we *would* pay for Berkshire's float, the 'mutual fund,' which is up to $24.5 billion now. I may as well say right now that the point of this exercise is to see the range of values an investor can put on a business, depending on how aggressive he or she wants to be. This post does not aim to pick one value.

The profits: Today they are low because most of the float is in bonds and cash, but that portfolio may change. As shown in the tables below, the profits, even at moderate rates of return, can produce a fine result. The other thing that counts in predicting profits—the cost of the float—is running at 1.7% this year. Historically, when you even out all the ups and downs of the insurance game, Gen Re's cost has averaged less than 1%; Berkshire's has been well under zero. (Changes in the nature of the contracts Berkshire writes may produce a higher cost of float in the future, but along with that will come an even higher investment return.) One last thing to keep in mind is the extra tax burden of 1% that comes with the territory of earning money through an insurance company.

The growth: This year the float has grown at 7.5% so far. Buffett and Munger have said they don't know how fast it will grow over time. They have relayed some of their expectations for the next 10–15 years, and from those comments we might predict an 8% growth rate for the next decade or so. But we are about to do a perpetuity calculation—you have to pick a rate that is sustainable *forever*. One way to be safe is to pick a low rate that trudges along with your outlook for GDP, more or less.

What to pay: Let's say first that this is only *one* method of looking at the value and is only meant to give people an idea of what assumptions go hand in hand with any particular multiple of float, using this method. I'd be happy to see this post spark others that show alternate methods that do not rely on a perpetuity calculation. What all will have in common is that they value the business behind the $24.5 billion in float today. That obvious necessity is left out of some valuations of Berkshire we see.

Below are two tables. The first uses a discount rate of 10%. In a world of 6% government bonds, a 10% return is good. The second uses a discount return of 15%—what many of us, along with WEB, shoot for. But a bargain and a fair market price are two different things.

Using a discount rate of 10%, here are the multiples of float that are appropriate to pay, depending on the assumptions made. A multiple of 2, for example, means 2x$24.5 billion in Berkshire's case or $49 billion.

		Growth				
		3%	**4%**	**5%**	**6%**	**7%**
	7%	1	1.2	1.4	1.7	2.3
P	**8%**	1.1	1.3	1.6	2	2.7
r	**9%**	1.3	1.5	1.8	2.2	3
o	**10%**	1.4	1.7	2	2.5	3.3
f	**11%**	1.6	1.8	2.2	2.7	3.6
i	**12%**	1.7	2	2.4	3.1	4
t	**13%**	1.9	2.2	2.6	3.2	4.3
s	**14%**	2	2.3	2.8	3.5	4.7
	15%	2.1	2.5	3	3.7	5

And for a discount rate of 15%:

		Growth				
		3%	**4%**	**5%**	**6%**	**7%**
	7%	.6	.7	.7	.8	.9
P	**8%**	.7	.7	.8	.9	1
r	**9%**	.7	.8	.9	1	1.1
o	**10%**	.8	.9	1	1.1	1.2
f	**11%**	.9	1	1.1	1.2	1.4
i	**12%**	1	1.1	1.2	1.3	1.5
t	**13%**	1.1	1.2	1.3	1.4	1.6
s	**14%**	1.2	1.3	1.4	1.6	1.7
	15%	1.2	1.4	1.5	1.7	1.8

The math: The perpetuity formula goes like this...

An appropriate multiple of distributable cash = divided by (the discount rate less the growth rate)

An example: profits of 8%, growth of 4% annually...1 divided by (.10–.04)=16.67

Then, the multiple of 16.67 times profits of .08 equals 1.33, which is the appropriate multiple of float. For Berkshire today, using those particular assumptions, that would mean the appropriate price to pay to earn 10% is $24.5 billion times 1.33. That comes to $32.6 billion."

"Neuroberk" (Sam Park) posted this on November 10, 1999:

"Iko's great post on the valuation of float will remain as a reference for me.

WEB said in his 1997 letter, "Though our float is shown on our balance sheet as a liability, it has had a value to Berkshire *greater than an equal amount of net worth would have had.*"

What Iko tried in his post was to show how much *greater than an equal amount of net worth* the insurance float could be under different assumptions of growth rate, cost and investment return of float.

From what WEB said, we know that float is at least as valuable as net worth, meaning the float multiplier in Iko's table should be at least 1. This means that a minimum $24.5 billion should be added to BRK's accounting net worth in order to show its economic net worth.

One caveat, however, is that current book value of BRK has $18 billion worth of goodwill, a major part of which represents the value of Gen Re's float.

To avoid the double counting, I like to use the invested assets as the basis, since it includes the float but not the goodwill. For example, if I think the float is equally valuable as equity (multiplier 1 in Iko's table), then I can regard the amount of invested assets representing the value of BRK insurance business and its liquid capital, but *not including* the value of other operating businesses. One might argue that the value of GEICO's underwriting profits should be a separate item, depending on the future trend of GEICO and the other insurance results.

I personally think the value of BRK insurance float should be

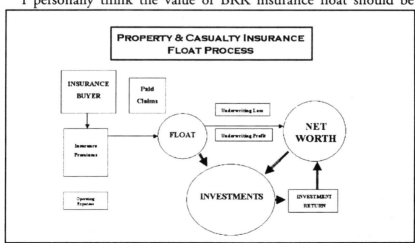

(Source: Fairholme Capital Management)

between one to two times the current amount of float, probably closer to two times.

153

WHAT'S BERKSHIRE REALLY WORTH?

AN ABE LINCOLN SIGNATURE

I f you ever tire of Buffett and Munger saying they won't reveal their exact idea of Berkshire's worth, here's a way to get an even more precise estimate than they can offer. Look in the newspaper.

An equally good way may be to use this formula:

Establish the worth of this rare collectible note signed by Abe Lincoln when he was the 16th President of the United States, and there you have it:

"Sec. of the Treasury, please see this lady, (wife of a wounded soldier) who seeks employment. April 25, 1863. A. Lincoln."

Over time the price of the note and a Berkshire share have been almost precisely the same, according to Tim Burton, of Milwaukee, Wisconsin, citing Steven M. Berez's *Profiles in History.*

The following lists the data:

(AP/Wide World Photos)
Abe Lincoln:, "It is best not to swap horses when crossing streams.

Buffett: "The best time to sell a stock is never."

	Lincoln's signature	Berkshire share
1982	$1,000	$965
1986	$3,000	$2,925
1992	$9,500	$9,275
1993	$12,000	$11,750

	Lincoln's signature	Berkshire share
1995	$25,000-$30,000	$32,100
Early 1996	$29,500-$33,000	$33,000
December 10, 1996: (Ad in the *Wall Street Journal*): Abraham Lincoln. Splendid Civil War Document signed, 10/10/1863, overturning death sentence of convicted Union army deserter, Handsomely framed w/19th century engraved portrait of the compassionate President.	$32,500	$33,200
Early 1997	$35,000	$36,000
Early 1998	$75,000	$70,000

With runaway inflation, however, Lincoln's signature and perhaps a BMW might beat the pants off Berkshire.

On June 15, 1993, someone called Burton to sell him a Lincoln signature for $15,700. Berkshire closed that day at $15,825. "I almost dropped the phone," Burton said.

What Berkshire shareholders really want to witness is the stock trading at the recent price of an Abe Lincoln letter and signature: $420,000.

Just to keep Berkshire shareholders on edge, Sotheby's in recent times has sold a document signed by Lincoln appointing an assistant paymaster in the Navy for only $3,850. But keeping Berkshire's shareholders in high spirits, a page of Lincoln's 1858 handwritten "House Divided" speech has commanded $1.5 million.

154

GOING ONLINE WITH
YELLOW BRKERS

"WANNA COME UPSTAIRS AND SEE MY A SHARE?"

S everal years ago a few Berkshire shareholders began getting together through the America Online ("America On Hold" sometimes) service to talk to one another about every facet of Berkshire.

The board developed out of the camaraderie of some hard core Berkshire fans about 1996. "Pagewrite," who is Charles Page of Carmel, California, said: "Gartmann suggested that we needed a moniker, a name for the group and offered a prize for the one who came up with the name which we adopted. Loving word play I suggested that since Buffett was the Wizard of Om (Omaha) and that we were all going to find the wizard along the BRK road we should call ourselves the Yellow BRKers. I knew nothing about Doshoes and WEB's interest in the Wizard of Oz. Gartmann liked the name and the concept and sent me the prize, a glass paperweight with Berkshire Hathaway on it which he had bought at Borsheim's.

(Photo by John Gartmann)

Some Yellow BRKers got together at Gorat's September 15, 1998 before Berkshire's special meeting the next day. At the big table, from the left, clockwise, are David and Cathy Hayden, Carol Meduna, Jim Maves, John Gartmann, Frank Fitzpatrick, Bryan Sedway, Jill Silverman, Dr. Sam Park, Michael Rhodes, and Lyle McIntosh.

"Gartmann also suggested that since we did not know each other and needed to have a way of recognizing the group he would wear a yellow hat. So he went to some novelty store and bought the massive hat, which is foam, but it wasn't yellow. So he bought some yellow spray paint and sprayed the hat, not thinking about the fact that it was porous. Apparently he had a soggy mess with paint all over and it took forever to dry."

In any event, the Yellow BRK Club came into being named after the yellow brick road that led to the Wizard of Oz. The group stays in touch electronically on Berkshires's message board on AOL.

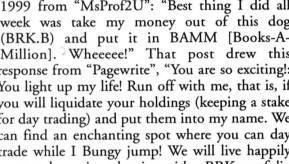

(Photo by Pat Kilpatrick)

This is Buddy Clinton. Buddy is a dog. Berkshire Hathaway is a corporation, not a dog.

For many shareholders going electronic and tracking every nuance of Berkshire is real fun.

You get an occasional message like this one in 1999 from "MsProf2U": "Best thing I did all week was take my money out of this dog (BRK.B) and put it in BAMM [Books-A-Million]. Wheeeee!" That post drew this response from "Pagewrite", "You are so exciting!: You light up my life! Run off with me, that is, if you will liquidate your holdings (keeping a stake for day trading) and put them into my name. We can find an enchanting spot where you can day trade while I Bungy jump! We will live happily ever after, rather than spend our time sleeping with a BRK portfolio which just compounds at a boring rate of 30% a year! Who needs WEB! I have been searching for a companion just like you. Please send a photo of your stock certificates! Upon receipt of the photo I will file for divorce and meet you on the yellow brick road."

Some weeks later when Berkshire's stock rocketed up about $11,000 in three days Page offered this post: "This stock is a dog. Remember that comment. Well, that dog is running and hunting! Go Rover."

When the stock dropped a lot in 1999, Berkshire's message board often sounded like a pack of dogs barking:

"Ruffruff. What a dog!" was typical of a number of posts.

"We used to fool around," Debbie Cohen told *Newsweek* (May 19, 1997). "Now he (former boyfriend and now husband Larry Oberman, a money manager in Chicago) just wants to go on America Online to talk about Berkshire stock."

Oberman concurs, "We're like a cult. But instead of Kool Aid and pudding, we have Coca-Cola and See's Candy, and to date Warren hasn't told us to take the poison yet." After all, Berkshire has been dismissed as a "cult stock." At annual meetings, Larry and his poor wife take the cake for early attendance. As of 1999 he had been first in line six of the previous seven years. "We arrived at 4:30 a.m. this year [1999] and 12 minutes later someone else showed up."

Over time the online discussions have included sophisticated looks at intrinsic value. Discussions about how to value float and general camaraderie among fellow cult members abound, and tend to reach a fever pitch around annual meeting time.

At annual report and annual meeting time e-mails fly furiously reminding one of the Irish poet John O'Donohue's comment: "E-mail is like coming home at night after a long day and finding 70 people in your kitchen."

Shortly before Berkshire's Annual Meeting in 1997, someone with the code name of "Doshoes" penned some postings. Doshoes? Doshoes had mysterious powers. Doshoes could even get impossible- to-obtain reservations at Gorat's.

Who was Doshoes? Doshoes offered a few hints. Quickly Berkshire shareholders could spot it was someone pretty close to Buffett.

A Doshoes posting to a request for a table at Gorat's: "Your timing is amazing. I just stopped at Gorat's and the doors were locked. So I'll be stopping by again in an hour or so. Think positive—this might take some begging. I will be at a different table, but I'll be there. You guys sound like a lot more fun than my group—since three rounds sounds like only a beginning. The table I'm at focuses solely on Coca-Cola products..."

More hints. Something about the Wizard of Omaha and being a fan of the Wizard of Oz. Finally her name was revealed as a shortened version of "Dorothy's Ruby Shoes." (BUT NEVER FORGET THAT IN THE ORIGINAL BOOK DOROTHY'S SHOES WERE MADE OF *SILVER!)* Finally it turned out that "Doshoes" was Buffett's daughter, Susan!

Page says that Buffett loves the *Wizard of Oz* and used to read it to Susie when she went to bed. "She has a big collection of *Oz* paraphenalia."

Later she invited those on the Yellow Brick Road—Yellow BRKers—to Mr. Toad's watering hole near the stadium where Buffett throws the first pitch of a baseball game as part of annual meeting festivities.

She has been monitoring the comments on AOL and showing them to her father who said, "These guys know more about

Berkshire's intrinsic value than I do."

Buffett stopped in briefly at Mister Toad's where his daughter and some of her family and friends and a clan of "Yellow BRKers" had gathered. Buffett, dressed in a baseball jacket, said, "Hi, everybody, I'm her dad." He shook hands with folks and dashed off to his baseball game.

(Photo by Mary Houbolt)

Buffett's assistant, Debbie Bosanek, receives a "Ms.Sec2U" shirt from yellow BRKer Lyle McIntosh at annual meeting festivities in 1999.

At the Mr. Toad's gathering in 1999, the Yellow BRKers presented Debbie Bosanek with a T-shirt that said, "Ms.Sec2U", as in Ms. Secretary to you—a spoof on the cantankerous "Ms.Prof2U." On the back of Debbie's shirt was inscribed: "My secret...I read all WEB's mail." When Buffett and Susie arrived, Buffett was given a shirt that said: "5 Cokes a Day will Keep the Hair Away" and featured a picture of a bald Buffett as he appeared as Daddy Warbucks in a local rendition of "Annie".

Among the most avid yellow BRKers is Berkshire shareholder John Gartmann, a 66-year-old retired mechanical and electrical engineer from Delran, New Jersey. He still owns apartment buildings and runs an aviation mail order business. Gartmann occasionally has posted the board to please "send money so I can get to Omaha. (Will work for food—I mean A shares.)"

Certainly the bias on the AOL message board is toward owning Berkshire although there is plenty of skepticism tossed in about whether Berkshire or some of its holdings are overvalued.

One of the more lucid series of "postings" has come from "Tode" who in real life is Michael Rhodes, a lawyer in Kansas City.

Here are portions of Tode's first entry of December 1, 1996: "I am new to this posting board but have been a BRK shareholder since 1985. Just spent part of this weekend reviewing the messages from this group since last May. Lots of interesting analysis about what the intrinsic value of BRK is—a question I have been very much interested in for a long time.

"I saw a lot of argument on how to value the insurance float. It appears this group has reached a consensus—the float is worth some-

(Photo by Nancy Line Jacobs)

Yellow BRKer John Gartmann in uniform. He says he's "Berkshire rich and cash poor."

where between a negative $6.9 billion and a positive $15 billion.

"May I offer my two cents worth. The float is very valuable, but its value is reflected in the look through earnings. That is, the total look through earnings per share includes the earnings generated from both assets that are owned by shareholders (equity) and assets that are 'owned' by others (float and deferred taxes). The look through earnings also reflect the cost of the OPM that the shareholders get to use, i.e., if the float is generated with an underwriting loss, the loss reduces the look through earnings, and if it generates an underwriting profit, the profit shows up in look through earnings as well...

"Rather than trying to specify a number for the value of the float per se (which results in confusion at best and double-counting at worst), it is better to accept the fact that all of the factors which determine the float's value will be reflected in the multiplier on this company. 25 times 1,400 look-through earnings for 1996 gives you $35,000 a share. Another useful benchmark is twice book. Book value on 9/30/96 was 17,500 and now is north of 18,000. Twice book puts you over $36,000 a share. The stock is a buy..."

In later postings Tode says he thinks Buffett's method of calculating look-through earnings is too conservative, "mainly because he ignores the retained earnings of the $5 billion of equities not identified, and the subtraction he does for the tax that would be owed by BRK if all earnings were paid out in dividends ignores the fact that the earnings are actually being plowed back into the business and inuring to BRK's benefit."

Another chat liner wrote: "Actually, without the $6.9 billion of float Berkshire's investment portfolio would perhaps be $15 billion less since the float increments have historically been reinvested and grown just like any other component net cash inflow, but in the case of float, the corresponding cash flows have been generated at zero cost and so represent a pure and undiluted free cash flow."

Yet another posting: "Thanks for the scoop on MCD [McDonald's]. I wouldn't be surprised if Buffett has been buying more since 9/30/95 since MCD has been an underperformer this year and the international growth story is more compelling than ever. It will be interesting to see if it shows up [it did] as a disclosed position in the annual report next spring. He's obviously been buying something because the cost of equities owned has increased from $7.1 to $8.7 billion from 12/31/95 to 9/30/96...

"One of the early no-brainer valuation methods I used was future look-through earnings. Keep things simple. My best guess for 1996 look-through earnings is about $1,400 per share. Just multiply this number by the correct P/E multiple and presto, you have the intrinsic value.

"What's the correct multiple? Reasonable minds differ, of course. If KO and G are worth 30 times next year's earnings, the same multiple should apply to their share of the 1,400 total (which you can compute easily enough). Other holdings are worth maybe 10 to 15 times earnings. You could calculate the average weighted P/E ratio for the entire equity portfolio if you are feeling energetic enough. Then you have to add something to reflect the leverage on the balance sheet from float and deferred taxes. This is BRK's secret weapon and it is much more valuable now than it was five years ago. A lot of Wall Street experts just don't get it—they say BRK is a closed end fund and therefore should sell at a discount to its net assets. A better analysis is a margin account with Buffett investing two dollars of assets for every dollar of equity. But even this analogy falls short of describing reality because the margin debt is interest-free (the deferred taxes cost nothing and with the addition of GEICO the float will likely be generated at an underwriting profit for the foreseeable future). PLUS, the pool of OPM is constantly growing—the float should increase about a billion dollars a year. Don't forget that GEICO's share of the auto insurance market is tiny and they have only begun to tap the standard and non-standard driver markets where they are now growing at a rate of 29%...

"One of the early no-brainer valuation methods I used was simply to take total assets (as shown on the balance sheet with no adjustments) per share. It has the virtue of simplicity and in a rough way tracks with the arguments that have been presented in these postings, i.e., that the liabilities are not real and should be ignored. If you ignore the float liability and heavily discount the deferred tax liability, the only liabilities that remain roughly correspond to the "asset" value of the future float growth. As of 9/30/96, BRK has $32,671 assets per share. Here are the numbers going back several years, all at year-end:

1995	$25,214
1994	$18,114
1993	$16,570
1992	$14,909
1991	$12,618
1990	$ 9,310
1989	$ 8,253

Compared to the highs each year for BRK's stock price:

1995	$33,400
1994	$20,800
1993	$17,800
1992	$11,750
1991	$ 9,130
1990	$ 8,730
1989	$ 8,900

"There has been a rough correlation over time. Buffett's infamous 'do not buy my stock' remark last spring should not have come as a shock to anybody. It was grossly out of its normal range, measured by assets per share, book value per share, look-through earnings per share or any other measure. I would argue it is now back in the normal range..."

Here's a posting from JTayan from February 21, 1997: "I think the comment by WEB ("I never give stock tips, but if I die, buy the stock.") was in response to numerous comments from numerous people asking what would happen to the stock if he died. He was trying to say that there was value in the company without his being there...I think if he died the stock would fall, at least initially, more than 25%. I think it would fall below book value. However, his next in command would probably use the large cash flow to buy back stock at that severely discounted price and I would see it eventually recovering to at least 80 or 90% of intrinsic value. That is why it is important to keep an eye on intrinsic value."

A posting just hours later from John Gartmann read: "Warren was born August 30, 1930 in Omaha, Nebraska. Warren will outlive us all as he has no worries other than whether it may rain on May 3, 1997 and cancel the baseball game and his first pitch at the annual meeting outing."

A posting from "Grahdodd" of March 16, 1997 after Berkshire's 1996 Annual Report was issued: "A brilliant annual report, more great lessons on stock selection process, interesting observations on the general stock market (unfortunately the headline for the national-al media is that stocks are overpriced).

"The big surprise here is the McDonald's position. And the average price (at $42 per share) is substantially higher than when WEB first started buying the stock—so a lot of that could be late '96-year and continuing.

"Okay—how about a quick back-of-the envelope sketch of BRK's value: Let's use the 12/31/96 numbers which understate the large equity positions which have run up considerably since then (all per-share numbers)

a.) You get $28,500 in securities

b.) You get $421 pre-tax, $273 after tax of operating earnings. Let's give this a market multiple of trailing 12/31 at 19x of $4,301 (I think this is also very conservative because these businesses are better than average enterprises.)

c.) Let's value float conservatively at 1.2x which gives us $6,660.

d.) Let's take this number and subtract from it for deferred taxes on cap gain $1,530 which represents a 10% tax on the per-share equivalent of $18.59 billion unrealized portfolio gain. This is a fair number because the annual certainly leads one to believe that none of the 'Inevitables' are going to be sold anytime soon.

"That gets us to $38,817 and it excludes all equity appreciation this year, and probably understates the value of the operating subsidiaries and the insurance float, and values management by the smartest investor of all-time working around the clock for 9 cents per year per share—at zero.

"Conclusion? You can safely buy this business for anything under $40,000."

"Pagewrite" offered this posting on April 9, 1997: ... "I had a friend who was a successful investor and once I asked (after I heard of Buffett and BRK) if he knew of Buffett. He said: 'Please don't ever mention that name to me.' Why not? I said. His response: 'Someone told me about Buffett and how smart he was in 1965 and said how he now has gone public. You can buy shares in his company. I bought 5,000 shares at $12 a share. My broker who had helped me make a lot of money said the way to lose money is to get greedy. So if a stock doubles in value sell and get out. So when BRK hit 28 I sold, had more than doubled my money. I was happy. Please don't talk to me about Buffett and BRK!' "

(Photo courtesy of Charles Page)

Charles Page: Actually this is a nude photo of Page from the neck up. He looks like a cross between Mark Twain and Wall Street Journal's Al Hunt. Page was a good friend of Frank Wells, the highly regarded No. 2 man at Disney who died in a helicopter crash in 1994. Wells was a year behind Page at Stanford Law School.

Here's an unusual posting. It comes from RAD4IU (Robert Dykstra, of Fort Wayne, Indiana) on May 7, 1997: "Since I am not able to add anything to the intrinsic value discussion (I feel a little bit like Charlie Munger after WEB answers a question at the meeting—'I have nothing to add.'), I will attempt to interject a bit of humor. If this offends anyone let me know. Here goes:

Top Ten Reasons to Own Berkshire Hathaway Stock:
- 10. Between your shares and WEB's you control the company.
- 9. Omaha Steaks
- 8. Feel good everytime you shave, drink a Coke, or have a burger.
- 7. 900 million servings of Coke products sold every day.
- 6. Buffett family are great people.
- 5. High dividend yield on stock—one hot dog and Coke per year.
- 4. Frees up time to play golf.
- 3. Never have to pay a seller's commission

on stock.

2. Charlie Munger's dry wit.

1. WEB is your partner!

You think Letterman would use this material?"

One fellow wrote that his mother had the good sense to buy Berkshire early on, that basically Berkshire was their entire net worth. Suddenly there were messages from folks saying they wanted to marry her.

The son finally revealed her portfolio as follows:

SECURITY	WEIGHT
Cash	0%
Bonds	0%
International equities	0%
Coke	.023%
Gillette	.0137%
Berkshire	99.633%
Cherry Coke	6 cases

And it's fun to watch beginners start to learn about Berkshire with such questions as:

Is Katharine Graham related to Ben Graham? (No)

Another one-liner was thrown by all the references to "WEB," saying: "I'm new to online. What is a WEB? Is it online talk or an index on the American Stock Exchange or none of the above?"

Another onliner helped out immediately: "WEB=Warren E. Buffett, Chairman of Berkshire Hathaway."

On July 26, 1997, Tode weighed in with:

"It sounds simplistic and obvious that the true value of BRK is the confidence shareholders have that cash flows will be reinvested at returns that far exceed the LTGB [long term government bond] rate. But that's it. What other company can provide this same assurance for the long term? Compare BRK to a zero coupon treasury bond with a 12% coupon. I have always felt BRK to be superior. First, there is the tax advantage of being able to defer taxes until you decide to sell. Second, while there is no 'guarantee' BRK will achieve 12% return on reinvested cash flow, it seems highly probable. Third, it is impossible for a 12% zero treasury bond to earn MORE than 12% if held to maturity, while BRK historically has done far better than 12% and has a very good chance in my opinion of achieving WEB's goal of 15%. And yes, there is a real possibility, more than a pipe dream, that despite WEB's disclaimer, it just may beat 15%.

"Most importantly, a zero coupon bond has zero brains. There is no intellect to guide the reinvestment of capital every six months. No matter what opportunities Mr. Market may serve up, the zero coupon bond will pass them up and

(Photo courtesy of Marlin Stockwell)

Buffett's daughter Susie, Charles Page, and Marlin Stockwell at a Yellow BRKer reunion the weekend before Berkshire's annual meeting in 1999.

mindlessly compound at the guaranteed rate until maturity. While no-brainer investments have their place in the investment universe (no brains often are preferable to the average professional money manager,) you pay a very heavy price for the certainty that you will do no worse than the coupon rate.

"With BRK, you have the best brains in the business world scouring Mr. Market every day looking for a mispriced bet. You have buckets of free cash flow cascading in every morning. You have lots of dry powder (GEICO's bond portfolio) available to deploy if a mispriced bet appears. You have WEB tap-dancing to work every morning, a man on a mission who is doing what he loves to do. Almost unbelievably, you not only have the best brains and complete focus on the task at hand, you also get a very rare commodity in today's business world—INTEGRITY. You can be certain that management will not dilute future shareholder returns by lining their own pockets with excessive compensation and stock options, and you can be certain management will not try to mislead shareholders.

"Put it all together and it's worth a lot. A whole lot. Name another company that can compare. Despite what we read about Buffettmania, what is amazing is that intelligent people who spend a lot of time studying the menu of investment selections day in and day out, almost invariably pick Company X over BRK. Perversely, the smarter they think they are, the greater the odds they will make the wrong decision."

After Berkshire's announcement of its huge silver purchase in early

1998, "Marlinls" (Marlin Stockwell of New Port Rickey, Florida), who has a Yellow Berkshire Club website at http://www.geocities.com/marlinls.geo, filed this posting:

"We were shocked about zeros and now the silver. Forget the closing price for the end of '98. I think it would be more fun to guess what's next. Will he buy farm land, pork bellys, a country, a Caribbean island, Trump's casinos, a cruise ship line, a national football team, hotels. The possibilities are endless." Yellow BRKer Rich Rockwood of Indianapolis, Indiana operates two websites—www.focusinvestor.com which has to do with focus investing and sells used business books. Rockwood's other site (www.geocities/rrockw) has information about Buffett and value investing.

Here's an entry from August 5, 1997: "I love this reoccurrence. For 14 years I have been asking stockbrokers and investment counselors if BRK would be an attractive purchase. To a man and woman, every time, at every level, the response has remained the same. 'No, it's too pricey, overvaluated [sic], overrated, ridiculous, and at insane levels.' I have never, not once, been told the opposite."

Amidst the slew of online well wishes at Thanksgiving 1997, came a posting from Doshoes who predicted Nebraska would beat Colorado in their football game. She added "Happy Thanksgiving to all of you. I'll keep an eye on the Chairman's gravy intake—it's sometimes a bit excessive." Months later she made this posting: "It took me until the age of 20 to realize gravy is not a beverage."

On December 5, 1997, someone e-mailed the Berkshire message board: "What is Berkshire Co? Saw this stock for the first time last night and it was selling for 46,600."

These were among the answers:

1) "One must discover Berkshire for himself. Nobody can explain the price!"
2) [The price] "is the sound of the stock clapping."
3) "Berkshire is an experience of the mind."
4) "Check out www.berkshirehathaway.com. *It'll be like getting a drink of water ... from a fire hydrant.*"

The Berkshire message board on AOL has even had postings about how to have a successful marriage. This is from "Pagewrite."

"People often ask me and my wife our secret of being married for

46 years and having four wonderful children and five grandchildren. My wife told a friend that what has kept our marriage together is that we go out to dinner twice a week, every week. A good restaurant, soft music, candlelight, special food then a walk home in the moonlight. That is what does it.

"She goes on Tuesday nights and I go on Thursday nights."

Here's a posting on the "Berkshire message board" from Don Danly:

"I agree...that the price has gotten well ahead of the historical trend line. A least-squares regression line for the logarithm of the year-end BRK price versus the year for the period 1982-1996 leads to the following equation:

$$\text{Year-end price} = 10\verb|^|(3.7636-0.1148\,(\text{year}-1989))$$

The predicted prices are:

Year	Predicted Price	Actual Price	Error (P-A)/A
1982	912	775	17.7%
1983	1188	1310	-9.3%
1984	1547	1275	21.3%
1985	2015	2480	-18.7%
1986	2625	2820	-6.9%
1987	3420	2950	15.9%
1988	4454	4700	-5.2%
1989	5802	8675	-33.1%
1990	7558	6675	13.2%
1991	9844	9050	8.8%
1992	12823	11750	9.1%
1993	16703	16325	2.3%
1994	21757	20400	6.7%
1995	28341	32100	-11.7%
1996	36917	34400	7.3%
1997	48087	46000	4.5%
1998	62637		

"The predicted price is within 13% of the actual for the past eight years. There is a big deviation in 1989 (and maybe the same will occur in 1998), but the historical trend line predicts a year-end price of 62637 for this year. This ain't all bad—it works out to 30% APR over the 16-year period."

Danly quickly made this amendment:

"In case anyone actually tries to use my regression equation for the BRK. A price, I need to correct a typo I made. I gave the equation as

$$\text{Year-end price} = 10\verb|^|(3.7636-0.1148(\text{year}-1989))$$

The minus sign was a typo; try

Year-end price = 10^(3.7636 + 0.1148(year - 1989))
(note 10^p denotes 10 raised to the p power)

The first equation will give a BRK. A price of $22.53 in the year 2010, while the correct equation gives $1,494,170. Sorry for the minor discrepancy."

The posting drew this response from Michael Rhodes:

"Donald D—I confess that my education so far has not included least square regressions and logarithms. But thanks anyhow. I agree with your conclusion that the price is ahead of its long-term trend, even if I don't understand your advanced math (anything beyond counting bunnies and the Rule of 72 is advanced in my book)."

After word in 1998 that Berkshire would buy General Re, one posting requested the origin of the H. in Jesus H. Christ.

Answer: Hathaway.

A posting on July 16, 1998 offered:

10 Questions Never To Ask on the AOL BRK Board (or at the annual meeting):

10. When will the stock split?
9. Isn't it too late to buy Berkshire shares?
8. Buffett's just been unusually lucky, hasn't he?
7. Isn't Buffett an idiot for not buying technology stocks?
6. Shouldn't I wait to buy until the price drops? It's so high right now!
5. Isn't Berkshire Hathaway just a glorified mutual fund?
4. Why don't any brokers recommend Berkshire shares? That CAN'T be good!
3. Doesn't the high PE ratio mean the stock is overvalued?
2. Buffett's success is due to insider information and other sleazy tactics, right?

And the one question which must NEVER, EVER be asked:

1. What happens when Warren Buffett dies?

Even Buffett, through Debbie Bosanek, has posted the board.

After a group of Yellow BRKers sent him a box of See's candy for his birthday, Buffett told the board: "Many thanks for the box of See's. You're definitely off to a good start. Next year, may I suggest an Executive Jet gift certificate. Warren Buffett."

Later a group of yellow BRKers sent Buffett some peanut brittle. Here's the thank you from Debbie Bosanek posted on the board: "Warren and I have just received a generous supply of peanut brittle. We want to thank all of you for this much needed (and appreciated) nourishment. Productivity at headquarters has leaped to a new high, thanks to you."

Yet another message from Buffett was posted on November 5, 1998: "I've received the yellow roses (through Don and Vera [Danly]) and want to pass along my thanks. It was nice to have my old Rolls Royce chauffeur remember me."

(Photo by John Gartmann)
Neurologist Dr. Sam Park and thus his Internet name of "Neuroberk"

In the midst of the gloom and doom of the financial crises of 1998 "Neuroberk" (Dr. Sam Park of Tulsa, Oklahoma) wrote:

"Imagine you have just returned from a nine months' trip to a remote location and looked up the financial news for the first time in nine months.

"You would be pleased to find out that BRK went up by 29.3% while DJIA went down by 1.6% and S&P 500 went up by 3.3% so far this year.

"To your pleasant surprise, you found out that BRK is acquiring GRN, increasing invested insurance assets by $25 billion, and per share book value by $12,902.

"You are also excited to learn that WEB is sitting on a cash horde of $9 billion, not including the newly available investible funds from GRN, and the proverbial buying opportunity for WEB is on hand with the general pessimism in the financial market.

"Wouldn't you be puzzled if you find some BRK shareholders worrying about 'inverted yield curve', '25% paper loss in the last 2 months' or the 'Y2K problem' instead of rejoicing their luck?"

The Berkshire board posters even include a farmer—BRKFarmer1 is his net name. He is Lyle McIntosh, president of Rockford Farms, an area covering 15 miles, in Missouri Valley, Iowa. Basically he grows corn and soybeans and has a Pioneer seed sales and farm real estate business. A portion of the money from those enterprises goes to buy Berkshire.

It was BRKFarmer who posted the board with this account of Buffett playing Daddy Warbucks in "Annie" December 14, 1998:

"It's all over folks. We've lost WEB. His new career started last night at the Rose Blumkin Performing Arts Center. His singing and performance as Daddy Warbucks in 'Annie' had critics marveling and the teenage girls in the audience shrieking with delight. I doubt any entertainer since 'ole blue eyes' has created such a stir among the female gender. (And that was even with his 'skin head' wig.) When he stepped up and belted out strains of 'Tomorrow' security had to restrain the more excitable ones.

"Seriously, it was great fun. He was joined, among others by Susan Jacques of Borsheim's, Chris Blumkin of the Furniture Mart, and Senator Bob Kerrey as Franklin Roosevelt.

"The Rose is a magnificent landmark work of art. The restoration of the old theater and the intricate carvings and designs are worth stopping by and seeing if you get the chance. It is the home of the Omaha Theater Company for Young People, and was initiated by a large grant by Rose Blumkin. Our own Doshoes was responsible for the successful fund raising campaign.

"Looks like BRK may now be leaderless, as after the show WEB was surrounded by a score of talent scouts and agents, each trying to sign him up."

A post from Jack Benvent addressed the problems of Berk Heads and their dating life:

"St. Valentine's Day has brought a big issue into focus. As a single male out there in the dating world I am wondering—just how do you explain to potential significant others about Berkshire and Buffett? I've met a couple of nice women lately and I'm certain they'll think I'm certifiable. I'm afraid that if the topic of Berkshire and Buffett comes up (I avoid the topic at all costs) I'll come across like one of those Star Trek people who attend conventions wearing Spock ears or full Capt. Kirk attire.

"I think it is probably best if I don't 'come out of the closet.' How do you explain the shelf full of annual reports that you won't let them touch? How do you explain that you have to be online on a Saturday in March because it's 'really important'? "How do you explain that you HAVE to go to Omaha every year? How do you explain the closet full of Berkshire Hathaway active wear? (Forget even trying to explain the guy in the yellow hat—that defies explanation!)

"My mother (who is convinced I'll never get married) and I thank you in advance for any advice."

Signed, "Sleepless in NJ"

Two days later he posted a possible solution: "I'm thinking about changing my pick-up line to, 'Wanna come upstairs and see my A share?' "

Berkshire reported profits of $2.8 billion on March 9, 1999 for 1998 and the stock dropped triggering this post from

"MrDougFLA": "So why is it DOWN on the news? Because profits are bad, losses are good:"

Net annual profits:

BRK	$2,830,000,000.00
AMZN [Amazon.com]	$0.00
BAMM [Books-A-Million]	$34.79

A post from Finnigan1 suggested some new chapter titles for this book:

"Yellow Hats and Spam"
"Day of the Yellow Hat"
"Mr. Secret CGMI" [a stock John Gartmann likes]
"Hats in Love"
"The Bonfires of Yellow Hats"
"Little Hats"
"The Right Hats"
"100,000 Yellow Hats or Bust"
"The Old Man and the Hat"
"Anna Kayellowwhatya"
"The Great Hatsby"
"The Hunt for Yellow October"
"The Hatling"
"The Electric Kool Aid Hat Test"
or my favorite
"Gorillas of the Omaha Mist"

(Photo courtesy of John Gartmann)

Tom McIntosh, John Gartmann, and Lyle McIntosh. Brothers Tom and Lyle played hosts to John Gartmann at their farm one day in 1998.

The board also has been a place where some signing on with aliases say things they might not under their own name. And it's been a place rampant with rumors that Buffett was buying Qualcom or Amazon.com. Perhaps the most egregious act was a post on the Yahoo board purporting to be a Berkshire press release saying Berkshire planned to sell 200,000 shares because the stock was overvalued. The boiler plate information was typical of a real Berkshire release. Close inspection showed the poster to be "Mr. and Mrs. BS" and the item was released well before its posted time of release. The bogus item was designed to look like an authentic Berkshire release.

Another message posing as an official Berkshire release said the company was planning to buy back 200,000 shares.

One report, which apparently originated on the Yahoo message board on February 8, 2000, said Buffett was in an Omaha hospital in severe condition. At first Berkshire said it didn't comment on rumors. Soon the *Omaha World-Herald* said Buffett's friends said he was fine and then on February 10, 2000 Berkshire released a press release saying:

"Recently certain rumors have surfaced on the Internet regarding share repurchases and Mr. Buffett's health. While it has been a long standing Berkshire policy to not comment on rumors, we are making an exception with respect to these recent rumors. **All rumors regarding share repurchases and Mr. Buffett's health are 100% false**. We encourage shareholders and others who are interested in obtaining information about Berkshire to visit our Web site (berkshirehathathway.com) where all press releases are posted concurrent with their release to the media."

After the rumors of her father's ill health, his daughter, Susie, showed up to a charity benefit sporting a badge which said, "My Father is Fine." (*Omaha World-Herald*, February 17, 2000) Buffett himself said, "That was something. I should have been checking my pulse all through this thing to see if I'm still here...I feel terrific."

(Photo by Dara Zapata)

Here, young Andy Zapata, son of Yellow BRKer Dara Zapata, appears as young Warren Buffett in a "Living History Museum" project. Students had to read at least one book about the person they portrayed in a paper and a speech for a sixth grade class at John D. Runkle School in Brookline, Massachusetts. CBS's Mike Wallace is a graduate of the school, as is Pulitzer Prize winner Jared Diamond, author of Guns, Germs and Steel, and The Third Chimpanzee, books that Munger recommends.

(Photo courtesy of Whitney Tilson)

Yellow BRKers Unite!
Ken Shubin Stein and Stefan Rosen of Compo Asset Management, Dale Wettlaufer, of Legg Mason Fund Advisors, Whitney Tilson of Tilson Capital Partners, and Jack Benvent at a New York Security Society Analysts meeting about Berkshire Hathaway December 3, 1999.

967

(Photo by Marlin Stockwell)   (Photo courtesy of Mary Houbolt)

PaineWebber analyst Alice Schroeder at the Yellow BRK party April 28, 2000 where Berkshire shareholder Lyle McIntosh was the master of ceremonies.

Yellow BRKer Marlin Stockwell jokes that Buffett begged to be in this photo with him. Dr. John Houbolt is to the right.

This cartoon by Mark Parisi with Atlantic Feature Syndicate originally ran June 27, 1997 with a caption saying: "Slight change of plans, folks... From now on, we follow the Yellow Brick Sidewalk." Some Yellow BRKers asked him to revise it to reflect Berkshire's misfortunes of 1999. Yellow BRKers gave Buffett a copy of the cartoon at their party April 28, 2000.

155

OPEN LETTER TO BUFFETT

J ack Benvent, of Haworth, New Jersey, who works in his family's
real estate business, penned this "open letter" to Buffett March
6, 2000:
*A few years ago, I could have posted this without a disclaimer. Times
have changed, have they not? What follows is intended as a joke, a spoof,
to maybe get a few chuckles. I just started imagining all of the mail WEB
must be getting these days—and what the questions are going to be like
at this year's meeting—and this sort of sprung to mind. As the fictional
author of this fictional letter might say, "Laugh a little, you'll live
longer." Enjoy.*

To: Warren Buffett
Chairman, Berkshire Hathaway
Kiewit Plaza
Omaha, Nebraska

Dear Sage of Omaha:

Let's be honest, our stock price ain't doing so good. And now, with
the annual report and the annual meeting coming up, I would like
to, with all due respect, make the following suggestions to you, our
beloved chairman, in an effort to help light this candle.

1. Charlie Cam

Did you read this in *Barron's* last week?
*OpenFund is a $28 million mutual fund that runs stark naked.
Window dressing is impossible. That's because the South San Francisco-
based manager of the fund, MetaMarkets Investments, posts the entire
portfolio on its Website, www.openfund.com , along with every trade—
and even a constant Web-cam view of the trading desk.*

I checked out the web site and thought EUREKA! This is a gold
mine. Mungercam.com, BRK's first foray into the Internet media.

First off, Charlie doesn't move real quickly, so we can save money
and buy a really cheapo web camera. No streaming media needed;
the guy barely moves. Secondly, Charlie makes about one trade a

decade, so it isn't as if he is going to give away some big company secret on a daily basis. Finally, we can rake in the money selling books. Subscribers will watch him reading some highly intellectual book on the web cam and click on the link to Amazon.com to directly order the book. We'll make 10% per order! As I see it, the only person who is going to get hurt in this deal is the bookseller at Eppley Airfield and he sells those big red foam "Cornhusker's #1" fingers for about $10 a pop so I don't feel all that sorry for him. Besides, MungerTV might help get that pain in the neck at the SEC, Arthur Levitt, off your back.

2. It's time for a New Look

All this Old Economy vs. New Economy stuff has me batty too. So I say the heck with it—if you can't beat them, join them. And it seems to me nothing says "Old Economy" more than a clean shaven face, a nice suit, a white shirt and a red tie. Grow a goatee Warren! I know the folks at Gillette may not like it, but if you want to be a winner you have to look like one, and all the hip money guys I see on CNBC & Fox have goatees. Lose the white shirt; a nice lavender one screams "Success" these days. And those glasses! Geesh! Get Doshoes to hop on an Executive Jet to New York, head down to Soho, and buy you some really little glasses with oval black frames. Or even better, maybe you can dig out the old square glasses and skinny neckties you wore back in your Columbia days with Ben Graham. On the east coast, the nerdy look is back in style baby.

On the west coast, all of the newly minted Internet billionaire dudes dress irreverently and surf before they go to work. So, for the new BRK movie, see if you can get a video of Charlie driving a convertible Porsche, wearing a backwards baseball cap on his head and "hanging ten" at Malibu. (Tell him I think Ben Franklin invented the surfboard.) Having Charlie yell "Cowbunga! The surf is gnarly!" into the camera might be a good idea too. Investors love a surfing rich guy with expensive taste and a wacky sense of humor. It inspires confidence.

3. Run up some debt already

So what if Berkshire's got more cash than Fort Knox. As we say here in New Jersey, "big deal." You want to make Berkshire a big winner on Wall Street? Run up some huge debt. Go nuts. Borrow like there is no tomorrow. Investors love debt. We are already losing money at Gen Re—that's a good start. Now let's go gaga with debt and tell the world that it is all a part of your business model. Borrow a coupla' bil, go on CNN, look Willow Bay directly in her baby blues, and repeat after me: "This time it's different. You just gotta believe in the business model. There is a huge untapped market out there, and my partner surfs every morning. So, Willow, how do you like my goatee?"

4. It's razzle dazzle time

I always heard you have one of the greatest financial minds of all time. Start using it already! Here's a clue: No one is buying your Intrinsic Value mumbo jumbo anymore. Sure, Intrinsic Value was all the rage for awhile and you deserve a little credit, but heck, no one cares anymore. In fact, I read it officially in *Barron's* last week. It said:

Warren Buffett's Berkshire Hathaway has taken hefty stakes in two apparel companies whose shares have been clobbered almost as badly as its own. The market doesn't care.

Intrinsic Valuations have gone the way of the Pet Rock and the Mood Ring. No one is buying either one of those anymore either. This market wants IPOs, spin-offs, tracking stocks, and Internet stock incubators. It's time to give the market what it wants.

First I saw Lucent spun off two of their deadbeat companies and the market absolutely loved it. LU jumped 10% in a day. That's an easy one for us—let's spin off the shoe division and World Book. Bingo, we're up to 10%. Next, we need a really cool tracking stock. You never actually have to spin off the tracking company. We just need something sexy to give analysts something fun to banter about on CNBC. You know what GM does with Hughes Satellite? Same idea. Again this is easy—issue a tracking stock for Executive Jet. Here's a formula for you: Pro golf + private jets + tracking stock = lots of sexy banter with Joe Kernen and David Faber. None of this will add any real long term value to the company, but who cares. Sexy banter drives stock prices.

5. Move your assets

Warren, you probably don't even realize what BRK's greatest asset is. Here's a hint: what was the key to the AOL/Time Warner deal? Content, my friend, content. I see all of these pip-squeak investment counselors charging big bucks for newsletters and fancy schmancy conferences and do you know what they do? They quote you. Heck, half of these guys wouldn't even know how to spell "PE" if it weren't for you. Enough already! It's time we start selling your content. You know the annual report? I say you charge $250 apiece for them. The annual meeting? Admission should run about $2000 a head. Want to visit the official BRK home page? That's $20 a month. Look, I own stock in Disney too, but you don't see Eisner sending me a free Snow White DVD every year and handing me the keys to the Magic

Kingdom. No, he sells content. We have to do the same thing.

And, while we're on this topic, I don't want to get any more spam e-mails from Internet wannabes trying to sell me some crummy software that will screen stocks just like you without us at BRK getting some of the vig. That's called "licensing." And the same goes for Gorat's. You think those hash slingers would sell one lousy steak without you? Every mention you give them in an annual report costs them 50% off the top from now on. That's called an "endorsement deal". Capishe?

And in conclusion ...

Have you considered putting BRK into some sort of global-wireless-broadband-fiber-optic-packet-switching-b2b-internet-e.commerce venture? They're hot now. Listen, I know you have this little "investing philosophy" thing, but lately I think you are a little too hung up on the "businesses I understand at reasonable prices" part of the equation. Nobody understands anything about anything these days. So what. Buy some tech stock, make some money. What's there to understand? Nothing unreasonable about that.

Warren, I have plenty of other good ideas but I have my own business to run; I depend upon you and Charlie to run BRK all on your own. You've done a pretty decent job so far but, if you should need any more great free advice like this, you might want to try surfing the Internet once in a while.

(With permission of Jack Benvent)

156

A BERKSHIRE SHAREHOLDER
SCORES A PERFECT
1,600 ON HER SATS.
HARVARD IT IS.

S arah Park, daughter of Dr. and Mrs. Sam Park, of Tulsa, Oklahoma, scored a perfect 1,600 on the Scholastic Aptitude Test (SAT) in 1998—800 in both math and verbal tests.

What's more, she did it as a junior and at a public high school—Washington High School in Tulsa.

The SAT was taken by 1.2 million students in 1997-98. Of those, 673 achieved a perfect score on the tests. (*Tulsa World*, December 19, 1998)

(Photo courtesy of Dr. Sam Park)

This photo, from left, shows Mrs. Eunna Park, Daniel Park, Dr. Sam Park, Sarah Park, Washington Post's Katharine Graham and Buffett. The photo was shot at Berkshire's annual meeting in 1997 and Park got Buffett's autograph on the photo in 1998 at Gorat's.

"I was not expecting a 1,600," Miss Park, 16 at the time, told the newspaper. "I had hoped to do well, but I know it's easy to make a mistake on the SAT. To be honest, I had hoped to get the SAT over with before next year so it would not be something I would worry about."

Miss Park was in the middle of four Advanced Placement courses, calculus II, an art elective and pursuing interests in French, Spanish, painting and fencing. Oh, and she found a little extra time to start a student literary magazine, "The Sting."

Sarah, who is now a student at Harvard, owns one share of Berkshire's Class A stock. That's pretty smart.

157

"GUTSYOK"

Marsha Tate of Los Angeles ("GutsyOK" on the AOL Berkshire message board) wrote to Buffett in August 1998 that she hoped one day to be a Berkshire shareholder. In the meantime, she said, she was working five jobs.

"I was turning 40 and I was upset with myself because I didn't buy two shares of Berkshire A when I had the money. I got greedy playing options. I was on a roll. I thought maybe I could make enough money to buy four shares. However, I was wrong, the market took a turn for the worse," she said.

"I'm a teacher and I've always taught my students to go after their goals, not to be content. I dreamed of owning an A share.

"It was 2 a.m. one morning when I wrote him a letter," she added. She explained how she had been working as a teacher for 17 years, a tutor, a governess (who kept one child seven years), ran an import-export business and was in sales part-time for I. Magnin.

"I went away and came back and almost didn't realize Buffett had replied. I expected some big item saying Berkshire Hathaway. I almost threw it away. He invited me to the annual meeting and sent me a ticket to get into the meeting. It was the most incredible trip of my life.

Although her dream had been to buy an A share, she went ahead and bought some B shares right after the meeting.

"In March 1998, I had a dream that I was going to meet Warren Buffett. I didn't know when or how. Last August, I decided to write Warren Buffett a letter, to ask whether or not a non-shareholder could attend his annual meeting, just in case I wasn't a shareholder by May of 1999. I explained to him how hard I worked to become a shareholder. I was embarrassed to tell him that I lost money playing options!" she added.

Marsha Tate and Buffett at Berkshire's annual meeting festivities in 1999. Good book, Marsha!

158

SUICIDE WATCH IN THE "BUMMER OF '99"

Berkshire's stock price took a big blow in 1998-1999 after the announcement of the purchase of General Re. The insurance cycle suddenly went soft and great companies such as Coke, Gillette and Disney seemed to falter all at once. The stock plunged from about $80,000 in mid-1998 to $52,000 in late 1999, closing the year at $56,100.

Some shareholders spoke about a suicide watch and the endless agony. The tone of some of the messages on the Internet took a decidedly sour tone:

• "Many shareholders are staring at significant paper losses (myself included). An earlier post mentioned how WEB (and many other BRK millionaires) are not bothered by a large BRK decline because it doesn't affect their lifestyles. This may be true, but for a working class stiff (janitor) like myself who tries to save money to take care of my wife and my new millennium baby, a BRK decline represents a real loss of money. I just want Warren to explain what the heck is going on with Berkshire's depressed prices. If the price action is nothing more than Mr. Market being irrational, then let us know! SAY SOMETHING WARREN! SOME OF US WORKING CLASS STIFFS DEPEND ON YOU!!!"

• "Another earnings warning from Gillette. I wasn't surprised. Offended yes. At least now we know why BRK went down today. The informed sold. I don't know the right thing to do, however. Gillette is a component of the overall picture, but who knows how big that component is? I think the shareholder meeting will be a little different this time around. I wonder if the responses to questions will be standard, canned, noninstructive or just plain dismissive."

• "Comment has been made about the shrinking volume of postings of this board. There is such a pro-WEB mindset on the board that anyone suggesting anything critical that they are so attacked with emotional arguments that add little light to the subject. For instance I think WEB wasn't thinking much about his shareholders when he bought General Re and has essentially kept quiet about it since. If he cared about his shareholders he would discomode (sic) himself and give us some encouragement. I know such is beneath him, but then actions speak louder than the lack of words. I know such comments are inflammatory and much like attacking the flag but until criticism can be treated as something other than the ravings of a mad man then there aren't going to be many new folks wasting their time on this board."

• "I guess what I don't understand is why Mr. Buffett doesn't make some kind of statement to his shareholders. Surely he must realize this isn't just about a stock price going down. It is about people's hopes and dreams being shattered...retirement dreams, a child's wedding, a child's education, a new home. Maybe when you already have billions you don't think of something like that."

• "I'm really furious...in this ongoing long-term."

159

POINT COUNTERPOINT

Forbes columnist Martin Sosnoff was among those critical of Buffett during Berkshire's rocky year of 1999. His article (December 13, 1999) entitled "Buffett: What Went Wrong?" made these points.

• "The fall-off [in Berkshire's stock price] demonstrates the painful limitations of his philosophy: Buy good companies he understands and hold them forever."

• He criticized Buffett's Coca-Cola investment: "Staying married for life to a group of stocks risks big problems. Look at Coke's gyrations."

• He criticized Buffett for not buying drug stocks during the Clinton health plan scare [actually Buffett bought Bristol-Myers during that time].

• He criticized Buffett for not buying technology companies [perhaps a fair criticism since he knows Bill Gates].

• He criticized GEICO's rapid growth strategy. "This situation dredges up unhappy memories about the carrier from the 1970s [seems a slight stretch to compare GEICO of the late 1990s to the 1970s].

• General Re is stalled out in a worldwide insurance market suffering from large overcapacity [correct for the moment].

• Sosnoff's final overall criticism: "Berkshire diehards need to deal with two sobering issues: Buffett's age, 69 [not talking about age discrimination, are we?] and the company's sizable premium over aftertax liquidating value [Are you sure, Mr. Sosnoff?]. The Sage of Omaha is a great man, but he does not walk on water."

One poster replied on the Berkshire message board:

Here are the facts: In just the past few weeks, Coke has appreciated 45% adding $4.2 billion to our portfolio. At the same time Gillette has gone up about 25%. You know about American Express—it's been a moonshot.

You mention Freddie Mac...the company is growing its earnings way above trend line—about 27% gain this year on top of upper teens—low 20% annual growth the past decade. Next year estimates call for upper teens growth. Problem loans have plummeted and earnings are accelerating. A "dog" you say?

Dairy Queen is a pure and simple cash cow. It's done its job. Policy growth at GEICO has been nothing short of astounding. We knew earnings would decline this year because of the expense of all the new business (new policies cost us money in year one—we think its a good investment).

FlightSafety ROE is way above 17% now—its one of the fastest growing privately held businesses we own.

Sure, Gen Re's losses have been a disappointment. But remember we bought this for (a) float expansion (now $24 1/2 billion) and (b) insurance synergies which would hopefully be realized a few years down the line.

Sosnoff's observations are off the mark, and frankly old news. You say Berkshire is a "turnaround" and you know you might be right.

Coke and Gillette are rebounding from overseas and currency challenges. The marketplace clearly acknowledges that now.

The GEICO business will be more profitable each year looking out. Re-insurance is on track and we are now the dominant player in the world. Simply—we can make great bets that others can't.

And we've got to hope that the Gen Re situation at least doesn't get worse. I think that's a good bet...we know about the lumpiness of this business.

All in all—I like where we are.

Another poster wrote:

I have a lot of respect for Buffett, but let's face the facts—the guy is in one hell of a slump. His equities (minus AXP) have performed miserably for two consecutive years. He sold his McDonald's only to watch it double. He bought Gen Re at the top of the market and has now lost $1.25 billion in earnings. GEICO's earnings have plunged in the cut throat car insurance market. KO, G, FRE and DIS have tanked, while the Post always underperforms. He sold Citigroup way too early. The shoe biz continues to be killed by cheap imports. His silver position is a DOG. Dairy Queen only does about $200,000 per store compared to $1,250,000 for McDonald's. Why sell the winner and hang on to the loser? He sits on a ton of low earning cash dragging down ROE. His big bond position has gone down since he purchased it. Executive Jet is spending billions with no great returns to show yet. FlightSafety had fairly low returns on equity when he purchased it—about 17%. His stock has not beaten the S&P 500 over the last five year period. What is his jewelry division doing about cheaper Internet competition?

Helzberg's looks dead to me as Zales knocks the cover off the ball. When was the last time you heard a commercial for them? Borsheim's has a chance on the Internet, but they need to advertise, which they are not doing. Someone else will end up beating them on Internet sales, which will be huge. The last time Sosnoff bashed Buffett was January of 1999, which looks like a great call by him. Go read the article again and you will see how perfect his predictions turned out to be. Oh yea, Scott and Fetzer was the target of a very negative front page article in the *Journal* two months ago. Let's face it, almost every major business that Berkshire has is going through a tough time. I would not criticize Sosnoff for pointing that out. He could have saved all of us some money in 1999. It's kind of ironic that a guy like Buffett who hates turnaround situations now has a big one on his hands—Berkshire Hathaway! Let's hope he hasn't lost his touch.

Saudi Arabian Prince Alwaleed Bin Talal wrote *Forbes* (January 24, 2000)..... "Although companies like Coke and Gillette may be considered part of the 'old economy' that 'old' system is not going to suddenly evaporate. I may not be in full agreement with Mr. Buffett's avoidance of tech investments, but I strongly believe in his decades of philosophy and strategies that have acted as a beacon for other investors."

160

A MESSAGE FROM BUFFETT'S DAUGHTER

"Doshoes New Shoes"

This photo of an oil painting on canvas panel by Dara Zapata of Boston of Buffett's daughter ("Doshoes" on the Internet) depicts a shoe box which says color Ruby/Silver; Style 75,500 (the artist's target for Berkshire's stock price in May 1998). On the monitor, there's the Berkshire fistful of dollars, the AOL logo, Nebraska logo and the Yellow BRKer group at Mr. Toad's, including John Gartmann in the yellow hat.

Here is a message from Buffett's daughter, Susan, of February 12, 1998, about Berkshire's Annual Meeting:

The annual report will be mailed no later than March 15th.

Here are the answers to the questions you have asked about the meeting:

The Embassy Suites is located in the Old Market area. This is the best area to walk around, shop, eat and drink. It's also across the street from Mr. Toad's.

The Marriott is across the street from Borsheim's ....

The Westin Aquila is a nice hotel in the downtown area. Also, the Radisson Redick and the Doubletree are downtown. (I'm not trying to sell you on downtown—this is information only!)

There is no hotel that is within walking distance of AkSarBen...

I really recommend renting a car. There are about five cabs in this city.

There are plenty of things to do when you're finished at

Borsheim's and the Furniture Mart. The Joslyn Art Museum is beautiful—I'm not sure if the Degas exhibit will still be here, but it's a great place to visit. The Western Heritage Museum is the old Union Station and it's really great—it's also the site of your Chairman's weekly Sunday lunches with my brothers and me when we were kids. We have an incredible zoo—it's across the street from the baseball stadium on 10th Street. Don't miss the jungle, the aquarium and the IMAX theater.

If you're bringing kids, we have a nice Children's Museum on 20th Street. And the Children's Theater at 20th and Farnam will be presenting "Charlotte's Web." One personal comment here—the Children's Theater is in the Rose Blumkin Performing Arts Center. This is a renovated vaudeville theater that you should all see—just because it's so great. The building was bought by Mrs. B. in 1980 so that it wouldn't be torn down. It was renovated and reopened about two years ago. At the black-tie opening gala, Warren played the ukulele while Frances Batt (Mrs. B.'s daughter) sang "Am I Blue." This is because she won a five-dollar gold piece when she was five years old for singing that song on that very stage. It was one of the first wonderful experiences that Mrs. B. had in the U.S. and that's why she saved the building. Isn't that a great story?

Some good restaurants are (and these are in no particular order)—Vivace, The French Cafe, V. Mertz, the Indian Oven, Ahmad's, The Flatiron Grill, M's Pub, Spanna, Jams, Yo Yo Grille, Jaipur. I'll keep thinking and let you know if I come up with others. The best steaks are at Gorat's—be careful of some of the restaurants listed (especially in the steak department) on the information sheet that comes from Berkshire Hathaway.

The weather question is really hard to answer. Most likely, it will be pretty nice—around 60 to 70 degrees. It's very possible that it will rain and it's even possible that we will have a tornado. A few years ago there was a tornado warning right after the meeting and some people had to take shelter in the vault at Borsheim's.

For those of you who don't know, the meeting lasts until around 3:30. There's a break for lunch (about 20-30 minutes) and then the "hard core" (which seems to be about 6000 people) stay for the afternoon. There are a bunch of booths in AkSarBen where you can buy all kinds of stuff to help the stock price rise. You will have an opportunity to buy the NEW shirts for 1998, along with a lot of other fun things.

The baseball seating looks like it will work well. The meeting seating could get tricky. I'm still not sure I've figured out how to make it work. But I'll keep you all informed. We might need someone to stand guard at the reserved area—this job would start when the doors open. And, any empty seats would have to be released around 8:15.

If I've forgotten anything, please e-mail or post it and I'll try to answer.

161

THE BUNNY FARM
(A LESSON IN RATIONAL EXUBERANCE)

Here are missives on the "Berkshire message board" from Berkshire shareholder Michael Rhodes of Kansas City, Missouri:

January 1997:

Think of BRK as 3 pieces:

1. A closed end fund owning stocks and bonds
2. A group of non-insurance operating businesses that produce cash for WEB to deploy
3. An insurance operation that generates cash for WEB to deploy

Piece 1 is easy to value since it is all publicly traded. It's worth about $35.5 billion ($6.5 billion bonds, $24.1 billion for 6 disclosed equities and $4.9 billion conservative estimate for the other equities.)

Piece 2 is worth about $5 billion (I take [a] valuation of 3.3 billion, add the $1.5 billion for FlightSafety, and round up another $0.2 billion because WEB paid FlightSafety... this much below its intrinsic value.)

So 1+2 = $40.5 billion

Now the fun part. But first note at $34,100 a share BRK's market cap is $41.3 billion. Only $0.8 billion more than the first two pieces alone.

While the float debate is ongoing, I will stick my neck out and predict that the consensus that will emerge is that the float is worth around $12 billion...

This puts us at $52.5 billion. From this I would subtract something for the present value of deferred taxes—to be very conservative let's call it $2.5 billion. Thus we have BRK worth an even $50 billion, comfortably above Mr. Market's $41.3 billion valuation. The part I really like is the above analysis does not add anything for WEB's magic multiplier effect. Piece 1 is worth what the market says with or without WEB. Piece 2 does not need WEB in order to sustain the cash flows available to redeploy, nor does Piece 3.

Think of BRK as a big bunny farm. The $12 billion valuation for

(Illustration by Nancy Line Jacobs)

the float is just the first generation of bunnies (the present value of the float cash that comes in the door each year). What WEB brings to the table is his ability to make these little bunnies multiply. By the time next year's truckload of 840 million (annual float increment) bunnies arrive at the farm, last year's bunnies have produced new generations.

The dividend and interest income from Piece 1 and the cash flow from Piece 2 also bring in truckloads of new bunnies annually.

After a while, you've got a mighty big bunny farm. You can buy a piece of the farm today for about 83 cents on the dollar.

🐰🐰🐰🐰🐰🐰🐰🐰🐰🐰🐰🐰🐰🐰🐰🐰🐰🐰🐰🐰🐰🐰

August 30, 1997

I spent some time this morning out in the bunny pen updating the census taken last January that showed the farm was then on sale for about 83 cents on the dollar. After reading that census again last night, I wondered what today's quote would look like, with Mr. Market suddenly worried that the proprietor/birthday boy has lost his ability to motivate bunnies to do what they do best.

It turns out the first bunnies in the insurance pen are totally out of control. Last January I was assuming $840 million in new float for 1997. For the first half alone the farm needed a shipment of 500 million new float bunnies. The second quarter shipment was 400 million. And when doing the January census, I didn't count on any underwriting profit bunnies arriving. It turns out 118 million arrived in the first half. So assuming the same second half of 1997 brings the same shipments as the first half, the new insurance bunny shipments will be over 1.2 billion for 1997.

Of course, one bad hurricane or earthquake could destroy up to 600 million bunnies, a sad fact that bunny farm owners must keep in mind at all times. But that potential tragedy notwithstanding, the fact remains that the insurance bunny pen is more crowded than I had anticipated eight months ago. And looking out at the front gate, the incoming trucks are lined up a mile down the lane. Maybe the valuation of the insurance bunny pen ($12 billion in January) needs to be adjusted for overcrowded conditions. Using the same multiple used in January (14.3 which was the 7% long bond yield inverted), and updating the 1997 new insurance bunny count to 1.2 billion invested over 840 million, the new valuation would be about $17.2 billion...

The rest of the farm is also doing fine. Cash and securities about $40 billion, compared to $35.5 billion in the January count.

Assuming the owned non-insurance businesses are conservatively worth $5 billion and assuming a deduction of $2.5 billion for deferred taxes (both the same assumptions used in January), the total farm valuation comes to about $59.7 billion.

Today Mr. Market says the farm is worth $51.1 billion. The farm is on sale, marked down to 85 cents on the dollar. And the birthday boy is still spiking the bunny feed with aphrodisiac.

Rhodes offered this update on October 24, 1999:

I know it is wearisome for some to keep reading that BRK is cheap while watching it get cheaper every day, but here's a quick and dirty addition exercise.

$71B	Investments/Cash
$10B	Non-insurance businesses IV
$83B	Market cap of BRK
- 81B	Total of above two parts
2B	Market's valuation of BRK's $23B-24B Float

This is beyond cheap.

162
WASHINGTON AND LEE
UNIVERSITY GETS
1,000 SHARES OF BERKSHIRE
"THAT'S WHAT WARREN BUFFETT DID FOR ME."

Ernie Williams, Class of '38 at Washington and Lee University in Lexington, Virginia, long has been a benefactor of the school he and three generations of his family love. But with Williams' recent gift to the school, he outdid himself when he and his wife, Marjorie, handed over 1,000 shares of Berkshire to W&L for professorships and scholarships. The gift was the second largest in W&L history.

"I was certainly surprised at the amount of capital gains he had in the Berkshire stock," said David R. Long, director of planned giving at W&L.

"I had known for some time he had a large position in the stock and was thinking about giving some of it to W&L...All along Ernie had wanted it to be anonymous but we convinced him to make an announcement to help with publicity in the fundraising campaign. He's very emotional when it comes to helping W&L."

So how did Williams come by 1,000 shares of Berkshire stock?

"I read a story in the October 1977 issue of *Fortune* magazine by Warren Buffett," Williams recalled. "The logic of it overwhelmed me. I must have read it three, seven or ten times." Williams noticed in the "pink sheets" that a friend of his made a market in Berkshire stock. Soon Williams bought some Berkshire shares at about $80 each. Then he headed for Berkshire's Annual Meeting in April 1978, and met Buffett. "I had about 150 shares and I really went out to see if I should buy more.

"There were 17 people at the meeting held in the National Indemnity headquarters building. Buffett was sitting one chair from me and never left and never said a word. There was a clock there on the wall behind Ken Chace who conducted the meeting. The meeting started exactly at 10 a.m. and it was over in exactly 10 minutes and he left.

"I got him out in the hall and said I'd flown all the way out and

(Photo courtesy of Ernie Williams)

Ernie Williams

would he talk to me. We talked. I doubt it was more than 15 minutes. Mainly he told me that short-term there would be some problems at the *Buffalo News* but that things might work out well there in the long run. That was before the other paper—*The Courier*—folded."

Williams said there wasn't anything specific that Buffett said that made him realize Buffett was special. Still, something about Buffett struck him so much that Williams immediately called his office to buy more Berkshire stock.

Williams, former president of the old Mason & Lee brokerage house in Lynchburg, Virginia, called his office and put in an order to buy Berkshire shares, saying: "I want you to clean up the market for Berkshire."

When his office called back to say they had filled his order, he said, "Now I want you to go out and buy more Berkshire."

"I then flew on to Chicago in a snowstorm that day and I got there about 2:30 and I called my office and said I wanted to buy more Berkshire. I was told it was trading at a higher price. I said I want you to go out and buy," he said.

At the time the stock was trading without any fanfare in the pink sheets.

In those transactions that day of the Berkshire meeting, Williams picked up about 150 shares at an average cost of about $152 a share.

From that day forth until 1983 when Berkshire was trading at more than $1,300 a share, Williams continued to buy. At that point, Williams held about 1,500 Berkshire shares and became a multi-millionaire.

All of Williams' family members are wealthy, and W&L is a major beneficiary of his farsighted investment in Berkshire.

"That's what Warren Buffett did for me," he said.

Over the years, he followed Buffett into certain Berkshire investments such as GEICO.

For many years, Williams lived at Hilton Head Island, South Carolina, on Laughing Gull Road. Buffett and Williams occasionally were in touch. "He joked with me about my address," said Williams, who now lives in Village of Golf, Florida, near Delray Beach.

Williams relates another Buffett story of buying his first shares through his friend, Archie MacAllaster. MacAllaster is chairman of MacAllaster Pitfield, a firm specializing in over-the-counter securities, mainly bank and insurance issues.

Williams says that MacAllaster, who is often interviewed by *Barron's* magazine, was well regarded for his knowledge of insurance stocks, and that MacAllaster once met Buffett and talked about insurance stocks.

Williams said, "MacAllaster came away from a luncheon thinking he didn't know a thing about insurance company stocks compared to Buffett. He said Buffett knew more about insurance stocks than anyone he'd ever met."

That's right, says MacAllaster, who notes he was a market-maker in Berkshire stock at a time when Williams was putting in buy orders for Berkshire. "I was a little nervous about holding Berkshire."

As for Buffett, Berkshire shareholder MacAllaster said, "I talked to him way back. He knew all about insurance and financial stocks. He is one smart financial person. He understood insurance stocks in Nebraska and he understood them nationwide...He understood balance sheets."

The real hero of the story, Williams says, was Fitz Fitzgerald, MacAllaster's trader. "He didn't want to inventory any Berkshire. And he would call me and say, 'Look, I hate to see Berkshire break 300. I've got 300 shares you can have at that price.' And he did that every time he would take stock in. He didn't mean to be so good to me...I always bought it on the offered side. Good Old Fitz."

At the dedication of the Ernest Williams II School of Commerce, Economics and Politics at W&L in 1995, J. Alfred Broaddus, of W&L's Class of '61 and president of the Federal Reserve Bank of Richmond, praised Williams for his purchase of property on Hilton Head Island, South Carolina, in the 1950s and Berkshire stock in the 1970s.

"The audience knows these things, Ernie, and consequently and undoubtedly they would much rather have you up here giving them business advice and investment tips than some guy from the Fed," Broaddus said. (*The Washington and Lee Alumni Magazine*, Fall, 1995)

There's little doubt Washington & Lee will stay in touch with Williams. He told *Forbes* (October 12, 1998) he and his family have more than 4,000 shares of Berkshire Class A stock.

163

"SIR, WHAT IF YOU DIE?"
"IT WOULDN'T BE AS NEGATIVE FOR THE HOLDERS AS IT WILL BE FOR ME."

"Sir, what if you die?"

This touchy question gets posed to Buffett almost every year, although usually more subtly.

At a discussion about how Buffett's death might affect his company's stock, Buffett quipped, "It wouldn't be as negative for the holders as it will be for me." He made that comment from his front row seat at a conference held October 27, 1996, at the Benjamin Cardozo School of Law at Yeshiva University in New York City (where 150 people stood in line for 2 days to get into the conference). How would you like it if you were asked in public every year about walking into a Mack truck?

"Here comes the 'if I get hit by a truck question,'" Buffett has said under his breath when he gets it at annual meetings.

Rob Sullivan, who runs Sullivan Consolidation, Inc. in Springfield, Massachusetts, jokes that he takes exception to the "hit by a truck question."

"I run a trucking company and I've instructed our drivers to be careful not to hit [Buffett and Munger] because they have Berkshire and Wesco in their pension plan."

Buffett wrote Sullivan after the annual meeting in 1995: "Thanks for your note and the bunnies you sent. They were a big hit with the little kids at home and also the big kids here in the office.....P.S. No more mention of 'truck'!"

It's a near certainty that Buffett will not die by being hit by a truck. Tooth decay, maybe.

"All in all, we're prepared for 'the truck,'" Buffett wrote in the 1993 Annual Report after explaining his stock will not be sold at his death, but will go either to his wife or his foundation. And he said there are plans for strong management.

"After my death, all of my stock will go to my wife Susie should she survive me, or to a foundation if she dies before I do. In neither case will taxes and bequests require the sale of consequential amounts of stock," Buffett wrote.

"Nothing will be forced by estate taxes. I owe that to people in case I step in an elevator shaft absent-mindedly," Buffett said at the

Berkshire Annual Meeting in 1986.

Asked at the annual meeting in 1991 what would happen to Berkshire if he died, Buffett deadpanned, "Our businesses are run as if I am not there. So the exact location of my body shouldn't matter."

Buffett has assured shareholders that nothing will happen to his Berkshire stock. "Not a single share of my stock will be sold," he has said. Almost all his Berkshire stock is going to The Buffett Foundation.

"It's a marvelous society that lets me do what I do. I wouldn't be worth a damn in Bangladesh or Peru or some place. The fact that I have a lot of fun with it and can consume some of it, I think I should give it back to society. I see no reason why I should create some dynasty of wealth that can go around fanning themselves," he said on Adam Smith's *Money World* show in connection with Berkshire's annual meeting in 1990.

Here's how he puts things in the 1990 Annual Report: "I feel strongly that the fate of our businesses and their managers should not depend on my health which, it should be added, is excellent—and I have planned accordingly. Neither my estate plan nor that of my wife is designed to preserve the family fortune; instead, both are aimed at preserving the character of Berkshire and returning the fortune to society."

Precisely how all this will work has not been publicly spelled out. "The sequence of its disposition depends on the order of death. But ultimately, it will go back to society," Buffett said at the annual meeting in 1991. Nor has it been detailed what will happen to Buffett's substantial personal portfolio.

What has been communicated is that the Berkshire shareholders should not lie awake at night and worry that Berkshire is going back to $12 a share the day Buffett goes.

"I don't do the normal exercise and I don't eat a normal diet. But we do have someone in mind who would be our successor if Charlie and I were to die at once. And on my death, not a share of stock has to be sold. I have promised people that my affairs will not cause people any surprises," Buffett said at the annual meeting in 1988.

At the meeting in 1991 he said, "You have two questions as shareholders that you have to think about: Will the owners behave any different as owners? And will the managers behave any different as managers?" He made it clear the answer to both questions is no.

Munger said, "I think it's obvious that if Warren died tomorrow the prospects of the company would be somewhat reduced.

Certainly the capital allocation process couldn't be made better under any foreseeable scenario. However, I do think a company like Berkshire would have a lot of time to find a successor. And you only need one." Buffett: "Maybe less."

Munger: "And I don't think that you should assume that the personality who put the whole thing together would be incapable of finding a successor."

Buffett: "It's an easy company to run. And the capital allocation process may be self-defeating anyway over time. And there's nothing that says we can forever allocate the capital better than you.

"So as the years go by, it's not inconceivable that we could have a policy on dividends that would be dramatically different than the present one because we believed you could do a better job of allocating the capital than we could—partly because the sums would be so large. And Charlie says we're looking forward to that day."

But even if Buffett were to step into an elevator shaft tomorrow, his current investments would live on. People will go on drinking Coca-Cola, shaving with Gillette and buying *World Books* using their American Express cards.

Berkshire probably would hit some air pockets if Buffett were to depart, and some suggest a huge stock price drop, knocking out what many observers call "a Buffett premium."

Such fears are summarized by *Newsday's* Allan Sloan: "I'd sure hate to find buyers for large blocks of Berkshire stock if Buffett weren't there." Still, that might be a moment to buy.

At the annual meeting in 1987, Buffett made a remarkable comment after an explanation about how if he should go, then Munger would run things "and we have a provision beyond that." What he said next is that he had almost never given a stock tip in his life.

Then he gave one: "When I die, buy the stock."

He suggested the stock price might drop, making Berkshire a real buy. He repeated his standard remark that none of his stock will be sold.

At the annual meeting in 1986, Buffett said, "Charlie will be running it. No Berkshire holding will be sold. It will be kept intact. Capital Cities, Gillette and GEICO will continue. There will be no surprises for management."

He said that when he dies the stock price shouldn't change much, wisecracking, "I'll be disappointed if it goes up a lot," a reference to some stocks rising in relief when certain CEOs leave the scene. "No you won't," Munger quipped.

Buffett said of Munger, "He'll be flattered," by Berkshire rising in anticipation of Munger's reign.

Should Buffett go, Berkshire would be run by Munger who for years has allocated the capital with Buffett. Would things be as good as under Buffett, the true glue that keeps the disparate parts of Berkshire together? No. They would not. Buffett is an original, one of a kind. Would they be bad? Not at all.

As Munger has put it, "Capital allocation would not be as good as under him. But it would not be bad, either."

Says one Berkshire shareholder, "One of the most significant questions about Berkshire is what will happen when Buffett dies."

Munger has said, "Berkshire's chairman may get older, but the assets aren't going anywhere. And the nature of the Berkshire game is that we do not have to replace armies to make it work well. We've run so lean over the years that over time we've only got two or three crucially important bodies to replace."

"We'll get somebody like Warren," Munger has said. There's the rub, of course.

Says one Berkshire shareholder, "Munger can do everything Buffett does except be funny at the annual meeting."

Beyond Munger, will Berkshire find some superb individual to allocate the capital? Sure. But just who had long been a mystery.

In Berkshire's 1995 Annual Report Buffett indicated that person "immediately available" is GEICO's Lou Simpson, calling him someone who could handle Berkshire's investments were anything to happen to him and Munger.

Buffett always means what he says and says what he means.

"When I die, buy the stock." What does that mean? No one knows for sure. But, with Buffett saying it, it means what it says.

One shareholder says, "He probably means that if Berkshire took a big dip upon his death, the stock would be undervalued and be a buy."

Buffett never makes idle comments, and his comment about buying the stock means something, but it's unclear just what.

Buffett's comment certainly seems to suggest some finale. Expect a surprise when his estate passes to The Buffett Foundation.

Berkshire shareholder Judith Goodnow Prus believes Berkshire's denouement to the Buffett era will strike a theme of Buffett-as-teacher. Ever since Buffett taught investment courses in his early days in Omaha, he has been a teacher of sorts. His occasional talks, his writings, his fielding of questions at annual meetings all show characteristics of a teacher.

Indeed Mrs. Prus thinks Buffett may have accepted the Salomon post in part because of his love of teaching. "It seems to me the reason he was so quick to accept the Salomon challenge...it was a made-to-order opportunity to teach some ethical as well as economic lessons. I think he seized the opportunity for this reason, not just to protect an investment...

"I think he is so intelligent and so rational and so realistic, that he must understand that he is in a unique position to teach and has a responsibility to do so...Perhaps it doesn't make any sense for him to teach in the usual sense, that is one teacher, with a few pupils, but perhaps some day soon, with the new methods of communication, he would be able to invest some limited amount of time and reach a lot of people at once.

"Anyway, perhaps the denouement will be one big lesson. I hope so," Mrs. Prus said.

Buffett's net worth of about $30 billion would make his foundation the largest charity in the nation; the Ford Foundation is now the largest with assets of about $10 billion. Buffett's children are each to receive a relative pittance of roughly $5 million. (*Wall Street Journal*, November 8, 1991) When the day is done, Buffett is a giver, not a taker.

"The other significant question about Berkshire is to figure out how to recognize the next Warren Buffett," said a Berkshire shareholder, adding that he has often tried to convince others of the appeal of Berkshire with almost no results.

"I have seen so many people pass it up," said one Berkshire shareholder. "I would like for my children to be able to recognize the next Berkshire that comes along."

Of course, one answer is to recognize this one and not worry too much about searching out another one. It's the same proposition for those investors who try to figure out where Buffett is investing or how to copycat his investments.

The way to be sure you are doing what Buffett is doing when he is doing it is simply to be a Berkshire shareholder, that is just sit back and leave the driving, the investing, to him. Why try to second-guess Buffett? Why not just enjoy what he's doing?

Occasionally, there are rumors that Buffett is up for a government job or is under consideration to head the New York Stock Exchange, but he has sidestepped all that with the assurance, "I'll keep doing this as long as I live." (*Los Angeles Times*, Linda Grant, April 7, 1991)

"I think he's an American genius...He has a sterling reputation," said Kahn Brothers' Irving Kahn, who adds that his only bone to pick with Buffett is why, as he's gotten older, Buffett has continued to concentrate on amassing wealth rather than giving more consideration to what that wealth can do for society. Kahn said:

> After all, it's money he's made from other people. He didn't create the telephone or invent something...Sooner or later some of that money should go back to society. Warren Buffett looks good versus the other nefarious collectors of corporate shares. Yet his gains equal the losses of all who sold to him...Maybe after so many brilliant achievements, Warren Buffett will use his energy and brains for broader and deeper national problems.

Sequoia Fund President Bob Goldfarb said at Sequoia's Annual Meeting in 1998: "Periodically, you read about a company that is characterized as the next Berkshire Hathaway. There is no next Berkshire Hathaway."

At Sequoia's 1999 Annual Meeting Goldfarb's similar thought was: "A friend of mine has commented that everybody is always looking for the next Warren Buffett. The fact is that there is no next Warren Buffett."

We shall see whether Buffett has given full thought to how that money will be used.

Buffett may feel that the more wealth he can accumulate, the more he can help the world. And of course Buffett has offered a lot in human terms already, setting examples in human and financial behavior for all. And the Buffett/Berkshire story is unfinished.

Almost everyone's first question about Berkshire is what happens when Buffett passes on. The query persists though Buffett is most assuredly not on his deathbed. It may well be that Buffett plans on surprising people by doing what he's doing until a very late age.

Perhaps a good response to the "what if he dies" question is, "What if he lives?"

He seems to be a healthy, happy and energetic man, and he just may live beyond the next quarter's earnings statement.

And how might Berkshire do if Buffett lives a long life? "Berkshire will generate significant sums of investable capital and Buffett will deploy this money successfully. Unfortunately, we can't put a number on this success. There's every reason to think the investments will do better than average, but there's no telling how much better, or what average will be," says Steve Wallman, who heads Wallman Investment Counsel in Madison, Wisconsin.

"Most people looking at Berkshire seem to suffer from a lack of imagination. They don't have the vaguest idea of where Buffett is taking the company, so they conclude that Buffett doesn't know where he's going either."

Buffett himself has given every indication that he has a few more chapters in his book, more painting to do on his Berkshire canvas.

Beyond that, things are not spelled out. But it is assumed that Buffett has researched the matter thoroughly and will leave his wealth to society in the least disruptive way to Berkshire shareholders.

"His integrity seems to me to be involved in his plans for the ultimate future of the company, when he is not there. Everyone who knows him seems to feel comfortable about whatever plan he might have for the company; we all seem to feel that it will be right, honorable and good. We trust his goodness," Mrs. Prus said.

The better Berkshire does, the more the foundation can do to achieve its lofty aims. One Berkshire shareholder has said that Buffett is not so much about money as he is about love.

What Buffett has reaped from society will be entirely given back to it. Buffett has an admiration for those who take a little from society and give a lot back.

In a letter to the *Omaha World-Herald*, January 20, 1980, reprinted in part in the *The Kiewit Story* by Hollis J. Limprecht, Buffett eulogized Peter Kiewit, the former head of Peter Kiewit Sons', Inc.:

> Pete Kiewit was overwhelmingly a producer, not a consumer. Profits went to build the capacity of the organization, not to provide opulence for the owner. In essence, one who spends less than he earns is accumulating 'claim checks' for future use. My guess is that he left claim checks worth some $150 million at the time of his death.
>
> During his lifetime, he and his family probably personally redeemed something like 3% of the claim checks that he produced. Upon his death, he left another 5% or so to his family. The balance was left to his community through a foundation whose intent, I believe, is to utilize a significant portion of those claim checks—stored-up consumption, in reality—for the benefit of the people of the Midlands.
>
> The bricklayer of 1920 turned out to be an extraordinary endowment manager, indeed. And now, at his death, that estimated $150 million endowment has been turned over to a group of foundation trustees who are likely to achieve Kiewit-type results in maximizing the flow of benefits to society from those funds. Peter Kiewit could not have better

served his community and his compatriots. (p. 276)

That last line could someday be a well-deserved epitaph for Buffett.

Munger sheds some light on this question in his 1990 letter to Wesco shareholders.

> This eccentric, who heads Berkshire Hathaway, Wesco's parent corporation, believes for some reason that accumulated wealth should *never* be spent on oneself or one's family, but instead should merely serve, before it is given to charity, as an example of a certain approach to life and as a didactic platform.
>
> These uses, plus use in building the platform higher, are considered the only honorable ones not only during life but also after death. Shareholders who continue in such peculiar company are hereby warned by our example in writing this section: some of the eccentricities of this fellow are contagious, at least if association is long continued.
>
> If Warren were a homespun philosopher running a small creamery, who'd pay attention to what he says? The money gives him the base to communicate his ideas. Berkshire is, in many ways, an exercise in didacticism. (*U.S. News & World Report*, June 20, 1994)

Herein is the permanent value that Buffett and Munger have so brilliantly created.

As for Berkshire, surely it will pass into competent hands and continue to flourish whether or not Buffett is running it.

And Buffett plans to keep running it for some time. Once at Harvard Business School he was asked when he planned to retire. "About five to ten years after I die," he replied.

And he told Columbia business students October 27, 1993:

> Berkshire would be pretty easy to run. It's in marvelous financial shape, has a great set of managers in the operating businesses.
>
> The person that ran it would have to do two things. They would have to basically keep the present managers motivated and happy doing what they're doing. And that basically means leaving them alone and judging them by the right standards.
>
> And then they'd have to allocate capital. They could partially solve the capital allocation by simply establishing a significant dividend policy for one thing.

They'd have to get one good idea a year on capital allocation. And the managing would be very simple.

Buffett wrote in Berkshire's "Owner's Manual" in June, 1996:

Charlie and I mainly attend to the capital allocation and
the care and feeding of our key managers. Most of these
managers are happiest when they are left alone to run their
businesses, and that is customarily just how we leave them.
That puts them in charge of all operating decisions and of
dispatching the excess cash they generate to headquarters.
By sending it to us, they don't get diverted by the various
enticements that could come their way were they responsible for deploying the cash their businesses throw off.
Furthermore, Charlie and I are exposed to a much wider
range of possibilities for investing these funds than any of
our managers could find in his or her own industry.

Most of our managers are independently wealthy, and it's
therefore up to us to create a climate that encourages them
to choose working with Berkshire over golfing or fishing.
This leaves us needing to treat them fairly and in the manner that we would wish to be treated if our positions were
reversed.

As for the allocation of capital, that's an activity both
Charlie and I enjoy and in which we have acquired some
useful experience. In a general sense, grey hair doesn't hurt
on this playing field: You don't need good hand-eye coordination or well-toned muscles to push money around (thank
heavens). As long as our minds continue to function effectively, Charlie and I can keep on doing our jobs pretty much
as we have done in the past.

On my death, Berkshire's ownership picture will change
but not in a disruptive way: First, only about 1% of my
stock will have to be sold to take care of bequests and taxes;
second, the balance of my stock will go to my wife, Susan, if
she survives, or to a family foundation if she doesn't. In
either event, Berkshire will possess a controlling shareholder
guided by the same philosophy and objectives that set our
course.

At that juncture, the Buffett family will not be involved in
managing the business, only in picking and overseeing the
managers who do. Just who those managers will be, of
course, depends on the date of my death. But I can anticipate what the management structure will be: Essentially my

job will be split in two parts, with one executive becoming responsible for investments and another for operations. If the acquisition of new businesses is in prospect, the two will cooperate in making the decisions needed. Both executives will report to a board of directors that will be responsible to the controlling shareholder, whose interest will in turn be aligned with yours.

Were we to need the management structure I have just described on an immediate basis, my family and a few key individuals know who I would pick to fill both posts. Both currently work for Berkshire and are people in whom I have total confidence.

I will continue to keep my family posted on the succession issue. Since Berkshire stock will make up virtually my entire estate and will account for a similar portion of the assets of either my wife or the foundation for a considerable period after my death, you can be sure I have thought through the succession question carefully. You can be equally sure that the principles we have employed to date in running Berkshire will continue to guide the managers who succeed me.

Lest we end on a morbid note, I also want to assure you that I have never felt better. I love running Berkshire, and if enjoying life promotes longevity, Methuselah's record is in jeopardy.

In any event, one should not wish Buffett to be in any hurry to leave. Rather, we should wish him immortality as he has wished it for his managers.

We should fully enjoy the presence of this genius while we can.

As John Buchan wrote in *Pilgrim's Way*, of Lawrence of Arabia: "If genius be, in Emerson's phrase, a 'stellar and undiminished something,' whose origin is a mystery and whose essence cannot be defined, then he was the only man of genius I have ever known."

164

"YESTERDAY I DIED."

Buffett was asked the "If you get hit by a truck" question one more time in 1998 when he and Bill Gates appeared at a symposium at the University of Washington.

The question was even more directly posed under the assumption that Berkshire's success depends on Buffett. The question ended: "What will happen when you're gone?"

Buffett replied (*Fortune*, July 20, 1998): "Your assumption is wrong. I will keep working until about five years after I die, and I've given my directors a Ouija board so they can keep in touch. But if the Ouija board doesn't work, we have outstanding people who can do what I do. People are not going to stop drinking Coca-Cola if I die tonight, they're not going to quit shaving tonight, they're not going to eat less See's candy, or fewer Dilly Bars, or anything of the sort. Those companies have terrific products, they've got outstanding managers, and all you'll need at the top of Berkshire is someone who can allocate capital and make sure you have the right managers down below. We've got the people identified to do that, and the board of directors of Berkshire knows who they are.

"In fact, I've already sent out a letter that tells what should be done, and I've got another letter addressed that will go out at the time, and it starts out, 'Yesterday I died,' and then tells what the plans of the company are."

The end of his letter says: "dictated but not read."

165
THE BUFFETT FOUNDATION
TO BE THE WORLD'S LARGEST CHARITY

B uffett's wealth, the fruits of his lifetime of long-term investing, is slated to go to The Buffett Foundation and then back to society.

Buffett's foundation could easily wind up as the largest on earth dwarfing even the legacies of Rockefeller and Ford. The largest foundations in the U.S., according to *The New York Times* (September 12, 1999) citing *The Chronicle of Philanthropy:*

The 10 wealthiest private foundations in the United States.

Foundation Location and Year Established	Assets in Billions	Estimated 1999 giving in Millions
Bill & Melinda Gates Foundation, Seattle, 1994*	$17.1	$500
David and Lucile Packard Foundation Los Altos, California, 1964	13.0	440
Ford Foundation, New York, 1937	11.4	550
Lilly Endowment Indianapolis, 1937	11.1	500
Robert Wood Johnson Foundation Princeton, New Jersey, 1936	8.1	440
W. K. Kellogg Foundation Battle Creek, Michigan 1930	6.2	221
Pew Charitable Trusts Philadelphia, 1948	4.8	230
John D. and Catherine T. MacArthur Foundation Chicago, 1978	4.2	168
Andrew W. Mellon Foundation New York, 1969	3.5	153
Rockefeller Foundation New York, 1913	3.5	175

*This foundation was created in 1999 by the merger of two other Gates' foundations, founded in 1994 and 1997.

Asset values between June 30, 1999 and August 16, 1999.

There is always a good debate over whether to leave a fortune to society sooner or later. *Fortune* summarized the issue (March 15, 1999): "Buffett says it's a good thing Gates waited as long as he did. 'If he had given away 90% of his money ten years ago, it would have been at a huge cost to society,' says Buffett. 'Giving away that money early on might have cheated the world out of $100 billion. Instead he has been running the best-performing endowment fund in the world.' The counter-argument is that there is a time value of money to charity as well. That is, if Gates had given away, say, $50 million ten years ago to eradicate a disease, and that money had found a cure, and the cure had saved 100,000 lives, let alone saved $1 billion in health-care costs, how do you assign a value to that? There is no right answer of course."

Buffett calls his fortune, "a fund that's not yet activated." (*Omaha World-Herald*, October 4, 1993)

The thrust of The Buffett Foundation's giving currently is for planned parenthood, reducing the risk of nuclear war, and education. Currently the foundation gives away about $11 million to $12 million a year with most of the money going to family-planning services, including abortions. (*Business Week*, July 5, 1999)

"His big interest has always been the problem of world population growth. He thinks it's a danger to the world...that you can have it all but if you have overpopulation the world will struggle with problems like housing," says his sister, Doris Bryant.

With the exception of some grants made in Omaha, the focus of the foundation is largely family planning, both domestic and international.

The foundation, with assets in 1998 of about $22 million [Berkshire contributed about $8 million to the foundation in 1998], has no grant guidelines except for its college scholarship program which provides scholarships to University of Nebraska students. The foundation doesn't accept applications for grants.

The foundation is run out of a one-person office in Kiewit Plaza, 12 floors below Berkshire's headquarters, by Allen Greenberg, the former husband of Buffett's daughter Susan. Greenberg took the job in 1987.

Greenberg was raised in New York City where his father owned a newspaper distribution business. After graduating from New York University Law School, he began a career in public-interest law and worked as a legislative aide to Representative Charles Schumer, now senator of New York. The marriage pleased Susie's parents, who took to calling Greenberg "Allen-the-perfect-son-in-law." Aside from a part-time secretary, Greenberg remains the foundation's only employee—at a salary of $120,000.

"Of the $17.6 million that the Buffett Foundation donated in the fiscal year ended June 30, nearly $3.8 million went to Planned Parenthood. This ranked the foundation among the federation's top three contributors. But what truly sets the Buffett Foundation apart is that it involves itself directly at the clinic level by making project grants to local affiliates across the country—17 of them this year alone. Over the years, Buffett money has enabled dozens of Planned Parenthood clinics to add abortion to their panoply of services." (*Business Week*, October 25, 1999)

"Buffett indicated a new willingness to make a large, direct gift to the foundation before his death. 'If my wife and Allen had projects they felt were tenable right now, I would consider it,' Buffett says. Indeed, the foundation's annual giving has risen, of late, to a level that may soon force the issue. The $17.6 million in donations made in fiscal 1999 represented a 41% increase over the previous year. If Greenberg maintains this pace the existing endowment might well be exhausted within a year.

"But even if Buffett were persuaded to ratchet up his annual giving above the $25 million or even the $100 million mark, the time will come when Greenberg will have to operate on an incomparably larger scale. By law, a foundation is required to give away at least 5% of its endowment every year. Even if the Buffetts were to leave an estate no larger than it is today, Greenberg would have to distribute a staggering $1.8 billion a year.

Greenberg would not be quoted for this article, but has told friends that he tries

(Photo courtesy of Omaha World-Herald)

Buffett Foundation's Allen Greenberg

not to dwell on the future lest he become "paralyzed with fear."
(*Business Week*, October 25, 1999)

Buffett's daughter, Susan, and Allen Greenberg were married 12 years until their divorce in 1995.

"I've given no thought at all to replacing Allen since he and my daughter divorced. I think he is the best person in the U.S. to run the foundation," Buffett has said. (*Business Week*, October 25, 1999)

Buffett has decided not to dictate from the grave how the foundation should operate, saying that high-grade people living after him will be better judges of how best to use the money for mankind.

He has shied away from saying too much about the foundation, formed in 1964, but Buffett has said that most of his money will go back to society and that the conduit for building a better world is the foundation.

The foundation is still quite small and waiting for Buffett's vast wealth to multiply into a force for the betterment of mankind. "The foundation will be funded in a big way at my death and I've told the trustees that they can do anything they think is the thing to do at the time. I do not restrict them in any way. I will tell them that their decisions above ground will be a lot better than mine 6 feet under-ground....You don't know what the major problems of the world will be or what the funding sources will be or anything. So they [the foundation's trustees] have total discretion." Buffett said. (*Omaha World-Herald*, May 25, 1997)

The foundation's assets are currently a hodgepodge of stocks. Warren and Susan Buffett have made donations through Berkshire's charitable giving program. So far the foundation has been the recipient of millions of the Buffett's billions.

The Buffett Foundation assets of only $1.4 million in 1981 grew to $8.4 million in 1986, largely because of good return on investments and Buffett's own contributions through Berkshire's shareholder-designated contributions program.

The *Forbes* story about Buffett being the richest person in the country in October 1993, figured that the Buffett estate could be worth $100 billion in 20 years, dwarfing the legacies of Rockefeller, Ford and Carnegie.

Buffett, sometimes criticized for not giving away his money now, said, "I wouldn't want to transfer Berkshire Hathaway shares to anyone while I'm alive. If I owned a wide portfolio of securities I could give them away. But, I don't want to give up control of Berkshire Hathaway...I've got this fund that's not yet activated, and it is building at a rate greater than other endowments, like Harvard's. It's growing at 25% to 30%."

The Buffett Foundation on June 30, 1990, had assets of $15,210,316, according to Foundation Incorporation records. In the 12 months ending then, the foundation made contributions and paid grants totalling $1,417,895 to more than 80 entities. Operating and administrative expenses during this period totalled $131,382. The largest of the grants was $200,000, and the smallest was $280 to Rudyard Theatre. Average amounts fell in the $1,000 to $10,000 range.

If that doesn't tell a whole lot, it still serves as a tantalizing blueprint of future giving.

What is known about the foundation is that, on the asset side, its stockholdings show Buffett to be a stock market junkie.

The foundation's Form 990-PF for the year ended June 30, 1990, shows about 200 stock positions ranging from 200 shares of Abbott Laboratories to 110 shares of Zenith National Insurance Co. Berkshire itself also owns stocks from A to Z: Arrow Electronics to Zenith National Insurance.

And in the foundation there was everything in between from 200 shares of American Brands, 10 shares of Cap Cities, now Disney, 75 shares of CBS, 600 of Coca-Cola, 200 Freddie Mac, 100 GE, 100 J&J, 100 Eli Lilly, 750 Loews, 200 Melville Corp., 150 Morgan Stanley Group, 800 Philip Morris, 100 Playboy Enterprises, 100 Ralston Purina, 100 Rockefeller Center Properties, 100 Salomon, 100 Sears Roebuck, 100 Tiffany, 100 Torchmark, 200 Wal-Mart Stores, 10 Washington Post Co., 100 Wells Fargo, and many others.

The recipients are equally eclectic. Form 990-PF report shows the following were among the recipients of the foundation's contributions and grants:

> ACLU Reproductive Freedom Project—$15,000
> Alan Guttmacher Institute—$100,000
> Cancer Research Institute—$1,000
> Caring for Children—$1,000
> Girls, Inc. of Omaha—$20,000
> International Projects Assistance Services $200,000
> Omaha Zoo Foundation—$9,500
> Planned Parenthood of Mid-Iowa—$30,000
> Planned Parenthood of New York City—$100,000
> Salem Baptist Church—$5,000
> Sex Information and Education Council of U.S.—$15,000
> United Way of the Midlands—$122,411

Alice Buffett Outstanding Teacher Awards—$10,000 each to 15

recipients which the foundation gives each year. Alice Buffett was Buffett's aunt who taught in Omaha for 35 years.

In fiscal 1991–92, the foundation gave 73% of its donations, totaling $2.2 million, to groups involved in limiting population. (*Omaha World-Herald*, July 24, 1992)

The largest recipients were the Center for Reproductive Law and Policy, New York, $500,000, and International Projects Assistance Services, Carrboro, North Carolina, which trains doctors and health professionals and provides equipment for medical clinics in developing countries, received $250,000.

A story in *The New York Times* (December 3, 1995) gave a good look at the Buffett Foundation. "On June 30, 1995, the Buffett Foundation had assets of $21.6 million, according to the latest tax returns. About $7 million of that was invested in a smorgasboard of 184 stocks.

"But despite the variety, one stock, General Dynamics, dominated the foundation's equities, accounting for $5.63 million, or more than 80% of their total worth. Loews was the far-distant, second-largest holding, with a value of $90,750 as of June 30."

The other main holdings were 1,200 shares of Coca-Cola, 800 shares of Philip Morris, 375 shares of American International Group, 900 shares of Pepsico, 800 shares of Campbell Soup, 600 shares of Anheuser-Busch, 600 shares of Hershey Foods and 600 shares of Leucadia National.

The cost of three major holdings was $2.65 million and the worth on June 30, 1995, was $6.08 million.

The *Times* story said:

> Aficionados speculate that the foundation... may be [Buffett's] research vehicle, a means of keeping track of annual reports from companies he likes to follow.
>
> The nation's best known investor keeps only 32% of his foundation's money in stocks. Most of the money, 57%, is in Treasuries, with the balance in cash and other assets... Companies can deduct the full value of an appreciated stock without paying capital gains on the appreciation, up to 10% of their taxable income. For example, two years ago, at Mr. Buffett's election, Berkshire donated 110,485 shares of Torchmark, an insurance company, to the foundation. The stock cost Berkshire $2.1 million, but the company got to deduct from taxes $4.8 million, the shares' value at the time of the donation, and did not have to pay the 35% tax on the gain.

The nonprofit foundation, which then sold the stock, paid just the 2% gains tax to which it is subject. To top it off, Mr. Buffett got to direct the flow of nearly 5 million philanthropic dollars at a cost to Berkshire of just $2.1 million.

Buffett often speaks of working with people he likes, admires and trusts, so it's not at all surprising that he has chosen people close to him as officers and directors of his foundation.

The officers of The Buffett Foundation are:

Susan T. Buffett, president
Warren E. Buffett, vice president & treasurer
Gladys Kaiser, secretary
Allen Greenberg, Buffett's former son-in-law, executive director

The directors of the foundation: Buffett and his wife, their daughter, Susan, Carol Loomis and Tom Murphy.

Also Buffett had the tiny Sherwood Foundation directed by his children and Astrid Menks. For the year that ended July 30, 1993, it had assets of $584,000 and gave away about $370,000. (*New York Times*, December 3, 1995) "Buffett contributes $500,000 a year to a Sherwood Foundation so that each of his children and his companion Astrid Menks can make contributions of their own totalling $100,000 a year or so. Buffett does not check how the contributions are made." (*Warren Buffett Speaks*, Janet Lowe, 1997, p. 51)

In late 1999 Buffett's three children formed separate foundations to replace their shared Sherwood Foundation. The Howard Buffett Foundation held 500 A shares, a gift from Mrs. Susan Buffett. Howard Buffett said (*Omaha World-Herald*, February 16, 2000) that the new foundations simply allow contributions to be made individually rather than by committee. "Not a lot has changed. This gives us the ability to do things a little bit more on our own, that's all."

Buffett said most of the contributions he will make will go to "conservation, education and kids." Beneficiaries include Ecotrust, a Portland, Oregon, conservation group; the World Wildlife Fund, the DeWildt Cheetah Sanctuary in South Africa as well as other groups including a teacher awards program in Decatur, Illinois.

The Buffett foundation paid more than half the first-year costs for tests needed to bring the French abortion pill, RU-486, to the U.S. market, according to the *Omaha World-Herald*. (Cindy Connolly, April 21, 1996)

"The Buffett Foundation gave $2 million in 1994 to fund clinical trials for the pill, which is called mifepristone in the United States. The money went to Population Council, a nonprofit research group in New York that holds the U.S. patent rights to the pill," the story said.

"The $2 million the Buffett Foundation gave for the clinical trials was in addition to more than $5 million it contributed in 1994 to various organizations that work to limit population growth."

In 1997 the foundation gave about $8 million to family-planning causes. *(Barron's,* December 8, 1997)

The story also said that since 1988 the foundation has been primarily devoted to limiting population growth.

In 2000 the foundation gave Family Health International a $2 million grant to seek approval to market quinacrine as a nonsurgical sterilization method.

The foundation owns 100 shares of Lynch Corporation, trading on the American Stock Exchange, according to Samuel Yake, of Paoli, Pennsylvania. "Our family and some friends own a large stake in Lynch, so we naturally ask brokers and others if they've ever heard of it. Only one person has ever said 'yes.' That was Warren Buffett, whom we met at the Coca-Cola meeting earlier this year [1996]. When I asked him if he'd ever heard of Lynch, he immediately said, 'Oh, you mean Mario Gabelli's company.' I was astounded that a fellow of his wealth would have space in his mind for this little company."

Lynch, run by Gabelli, owns stakes in Spinnaker Industries and has interests in multimedia, transportation services and manufacturing.

The company was featured in a piece in *Forbes* (July 24, 1989) under the headline: "Berkshire Hathaway II?"

A *Barron's* story (December 8, 1997) suggesting that problems other than overpopulation needed Buffett's attention, quoted Buffett as saying: "Certainly I consider population and reproductive rights to be important issues, and I may write about them one day. But until then, I don't want to comment on the question or become a spokesman. I'd end up getting 50 letters a day. It would change my life too much."

On March 2, 1999, Buffett told "Nightline's" Ted Koppel: "I enjoy the idea of building an endowment fund up for society. I mean I enjoy the process by itself. But if you think about it, if I'd done all of that 15 years ago society would have had a few hundred million dollars of claim checks and now if I died tonight they'd have $30 billion of claim checks. So it's not a bad endowment fund. I have six very bright, high grade people whose thinking above ground will be a lot better than my thinking six feet underground and I've given them a few guidelines but nothing that ties their hands in any way. I want them to tackle big problems. I want them to tackle problems that generally don't have a funding constituency so that they're not the kind of things that government can attack well and that are not being attacked by philanthropy generally. I want them to try and do something big."

Buffett has said increasing his wealth has little effect on his life. "It just doesn't make any difference. It will make a difference to the size of my foundation when I die. It has no consequence for me whatso-ever." (*Financial Times,* May 17, 1999)

In a statement December 27, 1999 Buffett said that he and his wife have donated 2,500 Class A shares worth about $134 million at the stock price then, to four unnamed charities.

He said he was disclosing the fact so that investors did not think he was selling.

"Mr. and Mrs. Buffett are making this announcement because there have been occasions when gifts by them have been reported in the media as sales," the statement said. "Mr. and Mrs. Buffett have never sold any Berkshire shares."

The statement said the charities receiving the stock have agreed not to sell more than 10 shares during any one-week period.

One Berkshire shareholder noted on AOL's Berkshire message board that he was notified by his designated charity it had received the donation from Berkshire in General Dynamics stock.

Another shareholder posted: "I didn't realize Berkshire ever made stock contributions instead of cash, but this makes sense for the same reason it makes sense for an individual to donate appreciated securities. You effectively sell the stock and avoid the capital gains tax.

"For years we have debated how to handle the deferred tax liability in intrinsic value calculations. Now we see that with this nifty trick the tax liability on Coke and others can be avoided—just give all 200 million shares of Coke away to charity in annual increments spread over the next 10,000 years and voila, the capital gains tax liability is zero!! Cool."

166

SECOND CHANCE

The Buffett Foundation gives $250,000 annually to support "Second Chance," an effort led by Retired Air Force General Lee Butler to reduce nuclear weapons. However, this is what was mistakenly reported by a national business publication:

"Renowned investor and billionaire Warren Buffett is close to announcing the creation of a new foundation devoted to disarmament and nuclear issues paid for with a personal check for $1 billion. 'The Omaha Project'—it's a tentative name -- would be based in the Nebraska city that is home to Buffett's Berkshire Hathaway Inc. Retired Air Force Gen. Lee Butler, an advocate of cutting nuclear weapons, and the former head of the U.S. Strategic Command based near Omaha, is the leading candidate to head the project, sources tell our Warren P. Strobel," according to *U.S. News and World Report* (January 4, 1999).

Dr. Sam Park "Neuroberk" was the first with the dramatic (but mistaken) report on the AOL message board on December 29, 1998.

Almost immediately a poster wrote: "I had no idea. I have been an admirer of Warren Buffett for a long time, and have made a lot of money investing in Berkshire. If this is true, I will sell my Berkshire shares immediately because I have no desire to be mixed up with someone having the communist sympathies that this would indicate."

Buffett confirmed he had given some money to the Lee Butler effort during an interview with "Nightline" anchor Ted Koppel (March 2, 1999). Buffett told Koppel he wanted his fortune to go to society to attack big problems that are not funded by government.

Buffett told "Nightline's" Ted Koppel (March 2, 1999): "The number one problem of mankind, but I don't know how to attack it with money, I think is the spread of nuclear knowledge. I mean I think that the greatest danger that mankind faces is the fact that more and more people will know how to build weapons of incredible destruction and the knowledge won't go away. I don't know how to attack that problem with money.

"There's an organization formed that's in the process of being formed by Lee Butler, who was the former commander-in-chief of what was the strategic air command, now is STRATCOM. He calls it Second Chance. He's devoting his energies and I'm devoting some money to working on that problem. There's nobody better qualified than Lee to be working on it."

167

DORIS BUFFETT BRYANT
THE SUNSHINE LADY FOUNDATION

Buffett's sister, Doris Buffett Bryant, has her own foundation which is giving money to worthy causes.

Since 1996 at the death of her mother and an inheritance in a stock controlled by her brother, she's been looking for "sunbeams" to help her decide how best to give the money away. Each sunbeam agrees to give away $10,000 in a manner they best see fit.

Mrs. Bryant's Sunshine Lady Foundation, created with the windfall inheritance her mother bequeathed, has been searching the Davidson College campus for some of its sunbeams. The students selected have a year to give $10,000 to spread a kindly light in the world.

So far, according to an Associated Press story in the Charlotte, North Carolina *News and Record* (September 20, 1998), the philanthropists have showered donations on community centers, elementary schools and a rape intervention agency. And they've helped a bedridden polio patient, a child with brain-stem cancer, a woman in an abusive relationship and a family with a disabled son. "I like the idea of bringing sunshine to people's lives," Mrs. Bryant said.

(Photo by Nancy Line Jacobs)

Buffett's sisters, Mrs. Doris Bryant, left, and Mrs. Bertie Bialek, right, with daughter, Susie Buffett, in middle, at Berkshire Annual Meeting festivities in 1999

She and her husband, lawyer Al Bryant, continue to drive sec-
ondhand cars and live in their cottage on the North Carolina coast.

"We're fortunate because he [Warren] loves to make money. And
I love to give it away." she added.

As of 1998, she had handed out $3 million.

In Carteret County, North Carolina, Mrs. Bryant has sent 48
youngsters to college with annual scholarships ranging from $200 to
$10,000. There are strings attached. They must keep up a 3.0 grade
point average and refrain from any "self-destructive" activities,
including body piercing, tattooing, drinking, smoking or taking illegal drugs.

Mrs. Bryant says of her philanthropy: "I can't get all puffed up
about this. I'm simply passing along the luck."

Mrs. Bryant started with an inheritance of $10 million. There was
a trust that Buffett's father set up in his will that started distributing
its assets to Buffett's sisters after the death of their mother. The foundation has given away $4.4 million and still has a worth $16 million.

Worth magazine (October, 1999) said Mrs. Bryant operates the
foundation from the living room of her modest cottage in Morehead
City, North Carolina, and the foundation has a one room office in
the city's "Don't blink downtown."

Doris Bryant is the sister who early on invested with her brother
in Cities Service preferred stock. She sold only to see the stock
become a winner later.

According to *Worth*:

"She reformed with his next advice to buy Government
Employees Insurance Co., or GEICO, now a subsidiary of
Berkshire Hathaway. She bought $500 worth of the stock and
hung on, and a few years later her investment served as the
down payment on her first home..."

"She held $20,000 of Berkshire Hathaway in the mid-1960s,
but she's, regrettably, not worth $102 million at present. She
took some money out for living expenses along the way and,
during the 1980s, did the unthinkable. She started to play the
market herself with high-risk investments known as market
options, and as she once related to an interviewer, she got
'cleaned out' in the 1987 crash, ending $2 million in debt.

"Warren was worth billions at the time, of course, but chose
not to bail her out. 'Warren can be unbending,' says a friend
who knows both siblings. It took the hard work of her lawyer
to get Bryant back on her feet financially. That was Al Bryant,
and she married him..."

Bryant says she was inspired by a helpful friend, Josephine Travis, to start her foundation. When Bryant asked Travis what she could do in return for her favors, Travis said: "Just pass it on." To eliminate a lot of complicated grant work, she gets her ideas from her sunbeams and has given to a quadriplegic who was in a car crash, a deaf four-year-old and a family made homeless by a tornado and a policeman who needed a bone-marrow transplant to fight leukemia.

The *Worth* story said: "Determined to run through as much of the foundation money as she can before she dies, Bryant is thinking bigger and bigger, as with her plans to redecorate every safe house for battered women in the country. 'Too many of them seem like early Salvation Army,' Bryant says, horrified. 'They reinforce the idea that women are worth nothing.' "

The *Worth* story entitled "Virtue Capital" ended by saying: "Just pass it on."

168

DONALD AND MILDRED OTHMER

In 1998 Mildred Topp Othmer, a longtime Berkshire investor, left a fortune of about $450 million to charity. For example, more than $100 million went to the University of Nebraska-Lincoln. Her niece, Mary Siena, challenged her will on grounds that Othmer was not competent late in her life.

The case was settled and as things turned out the University of Nebraska wound up with a $125 million gift, according to the university's *Reporter* (Fall 1998).

It said the Othmer gift will be held in an endowment fund with about 75% of the income from that fund to be used to support chemical engineering programs at the university and to help upgrade technology on the Lincoln campus. An additional 12.5% was earmarked for academic programs and the other 12.5% was to back other university projects.

(AP Photo)

Donald and Mildred Othmer in 1983

1023

"I see this as an excellent fund, which will allow the University of Nebraska-Lincoln to rise to a whole new level of excellence, especially in the areas of research and graduate studies," said James Moeser, Chancellor of the University of Nebraska-Lincoln. He said the gift was probably the most important asset ever to come to the university. "The impact of their gift will be felt 50 and 100 years from now," Moeser was quoted.

The *New York Times* reported in a front page story (July 13, 1998) that Donald and Mildred Othmer were an ordinary seeming couple that left a staggering $750 million to charity.

He was a professor of chemical engineering at Polytechnic University in Brooklyn, "a workaholic with scores of patents and a sideline in consulting. She was a former teacher and buyer for her mother's dress store who volunteered at the Brooklyn Botanical Garden and Planned Parenthood. They had no children, unless you count the students he invited to have dinner."

"When they died—he in 1995 and she in April [1998], both in their 90s—they left their money to many of their favorite charities..."

"Some decades ago they invested most of their savings with an old family friend from Omaha: Warren E. Buffett..."

"Polytechnic, for instance, stands to receive nearly $200 million, a sum about four times the school's entire endowment. Long Island College Hospital, also in Brooklyn, is in line for about $160 million. The University of Nebraska and the Chemical Heritage Foundation, in Philadelphia, also expect to get more than $100 million each..."

"After initially investing $25,000 each in a partnership with Mr. Buffett, in the early 1960s, the couple received shares of Berkshire Hathaway in 1970 at $42 a share..."

"Lawyers say that Mrs. Othmer's estate contains about 7,500 shares of Berkshire Hathaway stock; her husband's approximately 7,000 shares were sold after his death in 1995, at just under $30,000 a share.

"Mid was very smart and a full participant in decision-making," *The Times* quoted Buffett as saying.

"As Mr. Buffett recalls it, Mrs. Othmer's mother, Mattie Topp, first approached him about investing for the family around 1958, when he was 27 and managing less than $1 million. She had used Mr. Buffett's father as her broker before he became a United States Representative."

The Othmers had no children. They sat in the same Congregational church pew every Sunday. The Brooklyn area was the real beneficiary of the Othmer gifts with substantial sums going to Polytechnic University there, which once faced bankruptcy, as well as Long Island Hospital, the Brooklyn Historic Society, their Plymouth Church and the Brooklyn Botanical Garden.

According to *The New York Times* (February 4, 1999), the Brooklyn area was to receive about $240 million. "By comparison, if Brooklyn's application to become an empowerment zone is approved, the federal funds will total $330 million."

The Times (July 13, 1998) quoted Buffett as saying: "They were such high-quality, nice people, who had no children and wanted to translate their wealth into something beneficial to society."

Mrs. Othmer, a graduate of the University of Nebraska, received a master's degree from Columbia University Teachers College in 1945. Mr. Othmer held a number of patents from his research in chemical engineering and was co-editor of the *Kirk-Othmer Encyclopedia of Chemical Technology.*

169

ALL-AMERICAN ALABAMA FOOTBALL PLAYER KERMIT KENDRICK TACKLES BUFFETT FOR AN AUTOGRAPH

One day I went to a bookstore and bought a couple of copies of my first book about Buffett and gave one to a friend. As we were talking, a stranger happened by, saw the book and—entirely unsolicited—said he liked the book.

He said he had read every word and that we were really going to enjoy reading it.

When he found I was the author, he was surprised.

I was so taken with his compliment (the fellow praised the book and said Buffett was his hero) that I gave him my copy.

He turned out to be Kermit Kendrick, an all-American defensive back for the University of Alabama football team in the late 1980s and is now a law student.

I autographed the book and then he asked if there were any way to get Buffett's autograph. Not likely, I indicated.

Back at the office, I felt troubled about it and called Kermit, saying, "You really want that book signed by Warren Buffett?" We met immediately, he returned the book to me, and I sent it to Buffett.

A few days later, even though I had sent a return envelope with regular postage, Buffett via Federal Express on Christmas Eve—in a random act of kindness—returned the book, autographed.

My note to Kermit said, "Many thanks for your unsolicited compliment about the book. I really do appreciate it. I hope your finances wind up in *better* shape than Warren Buffett's. All the best and happy investing! Roll Tide!"

Buffett's note to him read, "Kermit, Best wishes for a great career in investments. And good luck to the Tide unless the Cornhuskers are the opponent."

Said Kendrick, "This is probably the most exciting day of my brokerage career.

"...Just one other thing. Is there any way to meet him?"

Kendrick finally met Buffett at the Berkshire Annual Meeting in 1996. Kendrick got in touch with Alabama's former offensive coach,

Crimson Tide's Kermit Kendrick tackles Buffett for an autograph.
(Photo courtesy of the University of Alabama)

(Photo by Pat Kilpatrick)

Here's a photograpic response from former Alabama Coach Gene Stallings and Kermit Kendrick. Author—the fellow with the biggest shoulders—is at the left. Actual photo of God can be seen in upper left area even though it looks like Coach Paul "Bear" Bryant.

(Photo by Tom Conrad)

Buffett and Kendrick finally meet at Berkshire's Annual Meeting in 1996.

Homer Smith, who wrote Buffett about Kendrick. Buffett wrote back to Smith sending Kendrick a ticket to the annual meeting.

Buffett is a well-known Huskers football fan and like many fans in Nebraska, Alabama and Tennessee, for example, may see football through View No. 1 which is that Football is Life.

View No. 2, as expressed by George Will, is that "football combines the two worst things about America. It is violence punctuated by committee meetings."

170

BUFFETT PICKS UP A PENNY
"THE BEGINNING OF THE NEXT BILLION."

This book has bandied about the B word—billion.

One day in the mid-1980s, Buffett got on the elevator at Kiewit Plaza in midtown Omaha. He was going to his office on the 14th floor.

On the floor of the elevator was a penny. None of the employees of Peter Kiewit Sons', the construction conglomerate, paid any attention. Buffett leaned over, reached down and picked up the penny.

To the Kiewit executives, stunned that he would bother with a penny, the fellow who would one day be the richest person in the world quipped, "The beginning of the next billion."

(Photo courtesy of *Midlands Business Journal* in Omaha)

Buffett Wannabe (as in I "wanna be" like Buffett) George Morgan, an Omaha stockbroker, explains what $1 billion is: "A man gave his wife $1 million to spend at the rate of $1,000 per day. In three years she returned for more. So he gave her $1 billion and she didn't come back for 3,000 years." Buffett could send his wife on a shopping spree for about 90,000 years. That's called shopping after you've dropped.

Buffett picking up a penny at Omaha's Bookworm store November 4, 1994.
Maybe the beginning of yet another billion.

171

HARVARD-REJECTEE RETURNS IN TRIUMPH

HARVARD FLUNKS SPELLING TEST

Buffett, who as a teenager was rejected at Harvard Business School, spoke to Harvard in early 1996 before a standing-room-only crowd.

Predictably, *The Harbus*, Harvard Business School's student newspaper, wrote an intelligent, sophisticated article, although it left out a "t" in Buffett's name.

Comparing the merits of a Harvard Business degree or just investing the tuition money with Buffett early on, the story began:

"$45,000,000. This is the fortune a 1956 Harvard Business School graduate would have amassed today had he traded in his tuition money and degree back then and given it instead to Warren E. Buffett of Omaha, Nebraska."

Buffett gave a short talk about honesty and integrity, mentioning the personal qualities of Tom Murphy, the former chairman of Cap Cities/ABC and a graduate of Harvard Business School's Class of 1949.

"In the 20 years I've known him, he has never done anything he couldn't put on the front page of the newspaper," Buffett said.

Then he threw it open for questions. *The Harbus* said:

Students questioned Buffett on topics ranging from technical issues of valuation and finance to personal philosophies of success and fulfillment...Buffett stood steadfast by his well-known policy of never discussing current or future investment targets. He also shunned discussion of business school finance topics such as the Black-Scholes model and the efficient market hypothesis in favor of strike zones and fat pitches.

He stressed common sense, discipline, and patience, as opposed to IQ, as the keys to good investing. When asked what is the key to picking good stocks, Buffett responded, "understanding and picking good businesses..."

At the conclusion of the talk, fans rushed the stage with cameras flashing, while Buffett autographed dollar bills, T-shirts, annual reports and assorted unauthorized biographies...

After a 15 minute post-speech melee, Buffett excused himself and was hurried off to his private jet which was waiting to whisk him home in time for work the next day.

172

"Something's happened, Doug. I've lost touch with the Warren Buffett in me."

Drawing by Weber; © 1995
The New Yorker Magazine, Inc.

173
THE WIT OF WARREN BUFFETT
"TESTING...TESTING...
ONE MILLION...TWO MILLION...THREE MILLION."

(**Author's note:** to paraphrase: There is faith, hope and charity—and the greatest of these—is a sense of humor.)

"I...prefer the iceberg approach toward investment disclosure." (*Buffett Partnership letter, July 22, 1966*)

"These conditions will not cause me to attempt investment decisions outside my sphere of understanding (I don't go for the 'If you can't lick 'em, join 'em philosophy'—my own leaning is toward 'If you can't join 'em, lick 'em')." (*Buffett Partnership letter, January 25, 1967*)

"Our experience in workouts this year has been atrocious—during this period I have felt like the bird that inadvertently flew into the middle of a badminton game." (*Buffett Partnership letter in 1969*)

"With value like that [Walt Disney at the time], I know I'm not going to get stuck with a Kentucky Fried Computer when it goes out of fashion." (*Forbes, November 1, 1969*)

"I, in fact, indirectly own some Ford convertibles (bonds, not cars)." (*Article by Buffett for the Wall Street Journal, August 15, 1977*)

Quoting Yogi Berra: "It will be déjà vu all over again." (*1983 Annual Report*)

"Because my mother isn't here tonight, I'll even confess to you that I've been an arbitrageur." (*Columbia Law School's Center for Law and Economic Studies in 1985*)

"Our gain in net worth during the year was $613.6 million or 48.2%. It is fitting that the visit of Halley's Comet coincided with this percentage gain; neither will be seen again in my lifetime." (*1985 Annual Report*)

Buying bonds in inflationary times: "In runaway inflation, what you've bought is wallpaper." *(Fortune, April 25, 1985, and quoted in the Anagnos thesis in 1986)*

Here's Buffett's letter to Maria Anagnos after she sent him her thesis:

Berkshire Hathaway, Inc.
1440 Kiewit Plaza
Omaha, Nebraska 68131
Telephone (408) 346-1400

Warren E. Buffett, Chairman

July 3, 1986

Ms. Maria Anagnos,
300 East 62nd Street,
New York, New York 10021

Dear Maria:

Thanks for sending the thesis, which I enjoyed immensely. (Dale Carnegie once said that, next to "Would you like a drink?", a person's name is the most welcome sound in the English language). I'm glad NYU gave you an "A"; so do I.

It probably is a good thing you finished your thesis when you did. A few more years of markets like this and we won't look so good—at least on a relative basis.

We're writing a portion of Continental Illinois's Director's and Officer's Liability Insurance this year, so be sure to keep everybody on their toes. And if you are out this way, stop by and bring me up to date.
Best wishes.

Sincerely,
Warren E. Buffett

WEB/gk

"When ideas fail, words come in handy." *(Buffett quoting Goethe)*

"The future isn't what it used to be." *(Buffett quoting Pogo)*

"All men's misfortunes spring from the single cause that they are unable to stay quietly in one room." *(Buffett quoting Pascal)*

"So convenient a thing it is to be a reasonable creature, since it enables one to find or make a reason for everything one has a mind to do." *(Buffett quoting Ben Franklin)*

"The term 'institutional investor' is becoming one of those self-contradictions called an oxymoron, comparable to 'jumbo shrimp,' 'Lady mudwrestler' and 'inexpensive lawyer.' " *(widely quoted)*

The hunt for acquisitions is like "bagging rare and fast-moving elephants." *(widely quoted)*

Establishing criteria for acquisitions of companies is "a lot like selecting a wife. You can thoughtfully establish certain qualities you'd like her to have, and then all of a sudden, you meet someone and you do it." *(Annual Meeting in 1986)*

"You may quit having children if you keep having clunkers. But you just don't cast them out." *(Annual Meeting in 1986)*

On the advanced age of many Berkshire managers: "We find it's hard to teach a young dog old tricks. But we haven't had lots of problems with people who hit the ball out of the park year after year. Even though they're rich, they love what they do. And nothing ever happens to our managers. We offer them immortality." *(Annual Meeting in 1987)*

"We do not have, never have had, and never will have an opinion about where the stock market, interest rates or business activity will be a year from now." *(Forbes, October 13, 1997 from 1987 quote)*

"If any of you would like to withdraw your proxy at this time, just raise your hand. As soon as we can get around to you, you will be ejected from the meeting." *(Annual Meeting in 1988)*

"If you want to be loved, it's clearly better to sell high-priced corn flakes than low-priced auto insurance." *(1988 Annual Report)*

Adam Smith: "Where do you get these aphorisms that you've gotten so well known for?"
Buffett: "Well, I don't know. They're about the limit of my intellectual capacities, so I have to work with one sentence." *(Adam Smith's "Money World" show, June 20, 1988)*

Talking about excesses in the takeover field that year: "Toto, I have a feeling we're not in Kansas any more." Buffett quoting Dorothy from *The Wizard of Oz. (1988 Annual Report)*

"After ending our corporate marriage to Hochschild Kohn, [a

Baltimore department store Buffett bought for a bargain price] I had memories like those of the husband in the country song, 'My Wife Ran Away With My Best Friend and I Still Miss Him a Lot.' " *(1989 Annual Report)*

On how he handles so many requests from people. "Well, I just use the Nancy Reagan policy. I just say no." *(Annual Meeting in 1989)*

"FSLIC has essentially allowed crooks and dopes to print money. Otherwise it's an unqualified success." *(Annual Meeting in 1989)*

"A takeover (of Coca-Cola) would be like Pearl Harbor." *(Fortune, April 10, 1989)*

How Berkshire handles macroeconomic forecasts: "Charlie (Munger) is our macroeconomics expert. Actually, I handle Omaha and Council Bluffs and Charlie handles the rest of the country." *(Annual Meeting in 1990)*

Munger's note: "Berkshire has not thrived in the past from making macroeconomic predictions. Therefore, we don't think a lot about it. We just try to do sound things and we figure economic trends will average out over the long run. We're agnostics on the economy." *(Annual Meeting in 1990)*

Value investing: "The fact that it's so simple makes people reluctant to teach it. If you've gone and gotten a Ph.D. and spent years learning how to do all kinds of tough things mathematically, to have to come back to this is—it's like studying for the priesthood and finding out that the Ten Commandments were all you needed." *(New York Times Magazine, L.J. Davis, April, 1990)*

About making money: "I enjoy the process far more than the proceeds, though I have learned to live with those, also." *(Forbes, October 22, 1990)*

In the midst of the 1990 stock market slump after Berkshire had fallen 36% from $8,675 to $5,500 and *Fortune* magazine estimated that Buffett had a paper loss so far for the year of $1.5 billion or $215,450 an hour: "I have not cut back from double hamburgers to single hamburgers." *(Fortune, November 5, 1990)*

How about the corporate jet, he was asked. "That'll be the last thing to go." *(Fortune, November 5, 1990)*

His observation that if you could simply extrapolate the past into the future, "the richest people all would be librarians." *(widely quoted)*

On once contemplating shorting a $1 stock, Buffett said he was told by a friend, "Isn't that like jumping off a pancake?" *(Annual Meeting in 1990)*

"Wall Street is the only place that people ride to in a Rolls-Royce to get advice from those who take the subway." *(Los Angeles Times Magazine, April 7, 1991)*

"Elephant bumpers,"—Buffett's term for bosses blinded by the limelight. "If they're bumping into elephants at industry meetings, they think they're elephants too." *(Fortune, April 22, 1991)*

"If you can eliminate the government as a 46% partner, the business will be far more valuable." *(widely quoted)*

Of preparation for the celebrity tennis match (February 9, 1992) in which Buffett teamed with Martina Navratilova to play Pam Shriver and former Dallas Cowboys quarterback Danny White: "I think that the majority of my training for this event is to learn how to say 'yours' in Czechoslovakian." *(Omaha World-Herald, January 21, 1992)*

"We believe that according the name 'investor' to institutions that trade actively is like calling someone who repeatedly engages in one-night stands a romantic." *(1991 Annual Report)*

On longevity: "We take as our hero Methuselah." (Noah's ancestor is said to have lived 969 years). *(Annual Meeting in 1992)*

Once (September 2, 1992) Omaha stockbroker George Morgan walked up to Buffett, addressing him as "Mr. Buffett." "I know," said Buffett.

Acquisitions as frog-kissing: "I've observed that many acquisition-hungry managers were apparently mesmerized by their childhood reading of the story about the frog-kissing princess. Remembering her success, they pay dearly for the right to kiss corporate toads, expecting wondrous transfigurations...Initially, disappointing results deepen their desire to round up new toads. (Fanaticism, said philosopher Santayana, consists of redoubling your effort when you've forgotten your aim).
"Ultimately, even the most optimistic manager must face reality. Standing knee-deep in unresponsive toads, he announces an enormous 'restructuring' charge. In this corporative equivalent of a Head Start program, the CEO receives the education but the stockholders pay the tuition.

"In my early days as a manager, I, too, dated a few toads. They were cheap dates—I've never been much of a sport—but my results matched those of acquirers who courted higher-price toads. I kissed and they croaked." *(1992 Annual Report)*

Tighter accounting: Managers thinking about accounting issues should never forget one of Abraham Lincoln's favorite riddles: "How many legs does a dog have if you call his tail a leg?" The answer: "Four, because calling a tail a leg does not make it a leg." *(1992 Annual Report)*

"We've long felt that the only value of forecasters is to make fortune-tellers look good." *(1992 Annual Report)*

"Our...conclusion that an increased capital base will act as an anchor seems incontestable. The only open question is whether we can drag the anchor along at some tolerable, though slowed, pace." *(1992 Annual Report)*

Berkshire is one of the largest "super-cat" writers of insurance for catastrophes such as hurricanes and earthquakes: "Now you know why I suffer eyestrain: from watching the Weather Channel." *(1992 Annual Report)*

After introducing himself and Munger, he said he'd like to introduce the rest of Berkshire's board—"the entire three." *(Annual Meeting in 1993)*

After adjourning the meeting in about five minutes, Buffett said, "You can see I don't get paid by the hour." *(Annual Meeting in 1993)*

"I'd like to introduce Berkshire's managers, except Mrs. B. couldn't take time off from work for foolishness like a shareholders' meeting." *(Annual Meeting in 1993)*

"I was looking through the shareholder list recently and saw the name of someone not even born. I knew the mother was having a difficult pregnancy. I checked into it and found that the baby was our youngest shareholder. He was a shareholder two weeks before he was born. He's Riley Timothy Guerin (Rick Guerin's son)." At that moment a cartoon flashed on the screen of a baby saying, "What do you mean I have only two shares of Berky?" *(Annual Meeting in 1993)*

Buffett is known for advocating executive compensation based strictly on performance: "I've sat on 15 different boards and the only one in which I was invited on the compensation committee was at Salomon and we all know how that one turned out." *(Annual Meeting in 1993)*

After answering a question, Buffett asked Munger for his thoughts. Munger said, "I've got nothing to add." Quipped Buffett, "Sometimes he subtracts." Later during one of Munger's long pauses, Buffett said, "I feel a rebuttal coming on here." *(Annual Meeting in 1993)*

Munger launched into a long lesson about owning too many stocks, saying no one can follow 40 stocks in 30 different industries. "Can you?" he asked Buffett. "Not after that speech!" said Buffett. "You may only need one." *(Annual Meeting in 1993)*

Rick Berkshire, son of Robert Berkshire, asked if there were any plans to change Berkshire's name. "You don't have to worry about us changing anything at Berkshire," Buffett said. *(Annual Meeting in 1993)*

"How do you read an annual report?"..."Well, I start at the front and read to the back." *(Annual Meeting in 1993)*

Late in the meeting, Buffett launched into heavy criticism of business consultants, saying they were a form of intellectual prostitution. About that time a number of people began leaving the meeting. Said Buffett, "The consultants are now leaving the room." *(Annual Meeting in 1993)*

"In the early 1900s, a reporter was sent over from Europe to do a story on Andrew Carnegie. And he cabled back to his editors, 'I never realized that there was so much money in libraries.' That fellow might have had a career in writing investment reports." *(Annual Meeting in 1993)*

Lights! Camera! Cash Flow! Capital Cities/ABC Chairman Thomas Murphy and investor Warren Buffett, whose Berkshire Hathaway owns about 20% of the network's stock, will appear on the August 27 episode of the ABC soap *All My Children*, returning after their cameos of two years ago. The network shells out $300 or so to each, about right considering their performances. When handed his check, Murphy said, "I'm going to frame this." Said Buffett: "I'm going to frame the stub." *(Fortune, September 6, 1993)*

"All these little kids came up to me wanting my autograph (at a College World Series event where Buffett threw out the first pitch), so I wanted to look like Nolan Ryan"...Buffett describes bungling the pitch... "I looked up and saw these same kids erasing my signature." *(Interview by Sue Baggarly of WOWT-TV in Omaha, October 14, 1993)*

"My health is terrific. I just went for the first time in six or seven years for a general checkup. The doctor asked me about my diet and said, 'You're counting rather heavily on your genes, aren't you?'" *(Interview by Sue Baggarly, WOWT-TV in Omaha, October, 14, 1993)*

"Going short is betting on something that'll happen. If you go short for meaningful amounts, you can go broke. If something is selling for twice what it's worth, what's to stop it from selling for 10 times what it's worth? You'll be right eventually, but you may be explaining it to somebody in the poorhouse." *(Talk to Columbia business students, October 27, 1993)*

Buffett to Delta chairman Ronald Allen: "The airline industry is to the free-enterprise system what hell is to heaven." *(The Atlanta Journal/The Atlanta Constitution, July 23, 1994)*

"I gave this advice one time at Harvard when somebody asked me, 'Who should I work for?' I said, 'Well, go work for somebody you admire. You're bound to get a good result.' A couple of weeks later, I received a call from the Dean, and he said, 'What did you tell that group? They've all decided to become self-employed!' " *(Talk to University of Nebraska students, October 10, 1994)*

Munger's fear of flying: "He's a guy who has a prayer session before he takes a bus." *(Omaha World-Herald, October, 1994)*

When he was 17, Buffett got $5 from *Barron's* for writing a piece about odd lot statistics. "Five dollars was the only money I ever made from using odd lot statistics." *(New York Society of Security Analysts, December 6, 1994)*

There was only about $12 million in capital at Graham-Newman when Buffett worked there. "That's a rounding error now at Magellan." *(New York Society of Security Analysts, December 6, 1994)*

"Ben (Graham) used to say he wanted to do three things every day— something foolish, something creative and something generous. He usually got the foolish done before breakfast. That was typical of Ben." *(New York Society of Security Analysts, December 6, 1994)*

Higher math talent is not really necessary to be an investor. "You've got to figure out the worth of the company and divide by the number of shares outstanding so it does require division." *(New York Society of Security Analysts, December 6, 1994)*

Commenting on the unprofitable airline industry, talking about when the Wright Brothers flew at Kitty Hawk: "If there had been a capitalist down there, the guy should have shot Wilbur." *(Fortune, April 3, 1995)*

"Charlie and I, at 71 and 64, respectively, now keep George Foreman's picture on our desks. You can make book that our scorn for a mandatory retirement age will grow stronger every year." *(1994 Annual Report)*

Of selling some Berkshire products like See's Candies and Dexter shoes at the Berkshire annual meeting: "Though we like to think of the meeting as a spiritual experience, we must remember that even the saintliest of religions includes the ritual of the collection plate." *(1994 Annual Report) (Note: Some Berkshire shareholders call Omaha, "The spiritual capitol of the world.")*

"Of course, what you really should be purchasing is a video tape of the 1995 Orange Bowl. Your Chairman views this classic nightly, switching to slow motion for the fourth quarter. Our cover color this year is a salute to Nebraska's football coach, Tom Osborne, and his Cornhuskers, the country's top college team. I urge you to wear Husker red to the annual meeting and promise you that at least 50% of your managerial duo will be in appropriate attire." *(1994 Annual Report)*

Munger: "Our chief contribution to the businesses we acquire is what we don't do." Buffett: "He has spoken." *(Annual Meeting in 1995)*

Shareholder: "You've repeatedly said that you see many wonderful stock ideas, but can't invest because they're too small. Given the fact that many in the audience today have a lower dollar investment threshold..." Buffett: "In other words, do these stocks have names?" *(Annual Meeting in 1995)*

Buffett: "The government has a 35% interest - a profits interest - in the earnings of all corporations. So at a tax rate of 35%, they in effect own 35% of the stock of American business. And they own a significant share of Berkshire - we write them a check every year. We

U.S. Senator Bob Kerrey, Debra Winger and Buffett
"The real trick to this is having Debra (Winger) as a co-host. Otherwise, this room
would be empty," Buffett said at a fundraiser for Kerrey that Buffett and Miss
Winger co-hosted.

don't write you a check, but we write them a check. And we plow your earnings back to create more value for them." Munger: "Are you trying to cheer these people up?" *(Annual Meeting in 1995)*

"To paraphrase President Kennedy, a rising tide lifts all yachts." *(1995 Annual Report)*

"Soon after our purchase of the Salomon preferred in 1987, I wrote that I had 'no special insights regarding the direction or future profitability of investment banking.' Even the most charitable commentator would conclude that I have since proven my point." *(1995 Annual Report)*

"At Borsheim's we will also have the world's largest faceted diamond on display. Two years in the cutting, this inconspicuous bauble is 545 carats in size. Please inspect the stone and let it guide you in determining what size gem is appropriate for the one you love." *(1995 Annual Report)*

Reply to a suggestion that Buffett was getting as famous as the Pope or the President: "My first reaction is that maybe I should tell my barber that we should save the clippings and sell them." *(Annual Meeting in 1996)*

Munger told Buffett he had never actually seen him run formulas discounting future cash flows. "Well, some things you only do in private," Buffett replied. *(Annual Meeting in 1996)*

Buffett of Munger: "I can see. He can hear. We make a great combination." *(Annual Meeting in 1996)*

"Your board has collectively lost 100 pounds in the past year. They must have been trying to live on their director's fees." *(Annual Meeting in 1996)*

"I only invest in companies which can be run by idiots because sooner or later one will." *(widely quoted)*

"I was recently studying the 1896 report of Coke (and you think you're behind in your reading!)" *(1996 Annual Report)*

On being lucky enough to live in a time your talents are recognized: "If I'd been born a few thousand years ago, I'd probably have been some animal's lunch." *(From a column by Bill Gates which ran in the Omaha World-Herald, March 16, 1997)*

"Happiness does not buy money." *(Forbes, April 21, 1997)*

"You might want to invest where we invest, but don't eat where we eat." *(Annual Meeting in 1997)*

"If you gave me $100 billion—and I would encourage you to do that—I don't know how to displace Coke." *(Annual Meeting in 1997)*

Of 18 holes of golf with Bill Gates at the Omaha Country Club: "We had a small wager. But the outcome did not affect the *Forbes* rankings." *(Omaha World-Herald, June 2, 1997)*

"I can understand Dairy Queen. It's pushing the envelope for me, but I can get there." *(talk to students at Mary Washington College, November 11, 1997)*

"We will not ask you to adapt the philosophy of the Chicago Cubs fan who reacted to a story of a lackluster season by saying, 'Why get upset? Everyone has a bad century now and then.' " *(1997 Annual Report)*

"Try to think kindly of us when we blow one. Along with President Clinton, we will be feeling your pain: The Munger family has more than 90% of its net worth in Berkshire and the Buffetts more than

99%." *(1997 Annual Report)*

Growing crowds at the annual meeting: "Maybe it's a tracking device on the price of Berkshire stock." *(Annual Meeting in 1998)*

Shareholder: "I'm very concerned about your health, seeing your diet [of Cokes, See's Candy and Dilly Bars] throughout the annual meeting." "And that's just what I do in public," Buffett replied. *(Annual Meeting in 1998)*

"Charlie and I are both very healthy. If you were in the life insurance business, you would be happy to write us a standard rate." *(Annual Meeting in 1998)*

"I think I am undertaxed, but I do not send along any voluntary payments." *(Annual Meeting in 1998)*

How to teach in business schools: "I would say for a final exam, here's the stock of any Internet company, what's it worth? And anybody who gave an answer, flunks." *(Annual Meeting in 1998)*

Munger: "I've always said the best way to get what you want is to deserve what you want."
Buffett: "I want some more peanut brittle." *(Annual Meeting in 1998)*

Q. Year 2000 problem?
Buffett: "I don't think it has any investment consequences for Berkshire...maybe the government won't find our tax return." *(Annual Meeting in 1998)*

Observation that Buffett's net worth has increased in the past decade. "I have noticed." *(Adam Smith's "Money Game" show, May 18, 1998)*

I thought I ought to start off this by announcing that Bill [Gates] and I have a small bet as to who would get the most applause. I suggested that I bet my house against his. We settled on a small sum, but evidently it isn't such a small sum to Bill, because just before we came out he gave me this Nebraska Cornhusker shirt to wear, and then he puts on this purple University of Washington shirt himself." *(Fortune, July 20, 1998, reporting on an appearance by Buffett and Gates at the University of Washington)*

After Gates talked about great advances in software, Buffett said: "Don't you think Dairy Queen is more important than that?" Gates: "You can manage Dairy Queen Warren. I'll go and buy Dilly Bars."

Buffett: "We'll raise the price when you come." *(Fortune, July 20, 1998)*

"Actually the two of us [Bill Gates and Buffett] have a small announcement we would like to make." *(Fortune, July 20, 1998, in a response to a question about mergers.)*

"I always say if a traffic cop follows you for 50 miles, you're going to get a ticket. Clinton has been in somewhat the same position [in his relations with Monica Lewinsky]. But, unfortunately, he went 100 miles an hour." *(The Buffalo News, September 10, 1998)*

"We want a maximum amount of stupid people in the market as possible." (Berkshire special meeting, September 16, 1998)

An agnostic is a person who says, "At least I'm not an atheiest, thank God." *(Berkshire special meeting, September 16, 1998)*

Are rich people jerks? Buffett has said that being rich makes you more of whatever you are—in some cases—a bigger jerk. "I don't think Warren's a big jerk," said Senator Bob Kerrey. "But I could be," Buffett said. *(Omaha World-Herald, December 13, 1998)*

Moats around business franchises: "In my moat, I'd throw in a couple of sharks—or a few gators." *(Miami Herald, December 27, 1998, quoting a talk to the University of Florida)*

"There are really only three kinds of people in the world: Those who can count and those who can't." *(1998 Annual Report)*

"One beneficiary of our increased size has been the U.S. Treasury. The federal income taxes that Berkshire and General Re have paid, or will soon pay, in respect to 1998 earnings total $2.7 billion. That means we shouldered *all* of the U.S. Government's expenses for more than a half-day.   Follow that thought a little further. If only 625 other U.S. taxpayers had paid the Treasury as much as we and General Re did last year, no one else—neither corporations nor 270 million citizens—would have had to pay federal income taxes or any kind of federal tax (for example, social security or estate taxes). Our shareholders can truly say that they 'gave at the office.' " *(1998 Annual Report)*

"In connection with General Re merger, we wrote a $30 million check to the government to pay our SEC fee tied to the new shares created by the deal. We understood that this payment set an SEC record. Charlie and I are enormous admirers of what the

Commission has accomplished for American investors. We would rather, however, have found another way to share our admiration." *(1998 Annual Report)*

"I brought along my briefcase indicator here for you. I knew you'd be interested in that." *(CNBC interview before Berkshire's annual meeting in 1999)*

CNBC: "You have about $15 billion in cash?" Buffett: "Well I don't have it all on me right now!" *(CNBC interview before Berkshire's annual meeting)*

What he thinks of being called the Oracle of Omaha: "Well, what it has in alliteration, it lacks in accuracy." *(Annual Meeting weekend in 1999)*

Said he'd answer questions, "about six hours, or until we run out of candy." *(Annual Meeting in 1999)*

Meeting adjournment: All those in favor say, 'Aye.' All those opposed say 'I'm leaving!... I ask you, was Joe Stalin ever any better?" *(Annual Meeting in 1999)*

Academic requirements to get a star football player through school. Here's the player's answer to the two questions he had to pass:
Q: "What did old McDonald have?"
A. "Farm."
Q. "How do you spell farm?"
A. "E-I-E-I-O."
(Annual Meeting in 1999)

"We ask them [Berkshire subsidiaries] to mail the money to Omaha. We'll even send them a stamp." *(Annual Meeting in 1999)*

"I tell college students we live about the same. We eat about the same, dress about the same, have a car and TV and air conditioning, but I travel a lot better on NetJets." *(Annual Meeting in 1999)*

Munger: "Continuity in corporate culture is more likely to continue at Berkshire than at most public corporations. I think the captial would be allocated less well, but that's just too damn bad!'
Buffett: "That's why we don't have a PR department!"
(Annual Meeting in 1999)

Question from a student about how to form a nonprofit organization: "I've always tried to avoid forming a nonprofit organization." *(Omaha World-Herald, October 12, 1999)*

Advice to students: "If you can't pay for it, don't buy it. Get yourself into a situation where you can buy anything, then we'll be happy to see you at Borsheim's or the Nebraska Furniture Mart." *(Omaha World-Herald, October 12, 1999)*

"When I issue stock, I tend to break out into a rash." *(Omaha World-Herald, November 3, 1999)*

"I'm 69, but I have the mind of a 12-year-old." *(St. Petersburg Times, December 15, 1999)*

"If the stock goes down a lot the day I die, it's probably a very good buy. If it goes up a lot, I'm really going to be sore." *(Omaha World-Herald, February 22, 2000 from a talk to Midland Lutheran College business students in Fremont, Nebraska)*

His dismal 1999: "My performance reminds me of the quarterback whose report card showed four Fs and a D but who nonetheless had an understanding coach. 'Son,' he drawled, 'I think you're spending too much time on one subject.' " *(1999 Annual Report)*

"Neither my wife nor I have ever sold a share of Berkshire and—unless our checks stop clearing—we have no intention of doing so." *(1999 Annual Report)*

"My annual outlays at EJA [Executive Jet] and Borsheim's, combined, total about ten times my salary. Think of this as a rough guideline for your expenditures with us." *(1999 Annual Report)*

"I'd write life insurance in an emergency room provided the premiums are high enough." *(widely quoted)*

On being offered the job of chairman of the Federal Reserve Board:
"I would say no in in a hurry."—*Warren Buffett*
"I would say no quicker."—*Charlie Munger*
"You notice that we gave answers unequivocally. That alone would disqualify us." *(Annual Meeting in 2000)*

On being hit by a bus or truck—"Well, just so it's not a GEICO driver." *(Annual Meeting in 2000)*

On making investment decisions: "We have no master plan. We're just thinking all the time and every now and then something sort of bubbles up to the level of making a telephone call. It would be very depressing for you to see it in action." *(Press conference, April 30, 2000)*

174
THE WISDOM OF WARREN BUFFETT
"THE FACT THAT PEOPLE WILL BE FULL OF GREED, FEAR OR FOLLY IS PREDICTABLE. THE SEQUENCE IS NOT."

Visualizing success at age seven: "I don't have much money now but someday I will and I'll have my picture in the paper." (Attributed to his mother Leila Buffett about 1937. *Thoughts of Chairman Buffett, Simon Reynolds*)

"The investor of today does not profit from yesterday's growth." *(The Commercial and Financial Chronicle, December 6, 1951)*

The joys of compounding: "One story stands out. This, of course, is the saga of trading acumen etched into history by the Manhattan Indians when they unloaded their island to that notorious spendthrift, Peter Minuit in 1626. My understanding is that they received $24 net. For this, Minuit received 22.3 square miles which works out to about 621,888,320 square feet. While on the basis of comparable sales, it is difficult to arrive at a precise appraisal, a $20 per square foot estimate seems reasonable given a current land value for the island of $12,433,766,400 ($12½ billion). To the novice, perhaps this sounds like a decent deal. However, the Indians have only had to achieve a 6½% return (the tribal mutual fund representative would have promised them this) to obtain the last laugh on Minuit. At 6½%, $24 becomes $42,105,772,800 (42 billion) in 338 years, and if they just managed to squeeze out an extra half point to get to 7%, the present value becomes $205 billion." *(Buffett Partnership letter, January 1965)*

"The course of the stock market will largely determine...when we'll be right, but the accuracy of our analysis will determine whether we'll be right. In other words, we...concentrate on what should happen, not when it should happen...If we start deciding, based on our guesses or emotions, whether we will...participate in a business where we...have some long-run edge, we're in trouble. We will not sell our interests in businesses when they are attractively priced just because some astrologer thinks the quotations may go lower even

1053

though forecasts...will be right some of the time...The availability of a quotation for your business interests should always be an asset to be utilized if desired. If it gets silly enough in either direction, you take advantage of it. Its availability should never be turned into a liability whereby its periodic aberrations in turn form your judgments." *(Buffett Partnership letter, July, 1966)*

"All of our investments usually appear undervalued to me—otherwise we wouldn't own them." *(Buffett Partnership letter, July, 1966)*

"I am not in the business of predicting general stock market or business fluctuations. If you think I can do this, or think it is essential to an investment program, you should not be in the partnership." *(Buffett Partnership letter, July, 1966)*

"As Ben Graham said: 'In the long run, the market is a weighing machine—in the short run, a voting machine.' I have always found it easier to evaluate weights dictated by fundamentals than votes dictated by psychology." *(Buffett Partnership letter in 1969)*

"Maybe grapes from a little 8-acre vineyard in France are really the best in the whole world, but I have always had a suspicion that about 99% of it is in the telling and about 1% of it is in the drinking." *(Warren Buffett Speaks, Janet Lowe, p. 36 quoting SEC file No. HO-784, Blue Chip Stamp et al/Warren Buffett, letter to Charles N. Huggins, December 13, 1972)*

"The sillier the market's behavior the greater the opportunity for the business-like investor. Follow [Ben] Graham and you will profit from folly rather than participate in it." *(Preface to the fourth edition of The Intelligent Investor, 1973)*

"I shave my face on the same side every morning and put on the same shoe first and people are creatures of habit." *(Courier Express v. Evening News testimony, November 4, 1977)*

"We ordinarily make no attempt to buy equities anticipating favorable short-term price behavior. In fact, if the business experience continues to satisfy us, we welcome lower prices as an opportunity to acquire even more of a good thing." *(1977 Annual Report)*

"When companies with outstanding businesses and comfortable financial positions find their shares selling far below intrinsic value in the marketplace, no alternative action can benefit shareholders as surely as repurchases." *(widely quoted)*

"(The) argument is made that there are just too many (investment) question marks about the near-term future; wouldn't it be better to wait until things clear up a bit? You know the prose: 'Maintain buying reserves until current uncertainties are resolved,' etc. Before reaching for that crutch, face up to two unpleasant facts: the future is never clear; you pay a very high price in the stock market for a cheery consensus. Uncertainty actually is the friend of the buyer of long-term values." *(Forbes, August 6, 1979)*

"Your charitable preferences are as good as mine." (1981, announcing that Berkshire shareholders could designate their choice of charitable contributions.)

"We do not need more people gambling in non-essential instruments identified with the stock market in this country, nor brokers who encourage them to do so. What we need are investors and advisers who look at the long-term prospects for an enterprise and invest accordingly. We need intelligent commitment of investment capital, not leveraged market wagers. The propensity to operate in the intelligent, pro-social sector of capital markets is deterred, not enhanced, by an active and exciting casino operating in somewhat the same arena, utilizing somewhat similar language and serviced by the same work force." *(From a letter Buffett wrote to John Dingell, Chairman of the House Subcommittee on Oversight and Investigations, in March 1982, when Congress was considering whether to allow the Chicago Mercantile Exchange to trade futures contracts.)*

"Geometric progressions eventually forge their own anchors." *(1982 Annual Report)*

"The market, like the Lord, helps those who help themselves. But unlike the Lord, the market does not forgive those who know not what they do." *(1982 Annual Report)*

"Although our form is corporate, our attitude is partnership. Charlie Munger and I think of our shareholders as owner-partners, and of ourselves as managing partners. (Because of the size of our shareholdings we also are, for better or worse, controlling partners.) We do not view the company itself as the ultimate owner of our business assets but, instead, view the company as a conduit through which our shareholders own the assets." *(1983 Annual Report)*

Quoting John Maynard Keynes: "The difficulty lies not in the new ideas but in escaping from the old ones." *(1983 Annual Report)*

"I heard a story recently that is applicable to our insurance accounting problems: a man was traveling abroad when he received a call from his sister informing him that their father had died unexpectedly. It was physically impossible for the brother to get back home for the funeral, but he told his sister to take care of the funeral arrangements and to send the bill to him. After returning home he received a bill for several thousand dollars, which he promptly paid. The following month another bill came along for $15, and he paid that too. Another month followed, with a similar bill. When in the next month, a third bill for $15 was presented, he called his sister to ask what was going on. 'Oh', she said. 'I forgot to tell you. We buried Dad in a rented suit.' " (1984 Annual Report)

"I have seen no trend toward value investing in the 35 years I've practiced it. There seems to be some perverse human characteristic that likes to make easy things difficult." *(Talk to Columbia Business School in 1985)*

"Complete anonymity would be the best way for me to operate, but because of size that's not possible anymore." *(Financial Review, December 9, 1985)*

"All I want is one good idea every year. If you really push me, I'll settle for one good idea every two years." *(Financial Review, December 9, 1985)*

"The failure of business schools to study men like Teledyne's Henry Singleton is a crime. Instead they insist on holding up as a model executives cut from McKinsey & Company cookie cutters." *(Talk to Columbia Business School in 1985)*

"When I get an investment proposal, I can look at it in five minutes or less. I can filter out 99% of the ideas in five minutes." *(Financial Review, December 9, 1985)*

"The fact that people will be full of greed, fear or folly is predictable. The sequence is not predictable." *(Channels magazine, talk to Patricia Bauer, 1986)*

"Money, to some extent, sometimes lets you be in more interesting environments. But it can't change how many people love you or how healthy you are." *(Channels magazine, talk to Patricia Bauer, 1986)*

Author's note: of course others say: "Money cannot buy happiness, but then happiness cannot buy groceries" or "I'm tired of love, I'm still tired of rhyme, but money gives me pleasure all the time."

Business schools "reward complex behavior more than simple behavior; but simple behavior is more effective." *(Channels magazine, talk to Patricia Bauer, 1986)*

"The idea that you get a lifetime supply of food stamps based on coming out of the right womb strikes at my idea of fairness." *(Channels magazine, talk to Patricia Bauer, 1986)*

Arms control and population growth problems: "If we don't solve them, we don't have a world." *(Channels magazine, talk to Patricia Bauer, 1986)*

"The key in life is to figure out who to be the batboy for." *(Broadcasting, June 9, 1986)*

Patience: "You don't trade in houses, children and wives every year, so why trade companies around. I want to have fun with the companies, see them grow and develop. And also, I want to enjoy life. I can't understand the Carl Icahn's, Victor Posner's and Ted Turner's of the world. In the end all my money is going to charity. So it's crazy to live by being in uncomfortable situations, or being unpleasant towards others. What's the difference anyway, if the Buffett Foundation is worth "X" or "2X" at the end..." *(Anagnos thesis, 1986, quoting Buffett)*

"I do what I like to do. I don't spend five minutes a year doing what I don't like. And fortunately I have the luxury to do so. I don't care what anyone else does. I like people, and I like the people I associate with. I care about them and their businesses. And besides, I want to have fun!" *(Anagnos thesis, 1986, quoting Buffett)*

"Would anyone say the best way to pick a champion Olympic team is to select the sons and daughters of those who won 20 years ago? Giving someone a favored position just because his old man accomplished something is a crazy way for society to compete." *(Fortune, September 29, 1986)*

"Love is the greatest advantage a parent can give." *(Fortune, September 29, 1986)*

"We like to buy businesses, but we don't like to sell them." *(Annual Meeting in 1987)*

"Anything that can't go on forever will end." *(Annual Meeting in 1987, paraphrasing Herb Stein)*

"I like the fact it's a big transaction. I can't be involved in 50 or 75 things. That's a Noah's Ark way of investing—you end up with a zoo that way. I like to put meaningful amounts of money in a few things." *(Wall Street Journal, September 30, 1987, shortly after Berkshire's $700 million investment in Salomon)*

"The public school teacher is probably the most under-compensated and under-appreciated person in the public arena." *(Omaha World-Herald, October 1, 1987)*

"There's no reason in the world you should expect some broker to be able to tell you whether you can make money on index futures or options or some stock in two months. If they knew how to do that, he wouldn't be talking to investors. He'd have retired long ago." *(Money, Fall 1987)*

"It looks...impressive if it comes out of a computer. But it's frequently nonsense. The person who's making the decision is far more important." *(Outstanding Investor Digest, October 7, 1987)*

"I'm an analyst basically. I try to figure out what businesses are worth, then divide by the number of shares outstanding." *(Omaha World-Herald, October 18, 1987, quoting Money magazine)*

"There's something about smart people explaining ideas to an orang-utan that makes their decision-making better." *(Fortune, October 26, 1987)*

"We're far from believing that there is not a fate worse than debt. We are willing to borrow an amount that we believe—on a worst-case basis—will pose no threat to Berkshire's well-being." *(1987 Annual Report)*

"What I am is a realist. I always knew I'd like what I'm doing. Oh, perhaps it would have been neat to be a major league baseball player, but that's where the realism comes in." *(US West, Autumn, 1987)*

"I keep an internal scorecard. If I do something that others don't like but I feel good about, I'm happy. If others praise something I've done, but I'm not satisfied, I feel unhappy." *(US West, Autumn, 1987)*

"The market is there only as a reference point to see if anybody is offering to do anything foolish. When we invest in stocks, we invest in businesses. You simply have to behave according to what is rational rather than according to what is fashionable." *(Fortune, January 4, 1988)*

"Our goal is to attract long-term owners who, at the time of purchase, have no timetable or price target for sale but plan instead to stay with us indefinitely." *(1988 Annual Report)*

"I want to be in businesses so good that even a dummy can make money." *(Fortune, April 11, 1988)*

"We don't go into companies with the thought of effecting a lot of change. That doesn't work any better in investments than it does in marriages." *(Fortune, April 11, 1988)*

"If we get on the main line, New York to Chicago, we don't get off at Altoona and take side trips." *(Fortune, April 11, 1988)*

"It's far better to buy a wonderful company at a fair price than a fair company at a wonderful price." *(widely quoted)*

On turnarounds: "The projections will be dazzling—the advocates will be sincere—but in the end, major additional investment in a terrible industry usually is about as rewarding as struggling in quicksand." *(widely quoted)*

"I don't know what it'll (the stock market) do tomorrow or next week or next year. But I do know that over a period of 10 to 20 years you'll have some very enthusiastic markets and some very depressed markets. The trick is to take advantage of the markets rather than letting them panic you into the wrong action." *(widely quoted)*

"It's just not necessary to do extraordinary things to produce extraordinary results." *(widely quoted)*

The importance of a franchise business: Adam Smith: "So it's the power of the franchise?" Buffett: "It's the power of the franchise." *(Adam Smith's "Money World" show, June 20, 1988)*

"The most important quality for an investor is temperament, not intellect. You don't need tons of IQ in this business. You don't have to be able to play three-dimensional chess or duplicate bridge. You need a temperament that neither derives great pleasure from being with the crowd or against the crowd. You know you're right, not because of the position of others, but because your facts and your reasoning are right." *(Adam Smith's "Money World" show, June 20, 1988)*

"Our outlook for inflation is always the same. We feel there's a big bias toward inflation—both in the U.S. and around the world...It's a world where prices are going to go up. It's just a question of how much. You could definitely have some explosive inflation at some point. Printing money is just too easy. I'd do it myself if I could get away with it." *(Annual Meeting in 1988)*

"We don't view precious metals and precious stones as great inflation hedges. But we don't bring anything to that game, so we don't play it." *(Annual Meeting in 1988)*

"It's hard enough to understand the peculiarities and complexities of the culture in which you've been raised, much less a variety of others. Anyway, most of our shareholders have to pay their bills in U.S. dollars." *(Annual Meeting in 1988)*

"We wouldn't care if the market closed for a year or two. It closes on Saturday and Sunday and we do just fine." *(Annual Meeting in 1988)*

"If principles are dated, they're not principles." (Annual Meeting in 1988)

On properly valuing a business: "To properly value a business, you should ideally take all the flows of money that will be distributed between now and judgment day and discount them at an appropriate discount rate. That's what valuing businesses is all about. Part of the equation is how confident you can be about those cash flows occurring. Some businesses are easier to predict than others. For example, water companies are generally easier to predict than building contractors. We try to look at businesses that are predictable." *(Annual Meeting in 1988)*

Something Buffett doesn't lose sleep over: "We're actually prohibited from buying other savings and loans. But that's not a prohibition that keeps us up at night." *(Annual Meeting in 1988)*

Money: "I think if you found an athlete that was doing well—and I'm not comparing myself—but a Ted Williams or an Arnold Palmer or something—after they have enough to eat, they're not doing it for the money. My guess is that if Ted Williams was getting the highest salary in baseball and he was hitting .220, he would be unhappy. And if he was getting the lowest salary in baseball and batting .400, he'd be very happy. That's the way I feel about this job. Money is a byproduct of doing something I like doing extremely well." *(Annual Meeting in 1988)*

"Anything can happen in stock markets and you ought to conduct your affairs so that if the most extraordinary events happen, that you're still around to play the next day." *(Buffett on Adam Smith's*

"Money World" show, June 20, 1988)

"Valuing a business is part art and part science." *(Esquire, October, 1988)*

Quoting Casey Stengel, who once described his job as "getting paid for the home runs the other fellows hit." *(widely quoted)*

"Great investment opportunities come around when excellent companies are surrounded by unusual circumstances that cause the stock to be misappraised." *(Fortune, December 19, 1988)*

IMAGINARY NEWS ADVISORY: Buffett steps into elevator shaft July 4, 2084, leaving twenty trillion to the Buffett Foundation. Berkshire drops 23% in the first minute of trading to $99 million a share. Munger steps up to the easel. Lou Simpson, named vice chairman, initiates massive stock buy-back. Consults Gates. Starts talks to buy China. Berkshire ends trading session at $123 million as investors recall Buffett's famous words of December 19, 1988.

"Take the probability of loss times the amount of possible loss from the probability of gain times the amount of possible gain. That is what we're trying to do. It's imperfect, but that's what it's all about. We compete only within the circle of what we understand, which eliminates a lot." *(Annual Meeting in 1989)*

"Time is the friend of the wonderful business, the enemy of the mediocre." *(1989 Annual Report)*

"It's no sin to miss a great opportunity outside one's area of competence." *(1989 Annual Report)*

"I found in running businesses that the best results come from letting high-grade people work unencumbered." *(Fortune, September 11, 1989)*

On why Berkshire borrowed $400 million and put the cash into Treasuries: "The best time to buy assets may be when it is hardest to raise money." *(Fortune, October 23, 1989)*

"I've often felt there might be more to be gained by studying business failures than business successes. It's customary in business schools to study business successes. But my partner, Charlie Munger, says all he wants is to know where he's going to die—so he won't ever go there." *(Talk to Emory Business College, November, 1989)*

"I'm not like a steel executive who can think only about how to invest in steel. I've got a bigger canvas, simply because I have spent my life looking at companies, starting with Abbott Labs and going through to Zenith." *(Fortune, January 29, 1990)*

"I think it's a saner existence here [Omaha]. I used to feel when I worked back in New York that there were more stimuli just hitting me all the time, and if you've got the normal amount of adrenaline, you start responding to them. It may lead to crazy behavior after a while. It's much easier to think here." *(New York Times Magazine, L.J. Davis, April 2, 1990)*

"I love what I do. I'm involved in a kind of intellectually interesting game that isn't too tough to win, and Berkshire Hathaway is my canvas. I don't try to jump over seven-foot bars: I look around for one-foot bars that I can step over. I work with sensational people, and I do what I want in life. Why shouldn't I? If I'm not in a position to do what I want, who the hell is?" *(New York Times Magazine, L.J. Davis, April 2, 1990)*

"Any young person who doesn't take up bridge is making a big mistake." *(New York Times, May 20, 1990)*

"Stocks are simple. All you do is buy shares in a great business for less than the business is intrinsically worth, with management of the highest integrity and ability. Then you own those shares forever." *(Forbes, August 6, 1990)*

Buffett's description of some of the ground rules for the Buffett Partnership. "I told them (limited partners), 'What I'll do is form a partnership where I'll manage the portfolio and have my money in there with you. I'll guarantee you a 6% return, and I get 25% of all profits after that. And I won't tell you what we own because that's distracting. All I want to do is hand in a scorecard when I come off the golf course. I don't want you following me around and watching me shank a three-iron on this hole and leave a putt short on the next one.' " *(1990 Investors Guide/Fortune)*

"A hyperactive stock market is the pickpocket of enterprise." *(widely quoted)*

"You don't need to be a rocket scientist. Investing is not a game where the guy with the 160 IQ beats the guy with a 130 IQ. Rationality is essential." *(widely quoted)*

"In a sense Berkshire Hathaway is a canvas, and I get to paint anything I want on that canvas. And it's the process of painting that I really enjoy, not selling the painting." *(widely quoted)*

"You can't be smarter than your dumbest competitor. The trick is to have no competitors." *(widely quoted)*

"In the insurance business, there is no statute of limitations on stupidity." *(1990 Annual Report)*

"The most common cause of low prices is pessimism—sometimes pervasive, sometimes specific to a company or industry. We want to do business in such an environment, not because we like pessimism but because we like the prices it produces. It's optimism that is the enemy of the rational buyer. None of this means, however, that a business or stock is an intelligent purchase simply because it is unpopular; a contrarian approach is just as foolish as a follow-the-crowd strategy. What's required is thinking rather than polling." *(1990 Annual Report)*

"The most important thing to do when you find yourself in a hole is to stop digging." *(1990 Annual Report)*

How a corporation (specifically Salomon) should behave: "Anything not only on the line, but near the line, will be called out." *(Wall Street Journal, August 19, 1991)*

"In the end we must have people to match our principles, not the reverse." *(Salomon report to shareholders, third quarter, 1991)*

"Someone's sitting in the shade today because someone planted a tree a long time ago." *(NewsInc., January, 1991)*

"Our stay-put behavior reflects our view that the stock market serves as a relocation center at which money is moved from the active to the patient." *(1991 Annual Report)*

"The best CEOs love operating their companies and don't prefer going to Business Roundtable meetings or playing golf at Augusta National." *(Fortune, April 22, 1991)*

"To swim a fast 100 meters, it's better to swim with the tide than to work on your stroke." *(Annual Meeting in 1991)*

"There are a lot of profitable things you can do but you have to stick to what you can do. We can't find a way to knock out Mike Tyson." *(Annual Meeting in 1991)*

"We're not pure economic creatures...And that policy penalizes our results somewhat, but we prefer to operate that way in life. What's the sense of becoming rich if you're going to have a pattern of operation where you continually discard associations with people you like, admire and find interesting in order to earn a slightly bigger figure? We like big figures, but not to the exclusion of everything else." *(Annual Meeting in 1991)*

On the desire for big positions in the right business: "We own fewer stocks today at $7 billion than we did when our total portfolio was $20 million." *(Annual Meeting in 1991)*

No frills. "Whatever colors were on the corporate jet when we bought it are the ones that are on it today. There's no 'WB' or 'BH.' And that's not likely to change." *(Annual Meeting in 1991)*

On not second-guessing the managers of his business: "If they need my help to manage the enterprise, we're probably both in trouble." *(Outstanding Investor Digest, May 24, 1991)*

"For me, it's what's available at the time. We're not interested in categories per se. We're interested in value." *(Business Week, August 19, 1991)*

"Easy access to funding tends to cause undisciplined decisions." *(Salomon conference with clients, September 13, 1991)*

On learning from mistakes: "I guess I had too much inclination originally to buy mediocre, or worse than mediocre, businesses at a very cheap price. That works OK, in the sense that you never lose money; but you never end up with a great business that way either. So that emphasis has shifted over the years. We don't want to buy the worst furniture store in town at the cheapest price; we want to buy the best one at a fair price." *(widely quoted)*

His biggest strength: "I'm rational. Plenty of people have higher IQs, and plenty of people work more hours, but I am rational about things. But you have to be able to control yourself; you can't let your emotions get in the way of your mind.
"In 1986, my biggest accomplishment was not doing anything stupid. There is not much to do; there is not much available right now. The trick is, when there is nothing to do, do nothing.
"I love what I do. All I want to do is do what I'm doing as long as I can. Every day I feel like tap dancing all through the day. I really do." *(widely quoted)*

Advice to graduating MBA students. "Go to work for whomever you admire the most. You'll be turned on; you'll feel like getting out of bed in the morning; and you'll learn a lot.

"That is what I did. I wanted to work for Ben Graham, but he didn't hire me immediately. I offered to go to work for him for nothing too, so it's even worse than it sounds. So I started trying to be useful to him in various ways. I did a number of studies I dreamt up. I tried to suggest ideas.

"If I were a student today, I would probably try to show the people where I worked what I could do. If I wanted to be starting quarterback on the Washington Redskins, I'd try to get them to watch me throw a few passes.

"As a corollary, I would never go to work for an operation that I had any negative feelings about." *(widely quoted)*

"Investment must be rational; if you don't understand it, don't do it." *(Forbes, October 19, 1992)*

Restaurants as investments: Not good, because "a similar one can open up across the street." *(Business Week, Robert Stoval column, January 5, 1993)*

"Growth is always a component in the calculation of value, constituting a variable whose importance can range from negligible to enormous and whose impact can be negative as well as positive." *(1992 Annual Report)*

"What counts for most people in investing is not how much they know, but rather how realistically they define what they don't know. An investor needs to do very few things right as long as he or she avoids big mistakes." *(1992 Annual Report)*

"If options aren't a form of compensation, what are they? If compensation isn't an expense, what is it? And if expenses shouldn't go into the calculation of earnings, where in the world should they go?" *(1992 Annual Report)*

"Mrs. Blumkin recently sold her Mrs. B's Warehouse to the Mart and announced plans to operate her carpet business alongside a new store operated by the Mart. I am delighted that Mrs. B has again linked up with us. Her business story has no parallel and I have always been a fan of hers, whether she was a partner, or a competitor. But, believe me, partner is better." *(1992 Annual Report)*

"Overhead costs are under 1% of our reported operating earnings and less than $1/2$ of 1% of our look-through earnings. We have no legal, personnel, public relations, investor relations, or strategic planning departments. In turn this means we don't need support personnel such as guards, drivers, messengers, etc." (1992 Annual Report)

Two kinds of information: "Those things you can know and those things important to know. Those things you can know that are important constitute an extremely small percentage of the total known." *(widely quoted)*

On investing: "Investing is not that complicated. You need to know accounting, the language of business. You should read *The Intelligent Investor*. You need the right mindset, the right temperament. You should be interested in the process and be in your circle of competence...Avoid overstimulation. Read Ben Graham and Phil Fisher, read annual reports and trade reports, but don't do equations with Greek letters in them." *(Annual Meeting in 1993)*

"I read annual reports of the company I'm looking at and I read the annual reports of the competitors...That's the main source material." *(Annual Meeting in 1993)*

Munger: "We like to keep things simple...so the chairman can sit around and read annual reports." *(Annual Meeting in 1993)*

Berkshire's price: "At no time has Berkshire's price been ridiculously out of line from intrinsic value. All along it's been reasonably priced." *(Annual Meeting in 1993)*

On selling off businesses: "We try not to sell the flowers to water the weeds." *(Annual Meeting in 1993, quoting Peter Lynch)*

"If you advertise for an opera and a rock concert, you get a different audience...We try to attract the long-term shareholder. We don't want a lot of seat-changing. If you get the wrong shareholder, he'll leave you in six months...We're very unlikely to split the stock." *(Annual Meeting in 1993)*

On media reports of what he's buying: "Some are erroneous...We don't announce our acquisitions (unless legally required). Everyone in this room is a little richer because of that policy." *(Annual Meeting in 1993)*

"Daily newspapers are still good businesses, just not as good as before." *(Annual Meeting in 1993)*

On giving: "My feeling is you pick high-grade younger people to do it...I'm not going to give a tightly drawn document about it. You hope that they are a lot smarter above the ground than you are below ground. You should concentrate your shots in death as well as life." *(Annual Meeting in 1993)*

Inflation prospects: "It's basically just in remission." *(Annual Meeting in 1993)*

Restructurings—"That's a word for mistakes." *(Annual Meeting in 1993)*

The investment professional as a whole doesn't add value: "One factor people have not focused on enough is that obviously professional investment management in aggregate will deliver a poorer return than a simple indexed investment because of the frictional costs Charlie mentioned. Such a significant percentage of the $4 trillion equity market is managed by managers who are getting paid to do the job that their aggregate performance has to be a little less than average simply because of frictional costs. So therefore you have a profession where practitioners as a whole can add nothing to what you can do yourself. In fact, they subtract from it." *(Annual Meeting in 1993)*

"There's good money out of cigarettes which in turn kill people." *(Annual Meeting in 1993)*

Berkshire's future: "I see a lot of interesting things happening, but I haven't the faintest idea what they'll be." *(Nightly Business Review, April 26, 1993)*

On the wealthy paying a fair share under President Clinton's deficit reduction proposal: Buffett, who makes a $100,000 annual salary and $148,000 in director's fees, said, "If I make it into the top 1% (of taxpayers), I don't mind at all. It would be bad for America if we didn't do anything. We can't sit there and choose among 20 bills. I like the idea of more progressivity on the tax rates. I just wish it had been achieved more in spending cuts." *(USA Today, August 6, 1993)*

Where will you take your next vacation? "There's nothing to get away from." *(Forbes reporter Robert Lenzner's query of Buffett for an October 19, 1993 story)*

How's the 1993 stock market? "Common stocks look high and are high, but they are not as high as they look." Buffett quoting Ben Graham's response before the 1955 Fulbright hearings in Washington, D.C. *(Forbes, October 19, 1993)*

Buffett as admirer of the British economist and investor John Maynard Keynes: "Keynes essentially said don't try and figure out what the market is doing. Figure out businesses you understand, and concentrate. Diversification is protection against ignorance, but if you don't feel ignorant, the need for it goes down drastically." *(Forbes, October 19, 1993)*

Summing up Ben Graham's teachings: "When proper temperament joins with proper intellectual framework, then you get rational behavior." *(Forbes, October 19, 1993)*

International portfolio: "I get $150 million earnings pass-through from international operations of Gillette and Coca-Cola. That's my international portfolio." *(Forbes, October 19, 1993)*

"I am a better investor because I am a businessman, and a better businessman because I am an investor." *(Forbes, October 19, 1993)*

"Children should be given enough to do what they want to do, but not enough to be idle." *(WOWT-TV in Omaha, October 14, 1993)*

Advice for someone coming into the investment field: "If he were coming in with small sums of capital, I'd tell him to do exactly what I did 40-odd years ago, which is to learn about every company in the United States that has publicly traded securities and that bank of knowledge will do him or her terrific good over time." Adam Smith: "But there's 27,000 public companies." Buffett: "Well, start with the A's." *(Adam Smith's "Money World," October 21, 1993)*

"The smartest side to take in a bidding war is the losing side." *(Fortune, November 29, 1993, quoting Buffett's talk to Columbia Business School students October 27, 1993)*

Picking the right business for a long-term holding: "If you're going to have a Catholic marriage, you'd better do it right." *(Omaha World-Herald, October 28, 1993, quoting from the same talk)*

"I feel competent...in a very few cases. I think that Bill Gates is one of the best managers in the world, but I don't have the faintest idea of how to evaluate what the stream of coupons will look like on a bond called Microsoft. *(Omaha World-Herald, October 28, 1993, quoting from the same talk)*

"It may be a sensational stream of coupons, but I just don't know enough about it to evaluate that. But if I can't evaluate it...then I'm not investing. I'm betting on whether a stock will go up or down tomorrow or next week or next month...I put a heavy weight on certainty." *(Omaha World-Herald, October 28, 1993, quoting from the same talk)*

"Risk is not knowing what you're doing." *(Omaha World-Herald, October 28, 1993, quoting from the same talk)*

"I would think very hard about getting into a business with fundamentally good economics. I would think of buying from people I can trust. And I'd think about the price I'd pay. But I wouldn't think about price to the exclusion of the first two. And that essentially, is what we're trying to do at Berkshire. And if I did that, would I think about whether I could buy it cheaper on Monday rather than on Friday or would I think about the January effect or other nonsense?" *(Omaha World-Herald, October 28, 1993, quoting from the same talk)*

Communications investments: "I don't like businesses where the technology is changing fast. Basically, I don't think I'm a great one for seeing the future when the future looks way different than the present. Generally, anything that is subject to a lot of change and technology, I tend to be critical of rather than excited by." *(Omaha World-Herald, October 28, 1993, quoting from the same talk)*

On common sense and believing in yourself: "In the end, I always believe my eyes rather than anything else." *(Omaha World-Herald, October 28, 1993, quoting from the same talk)*

"Invest within your circle of competence. It's not how big the circle is that counts. It's how well you define the parameters." *(Fortune, November 29, 1993)*

Taxes: "Speaking for our own shares, Charlie and I have absolutely no complaint about these taxes. We know we work in a market-based economy that rewards our efforts far more bountifully than it does the efforts of others whose output is of equal or greater benefit to society. Taxation should, and does, partially redress this inequity. But we still remain extraordinarily well-treated." *(1993 Annual Report)*

"Diversification is a hedge against ignorance." *(widely quoted)*

Diversification: "The strategy we've adopted precludes our following standard diversification dogma. Many pundits would therefore say the strategy must be riskier than that employed by more conventional investors. We disagree. We believe that a policy of portfolio concentration may well decrease risk if it raises, as it should, both the intensity with which an investor thinks about a business and the comfort level he must feel with its economic characteristics before buying into it. In stating this opinion, we define risk, using dictionary terms, as 'the possibility of loss or injury.'

"Academics, however, like to define investment 'risk' differently, averring that it is the relative volatility of a stock or a portfolio of stocks—that is, their volatility as compared to that of a large universe of stocks. Employing databases and statistical skills, these academics compute with precision the 'beta' of a stock—its relative volatility in the past—and then build arcane investment and capital allocation theories around this calculation. In their hunger for a single statistic to measure risk, however, they forget a fundamental principle: It is better to be approximately right than precisely wrong." *(1993 Annual Report)*

"The pleasant but vacuous director need never worry about job security." *(1993 Annual Report)*

"There's no use running if you're on the wrong road." *(1993 Annual Report)*

"We know who the best baseball players are; why not know who the best teachers are?" *(Interview with Tom Brokaw of NBC News, April 12, 1994)*

"You can't get rich with a weathervane." *(Annual Meeting in 1994)*

"We'd rather multiply by three than pi." *(Annual Meeting in 1994)*

"Charlie and I never have an opinion about the market because it wouldn't be any good and it might interfere with the opinions we have that are good." *(Annual Meeting in 1994)*

"Virtually everything we've done has been by reading public reports and then maybe asking questions around and ascertaining trade positions and product strengths or something of that sort." *(Annual Meeting in 1994)*

Coca-Cola! "Coke in 1890 or thereabouts—the whole company-sold for $2,000. Its market value today is $50—odd billion. Somebody could have said to the fellow who was buying it in 1890, 'We're going to have a couple of great World Wars. There'll be a panic in 1907. All of these things are going to happen. Wouldn't it be better to wait?' We can't afford that mistake." *(Annual Meeting in 1994)*

"There's nothing that I know about that product or its distribution system, its finances or anything that hundreds of thousands or millions of people don't know, too. They just don't do anything about it." *(Annual Meeting in 1994)*

"So the important thing that we do as managers generally is find the .400 hitters and then not tell them how to swing...And the second thing we do is allocate capital. Aside from that, we play bridge. That's Berkshire." *(Annual Meeting in 1994)*

"There's a huge difference between the business that grows and requires lots of capital to do so and the business that grows and doesn't require capital." *(Annual Meeting in 1994)*

"We don't have any meetings of any kind at Berkshire, but we'd never have an asset allocation meeting." *(Annual Meeting in 1994)*

"I buy expensive suits. They just look cheap on me." *(Annual Meeting in 1994)*

Thinking for yourself: "You have to think for yourself. It always amazes me how high-IQ people mindlessly imitate. I never get good ideas talking to other people." *(U.S. News & World Report, June 20, 1994)*

A good business: "Look for the durability of the franchise. The most important thing to me is figuring out how big a moat there is around the business. What I love, of course, is a big castle and a big moat with piranhas and crocodiles." *(U.S. News & World Report, June 20, 1994)*

"Compound interest is a little bit like rolling a snowball down a hill. You can start with a small snowball and if it rolls down a hill long enough (and my hill is now 53 years long - that's when I bought my first stock), and the snow is mildly sticky, you'll have a real snowball at the end." *(Talk to University of Nebraska students, October 10, 1994)*

"I spend an inordinate amount of time reading. I probably read at least six hours a day, maybe more. I spend an hour or two on the telephone, and the rest of the time I think. We have no meetings at Berkshire. I hate meetings." *(Omaha World-Herald, October 11, 1994)*

"I'm sort of a Republican on the production side, and I'm sort of a Democrat on the distribution side." *(Associated Press, October 16, 1994)*

"All these people who think that food stamps are debilitating and lead to a cycle of poverty, they're the same ones who go out and want to leave a ton of money to their kids." *(Associated Press, October 16, 1994)*

"All we want is to be in businesses that we understand, run by people whom we like, and priced attractively relative to their future prospects." *(Fortune, October 31, 1994)*

"We don't know and we don't think about when something will happen. We think about what will happen." *(Fortune, October 31, 1994)*

"You're lucky in life if you pick the right heroes. Ben was mine." *(New York Society of Security Analysts, December 6, 1994)*

About Ben Graham being generous with his ideas: Quoting Oscar Hammerstein, "A bell's not a bell until you ring it. A song is not a song until you sing it. And love in the heart isn't put there to stay. Love isn't love 'til you give it away." *(New York Society of Security Analysts, December 6, 1994)*

"The professional in almost any field achieves a result which is significantly above what the layman in aggregate achieves. It's not true in money management." *(New York Society of Security Analysts, December 6, 1994)*

The basic ideas of investing are to look at stocks as businesses, use market fluctuations to your advantage and seek a margin of safety. "That's what Ben Graham taught us...A hundred years from now they will still be the cornerstones of investing." *(New York Society of Security Analysts, December 6, 1994)*

"We just try to buy businesses with good to superb underlying economics, run by honest and able people and buy them at sensible prices. That's all I'm trying to do. When I see a seven-footer, I think, 'Is the guy coordinated, can I keep him in school and all those things. And then some guy comes up to me and says, 'I'm 5-6, but you ought to see me handle the ball.' " Says Buffett: "I'm not interested." *(New York Society of Security Analysts, December 6, 1994)*

On being named pitchman for economic development in Nebraska: "Easiest job I ever had." *(Omaha World-Herald, January 11, 1995)*

"The best time to sell a stock is never." *(USA Today, February 17, 1995)*

"When you find a really good business run by first-class people, chances are a price that looks high isn't high." *(London Independent, February 19, 1995)*

"I'd be a bum on the street with a tin cup if the market were efficient." *(Fortune, April 3, 1995)*

"Thirty years ago, no one could have foreseen the huge expansion of the Vietnam War, wage and price controls, two oil shocks, the resignation of a president, the dissolution of the Soviet Union, a one-day drop in the Dow of 508 points, or treasury bill yields fluctuating between 2.8% and 17.4%." *(1994 Annual Report)*

"Fear is the foe of the faddist, but the friend of the fundamentalist." *(1994 Annual Report)*

"It's far better to own a significant portion of the Hope diamond than 100% of a rhinestone." *(1994 Annual Report)*

Quoting Wayne Gretzky, "Go to where the puck is going to be, not where it is." *(1994 Annual Report)*

"We try to *price*, rather than *time*, purchases. In our view, it's folly to forego buying shares in an outstanding business whose long-term future is predictable, because of short-term worries about an economy or a stock market that we know to be unpredictable. Why scrap an informal decision because of an uninformed guess?" *(1994 Annual Report)*

"If I can't make money in a $5 trillion market, it may be a little bit of wishful thinking to think that all I have to do is get a few thousand miles away and I'll start showing my stuff." *(widely quoted)*

"You don't have to make money back the same way you lost it." *(Annual Meeting in 1995)*

"We believe in managers knowing money costs money." *(Annual Meeting in 1995)*

"A stock doesn't know who owns it. You may have all of these feelings and emotions as the stock goes up or down, but the stock doesn't give a damn." *(Annual Meeting in 1995)*

"We try to find businesses with wide and long moats around them protecting a castle with an honest lord of the castle...all moats are subject to attack in a capitalistic society." *(Annual Meeting in 1995)*

"We like stocks that generate high returns on invested capital where there is a strong likelihood that it will continue to do so. For example, the last time we bought Coca-Cola, it was selling at about 23 times earnings. Using our purchase price and today's earnings, that makes it about five times earnings. It's really the interaction of capital employed, the return on that capital, and future capital generated versus the purchase price today." *(Annual Meeting in 1995)*

"There are certain kinds of businesses where you have to be smart once and the kind where you have to stay smart every day to defend it. Retailing is one of them. If you find a retailing concept that catches on, you have to defend it every day." *(Annual Meeting in 1995)*

Advice to managers: "Think like an owner and give us the bad news early." *(Annual Meeting in 1995)*

"I have no use whatsoever for projections or forecasts. They create an illusion of apparent precision. The more meticulous they are, the more concerned you should be. We never look at projections, but we care very much about, and look very deeply at, track records. If a company has a lousy track record, but a very bright future, we will miss the opportunity." *(Annual Meeting in 1995)*

First thing Buffett thinks about when buying a business: "Can I understand it?" *(Annual Meeting in 1995)*

"If the accounting confuses you, don't do it." *(Annual Meeting in 1995)*

"I look for what's permanent, and what is not." (Annual Meeting in 1995) **[Author's note: see there!]**

Coca-Cola: "It's not a bad measuring stick against buying the things. I don't have any plans to buy more right now, but I wouldn't rule it out. And when I consider buying another business, I'll say, 'Why would I rather have this than Coca-Cola?' " *(Annual Meeting in 1995)*

"If you have to choose between a terrific management and a terrific business, choose the terrific business." *(Annual Meeting in 1995)*

Management: "If the company cannot be expected to stand on its own two feet for years after the ink is dry, we would not be interested." *(Annual Meeting in 1995)*

"It's not that I want money. It's the fun of making it and watching it grow." *(Time, August 21, 1995)*

Selling a familiar stock is "like dumping your wife when she gets old." *(Business Week, August 21, 1995)*

"Chains of habit are too light to be felt until they are too heavy to be broken." *(PBS TV program produced by the University of North Carolina, Center for Public Television, 1995)*

On waiting until the last minute to decide whether to take stock, cash or a combination in connection with the Disney/Cap Cities merger: "I never swing at a ball while it's still in the pitcher's glove." *(Fortune, March 4, 1996)*

"In the early years, we needed only good ideas, but now we need good *big* ideas." *(1995 Annual Report)*

A man with an ailing horse: "Visiting the vet, he said: ' Can you help me? Sometimes my horse walks just fine and sometimes he limps.' The vet's reply was pointed: 'No problem—when he's walking fine, sell him.' In the world of acquisitions, that horse would be sold as Secretariat." *(1995 Annual Report)*

"We do have a few advantages, perhaps the greatest being that we don't have a strategic plan." *(1995 Annual Report)*

"We avoid the attitude of the alumnus whose message to the football coach is, 'I'm 100% with you—win or tie.' " *(1995 Annual Report)*

A question folks at Berkshire always should ask: "And then what?" *(Annual Meeting in 1996)*

"There is no formula to figure (intrinsic value) out. You have to know the business." *(Annual Meeting in 1996)*

"If you find three wonderful businesses in your life, you'll get very rich." *(Annual Meeting in 1996)*

"We like businesses which are fundamental, simple and where the rate of change is not very fast." *(Annual Meeting in 1996)*

"If the business and the manager are right, you should probably forget the quote." *(Annual Meeting in 1996)*

"The definition of a great company is one that will be great for 25 or 30 years." *(Annual Meeting in 1996)*

"We do not view Berkshire shareholders as faceless members of an ever-shifting crowd. But rather as co-venturers who have entrusted their funds to us for what may well turn out to be the remainder of their lives." *(Berkshire's Owner's Manual, June, 1996)*

"Overall, Berkshire and its long-term shareholders benefit from a sinking stock market much as a regular purchaser of food benefits from declining food prices. So when the market plummets—as it will from time to time—neither panic nor mourn. It's good for Berkshire." *(Berkshire's Owner's Manual, June, 1996)*

An added principal: "To the extent possible, we would like each Berkshire shareholder to record a gain or loss in market value during his period of ownership that is proportional to the gain or loss in per-share intrinsic value recorded by the company during the holding period. For this to come about, the relationship between the intrinsic value and the market price of a Berkshire share would need to remain constant, and by our preferences at 1-to-1. As that implies, we would rather see Berkshire's stock price at a fair level than a high level. Obviously, Charlie and I can't control Berkshire's price. But by our policies and communications, we can encourage informed, rational behavior by owners that, in turn, will tend to produce a stock price that is also rational. Our it's-as-bad-to-be-overvalued-as-to-be-undervalued approach may disappoint some shareholders, particularly those poised to sell. We believe, however, that it affords Berkshire the best prospect of attracting long-term investors who seek to profit from the progress of the company rather than from the investment mistakes of others." *(Berkshire's Owner's Manual, June, 1996)*

"You can gain some insight into the difference between book value and intrinsic value by looking at one form of investment, a college education. Think of the education's cost as its 'book value.' If the cost is to be accurate, it should include the earnings that were foregone by the student because he chose college rather than a job. For this exercise, we will ignore the important non-economic benefits of an education and focus steadily on its economic value. First, we must estimate the earnings that the graduate will receive over his lifetime and subtract from that figure an estimate of what he would have earned had he lacked his education. That gives us an excess earnings figure, which must then be discounted, at an appropriate interest rate, back to graduation day. The dollar result equals the intrinsic economic value of the education.

"Some graduates will find that the book value of their education exceeds its intrinsic value, which means that whoever paid for the education didn't get his money's worth. In other cases, the intrinsic value of an education will far exceed its book value, a result that proves capital was wisely deployed. In all cases what is clear is that book value is meaningless as an indicator of intrinsic value." *(Berkshire's Owner's Manual, June, 1996)*

"That which is not worth doing is not worth doing well." *(widely quoted)*

"The much maligned idle-rich have received a bad rap: they have maintained their wealth while many of the energetic rich—aggressive real estate operators, corporate acquirers, oil drillers etc.—have their fortunes disappear." *(widely quoted)*

"It's the big, dumb acquisitions that are going to cost shareholders far, far more than all other things." *(October 27, 1996 at Yeshiva University's Benjamin N. Cardozo School of Law)*

"There is no question the leeway I have to report earnings as CEO of Berkshire is enormous. I don't know how to quantify it precisely, and some of it would catch up with you later on, in terms of insurance reserves, for example. In an insurance company, the long-tail business in particular, you can paint any picture you want, for a period that probably encompasses enough time to either buy out the public or to effect a major public offering." *(Conversations from the Warren Buffett Symposium October 27, 1996 at Yeshiva University's Benjamin N. Cardozo School of Law)*

"With enough inside information and a million dollars, you can go broke in a year." *(widely quoted)*

Buffett to Katharine Graham about the tough days in the 1970s at the Post: "When you're down for one day it doesn't change anything. If you're down for a year, you've lost the whole enterprise. Where in between do the lines cross?" What he was watching for was that line-crossing point. Looking back, he admitted, "You didn't come near that point where you were in serious danger of losing the company, but it's like looking for a cure for cancer; you either find the cure or you die in six months. And if you find one in the fourth month, you say there was nothing to it." *(Personal History, Katharine Graham, p. 552)*

"I would not want you to panic and sell your Berkshire stock upon hearing that some large catastrophe had cost us a significant amount. If you would tend to react that way, you should not own Berkshire shares now, just as you should entirely avoid owning stocks if a crashing market would lead you to panic and sell." *(1996 Annual*

Report)

Taxes: "In 1961, President Kennedy said that we should ask not what our country can do for us, but rather what we can do for our country. Last year we decided to give this suggestion a try—and who says it never hurts to ask? We were told to mail $860 million in income taxes to the U.S. Treasury.

"Here's a little perspective on that figure: If an equal amount had been paid by only 2,000 other taxpayers, the government would have had a balanced budget in 1996 without needing a dime of taxes—income or Social Security or what have you—from any other American. Berkshire shareholders can truly say, 'I gave at the office.' Charlie and I believe that large tax payments are entirely fitting. The contributions we thus make to society's well-being is at most only proportional to its contribution to ours. Berkshire prospers in America as it would nowhere else." *(1996 Annual Report)*

"Inactivity [in investing] strikes us as intelligent behavior." *(1996 Annual Report)*

"If you aren't willing to own a stock for ten years, don't even think about owning it for ten minutes." *(1996 Annual Report)*

"I would rather be certain of a good result than hopeful of a great one." *(1996 Annual Report)*

In comparison to 1% fees of most mutual funds: "We are here to make money with you, not off you." *(1996 Annual Report)*

"In the securities business, whatever can be sold will be sold." *(1996 Annual Report)*

"To invest successfully, you need not understand beta, effcient markets, modern porfolio theory, option pricing or emerging markets. You may, in fact, be better off knowing nothing of these. That, of course, is not the prevailing view at most business schools, whose finance curriculum tends to be dominated by such subjects. In our view, though, investment students need only two well-taught courses—How to Value a Business, and How to Think About Market Prices." *(1996 Annual Report)*

"If you were a jerk before, you'll be a bigger jerk with a billion dollars." *(Forbes, April 21, 1997)*

"I like guys who forget that they sold the business to me and run the show like proprietors. When I marry the daughter, she continues to live with her parents." *(Warren Buffett Speaks, Janet Lowe, 1997, p. 80)*

"I used to be too price-conscious. We used to have prayer meetings before we'd raise the bid an eighth and that was a mistake." *(Annual Meeting in 1997)*

"The single biggest recurring mistake I've made has been my reluctance to pay up for outstanding businesses." *(Annual Meeting in 1997)*

"I've got 99% of my money in Berkshire, but it was bought at a different price." *(Annual Meeting in 1997)*

"We like the idea of having it all in Berkshire, but we don't recommend it." *(Annual Meeting in 1997)*

"It's our job to focus on what we know and that makes a difference." *(Annual Meeting in 1997)*

"Money management is one field where you can get something for nothing. Money managers in aggregate have gotten something for nothing—stockholders' money—and the investors have paid for it." *(Annual Meeting in 1997)*

"Do something you enjoy, not to get money so you can do something you like later. If we were in this only for the money, we would have quit years ago." *(Annual Meeting in 1997)*

"Investment is about putting out money today to get more money back later on from the asset—and not about selling it to somebody else." *(Annual Meeting in 1997)*

"Regarding learning from your mistakes, the best thing to do is to learn from the other guys' mistakes. As Patton used to say, 'It's an honor to die for your country, but make sure the other guy gets the honor.' Our approach is really to try and learn vicariously." *(Annual Meeting in 1997)*

"Our job really is to focus on things that we can know that make a difference. If something can't make a difference or if we can't know it, then we write it off." *(Annual Meeting 1997)*

"Price is what you pay; value is what you get." *(widely quoted)*

"Financial success is not a matter of genius. It's a matter of having the right habits." *(Omaha World-Herald, November 12, 1997)*

Credit cards are a bad idea unless people pay the full balance each month to avoid interest. "Nobody's ever gotten rich paying 18 to 21% on their money." *(Omaha World-Herald, November 12, 1997)*

Acquisitions often are described as " buyer buys seller." Buffett says what's actually happening is: "buyer sells part of itself to acquire seller." *(The Essays of Warren Buffett: Lessons for Corporate America, Lawrence A. Cunningham, Cardozo Law Review, 1997)*

"Act like owners." Advice to Dow Jones & Co. dissident shareholders. *(Fortune, March 2, 1998)*

"For anyone deploying capital, nothing recedes like success." *(1997 Annual Report)*

"At our present size, any performance superiority we achieved will be minor." *(1997 Annual Report)*

"Smile when you read a headline that says 'investors lose as market falls.' Edit in your mind to 'Disinvestors lose as market falls—but investors gain.' Though writers often forget this truism, there is a buyer for every seller and what hurts one necessarily helps the other. (As they say in golf matches: 'every putt makes *someone* happy.')" *(1997 Annual Report)*

"Catastrophe bonds...may well live up to their name." *(1997 Annual Report)*

Options: "Their reported costs (but not their true ones) will rise after they are bought by Berkshire if the acquiree has been granting options as part of its compensation packages. In these cases, 'earnings' of the acquiree have been overstated because they have followed the standard—but, in our view, dead wrong—accounting practice of ignoring the cost to a business of issuing options. When Berkshire acquires an option-issuing company, we promptly substitute a cash compensation plan having an economic value equivalent to that of the previous option plan. The acquiree's true compensation cost is thereby brought out of the closet and charged, as it should be, against earnings." *(1997 Annual Report)*

"I paid my first tax at 13 years old and I'm not that bothered—I'd rather be a big taxpayer than need government help." *(Annual Meeting in 1998)*

"It's much more fun to have a company that's largely owned by individuals than institutions. Neither Charlie nor I are working for the money. [Our success as managers] translates into changes in people's lives not some institutional manager's performance figures." *(Annual Meeting in 1998)*

"We will wait until we find something we like. We will love it when we can swing in a big way. That's our style." *(Annual Meeting in 1998)*

"An occasional dry stretch in new buying? This is no great tragedy in an investing lifetime." *(Annual Meeting in 1998)*

"I tap dance to work, and when I get there I think I'm supposed to lie on my back and paint the ceiling." *(Fortune, July 20, 1998)*

"If you look at the history of markets, you see everything under the sun." *(Annual Meeting in 1998)*

"We centralize money. Everything else is decentralized." *(Annual Meeting in 1998)*

"We try to think about things that are both important and knowable. There are important things that are not knowable...And there are things knowable but not important—and we don't want to clutter up our minds with those." *(Annual Meeting in 1998)*

"I really don't know what Berkshire is selling for today. It just doesn't make any difference. I can't tell you what it was selling on May 4th, 1983 or May 4th, 1986. And I don't care what it sells for on May 4, 1998. I do care what it sells for 10 years from now. That's what counts. And that's where all our focus is." *(Annual Meeting in 1998)*

On planning ahead: "It wasn't raining when Noah built the ark." *(After Berkshire announced it would acquire General Re, in June 1998)*

"In most acquisitions, it's better to be the target than the acquirer. The acquirer pays for the fact that he gets to haul back to his cave the carcass of the conquered animal." *(Fortune, July 20, 1998)*

His beef with EBITDA (earnings before interest, taxes, depreciation and amortization): "Why not report earnings before wages? Why not report earnings before rent? In fact, why not report earnings before all expenses? That's called sales." *(Berkshire's special meeting, September 16, 1998)*

"We're risk adverse, not volatility adverse." *(Berkshire's special meeting, September 16, 1998)*

"I was in no position to offend anyone." On taking no role in 1992 presidential politics when he was involved in salvaging Salomon. *(Omaha World-Herald, December 13, 1998)*

The job of government, it seems to me, is to promote trade that will raise the standard of living of the country and at the same time have a safety net for those who are dislocated...You need a policy that takes care of people who lose jobs through no fault of their own." *(Omaha World-Herald, December 13, 1998)*

"After you graduate, take a job you like, not one you think will look good on your resume. Take one that you would take if you were independently wealthy. Money isn't everything. Liking the people you work with is." *(Miami Herald, December 27, 1998, quoting a talk at the University of Florida)*

"I buy businesses, not stocks...businesses I would be willing to own forever. For a good diversified portfolio, you don't need to own pieces of a large number of businesses. If you can identify six good ones, that should be enough. If you go into a seventh, you may be stretching too far." *(Miami Herald, December 27, 1998, quoting a talk at the University of Florida)*

Macroeconomics: "If I were at a dinner with Alan Greenspan on one side of me and Robert Rubin on the other, what they said would mean nothing to me." *(Miami Herald, December 27, 1998, quoting a talk at the University of Florida)*

Low expectations is what you want. "I mean I've never told anybody to buy Berkshire stock. And if I were to give advice to somebody about how to have a marriage that would last and they could only seek one quality in their spouse, now, if the only thing you're interested in is having the marriage last....then you want low expectations." *(Interview on "Nightline," March 2, 1999)*

"You should understand just what an average gain of 15% over the next five years implies: It means we will need to increase net worth by $58 billion. Earning this daunting 15% will require us to come up with big ideas: Popcorn stands just won't do. Today's markets are not friendly to our search for 'elephants,' but you can be sure that we will stay focused on the hunt." *(1998 Annual Report)*

"A majority of our shares are held by investors who expect to die still holding them. We can therefore ask our CEO's to manage for maximum long-term growth, rather than for next quarter's earnings."

(1998 Annual Report)

"Money managers purposely work at manipulating numbers and deceiving investors. And, as Michael Kinsley has said about Washington: "The scandal isn't in what's done that's *illegal* but rather in what's *legal*." *(1998 Annual Report)*

"I like a company I can understand, management that I like and trust and a price that is sensible. But with the Dow near 10,000 points, I will have trouble finding No. 3." *(San Antonio Express-News, March 20, 1999)*

"Capitalism is brutal. We could all go count the restaurants for the next three miles, and in five years, many of them will not be there with the same names. There are no prizes if you don't run them right. That's why I buy good businesses to begin with." *(San Antonio Express-News, March 20, 1999)*

"I don't want a boat or 10 cars. I can drive only one car at a time. I might as well buy an auto dealership and say they're all mine. I don't want a 300-room house either. After awhile, the possessions possess you." *(San Antonio Express-News, March 20, 1999)*

"When we can't find things to invest in, the money piles up. When we can find something, we pile in." *(Annual Meeting in 1999)*

"Stocks are not items that wiggle around in the paper and have charts attached to them." *(Annual Meeting in 1999)*

"Essentially, you're being a reporter. It's very much like journalism. If you ask enough questions...It's an investigative process—a journalistic process. And in the end, you want to write the story." *(Annual Meeting in 1999)*

"There's a lot of difference between making money and spotting a wonderful industry." *(Annual Meeting in 1999)*

"Why do smart people do dumb things that are against their self interest? Our success has probably been driven mostly by avoiding mistakes." *(Annual Meeting in 1999)*

"I read the *Financial Times* every day, but if there is something in their headline, 'What I think the world will look like next year' by anybody prominent in the world of economics, I don't read the article. The time spent doing that I could spend looking at businesses. I'm not interested in soothsaying." *(Financial Times, May 17, 1999)*

"You tell me who somebody's heroes are, and I will tell you how they will turn out. If you get the right heroes, it gets you through a tremendous amount." *(Financial Times, May 17, 1999)*

"I was lucky to be wired the way I am...I happen to fit very well into a big market economy, where allocation of capital is an important and well-paid function...If the money was in high-jumping, I couldn't be making any money....If the money was in spelling, I probably wouldn't be making any money. I was lucky. I applied myself to it but it has been a lot of fun, so why shouldn't I? It doesn't make me superior to anybody who is leading a boy scout troop in Omaha in terms of helping the community. I was just in the right place at the right time." *(Financial Times, May 17, 1999)*

"I'm comfortable with myself. I can afford it. I've never been tested. Who knows how I would behave if I had a kid who needed an operation next week and I didn't have any money?" *(Financial Times, May 17, 1999)*

On being a good investor: "I was born at the right time and place, where the ability to allocate capital really counts. I'm adapted to this society. I won the ovarian lottery. I got the ball that said, 'capital allocator—United States.' " *(Business Week, July 5, 1999)*

"Success in investing doesn't correlate with I.Q. once you're above the level of 125. Once you have ordinary intelligence, what you need is the temperament to control the urges that get other people into trouble in investing." *(Business Week, July 5, 1999)*

On identifying good companies: "The best thing that happens to us is when a great company gets into temporary trouble...We want to buy them when they're on the operating table." *(Business Week, July 5, 1999)*

On the size of his stock portfolio: "If I was running $1 million today, or $10 million for that matter, I'd be fully invested. Anyone who says that size does not hurt investment performance is selling. The highest rate of return I've ever achieved were in the 1950s. I killed the Dow. You ought to see the numbers. But I was investing peanuts then. It's a huge structural advantage not to have a lot of money. I think I could make you 50% a year on $1 million. No, I know I could. I guarantee that." *(Business Week, July 5, 1999)*

"Up until a few years ago, we sold things to buy more because I ran out of money. I had more ideas than money. Now I make more money than ideas." *(Business Week, July 5, 1999)*

On holding cash: "Today we have $15 billion in cash. Do I like getting 5% on it? No. But I like the $15 billion, and I don't want to put it in something that's not going to give it back and then some. The nature of markets is that at times they offer extraordinary values and at other times you have to have the discipline to wait." *(Business Week, July 5, 1999)*

"If you think about it [i.e., the markets], you get these huge swings in valuations. It's the ideal business arrangement, as long as you don't go crazy. The 1970s were unbelievable. The world wasn't going to end, but businesses were being given away. Human nature has not changed. People will always behave in a manic-depressive way over time. They will offer great values to you." *(Business Week, July 5, 1999)*

On the Internet's impact on business: "The Internet as a phenomenon is just huge. That much I understand. I just don't know how to make money at it...I don't try to profit from the Internet. But I do want to understand the damage it can do to an established business. Our approach is very much profiting from lack of change rather than from change. With Wrigley chewing gum, it's the lack of change that appeals to me. I don't think it is going to be hurt by the Internet. That's the kind of business I like." *(Business Week, July 5, 1999)*

On Internet stock valuations: "There will be enormous amounts of disappointment. The numbers of people buying these stocks to hold them are very few. I think 98% of them are being bought by people because they are going up. If these stocks stop going up, they'll get out. Very few of these companies will be big winners in the long run. It's the nature of capitalism not to get a lot of winners. You get a few." *(Business Week, July 5, 1999)*

"With Coke I can come up with a very rational figure for the cash it will generate in the future. But with the top 10 Internet companies, how much cash will they produce over the next 25 years? If you say you don't know then you don't know what it is worth and you are speculating, not investing. All I know is that I don't know, and if I don't know, I don't invest." *(Business Week, July 5, 1999)*

On technology stocks: "How do you beat Bobby Fischer? You play him at any game but chess. I try to stay in games where I have an edge, and I never will in technology investing." *(Business Week, July*

5, 1999)

On macro-economic forecasting: "I don't read economic forecasts. I don't read the funny papers." *(Business Week, July 5, 1999)*

On PaineWebber analyst Alice Schroeder's research showing that Berkshire Hathaway is selling at a sizable discount: "I think she did a very thorough job. It seems to me she varied from the standard approach of securities analysts. But I don't comment on the value. I don't want anybody to come into Berkshire based on what I'm saying about the value of the stock. Our goal is to have the stock sell as close to the intrinsic value as possible, so that people come in and go out on the same basis." *(Business Week, July 5, 1999)*

On daytraders and speculators: "We try to communicate in a way that turns people off who have a crazy approach to stocks. It matters as much who you repel as who you attract. If we were sizably owned by daytraders, we'd have crazy valuations in no time—and in both directions." *(Business Week, July 5, 1999)*

On Coca-Cola: "I have a very strong feeling that Coca-Cola will dominate a much larger soft drink business 10 years from now than today. But in terms of the short run, I have no idea what will happen." *(Business Week, July 5, 1999)*

On past mistakes: "My biggest lost opportunity was probably Freddie Mac. We owned a savings and loan, and that entitled us to buy 1% of Freddie Mac stock when it first came out. We should have bought 100 S&Ls and loaded up on Freddie Mac. What was I doing? I was sucking my thumb." *(Business Week, July 5, 1999)*

"The biggest cause of that kind of mistake [here, failing to buy more Citicorp in 1991] is that I stop buying when the stock starts moving up. I got so enamored of how cheap it was when I started buying that I stopped. I have often folded my tent. I believe in loading up on these things. There wasn't anyone who thought Citibank was going to disappear. And there wasn't anyone who thought it wasn't cheap at $9 a share." *(Business Week, July 5, 1999)*

"We've lost very little on errors of commission. The errors of omission are the big ones." *(Business Week, July 5, 1999)*

"I close my eyes and think about what a company's going to look like in ten years before I invest." *(Disney's Michael Eisner quoting Buffett. Fortune, September 6, 1999)*

"Now, to get some historical perspective, let's look back at the 34 years before this one—and here we are going to see an almost Biblical kind of symmetry, in the sense of lean years and fat years—to observe what happened in the stock market. Take, to begin with, the first 17 years of the period, from the end of 1964 through 1981. Here's what took place in that interval:

Dow Jones Industrial Average

Dec. 31, 1964: 874.12

Dec. 31, 1981: 875.00

Now I'm known as a long-term investor and a patient guy, but that is not my idea of a big move." *(Fortune, November 22, 1999)*

"Every time the risk-free rate moves by one basis point—by 0.01%—the value of every investment in the country changes. People can see this easily in the case of bonds, whose value is normally affected only by interest rates. In the case of equities or real estate or farms or whatever, other very important variables are almost always at work, and that means the effect of interest rate changes is usually obscured. Nonetheless, the effect—like the invisible pull of gravity—is constantly there." *(Fortune, November 22, 1999)*

"The absolute most that the owners of a business, in aggregate, can get out of it in the end—between now and Judgment Day—is what that business earns over time." *(Fortune, November 22, 1999)*

"Well I thought it would be instructive to go back and look at a couple of industries that transformed this country much earlier in this century: automobiles and aviation. Take automobiles first: I have here one page, out of 70 in total, of car and truck manufacturers that have operated in this country. At one time, there was a Berkshire car and an Omaha car. Naturally I noticed those. But there was also a telephone book of others. All told, there appear to have been at least 2,000 car makes, in an industry that had an incredible impact on people's lives. If you had foreseen in the early days of cars how this industry would develop, you would have said, 'Here is the road to riches.' So what did we progress to by the 1990s? After corporate carnage that never let up, we came down to three U.S. car companies—themselves no lollapaloozas for investors. So, here is an industry that had an enormous impact on America—and also an enormous impact, though not the anticipated one, on investors." *(Fortune, November 22, 1999)*

"Move on to failures of airlines. Here's a list of 129 airlines that in the past 20 years filed for bankruptcy. Continental was smart enough to make that list twice. As of 1992, in fact—though the picture would have improved since then—the money that had been made since the dawn of aviation by all of this country's airline companies was zero. Absolutely zero. Sizing all this up, I like to think that if I'd been at Kitty Hawk in 1903 when Orville Wright took off, I would have been farsighted enough, and public-spirited enough—I owed this to future capitalists—to shoot him down. I mean, Karl Marx couldn't have done as much damage to capitalists as Orville did." *(Fortune, November 22, 1999)*

"The key to investing is not assessing how much an industry is going to affect society, or how much it will grow, but rather determining the competitive advantage of any given company and, above all, the durability of that advantage. The products or services that have wide, sustainable moats around them are the ones that deliver rewards to investors." *(Fortune, November 22, 1999)*

"I focus on the absence of change. I don't think the Internet is going to change how people chew gum." *(Fortune, December 20, 1999)*

"Most people get interested in stocks when everyone else is. The time to get interested is when no one else is." *(Fortune, December 20, 1999)*

"I never met a man who could predict the market." *(widely quoted)*

On buying companies: "I look at what their long-term competitive advantage is and that's something that's enduring. I have to understand what they sell, why people buy it, why people might buy something else." *(St. Petersburg Times, December 15, 1999)*

About not talking about Berkshire's problems in 1999: "You don't talk about Father on Mother's Day, and today, GEICO is Mother's Day." *(at an appearance in Lakeland Florida to open a new GEICO call center, St Petersbug Times, December 15, 1999)*

"Once again, I would like to make some comments about accounting, in this case about its application to acquisitions. This is currently a very contentous topic and, before the dust settles, Congress may even intervene (a truly terrible idea)." *(1999 Annual Report)*

On buying companies: "We like to think that we're the Metropolitan Art Museum of business." *(Annual Meeting in 2000)*

"We buy into success stories." *(Annual Meeting in 2000)*

"A casino is a much more exciting place than a church, "but the by products are much worse. *(Press conference April 30, 2000)*

"It would be a nightmare if there was a speculative surge in Berkshire. Then you'd get all kinds of people coming in, and if the stock went up to $200,000, I would say to Charlie, 'It's all yours.' " *(Press conference April 30, 2000)*

How to think about investing: "The first investment primer was written by Aesop in 600 B.C. He said, 'A bird in the hand is worth two in the bush.' Aesop forgot to say when you get the two in the bush and what interest rates are; investing is simply figuring out your cash outlay (the bird in the hand) and comparing it to how many birds are in the bush when you get them." *(Annual meeting in 2000)*

The impact of technology on the Internet: "For society, the Internet is wonderful, but for capitalists, it will be a net negative. It will increase efficiency, but lots of things increase efficiency without increasing profits. It is way more likely to make American business less profitable than more profitable." *(Annual meeting in 2000)*

"I can give you an argument, but I can't give you understanding." *(Annual meeting in 2000)*

MUTUALLY UNDERSTOOD

BUFFETT DECODES FUND PROSPECTUS

The Securities and Exchange Commission warns mutual funds to write their prospectuses in plain English (story 1B). To show mutual fund lawyers how to do it, SEC Chairman Arthur Levitt asked Warren Buffett, the legendary investor and CEO of Berkshire Hathaway to rewrite a typical mutual fund prospectus paragraph. Here is the paragraph—and Buffett's version.

By Marcy Nighswander, AP

The original:

Maturity and Duration Management

Maturity and duration management decisions are made in the context of an intermediate maturity orientation. The maturity structure of the portfolio is adjusted in the anticipation of cyclical interest rate changes. Such adjustments are not made in an effort to capture short-term, day to day movements in the market, but instead are implemented in anticipation of longer term, secular shifts in the levels of interest rates (i.e. shifts transcending and/or not inherent to the business cycle). Adjustments made to shorten portfolio maturity and duration are made to limit capital losses during periods when interest rates are expected to rise. Conversely, adjustments made to lengthen maturation for the portfolio's maturity and duration strategy lies in analysis of the U.S. and global economies, focusing on levels of real interest rates, monetary and fiscal policy actions and cyclical indicators.

Buffett's version:

Maturity and Duration Management

We will try to profit by correctly predicting future interest rates. When we have no strong opinion, we will generally hold intermediate-term bonds. But, when we expect a major and sustained increase in rates we will concentrate on short-term issues. And, conversely, if we expect a major shift to lower rates, we will buy long bonds. We will focus on the big picture and won't make moves based on short-term considerations.

(USA Today, October 14, 1994)

1090

175

LUNCH WITH WARREN BUFFETT

"I'LL HAVE A COKE." "ATTABOY!"

After *Warren Buffett: The Good Guy of Wall Street* (my first Buffett book) came out in 1992, I received a short letter from him saying, in part, "You've treated me better than I deserve but as Charlie and I have repeatedly said, 'Who the hell wants only what they deserve?' "

Later I went to Omaha for some book-signings; at the first one at Village Bookstore, Buffett's daughter Susan came by and I autographed a copy for her daughter, Emily.

When I returned to the Red Lion hotel I was surprised to find a message from Susan. I returned her call and she said she had talked with her father and that he'd be glad to see me the next day.

"He's there all day. Just go up anytime," she said.

In the morning (October 2, 1992), I called Gladys Kaiser who said lunch would be a good time to come. My wife Pat and I parked in the Kiewit Plaza parking deck, talked to the guard who called Mrs. Kaiser, and we were told to take the elevator to the 14th floor to 1440.

We were buzzed through the security system and met the receptionist, who was answering calls. There was at least one request for a Berkshire annual report, a request that is transferred to a tape recording. We were told Mr. Buffett was on the phone but would be with us soon.

Pat and I sat and looked about at the tiny headquarters. There was a collage that had the symbol BRK on it and other items such as *The Buffalo News*; to our left at the entrance was a small sign: "A fool and his money are soon invited everywhere."

Debbie Bosanek came out and introduced herself and then Gladys Kaiser. Marc Hamburg, Berkshire's treasurer happened by. And in less than five minutes—about the time it takes him to conduct the annual meeting—Buffett, dressed in a purple tie and dark conservative suit came ambling down the hallway, saying, "Hi, Andy. Hi, Pat."

"Have you given them a tour?" he asked Mrs. Kaiser, realizing he was stuck with showing us around.

(Photo by Pat Kilpatrick)

The locked doorway into Berkshire headquarters. This writer had arrived for a meeting with Buffett. At lunch he asked for a Coke and Buffett said, "Attaboy!"

He gave a several-minute tour, walking down a narrow hallway pointing to old front pages of the *Wall Street Journal*: "This was the high in 1927 and the low in 1932 in the Depression. We have them because they cost just a dollar." He showed us the document for the original Buffett Partnership.

Mrs. Kaiser pointed out the "library"—just a few books—and Buffett pointed out the "conference room"—two chairs and a small table.

He showed us an old-time Coke machine and his supply of Cokes.

The pale green-walled headquarters was a short line of offices, several groupings of filing cabinets and not much else. The offices, smaller and more cramped than advertised, reminded me of the narrow corridors of a Navy destroyer.

Buffett showed us some old leather-bound ledgers of the Berkshire and Hathaway textile firms, trying to find the signature of early shareholder Hetty Green, known for her wealth and uninviting personality. He couldn't find it.

The tour was suddenly over and we were following him out and down the elevator two floors to the Kiewit Plaza Club dining room.

I asked, "Where are the hamburgers and potato chips?" and he replied, "Oh, we have those, too."

So what would everyone have? He ordered a bacon, lettuce and tomato sandwich, a salad and iced tea. When I started by ordering a Coke, he said, "Attaboy!"

He looked fine, was energetic, talked fast, and was walking with an ever-so-slight limp. He was pale and looked as though he had been in a library all his life, never a minute in the sun. Still, he gave the impression of tremendous energy, genuine interest in everything about life, dominating conversations with stories and jokes.

"I saw your father's byline on the presidential series. In fact, I stopped the VCR to look at it...I watched it on a VCR so I could stop and not miss anything because the phone rings."

I asked him about his early purchase of Washington Post Co. stock. He said he'd gotten to know Katharine Graham, knew of the business from his paperboy days, had watched the stock go public in 1971 and then watched it decline.

"I knew The *Post* was going to outdo The *Star*, not necessarily that the *Star* would fold." He explained he bought his Post Co. stock quickly over a several-month period.

He also told a story about how Peter Kiewit once saved the *Omaha World-Herald* from the clutches of the Newhouse chain, which was after it. "Kiewit bought it over a weekend," Buffett said.

He asked all about the book—the editing, publishing and finances of it. He thought it was very difficult to keep track of things in the publishing world, and said that one of his sons was in the music business, and knew that it was difficult to keep exact tabs on sales.

He was aware that a book about himself by Roger Lowenstein was coming out.

He still plans his own book, but maybe not right away, saying he thought he ought not to write two books, just one, and that there was still a lot left to do yet. "Of course, you don't want to wait until you're 98, or something."

He added, "Frankly, I haven't kept that many notes," to which Mrs. Kaiser said, "He has it all up here," pointing to her head.

Buffett repeated his joke about wanting Carol Loomis to do most of the work on the book.

I asked Buffett if I were to see the list of Berkshire shareholders, would there be more high-profile names than I had listed in my book. "You had a pretty good list, but, yes, there would be a lot of names you'd recognize." He gave only one vague hint. "There's a movie star who has been buying lately."

He told us a story about Paul Newman, with no suggestion Paul Newman was the movie star doing the buying.

Years back, he said, he once sat at a dinner table with Paul Newman, and Senator Charles Percy's wife was between them. "She never looked at me the whole time. I could have been an empty seat." I asked Buffett if he had a chance to talk to Paul Newman, and he said he did a little. "But I practically had to knock her over to talk to him."

Later Buffett said he thought a book ought to be done about Don Keough, Coke's president. "There have been a lot of books done about Coca-Cola, but not about him."

He said that over the past weekend he had been to Seattle to see the Washington-Nebraska football game and had been with a group that included Bill Gates. "He read a book during the game," Buffett said.

"I met him through Meg Greenfield (editorial page editor of the Washington Post who died in 1999). About a year and half ago, she asked me to check on the affordability of her building a house," he said. But Buffett said he already knew the answer. "When you ask if you can afford it, you can. Otherwise you don't ask."

Buffett also said, "I'm for people doing what they want to with their money."

Buffett said Gates' late mother, Mary, was a Berkshire shareholder.

Toward the end of lunch he asked about my career change, and I told him I was studying for the Series 7 exam to be a stockbroker, and he related his Series 7 experience: "When I took over Salomon there was a requirement, as an officer of a securities firm, that I take the Series 7. But I kept delaying it until I left because I was afraid I wouldn't pass it."

Also, he said, because Salomon trades commodities and has foreign businesses there were many rules requiring his fingerprints. "They took 12 sets of my fingerprints."

After lunch we all went back up the elevator (I did not see him check for pennies on the floor) two floors to Berkshire headquarters. The elevator did not magically open when he came up. We had to wait a minute.

I thought things were coming to an end without seeing his office, but then he motioned us to come on back at the same moment I said I'd love (read kill) to see mission control.

We walked in and I pointed to the two black phones behind his desk, and I asked if that was the "bank" of phones where he placed orders. "Yes," he said.

His office featured his rather small desk with another phone, and two small couches. He showed us a framed photo on the wall (his cameo appearance on ABC's soap opera *All My Children*), and with pride pointed to a notice of payment of $10 for his wardrobe fee. "My daughter says that's about what it's worth."

There was a photo of his father and there was an old ticker tape, but really very few things in the way of mementos.

(Photo by Michael O'Brien)

Buffett in his office at "The Pleasure Palace." "We read. That's about it," says Buffett.

Lining a shelf near his desk were some books, including a row of census books.

We thanked him for his hospitality and he walked us to the hallway, waved nonchalantly, and said for me to stay in touch about the progress of the book.

The little more than one-hour trip to the mountaintop was over.

176

LOUIS RUKEYSER HAS LUNCH WITH WARREN BUFFETT

Louis Rukeyser, the noted economic commentator whose *Wall $treet Week With Louis Rukeyser* has been the world's most widely watched television program about money since its inception in 1970, has had a longtime friendly correspondence with Warren Buffett. They had lunch together in Omaha on October 28, 1997, and Rukeyser wrote about it in the December, 1997 issue of his best-selling financial newsletter, *Louis Rukeyser's Wall Street*. His revealing piece follows:

On the morning [October 28, 1997] after the stock market played its latest pre-Halloween trick to frighten investors, with the Dow plunging 554 points and the New York Stock Exchange adding to the terror via two extended trading halts, I happened to be in Omaha for a speaking engagement and was scheduled to have lunch with Warren Buffett. Hollywood could not have arranged more suspenseful timing.

At 67, Warren is already an American myth: the world's most successful investor; the second-richest man in the U.S. (after his younger pal, Bill Gates); the genius of Berkshire Hathaway, the holding company whose original shares are the most expensive on any stock exchange in history, currently going for more than $45,000 a unit. I didn't expect Warren to be falling to pieces, like most of the pseudo-experts I had been watching and reading about the past few hours, but I was certainly anxious to hear whatever he had to say.

In the event, we were perhaps the two calmest people in Omaha, if not the entire world of finance. I

(AP/Wide World Photos)

Louis Rukeyser

1097

called on Warren in his modest office suite, and found him slightly less of a technophobe than rumor would have it. A cable-TV ticker show was on—with the sound turned off, of course; he hasn't gone loony—and he confessed that he does fool around a bit on the Internet, though chiefly to play long-distance bridge games. With unfailing graciousness, he showed me some memorabilia of the humble beginnings of his investment career, and we talked of his old mentor, Benjamin Graham, who had been scheduled to be my guest on *Wall $treet Week With Louis Rukeyser* when he contracted his final illness. Then, because Warren had to fly that afternoon to what would be the last directors' meeting of Salomon Brothers (prior to its merger with Smith Barney), we moved on to lunch at a club within the building.

Here I had another surprise. The one thing I had been told to view as an absolute certainty was that Buffett, a famously large stockholder of Coca-Cola, never drank anything but Cherry Coke. But when I ordered an iced tea, he immediately said: "That sounds good. Let me have an iced tea, too." A subtle investment tip? Nope; just evidence that he is a nice—and not wholly predictable—guy, two qualities that have surely helped him mightily along the way.

Similarly, when I mentioned that there was now at least one Web site providing a "Warren Buffett screen," supposedly listing stocks he might buy, and that the proprietor had chortled publicly after Berkshire Hathaway announced Oct. 21 that it would purchase one of the companies on the list, International Dairy Queen, for $585 million, Buffett's response was instructive: "Oh, we never would have bought that as a stock, Lou. But buying the whole business made some sense to us; it would only have to be two-thirds as attractive on that basis [primarily for tax reasons]."

His reaction to the overall market panic was in the same almost-disdainful vein. "If you can't buy a stock and not even worry about whether the market is going to shut for the next three years," he told me, "you shouldn't buy the stock at all." The intense volatility that had so many lesser investors gulping down heart medicine was merely further evidence of what Ben Graham had dubbed "Mr. Market": a hysterical fellow from whose day-to-day behavior you should separate yourself whenever possible. The sensible way to buy a stock, Warren reiterated, was to think of it not as a piece of paper but a piece of a business. If you buy on that basis, you'll make sounder choices (eschewing what's hot that fortnight) and find it easier to show patience and perseverance when "Mr. Market" periodically goes crazy.

There was nothing new about Buffett's reaction, which is perhaps why he continues to make so much money not just for Berkshire Hathaway shareholders but for all who follow his down-home, common-sense advice. In the most recent annual report of his $43 billion multi-stock holding company, he wrote words that have front-page timeliness today: "You should entirely avoid owning stocks if a crashing market would lead you to panic and sell...Selling fine businesses on 'scary' news is usually a bad decision."

Warren Buffett is often described as a simple man. He lives in the house where his children were born, he drives himself to work, he would never be mistaken for an international gourmet (he likes ice cream with malted-milk powder for breakast, and a major feast would be hamburgers, popcorn and—of course—Cherry Coke). But it is the simplicity of a man who knows what he knows and what he doesn't, and is content to stick to the former—which means, by the standards of our celebrity society, where every new millionaire or movie star claims to have the answer to every problem on the planet, that his is a very profound simplicity indeed.

One of the things he knows is how silly it would be to panic about investing in the fall of 1997. Warren Buffett won't do it, and neither should you.

In the July, 1998 issue of his newsletter, Rukeyser wrote:

How $10,000 Ballooned into $272 Million

The winner's game is buying and holding good businesses with strong enduring qualities. That's Warren Buffett's approach and its done pretty well by him. He's #2 on the *Forbes* list, and he got there by buying stocks in solid companies and *holding* them—not by wasting time trading in and out to make a point here and there.

Anyone with the good judgement to invest $10,000 in Buffett's partnership at its inception in 1956 (and to transfer into Buffett's Berkshire Hathaway at the partnership's termination) would today be sitting on an astonishing $272 million—after all fees and expenses. What's more, the lucky investor would have incurred only about $54,000 in income taxes during the entire 42-year period! No PR man alive could dream up a better testimonial for buying and holding shares of quality American businesses than that.

177

"I'VE MADE MORE MONEY WITH MY REAR END THAN WITH MY HEAD."

Not so very long before, on November 16, 1992, Berkshire had hit $10,000 closing at $10,200 on volume of 210 shares. That last trade came from the Omaha brokerage firm of Kirkpatrick, Pettis where someone said: "Nobody's ever paid $10,200 for it." Replied a trader: "You just did!"

Suddenly Berkshire was a $10,000 stock! It was the highest price at which any equity had ever traded on the New York Stock Exchange. One person asked a Berkshire shareholder: "How can a stock go above $10,000?"

The five digit price fouled up stock quotes everywhere. Some quote machines didn't record that Berkshire was over $10,000. The Bloomberg service, for example, said the stock closed at $9,950. Other services carried the bid and asked at $9,900 by $9,950. Others carried quotes from $200 to $950. Buffett later joked that *The New York Times* printed "all the news fit to print in four digits."

One broker called a Berkshire shareholder saying: "Did Berkshire split or what?"

Some of the lower quotes were recorded in the accounts of some Berkshire shareholders, really gumming up the works.

A broker explained that a purchase of Berkshire shares that day went unrecorded for a time because, "It had to have special handling to accommodate the five digits." The Big Board had to give Berkshire stock quotes by means of an old-fashioned electronic messaging system to financial news services as technicians worked to accommodate the five-digit number.

LaVerne Ramsey, a stockbroker with Prudential Securities in Birmingham, Alabama, sent the following memo to Berkshire shareholders: "There is good news and bad news. The good news is that Berkshire went over $10,000...The bad news is that the 'broker book' system, along with many other financial services, has been unable to handle a five-digit stock price. Therefore the unrealized gain figure is way off because the system drops a digit. Our operations people are working on the problem.

"In the meantime, here is the incorrect copy for the month of November, 1992. It can be a souvenir of the historic milestone for Berkshire Hathaway."

The *Wall Street Journal*, reaching Buffett, got this comment: "What tickles my fancy is when the intrinsic value improves. I focus on what's happening on the playing field, not what's on the scoreboard."

The *Omaha World-Herald* got an even better quote when it asked about a stock price of $10,000 based on long-term holdings: Buffett, apparently enjoying things more than he was letting on, said: "I've made more money with my rear end than my head."

"It proves what Woody Allen said is true: '90% of life is just showing up.'"

George Morgan, of Kirkpatrick, Pettis thinks Berkshire shareholders should show up for life for at least another decade or so because if Buffett can manage an annual 20% net worth growth, the stock may be trading at $200,000 a share. Berkshire now needs roughly a three fold increase to get there.

Charles Schwab & Co. wrote to its Berkshire shareholders: "You are probably already aware of the difficulty financial institutions such as Schwab have had in reporting transactions involving Berkshire Hathaway Inc. since the price of its stock rose above $10,000 per share. In particular, your Schwab statements, confirmations, and other forms of account information are unable to reflect a price-per-share above $9,999.00.

"In order for our systems to correctly calculate your account, summary balances, your statements, trade confirmations, and other account and trade information will report one (1) share of BRK as 10 'fractional shares,' each with a price of one-tenth ($\frac{1}{10}$) of the actual value of one share of BRK.

"For example, if you own or trade two shares of BRK when the price-per-share is $15,000, the quantity, or the number of shares, will be shown as 20 (2 x 10 fractional shares) and the latest price will appear as $1,500 ($\frac{1}{10}$ of $15,000). Total amount on confirmations and market value on statements will be shown as $30,000, the correct total for 2 shares..."

Berkshire shareholders were calling it the New Math.

In 1994, seven years to the day after October 19, 1987, when Berkshire and everything else was crashing, Berkshire traded for a brief time at $20,000 a share.

In early 1996 Berkshire's stock price hit a high of $38,000 before falling back, taking about a year to return to that level.

In May 1997, the stock smashed through $40,000 and ended the year at $46,000. Soon it hit $50,000. On March 11, 1998, it closed at $60,000 and on April 9, 1998, the stock closed at $70,000 and went slightly above $80,000 in June 1998 when Berkshire said it would buy General Re.

Shareholders began musing about a $100,000 celebration party. It reminded one of a bumper sticker that says: "In case of rapture, this car will be unmanned."

But in late 1998, and all of 1999, the rain poured on everyone's parade with the stock closing the millennium at $56,100.

178

"A DO-IT-YOURSELF STOCK SPLIT"

"We're giving shareholders a do-it-yourself split, if they care to," Buffett said in a rare conference call with reporters.

Buffett came up with an unusual split not because he wanted to split the stock, but because he was ticked at unit investment trusts. The unit trusts were trying to piggyback Berkshire's success and exploit his reputation, selling units—with high commissions and management fees—of Berkshire and Berkshire-related stocks for $1,000 units.

In offering a Class B share worth 1/30 of the original, now Class A shares (symbol BRKA), Buffett not only undercut the business of unit trusts, he also provided more flexibility to those trying to get Berkshire into their IRAs or giving up to $10,000 a year tax-free to children.

Buffett could have simply split the stock but said that might have led to a "slightly more speculative bunch," and he did not want a new shareholder base that might be "uninformed or have unrealistic expectations."

Buffett said Class B shareholders would not be allowed to participate in Berkshire's charitable giving program. In 1995 Berkshire shareholders could designate $13 a share to charity, but that would amount to 43 cents a share for a Class B shareholder. "It would be crazy to make 43-cent designations," Buffett said.

However, "unlike the indirect investments offered by the trusts, shares of Class B Common Stock entitle holders to the attributes of Berkshire shares, such as the power to vote on matters put to Berkshire shareholders, the right to receive Berkshire's annual report and other communications to shareholders, and the right to attend meetings of Berkshire's shareholders." (Prospectus for the Class B offering)

The stock offering was Berkshire's first, although there once was a zero-coupon bond convertible into stock. Knowing there would be heavy demand for the issue, Buffett joked that there would be "less of a road show" associated with the Class B offering than most other offerings. "We've never felt any need to have a public offering," he said. "We're not trying to attract the most people, only the people attracted to us."

Buffett ended the conference call saying, "I look forward to reading your stories tomorrow."

Originally Berkshire planned to issue 100,000 shares, but sensing heavy interest it raised the offering to 250,000 shares, then to 350,000 shares and finally to 450,000 shares. So Berkshire raised $565 million.

Under the symbol BRKB, the Class B shares started trading May 9, 1996 at $1,110, closing up $50 to $1,160.

Buffett told *Barron's* (May 13, 1996): "I am more than pleased [with the offering]. We had some unconventional objectives in the offering, and when those were explained to Salomon, they figured out ways they thought would best achieve those objectives. I think maybe they got just exactly the kind of investor we want. We wanted people who are going to be with us for an indefinite future, and to design an offering in this kind of market, with a hot IPO market as a backdrop, that succeeds in getting these kinds of investors is a great credit to Salomon."

"Through the use of Salomon as underwriter, the total underwriting cost was only $7.8 million, about 1.5% of the capital raised (an unusually small figure since 7% is the average underwriting cost of such an issue.") (*The Essays of Warren Buffett: Lessons for Corporate America*, Cardozo Law Review, September-November, 1997, p. 502)

Berkshire's Class B shares are the second highest priced stock trading on the New York Stock Exchange after the Class A shares. The shares of The Washington Post Co. are the third highest.

A group of shareholders at dinner the night before Berkshire's annual meeting in 1996—obviously in a good mood—agreed that Berkshire might hit $40,000 in 1997. A fellow at the bar getting a drift of the conversation said: "Yeah, that's for the Class B share!"

Buffett wrote in the *Owner's Manual* in June, 1996:

"When we sold the Class B shares, we stated that Berkshire stock was not undervalued—and some people found that shocking. That reaction was not well-founded. Shock should have registered instead had we issued shares when our stock was undervalued. Managements that say or imply during a public offering that their stock is undervalued are usually being economical with the truth or unecomonical with their existing shareholders' money. Owners unfairly lose if their managers deliberately sell assets for 80¢ that in fact are worth $1. We didn't commit that kind of crime in our recent offering and we never will."

In 1996 5,120 Class A shares were converted to Class B shares and in 1997 10,048 Class A shares were converted to Class B shares. On

March 3, 1999 there were 1,341,174 A shares and 5,385,320 B shares outstanding.

Buffett said at Berkshire's special meeting September 16, 1998: "I don't see creating a C stock."

Sometimes the B share trades at less than $\frac{1}{30}$ of the A share. Here's what Buffett said about why that may happen from this memo to the Berkshire home page February 2, 1999:

"The Class B can *never* sell for anything more than a tiny fraction above $\frac{1}{30}$ the price of A. When it rises above $\frac{1}{30}$, arbitrage takes place in which someone—perhaps the NYSE specialist—buys the A and converts it into B. This pushes the price back into a 1:30 ratio.

On the other hand, the B can sell for less than $\frac{1}{30}$ the price of the A since conversion doesn't go in the reverse direction. All of this was spelled out in the prospectus that accompanied the issuance of the Class B.

When there is more demand for the B (relative to supply) than for the A, the B will sell at roughly $\frac{1}{30}$ of the price of A. When there's a lesser demand, it will fall to a discount.

In my opinion, most of the time, the demand for B will be such that it will trade at about $\frac{1}{30}$ of the price of the A. However, from time to time, a different supply-demand situation will prevail and the B will sell at some discount. In my opinion, again, when the B is at a discount of more than say, 2%, it offers a better buy than the A. When the two are at parity, however, anyone wishing to buy 30 or more B should consider buying A instead."

The chatter about coverting A shares to B shares and why the B doesn't always trade at exactly $\frac{1}{30}$ of the A triggered this post from one shareholder." "I'm reminded of Mae West's comment when asked, 'You're shipwrecked on a desert island. You see a life boat washing ashore with seven sex-starved sailors aboard. What would you do?' She replied, 'I understand the situation, but I don't see the problem.' "

179

ONE OF THE RICHEST PEOPLE
IN THE WORLD

In the spring of 1993, Buffett became one of the richest people in America as Berkshire's rising stock price carried Buffett's worth above that of his closest rival, Microsoft's Bill Gates.

By that summer, Buffett's net worth exceeded $8 billion. For a man who inherited nothing, the achievement spoke volumes.

In its June 28, 1993 issue, *Fortune* (with photos of billionaires Sultan of Brunei, Queen Elizabeth II, Ross Perot, Buffett and Bill Gates on the cover) ranked Buffett as the thirteenth-richest person in the world and the third-richest American, with $6.4 billion, behind Metromedia's John Kluge with $8.8 billion and Gates with $6.7 billion.

Then the *Forbes'* July 5, 1993 issue listed Gates as worth $7.4 billion, Buffett $6.6 billion and Kluge, $5.5 billion.

On September 4, 1993, the *Washington Post* reported that Buffett appeared to be the richest person in the U.S.

And the *Forbes* issue of October 18, 1993, said Buffett was indeed the richest person in the country with a net worth of $8.3 billion, topping Bill Gates at $6.3 billion, John Kluge at $6.2 billion and Sumner Redstone at $5.6 billion.

Forbes' five-page story about America's richest person carried photos of Buffett at an Omaha Royals game at Omaha's Rosenblatt Stadium. Buffett wore a bright red, short-sleeve shirt saying "Nebraska." He was eating from a Cracker Jack box and drinking a Coke.

There he was—the richest person in the country, largely because of his stock-picking and long-term holding preference in investing.

The news led to a flurry of headlines such as, "The Sage of Omaha deposes Dollar Bill" and "Gates gets Buffetted."

In an interview, Buffett told *Forbes*, "I have in life all I want right here [Omaha]. I tap dance in here [his office] and work with nothing but people I like. I don't have to work with people I don't like."

Forbes said that when Buffett dies he probably will have "set the stage for the biggest charitable foundation ever, one that easily, as suggested earlier, will dwarf the legacies of Rockefeller, Ford and Carnegie. Over the past 23 years, Buffett's investments have compounded his wealth at an average annual rate of 29%. He probably can't keep that up. But give him 15%. If he lives another 20 years and does 15%, the Buffett Foundation will have well over $100 billion. If, as is quite possible, he lives a good deal longer...well, you get the picture."

Omaha World-Herald columnist Robert McMorris wrote at the time that he enjoyed claiming Buffett, who lived a mile away, as a neighbor. "Some day somebody will say to me, 'You're from Omaha? Isn't that where Warren Buffett lives?'

"And I'll say, "Oh, sure, I know Warren. He's practically a neighbor of mine.

"I may even allow that I've discussed investment strategy with him.

"That's more or less true. I once asked him what advice he gives investors who ask for tips on the stock market.

"He said he tells them: 'Buy low, sell high.'"

Later in the story McMorris wrote, "He doesn't have a computer in his office or home. No calculator, for that matter.

"Such toys are unnecessary, he told me, because his line of work is 'not that complicated.'

"For years, though, he had a dart board in his outer office that he claimed was his stock selector.

"He said he has since lost faith in it. 'It doesn't work any more, so I'm going to give it to Bill Gates.' "

"I'll let him have the dart board so we can keep him in second place," Buffett said.

But that hasn't worked. In recent years Microsoft, with its grip on the Information Age, has soared, vaulting Gates to the post of the richest person in the world, the first person to claim a 12-figure fortune. Microsoft co-founder Paul Allen has surpassed Buffett as have Microsoft's Steve Ballmer and several hi-tech mogels around the world.

All three multi-billionaires apparently agree with George Bernard Shaw's adage: "The lack of money is the root of all evil."

180

SO LONG JOHN JACOB ASTOR, ANDREW CARNEGIE, JOHN D. ROCKEFELLER; HELLO, BILL GATES.

Gates, Paul Allen, Steve Ballmer and Buffett are now the richest people ever in America, in real terms—in dollars adjusted for inflation over the years.

John Jacob Astor, who built his wealth in fur trading and real estate ("Buy the acre; sell the lot") and Andrew Carnegie, whose Carnegie Steel Co. produced a quarter of the steel in the U.S. ("There's no idol more debasing than the worship of money."), were among the richest of their time. They were worth several hundred million dollars. Even if those fortunes were inflation-adjusted for today's values, Buffett would still be richer by far.

In its 1992 Richest 400 edition, *Forbes* said that Standard Oil founder John D. Rockefeller, the richest man of his day, would have a fortune of slightly more than $10 billion in today's dollars.

Gates, Allen, Ballmer and Buffett have now far surpassed that figure. Gates has even passed the $100 billion barrier, before slipping back as Oracle Corp.'s Larry Ellison surged to about even with Gates.

Still, by one measure Rockefeller was the richest, according to *The Wealthy 100* by Michael Klepper and Robert Gunther. It ranked the richest Americans by comparing the person's net worth to the country's GNP in their day. Rockefeller, with $1.4 billion in his day took the number one ranking compared to 31st for Gates and 39th for Buffett in 1996.

Biographer Ron Chernov wrote in *Titan* (p. 556), a biography of John D. Rockefeller: "Rockefeller's net worth reached a lifetime peak of $900 million in 1913—more than $13 billion in 1996 dollars." That figure, about $15 billion today, amounted to 2.5% of the gross national product of the time.

Also, for all the controversy of how Rockefeller made his millions, he did become one of the greatest philanthropists (His philanthropy totaled $500 million, about $8 billion in today's dollars.) in American history, backing many medical and educational efforts.

Carnegie made great gifts to libraries.

But certainly in dollar amounts, and after inflation, Gates, Ellison, Allen, Ballmer and Buffett, in real terms, have the most chips.

181

"IS IT OKAY WITH YOU IF HE SHOWS UP AT YOUR BOOK SIGNINGS?"

In late October 1994, I sent a copy of my second book to Buffett via Federal Express's 10:30 a.m. delivery. In about an hour, no more than an hour and a half, I got a call from Buffett's assistant, Debbie Bosanek.

"He's read your book. He likes your book....would it be okay with you if he shows up at your book signings?" she asked of three signings I had scheduled in Omaha.

I flew to Omaha, but because my plane was delayed an hour in Atlanta, arrived just in the nick of time for the first signing at the Bookworm store. "Oh, USAir?" Buffett quipped.

Just outside the store, I ran into Gladys Kaiser and stopped to talk, not realizing anyone was in the store. When I walked in, I saw the place was full of people.

"We're sold out," the owner said, explaining people had either bought the book there or had phoned in orders.

Before going to Omaha, I had two book signings in Birmingham and had sold 25 and 71 books.

At the Bookworm, more than 100 were sold before Buffett showed up.

After signing books, Buffett and I signed book plates to go in more books that would be shipped to the store.

Buffett set the tone for the afternoon by handing me a photo of himself dressed in a Nebraska football uniform with a big number 1 on the jersey. And he gave me a photo for Kermit Kendrick.

Later he tossed a penny on the floor and asked if I wanted a photo of him picking it up.

Gladys Kaiser was one of the first people to get Buffett's autograph. "And keep on brushing" he wrote in reference to the joke she and I had started about how often she brushes her teeth.

Later a woman said she hoped her son would grow up to be like him. "Well, tell him not to eat quite so much," Buffett replied.

Then he was asked to hold a baby girl for a photo and the baby cried. Then someone asked Buffett to give her his wallet and when he started to, the girl howled. "Well, she behaves better than most women who've asked for my wallet."

Later in the afternoon we did a signing at Village Books where again the store immediately sold out. Again, Buffett had a quip for many and after a "Thank you" would say, "My pleasure."

When people started asking him to sign dollar bills, he said, "Can I keep half?"

For four hours that day he signed books. He seemed to enjoy it, but confessed at the end, "Well, it's gotten a little out of hand," as he stayed until 6:30 p.m. so everyone who came got his autograph. He said he had signed so many books, his autograph was becoming "devalued."

But even at the bookstore, you could get a glimpse of a mind still trying to learn. He asked the owners how much theft they had, what they did about it and later asked, "How well is *The Bell Curve* selling?"

Toward the end of the day, I really got to talk to him and asked him what the markets had done that day. He told me the stock market had been off about 40 points and that the long bond had sold off sharply.

I asked him how Berkshire fared. "I don't know. I didn't ask."

Because he didn't have a computer, I asked how he keeps abreast of the market. He said, "I pick up the phone and call Salomon and they tell me about the market or some stock I'm interested in."

He talked about his reading and said he had 50 books at home he needed to get to. "I'm getting behind," he said.

The next day he showed up at Waldenbooks to cheers. He was citing the statistics of the first quarter of the Nebraska-Kansas football game.

One lady asked for a picture and Buffett said, "Well, the backside's better."

Not knowing Buffett was going to show, I had only sent 700 books to Omaha by our self-publishing unit. They were delivered to the stores by a friend, Don Pippen of Southern Publishers Group, just in time.

Defying any of Ben Graham's formulas Buffett managed to sell 1,000 of the 700 books, including nameplates for future books.

The man can sell books.

After I told Michael Assael that, he wrote: "You'd make even Ben Graham's eyes pop out with your new book statistics: Selling 1,000 of 700 books! Ben might call that, 'selling your books short against their box.' "

About a month later I tried to get a book signing in New York, but was turned down by every book store there I could think of. "We don't do signings for self-published books; we don't buy books from you; we're too busy," were some of the objections.

Thanks to Pippen, who made calls from a phone booth in Florence, Alabama, I wound up with a signing in the lobby of the Millenium Hilton.

When I told Debbie Bosanek I had a signing there, she said, "The Millenium Hilton? That's where he's staying."

The morning of one of the signings I walked through the lobby and saw a man reading the *New York Times*. He looked like Buffett. He *was* Buffett. I sat and talked (stalking again?) with him several minutes. Later he went to speak to a Ben Graham commemorative luncheon sponsored by the New York Society of Security Analysts.

Afterwards he dropped by my signing, but I didn't have much business and he stayed only a short time. He signed a few books,

(Photo by Nancy Line Jacobs)

Buffett at a book signing at Village Books in Omaha November 4, 1994. The man can sell books.

changed a $100 bill at the counter and was gone.

After the 1996 version of this book came out, I sent it along to him. It arrived on his birthday.

Buffett replied: "What a great present on my 66th. I plan to show Tom Osborne the back cover so he can re-think his starting lineup." Later he wrote, "Thought this book was a little abbreviated, please try to flesh out a bit the next edition (due in December)."

When the 1998 edition came out, he wrote that he enjoyed the book, but thought it was "a little skimpy."

182

THE RECORD

"THE BEST IS YET TO COME."

Here's Berkshire's record for annual per-share increase in book value over the years, compared to the S&P 500 Index, which includes dividends.

Berkshire shareholder Ed Prendeville says, "The record is spectacular, and if you adjust some way for the low risks Buffett has taken, his record probably stands alone."

Relative results, in percentage terms, are shown in the third row. Has Guinness thought about this one? (Losses are in parentheses.)

	Berkshire	S&P	Relative results
1965	23.8	10.0	13.8
1966	20.3	(11.7)	32.0
1967	11.0	30.9	(19.9)
1968	19.0	11.0	8.0
1969	16.2	(8.4)	24.6
1970	12.0	3.9	8.1
1971	16.4	14.6	1.8
1972	21.7	18.9	2.8
1973	4.7	(14.8)	19.5
1974	5.5	(26.4)	31.9
1975	21.9	37.2	(15.3)
1976	59.3	23.6	35.7
1977	31.9	(7.4)	39.3
1978	24.0	6.4	17.6
1979	35.7	18.2	17.5
1980	19.3	32.3	(13.0)
1981	31.4	(5.0)	36.4
1982	40.0	21.4	18.6
1983	32.3	22.4	9.9
1984	13.6	6.1	7.5
1985	48.2	31.6	16.6
1986	26.1	18.6	7.5
1987	19.5	5.1	14.4
1988	20.1	16.6	3.5

1989	44.4	31.7	12.7
1990	7.4	(3.1)	10.5
1991	39.6	30.5	9.1
1992	20.3	7.6	12.7
1993	14.3	10.1	4.2
1994	13.9	1.3	12.6
1995	43.1	37.6	5.5
1996	31.8	23.0	8.8
1997	34.1	33.4	.7
1998	48.3	28.6	19.7
1999	.5	21.0	(20.05)

Shortly before an Omaha Royals (now Omaha Golden Spikes) baseball game the weekend prior to Berkshire's Annual Meeting in 1994, *Toronto Star* reporter Jade Hemeon talked briefly with Buffett about Berkshire. "It's a painting in progress. The best is yet to come," he told her.

183

BERKSHIRE'S STOCK TABLES:
"SHOW ME THE MONEY!"
CUBA GOODING—*JERRY MAGUIRE*

1965	High	Low	1970	High	Low
First Quarter	16	12	First Quarter	47	40
Second Quarter	21	16	Second Quarter	47	32
Third Quarter	19	17	Third Quarter	43	35
Fourth Quarter	22	18	Fourth Quarter	43	39
1966			**1971**		
First Quarter	27	20	First Quarter	51	40
Second Quarter	27	21	Second Quarter	55	48
Third Quarter	23	18	Third Quarter	53	51 ★
Fourth Quarter	18	17	Fourth Quarter	74	70 ★
1967			**1972**		
First Quarter	20	17	First Quarter	76	73 ★
Second Quarter	19	17	Second Quarter	78	78 ★
Third Quarter	21	18	Third Quarter	84	80 ★
Fourth Quarter	21	19	Fourth Quarter	80	80 ★
1968			**1973**		
First Quarter	24	20	First Quarter	93	80
Second Quarter	31	23	Second Quarter	87	85
Third Quarter	33	26	Third Quarter	88	83
Fourth Quarter	39	32	Fourth Quarter	87	71
1969			**1974**		
First Quarter	40	34	First Quarter	76	72
Second Quarter	45	35	Second Quarter	76	64
Third Quarter	39	31	Third Quarter	64	49
Fourth Quarter	44	34	Fourth Quarter	49	40

1975	High	Low	1981	High	Low
First Quarter	51	38	First Quarter	505	425
Second Quarter	51	45	Second Quarter	525	485
Third Quarter	60	41	Third Quarter	520	460
Fourth Quarter	43	38	Fourth Quarter	590	460
1976			**1982**		
First Quarter	56	38	First Quarter	560	465
Second Quarter	60	55	Second Quarter	520	470
Third Quarter	73	61	Third Quarter	550	430
Fourth Quarter	95	66	Fourth Quarter	775	540
1977			**1983**		
First Quarter	97	85	First Quarter	965	775
Second Quarter	100	95	Second Quarter	985	890
Third Quarter	107	100	Third Quarter	1,245	905
Fourth Quarter	139	107	Fourth Quarter	1,385	1,240
1978			**1984**		
First Quarter	142	134	First Quarter	1,360	1,240
Second Quarter	180	142	Second Quarter	1,345	1,220
Third Quarter	180	165	Third Quarter	1,305	1,230
Fourth Quarter	189	152	Fourth Quarter	1,305	1,265
1979			**1985**		
First Quarter	185	154	First Quarter	1,930	1,275
Second Quarter	215	185	Second Quarter	2,160	1,725
Third Quarter	350	215	Third Quarter	2,235	2,005
Fourth Quarter	335	240	Fourth Quarter	2,730	2,075
1980			**1986**		
First Quarter	360	260	First Quarter	3,250	2,220
Second Quarter	340	250	Second Quarter	3,160	2,640
Third Quarter	415	305	Third Quarter	3,100	2,525
Fourth Quarter	490	385	Fourth Quarter	2,925	2,620

1987	High	Low
First Quarter	3,630	2,800
Second Quarter	3,530	3,330
Third Quarter	4,220	3,420
Fourth Quarter	4,270	2,550

1988	High	Low
First Quarter	3,500	3,000
Second Quarter	4,150	3,400
Third Quarter	5,000	4,040
Fourth Quarter	5,050	4,600

1989	High	Low
First Quarter	5,025	4,625
Second Quarter	7,000	4,950
Third Quarter	8,750	6,600
Fourth Quarter	8,900	7,950

1990	High	Low
First Quarter	8,725	6,675
Second Quarter	7,675	6,600
Third Quarter	7,325	5,500
Fourth Quarter	6,900	5,500

1991	High	Low
First Quarter	8,275	6,550
Second Quarter	8,750	7,760
Third Quarter	9,000	8,325
Fourth Quarter	9,125	8,150

(Year-end 1991: 9,050)

1992	High	Low
First Quarter	9,000	8,575
Second Quarter	9,300	8,850
Third Quarter	9,950	9,050
Fourth Quarter	11,750	9,150

(Year-end 1992: 11,750)

1993	High	Low
First Quarter	13,200	11,350
Second Quarter	16,200	11,800
Third Quarter	17,800	15,100
Fourth Quarter	17,800	16,200

(Year-end 1993: 16,325)

1994	High	Low
First Quarter	16,900	15,150
Second Quarter	16,700	15,400
Third Quarter	19,750	16,425
Fourth Quarter	20,800	19,200

(Year-end 1994: 20,400)

1995	High	Low
First Quarter	25,200	20,250
Second Quarter	24,450	21,500
Third Quarter	30,600	23,400
Fourth Quarter	33,400	28,850

(Year-end 1995: 32,100)

1996	High	Low
First Quarter	38,000	29,800
Second Quarter	36,000	30,000
Third Quarter	33,500	30,500
Fourth Quarter	36,500	31,000

(Year-end 1996: 34,100
Class B: 1,112)

1997	High	Low	1999	High	Low
First Quarter	37,900	33,000	First Quarter	81,100	61,900
Second Quarter	48,600	35,900	Second Quarter	78,600	68,300
Third Quarter	48,300	41,300	Third Quarter	73,000	54,000
Fourth Quarter	47,200	42,500	Fourth Quarter	66,900	52,000

(Year-end 1997: 46,000
Class B: 1534)

(Year-end 1999: 56,100
Class B: 1,830

1998			2000	High	Low
First Quarter	69,500	45,700	First Quarter	56,500	40,800
Second Quarter	84,000	65,800			
Third Quarter	78,500	57,000			
Fourth Quarter	71,000	57,700			

(Year-end 1998: 70,000
Class B: 2,350

These figures were provided by the National Quotation Bureau but they only show the price on the last day of the quarter at a time when Berkshire was not listed in the National Association of Securities Dealers Automated Quotation (NASDAQ) system. Instead Berkshire was listed in the "pink sheets" and it was not a marginable security. The National Quotation Bureau has only end-of-the-month listings from that time.

184

A WORD FROM THE DIRECTOR OF TECHNOLOGY

OF THE WILSON COIN-OPERATED MACHINE CO.

Don Danly, Buffett's teenage partner in the Wilson Coin-Operated Machine Co., offered this post on the AOL Berkshire message board July 24, 1998:

I've noted various figures quoted for the past performance of BRK stock price. The number obviously depends on how many years you go back in time. Listed below are the geometric average returns for the past one-year through 28-years using the closing price in 1997 as the final number (46,000).

Year	BRK Year-End Price	No. Of Years Data	Average Price Increase Through 12/97
1969	42		
1970	40	28	28.4%
1971	48	27	29.8%
1972	78	26	30.2%
1973	80	25	29.1%
1974	50	24	30.3%
1975	40	23	34.5%
1976	94	22	37.8%
1977	134	21	34.3%
1978	158	20	33.9%
1979	320	19	34.8%
1980	420	18	31.8%
1981	560	17	31.8%
1982	775	16	31.7%
1983	1310	15	31.3%
1984	1275	14	28.9%
1985	2480	13	31.8%
1986	2820	12	27.6%

1987	2950	11	28.9%
1988	4700	10	31.6%
1989	8675	9	28.8%
1990	6670	8	23.2%
1991	9050	7	31.8%
1992	11700	6	31.1%
1993	16320	5	31.5%
1994	20400	4	29.6%
1995	32100	3	31.1%
1996	34100	2	19.7%
1997	46000	1	34.9%

For example, the average increase over the past five years was 31.5%; over the past ten years the figure is 31.6%. The 28-year average is 28.4%. These averages don't include the large rise experienced in 1998. It seems safe to say the historical increase in stock price has been a shade over 30%—mighty good!

Don, Director of Technology
Wilson Coin-Operated Machines

185

"OUR PEANUT MACHINERY SUBSIDIARY HAD GROSS REVENUES OF ONE PENNY AND A BIG LAWSUIT."

Buffett gave a talk to the "Yellow BRK" party April 28, 2000:

MR. BUFFETT: I saw Don Danly as I came in. Would he come up? There he is. I see him. Come on up. Because we have to straighten things out about the golf ball business.

Don, as many of you know, was my partner in the Wilson Coin-Operated Machine Company, which was an incredible success. And we started with one $25 pinball machine which we put over at Frank Arago's Barber Shop, and we built the route to seven as I remember, including a huge winner down by Griffith Stadium.

We were bothered at one point by Frank actually, who wanted us to put in a peanut machine. And we didn't like that, because the nice thing about the pinball machine business was it was a nickel thing, but it was all profit, there was no cost of goods sold whatsoever, whereas peanuts you had to actually give people something. That went against the grain.

But then Frank told us that we were going to have to remove our pinball machine unless we put in a peanut machine. So, we bought a Northwestern peanut machine for about eleven bucks or something like that, ten or eleven bucks. And we bought five pounds of Spanish peanuts as I remember. And we took it out to the barber shop and placed it in the barber shop and then drove back to my house.

And my mother was at the door looking panicked. She said there was some fellow screaming on the phone. So I took the phone, and I couldn't completely understand it but I figured out it was Frank, and I thought we better get back to the barber shop fast.

So we went back to the barber shop. We had now been in the

peanut business probably twenty minutes. There was a fellow there bleeding from the mouth. And it turned out that the peanut machine we bought had some little glass shavings down at the bottom. At that point our pinball subsidiary—I mean our peanut machine subsidiary had gross revenues of one penny and a big lawsuit. So we gave the machine to Frank and told him it was all his, peanuts and everything.

But then they mentioned the used golf ball business. And we did go into the golf ball business because there was a fellow named Bob Kerlin who had heard rumors from us of our incredible success in the pinball business so he wanted to go into our next deal. He was sort of like an IPO free rider or something like that. He kept insisting.

And finally we decided to go into the used golf ball business and we decided to make Kerlin a partner, and you will see why in a second. Because our idea of going into the used golf ball business was to go over to, as I remember, a course over in Virginia. We would go out early in the morning before anybody was there. And there was this lake and we were going to retrieve these balls from the lake. And I used to count the money and Don would fix the machines, but neither one of us wanted to go into that damn lake. So we decided to take Kerlin in as a full-fledged, one-third partner.

And to do that we felt we wanted to buy the best of equipment. So Don went down to an Army surplus store, around 9th and D, and bought a gas mask. And we hooked that up to a garden hose and we tested it in about three inches of water in our bathtub to see whether it would work, that you could breathe. We decided that was enough for Kerlin. Then we had to make sure he stayed down, so we got my Washington Post newspaper bag and we stuck in a bunch of barbell plates.

We went out to this course and Kerlin stripped down and he put on this Washington Post thing and a gas mask and weighted down by plates, and we told him, you know, "Now is the time to earn your third of the deal." We sent him into this lake.

And unfortunately there were a couple of things that -- I wasn't supposed to know anything, I mean Don is the guy that took up physics and chemistry and all that stuff; I just knew how to count money. But he forgot to think about what would happen once Kerlin got underneath and couldn't see a damn thing and he was having trouble breathing.

And then just about this time the guy with the truck came along who was going to fill up the sand traps. And we got this guy on this hose, he is down there in the lake. We started pulling back on the hose trying to get him back. And then the man stopped us and asked us what we were doing. I'm not sure which one of us came up with the answer that we were doing an experiment for our physics class. That was our used golf ball business. I just thought you were entitled to the full story.

I will save the rest of my stories for tomorrow at the meeting. I don't want to blow all my lines tomorrow.

MR. DON DANLY: I can't top that. I have never even told that story, and you can understand why. It was a tremendous embarrassment after being considered as the technical man by these people. Thank you.

MR. LYLE MCINTOSH: Okay, thanks a lot, Warren. We appreciate it. We know you've got a busy day and we really appreciate it.

(Photo by Pat Kilpatrick)

Buffett and Don Danly at "Yellow BRK Club" party April 28, 2000.

186

"WHAT'S THE COMBINED IQ OF WARREN BUFFETT AND CHARLES MUNGER?"

EXPANDING OR "SHRINKING"?

Berkshire shareholder Bill Scargle says he's wondered all along how smart Buffett and Munger really are.

"I've often asked myself what's the combined IQ of Warren Buffett and Charles Munger?

"I've finally decided what the answer is. It's the stock price of Berkshire." So if you had asked, for example, what's the combined IQ of the two men in 1998, then the answer was 70,000.

Actually the subject of Buffett's IQ has been the frequent topic of uninformed discussion. And there's no new light to be found here. Some say the average IQ of those in Harvard Law School is 150. Buffett's IQ is believed to be substantially higher. Leonardo da Vinci is believed to have had an IQ of 200. But were there IQ tests back then or even true false tests in Leonardo's day? Maybe it was all about how well you could paint or draw. In any event, Buffett has done okay with his canvas.

Press accounts have pegged Bill Gates' IQ at about 170 and author Norman Mailer's at 165.

A former Harvard business school student, who does not know Buffett's IQ, conjectures it's far above 150, saying his math ability and memory clearly are at genius levels.

Buffett has been quoted as saying he doesn't know his IQ. To get to the bottom of things, this courageous reporter once asked Buffett pointedly about his IQ, hoping to elicit a 700-page thesis, or better, a 30 billion pound, 1,000-page gorilla. His reply was one word: "shrinking."

187
A $210,000 WALLET

Buffett auctioned his 20-year-old wallet on December 3, 1999 and received a high bid of $210,000 which went to a charity, Girls Incorporated of Omaha.

The story about the battered old black billfold broke in *The Wall Street Journal* (December 2, 1999). "I've never gone for the top of the line," Buffett was quoted.

The wallet survived the dunking in a Minnesota lake after a fishing boat capsized leaving Buffett, Munger and Rick Guerin dog-paddling.

Buffett didn't include his credit cards, driver's license or a pass for free McDonald's hamburgers. He did include an expired half-price pass from Hooter's restaurant chain given him for allowing the chain to note Buffett's birthday on their calendar.

"I plan to leave the name of a stock tip in it for whoever buys it," Buffett told the *Journal*. It turned out to be First Industrial Realty Trust.

Television interviewer Bob McCartney of KETV in Omaha asked

(Photo courtesy of Girls, Inc.)

Buffett's wallet was auctioned off for $210,000 which went to Girls Inc.

Buffett if he thought the wallet bidding would get to the seven figure mark. "No, no, I don't think so...if it got that high, I'd be sorry I didn't sell it myself."

When the subject came up of the Hooter's pass, Buffett said: "It expired, and they didn't offer me a renewal."

As for the stock tip, Buffett said there might be "a little mention" of a company Berkshire bought that wasn't public knowledge yet.

(Photo courtesy of John Morgan)

John Morgan was the top bidder for Buffett's billfold

John Morgan of Wayzata, Minnesota, won the wallet with a $210,000 bid. Morgan was born and raised in Omaha in an area that was served by Girls, Inc.

Reports said Morgan would share the stock's name with people who gave $1,000 or more to Girls Inc., whose board is headed by Buffett's daughter, Susie, who came up with the auction idea.

So what's her next auction item proposal? Buffett told the *Omaha World-Herald* (December 2, 1999): "I can't talk to her anymore. I've got to watch it. It may be my underwear next time."

Morgan, 58, is a successful businessman who co-founded an equipment-leasing company, took Winthrop Resources public and in 1997 sold it to Minneapolis-based TCF Financial Corp. Morgan and two partners sold the business for $325 million. Each of the three partners received about $60 million each. In January 1999 the three partners formed Rush River Group to invest in over-the-counter stocks. Rush River has a stake in Grow Biz and Morgan is now the CEO of Grow Biz which owns a large number of retail stores.

Morgan serves on the boards of African-American Family Services and Page Education Foundation which gives aid to minorities. "If people ask me the reason for my success, I say "I'm white and I'm male," Morgan said. (*Detroit Free Press*, December 15, 1999)

Morgan, the first graduate from high school in his family, was told by his guidance counselor, that he should be a bricklayer. Instead he worked his way through college.

The secret stock tip of First Industrial Realty Trust, a REIT that owns warehouses and distribution facilities was revealed in a *Wall*

Street Journal story (December 17, 1999). Fred Henry, a 40-year-old well-digger in Oakland, Iowa, who contributed to Girls Inc. and received the tip from Morgan confirmed the name of the stock to the *Journal*. How often do well-diggers source the *Journal* about a stock tip in an old billfold?

After Morgan won the wallet, Buffett took him to dinner. (I met Morgan at Berkshire's annual meeting festivities in 2000 and offered to sell him my wallet. He didn't express the slightest interest.)

(Photo courtesy of Sardar Biglari)

Here's a photo of Buffett's wallet when it was thick and in active use. It was taken when Buffett was in San Antonio visiting Star Furniture Chairman Melvyn Wolff. Wolff invited Sardar Biglari to meet Buffett. Biglari has sold two Internet companies and now heads the Biglari & Muzza Capital Management investment partnership in San Antonio. When Buffett pulled out his wallet, Biglari says, "I was afraid to know how much he carries with him so I said, 'I'll take stock instead.'" Maybe Biglari should have taken the wallet and auctioned it off for $210,000.

188

OVERHEARD

"WE WON'T BE IN OHIO THAT WEEKEND."

1   "I'm an investor. I've never heard of him."

2   "I've followed Buffett since the 1960s, but I'm into sectors now."

3   "Is this the book about the rock star?"

4   "Is this a book about football?"

5   "I'd like to order the book about William Buffett."

6   "Could I order the Jimmy Buffett book?"

7   "Could I get your pamphlet about Warren Buffett?"

8   "Do you collect books?"

9   "Could you call him to see if he'd contribute to my sorority?"

10 "Could you call him to see if we could have dinner with him?"

11 "He must have a very unhappy life."

12 "You must be rich because you've written a book."

13 "Would he marry me, if I proposed?"

14 "This is not a popular subject for a book."

15 Person professing in 1998 to follow Berkshire closely: "That stock price is between $200 and $300."

16 "What's his claim to fame?"

17 "Don't want the stock. I need to make some money fast."

18 "That stock doesn't meet the criteria I want."

19 Berkshire shareholder on hearing the stock hit $70,000: "Oh, no!"

20 "It couldn't go above $70,000. Who would buy it?"

21 "I've gone past feeling guilty. Son, is this illegal?"

22 "Do you follow Buffett? [apparently—but not for

certain—the listener didn't hear the question.] Reply: "I like the snow."

23 "What company is he with?"

24 "He's a bum."

25 CNBC: "Buffett is not where the action is."

26 Remainder buyer at bookstore chain: "There's no interest in this book" at any price.

27 "A Warren Buffett biography would not fit our wholesale list."

28 "Time to step down, Warren."

29 "Not to sound stupid but what is the reason for this stock to be so high?"

30 "Isn't that the stock that trades at $1 million a share?"

31 "Poor Warren Buffett."

32 "We won't be in Ohio that weekend."

189

A VIEW FROM GIFFORD COMBS

Gifford Combs, of Pacific Palisades, California, is the general partner of Chemin de Fer, Limited, an investment partnership. Chemin de Fer means *railway* in French and is also a French gambling game, roughly equivalent to Blackjack. "So an investment partnership named after a gambling game has a nice irony (pun intended) to it," Combs says. The partnership name stems from its origins which were to buy distressed debt of bankrupt railroads. "The first guy I bought bonds from was an old German man who had fled Nazi Germany in the 30s, and was very experienced in evaluating senior securities. He was Max Heine's partner. Heine founded Mutual Shares and later sold the business to his young protege, Michael Price. My friend, who was Max's partner, was also a friend and broker to a guy in Omaha named Warren Buffett," Combs said.

In journalism, a reporter usually needs a biography and a photo. Here's what I got when I e-mailed Combs for a "bio and pix":

First knowledge of Warren Buffett, 1972.
First telephone conversation with Warren Buffett, 1977.
First purchase of Berkshire Hathaway common, 1980.
A.B., magna cum laude, Harvard College, 1980.
First offer to have lunch, rebuffed by Warren Buffett, 1981.
Rotary Foundation International Scholar, University of Hong Kong, 1983.
M. Phil., with distinction, Cambridge University, 1983.
First growled at by Charles Munger, Esq., 1985
First Berkshire Hathaway meeting attended. Second to the last one at the Orpheum.

Combs writes:

To compound capital, one must first preserve it. For most investors such a truism seems so banal as to be a mere nostrum. Still, there is wisdom in most cliches, and this one is no exception. For taxable investors, the great bugbears are the three "T's"—turnover, transaction costs and taxes. Portfolio turnover creates frictional costs from trading and taxable events. The three combine to reduce the rate of compounding and with management fees create a substantial drag on performance for the typical money manager.

Because investment managers are generally compensated on a pre-tax basis under a "heads I win, tails you pay the difference" system, there tends to be an internal "institutional imperative" in most organizations to *transact*. Partially this is a function of human nature: investors, like most persons, suffer from some version of "the grass is greener syndrome". The new investment idea is almost always more intriguing than the stale one already sitting in the "IN" box or even the one in the portfolio. Consequently, many investors tend to behave like hummingbirds, searching constantly for sweeter nectar whilst maintaining high portfolio velocity.

Certainly, there are exceptions. Some money managers have demonstrated an admirable ability to build and manage portfolios over a long period with very little turnover. But it is a difficult task. And my personal observation and experience suggests that such restraint is imperfectly distributed among most mortals who are not candidates for canonization. It is not that such behavior is illegal, or immoral; but neither is it financially fattening.

For investors concerned about taxes and transaction costs, Berkshire Hathaway makes a great deal of sense. To be sure, an investor buying Berkshire today at around 60,000 dollars per share is not getting to the party early. Nevertheless, it may not be too late to have a great deal of fun. Berkshire now is selling around fair value. (My best estimate at present is approximately 66,000 dollars per share of intrinsic value.) That should not be a surprise, for Buffett's goal is that the share price be a close indicator of intrinsic value and his hope is that it not deviate greatly from that value.

At the price, one buys:
- A tax-efficient compounding vehicle
- A collection of some of the best business franchises available
- Arguably the best money-management talent in the world
- An opportunistic corporation focused on compounding share-holder wealth

In short, one buys into a very good hedge fund, albeit one with significant size, but also one with significant advantages.

A Great Investor

It is unnecessary to recite Warren E. Buffett's history and record. It should suffice to say that almost no serious observer would dispute the notion that he is the single best investor in the post-war period, and he may be one of the best of all time. Others may have compounded money at faster rates for some period of time, but no one to my knowledge has done so consistently over a long period of time employing substantial sums. As Buffett himself has said, "good money managers are self-liquidating." Eventually most players tire of the game and retire. Buffett is almost certainly unique in his desire to continue playing the game even after becoming one of the five wealthiest people in the world, and perhaps one of the twenty-five wealthiest of all time.

Naive observers of Berkshire often make the comment that it is nothing more than an investment company and as such should:

a) sell at a discount to the sum of its parts

b) is easily replicated by any investor

c) currently is priced at a significant premium to intrinsic value due to Buffett's cult-like status.

But Berkshire is much more than an investment company. It controls significant business enterprises and allocates capital among them. Futhermore, because of the mix of entities, it enjoys a favorable tax situation. Finally, it employs substantial non-interest-bearing leverage through its insurance reserves—its "float."

Capital Allocation and Great Businesses

Coupled with Buffett's singular dedication to the pursuit of compounding capital is an amazing assortment of businesses with superior operating characteristics. Buffett buys and holds on to businesses that generate huge amounts of cash and generate prodigious returns on unleveraged capital. This allows him, in turn, to reinvest in still more businesses. Of course it sounds easy, but few if any have employed such a strategy with the success of Berkshire. For most businesses, the achilles heel is capital allocation. Bad businesses take care of the problem by consuming ever-larger amounts of capital at relatively low rates of return. Good businesses generate lots of cash but often without commensurate opportunities to reinvest. Berkshire's holding company structure solves that problem for its subsidiaries. All cash is up-streamed to the parent company for Buffett to redeploy in the best way possible.

This ability to reinvest capital is no small advantage to be lightly dismissed. For an investor, there are three important considerations in evaluating a business: its operating profitability, its capital allocation, and its price. One can find businesses with generally good operating characteristics, and one can even find them at an attractive price from time to time, though not often in this recent market. Nevertheless, one is hardpressed to find such businesses where the capital allocation process is well-understood. The collection of businesses Berkshire owns simply could not be replicated by the average investor or even the well-heeled corporate buyer.

In addition to controlled businesses, Berkshire owns significant minority positions in a handful of companies, including Coca-Cola, The Washington Post Company, and American Express, and it is these large holdings which lend Berkshire its reputation as "merely an investment company." While Buffett prefers to own businesses outright, he would rather buy a piece of an excellent business at a good price than pay too much for total control. This willingness to own large minority positions and to sit with them for extended periods of time (nearly a quarter of a century in the case of the Washington Post) makes Buffett unique among the entrepreneurial asset accumulators (e.g. Hanson, Tisch, Murdoch). Also unique perhaps is the degree of influence Buffett is able to exercise in a minority role which allows him to improve his returns by changing the direction of investee companies in subtle ways. There is no doubt, for example, that it was Buffett who convinced the management of the Washington Post to repurchase so much of the company's stock over the past twenty-five years, to such good result.

For Buffett, cash flows are all alike, assuming they emanate from a business he feels he understands that is run by someone he trusts. Those cash flows are the equity equivalent of the coupon on a bond, and the question is what will those coupons be over a long period of time and how much must one pay for that "bond" today. Whether a dollar of earnings is controlled by Berkshire itself in a wholly owned business or retained by an investee company in which Berkshire owns a stake is of no consequence to Buffett. He is merely interested in maximizing the long-term return to Berkshire shareholders from the employment of its capital—in achieving the highest possible "equity coupon", as he refers to it.

An Insurance Franchise

Is Berkshire selling at a substantial premium to intrinsic value? No, unless one believes that the insurance business is likely to stop growing. The real secret to Berkshire is its float, and with the acquisition of General Reinsurance, Berkshire has a lot of it. If one assumes that Berkshire's new combined float (including all of its insurance entities) will grow at the rate of five percent per annum, and one further assumes that Berkshire can earn a return on its investment portfolio of 9.6 percent per annum[1], then the stock is probably fairly valued today, and will generate a very acceptable rate of return for its owners. And crucially, such returns are based on assumptions that require no genius at the helm, thus putting paid the criticism that Berkshire is a 'one-trick pony' entirely dependent upon the brilliance of a single individual.

Furthermore, there is reason to believe that Berkshire's insurance businesses will grow much faster than this. First, the acquisition of General Reinsurance has created the largest reinsurance company in the world, and has, for the first time, put Buffett's balance sheet strength into markets all over the world. There is simply no reinsurer that can compete with General Re over a similar range and depth of products.

Second, Berkshire's auto insurance subsidiary, GEICO, is growing extremely quickly and is taking market share from all of its major competitors, including Progressive, State Farm and Allstate. GEICO is probably the single most valuable consumer insurance franchise in the world today, and is worth many multiples the value that is carried on Berkshire's books.

The Buffett Premium

Although Berkshire once sold at a substantial discount to its intrinsic value, it does not at present. But neither does it sell at a premium reflecting Buffett's popularity with the public and the press, as some observers allege. Nevertheless, it is worth considering what is likely to happen in the event of Buffett's demise, an event which is after all postponable, but is not optional.

Given the holding company structure of Berkshire, the key variable will be who is in charge of allocating capital. Buffett himself has said that he gets involved in three areas: capital allocation (by far the most important), product pricing, and the compensation of the chief executives of the operating subsidiaries. Upon his death, this job is likely to be split in two, with one individual responsible for managing the operating businesses, in a traditional Chief Operating Officer model, and another responsible for capital allocation.

The latter is most likely to be Louis Simpson, who has been in charge of GEICO's investments for over a decade and has worked very closely with Buffett. Simpson invests in a style similar to Buffett. Will he be as good as Buffett? Probably not. After all, it's rather like asking whether Babe Ruth's replacement will be as strong a hitter. But it does not matter. Berkshire does not depend upon super-human feats to be successful. It merely needs to plod along, continuing on the path that Buffett has set for it. Berkshire the "machine" is strong enough that the particular driver need only keep it on course.

Upon Buffett's death, all of his stock will pass to his wife, and then to a charitable foundation. Virtually none of his stock will be sold.

There is likely to be some short-term price pressure on the stock, as panicky investors sell out. But over time, it seems more than likely that Berkshire will again sell at a price very close to its intrinsic value.

So, What's the Catch?

There isn't any catch. Which is exactly why it is so difficult for most money managers to recommend that their clients buy Berkshire! Indeed, in some sort of bass-ackwards way, there may be some part of human nature that actively works to prevent professional investors from buying Berkshire because it is so easy.

• Sell-side analysts on Wall Street do not want to "cover" Berkshire because management will not meet with analysts, except at the annual meeting, which is attended by more than ten thousand people. There's no "edge" to be gained there.

• Brokerage firms have no incentive to recommend Berkshire to their client because Berkshire shareholders tend to be remarkably loyal[2] and therefore generate few commission dollars.

• Investment "gate-keepers"—consultants who advise investors on which managers to hire—have great difficulty understanding a manager who holds Berkshire and are likely to criticize such holdings as lazy or dim-witted[3].

• Investors themselves are often ill-equipped to hold a position in Berkshire because it provides no "action". For many investors, the act of meeting with, the hiring and firing of investment managers is a *raison d'etre* unto itself. Holding a single position is unlikely to provide much satisfaction, no matter how profitable it may prove to be.

• Most importantly, investment managers must jump over two nearly-insurmountable psychological hurdles to buy and own Berkshire.

1. Buying Berkshire in some way means surrendering investment decision-making power to Buffett. It means admitting that he is better at the game. Few professionals, in a business where ego is stacked up like cordwood, are willing to do this.

2. The investor must admit that Berkshire, by virtue of its internal leverage generated through the insurance float, is a "better mousetrap" than most investors can offer their clients. Berkshire is simply better than a mutual fund or a hedge fund for virtually any US onshore taxable investor.

The manager of a Merrill Lynch mutual fund summed up this sentiment succinctly:

"Berkshire is probably a good stock, but I could never own it.

After all, I'm paid to DO something."

One wonders, of course, what he is being paid to do other than make money for his clients. Implicitly he is summing up the frustration a professional must necessarily feel in putting Berkshire in his portfolio—the mere act is a form of abdication and resignation. Even long-time Buffett observers are hard-pressed to hold large amounts of Berkshire in their portfolios for similar reasons, though their rationalizations may be more sophisticated, at least on the surface.[4]

For the wealthy, taxable investor, there are few, if any, investment vehicles with the characteristics of a position in Berkshire Hathaway. An investor with a long-term horizon, as family offices tend to have, would be well-advised to have a significant portion of its net worth stashed in such a holding.

(With permission of Gifford Combs)

—October 20, 1998

---

[1] These numbers are not chosen at random. They represent estimates of the growth of worldwide insurance premiums in nominal dollars and the long-term rate of return on equities in the US market from 1910 to 1980. Historically, of course, Berkshire has grown float much more quickly, and its historic return on its investment portfolio has been north of 25 percent per annum. The point is one need NOT make such heroic assumptions for Berkshire to be an attractive investment.

[2] The writer has held his shares for eighteen years.

[3] A manager of a "fund of funds" threatened to fire one of its sub-managers for holding too much Berkshire because the stock had appreciated too much over a three-year period, thus throwing the portfolio "out of balance".

[4] One money manager recently stated that he couldn't hold a large position in Berkshire because it was 'un-knowable'. Such rationalization borders on sophistry.

190

A POSSIBLE STOCK BUYBACK

As Berkshire's stock declined sharply in 1999-2000 there was much discussion about whether Buffett might buyback stock and he got letters from shareholders about it.

In Berkshire's 1999 Annual Report, Buffett wrote:

We will not repurchase shares unless we believe Berkshire stock is selling well below intrinsic value, conservatively calculated. Nor will we attempt to talk the stock up or down. (Neither publicly or privately have I ever told anyone to buy or sell Berkshire shares.) Instead we will give all shareholders — and potential shareholders — the same valuation-related information we would wish to have if our positions were reversed.

Recently, when the A shares fell below $45,000, we considered making repurchases. We decided, however, to delay buying, if indeed we elect to do *any*, until shareholders have had the chance to review this report. If we do find that repurchases make sense, we will only rarely place bids on the New York Stock Exchange ("NYSE"). Instead, we will respond to offers made directly to us at or below the NYSE bid. If you wish to offer stock, have your broker call Mark Millard at 402-346-1400. When a trade occurs, the broker can either record it in the "third market" or on the NYSE. We will favor purchase of the B shares if they are selling at more than a 2% discount to the A. We will not engage in transactions involving fewer than 10 shares of A or 50 shares of B.

(Photo by LaVerne Ramsey) 12-year-old looking Mark Millard handles fixed-income investments at Berkshire's headquarters.

Please be clear about one point: We will *never* make purchases with the intention of stemming a decline in Berkshire's price. Rather we will make them if and when we believe that they represent an attractive use of the Company's money. At best, repurchases are likely to have only a very minor effect on the future rate of gain in our stock's intrinsic value.

Berkshire did not buy back any of its shares, Buffett said at the annual meeting in 2000.

191

DEBBIE REYNOLDS

Debbie Reynolds, the 68-year old beloved actress who still entertains in Las Vegas, told *The Enquirer* (April 21, 1998) that after three failed marriages, she had had it with men.

The Enquirer said, "She's given up on love, marriage, and men entirely—unless she could have multibillionaire investor Warren Buffett...

"I've just been reading a book about Warren [if it's *Of Permanent Value*, Debbie, please call right away!] He'd be perfect. A fascinating man. He's one of the most outstanding business men in America.

(Photo by Paul Fleetwood)

Bank of Granite Chairman John Forlines, left, Debbie "Singing in the Rain" Reynolds and Buffett in front of the Omaha Marriott hotel April 30, 2000.

"Now if I were to meet him, that would be a different story! He seems to be so smart in business like I have never been. It would be interesting to be around a person that was the opposite of myself.

"But he's married, so of course I'm joking."

Well, Reynolds showed up at some of Berkshire's annual meeting festivities in 2000. No comment.

192

WHO WANTS TO BE A JILLIONAIRE?

In a spoof on the popular TV quiz show *Who Wants to Be a Millionaire*, Buffett, Ameritrade's Joe Ricketts and Kiewit's Walter Scott participated in a show in early March 2000, at the Omaha Press Club for the benefit of journalism students.

On tape host Regis Philbin said the three Omaha billionaires "qualified for tonight's show by having the fastest fingers in the financial sector." (*Omaha World-Herald*, March 4, 2000).

When Regis mentioned "millionaire" the three stormed off the stage unwilling to play for such a penny stake. When Regis asked "Who Wants to Be a Jillionaire?" they came back to play.

The game came down to Buffett's last multiple-choice question: "Which of the following of these is a sure-fire investment in the new millennium?"

(Photo courtesy of the Omaha World-Herald)

A videotaped Bill Gates, on monitor at right, replies to Buffett's "phone-a-friend" call for help answering a question during a rehearsal for the Omaha Press Club's Annual Show in 2000. The segment was called "Who Wants to Be a Jillionaire." The other contestants were fellow Omaha billionaires Joe Ricketts and Walter Scott.

A.   Cherry Coke futures
B.   Anything with "Dot Com" in the name
C.   Blackjack at Harvey's Casino
D.   Value Investing with the Wizard of Omaha

"It's a tough one," Buffett agonized. "I don't like futures trading and the Internet is a passing fad. Blackjack is just gambling, unless you can count the cards, and value investing hasn't been working for me lately."

Buffett decided on a "lifeline" and phoned a friend for help, calling on Bill Gates.

When Gates was told Buffett was calling for help, Gates said:

"Not again!"

In the end, Buffett won. Asked what he would do with the money Buffett said: "At times like this, you think of your family. I think I'll give each of my kids $300. Then maybe I'll buy a second suit. And a comb."

That was Buffett's final answer.

193

"LOOK, HE'S MOVING!"

The NBC affiliate in Omaha, WOWT-TV, Channel 6, on October 14, 1993, aired an interview with Buffett.

Reporter Sue Baggarly had asked him how others could be successful investors, and he had quipped that living a long life was one ingredient because of the effect of compounding money over time.

At the end of the half-hour session she asked, "How would you like to be remembered?" and Buffett shot back, "Well, I'd like for the minister to say, 'My God, he was old.' "

And surely Buffett would like the minister to add: "Look, he's moving!"

194

"HE RESTS...HE HAS TRAVELED."
JAMES JOYCE
"MAYBE JUST ONCE." AN EXALTED JOURNEY

There are three seminal works in literature using Homer's Odysseus as hero. There is the original, Homer's *Odyssey*, the story of a hero who longs to return home to restore order in Ithaca after the Trojan War.

In our century, the two most comprehensive works based on Homer's work are *The Odyssey: A Modern Sequel* by a Greek poet and novelist, Nikos Kazantzakis, and *Ulysses* by the Irish novelist, James Joyce.

Each work portrays a hero—facing travels, adventures, and setbacks—who somehow prevails.

Odysseus was trying to return home; the Kazantzakis hero is a self-propelled, centrifugal soul trying to abandon his home and seek a bold new life beyond; and Joyce's Leopold Bloom was trying to survive the day in a small, imperfect, real world of work and home in Dublin, Ireland, and still he wins everyday, yet bold victories.

Homer's Odysseus and Joyce's Leopold Bloom are centripetal heroes; throughout their travels and adventures, they seek to arrive safely at home. Kazantzakis' Odysseus rejects his home and hunts new worlds to conquer in search of freedom.

Each hero, in whatever setting, provides hope that although humankind faces a hostile world, one can master it and even extend man's boundaries.

And when the day is done, there is no higher salute than Joyce's toward Leopold Bloom: "He rests...He has traveled."

Buffett, who has hunkered down in his modest home and office in Omaha most of his life, and yet has also seen the bright lights of the world, has chalked up extraordinarily vast achievements, and riches, all of which he will generously hand back to our society.

He has lived in some ways an ordinary existence in Omaha, leaving at times to score brilliant achievements. His life is analogous to a life suggested by a cartoon on James Joyce's refrigerator:

(Photo by Michael O'Brien)

Warren Buffett atop Kiewit Plaza and the world, looking out over his beloved Omaha. Buffett says he can think more clearly about the stock in front of him in Omaha than he can on Wall Street.

1. Call bank.
2. Dry cleaner.
3. Forge in the smithy of my soul the uncreated conscience of my race.
4. Call Mom.

Wallman Investment Counsel's Steve Wallman says:

In some respects, there never will be another Warren Buffett for the same reason there will never be another Babe Ruth. They're both far larger than the sum of their total skills and records. They're heroes in the true sense of the word. People may break Ruth's records, and Buffett's, too, but it will be generations before a player, or investor, captures the public's imagination the way Ruth and Buffett have.

Babe Ruth was the first great home run hitter. I think Buffett is much the same—the first great stock market investor.

Even if someone rivals Buffett's talents, he'll have trouble with the longevity issue. Ted Williams may have been the best hitter who ever lived (certainly the best old hitter), but his career was interrupted by military service twice. Very few investors will have the personality to keep playing the game as long as Buffett has. Even fewer will break into the big leagues at 25.

In the same vein, two Berkshire shareholders once engaged in the following conversation about Buffett:

Shareholder 1: "He's the kind of investor who comes along just once in a generation."

Shareholder 2. "Yeah, he's an original."

Shareholder 1. "Maybe, it's more than just once in a generation."

Shareholder 2. "Yeah, maybe just once."

A great student and teacher, Buffett has taught us that honesty and traditional values can prevail.

Buffett has made us think, has made us laugh and has amply enriched the world, creating great permanent value in many ways.

By any measure for heroes, Warren Buffett has made a transcending journey, indeed an exalted odyssey. He is the Odysseus for our time.

195

BACK TO BEN GRAHAM

Ben Graham, the creator of value investing and Buffett's beloved teacher, turned 80 years old on April 11, 1974, and died in 1976.

At a seminar in 1974 Graham said:

> Let me close with a few words of counsel from an 80-year-old veteran of many a bull and many a bear market. Do those things as an analyst that you know you can do well, and only those things. If you can really beat the market by charts, by astrology or by some rare and valuable gift of your own, then that's the row you should hoe. If you're really good at picking the stocks most likely to succeed in the next 12 months, base your work on that endeavor. If you can foretell the next important development in the economy, or in technology, or in consumers' preferences, and gauge its consequences for various equity values, then concentrate on that particular activity. But in each case you must prove to yourself by honest, no-bluffing self-examination and by continuous testing of performance, that you have what it takes to produce worthwhile results.

On his 80th birthday Graham gave a summing-up speech which appears as the epilogue of *Benjamin Graham*, the memoirs of Ben Graham, published by McGraw-Hill and edited by Seymour Chatman in 1996:

> ...It is strange that the *Odyssey* has meant so much to me, since Ulysses' character is so different from my own. He was a great fighter and plunderer, while I have never fought with anyone or plundered anything in my life. He was crafty and devious, while I pride myself on being straightforward and direct. Yet he has attracted me all my life, as he has attracted countless readers for the past 2,500 years.
>
> Now for my final message. What better one can I choose than the closing lines of Tennyson's *Ulysses* (p. 315), those words well loved and oft repeated in the Graham family:

Come, my friends, 'tis not too late to seek
A newer world. Push off, and sitting well in order, smite
The sounding furrows; for my purpose holds
To sail beyond the sunset and the baths
Of all the western stars, until I die.
It may be that the gulfs will wash us down:
It may be we shall touch the Happy Isles,
And see the great Achilles, whom we knew.
Though much is taken, much abides; and though
We are not now that strength which in old days
Moved earth and heaven; that which we are, we are;
One equal temper of heroic hearts,
Made weak by time and fate, but strong in will
To strive, to seek, to find, and not to yield.

Warren Buffett, history's greatest stockpicker, rings the opening bell for trading at the New York Stock Exchange May 9, 1997. From the left are Jim McGuire, the specialist for Berkshire's stock, New York Stock Exchange Chairman Richard Grasso, Buffett and Buffett's daughter, Susan. Buffett's wife, Mrs. Susan Buffett, is to the far right although only the top of her head is visible.

Warren Buffett revealed! Berkshire's quarterback likes the Nebraska football team and Berkshire's finances to be No. 1.

(Photo courtesy of Warren Buffett)

Off to the races. Buffett learns what Winston Cup driving is like at Disney World. Maybe the unidentified driver is really Charles Munger. Maybe Lou Simpson is in the back seat.

Reader(s):

Hope to write to you in Y3K, but I'll start in 2002 and it won't be by postcard.

All the best,

Andy

Index

Index

Andrew Kilpatrick is a 1965 graduate of Washington and Lee University. He served in the Peace Corps in India for two years, earned a master's degree in English from the University of Vermont and was a U.S. Navy officer for three years.

His 20-year career with newspapers in Birmingham included eight years as a business reporter. He is a stockbroker with Prudential Securities in Birmingham.